IMPORTANT.

HERE IS YOUR REGISTRATION CODE TO ACCESS YOUR PREMIUM McGRAW-HILL ONLINE RESOURCES.

For key premium online resources you need THIS CODE to gain access. Once the code is entered, you will be able to use the Web resources for the length of your course.

If your course is using **WebCT** or **Blackboard**, you'll be able to use this code to access the McGraw-Hill content within your instructor's online course.

Access is provided if you have purchased a new book. If the registration code is missing from this book, the registration screen on our Website, and within your WebCT or Blackboard course, will tell you how to obtain your new code.

Registering for McGraw-Hill Online Resources

To gain access to your McGraw-Hill web resources simply follow the steps below:

1. USE YOUR WEB BROWSER TO GO TO: **www.mhhe.com/alloy9**
2. CLICK ON **FIRST TIME USER**.
3. ENTER THE REGISTRATION CODE* PRINTED ON THE TEAR-OFF BOOKMARK ON THE RIGHT.
4. AFTER YOU HAVE ENTERED YOUR REGISTRATION CODE, CLICK **REGISTER**.
5. FOLLOW THE INSTRUCTIONS TO SET-UP YOUR PERSONAL UserID AND PASSWORD.
6. WRITE YOUR UserID AND PASSWORD DOWN FOR FUTURE REFERENCE. KEEP IT IN A SAFE PLACE.

TO GAIN ACCESS to the McGraw-Hill content in your instructor's **WebCT** or **Blackboard** course simply log in to the course with the UserID and Password provided by your instructor. Enter the registration code exactly as it appears in the box to the right when prompted by the system. You will only need to use the code the first time you click on McGraw-Hill content.

Thank you, and welcome to your McGraw-Hill online resources!

McGraw-Hill Higher Education

* YOUR REGISTRATION CODE CAN BE USED ONLY ONCE TO ESTABLISH ACCESS. IT IS NOT TRANSFERABLE.

0-07-294310-6 T/A ALLOY: ABNORMAL PSYCHOLOGY, 9E

REGISTRATION CODE

ZJC5-VLBP-9FR6-FO11-2RS7

Higher Education

McGraw-Hill

Abnormal Psychology

CURRENT PERSPECTIVES

NINTH EDITION

Lauren B. Alloy
Temple University

John H. Riskind
George Mason University

Margaret J. Manos

Boston Burr Ridge, IL Dubuque, IA Madison, WI New York San Francisco St. Louis
Bangkok Bogotá Caracas Kuala Lumpur Lisbon London Madrid Mexico City
Milan Montreal New Delhi Santiago Seoul Singapore Sydney Taipei Toronto

The McGraw-Hill Companies

Higher Education

Abnormal Psychology
Current Perspectives

Published by McGraw-Hill, an imprint of The McGraw-Hill Companies, Inc., 1221 Avenue of the Americas, New York, NY 10020.

1 2 3 4 5 6 7 8 9 0 WCK WCK 0 9 8 7 6 5 4

ISBN 0-07-242298-X

Vice president and Editor-in-chief: *Thalia Dorwick*
Publisher: *Stephen D. Rutter*
Director of development: *Judith Kromm*
Senior sponsoring editor: *John T. Wannemacher*
Senior marketing manager: *Melissa Caughlin*
Lead production editor: *David M. Staloch*
Senior production supervisor: *Richard DeVitto*
Art director: *Jeanne M. Schreiber*
Design manager: *Cassandra Chu*
Art editor: *Emma Ghiselli*
Interior designer: *Glenda King*
Cover designer: *John Greenfield*
Photo research coordinator: *Nora Agbayani*
Photo researcher: *Toni Michaels*
Compositor: *The GTS Companies/LA Campus*
Typeface: *10/12 Sabon*
Printer and binder: *Quebecor World Color, Versailles*

Cover image: © *Diana Ong/SuperStock*

Text and photo credits begin on page C-1 and constitute an extension of the copyright page.

LIBRARY OF CONGRESS CATALOGING-IN-PUBLICATION DATA

Alloy, Lauren B.
Abnormal psychology: current perspectives / Lauren B. Alloy, John H. Riskind, Margaret J. Manos.—9th ed.
p. cm.
Includes bibliographical references and index.
ISBN 0-07-242298-X
1. Psychology, Pathological. I. Riskind, John H. II. Manos, Margaret, J. III. Title.
[DNLM: 1. Psychopathology. WM 100 A441a2004]

RC454.B577 2004
616.89—dc22 2003059304

www.mhhe.com

ABOUT THE AUTHORS

Lauren B. Alloy is an internationally recognized researcher in the area of mood disorders. Her work on depression has had a major impact on the fields of clinical, personality, social, and cognitive psychology. She is currently Professor of Psychology at Temple University. Previously at Northwestern University, she became the youngest Professor in the university's history and the first woman to become a Professor in Northwestern's psychology department. She received both her B.A. and Ph.D. in psychology from the University of Pennsylvania. Dr. Alloy was awarded the American Psychological Association's Young Psychologist Award in 1984, won the American Psychological Association's Division 12 Distinguished Scientific Contribution Award in 2003 (jointly with Dr. Lyn Abramson) and named the APA's Master Lecturer in Psychopathology in 2002 (jointly with Dr. Lyn Abramson). In 2001, she received Temple University's Paul W. Eberman Faculty Research Award. She was also recognized by Northwestern University's College of Arts & Sciences with the Great Teacher Award in 1988 for her classroom teaching and mentoring of students. She is a Fellow of the American Psychological Association and American Psychological Society. Dr. Alloy is the author of more than 130 scholarly publications, including a book (co-edited with Dr. John Riskind) entitled *Cognitive Vulnerability to Emotional Disorders.* She has served on the editorial boards of the *Journal of Abnormal Psychology, Journal of Personality and Social Psychology, Journal of Consulting and Clinical Psychology, Clinical Psychology: Science and Practice, Cognitive Therapy and Research,* and the *Journal of Cognitive Psychotherapy: An International Quarterly,* and has served as Guest Editor for the *Journal of Abnormal Psychology, Cognitive Therapy and Research, Journal of Cognitive Psychotherapy: An International Quarterly,* and *Journal of Social and Clinical Psychology.* She regularly teaches courses on psychopathology.

Dr. Alloy's research focuses on cognitive, interpersonal, and biopsychosocial processes in the onset and maintenance of depression and bipolar disorder. Along with her colleagues, Lyn Abramson and Gerald Metalsky, she is the author of the hopelessness theory of depression and she discovered, with Lyn Abramson, the "sadder but wiser," or "depressive realism," effect. In her leisure time, she enjoys sports, the theater, good restaurants, and she is a movie fanatic. But most of all, she loves being with her husband, Daniel, and daughter, Adrienne.

John H. Riskind received his doctorate in psychology from Yale University in 1977. He had a postdoctoral fellowship at the University of Pennsylvania Center for Cognitive Therapy in the Department of Psychiatry, where he trained with Aaron Beck and served as his Director of Research for two years. He has held faculty positions at several universities and is now Professor of Psychology in the clinical psychology program at George Mason University. An associate editor of the journal *Cognitive Therapy and Research* and the *Journal of Cognitive Psychotherapy,* Dr. Riskind is also the author of approximately 70 published articles and chapters in professional journals. His research interests center on cognitive vulnerability factors for anxiety and depression and on the nature of distinct and overlapping features of anxiety and depression. Dr. Riskind conducts a private clinical psychology practice in cognitive therapy in Fairfax, Va.

Margaret J. Manos is a New York City-based writer and editor. She has contributed to a number of textbooks in the social sciences. She also writes about theater.

CONTENTS IN BRIEF

Preface xi

PART ONE Introduction to Abnormal Psychology

1 Abnormal Psychology: Historical Perspectives 1
2 Diagnosis and Assessment 26
3 Research Methods in Abnormal Psychology 54

PART TWO Theoretical Perspectives

4 The Behavioral, Cognitive, and Sociocultural Perspectives 75
5 The Psychodynamic, Humanistic-Existential, and Interpersonal Perspectives 105
6 The Neuroscience Perspective 130

PART THREE Emotional and Behavioral Disorders

7 Anxiety Disorders 150
8 Dissociative and Somatoform Disorders 179
9 Stress and Physical Disorders 211
10 Mood Disorders 245
11 Personality Disorders 286
12 The Nature of Substance Dependence and Abuse 312
13 Sexual Dysfunctions, Paraphilias, and Gender Identity Disorders 355

PART FOUR Psychotic and Neuropsychological Disorders

14 Schizophrenia and Delusional Disorder 389
15 Neuropsychological Disorders 431

PART FIVE Developmental Disorders

16 Disorders of Childhood and Adolescence 458
17 Mental Retardation and Autism 484

PART SIX Legal and Ethical Issues in Abnormal Psychology

18 Legal and Ethical Issues in Abnormal Psychology 510

Glossary G-1
References R-1
Credits C-1
Indexes I-1

CONTENTS

Preface xi

PART ONE Introduction to Abnormal Psychology

CHAPTER 1
Abnormal Psychology: Historical Perspectives 1

Abnormal Behavior and Society 2
- Defining Abnormal Behavior 2
- Relating Abnormal Behavior to Groups 4
- Explaining Abnormal Behavior 6

FOCUS ON: *Culture-Bound Syndromes* 7
- Treating Abnormal Behavior 9
- Preventing Abnormal Behavior 9

FOCUS ON: *The Mental Health Professions* 10

Conceptions of Abnormal Behavior: A Short History 11
- Ancient Societies: Deviance and the Supernatural 11
- The Greeks and the Rise of Science 12
- The Middle Ages and the Renaissance: Natural and Supernatural 12
- The Eighteenth Century and After: The Asylums 13
- The Rise of the Prevention Movement 17

FOCUS ON: *The Homeless and Mentally Ill* 18
- The Rise of Managed Behavioral Health Care 19
- The Foundations of Modern Abnormal Psychology 20
- Non-Western Approaches to Abnormal Behavior 22

A Multiperspective Approach 23

CHAPTER 2
Diagnosis and Assessment 26

Diagnosis and Assessment: The Issues 27
- Why Assessment? 27
- The Diagnosis of Mental Disorders 28

RESEARCH HIGHLIGHTS: *On Being Sane in Insane Places* 30
- Assessing the Assessment: Reliability and Validity 32

RESEARCH HIGHLIGHTS: *Comorbidity: Disturbance as a Package* 35
- Problems in Assessment 35

Methods of Assessment 37
- The Interview 37

FOCUS ON: *A Sample SCID Interview* 38
- Psychological Tests 38

FOCUS ON: *The Mini Mental Status Exam* 39
- Laboratory Tests 48
- Observation in Natural Settings 49

Cultural Bias in Assessment 50

CHAPTER 3
Research Methods in Abnormal Psychology 54

Characteristics of the Scientific Method 55
- Skeptical Attitude 55
- Objectives 55
- Scientific Procedures 57

FOCUS ON: *The Case Study* 58

RESEARCH HIGHLIGHTS: *Treatment Development: An Example of Hypothesis Generation* 60

Ethical Issues in Research 62

Research Designs 64
- Correlational Research 64

FOCUS ON: *The Correlation Coefficient: A Measure of Predictive Strength* 65
- Epidemiological Studies 66
- Experimental Designs 67
- The Single-Case Experiment 69

PART TWO Theoretical Perspectives

CHAPTER 4
The Behavioral, Cognitive, and Sociocultural Perspectives 75

The Behavioral Perspective 75
- The Background of Behaviorism 76
- The Assumptions of Behavioral Psychology 78
- The Basic Mechanisms of Learning 78
- Other Mechanisms Associated With Learning 80
- Abnormal Behavior as a Product of Learning 83
- The Behavioral Approach to Therapy 83

FOCUS ON: *The Limitations of Change: An Acceptance-Based Approach to Couple Therapy* 86
- Evaluating Behaviorism 87

The Cognitive Perspective 88
- The Background of the Cognitive Perspective 88

Cognitive Behaviorism 89
Cognitive Appraisal 90
Information Processing 93
The Cognitive Approach to Treatment 94
Evaluating the Cognitive Perspective 97

The Sociocultural Perspective 98
Social-Situational Influences on Behavior 98
Mental Illness and Social Ills 99
Mental Illness and Labeling 99
Class, Ethnicity, and Diagnosis 99

RESEARCH HIGHLIGHTS: *The Stigma of Psychiatric Labels* 100

Sociocultural Factors, Help-Seeking, and Treatment 101
Prevention as a Social Issue 101
Evaluating the Sociocultural Perspective 102

CHAPTER 5
The Psychodynamic, Humanistic-Existential, and Interpersonal Perspectives 105

The Psychodynamic Perspective 105
The Basic Concepts of Freudian Theory 106
The Descendants of Freud 111

FOCUS ON: *Psychodynamic Theory and Female Development* 112

The Psychodynamic Approach to Therapy 117

RESEARCH HIGHLIGHTS: *A Cognitive Approach to Transference* 119

Evaluating the Psychodynamic Perspective 120

The Humanistic-Existential Perspective 123
Basic Assumptions 123
Humanistic Psychology 123

FOCUS ON: *Positive Psychology* 124

Existential Psychology 126

The Interpersonal Perspective 127

Integrating the Perspectives 127

CHAPTER 6
The Neuroscience Perspective 130

Behavior Genetics 131
Clinical Genetic Studies 131

RESEARCH HIGHLIGHTS: *The Minnesota Study of Twins Reared Apart* 134

Molecular Genetics Studies 135

The Central Nervous System 135
Neurons 136
Neurotransmitters 137
The Anatomy of the Brain 139
Measuring Brain Activity and Structure 141
Lateralization: Effects on Language and Emotion 143

The Peripheral Nervous System: Somatic and Autonomic 144
The Somatic Nervous System 144
The Autonomic Nervous System 144

The Endocrine System 146

Evaluating the Neuroscience Perspective 146
Integrating the Neuroscience and Psychological Perspectives 147

PART THREE Emotional and Behavioral Disorders

CHAPTER 7
Anxiety Disorders 150

Anxiety Disorder Syndromes 151
Phobias 152
Generalized Anxiety Disorder 153
Obsessive-Compulsive Disorder 154

FOCUS ON: *Animal Hoarding and Obsessive-Compulsive Disorder* 155

Posttraumatic Stress Disorder 157

FOCUS ON: *Terrorism from the Skies: Communal Posttraumatic Stress* 160

Panic Disorder 161

Anxiety Disorders: Theory and Therapy 163
The Cognitive Perspective: Overestimation of Threat 163

FOCUS ON: *A Panic Attack* 167

PREVENTION: *Cognitive-Behavioral Intervention To Prevent Anxiety Disorders* 168

The Behavioral Perspective: Learning To Be Anxious 168
The Psychodynamic Perspective: Neurosis 170
The Neuroscience Perspective: Biochemistry and Medicine 171

CHAPTER 8
Dissociative and Somatoform Disorders 179

Dissociative Disorders 180
Dissociative Amnesia 181
Dissociative Fugue 182

FOCUS ON: *Dissociative Identity Disorder and the Law: Who Committed the Crime?* 183

Dissociative Identity Disorder 184

PREVENTION: *Educating Children About Child Abuse* 187

Depersonalization Disorder 188

RESEARCH HIGHLIGHTS: *Recovered Memory of Childhood Abuse: A Modern Dilemma* 190

Dissociative Disorders: Theory and Therapy 192
The Psychodynamic Perspective: Defense Against Anxiety 192
The Behavioral and Sociocultural Perspectives: Dissociation as a Social Role 193
The Cognitive Perspective: Memory Dysfunction 195
The Neuroscience Perspective: Brain Dysfunction 197

Somatoform Disorders 197
Body Dysmorphic Disorder 198
Hypochondriasis 199

Somatization Disorder 200
Pain Disorder 201
Conversion Disorder 201

Somatoform Disorders: Theory and Therapy 204
The Psychodynamic Perspective: Defense Against Anxiety 204
The Behavioral and Sociocultural Perspectives: The Sick Role 205
The Cognitive Perspective: Misinterpreting Bodily Sensations 207
The Neuroscience Perspective: Brain Dysfunction 208

CHAPTER 9
Stress and Physical Disorders 211

Mind and Body 212

Stress 214
Defining Stress 214
What Determines Responses to Stress? 214

How Stress Influences Illness 215

RESEARCH HIGHLIGHTS: *Minor Stress and Illnesses* 216

Changes in Physiological Functioning 216
Changes in High-Risk Behavior 220

Psychological Factors and Physical Disorders 221
Coronary Heart Disease 221
Hypertension 224
Cancer 225
AIDS 228
Headache 230
Obesity 231
Sleep Disorders 233

Stress and Illness: Theory and Therapy 236
The Behavioral Perspective: Learning and Unlearning Responses to Stress 236
The Cognitive Perspective 238
The Psychodynamic Perspective 239

PREVENTION: *The Role of Spirituality in Well-Being* 240

The Interpersonal Perspective 241
The Sociocultural Perspective 242
The Neuroscience Perspective 242

CHAPTER 10
Mood Disorders 245

Depressive and Manic Episodes 246
Major Depressive Episode 246
Manic Episode 247

Mood Disorder Syndromes 248
Major Depressive Disorder 248

RESEARCH HIGHLIGHTS: *Gender Differences in Depression* 250

Bipolar Disorder 251
Dysthymic Disorder and Cyclothymic Disorder 252
Dimensions of Mood Disorder 253

FOCUS ON: *Bipolar Disorder and Creativity: Streams of Fire* 254

Comorbidity: Mixed Anxiety-Depression 257

Suicide 257
The Prevalence of Suicide 257
Myths about Suicide 260
Suicide Prediction 260
Suicide Prevention 262

Mood Disorders: Theory and Therapy 263
The Behavioral and Interpersonal Perspectives 263
The Cognitive Perspective 264
The Psychodynamic Perspective 269

PREVENTION: *The Penn Optimism Project* 270

The Sociocultural Perspective 272
The Neuroscience Perspective 273

FOCUS ON: *Drug Therapy Versus Psychotherapy* 281

CHAPTER 11
Personality Disorders 286

Odd/Eccentric Personality Disorders 287
Paranoid Personality Disorder 287
Schizotypal Personality Disorder 288
Schizoid Personality Disorder 289

Dramatic/Emotional Personality Disorders 290
Antisocial Personality Disorder 290

RESEARCH HIGHLIGHTS: *Are There Two Types of Psychopath—Successful and Unsuccessful?* 292

Borderline Personality Disorder 293

FOCUS ON: *Serial Killers* 294

Histrionic Personality Disorder 296
Narcissistic Personality Disorder 297

Anxious/Fearful Personality Disorders 298
Avoidant Personality Disorder 298
Dependent Personality Disorder 299

FOCUS ON: *Impulse-Control Disorders* 300

Obsessive-Compulsive Personality Disorder 301

Personality Disorders: Theory and Therapy 303
The Psychodynamic Perspective 303

PREVENTION: *Childhood Intervention To Prevent Personality Disorders* 305

The Behavioral Perspective 305
The Cognitive Perspective 306
The Sociocultural Perspective 308
The Neuroscience Perspective 308

CHAPTER 12
The Nature of Substance Dependence and Abuse 312

The Difference Between Dependence and Abuse 313

Alcohol Dependence 314
The Social Cost of Alcohol Problems 315
The Personal Cost of Alcohol Dependence 316
The Development of Alcohol Dependence 318

FOCUS ON: *Binge Drinking on Campus* 322

Treatment of Alcohol Dependence 322

Nicotine Dependence 326

The Antismoking Movement 326

Legal Remedies 327

Nicotine Dependence: Theory and Therapy 327

Other Psychoactive Drugs 329

Depressants 330

Stimulants 333

Hallucinogens 335

Marijuana and Hashish 336

FOCUS ON: *Anabolic Steroids and Athletes* 339

Substance Dependence: Theory and Therapy 340

The Psychodynamic Perspective 340

The Behavioral Perspective 341

The Interpersonal Perspective 342

The Cognitive Perspective 343

The Neuroscience Perspective 345

The Sociocultural Perspective 349

PREVENTION: *Early Intervention With Children at Risk for Substance Abuse* 350

CHAPTER 13
Sexual Dysfunctions, Paraphilias, and Gender Identity Disorders 355

Classifying Sexual Behavior 356

Sexual Dysfunctions 358

Forms of Sexual Dysfunction 358

FOCUS ON: *Sex in America: Myths and Reality* 359

FOCUS ON: *What Is Normal Sexual Response in a Woman?* 361

Diagnosing Sexual Dysfunction 362

Sexual Dysfunction: Theory and Therapy 364

The Psychodynamic Perspective 364

The Behavioral and Cognitive Perspectives 365

Multifaceted Treatment 367

The Neuroscience Perspective 369

Paraphilias 370

Fetishism 371

Transvestism 372

Exhibitionism 373

Voyeurism 374

Sadism and Masochism 374

Frotteurism 376

Pedophilia 376

Rape 378

Paraphilias: Theory and Therapy 379

The Psychodynamic Perspective 379

The Behavioral Perspective 380

The Cognitive Perspective 381

The Neuroscience Perspective 381

PREVENTION: *Pedophilia and Child Sexual Molestation* 382

Treatment Efficacy 383

Gender Identity Disorders 383

Patterns of Gender Identity Disorder 384

The Psychodynamic Perspective 384

The Behavioral Perspective 385

The Neuroscience Perspective 385

Gender Reassignment 385

PART FOUR Psychotic and Neuropsychological Disorders

CHAPTER 14
Schizophrenia and Delusional Disorder 389

Schizophrenia 390

The Prevalence of Schizophrenia 390

The History of the Diagnostic Category 390

The Symptoms of Schizophrenia 391

The Course of Schizophrenia 399

The Subtypes of Schizophrenia 400

The Dimensions of Schizophrenia 403

Delusional Disorder 405

The Symptoms of Delusional Disorder 405

Problems in the Study of Schizophrenia 406

Schizophrenia: Theory and Therapy 407

The Neuroscience Perspective 407

FOCUS ON: *Eye Tracking as a Marker for Schizophrenia* 411

RESEARCH HIGHLIGHTS: *Is Schizophrenia an Infectious Disease? The Viral Hypothesis* 415

PREVENTION: *The Schizophrenia Prodrome: Implications for Prevention* 418

The Cognitive Perspective 418

The Interpersonal Perspective 422

The Behavioral Perspective 425

The Sociocultural Perspective 427

Unitary Theories: Diathesis and Stress 427

CHAPTER 15
Neuropsychological Disorders 431

Problems in Diagnosis 432

Identifying an Acquired Brain Disorder 432

Specifying the Type of Disorder 433

Specifying the Site of the Damage 436

Types of Acquired Brain Disorders 436

Cerebral Infection 436

Traumatic Brain Injury 439

Cerebrovascular Accidents: Strokes 441

PREVENTION: *Preventing Traumatic Brain Injuries* 442

Brain Tumors 444
Degenerative Disorders 444

FOCUS ON: *Caregivers: The Hidden Victims of Dementia* 450

Nutritional Deficiency 451
Endocrine Disorders 451
Toxic Disorders 452

The Epilepsies 453
Causes of Epilepsy 453
Types of Seizures 453
Psychological Factors in Epilepsy 454
Treatment of Epilepsy 455

PART FIVE Developmental Disorders

CHAPTER 16 Disorders of Childhood and Adolescence 458

Issues in Child Psychopathology 459
Prevalence 459
Classification and Diagnosis 459
Long-Term Consequences 460

Disruptive Behavior Disorders 461
Attention Deficit Hyperactivity Disorder 461
Conduct Disorder 463

FOCUS ON: *Antisocial Adolescents: Are There Two Types?* 465

Disorders of Emotional Distress 466
Anxiety Disorders 466
Childhood Depression 468

Eating Disorders 469
Anorexia Nervosa 469
Bulimia Nervosa 470
Childhood Obesity 470

Elimination Disorders 471
Enuresis 472
Encopresis 472

Childhood Sleep Disorders 472
Insomnia 472
Nightmares and Night Terrors 473
Sleepwalking 473

Learning and Communication Disorders 474
Learning Disorders 474

FOCUS ON: *Recognizing Learning Disorders: Some Signs* 475

Communication Disorders 476

Disorders of Childhood and Adolescence: Theory and Therapy 476
The Behavioral Perspective 477

PREVENTION: *The FRIENDS Program for Preventing Childhood Disorders* 478

The Cognitive Perspective 478
The Interpersonal Perspective 480
The Sociocultural Perspective 480
The Psychodynamic Perspective 480
The Neuroscience Perspective 481

CHAPTER 17 Mental Retardation and Autism 484

Mental Retardation 485
Levels of Mental Retardation 485
Genetic Factors 486
Environmental Factors 488
Mental Retardation in Adults 492

Autism 493
Symptoms of Autism 494

FOCUS ON: *Savant Syndrome* 495

Theories of Autism 497

Society and People with Developmental Disorders 500
Public Policy 500
Community Integration 502
Quality of Life 502
Support for the Family 503
Employment 503

Prevention and Therapy 504
Primary Prevention 504
Secondary Prevention 504
Behavioral Therapy 505
Cognitive Therapy 506
Pharmacological Therapy 507
Psychotherapy 507

PART SIX Legal and Ethical Issues In Abnormal Psychology

CHAPTER 18 Legal and Ethical Issues in Abnormal Psychology 510

Psychological Disturbance and Criminal Law 510
The Insanity Defense 511

FOCUS ON: *Evolution, Misfortune, and Criminal Responsibility* 514

Competency to Stand Trial 517

Civil Commitment 518
Procedures for Commitment 518

PREVENTION: *The Mental Health Court* 520

Standards for Commitment 522

FOCUS ON: *The Limits of Confidentiality* 523

Patients' Rights 527
The Right to Treatment 527
The Right to Refuse Treatment 529
The Right to a Humane Environment 529

FOCUS ON: *Sex, Lives, and Mental Patients: The Hospital's Dilemma in the Age of AIDS* 530
Behavior Therapy and Patients' Rights 531
Ethics and the Mental Health Profession 532
Confidentiality in Psychotherapy 532
Informed Consent for Psychotherapy 534
Multiple and Exploitative Relationships in Psychotherapy 534
Glossary G-1
References R-1
Credits C-1
Indexes I-1

PREFACE

From its inception, *Abnormal Psychology: Current Perspectives,* has provided a balanced, contemporary introduction to the symptoms, theory, and treatment of psychological disorders. The ninth edition continues this commitment and, with the addition of video case studies on a new student CD-ROM video, gives a human face to the clinical portraits drawn in the text.

The balanced approach taken by this text acknowledges that a variety of psychological perspectives can be brought to bear on a given disorder. At the same time, some perspectives have been shown empirically to be more effective for certain disorders than others. Therefore, the breadth and depth of discussion of each perspective in the disorders chapters is proportional to its contribution to the understanding and treatment of that particular group of disorders. This approach makes sense from an instructional point of view, although it can be difficult for students taking the introductory course in abnormal psychology to grasp the theoretical differences while trying to differentiate among the disorders and their treatments. For this reason, we provide three chapters devoted to the theoretical perspectives near the beginning of this text (Chapters 4–6). A solid theoretical foundation makes the study of the psychological disorders more manageable for students.

Abnormal Psychology: Current Perspectives is unique in that each edition is prepared with input from experts in the various disorders, making it as accurate and as up-to-date as possible. Many of the changes in this edition (such as the addition of a separate chapter on the neuroscience perspective) reflect new discoveries about the causes of particular disorders and promising new treatment approaches. Research Highlights boxes call additional attention to the essential contributions of research to a better understanding of psychological disorders and a better future for the people who live with them.

A new theme in this edition is prevention. Introduced from a historical perspective in Chapter 1, prevention features prominently in the disorders chapters. Each of the disorders chapters, as well as Chapter 18, Legal and Ethical Issues, includes a Prevention box profiling an outreach program designed for people at risk for one of the disorders described in the chapter. For example, in Chapter 10, the Prevention box discusses the Penn Optimism Project for preventing depression.

Case studies have long been used to give students a window on the manifestations of psychological disorders. Now, through the use of the *MindMAP Plus* CD-ROM packaged with the book, students can observe for themselves the symptoms and suffering of real people with the disorders described in the text. Excerpted from McGraw-Hill's *Faces of Abnormal Psychology,* volumes I and II, and from footage licensed from The Discovery Channel, the video interviews found on the CD powerfully convey what it is like to live with a psychological disorder. Contextualized with a short text preview and several follow-up questions, these videos add a much-needed human dimension to a subject with which many students have little or no experience.

Highlights of This Edition

Continuing the trend started with the eighth edition, we have reduced the number of chapters in the book to 18, down from 19. In response to feedback from instructors, we have redistributed the coverage of antisocial behavior into the chapters on anxiety disorders, personality disorders and sexual disorders and integrated material on prevention in Chapter 1 and in each of the disorders chapters. Also, in recognition of the growing body of neuroscience research, we have added a third perspectives chapter devoted to the neuroscience perspective. The other two perspectives chapters now cover the behavioral, cognitive, and sociocultural perspectives (Chapter 4) and the psychodynamic, humanistic and interpersonal perspectives (Chapter 5). The entire text has undergone significant updating, including the addition of more than 200 new references and many empirical studies. All terminology and diagnostic information have been revised to be consistent with the *Diagnostic and Statistical Manual of Mental Disorders,* Fourth Edition, Text

Revision (*DSM-IV-TR*). Other key changes include the following:

Chapter 1: Abnormal Behavior: Historical Perspectives

- A new section describes the rise of the prevention movement.
- A new section discusses the effects of managed care on mental health care.
- A new table highlights ethnic differences in rates of depression.

Chapter 2: Diagnosis and Assessment

- The discussion of diagnosis reflects *DSM-IV-TR*.
- A revised discussion of IQ tests addresses the issue of cultural bias.
- The section on the Rorschach test now covers the controversy surrounding its use and interpretation.

Chapter 3: Research Methods in Abnormal Psychology

- A new section on research ethics appears in this chapter.

Chapter 4: The Behavioral, Cognitive, and Sociocultural Perspectives

- This new chapter places the behavioral, cognitive, and sociocultural perspectives in a broader historical context.
- The discussion of cognitive appraisal was expanded to better explain the concept of cognitive vulnerability.
- A new section discusses the relationship between socioeconomic status and ethnicity and willingness to seek help for mental health problems.

Chapter 5: The Psychodynamic, Humanistic-Existential, and Interpersonal Perspectives

- The humanistic-existential perspective was restored and its relation to the psychodynamic perspective is explained.
- A new section on the interpersonal perspective replaces the discussion of the family systems approach.

Chapter 6: The Neuroscience Perspective

- This new chapter emphasizes the role of neuropsychological processes in abnormal behavior.
- A new section discusses the integration of the neuroscience perspective with the psychological approaches as a way of arriving at a more complete explanation of a number of psychological disorders.

Chapter 7: The Anxiety Disorders

- The chapter has been reorganized to focus first on the disorders involving fear of an identifiable object or situation, which students can understand more readily than disorders having no specific stimulus.
- A new Focus box discusses the relationship of animal hoarding to obsessive-compulsive disorder.
- A new Focus box explores the communal trauma that can result from experiencing an act of terrorism, such as the 9/11 attacks in New York, Pennsylvania, and Washington.

Chapter 8: Dissociative and Somatoform Disorders

- A new Prevention box focuses on educational programs designed to teach children to recognize and avoid abusive situations.

Chapter 9: Psychological Stress and Physical Disorders

- The discussion of cancer has been rewritten to explore in greater depth the importance of psychological factors to the body's ability to defend against cancer.
- The discussion of HIV and AIDS has been updated and clarified.
- Updated information on gender, ethnic, and socioeconomic differences in the effects of stress on cardiovascular health was added to the discussion of groups at risk for heart disease.
- New material on the effects of spirituality on the stress response appears in a Prevention box.

Chapter 10: Mood Disorders

- The section on theory and therapy was reorganized and updated to reflect the greater influence of the behavioral/interpersonal and cognitive perspectives in understanding and treating depression and bipolar disorder.
- Recent findings indicating that behavioral and cognitive models might be applicable to bipolar disorder are discussed.
- A new Prevention box profiles the Penn Optimism Project.

- New information added to the section on the neuroscience perspective points to a therapeutic effect of sleep deprivation on patients with bipolar disorder and on IPSRT as an adjunctive treatment for bipolar disorder.
- Coverage of transcranial magnetic stimulation (TMS) was added to the neuroscience section.

Chapter 11: Personality Disorders

- The updated chapter now includes antisocial personality disorder.
- A new Research Highlights box compares "successful" and "unsuccessful" psychopaths.

Chapter 12: Substance-Abuse Disorders

- The section on Genetic Studies includes a discussion of the interaction of genetic and environmental factors on alcohol dependence.
- Updated material on possible changes in the brain and on the involvement of serotonin and GABA in substance abuse was added.

Chapter 13: Sexual Dysfunctions, Paraphilias, and Gender Identity Disorders

- The discussion on treatment of sexual dysfunction was revised to include Viagra and the latest prosthetic treatments
- The paraphilias section now includes coverage of rape.
- New material on the efficacy of treatment for paraphilias was added.

Chapter 14: Schizophrenia and Delusional Disorder

- A new Prevention box discusses the prodrome syndrome and RAPP, a program created to establish prospective criteria that can be used to identify adolescents at risk for schizophrenia and treat them before symptoms develop.

Chapter 15: Neuropsychological Disorders

- The discussion of epilepsy has been substantially expanded and updated.

Chapter 16: Disorders of Childhood and Adolescence

- A new introduction outlines the developmental approach to child psychopathology.
- A new Prevention box discusses the FRIENDS program for anxiety reduction in children.

Chapter 17: Mental Retardation and Autism

- Revisions clearly separate mental retardation and autism, while making the point that there is some overlap with respect to symptoms, age of onset, prognosis, etiology, and treatment.
- The discussion of the institutionalization of people with mental retardation has been rewritten to focus on the positive effects of deinstitutionalization.

Chapter 18: Legal and Ethical Issues in Abnormal Psychology

- The chapter now includes a discussion on ethics and the mental health profession.
- A new section discusses issues involving involuntary commitment, outlines new laws on the commitment of sexually violent predators, increasing use of involuntary outpatient commitment to insure treatment compliance, and the effectiveness of coerced treatment.

Supplements

The supplements listed here are intended to be used with *Abnormal Psychology*, Ninth edition. Please contact your local McGraw-Hill representative for details concerning policies, prices, and availability, as some restrictions may apply.

The McGraw-Hill Casebook in Abnormal Psychology, Fifth Edition, by John Vitkus, The Cleveland Clinic Foundation. This casebook features 22 case studies from the files of mental health professionals. The cases cover a broad range of disorders and therapies, from phobias to road rage.

***MindMAP Plus* Student CD-ROM.** A new learning tool packaged with new copies of *Abnormal Psychology*, this CD includes video clips from McGraw-Hill's exclusive *Faces of Abnormal Psychology* series and the Discovery Channel video sources illustrating key concepts and featuring real people discussing their disorders. Images in the text key the videos to specific topics. Each video is contextualized with pedagogy, including follow-up questions and web connections. Additionally, a short self-test section for each chapter provides a valuable study aid.

Student Study Guide by Michele Catone-Maitino, Hudson Valley Community College. Learning objectives, key terms, and important names begin each chapter. A guided self-study helps students to review concepts in the chapter, and multiple-choice practice tests enable students to assess their learning. A "Helpful Hints" section provides studying tips and assists students with the chapter's most difficult concepts. An answer key, complete with feedback, is also included.

Online Learning Center with PowerWeb (**http://www.mhhe.com/alloy9**). Practice tests and key terms are available online, as part of comprehensive website for *Abnormal Psychology*, Ninth Edition. PowerWeb, a password-protected section of the website, is available free with the purchase of a new copy of the text. PowerWeb articles and in-depth essays direct students to more than 6,000 high-quality references. The password can be found on the card that is bound into the front of each new text.

Instructor's Resource CD-ROM. In addition to the complete Instructor's Manual, PowerPoint slides, and Test Bank, the Instructor's Resource CD-ROM contains an image gallery of illustrations from the book. An easy-to-use interface facilitates the design and delivery of multimedia classroom presentations.

Instructor's Manual by Joseph A. Davis, San Diego State University. Each chapter of the manual provides many ideas for lectures, demonstrations, activities, and classroom assessment techniques, as well as Talking Points to stimulate class discussion. The Instructor's Manual also includes descriptions of the videos found on the *MindMAP Plus* Student CD and suggestions for using them in class. The Instructor's Manual can be found on the Instructor's Resource CD-ROM and on the password-protected instructor's side of the Online Learning Center.

PowerPoint Slides by Joseph A. Davis, San Diego State University. To enhance lectures and classroom presentation of materials, full-color images from the book are integrated with summaries and main points of each chapter. The PowerPoint slides can be found on the Instructor's Resource CD-ROM and on the password-protected instructor's side of the Online Learning Center.

Test Bank by Michele Catone-Maitino, Hudson Valley Community College. Written by the author of the Student Study Guide, the Test Bank is correlated with the Study Guide. The Test Bank contains nearly 2,000 multiple-choice items and essay questions. Items that test knowledge of material in the text's boxes are called out for easy reference in the answer keys. The Test Bank can be used on all the major computer platforms and is available on the Instructor's Resource CD-ROM in both text files and computerized format.

Faces of Abnormal Psychology, volumes I and II. Available to adopting instructors on DVD as well as in VHS format, each volume presents ten 8-10 minute clips suitable for classroom viewing. Each video features an interview with someone who has experienced a psychological disorder. Schizophrenia, posttraumatic stress disorder, obsessive-compulsive disorder, and Asperger's syndrome are some of the disorders covered.

Taking Sides: Clashing Views on Controversial Issues in Abnormal Psychology. This debate-style reader introduces students to controversial viewpoints on important issues in the field. Each topic is carefully framed for the students, and the pro and con essays represent the arguments of leading scholars and commentators in their fields. An Instructor's Guide containing testing materials is also available.

PageOut is a tool designed to let an instructor build his or her own website in less than an hour. PageOut requires no prior knowledge of HTML, no long hours of coding, and no design skills. Even the most inexperienced computer user can quickly and easily create a professional-looking course website with PageOut by filling in templates with information and with content provided by McGraw-Hill. Visit **http://www.pageout.net** for more information.

Populated ***WebCT*** and ***Blackboard*** course cartridges are also available to instructors.

For information on any component of the teaching supplements, instructors should contact their McGraw-Hill representative.

Acknowledgments

Several experts have contributed material that was used to prepare this edition of *Abnormal Psychology: Current Perspectives,* insuring that it continues to represent the most current scholarship, coverage, and thinking in the field. We gratefully acknowledge the following people for their contributions to the chapters for which they shared their expertise:

Julie Lynch, Albany Psychological Associates (neuropsychological disorders)

Grant Benham, University of Texas, Pan American (stress and physical disorders)

Edward Chang, University of Michigan (media integration)

Kevin S. Douglas, Florida Mental Health Institute, University of South Florida (legal issues)

Richard G. Heimberg, Temple University (ethical issues)

Christopher A. Kearney, University of Nevada, Las Vegas (childhood disorders, mental retardation, and autism)

Catherine Stoney, Ohio State University (stress and physical disorders)

Marcello Spinella, Richard Stockton College of New Jersey, (neuropsychological disorders)

Our appreciation also goes to the reviewers who provided valuable feedback on the eighth edition and on the ninth edition during its development. They are:

Brad A. Alford, *University of Scranton*
Carol Austad, *Central Connecticut State University*
Mitchell E. Berman, *University of Southern Mississippi*
Charles M. Borduin, *University of Missouri*
Robert F. Bornstein, *Gettysburg College*
Kevin Byrd, *University of Nebraska at Kearney*
Julie Deisinger, *Saint Xavier University*
Peter A. DiNardo, *State University of New York, Oneonta*
Jean E. Dumas, *Purdue University*
Claudia Evarts-Kittock, *Cambridge Community College (MN)*
Marc D. Feldman, MD
Diane Finley, *Prince Georges Community College*
Michael Friedman, *Rutgers University*
Howard Garb, *V. A. Medical Center, Pittsburgh*
Morton G. Harmatz, *University of Massachusetts, Amherst*
Richard G. Heimberg, *Temple University*
R. J. Huber, *Meredith College*
Michael Ichiyama, *University of San Diego*
Rick E. Ingram, *Southern Methodist University*
Kenneth Jackson, *Saint Xavier University*
Connie Kasari, *University of California, Los Angeles*
Christopher A. Kearney, *University of Nevada, Las Vegas*
Carolin Keutzer, *University of Oregon*
Kent Kiehl, *Yale University*
Herbert Krauss, *Hunter College*
Patricia Levy, *University of Southern Colorado—Pueblo*
Joseph LoPiccolo, *University of Missouri—Columbia*
Arthur Lyons, *Moravian University*
David M. McCord, *Western Carolina University*
Benay A. McCue, *Kankakee Community College*
Lee M. Marcus, *University of North Carolina, Chapel Hill*
Eleanor Midkiff, *Palomar College*
Joni L. Mihura, *University of Toledo*
Robert L. Moore, *Marshalltown Community College (IA)*
Peter E. Nathan, *University of Iowa*
Michael T. Nietzel, *University of Kentucky*
Maribeth Palmer-King, *Broome Community College*
Sohee Park, *Vanderbilt University*
Thomas Pruzinsky, *Quinnipiac College*
Cecil R. Reynolds, *Texas A & M University*
Barry Rosenfeld, *Fordham University*
Randall T. Salekin, *University of Alabama*
Philip Schatz, *Saint Joseph's University*
Brad Schmidt, *Ohio State University*
Wendy Silverman, *Florida International University*
Jefferson A. Singer, *Connecticut College*
Donald S. Strassberg, *University of Utah*
Bryce Sullivan, *Southern Illinois University at Edwardsville*
Samuel M. Turner, *University of Maryland, College Park*
Erik Willcutt, *University of Colorado—Boulder*

We also want to thank Torrey Creed for updating the *DSM* content to accurately reflect *DSM-IV-TR.*, as well as the staff of McGraw-Hill who helped to produce this edition.

Lauren B. Alloy
John H. Riskind
Margaret J. Manos

CHAPTER

1

Abnormal Behavior and Society

Defining Abnormal Behavior

Relating Abnormal Behavior to Groups

Explaining Abnormal Behavior

Treating Abnormal Behavior

Preventing Abnormal Behavior

Conceptions of Abnormal Behavior: A Short History

Ancient Societies: Deviance and the Supernatural

The Greeks and the Rise of Science

The Middle Ages and the Renaissance: Natural and Supernatural

The Eighteenth Century and After: The Asylums

The Rise of the Prevention Movement

The Rise of Managed Behavioral Health Care

The Foundations of Modern Abnormal Psychology

Non-Western Approaches to Abnormal Behavior

A Multiperspective Approach

Abnormal Psychology: Historical Perspectives

Before we can begin a study of abnormal psychology, we need to think about what kind of behavior deserves to be called "abnormal." Consider the following examples:

- A woman becomes seriously depressed after her husband's death. She has difficulty sleeping and loses her appetite. Does she have a psychological disorder, or is this just a case of normal grieving?
- A young man tries to force his date to have sexual intercourse, even though she says no and resists him physically. Is this evidence of psychological disturbance, or is it just a crime?
- A man will not use airplanes for long-distance travel. He insists that his family take trains on vacations. Should we call this abnormal or just unusual and inconvenient?
- A young woman occasionally indulges in binge eating, after which she forces herself to vomit. Does she have a psychological disorder, or is she just responding to the society's unreasonable standards for body weight?
- A teenaged girl in Africa makes cuts in her arms and face in order to produce decorative scars. Is this pathological self-mutilation, or is it a normal practice of the girl's culture?

Abnormal Behavior and Society

Defining Abnormal Behavior

When we ask how a society defines psychological abnormality, we are asking, first, where that society draws the line between acceptable and unacceptable behavior and, second, which unacceptable behaviors the society views as evidence of "disorder" rather than simply as undesirable characteristics. The most common standard for answering these questions is the society's norms.

Norm Violation Every human group lives by a set of **norms**—rules that tell us what it is "right" and "wrong" to do and when, where, and with whom. Such rules circumscribe every aspect of our existence. They are taken for granted by people within a culture, but they can differ widely between cultures.

Consider, for example, a study of problem behavior among schoolchildren in Thailand and the United States. Because of the cultural norms of humility, obedience, and respect in Thailand, Thai teachers set a lower threshold than American teachers for identifying problem children in their classrooms. As a consequence, Thai teachers describe Thai children as showing problem behavior (conduct problems, inattention, etc.) at a higher rate than American teachers describe American children showing these behaviors. And yet, objective observers rating the same children, in the same classes, on the same problem items, report just the opposite result. According to Weisz, Chaiyasit, Weiss, et al. (1995),

> [American and Thai] teachers . . . reported levels of problem behavior that were twice as high for Thai children as for their American age-mates. By contrast, direct observations in the present study showed the reverse pattern: Twice as much problem behavior among American children as among Thai children, a difference so large that it accounted for 43% of the variance in problem scores.

Thus, Thai children who violate cultural norms even a little bit are seen as problematic or abnormal, even though the same behavior is judged as normal by American standards.

The second and third examples at the beginning of this chapter involve norm violation. In our culture, men are not supposed to force women to have sex, and we expect people traveling long distances to take planes. The last example involves conformity to the norms of an African culture, but if someone in the United States were to engage in this behavior, it would probably be viewed as norm violation.

From culture to culture, definitions of normal and abnormal behavior vary. While this Kikuyu woman's dress is traditional in Kenya, a woman dressed in this fashion in the United States might be considered to be violating societal norms.

In small, highly integrated cultures, disagreement over norms is rare. In a large, complex society, on the other hand, there may be serious conflicts over norms. For example, the gay liberation movement can be conceptualized as the effort of one group to persuade the society as a whole to adjust its norms so that homosexuality will fall inside rather than outside the limits of acceptability.

Because norms are so variable, norm violation may seem a weak basis for judging mental health. It can also seem an oppressive standard, one that enthrones conformity as the ideal pattern of behavior. Nevertheless, norms remain a very important criterion for defining abnormality. Though they may be relative, they are so deeply ingrained that they seem absolute; therefore, anyone who violates them seems abnormal.

Norms, however, are not the only standard for defining abnormal behavior. Other criteria are statistical rarity, personal discomfort, and maladaptive behavior.

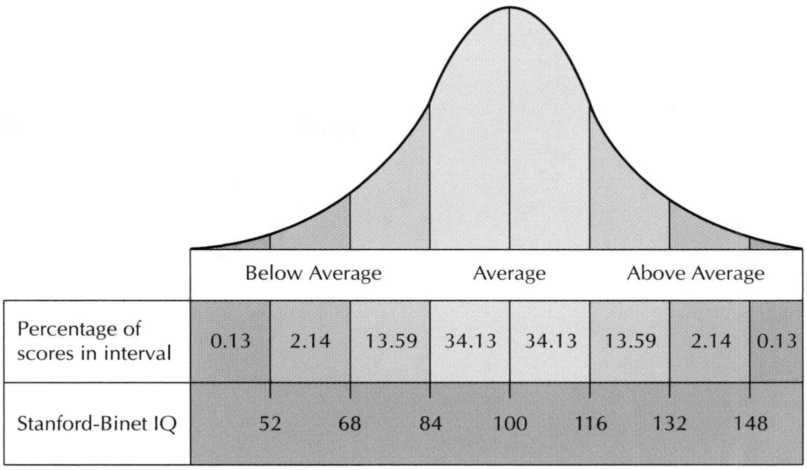

FIGURE 1.1 The distribution of IQ scores in the United States. More than 68 percent of the population scores between 84 and 116 points on the Stanford-Binet IQ test. Using the statistical approach to abnormality, diagnosticians designate as mentally retarded those falling below approximately 68 points. As the figure indicates, this group is statistically rare, representing only about 2 percent of the population.

Statistical Rarity From a statistical point of view, abnormality is any substantial deviation from a statistically calculated average. Those who fall within the "golden mean"—those who do what most other people do—are normal, while those whose behavior differs from that of the majority are abnormal. This criterion is used in some evaluations of psychological abnormality. The diagnosis of mental retardation, for instance, is based in large part on statistical accounting. Those whose tested intelligence falls below an average range for the population, and who also have problems coping with life, are labeled "mentally retarded" (see Figure 1.1).

The statistical-rarity approach makes defining abnormality a simple task. One has only to measure a person's performance against the average performance. If it falls outside the average range, it is abnormal. There are obvious difficulties with this approach, however. As we saw earlier, the norm-violation approach can be criticized for exalting the shifting values of social groups, yet the major weakness of the statistical-rarity approach is that it has *no* values—it makes no distinction between desirable and undesirable rarities. Such a point of view is potentially dangerous. For example, not only mentally retarded people but also geniuses—and particularly geniuses with new ideas—might be considered candidates for psychological treatment.

Personal Discomfort Another criterion for defining abnormality is personal discomfort: If people are content with their lives, then they are of no concern to the mental health establishment. If, on the other hand, people are distressed over their thoughts or behavior—as the grieving widow mentioned at the beginning of this chapter might be—then they require treatment.

This is a more liberal approach than the two we just discussed, in that it makes people the judges of their own normality, rather than subjecting them to the judgment of the society or diagnostician. And this is the approach that is probably the most widely used in the case of the less severe psychological disorders. Most people in psychotherapy are there not because anyone has declared their behavior abnormal but because they themselves are unhappy.

Reasonable as it may be in such cases, the personal-discomfort criterion has an obvious weakness in that it gives us no standard for evaluating the behavior itself. This is especially problematic in the case of behaviors that cause harm. Is teenage drug addiction to be classified as abnormal only if the teenager is unhappy with the addiction? Furthermore, even if a behavior pattern is not harmful, it may still seem to require psychological attention. People who believe that their brains are receiving messages from outer space may inflict no pain on others, yet most mental health professionals would consider them in need of treatment.

Maladaptive Behavior A fourth criterion for defining a behavior as abnormal is whether it is maladaptive. Here the question is whether a person, given that behavior pattern, is able to meet the demands of his or her life—hold down a job, deal with friends and family, pay the bills on time, and the like. If not, the pattern is abnormal. This standard overlaps somewhat with that of norm violation. After all, many norms are rules for adapting our behavior to our society's requirements. (To arrive for work drunk is to violate a norm; it is also maladaptive, in that it may get you fired.) At the same time, the maladaptiveness standard is unique in that it concentrates on the practical matter of getting through life successfully. If the man with the fear of flying has a job that requires long-distance travel, his behavior (avoiding air travel) could be considered maladaptive.

Whether a behavior is maladaptive is one of the criteria for defining abnormality. Many people, like those pictured here, gamble occasionally for fun. However, if someone's gambling leads to unmanageable debt and neglect of family and friends, it could be viewed as maladaptive.

This practicality makes the maladaptiveness standard a useful one. Also, many professionals favor the maladaptiveness standard for its elasticity: Because it focuses on behavior *relative to life circumstances,* it can accommodate many different styles of living. But, as with the personal-discomfort criterion, this liberalism is purchased at the cost of values. Are there not certain circumstances to which people should *not* adapt? Of course, any responsible professional using the maladaptiveness standard would also assess the situation to which the person is failing to adapt. If a child whose parents leave her alone in the house at night is brought to a therapist with sleeping problems, the therapist is likely to direct treatment at the parents rather than at the child. Nevertheless, the maladaptiveness standard, like the norm-violation standard, raises the possibility of bias in favor of "fitting in."

A Combined Standard The questions raised by these criteria for defining abnormality can be summarized as one question: Should our standard be *facts,* such as statistical rarity or a clearly dysfunctional behavior (e.g., failure to eat), or should it be *values,* such as adaptation or adherence to norms? Many professionals feel that the question cannot be decided one way or the other but that the definition of *mental disorder* must rest on both facts and values. Jerome Wakefield (1999), for example, has proposed that mental disorder

> means *harmful dysfunction,* where dysfunctions are failures of internal mechanisms to perform naturally selected functions. The harmful dysfunction (HD) analysis rejects both the view that disorder is just a value concept referring to undesirable or harmful conditions and the view that disorder is purely a scientific concept. Rather, the HD analysis proposes that a disorder attribution requires both a scientific judgment that there exists a failure of designed function and a value judgment that the design failure harms the individual. (p. 374)

People diagnosed as having schizophrenia, for example, often cannot think or speak coherently. To use Wakefield's terms, their "internal mechanisms" are failing to perform "their naturally selected functions." And these disabilities in turn harm the individual—for instance, their ability to hold down a job or raise children. As we shall see, the current edition of the *Diagnostic and Statistical Manual of Mental Disorders,* the American Psychiatric Association's guidebook to identifying mental disorders, also rests on a combined standard of facts and values.

However much dispute surrounds the definition of abnormal behavior, it should be kept in mind that most societies identify the same *categories* of behavior as indicative of mental disorder. As Maher and Maher (1985) point out, there are four basic categories:

1. Behavior that is harmful to the self or that is harmful to others without serving the interests of the self
2. Poor reality contact—for example, beliefs that most people do not hold or sensory perceptions of things that most people do not perceive
3. Emotional reactions inappropriate to the person's situation
4. Erratic behavior—that is, behavior that shifts unpredictably

Relating Abnormal Behavior to Groups

The process of defining abnormality becomes more complex when we factor in differences among groups. Even in one small neighborhood—in Los Angeles,

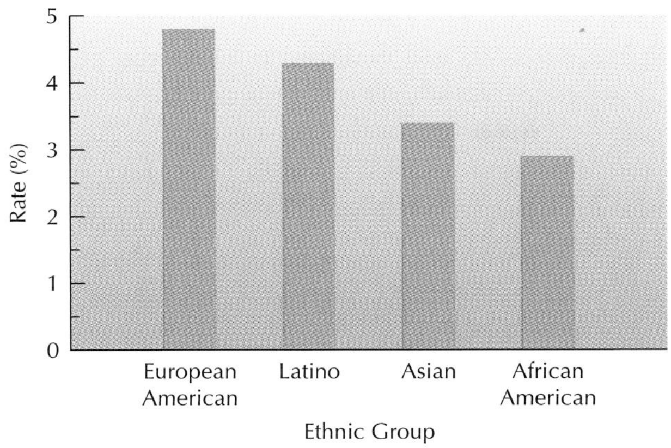

Source: Data from Zhang, A.V. and Snowden, L.R. (1999). Ethnic characteristics of mental disorders in five U.S. communities. *Cult. Diversity & Ethnic Minority Psych, 5, 134–46.*

FIGURE 1.2 Lifetime prevalence rates per 100 for major depression in the U.S. by ethnic group.

say—psychological disturbance affects the men and the women, the teenagers and the old people, the Korean Americans, the African Americans, and the European Americans in different ways. First, as revealed by epidemiology (to be discussed in Chapter 3), the study of the distribution of disorders within populations, various groups are at greater and lesser risk for specific disorders. Second, groups differ in how they experience and express psychological disorders. Finally, because groups vary in their norms, behavior that seems unremarkable to one group may appear bizarre to another, and this can affect diagnosis, the process by which abnormal behavior is identified and classified.

In the chapters that deal with specific disorders, we will discuss these matters under the heading "Groups at Risk." As you will see, there are many kinds of groups—defined by gender, age, cultural and ethnic origin, social class, religion, place of residence (urban or rural), and other factors—that are differently affected. For the moment, we will focus on groups defined by ethnicity and gender.

Cultural and Ethnic Group Differences Depression offers a good illustration of the fact that psychological disorders strike different cultures at different rates. In the United States, the lifetime prevalence rate for major depression is more than four times the rate in Taiwanese villages. In turn, the rate in New Zealand is almost triple the U.S. rate (Kaelber, Moul, & Farmer, 1995). Within a society, as well, risk varies according to ethnic origin. Look at Figure 1.2. In the United States, African Americans show significantly lower rates of major depression than European Americans or Latinos (Zhang & Snowden, 1999).

Different cultural groups also have their own ways of experiencing and managing psychological distress (Rogler, 1999). Richard Castillo, in his book *Culture and Mental Illness,* offers this case of an American-style depression:

> During his medical training, Bill experienced a four-month depression following the death of his father. He saw a psychiatrist, was put on antidepressant medication, and recovered. He graduated from medical school with honors, married, and soon became a successful pediatrician. Then, when he was 35, his wife was diagnosed with liver cancer. Watching her die, and wondering how he would raise their two daughters (aged 2 and 4) without her, he again succumbed to depression and had to be hospitalized for a month. Later he remarried and was happy for a while, until his new wife demanded an "open marriage." A divorce followed, but his ex-wife went on living in the same town as Bill. One night, after seeing her with another man at a restaurant, Bill got drunk, drove to her apartment, and banged on the door, demanding to speak to her. She called the police, and he was arrested. This scandal plunged him into another depression. He was hospitalized and given drugs and electroshock treatment. Upon his release, he was informed that the state medical board had decided to suspend his license because of his mental illness. When he appealed the board's decision, the story was picked up by the local newspapers and television, so that all his personal troubles were broadcast to the community. Bill won his appeal, but, two weeks later, at age 45, he committed suicide. (Adapted from Castillo, 1997a, pp. 25–26.)

By way of contrast, Castillo tells the story of a man he interviewed in India, a clothing merchant named Mr. Sinha. Mr. Sinha had a disorder that in India is known as "dhat syndrome" and that is said to be caused by excessive loss of semen. Its symptoms are fatigue, body aches, sadness, anxiety, loss of appetite, insomnia, and suicidal feelings. That pattern indicates what we in the West call major depression. But Mr. Sinha, like other Indians, called it dhat syndrome, and he believed it was due to his having masturbated too much as a teenager. He explained this to Castillo:

> During my high school days I was—well—I will put all the facts very open before you. I was in the acute habit of masturbation. . . . All the time I used to be indulged in sexual feelings—thinking about that. Always, you can say, daydreaming—doing masturbation. *Extremely.* So all this made me very weak, much more weak mentally than physically. And I connect the causes of the mental illness with that. (Castillo, 1997a, p. 29)

In Bill and Mr. Sinha, both of whom probably had the same disorder, we can see how culture shapes psychological disturbance. To begin with, the two men had different subjective experiences of their symptoms. Bill, as an American and a doctor, saw his disorder as biologically based. Mr. Sinha, as an Indian, viewed his illness as a moral and religious problem. The two men also responded differently. Every culture has what is called its "idiom of distress," the pattern of behavior by which people in that culture signify that they are ill. Bill, using the American idiom, went to a medical doctor to get medical treatments: drugs and shock therapy. Mr. Sinha went to a Hindu religious healer, and he tried to avoid having sex with his wife, though he often slipped and felt guilty about this. Interestingly, neither treatment succeeded.

Culture impinges on abnormal psychology also in that the norms of different cultures can produce behavior that, while appropriate for people of that culture, may seem pathological to people of other cultures. If Mr. Sinha had emigrated to the United States and had tried to explain the sexual cause of his disorder to an American psychiatrist, the psychiatrist might have decided that this man was suffering from delusions (irrational beliefs) and, therefore, he was not just depressed but psychotic, or very drastically impaired. Likewise, many people from non–European American cultures report perceptual experiences such as seeing the Virgin Mary or hearing the voice of God. An American diagnostician may view these reports as evidence of hallucinations (false sensory perceptions)—again, a symptom of psychosis. Meanwhile, for the person in question, such perceptions are a normal part of religious experience (American Psychiatric Association, 2000). Norm clashes of this kind have been a persistent problem in the psychological treatment of immigrant populations. The *Diagnostic and Statistical Manual of Mental Disorders* now specifically requires that mental health professionals take the patient's cultural background into account before deciding which psychological disorder, if any, he or she has. (See the box on page 7.)

Gender Differences Gender, like culture, affects the expression of psychological disorders. Depressed men are more likely to be withdrawn; depressed women are more likely to be dependent. Gender also affects susceptibility to a disorder. Depression, eating disorders, and anxiety disorders are more common in women; substance abuse, antisocial behavior, and paranoia are more common in men (Kohn, Dohrenwend, & Mirotznik, 1998). What accounts for these gender differences in rates of specific disorders remains to be answered. Are these differences due to biological or sociocultural factors or a combination of the two? We will consider some of the possible causes of gender differences in the chapters on specific disorders.

Explaining Abnormal Behavior

Since antiquity, people have developed theories as to the causes of abnormal behavior. These theories have a common base in that they are all naturalistic; that is, they seek to account for abnormal behavior in terms of natural events—disturbances in the body or disturbances in human relationships. Beyond this, however, they differ greatly. Because they will figure importantly in the later chapters of this book, it is worth examining them briefly at this point.

The Medical Model According to what is loosely called the **medical model** (or *disease model*), abnormal behavior is comparable to disease: Each kind of abnormal behavior, like each disease, has specific *causes* and a specific *set of symptoms*. In its strictest sense, the medical model also implies that the abnormal behavior is **biogenic**—that is, it results from a malfunction within the body. However, even those who do not think that all abnormal behavior is biologically based are still thinking in medical terms when they speak of overt "symptoms" and underlying causes.

Biogenic theories of abnormal behavior have been with us since ancient times. In the Middle Ages and the Renaissance, biogenic theories coexisted with supernatural theory, the belief that abnormal behavior was caused by God or, more often, the devil. But, in the eighteenth and early nineteenth centuries, religious explanations were gradually eclipsed by biological explanations. This newly dominant medical approach was soon rewarded by a series of important breakthroughs. Several previously unexplained behavior patterns were found to result from brain pathologies—infection, poisoning, and the like. Such discoveries brought immense prestige to the biogenic theory of abnormal behavior. Medicine, it was assumed, would ultimately conquer madness. On this assumption, madness was increasingly turned over to the medical profession.

There remained many patterns of abnormal behavior—indeed, the majority—for which no medical cause had been discovered, yet, because researchers were confident that such causes would eventually be found and because abnormal behavior was by then the province of medicine, these patterns were treated *as if* they were biologically based. In other words, they were treated according to a medical "model." (In scientific terms, a *model* is an analogy.) This

Focus On... Culture-Bound Syndromes

Although many types of psychological disorders occur across cultures, a number of syndromes appear to be unique to certain cultures and societies. These culture-bound syndromes often entail dramatic symptoms and occur within a brief time period. Although these syndromes may seem bizarre to someone from a different culture, they are clearly recognized within their culture as the troubled reactions of people in distress, who need the help of others (Littlewood & Lipsedge, 1986; Rogler, 1999).

Culture-bound syndromes occur throughout the world. Indeed, the fourth edition of the *Diagnostic and Statistical Manual of Mental Disorders (DSM-IV-TR)* recognizes the need to consider non–European American syndromes when evaluating the behavior of people from other cultures. Some examples of these syndromes, as recognized in *DSM-IV-TR* (American Psychiatric Association, 2000), include the following:

- *Amok:* A predominantly male reaction characterized by brooding and sudden outbursts of aggressive or violent behavior. The episode often seems to be a reaction to an insult or a slight and is accompanied by feelings of persecution. It is often followed by withdrawal and fatigue. The syndrome is found in people from Southeast Asia and the Caribbean and in some Native American cultures (e.g., the Navajo).
- *Koro:* A sudden and intense fear that sex organs (the penis or nipples) will recede into the body and cause death. It is reported in South and East Asia, as well as in China. There have been reports of local epidemics of the syndrome.
- *Nervios:* A very broad expression of distress that includes headaches, upset stomach, nervousness, dizziness, and inability to sleep. It is found in many cultures but is common in Latino communities. It tends to persist over time following periods of stress.
- *Pibloktoq:* An attacklike syndrome that can last up to 30 minutes, involving behavior such as tearing off clothing, shouting, becoming violent, and fleeing. It is often followed by convulsive seizures and a period of coma. Upon recovery, the afflicted individual seldom recalls the episode. The syndrome is primarily found in Eskimo communities.
- *Susto:* A fright reaction that can last for days or years, often occurring in Latin America and in Latino communities, although variations of the syndrome have been observed in many other cultures. The reaction is often attributed to the soul leaving the body (*susto* means soul-less), with severe consequences for the person. In some cases, death is attributed to the condition. Many of the symptoms resemble major depressive disorders.

These examples illustrate some forms of psychopathology that are unusual in European American culture. However, it is important to recognize that some forms of illness are also unique to our experience. Many of them are also more likely to affect only one gender. The following are examples of these culture-bound syndromes (Castillo, 1997a; Littlewood & Lipsedge, 1986):

- *Agoraphobia:* An intense anxiety reaction upon leaving the home or entering a public space that is experienced primarily by women. It can be extremely debilitating in that the person is unable to carry on normal activities outside the home.
- *Anorexia nervosa:* A syndrome of intense dieting to achieve weight loss, primarily displayed by adolescent girls concerned about their physical appearance. First noticed in the 1800s in Europe, the syndrome has reached epidemic proportions in many industrialized countries.
- *Shoplifting:* A primarily female syndrome of stealing goods from stores even though the person can afford to purchase them. It is seen as an obvious attempt to gain attention.
- *Flashing:* A primarily male syndrome of brief but dramatic display (exhibitionism) of the naked body to a female onlooker.

meant not only that abnormal behavior was best handled by physicians, in hospitals, and by means of medical treatments such as drugs but also that the entire problem of deviant behavior should be conceptualized in medical terms such as *symptom, syndrome, pathology, mental illness, patient, diagnosis, therapy, treatment,* and *cure* (Price, 1978). Although this book is not based on the medical model, such terms will occur here repeatedly. They are part of the language of abnormal psychology.

Not everyone accepted the medical model, however. Indeed, it was sharply criticized. As many psychological writers pointed out, biological causes had *not* been found for most patterns of abnormal behavior; therefore, it was wrong to think of such patterns as illnesses. Perhaps the most prominent critic of the medical model was American psychiatrist Thomas Szasz. In a book called *The Myth of Mental Illness* (1961), Szasz claimed that most of what the medical model called mental illnesses were not illnesses at all but, rather, "problems in living," expressed as violations of moral, legal, and social norms. To label these deviations "sick" was, according to Szasz, not only a falsification of the conflict between the person and the society but also a dangerous sanctification of the society's norms. As others showed, the "sick" label also deprives people of responsibility for their behavior (they can't help it—they're sick) and relegates them to a passive role that makes it hard for them to return to normal behavior. In other words, the medical model can foster serious abuses.

Many psychological professionals now take a neutral position as to the ultimate causes of abnormal behavior. But biological research in abnormal psychology

During the Middle Ages and the Renaissance, abnormal behavior was often believed to be caused by the devil. In this late-fifteenth-century painting, St. Catherine of Siena is casting the devil out of a possessed woman. It can be seen as a tiny imp flying out of the woman's mouth.

has made great strides in the past three decades, and as a result biogenic theories are viewed respectfully today.

In the chapters that follow, we will discuss some of this research, which we have grouped together as the **neuroscience perspective** within abnormal psychology. Like the medical model, the neuroscience perspective focuses on the biological or neurological components of abnormal behavior. Unlike the medical model, however, it does not suggest that all or even most abnormal behavior patterns are merely symptoms of biological abnormalities, or even that such patterns are best treated in a medical setting. Rather, the neuroscience perspective simply concentrates on the neurological aspects of a disorder in an effort to understand its characteristics. Consider sadness, for example. Sadness can be studied at many different levels of analysis. One can analyze the thoughts that accompany it, and that is what cognitive psychologists do (see Chapter 4). Another approach is to use brain imaging techniques to study the changes in brain cell activity that accompany reported states of sadness, and that is what neuroscience researchers do. Both the thoughts and the brain changes are part of sadness and may, at various levels, cause it. Neuroscience researchers do not claim that biological changes are the root cause, only that they constitute an important level of analysis. The neuroscience perspective has thus retained the medical model's biological focus without expanding it into an all-embracing medical approach to abnormal behavior.

Psychological Approaches Complementing the medical model are the psychological theories of abnormal behavior. Such theories attribute disturbed behavior patterns not to biological malfunction but to psychological processes resulting from the person's interaction with the environment. Thus, disturbed behavior may be explained by negligent upbringing, by traumatic experiences, by inaccurate social perceptions, or by too much stress.

There are dozens of competing psychological theories of abnormal behavior. Still, it is possible to identify a few fairly unified *perspectives*—broad schools of thought based on the same fundamental assumptions. In this book, we will refer repeatedly to the following psychological perspectives:

1. *The psychodynamic perspective,* which assumes that abnormal behavior issues from unconscious psychological conflicts originating in childhood
2. *The behavioral perspective,* which holds that a primary cause of abnormal behavior is inappropriate learning, whereby maladaptive behaviors are rewarded and adaptive behaviors are not rewarded
3. *The cognitive perspective,* which maintains that abnormal behavior is an outgrowth of maladaptive ways of perceiving and thinking about oneself and the environment
4. *The interpersonal perspective,* which views abnormal behavior as the product of disordered relationships
5. *The sociocultural perspective,* which views abnormal behavior as the product of broad social and cultural forces. It also examines the biases that can influence diagnosis

In addition to considering these psychological viewpoints, we will pay close attention to the neuroscience approach:

6. *The neuroscience perspective,* which analyzes abnormal behavior in terms of its neurochemical, neuroanatomical, and neurohormonal components

Each of these perspectives has made substantial contributions to the study of abnormal psychology, and each has shortcomings as a comprehensive approach to human behavior. The six perspectives will be discussed in detail in Chapters 4, 5, and 6. In addition, the perspectives will be featured as explanations of abnormal behavior and approaches to treatment in the chapters on specific disorders. There, they will be discussed in proportion to their usefulness in understanding each group of disorders.

Another perspective that commanded much attention for many decades is the humanistic-existential perspective—not a single perspective but a collection of the belief systems of well-known thinkers as diverse as Carl Rogers, Abraham Maslow, Rollo May, Viktor Frankl, and R. D. Laing. Although some key premises of both the humanists and the existentialists overlap principles of the aforementioned psychological theories, the humanistic and existential schools are not primarily based on the methods of natural science; therefore, we will only discuss them briefly in this book.

Treating Abnormal Behavior

However they explain abnormal behavior, most societies feel that something must be *done* about it. How do human groups arrive at a way of treating the deviant in their midst?

This depends on many factors. One is the nature of the society. In a small, traditional community, deviant persons are likely to remain at home. Typically, they are prayed over, relieved of responsibilities, and treated with mixed kindness and ridicule. A large, technological society, on the other hand, tends to isolate deviants so as to prevent them from disrupting the functioning of the family and the community.

A second factor influencing the society's treatment of abnormal behavior is its explanation of such behavior. If the deviant is seen as possessed by evil spirits, then the logical treatment is to draw out such spirits—by means of prayer, potions, or whatever. If, in keeping with the medical model, abnormal behavior is assumed to be the result of neurological pathology, then it is handled by medical treatments: drugs, hospitalization, perhaps even surgery. If abnormal behavior is interpreted according to psychological theories, it is treated via psychological therapies. As we have seen, many psychological professionals today feel that, whatever its ultimate cause—if, indeed, ultimate causes can be found—abnormal behavior has psychological *and* neurological components. Accordingly, in recent years there has been increased interest in *multimodal treatments,* the combining of two or more kinds of therapy—for example, "talk" psychotherapy and drugs. In the box on page 10, we describe the kinds of therapists who provide these treatments.

Preventing Abnormal Behavior

Prevention, the process of keeping disorders from beginning in the first place, became popular within the mental health professions in the 1960s as clinical psychologists began to understand how social, economic, and political circumstances shape mental health. Prevention goals might focus on changing the environment, the family, or the individual and could include such programs as setting up an after-school program for teenagers in an underserved community, assisting an entire family by enrolling the parents in a class on parenting techniques, or teaching an individual coping skills for dealing with stress.

Today, as it becomes apparent that many disorders are almost impossible to cure after onset, advocates continue to explore prevention alternatives. Prevention has become a priority for research and treatment in government, as manifested in the funding of large-scale, community-based, public health projects by the National Institutes of Health, Mental Health, Alcohol Abuse and Alcoholism, Drug Abuse, and Child Health and Human Development.

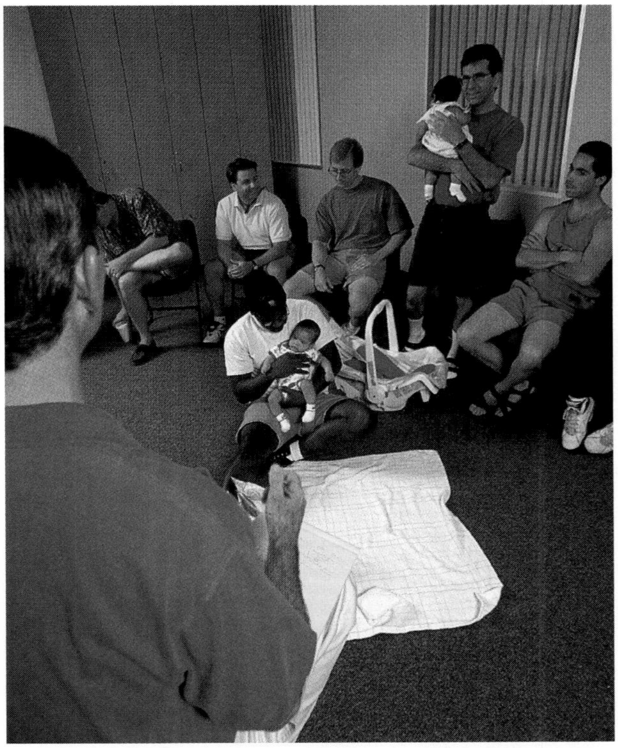

Many mental health professionals believe that offering classes that teach better parenting techniques, like the one pictured here, is one way to prevent the onset of disorders.

Focus On... The Mental Health Professions

Psychotherapy is a relatively formal relationship between a trained professional and a person (or family) who seeks help with psychological problems.

There are four main types of mental health professionals. A **psychiatrist** is an M.D. who specializes in diagnosing and treating mental disorders. Because of their medical degree, psychiatrists can also prescribe psychoactive drugs, medications that can improve the functioning of people with mental disorders. Some psychiatrists, called psychopharmacologists, specialize in medical treatments. A **clinical psychologist** is a Ph.D. or Psy.D. who has spent four to six years in graduate school and has completed a one-year clinical internship. Clinical psychology programs train people to do diagnosis, therapy, and research. A **psychiatric social worker** has earned an M.S.W. (master of social work), with special training in psychological counseling. A **psychoanalyst** has had postgraduate training at a psychoanalytic institute and has undergone psychoanalysis. Most psychoanalysts are psychiatrists, but other mental health professionals may undertake this training.

There are as many as 1,000 distinct forms of psychotherapy. Which approach a therapist takes depends on his or her theoretical perspective, though there are growing trends toward eclecticism, or combining techniques from different schools, and toward combining medication with therapy sessions.

What Is Prevention? Psychologists distinguish between primary and secondary prevention. Kaplan (2000) includes a third type of prevention, called tertiary prevention, but it simply involves doing therapy once a disorder has developed.

Primary prevention is concerned with preventing mental disorders from developing in the first place by creating environments that are conducive to mental health, by making individuals strong enough to avoid the factors that would put them at risk for mental illness, and by teaching people skills that aid them in coping with risk factors, such as stress. Primary prevention is therefore designed to have an impact on the entire population. For example, ensuring that every pregnant woman gets adequate prenatal and postnatal health care would probably have a major impact on depression, schizophrenia, and antisocial behavior, as we will see in Chapters 10, 11, and 14.

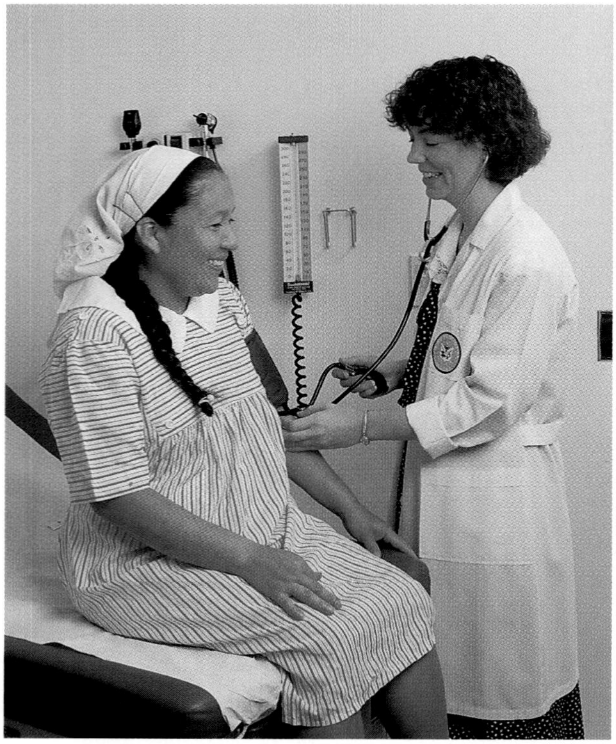

Ensuring that all pregnant women receive adequate prenatal and postnatal health care is one example of primary prevention.

Secondary prevention focuses on reducing the risk for a particular mental disorder in individuals who are most likely to develop that disorder. For example, adolescents with conduct disorders are at high risk for becoming antisocial adults, as we will see in Chapter 16 (Loeber & Farrington, 2000). A secondary prevention program would work to identify such adolescents and apply an intervention aimed at preventing antisocial personality disorder.

Prevention goals have broadened since the 1960s. Although the ideal is still preventing the onset of a particular disorder, other outcomes are often considered worthwhile from a public health perspective, such as decreasing the severity of a disorder or delaying its onset, as when prevention programs for suicidal adolescents delay the onset of depression until the twenties. These goals can have ramifications for mental health beyond the individual; for example, delaying the onset of depression in new mothers can make a difference in whether or not their children develop a vulnerability to depression.

In the past 30 years, prevention has also come to be viewed as part of a continuum with treatment. At one extreme, universal prevention, in which everyone benefits from the intervention, targets the entire population; an example would be high-quality prenatal care that is universally available to all socioeconomic classes. Selective preventive interventions are aimed at a subgroup whose risk for developing a particular disorder is higher than average, such as adolescents with conduct disorder. Further along the treatment continuum are indicated preventive or "early" interventions, as when aggressive young children are treated because they show early signs of conduct problems or because of a biological marker indicating a risk for a disorder.

The Art of Prevention Science Prevention science means both reducing risks (the goal of secondary prevention) and strengthening resilience (the goal of primary prevention programs). In theory, reducing the onset of mental disorders is more efficient and cost-effective than attempting to eliminate mental disorders once they appear. Even the most expensive prevention programs are far less costly to society than a lifetime of mental illness, which affects physical health, lowers work productivity, and creates human suffering that is virtually impossible to quantify. As researchers learn more about the factors that predict the onset of mental disorders, more programs can be developed for high-risk populations. These programs, implemented in the schools, homes, and communities of high-risk individuals, typically focus on early intervention. By identifying risk factors early in the lives of potential victims, such programs can focus on high-risk children and adolescents. In fact, prevention programs aimed at children and adolescents are the most lasting legacy of the prevention movement (Dulmus & Rapp-Paglicci, 2000). We will discuss specific work on prevention in the chapters that cover particular disorders.

Conceptions of Abnormal Behavior: A Short History

Changing Historical Views and Treatments of Abnormal Behavior

On the MindMAP CD-ROM that came with your text, the video "History of Mental Illness" explores the changing perceptions and treatments of abnormal behavior from ancient times into the twentieth century. Do you think people's perceptions will have changed much by the end of the twenty-first century? How?

Our modern approaches to treatment and prevention are not new. They are the result of centuries of trial and error. In this section, we will present a brief history of our ancestors' handling of abnormal behavior.

Ancient Societies: Deviance and the Supernatural

We know little about the treatment of deviant behavior in prehistoric and ancient societies. What we do know suggests that our early forebears regarded deviant behavior, like most other things they did not understand, as the product of remote or supernatural forces—the movements of the stars, the vengeance of God, the operation of evil spirits. This idea seems to have endured for many centuries. References to possession can be found in the ancient records of the Chinese, the Egyptians, the Hebrews, and the Greeks. In the New Testament, Jesus is reported to have drawn out devils from the possessed.

The cure for possession was to coax or force the evil spirits out of their victim—a practice called **exorcism.** Many exorcisms were confined to prayer, noisemaking, and the drinking of special potions. In more difficult cases, the possessed person might be submerged in water, whipped, or starved in order to make the body a less comfortable habitation for the devil. Not surprisingly, some people died in the course of exorcism. But most treatments were probably far less dramatic. For example, the person might simply be sent home to rest and given special mention in the community's prayers. Such remedies are common in small, traditional societies today, and they were probably common in ancient societies as well.

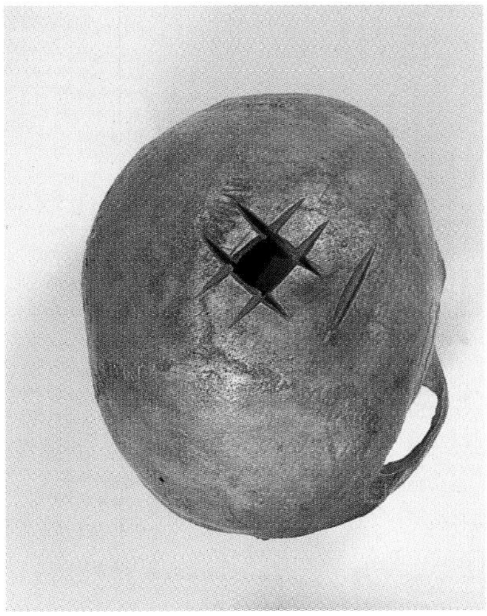

The hole in this prehistoric skull was surgically produced, possibly in an effort to curb abnormal behavior. This procedure is called trephination.

The Greeks and the Rise of Science

The evolution of a naturalistic approach to abnormal behavior began in ancient Greece and China. The earliest surviving evidence of this trend is found in the writings attributed to Greek physician Hippocrates (c. 460–c. 360 B.C.E.). In opposition to current supernatural theories, Hippocrates set about to prove that all illness, including mental illness, was due to natural causes. For example, in his treatise on epilepsy, known at the time as the "sacred disease," Hippocrates curtly observed: "If you cut open the head, you will find the brain humid, full of sweat and smelling badly. And in this way you may see that it is not a god which injured the body, but disease" (cited in Zilboorg & Henry, 1941, p. 44).

Hippocrates undertook a number of reforms. First, he set himself the novel task of actually observing cases of mental disturbance and of recording his observations as objectively as possible. Consequently, his writings are the first in Western scientific literature to contain empirical descriptions (descriptions based on observation) of mental disorders such as phobia and epilepsy.

Greek physician Hippocrates rejected the supernatural theories of abnormal behavior that were prevalent in his time. Asserting that mental illness was due to natural causes, he developed the influential biogenic theory of the four humors.

Second, Hippocrates developed several of the earliest biogenic theories of abnormal behavior. For example, he believed that many disorders were due to an imbalance among four **humors**, or vital fluids, in the body: phlegm, blood, black bile, and yellow bile. An excess of phlegm rendered people phlegmatic—indifferent and sluggish. An excess of blood gave rise to rapid shifts in mood. Too much black bile made people melancholic, and too much yellow bile made them choleric—irritable and aggressive. Primitive as this theory may seem, it foreshadowed today's biochemical research in abnormal psychology.

The Middle Ages and the Renaissance: Natural and Supernatural

In the second century C.E., Galen, another Greek physician who practiced in Rome, showed that the body's arteries contained blood—not air, as was commonly thought. This discovery led to the practice of bleeding the mentally disturbed, in the hope of restoring the proper balance among the humors of the body. (Bleeding persisted as a treatment for emotional and physical disorders into the nineteenth century.) But, with the fall of Rome in the fifth century, the study of mental illness, together with other branches of learning, shut down, not to be reborn until later, during the Middle Ages.

Medieval Theory and Treatment The Middle Ages were characterized by ardent religiosity. Insanity, like all other things, was thought to be controlled by supernatural forces, and many of the insane were handled accordingly. Some were taken to shrines, prayed over, and sprinkled with holy water. Others were starved and flogged, to harass the devil within.

Nevertheless, English legal records show that, when medieval officials examined deranged people, they often recorded natural, commonsense explanations for the derangement. One man, examined in 1291, was said to have lapsed into insanity after a "blow received on the head." The uncontrollable violence of another man, examined in 1366, was reportedly "induced by fear of his father" (Neugebauer, 1978). These are the kinds of causes that might be cited today.

Furthermore, whether insanity was attributed to natural or supernatural forces, it was often treated as a form of illness (Kemp, 1990). Windows of medieval churches show the saints curing the insane alongside the lame and the blind. Many of the insane were admitted to the same hospitals as other sufferers.

Politics, Religion, "Witchcraft," and the Treatment of Mental Illness in the Renaissance The Renaissance, stretching from the fifteenth to the seventeenth century, has long been regarded as a glorious chapter in the history of Western culture, yet it is during this period that occurred one of the ugliest episodes in European history: the witch hunts. Women (and a few men) whose behavior gave offense to church authorities were accused not just of being in league with the devil but of committing heinous acts—eating children, staging orgies, and the like. The charges soon spread, creating a climate of fear and hysteria, in which anyone who behaved strangely, or who behaved in a way that someone in power did not like, stood in danger of being executed for witchcraft. It is estimated that, from the middle of the fifteenth century to the end of the seventeenth, 100,000 people were executed as witches (Deutsch, 1949).

Some have argued (e.g., Spanos, 1994) that the witch hunts may have had little connection with the history of mental illness, as most of the accused were probably not mentally ill. In large communities, witch hunting apparently had less to do with bizarre behavior than with political and economic interests; that is, the trials were used to confiscate property and to eliminate political troublemakers. (Recall that Joan of Arc, who helped the French expel the English invaders in the early fifteenth century, was burned as a witch.) In smaller communities, however, the accused were often poor, old, socially marginal women or simply socially disreputable types—and some of the mentally ill no doubt fell into this group (Spanos, 1994).

The fact that the mentally ill suffered from the witch hunts is also clear from the writings of those who protested against the craze. In 1563, for example, German physician Johann Weyer, the first medical practitioner to develop a special interest in mental illness, published a treatise, declaring that those who were being burned as witches were actually mentally unbalanced and not responsible for their actions. Weyer was soon followed by an Englishman named Reginald Scot, who in 1584 published his *Discovery of Witchcraft,* a scholarly work pointing out, among other things, the evidence of mental illness in those being persecuted by the witch hunters.

It seems likely, then, that some of the "witches" were psychologically disturbed. At the same time, the evidence suggests that in the Renaissance most of the mentally ill were of little interest to the witch hunters. Instead, as in the Middle Ages, they were seen as sick people whose problems could be explained in natural terms (Kemp, 1985) and whose care, in any case, had to be seen to by the community. Some were apparently kept in almshouses (institutions for the poor), others in general hospitals. Indeed, London's Bethlem hospital, founded in 1247, was given over almost exclusively to the insane by the fifteenth century. It is also in the Renaissance that we see the first major efforts to institutionalize the practice of community care (Allderidge, 1979)—that is, supervision of the mentally ill within the community but outside the hospital. The "poor laws" of seventeenth-century England required that "lunaticks," along with the aged, the blind, and other unfortunates, be provided for by their local government or parish. Some patients were kept at home, while money for their maintenance was paid out of parish funds. Homeless patients might be boarded with families in the community. As we shall see, the practice of housing the psychologically disabled with willing families is being experimented with in the United States today.

The Eighteenth Century and After: The Asylums

The Early Asylums The practice of hospitalizing the psychologically disturbed is an old one. In Arab countries, general hospitals provided wards for the mentally ill as early as the eighth century (Mora, 1980). The first hospital exclusively for the insane opened in Spain in the early fifteenth century. This example was eventually followed in London, Paris, Vienna, Moscow, Philadelphia, and other major cities. More and more, the insane were removed to institutions.

Most of the early mental asylums opened with the best of intentions, but the conditions in which their patients lived were often terrible. London's Bethlem hospital, mentioned earlier, became so notorious for the misery within its walls that it gave rise to the word *bedlam,* meaning "uproar." A writer in the seventeenth century described Bethlem as follows:

> It seems strange that any should recover here, the cryings, screechings, roarings, brawlings, shaking of chains, swarings, frettings, chaffing, are so many, so hideous, so great, that they are more able to drive a man that hath his witts, rather out of them, than to help one that never had them, or hath lost them, to finde them againe. (Allderidge, 1985)

Historians have produced many chilling descriptions of the early mental hospitals (Foucault, 1965; Scull, 1993), often with the suggestion that these institutions did not aim to cure, but only to isolate and humiliate the insane. Other writers have taken a more balanced view. In a study of the archives of

Bethlem, for example, Allderidge (1985) has pointed out that the bedlam therein was almost certainly due to the difficulty of handling violent patients in the days before psychiatric medication. The hospital had rules against beating patients, and the archives show that some patients enjoyed privileges that would not be commonly found today in a public charity, which is what Bethlem was. Indictments of Bethlem, for example, often cite the case of James Norris, who was kept in chains there for nine years in the early nineteenth century. But the records on Norris show that he was an extremely violent patient who had attacked a number of attendants and fellow patients before the staff resorted to chaining him. The records mention, furthermore, that while chained Norris occupied himself mainly by reading books and newspapers and by playing with his pet cat. Obviously, though he was in chains, someone on the staff remembered that he was a human being, with human needs.

The Reform of the Asylums The first serious efforts to improve treatment in the large hospitals began in the late eighteenth century. The reforms were begun by Vincenzo Chiarugi, superintendent of an asylum called the Ospedale di Bonifazio in Florence and by Jean-Baptiste Pussin, who directed the "incurables" ward at La Bicêtre, a large hospital in Paris. Pussin, for example, forbade his staff to beat the patients—an innovation that caused a near revolt among the attendants. He also gave orders to unchain a group of patients who, having been declared "furious," had lain in shackles for years—in some cases, for decades. Without their chains, these patients could move about on the grounds, take the fresh air, and feel some sense of personal liberty. As Pussin had hoped, many of them became more manageable.

Pussin's reforms were extended by Philippe Pinel, who became chief physician of La Bicêtre's ward for the mentally ill in 1793. Pinel's position was that the mentally ill were simply ordinary human beings who had been deprived of their reason by severe personal problems. To treat them like animals was not only inhumane but also impeded recovery. Pinel replaced the dungeons in which the patients had been kept with airy, sunny rooms and did away with violent treatments such as bleeding and cupping (blistering the skin with small hot cups). He also spent long hours talking with the patients, listening to their problems, and giving them comfort and advice. He kept records of these conversations and began to develop a case history for each patient. This practice of recordkeeping, introduced by Pinel, was an extremely important innovation, for it allowed practitioners to chart the patterns that emerge in the course of various disorders—when and how the disorder first appears, which symptoms develop in which order, and so on. Knowledge of these patterns became the basis for classification of disorders, research into their causes, and treatment. After Pinel's retirement, his student and successor, Jean Esquirol, founded 10 new mental hospitals in various parts of France, all based on the humane treatment developed by Pussin and Pinel.

At the same time that Pussin and Pinel were working in Paris, a Quaker named William Tuke was attempting similar reforms in northern England. Convinced that the most therapeutic environment for the mentally ill would be a quiet and supportive religious setting, Tuke in 1796 moved a group of mental patients to a rural estate, which he called York Retreat. There they talked out their problems, worked, prayed, rested, and took walks in the countryside.

Though vigorously resisted by Pinel's and Tuke's contemporaries, these new techniques eventually

These woodcuts from 1875 show male patients (left) let out of their rooms to "take the air" in the corridor and female patients (right) eating a meal in Philadelphia's Blockley Hospital.

Philippe Pinel supervises the unchaining of inmates at La Salpêtrière, the hospital he directed after his work at La Bicêtre. The reforms of Pussin, Pinel, and Tuke led to the movement called moral therapy, which was widespread in the eighteenth and nineteenth centuries.

became widespread, under the name of **moral therapy.** Based on the idea that the mentally ill were simply ordinary people with extraordinary problems, moral therapy aimed at restoring their "morale" by providing an environment in which they could discuss their difficulties, live in peace, and do some useful work. Apparently, this approach was extremely successful. Records show that, during the first half of the nineteenth century, when moral therapy was the only treatment provided by mental hospitals in Europe and America, at least 70 percent of those hospitalized either improved or actually recovered (Bockoven, 1963).

The Reform Movement in America The leader in the development of the American mental health establishment was Benjamin Rush (1745–1813), known as the "father of American psychiatry." Rush advanced the cause of mental health by writing the first American treatise on mental illness, by organizing the first medical course in psychiatry, and by devoting his attention, as the foremost physician at Pennsylvania Hospital, exclusively to mental problems.

Today, some of Rush's thinking seems primitive: He believed that mental illness was due to an excess of blood in the vessels of the brain. To relieve the pressure in the blood vessels, he relied heavily on bleeding. He also had patients dropped suddenly into ice-cold baths or strapped into a device called the "tranquilizer." These procedures, however, were accompanied by a number of humane practices. Rush recommended that doctors regularly bring little presents, such as fruit or cake, to their patients. He also insisted that Pennsylvania Hospital hire kind and intelligent attendants—people who could read to patients, talk to them, and share in their activities. In sum, Rush guided American psychiatry in the direction of a humane therapy.

The task of extending these reforms fell to a Boston schoolteacher named Dorothea Dix (1802–1887). At the age of 40, Dix took a job teaching Sunday school in a prison. There she had her first exposure to the gruesome conditions suffered by the mentally ill. Later she went abroad, visiting York Retreat, as well as other moral therapy institutions, and became

Dorothea Dix worked to expose the maltreatment of the mentally ill and to establish mental hospitals devoted to their care.

convinced of the need to reform mental health care (Rosenblatt, 1984). Soon she was traveling across the country, examining the squalid jails and poorhouses in which the mentally ill were confined and lecturing state legislators on their duty to these people. Dix called for the mentally ill to be removed to separate, humane facilities geared to their special needs. Carrying her campaign across the United States and eventually to Canada and Scotland as well, she was responsible for the founding and funding of 32 mental hospitals.

Hospitalization and the Decline of Moral Therapy Dix's reforms had one unfortunate result that she could not have anticipated: They contributed to the decline of moral therapy (Foucault, 1965). As hospital after hospital opened, there were simply not enough advocates of moral therapy to staff them. Indeed, there were not enough staff of any kind, for, though the state governments were willing to build mental hospitals, they still did not consider mental health as important as physical health. This meant less money for mental hospitals, and less money meant fewer employees. At the same time, the patient populations of these institutions grew year by year. With many patients and few attendants, the hospitals could not provide the sort of tranquil atmosphere and individual care essential to moral therapy.

There were other reasons for the decline of moral therapy (Bockoven, 1963). To begin with, its first-generation advocates—people such as Pussin, Pinel, and Tuke—were not succeeded by an equally powerful second generation. Second, by the turn of the century, many of the indigent patients who filled the mental hospitals were Irish Catholic immigrants, against whom there was considerable prejudice. The Protestant establishment might be willing to pay for these patients' hospitalization but not for the luxury of moral therapy. Finally, the growth of the state mental hospital system occurred at the same time as the rise of the medical model. The early successes of the medical model convinced psychiatric professionals that their efforts should be directed toward biological treatments rather than toward the psychological attentions of moral therapy.

Thus, during the second half of the nineteenth century, moral therapy was increasingly replaced by custodial care. Throughout this period, communities showed less and less willingness to tolerate mentally ill people in their midst (Luchins, 1993). Therefore, many people whose behavior was merely eccentric, but not seriously disruptive, were sent off to the institutions. There they were no longer pressured to act normal, as they had been in the community. Meanwhile, all the effects of hospitalization—the social stigma, the damage to self-esteem, the loss of moorings in reality, the temptation of the "sick" role—pushed them toward permanent patient status. Recovery rates dropped (Bockoven, 1963; Dain, 1964). Care was custodial, not remedial.

This situation continued into the middle of the twentieth century, often with dreadful consequences, particularly in the area of patient control. In the 1940s and 1950s, for example, thousands of mental patients who were considered uncontrollable in one way or another were subjected to a crude form of brain surgery called **prefrontal lobotomy.** In this procedure, an instrument is inserted into the brain's frontal lobe, immediately behind the forehead, and rotated, thus destroying a substantial amount of brain tissue. Many people emerged from their lobotomies in a permanent vegetative state; others died (Redlich & Freedman, 1966). It was thus with considerable relief that mental health professionals greeted the introduction, in the 1950s, of the phenothiazines, a new class of drugs that was highly effective in calming the severely disturbed.

The Exodus from the Hospitals In the 1950s and 1960s, evidence of the damage that hospitalization did to patients was mounting fast (Goffman, 1961; Scheff, 1966). Around the same time came the phenothiazines, calming patients to the point where, it seemed, they could be released from the hospital. The state legislatures were willing; hospitalization was expensive. Thus began the **deinstitutionalization** movement. Starting in the late 1950s, hundreds of thousands of patients, some of whom had been in the hospital for 20 or 30 years, were given bottles of pills and discharged (Cohen, 2000). By the end of the twentieth century, the number of psychiatric patients in hospitals had dropped to a small fraction of what it had been in 1955 (see Figure 1.3).

Clearly, they still needed some sort of care, and so did new patients, if they were not going to be hospitalized. In 1963, Congress passed the Community Mental Health Centers Act, providing for the establishment, across the country, of mental health services that people could use without being uprooted from their normal lives. The new **community mental health centers** offered several kinds of care. One was **outpatient** (outside-the-hospital) psychological counseling. Between 1955 and 1975, the rate of outpatient counseling in the United States increased twelvefold (Kiesler, 1982a). Another service was **inpatient** (in-the-hospital) care, but modified. There were day hospital programs, in which patients stayed in the hospital only from nine to five, returning home at night; there were also night hospital programs, in which patients went to work or school during the day and then

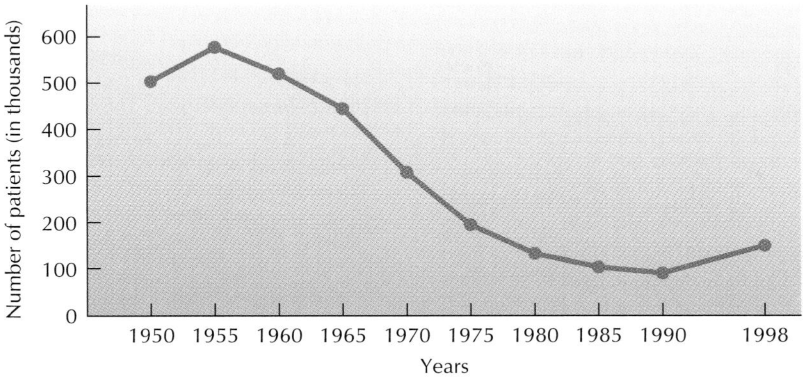

FIGURE 1.3 Since the late 1950s the number of patients in mental hospitals has dropped considerably. (U.S. Bureau of the Census, 2001)

came back to the hospital at night. Some community mental health centers also offered improved emergency services—for example, 24-hour storefronts where people in crisis could go to have a talk (and possibly a tranquilizer) and to make an appointment for outpatient counseling. Outside the community mental health centers, some patients were placed in halfway houses, or residences for people who, no longer requiring hospitalization, still needed help in readjusting to community life. In a halfway house, residents live together, talk out their problems, and relearn social skills.

Many of these community services are still in operation today, and some are excellent, but they are the rare ones. In 1981, a system of block grants to the states replaced the Community Mental Health Centers Act (see below), shifting the responsibility for funding to state legislatures. In most cases, the state legislatures have not provided sufficient funds for the community mental health centers to give mental patients the support they need. Some community services offer nothing more than custodial care under a new name. Many of the people returned to the community via deinstitutionalization are receiving no services at all. Of the million or so homeless people nationwide, about one fourth are estimated to have a serious mental illness and about one half to have a history of substance abuse (Dickey, 2000). By day, they walk the streets; by night, they sleep in doorways. Many might be better off in the hospital, with a clean bed. (See the box on page 18.)

Some do go back to the hospital. It is still true that the population of the state mental hospitals is low compared with pre-1960s figures, for patients are now discharged quickly. Indeed, the number of hospitalized mental patients in New York State has dropped from over 93,000 in 1955 to under 5,000 today (Cohen, 2000). Even in settings where, in earlier decades, people often stayed for life (e.g., public hospitals, Veterans Administration psychiatric hospitals), the current length of stay is less than one week (Kessler, 1998). On the other hand, a number of patients are no sooner discharged than they are readmitted—a situation called "revolving door syndrome"—because of the lack of services outside the hospital. While the inpatient population has decreased, the number of admissions has actually increased (Kiesler, 1982b).

The Rise of the Prevention Movement

Forty years ago, people with mental illnesses received humane treatment if they could afford it; if they could not, they were hospitalized in the sorts of squalid and overcrowded facilities described above. When mental health professionals began to talk, in the 1960s, of identifying disorders before they began and preventing their onset, they also sought to offer prevention services to all who needed them, regardless of wealth or social status.

In 1959, an influential book by George Albee, *Mental Health Manpower Trends,* pioneered the idea that mental health professionals should be accessible to everyone, rich and poor. Albee noted that treatment providers tended to be concentrated in urban areas and that most of them were engaged in private practice, seeing one client per hour. He also observed that the services tended to follow money and privilege, abandoning the inner cities and rural areas where poor people lived. Albee argued persuasively that private practice cannot be a sound basis for a national mental health policy and that the single-patient, 50-minute hour consumed far too many resources while leaving the most severely disordered people untreated.

With society beginning to view mental illness as a reflection of "problems in living," rather than as a disease, Albee asserted that mental health professionals needed to change to accommodate the increased demand for services. He imagined a number of professions, including public health, education, law, religion, social welfare, and urban planning,

Shifting the care of chronic mental patients from state hospitals to the community is called deinstitutionalization, but many city dwellers call it "dumping." In cities across the country, hundreds of thousands of patients considered capable of functioning on medication outside the institution have been released.

Of the million or so homeless people nationwide, approximately one fourth are thought to be suffering from severe mental disorders and one half from substance abuse (Dickey, 2000; Sullivan, Burnam, & Koegel, 2000). In a study of homeless shelters in Massachusetts, up to a third of the residents exhibited mental illness (Mosher-Ashley, Henrikson, & French, 2000).

Community services in every city are insufficiently staffed and funded to see that the mentally ill are housed, put to work, or looked after. Some live in inexpensive single-room-occupancy (SRO) "hotels"—often warrens of tiny, filthy rooms. Community services for the chronic mentally ill may consist of a welfare check and occasional visits by a social worker dispensing tranquilizers. Otherwise, they are typically on their own, sitting in their rooms or drifting through the streets. When they die, they are rarely missed.

Still worse, some of the mentally ill have no housing at all, since they lack the money even for the cheapest flophouse. Many have essentially no income and are dependent on city shelters and soup kitchens. Some spend their days wandering from neighborhood to neighborhood; others travel around one or a few blocks. They sleep where they can—if not in shelters, then in doorways, in parks, and in subways and train stations. They carry their belongings in shopping bags or roll grocery carts along the sidewalks.

For people with homes and jobs, it can be difficult to understand that the mentally ill "street person," ragged and dirty, once had a normal life. In 1991, composer and writer Elizabeth Swados wrote about the descent of her brother Lincoln Swados into schizophrenia and eventually life on the street. The Swados family was privileged, and Lincoln grew up intelligent and talented. But he was eccentric, and he often misbehaved at school. When he went away to college, he broke down. As Swados (1991) describes it:

> He never made it through his freshman year at Syracuse. . . . Lincoln promised to write, but he never did. Several months later, my father received an almost booklength letter from my brother describing himself as in a helplessly disoriented state. He was unable to go to classes, unable to leave his room. The voices in his head were directing him to do too many different things. My father showed the letter to several psychiatrists, who recommended that Lincoln be hospitalized immediately. (p. 18)

Released from the hospital after lengthy treatment, Lincoln again deteriorated. In a suicidal period, he tried to kill himself by jumping in front of a subway train. This resulted in the amputation of his right arm and leg. Then, disabled physically as well as mentally, Lincoln Swados went to live on the Lower East Side of New York, a poor and dangerous neighborhood. Repeatedly rejecting the efforts of family and friends to help him—he refused to answer the door when they came to see him—Swados sank further into mental and physical illness. His sister eventually found him dead in his shabby apartment. He was 46.

Compared with many people with schizophrenia, Lincoln Swados was fortunate—he had financial resources and a family that tried to help him. Given his fate, it is easier to understand how others with serious disorders end up on the street, penniless and in desperate need of care.

The deinstitutionalization movement of the past quarter century has sought to release many mentally ill people from hospitals. Often, however, government funding has not followed the released patients into the community. As a result, adequate pro-grams do not exist for the treatment and supervision of the thousands of homeless mentally ill people who now roam the streets of American cities.

training a new breed of clinician in creating a society that maximized human potential. Albee recommended that psychologists develop programs and train other, less expensive paraprofessionals to do the therapy, both to save money and to reduce the demand for Ph.D.'s.

These were the blueprints to create a society that prevented mental illness. However, barriers—political, organizational, and social—arose almost immediately (Broskowski & Baker, 1974).

The first blow came in 1961, when the Joint Commission on Mental Health and Illness recommended a continued emphasis on treatment and rejected "visionary" primary prevention. The commission felt that the public health model, on which prevention was based, had already been tried and failed. However, a few years later (1963), Congress passed the Community Mental Health Centers Act, which gave primary prevention a temporary boost. Community mental health centers were indeed formed, as noted above, and mental health care included ideas about prevention and social change.

As we have seen, secondary prevention has become dominant in much of the mental health field today. Early interventions with high-risk populations have become the most promising methods for treating intractable disorders. The focus on social context in secondary prevention led to **community psychology**, an area of psychology that examines communities rather than individuals. Community psychology has become a vital field of study, and it has also promoted a much more multicultural and multiethnic perspective within clinical training programs.

However, community and clinical psychologists have had a difficult time finding ways to implement and even define primary prevention programs. No road map was ever provided for clinical psychologists to make the transition from scientist-practitioners to agents of social change. Clinical psychology was unable or unwilling to move from a "defect" model of mental illness, one that sees mental illness as resulting from defects within the individual, to a contextual model emphasizing growth and development (Cowen & Durlack, 2000). A contextual model looks at mental disorders as problems in living, generated by stressful environments. The goal of such a model is not simply to eliminate mental illness but also to create mental health. Primary prevention has historically been linked to the goal of creating a society oriented toward personal growth. But how can we define the success of a prevention program when the criteria used to measure it are based on a defect model of abnormal behavior?

Since the 1990s, mental illness has once again come to be perceived as a disease, rather than simply a reflection of "problems in living." Today's prevention scientists consider mental disorders to be brain diseases, and they attempt to reduce the risk in populations vulnerable to such disorders, which they usually attribute to genetic or brain deficiencies (Mrazek & Haggerty, 1994). New opportunities to prevent biologically based disorders range from medication administered before symptoms appear to genetic engineering. However, predicting—and, thus, preventing—disorders based on physical signs is far from easy. It is doubtful that researchers will ever find a single biological or environmental agent that triggers mental illness; prevention must involve both types of factors to be effective.

The Rise of Managed Behavioral Health Care

Managed care is an umbrella term for the variety of organizational structures, insurance benefits, and regulations that both provide for and control the cost of health care procedures. **Managed behavioral health care (MBHC)** is the term most often used to describe managed mental health care. MBHC entered the mental health care delivery system in the 1980s. In the past ten years, it has become the dominant force in mental health care (Cushman & Gilford, 2000).

The goal of managed care is to control the cost of treatment, primarily by limiting the use of services and by imposing restrictions on the kinds of services covered and on which practitioners may be selected. MBHC is most often provided through one of two types of organizations: staff model health maintenance organizations (HMOs), and MBHC organizations. Staff model HMO enrollees receive mental health treatment from specialist in-house staff providers, and their overall treatment is consolidated among one provider group. MBHC organizations, also called "carve-out vendors," are managed care organizations that have been hired by employers to organize specialized mental health treatment for enrollees independently ("carved out") from their overall health care. These MBHC organizations employ specialists to assess and monitor each patient's access to and use of mental health treatment within the network.

The growth in managed care has significantly changed the way mental health care is provided in the United States. The for-profit corporations that provide managed care usually favor behavioral descriptions of patient symptoms, treatment focused on relief of those symptoms, the use of medication, and concrete, directive interventions within a short-term format (Cushman & Gilford, 2000). Statistics on the decline in number of treatment days and benefit costs help illuminate the changes in behavioral health benefits under managed care. Inpatient days—the number of hospital days used per 1,000 people—has declined from approximately 150 per 1,000 in 1983 under traditional fee-for-service insurance, to 25 in 1998 under HMOs (Kessler, 1998). The cost of benefits paid, expressed in dollars per member per month, has declined as well, from approximately $9 per member per month in 1983 to $2 to $2.75 per member per month in 1998 (Kessler, 1998). The number of visits to mental health care providers has also been curtailed under managed care. In 1988, 26 percent of plans limited enrollees to a certain number of visits to their mental health care providers annually; in 1997, 48 percent of plans were imposing such visit limits—and the visit limit had decreased from an average of 50 per year in 1988 to just 20 a year in 1997 (Rothstein, Haller, & Bernstein, 2000).

Managed behavioral health care has raised a number of concerns for mental health care providers, especially over maintaining control of professional decisions, length and adequacy of treatment, and practitioner-client confidentiality (Rothstein, Haller, & Bernstein, 2000). Despite practitioners' concerns, however, managed behavioral health care is firmly entrenched in the American health care system today.

The Foundations of Modern Abnormal Psychology

In the late nineteenth century, as the new mental hospitals were opening throughout the United States, the study of abnormal psychology was rapidly expanding in both Europe and America. New theories were being introduced and tested, while opposing theories arose to challenge them.

The Experimental Study of Abnormal Behavior In 1879, Wilhelm Wundt, a professor of physiology at the University of Leipzig, Germany, established a laboratory for the scientific study of psychology—that is, the application of scientific experimentation, with precise methods of measurement and control, to human thought and behavior. The opening of Wundt's laboratory is often cited as the beginning of modern psychology. Among Wundt's students was Emil Kraepelin (1856–1926), who eventually established his own psychological laboratory, devoted primarily to the study of **psychopathology,** or abnormal psychology. There Kraepelin and his students investigated how psychopathology was related to movement, to fatigue, to emotion, to speech, and to memory (Maher & Maher, 1985).

Kraepelin's approach was copied elsewhere. In 1904, the first American laboratory for experimental work with mental patients opened at the McLean Hospital in Massachusetts, and other hospitals soon followed McLean's example (Taylor, 2000). In 1906, Morton Prince, an American physician specializing in mental disorders, founded the first journal specializing in experimental psychopathology, the *Journal of Abnormal Psychology.* (It remains the foremost journal on this subject today.) In all, experimental abnormal psychology made substantial strides in the first two decades of the century.

Kraepelin and Biogenic Theory Biogenic theory, as we have seen, originated in ancient times and persisted, though sometimes obscured by supernaturalism, through the Middle Ages and Renaissance. Then, in the late eighteenth and early nineteenth centuries, when medical research was making rapid advances, it again became dominant. Kraepelin, the founder of experimental abnormal psychology, was the person who first placed biogenic theory in the forefront of European psychiatry. In his *Textbook of Psychiatry* (1883/1923), Kraepelin not only argued for the central role of brain pathology in mental disturbance but furnished psychiatry with its first comprehensive classification system, based on the biogenic viewpoint. He claimed that mental illness, like physical illness, could be classified into separate pathologies, each of which had a different organic cause and could be recognized by a distinct cluster of symptoms, called a **syndrome.** Once the symptoms appeared, the mental disturbance could be diagnosed according to the classification system. And, once it

Emil Kraepelin, a German psychiatrist who founded experimental abnormal psychology, believed that mental illness could be classified into separate pathologies based on their symptoms.

was diagnosed, its course and outcome could be expected to resemble those seen in other cases of the same illness, just as one case of measles could be expected to turn out like other cases of measles.

Kraepelin's biogenic theory and his classification system received widespread publicity and generated high hopes that the mysteries of mental illness would be solved in commonsensical, natural ways. At the same time, the neurological and genetic components of psychopathology were gaining attention through the writings of another German physician, Richard von Krafft-Ebing (1840–1902), who emphasized biological and hereditary causation in his *Textbook of Psychiatry* (1879/1900) and in his pioneering encyclopedia of sexual disorders, *Psychopathia Sexualis* (1886/1965). It was from the work of these theorists that the modern medical model of psychological disturbance evolved.

The most stunning success of the medical model was the discovery that **general paresis,** a mysterious syndrome involving the gradual and irreversible breakdown of physical and mental functioning, was actually an advanced case of syphilis. This breakthrough had an immense impact on the mental health profession and helped to establish the medical model in the lofty position it still occupies today.

However, at the same time that neurological research was nourishing biogenic theory, other findings were laying the foundation for a comprehensive **psychogenic theory,** the theory that psychological disturbance is due primarily not to biological dysfunction but to emotional stress.

Mesmer and Hypnosis The history of modern psychogenic theory begins with a colorful figure, Franz Anton Mesmer (1733–1815). With the late eighteenth century came exciting discoveries in magnetism and electricity. Mesmer, an Austrian physician, tried to apply this new knowledge to the study of mental states. His theory was that the movement of the planets controlled the distribution of a universal magnetic fluid and that the shiftings of this magnetic fluid were responsible for the health of mind and body. Furthermore, he was convinced that this principle of "animal magnetism" could be used in the treatment of **hysteria,** a disorder involving the impairment of normal function—for example, a person would suddenly become blind or paralyzed—with no apparent organic cause. Hysteria was a common complaint at the time, especially in women.

Mesmer's treatment for hysteria was rather exotic. The patients sat around a huge vat containing bottles of fluids from which iron rods protruded. The lights were dimmed and soft music was played. Then Mesmer appeared, "magnetic" wand in hand, and went from patient to patient, touching various parts of their bodies with his hands, with his wand, and with the rods protruding from the vat, in order to readjust the distribution of their magnetic fluids. The most striking aspect of this treatment is that in many cases it worked.

Mesmer's theory of animal magnetism was later investigated and declared invalid, yet even if his theory was wrong, his treatment was somehow right. What Mesmer had discovered, accidentally, was the power of suggestion to cure mental disorder. He is now regarded as the first practitioner of **hypnosis** (originally known as "mesmerism"), an artificially induced trance in which the person is highly susceptible to suggestion.

The Nancy School Some years after Mesmer's death, his findings were reexamined by two enterprising French physicians, Ambrose-Auguste Liébeault (1823–1904) and Hippolyte-Marie Bernheim (1840–1919), both practicing in Nancy, in eastern France. For four years Bernheim had been treating a patient, with no success. Finally, after hearing that a certain Dr. Liébeault was having considerable success with unconventional methods, Bernheim sent the patient to him. When the patient returned completely cured, Bernheim called on Liébeault to ask what he had done. What Liébeault had done was simple: He had hypnotized the patient and told him that, when he awakened, his symptoms would be gone (Selling, 1940).

Bernheim was persuaded, and thereafter the two physicians worked as a team. Together they discovered that hysteria could be not only cured but also induced by hypnosis. For example, if a hypnotized person were told that she had no feeling in her hand, the hand could then be pricked with a needle without producing any response. On the basis of such findings, Liébeault and Bernheim evolved the theory that hysteria was actually a form of self-hypnosis and that other mental disorders might also be due to psychological causes.

This view won a number of adherents, and the group became known as the "Nancy school." The Nancy school soon came under attack by a formidable challenger, Jean-Martin Charcot (1825–1893), a famous neurologist who at that time was director of La Salpêtrière hospital in Paris. Charcot had also experimented with hypnosis, but he had abandoned it, concluding that hysteria was due to biogenic causes after all. The debate between the Paris school, consisting of Charcot and his supporters, and the Nancy school was one of the earliest major academic debates in the history of modern psychology. Eventually, the insurgent Nancy school triumphed, and Charcot himself was later won over to the psychogenic theory of hysteria. But this debate extended far beyond the specific problem of hysteria, for it raised the possibility that any number of psychological disorders might be due to emotional

The French neurologist Jean-Martin Charcot is shown here, with a patient on his arm, giving one of his famous lectures on hysteria. Charcot was at the center of the late-nineteenth-century debate between psychogenic and biogenic theories of hysteria.

states rather than (or as well as) to neurological causes. The work of the Nancy school had a profound influence on the developing field of experimental psychopathology in the United States, leading American pioneers, William James and James Jackson Putnam of Harvard, Morton Prince of Tufts, and Adolph Meyer of Clark, to focus on the study of altered emotional states, such as trances, hypnosis, and hysteria (Taylor, 2000).

Breuer and Freud: The Beginnings of Psychoanalysis

One of the many people affected by the debate over hysteria was a young Viennese physician named Sigmund Freud (1856–1939). Early in his career, Freud worked with Josef Breuer, a physician who was experimenting with hypnosis. A few years earlier, Breuer had treated a woman, later known to medical history as "Anna O.," who had various hysterical symptoms—partial paralysis, inability to swallow, and so on. Somewhat by chance, Breuer discovered that under hypnosis Anna O. was able to discuss her feelings uninhibitedly and that, after doing so, she obtained some relief from her symptoms. Anna O. called this the "talking cure."

Together Breuer and Freud experimented with talking cures. They soon became convinced that hysteria and other disorders were caused by "unconscious" conflicts; once aired via hypnosis, the conflicts lost their power to maintain the symptoms. In 1895, Breuer and Freud published their findings in a volume titled *Studies in Hysteria*. This book, in which the authors put forth their theory of the unconscious, was a milestone in the history of psychology.

Later, working independently, Freud abandoned hypnosis in favor of a technique he called **free association:** He asked patients to relax on a couch and simply pour out whatever came to mind. Freud also encouraged his patients to talk about their dreams and their childhoods. He then interpreted this material to the patients according to the theories he was constructing about the unconscious. To this form of therapy, in which patients are cured through the gradual understanding of unconscious conflicts, Freud gave the name **psychoanalysis.** Freud's theories were very controversial at first. Eventually, however, they became the basis for the psychodynamic perspective (Chapter 5) and exerted a profound influence on twentieth-century thought (Fancher, 2000).

Non-Western Approaches to Abnormal Behavior

The history just outlined describes only one tradition, that of the West—of Europe and America. Asia and Africa have their own ways of handling abnormal behavior. Their traditions, thousands of years old, are impossible to summarize briefly, but they do share certain principles that distinguish them from Western abnormal psychology. First, Asians and Africans do not separate psychology from spiritual matters. In the West, psychology is part of science. In Africa, psychology is part of religion. Second, in psychology, as in other areas of life, Asians and Africans do not prize individualism as much as Westerners do. Rather, they see human beings as part of a network of relationships, and those relationships are often the focus of psychological treatment.

Africa In Africa, a person who lives alone is likely to be considered odd. People lead their lives within large, extended families, and it is the family that is expected to handle psychological crises. When that fails, the troubled person goes to a psychological healer, who may well be the community's healer of physical problems as well. Generally, the healer attributes the problem to a disruption in the person's relationship with the spirit world—a situation that may be due to sorcery, the evil eye, the breaking of a taboo, or the failure to perform required rituals. Physical causes are also taken into account, and many healers recommend physical treatments such as herbs. But often the treatment, like the presumed cause, is spiritual: rituals, animal sacrifices, incantations, the wearing of amulets, and the use of special objects.

Such treatments may be very pragmatic. T. Asuni offers the following example:

> An African woman from a polygamous tribe went to a healer, complaining that her husband was threatening to send her back to her family because she was constantly having violent arguments with one of her co-wives, whom the husband seemed to favor. The healer gave her a small object and told her that it embodied the spirit of the other wife. Whenever she began to quarrel with the other wife, she was to put this object in her mouth and bite it. This, he said, would solve her problem. The woman returned several weeks later to thank the healer, saying that not she, but the other wife, had been sent away. (Adapted from Asuni, 1986, p. 313.)

Asuni speculates that the healer felt it was unrealistic to tell the woman not to quarrel with the co-wife. Instead, he gave her a less direct way of getting back at her rival, by biting the object. At the same time, the object-biting kept the patient from quarreling—she couldn't bite and argue at the same time—so the cause of her husband's anger with her was removed.

Here we see many of the same principles used in Western psychological treatment: suggestion, reassurance, and manipulation of the environment. Other techniques shared by Western and African psychotherapy are emotional venting and group treatment. (The previous case is unusual in that the woman went to the healer alone. Most African patients arrive with a large delegation of family members, and the prescribed rituals are performed by the whole group, with the healer as a sort of master of ceremonies.) What is not shared is Western psychotherapy's goal of insight. African patients are not asked to analyze themselves. This would be considered a distraction from the main goal of treatment, correcting the person's relationship to family and to ancestral spirits.

Asia Asian religious philosophies, such as Hinduism and Buddhism, emphasize self-awareness: People are taught to pay close attention to their inner states and thereby, in some measure, separate themselves from their own thought processes. The most common method of achieving this is meditation. Meditation is now widely used in the West for stress reduction. In Asia, where it has been practiced for thousands of years, it is used to relieve a wide variety of psychological problems—for example, phobias, substance abuse, and insomnia—and medical problems such as asthma and heart irregularities (Walsh, 1999).

Like meditation, other Asian psychotherapies tend to be "quiet therapies," in which patients deal mainly with themselves, though under the guidance of a professional. An example is Naikan therapy, a popular Japanese treatment that was developed in the 1950s. The fundamental principle of Naikan therapy is that many psychological problems are due to self-centeredness. Patients, therefore, are taught to engage in long periods of "self-observation"—16 hours a day, in the hospital, for the first week of treatment and a few hours a day thereafter—during which they examine their relationships with others (especially their parents), asking themselves what they received from these people, what troubles they caused them, and what they gave back to them (Reynolds, 1993). The aim is to make patients more accepting and appreciative of those around them.

Another treatment widely used in Japan, particularly for anxiety disorders, is Morita therapy. Here again, patients are hospitalized, this time for four to five weeks, and required to engage in prolonged reflection. At first they remain inactive; then, gradually, they are allowed to take up tasks and mix with people again. The object is to clear the mind of anxiety-producing perfectionism and to make the patient yearn again for practical activity.

Though used for psychological purposes, these Asian therapies are all rooted in religion, in the Zen Buddhist goal of freeing oneself of thoughts that disrupt the harmony between the self and the universe. In all three, one detaches oneself from the world in order to return to it—to practical activity and social responsibility (Sharf, 1996).

A Multiperspective Approach

This book rests on three basic assumptions. The first is that *human behavior can be studied scientifically;* that is, scientists can observe objectively both behavior and the environment in which it occurs. From these observations, they can draw conclusions about the causes of behavior; knowing these causes, they can predict and influence behavior.

Second, this book assumes that *most abnormal behavior is the product of both psychological and biological processes.* The unobservable events of the mind, such as attitudes, memories, and desires, are unquestionably involved in most forms of psychopathology. Psychopathology, in turn, is connected to biological events: the secretion of hormones by the glands, the movement of electrical impulses across the brain, and so forth. How these two kinds of events hook together in the web of causation is, as we shall see, a maddeningly complex question.

The third assumption of this book is that *each human being is unique.* Human behavior may be discussed in general terms, but it still issues from individuals, each of whom has a unique set of memories, desires, and expectations, and each of whom has some ability to control his or her behavior.

In the following chapters, we will stress the perspectives on abnormal behavior described earlier: the psychodynamic, behavioral, cognitive, interpersonal, sociocultural, and neuroscience perspectives. Each of these viewpoints is narrower and more specific than the broad approach just defined, and more often than not they disagree with one another. But, taken together, they provide a comprehensive view of modern abnormal psychology.

Key Terms

biogenic, 6
clinical psychologist, 10
community mental health centers, 16
community psychology, 19
deinstitutionalization, 16
exorcism, 11
free association, 22
general paresis, 21
humors, 12
hypnosis, 21
hysteria, 21
inpatient, 16
managed behavioral health care, 19
managed care, 19
medical model, 6
moral therapy, 15
neuroscience perspective, 8
norms, 2
outpatient, 16
prefrontal lobotomy, 16
prevention, 9
primary prevention, 10
psychiatric social worker, 10
psychiatrist, 10
psychoanalysis, 22
psychoanalyst, 10
psychogenic theory, 21
psychopathology, 20
secondary prevention, 10
syndrome, 20

Summary

- Definitions of abnormal behavior vary from century to century and from society to society. A common basis for defining behavior as abnormal is violation of the society's norms, or rules for correct behavior. Behavior that is statistically rare, causes personal discomfort to the person who exhibits it, or is maladaptive, may also be considered abnormal.
- Psychological disturbance has different effects on different social groups, defined by cultural and ethnic origin, gender, age, and other factors. Such groups are at differing risk for various disorders, and they experience and express the disorders differently. They may also embrace different norms, which affect diagnosis.
- Just as there are many definitions of abnormal behavior, so are there many explanations. According to the medical model, abnormal behavior is *like* a disease: Even if the condition is not the result of organic dysfunction, it should be diagnosed and treated as an illness. A refinement of the medical model, the modern neuroscience perspective seeks to identify the organic components of mental disorders but does not insist on an exclusively biological cause.
- Psychological theories trace abnormal behavior to a person's interactions with the environment. The most prominent psychological theories include the psychodynamic approach, which emphasizes unconscious conflicts originating in childhood; the behavioral perspective, which stresses inappropriate conditioning; the cognitive perspective, which focuses on maladaptive ways of perceiving the self and the environment; and the interpersonal perspective, which views abnormal behavior as the product of disordered relationships. The sociocultural perspective examines the influence of social forces on behavior and diagnosis.
- The treatment of abnormal behavior depends on the nature of the society, the criteria used to identify abnormality, and the society's explanation of abnormal behavior.
- Since the 1960s, psychologists have investigated prevention, or ways to keep disorders from beginning by changing the environment, the family, and the individual. These efforts have included primary prevention, which is intended to affect the entire population, and secondary prevention, which is aimed at reducing risk among a targeted high-risk population.
- Prevention is part of the treatment continuum. Universal prevention involves the entire population; selective preventive interventions are aimed at subgroups with a higher-than-average risk for a disorder; and indicated preventive interventions are designed for individuals who either show early signs of a disorder or have a biological marker for that disorder.
- Over time, prevention goals have broadened. Prevention programs are intended not only to prevent the onset of a disorder but also to decrease the severity or delay the onset of disorders.
- Prehistoric and ancient societies apparently viewed abnormal behavior as a product of supernatural forces. Treatment consisted of various forms of exorcism.
- The naturalistic approach to abnormal behavior in Western culture dates from ancient Greece. Hippocrates

observed and recorded cases of mental disturbance and developed a biogenic theory of abnormal behavior.

- In the Middle Ages, supernatural explanations of abnormal behavior were again dominant, though naturalistic theories also persisted.
- During the Renaissance, despite a growing trend toward regarding abnormal behavior as an illness, thousands of people, mostly women, were burned in witch hunts. Some of these people were probably psychologically disturbed.
- In the eighteenth and nineteenth centuries, hospitalization of the mentally disturbed became increasingly common. Conditions in the asylums were typically cruel and degrading. In the late eighteenth century, people such as Philippe Pinel and William Tuke began the reform of institutional care. The new approach, stressing a peaceful environment, useful work, and dignified treatment, came to be known as moral therapy.
- With the efforts of Dorothea Dix and others, many mental hospitals were built in the nineteenth century, but these institutions did not live up to the reformers' hopes. Moral therapy was replaced with custodial care. People with psychological disturbances were isolated in prisonlike institutions, sometimes for life—a pattern that continued into the mid–twentieth century.
- In the 1950s, with the introduction of a new class of tranquilizers, the phenothiazines, the deinstitutionalization movement began. But because of lack of funding, deinstitutionalization was not accompanied by sufficient growth in community services. Today, hospital stays are brief, but rates of admission remain high.
- The prevention movement began in the 1960s when researchers observed that poor rural and inner-city residents were underserved by the existing mental health system. The movement demanded access to mental health care for the poor and encouraged psychologists to change society to maximize human potential. The field of community psychology grew out of this movement.
- Many modern primary prevention programs attempt to enhance people's resilience, or the ability to cope with stressful environments. These programs involve working with the population as a whole, not just with a high-risk population.
- In the late nineteenth century, experimental psychology, initiated by Wilhelm Wundt, was extended to the study of psychological disturbance. Emil Kraepelin's biogenic theory, together with breakthroughs in biological research, pushed the medical model to the forefront.
- With Franz Anton Mesmer's discovery of hypnosis in the eighteenth century, it became clear that some psychological disorders could be cured by suggestion. This laid the groundwork for psychogenic theory. At the end of the nineteenth century, Sigmund Freud began developing his pioneering theory, psychoanalysis, which argued that psychological disorders were caused by unconscious conflicts.
- In contrast to the modern Western tradition, African and Asian approaches to psychological disturbance tend to be more closely connected to religion. They also place less emphasis on individualism and greater emphasis on social relationships.
- This book is based on three assumptions: Human behavior can be studied scientifically; most abnormal behavior is the product of *both* psychological and biological processes; and each human being is unique. To present a comprehensive view of abnormal psychology, we will draw on all the theoretical perspectives described earlier.

CHAPTER

2

Diagnosis and Assessment: The Issues

Why Assessment?

The Diagnosis of Mental Disorders

Assessing the Assessment: Reliability and Validity

Problems in Assessment

Methods of Assessment

The Interview

Psychological Tests

Laboratory Tests

Observation in Natural Settings

Cultural Bias in Assessment

Diagnosis and Assessment

Most of this book is devoted to the common categories of abnormal behavior. As categories, such disorders are easy to discuss. We chart the symptoms, weigh the possible causes, and review the suggested treatments. It is only in the vocabulary of psychology, however, that abnormal behaviors exist as categories. In reality, they are the complex and ambiguous things that people do and say. And the first job of the mental health profession is to look at what people say and do and to make some sense out of it. This process is called **psychological assessment,** which may be defined as the collection, organization, and interpretation of information about a person and his or her situation.

Psychological assessment is not a recent invention. Throughout history, people have been developing systems for sorting people into categories so as to predict how they will behave. The first assessment system was probably astrology, developed by the ancient Babylonians and later disseminated to Egypt, Greece, India, and China (Kemp, 1990). Initially, the stars were read only for clues about matters of public concern—wars, floods, crop failure. By the fifth century B.C.E., however, astrology was also being used as the basis of personal horoscopes, revelations of individual character and destiny.

Ancient societies also practiced psychiatric classification. By 2600 B.C.E., the Egyptians and the Sumerians had recognized what would later be called melancholia, hysteria, and senile dementia. By 1400 B.C.E., India had developed a psychiatric classification system in which seven kinds of demonic possession produced corresponding types of abnormal behavior. As mentioned in Chapter 1, Hippocrates, in fifth-century B.C.E. Athens, insisted on natural causes, as opposed to possession. In addition to his four humors, he and his followers devised a six-part system for

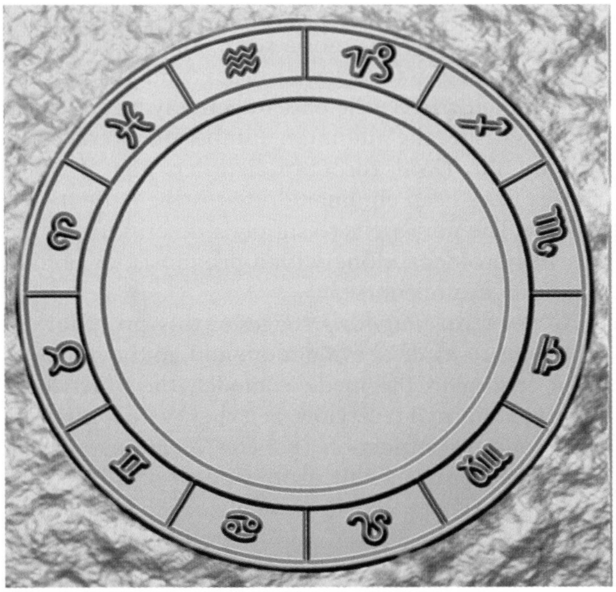

Astrology represents the first method of psychological assessment, developed by the ancient Babylonians. Although personal horoscopes continue to be popular, astrology is generally not considered a valid means of assessment today.

classifying mental disorders: phrenitis (mental disturbance with fever), mania, melancholia, epilepsy, hysteria, and "Scythian disease," similar to what we call transvestism (Mack, Forman, Brown, et al., 1994).

It is important to note that each of these assessment systems is based on a theory of human behavior. To the astrologists, behavior was determined by the positions of the stars at one's birth. To the ancient Indians, it was controlled by spirits. Modern assessment procedures, in turn, are based on psychological theories, biogenic and psychogenic. These theories, too, will change. With assessment, as with the definition of abnormal behavior, we are looking at something that is the product of each generation's and each culture's efforts to make sense of the way people act.

In this chapter, we will first discuss the issues surrounding assessment: what it aims to do, how well it succeeds, and what can cause it to fail. Then we will describe the most commonly used assessment techniques and their relation to the major psychological perspectives.

Diagnosis and Assessment: The Issues

Why do people undergo psychological assessment? In what cases, and why, does such assessment involve diagnostic labeling? How useful are diagnostic labels? How can we tell a good assessment technique from a bad one? These questions have no easy answers. The entire enterprise of diagnosis and assessment is surrounded by controversy.

Why Assessment?

All psychological assessment has two goals. The first is description, the rendering of an accurate portrait of personality, cognitive functioning, mood, and behavior (Meyer, Finn, Eyde, et al., 2001). This goal would be important even if there were no such thing as abnormal psychology. Science aims to describe; and psychology, the science of human personality and behavior, aims to describe personality and behavior, simply for the sake of increasing our understanding of reality.

However, such descriptions may also be needed for decision-making purposes. This brings us to the second goal of psychological assessment: prediction. Again, prediction need serve no practical purpose. The mere desire to advance human knowledge could motivate a psychologist to try to predict, for example, whether children of divorced parents are likely to become divorced themselves. Within abnormal psychology, however, assessment often has important practical applications. Should this child be put in a special education program? Is this person psychologically fit to stand trial? Would that patient benefit from drugs? Should he be hospitalized—even against his will? These are the questions that clinical assessment addresses (Meyer, Finn, Eyde, et al., 2001). The answers may determine the direction of the person's entire future.

Patients must also be reassessed to see if they are improving. Today, in the cost-conscious atmosphere of managed health care, insurers are asking for evidence that the treatments they are paying for are actually working. Because this evidence can be provided only by assessing the patients, psychological assessment is likely to be even more important in the coming years (Beutler, Kim, Davison, et al., 1996).

In this chapter, we will be tracking the psychological assessment of a patient named Joe, who is 23 years old. Joe has mild mental retardation and many related problems, such as impulsiveness and fits of anger. He had been placed in a "group home," a fairly nonrestrictive setting with professional counselors present only during the day, but because of his disruptive behavior he had been asked to leave the group home. He is now in the hospital, and the purpose of the assessment is to decide where he should be placed. Does he need to stay in the hospital longer? Could he go back to the group home? Or should he be placed in an intermediate setting, a "residential home," with 24-hour staff? Joe's assessment will be described throughout the chapter.

The Diagnosis of Mental Disorders

In nonclinical contexts, assessment may involve no labeling. When job applicants take psychological tests, one person is chosen for the job, while the others are not, and that is the end of it. Clinical assessment, however, often includes **diagnosis,** in which the person's problem is classified within one of a set of recognized categories of abnormal behavior and is labeled accordingly.

The Classification of Abnormal Behavior All sciences classify—that is, they order the objects of their study by identifying crucial similarities among them and sorting them into groups according to those similarities. Astronomers classify heavenly bodies according to color, size, and temperature. Physicians classify diseases according to the organ or system affected. And mental health professionals classify mental disorders according to patterns of behavior, thought, and emotion.

As we saw in Chapter 1, in the late nineteenth century, Kraepelin developed the first truly comprehensive classification system for severe mental disorders. All later systems were influenced by this one. Eventually, in 1952, the American Psychiatric Association (APA) published its own version of the system, under the title *Diagnostic and Statistical Manual of Mental Disorders,* or *DSM.* Since that time, the *DSM* has undergone several revisions. There was a *DSM-II,* followed in turn by *DSM-III, DSM-III-R* (revised), *DSM-IV,* and, most recently, *DSM-IV Text Revision* ***(DSM-IV-TR),*** which was published in 2000. *DSM-IV-TR* contains the same criteria for each category as *DSM-IV,* but updates the description of what is known about each disorder based on research conducted since the publication of *DSM-IV. DSM-IV-TR*'s listing of diagnostic categories can be seen inside the cover of this book.

Another classification system is the mental disorders section of the *International Classification of Diseases (ICD),* published by the World Health Organization (WHO). All members of the WHO, including the United States, use the *ICD,* though each member can, for some purposes, adopt other criteria for disorders, such as *DSM-IV-TR,* to reflect diagnostic practices within that country. Most revisions of the *DSM* have been coordinated with revisions of the *ICD. DSM-IV-TR* is consistent with the *ICD*'s current, tenth edition, *ICD-10* (Nathan & Langenbucher, 1999).

The Practice of Diagnosis The *DSM* provides the foundation for diagnosing mental disorders. Each *DSM* category is accompanied by a description of the disorder in question, together with a set of specific criteria for diagnosis. Faced with a patient, the assessor decides which diagnosis seems most likely, consults the criteria for that disorder, and then determines which criteria the patient actually meets. If the patient satisfies the minimum number of criteria specified by the *DSM* for that disorder, and if other choices have been eliminated, that is the patient's diagnosis. The purpose is to supply a description of the patient's problem, along with a prognosis, or prediction of its future course.

As the term *diagnosis* suggests, this procedure is analogous to medical evaluation; and, in the minds of some, it implies the medical model, the practice of treating abnormal behaviors as if they were symptoms of biological dysfunction (Follette & Houts, 1996). However, mental health professionals of all persuasions, including those who strongly object to the medical model, use diagnosis, and for good reasons.

To begin with, research depends on diagnosis. For example, in order to find out the causes of schizophrenia, researchers need to have groups of people with schizophrenia to study, and it is only through diagnosis—that is, giving certain people the label of schizophrenia—that they can gather such groups. Even apart from research requirements, mental health professionals, like other professionals, need a vocabulary in order to discuss their subject. If they did not establish a common vocabulary, such as that provided by the *DSM,* they would develop their own, idiosyncratic terms and definitions, with much resulting confusion. Finally, psychology is tied in with many other institutions in our society, and all of these institutions require the use of diagnostic labels. To get funding for its special education program, a school system has to say how many children with mental retardation or autism it is handling. When hospitals apply for funds, they have to list the number of people with schizophrenia, alcoholism, and so on, that they are treating. Insurance companies require a diagnosis before they will pay the bills. Thus, diagnosis is practiced, and its vocabulary—that of the *DSM*—has become our society's primary means of communicating about abnormal behavior.

Criticisms of Diagnosis The major criticism of diagnosis has to do with what some perceive as its tie to the medical model. As noted in Chapter 1, Szasz (1961) and many other writers have vigorously attacked the medical model, and they have attacked the diagnosis of mental disorders on the same grounds—namely, that its purpose is to give psychiatrists control over other people's lives (Sarbin, 1997). In addition to this argument, four other criticisms of diagnosis merit consideration.

The first is that diagnosis falsifies reality by implying that most abnormal behavior is qualitatively different from normal behavior. *DSM-IV-TR,* for example, lists a condition called "nightmare disorder," with, as usual, specific criteria for diagnosis: The person's nightmares must be "extended and extremely frightening," and they must occur repeatedly. One person with nightmares will meet these criteria, while another will not. But the application of the diagnosis to one and not the other suggests that there is a difference in kind between their two conditions, whereas, to all appearances, the difference is simply one of degree. Likewise, most forms of psychopathology are at the far end of a long continuum from normal to abnormal, with many gradations in between (Nathan & Langenbucher, 1999). In response to the criticism that the *DSM* criteria are overly inclusive, a clinical significance criterion was added to many categories in *DSM-IV-TR* (Spitzer & Wakefield, 1999). This criterion requires that symptoms cause "clinically significant distress or impairment in social, occupational, or other important areas of functioning" (American Psychiatric Association, 2000) and is designed to separate cases that reflect disorder from cases that reflect normal reactions to stress.

If diagnosis discounts the gradations between normal and abnormal, it is even more likely to discount the gradations between different forms of abnormality—a second major criticism. Many people with "depression" suffer the same problems as people with "schizophrenia"; others have much in common with "anxiety disorder" patients. In other words, behavior is far less clear-cut than the diagnostic system, and, in imposing this artificial clarity, critics claim, diagnosis distorts human truth.

A third criticism is that diagnosis gives the illusion of explanation (Carson, 1996). For example, the statement "She is hallucinating because she has schizophrenia" *seems* to have explanatory value. In fact, it has none. "Schizophrenia" is simply a term that was made up to describe a certain behavior pattern involving hallucinations—a behavior pattern of which the cause is still largely unknown. Likewise, "depression," "phobia," "paranoia," and other diagnostic labels are not explanations but terms used so that researchers can do the work necessary to find explanations. This fact is often forgotten.

A fourth criticism is that diagnostic labeling can be harmful to people. As some theorists have argued, the label obscures the person's individuality, inviting mental health professionals to attend to the "phobia" or "depression" rather than the human being—or, for that matter, the family or the society, which may be the true source of the disorder (Sarbin, 1997). In addition, others' reactions to diagnostic labels can do concrete harm, damaging people's personal relationships, making it hard for them to get jobs, and in some cases depriving them of their civil rights. Furthermore, sociocultural theorists such as Scheff (1975) claim that diagnostic labels encourage people to settle back into the "sick" role and become permanent mental patients.

According to some writers, the shortcomings of *DSM*-based diagnosis are so serious that the system should be abandoned altogether. In a classic 1975 paper, for example, Rosenhan argued that a diagnostic system must demonstrate that its benefits (in indicating appropriate treatments, for instance, or in leading researchers to causes) outweigh its liabilities in order to justify its use. As causes and effective treatments had not yet been discovered for so many of the *DSM* categories, there

This man is filing for unemployment. One criticism of diagnostic labeling is that it stigmatizes people, making it difficult for them to get jobs or establish personal relationships.

Research Highlights: On Being Sane in Insane Places

Can the sane be distinguished from the insane via *DSM*-based diagnosis? In the early 1970s, D. L. Rosenhan (1973) set up an experiment whereby eight psychologically stable people, with no history of mental disorder, tried to get themselves admitted to mental hospitals. The eight "pseudopatients"—three psychologists, a psychiatrist, a graduate student in psychology, a pediatrician, a painter, and a homemaker—presented themselves at separate hospitals in five states. They all went under assumed names, and those involved in mental health lied about their professions. Otherwise, they gave completely accurate histories, adding only one false detail: each of them claimed that he or she had been hearing voices that seemed to say something like "hollow," "empty," or "thud."

The pseudopatients' greatest fear in embarking on their experiment was that they would be unmasked as frauds and thrown out of the hospital. As it happened, they were diagnosed as schizophrenic and were all admitted as mental patients.

Once admitted, the pseudopatients made no further reference to the voices. They behaved completely normally, except that they made special efforts to be courteous and cooperative, yet none of them was ever exposed as a fraud. In Rosenhan's opinion, the staff simply assumed that, because these people were in a mental hospital, they were disturbed. This assumption persisted, despite the fact that all the pseudopatients spent a good part of the day taking notes on what went on in the ward. The staff either ignored the note taking or interpreted it as an indication of pathology. On one pseudopatient's hospital record, the nurse, day after day, noted this symptom: "Patient engages in writing behavior" (Rosenhan, 1973, p. 253). The genuine mental patients were apparently not so easy to fool. According to Rosenhan, they regularly accused the pseudopatients of being sane and speculated out loud that they were journalists sent in to check up on the hospital.

All the pseudopatients were eventually discharged. Their stays ranged from 7 to 52 days, with an average of 19 days. Upon discharge, they were classified not as being "cured" or as showing no behavior to support the original diagnosis but, rather, as having psychosis "in remission." In other words, their "insanity" was still in them and might reappear.

The evidence of this study led Rosenhan to conclude that, while there might in fact be a genuine difference between sanity and insanity, those whose business it was to distinguish between them were unable to do so with any accuracy. The focus of his criticism was the fact that, once the pseudopatients were admitted and began behaving normally, their normality was not detected. In his view, the reason for this was that in diagnosis the initial evaluation—which, as in this case, may be based on a single symptom—distorts all future evaluations of the patient, making it impossible for diagnosticians to see the person otherwise than in the role of "schizophrenic" or whatever he or she has been labeled. As a result, the sane cannot be distinguished from the insane.

Rosenhan's conclusion has been contested by a number of other investigators. Spitzer (1976), for example, argued that the fact that the pseudopatients were able to lie their way into the hospital was not proof that the diagnostic system was invalid. (If a person swallows a cup of blood and then goes to an emergency room and spits it up, and if the physician on duty diagnoses the person's condition as a bleeding ulcer, does this mean that the diagnostic criteria for bleeding ulcer are invalid?) As for the hospital staff's failure to detect the pseudopatients' normality once they were in the hospital, Spitzer again argued that this was no reflection on the diagnostic system. People are not diagnosed solely on the basis of how they are behaving at the moment but also on the basis of their past behavior. If a person reports having repeated hallucinations and then reports no hallucinations for 2 weeks, this does not necessarily—or even probably—mean that no psychiatric abnormality exists, much less that none ever existed. In the absence of alcoholism or other drug abuse, hallucination is ordinarily a sign of severe psychological disturbance; for a diagnostician to discount this symptom simply because it had not appeared for a few weeks would be extremely careless. Indeed, as Spitzer pointed out, the fact that the hospitals released the pseudopatients in an average of 19 days actually shows a rather rapid response to their failure to produce any further symptoms. And the fact that they were released as being "in remission," an extremely rare diagnosis, suggests that the hospital staff recognized that they were atypical, if not faked, cases; in any case, they were not just lumped together with all other people diagnosed with schizophrenia.

Rosenhan's study was widely debated in the 1970s. Whatever the validity of its conclusions, it added to the general dissatisfaction with *DSM-II*, which led to the continuing tightening of the diagnostic criteria and the effort to base those criteria on empirical evidence. In fact, under the current criteria in *DSM-IV-TR*, an individual would not be diagnosed as having schizophrenia only on the basis of auditory hallucinations.

---

was no justification, as Rosenhan saw it at that time, for continuing to use these labels. (For further discussion of Rosenhan's position, see the box above.)

Categorical vs. Dimensional Classification One proposed solution is that **categorical classification**—the sorting of patients into diagnostic categories, as per the *DSM*—be replaced by **dimensional classification.** In this method, the diagnostician would not try to pinpoint the person's "defining" pathology; instead, he or she would be scored on different dimensions of pathology. Essentially, the difference is between a qualitative and a quantitative analysis. In categorical classification, a patient might be given the diagnosis "major depressive episode." In dimensional classification, there would be no such diagnosis but, rather, a series of scores on depression, anxiety, sleep disturbance, and so forth.

Dimensional classification is not as simple as categorical classification, but, as its defenders point out, simplicity is not a virtue if it distorts reality. The *DSM* categories, they say, are based on arbitrary cut-off points. For example, to be diagnosed with schizophrenia, a person must have had the characteristic symptoms for at least six months. If the six-month requirement is not met, the person is said to have "schizophreniform disorder." These rules have resulted in a proliferation of mini-categories that may, in the end, tell us little about the patients (Nathan & Langenbucher, 1999). In the words of Widiger and Trull, "Rather than wrestle with the arbitrary distinctions between schizophrenia, simple schizophrenia, schizophreniform, schizoaffective, schizotypal, and schizoid . . . it might be preferable to assess patients along the dimensions that underlie these distinctions (e.g., severity, course, content, and pattern of schizophrenic symptomatology)" (1991, p. 124).

Other writers have pointed out how much more information dimensional classification could offer. As we saw in Chapter 1, many disorders take different forms depending on gender and age. In dimensional classification, males and females, children and adults, could be graded within their own groups—on the curve, so to speak. Dimensional classification could also specify differences in information between different sources: what the child's teachers say about his disruptiveness, as opposed to what his parents say (Achenbach & McConaughy, 1996). According to some defenders of dimensional classification (Nathan & Langenbucher, 1999), the only things standing in the way of conversion to this system are tradition and professional vanity. (Rendering a diagnosis, saying, "This patient has schizophrenia," implies a kind of authority that totaling up dimensional scores would not.) Adherents of categorical classification answer that the dimensional system is too complicated. At the same time, many of the *DSM* categories have been revised in order to allow for dimensional distinctions. In a number of categories, such as conduct disorder and substance abuse, diagnosticians are now asked to give severity ratings.

Defending Diagnosis Experienced diagnosticians harbor no hopes that *DSM-IV-TR* is foolproof, yet most mental health professionals today would not side with the arguments that Rosenhan mounted against the *DSM* system in the 1970s. The crucial point is, again, that research depends on diagnosis. As Spitzer (1976) wrote in response to Rosenhan's challenge:

> Is Rosenhan suggesting that prior to the development of effective treatments for syphilis and cancer, he would have decried the use of these diagnostic labels? Should we eliminate the diagnoses of antisocial personality, drug abuse, and alcoholism until we have treatments for these conditions whose benefits exceed the potential liabilities associated with the diagnosis? How do we study the effectiveness of treatments for these conditions if we are enjoined from using the diagnostic categories until we have effective treatments for them? (p. 469)

Such arguments have had their effect. Since the seventies, *DSM*-based diagnosis has become more widely used and, with successive improvements in the manual, less controversial.

In order to aid research, however, diagnosis must be consistent and meaningful. It must *mean* something—and it must mean the same thing to everyone—that a patient is given the label of "schizophrenia" or "phobia." In this respect, diagnosis made a poor showing in the past. Earlier editions of the *DSM* offered relatively brief and vague descriptions of the disorders listed. As a result, there was a good deal of inconsistency in diagnosis, with the further result that diagnostic groups were disappointingly heterogeneous; that is, the symptoms of the patients assigned to many of the categories were not similar enough to make the label truly useful. Furthermore, the early editions of the manual explicitly or implicitly ascribed numerous disorders to causes that had not been definitely established, thus further complicating diagnosis and impeding research.

DSM-IV-TR Beginning with *DSM-III* in 1980, revisions of the manual have been, in large part, an effort to remedy these problems. In *DSM-IV* and *DSM-IV-TR* the major innovation was a concerted effort to base the manual on research (Nathan & Langenbucher, 1999). The revision team did a systematic study of the research findings on each disorder and in some cases even had research data reanalyzed. The team also conducted field trials, comparing the usefulness of the new diagnostic criteria with those in previous editions. Let us look at the changes that have been made in the manual over the past 20 years, as reflected in *DSM-IV-TR*.

Specific Diagnostic Criteria First, the criteria for diagnosis are highly detailed and specific, including the following:

- *Essential features* of the disorder: those that "define" it
- *Associated features:* those that are usually present
- *Diagnostic criteria:* a list of symptoms (taken from the lists of essential and associated features)

that *must* be present for the patient to be given this diagnostic label
- Information on *differential diagnosis:* data that explain how to distinguish this disorder from other, similar disorders

In addition, the descriptions offer information on the course of the disorder, age at onset, degree of impairment, complications, predisposing factors, prevalence, family pattern (that is, whether the disorder tends to run in families), laboratory and physical exam findings, and relationship of the disorder to gender, age, and culture. The most important feature of the descriptions, however, is the highly specific quality of the diagnostic criteria.

Five Axes of Diagnosis A second important feature of *DSM-IV-TR* is that it requires the diagnostician to give a substantial amount of information about patients, evaluating them on five "axes," or areas of functioning:

Axis I—Clinical syndrome: the diagnostic label for the patient's most serious psychological problem, the problem for which he or she is being diagnosed

Axis II—Personality disorders or mental retardation: any accompanying long-term disorder not covered by the Axis I label.*

Axis III—General medical disorders: any medical problem that may be relevant to the psychological problem

Axis IV—Psychosocial and environmental problems: current social, occupational, environmental, or other problems that may have contributed to or are resulting from the psychological problem

Axis V—Global assessment of functioning: a rating, on a scale of 1 to 100, of the patient's current adjustment (work performance, social relationships, use of leisure time) and of his or her adjustment during the past year†

To return to our case of Joe, his diagnosis was as follows:

Axis I: Adjustment disorder with mixed disturbance of emotions and conduct

Axis II: Mild mental retardation (principal diagnosis)

Axis III: No medical problems

Axis IV: Dismissed from group home

Axis V: Current—major impairment (40), in past year—moderate difficulty (60)

Thus, instead of simply writing down "depression," today's diagnostician must create a little portrait, the features of which may then be useful in devising a treatment program. Furthermore, it is hoped that this five-part diagnosis will help researchers in their exploration of connections between psychological disorders and other factors, such as stress and physical illness.

Unspecified Cause A final important feature of *DSM-IV-TR* is that it avoids any suggestion as to the cause of a disorder unless the cause has been definitely established. This feature, introduced with *DSM-III* in 1980, necessitated substantial changes in the classification system. The term *neurosis,* for example, was dropped altogether, as it implies a Freudian theory of causation (i.e., that the disorder is due to unconscious conflict). Since 1980, the manual has simply named the disorders and described them as clearly and specifically as possible. Their causes, if they are not known, are not speculated upon. This change was not without cost, however. All successful classification systems in other sciences have been based on theory, and theory is the motor of research: It specifies what questions need answering (Follette & Houts, 1996). But only by removing causal assumptions was it possible to produce a manual that can be used by all diagnosticians, regardless of what theories they hold.

The major goal of the 1980 revision was to improve the reliability and validity of psychiatric diagnosis. Reliability and validity will be discussed as general scientific concepts in Chapter 3. Here we will see how they apply to the diagnosis of mental disorders.

Assessing the Assessment: Reliability and Validity

Reliability The **reliability** of any measurement device is the degree to which its findings can stand the test of repeated measurements. Thus, in its simplest sense, reliability is a measure of the consistency of such a device under varying conditions. A 12-inch ruler is expected to produce the same measurements whether it is used today or tomorrow, in Salt Lake

*Axis II is confined to disorders that generally date from childhood. They are separated from the Axis I "clinical syndromes" to give the diagnostician a chance to note not just the primary problem (Axis I) but also any other, chronic condition (Axis II) that accompanies the primary problem and perhaps contributes to it. In some instances, a chronic condition *is* the patient's primary problem, in which case it is still listed on Axis II but is marked "principal diagnosis."

†Reprinted with permission from the *Diagnostic and Statistical Manual of Mental Disorders,* Fourth Edition, Text Revision. Copyright © 2000 American Psychiatric Association.

City or New Orleans, by you or by me. Likewise, a psychological assessment technique, to be considered reliable, must produce the same results under a variety of circumstances.

There are three criteria for reliability in psychological assessment:

1. *Internal consistency.* Do different parts of the test yield the same results?
2. *Test-retest reliability.* Does the test yield the same results when administered to the same person at different times?
3. *Interjudge reliability.* Does the test yield the same results when scored or interpreted by different judges?

Each of these three criteria applies with particular force to certain kinds of tests. Test-retest reliability is most important in assessments of stable individual difference characteristics—for example, IQ tests. Internal consistency is most important in tests that use many items to measure a single characteristic—for example, a 60-item test for anxiety. In the diagnosis of mental disorders the most crucial criterion is interjudge reliability, the degree of agreement among different diagnosticians as to what specific disorder any given patient has.

As indicated earlier, the rate of agreement has been very low in the past. Indeed, Spitzer and Fleiss (1974), in a review of research on the reliability of psychiatric diagnosis, found that interjudge reliability was satisfactory in only *three* diagnostic categories: mental retardation, organic brain syndrome, and alcoholism. And these are broad categories.

When detailed, specific diagnostic criteria were first introduced in *DSM-III,* this problem was solved to some degree (Nathan & Langenbucher, 1999). In one study, with diagnosticians trained in the use of *DSM-IV,* the rate of agreement on some disorders, such as alcohol and substance abuse and dependence, was high (Langenbucher, Morgenstern, Labouvie, et al., 1994); yet, for certain *DSM-IV* categories, notably the personality disorders, interjudge reliability was still problematic (Nathan & Langenbucher, 1999). This is one area of weakness that later editions of the *DSM* have been trying to address. As we shall see when we examine the personality disorders, the criteria for these diagnoses are now highly specific.

Increased interjudge reliability is not achieved without costs, however. As Blashfield and Draguns (1976) have pointed out in a classic paper, reliability is not the only consideration in creating a diagnostic system. Ideally, the system should also have high "coverage"—that is, most cases of abnormal behavior should qualify for one of its categories. Earlier editions of the *DSM* achieved high coverage by having loose diagnostic criteria; because the behavioral descriptions were so broad, almost any patient could be made to fit somewhere. The later editions, with their stricter criteria, have lower coverage, with the result that more patients are swept into residual categories—some writers call them "wastebasket diagnoses"—such as "psychotic disorder not otherwise specified." This problem, in turn, has been addressed by adding new categories. The number of categories has more than tripled since the introduction of the diagnostic manual. (See Figure 2.1.) Even so, the diagnostic criteria are so strict that many patients

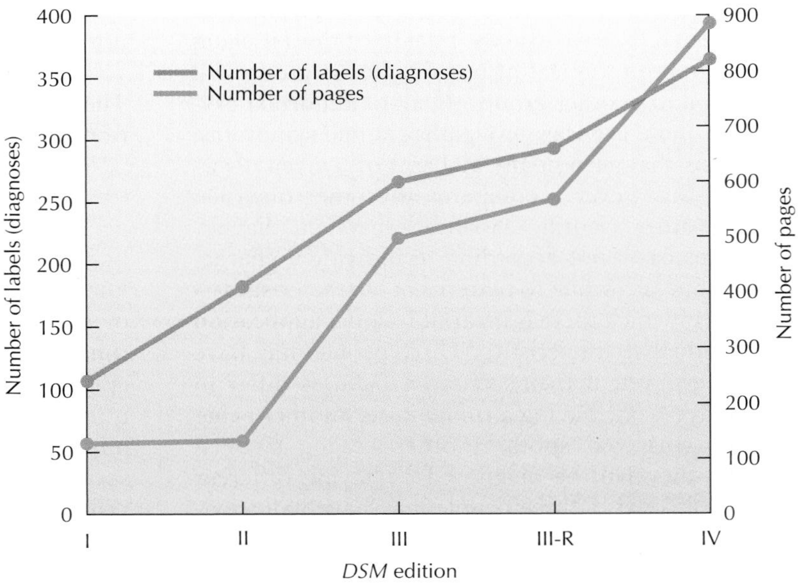

FIGURE 2.1 The growth of successive editions of the *DSM*. Versions I, II, III, III-R, and IV are the first, second, third, revised third, and fourth editions, respectively. (Adapted from Follette & Houts, 1996, p. 1125.)

still end up with "not otherwise specified" (NOS) diagnoses. In certain categories, such as the dissociative disorders (Chapter 8), the *majority* of patients are given NOS diagnoses (Mezzich, Fabrega, Coffman, et al., 1989; Saxena & Prasad, 1989). Thus, as diagnostic groups have become purer, they have become smaller, leaving researchers less to work with.

Validity Whereas reliability refers to the consistency of a measuring instrument under varying conditions, **validity** refers to the extent to which the test measures what it is supposed to measure. Do people who score high on a typing test really type better than people who score low? If so, the test is valid.

As with reliability, there are several kinds of validity. Because the major purpose of any assessment system is to describe and predict behavior, we will discuss the two kinds of validity that are most relevant to the diagnosis of mental disorders: descriptive validity and predictive validity.

Descriptive Validity The **descriptive validity** of an assessment device is the degree to which it provides significant information about the current behavior of the people being assessed. A frequent criticism of the diagnosis of mental disorders is that it has little descriptive validity—that it does not tell us much about the people diagnosed. Proponents of this view point to the fact, mentioned earlier, that people assigned to the same diagnostic group may actually behave quite differently, while people assigned to different diagnostic groups may show many of the same behavioral oddities—a problem that was not solved by *DSM-IV* or *DSM-IV-TR* (Frances, First, & Pincus, 1995; Follette & Houts, 1996). But diagnosis does not claim to produce groups that are completely homogeneous; this would be impossible, for no two people, normal or abnormal, behave exactly alike. Nor does it claim that a symptom typical of one diagnostic group will not be found in other groups. In all of abnormal psychology, there are very few pathognomic symptoms, symptoms that accompany all cases of a given disorder and that never accompany any other disorder. Like any other scientific classification system, diagnosis groups cases not according to individual characteristics but according to patterns of characteristics—patterns in which there is invariably some duplication of individual characteristics. Three people may have high fevers, yet, if their symptom pictures differ in other ways—one having a runny nose, another being covered with red spots, another having swollen cheeks—they will be diagnosed as having different diseases. Likewise, three people may have hallucinations, yet if they differ in other important respects—one having a long history of alcohol abuse, the second showing severe depression, and the third believing that her thoughts are being broadcast so that everyone in the room can hear them—then they are likely to be given three different diagnoses: alcoholism, depression, and schizophrenia, respectively. In other words, research would have to show that the pattern of symptoms—not just individual symptoms—is substantially different within categories and substantially similar between categories before the diagnosis of mental disorders could be said to have poor descriptive validity.

A more serious challenge to the descriptive validity of diagnosis is the fact that most patients (Kessler, McGonagle, Zhao, et al., 1994; Nathan & Langenbucher, 1999) show **comorbidity;** that is, they meet the diagnostic criteria for more than one Axis I disorder. In such cases, the person is usually given more than one diagnosis, but such multiple diagnoses, implying that the person has two (or more) independent disorders, may not be accurate descriptions of the case. Comorbid conditions generally have a more chronic course, a poorer response to treatment, and a poorer prognosis than single disorders. In other words, they may represent a different, unrecognized disorder, rather than a combination of recognized disorders. (See the box on page 35.) Recent editions of the *DSM* have struggled with the question of comorbidity—some of the new categories cover what, earlier, would have been called comorbid conditions—but this problem will remain an issue for those revising the manual.

Predictive Validity An assessment tool with high descriptive validity is one that helps us describe the person's current behavior. An assessment method with high **predictive validity** is one that helps us answer important questions about that behavior. In abnormal psychology, the most important questions involve determining cause, prognosis, and treatment. The extent to which a diagnosis answers those questions is the extent of its predictive validity.

Some diagnostic labels have high predictive validity in some respects. We know, for example, that people diagnosed with mania or schizophrenia are likely to respond to certain drugs. Likewise, we know that many people diagnosed with either mania or depression will probably recover within a short time—and that they will probably have further episodes of mood disturbance. Diagnostic labels offer less information, however, as to the course of milder disturbances or the treatment they will respond to.

It is possible that the limited predictive validity of diagnosis is due primarily to its limited reliability. While an assessment technique that has high reliability

Research Highlights: Comorbidity: Disturbance as a Package

One of every two people in this country has had or will have a serious psychological disorder, and one of three has had to cope with such a disorder within the past year. These sobering figures were the product of a survey of over 8,000 people, ages 15 to 54—the first survey ever to administer a structured face-to-face mental health interview to a representative sample of the population of the United States (Kessler, McGonagle, Zhao, et al., 1994).

The participants were questioned as to whether they had suffered any 1 of 14 major disorders described in the *DSM* and, if so, what treatment they had received. Leading the list were major depression, alcohol dependence, and phobias. As surprising as the prevalence was the rate of treatment. Less than 40 percent of those who reported having had a disorder had ever sought or received treatment.

The primary focus of this study was comorbidity—two or more disorders occurring simultaneously—and the results were eye-opening. The National Comorbidity Survey (NCS) discovered that having two or more psychological disorders at the same time is more common than having just one. Almost 80 percent of the disorders reported to the NCS coexisted with at least one other disorder. Interestingly, these comorbid disorders tended to be concentrated in a relatively small sector of the population. More than 50 percent of all the reported disorders occurred in the 14 percent of the participants who had a history of three or more comorbid disorders. This group—which also tended to have the most serious disorders—tended to be urban, low-income, poorly educated, white, female, and aged 20 to 40. (In general, the more years, the more money, and the more education a person had, the less likely he or she was to report a current disorder.)

Perhaps the most important question about cases of comorbidity is whether, in fact, they represent comorbidity. When a person shows symptoms of two different disorders, does he or she really have two disorders—or just one complex disorder that our diagnostic system is wrongly separating into two?

Consider the relationship between antisocial personality disorder (a long-standing pattern of violating the rights of others—see Chapter 11) and substance dependence. These two disorders often turn up in the same person—so often, indeed, that each is mentioned in the *DSM's* description of the other. But *are* they two different disorders? Sometimes it is possible, from the person's history, to see how one seemed to give rise to the other—how, for example, a heroin addiction eventually led the person into antisocial acts (theft, betrayal of friends, abandonment of children) or, conversely, how a long-standing pattern of antisocial behavior eventually came to include heroin addiction. But very often the two patterns develop simultaneously. Furthermore, even if one precedes the other, this does not prove that it caused the other. Possibly, both were caused by something else altogether.

The comorbidity question, then, has to do with more than terminology. How we define a disorder affects our theories of causation. It also affects treatment decisions. Consider, for example, a person whose heroin dependence developed as part of a long-standing pattern of antisocial behavior. If he is diagnosed as having two comorbid disorders—substance dependence and antisocial personality disorder—this may obscure the fact that what he really needs to be treated for is antisocial personality disorder and that, without such treatment, any therapy for the drug problem is likely to be a waste of time.

On the other hand, it might still be useful to provide both diagnoses; whether or not each represents a separate disorder, each may require separate treatment. In the case above, the fact that the drug dependence seemed to develop as a consequence of the antisocial personality disorder does not mean that it will automatically clear up if the person is treated for antisocial personality disorder. By that point, the drug habit may have developed a life of its own, creating the conditions for its continuance. Furthermore, a drug problem will seriously affect the person's chances of responding to treatment for antisocial personality disorder (just as, conversely, antisocial tendencies will undermine drug treatment).

Antisocial personality disorder and drug dependence are not the only pair of disorders involved in the comorbidity question. There are a number of such pairings, and the list will no doubt lengthen as research continues. In light of the NCS finding that most cases of psychological disorder are actually cases of more than one disorder, our current way of viewing psychological abnormality—as a matter of discrete syndromes—may have to be revised. Even if the syndromes remain separate, we will need to study them not in isolation but in interaction.

may have low validity,* the reverse is not true. To have high validity, a system must have high reliability. The improved reliability of the recent editions of the *DSM* may result in improved validity.

*For example, astrology has high reliability. People can be grouped according to birth date with great consistency and accuracy. But, in order to have high validity as well, these groupings would have to reflect what the astrologers claim they reflect—namely, individual personality traits. Because there is no evidence that they do, the system has low validity.

Problems in Assessment

The reliability and validity of any assessment tool can be affected by a number of problems, some having to do with the administration of the measure, others with its interpretation. One such problem is the assessor—his or her personal manner and how it affects the person being assessed (Garb, 1998). If a diagnostician tends to be very formal and businesslike during a diagnostic interview, the respondent—

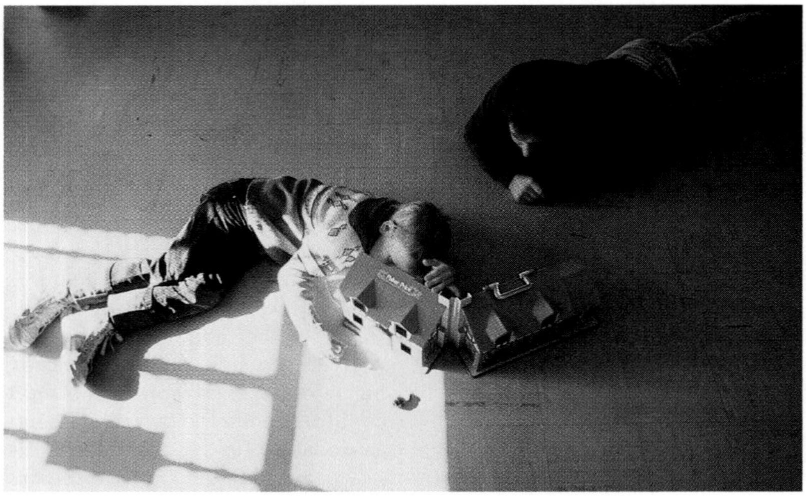

Assessment techniques must be geared to the capabilities of the subject. Some children will not respond well to a formal interview. The assessor may find it more effective to let the child's concerns emerge through play in an informal setting.

particularly a child or a troubled adult—may respond in a guarded way. If the diagnostician interprets this behavior as a reflection of paranoid or depressive leanings and diagnoses accordingly, how are the people who later treat the patient to know that the "paranoia" or "depression" was, in part, a response to the diagnostician? Even attributes that the examiner cannot control, such as physical appearance, ethnicity, and gender, may affect the respondent's performance.

Assessors affect examination results more directly through their interpretation of the evidence. People present many different sorts of information; diagnosticians must filter all of it through their own minds, selecting what seems most important. In the process, they are bound to be influenced by their own biases. For example, some diagnosticians favor certain diagnoses over others. Indeed, there have often been marked differences in diagnosis between hospitals, between communities, and between countries (Garb, 1998). For years, what was called psychotic depression in England was often called schizophrenia in the United States (Cooper, Kendell, Gurland, et al., 1972). Likewise, one hospital may have long experience treating manic episodes, while a neighboring hospital has equally long experience with paranoid schizophrenia—largely because those are the diagnostic labels favored by their respective staffs. On a more comprehensive level, many critics feel that diagnosticians in general have a "pathological bias"—a tendency to see sickness instead of health (Garb, 1998). Diagnosticians often have neither the tools nor the training to assess areas of strength, whereas they are carefully trained to spot signs of weakness and deviance (Seligman & Csikszentmihalyi, 2000). Consequently, it is weakness and deviance that they tend to find. (See the box on page 30.)

Finally, pragmatic considerations may interfere with accurate evaluation. When psychological treatment is paid for through company insurance, word of the patient's "condition" may reach the ears of his or her coworkers. Anticipating such gossip, diagnosticians may apply a label that indicates a milder disturbance than they feel the patient actually has. In other instances, they may exaggerate a patient's disturbance—again, for practical reasons. The Veterans Administration, for example, pays higher benefits to veterans diagnosed as psychotic than to those with less severe diagnoses. Thus, when a patient's financial circumstances are particularly bad, psychiatrists may favor the evidence for psychosis.

Recent editions of the *DSM* have tried to minimize these interferences in various ways, principally by making the criteria for a diagnosis very specific and by establishing for each disorder a fixed "decision rule," or minimum number of symptoms that must be present for a patient to receive that diagnosis. Under "major depressive episode," for example, the manual lists nine symptoms (Chapter 10) and then specifies that, for that diagnosis to be given, the person must have shown five of the symptoms during the same two-week period. Such a rule is harder to interpret freely than the vaguer descriptions in earlier editions of the manual.

Another suggestion that has been offered for minimizing assessment interferences is that diagnosticians should rely more on statistical relationships, or actuarial judgment, than on their own clinical judgment. Insurance companies, for example, use actuarial judgment to calculate risks. Given an applicant who is male, 50 years old, married, and the survivor of one heart attack, they use tables based on the histories of other such people to calculate what this person's life expectancy is and what his medical expenses are likely to be. Because research has shown that actuarial judgment is frequently superior to clinical judgment (Garb, 1998), it has been proposed that particularly in making treatment decisions—whether a patient should be given psychotherapy, put on drugs, or hospitalized—diagnosticians should turn to the actuarial method. Statistical rules are available to predict violence, child abuse, and repeat offenses among juvenile offenders. However, as yet, there are no well-validated actuarial methods for making diagnoses or treatment decisions (Wood, Garb, Lilienfeld, et al., 2002).

Even if the diagnostic system were flawless, however, there would still be a problem, because a certain percentage of diagnosticians simply do not follow the rules. A study of *DSM-III-R* personality disorder diagnoses made by psychiatrists and psychologists found that 72 percent of the clinicians gave patients diagnoses that didn't satisfy the diagnostic criteria for the disorders ascribed to them (Davis, Blashfield, & McElroy, 1993). Some therapists whose patients tend to have the normal run of middle-class sorrows fall back repeatedly on certain diagnoses (anxiety disorder and adjustment disorder are particular favorites) that they feel are specific enough to satisfy the insurance company but "harmless" and vague enough not to invade the patient's privacy. Consequently, they seldom even open the diagnostic manual.

Methods of Assessment

Assessment techniques fall into four general categories: the interview, psychological tests, laboratory tests, and observation in natural settings.

The Interview

Of all the methods of assessment, the **interview,** consisting of a face-to-face conversation between participant and examiner, is the oldest, the most commonly used, and the most versatile. It may be highly structured, with the participant answering a prearranged sequence of questions, or it may be unstructured, giving participants the chance to describe their problem in their own way. The evaluation method also varies from structured to unstructured. Even after a highly structured question-and-answer session, examiners may rely primarily on their own subjective impressions in evaluating participants. Alternatively, they may follow a detailed manual to score participants' responses, giving 1 point for one type of response, 2 points for another type of response, and so forth.

The degree of structure in the interview and the questions asked depend on the interviewer's purpose. If the aim is simply to put the client at ease, in an effort to promote trust and candor, then the structure will be loose. This is usually the case, for example, with the intake interview at the beginning of psychotherapy. However, interviewers often have a clear idea of what kind of information they need and cannot waste too much time obtaining it. Therefore, most interviews have a definable structure.

The major pitfall of assessment by interview is that it can give uncontrolled play to interviewers' subjectivity and biases. Interviewers, like most of the rest of us, have feelings about Blacks and Whites, women and men, handsome people and plain people, even short people and tall people, and such feelings, not to speak of more specific biases, can influence the results of the interview.

For this reason, a fairly structured interview and scoring system are often recommended, even though the individual's responses and the interviewer's intuitive powers are thereby restricted. When the purpose of the interview is diagnosis, and particularly when the diagnosis is to be used in research—for example, to assemble a study group—researchers use highly structured interviews. One such interview is the Schedule for Affective Disorders and Schizophrenia, or SADS (Endicott & Spitzer, 1978), which, with its own special scoring system, has proved highly reliable (Andreasen, McDonald-Scott, Grove, et al., 1982). Another is the Structured Clinical Interview for *DSM-IV,* or SCID, widely used by clinicians to help in providing *DSM*-based diagnoses. (See the box on page 38.) A third is the Diagnostic Interview Schedule, or DIS, of the National Institute of Mental Health (Robins, Helzer, Croughan, et al., 1981), which yields diagnoses by computer. Such diagnostic tools do not have high coverage, but that is not their purpose. Their goal is to give diagnoses as precisely as possible so that, when a team of researchers says that a new drug worked or didn't work with a group of people with schizophrenia, they can be fairly certain that it was, in fact, tested on a group of people with schizophrenia. A number of researchers (e.g., Garb, 1998) have shown that structured diagnostic interviews do greatly improve the reliability of diagnosis.

A very widely used form of interview is the **mental status exam,** or **MSE.** The MSE is to mental problems what a physical checkup is to medical problems—that is, a very broad examination aimed at turning up any sign of disorder. Through observation and questioning, the diagnostician rates the patient on appearance, speech, mood, perception, thought content, and cognitive processes (Ginsberg, 1985). The purpose is not just to detect disorders but, above all, to spot dementia (severe mental deterioration) and other neurological disorders. A shorter form of the MSE is the **mini mental status exam,** or **MMS.** (See

Focus On... A Sample SCID Interview

In this section of the SCID interview, the diagnostician is evaluating the participant for major depressive disorder. Note how structured the interview is. The questions are specified, and they deal with six symptoms of the disorder. (See the sentences in italics.) Depending on the answers, the diagnostician will give the person a score of 1 (symptom absent), 2 (symptom mild), or 3 (symptom pronounced) for each of the six items.

Now I am going to ask you some more questions about your mood.

- In the last month . . .

  Has there been a period of time when you were feeling depressed or down most of the day nearly every day? (What was that like?)

  IF YES: How long did it last? (As long as two weeks?)

- *What about losing interest or pleasure in things you usually enjoyed?*

  IF YES: Was it nearly every day? How long did it last? (As long as two weeks?)

- During the worst two weeks of last month . . .

  Did you lose or gain any weight? (How much?) (Were you trying to lose weight?)

  IF NO: How was your appetite? (What about compared to your usual appetite?) (Did you have to force yourself to eat?) (Eat [less/more] than usual?) (Was that nearly every day?)

- *How were you sleeping?* (Trouble falling asleep, waking frequently, trouble staying asleep, waking too early, OR sleeping too much? How many hours a night compared to usual? Was that nearly every night?)

- *Were you so fidgety or restless that you were unable to sit still?* (Was it so bad that other people noticed it? What did they notice? Was that nearly every day?)

  IF NO: What about the opposite—talking or moving more slowly than is normal for you? (Was it so bad that other people noticed it? What did they notice? Was that nearly every day?)

- *What was your energy like?* (Tired all the time? Nearly every day?)

Source: Adapted from *SCID Newsletter*, vol. 1, issue 1.

the sample questions in the box on page 39.) The MMS is the world's most widely used screening method for dementia (Mohs, 1995). Our sample patient, Joe, was given a clinical interview and a mental status exam. Here are the examiner's "behavioral observations":

EVALUATION OF JOE: Behavioral Observations

Joe was a 23-year-old White male, heavyset. He was dressed in a T-shirt, shorts, and basketball shoes without laces. His movement was rather sluggish. He had a constant hand tremor, and his legs shook vigorously when he was nervous. His speech, though coherent, was hesitant and poorly articulated. He seemed proud and at ease when he was responding correctly; when confronted with failure, he became uncomfortable and embarrassed. His comprehension of the instructions was adequate, and he asked for clarification when he needed it. His concentration was satisfactory in general, but his attention wandered when he was having a hard time with a question. He was quick to establish rapport with the examiner and was cooperative throughout the examination.

Psychological Tests

More structured than the normal interview, the **psychological test** is a standard procedure in which persons are presented with a series of stimuli to which they are asked to respond. Such a test, like the highly structured interview, gives the individual little freedom in responding, but, because of its restrictive quality, the psychological test can be scored more easily and more objectively. In fact, many psychological tests are scored by computer and then interpreted by a psychologist.

For decades, the dominant method of psychological testing has been the **psychometric approach.** The aim of this method is to locate stable underlying characteristics, or **traits** (e.g., anxiety, passivity, aggression, intelligence), that presumably exist in differing degrees in everyone. Because it assumes the existence of stable traits and aims to measure them, the psychometric method considers response variability due to situational influences to be simply a source of error and makes every effort to screen out such influences. For example, instead of leaving it to examiners to give the test instructions in their own words—words that might vary in substance and tone from one examiner to the next—most psychological tests now provide extremely precise directions that the examiner reads aloud to the participants, just as with the Scholastic Assessment Test (SAT).

There are many kinds of psychological tests. We will discuss intelligence tests, projective personality tests, self-report personality inventories, and tests for cognitive impairment.

Intelligence Tests **Intelligence tests** were the first of the psychological assessment techniques to be widely used. Modern intelligence tests are based on the work

Focus On... The Mini Mental Status Exam

ORIENTATION:
- What is the year?
- What is the season?
- What is the day of the week?
- What is the month?
- Can you tell me where we are? (residence or street name required)
- What city/town are we in?

REGISTRATION:
- I am going to name three objects. After I have said them, I want you to repeat them. Remember what they are because I am going to ask you to name them again in a few minutes. "Apple . . . Table . . . Penny."

ATTENTION AND CALCULATION:
- Can you subtract 7 from 100, and then subtract 7 from the answer you get and keep subtracting 7 until I tell you to stop?
- Now I am going to spell a word forwards and I want you to spell it backwards (in reverse order). The word is WORLD. W-O-R-L-D.

RECALL:
- Now what were the three objects I asked you to remember?

LANGUAGE:
- What is this called? (Show watch.)
- What is this called? (Show pencil.)
- Now I would like you to repeat a phrase after me: "No ifs, ands, or buts."
- Take this paper in your right hand, fold the paper in half using both hands, and put the paper down, using your left hand.
- Pick the paper up and write a short sentence on it for me. (Sentence must have subject and verb and make sense.)
- Please turn to page 8 in your booklet. Now copy the design that you see printed on the page. (Design is interlocking pentagons. The result must have five-sided figures, with intersection forming a four-sided figure.)

Source: Adapted from Holzer, Tischler, Leaf, et al., 1984, p. 6.

of Alfred Binet, the French psychologist who in 1905 introduced the first intelligence test into the French school system to help teachers determine which children would require special education. Later revised by Lewis Terman of Stanford University and now known as the Stanford-Binet Intelligence Scale, the test measures a child's ability to recognize objects in a picture, to remember a series of digits, to define simple words, to complete sentences in a logical fashion, and so forth. There is also an adult version of the test, with comparable tasks scaled to adult abilities. The person's final score on the test is rendered as an **intelligence quotient**, or **IQ.**

Also widely used are the Wechsler Intelligence Scales. Developed by American psychologist David Wechsler, these tests, unlike the Stanford-Binet tests, yield not only a general IQ but also a Verbal IQ, measuring verbal ability, knowledge, and comprehension, and a Performance IQ, measuring problem solving and intelligence in a way that does not depend upon verbal ability (see Figure 2.2, page 41). When Verbal IQ is being assessed, adults might be asked how many days there are in a year or how many state capitals there are in the United States. When Performance IQ is being assessed, they might be asked to transcribe a code or to reproduce a design with colored blocks. There are three Wechsler tests, each geared to a different age group: the Wechsler Adult Intelligence Scale–III (WAIS-III), the Wechsler Intelligence Scale for Children (WISC-III), and the Wechsler Preschool and Primary Scale of Intelligence–Revised (WPPSI-R) (Tulsky & Ledbetter, 2000). Joe was given the WAIS, together with two other intelligence tests. His results are summarized here:

EVALUATION OF JOE: Intellectual Functioning

Joe is functioning at a level of mild mental retardation (Full Scale IQ: 59; Verbal Scale IQ: 61; Performance Scale IQ: 56). His results on a school achievement test placed him at a third-grade level. His performance on a picture vocabulary test was equivalent to that of a 10-year-old. His main cognitive difficulties seem to be in perceptual accuracy, visual-motor-spatial integration, and information processing. This is probably due to an organic brain impairment.

Such cognitive problems are obviously an important factor in his current poor adjustment. His thinking is simple and concrete; therefore, he is at a loss, and becomes disorganized, in complex or ambiguous situations. In particular, he has difficulty understanding cause-and-effect relationships. He acknowledges, for example, that his temper and his drug use were the reasons for his dismissal from the group home, but he doesn't see why. His ability to distinguish right from wrong is at a very superficial level.

The potential influence of intelligence tests is very great. Not only do they play an important part in the diagnosis of mental retardation and brain damage, but, unlike all other psychological tests, they are routinely given to schoolchildren across the country, often with serious consequences. Ability tests can determine whether students are placed in special education or "gifted" classes, what high schools and colleges they will attend, and in turn what kind of education they will receive.

The Wechsler Intelligence Scales measure a number of dimensions of intelligence, including Performance IQ. In the segment of that test shown here, this boy is being timed as he tries to reproduce a pattern of blocks.

Because of their importance, intelligence tests are very carefully designed. They have been shown to have high internal consistency: A person will do approximately the same on different items measuring the same kind of ability (Sparrow & Davis, 2000). They also have high test-retest reliability: A person who takes the same IQ test twice, several years apart, will score approximately the same both times (Sparrow & Davis, 2000). Finally, the validity of the major IQ tests has been shown to be relatively high in that there is a strong correlation between children's IQ scores and their later performance in school (Sparrow & Davis, 2000).

But is the ability to do well in our school systems the most important measure of intelligence? As Wechsler (1958) pointed out, intelligence is not an existing thing, such as heart rate or blood pressure, that can be objectively quantified. Rather, it is an inferred construct. We infer what we call intelligence from what we consider correct behavior in response to various problems. For a number of years, it has been charged that both our schools and our IQ tests are culturally biased—that they interpret as intelligence what is actually just familiarity with middle-class culture (Suzuki & Valencia, 1999; Tulsky & Ledbetter, 2000). A test question that asks whether a cup goes with a bowl, a spoon, or a saucer will not be easy for a lower-income child who has never seen a saucer. In response to such criticism, efforts have been made in recent years to remove inadvertent cultural bias from the major IQ tests (Tulsky & Ledbetter, 2000).

Another, more general challenge to IQ testing is that conventional IQ tests—the Stanford-Binet and the WAIS—are "static" measures of existing abilities and knowledge levels that do not assess a person's capacity to learn. In contrast, dynamic intelligence testing measures the learning potential of individuals during the acquisition of new cognitive operations (Grigorenko & Sternberg, 1998). Unlike conventional IQ tests, dynamic testing emphasizes the psychological processes involved in learning, uses feedback from the examiner, and takes place in an atmosphere of teaching (Grigorenko & Sternberg, 1998).

A second general challenge to IQ testing is whether it reflects too narrow a view of mental ability. Psychologist Howard Gardner (1998; Gardner & Hatch, 1989) has argued that traditional IQ tests measure only three components of intelligence: verbal ability, mathematical-logical reasoning, and spatial-perceptual skills. In Gardner's view, there are at least five other important kinds of intelligence: musical ability, physical skill, interpersonal ability (the capacity to understand others), intrapersonal ability (the capacity to understand oneself), and naturalist ability (the capacity to discern patterns in nature). Other researchers cite evidence of "practical intelligence" (the ability to implement solutions in real-

One criticism of IQ testing is that it fails to measure all components of intelligence. For example, traditional IQ tests would not account for the musical talent demonstrated by this violinist. Howard Gardner proposed a broader view of mental ability, naming eight important kinds of intelligence, of which musical ability is one.

Paraphrased Wechslerlike Questions

General Information

1. How many wings does a bird have?
2. How many nickels make a dime?
3. What is steam made of?
4. Who wrote "Paradise Lost"?
5. What is pepper?

General Comprehension

1. What should you do if you see someone forget his book when he leaves his seat in a restaurant?
2. What is the advantage of keeping money in a bank?
3. Why is copper often used in electrical wires?

Arithmetic

1. Sam had three pieces of candy and Joe gave him four more. How many pieces of candy did Sam have altogether?
2. Three men divided eighteen golf balls equally among themselves. How many golf balls did each man receive?
3. If two apples cost 15¢, what will be the cost of a dozen apples?

Similarities

1. In what way are a lion and a tiger alike?
2. In what way are a saw and hammer alike?
3. In what way are an hour and a week alike?
4. In what way are a circle and a triangle alike?

Vocabulary

This test consists simply of asking, "What is a ______ ?" or "What does ______ mean?" The words cover a wide range of difficulty or familiarity.

Block Design

Simulated items similar to those in the Wechsler Intelligence Scales for Adults and Children.

FIGURE 2.2 These test items are similar to those included in the various Wechsler Intelligence Scales. *(Left)* Sample questions from five of the verbal subtests. *(Right)* A problem in block design—the subject is asked to arrange a set of blocks to match a pattern like the one shown.

world environments, Wagner, 2000) and "emotional intelligence" (the capacity to perceive accurately, appraise, and express emotion; Mayer, Salovey, & Caruso, 2000) as important contributors to success. The empathy of a friend, the physical skills of a Venus Williams or a Tiger Woods—in our culture these are not considered components of "intelligence," and they are not what IQ tests aim to measure. According to Gardner, they should be, for they are controlled by the brain and help to determine an individual's success in life.

Projective Personality Tests **Projective personality tests** are based on the psychodynamic assumption that people's true motives, because they are largely unconscious, must be drawn out indirectly (Dosajh, 1996). Accordingly, projective tests expose individuals to ambiguous stimuli into which they must "read" meaning. Whatever meaning they give to the stimulus is thought to contain clues to their unconscious processes—clues that the interviewer must interpret.

The Rorschach Most famous of the projective tests is the **Rorschach Psychodiagnostic Inkblot Test** (Rorschach, 1942), in which participants are asked to respond to 10 cards, each showing a symmetrical inkblot design. The designs vary in complexity and coloring. The test is administered in two phases. In the first phase, the "free-association" phase, participants are asked to describe as specifically as possible what each card reminds them of. In the second phase, called the "inquiry" phase, participants are asked which characteristics of each inkblot contributed to the formation of their impression of that inkblot.

As we pointed out earlier, highly unstructured interviewing methods may be combined with highly structured scoring methods. This is the case with the Rorschach. The subjective material elicited by the inkblots is generally evaluated according to a detailed manual, indicating how specific responses are to be interpreted (Beck, 1961; Exner, 1978; Exner & Weiner, 1995). For example, an important aspect of the evaluation depends on the extent to which the

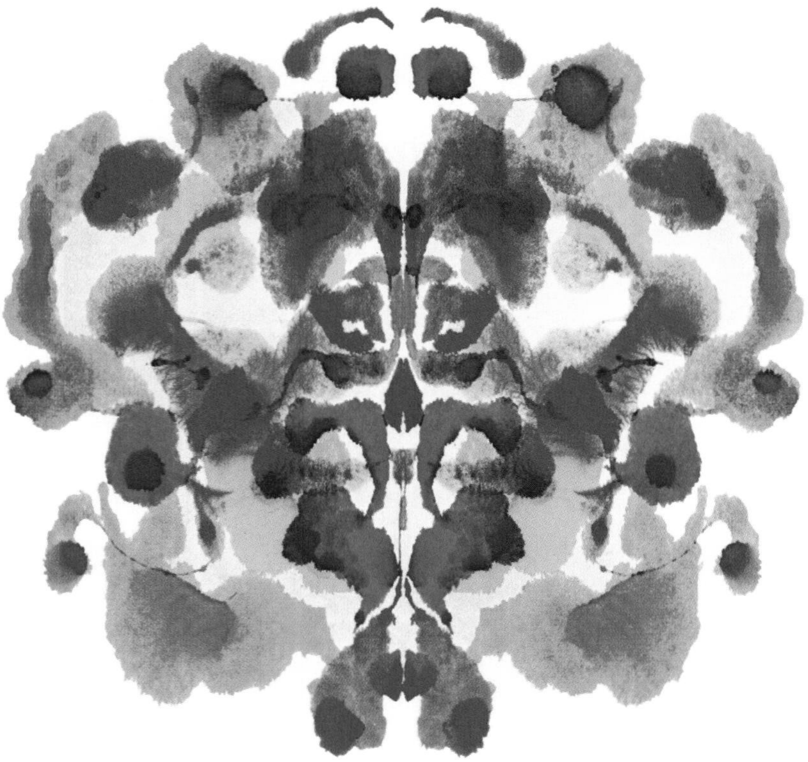

FIGURE 2.3 An inkblot similar to those used in the Rorschach test. In this test, the participant is asked to describe what he or she "sees" in the design, and why.

individual's responses represent what is called "good form"—that is, how plausible the individual's interpretation of a picture is in view of the shapes contained in it. Consider, for example, the inkblot in Figure 2.3, which might reasonably be interpreted as an elaborate flower or insect. Many other readings are plausible as well, but if an individual claimed that what he or she saw in this picture was a small boy crouching in a corner—something that actually contradicts the form of the inkblot—then the interviewer might conclude that the response reflected an inner conflict and distortion of reality (or that the individual was not taking the test seriously). Here is Joe's response to a Rorschach card:

EVALUATION OF JOE: The Rorschach Test

The assessor (A) showed Joe (J) a card and asked him what it looked like:

J: A forest and a fire around it.

A: [Repeats Joe's response.]

J: Here is the fire.

A: What makes it look like a fire?

J: How the flames are up in the air.

A: What makes it look like flames?

J: Because it's burning the tree.

A: What makes it look like it's burning the tree?

J: Someone started it. You can tell by the bushes in flames.

A: What makes it look like flames to you?

J: How it's colored, because fire is yellow.

A: What makes it look like bushes to you?

J: Because you got the tree standing.

A: What makes it look like a tree to you?

J: Because it's big, and it has leaves on it.

A: What makes it look like leaves to you?

J: The way how it's shaded.

The examiner also weighs the content of the individual's responses. If a certain theme keeps reappearing in the individual's interpretations, then, depending on the nature of the theme, the examiner may take it as a clue to underlying conflicts. Water, for example, may be interpreted as a sign of alcoholism; eyes as indicative of paranoid suspicion; and so forth.

The TAT A second popular projective technique is the **Thematic Apperception Test, or TAT.** In this test, the participant is presented with a series of pictures.

FIGURE 2.4 Picture similar to those used in the Thematic Apperception Test (TAT). In this test, the participant is asked to tell a story about what is being shown in the picture.

Unlike the abstract Rorschach inkblots, most of the TAT pictures show a person, or possibly two or three people, doing something. The scenes are ambiguous enough to allow for a variety of interpretations, yet they nudge the participant in the direction of certain kinds of associations. For example, the picture in Figure 2.4, showing a younger woman and an older woman, might tap the participant's feelings about his or her mother. Some researchers (e.g., Rapaport, Gill, & Shaefer, 1968) claim that certain cards are particularly useful in eliciting specific kinds of information, such as the presence of underlying depression, suicidal thoughts, and strong aggressive impulses. Following are Joe's responses to three of the TAT cards. Most of his responses contained themes of violence.

As with the Rorschach, individuals go through the cards one by one. With each card, they are asked to describe what has led up to the scene presented in the picture, what is going on in the picture, what the characters are thinking and feeling, and what the outcome will be. Like the Rorschach, the TAT includes an inquiry phase to clarify ambiguous responses. Then, through a complex scoring system, the individual's responses are converted into an interpretation of his or her unconscious conflicts and motivations.

EVALUATION OF JOE: The TAT Test

Card 1 This is a boy who is looking at a gun. Don't know if it's loaded or not. He's thinking about using it on himself, like killing himself. He tries to find some bullets for the gun in his dad's room, and he will find the bullets and will shoot himself three times in the head.

Card 14 This is a man who looks like he's escaping from prison because of a murder that he committed. So he asks his friend to go with him, and the friend goes with him, and they will run into the forest. The guards are chasing them with their dogs, and they get caught.

Card 13 This is John and his wife, Mary. John has been married to Mary for about 6 years. One day John came home from work and found Mary in bed dead. He was shocked, terrified. Police came to their home and questioned John, and he said he didn't do it. He was framed for murder, so then John had to go to jail because he was framed, and his lawyer talked to him. Then they went to court, and the jury decided that he was not guilty.

There are other projective tests as well, including the Sentence Completion Test, in which the interviewer reads the first part of a sentence and the participant supplies the rest. This is a sampling of Joe's responses to the Sentence Completion Test. His words are in italics.

EVALUATION OF JOE: Sentence Completion Test

He felt held back by *his anger.*

Because of his mother, *he ran away.*

Most women *should realize that they love their children.*

His family treats him as *dirt.*

Most of all he wants *another home.*

He got sore when *he started drinking.*

He would be happy if *he was more smarter.*

Most men act as though *they are rich.*

Ever since he got sick, *he got better.*

When others have to rely on him he *gets upset.*

When they turned him down for the job he *got mad.*

He is afraid of *himself.* [Interviewer asks why.] *Sometimes I feel like I'm in a different world.*

He is ashamed of *himself.* [Interviewer asks why.] *Because he can't get the attention that he needs.*

Whenever he was with his mother he felt *nervous.*

He thinks of himself as *mature.*

The main thing in his marriage is *money.*

His first sexual experience *was when I was about 16. I didn't get her pregnant.*

In the company of women he feels *happier.*

What he really thought would help him *is going for help, getting some help.*

When they left him flat, *he got an attorney.*

It makes him nervous when *he has to talk about different things that upset him.*

Following the sexual act he usually feels *embarrassed.*

He felt to blame when *it was his own fault.*

Taking orders, *couldn't take them good.*

When he saw that he was not getting ahead *he worked on it.*

Compared to most men he *hurts.*

The main thing in his life *is that he will get his life back together.*

Anybody would be angry if *I tried to kill myself.*

Evaluation of Projective Tests Of all the forms of psychological testing, the projective techniques allow individuals the greatest freedom in expressing themselves. However, these tests also allow the interviewer the greatest freedom in interpreting the responses, and herein lies their major problem. Opponents of the projective tests claim that the chain of inference leading from the individual's response to the interviewer's report is simply too long, too complex, and too subjective, with the result that the report may tell more about the interviewer than about the individual. This argument has been supported by numerous studies (Lilienfeld, Wood, & Garb, 2000) showing poor interjudge reliability for the projective tests. And, as may be expected when a method lends itself to many different clinical interpretations, many researchers have found the validity of many of the scores on the projective tests to be disturbingly low (Lilienfeld, Wood, & Garb, 2000). It was partly in response to such findings that empirically based scoring systems were developed for the projective tests. The Exner scoring system for the Rorschach is a highly detailed procedure in which the person's responses are reduced to a numerical pattern, which is then compared with patterns derived from a variety of normative groups. This system has led to improved validity of the Rorschach for some purposes, such as the evaluation of thought disorder (Lilienfeld, Wood, & Garb, 2000).

However, the Rorschach (and TAT) continues to be surrounded by controversy (Wood, Nezworski, & Stejskal, 1996; Lilienfeld, Wood, & Garb, 2000). Studies claiming to support the reliability and validity of Exner's scoring system for the Rorschach are largely unpublished and have not been made available to independent investigators (Wood, Nezworski, & Stejskal, 1996). Moreover, a number of problems with the groups on which Exner's scoring system was standardized have come to light (Exner, 2002; Wood, Nezworski, Garb, et al., 2001). And most important, the use of Exner's normative data may lead to the overperception of psychopathology in respondents (Hamel, Shaffer, & Erdberg, 2000; Wood, Nezworski, Garb, et al., 2001). For example, in one study the Rorschach was administered to 100 normal school children with no history of mental disorder (Hamel, Shaffer, & Erdberg, 2000). The results suggested that most of the children in the sample suffered from reasoning so faulty that it approached psychosis and from a mood disorder.

Whatever the scientific standing of projective testing, its supporters claim that this is the only assessment method that is open and flexible enough to provide information about the individual's unconscious processes (Weiner, 1999). Because of these features, the Rorschach and the TAT are among the most frequently administered psychological tests (Watkins, Campbell, Nieberding, et al., 1995), but their popularity is starting to wane (Piotrowski, Belter, & Keller, 1998). Indeed, given that projective tests require extensive training and are time-consuming to administer, score, and interpret, and that recent evidence suggests they may not have much predictive validity beyond the easier-to-administer self-report inventories, their popularity is likely to continue declining (Lilienfeld, Wood, & Garb, 2000). It was on the basis of projective tests, together with the clinical interview and the mental status exam, that Joe's assessor drew up the following personality profile:

EVALUATION OF JOE: Personality Profile

Joe's stress tolerance is far lower than the average. At the same time, he is faced with extraordinary stress in the form of neglect by his family, who essentially abandoned him four years ago. (See his sentence completion: "His family treats him as *dirt*.") He has a hard time controlling his emotions and tends to respond in an intense and impulsive manner. This causes him to be rejected by others, which makes him even more desperate and uncontrolled, which in turn provokes further rejection—a vicious cycle.

His poor perception of reality, due to his intellectual handicap, makes it even harder for him to respond appropriately. When frustrated, he becomes overtly aggressive. He seems to have a considerable amount of anger. Nearly all his TAT stories had to do with violence. His obsession with injury to himself and others should be taken seriously. He has been injured in the past. By his account, he was sexually molested by his stepfather on numerous occasions.

His self-image is both positive and negative. He sees himself as kind and generous, and on the Sentence Completion Test he describes himself as mature. He says that he wants to join the police force. On the other hand, he is aware of his intellectual shortcomings (see sentence completion: "He would be happy if *he was more smarter*"), and much of the time he feels inadequate, insecure, and confused. ("Sometimes I feel like I'm in a different world.")

Self-Report Personality Inventories Unlike projective tests, **self-report personality inventories** ask the respondents direct questions about themselves. Such a test may instruct respondents to rate a long list of descriptive statements—such as "I am afraid of the dark" or "I prefer to be alone most of the time"—according to their applicability to themselves. Or the test may consist of a list of things or situations that respondents are asked to rate according to whether they are appealing or frightening. In any case, in the self-report inventory, as the name indicates, respondents assess themselves. This self-assessment may not be taken at face value by the testers, but it is given some weight.

The MMPI-2 The most widely used self-report personality inventory is the **Minnesota Multiphasic Personality Inventory-2**, or **MMPI-2** (Hathaway & McKinley, 1943, 1989). One purpose of the MMPI-2 is to simplify differential diagnosis by comparing self-descriptive statements endorsed by new patients to those endorsed by groups of people already diagnosed with schizophrenia, depression, and so forth. Thus, it is important to note that an evaluation produced by the MMPI-2 is not derived directly from the person's self-description. A person who answers yes to such statements as "Someone is pouring dirty thoughts into my head" is not automatically judged to have schizophrenia. Rather, the evaluation depends on whether responses to these and other statements show a *pattern* similar to that seen in the MMPI-2 responses of people already diagnosed with schizophrenia. In addition to helping clinicians to make diagnoses, the MMPI-2 is also used to gather descriptive information about a person's psychiatric symptoms, cognitions, and interpersonal relationships, as well as to aid in treatment planning.

The test items range from statements of ordinary vocational and recreational preferences to descriptions of bizarre thoughts and behaviors. We have already given one example of the latter. Other items similar to those on the MMPI-2 checklist are:

"I go to a party every week."
"I am afraid of picking up germs when I shake hands."
"I forgive people easily."
"I sometimes enjoy breaking the law."

The test items were originally compiled from a variety of sources—psychiatry textbooks, directions for psychiatric and medical interviews, and previously published personality tests (Graham, 2000). These items were tried out on groups of patients hospitalized for schizophrenia, depression, and so on, and then given to normal individuals. Only those items on which the pathological groups substantially diverged from the normal groups were retained. In the end, the test was made up of over 500 statements, yielding a rating of the individual on 10 clinical scales. The following are the 10 scales, along with the characteristics that might be inferred from a high score on any one of them:

Hypochondriasis: anxious over bodily functioning
Depression: hopeless
Hysteria: immature, suggestible, demanding
Psychopathic deviate: amoral, unscrupulous, rebellious
Masculinity-femininity: characterized by traits and interests typically associated with the opposite sex
Paranoia: suspicious, jealous
Psychasthenia: fearful, unconfident
Schizophrenia: withdrawn, disorganized in thought processes
Hypomania: impulsive, distractible
Social introversion: shy, self-effacing

In addition to the clinical scales, the MMPI-2 uses a number of control scales designed to measure the validity of the individual's responses (Graham, 2000). The *L (Lie) scale* indicates the degree to which the individual appears to be falsifying responses in a naive way in order to "look good." For example, if the individual checks "false" next to a statement such as "I do not always tell the truth," this will boost his or her score on the L scale. The *K (Subtle Defensiveness) scale* measures less obvious kinds of defensiveness. Most educated people would know better than to claim on a psychological test that they never told a lie, but if, for example, they were involved in a child-custody case, they might be motivated to distort the truth about their moral character in subtler ways. This is what the K scale is designed to detect. Roughly the opposite of the L and K scales is the *F (Infrequency) scale,* which measures the individual's tendency to exaggerate his or her psychological problems. Included on the MMPI-2 are a number of statements (e.g., "Someone has been trying to rob me," "Evil spirits possess me at times") that are very infrequently endorsed by normal people and that people with mental disorders endorse only selectively, in a manner consistent with their symptoms. People who frequently and unselectively endorse these statements receive a high F-scale score, which may mean that they are trying to fake mental illness—for example, for the sake of a lawsuit claiming psychological injury—or that they are very distressed and trying to get help. (Alternatively, it may mean that they have reading problems or are responding randomly.) When the MMPI was revised in 1989, several additional control scales were added (Graham, 2000).

The usual procedure for evaluating an MMPI-2 is to arrange the individual's scores on the various scales in numerical order, from the highest to the lowest score, and then to interpret the pattern of scores by comparison with patterns seen in normal and pathological groups, rather than to interpret any one scale separately. Some clinicians do draw diagnostic conclusions from scores on individual scales. A clinician may assume, for example, that a person who scores high on the depression scale is a good candidate for the psychiatric diagnosis of depression—that is, that he or she will show not only sadness but also guilt, lack of motivation, sleeping and eating problems, and other symptoms of depression. Such one-scale diagnoses are apparently not very meaningful, however. Although many of the MMPI scales are related to the expected symptoms, these symptoms are usually related to several (in some cases, almost all) of the other scales as well. (Graham, Ben-Porath, McNulty, 1999). Thus, scores on individual scales cannot, in general, yield sound diagnoses. Indeed, there is some doubt as to whether even the pattern of scores is a valid source of diagnostic information. The major value of the MMPI-2 is probably in communicating the degree of overall disturbance (mildly troubled, deeply troubled, etc.) rather than in pinpointing the exact nature of the disturbance.

Even as a measure of the degree of disturbance, the MMPI-2 is not an infallible instrument. A concern about the original edition of the test was the narrowness of the group of normal participants on whom it was standardized. All were White, and most were young married people living in small towns or rural areas near Minneapolis, where the test was being devised. With the revision, the test was standardized on a much more representative sample (Graham, 2000) and modernized in other ways as well. Sexist language was removed, as were test items that seemed aimed at identifying people's religious beliefs.

However updated, the test still has many of its original shortcomings (Helmes & Reddon, 1993). Most important, it is still a self-report test and is thus faced with the problem that many people do not give accurate reports about themselves. Some will lie; others will fall into what are called **response sets,** test-taking attitudes that lead them to shade their responses one way or another, often unconsciously (Butcher, 1999). One such response set is the "social desirability set," the tendency to try to make oneself look good; another is the "acquiescence set," the tendency to agree with statements whether they apply to oneself or not (Butcher, 1999; Huang, Liao, & Chang, 1998). The control scales, as we saw, were designed to detect such distortions, but no one pretends that they eliminate all inaccuracy. In clinical settings, where people are usually taking the MMPI-2 because they have problems and want help, deliberate falsification is less likely, but it can easily occur in other

TABLE 2.1 Differences Between the Self-Report (MMPI-2) and the Projective Method of Personality Assessment

CHARACTERISTICS OF THE SELF-REPORT METHOD	CHARACTERISTICS OF THE PROJECTIVE METHOD
1. Expectations are well defined.	1. Expectations are minimally defined.
2. Stimuli are familiar.	2. Stimuli are novel.
3. It has a narrow range of response options.	3. It has a wide range of response options.
4. Task requires patient to consider self, decide if traits are characteristic, decide how to present self, and then indicate decisions on paper.	4. Task requires patient to formulate perceptions, decide which perceptions to articulate to the examiner, and then respond to further questions.
5. Administration and scoring require minimal skill.	5. Administration and scoring require considerable skill.
6. Patients are assumed to use a similar benchmark for deciding if trait is characteristic of themselves.	6. Examiner provides stable benchmark for classifying patient characteristics.
7. Measure is completed alone.	7. Measure is completed with an examiner.
8. It requires an in vitro description of personal characteristics.	8. It requires an in vivo demonstration of personal characteristics.
9. At best, raw data are dependent on conscious awareness and complexity of self-representations.	9. At best, raw data are dependent on engagement with the task and ability to articulate perceptions and their determinants.
10. Dissimulation and impression management affect reported symptoms.	10. Dissimulation and impression management affect engagement with task.
11. It is a better tool for obtaining information about specific overt symptoms, events, and experiences.	11. It is a better tool for assessing personality predilections that may or may not be evident in overt behavior or consciousness.

Source: Meyer, 1997, p. 299.

situations, such as the screening of job applicants. As for unconscious falsification, it is probably common in all settings. The differences between the self-report method and the projective method are summarized in Table 2.1.

The major argument in support of the MMPI-2 is that there is a large body of research that supports its validity (Graham, 2000). In addition, because it can be scored by computer, it enables examiners to measure a given person against previously tested respondents with great precision (Butcher, 1999)—and with great speed. The computers that now analyze the answer sheets and make up the profiles can do so in less than 1½ seconds. Furthermore, although the test is not immune to error, it has been found to agree moderately with personality ratings by parents, spouses, and clinicians (Meyer, 1996; Graham, 2000).

Cognitive-Behavioral Questionnaires Today, probably more psychologists practice cognitive behavioral therapy than any other type of treatment approach. They use self-report instruments to assess their clients' symptoms, cognitions, behaviors, and functioning at the beginning of treatment and then readminister these measures at various stages of therapy to assess their clients' progress (Antony & Barlow, 2001). For example, a cognitive-behavioral therapist working with a depressed client is likely to use questionnaires that will describe (1) the severity and frequency of depressive symptoms, (2) cognitions or beliefs that may maintain the depressive symptoms, (3) behaviors used to cope with the depressive symptoms, and (4) social and occupational functioning. The Automatic Thoughts Questionnaire–Revised (ATQ-R) (Kendall, Howard, & Hays, 1989) is an example of a commonly used measure of cognitions associated with depression. The ATQ-R assesses positive and negative thoughts that pop into a person's head. Respondents indicate whether they have experienced the thought "not at all," "sometimes," "moderately often," "often," or "all the time" over the previous week. Sample thoughts are:

> "I feel like I'm up against the world."
> "I'm no good."
> "I'm proud of myself."
> "Why can't I ever succeed?"

The ATQ-R has good reliability and validity, and because it is brief and easy to complete, it has excellent utility in clinical settings (Nezu, Ronan, Meadows, et al., 2000).

Psychological Tests for Neuropsychological Impairment Psychological disturbance may be due to neurological problems rather than, or as well as, "life"

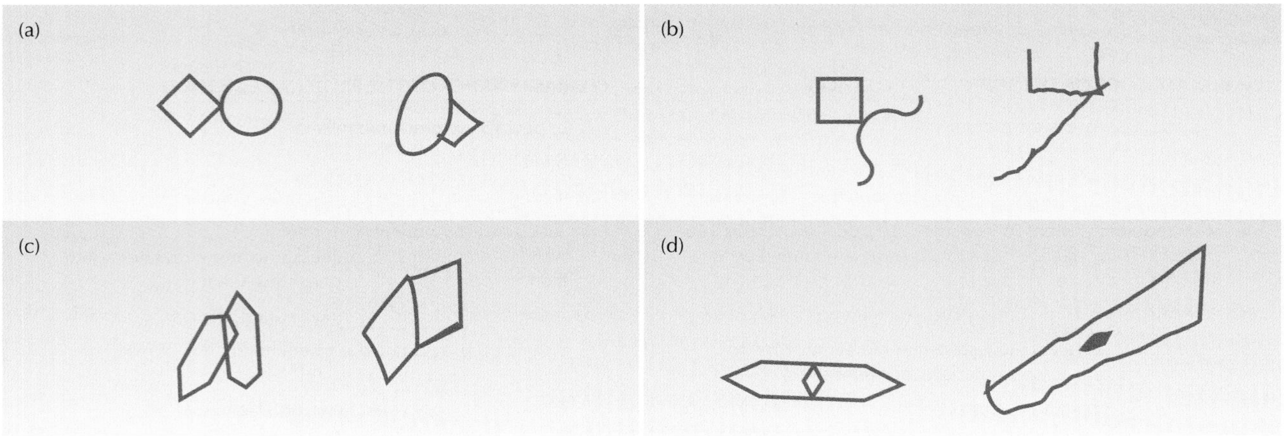

FIGURE 2.5 Joe's responses to the Bender Visual-Motor Gestalt Test. In each box, the design to be copied is at the left, and Joe's attempted copy is at the right. Brain impairment is indicated by certain characteristics of Joe's drawings: rotation, or turning a figure around *(a);* "impotence," or inability to complete the figure *(b);* difficulty in overlapping *(c);* and simplification *(d).*

problems. Thus, a major task of psychological assessment is to distinguish biogenic from psychogenic cases and, in biogenic cases, to determine what the neurological problem is.

In addition to the mental status exam, described earlier, certain pencil-and-paper tests have proved valid measures of neurological damage. One device that is widely used to screen patients for neurological malfunction is the *Bender Visual-Motor Gestalt Test* (Bender, 1938). The person is shown nine simple designs, each printed on a separate card, and is asked to reproduce the designs on a piece of paper. If certain errors, such as rotation of the figures or rounding of the corners, consistently appear in the person's drawings, the examiner is likely to suspect neurological impairment. (See Figure 2.5 for Joe's drawings.) In some cases, the test involves a second phase, in which the examiner asks the person to reproduce the designs from memory. Failure to reproduce more than two designs is generally viewed as further evidence of impairment.

More helpful in providing specific information is a coordinated group of tests called the *Halstead-Reitan Neuropsychological Battery.* These tests are based on our (still imperfect) knowledge of which areas of the brain control which intellectual and motor functions. The individual is confronted with a variety of tasks—several performance measures, including those of the Wechsler Adult Intelligence Scale, along with tests of perception and rhythm, a test measuring the individual's ability to fit various wooden forms into receptacles of the same shapes while blindfolded, and so forth. (The test takes two to eight hours to administer.) Each of these tasks was originally designed to assess the functioning of a specific area of the brain, so failure at any one task can presumably help the diagnostician pinpoint the site of the neurological damage. However, given the complex crisscrossings of the neural pathways—together with the equally complex interaction between the brain and behavior—such decisions are still not easily made (Milberg, 1996; Horton, 1997).

Laboratory Tests

While psychological measures can be of help in diagnosing brain dysfunction, the primary means of detecting such problems is direct testing of the structure and function of the nervous system through laboratory methods. A standard test is the **electroencephalogram (EEG)**, in which the electrical activity in the brain cells is picked up by electrodes attached to the skull and recorded in oscillating patterns called brain waves. The EEG can detect tumors and injuries in the brain. Researchers have recently developed more sophisticated means of testing for brain dysfunction, such as computerized tomography (CT), which is essentially a series of computer-enhanced X rays of the brain, and positron emission tomography (PET), which involves tracing the progress of radioactive particles through the brain. Both techniques have already produced new findings about schizophrenia and other disorders. A newer method is magnetic resonance imaging (MRI). Through the use of magnetic fields, MRI yields a highly precise picture of the brain from more vantage points than other methods.

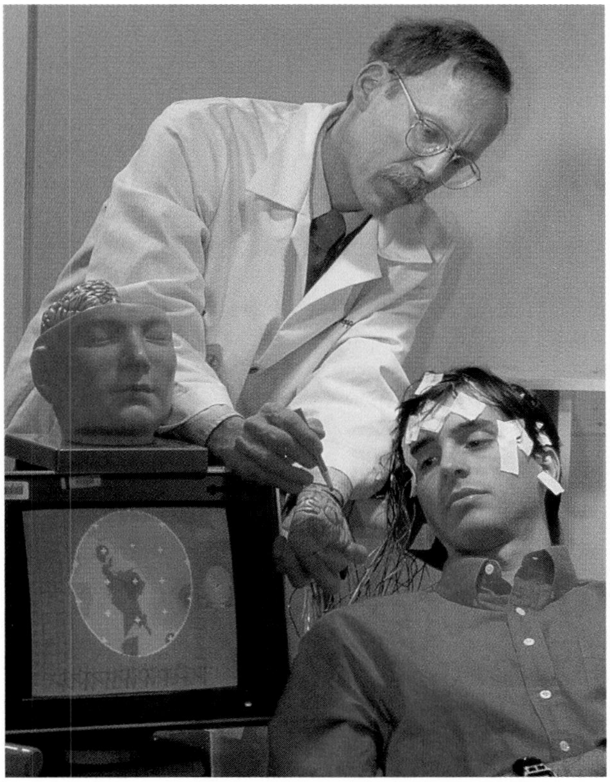

Here, a doctor uses an EEG to measure brain waves. The EEG, one of the laboratory methods used to test the structure and function of the nervous system, can detect tumors and injuries in the brain.

Functional MRI: Mapping How the Brain Works Across Space and Time

On the MindMAP CD-ROM, the video "Brain Structures and Imaging Methods" shows how the development of the functional MRI has led to a better understanding of how the brain works and looks at an even newer technique called magnetoencephalography (MEG). How might these techniques and the other laboratory tests described in this section lead to improved treatment of psychological disorders?

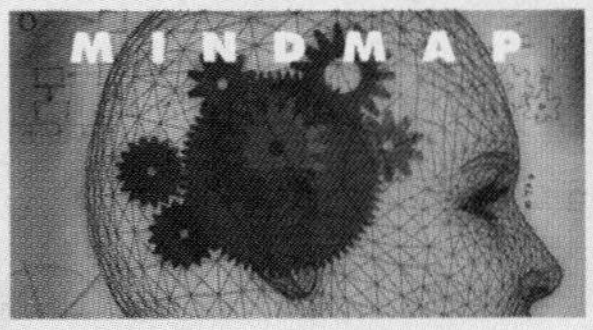

Laboratory tests can also be used to identify psychogenic disorders. There is an intimate relationship between emotion and physiological functioning. When a person's anger level rises, so may the blood pressure. When a person's anxiety level rises, so may the activation level of the sweat glands. Such changes can be monitored by physiological recording devices such as the **polygraph,** a machine equipped with a number of sensors, which, when attached to the body, can pick up subtle physiological changes. These fluctuations, in the form of electrical impulses, are amplified within the polygraph and activate pens that then record the changes on a continuously moving roll of paper. When the sensor measures changes in the electrical resistance of the skin—an indication of sweat gland activity—the result is a reading of **galvanic skin response (GSR).** When the sensor is used to pick up subtle changes in the electrical activity of muscles, the result is an **electromyogram (EMG).** The polygraph can also measure a number of other physiological responses, such as heart rate, blood volume, and blood pressure.

Either the polygraph as a whole or its separate measures can be used as indicators of emotional responses to specific stimuli and, thus, can aid in assessment. For example, patients with high blood pressure may be fitted with a portable blood-pressure recorder so that they can take their own blood pressure at regular intervals during the day, at the same time recording in a notebook what they are doing at the time of each reading. When the two records are compared and elevations in blood pressure correlate consistently with a specific environmental stimulus, such as the family dinner hour, then the diagnostician has at least some preliminary clue as to the source of the patient's stress.

Psychophysiological tests have a number of advantages. First, they tap into processes that the person is usually unaware of and therefore cannot report on. Second, they are often more precise than other measures and can provide information on the timing of complex psychological processes. Many of them show reasonably good internal consistency and test-retest reliability. The only problem with them is in interpreting the psychological significance of the results (Tomarken, 1999). For example, the polygraph may be a good test of anxiety, but it is not a reliable test of whether a person is lying. (Many liars have passed, and many truth-tellers have failed, the polygraph.) For this reason, attempts to use polygraph test results in law courts as an index of truthfulness have always been surrounded by controversy.

Observation in Natural Settings

As noted earlier, the psychometric approach aims to measure what are presumed to be the person's stable personality characteristics. Supporters of this approach would not deny that behavior is influenced by **situational variables,** the environmental stimuli that precede and follow any given action. No one disputes, for example, that children who are coddled by their parents after temper tantrums are likely to have more temper tantrums. Nevertheless, adherents of the psychometric approach assume that behavior issues primarily from **person variables,** the person's stable traits.

Behavioral psychologists take essentially the reverse position. They claim that the major determinants of behavior are the situational variables—the physical and social settings in which the behavior takes place. From this point of view, it follows that abnormal behavior cannot be accurately assessed in a clinician's office. People must be observed in their natural settings—the classroom, the home, wherever the diagnostician can unobtrusively follow them—so that the connections between behavior and situation will be revealed.

Actually, a diagnostician need not subscribe to behavioral theory in order to value this method of assessment. It has been used for a long time by clinicians of many persuasions, especially in treating children. Its value is that it allows the diagnostician to pinpoint circumstances that elicit the problem behavior—information that is useful no matter what the behavior is ultimately ascribed to (Cone, 1999). Consider, for example, a child who is having discipline problems in school. An observer may be sent into the classroom to analyze precisely what environmental conditions provoke her outbursts—teasing by other children, difficult academic tasks, or whatever. Once this information is collected, the diagnostician is in a better position to determine what the child's problem actually is.

Direct observation has a number of advantages over other assessment techniques (Cone, 1999). For one thing, it does not depend on self-report, which, as we have seen, may be inaccurate. While the parents of an aggressive boy may state that he is *always* making trouble, and while the child may report that he makes trouble only when someone hits him or takes his things, the observer has a better chance of finding out where the truth lies. Second, observation cuts down on assessment errors caused by the person's response to the examiner or by the examiner's overly subjective interpretations. Finally, observation tends to provide workable answers to behavioral problems. Situational observation may reveal that a child's aggression surfaces only during certain kinds of interaction with his parents—a variable that is much easier to deal with than unconscious conflict. Furthermore, if an underlying conflict does exist, it is possible that adjustment of the parent-child interaction will help resolve it.

Observation is not without its problems, however (Cone, 1999). In the first place, it requires a great investment of time. Second, the presence of observers may be "reactive"; that is, the person being observed may act differently because he or she is being observed. "Problem" children (and "problem" parents and teachers) often show speedy improvement once they realize they are being watched by a person with a clipboard. Sometimes this problem can be solved through surreptitious observation. The assessor can watch through a one-way mirror or, in the case of a classroom, can be introduced as the "teacher's helper" for the day. However, such teacher's helpers often fool nobody, and surreptitious observation is ethically questionable in any case. An alternative, though it also presents ethical problems, is to use recording equipment rather than human beings to do the observing. Unlike a human observer, a video camera can be set up to operate continuously, with the result that the people being observed eventually forget its presence and resume their accustomed behavior.

A one-way window can be useful in assessing behavior in natural settings. Individuals are usually informed that they are being watched, but they are less aware of being observed and thus behave more naturally, because they cannot see the assessor.

Cultural Bias in Assessment

A major concern in diagnosis and assessment is the problem of cultural bias. We have already considered this matter in relation to IQ testing. Various studies have also revealed bias in diagnosis. For example, when diagnosticians are shown case studies identical in every respect except for skin color, Blacks are more likely to be labeled with alcoholism or schizophrenia, while Whites tend to receive the less stigmatizing diagnosis of depression (Garb, 1998).

These, however, are only the most blatant examples of cultural bias in assessment. Researchers have revealed subtler distortions as well (Okazaki & Sue, 1995). For instance, several studies have shown that bilingual patients receive drastically different diagnoses, depending on whether the interview is conducted in the patient's first or second language. De Castillo (1970), the first researcher to raise this problem, and a Spanish speaker, described the following case:

> R. A. was a 28-year-old Cuban patient charged with murder. During his rather lengthy hospitalization he was under the care of a Spanish-speaking physician who found him to be psychotic, suffering from terrifying imaginary experiences. Occasionally he was interviewed by an English-speaking psychiatrist, in whose judgment the patient was coherent, factual, and free from overt psychotic manifestations. I was asked to evaluate his mental status on a few different occasions and encountered exactly what the other Spanish-speaking physician had found. (p. 161)

Later researchers (Malgady & Costantino, 1998) have likewise shown that diagnosticians find less pathology in patients speaking a second language, and they explain the phenomenon as De Castillo did: Using the second language requires patients to organize their thinking better, with the result that their thoughts seem less disturbed. Curiously, other researchers have found the opposite effect, that diagnosticians find *more* pathology in patients speaking a second language (Marcos, Alpert, Urcuyo, et al., 1973). (They explain this as the diagnostician's response to the patient's language problems—misunderstood questions, misused words, speech hesitations, etc.) How can we evaluate such contradictory evidence? For Cuellar (1998), the opposing findings suggest that several kinds of distortion can affect the assessment of bilingual patients. If you consider that most diagnostic interviews with nonnative English speakers are conducted in English, this could be a serious problem.

The broader matter of cultural bias was acknowledged in the latest revision of the *DSM*. Earlier editions of the manual contained very little information on how behaviors thought normal in one ethnic group, age group, or gender might be misinterpreted as abnormal by a diagnostician of a different gender, age, or ethnic background. Now, in *DSM-IV-TR*, most of the diagnostic categories include such information (Cuellar, 1998). For example, the diagnostic criteria for "conduct disorder" (a pattern of antisocial behavior—aggression, destructiveness, deceitfulness—beginning in adolescence) are accompanied by a warning that this diagnosis may be "misapplied to individuals in settings where patterns of undesirable behavior are sometimes viewed as protective (e.g., threatening, impoverished, high-crime)" (American Psychiatric Association, 2000, p. 96). In other words, gang members in ghetto neighborhoods may have social, more than psychological, reasons for delinquency. Likewise, under "schizophrenia," the manual cautions that "in some cultures, visual or auditory hallucinations with a religious content may be a normal part of religious experience (e.g., seeing the Virgin Mary or hearing God's voice)" (p. 306) and therefore should not automatically be taken as symptoms of psychosis. As we saw in Chapter 1, the manual also has a new "Glossary of Culture-Bound Syndromes," including conditions such as "ghost sickness" ("a preoccupation with death . . . observed among members of many American Indian tribes" [p. 900]) and the "evil eye" ("a concept widely found in Mediterranean cultures" [p. 901]) that may or may not warrant diagnosis.

Individuals living in poor and crime-ridden neighborhoods may have social, rather than psychological, reasons for delinquency. Unlike prior editions of the manual, the DSM-IV-TR *advises diagnosticians to take culture, ethnicity, age group, and gender into account to avoid misapplying diagnoses.*

Such cautionary information may help people from various subgroups to receive less biased diagnoses. Or, ironically, it may not. Remember that the best diagnosis is not the mildest diagnosis but the most accurate diagnosis, which will presumably lead to the most appropriate treatment. In a large-scale study of California clinicians, Lopez and Hernandez (1986) found that some of these therapists, in an attempt to be sensitive to "cultural diversity," underestimated the seriousness of their patients' symptoms. One clinician, for example, had a patient who was hallucinating, but he did not consider the diagnosis of schizophrenia because the patient was Black, and Black people, he reasoned, were culturally more prone to hallucinations than White people. His conclusion was not inconsistent with *DSM-IV-TR*'s warning that hallucinations are a normal part of religious experience in "some cultures." Nevertheless, as the researchers point out, the woman may indeed have had schizophrenia—and been deprived of appropriate treatment as a result of her therapist's scruples regarding cultural bias.

Still, as with the conflicting evidence about assessments in a second language, this does not mean that diagnosticians should give up trying to correct bias. Fifty years ago, many diagnostic practices were patently racist. If, today, the effort to solve that problem involves some error and overcompensation, the effort is still necessary.

Key Terms

categorical classification, 30
comorbidity, 34
descriptive validity, 34
diagnosis, 28
dimensional classification, 30
DSM-IV-TR, 28
electroencephalogram (EEG), 48
electromyogram (EMG), 49
galvanic skin response (GSR), 49
intelligence quotient (IQ), 39
intelligence tests, 38
interjudge reliability, 33
internal consistency, 33
interview, 37
mental status exam (MSE), 37
mini mental status exam (MMS), 37
Minnesota Multiphasic Personality Inventory-2 (MMPI-2), 45
person variables, 50
polygraph, 49
predictive validity, 34
projective personality tests, 41
psychological assessment, 26
psychological test, 38
psychometric approach, 38
reliability, 32
response sets, 46
Rorschach Psychodiagnostic Inkblot Test, 41
self-report personality inventories, 45
situational variables, 49
test-retest reliability, 33
Thematic Apperception Test (TAT), 42
traits, 38
validity, 34

Summary

- Psychological assessment has two goals. The first is to describe the personality and behavior of the person being assessed. The second is to predict that person's psychological functioning in the future. Psychological assessment is used for such practical purposes as school placement and job screening. In the clinical context, it helps clinicians determine the most effective treatment; reassessment helps practitioners determine whether treatment is working.
- Clinical assessment is a form of diagnosis, in which mental health professionals label an individual's problems according to criteria specified in the *DSM* and suggest his or her prognosis. This classification provides an essential common vocabulary for researchers, practitioners, and public health officials. Critics argue that psychiatric diagnosis falsely implies that abnormal behavior is qualitatively different from normal behavior; that there are clear-cut differences between different diagnostic categories; that diagnostic labels may be mistaken for explanations; and that the person may be stigmatized. Some have proposed dimensional classification as a replacement for categorical classification, with the goal of making diagnosis more qualitative than quantitative.
- ***DSM-IV-TR*** attempts to remedy these problems by offering detailed, specific criteria for a diagnosis and by requiring data on five dimensions or axes: the specific clinical syndrome being diagnosed, long-standing personality disorders (or, for children, mental retardation), relevant medical problems, psychosocial and environmental problems, and a numerical assessment of the patient's recent levels of adjustment and of the current degree of impairment. *DSM-IV-TR* deliberately avoids reference to the causes of a disorder. Ideally, the result of assessment is a portrait, not a label.
- The usefulness of an assessment depends on reliability, or the consistency of measurement under varying conditions, and validity, or whether the assessment tool measures what it is supposed to measure. Diagnoses based on early editions of the *DSM* have shown low interjudge reliability and, perhaps for this reason, poor predictive validity. The more detailed, specific criteria and categories of recent editions of the *DSM* have corrected these problems to some degree. But growing recognition of comorbidity has presented a challenge to the descriptive validity of diagnosis according to *DSM*.
- Other problems relate to the assessor. The influence of the clinician's behavior and appearance on the subject's behavior and responses, the assessor's personal and professional biases, and pragmatic considerations all may interfere with accurate psychological assessment.

The stricter criteria of recent editions of the *DSM* correct some problems but may also encourage clinicians to overuse residual diagnoses (such as anxiety disorder).

- There are four common methods of assessment. The first is the interview, which may be structured or unstructured. Highly structured interviews—such as the SCID, the DIS, and the MSE—are called for when an unambiguous diagnosis is required.
- A second method is psychological testing. Intelligence tests (e.g., the Stanford-Binet and Wechsler scales) have high internal consistency and reliably predict performance in school, but they may be culturally biased and measure too narrow a range of mental abilities. Projective personality tests (e.g., the Rorschach, the TAT, and the sentence completion test) allow individuals freedom of expression but also permit variable interpretations, which led to the development of empirical scoring. Self-report personality inventories such as the MMPI-2, likewise, are scored against norms (how people with known disorders responded). Despite controls against false answers, these tests are not foolproof.
- A third type of assessment is designed to detect neurological impairment. Today paper-and-pencil tests that assess functions mediated by different areas of the brain are invaluable for explaining relations between the brain and behavior. These tests are supplemented by sophisticated laboratory tests which produce detailed pictures of the brain at work and physiological measures of emotional arousal (the polygraph) and sleeping patterns. Psychophysiological tests tend to yield superior consistency of results, but the significance of the results is often difficult to interpret.
- A fourth method of assessment is observation of subjects in natural settings, either directly or surreptitiously, with one-way mirrors or video cameras.
- Biases based on language, ethnicity, and culture have long been known to compromise the accuracy of psychological assessment and diagnosis. Such biases have been a subject of much research in recent decades, although some error still persists. A more recent hazard is error based on overcompensation to avoid possible bias.

CHAPTER

3

Characteristics of the Scientific Method

- Skeptical Attitude
- Objectives
- Scientific Procedures

Ethical Issues in Research

Research Designs

- Correlational Research
- Epidemiological Studies
- Experimental Designs
- The Single-Case Experiment

Research Methods in Abnormal Psychology

Though it is doubtful that Isaac Newton really stumbled upon the law of gravitation by being hit on the head by a falling apple, the principle behind the story is sound. Scientific discovery sometimes occurs in a very unmethodical way, through accidents, hunches, and intuition. The earliest antipsychotic drug, for example, was developed by accident. Called chlorpromazine, it was first introduced as a treatment for surgical shock. Actually, it did little to reduce surgical patients' risk of going into shock, but, strange to say, it made them calm. The drug was then tested, quite successfully, on people with schizophrenia. It reduced their hallucinations and thought disorders. Chlorpromazine is still used today, and its discovery has led to the development of other, more effective treatments for schizophrenia.

Thus, scientific discovery involves chance. But any discovery, in order to be confirmed, must be tested via meticulous, systematic research, often over long periods of time. This chapter describes the general principles of scientific research. First, we will examine the characteristics of the scientific method. Then we will look at the research designs that scientists use in the study of abnormal behavior.

Characteristics of the Scientific Method

Skeptical Attitude

More than anything else, scientists are skeptical. Not only do they want to see it before they believe it, but they also want to see it again and again, under conditions of their own choosing. Scientists are skeptical because they recognize two important facts. First, they know that behavior is complex: that many factors are often needed to explain any psychological phenomenon. They also know that it is usually quite difficult to identify those factors. Explanations are often premature or incomplete; not enough factors may have been considered. While it may seem that a child's asthma attacks always follow an emotional upset, for example, it is possible that cat hair, pollen levels, and the child's history of respiratory infection are also involved. Single-cause explanations, because they are simple, are appealing, but in the study of behavior they are rarely accurate.

The second reason for skepticism is that science is a human endeavor. Scientists are not simply passive observers of the phenomena they study. It is they who decide how to define the thing they are measuring, which questions to ask about it, and how to collect, analyze, and interpret the data. These decisions are subjective; reasonable minds may disagree about them. Therefore, scientists have to be skeptical about new discoveries, even after they are tested. In the field of abnormal psychology, findings often raise as many questions as they answer.

Why a Skeptical Attitude Is a Good Thing To Have

To appreciate the value of a skeptical attitude, watch the video "When Eyes Deceive" on the MindMAP CD-ROM. How would a skeptical attitude help mental health professionals to assess and diagnose individuals experiencing abnormal behavior? Can you think of situations in which a skeptical attitude would not be helpful?

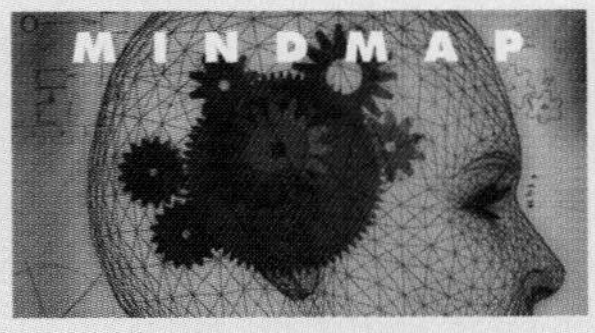

Objectives

Ideally, the scientific method is intended to meet four objectives: description, prediction, control, and understanding (Figure 3.1). **Description** is the defining and classifying of events and their relationships. To be useful, a description must have reliability (Chapter 2)—that is, it must be stable over time and under different conditions. Suppose, for example, that a person is given an IQ test and scores very high; then he is given the same IQ test two days later and scores very low. Because intelligence is unlikely to change in the course of two days, we would assume that the test was unreliable. A useful description must also have validity (Chapter 2)—that is, it must measure what it claims to measure. If that IQ test actually

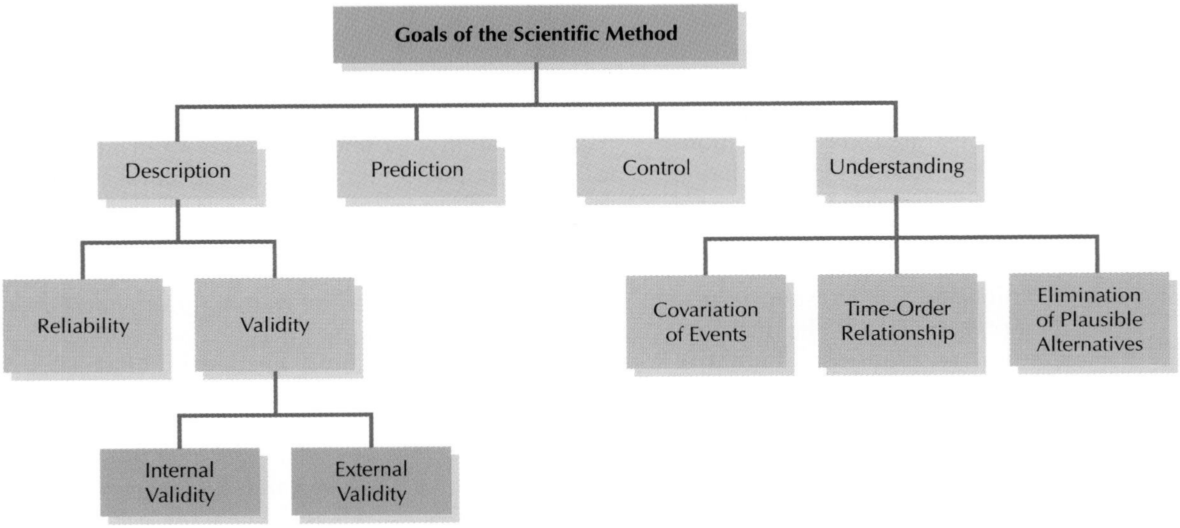

FIGURE 3.1 The four objectives of the scientific method, together with their individual requirements.

measured social skills rather than intelligence, then it would not be valid. Assessment techniques have been developed to provide reliable and valid descriptions of a wide range of concepts, from extroversion to depression.

A description of events and their relationships often serves as a basis for **prediction.** If a description of schizophrenia notes that children of parents with schizophrenia are 10 times more likely to develop schizophrenia than are children of nonschizophrenic parents, it can reasonably be inferred that one cause of schizophrenia is having parents with schizophrenia.

Successful prediction doesn't always pinpoint a cause, however. In the case of schizophrenia, for example, the fact that children of parents with schizophrenia are at risk for schizophrenia does not tell us whether this relationship is due to genes or the stresses of growing up with such parents—or to another factor. Still, it is useful to know that these children are at risk, for such predictive knowledge can guide research into causes and can help in treatment and prevention.

Indeed, it is the development of treatment and preventive strategies that forms the basis of the third goal of science—**control.** When scientists can control behavior, they may be able to change it for the better. For example, there is a body of research showing that certain types of poor communication are highly predictive of relapse in adolescents and adults with schizophrenia who are recovering from a psychotic episode. Guided by that research, psychologists have tried to teach family members of people with schizophrenia better communication skills, in order to prevent relapses.

If we ever find out how much responsibility can be assigned to each of the factors thought to lead to schizophrenia, we will have achieved the fourth goal of the scientific method: **understanding,** the identification of the cause or causes of a phenomenon. Before causality can be demonstrated, three conditions must be met (Kazdin, 1999). First is the **covariation of events:** If one event is to be accepted as a cause of another, the two events must vary together—that is, when one changes, the other must also change. Second is a **time-order relationship:** The presumed cause must occur *before* the presumed effect. The final condition is the **elimination of plausible alternative causes:** The proposed causal relationship can be accepted only after other likely causes have been ruled out. For most types of abnormal behavior, we will probably never be able to isolate one factor as *the* cause. As we shall see in later chapters, complex behaviors, normal and abnormal, are usually the product of many causes.

Internal and External Validity Scientists are often faced with a problem called confounding. **Confounding** occurs when two or more causal factors exert an effect on the same thing at the same time, thus interfering with accurate measurement of the causal role of either one. A classic example is the infamous "executive monkey" study of vulnerability to ulcers (Brady, 1958). In this study, 4 pairs of monkeys were wired to receive electric shocks every 20 seconds. In each pair, however, 1 monkey, the so-called executive monkey, could turn off the coming shock if at any time in the intervening 20 seconds it pressed a lever near its hand. The second monkey in each pair, called the "yoked" monkey, had no such control. It simply received whatever shocks the executive received. The results of this study were dramatic. All 4 executive monkeys developed ulcers and died, while the yoked monkeys showed no signs of ulcer. The conclusion seemed clear: Being in charge is stressful and can be hazardous to health.

However, after several researchers redid the experiment and got different results, people began to look more closely at the procedures followed in the original experiment. Rather than being chosen at random, the 4 executive monkeys had been selected because, on a preliminary test, they had shown higher rates of responding than their yoked partners. Subsequent research (Weiss, 1977) showed that animals with higher response rates have an increased likelihood of developing ulcers. (In fact, the more recent research findings suggest that being in charge *decreases* the likelihood of developing ulcers.) Thus, in the original study, the difference in response rates confounded the relationship between having control and developing ulcers. Studies that are free of confounding are said to have **internal validity** (Kazdin, 1999).

The internal validity of a study can be distinguished from its external validity. **External validity** is the extent to which research results can be generalized. **Generalizability**—a finding's ability to be applied to different populations, settings, and conditions—in turn depends on the **representativeness** of the sample from which the finding was gathered: the degree to which this sample's essential characteristics match those of the population we want to generalize about. An internally valid study may show, for example, that depressed women are more likely than nondepressed women to have suffered recent declines in social support. Their marriages may have become strained, or their relationships with friends or family may have deteriorated. But, if the research sample is not representative of men as well as women, the finding is not generalizable to men. It is possible that in men the precursors of depression have more to do with

Most natural populations show demographic differences—variations in age, gender, ethnicity, and so on. Random sampling is the best technique for ensuring that variation within a population is adequately reflected in a research sample. This representativeness, in turn, helps ensure a study's external validity.

failures at work than with social relationships. As pointed out in Chapter 1, gender differences turn up in many disorders.

The representativeness of a sample depends on how carefully the participants, settings, and conditions of the study have been selected. The best way to achieve a representative sample is to use random sampling. In a **random sample,** every member of the population has an equal likelihood of being included. Given that the sample is large enough, random sampling makes it likely that the characteristics of the sample will generally match the characteristics of the population.

A common problem in studies of abnormal behavior is that they tend to rely on samples of convenience—for example, all the depressed women in the hospital where the researcher works or all the test-anxious students in a certain university clinic—rather than on more representative samples (Kazdin, 1999). In order to generalize the findings of such studies to the population as a whole (for instance, all depressed women, all test-anxious college students), we must repeatedly **replicate** them; that is, the study must be redone, producing similar findings, with another sample.

Scientific Procedures

Scientific methods should be put to use every time researchers perform a study. In any well-conducted study, the key elements are the generation of hypotheses, the formulation of operational definitions, and the establishment of methods of control.

The Hypothesis A **hypothesis** is a tentative explanation for behavior; it attempts to answer the questions "How?" and "Why?" The object of research is to test hypotheses; however, before a hypothesis can be tested, it must be generated. Intuition often plays an important role here. Psychologist Neal Miller (1972) describes his state of mind during exploratory work and hypothesis generation:

> During this phase I am quite freewheeling and intuitive—follow hunches, vary procedures, try out wild ideas, and take shortcuts. During it, I am usually not interested in elaborate controls; in fact, I have learned to my sorrow that one can waste a lot of time on designing and executing elaborate controls for something that is not there. (p. 348)

A hypothesis often begins as a hunch, which in turn can come from various sources. Sometimes, in the course of an experiment, researchers notice something that they didn't expect, and this leads them down a new path, toward a new hypothesis. Recently, for example, two researchers, Jacobson and Gottman (Gottman, Jacobson, Rushe, et al., 1995; Jacobson, Gottman, & Shortt, 1995), were studying the physiological processes of men who beat their partners. As they analyzed their findings, they noticed something curious: Some of the violent men tended to show internal calm the more outwardly aggressive they became. For example, although it is natural for heart rate to go up during an argument, for these unusual men it went down. The researchers hypothesized that such internal calm constituted a "marker" for the most severe types of wife-beaters.

For researchers who are also **clinicians,** or providers of treatment, hypotheses often arise from watching patients' reactions to treatment. That was the case, for example, with the development of chlorpromazine. As noted at the opening of this chapter, chlorpromazine was introduced as an aid to surgery. It took a sharp-eyed clinician to notice that the drug had the effect of

Focus On... The Case Study

A **case study** is a detailed account of the treatment of a single patient. In its classic form, the case study begins with a description of the person, including test results, interview impressions, and physical and psychological history. Then it describes the treatment of that person and the treatment outcome. Such studies have been instrumental in encouraging therapists to try new treatments. The vividness of the case study is itself inviting—clinicians can imagine themselves implementing the same procedure—and the amount of detail instructs clinicians as to exactly how the treatment is applied. Freud's famous case studies—of Little Hans (1909/1962), a child with a phobia; of Anna O. (1895/1962), a woman with hysteria (Chapter 1); of the Rat-Man (1909/1962), a patient with obsessional thoughts—did as much as his general writings to gain followers for his new psychoanalytic method. The same has been true of behavioral treatment. One of the crucial factors in the spread of behavioral therapy in the 1960s and 1970s was the publication, in 1965, of Leonard Ullmann and Leonard Krasner's *Case Studies in Behavior Modification*.

The case study is also a good way to describe rare phenomena. Tourette's disorder, for example, is a very rare condition involving motor and vocal tics. People with Tourette's disorder jerk their bodies this way and that; they also make involuntary sounds—clicks, grunts, barks, and snorts. To their embarrassment, they may shout insults or obscenities. Because the disorder strikes only 4 or 5 people out of 10,000, most clinicians will never see a patient with Tourette's disorder. Therefore, the case study included in neurologist Oliver Sacks' *An Anthropologist on Mars* is a useful contribution to the literature of abnormal psychology.

The limitations of the case study method are quite obvious. Because many variables are not controlled, cause-and-effect conclusions can rarely be drawn. Furthermore, it is impossible to generalize safely from one person. Who can say that the progress of a dog phobia in patient X is representative of people with phobias in general? However, case studies do have the unique advantage of immediacy. In reading a case study, one can actually feel what it is like to live with that disorder. In view of these strengths and weaknesses, case studies are regarded as most valuable when they are used to complement experimental research. That is how they will be used in this book.

calming patients and, thus, to hypothesize that it could be an effective tranquilizer. The same rules operate in psychotherapy. In responding to the patient, the therapist may say something that has an unexpectedly helpful effect. Suddenly, the patient is able to register for school, get a full night's sleep, or talk about a problem that she was unable to discuss before. The alert therapist notices this and tries that response again, perhaps with other patients. If it goes on working, the therapist can use it to generate a new hypothesis about treatment. Such hypotheses can also originate from accounts of other clinicians' patients. Case studies (see the box above) have given many therapists good ideas. Today researchers are paying more and more attention to the development of effective treatments, an area in which hypothesis generation plays a major role. (See the box on page 60.) That effort, in turn, may result in the development of an actual methodology, or systematic procedure, for generating hypotheses.

Operational Definitions For a hypothesis to be testable, it must be falsifiable; that is, it must be stated in such a way that it can be proven untrue. To this end, the concepts in the hypothesis must be "operationalized," or given **operational definitions**—that is, they must be defined in terms of operations that can be observed and measured. "Depression," for example, could be operationalized by defining it in terms of the Beck Depression Inventory, a test in which participants circle, as applicable or inapplicable to themselves, statements about sadness, discouragement, sleeping problems, and so forth. Their endorsement of these statements is an observable operation. It is also measurable. Participants receive a score based on which statements they circle. A very low score indicates no depression, and a very high score means severe depression. The score serves as the operational definition of depression. Thus, in a study of nondepressed versus severely depressed people, the researchers might operationally define these two conditions as Beck inventory 5-or-below (no depression) and Beck inventory 28-or-above (severe depression), respectively. In doing so, they would be ensuring that everyone involved in that research, and everyone reading about it, understood these concepts in the same way.

Methods of Control In setting up experiments to test their hypotheses, researchers need to **control** events that might influence the behavior they are studying. An experiment usually involves the manipulation (deliberate changing) of one or more factors and the measurement of the effects of that manipulation on behavior.

Independent and Dependent Variables The **independent variable** is the factor that is manipulated by the experimenters in an effort to measure its effects. The **dependent variable** is the factor (or, in psychological research, the behavior) that will presumably be affected by the manipulation of the independent variable and whose changes the experiment aims to measure. If a hypothesis is to receive a fair trial, the experiment must be internally valid; that is, the cause of any obtained outcome must be the independent variable. The internal validity of a study is ensured if **control techniques** are used properly. The three methods of control are manipulating, holding conditions constant, and balancing. These three methods can be illustrated by a hypothetical experiment. Let us say that we are going to examine the effect of alcohol consumption on tension.

In the simplest of experiments, the independent variable is manipulated at two levels. These two levels usually represent the presence and absence of some treatment. The condition in which the treatment is present is commonly called the experimental condition; the condition in which the treatment is absent is called the control condition. In the experimental condition in our hypothetical research project, participants are given 0.5 gram of alcohol per kilogram of body weight. The alcohol is administered as a mixture of vodka and tonic water. In the control condition, participants are given the tonic water plain—no vodka. Thus, the alcohol is the independent variable; its presence or absence is manipulated by the researcher. The dependent variable is the participant's heart rate, which is the operational definition of tension in this study.

Other factors in the experiment that could influence the participants' heart rate are controlled by being held constant. For instance, the instructions given for performing the tasks in the experiment, the tone of voice used by the experimenter in giving these instructions, the setting and the length of time in which the participants are allowed to consume the drink, and other factors that can be held constant are identical in the two conditions. When all factors that could possibly be independent variables are held constant, no confounding is possible.

At least one set of factors cannot be held constant in this or any other experiment—the characteristics of the participants tested. Researchers control factors that cannot be held constant by trying to balance the influence of these factors among the different experimental conditions. The most important balancing technique, **random assignment,** involves assigning participants randomly to the different groups in the experiment. For example, if our hypothetical researchers were to assign all the male participants to the vodka group and all the female participants to the no-vodka group, gender differences would confound the experiment. If, however, the participants were assigned randomly—by drawing lots, for example—then the researchers would maximize the likelihood that the two groups were equivalent on all measures other than the independent variable. (Note the difference between random assignment and random sampling, described earlier. In random sampling, participants are chosen at random from a population, the goal being representativeness. In random assignment, already-chosen participants are sorted at random into different experimental groups, the goal being balance among the groups.) It was the lack of random assignment that confounded the "executive monkey" experiment, discussed earlier.

In a properly conducted experiment, then, all variables other than the independent variable are either held constant or balanced. If it were not for the manipulation of the independent variable (the presence or absence of alcohol in the drink), the groups would be expected to perform similarly. Therefore, if the groups perform differently, the researchers can assume that the independent variable is responsible for the difference.

Minimizing the Effects of Expectations A further problem in conducting experiments is that both the experimenter and the participants may expect a certain outcome and act accordingly. For example, if participants know that they are drinking alcohol, they are likely to expect certain effects: that they will feel relaxed, giddy, and so on. If participants respond according to these expectations, called **demand characteristics,** it will be difficult to determine the effect of the alcohol. Similarly, the experimenters may have expectations and, consequently, may treat the participants who have received alcohol differently than they treat those who are drinking plain tonic. For example, the experimenter may read the instructions more slowly to the "drinkers." The experimenter's observations of behavioral results may also be biased by the knowledge of the experimental conditions. For instance, the experimenter, in observing the "drinking" group, may be more likely to notice any unusual motor movements or slurred speech. The term used to describe these biases is **experimenter effects.**

Scientists have developed procedures to control for both demand characteristics and experimenter effects. One is the use of a placebo control group. A **placebo** (Latin for "I shall please") is a substance that looks like a drug or other active substance but is actually an inert, or inactive, substance. In our alcohol example, a placebo control group would receive a drink that would look, smell, and taste like the alcoholic drink but would contain no alcohol. Thus, if "alcoholic" effects could be noted in these participants' behavior after they had had their drinks, the

Research Highlights

Treatment Development: An Example of Hypothesis Generation

One area of mental health in which hypothesis generation is receiving increasing attention is treatment development. In fact, beginning in 1992, the National Institute of Mental Health (NIMH), the federal agency that provides funding for mental health research, initiated a program to help recognize treatment development as a legitimate type of research investigation, one that could be funded as a separate phase of scientific inquiry. This is the first example of official recognition that hypothesis generation constitutes a legitimate phase of research design.

There is no universally recognized methodology for treatment development. However, as an example of how treatment development methodology can be applied, Robert Kohlenberg (2000) received funding to develop a treatment to enhance the effectiveness of a new variant of cognitive-behavioral therapy (CBT) for depression. The purpose of this treatment development study is to (1) show that the new version of CBT is promising, (2) demonstrate that it is clearly distinguishable from traditional CBT, and (3) develop a treatment manual that can be used for hypothesis testing once the treatment is developed.

CBT for depression is described in Chapter 10. It was developed by Beck and his associates to treat depression by changing the way depressed people think. The cognitive theory underlying CBT is that depression is at least partly caused by faulty thinking and that, by correcting this faulty thinking, depressed people not only recover but leave therapy with permanent changes in their thinking such that they are inoculated against subsequent relapse. Research suggests that CBT is moderately effective. The purpose of Kohlenberg's research is to enhance both the short- and long-term effectiveness of CBT.

The NIMH treatment development project is designed to integrate CBT with a treatment developed by Kohlenberg and Tsai (1992), functional analysis psychotherapy (FAP). Standard CBT uses incidents primarily from the natural environment as "material" to examine and work on in therapy, whereas FAP focuses on correcting the abnormal behavior that takes place right in the therapy session, drawing on the intense relationship between therapist and client.

According to the theoretical rationale for FAP-enhanced CBT (or FECT), if depressed clients engage in behavior that makes them depressed in the therapy session and the therapist notices it, avoids reinforcing it, and instead reinforces behavior conducive to helping the clients overcome their depression, the therapist-client transactions will automatically generalize to the natural environment. For example, consider the following dialogue between client and therapist:

C: Our time will be up in 5 minutes. Then your next client will come in. I'm just part of your assembly line.

T: What do you mean? Are you thinking that you are just one of many clients and that, even though this hour is special to you, it isn't special to me?

C: Yeah. And it makes me angry. And you seem like a phony.

T: I can see why you might feel that way. What impresses me is that you were able to say it.

experimenters would know that demand characteristics played an important role in the participants' behavior.

Placebo control groups are traditionally used for evaluating drug treatments, but they have also been used to assess various forms of psychotherapy. While other groups undergo specific therapies, the placebo control group receives a "theoretically inert" treatment (Haaga & Stiles, 2000); that is, the placebo control group is taken through a procedure that, while sufficiently complicated to seem like psychotherapy, is unrelated to any recognized form of psychotherapy. If, as has happened, this group shows improvement comparable to that of participants receiving recognized treatments, experimenters are at least alerted to the fact that therapeutic outcome is being affected by nonspecific (non-theory-related) factors, such as attention from the therapist.

Another way to minimize the influence of participants' and experimenters' expectations is to use a **double-blind** procedure. In this technique, both the participant and the experimenter are kept unaware (blind) as to which treatment is being administered. In our alcohol study, we could achieve double-blind

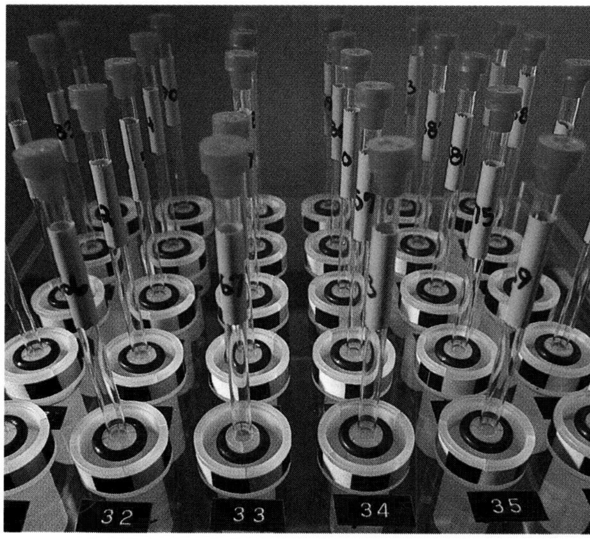

In a double-blind study, the experimental substance and the placebo control are administered from coded containers. This procedure keeps both the experimenters and the participants from knowing until afterward which participants received which substance. The purpose is to prevent the expectations of the experimenter and of the participants from affecting the study's results.

While the therapist might have tried to persuade the client that he was special or directed the discussion back to relevant issues in the environment, in FECT this would be a golden opportunity for the therapist to reinforce the client for his assertiveness. Because lack of assertion is a major part of this client's problem, his ability to be assertive with the therapist is significant. Equally significant is the FECT therapist's ability to recognize the clinically relevant behavior and reinforce it.

By training therapists to use FAP along with CBT, Kohlenberg hopes to enhance therapists' ability to use examples of faulty thinking in therapy sessions to modify depressive behavior. Therapists have been hired to be trained in both approaches, and experts in each are being used as supervisors. As depressed clients are randomly assigned to CBT (the control group) and FECT (the experimental group), the investigators will be able to assess the promise of FECT. Although only a handful of clients will be treated—not enough to apply the kind of statistical inference used in hypothesis testing—if FECT performs well relative to CBT, one can infer that FECT is promising and, therefore, worthy of formal hypothesis testing. Kohlenberg has also developed a system for coding therapist behaviors in the session, so that raters can be trained to code tapes of FECT and CBT and determine whether the therapists are restricting their FAP interventions to the FECT conditions. The coders are blind to which condition they are coding. This coding will determine the discriminability of the two treatments and lead to a system that can be used to code tapes in future studies comparing the two treatments.

Unlike formal experiments, in which the independent variable (in this case, treatment condition) must be kept constant throughout the duration of the study, it is expected that during treatment development, the FECT treatment will change as each case is intensely scrutinized. Regular observation of tapes by supervisors, meetings to discuss the cases, and information gleaned from informal observations will gradually shape a new, integrative manual for the FECT treatment. Thus, at the conclusion of the treatment development study, a new independent variable will emerge; and if the experimental treatment is promising enough, it will be ready to be tested under formal experimental conditions.

Treatment development is an example of a type of pilot study. Pilot studies are usually preparatory investigations, preliminary inquiries, which are less time consuming and less expensive than full-blown experiments. They are designed to help prepare the investigators for formal hypothesis testing, by perfecting both independent and dependent variables so that, when the experiment occurs, the hypothesis will receive an optimal, internally valid test.

Pilot studies often make up an important part of the treatment development process. But it is the interaction between scientists, therapists, and supervisors and the insights gleaned from this collaboration that are the most important components of the development of a new treatment.

control by having two researchers: one to prepare the drinks and to code the glasses, and a second researcher to pass them out, recording which participant got which glass. As long as the first researcher did not know who got what drink and the second researcher did not understand the coding system, neither of them would know, when they got to the stage of observing the participants' behavior, who was a "drinker" and who was not. The drinkers would be identified only later, when the code was compared with the record of who received what. At the same time, the drinkers would have no way of knowing whether they were receiving the alcohol or the placebo, hence the term "double-blind": Both parties are in the dark.

Statistical Inference Suppose that we have completed the alcohol study just described. Can we be reasonably confident that the results are real, rather than simply the product of chance? To be confident that results are not due to chance, scientists often rely on **statistical inference.** They begin by assuming the **null hypothesis,** which, as the term implies, is the assumption that the independent variable has had no effect. Then they use probability theory to determine the likelihood of obtaining the results of their experiment if the null hypothesis were correct—that is, if the independent variable had had no effect. If the likelihood is small (conventionally, less than 5 times out of 100, or .05), they judge the result to be "statistically significant," reject the null hypothesis, and conclude that the independent variable did have an effect.

You can appreciate the process of statistical inference by considering the following situation. You and a friend have dinner together once a week, and you always toss a coin to see who will pay the bill. Curiously, your friend always has a coin ready, and so she always does the tossing. Now, it would be convenient if you could examine the coin to see if it is unfairly weighted. But since this might cause a problem in your relationship, the best you can do is test her coin indirectly by using the null hypothesis; that is, you assume that the coin is unbiased and then wait to see the results. If, over time, the coin tossing deviates from the expected 50–50 split of heads and tails more than chance would predict, you might conclude that there is something funny about your friend's coin. You don't know for sure that her coin is unfairly weighted, but you do know that the likelihood of your losing that often with a fair coin is less than 5 times out of 100, or .05. Similarly, researchers would like to test any obtained result directly for significance, but usually the best they can do is compare their outcome to the outcome expected if chance alone were operating.

Statistical inference tells us only that a finding is believable. It does not tell us whether the finding is important. It is possible to obtain statistically significant differences between groups even when there is no substantial difference between those groups in the natural environment. This can be done, for example, simply by using very large numbers of participants. If, in the alcohol study, we were to assign 5,000 participants to the experimental group and 5,000 to the control group, almost any difference between the two groups would test out as statistically significant, though it might have no scientific meaning whatsoever (Jacobson, Roberts, Berns, et al., 1999; Kendall, Marrs-Garcia, Nath, et al., 1999).

Even if a statistically significant finding does represent a true difference between groups, that does not mean that the difference is great enough to have any practical consequence. When therapists read about research on new treatments, they want to know not just whether the findings are statistically significant, but also whether they have **clinical significance**—that is, whether they can be of real help in treatment. Imagine, for example, a study of a new treatment for obesity, using participants weighing about 300 pounds. If the experimental participants (those trying the new treatment) lost an average of 10 pounds apiece and the control participants lost no weight at all, that would be a statistically significant finding, but it would not be of much help to an obesity therapist's 300-pound patients.

This does not mean that tests of statistical significance are a waste of time. In some cases, they are a crucial protection against mistaking chance conjunctions for important relationships, but statistical significance is a minimum standard.

Ethical Issues in Research

The goals of research are to benefit society by increasing scientific understanding, but because a psychologist's actions carry much more weight than the actions of most other people, researchers can do damage. For instance, if a waiter calls a customer crazy, the remark can be shrugged off as the comment of a rude or stressed worker who has been on his feet too long. But if a psychologist calls a participant in a research study the equivalent of crazy (for example, by providing false feedback on a fake personality test), the individual is likely to accept it as a diagnosis based on scientific evidence and suffer emotionally as a result (Bersoff & Bersoff, 1999). Consequently, any psychological study involving human subjects must meet stringent ethical standards.

Ethical considerations go hand in hand with methodological decisions in planning research; often, proper ethics requires trade-offs with experimental design. Here we will discuss the most important ethical issues in clinical research.

First, participation in scientific research must be voluntary. It is unethical to use undue inducement or any type of force, fraud, deceit, duress, or other form of constraint or coercion when recruiting research participants (American Psychological Association, 1992, section 6.14). For instance, while it is common to offer research participants financial compensation for their time and effort, too much money might constitute an undue inducement. Or, for instance, in institutional settings such as schools, prisons, or mental hospitals, potential participants may feel coerced to participate in order to comply with the expectations of authority figures. One way around this problem is for researchers to refrain from direct solicitation and instead recruit participants passively—for example, through sign-up sheets posted on bulletin boards (Bersoff & Bersoff, 1999).

In addition, *who* is recruited matters. Historically, psychological research has been conducted primarily in Caucasian populations (Hall, 1997). However, today approximately one third of the U.S. population consists of people of color (U.S. Census Bureau, 1995). As we saw in Chapter 1, there are ethnic and cultural differences in the prevalence, expression, and treatment of different mental disorders. Thus, a failure to include demographically diverse samples in clinical research can lead to the misdiagnosis and mistreatment of minority group members (Bersoff & Bersoff, 1999).

The principle of **informed consent** is the backbone of ethics in clinical research. Before a potential participant consents to volunteer for medical research, he or she should be informed as to what that research might involve. A proper consent form includes the following elements (Bersoff & Bersoff, 1999):

1. An explanation of the purpose, procedures, and duration of the research that is complete enough to allow the potential participant to make an informed decision about choosing to participate
2. Disclosure of any appropriate alternative procedures that might be advantageous to the participant

3. An offer to answer any questions concerning study procedures
4. An instruction that the participant is free to withdraw consent and stop participating in the project at any time
5. A statement describing the extent, if any, to which the data collected will be kept confidential
6. Information regarding whom to contact if the potential participant has any questions regarding the experiment

Two ethical issues involving informed consent are especially relevant to research in psychological disorders. First, certain individuals, such as children or people with severe mental illness, may be considered legally incompetent to provide informed consent. In these cases, informed consent must be provided by a legal guardian. Even with the guardian's consent, however, unless the potential participant is extremely young or very cognitively impaired, the researcher is still required to obtain his or her agreement (Bersoff & Bersoff, 1999).

The second issue concerns studies that use deception. Deception in psychological research is legal and in some cases necessary in order to avoid compromising the outcome of the study. Imagine, for example, if the individuals in the placebo control group in the alcohol study described earlier were told the truth, that their drink contained no alcohol. Nonetheless, even though necessary to the research, such deception is a breach of trust between investigator and participant. Moreover, without knowing the true purpose of the study and the actual procedures taking place, is the participant really providing fully informed consent? The breach of trust inherent in deception research can be mitigated somewhat by withholding information, rather than lying outright, in consent forms. In addition, researchers could choose never to withhold risk-related information and actually inform participants that they might be deceived at some time during the study, without telling them what the deception might be. If such information would invalidate the study, an alternative would be to offer participants the chance to withdraw consent to use their data at the end of the experiment, after they have been fully informed about the deception (Bersoff & Bersoff, 1999).

In considering a research project, investigators must also weigh the potential benefits to participants and society with the risk to participants. Risk involves not just the potential for physical harm, but also psychological risks, such as invasion of privacy, loss of self-esteem, negative mood, stress, and physical or emotional discomfort. And there are costs for people who are only indirectly involved. For example, a study that investigates family history of schizophrenia may be an invasion of the privacy of family members who are not directly participating in the study and have not given informed consent to having their mental illness history discussed (Bersoff & Bersoff, 1999). The other side of the equation is the benefit. For most research studies, the benefit may consist of payment for time and effort expended or the more indirect benefit of knowing that one has contributed to the advancement of science. In applied research, the benefit may consist of receiving an experimental intervention to treat a particular disorder.

The use of **control groups**, groups that do not receive the experimental treatment, is essential to good research design. If there is no known effective treatment for a disorder or psychological problem under study, then the use of control groups does not raise an ethical issue; the participants in the control group are not being deprived of standard care for the sake of the research project. However, if effective treatments are available, an ethical problem arises when some participants are randomly assigned to a no-treatment control group in order to compare the effectiveness of the experimental treatment to no treatment. To circumvent this problem, the researcher can use a wait-list control group, consisting of people who are signed up for the experimental treatment but who have not yet received it because there is currently no room available in the program. While waiting for the treatment, these individuals can serve as a control group.

Researchers also have the ethical obligation to protect the privacy or confidentiality of the data provided by participants, with the exception of information that must be reported as required by law. For example, many states have mandatory reporting statutes for child abuse. In addition, researchers have an ethical obligation to inform parents about suicidal plans, serious drug use, or other risky behavior reported by a child in a research study. One concern raised by disclosure of the exceptions to confidentiality, of course, is that participants may be less likely to provide sensitive information in a research study (Bersoff & Bersoff, 1999).

A related concern in research is the obligation to intervene when participants provide information suggesting that they might harm themselves or others or are in serious distress (Bersoff & Bersoff, 1999). Under these circumstances, investigators should follow up and provide the option of treatment or referral for treatment to an appropriate facility. In emergency situations, researchers may need to break confidentiality and take the participant to a hospital emergency room for immediate treatment.

The final ethical obligation in a research study is debriefing: At the end of the project, the researchers must give participants a complete and accurate explanation of the study's purpose. An adequate debriefing is especially important in studies that involve deception, negative mood manipulations, or stress-inducing experiences. However, in some circumstances a complete debriefing might do more harm than good, such as when participants are selected for a study based on some deficit or risk for a disorder or when they have unknowingly displayed some potentially embarrassing or undesirable behavior during the course of the study. In such cases, full disclosure of this information during the debriefing is unwarranted; a more general description of the study may be provided instead (Bersoff & Bersoff, 1999).

"DO PEOPLE HATE US BECAUSE WE DRESS THIS WAY, OR DO WE DRESS THIS WAY BECAUSE PEOPLE HATE US?"

Research Designs

Research designs are the tools experimenters use to test hypotheses. Each design has its advantages and disadvantages. Asking a researcher whether one design is better than another is like asking a carpenter whether a screwdriver is better than a hammer. Which tool is best depends on the job to be done and the theory to be tested (Alloy, Abramson, Raniere, et al., 1999).

Correlational Research

In abnormal psychology, as in all science, the choice of research design involves ethical and practical considerations. For example, if we were interested in whether divorce increases a person's risk for depression, we could not randomly assign a group of people to get divorced and then wait to see if they developed depression.

A common solution to this problem is to examine groups that have been "treated naturally"; that is, people who are divorced can be compared, as to their rate of depression, with those who have remained married. Such studies have been done, and they have shown that people who are separated or divorced are indeed much more likely than married people to become depressed (Bruce & Kim, 1992). Because this kind of research involves looking for correlations, or relationships, between participants' characteristics and their performance, it is called **correlational research.**

One correlational design frequently used in research on abnormal behavior is the **case-control design,** in which people diagnosed as having a particular mental disorder—the "cases"—are compared with "controls," or people who have not been diagnosed as having the disorder (Alloy, Abramson, Raniere, et al., 1999). For example, if people with schizophrenia and people chosen from the general population differ according to a specific measure of behavior, the difference may be an indicator of schizophrenia, as long as other characteristics are balanced across the two groups.

Correlational research designs are highly effective in meeting the first two objectives of the scientific method, description and prediction. Unfortunately, serious problems arise when the results of correlational studies are used as a basis of causal inference. People tend to assume that all three conditions for a causal inference (covariation of events, a time-order relationship, and elimination of plausible alternative causes) have been met when really only the first condition, covariation, has been met. For instance, the evidence that divorced people are more likely than married people to become depressed shows that these two factors are correlated. Such a finding could be taken to mean that divorce causes depression. Before reaching that conclusion, however, we must be sure that the time-order condition has been met—namely, that divorce preceded the depression. Perhaps depressed people are more likely to get divorced because of the strain placed on the relationship by the depression. In other words, a demonstration of covariation offers no indication of the direction of a

Focus On... The Correlation Coefficient: A Measure of Predictive Strength

The **correlation coefficient** *(r)* is a measure of how well we can predict one variable if we know the value of another variable. For example, we might want to know how accurately we could predict students' success in college on the basis of their SAT scores.

The correlation coefficient has two characteristics, a direction and a magnitude. The direction can be either positive or negative. A positive correlation indicates that, as the value of one variable (*X*) increases, the value of the other variable (*Y*) also increases (see Figure 3.2a). The correlation between SAT scores and success in college should be a positive one. In a negative correlation, as the value of *X* increases, the value of *Y* decreases (see Figure 3.2b). The higher a person's social class, the less likely that person is to be admitted to a mental hospital; social class and admission to mental hospitals are negatively correlated. Figure 3.2c shows what happens when two variables are neither positively nor negatively correlated: As the value of *X* increases, the value of *Y* changes unpredictably. Because we have no ability to predict *Y* on the basis of *X*, the correlation coefficient in this situation is zero. For example, the relationship between eye color and mental illness represents a zero correlation; we could not predict the likelihood that a person would become mentally ill by knowing the person's eye color.

The magnitude of the correlation coefficient can range from 0 to 1.00. A value of +1.00 indicates a perfect positive correlation, and a value of −1.00 indicates a perfect negative correlation. Values between 0 and 1.00 indicate predictive relationships of intermediate strength. Remember, the sign of the correlation signifies only its direction. An *r* value of −.46 indicates a stronger relationship than an *r* of +.20.

One final word of caution: The correlation coefficient represents only the linear relationship between two variables. The linear correlation of *X* and *Y* in Figure 3.2d is zero, but the two variables are obviously related. A curvilinear relationship like that shown in Figure 3.2d exists between level of arousal and performance. Performance first increases with increasing arousal but then declines when arousal exceeds an optimal level.

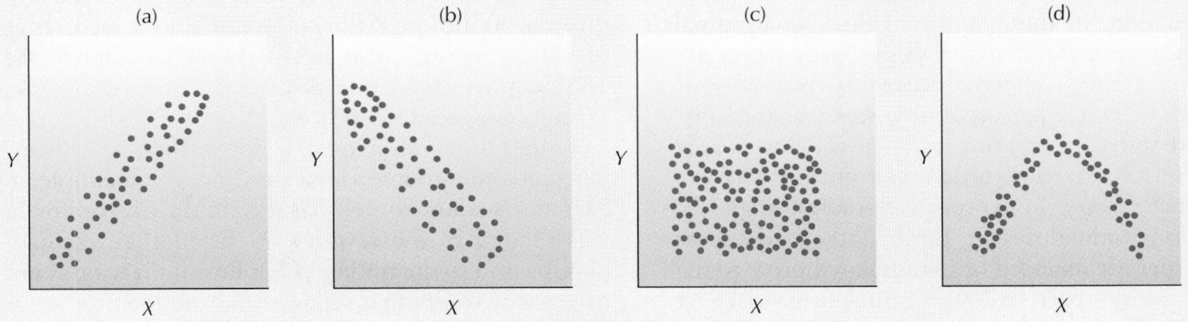

FIGURE 3.2 (a) Positive linear correlation. (b) Negative linear correlation. (c) No correlation. (d) No linear correlation, but evidence of a relationship between X and Y.

causal relationship. (For a discussion of the most common measure of covariation, the **correlation coefficient,** see the box above.)

Nor does covariation eliminate plausible alternative causes. The fact that two factors covary does not mean that one is the cause of the other. Perhaps they are both dependent on another factor altogether—the so-called **third-variable problem.** Perhaps the situation is not that divorce causes depression or vice versa but, rather, that both are caused by the stresses of poverty. The directionality and third-variable problems make it a treacherous enterprise to infer causation from correlations.

One partial solution to the third-variable problem is matching, or choosing participants who are similar with regard to potentially relevant factors other than the factor of interest. The divorced and nondivorced participants could be matched, for example, on income level. The idea, of course, is to end up with two groups that differ only in the matter of divorce. In a sense, matching is an application of the control technique of holding conditions constant. One problem with this approach is that matching may lead to such a restriction of the people included in the study that the groups may no longer be representative of the general population (Alloy, Abramson, Raniere, et al., 1999). If you were to compare the emotional disorders of college students with those of elderly people who had been matched with the students for general health and amount of education, you would probably be studying a very unrepresentative group of elderly people. A more serious problem with matching, however, is that the number of potentially relevant factors is usually so large that it is impossible to select two or more groups equal in all characteristics except the one of interest. In the divorce study, one might want to control many factors besides income— for example, gender, educational level, religion, ethnic origin, and number of children. Nonetheless, matching can be useful. If a relationship between divorce and depression persisted after divorced and married groups were matched on income level, then the researcher could reasonably conclude that income level alone was not responsible for the difference.

Alternatively, the researcher could revert to random selection. When there are many potentially confounding factors, the best choice is usually careful random selection or random selection within certain broad restrictions—in this case, for example, married people with family incomes of $50,000 to $100,000 versus divorced people whose predivorce family income was $50,000 to $100,000.

Longitudinal Studies One type of correlational research design is sufficiently distinct to warrant separate discussion. In these studies, called **longitudinal studies,** the behaviors of the same participants are studied on several different occasions over what is usually an extended period of time. Because the same people are tested several times, it is possible to specify more precisely the time-order relationship between factors that covary. In **prospective studies,** a specific kind of longitudinal design, the hypothesized causes of a disorder are assessed or manipulated prior to the onset of the disorder (Alloy, Abramson, Raniere, et al., 1999). Thus, these studies allow for the unambiguous conclusion that the hypothesized causes preceded the disorder.

One of the most important forms of prospective research is the **high-risk design,** which involves the study of people who have a high probability of developing a disorder (Alloy et al., 1999). For several decades, Sarnoff Mednick and his research team (e.g., Olin & Mednick, 1996) have been studying the development of people who are at high risk for schizophrenia because their mothers had schizophrenia and because this disorder seems to have a strong genetic component. The findings of Mednick's team will be discussed in detail in Chapter 14, but two points are worth noting here, as examples of what high-risk research can produce. First, the mothers with schizophrenia whose children also developed schizophrenia were more severely disturbed than were the mothers with schizophrenia whose children did not develop schizophrenia. Second, the mothers of the high-risk children who developed schizophrenia were hospitalized—and, thus, separated from their families—while their children were young.

Mednick's longitudinal studies are an example of **genetic high-risk design:** The participants are chosen because they are thought to be genetically predisposed to the disorder. Another type of high-risk design that has been used increasingly in research on abnormal behavior is the **behavioral high-risk design.** Here, participants are chosen not because of genetic vulnerability but because they show a behavioral characteristic, of whatever origin, that is thought to make them vulnerable to a disorder. An example of this design comes from the research of Lauren Alloy and Lyn Abramson and their associates (Alloy & Abramson, 1999; Alloy, Abramson, Whitehouse, et al., 1999; Alloy, Abramson, Hogan, et al., 2000). Alloy and Abramson selected a group of college freshmen who, based on negative thinking patterns identified by two tests, were considered vulnerable to depression. Another, low-risk, group of freshmen exhibited positive thinking patterns. After only a 2.5-year follow-up, the 173 people in their high-risk group had developed a first onset of major depressive disorder at almost 8 times the rate and a recurrence of major depression at over 3 times the rate of the 176 people in the low-risk group (Alloy, Abramson, Whitehouse, et al., 2003).

Longitudinal designs are not without problems when it comes to inferring causation. For example, in Mednick's study, to say that the child's schizophrenia was related to the severity of the mother's schizophrenia and to the timing of her hospitalization is not necessarily to say that separation from the mother or the degree of her psychopathology caused the disorder in the child. Perhaps the children who were later diagnosed with schizophrenia were already, in their early years, sufficiently impaired to cause increased emotional distress in their mothers, which in turn could have caused these mothers to be more severely disturbed and to be hospitalized sooner. Longitudinal studies, then, do not eliminate the question of causality, but they do enable researchers to gain a better understanding of the time course of the development they are investigating.

Epidemiological Studies

Epidemiology is the study of the frequency and distribution of disorders within specific populations. Key concepts in epidemiology are **incidence,** the number of new cases of the disorder in question within a given time period, such as a year; **prevalence,** the percentage of the population that has the disorder at a particular time; and duration, the average length of a given disorder. The simple formula is prevalence = incidence × duration. Thus, acute depression is a

These children spent their early years amid random violence in Belfast, Northern Ireland. Epidemiological studies would reveal the incidence of depression and anxiety disorders among children in this community. Such studies might also identify the kinds of buffers that protect children psychologically from extreme stress.

brief disorder with a high incidence, while schizophrenia is a lengthy disorder with a low incidence. Both have fairly high prevalence, but for different reasons. Epidemiological data, then, tell us how common a disorder is. They may also point researchers to significant relationships between the disorder and other variables, such as age, gender, and life circumstances. Such findings, in turn, may suggest causes. For example, the epidemiological finding that depressed people have higher rates of negative life events than do nondepressed people (Kohn, Zislin, Agid, et al., 2001) has led to what is now the widely held hypothesis that life stresses may trigger depressive episodes in vulnerable people.

Epidemiological surveys, like other research designs, are prone to certain pitfalls. The most serious concern is that descriptions of a population based on a sample are dependent on the representativeness of the sample. Random sampling is the best technique currently available to ensure representativeness, but random sampling guarantees representativeness only when all the selected respondents take part in the survey. In one study, for example, a random sample of Detroit-area residents between the ages of 18 and 45 was surveyed in order to obtain information on the prevalence of exposure to traumatic events and posttraumatic stress disorder (Breslau, Kessler, Chilcoat, et al., 1998). But, as the research report points out, about 13 percent of the individuals selected refused to participate. We have no way of knowing whether these people were more likely or less likely to have experienced traumas than were the people who agreed to participate. Perhaps the nonparticipants were generally more traumatized and fearful and, therefore, unwilling to talk to a stranger. Or perhaps they were generally *less* traumatized and fearful and, thus, able to be assertive in refusing to be questioned. Although the representativeness of a survey is compromised whenever the response rate falls below 100 percent, the fact is that the usual response rate is about 50 to 60 percent, and it is usually men, low socioeconomic status (SES), and minority individuals who are less likely to participate (Fischer, Dornelas, & Goethe, 2001).

Experimental Designs

A "true" experimental design is one in which an independent variable is manipulated by the experimenter and a dependent variable is measured. Most research on the causes of abnormal behavior does not involve true experiments, for the reason stated earlier: Ethical and practical considerations forbid our imposing the suspected cause (independent variable) on experimental participants. However, there are types of true experiments that have advanced our understanding of abnormal psychology.

Clinical Trials **Clinical trials** are studies of the effectiveness of treatments. In randomized clinical trials, patients with a particular disorder are randomly assigned to one or more treatments, or to a treatment group versus an untreated control group. For example, researchers might assemble a group of people with dog phobias and randomly assign them to one of two treatment conditions, behavioral or psychodynamic therapy. The treatment would be the independent variable. The dependent variable might be a test, rating the severity of dog phobia. The test would be administered before and after treatment to determine which therapy is more effective (Haaga & Stiles, 2000).

Sometimes in clinical trials, researchers use no-treatment control groups, which offer advantages over alternative-treatment control groups. Without a no-treatment control group for comparison, researchers who found reduced dog phobias after 3 months of behavioral therapy, for example, would not know whether the therapy contributed to the effect or if the reduction in phobia was caused by something else entirely (Haaga & Stiles, 2000). No-treatment control groups are especially useful when a treatment's effectiveness is unknown. For example, if researchers do not know whether behavioral therapy is useful for treating dog phobias, then the first task would be to discover whether such therapy is more effective than no treatment at all, by experiments on a group receiving behavioral therapy alongside a control group receiving no therapy.

No-treatment control groups have limitations, however. When there is already strong evidence that at least one effective treatment exists for a condition, as is the case with many psychological disorders, then demonstrating a treatment's superiority to no treatment has little value for deciding which therapy to use. It is also not easy to sustain absolutely pure "no treatment" conditions. Participants in the no-treatment group may go elsewhere (to books, friends, the Internet, etc.) for assistance and thus turn the research project into a comparison between active treatment versus an amalgam of other forms of help (Haaga & Stiles, 2000). As well, it is generally considered unethical to withhold treatment from people who need it. Consequently, no-treatment control groups do not usually remain untreated long enough to tell researchers anything about long-term effects (Haaga & Stiles, 2000).

A randomized controlled clinical trial by Heimberg, Leibowitz, Hope, et al. (1998) comparing cognitive-behavioral group therapy and drug treatment for social phobia used both an alternative-treatment control group and two no-treatment control groups in the same study. Participants received one of the following types of treatment: cognitive-behavioral group therapy, drug therapy, pill placebo administration, or attention-placebo group therapy. Results showed both cognitive-behavioral group therapy and drug therapy to be more effective than either of the placebo control conditions.

Several forms of psychotherapy and drug treatment have been subjected to hundreds of clinical trials; and when they pass the test, they are said to be "empirically supported" by controlled experimental research. Unfortunately, such research seldom pays enough attention to the matter of clinical significance. Though a treatment may, technically speaking, be "empirically supported," that does not mean it is really effective enough that therapists should drop the methods they are using and switch to this one. Still, clinical trials do constitute a form of true experiment—one that may suggest not only useful treatments but also possible causes.

Analogue Experiments Another type of true experiment often used in psychopathology research is the **analogue experiment.** The researcher designs an experimental situation that is analogous to "real life" and that may serve as a model for how psychopathology develops and how it can be alleviated. The critical advantage of analogue experiments is that they permit the kinds of control necessary to identify causal relationships and therefore have high internal validity.

Wegner and his colleagues, for instance, used an analogue experiment to test the hypothesis that active attempts to suppress an unwanted thought lead the thought to become more intrusive subsequently, as in obsessive-compulsive disorder (OCD) (Wegner, Scheider, Carter, et al., 1987; Wenzlaff & Wegner, 2000). One group of students focused on the target thought (a white bear) from the start, whereas the other group first tried to suppress thoughts of a white bear. Compared with the group that thought about a white bear at the outset, the group that initially suppressed the target thought reported a higher rate of white bear thoughts during a subsequent expression period. This paradoxical finding suggested that OCD patients' attempts to suppress their unwanted, obsessive thoughts may actually have led these obsessions to become more intrusive and maintain their OCD (Wenzlaff & Wegner, 2000).

Another important advantage of analogue research is that, in the artificial, analogue setting, the experimenter can test variables that could not be manipulated with genuinely distressed people. To cause ordinary college students to temporarily have intrusive thoughts, as was done in the experiment just described, is ethically permissible, but one cannot risk making OCD patients more obsessive. On the other hand, the kinds of psychological problems that one can ethically induce in an experiment may *not* be analogous to mental disorders (Suomi, 2000). In general, the more ethical an analogue experiment in abnormal psychology, the less analogous it is likely to be, but one cannot, for that reason, ignore ethics. This problem can be partially solved by developing animal models of psychopathoogy. For example, uncontrollable electric shock has been used with animal subjects as an analogue of the types of stressful experiences that are

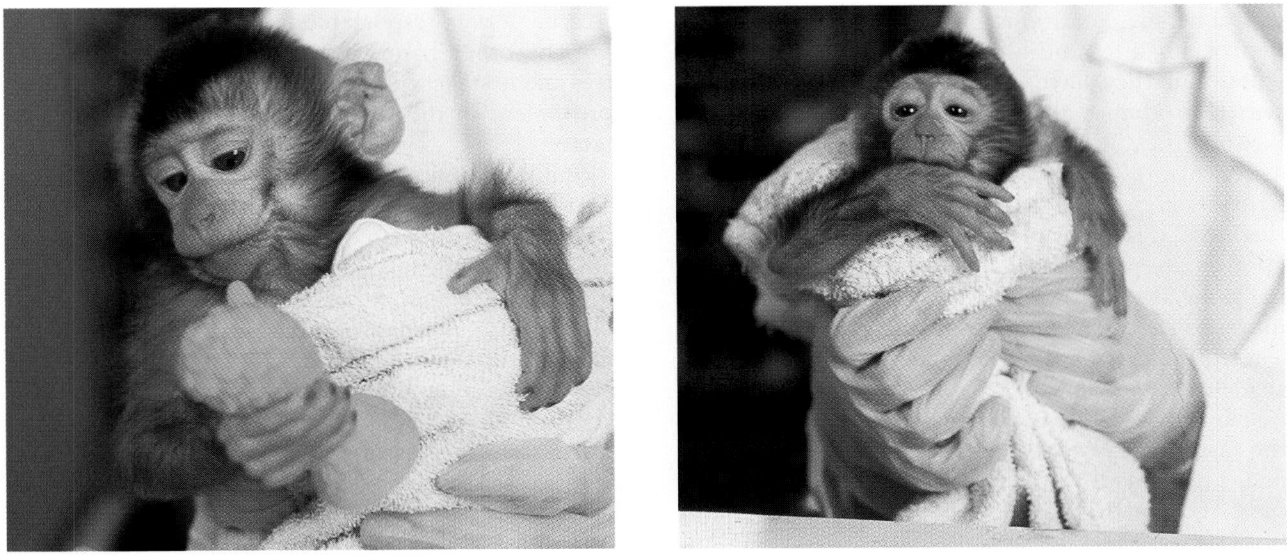

The baby macaque on the left exhibits normal curiosity, while the one on the right, suffering from induced fetal alcohol syndrome, is listless and unresponsive. Such animal models of human pathology can make valuable contributions to our understanding of various disorders. Though animal research presents ethical problems, it will probably remain an important tool in determining the causes of psychopathology.

thought to cause ulcers and depression (Peterson, Maier, & Seligman, 1993). We saw this technique in the executive monkey experiment discussed earlier in this chapter.

Animal models offer several advantages (Ferguson, 2001; Suomi, 2000). Not only can researchers more closely mimic the severity of naturally occurring events, but they can also gain almost complete control over the subject's developmental history (e.g., diet and living conditions) and even, through controlled breeding, its genetic endowment. Many important variables can be held constant and thus can be prevented from confounding the experiment. Further, many behavioral and physiological procedures considered too intrusive to be used with human participants (e.g., sampling brain neurotransmitters or cerebrospinal fluid) can be performed on animals. Also, because laboratory animals develop more rapidly and have shorter life spans than do humans, the long-term consequences of pathology and effectiveness of treatment can be assessed quickly. Animal models have been developed for drug addiction, anxiety disorders, depression, and various other forms of psychopathology (King, Campbell, & Edwards, 1993). It should be added, however, that experimentation with animals has also become increasingly controversial on ethical grounds.

Though analogue experiments cannot be exactly like the real thing, they can come close to it, and it is on the degree of likeness that they are evaluated: How close to reality did they come? The answer to this question depends on how much we know about the real thing (Bourin, Fiocco, & Clenet, 2001; Suomi, 2000). We still do not know the causes of many psychological disorders, let alone the cures. Consequently, many models can be validated only partially—in terms of the symptoms they reproduce, for instance. Even though, by manipulating certain variables, experimenters may reproduce the symptoms of a naturally occurring disorder, they still have not proved that the naturally occurring disorder issues from those same variables (Suomi, 2000). When animal subjects are used, a nagging question is always present: Just how similar is the behavior of any other animal species to that of the human species? In addition, it is unlikely that all forms of human psychopathology can be induced in animals.

The internal validity provided by analogue experiments must be weighed against the cost to external validity. As a general rule, experimental procedures that increase internal validity tend to decrease external validity (Kazdin, 1999). Nevertheless, the search for causal relationships is best conducted under the tight controls of experiments with high internal validity.

The Single-Case Experiment

Experiments with multiple groups, particularly those in which participants are randomly assigned to experimental conditions, are often considered the best means of establishing cause-and-effect relationships. But they have certain disadvantages for research in abnormal psychology (Gaynor, Baird, & Nelson-Gray, 1999). For example, ethical problems arise when researchers withhold treatment from participants in order to provide a "control" group. Furthermore, it is sometimes difficult to assemble enough appropriate participants for a group experiment. Finally, the average response of a group of participants may not be representative of any one participant. These problems have led some researchers to turn to single-case experiments.

The **single-case experiment** resembles its cousin, the case study, in that it focuses on behavior change in one person. However, it differs from the traditional case study in that it methodically varies the conditions surrounding the person's behavior and continuously monitors the behavior under those changing conditions. When properly carried out, the single-case experimental design has considerable internal validity (Morgan & Morgan, 2001).

The first stage of a single-case experiment is usually an observation, or baseline, stage. During this stage, a record is made of the participant's behavior before any intervention. A typical measure is frequency of behavior over a period of time, such as an hour, a day, or a week. For example, a record might be made of the number of tantrums thrown by a child or the number of panic attacks reported by a person with an anxiety disorder. (A potential drawback to this approach is that the mere fact of observation can change the behavior if the participant knows he or she is being observed, a problem known as the Hawthorne effect.) Once behavior is shown to be relatively stable—that is, once there is little fluctuation between recording intervals—a treatment is introduced. The effect of the treatment is ordinarily evaluated by comparing baseline behavior with after-intervention behavior (Gaynor, Baird, & Nelson-Gray, 1999).

Single-case experiments can be set up in a number of ways, but the most common designs are described here.

ABAB Design In the **ABAB design,** an initial baseline stage (A) is followed by a treatment stage (B), a return to baseline (A), and another treatment stage (B). Because treatment is removed during the second A stage, this design is also referred to as a "reversal design." If behavior, after improving in the first treatment stage, reverts to baseline when the treatment is withdrawn and then improves again in the second treatment stage, it is fair to assume that the treatment was responsible for the behavior change. On the other hand, if only one baseline and one treatment stage were used (an AB design), any improvement in the B stage might be due to another factor.

Bulik, Epstein, and Kaye (1990) used an ABAB design when they worked to modify the behavior of a female inpatient diagnosed with bulimia and laxative abuse. The patient was allowed to self-administer up to 6 doses of either an active drug laxative or a placebo in alternating phases. In this case, the placebo was the treatment for the girl's laxative abuse. Outcome measures included the number of laxative doses administered daily and the participant's own reports of her cravings for the laxative. Figure 3.3 shows the changes in the participant's behavior through alternating baseline and treatment conditions. As the graph shows, the number of doses administered was high and steady during the active laxative phase (the first A stage) and decreased during the placebo phase (the first B stage). This rate increased when the active drug was reintroduced during the second A phase and finally decreased substantially in the second, and last, B phase. A similar pattern was noted in the girl's own reports of cravings. This study demonstrates that when the cues associated with laxative use (placebo phase) appeared without the accompanying reinforcer (active laxative), reports of cravings for the drug disappeared, and the rate of self-administration decreased as well (Gaynor, Baird, & Nelson-Gray, 1999). In other words, when the placebo laxative did not have an actual laxative effect, the patient lost her craving for it, and reduced her use of the drug.

Treatment withdrawal in the ABAB design may pose ethical problems. While the girl's return to using laxatives in the second A stage was not cause for alarm, there are certain behaviors—such as self-mutilation in severely disturbed bulimic patients—for which it is not appropriate to halt effective treatment. In such cases, other, single-case experimental designs must be considered.

Multiple-Baseline Design An experimental design that does not depend on interrupting treatment is the **multiple-baseline design.** In this procedure, the same treatment is aimed successively at several targets—usually several participants, several behaviors in one participant, or several situational variants for one behavior. When the design is used across participants, a baseline is first established for each participant; then the intervention is introduced, first for one participant, then for the next, and so on. If the intervention is responsible for changing behavior, then an effect

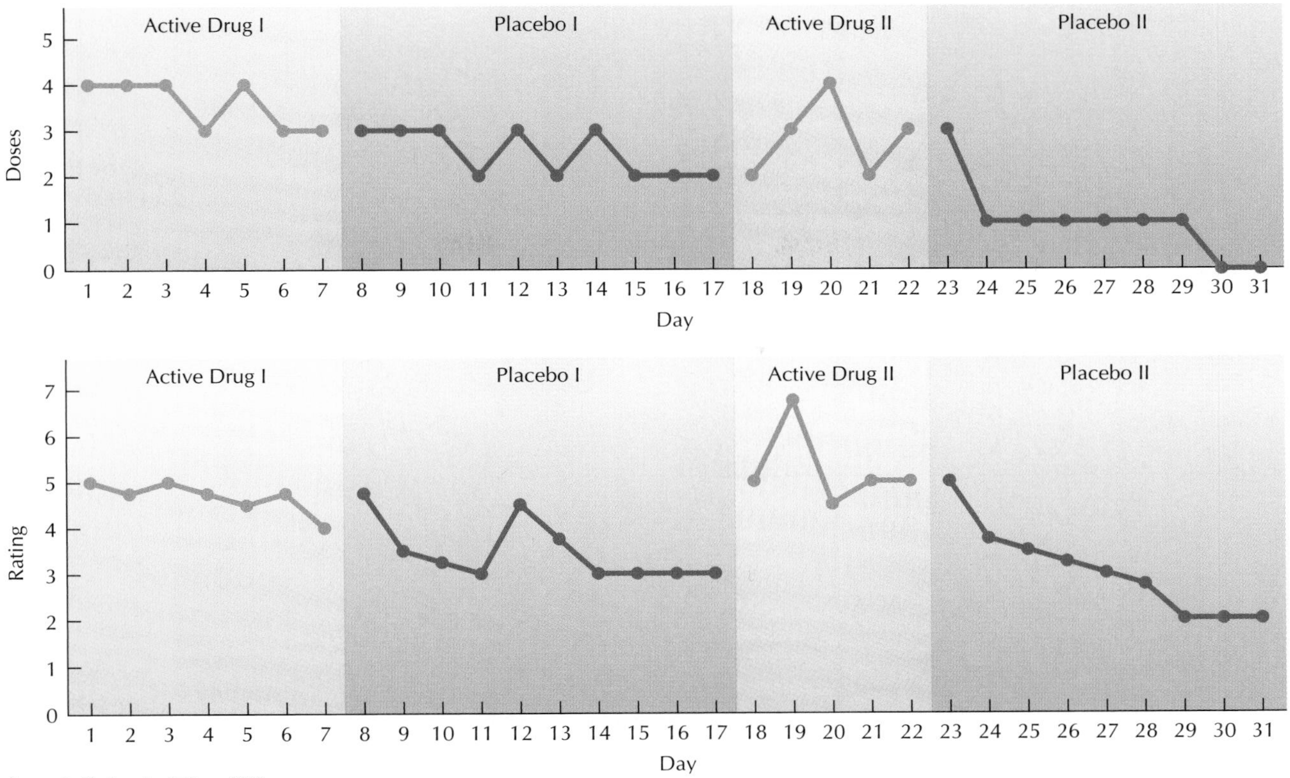

Source: Bulik, Epstein, & Kaye, 1990

FIGURE 3.3 The ABAB procedure helped a girl with bulimia learn to stop abusing laxatives. The top panel shows the daily doses of laxative or placebo. The bottom panel is a graphic display of the participant's daily cravings. As the graphs show, administering a placebo laxative discouraged the participant's habit as well as her cravings (Placebo I). When the placebo treatment was temporarily halted, her habit gained strength again (Active Drug II), but then it declined once more when the placebo was reapplied (Placebo II).

should be observed in each participant immediately following treatment. Like the ABAB design, the multiple-baseline design rules out alternative explanations for behavior change by demonstrating that behavior responds systematically to the introduction of the treatment.

Ollendick (1995) used a multiple-baseline design to treat 4 adolescents diagnosed with panic disorder with agoraphobia. Gaynor, Baird, and Nelson-Gray (1999) describe the study, in which all 4 adolescent clients reported experiencing panic attacks for the previous 6 months, 2 years, 6 years, and 6 years, respectively, indicating the presence of a long-standing problem in each child. All showed a decline in panic attacks during Ollendick's treatment, such that in the final 2 weeks of treatment no one described having had any panic attacks at all (Figure 3.4). All 4 adolescents maintained the effect at a 6-month follow-up.

Limitations of the Single-Case Design Like the traditional case study, the single-case experiment design is weak in external validity. As each person is unique, it can be argued that there is no way of knowing whether the effect of a particular treatment on one person can predict its effect on other people. This problem may not be as serious as it appears, because the efficiency with which data can be collected from one participant often makes it easy to repeat the procedures with other participants (Morgan & Morgan, 2001). Therefore, while generalizability is in no way guaranteed by the single-case design, it can easily be tested. Moreover, external validity can be enhanced by the use of a single group of participants in a single-case experimental design, such as ABAB. Then it is possible to draw conclusions about the effect of the experimental variable not just on the individual participants but on the population from which the sample was drawn.

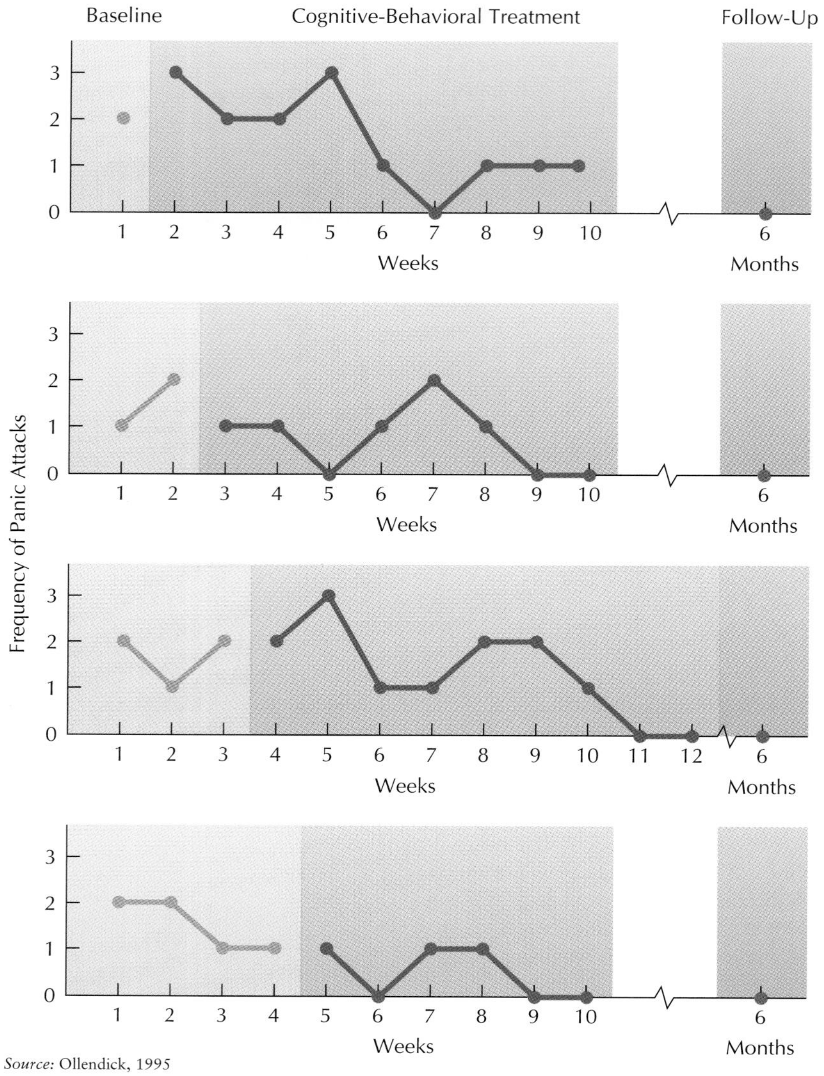

Source: Ollendick, 1995

FIGURE 3.4 Frequency of weekly panic attacks for 4 adolescents, listed from top to bottom. The multiple-baseline design has an important advantage over the ABAB design: It does not require the experimenter to interrupt a treatment that seems helpful.

Key Terms

ABAB design, 70
analogue experiment, 68
behavioral high-risk design, 66
case-control design, 64
case study, 58
clinical significance, 62
clinical trials, 67
clinicians, 57
confounding, 56
control, 58
control group, 63
control techniques, 59
correlation coefficient, 65
correlational research, 64
covariation of events, 56
demand characteristics, 59
dependent variable, 58
description, 55
double-blind, 59
elimination of plausible alternative causes, 56
epidemiology, 66
experimenter effects, 59
external validity, 56
generalizability, 56
genetic high-risk design, 66
high-risk design, 66
hypothesis, 57
incidence, 66
independent variable, 58
informed consent, 62
internal validity, 56
longitudinal studies, 66
multiple-baseline design, 70
null hypothesis, 61
operational definitions, 58
placebo, 59
prediction, 56
prevalence, 66
prospective studies, 66
random assignment, 59
random sample, 57
replicate, 57
representativeness, 56
single-case experiment, 70
statistical inference, 61
third-variable problem, 65
time-order relationship, 56
understanding, 56

Summary

- The scientific method is characterized by the skeptical attitude of those who use it; by the objectives it is intended to meet (namely, reliable and valid description, prediction, control, and understanding of behavior); and by the specific procedures used to meet those objectives (hypothesis testing, definition formulation, and methods of control).
- Research that fails to eliminate alternative explanations of a phenomenon is said to be confounded. Only when no confounding is present is a study internally valid.
- The external validity of research depends on whether the findings can be generalized, or applied, to different populations, settings, and conditions. External validity increases as the representativeness of a sample increases. The best way to achieve a representative sample is to use a random sampling procedure. External validity also increases with frequent, successful replication of a study.
- Research often begins with the development of a testable, or falsifiable, hypothesis. To be testable, a hypothesis must be formulated with operational definitions that can be observed and measured.
- Generally, a hypothesis is tested in an experiment, in which three control techniques are used: manipulating the independent variable in order to measure its effects on the dependent variable, holding all other variables constant, and balancing uncontrollable factors—the personal characteristics of the subjects being tested—among all conditions.
- Often, the response of a placebo control group can either support or cast doubt on the supposed relationship between an independent and a dependent variable.
- Double-blind experiments, in which neither the subjects nor the experimenters know what treatment is being administered to whom, are used to minimize the effect of expectations on the study's results or on their interpretation.
- Any psychological study involving human subjects must meet strict ethical standards. Above all, participation in scientific research must be voluntary. It is unethical to use undue inducement or any element of force or duress when recruiting research participants.
- Informed consent is the most important ethical principle in clinical research. Essential elements of a consent form are an explanation of the purpose and duration of the research, disclosure of appropriate alternative procedures that might be more advantageous to participants, an offer to answer any questions about the study, an understanding that the participant is free to withdraw consent at any time, a statement regarding the confidentiality of the data collected and information about whom to contact if the participant has questions. Unless a potential participant is extremely young or extremely cognitively impaired, researchers must still obtain his or her agreement; otherwise, consent must be provided by a legal guardian.
- Although deception in psychological research constitutes a breach of trust between researcher and participant, it is legal and sometimes necessary to validate the results. Such a breach can be reduced somewhat by withholding information, rather than outright lying, in consent forms; by informing participants that they may be deceived during the study, without telling them how; or by offering participants the chance to withdraw their data from the project at the end of the experiment, after they have been fully informed of the deception.
- The use of control groups is essential to good research design. However, ethical problems arise when some participants are randomly assigned to no-treatment control groups in order to compare the effectiveness of an available experimental treatment against no treatment at all. One alternative is to use individuals who are on a waiting list for the experimental treatment as controls while they are waiting to receive the treatment.
- Researchers are ethically bound to maintain the confidentiality of the data they gather, with the exception of information that must be reported as required by law, such as evidence of child abuse. Researchers are also ethically obliged to tell parents about a child's suicide plans or other risky behavior if it is reported in a study and to intervene when study participants suggest that they might harm themselves or others or are otherwise in serious distress.
- Many different research designs are used to investigate abnormal behavior. Prior to the testing of hypotheses, a phase of exploration, discovery, and observation is used to generate the hypotheses. One basis for hypothesis generation is the case study, the intensive description and analysis of a single person. Treatment development is also gaining recognition as a method of informal observation that is useful for generating hypotheses and the experimental methods for testing them.
- Correlational, or natural, group designs examine whether systematic differences exist between groups of people who have been treated "naturally." Major tasks in evaluating the results of correlational studies are to determine the direction of the causal relationship and to eliminate possible third variables that may cause differences between groups.
- Longitudinal studies examine the behavior of people over time. Although this design does not solve the problem of determining causality, it is more powerful than a correlational design, because assumptions of covariation and time-order relationships can be more easily tested.
- The high-risk design is a type of longitudinal research that follows people who are thought to be vulnerable to developing a disorder in the future.

- Epidemiological studies examine the incidence and prevalence of a behavioral disorder in a population. Such studies can help to determine whether the frequency of a particular disorder is related to other variables, which may be causes. A major concern in epidemiological surveys is the representativeness of the sample.
- In experimental designs, the experimenter manipulates an independent variable and measures a dependent variable.
- Analogue experiments, which place subjects in artificial situations that are analogous to real-life situations, permit the kind of experimental control that is useful in identifying causal relationships.
- Clinical trials are experimental designs used to evaluate treatments for behavior disorders. They involve randomly assigning patients to either experimental or control groups and examining whether or not the experimental treatment outperforms the comparison one.
- Single-case experimental designs monitor behavior change in an individual following an intervention that was introduced after a baseline (no-treatment) observation. Evidence for a causal relationship is obtained if the person's behavior changes systematically with the introduction of the treatment.

CHAPTER

4

The Behavioral Perspective
- The Background of Behaviorism
- The Assumptions of Behavioral Psychology
- The Basic Mechanisms of Learning
- Other Mechanisms Associated With Learning
- Abnormal Behavior as a Product of Learning
- The Behavioral Approach to Therapy
- Evaluating Behaviorism

The Cognitive Perspective
- The Background of the Cognitive Perspective
- Cognitive Behaviorism
- Cognitive Appraisal
- Information Processing
- The Cognitive Approach to Treatment
- Evaluating the Cognitive Perspective

The Sociocultural Perspective
- Social-Situational Influences on Behavior
- Mental Illness and Social Ills
- Mental Illness and Labeling
- Class, Ethnicity, and Diagnosis
- Sociocultural Factors, Help-Seeking, and Treatment
- Prevention as a Social Issue
- Evaluating the Sociocultural Perspective

The Behavioral, Cognitive, and Sociocultural Perspectives

In Chapter 1, we spoke briefly of the perspectives, or schools of theory and practice, in abnormal psychology. Those perspectives are the subject of this and the next two chapters. In this chapter, we focus on the behavioral, cognitive, and sociocultural perspectives. The behavioral perspective emphasizes factors in the environment that influence behavior. The cognitive perspective looks at the role that subjective thought and mental processes (such as attention, memory, and interpretation) play in abnormal behavior. The sociocultural perspective focuses on the individual's social context and on the importance of considering differences in cultural and ethnic values when thinking about the causes and treatments of abnormal behavior.

All three perspectives are products of the twentieth century, and all arose in reaction to earlier philosophies of behavior—behaviorism as a reaction to psychodynamic theory and the introspective method, which we will discuss in Chapter 5; cognitive theory as a reaction, in some measure, to the extreme focus on observable behavior of classical behavioral theory; and sociocultural theory as a reaction to psychology itself, with its habit of viewing abnormal behavior as a problem in the person rather than in the social context.

The Behavioral Perspective

The **behavioral perspective** views behavior (except for genetically determined behavior) as the result of environmental experience. Environmental experience, also called learning, is the sum total of all life experiences that the individual has been subjected to and that continue to impinge on his or her behavior—modifying it, refining it, and changing it. For the behaviorists, the only causes of behavior other than genes are in the environment (Skinner, 1953). Faced with a student who is depressed after failing an exam, the behavioral theorist would be interested in

Ivan Pavlov (center) discovered a basic mechanism of learning, the conditioned reflex, while doing research on digestion. The dog in Pavlov's experiment learned to salivate at the sound of a tone by associating it with being fed. With this accidental discovery, Pavlov laid the theoretical foundation of behaviorism.

proximal, or nearby, causes, causes in the current environment: What were the consequences for the student of failing the exam? What circumstances in her current life situation may have caused the failure, and what current circumstances may now be operating to encourage the response of depression?

The behaviorists' proximal focus is in part the result of their insistence on scientific method, more specifically on a method known as the experimental analysis of behavior.

The Background of Behaviorism

An important component of many psychological theories in the late nineteenth century was introspection, the study of the mind by analysis of one's own thought processes. Behaviorism arose in reaction to this trend, claiming that the causes of behavior were not in the mysterious (and untestable) depths of the mind but in the environment, first in people's learning histories, then in the more proximal stimuli that elicited, shaped, reinforced, and punished certain of their responses. The explanation, in other words, lay in **learning,** the process whereby behavior changes in response to the environment.

Actually, psychological theorists had long recognized the influence of learning on human behavior. But not until the early twentieth century did scientists begin to uncover the actual mechanisms of learning, thereby laying the theoretical foundation for behaviorism. Especially crucial were the contributions of four scientists: Ivan Pavlov, John B. Watson, Edward Lee Thorndike, and, most important, B. F. Skinner.

Pavlov: The Conditioned Reflex In conducting research with dogs, Ivan Pavlov (1849–1936), a Russian neurophysiologist, found that, if he consistently sounded a tone at the same time that he gave a dog food, the dog would eventually salivate to the sound of the tone alone. Thus, Pavlov discovered a basic mechanism of learning, the **conditioned reflex:** If a neutral stimulus (e.g., the tone) is paired with a nonneutral stimulus (e.g., the food), the organism will eventually respond to the neutral stimulus as it does to the nonneutral stimulus.

Pavlov's discovery had profound implications. Whereas it had always been assumed that human beings' reactions to their environment were the result of complicated subjective processes, Pavlov's finding raised the possibility that many of our responses, like those of the dogs, were the result of a simple learning process. In other words, our loves and hates, our tastes and distastes, might be the consequences of nothing more mysterious than a conditioning process whereby various things in our environment became "linked" to other things to which we respond instinctively, such as food, warmth, and pain. Along with this different view of psychology came the possibility of testing such processes empirically, under controlled conditions.

Watson: The Founding of Behaviorism It is John B. Watson (1878–1958), an American psychologist, who is credited with founding the behavioral movement. In a now-famous article, "Psychology as the Behaviorist Views It," Watson (1913) made his position clear: "Psychology, as the behaviorist views it, is a purely objective, experimental branch of natural science which needs introspection as little as do the sciences of chemistry and physics" (p. 176). Watson argued that introspection was, if anything, the province of theology. The province of psychology was behavior—observable and measurable responses to specific stimuli. And the goal of psychology was the prediction and control of behavior.

Watson supported his rejection of the introspection method by demonstrating, in a classic experiment, that a supposedly subjective emotion such as

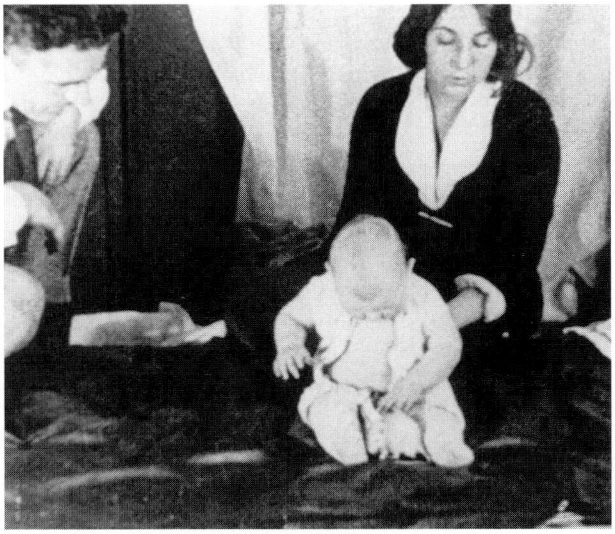

To support his claim that psychology is an objective science, John B. Watson and his colleague Rosalie Rayner conducted an experiment to condition "Little Albert" to fear rats. Watson's experiment is considered unethical by today's standards.

fear could, like the salivation response of Pavlov's dogs, result from a simple, objective conditioning process. With the help of a colleague, Rosalie Rayner, Watson conditioned a fear of rats in an 11-month-old boy, Albert B. (Watson & Rayner, 1920). Before the experiment, Albert had no fear of the tame laboratory rats. On the first day of the experiment, the boy was shown a white rat. Watson then struck an iron bar with a hammer, producing a very loud noise. The first time this happened, Albert was simply startled. As it happened again and again, he began to show signs of fright—crying, falling over, and crawling away from the rat. After 7 pairings of the rat and the noise, Albert showed these reactions in response to the rat alone, without the noise. Thus, a conditioned fear reaction had been established. Later tests showed that, without further conditioning, Albert produced these sorts of behaviors in response to a variety of stimuli similar to the rat: a rabbit, a dog, a sealskin coat, and a bearded Santa Claus mask. Commenting on these results, Watson argued that many of our "unreasonable" fears are established in the same way that Albert's was—through conditioning.

Thorndike: The Law of Effect Another psychologist of Watson's time was Edward Lee Thorndike (1874–1949), whose early experiments with animals had a decisive influence on learning theory. Unlike Pavlov and Watson, who had studied the relationships between behavior and the stimuli that preceded it, Thorndike was interested in the relationship between behavior and its consequences. If an organism is repeatedly presented with a pleasant or painful stimulus after making a given response, how will this affect the response?

In one experiment, Thorndike placed a hungry cat in a box equipped in such a way that, if the cat pulled a cord or pressed a lever, the door of the chamber flew open. When the cat escaped, it was given a piece of salmon to eat. In early trials, the cat often took a long time to get out of the box. Gradually, however, the escape time grew shorter and shorter until finally the cat was no sooner placed in the box than it exited and collected its reward. Thorndike concluded that the reason the cat learned the proper escape response was that this response had become associated with the food, which was the consequence of escaping. From this conclusion, Thorndike formulated what he called the **law of effect,** which states that responses that lead to "satisfying" consequences are strengthened and therefore are likely to be repeated, whereas responses that lead to "unsatisfying" consequences are weakened and therefore are unlikely to be repeated.

Skinner: Radical Behaviorism Psychologist B. F. Skinner (1904–1990) created a version of behaviorism that was revolutionary in its implications and applicable to everyday life. First, he broadened behaviorism. Watson had declared that psychologists should study only what they could observe. Skinner referred to this as "methodological behaviorism" and set out to expand it. In his approach, which he called **radical behaviorism,** everything a person does, says,

B. F. Skinner, the founder of radical behaviorism, extended earlier behavioral theories and demonstrated their applicability to everyday life.

and feels constitutes behavior and, even if unobservable, can be subjected to experimental analysis. The skin, he said, was an arbitrary boundary. Whether behavior was public or private, it was still of interest to psychology.

Second, Skinner insisted on the practical applications of experimental analysis. He took Thorndike's law of effect and developed a method for predicting and influencing human behavior that focused on the association between action and consequences. He demonstrated that our social environment is filled with reinforcing and punishing consequences, which mold our behavior as surely as the piece of salmon molded the behavior of Thorndike's cat (Skinner, 1965). Our friends and families influence us with their approval or disapproval. Our jobs influence us by offering or withholding money. Our schools influence us by passing us or failing us, thus affecting our access to jobs. Skinner stated outright what Pavlov had merely suggested: Much of our behavior is based not on hypothetical processes occurring beneath the skin but on external contingencies. Furthermore, precisely because they *are* external, these contingencies can be altered to change our behavior. As we will see, this is a fundamental principle of behavioral therapy.

The Assumptions of Behavioral Psychology

Before we go on to discuss the mechanisms of learning, we will review the basic assumptions of behaviorism as it developed in the hands of the scientists whose work we just discussed.

The first assumption is that the task of psychology is, as Watson claimed, the study of behavior—the study of the responses that an organism makes to its learning history, to the aggregate of experiences that it has been subjected to throughout its life. Such experiences may be imposed from the outside, by the people, objects, and events in the organism's environment. They can also be internal, such as back pain, which may elicit the response of taking a pill. Likewise, responses may be external (e.g., pounding a table in anger) or internal (e.g., thinking "I'm not going to show her I'm angry").

A second basic assumption has to do with methodology. According to methodological behaviorism, both stimuli and responses are objective, empirical events that can be observed and measured and that *must* be observed and measured in order to qualify as scientific evidence. Hence, behavioral studies since Pavlov's time have always attempted to include careful measurement of responses.

A third assumption, formulated by Watson, is that the goal of psychology is the prediction and control of behavior. For behaviorists working in a laboratory, where they can set up and manipulate environmental circumstances, prediction and control are relatively easy to obtain. But when the behaviorist moves out of the laboratory into the world at large, these goals become more elusive. The environmental stimuli of everyday life are infinitely more varied, complex, and uncontrollable than those of the laboratory; and individuals, even when studied under controlled conditions, have genetic constraints and learning histories that limit the influence of the scientist.

The final basic assumption of contemporary behaviorism is that the place to look for the real causes of behavior, at least those that are not genetically determined, is outside rather than inside the organism. Predictors of behavior that lie within the organism are not held to be causes; rather, they are the mechanisms by which the environment exerts its effects. This assumption is an article of faith. Thus, contemporary behaviorism is really less a theory than a method, one that makes possible the experimental analysis of behavior. That analysis is stated in terms of the mechanisms of learning, to which we will now turn.

The Basic Mechanisms of Learning

Respondent Conditioning According to behaviorists, all behavior that is not genetically determined is a function of either respondent or operant conditioning. Unconditioned responses are innate reflexes, such as blinking and salivation, that occur automatically when elicited by certain stimuli. It is possible, however, through the pairing of stimuli, to condition people to respond reflexively to an initially neutral stimulus, one that would not naturally have elicited the response. The learning of such a conditioned response is what is commonly referred to as **respondent conditioning** (or classical conditioning). An excellent example is Pavlov's dog experiment. Because a hungry dog salivates naturally—that is, without conditioning—when presented with food, the food is designated as an **unconditioned stimulus** (UCS) and the natural response of salivation as the **unconditioned response** (UCR). And, because the dog's salivation to the tone was the result of conditioning, the tone is called the **conditioned stimulus** (CS) and the salivation to the tone alone, without the food, the **conditioned response** (CR).

As we proceed up the evolutionary scale from animals to humans, classical conditioning plays less of a role. Even in humans, however, many behaviors can be attributed to classical conditioning. For example, adolescent and adult humans respond reflexively to erotic stimulation with sexual arousal. However, through the pairing of erotic and neutral stimuli, humans can learn to become sexually aroused by stimuli that would otherwise have posed no erotic potential. Verbal references to sex are one example. This makes the study of sexual behavior complicated, because everyone has a different learning history. One person's sexual fantasy may be another person's basis for disgust.

Operant Conditioning In respondent behavior, the organism responds passively to the environment; in operant behavior, as the name suggests, the organism *does* something because in the past that action was associated either with desirable outcomes or with the avoidance of undesirable outcomes. Unlike respondent behavior, however, all operant behavior is the result of conditioning. In **operant conditioning** (also called instrumental conditioning), the likelihood of a response is increased or decreased by virtue of its consequences. Having taken a certain action, the individual learns to associate that action with certain consequences. This association between action and consequence is called a **contingency,** and it will direct the individual's behavior in the future: The person will repeat the behavior, or cease to engage in it, in order to obtain or avoid the consequence. This, of course, is Thorndike's law of effect, and a good example is Thorndike's cat. Human beings, like the cat, learn to do things as a function of their consequences.

Were it not for the salmon, Thorndike's cat would not have learned to press the lever. Were it not for the paycheck, some people would not go to work. Operant conditioning depends on **reinforcement,** the process by which events in the environment increase the probability of the behavior that preceded it. As Skinner pointed out, the world is full of reinforcers. The simplest type, the **primary reinforcer,** is one to which we respond instinctively, without learning, under the right conditions—for example, food (when we are hungry), water (when we are thirsty), warmth (when we are cold), and sex (when we are aroused). Most of the reinforcers to which we respond, however, are not simple primary reinforcers but, rather, **conditioned reinforcers** (also called secondary reinforcers), stimuli to which we have learned to respond through their association with primary reinforcers. Money is a good example of a conditioned reinforcer. We respond to it positively not because we have an instinctive liking for green pieces of paper printed with symbols but because those pieces of paper are associated with past reinforcers and signal the future delivery of further reinforcers.

Environmental contingencies operate on behavior in three basic ways. In **positive reinforcement,** a response followed by a consequence in the environment results in a strengthening of the response. Suppose a child dresses herself for school for the first time. Her parents praise her, and, following this praise, she dresses herself the next morning. Let us further suppose that later the praise stops, and the child stops dressing herself. It appears that the praise is functioning as a positive reinforcer. The evidence would be even stronger if a reinstitution of praise were to result in a resumption of self-dressing.

A second type of reinforcement process is **negative reinforcement.** In this case, the response is strengthened by the avoidance or removal of an aversive stimulus. To understand negative reinforcement, let us imagine that a student fails to study for an exam and, consequently, receives an *F.* If he studies for the next exam, avoids an *F,* and then goes on studying for exams in the future, it appears that receiving an *F* constituted a negative reinforcer.

This process, also called escape or avoidance learning, can teach us some very useful behaviors, as in the example just cited. However, behaviorists feel that it may also be responsible for many patterns of abnormal behavior. For example, a little boy who is bitten by a dog may develop a dog phobia, a fear of all dogs. From that point on, he may simply run the other way whenever he sees a dog; and, every time he flees, the avoidance of being bitten will reinforce the running away. As a result, the dog phobia will be maintained indefinitely, because the boy never has a safe, happy experience with a dog to counteract the phobia.

Whereas reinforcement involves the strengthening of behavior, **punishment** describes the suppression of behavior. Typically, punishment is a process whereby behavior decreases in frequency following aversive consequences. For example, when we scold a child for hitting another child, we are hoping that scolding will function as a punisher. If the child subsequently hits less frequently, we have probably succeeded in finding an effective punisher.

Negative reinforcement and punishment are sometimes confused, for a number of reasons. First, similar consequences do not have similar effects on all people. For example, we think of scolding as a punishment, and when we scold a child for aggressive behavior, we would expect the aggression to decrease. But, in some families, parental scolding actually results in *increased* aggression, a phenomenon called the negative spiral (Patterson, 1982). Thus, while the parent is trying to punish the child, the child is actually reinforced by the scolding. Another reason for confusion between the categories is that people find it hard to think of reinforcement as negative, so they just call "pleasant" situations reinforcement and "unpleasant" situations punishment. Keep in mind that behaviorists avoid defining reinforcers and punishers according to their apparent rewarding or punishing properties. Instead, reinforcers and punishers are determined empirically, by observing how they function in strengthening or weakening behavior. *Reinforcement increases the likelihood of a response; punishment decreases the likelihood of a response.*

The process of identifying reinforcing and punishing consequences is what behaviorists call functional analysis. Functional analysis is the primary method for determining which variables control behavior. If the behavior systematically varies according to your presenting and withholding certain consequences, you are demonstrating a functional relationship between the two. Such demonstrations are the hallmark of a behavior analysis.

Other Mechanisms Associated With Learning

In addition to defining respondent and operant conditioning, psychologists have identified a number of other mechanisms associated with learning. These mechanisms identify some of the processes involved in learning, help to explain its scope and complexity, and delineate the conditions under which it occurs.

Extinction One of the most important of these mechanisms is **extinction,** the elimination of a response by withdrawing whatever reinforcer was maintaining it. In respondent conditioning, as we saw, a CS comes to be paired with a UCS, creating a CR. By the same token, the CR will extinguish if the CS is repeatedly presented *without* the UCS. Take, for example, the case of the dog-phobic child. Just as his fear was created by the pairing of the dog (CS) with the bite (UCS), so it will dissipate if he repeatedly encounters dogs that don't bite. (And that is how dog phobias are treated by behavioral therapists. The key is to get the phobic person to play with friendly dogs so that extinction can take place.) As for operant behaviors, extinction simply requires the removal of the reinforcement that is maintaining the response. Such a process is probably involved in the normal child's gradual abandonment of infantile behaviors. Because parental attention often reinforces temper tantrums, the ending of attention during a tantrum often leads to extinction.

Generalization Another important aspect of learning is **generalization,** whereby once an organism has learned to respond in a certain way to a particular stimulus, it will respond in the same way to similar stimuli without further conditioning. In other words, the conditioned response automatically "spreads," or generalizes, to things that resemble the conditioned stimulus. Once again, we have already seen an example: Albert B.'s spontaneous fear of rabbits, dogs, sealskin coats, and bearded Santa Claus masks once he was conditioned to fear the white rat.

Discrimination The opposite side of the coin from generalization is **discrimination**—that is, learning to distinguish among similar stimuli and to respond only to the appropriate one. Pavlov, for instance, found at first that a number of different tones, close in frequency, elicited his dogs' salivation response; however, when only one of those tones was consistently accompanied by food, the dogs learned to salivate to that tone only. Likewise, people learn to discriminate between similar environmental events—between a friendly smile and a malicious grin—when one has reinforcing consequences and the other does not.

Discrimination learning helps to explain complex learning in humans. A discriminative stimulus is a cue telling the individual that a particular response is likely to be reinforced. For example, at a high school dance, if Jim asks Pam for her phone number, the social norms at this high school might suggest that Jim finds Pam attractive. To the extent that "being found attractive" is a reinforcer, and to the extent that Pam has similar feelings about Jim, the request for the phone number functions as a discriminative stimulus for the response of providing the phone number, a response likely to be reinforced by a subsequent phone call from Jim. However, the same request, made by Frank, does not function as a discriminative stimulus for the same response. Why? Because, for whatever reason, Pam does not give her phone number to Frank. She may not find him attractive, or she may have heard things about him that make her wary of him.

In functional analysis, discriminative stimuli form an important piece of the puzzle. They can be narrow and discrete, as in the request for the phone number, or they can be broad and all-encompassing. For example, the entire learning history of an individual can be considered a discriminative stimulus. At any rate, the addition of the discriminative stimulus to the description of contingency generates a **three-term contingency:** Under certain conditions (e.g., certain learning histories, certain situations, all viewed as discriminative stimuli), certain responses are likely to be met with certain consequences (reinforcement, punishment, etc.). The addition of the discriminative stimulus complicates the relationship between behavior and its consequences, but all three terms are necessary for a complete behavior analysis.

Shaping A process critical to operant conditioning is **shaping,** the reinforcement of successive approximations of a desired response until it finally achieves the desired form. Shaping is involved in the development of many of our skills. Imagine a child learning to dive. First, she sits on the edge of the pool, puts her head down, and just falls into the water. For this first step, she receives a pat on the back (positive reinforcement) from the swimming teacher, and she may be further reinforced by the experience of successfully executing the act. Then she may start from a standing position and even hazard a little push as she takes off. This effort will be reinforced by further approval from the teacher, by the pleasure of a smoother descent into the water, and by her own feelings of achievement. Soon she will be ready for the diving board and then for fancier dives, with external and internal rewards at every step of the way. Thus, throughout the process there is positive reinforcement of successive approximations of the diving response.

Learning to Follow Rules: Instructions as Discriminative Stimuli Actually, it is unlikely that a swimming teacher would ask a child to learn by trial and error. Instead, the teacher would dive into the pool to show the child the proper technique and would then reward her with approval for imitating the performance. This type of learning—learning through imitation—is known as modeling (Bandura & Walters, 1963; Rosenthal & Bandura, 1978). Modeling is a common example of learning by exposure to **rules** or instructions. When behavior is governed by rules, following the rule is the behavior that is reinforced. Instructions are a type of rule. Modeling is a common form of instruction.

As in the diving lesson, so it is in human development in general: Rules normally accompany shaping—that is, we are rewarded for successive approximations of a response that conforms to the rule. But the converse is not necessarily true. Many children get no pats on the back as they are learning how to dive; they simply watch someone else do it, and suddenly they, too, are doing it. Thus, learning can occur without verbal specification of rules. A striking characteristic of rule-governed behavior is that, unlike many other forms of learning, it can—and often does—occur without any obvious external reinforcement (Hayes, 1989). Rules and instructions add to the child's learning history and provide a wealth of discriminative stimuli. They send signals to the child that certain responses are likely to be reinforced.

Modeling, like other rule-governed behavior, can occur without reinforcement. By watching his father use a lawnmower, this boy is learning his own skills.

Stimulus Equivalence Most of the mechanisms we have described so far involve directly training or reinforcing learned stimulus-response connections between observed stimuli and responses. For example, a parent who reinforces a child for brushing his teeth may teach the child to take responsibility for this task. However, researchers have discovered that people can learn stimulus-response connections without direct training (Follette & Hayes, 2000). Further, we can learn new connections that are not based on mere physical similarities between stimuli. Recall that in a simple stimulus generalization effect, a child might generalize a conditioned fear of rats to cats or other furry animals, based on the physical similarity of fur. Unlike such a generalization, which depends on shared physical characteristics, research on **stimulus equivalence** shows that people can learn new stimulus-response connections by transferring responses learned to one set of stimuli to another set of stimuli that have no physical similarities to the first set. For instance, people may come to transfer stimulus-response connections that they learned for a set of pictures of animals to a new set of stimuli, such as words that symbolically represent the same stimuli (e.g., the words "dog" and "horse"). It seems that this learning transfer happens because the mind learns to group together sets of different stimuli (e.g., pictures of objects and words for the objects). In this

TABLE 4.1 The Mechanisms of Learning

	DEFINITION	EXAMPLE
RESPONDENT CONDITIONING	Pairing a neutral stimulus with a nonneutral stimulus until the organism learns to respond to the neutral stimulus as it would to the nonneutral stimulus	A child who has seen a taxicab strike a pedestrian learns to fear all taxis.
OPERANT CONDITIONING	Rewarding or punishing a certain response until the organism learns to repeat or avoid that response in anticipation of the positive or negative consequences	See specific examples below.
Positive Reinforcement	Increasing the frequency of a behavior by rewarding it with consequences the organism wishes to obtain	Students praised by parents for studying study more and do better in school.
		AA programs reward alcoholics with praise, hugs, and medallions when they meet sobriety goals.
Negative Reinforcement	Increasing the frequency of a behavior by removing a stimulus the organism wishes to avoid	A person with claustrophobia goes on taking the stairs rather than the elevator, because he thereby avoids anxiety.
Punishment	Decreasing the frequency of a behavior by offering a consequence the organism wishes to avoid	A child molester, in treatment, views pictures of naked children, becomes aroused, then inhales ammonia and learns not to be aroused by this stimulus.
EXTINCTION	Decreasing the frequency of a behavior by unpairing UCS and CS, or behavior and reinforcement	A teacher decides to ignore the classroom disruptions of a child with autism, and the disruptions decrease.
GENERALIZATION	Spontaneously transferring a conditioned response from the conditioned stimulus to similar stimuli	A woman, after having been raped, begins to fear all men.
DISCRIMINATION	Learning to confine a response only to particular stimuli	In therapy, a person with severe depression learns to distinguish situations that can be changed from situations that cannot.
SHAPING	Reinforcing successive approximations of a desired response until that response is gradually achieved	A mentally retarded person is taught to make his bed by being praised first for pulling up the sheets and smoothing them down, then for pulling up the covers and smoothing them down, then for tucking them in.
RULE-GOVERNED BEHAVIOR	Learning by following instructions	A person with a phobia for heights watches a model climb a fire escape and gradually learns to climb one herself.
DERIVED STIMULUS RELATIONS	Learning by spontaneously grouping sets of stimuli, creating stimulus equivalence	A person who learns to respond to one kind of stimuli (such as objects) transfers learned stimulus-response connections to another set of stimuli (such as pictures of objects).

way, stimuli attain stimulus equivalence, and stimuli can acquire new stimulus-response connections, known as **derived stimulus relations.** This learning mechanism may help to explain why words and symbols acquire many of their psychological functions and come to affect behavior. For instance, by learning stimulus equivalences, people learn to respond to the word "money" much as they do to actual cash in the hand. The language symbols acquire many of the same psychological functions for future behavior as the stimuli they represent (Follette & Hayes, 2000).

Table 4.1 summarizes the various learning mechanisms we have discussed.

Abnormal Behavior as a Product of Learning

In the behavioral view, personality development is the result of the interaction between our genetic endowment and our experiences. And, according to the behaviorists, this is as true of abnormal development as it is of normal development. We have already seen how a dog phobia could develop through respondent conditioning and be maintained through negative reinforcement. Similarly, depression may be due in part to extinction: If significant positive reinforcements are withdrawn—a job lost, a marriage ended—many of a person's behaviors simply extinguish, and he or she becomes inactive, withdrawn, dejected, and depressed.

Contemporary, or radical, behaviorism emphasizes the importance of the three-term contingency and de-emphasizes the simple connection between stimulus and response. The extinction theory of depression, for example, arose in the 1970s, with P. M. Lewinsohn as its leading proponent. Today Lewinsohn claims that extinction theory is no longer sufficient to account for depression. Instead, he and his colleagues have put forth a vicious-cycle theory involving many components, with stress leading to a disruption of ordinary behavior patterns, leading to reduced positive reinforcement (extinction theory), leading to increased self-awareness and self-criticism (cognitive processing), leading to feelings of hopelessness, leading to self-defeating behaviors that occasion further stress, thus taking the person through the cycle again (Lewinsohn, Hoberman, Teri, et al., 1985). Such explanations, favoring complexity over simplicity and attempting to incorporate all recent experimental findings, represent the coming of age of behavioral explanations of abnormal behavior. A radical behaviorist would emphasize each phase of the cycle as adding to the life experience and learning history of the depressive. Nevertheless, the causal emphasis would remain on external circumstances. The internal experiences in this cycle—for example, the feelings of hopelessness—would be considered part of the depressive response rather than a separate component in the causal chain.

With more complex, radical behavioral views, the emphasis has shifted to the entire life history of the individual, rather than simply proximal causes. As a corollary, behaviorists avoid terms such as "normal" and "abnormal," because these words imply an absolute distinction between something healthy and something sick. In the behavioral view, there are no absolutes; behavior is defined within its context. The behaviorists also see all responses as united by the same principles of learning. At one end of the continuum we can, indeed, identify responses that make it difficult for people to conduct their lives successfully, but these responses do not differ qualitatively from more adaptive responses. Depressive behavior, as we just saw, may develop through the same mechanisms as any other category of behavior. Hence, behaviorists prefer to speak of "maladaptive" rather than "abnormal" behavior.

Likewise, behaviorists have traditionally been skeptical of the usefulness of labeling people according to diagnostic categories (e.g., phobia, schizophrenia, paranoia), because these categories, with their resemblance to medical diagnoses (e.g., pneumonia, cancer), seem to imply the medical model; that is, they suggest disease states—a suggestion that runs directly counter to the behaviorists' belief in the continuity of normal and abnormal. Furthermore, diagnostic categories group people based on similarities in form. For example, all those with similar depressive symptoms are called "depressed." However, to behaviorists, similar behaviors can serve a variety of functions, and one cannot assume that depressive behavior serves the same function for all people exhibiting it. Therefore, diagnostic labeling violates a basic tenet of behavior analysis: that the function of behavior, not the form, is the basis for prediction and influence. To the behaviorists, what is needed is not to put diagnostic labels on people but simply to specify as clearly as possible what the maladaptive behavior is, what contingencies may be setting the stage for and maintaining it, and how these contingencies may be rearranged in order to alter it (Hersen & Turner, 1984; Widiger & Costa, 1994).

In applying this sort of analysis to psychological abnormalities, the behaviorists do not claim that all such abnormalities are the result of learning alone, but only that learning may be an important contribution and that, *whatever the initial cause,* relearning may help to alter the behavior. For example, no one would claim that the basic cause of mental retardation is faulty learning, yet many mentally retarded people have been greatly helped by behavior therapies.

The Behavioral Approach to Therapy

One major influence of the behavioral perspective has been in the area of treatment. **Behavior therapy** attempts to alter abnormal behavior by making use of the same processes that presumably operate to produce normal behavior—reinforcement, punishment, extinction, discrimination, generalization, rules, and so forth.

Respondent Conditioning and Extinction Behavior therapy's respondent-conditioning techniques are aimed at changing how we feel—the degree to which we like, dislike, or fear certain aspects of the environment. All human beings, every day of their lives, are subject to respondent conditioning, and sometimes they develop fears and desires that interfere with their functioning. When this happens, the maladaptive response can be therapeutically unlearned, either by removing the stimuli that reinforce it (extinction) or by pairing it with incompatible positive or negative stimuli. Among the many techniques that employ these principles, we will describe two: systematic desensitization and exposure.

Systematic Desensitization First named and developed as a formal treatment procedure by Joseph Wolpe (1958), **systematic desensitization** is based on the premise that if a response antagonistic to anxiety (such as relaxation) can be made to occur in the presence of anxiety-provoking stimuli, the bond between these stimuli and anxiety will be weakened and the anxiety will extinguish. Systematic desensitization involves three steps. In the first step, the client is given relaxation training. In the second step, therapist and client construct a **hierarchy of fears**—that is, a list of anxiety-producing situations in order of their increasing horror to the client. The following, for example, is the hierarchy of fears (in this case going from most to least frightening) established for a patient who was plagued by fears of dying (Wolpe & Wolpe, 1981, p. 54):

1. Seeing a dead man in a coffin
2. Being at a burial
3. Seeing a burial assemblage from a distance
4. Reading the obituary notice of a young person who died of a heart attack
5. Driving past a cemetery (the nearer, the worse)
6. Seeing a funeral (the nearer, the worse)
7. Passing a funeral home (the nearer, the worse)
8. Reading the obituary notice of an old person
9. Being inside a hospital
10. Seeing a hospital
11. Seeing an ambulance

THE FAR SIDE© By GARY LARSON
© 1987 FarWorks, Inc. All Rights Reserved/Dist. by Creators Syndicate
Larson

"Now relax. ... Just like last week, I'm going to hold the red cape up for the count of 10. ... When you start getting angry, I'll put it down."

Once the relaxation response and the hierarchy of fears have both been established, then the two can be combined in the third step, the actual desensitization. In some cases, the desensitization is conducted *in vivo*—that is, the client practices relaxing while actually confronting the feared stimuli in the flesh. Most desensitization, however, takes place in the consulting office and relies on imagery. Clients are asked to relax and then to imagine themselves experiencing, one by one, the anxiety-producing stimuli listed in their hierarchies, starting with the least frightening and moving upward. When the client arrives at an item that undoes the relaxation response, he or she is asked to stop imagining the scene, rest, reestablish the relaxation, and then try the scene again. (If this doesn't work, intermediate scenes may have to be inserted into the hierarchy.) Depending on the severity of the problem, treatment generally takes 10 to 30 sessions (Wolpe, 1976), with a few in vivo sessions at the end to make sure that the relaxation response carries over from the imagined situation to the real one. Systematic desensitization has proved effective with a wide variety of problems, notably phobias, recurrent nightmares, and complex interpersonal problems involving various fears—of social and sexual intimacy, aggressive behavior, social disapproval, rejection, and authority figures (Kazdin & Wilson, 1978).

Exposure Despite its successes, systematic desensitization has now been largely replaced by exposure, which is simpler and apparently just as effective. **Exposure** is similar to systematic desensitization, except that the relaxation training is eliminated. Patients are simply confronted with the experiences they fear, but in the absence of reinforcement, so that the maladaptive response (anxiety, avoidance) can extinguish. In the original, "cold-turkey" version of exposure, called flooding, the patient undergoes a prolonged confrontation with the feared stimulus—or, if that is not possible, with vivid representations of it—in a situation that does not permit avoidance (Levis, 1985). This technique was found to be particularly useful in the elimination of obsessive-compulsive rituals (Rachman & Hodgson, 1980). As we will see in Chapter 7, obsessive-compulsive rituals usually have to do with one of two themes: contamination and checking. When the fear is contamination, flooding involves having clients actually "contaminate" themselves by touching and handling dirt or whatever substance they are trying to avoid. This ordeal is combined with response prevention: The clients are forbidden to carry out their anxiety-alleviating rituals (in this case, usually hand washing). The hoped-for result is that they will realize that the thing they fear actually poses no real threat. Flooding with response prevention apparently works well with anxiety-related disorders, but it is hard for patients to tolerate (Gelder, 1991). Today, instead of flooding, most behavior therapists use graded exposure. As in systematic desensitization, the client confronts the feared stimulus gradually, in steps. For example, people with dog phobias first watch videos of dogs, then enter a room where there is a caged dog, then stand in front of the cage, and so on, until, with the extinction of the fear, they are petting the dog.

Operant Conditioning Operant conditioning, as we have seen, is learning via consequences. Under certain stimulus conditions, we produce a certain response, and the fact that this response is followed by positive or negative consequences provides an incentive for us to repeat or avoid that same response when next we are faced with the same stimulus conditions. Operant behavior, then, has three components: (1) the learning history, discriminative stimulus, or cue for a certain response, (2) the response, and (3) the consequences. Behavior therapists have found that, by altering any of these components, they can change maladaptive patterns of behavior.

The manipulation of the consequences of a response in order to change the frequency of that response is called **contingency management.** An interesting example involved 40 participants in a 6-month behavioral program for cocaine dependence (Higgins, Delaney, Budney, et al., 1991). All the participants had to have their urine tested for cocaine traces 3 times a week. After the test, half simply received their test results. The other half received rewards as well as results: Every time their urine was "clean," they were given a voucher they could use to buy articles in local stores. For the first 3 months, the vouchers increased in value with each consecutive clean test. In the second 3 months, the vouchers were replaced by state lottery tickets. Both rewards worked very well. In the rewards group, 75 percent of the participants completed the whole 6-month program, as compared with 40 percent of the no-rewards group. Furthermore, the average length of continuous cocaine abstinence, as documented by the urine tests, was twice as long for the rewards group as for the no-rewards group. Clearly, behavior can be changed by managing its contingencies.

Multicomponent Treatment Most forms of behavior therapy are administered as part of multicomponent treatment. A psychological disorder typically has many facets, and as the person comes to live with the disorder, it develops more facets. Problem drinkers, for example, do not just have problems with drinking. Whether as a cause or a result of the drinking, they have problems with their marriages, their children, their jobs, their social skills, their expectations, and their self-esteem. The best treatments for substance dependence address all these difficulties, via different techniques. In the voucher program for cocaine abusers that we just described, the vouchers worked well, but their primary purpose was simply to keep the participants in the program, where, at the same time, they were receiving relationship counseling, instructions on avoiding cues for drug use, various kinds of skills training (drug refusal, problem solving, assertiveness), employment counseling, and help in developing new recreational activities. In such programs, the hope is that each kind of therapeutic change will bolster the others and thus, in a holistic fashion, free the person from the disorder.

The New Radical Behavioral Therapies: Integrating Acceptance With Change Over the past 15 years, radical and other behavior therapists have begun to emphasize "acceptance" as well as change, particularly in treating behavior disorders. In some cases, the approach is "integrative," combining behavioral principles with various philosophical perspectives. But what unites these approaches is recognition of the limits of direct attempts to change. These therapists show their patients that in many cases the harder you try to alter a behavior, the more entrenched it becomes. The key to change, they suggest, may be letting go of the goal of change. But, all the while that they are initiating patients into this supposedly fatalistic truth, they are also creating conditions that expose the patients to new, reinforcing contingencies, which may, in fact, generate change.

Perhaps the first acceptance-based version of behavior therapy was dialectical behavior therapy (DBT),

Focus On... The Limitations of Change: An Acceptance-Based Approach to Couple Therapy

Most couple therapies are based on a belief that partners who have weathered many years of severe conflict and incompatibility can still make major changes in their relationship. This optimistic view has been especially prevalent among behavior therapists, who inherited Watson's faith in the power of the environment to modify behavior. To subscribe to the behavioral position, however, one need not be optimistic about the human potential for change. Radical behaviorism is silent regarding the malleability of the human organism. It simply states that, to the extent that people change, they do so because environmental contingencies have changed.

Andrew Christensen and Neil S. Jacobson developed a promising approach called integrative behavioral couple therapy, or IBCT (Jacobson & Christensen, 1996). This therapy, derived from a radical behavioral perspective, takes as its starting point the apparently pessimistic view that couples who have suffered years of destructive interactions will find it hard, if not impossible, to change their relationship. But Christensen and Jacobson substituted a new kind of optimism. They said that if partners can learn to give up the struggle to change each other, paradoxically, many of the desired changes will emerge "spontaneously" as environmental contingencies alter and begin to support a more intimate relationship. Furthermore, through "acceptance work," areas of conflict can be turned into opportunities for intimacy. In the end, the couples are better off with those disagreements than they would be without them, or so the theory goes.

The therapeutic techniques used to foster acceptance fall into two basic categories: turning problems into strengths and tolerance. *Empathic joining* and *unified detachment* are both techniques for turning problems into strengths. In empathic joining, the effort is to change each partner's experience of the other's negative behavior from one of contempt or disgust to one of compassion and respect. For example, suppose John enters therapy convinced not only that Mary is uncommunicative, but also that she is uncommunicative because she is psychologically disturbed. Empathic joining techniques would give John opportunities to experience Mary's uncommunicativeness as just another endearing part of her and perfectly understandable, given Mary's experience with her own parents. Once John learns to love not just the parts of Mary he has always loved but even her communication difficulties, the environmental contingencies shape and reinforce her greater communicativeness.

Unified detachment serves the same purpose as empathic joining but comes at it from a different angle. In order to become more accepting of an area of conflict, partners are taught to regard the problem as an "it" rather than as something that one does to the other. In other words, they detach themselves from it and look at it together as a common enemy. In doing so, they become closer. For example, Frank had an extramarital affair. When his wife, Virginia, discovered this, she was both crushed and furious. Although Frank ended the affair and apologized, Virginia could not forgive him. Meanwhile, Frank, sensing her mistrust, found it difficult to be around her. The therapist gave Frank and Virginia the homework assignment of writing a joint letter to the third party, telling her together that the affair was over and explaining that they had decided to work together for a closer marriage. This joint effort both unified them and detached them from the shame and anger created by the betrayal.

In IBCT, turning problems into strengths is the ideal. The fallback strategy is tolerance, whereby partners simply learn to put up with the things they came into therapy wanting to change. An example of a technique used to promote tolerance is *role-playing negative behavior*. In the therapy session, the partners practice conflictual interactions that are likely to come up in the future, thus preparing themselves for the inevitable slip-ups. These practice exercises are analogous to exposure techniques used in behavior therapy: They desensitize couples to the occurrence of negative behavior in the future, so that, when it does occur, it will seem simply a problem, not a catastrophe.

How effective is IBCT? In a preliminary study reported by Jacobson, Christensen, and their colleagues (2000), couples were randomly assigned either to IBCT or to traditional behavioral couple therapy, or TBCT. Whereas TBCT improved the marriages of 64 percent of the couples, as it typically does, IBCT was successful in 89 percent of the cases. These results must be viewed with caution, however. The sample size was small (21 couples), and it was impossible to determine the reliability of the differences between the two groups' results. Still, these are by far the most impressive outcomes ever reported in couple therapy research. Furthermore, at a 1-year follow-up, 30 percent of the TBCT couples had separated, whereas all the ICBT couples were still together.

If the preliminary findings are confirmed, this will validate the notion that acceptance is key in a happy long-term relationship. Hard as it is to teach two old dogs new tricks, it may be easier if you stop trying.

developed by Marsha Linehan (1992) to treat borderline personality disorder (Chapter 11) and suicidal behavior. DBT integrates behavioral principles with Eastern religion and philosophy. It places a heavy emphasis on validation (i.e., acceptance) of the person and combines a variety of validation-fostering techniques with the traditional behavioral skills training.

The acceptance-based interventions have become popular alternatives to traditional behavior therapy in the past decade (Hayes, Jacobson, Follette, et al., 1994), and their influence is growing. It remains to be seen whether they will deliver on all they have promised.

Behavior Therapy and Prevention Behavioral techniques are often used in prevention programs, often as part of multicomponent treatments. For example, a Head Start program in Albuquerque, New Mexico, focuses on early detection and treatment of emotional or behavioral disorders in very young children (Forness, Serna, Nielsen, et al., 2000). The program includes teaching the children useful behavioral and social skills (in problem solving, following directions, sharing, for example) to improve their functioning.

Evaluating Behaviorism

Given the diversity of behavioral theories and approaches, behaviorism cannot be seen as a single, seamless perspective. Today, many behavioral therapists incorporate cognitive techniques in the treatment of maladaptive behavior.

Criticisms of Behaviorism Although behaviorism has had a huge impact on modern psychology, it has also had its critics. Much of the criticism has focused on charges that it oversimplifies the nature of psychological problems and their origins, is overly deterministic, and could be used by totalitarian political regimes for their immoral purposes.

Oversimplification A common objection to behavioral theory is that it constitutes a naïve simplification of human life. This criticism is based primarily on the work of early behaviorists such as Watson and Pavlov, which tended to reduce human existence to small measurable units of behavior. Thus, behavior therapy has been criticized for ignoring the whole person and focusing just on isolated stimulus-response connections. This criticism has merit when applied to early behaviorists, but not in regard to modern behavior therapy. The modern approach does not merely focus on isolated responses but also assesses all aspects of the interaction between the stimulus context and behavior, including thoughts, feelings, body sensations, and movements (Follette & Hayes, 2000; Kimble, 2000).

Another criticism has been that behavior therapy ignores cognitive processes and language that are distinct to humans and views humans as no different from other animals. Furthermore, critics claim that, by excluding the inner life from consideration, behaviorists have chosen to ignore all the deeper forces that distinguish human action from the behavior of experimental animals. Again, in the case of the early behaviorists, this charge has some justice, but not in the case of many modern behaviorists. The modern behavioral approach recognizes that humans are distinct in terms of language and cognition and that it is important to consider these distinctions. For instance, the concept of derived stimulus relations offers a way to understand symbolic processes and language.

A third version of the oversimplification charge holds that behavior therapy is shallow. Critics who feel that therapy should lead to greater self-acceptance and self-understanding view behavior therapy as shallow because it does not dwell on the patient's past (his or her childhood) and does not have self-insight as a primary goal. This criticism does not apply as much to the new acceptance-based treatments: Some of these treatments place as much importance on the patient's past as do psychodynamic theories (Jacobson & Christensen, 1996; Hayes, Strosahl, & Wilson, 1999). But as noted, the results of the acceptance-based treatments are not yet in. In the meantime, the criticism of shallowness does apply to traditional behavior therapy. Even though the early behavior therapists might have valued self-understanding for themselves, they felt it was too vague an idea to serve as a treatment goal. Traditional behavior therapy sought to provide people with skills to deal more effectively with problems in living.

Determinism The second major criticism of behaviorism is its assumption that behavior is controlled by reinforcement or other learning mechanisms, a view referred to as determinism. According to behaviorists, it is not "free will" but, rather, the interplay between life experience and genetic factors that determines what people do with their lives. Thus, Skinner (1953) argued that the notion of "the free inner man," and the capacity for human freedom, was obsolete. Whatever we do—whether it might be regarded as moral or immoral—we do because our evolutionary and learning histories have taught us to do it. Such ideas have been coldly received by theorists who emphasize free will and moral responsibility.

The Issue of "Control" Finally, critics of behavior therapy have expressed concerns about the possibility that behavior therapy condones coercion or could even become the basis for a totalitarian political regime in which reinforcers would be used to engineer, or control, behavior. The focus of behaviorists on life circumstances that can be manipulated to alter behavior has helped to fuel these "mad scientist" suspicions. Even so, all psychotherapies actually involve some control by the therapist, whether that control is directed toward insight or relearning. Behavior therapy simply seeks to identify basic mechanisms of learning that can allow individuals to improve their lives.

Some critics of behavior therapy have questioned whether behavior therapists can ultimately exercise effective control. Pointing to the high relapse rates among some disorders, such as substance abuse (Nicolosi, Molinari, Musicco, et al., 1991), such critics have suggested that behavioral techniques are futile without genuine cooperation from the patient. To behavior therapists, however, these research findings simply suggest that, for many clinical problems, we have not found effective ways to influence long-standing maladaptive behavior.

Finally, behavioral therapy has been accused of ignoring the therapeutic relationship. But today, most behavior therapists accept the importance of a strong therapeutic relationship for positive therapy outcomes (Follette & Hayes, 2000).

The Contributions of Behaviorism Behaviorism has been a dominant force in the development of modern psychology. Its impact on the study of abnormal behavior is evident in many ways, such as the emphasis on precise measurement of the features of presenting problems and empirical validation of the effectiveness of treatments.

How well, then, does behavior therapy do in achieving its goal of behavior change? According to the evidence, it does quite well. Behavior therapy has a relatively good record in treating anxiety and phobias (Emmelkamp, 1994); insomnia (Perlis, Aloia, Millikan, et al., 2000); obesity (Brownell & Wadden, 1992); alcohol and drug dependency (Nathan, Marlatt, & Loberg, 1978; Silverman, Svikis, Robles, et al., 2001); depression (Lewinsohn, Gotlib, & Hautzinger, 1998); marital problems (Jacobson, Christensen, Prince, et al., 2000); personality disorders (Linehan, Schmidt, Dimeff, et al., 1999); conduct disorders (Kazdin & Wassell, 1999); autism (McEachin, Smith, & Lovaas, 1993), and other problems. Aside from the fact that it often works, behavior therapy has other advantages as well. It tends to be faster and less expensive than other therapies. Its techniques can be taught to paraprofessionals and nonprofessionals, so that therapy can be extended beyond the consulting room to hospital wards, classrooms, and homes. Finally, because behavior therapy is precise in its goals and techniques, it can be reported, discussed, and evaluated with precision.

The Cognitive Perspective

Although the **cognitive perspective,** which views abnormal behavior as the product of mental processing, did not become important in abnormal psychology until the 1970s, cognitive functions such as memory, reasoning, and problem solving have been of interest to psychologists ever since psychology began (Craighead, Ilardi, Greenberg, et al., 1997). Cognition is important to abnormal psychology for two reasons. First, many psychological disorders involve serious cognitive disturbances (Beck & Rector, 2000; Clark, Beck, & Alford, 1999; Seligman, 1975). For example, severely depressed people usually cannot concentrate—a condition that makes them fail at tasks and thus feel more depressed. People with schizophrenia also have severe cognitive problems; typically, they cannot think or use language clearly. Second, certain cognitive patterns may not be symptoms but actual causes of their associated disorders—a possibility that has given considerable impetus to cognitive research in the past few decades.

The emergence of the cognitive perspective represented an important shift in abnormal psychology. Aaron Beck's (1967) cognitive model, which we will discuss below, shattered the traditional assumption that depression was simply an emotional disorder having a biological origin. Beck's model was based on the idea that systematic distortions in thinking about the self, world, and future help to trigger and maintain depression and other emotional disorders. In the past three decades, experimental cognitive traditions that deal with attention, memory, and information processing have been extended to a variety of psychiatric disorders (Mathews & MacLeod, 1994; Alloy & Riskind, in press).

The Background of the Cognitive Perspective

At a time when the stimulus-response position was endorsed by most learning theorists, other theorists questioned the exclusion of such mental processes as emotion, thought, expectation, and interpretation. How is it, they asked, that the same stimulus can produce different responses in different human beings? For example, some individuals might find New Age music exciting, but others might find it utterly boring. Some other factor, then, in addition to the stimulus, must be influencing the response. Presumably, that other factor was **cognition,** or the mental processing of stimuli.

Given the variability of responses, some behaviorists questioned not only stimulus-response theory (S-R theory) but also the very principle of reinforcement. For example, Edward Tolman (1948) held that human beings learned not by reinforcement of trial-and-error responses but by perceiving the relationship among various elements of the task. Reinforcement, Tolman argued, affected learning by creating expectancies, inner "predictions" as to which responses would lead to rewards and punishments in which situations. As for the responses themselves, they were learned through mental processes independent of reinforcement. Tolman and Honzig (1930) demonstrated this principle by showing that if rats were given a chance to explore a maze, without reinforcement, then later, when reinforcement was available, these rats would run the maze faster than other rats that had not had an opportunity to explore the apparatus. In other words, the rats had learned something without being rewarded for it.

Cognitive Behaviorism

Thus, behaviorism no sooner developed S-R theory than it produced a cognitive challenge to that theory. As we shall see, an alliance between these two, called **cognitive behaviorism,** has produced valuable results in the form of refined theories and treatments. Indeed, by 1990 the majority (69 percent) of the members of the Association for the Advancement of Behavior Therapy defined themselves as cognitive therapists, while only 27 percent called themselves behavioral (Craighead, 1990). The central claim of the cognitive behaviorists is that people's actions are often responses not so much to external stimuli as to their own individual mental processing of those stimuli. These theorists claim that, though cognitive events are not objectively observable, they are learned responses and thus are subject to the same laws as other behavior. Ultimately, theory and research on cognitive actors and their role in influencing behavior developed into a broader movement known as the cognitive perspective.

Besides its importance in providing new theories about behavior, the cognitive perspective has had a decided influence on the process of psychotherapy. In this chapter, we will see how two of the most influential cognitive theorists, Albert Ellis and Aaron T. Beck, developed their ideas about the role of cognition in abnormal behavior from working with clients in therapy. We will also briefly look at some of the principal techniques in cognitive therapy. More detail on cognitive therapies will be presented in chapters devoted to various disorders.

Albert Ellis: Irrational Beliefs Albert Ellis (b. 1913) developed what has come to be known as rational-emotive therapy, which is based on the idea that psychological problems are caused not by events in the outside world but by people's reacting to such events on the basis of irrational beliefs. Ellis (1962) has proposed an ABC system to explain how this process works: A is the activating experience; B, the beliefs or thoughts that irrationally follow; and C, the consequences for the person, both emotional and behavioral. Ellis (1980) suggests that most problems stem from certain core irrational beliefs, such as

Albert Ellis believes that people's irrational beliefs are the basis of psychological problems. He developed rational-emotive therapy to help change behavior by encouraging people to confront their irrational beliefs.

> I must do well and win approval, or I rate as a rotten person.
>
> Others must treat me considerately and kindly, or society and the universe should punish them.
>
> I should be able to get all the things I want easily and quickly.

Most people, when they see these beliefs stated so bluntly, are able to recognize their irrationality, yet they react to many events as if such statements were entirely true and reasonable. For example, a person may become extremely upset and depressed about some minor failing (reflecting the first irrational thought) or angry at some slight (reflecting the second irrational thought). Ellis' therapy involves confronting and disrupting the irrational beliefs (B) so that the emotional and behavioral consequences (C) will change accordingly.

Aaron Beck, shown here with his daughter and colleague Judith Beck, identified patterns of faulty thinking in people with depression and anxiety and developed a therapeutic approach in which clients are encouraged to replace faulty thoughts with more reasonable thoughts.

Aaron T. Beck: Cognitive Distortions In a number of influential books and articles, Aaron T. Beck (b. 1921) has pointed out that psychological disorders are often associated with specific patterns of faulty or distorted thinking (1967, 1999). In depression, for example, the distorted or faulty thoughts center on a pessimistic view of the self, the world, and the future—the "negative triad," as Beck calls it. In anxiety, the faulty thoughts center on threats of danger. The **cognitive distortions** Beck has identified include magnification (seeing minor events as far more important than they are), overgeneralization (drawing a broad conclusion from little evidence), and selective abstraction (paying attention to only certain kinds of evidence while ignoring other, equally relevant information). These faulty thoughts operate automatically, without the person's being aware of them. Thus, a person who becomes extremely depressed at not receiving a birthday card from one family member, while receiving cards from many other relatives and friends, would probably be engaging in all three kinds of cognitive distortion. In Beck's therapy, clients are led to discover their faulty thoughts and to replace them with more reasonable and valid thoughts.

We will refer to Ellis and Beck in other chapters in this book. Now let us consider some of the cognitive processes that they and other thinkers within this perspective have identified as crucial to abnormal behavior.

Cognitive Appraisal

Cognitive theorists argue that between stimulus and response comes the all-important process of **cognitive appraisal.** In cognitive appraisal, the person, before reacting, evaluates the stimulus in light of his or her own memories, beliefs, and expectations. This internal mental activity accounts for the wide differences in individual responses to the same external stimulus. For example, two people giving a lecture may react quite differently to the stimulus of seeing several members of the audience get up and walk out in the middle of the talk. One may say to himself, "Oh, I must be boring them to tears. I knew I would make a bad lecturer." And to this cognitive appraisal he will respond by becoming anxious, perspiring, and perhaps stumbling

Cognitive behaviorists believe that our cognitive appraisal of our competence affects our behavior in relevant situations. People who learn athletic skills in childhood are likely to feel confident about participating in sports—and perhaps other group activities—later in life.

over his words. Another lecturer, with a more positive view of herself and her speaking skills, may interpret the departures as due to circumstances external to herself. "They must have a class to catch. Too bad they have to leave; they will miss a good talk" (Meichenbaum, 1975, p. 358). And she will proceed, unruffled, with her lecture.

Cognitive theorists also believe that the extreme thoughts, beliefs, and feelings of people with psychiatric disorders are simply exaggerations of the thoughts, beliefs, and feelings of people without disorders. For example, triggering events such as a social rejection or a small increase in body weight are interpreted by some individuals as a brief setback and by others as decisive evidence of utter failure and personal defect. Thus, the cognitive perspective views diverse clinical disorders such as depression, panic disorder, eating disorders, and even schizophrenia and paranoid psychoses in terms of distorted or faulty cognitive processes (Beck & Rector, 2000; Haddock, Tarrier, Spaulding, et al., 1998; Riskind & Alloy, in press).

Some people develop habitual patterns of maladaptive appraisal (Alloy, Abramson, Hogan, et al., 2000; Weiner & Kukla, 2000; Riskind, Williams, Gessner, et al., 2000). Such patterns of interpretation can increase the risk that they will develop particular psychological disorders. Factors such as faulty beliefs (Ellis, 1962, 1980), faulty patterns for explaining life experiences, and faulty patterns of attention and mental self-regulation (Newman, Schmitt, & Voss, 1997; Mathews & MacLeod, 1994) can contribute to disorders. (A good analogy is to osteoporosis, a condition that causes brittle bones, which then break more easily when a person is bumped or falls.) Such faulty belief or explanatory patterns can work as cognitive vulnerability factors that increase the likelihood that a person will develop symptoms or episodes of clinical disorders when under stress. These long-standing cognitive vulnerabilities are called "distal" because they were often present long before the psychological problems developed (e.g., in the childhood or teenage years), in contrast to the "proximal" (nearby) factors, such as the ongoing stream of thoughts the person has during episodes of psychological problems (Alloy, Abramson, Raniere, et al., 1999; Riskind & Alloy, in press).

Stressful events can trigger the development of disorders for certain individuals (Alloy, Abramson, Raniere, et al., 1999), but the specific response can differ enormously from one person to another. For example, individuals who suffer from a variety of disorders such as depression, bipolar disorder, anxiety, and schizophrenia report higher levels of stressful events (e.g., recent family deaths, losses of employment or relationships) than other people do (Brown, Harris, & Eales, 1996; Zuckerman, 1998). Some individuals seem to be relatively resilient and even rise to the occasion when they encounter stressful events, whereas other individuals seem to be highly susceptible to even minor precipitating factors. In fact, most individuals who are exposed to stressful events do not develop clinically significant disorders. Moreover, the specific disorder that emerges is not determined by the precipitating stress alone but also by the pattern of faulty thinking. Cognitive **vulnerability-stress models** are useful in identifying not only which persons might be vulnerable to developing clinical disorders (individuals with a particular cognitive style) and when (after a stress), but even to which disorders they are vulnerable (depression, eating disorder, and so on).

If a person has developed cognitive vulnerability factors from childhood or other life experiences and these factors become triggered by recent events, the factors alter the person's response by biasing and filtering his or her thoughts and emotions (Clark, Beck, & Alford, 1999). This bias leads the individual to selectively notice or recall different things about the environment than he or she did before. The ways in which the bias is influenced can depend on the particular psychological disorders, a concept referred to as disorder specificity.

Disorder-specific biases are cognitive distortions that many cognitive theorists believe differ with different disorders (Beck & Clark, 1997; Mathews & MacLeod, 1994). For example, the disorder-specific bias in depression is for information relevant to the experiences of hopelessness and loss. In social anxiety (social phobia) the bias is for information relevant to the threat of public humiliation, accompanied by proximal thoughts such as "I'll make fool of myself." In panic disorder, the specific bias is for internal information relevant to unusual bodily sensations—such as those that might signal an impending heart attack or other feared calamity—and is associated with thoughts such as "I'm having a heart attack." Such biases are presumably triggered when cognitive vulnerabilities that were present long before the symptoms or episode are put into play. The specific mental-processing biases can, in turn, penetrate a range of basic information processes (e.g., selective attention, encoding and retrieval in memory, interpretation).

Conceptual Framework for Cognitive Vulnerability

As we can see in Figure 4.1, the cognitive perspective assumes that there are causal links between formative childhood or other earlier learning experiences and the development of cognitive vulnerability factors. These can then become activated by stressful events. Cognitive models can also integrate other factors—such as interpersonal factors—because such additional factors may influence whether cognitively vulnerable individuals develop disorders by either inhibiting or intensifying

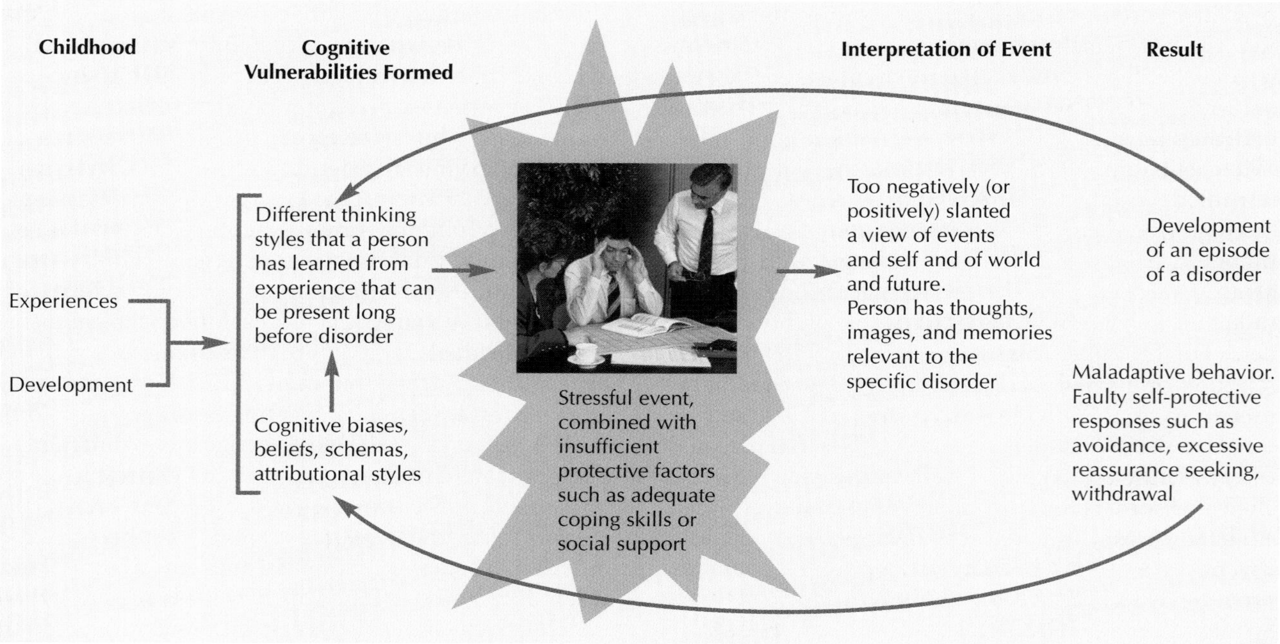

FIGURE 4.1 The cognitive perspective assumes causal links between childhood or other early learning experiences and the development of cognitive vulnerability factors. When a disorder develops, it can reinforce an individual's faulty thinking, as shown here with feedback loops.

their reactions to precipitating stresses. Cognitive models often portray some factors (e.g., social support, an intimate relation with a spouse or lover, effective coping mechanisms) as protective, working against the development of disorders (Brown & Harris, 1978).

Finally, vicious cycles contribute to the onset, maintenance, or recurrence of emotional disorders. Under the duress of the stress and intense symptoms, for example, cognitively vulnerable individuals tend to engage in various maladaptive self-protective or compensatory behaviors. Depressed individuals often create friction with others because of their heightened need for reassurance from them (Joiner, Alfano, & Metalsky, 1992). In other cases, individuals may inadvertently or unintentionally engage in self-fulfilling prophecies, called self-verification, that support negative concepts in a vicious cycle (Swan, Stein-Seroussi, & Giesler, 1992).

Attributions One form of cognitive appraisal is **attribution,** our beliefs about the causes of life events (Fiske & Taylor, 1991). Consider, for example, a woman who was recently fired. The way she explains this event to herself will affect her emotional state. Internal attributions ("I can't handle pressure") are much more damaging to self-esteem than external attributions ("My boss was impossible to work for!"). Likewise, broad-based, or global, attributions ("I'm incompetent") are more destructive than specific attributions ("I don't belong in sales"); and long-term, or stable, attributions ("I'll never get ahead") are more harmful than unstable attributions ("I picked the wrong job"). As we will see in Chapter 10, people who habitually attribute failures to global, stable, internal faults have a "depressive" attributional style that makes them more vulnerable to feelings of hopelessness and helplessness and ultimately more susceptible to depression (Abramson, Alloy, & Metalsky, 1995; Abramson, Metalsky, & Alloy, 1989).

Attributions in Everyday Life: The Fundamental Attribution Error

On the MindMAP CD-ROM, this video illustrates why attributions are so important in our everyday lives. After viewing this video, think about your own attributions. For example, how do you explain a high mark you received on an exam? How do you characterize classmates who also did well on the exam? Can you understand how a faulty internal attributions can lead to low self-esteem and a susceptibility to depression?

Self-Efficacy Albert Bandura (1977, 1986) sees behavior as regulated by cognitive expectancies. Bandura distinguishes between two kinds of expectancies: outcome expectancies, expectations that a given behavior will produce a certain result, and self-efficacy expectancies, expectations that one will be able to execute a given behavior successfully. In Bandura's view, self-efficacy expectancies are the chief determinant of coping behavior and they, in turn, are determined by performance feedback from prior experience. For example, a woman who is afraid of flying may know that the plane is likely to get her to another city for a job interview (high outcome expectancy). Despite this, she might not actually make the plane reservation because she has a low self-efficacy—that is, low confidence that she will be able to get on the plane and make the stressful trip without incident. Her lack of self-efficacy may be influenced by how well she has successfully managed similar stressful situations in the past.

Information Processing

Information processing is a broad area of cognitive research concerned with how the human mind takes in, stores, interprets, and uses information from the environment. Cognitive researchers have learned, for example, to make a distinction between what they call automatic processing and controlled processing of information. Automatic processing requires little attention and yields quick, well-learned responses that remain stable over time. Behaviors as diverse as the formulas or skills we use in driving a car in traffic or in scanning and identifying threats in the environment may become automatic, but only after prolonged practice and repetition. This latter kind of processing is called controlled processing. Controlled processing requires sustained concentration and logic as the mind integrates new information and devises a response (Bargh & Ferguson, 2000; Craighead, Ilardi, Greenberg, et al., 1997).

Many abnormal behavior patterns, such as anxiety disorders and depression, can be viewed as the result of inappropriate automatic processing (McNally, 1995). For example, a depression-prone woman may initially have had self-critical (depressing) thoughts as an intentional way to motivate herself to correct poor grades or faulty performance. This kind of controlled processing could become less controllable over time, as she repeats the behavior until it becomes automatic. Recent studies show that cognitive therapy is successful in teaching depressed people with these automatic negative biases to convert them to controlled processing (Segal, Gemar, & Williams, 1999).

Cognitive researchers also distinguish between what they call implicit and explicit cognitive processes. Implicit cognition is expressed in behaviors that indirectly indicate how a person is thinking (e.g., exaggerating the danger of injury) even though the person is not aware of thinking that way.

Explicit cognition involves intentional, conscious knowledge (such as consciously thinking about danger or intentionally trying to recall past threatening experiences). Both kinds of cognitive processes may influence abnormal behavior, but in different ways. For example, some anxious individuals show a memory bias for anxiety-related information on implicit memory tasks. An anxious person might complete the word stem fragment "kni" as "knife," while a nonanxious individual completes the word stem as "knight." However, when the anxious individuals are instructed to try to recall anxiety-related information (explicit cognition), they may show no greater memory bias than individuals who are not anxious. (Riskind, Williams, Gessner, et al., 2000).

Attention Attentional processes are an important aspect of cognitive biases because human beings cannot possibly attend to, let alone process, all the information that bombards their senses at any given moment. So they take in only the information that seems to them most important and filter out the rest. This mechanism, an indispensable adaptive function, is called **selective attention.**

Some forms of psychopathology may be due to a failure in selective attention. For example, many of the symptoms of schizophrenia, such as distorted perceptions and far-fetched, disorganized beliefs, may stem from a meltdown in selective attention, which allows the mind to be overwhelmed with disconnected information (Perry & Braff, 1994). In other cases, an attentional bias may contribute to psychological problems because it is too inflexible and slanted. For example, anxious individuals have a relatively habitual attentional bias—paying more attention to threat stimuli than do nonanxious people (Mogg & Bradley, 1998).

Organizing Structures The mind doesn't just choose what information it will take in. It also arranges that information in lasting and meaningful patterns, which then affect how other information will be taken in.

Cognitive psychologists define a **schema** as an organized structure of information about a particular domain of life—a structure that serves the person as a pattern for selecting and processing new information (Craighead, Ilardi, Greenberg et al., 1997). Many people have positive self-schemas, seeing themselves as successful, talented, and well liked. Such positive views can protect individuals' psychological and physical health (Taylor, Kemeny, Reed, et al., 2000), even if the self-schemas are slightly exaggerated, by helping them to remain optimistic about prospects for success and dismiss setbacks. So positive self-schemas lead people to view new information, including information about challenges or failures, more positively. By the same token, negative self-schemas are maladaptive, eroding hope and motivation, and causing people to focus on their failures.

According to cognitive theories, many psychological disorders have their origin in negative schemas developed in childhood. According to Aaron Beck, a potential for depression is due primarily to self-schemas dominated by themes of worthlessness, guilt, and deprivation. Anxiety, too, can derive from a faulty self-schema in which the individual views herself as extremely vulnerable to the threat of danger, physical injury, or social embarrassment.

Much of the power of schemas over cognitive processes hinges on the fact that they lead people to confirm or see what they were already prepared to expect to see. For example, a depression-prone person will be prepared to see failure or rejection and may distort events so that she interprets negative and even many neutral events in such terms. Such a person will also tend to cognitively distort positive outcomes by discounting or minimizing successes—for instance, by viewing a success experience as a fluke. This confirmation bias makes schemas resistant to change (Fiske & Taylor, 1991), because people tend to remember information that supports their schemas. For example, depressed individuals remember negative, discouraging information better than they do positive information. This is in contrast to most individuals who tend to remember positive information better. Additional biases, including a "self-verification" tendency to behave or interact with others in ways that unintentionally support one's negative beliefs (e.g., acting in ways that are likely to ensure social rejection), can also help maintain schemas (Swan, Stein-Seroussi, & Giesler, 1992).

The Cognitive Approach to Treatment

If cognitions are an important cause of abnormal behavior, it follows that such behavior can be treated by changing those cognitions. Cognitive approaches to treating psychological disorders assume that disorders persist as long as the cognitive components of the disorders continue to be active and that they improve when the cognitive components are altered. Furthermore, durable (lasting) improvement requires changes in the underlying mechanisms or cognitive vulnerabilities (e.g., beliefs or attributional patterns) that produce dysfunctional thoughts and biases in the ways individuals process information (Alford & Beck, 1997). The cognitive approach assumes that the way in which individuals process and interpret internal and external information must be modified to bring about enduring change in their psychological functioning and to prevent the recurrence of psychological problems (Dobson, Backs-Dermott, & Dozois, 2000).

Self-Instructional Training Developed by Donald Meichenbaum and his colleagues (Meichenbaum, 1977), self-instructional training (SIT) is a straightforward approach designed to help individuals overcome cognitive deficits in self-control, problem solving, and information seeking (Dobson, Backs-Dermott, & Dozois, 2000). Originally developed for use with behaviorally disordered or impulsive children, SIT concentrates on "self-talk," the things that people say to themselves before, during, and after their actions. For example, Meichenbaum (1977) believed that impulsive children wielded less effective control over their behavior with their private speech than less impulsive children. Using SIT, children would observe the therapist or trainer provide oral instructions, then perform the task while the trainer coached them, and finally perform the task while speaking aloud with self-instructions. Thus, the children were trained to engage in self-verbalizations when performing a task ("What is the problem to work on now?" "What is the way to solve this problem?") and to engage in positive self-statements for appropriate responses ("Good, I did a nice job").

Ellis' and Beck's Cognitive Therapies Other kinds of cognitive therapy call on the client to identify and analyze self-defeating cognitions, as well as to revise them. Perhaps the oldest such treatment is Albert Ellis' **rational-emotive therapy.** As we saw earlier, Ellis' basic contention is that emotional disturbances are the result not of objective events in people's lives but of the irrational beliefs that guide their interpretations of those events. To combat such beliefs, Ellis and his followers point out in blunt terms the irrationality of the client's thinking, model more realistic evaluations of the client's situation (e.g., "So what if your mother didn't love you. That's *her* problem!"), instruct the client to monitor and correct his thoughts, rehearse the client in appraising situations realistically, and give homework assignments so that new ways of interpreting experience can be strengthened.

Similar in theory if not in tone is the version of cognitive therapy developed by Aaron Beck (1976).

We have already discussed Beck's theory of depression: that it is caused by a "negative triad" of faulty thoughts about the self, the world, and the future. To change such cognitions, Beck adopts a less didactic and more Socratic approach than Ellis, questioning patients in such a way that they themselves gradually discover the faulty nature of their thoughts. We will discuss Beck's treatment for depression in detail in Chapter 10.

Constructivist Cognitive Therapy A slightly different version of cognitive therapy has been proposed by Michael J. Mahoney (1995). He calls his approach constructivist cognitive therapy, as opposed to the Beck and Ellis approaches, which he calls "rationalist." To Mahoney, rationalist cognitive therapy depends too much on conscious, rational, verbal analysis and does not take sufficient account of emotions and other seemingly irrational components of behavior. According to Mahoney, people begin in childhood to construct their worlds from their experience: their actions and the feedback from those actions. If the cognitive patterns developed in this way are self-defeating, then constructivist cognitive therapy provides a chance to construct new patterns. Self-exploration is an important part of the process. Among the techniques Mahoney recommends are writing (poems, journals, stories, letters, not to be mailed), observing oneself sitting in front of a mirror, and speaking in a "stream-of-consciousness" manner in the therapeutic setting. These techniques all aim at helping the client understand, and change for the better, his characteristic way of viewing the world, called a narrative (or life story). Constructivist techniques seek to help the client create a more meaningful, empowering, and coherent narrative for understanding his life.

Cognitive therapists today emphasize getting clients to empirically test their hypotheses, which is quite unlike Mahoney's approach. Mahoney's constructivist approach, however, adopts the view of postmodernist thinkers who emphasize that we live in a world of multiple social realities. He does not assume that there is any objective reality to test beliefs against, because different people, cultures, and ethnic groups have different constructions, or ways of perceiving social reality (Neimeyer & Stewart, 2000).

Cognitive Therapy in Clinical Practice In actual application, cognitive therapy proceeds through a series of stages. In the first session(s) the therapist gathers information about the client's current problems, including the situational triggers for the client's feelings, thought patterns, and responses. This process organizes the therapist's and client's understanding of the interrelationships among developmental experiences (e.g., childhood events), core beliefs that constitute cognitive vulnerabilities, and faulty coping patterns (e.g., avoiding problems), and how they are reflected in the client's automatic thoughts, emotional responses, and behavior in different situations. The **cognitive case conceptualization** is used to coordinate, plan, and guide all aspects of the treatment (Persons & Davidson, 2001; Beck, 1995), including specific "homework" assignments that can address the client's current needs.

The common element in all cognitive therapy is an attempt to identify and alter the pattern of thought that is causing a client's maladaptive behavior. Cognitive therapists teach clients to understand the relationship between cognitions and psychological problems and to experiment with more adaptive ways of responding and of perceiving themselves, the world, and the future (Dobson, Backs-Dermott, & Dozois, 2000). Together, client and therapist set an agenda of goals and problems during each therapy session and work together to check thoughts and beliefs against the evidence and to explore coping patterns. The therapy session itself might use various cognitive strategies, including **cognitive restructuring,** breaking down big problems into manageable pieces, generating alternative ways to handle problems, and identifying and responding to cognitive errors.

In the technique known as **decatastrophizing,** the client is asked to consider what would actually happen if his or her worst fear were realized. A client with a social phobia, for example, might say that he can't go to a party because he would feel foolish, no one would talk to him, and he would have a terrible time. "And what if that happened?" the therapist might ask. What is the *worst possible result?* That the client would leave the party early, without having spoken to anyone? And would that be a catastrophe or simply be embarrassing? Questions like these help clients realize that their fears are exaggerated.

Two major techniques in cognitive therapy are Socratic questioning and behavioral experiments. In **Socratic questioning,** the therapist asks a series of questions designed to get the client to look more objectively at thoughts, assumptions, and beliefs and to think about whether these are necessarily true. For example, the therapist might ask "What is the evidence for and against this belief?" and "Do you see any benefits to thinking this way?" In **behavioral experiments,** clients are urged to engage in **hypothesis testing** to "reality test" their assumptions. A depressed woman, for example, who insists that friends no longer want anything to do with her might be urged to call a few friends on the phone and suggest a get-together. The woman can then examine the result: Did the friends refuse to talk to her? Did they all refuse her invitation?

Cognitive therapy uses other behavioral techniques as well, such as social skills and assertiveness training. The following are examples of Socratic questioning and behavioral experiments.

COGNITIVE THERAPY: The Socratic Approach

The client, Susan, was a young, attractive, and intelligent woman who showed all the signs of social anxiety. She was afraid of being rejected by men. This dialogue from a cognitive therapy session illustrates the therapist's use of Socratic questioning to get the client to be more objective about her problems.

Therapist: You said that your evidence that you are unattractive is that you feel ugly and that Roger broke up with you.

Client: I just don't feel attractive.

Therapist: Right. You also said that the women in the magazines are more attractive than you are.

Client: That's right. They look like they're perfect.

Therapist: What do you think about the quality of your evidence in relation to the thought, "I'm ugly"? Would you be able to convince a jury that someone is ugly if they "felt ugly"?

Client: No. I guess they would require some kind of other information.

Therapist: You mean like some independent information—something other than the way you feel?

Client: Yeah. Like what other people think of that person.

Therapist: Are there some men who think you are attractive?

Client: Well, there have been a number of men who find me attractive. But I'm not interested in them.

Therapist: When you say that Roger broke up with you, you use that as evidence that you are not attractive. What were the reasons that you broke up?

Client: We weren't getting along. He just can't commit to anyone. And he lies.

Therapist: So you personalized his shortcomings and concluded that you are not attractive.

Client: That's true.

Therapist: I wonder if we could look at the evidence that you use to support your negative beliefs and see if the evidence is relevant and convincing or if it is characterized by these kinds of distortions.

BEHAVIORAL TESTING

Susan was afraid of being rejected by men. When she met a man at a party, she would look down, speak very softly, and say very little. Her automatic thoughts were "I have nothing to say" and "He won't find me attractive." The therapist concluded, from talking to her, that her "shy" behavior could be interpreted by men as "She's not interested in me" and "She doesn't find me attractive." The therapist shared this observation with Susan and asked her if she was willing to carry out a simple behavioral homework assignment.

Therapist: Let's test out this idea that men are unfriendly and don't like you. It seems to me that your tendency to avoid eye contact and to look away from men could be a signal to men that you don't find them attractive.

Susan: This never occurred to me.

Therapist: You know, men are very sensitive to rejection. I know, I'm a man.

Susan: I'm always thinking that they don't like me.

Therapist: Put your hands up and cover your eyes.

Susan: (does this)

Therapist: What color are my eyes?

Susan: I don't know for sure.

Therapist: What color is my tie and shirt?

Susan: I didn't notice.

Therapist: You're very focused on your own feelings and thoughts and so maybe you don't notice men. Men want to be noticed.

Susan: I never thought of it that way.

Therapist: Well, let's carry out an experiment and collect some information. When you are waiting for the subway or standing in the elevator, I'd like you to collect information for me. I'd like you to try to notice the color of each man's eyes and the color and design on his tie and shirt. This will help you pay attention to men.

Susan: OK, I'll try this.

Therapist: And I'd also like you to notice if any men look at you and if they ever smile.

This behavioral assignment forced Susan to give up her self-sabotaging, self-protective ("safety") behavior of avoiding eye contact with men. Her paying attention to men would keep her in the situation and allow her to collect information about whether men looked at her and smiled—perhaps addressing her belief that she was not attractive. The outcome of this homework assignment is that, a week later, she had recorded numerous times that men looked at her, smiled, and started conversations with her. It indicated to her that her shy attempts to protect herself—avoiding eye contact—actually kept her from finding out that men could be friendly. In this way, behavioral assignments allow individuals to "test out" their negative beliefs (from the files of Robert Leahy, American Institute of Cognitive Therapy, Manhattan).

Cognitive Therapy and Prevention Cognitive therapy techniques may be useful in helping to prevent mental disorders from developing in the first place. One study (Seligman, Schulman, DeRubeis, et al., 1999) involved a brief and inexpensive 8-week prevention workshop for university students who were at risk (cognitively vulnerable) for depression. Participants were followed for 3 years and compared to a control group that did not receive the prevention intervention. Findings indicated that workshop participants were less prone to depression, experienced fewer systems of physical illness, and had fewer doctors' visits than the control group (Seligman, Schulman, DeRubeis, et al., 1999; Buchanan, McClellan, Gardenswartz, et al., 1999).

Evaluating the Cognitive Perspective

Criticisms of Cognitive Theory Cognitive theory is open to the same criticism as any other theory that depends on inference—that it is unscientific—because we can't actually observe the forces under discussion. And, as critics have pointed out, the history of cognitive theory—memory theory in particular—has been one in which factors hypothesized as central were eventually replaced by other factors hypothesized to be central (Skinner, 1990; Watkins, 1990), inviting the question of how central they actually are, if they are so changeable. Whatever the hypothesized factors, noncognitive theorists are likely to deny not so much their existence as their centrality. According to behaviorists (Skinner, 1990; Follette & Hayes, 2000), cognitions may exist, but they are only a product of reinforcement or of larger patterns of learned responses (emotion, cognition, and behavior); therefore, what we have to study is not just cognition, but the larger context of learning. Likewise, psychodynamic theorists (see Chapter 5) would not deny the existence of cognitions or negative self-schemas, but they would say that they are the product of early troubled family relationships and that it is those relationships, not their cognitive consequences, that are the true root of the problem.

One major objection to the cognitive approach is that there are times when changing one's way of thinking about the world may not be the whole answer, or even appropriate. For example, with certain realities of life, such as a stressful work situation or an abusive marriage, simply changing one's view of the situation (but doing nothing else) might not be in the person's interest. Cognitive therapists counter that they seek to modify a combination of the internal (faulty thinking) and external (e.g., stressful work situations or marriages) problems; they don't just focus on changing thinking.

Likewise, an objection to some forms of cognitive therapy is that a dry, rational approach might not be the best way to change one's way of thinking about the self and the world. Many cognitive therapists today agree with the view that an experiential approach that involves intense feeling and emotion may often be necessary to change entrenched personal beliefs and schemas.

Another objection to cognitive therapy comes from constructivist theorists (Mahoney, 1991; Neimeyer & Stewart, 2000), who argue that different peoples and cultures have different realities, and no one view can claim to be more true than any other. These theorists reject the idea that cognitive therapists can help clients to "reality test" their beliefs or thinking, show them that beliefs are unrealistic, or supply them with more adaptive ways of responding or thinking, as defined by the therapist's own view of reality.

A final point about cognitive therapy, though not necessarily a shortcoming, is that we don't really know how it works (Dobson, Backs-Dermott, & Dozois, 2000). For example, does cognitive therapy actually reduce the frequency of dysfunctional thoughts; change distal cognitive vulnerabilities, such as dysfunctional beliefs or attributions; or just teach people a new set of skills for dealing with their thoughts or beliefs (Barber & DeRubeis, 1989)? There is some evidence that cognitive therapy works to prevent relapse by changing cognitions (Whisman, 1993; Hollon, DeRubeis, & Evans, 1996), but the evidence that it works by changing dysfunctional attitudes is mixed (Burns & Spangler, 2001). Thus, further research on the effects of cognitive therapy is clearly needed.

The Contributions of Cognitive Theory The cognitive approach has the virtue of focusing on specific, operationalized variables and of insisting on empirical evidence. At the same time, unlike other scientific approaches, such as behaviorism, it takes intangible processes—thoughts, emotions—into account. Using the cognitive approach, researchers have accumulated a large body of empirically based findings, with many useful models of the causes of abnormal behavior.

The cognitive perspective also supplies a particularly useful integrative framework for incorporating concepts and techniques—as well as approaches to therapy—from other parts of psychology (Alford & Beck, 1997). This is because cognitive therapy is built on a vulnerability-stress approach and accepts the idea that a role can be played by environmental, behavioral, sociocultural, and biological factors. In addition, cognitive theory has been more successful than some other approaches in developing disorder-specific formulations of causes and treatment.

Another advantage of cognitive therapy is the availability of manuals describing how to administer and evaluate it. Beck and his colleagues, for example, developed a detailed manual for the administration of cognitive therapy for depression (Beck, Rush, Shaw, et al., 1979). Such manuals have made it possible to train many therapists in this approach, as well as to conduct large numbers of large-scale outcome studies.

In the end, the strongest argument in favor of the cognitive approach to psychopathology is its therapy, which has been empirically validated by a particularly large number of controlled outcome studies (Chambless, Baker, Baucom, et al., 1998). Cognitive treatment is very practical. Its most notable successes so far have been in the treatment of depression and anxiety disorders, such as panic disorder, social phobia, and generalized anxiety disorder. Cognitive therapy has also proved helpful with substance dependence, eating disorders, and some personality disorders; and more recently, empirical support has even been found for cognitive therapy with schizophrenia (Beck & Rector, 2000) and delusional disorders (Haddock, Tarrier, Spaulding, et al., 1998).

The Sociocultural Perspective

Like the behavioral perspective, the sociocultural perspective studies abnormal behavior in an environmental context. But whereas the behavioral school confines its attention to the immediate environment, the **sociocultural perspective** views behavior as the product of broad social forces. It emphasizes the influence of cultural, gender, socioeconomic, and ethnic factors, along with identity, on behavior.

Social-Situational Influences on Behavior

One starting place for the sociocultural perspective is in the social-situational determinants of behavior, or how other people and the social environment influence our behavior. Some researchers have found that powerful situational forces (e.g., social pressures to conform to social roles) lead ordinary people to act in extreme ways that other people might label as "immoral," "mentally ill," or "abnormal" (Aronson, 1994). For instance, large proportions of otherwise normal people can often be induced to engage in incredibly injurious acts to others simply by being instructed to do so by a legitimate authority (Milgram, 1963), even when the victims beg them to stop.

In one influential study, Zimbardo and his students created a simulated prison in the basement of the psychology department at Stanford University (Zimbardo, 1971). A coin toss was used to randomly assign one half of the participants to be prisoners and

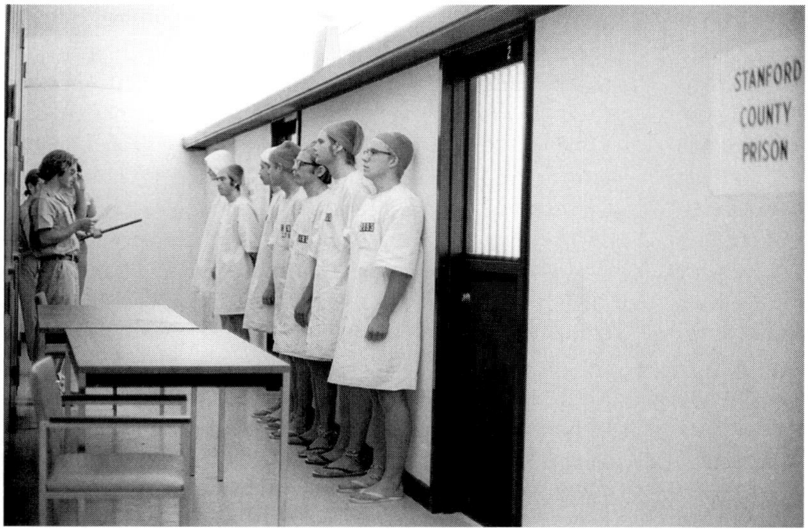

In Zimbardo's prison experiment, Stanford students assigned to be guards and prisoners so completely assumed their roles that researchers had to stop the study. Such experiments are deemed unethical today.

the other half to be guards. All participants were young men who had been carefully screened for psychological stability. After 6 days, Zimbardo had to close down his mock prison, because the young men began to take on their assigned roles and behave in increasingly frightening ways. As Zimbardo (1971, p. 3) put it, "In less than a week, the experience of imprisonment undid (temporarily) a lifetime of learning; human values were suspended, self-concepts were challenged, and the ugliest most base, pathological side of human nature surfaced. We were horrified" (as cited in Aronson, 1994, p. 10).

As these findings demonstrate, outsiders, even experts, often underestimate the power of situational forces and instead blame extreme behaviors entirely on problems in the person (Aronson, 1994). Powerful situational forces—such as poverty, racism, and even the label of mental illness itself—can create intense social adversity and stress, with psychological effects. They can also indirectly affect abnormal behavior by influencing how society comes to label behaviors as abnormal.

Mental Illness and Social Ills

Many injustices built into our society—poverty, the lack of any respected role for the aged, discrimination against minority groups and women, and homophobia (which in turn leads to condemnation of AIDS sufferers)—produce stress, which can lead to psychological disturbance. According to the sociocultural view, it should come as no surprise if a poor, ill-educated, and jobless teenager acts "wild" or if a lonely and idle 85-year-old woman is depressed. Rather than probe their psyches for an underlying psychological cause, say the socioculturalists, we should address the obvious social causes. For example, poverty is a significant risk factor for psychopathology (Eaton & Muntaner, 1999). In addition to experiencing more stress, the poor are less likely to have the personal resources and social support to cope with stress (Dohrenwend, Levav, Shrout, et al., 1998; Johnson, Cohen, Dohrenwend, et al., 1999). Epidemiological studies (Kessler, McGonagle, Zhao, et al., 1994) show that people in the lowest income groups have about *twice* the risk of developing an episode of a psychiatric disorder as people who are not poor.

Mental Illness and Labeling

Sociocultural forces can also influence how people define or label behavior as abnormal. As we saw in Chapter 1, the definition of abnormal behavior depends upon who is doing the defining. Adherents of the sociocultural approach claim that we may label people "mentally ill" not because of anything intrinsically pathological in their behavior but simply because they have violated social norms—a situation that the society cannot tolerate and that it handles by labeling and treating the people in question as though they were "sick." This theory has generated some interest in the process whereby people become labeled as mentally ill. How does the society choose which deviants it will designate as sick? And why do stigmatized people accept the label?

One theorist who has considered these questions at length is Thomas Scheff (1966, 1998). His analysis of the labeling process follows: Deviant behavior, whatever its cause, is extremely common. Most of it is transitory and is ignored by the society. However, certain forms of deviance, for one reason or another, come to the attention of the mental health care establishment and are singled out as "mental disorders." Once singled out and labeled in this way, a person exhibiting such deviance is placed in the social role of a "mentally ill" person. And it is extremely likely that the individual will accept that role, for, as with any other social role (e.g., teacher, student, wife, husband), society provides strong rewards for behavior consistent with the role and strong punishments for behavior inconsistent with the role. If, for example, a man who has once been labeled "mentally ill" tries to rejoin the world of the sane, he will find much to deter him—rejections from employment agencies, raised eyebrows from people who know about his "past," and so forth. Thus, according to Scheff, most people who are designated mentally ill ultimately embrace the role of mental patient. In short, the label becomes a self-fulfilling prophecy.

The Surgeon General's report on mental health (USDHHS, 1999) highlighted the perceived **stigma** of being labeled mentally ill as a powerful obstacle to seeking care. The effects of stigma on using mental health care services are particularly strong among certain segments of the population, such as older adults (Sirey, Bruce, Alexopoulos, et al., 2001). Other recent research has indicated that, for former mental patients, social rejection is a persistent source of social stress, which can lower self-esteem and confidence (Wright, Gronfein, & Owens, 2000).

Class, Ethnicity, and Diagnosis

What kinds of behavior are most likely to identify a person as mentally ill? What do socially learned stereotypes of mental illness consist of? A famous group of early studies, the so-called New Haven studies (Hollingshead & Redich, 1958; Myers & Bean, 1968), found that when people of lower socioeconomic levels suffered from behavior disturbances,

Research Highlights: The Stigma of Psychiatric Labels

People with mental illnesses bear a triple burden. First, they are challenged by disorders that are painful, disabling, and sometimes overwhelming. They must also deal with mental health care systems that are often fragmented, inadequately funded, and unresponsive to their needs. On top of this, they frequently encounter the negative attitudes of others toward individuals with psychiatric labels. Many mental health consumers (a term now widely used to refer to individuals who have been treated for psychiatric problems) have reported that this last burden may be the greatest.

Considerable research has established that people tend to associate mainly negative characteristics with mental illnesses—dangerousness, lack of motivation, and character weakness among them (Wahl, 1999). Studies have found that reported psychiatric treatment makes it less likely that a person will be offered a job, rented a room, or accepted for postgraduate study (Wahl, 1999). These public reactions, moreover, appear to be based not on the person's behavior or symptoms but on the psychiatric label itself. While improved identification of mental disorders has led to improved scientific understanding and treatment of these disorders, it is important to recognize that psychiatric labeling may also have significant negative consequences.

Wahl (1999) studied the day-to-day impact of negative public attitudes on people identified as having mental disorders. Almost 1,400 mental health consumers from every state in the United States responded to a written survey about their experiences of stigma and discrimination; 100 were interviewed at length. Social isolation and rejection was one of the common experiences reported by consumers in Wahl's sample; 60 percent reported that they had been shunned or avoided by others when their status as mental health consumers became known. Co-workers, friends, and even family, respondents said, became more distant when they found out about the respondent's mental health treatment history. Almost three quarters (70 percent) of survey respondents also indicated that they had experiences of being disregarded by others and treated as incompetent; people with college and graduate degrees found themselves being talked down to and given trivial work assignments when their mental illness was known. Consumers were often in the audience when others—including mental health caregivers—made jokes about mental illness or referred to people with psychiatric disorders in disparaging ways; 50 percent reported that this had happened to them often or very often. Consumers were also denied jobs, driver's licenses, medical insurance, and even opportunities to volunteer their time and expertise.

These experiences are not only painful but also undermine recovery. Many people, fearful of the public reactions that follow psychiatric labeling, are reluctant to seek mental health treatment; as many as half of those with psychiatric disorders, in fact, do not seek treatment. For those who do obtain psychiatric help, fear of being viewed unfavorably by others is a continuing worry, as 79 percent of the respondents in Wahl's study indicated. Furthermore, those who do undertake treatment may do so without the social support psychologists know to be an important factor in recovery from stresses of all kinds. At precisely the time they may most need understanding and support, then, those with mental illnesses instead experience isolation and rejection and are denied opportunities. Encounters with negative attitudes leave those individuals discouraged, depressed, and sometimes angry (emotions that are then often interpreted as symptoms of the person's illness, rather than as understandable reactions to mistreatment). Even more troubling, many mental health consumers internalize the negative attitudes that surround them, coming to accept the public's appraisal of them as deficient, unlikable, unworthy, and incapable of meaningful contributions to their communities.

Mental health consumers in Wahl's study pointed out the importance of looking beyond labels when responding to people who have had psychiatric treatment. In particular, they urged others to see them as not simply a bundle of symptoms leading to a psychiatric diagnosis, but as people who have many other characteristics—both positive and negative—beyond their mental illnesses. "Mental illness is just a piece of a person," said one study participant. "A person is composed of so many more pieces than mental illness. I am more than a diagnosis. I am a whole person, and I deserve to be treated like a whole person."

"Whenever [you] hear that somebody's got a mental illness," said another respondent, "don't act like they've died or like they're worthless or they're no good anymore, they're ruined. . . . Esteem them as valuable human beings."

they were more likely than middle-class people to be placed in state mental hospitals. The reasons were twofold. First, the lower-class people could not afford private outpatient care. Second, they tended to express their unhappiness in aggressive and rebellious behaviors. These behaviors, while acceptable to other lower-class people as "normal" signs of frustration, appeared unacceptable—indeed, bizarre—to the mental health professionals who were diagnosing them, because those professionals came from higher socioeconomic brackets and, accordingly, had different ideas about what constituted normal responses to stress. Hence, people with lower socioeconomic backgrounds were more likely to be labeled as psychotic and to be hospitalized as a result. In contrast, people of higher socioeconomic levels tended not to be hospitalized, not only because they could pay for outpatient care but also because their "style" of deviance (e.g., withdrawal and self-deprecation) seemed less bizarre to the doctors, who belonged to the same

Sociocultural theorists maintain that social conditions such as poverty and ethnic/cultural discrimination can lead to psychological disorders.

social class. Consequently, the individuals from higher socioeconomic backgrounds were diagnosed as having "neurotic" disorders—diagnoses that carry much less stigma—and, with the help of regular therapy, were able to return to their daily lives. Unlike the hospitalized and "psychotic" poor, they were given less of a "sick" role to fill and thus were more likely to improve.

This principle applies to ethnicity as well as to class (Aneshensel & Phelan, 1999; Hartwell, 2001). In one study (Luepnitz, Randolph, & Gutsch, 1982), experienced therapists were given sets of hypothetical patient profiles and were asked to provide diagnoses. From therapist to therapist, the profiles were the same except for one factor: ethnicity. Patients identified as white in one set were said to be African American in another. The study found that African Americans were more likely to be diagnosed as alcoholic or schizophrenic, whereas the whites *with the same symptoms* were more likely to be diagnosed as depressed. As in the New Haven studies, these different disorders carry different levels of stigma, have different prognoses, and lead to different treatments and chances of improvement.

Those charged with developing diagnostic criteria have not ignored these problems. One proposal is to replace the current diagnostic system with a dimensional system (Chapter 2), classifying patients not according to disorders but simply according to how they rate on variables such as depression or anxiety. Presumably, this would discourage stereotyping. Another possible solution, which has already been implemented in *DSM-IV-TR,* is to inform diagnosticians about cultural variations in normal and abnormal behavior and to warn them against specific biases.

Sociocultural Factors, Help-Seeking, and Treatment

Sociocultural forces can often influence whether individuals from different groups seek treatment as well as how they respond to treatment. For instance, Mexican Americans, particularly those who are recent immigrants, markedly underuse the mental health services available to them (Vega, Kolody, Aguilar-Gaxiola, et al., 1999). The cultural beliefs of these recent immigrants about the nature of psychological problems, and their customary patterns for dealing with them (i.e., through family support), can contribute to such underuse, as can the fact that community treatment centers may lack therapists who speak the immigrants' language. Sociocultural variations can also create differences in how people in different minority groups respond to the treatments they receive. For example, some groups can respond with significantly different physiological symptoms or side effects—even though they have the same standard pharmacological treatments (Herrera, Lawson, & Sramek, 1999).

Prevention as a Social Issue

Because sociocultural theorists are concerned with the social and economic causes of psychological disturbances, their approach to treatment revolves around community prevention programs. As we have seen (Chapter 1), three levels of prevention have been distinguished. The goal of primary prevention is to prevent the kinds of social ills that put people at risk for psychological disorders. Secondary prevention is aimed at modifying existing risk factors so that they do not lead to the development of disorders. Tertiary prevention is the treatment of disorders once they have developed.

A major consideration in all three levels of prevention is the need for greater sensitivity among mental health care providers to minorities and their circumstances, as well as greater recognition of culture-specific issues that can affect minorities' use of mental health services, diagnosis, and response to treatment.

Evaluating the Sociocultural Perspective

Almost no one in the mental health field would dispute the sociocultural theory that societal conditions contribute to psychological disturbance. Like all other perspectives, what distinguishes the sociocultural perspective from the other theories in this chapter is a matter of emphasis. Whereas sociocultural theorists claim that socially engendered stress is the primary cause, other theorists say that it is secondary to other factors, such as cognitive vulnerabilities or learning histories. In turn, most sociocultural theorists readily concede the importance of cognitive processes and learning histories, but argue that these are significantly influenced by social disadvantage.

The theory that psychological abnormality is a cultural artifact, maintained through labeling, is far more controversial. Differential labeling is not the only possible explanation for the disproportionate numbers of lower-class people who are diagnosed as psychotic. The phenomenon could be accounted for more simply with the social adversity, or socioeconomic-stress, theory: Because those who are poor have to cope with more serious stresses, they have more serious breakdowns. Another possible explanation is the social selection theory: Severely disturbed people slip downward on the socioeconomic ladder—they tend to lose their jobs, for example—so that, whatever their original socioeconomic status, they are members of the lower class by the time they are diagnosed (Aneshensel, Phelan, et al., 1999). Researchers are giving increasing attention to the role of these sociocultural factors.

Key Terms

attribution, 92
behavior therapy, 83
behavioral experiment, 95
behavioral perspective, 75
cognition, 88
cognitive appraisal, 90
cognitive behaviorism, 89
cognitive case conceptualization, 95
cognitive distortion, 90
cognitive perspective, 88
cognitive restructuring, 95
conditioned reflex, 76
conditioned reinforcers, 79
conditioned response, 78
conditioned stimulus, 78
contingency, 79
contingency management, 85
decatastrophizing, 95
derived stimulus relations, 82
discrimination, 80
disorder-specific bias, 91
exposure, 84
extinction, 80
generalization,80
hierarchy of fears, 84
hypothesis testing, 95
law of effect, 77
learning, 76
negative reinforcement, 79
operant conditioning, 79
positive reinforcement, 79
primary reinforcer, 79
punishment, 79
radical behaviorism, 77
rational-emotive therapy, 94
reinforcement, 79
respondent conditioning, 78
rules, 81
selective attention, 93
schema, 93
shaping, 80
sociocultural perspective, 98
Socratic questioning, 95
stigma, 99
stimulus equivalence, 81
systematic desensitization, 84
three-term contingency, 80
unconditioned response, 78
unconditioned stimulus, 78
vulnerability-stress model, 91

Summary

- The behavioral, cognitive, and sociocultural perspectives developed in reaction to established philosophies of behavior.
- The behavioral perspective stresses immediate causes of behavior, rather than deep-seated, unconscious ones. Behaviorism was developed in the early twentieth century as a result of discoveries about the mechanisms of learning. Pavlov demonstrated that learning could be the result of the conditioned reflex, or simple association; Watson believed that psychology should be a natural, empirical science; Thorndike's law of effect stated

that responses that lead to "satisfying" consequences are strengthened and likely to be repeated, while responses that lead to "unsatisfying" consequences have the opposite effect; and Skinner's radical behaviorism, held that behavior includes all that a person does, says, and feels, and asserts that any kind of behavior can be predicted and influenced through knowledge of relevant environmental contingencies.

- The basic assumptions of behaviorism are that psychology's task is to study behavior, or the responses an organism makes to stimuli on the basis of its learning history; that psychological research should be empirical, based on measurement; that the goal of psychology is the prediction and control of behavior; and that the real causes of any behavior that is not genetically determined lie outside the individual.
- According to behaviorists, there are two basic mechanisms of learning: respondent conditioning (an organism's learning to respond to a neutral stimulus as it would to a nonneutral one) and operant conditioning (an organism's learning to operate on the environment to obtain or avoid consequences).
- The frequency of behavior may be increased by positive or negative reinforcements or decreased through punishments.
- Related learning mechanisms include extinction (through repeated unpairing of a conditioned stimulus and an unconditioned stimulus); generalization (responding to related stimuli in similar ways); discrimination (learning to differentiate among related stimuli); shaping (reinforcing successive approximations to a desired response); and rule-governed behavior (learning by following rules and instructions).
- Behaviorists see all behavior as resulting in the same way from the interaction of our genetic endowment and our learning history. Thus, they prefer to speak of "maladaptive" rather than "abnormal" behavior and to avoid assigning people to specific diagnostic categories.
- Radical behaviorism has increasingly focused on complex rather than simple causes of maladaptive behavior (such as the depressive response)—that is, on an individual's entire life experience and learning history rather than on specific proximal causes.
- Behavior therapy uses the principles of learning to help patients change or unlearn maladaptive behavior, including self-defeating thoughts as well as inappropriate actions. Respondent-conditioning and extinction techniques (systematic desensitization, exposure) are used when the aim is to change emotional responses. Operant-conditioning techniques (such as contingency management) are used when the goal is to change overt behavior. Most forms of behavior therapy are administered as part of multicomponent treatment.
- New radical behavioral therapies, combining principles of behaviorism with elements of various philosophies, often emphasize acceptance or validation of an individual's maladaptive behavior. In doing so, they may open up indirect avenues to change.
- Behavior therapy is criticized for denying the client's freedom and uniqueness and for being superficial. However, it is effective in teaching people better skills to deal with life, it is often less expensive and faster than insight therapies, and it is precise in its goals and techniques.
- Behaviorism challenges not only other theories of abnormal behavior but also basic Western cultural notions. It has been criticized as oversimplified and deterministic and as a possible means of political coercion.
- At the same time, behavioral approaches to objectivity and experimentation have become the norm in psychological research, and behaviorism has largely destigmatized abnormal behavior. Behavior therapies have long been successful in achieving limited treatment goals, and radical behavioral therapists are now taking on the full range of clinical challenges.
- The cognitive perspective begins with an interest in cognition, or the mental processing of stimuli. The early cognitive behaviorists argued that variations in responses to the same stimuli could be explained only in terms of cognitive events. They argued that psychological problems arise from irrational beliefs (Ellis) or distorted thinking (Beck).
- The cognitive perspective holds that response to a stimulus reflects the way a person processes or appraises the stimulus, not the stimulus itself. Some attribution styles are more adaptive than others.
- The cognitive perspective has been criticized for being unscientific to the extent that it is based on inference, and for mistaking secondary for primary causes. At the same time, the cognitive perspective is more scientific than some other perspectives in that it emphasizes operationalized variables and empirical measures of memory, association, and anticipation.

- Cognitive therapy is based on the idea that, to change a pattern of maladaptive behavior, it is necessary to restructure the pattern of thoughts that maintains it.
- In self-instructional training, the client is taught to engage in more constructive self-talk. Rational-emotive therapy is aimed at identifying irrational assumptions that guide clients' interpretations of events and thus their behavior.
- Beck's cognitive therapy holds that emotional disorders are caused primarily by irrational, negative thoughts. Constructivist cognitive therapy uses self-exploration to gradually reveal new ways of thinking and feeling. Common strategies in cognitive therapy include cognitive restructuring, Socratic questioning, and behavioral experiments.
- Cognitive therapy is sometimes criticized for not recognizing that life can be irrational and that changing one's thinking is not always an appropriate response. On the other hand, it is very practical and often effective: Its techniques can be described forthrightly and summarized in a manual.
- The sociocultural perspective argues that the root of abnormal behavior lies not within the mind but in society. One theory is that social ills, such as poverty and discrimination, push people into psychopathology. Another theory holds that labeling people "mentally ill" tends to become a self-fulfilling prophecy. Additional research indicates that people's class and ethnicity influence the way in which their problems are diagnosed and the treatment they receive.
- No one disputes that socioeconomic factors and cultural variables may contribute to psychological disturbance, but the extent to which these are causes or effects of abnormal behavior is a matter of debate. Particularly controversial is the theory that labeling alone may be responsible for the disproportionate occurrence of psychological abnormality among the poor.

CHAPTER 5

The Psychodynamic Perspective
- The Basic Concepts of Freudian Theory
- The Descendants of Freud
- The Psychodynamic Approach to Therapy
- Evaluating the Psychodynamic Perspective

The Humanistic-Existential Perspective
- Basic Assumptions
- Humanistic Psychology
- Existential Psychology

The Interpersonal Perspective

Integrating the Perspectives

The Psychodynamic, Humanistic-Existential, and Interpersonal Perspectives

In this chapter we will discuss three influential schools of thought in abnormal psychology: the psychodynamic, humanistic-existential, and interpersonal perspectives. The psychodynamic perspective emphasizes the inner psychological processes that motivate behavior, such as unconscious conflicts over basic biological impulses. The humanistic-existential perspective began, in part, as a reaction to the psychodynamic perspective, although many of its leaders were trained in psychoanalysis, and some of its basic assumptions about the mind share features with psychoanalysis. The interpersonal perspective focuses on the individual's social environment and therefore is more empirical, less intuitive, than the psychodynamic and humanistic-existential schools. Of these perspectives, the psychodynamic has had the far greatest influence, particularly in our understanding of psychopathology, and therefore it receives the most coverage in this chapter.

The Psychodynamic Perspective

The **psychodynamic perspective** is a school of thought united by a common concern with the dynamics, or interaction, of forces lying deep within the mind. Different psychodynamic theorists emphasize different aspects of mental dynamics, but almost all agree on three basic principles. First is psychic determinism: Much of our behavior is not freely chosen but, on the contrary, is determined by the nature and strength of intrapsychic forces. Second is the belief that such forces usually operate unconsciously—in other words, we are unaware of the true motives of our behavior. Third, most psychodynamic thinkers assume that the form these forces take is deeply affected by childhood experience and particularly by relationships within the family.

The founding father of the psychodynamic perspective was Sigmund Freud, a neurologist who began his practice in Vienna in the 1880s. At that time, the most common complaint brought to the neurologist was hysteria, physical impairment—such as paralysis—for which no physical cause could be found. As we saw in Chapter 1, the idea that the origin of hysteria might be psychological rather than physiological had already been proposed. Convinced by this idea, young Freud set himself the task of discovering the specific psychological causes involved and of working out an effective cure. Within a few years, he had put forth the idea that hysteria constituted a defense against unbearable thoughts or memories. (The hand may be "paralyzed," for example, to overcome an urge to strike out.) From this seed grew his theory of **psychoanalysis,** by which, ultimately, he sought to explain not just hysteria but all human behavior, normal and abnormal. (It is important to note that the term "psychoanalysis" has two related meanings today: It refers to a theory of personality, which has evolved since Freud into several overlapping theories of human development, personality, and abnormal behavior [Lerner & Erlich, 2001]. "Psychoanalysis" also refers to a form of psychotherapy, a method for studying mental functioning.)

The psychodynamic perspective is by no means bounded by Freud's theory. It is a large and living school of thought, by now more than a century old, built of proposals and counterproposals, propositions and refinements contributed by many theorists other than Freud. It is impossible, however, in the space of this chapter, to give appropriate coverage to the full range of psychodynamic theory. Furthermore, Freud's theory, however much it has been revised, is still the foundation of psychodynamic thought. Therefore, we will give first and fullest consideration to Freud—that is, to the "classical" psychodynamic position. Then we will describe the ways in which later theorists have expanded this view.

The Basic Concepts of Freudian Theory

The Depth Hypothesis The key concept of psychoanalysis, and Freud's most important contribution to psychology, is the **depth hypothesis,** the idea that almost all mental activity takes place unconsciously. According to Freud, the mind is divided into two levels. At the surface is the perceptual conscious, consisting of the narrow range of mental events of which the person is aware at any given instant. Beneath the perceptual conscious lies the **unconscious,** consisting of all the psychological materials (memories, desires, fears, etc.) that the mind is not attending to at that moment.

It was Freud's belief that the things we forget do not disappear from the mind. They simply go into the unconscious. Furthermore, much of this material is not passively forgotten. It is actively forgotten, forced out of consciousness—a process called repression—because it is disturbing to us. These censored materials may erupt into consciousness when psychological controls are relaxed—for example, when we are under hypnosis or when we are dreaming. But, during our normal waking hours, the contents of the unconscious are kept tightly sealed from our awareness. At the same time—and this is the crucial point—these unconscious materials always play some role in determining our behavior. When we choose one profession over another or marry one person rather than another, we do so not only for the reasons that we tell ourselves but also because of events from our past that are now hidden from us—a fascinating and disturbing notion.

The Necessity of Interpretation If Freud was correct that the origins of our behavior are buried deep in the psyche, then psychology cannot confine itself simply to observing surface behavior. Rather, it must engage in **interpretation,** revealing the hidden, intrapsychic motives. Interpretation was Freud's primary tool. In all human behavior—actions, dreams, jokes, works of art—he saw two layers of meaning: the manifest content, or surface meaning; and the latent content, or true, unconscious meaning. The goal of his theoretical writings and of his therapy was to reveal, via interpretation, the latent content: the unconscious forces that cause people to do what they do.

In certain respects, this is an old and uncontroversial idea. For thousands of years, it has been understood that some decoding process, whether or not it is called "interpretation," is indispensable to human communication. When someone you have asked for a date replies that he or she is busy for the next month, you naturally understand the message. This person does not want to go out with you. The ability to get along in human society depends on our ability to decode such statements. Interpretation, then, was not invented by Freud. What Freud invented was the idea that interpretation could be used to identify unconscious motives for our behavior.

The Structural Hypothesis: Id, Ego, and Superego

Some years after his formulation of the depth hypothesis, Freud constructed a second, complementary psychic schema, the so-called **structural hypothesis.** As we have seen, the defining characteristic of psychodynamic theory, as handed down from Freud, is its concern with the interaction of forces within the mind. It is this interaction that the structural hypothesis describes. Briefly, it states that the mind can be divided into three broad forces—the id, the ego, and the superego—and that these three forces are continually interacting with one another, often in conflict.

The Id At birth, according to Freud's hypothesis, the energy of the mind is bound up entirely in primitive biological drives, to which Freud gave the collective term **id.** The id is the foundation of the psychic structure and the source from which the later developments of ego and superego must borrow their energy.

The drives that make up the id are of two basic types, sexual and aggressive—the former above all.* Freud saw the sexual drive as permeating the entire personality and subsuming, in addition to actual sexual behavior, a wide range of other life-sustaining pursuits, such as the need for food and warmth, the desire for the love of friends and family, and the impulse toward creativity. These and other positive desires, in Freud's view, were extensions and transformations of a basic sexual drive, which he named the **libido** and which he saw as the major source of psychic energy.

The id operates on what Freud called the pleasure principle; that is, it is utterly hedonistic, seeking only its own pleasure or release from tension and taking no account of logic or reason, reality or morality. Hungry infants, for example, do not ask themselves whether it is time for their feeding or whether their mothers may be busy doing something else; they want food, and so they cry for it. According to Freud, we are all, at some level, hungry infants.

The Ego While the id can know what it wants, it has no way of determining which means of dealing with the world are practical and which are not. To fulfill these functions, the mind develops a new psychic component, the ego. The **ego** mediates between the id and the forces that restrict the id's satisfactions. Ego functions begin to develop shortly after birth and emerge slowly over a period of years.

Whereas the id operates on the pleasure principle, the ego operates on the reality principle—to find what is both safe and effective. When the id signals its desire, the ego locates in reality a potential gratifier for the desire, anticipates the consequences of using that gratifier, and then either reaches out for it or, if that gratifier is ineffective or potentially dangerous, delays the id's satisfaction until a more appropriate gratification can be found.

In Freud's view, small children freely use aggression to get what they want because the id is not yet under the restraint of the ego and superego.

Imagine, for example, a 3-year-old girl playing in her room. The id signals that aggressive impulses seek release, and the girl reaches for her toy hammer. The ego then goes into action, scanning the environment. The girl's baby brother is playing nearby. Should she hit him over the head with her hammer? The ego, which knows from experience that this will result in the unpleasant consequence of punishment, says no and continues the scanning process. Also nearby is a big lump of clay. The ego determines that no harm will come from pounding the clay, and so the girl hits that instead. According to Freud, it is from the ego's weighing of these considerations that the mind develops and refines all its higher functions: language, perception, learning, discrimination, memory, judgment, and planning. All these are ego functions.

The Superego Imagine that three years later the same girl once again sits with hammer in hand, looking for something to pound. Again she considers her

*On the *number* of basic drives, Freud changed his theory many times. After 1920, he elevated aggression to the status of a basic drive, at least partly in response to the horrors of World War I.

brother's head, and again she rejects that possibility. This time, however, she rejects it not only because it would result in punishment but also because it would be "bad." What this means is that the child has developed a superego.

The **superego** is that part of the mind that represents the internalized moral standards of the society and, above all, of the parents. This superego, approximately equivalent to what we call "conscience," takes no more account of reality than the id does. Instead of considering what is realistic or possible, it embraces an abstract moral ideal and demands that the sexual and aggressive impulses of the id be stifled in order to conform to that ideal. It is then the job of the ego to find a way to satisfy the id without antagonizing the superego.

Thus, in the fully developed psychic structure, the ego has three fairly intransigent parties to deal with: the id, which seeks only the satisfaction of its irrational and amoral demands; the superego, which seeks only the satisfaction of its rigid ideals; and reality, which offers only a limited range of options.

When we consider the structural hypothesis, it is important to keep in mind that id, ego, and superego are not *things* in the mind or even parts of the mind, but simply names that Freud gave to broad categories of intrapsychic forces. It is difficult, in discussing these categories, not to speak of them as if they were actual entities—the id screaming for gratification, the superego demanding the opposite, and the ego running back and forth between them. But these are metaphors, nothing more.

The Dynamics of the Mind Through ego functions, as we have seen, the mind can usually mediate conflicts among id, superego, and reality. At times, however, either the id or the superego will threaten to overwhelm the ego's controls, resulting in unacceptable feelings or behavior. In response to this threat, the person experiences anxiety.

Anxiety, akin to what most of us call "fear," is a state of psychic distress that acts as a signal to the ego that danger is at hand. Anxiety can have its source in reality, as when you confront a burglar in your house. Or—and this was Freud's major concern—anxiety can originate in internal dynamics, in an id impulse that threatens to break through the ego's controls and cause the person to be punished, either by the superego (in the form of guilt) or by reality. Most anxiety is not experienced consciously. It is kept closeted in the unconscious, and the danger is dealt with through the ego's employment of defense mechanisms.

Freud's Model of the Human Psyche

This MindMAP video looks at Freud's structural hypothesis of the mind and discusses how conflict between the different forces of the psyche might lead to anxiety. In what ways would this three-part model be useful in explaining why people behave the way they do?

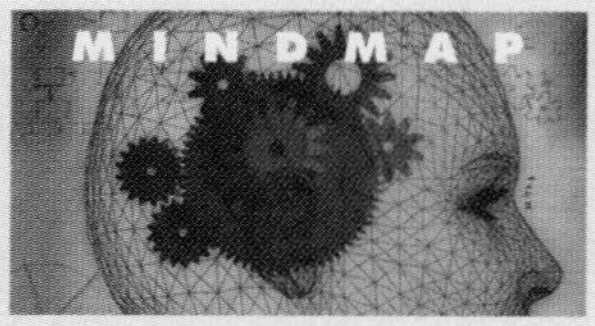

Defense Mechanisms The ego tends to distort or simply deny a reality (whether external or internal) that would arouse unbearable anxiety. This tactic is called a **defense mechanism,** and as long as it works, the anxiety will not be experienced consciously. According to Freud, we all use defense mechanisms all the time. If we did not, we would be psychologically disabled, for the facts they conceal—of the primitive drives of the id, of the condemnations of the superego—would produce intolerable anxiety if they were constantly breaking through into the conscious mind. The defense mechanisms, then, serve an adaptive function. They allow us to avoid facing what we cannot face and, thus, to go on with the business of living.

If they become too rigid, however, they can defeat adjustment. When defense mechanisms force us never to leave the house or—to use a more ordinary example—to transfer conflicts we have had with our parents onto our adult relationships or romantic partners, then we are sacrificing our adaptive capacities. Furthermore, if most of the ego's energy is tied up in the job of maintaining defenses, then the ego will have little strength left for its other important functions, such as perception, reasoning, and problem solving. Defense mechanisms, then, are adaptive only up to a point. Freud's daughter, Anna, who was also a prominent psychoanalyst, defined many of the defense mechanisms that are fundamental to psychodynamic theory (Freud, 1946).

Repression. In the process of repression, as we have already seen, unacceptable id impulses are pushed down into the unconscious and thereby robbed of their power to disturb us consciously. Thus, for example, a girl who is sexually attracted to her father will simply remove this intolerable thought from her consciousness. It may come up in her dreams, but in disguised form; and once she wakes up, the dreams, too, are likely to be repressed.

Sigmund Freud's daughter Anna was a psychoanalyst in her own right; she was largely responsible for defining the defense mechanisms. Here, father and daughter are pictured together in 1928.

One of the earliest of Freud's conceptualizations, repression is the most fundamental defense mechanism of psychodynamic theory. It is on the basis of this mechanism that Freud constructed his symbolic readings of human behavior, whereby a person's actions are viewed as masked representations of the contents of his or her unconscious. And Freud evolved his technique of psychoanalysis expressly in order to dredge up this repressed material—"to make the unconscious conscious," as he put it.

Repression is fundamental also in that it is the basis of all the other defense mechanisms. In every one of the defenses that we will describe, the "forbidden" impulse is first repressed; then, instead of acting on that impulse, the person engages in a substitute behavior that serves either as an outlet for the impulse, as an additional protection against it, or both.

Denial. Whereas repression is the refusal to recognize an internal reality or source of anxiety, such as a taboo impulse, denial is the refusal to acknowledge an external source of anxiety. In some cases, the person will actually fail to perceive something that is obvious. For example, a woman who has been diagnosed as terminally ill may go on planning a lengthy trip to be taken when she is well again. Because it involves a drastic alteration of the facts, denial is considered a "primitive" defense. It is usually resorted to by children or by people facing a very serious threat (e.g., terminal illness or the death of a loved one).

Projection. In projection, unacceptable impulses are first repressed, then attributed to others. Thus, an internal threat is converted into an external threat. For example, a man whose self-esteem is threatened by his own preoccupation with money may accuse others of being money-hungry. This relieves his own moral anxiety and simultaneously enables him to throw the guilt onto others.

Displacement. Like projection, displacement involves a transfer of emotion. In this case, however, what is switched is not the source but the object of the emotion. Afraid to display or even to experience certain feelings against whoever has aroused them, the person represses the feelings. Then, when the opportunity arises, he or she transfers them to a safer object and releases them. For example, a man may spend the day suffering humiliations at work for which he cannot retaliate; then he goes home, discovers that his son has failed to take out the trash, and on that pretext gives the boy a terrible dressing down.

Rationalization. Most defenses occur not in isolation but in combination (Erdelyi, 1985). In the example just cited, the pretext that the man used for yelling at his son illustrates another defense mechanism, rationalization. A person who engages in rationalization offers socially acceptable reasons for something that he or she has actually done (or is going to do) for unconscious and unacceptable motives. Rationalization is one of the most common defenses. According to Freud, we need to make ourselves "look good."

Isolation. We engage in isolation when we avoid unacceptable feelings by cutting them off from the events to which they are attached, repressing them, then reacting to the events in an emotionless manner. Isolation is a common refuge of patients in psychotherapy. Eager to tell the therapist what the problem is but unwilling to confront the feelings involved, patients will relate the facts in a calm, detached fashion ("Yes, my mother's death caused me considerable distress"), whereas it is actually the feelings, more than the facts, that need to be explored.

Intellectualization. Isolation is often accompanied by intellectualization: The person achieves further distance from the emotion in question by surrounding it with a smokescreen of abstract intellectual analysis ("Yes, my mother's death caused me considerable distress. Young children find it difficult to endure separation, let alone final separation, from their mothers," etc.).

Reaction formation. A person who engages in reaction formation represses the feelings that are arousing anxiety and then vehemently professes exactly the opposite. Thus, someone who claims to be disgusted by sexual promiscuity may be demonstrating a reaction formation against his or her own sexual impulses.

Regression. The mechanism of regression involves a return to a developmental stage that one has already passed through. Unable to deal with its anxiety, the ego simply abandons the scene of the conflict, reverting to an earlier, less threatening stage. In the extreme case, a regressed adult may be reduced to a babbling, helpless creature who has to be fed and toileted like a baby. On the other hand, well-adjusted adults often resort to minor regressive behaviors—whining, making childish demands, playing hooky from school or work—simply to take the edge off the pressures they are experiencing at the moment.

Undoing. In undoing, the person engages in a ritual behavior or thought in order to cancel out an unacceptable impulse. For example, some people with obsessive-compulsive disorder (Chapter 7) devise rituals, such as repeated hand washing, to dispel disturbing sexual thoughts.

Sublimation. Sublimation, the transformation and expression of sexual or aggressive energy into more socially acceptable forms, differs from all other defense mechanisms in that it can be truly constructive. The skill of a great surgeon, for example, may represent a sublimation of aggressive impulses. Likewise, Freud hypothesized that many of the beautiful nudes created by Renaissance painters and sculptors were the expression of sublimated sexual impulses.

The Stages of Psychosexual Development Freud's early psychoanalytic theory was heavily influenced by the evolutionary theories of Charles Darwin (Vakoch & Strupp, 2000). Freud assumed that evolutionary principles, including innate drives of sexuality and aggression, applied to human beings just as they do to other animals. In Freud's framework, biological drives are expressed as a function of **psychosexual development,** a series of stages in which the child's central motivation is to gratify sexual and aggressive drives in various erogenous (pleasure-producing) zones of the body: the mouth, the anus, and the genitals, in that order. The characteristics of the adult personality are a consequence of the ways in which conflicts over these id strivings are handled at each stage of development.

According to Freud, the oral stage is the first stage of psychosexual development. Infants put any and all objects they can into their mouths to gratify the urgings of the id.

The Oral Stage The **oral stage** begins at birth. As the name indicates, the mouth is the primary focus of id strivings. Infants must suck in order to live. Soon, however, they are using their mouths to satisfy not only their hunger but also their libidinal and aggressive impulses. Breast, bottle, thumb, pacifier, toys—infants suck, bite, and chew whatever they can find in their search for oral stimulation. According to Freud and his followers, unsatisfied oral needs can lead to dependency in adulthood.

The Anal Stage The **anal stage** usually begins in the second year of life. The libido shifts its focus to the anus and derives its primary gratification from the retaining and expelling of feces. The child's anal pleasures are barely established, however, before they are interfered with, through toilet training. Traditionally, Freudian theorists have regarded toilet training as a crucial event, since it is children's first confrontation with an external demand that they control their impulses. Suddenly their pleasures are brought under regulation. Toilet training, then, is the first difficult demand on the developing ego. If problems occur, the ego may experience considerable anxiety, and such anxiety can engender personality problems.

The Phallic Stage In the **phallic stage,** which extends from about the third to the fifth or sixth year, the focus is shifted to the genitals. The phallic stage is held to be particularly crucial because it is the scene of the **Oedipus complex,** named after Oedipus, the legendary king of Thebes, who unknowingly killed his father and married his mother. According to Freud (1905/1953), the child's extreme dependence on the mother during infancy culminates, during the phallic stage, in sexual desire for the mother. How this is resolved depends on whether the child is a boy or a girl. In boys, the incestuous desire leads to a recognition of the father's capacity for wrath, which in turn arouses **castration anxiety:** The boy fears that his father will punish him for his forbidden wishes by cutting off the guilty organ, his penis. This worry is supposedly confirmed by the boy's observations of female anatomy. Lacking penises, girls seem to him castrated, and he fears the same fate for himself. To allay his castration anxiety, he eventually represses the incestuous desire that aroused it. Instead of competing with the father, he identifies with him, internalizing the father's—and the society's—prohibitions against incest and aggression, thus building the foundations for the superego.

In girls, the situation is more complicated. In what has been called the **Electra complex,** a girl observes that she has been born without a penis. She experiences what Freud called penis envy, and this causes her to reorient her sexual interest toward her father. If she can seduce him, then at least vicariously she can obtain the desired organ. Of course, her desires are as futile as the boy's, and eventually she retreats back into her earlier, dependent identification with the mother.

Latency and the Genital Stage Usually between the ages of 6 and 12, the child goes through the **latency** period, during which sexual impulses seem dormant. Then, as the child enters puberty, sexual strivings are reawakened. Now, however, they are directed not at the child's own body, as in earlier stages, but toward others, in a new emotion combining altruistic feeling with the primitive sexual drive. This final phase of development, called the **genital stage,** ends with the attainment of mature sexuality, which to Freud meant not only heterosexual love but also maturity in a broad sense: "loving and working," as he characterized the hallmarks of healthy functioning.

Normal and Abnormal Behavior

Normal Personality Functioning In Freud's view, both the sane and the insane are motivated by the irrational id, with its reckless drives. Some people are simply more capable of controlling these drives. Their success in doing so depends largely on their psychosexual development, which, in the normal person, will have produced a healthy balance among the id, ego, and superego. This does not mean that the three forces coexist in perfect harmony. They are constantly conflicting, but the ego mediates. Thus, the key to adaptive behavior is ego strength. In times of stress, the ego may be weakened, in which case the defenses operate poorly, leaving us with a good deal of anxiety. Or, under the influence of alcohol or other drugs, the superego's functioning may become weak and thus allow id impulses the upper hand. But eventually the balance of power among the three psychic components is restored, and the person is once again able to satisfy the demands of the id without flying in the face of reality or morality.

Abnormal Personality Functioning Like normal functioning, abnormal functioning is motivated primarily by irrational drives and determined by childhood experiences. Indeed, one of the central principles of psychoanalytic theory is that normal and abnormal behavior lie on a continuum. Abnormality is a difference in degree, not in kind. Dreams, fantasies, works of art, psychiatric symptoms, hallucinations—these are simply different stops on the same road.

What, then, is the difference between normal and abnormal? The difference is ego strength. As we just saw, the ego may be weakened by conflict, but normally it bounces back. In some cases, however, the conflict continues, creating more and more anxiety, which in turn creates more and more rigid defenses in the form of behaviors that seriously impede adaptive functioning. After a car accident, a woman begins to feel anxious about driving; soon she can't ride in a car even if someone else is driving; eventually she refuses to leave her house. Freud called such conditions **neuroses.**

In extreme cases, the ego's strength may be severely depleted (or severely underdeveloped from the start), drastically curtailing adaptive functioning. Defenses break down, flooding the psyche with id impulses and attendant anxiety. Emotions are cut loose from external events. Speech loses its coherence. Inner voices are mistaken for outer voices. This condition of ego collapse, known as **psychosis,** is the furthest reach of the structural imbalance.

The Descendants of Freud

As Freud's theory gained acceptance, young people traveled to Vienna from many countries to be analyzed by Freud and his followers. They then took his theory back with them, disseminating it through Europe and the United States. As it spread, Freudian

Focus On... Psychodynamic Theory and Female Development

Freud, like all thinkers, reflected the values of his time. Nowhere is this more obvious than in his views on female development, which mirror—even defend—the sexual inequality of late-nineteenth-century Europe.

Freud's theory of female psychology rests on the fact that a girl does not have a penis. According to Freud, the moment a child notices this basic anatomical difference, he or she begins to become, psychologically as well as biologically, a male or a female. A girl's realization that she has no penis produces ineradicable jealousy, or "penis envy." As Freud (1932/1974) wrote, "The discovery that she is castrated is a turning point in a girl's growth" (p. 105). What she turns toward from that moment on is a position of inferiority.

The process may be summarized as follows. Because she considers herself already "castrated," a girl never experiences and then overcomes castration anxiety. Her Oedipal experience lacks the cathartic resolution of a boy's Oedipal crisis. As a result, her superego (the fruit of a successfully resolved Oedipus complex) is stunted. Throughout her life, she remains narcissistic, vain, and, above all, envious, for she can never overcome her bitterness over her castration. Furthermore, lacking a strong, mature superego, she is culturally inferior, since the ability to contribute to the advance of civilization depends on the mechanism of sublimation, which in turn depends on the superego. Thus, while men work at lofty pursuits, women remain mired in feelings of inferiority and efforts to compensate for it. If a woman is lucky, she will be rewarded with the ultimate compensation, a baby; if the baby is a boy, "who brings the longed-for penis with him" (Freud, 1932/1974, pp. 150, 154), all the better. But any baby is only a substitute: Because of women's perception of themselves as castrated, they remain, somehow, "other," a deviation from the norm of masculinity.

The opposition to this theory was first put forward in 1939 by post-Freudian theorist Karen Horney, who retorted that it is not little girls who perceive their condition as degraded. Rather, it is little boys—and the men they eventually become—who see their penisless counterparts as deficient. Horney also pointed out that, if girls are envious, what they probably envy is not a penis but, rather, the power that in most societies is reserved for men.

More recently, psychodynamic thinkers have proposed some sharply revised ideas of female development. What these thinkers have in common with Freud is the notion that the young child's attachment to its mother is of crucial importance to male or female development and that this attachment has a very different meaning for girls than for boys. Nancy Chodorow, in her book *The Reproduction of Mothering* (1978), stresses the differences between girls' and boys' early childhood environments. For both, the mother is the primary love object during early infancy. However, the girl's task is to internalize the feminine role, while the boy's task is to renounce an identification with femininity and differentiate from it in order to become masculine. Boys, therefore, place a premium on separation and individuation. Girls are less motivated to differentiate themselves and, consequently, have more difficulty with separation and individuation.

Another theorist in this mode is Carol Gilligan, author of *In a Different Voice* (1982), an influential book on girls' moral development. Like Chodorow, Gilligan sees boys' needs to separate from their mothers as responsible for a personality difference observable in adult men and women:

> For boys and men, separation and individuation are critically tied to gender identity since separation from the mother is essential for the development of masculinity. For girls and women, issues of femininity or feminine identity do not depend on the achievement of separation from the mother or on the progress of individuation. Since masculinity is defined through separation while femininity is defined through attachment, male gender identity is threatened by intimacy while female gender identity is threatened by separation. Thus males tend to have difficulty with relationships, while females tend to have problems with individuation. (p. 8)

In this view, the key crisis of early childhood is not the phallic conflict, but Margaret Mahler's "separation-individuation" crisis (see page 115). Girls, according to this theory, do *not* grow up into morally inferior penis enviers. They may, however, grow into adulthood with a greater need for close human attachments than many men have.

---

theory changed. Many of Freud's pupils and their pupils constructed new theories, extending and modifying his principles.

In this elaboration of Freud's theory, three trends are especially noteworthy. The first is the pronounced emphasis on the ego. Freud, while by no means ignoring the ego, gave special attention to the id. In general, later contributors to psychodynamic thought shifted the spotlight to the ego; that is, they deemphasized sex, instincts, and determinism and emphasized goals, creativity, and self-direction. Second, the post-Freudian thinkers tended to view the child's social relationships as the central determinant of normal and abnormal development. Again, this is hardly a subject ignored by Freud; the Oedipus/Electra complex is nothing if not a social drama. Still, Freud always viewed social interactions in relation to the strivings of the id. Later thinkers deemphasized the id and moved social interaction to center stage. Finally, later theorists tended to extend the period of critical developmental influences. Freud emphasized the phallic stages and especially the Oedipus/Electra complex.

Many subsequent thinkers have placed greater stress on infancy, while others see critical developmental junctures occurring well into adulthood.

Among the post-Freudian theorists, we will briefly consider two of Freud's students who dissented from his ideas—Carl Jung and Alfred Adler; two theorists who focused on interpersonal issues—Harry Stack Sullivan and Karen Horney; and two psychoanalysts who were pioneers in "ego psychology"—Heinz Hartmann and Erik Erikson. Finally, we will discuss Melanie Klein, Margaret Mahler, Heinz Kohut, John Bowlby, and Mary Ainsworth, whose theories have had a great impact on the field as it exists today.

Carl Gustav Jung Freud's most cherished pupil, Swiss psychiatrist Carl Gustav Jung (1875–1961), broke with him early in his career, claiming that Freudian theory was unduly negative and reductive. The main focus of the disagreement was the nature of the libido. Whereas Freud saw the energy of the psyche as primarily sexual, Jung viewed the libido as a much broader force, arguing (1935) that the mind contains not just the personal unconscious (that is, biological drives and childhood memories) but also a collective unconscious, a repository of "archetypes," or symbols, expressive of universal human experiences. This set of symbols, shared by all humankind, is the source of mythology and art, whose unity across cultures is explained by their common origin.

Alfred Adler Another member of Freud's inner circle who eventually broke with him was Alfred Adler (1870–1937). Like Jung, Adler believed that Freud had placed undue emphasis on sexual instincts. In Adler's view, the primary motivator of behavior is not the sexual drive but a striving to attain personal goals and overcome handicaps. (It was Adler who coined the term "inferiority complex.")

Adler's most important contribution, however, was his concern with the social context of personality. Psychological disturbance, he claimed, has its roots not so much in early childhood experiences as in people's present circumstances, particularly their relationships with others. Mature people are those who can resolve their power struggle and devote themselves selflessly to others.

Harry Stack Sullivan Like Adler, Harry Stack Sullivan (1892–1949), an American psychiatrist, believed that a person's psychological development is influenced by the surrounding social context. In particular, Sullivan considered the parent-child relationship crucial to the developing child's well-being. Children of rejecting parents develop severe anxiety about themselves—anxiety that makes it almost impossible to weather the threats to the self that are part of almost any close relationship. For people with disturbed family relationships, other human beings pose an overwhelming threat. In order to cope with this threat, the person either engages in rigid self-protecting behaviors (neurosis) or withdraws completely from other people (psychosis). In this view, psychological disturbance is an anxiety-motivated flight from human relationships.

In addition to elaborating the social theory of psychopathology, Sullivan was the first analyst to report significant success in the long-term psychoanalytic treatment of psychosis. The warm, supportive approach that he developed for this purpose has served as a model for later therapies that place people with psychosis in a benign environment for treatment (Chapter 14).

Karen Horney Another post-Freudian thinker who focused on social relationships was Karen Horney (1885–1952). According to Horney (1937), psychological disturbance is the result of basic anxiety, a pervasive view of the world as impersonal and cold.

Karen Horney diverged from Freud in her theory of female psychology. Horney asserted that men and women differ psychologically not because of penis envy, but because of the limited opportunities society affords to women.

This, in turn, is the product of a failed parent-child attachment. (Note how many post-Freudians conceptualize anxiety as stemming from a *lack* of parent-child intimacy, as opposed to the overintimacy postulated by the Oedipus/Electra complex.) Basic anxiety, as Horney saw it, leads to one of three "neurotic trends": moving away (shy, withdrawn behavior), moving toward (dependent, needy behavior), or moving against (hostile, aggressive behavior)—three patterns that cover most forms of psychopathology.

As the only woman among the early psychoanalytic thinkers, it was perhaps inevitable that Horney developed a theory of female psychology, one that departed from Freud's. (See the box on page 112.) Horney, like Freud, saw significant psychological differences between men and women, and competition between them, with men seeking to dominate women and women seeking to deceive and humiliate men. But, while Freud attributed this to penis envy, Horney proposed the more direct interpretation that it is due to men's greater prestige and wider opportunities in society.

Heinz Hartmann As noted, a critical trend in post-Freudian theory has been an increasing emphasis on ego functions. A milestone in this line of thought was Heinz Hartmann's *Ego Psychology and the Problem of Adaptation* (1939). Hartmann (1894–1970) argued that the ego develops independently of the id and has its own autonomous functions—in other words, functions that serve *ego* strivings, such as the need to adapt to reality, rather than id strivings. In particular, the mind's cognitive (mental-processing) operations, such as memory, perception, and learning, are, in Hartmann's (1939) view, "conflict-free" expressions of the ego. The id and the superego may help induce a child to go to school, for example, but only a relatively pure ego motivation can explain how the child learns to solve an algebra problem. Hartmann also felt that Freud overemphasized the role of conflict in mental life. If, in many of its basic operations, the ego is working for itself rather than mediating battles between the id and its opponents, then the life of the mind also has a "conflict-free sphere."

Hartmann's ideas were instrumental in the founding of a whole new school of **ego psychology,** which sees the development of personality as involving the formation of mental models of the world and how the world works (Vakoch & Strupp, 2000). Ego psychology has had a huge influence on psychoanalytic theory since World War II. Today many psychoanalytic writers focus on the ego and the interplay between its conflict-solving functions and its conflict-free functions, particularly cognitive processes. This shift has had the effect of bringing psychoanalysis closer to other branches of psychology, where cognitive processes have been commanding more attention in the past few decades.

Erik Erikson, shown with his wife Joan, proposed a theory of psychosocial development that extended and expanded Freud's psychosexual stages. According to Erikson, personality development continues throughout a person's lifetime.

Erik Erikson An important extension of ego psychology and of the social analysis of personality was the developmental theory put forth by Erik Erikson (1902–1994). To Erikson, the major drama of development is the formation of the ego identity, an integrated, unique, and autonomous sense of self. The ego identity is the product of what Erikson called psychosocial development. Like Freud's theory of psychosexual development, of which it is a deliberate revision, Erikson's psychosocial development proceeds through a series of chronological stages. But these stages differ from Freud's. In the first place, there are more of them. To Freud, the personality is essentially formed by the age of 6 or 7; to Erikson, personality development extends from birth to death. The second difference is the pronounced social emphasis of Erikson's theory, proclaimed in the term "psychosocial." While Freud saw the individual psyche in near isolation (except for the influence of parents and siblings), Erikson saw personality development as deeply affected not only by the family but also by teachers, friends, spouses, and many other social agents.

Third and most important is the central role of the ego in Erikson's developmental progression. Freud's stages have to do with challenges to id strivings; Erikson's stages have more to do with challenges to the ego. At each stage, there is a crisis—a conflict between the individual and the expectations now imposed by society. The ego is then called upon to

In Erikson's theory of psychosocial development, the primary task of the preschool child is to separate his or her identity from that of the mother. If successful, the child acquires the initiative to master a variety of skills.

resolve the crisis by learning new adaptive tasks. In the second year, for example, the child is faced with toilet training, a challenge that may lead to a new sense of self-reliance or, if the training is poorly handled, to feelings of shame and self-doubt.

Through this process of conflict resolution, the ego identity—the image of oneself as a unique, competent, and self-determining individual—is gradually formed. Or, if the ego fails to master the crisis, this failure will hamper identity formation and may generate psychological disorders. Erikson believed, however, that a failure at one stage does not guarantee failure at future stages. In his scheme, the ego is a resilient force, and there is always a second chance. Erikson's theory, thus, is more hopeful than Freud's scheme, where a serious childhood trauma can handicap a person for life.

Melanie Klein Certainly the most influential concept in contemporary psychodynamic thought is that of **object relations.** In psychodynamic terminology, "objects" are the people to whom one is attached by strong emotional ties. For the child, obviously, the chief object is the primary caretaker, usually the mother. And, according to object relations theorists, the most powerful determinant of psychological development is the child's interaction with the mother.

One founder of the object relations school, Melanie Klein (1882–1960), began to develop her ideas as she attempted to do psychoanalysis with children; Freud, in contrast, had worked primarily with adults. Using play therapy, Klein concluded that for children a major focus is developing models of the interpersonal world, particularly through their interactions with their mothers or primary caretakers. Central to this development of the self is the need to integrate conflicting feelings, such as love and hate, for the mother. If this process is successful, the child learns to react to the mother or caregiver with both love and hate, which provides the basis for the later development of empathy (as well as for feelings of guilt) (Vakoch & Strupp, 2000).

Margaret Mahler Another influential object relations theorist was Margaret Mahler (1897–1985). Mahler was concerned primarily with charting the process by which infants separate themselves psychologically from their mothers. Mahler saw newborns as having no sense of their own existence apart from their mothers. Then, at around 5 months, begins the long and sometimes wrenching process of separation-individuation. As conceptualized by Mahler, separation-individuation involves several stages, each marked by greater independence and greater ambivalence, as the child vacillates between pleasure and terror over his or her new separateness from the mother. This ambivalence is finally resolved between the ages of 2 and 3, when children achieve object constancy: They internalize the image of the mother—fix her in their minds so that she is no longer losable—and are thereby freed to consolidate a separate identity.

This, however, is the ideal scenario. Separation-individuation can be disturbed by many factors—above all by the mother, if she either hurries or resists the toddler's move toward independence. In any case, Mahler felt that the success with which the separation-individuation process is navigated determines the child's psychological future, since the features of

Margaret Mahler, like other object relations theorists, was interested in the process by which children gradually separate themselves psychologically from their mothers and become individuals in their own right.

this first, crucial relationship will be repeated in later intimate relationships.

Heinz Kohut Like Mahler, Heinz Kohut (1913–1981) was interested primarily in the psychological consequences of the parent-child relationship. In his practice as a therapist, Kohut encountered a great many patients who, though they shared similar problems—extreme demandingness and self-importance covering a very fragile self-esteem—seemed to fit no diagnostic category. He referred to this syndrome as narcissistic personality disorder (see Chapter 11). From his work with these patients, he built his so-called self psychology.

Kohut proposed that the development of the self, or core of the personality, depends on the child's receiving two essential psychological supports from the parents. One is the confirmation of the child's sense of vigor and "greatness." The other is a sense of calmness and infallibility: the feeling that there is nothing that the child can't handle. Parents communicate these things through the most ordinary daily behavior—by exclaiming over the artworks that their children bring home from school and by assuring them, when they are nervous over a test, that they can surely pass it. Thus the child will develop what Kohut and Wolf (1978) called a "healthy narcissism." But some parents cannot provide this support, and the result, for the child, is a damaged self. Thus, Kohut's theory, like Mahler's, differs from Freud's both in its interpersonal character and in its emphasis on cognitive and emotional rather than biological needs. Kohut and Mahler also place the critical events of early childhood well before the phallic stage, and this is the general trend in psychodynamic theory today.

John Bowlby and Mary Ainsworth One of the most influential forces in psychodynamic thought today is attachment theory, developed by English psychiatrist John Bowlby (1907–1991) with collaboration from psychologist Mary Ainsworth (b. 1913). Attachment theory is another example of the post-Freudian emphasis on social relationships. Bowlby was trained as a psychoanalyst, but eventually he discarded instinct theory and began adopting concepts from animal studies and cognitive psychology. In his influential trilogy *Attachment* (1969), *Separation* (1973), and *Loss* (1980), he put forth his theory that the basic determinant of adult personality is attachment, the affectional bond between the child and its primary caretaker. To grow up mentally healthy, he wrote, "the infant and young child should experience a warm, intimate, and continuous relationship with his mother (or permanent mother substitute) in which both find satisfaction and enjoyment" (1951, p. 13). In Bowlby's view, attachment is an emotional need, as opposed to the physical needs that Freud stressed, and it need not always be pleasurable. (The child might be firmly disciplined.) Basically, what the parent provided was a "secure base" of care to which the child could return, plus encouragement to explore the world beyond that base.

Bowlby estimated that as many as one third of all children did not have the kind of parenting that enabled them to form a secure attachment and that this predisposed them to problems in marriage and child rearing, for they would constantly perceive and interpret the behavior of those close to them according to the pattern of the old, faulty childhood attachment. He also believed that poor attachment led to adult disorders. For example, inadequate parental care could create the pattern of "anxious attachment" (insecurity, dependency), which in turn created a risk for phobias, hypochondriasis, and eating disorders. (People with "anxious attachment," Bowlby felt, were also apt to break down in the face of threats to later attachments.) Another pattern was "emotional detachment," the product not just of inadequate care but also of serious deprivation. Emotionally detached people, Bowlby felt, were at high risk for antisocial and hysterical personality disorders (Chapter 11).

Mary Ainsworth worked with Bowlby, beginning in the 1950s. Ainsworth (1967, 1982) conducted studies of infant-mother pairs in Uganda and the United States. Building on Bowlby's view, she theorized that a crucial component of attachment was the mother's sensitivity to the child's signals. Ainsworth also developed a reliable and valid method for testing attachment behavior: the so-called strange situation paradigm, in which children are observed as they are briefly separated from their mothers and exposed to strangers (Ainsworth & Wittig, 1969).

Prompted by attachment theory, researchers today are exploring the relationship between psychopathology and disturbed parent-child bonds. Recent research suggests that there is far more change or discontinuity in attachment patterns over the life span than Bowlby or Ainsworth expected. For example, early attachment patterns can improve when individuals experience later positive relationships or worsen after significant negative events (e.g., parental divorce or child abuse) (Waters, Merrick, Treboux, et al., 2000). Many researchers pay more attention to adult attachment patterns occurring close to the onset of psychological problems (Herzberg, Hammen, Burge, et al., 1999). For example, faulty adult attachment styles in romantic relationships are related to marital difficulties, problems in anger control, and difficulties in maintaining intimacy (Brennan & Shaver, 1998; Simpson, Rholes, et al., 1998). Faulty attachment patterns are also related to many personality disorders (Brennan & Shaver, 1998), mood disorders (Reinecke & Rogers, 2001; Rosenstein & Horowitz, 1996), and conduct or substance disorders (Allen, Hauser, & Borman-Spurrell, 1996), as well as to the severity of anxiety symptoms (Williams & Riskind, in press).

The Psychodynamic Approach to Therapy

Though psychoanalysis as practiced by Freud is rarely used today, it is, nevertheless, the grandfather of all psychodynamic therapies. Therefore, we will give this technique first consideration and then discuss its modern variants.

Freudian Psychoanalysis Freud's experience with his patients led him to conclude that the source of "neurosis" was anxiety experienced by the ego when unconscious material threatened to break through into the conscious mind. Thus, according to Freud, the proper treatment for neurosis was to coax the unconscious material out into consciousness so that the patient could at last confront it. Once acknowledged and "worked through," this material would lose its power to terrorize the ego. Self-defeating defenses could, accordingly, be abandoned, and the ego would then be free to devote itself to more constructive pursuits. As Freud succinctly put it, "Where id was, there shall ego be."

The client often lies on a couch, the better to relax, thus loosening the restraints on the unconscious, and the analyst typically sits outside of the client's field of vision. What the client then does is talk—usually for 50 minutes a day, 3 or 4 days a week, over a period of several years. The client may talk about his or her childhood, since it is there that the roots of the problem presumably lie, but present difficulties are also discussed. The analyst remains silent much of the time, so as not to derail the client's inner journey. When the analyst does speak, it is generally to interpret the client's remarks—that is, to point out their possible connection with unconscious material. This dialogue between client and therapist turns on four basic techniques: free association, dream interpretation, analysis of resistance, and analysis of transference (Vaughan & Roose, 1995).

Free Association Freud's primary route to the unconscious was free association, whereby the client simply verbalizes whatever thoughts come to mind, in whatever order they occur, taking care not to censor them either for logic or for propriety. The rationale is that the unconscious has its own logic and that, if clients report their thoughts exactly as they occur, the connective threads between verbalizations and unconscious impulses will be revealed. When such connections do become clear, the analyst points them out.

Dream Interpretation A second important tunnel to the unconscious is dream interpretation. Freud believed that, in sleep, the ego's defenses were lowered, allowing unconscious material to surface. But defenses are never completely abandoned; therefore,

This is the famous couch on which Freud's patients reclined while he analyzed them. Freud's chair was at the head of the couch, out of the patient's view. The comforts of the couch (note the pillows and coverlets) and the removal of the analyst from the patient's line of sight were intended to free the patient from inhibition in discussing intimate matters.

This painting by Henri Rousseau is titled The Dream. *Psychoanalytic methods encourage the client to report his or her dreams and then to free associate to the dream material. In light of the client's associations, the analyst interprets the dream, revealing its latent content, which will presumably center on unconscious conflicts.*

even in dreams repressed impulses reveal themselves only in symbolic fashion. Beneath the dream's manifest content, or surface meaning, lies its latent content, or unconscious understory. For example, one client, a depressed woman whose mother was verbally and physically abusive, reported a dream in which she saw a horse in a fenced-in area. A monkey kept jumping onto the horse's back, and the horse couldn't shake it off. According to the analyst, the latent content was that the horse was the client and the monkey on her back was her mother's constant criticism. The fenced-in area stood for her restricted self-esteem as a result of her domination by her mother (Glucksman, 1995, p. 189).

This is a simplified example, for dream interpretation normally involves free association. After the dream is reported, the analyst asks the client to free associate to its contents, and the resulting associations are taken as clues to the meaning of the dream.

Freud's Use of Dreams and Free Association

This MindMAP video focuses on how Freud studied the dreams of patients suffering from hysteria in order to uncover hidden trauma and used free association to elicit uncensored thoughts that might reveal unconscious impulses. Do you ever think that your dreams have hidden meaning?

Analysis of Resistance As clients are guided toward the unwelcome knowledge of their unconscious motivations, they may begin to show resistance, using various defenses to avoid confronting the painful material. They may change the subject, make jokes, or pick a fight with the analyst; they may even begin missing appointments. It is then the analyst's job to point out the resistance and, if possible, to interpret it—that is, to suggest what the patient is trying not to find out.

Analysis of Transference As psychoanalysis progresses, with the client revealing his or her secret life to the analyst, the relationship between the two partners becomes understandably complex. In his own practice, Freud noted that, while he tried to remain neutral, many of his patients began responding to him with very passionate emotions—sometimes with a childlike love and dependency, at other times with hostility and rebellion. Freud interpreted this phenomenon as a transference onto him of his clients' childhood feelings toward important people in their lives—above all, their feelings toward their parents.

Transference is an essential component of psychoanalysis. In fact, traditional analysts maintain that, in order for the therapeutic process to be successful, clients must go through a stage, called transference neurosis, of reenacting with the analyst their childhood conflicts with their parents, for it is these repressed conflicts that are typically undermining their adult relationships. The belief is that once these central emotions are brought out, clients have reached the core of the neurosis, which, with the analyst's help, they can then confront, evaluate realistically, and thereby overcome. This is a prime example of what psychoanalysts mean by the term "working through."

Research Highlights: A Cognitive Approach to Transference

According to psychodynamic theory, important people in our lives, such as our parents, are represented unconsciously in our memories and exert an influence on our thoughts and behavior. One such influence occurs in psychotherapy, where the conflicts and anxieties attached to these relationships can be unknowingly directed toward the therapist. Freud thought that his patients actually began to treat him as their father, a process that he called transference.

From the perspective of cognitive psychology, important people in our lives are represented in memory as schemas that contain not only memories of a person's appearance and identity but also potentially intense feelings toward the person. When we meet individuals who resemble people in our past, we assimilate the new people to the schemas we have formed from our past relationships. As a result, we expect people who resemble important others from our past to behave as those others did, and we experience feelings toward those individuals that are similar to the feelings associated with the people we already know. This expectation, based on cognitive psychology, is similar to the psychodynamic concept of transference. It has been tested in several experiments.

In one study, a pretest session was held 2 weeks before the experiment (Glassman & Andersen, 1999), during which 121 undergraduates (76 women and 45 men) were asked to describe an important person in their lives, someone who had been important to them for many years (e.g., a parent, another relative, or an old friend). Glassman and Andersen assessed the "significant-other representations" of the selected person by asking research participants to pick trait descriptors that they believed were good descriptors for that person (such as outgoing), poor descriptors (such as shy), or irrelevant to the description of that person (such as vain).

Unknown to these research participants, when they arrived for a presumably unrelated experiment a week later, they were actually taking part in an extension of the pretest session. In this second session, participants were told that they would play a computer game with a person seated at a terminal somewhere else in the building. In this game, participants were told, the other person would attempt to send them, over the computer, self-descriptive statements. (No other person was actually at another terminal.) While participants played the game, subliminal cues were flashed on the computer screen that either contained features from their own description of the selected important person in their lives or features from someone else's "significant other." Afterward, in an impression-rating task, participants whose screens had flashed cues describing their own significant other were more likely to ascribe additional significant-other features to their game partner, even though such features had not been presented subliminally. In other words, significant-other representations were activated without the participants' awareness and led participants to use the representations to infer unconsciously that their game partners had qualities that they might not in fact possess. In effect, participants seemed to confuse what they had objectively learned about the game partner with what they inferred on the basis of the activated significant-other presentation.

In many respects, these results reproduce the phenomenon of transference in a simple laboratory analogue to what might occur in psychotherapy. From the psychodynamic perspective, the question of whether transference has taken place in a therapist-client relationship can be answered only qualitatively or subjectively. Cognitive psychology, on the other hand, proposes that the evaluation of transference can be addressed through answers to specific questions—a hypothesis that can be tested through experiment.

Modern Psychodynamic Therapy Most of today's psychodynamic therapists practice a considerably modified form of psychoanalysis, often based not only on Freud's theory but also on the theories of his followers and of later thinkers (Brenner, 1982; Mitchell, 1988). They depart from orthodox psychoanalytic techniques in several important respects. First, they generally take a more active part in the therapy session, dealing with the client face-to-face (the couch is seldom used) and speaking and advising much more extensively than Freud would have considered appropriate. For example, a therapist in a psychoanalytic session might say something like the following:

> So far, what hits me between the eyes about your depression is how many losses you've had that you haven't mourned and how much your family discouraged your feeling sad by their criticism of your "feeling sorry for yourself." You might find you have some anger about that and other things that you haven't felt comfortable about admitting, and if we can access the grief and the anger, your depression may lift. Also, there is some evidence of a depressive streak that's congenital in your family and it doesn't sound like you've had anybody address that and help you cope by learning what situations tend to depress you and why. How does this sound to you?" (McWilliams, 1999, p. 43).

Second, as this example demonstrates, while the client's past is by no means ignored, modern psychodynamic therapists generally pay more attention to the client's present life, especially his or her personal relationships. Finally, most psychodynamic treatment today is briefer and less intensive than orthodox psychoanalysis. Therapist and client typically meet once or twice a week for anywhere from a few months to a few years. This broad category of therapy is probably the most common form of psychological treatment in the United States.

Evaluating the Psychodynamic Perspective

Research on Defense Mechanisms and Unconscious Processes The concepts of defense mechanisms and unconscious processes were long taboo in many areas of psychology, in part because many psychologists hesitated to accept the Freudian notion of unconscious mental processes. Today, due to evidence from research, there is more widespread acceptance of such processes, although they are understood in terms of cognitive automaticity, (Bargh & Ferguson, 2000), rather than as defense mechanisms over basic drives. Thus, the modern view of unconscious processes is not precisely the same as the view proposed by Freud.

The concept of defense mechanisms, too, has changed. In early psychodynamic theory, defenses had the rather limited function of managing anxiety about forbidden thoughts and impulses related to basic drives, such as sex and aggression. In contrast, contemporary psychodynamic theories define defense functions more broadly to include defenses of self-esteem and identity—and, in the extremes, the integration of the self (Cooper, 1998).

A major task in the study of defense mechanisms today is sorting out distinctions between different kinds of defenses (Norem, 1998). In effect, a classification system is needed for the hundreds of different defense mechanisms that have been proposed over the last century. It is often unclear how these defenses differ from each other and which distinctions are meaningful.

An important distinction is often drawn between defense mechanisms and coping (Lazarus & Folkman, 1984; Cramer, 1998). A defense mechanism is presumed to be an unconsciously motivated means of decreasing anxiety. Coping, on the other hand, entails conscious mental activity and has as its purpose solving objective problems realistically.

Defense mechanisms have been the subject of many studies. For example, researchers have found that individuals use more mature defenses over time. Vaillant (1976) examined Harvard men during late adolescence, in early adulthood (ages 20–35), and in midlife (over age 35). Consistent with psychodynamic theory, Vaillant found that the use of immature defenses (such as denial) decreased, and the use of mature defenses (such as humor and intellectualization) increased, with age. Vaillant and Drake (1985) have found support for the psychodynamic view that there are strong associations between levels of defense maturity and measures of psychological adjustment-maladjustment and of personality disorder.

Social psychologists also have found evidence for defense mechanisms. Baumeister, Dale, and Somer (1998) reviewed recent studies in social psychology for evidence of Freudian defense mechanisms. The work was done mainly in normal rather than in clinical populations, and researchers studied moderate rather than extreme forms of defense mechanisms. Even so, researchers concluded that reaction formation, isolation, and denial are consistently found and seem to serve defense functions. The Freudian defense of undoing, as reflected in imagining alternative scenarios to those that actually happened, is also amply documented, though it does not seem to serve a defensive function. Likewise, although researchers found evidence of projection, it seems to be a by-product of defense, and not a defense itself.

Criticisms of Psychodynamic Theory

Lack of Experimental Support The most common criticism of the psychodynamic position is that most of its claims have never been tested in scientifically controlled experiments. Freud's theories were based on clinical evidence—that is, observations of patients in therapy—and today psychodynamic writers still tend to rely on case studies to support their formulations. The problem with case studies is that they are open to bias. We can never know to what degree psychodynamic therapists' expectations color the patient's responses or their reporting of those responses.

The reason psychodynamic writers have depended on clinical evidence rather than controlled experiments is that most of the phenomena they deal with are too complex to be testable by current experimental techniques (Erdelyi & Goldberg, 1979). Furthermore, most of these phenomena are unconscious and, hence, inaccessible to direct testing. Nevertheless, some of Freud's most basic claims have been subjected to research and have been validated (Andersen, 1992; Fried, Crits-Christoph, & Luborsky, 1992; Holmes, 1978). Experiments have shown, for example, that dreams do allow people to vent emotional tension; that children do go through a period of erotic interest in the parent of the opposite sex, accompanied by hostile feelings toward the same-sex parent; that people do transfer feelings about those close to them in the past onto new people; and that bringing implicit perceptions and memories into conscious awareness does lead to more adaptive behavior. Likewise, recent research has shown that many of the basic methods of psychodynamic "insight" therapy do have the intended result of revealing core issues and fostering positive change (Anderson & Lambert, 1995; Bornstein, 1993a, 1993b; Grenyer & Luborsky, 1996).

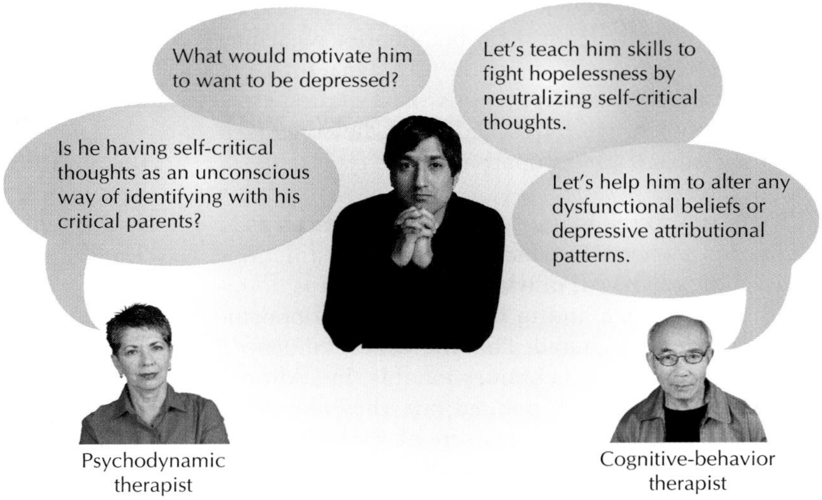

FIGURE 5.1 An example of how a psychotherapist and a cognitive-behavioral therapist might treat a person with symptoms of depression. Efforts by psychodynamic theorists and therapists to incorporate elements of the cognitive and behavioral approaches in the psychodynamic approach suggests that these schools might not be as far apart as psychologists once thought.

In other cases, the evidence contradicts Freudian theory. For example, there is little or no support for Freud's claim that dreams represent wish fulfillment or that women regard their bodies as inferior to men's because they lack penises. (Most of Freud's conclusions regarding specifically female sexuality have been contradicted by research [Fisher & Greenberg, 1977].) Likewise, little or no support has been found for Freud's proposed psychosexual stages of development. However, the important point is that psychodynamic theory is not altogether closed to empirical testing, and in some cases, it holds up well under such testing. Indeed, without intending to test psychodynamic theory, experimental psychologists have turned up evidence in support of many of Freud's positions—for example, that many of our mental contents are unconscious; that under normal conditions some of our unconscious mental contents are accessible to us, while others are not (Kihlstrom, 1987; Westen, 2000); and that many of the causes of our behavior are inaccessible (Bargh & Ferguson, 2000).

Recent social-cognitive studies are giving new life to some psychoanalytic concepts (see the box on transference, page 119). This work raises the tantalizing possibility of bringing these psychoanalytic/dynamic concepts and the cognitive perspective closer together over common ground. (See Figure 5.1 above.)

At the same time, psychodynamic psychologists have sought to find ways to reinvigorate or revitalize the approach. For example, Wachtel (1997) has emphasized the value of bringing behavioral techniques into psychodynamic therapy; Westen (2000) has highlighted the value of integrating social-cognition research with psychodynamic theory; and Kandel (1999) has urged that the theory be integrated with cognitive neuroscience (see Chapter 6).

Dependence on Inference A second, related criticism of the psychodynamic approach is that, because it assumes that most mental processes are unconscious, it must depend on inference, and inference can easily be mistaken. Indeed, the psychodynamic view of the relationship between behavior and mental processes is so complicated and indirect that behaviors could be taken to mean whatever the psychodynamic interpreter wants them to mean. If a 6-year-old boy expresses great love for his mother, it could be interpreted as a sign of Oedipal attachment. However, if the same 6-year-old boy expresses hatred for his mother, it could also be interpreted as an expression of Oedipal attachment, via reaction formation. It should be added, however, that responsible analysts rarely, if ever, draw conclusions on the basis of one piece of evidence alone.

Recent research by Luborsky and colleagues tries to address such criticisms (Luborsky & Crits-Christoph, 1998). Their method for independently coding what they call "core conflictual relationship themes" from transcripts of psychotherapy sessions has uncovered evidence suggesting that the more accurate therapists are in their interpretations—as defined by the agreement of independent raters with the therapists—the more positive the psychotherapeutic outcome.

Unrepresentative Sampling and Cultural Bias Another point on which psychodynamic theory has been criticized is that it is based on the study of a very limited sample of humanity. In most of Freud's published cases, the patients were upper-middle-class Viennese women between the ages of 20 and 44 (Fisher & Greenberg, 1977). Though these people were adults, Freud drew from them his theories regarding the child's psyche. (He never studied children in any systematic way.) Though they had serious emotional problems, he drew from them his theories regarding normal development. Though they lived in a time and place in which overt expressions of sexuality, especially by women, were frowned upon, he concluded that their sexual preoccupations were typical of all human beings.

There is also the matter of Freud's cultural biases. He lived in a society in which social-class distinctions were rigidly observed, in which the family was dominated by the father, and in which women's opportunities were strictly limited. That these facts influenced his patients' thoughts is unquestionable. In addition, as Erich Fromm (1980) pointed out, they may have influenced Freud's interpretation of that evidence, leading him to see more repression, more sexual motivation, and more "penis envy" than are actually universal properties of the human psyche.

Reductiveness It has been argued that psychodynamic theory has handed down to the twenty-first century an exceedingly dismal vision of human life—a reductive vision—in which the human being is driven by animal instincts beyond his or her conscious control, in which people are virtually helpless to change themselves after the die is cast in early childhood, in which acts of heroism or generosity are actually disguised outgrowths of baser motives, and in which all that most people can know of their own minds is the surface, while the true causes of their behavior remain sealed up in the dark chambers of the unconscious.

Many of these positions, it should be recalled, have been substantially modified by later psychodynamic theorists. Furthermore, even if that were not the case, it is not the duty of science to produce a comforting picture of life, only a true one. As it happens, Freud found much to admire in the human psyche he envisioned. If the ego could fashion civilization out of the base materials the id provided, then the ego was a heroic force, indeed.

Pessimism Psychodynamic theory is also seen as more pessimistic than many modern therapies, including cognitive-behavioral therapy, even by psychodynamic writers (Vakoch & Strupp, 2000; Westen, 2000). As Vakoch and Strupp (2000) point out, psychodynamic therapists tend to emphasize patients' deficiencies, compatible with their more "tragic vision" of life and "pessimistic view of the world." Likewise, psychodynamic therapists emphasize patients' feelings of guilt more often than cognitive-behavioral therapists do. A related criticism is that psychodynamic theory trends to rely too heavily on vague and often unspecified or unspecifiable concepts, such as "narcissistic vulnerability" or "self pathology" (Westen, 2000). Psychodynamic therapy has also been criticized for encouraging passivity and lack of responsibility in patients (May, 1990).

The Contributions of Psychodynamic Theory Psychodynamic therapy provided an extraordinary set of insights into the irrationality of human motivation (Kandel, 1999). At the same time, it helped to set the stage for modern views about the continuity between normal and abnormal behavior. By arguing that the most "crazy" behaviors have their roots in the same mental processes as the most "sane" behaviors, Freud contributed greatly to the modern effort to treat the mentally disturbed as human beings rather than as freaks. Furthermore, by pointing out what he called the "psychopathology of everyday life"—the ways in which irrational and unconscious impulses emerge in dreams, in jokes, in slips of the tongue, in our ways of forgetting what we want to forget—Freud showed that the mentally disturbed have no monopoly on irrationality. This aspect of psychodynamic theory helped to establish the concept of mental health as a continuum ranging from adaptive to maladaptive rather than as a dichotomy of "sick" and "healthy."

While modern thinkers are still arguing with Freud, no one can deny his impact on the contemporary conceptualization, assessment, and treatment of abnormal behavior. It is Freudian theory that is responsible for the widespread assumption that abnormal behavior stems from events in the individual's past and that it occurs in response to unconscious and uncontrollable impulses. In terms of psychological assessment, the widely used projective tests, such as the Rorschach (Chapter 2), are based on the Freudian notion that behavior is symbolic and that what a person reads into a picture or an event is actually a reading of his or her own psyche.

The impact of psychodynamic theory has been felt far beyond the field of professional psychology. Freud directed the attention of the twentieth century to the gap between the outer life and the inner life—to dreams, fantasies, and memory, as well as to how these factors guide our behavior. In doing so, he changed not only psychology but art, literature, history, and education. Indeed, he altered popular thinking. Today, people who have never read a word by Freud show no hesitation in explaining their problems in terms of their childhood experience, in viewing their own children's development as crucial prefigurations of their adult lives, or in using such terms as "repressed," "rationalization," and "ego." Freud radically altered the Western conception of the human mind. The same cannot be said of any other psychological theorist.

The Humanistic-Existential Perspective

The **humanistic-existential perspective** is both an outgrowth of and a reaction to the psychodynamic perspective. Indeed, many founders of the humanistic-existential movement were trained as psychoanalysts. However, they came to view psychodynamic theory as seriously inadequate. Many humanistic-existential thinkers were repelled by the Freudian idea that good adjustment means adapting to one's society, however questionable its values. Above all, many humanistic and existential thinkers took exception to the pessimistic determinism of the psychodynamic approach—the idea that human behavior is the product of forces beyond the conscious control (and often the knowledge) of the person. For these theorists, considering the "whole person" meant putting the spotlight on positive, more optimistic aspects of human potential for health, creativity, and constructive living.

Because these humanistic-existential theorists are highly individualistic and distinct, even from each other, they can only loosely be defined as a single school of thought, or even as two schools of thought. Our discussion will focus on the views of two humanistic theorists whose work laid the foundation for the contemporary humanistic-existential perspective: Carl Rogers and Abraham Maslow.

Basic Assumptions

The humanists and existentialists see a fundamental distinction between the natural sciences, which treat their subject matter as material "things," and the human sciences, which study subjective, dynamic processes. The humanists and existentialists believe that psychological theories of specifically human characteristics—such as authenticity and alienation—require a set of assumptions different from that of the natural sciences. To differing degrees, the humanists and existentialists agree on three basic premises and fault psychodynamic theories for failing to recognize them: the importance of understanding and entering into the patient's subjective world (the phenomenological approach); the promise of human potential and its uniqueness; and the importance of authenticity and its relation to freedom and responsibility.

The Phenomenological Approach Psychoanalytic theorists discount the significance of the conscious subjective world of the individual, seeing it as a surface that disguises the important hidden forces of the mind. Such thinkers accuse psychoanalytic therapists who engage in interpretation of the client's deep motivations and hidden conflicts of projecting their own interpretations, or even conflicts, onto patients. As existential theorist Rollo May asked (1959, p. 3), "Can we be sure . . . that we are seeing the patient as he really is, knowing him in his own reality; or are we seeing merely a projection of our own theories about him?" This question points to a central assumption of the humanistic-existential psychology: that the therapist cannot adequately understand the individual by interpreting the person with the detachment envisioned by psychodynamic theory, but must enter into, and understand, the patient's own perceptions and subjectively experienced world. This method, known as the **phenomenological approach,** means trying to see the world through clients' own perceptions and subjective experience.

Human Potential and Uniqueness The humanists and existentialists see the individual as a work in progress throughout life rather than as the unchangeable product of early childhood experiences. They place great emphasis on human potential—the ability of individuals to become what they want to be and fulfill their capabilities. Moreover, as each person experiences and perceives the world in a special way and participates in his or her own "self-creation," each person is unique. Hence, to reduce an individual to a set of formulas, whether behavioral or psychodynamic, is to see only a very limited portion of his or her being. While human behavior may follow certain rules, such rules can never define a human life.

Authenticity, Freedom, and Responsibility Humans, like other animals, are influenced by external realities beyond their control. But unlike other animals, people are gifted (and burdened) with self-awareness. This self-awareness allows us to transcend our biological impulses and to choose what we will ultimately make of our lives. By so doing, we can act as architects of our own destinies. The corollary of this freedom is that we are also ultimately responsible for the authenticity or inauthenticity of our lives. One branch of the existential movement emphasizes that authenticity requires being in touch with and experiencing one's own emotions and feelings in encounters with other people and life (Perls, 1973).

Humanistic Psychology

In contrast to the relatively pessimistic view of human potential adopted by psychodynamic theorists, the humanists put forward an emphatically positive vision of the human being. For example, whereas Freud saw the individual as motivated, from earliest

Focus On... Positive Psychology

The **positive psychology** movement, which focuses on helping people to live more fulfilling lives, has caught the attention of many practitioners today. The movement developed out of humanistic psychology and cognitive-behavioral therapy and contains elements of both.

Positive psychology is based on the belief that psychology is not just the study of disease, weakness, and damage; it is also the study of strength and virtue (Seligman & Csikzentmihalyi, 2000). Positive psychologists believe that psychology's preoccupation with identifying, undoing, and preventing damage has blinded practitioners to human strength. They call for a psychology that teaches people how to enhance the qualities that are the most likely buffers against mental illness: hope, resilience, persistence, future-mindedness, and courage (Gillham & Seligman, 1999).

As we saw in Chapter 4, a great deal of research indicates that positive outlooks and emotions are beneficial to psychological and physical health (Taylor, Kemeny, Reed, et al., 2000). The "nun study," a longitudinal study of the links between lifestyle and aging, provides additional interesting evidence for this idea.

Since 1986, David Snowdon and his colleagues have been studying 678 retired nuns living in Mankato, Minnesota. The women in the study are all School Sisters of Notre Dame who were born before 1917; when the study began, their average age was 85. Willing participants in the research project, the nuns granted open access to all of their medical and personal records and even agreed to donate their brains for study after their deaths.

When researchers analyzed the verbal content of the short autobiographies nearly 200 of the nuns had written on first taking their orders, they discovered a strong association between the positive emotional content in the nuns' early writings and their longevity six decades later (Danner, Snowdon, & Friesen, 2001). A significant association was also found between a high density of ideas (as evidenced by complex language structure) in the sisters' early writing and in their later experience of aging (Snowdon, Greiner, & Markesbery, 2000). Those sisters who, as young women, had more complex language structure and more positive emotions had increased longevity and less cognitive impairment with age. Further, nuns who had continued to teach most of their lives, and therefore presumably continued to exercise their intellectual functions, showed more positive outcomes than those who had not. The nun study demonstrates the exciting information that can be obtained by paying attention to the role an individual's strengths play in his or her mental health.

childhood, by basically selfish and irrational forces of the unconscious, humanists hold that if people are allowed to develop freely, without undue constraints, they will become rational, socialized, and constructive beings who are motivated to fulfill a higher vision of their capabilities. Of the humanists with this optimistic vision, the two most influential have been Carl Rogers and Abraham Maslow.

Rogers: The Motive To Self-Actualize Unlike psychodynamic theorists, who see behavior as a compromise among three opposing forces in the personality, Carl Rogers (1902–1987) saw all behavior as motivated by a single overriding positive force, the actualizing tendency. The actualizing tendency is the desire to preserve and enhance oneself. On one level, it includes the drive simply to stay alive, by eating, keeping warm, and avoiding physical danger. On the highest level, the actualizing tendency includes people's desire to test and fulfill their vision of their highest capabilities: to seek out new experiences, to master new skills, to find more fulfilling jobs and relationships, and so on. This process of exploring and fulfilling one's potential is called **self-actualization.**

In the course of pursuing self-actualization, people engage in what Rogers called the **valuing process.** Experiences that are perceived as enhancing to oneself are valued as good and are therefore sought after. Experiences perceived as not enhancing are valued as bad and are avoided. In other words, people know what is good for them.

Rogers believed that the degree of self-actualization that we achieve depends on the degree of congruence,

Carl Rogers, one of the architects of the humanistic perspective, emphasized the individual's capacity for personal growth and self-actualization.

or accurate fit, between our self-image (or self-concept) and our total perceptions of our experience, both internal and external. If the self-image is flexible and realistic enough to allow us to acknowledge and evaluate all our experience (such as anger and jealousy, as well as happiness and joy), then we are in an excellent position to pursue those experiences that are most enhancing and actualizing.

What determines whether we will become self-actualizing? The decisive factor is childhood experience. As children become aware of themselves, they automatically develop the need for what Rogers called **positive regard**—that is, affection and approval from the important people in their lives, particularly their parents. Invariably, however, positive regard comes with strings attached: To be loved, the child must be mild-mannered, assertive, boyish, girlish, or whatever. These extraneous values, dictating which of the child's self-experiences are "good" and which are "bad", are incorporated as **conditions of worth.** If the conditions are few and reasonable, then the child will entertain a variety of experiences. If, however, the conditions of worth are severely limiting, screening out large portions of the child's experience, then they will seriously impede self-actualization.

The latter situation is, according to Rogers, the source of abnormal behavior. As external conditions of worth come to control more and more of a person's behavior, a gap opens between the person's actions and his or her true self. The person automatically covers over this split with perceptual distortions, denying the conflict between self and reality. As in the case of Freudian defense, such distortions can lead to personality breakdown. Rogers (1980) cited the case of a woman who, raised to be gentle and docile, grew up denying to herself that she ever felt angry. When at last she discovered angry feelings in herself, it was as if an "alien" had taken over her consciousness; in fact, the alien was a screened-out part of herself.

To undo such damage, Rogers developed a technique that he called **client-centered therapy.*** Briefly, what the client-centered therapist does is create for the patient a warm and accepting atmosphere, by mirroring whatever feelings the patient expresses, by attempting to perceive the patient's world as he or she does, and most of all by offering the patient unconditional positive regard—respect and approval, with no conditions of worth. In this accepting atmosphere, the patient can at last confront feelings and experiences that are inconsistent with the self—a process that will result in the broadening of the self to include the total experience of the organism. The self and the organism are thereby brought back into congruence, and the patient is free to "*be,* in a more unified fashion, what he organismically *is*" (Rogers, 1955, p. 269). Thus freed, the patient can once again proceed with self-actualization.

Maslow: The Hierarchy of Needs Like Rogers, Abraham Maslow (1908–1970) started out with the premises that human beings are basically good and that all their behavior issues from a single master motive, the drive toward self-actualization. Maslow's special contribution to the humanistic program was his concept of the **hierarchy of needs,** a series of needs that must be met in the process of development before the adult can begin to pursue self-actualization. (See Figure 5.2.)

Maslow proposed five levels of needs, each of which must be satisfied before a person can proceed to the next level. First are the biological needs, the need for physical comfort and survival. Second are the safety needs, the need for a stable and predictable environment. The third level is the need for belongingness and love—that is, warm relationships with friends and family. At the fourth level are the esteem needs, which impel the person to seek the respect of others and eventually to create an internal fund of self-esteem. Finally, having fulfilled these prior needs, the person can proceed to the fifth level and begin fulfilling the need for self-actualization. "People who are at this level of motivational development . . . are in a very high degree spontaneous, guileless, open, self-disclosing, and unedited and therefore expressive" (Maslow, 1987, p. 66). Maslow also identified fourteen characteristics, called B-values (B for "being"), that he felt defined self-actualized people (see Table 5.1). For Maslow, as for Rogers, abnormality consists essentially of being blocked in the drive toward self-actualization.

This represents a unique outlook on psychopathology. What both Rogers and Maslow were concerned with was not really abnormality, but rather the failure to progress beyond the minimum acceptable standards of normality. According to Maslow, a man might hold down a job, take care of his children, differentiate between the real and the imaginary, and yet still feel lonely, alienated, and ineffectual—a situation Maslow called "the psychopathology of the normal." Human beings, Maslow argued, require a great deal more than mere "adjustment." Hence, psychology should address itself not just to repairing "breakdowns" but also

*"Client-centered" was Rogers' original term for his therapy, and since it is the familiar term, it is the one that will appear in this book. Rogers later began to call his approach *person*-centered rather than *client*-centered to indicate his belief that the same principles apply in all human interaction, not just in the relations between therapist and client.

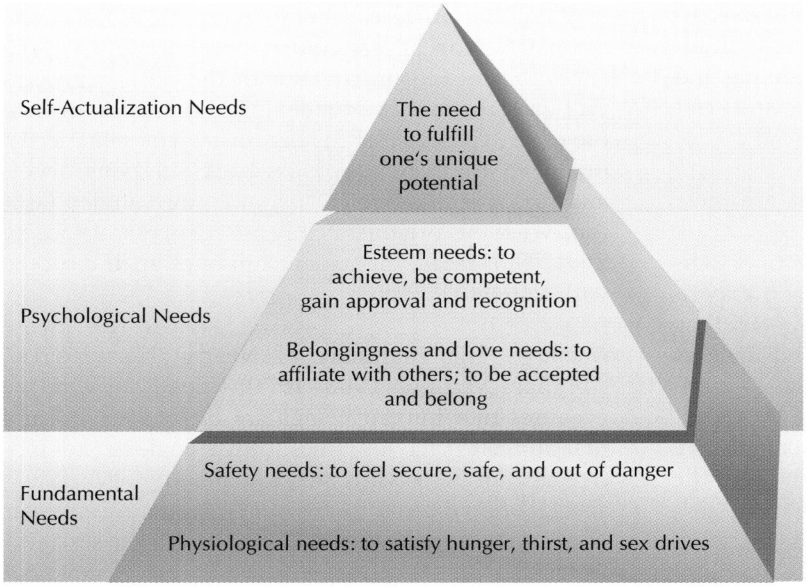
Self-Actualization Needs
The need to fulfill one's unique potential
Esteem needs: to achieve, be competent, gain approval and recognition
Psychological Needs
Belongingness and love needs: to affiliate with others; to be accepted and belong
Safety needs: to feel secure, safe, and out of danger
Fundamental Needs
Physiological needs: to satisfy hunger, thirst, and sex drives

FIGURE 5.2 Maslow's hierarchy of needs. According to Maslow, fundamental needs must be satisfied before a person is free to progress to psychological needs, and these in turn must be satisfied before a person can turn to self-actualization needs.

to helping people live rich, creative lives. This preoccupation with self-fulfillment, more than anything else, sets the humanistic school apart from other schools of abnormal psychology, most of which are chiefly concerned with repairing actual damage.

TABLE 5.1 Maslow's 14 B-Values

Aliveness	The desire to be part of the surrounding world and appreciate life
Autonomy	The need to direct one's own life
Beauty	The tendency to surround oneself with aesthetical, pleasing environments
Completion	The desire to persevere and see projects through to their end
Effortlessness	The preference for adopting straightforward, pragmatic solutions to problems
Goodness	A tolerance for others and a belief in the worth of all individuals
Humor	The ability to laugh at oneself and life's circumstances rather than belittling others
Justice	A belief in fairness and democratic principles
Perfection	The desire to do a task right, not to make do or settle for mediocrity
Simplicity	A preference for unpretentious, genuine lifestyles
Totality	A need to place oneself in a social context; a nonegotistical interest in others
Truth	An openness to novel ideas; a greater tolerance for ambiguity
Uniqueness	A desire to lead one's own life rather than follow social conventions or fads
Wholeness	The ability to accept the good with the bad and to accept all aspects of self

Existential Psychology

The views of existential psychologists such as Rollo May and Viktor Frankl were strongly influenced by European existential philosophy, with its emphasis on the difficulty of living authentically in the modern world. In the existentialist view, human beings, in their rush to obtain the material comforts offered by modern technology, have abandoned their values and lost their sense of personal responsibility. People in the modern world do not choose; they conform and follow. And by conforming, they fail to genuinely experience who they are and what they feel. The result is inauthenticity and a denial of the true self. This condition, which the existentialists call **alienation,** is a sort of spiritual death, in which the person is haunted by a sense of the ultimate meaninglessness of life and by terror over the nothingness that will come with death. Because it seemed to speak to the alienation of millions of people living in modern times, existential psychology gained considerable attention during the 1960s and 1970s.

The process-experiential approach is a recent offshoot of the humanistic-existential approach. It strongly emphasizes the role of emotion, and especially avoidance of painful emotions, in psychological maladjustment. Theorists focus on the need for curative, intense experiencing of unwanted and excluded, or overregulated, emotions, and their integration into the whole of the personality (Elliott & Greenberg, 1995). The goal of process-experiential therapy is to remove the blocks that prevent clients from experiencing emotions and facilitate change and greater integration of emotional experience.

The Interpersonal Perspective

The **interpersonal perspective** is actually not just one but several approaches. They all emphasize the importance of relationships with others for psychological adjustment. Although most therapeutic approaches deal in some way with the interpersonal dimensions of psychological problems, interpersonal theorists explicitly address, and place special emphasis on, interpersonal processes in abnormal behavior.

As we saw, Henry Stack Sullivan was one of the first theorists to systematically develop an interpersonal approach to psychiatric disorders. Other theorists have developed interpersonal approaches tailored to specific disorders, including schizophrenia (Bateson, Jackson, Halley, et al., 1956; Goldstein & Miklowitz, 1995) and depression (Coyne, 1990; Joiner, Alfano, & Metalsky, 1992).

Researchers have found ample evidence documenting the adverse effect unfavorable interpersonal environments can have on psychological well-being. For example, a variety of psychological disorders (e.g., substance abuse, depression, panic disorder) are associated with marital difficulties and inadequate support from social networks (Tiller, Sloan, Schmidt, et al., 1997; Gotlib & Schraedley, 2000).

Such findings on the psychological impact of disturbed relationships, and the seminal work of theorists such as Sullivan, have led to the development of several interpersonal approaches to psychotherapy. Here we will focus on one important approach, the interpersonal therapy (IPT) developed by Klerman and his colleagues (Klerman, Weissman, Rounsaville, et al., 1984).

Initially conceived for the treatment of depression, interpersonal psychotherapy has also been used to treat bulimia and several other disorders (Fairburn, Jones, Peveler, et al., 1993).

A cornerstone of the IPT approach is the belief that interpersonal functioning provides a primary therapeutic mechanism for improvement and relief from symptoms. IPT emphasizes several kinds of interpersonal problems that can affect current relationships. Thus, the focus is on the here and now, not the past. IPT is used with problems such as unresolved grief, role disputes, changes in roles, and interpersonal deficits. For example, unresolved grief over a prior loss is addressed in IPT by promoting a healthy grieving process and by encouraging the person to develop new relationships. The IPT approach to role disputes involves helping the patient negotiate disputes with other people, or learn to get beyond hostility when he or she is at an angry impasse with others. Role changes are dealt with by helping the patient to leave the old roles, mourn them if necessary, and view new roles in a positive light. For example, a mother who is faced with an "empty nest" could learn to see her new role without dependent children in the house as an opportunity to resume an interrupted career or cultivate interests for which she previously had little time. Interpersonal deficits are addressed by helping the individual deal with a lack of social skills, or with broader patterns of social isolation, that prevent him or her from having adequate relationships with others. Like cognitive-behavior therapy, IPT is designed as a time-limited, focused therapy that may last only 12 to 16 weeks.

Interpersonal therapy (IPT) can help "empty nesters" to adjust to life without dependent children by encouraging them to cultivate new interests or resume an interupted career.

Integrating the Perspectives

Although there are significant differences between the six theoretical perspectives described in Chapters 4 and 5, these approaches are not simply competing ways to look at abnormal behavior. In some cases, they are complementary or even convergent views. Echoes of the same core themes show up in different approaches, even if they have a different thrust. For example, ego psychology, object relations theory, cognitive therapy, and interpersonal therapy all emphasize mental representational models, or schema, of interpersonal relationships. A core thread concerned with the construction of personal meaning runs through the humanistic-existential perspective and some cognitive and psychodynamic perspectives. Finally, an interpersonal theme crops up in several modern perspectives, and some theorists have suggested that the interpersonal approach is a way to integrate the often quarrelsome perspectives (Kieseler, 1992).

Some theorists can be linked to more than one school. For instance, Henry Stack Sullivan is known as a post-Freudian, psychodynamic thinker—but he is also a father of the interpersonal school of psychotherapy. Finally, most modern perspectives in the field are not finished products, but continue to evolve even now, and reciprocally influence each other.

As we will see in Chapter 6, many of these theoretical perspectives can also be more broadly understood in terms of the "diathesis-stress model" (also called the vulnerability-stress model). This model recognizes that most disorders have a combination of internal and external causes.

Key Terms

alienation, 126
anal stage, 110
anxiety, 108
castration anxiety, 111
client-centered therapy, 125
conditions of worth, 125
defense mechanism, 108
depth hypothesis, 106
ego, 107
ego psychology, 114
Electra complex, 111
genital stage, 111
hierarchy of needs, 125
humanistic-existential perspective, 123
id, 107
interpersonal perspective, 127
interpretation, 106
latency, 111
libido, 107
neuroses, 111
object relations, 115
Oedipus complex, 111
oral stage, 110
phallic stage, 110
phenomenological approach, 123
positive psychology, 124
positive regard, 125
psychoanalysis, 106
psychodynamic perspective, 105
psychosexual development, 110
psychosis, 111
self-actualization 124
structural hypothesis, 107
superego, 108
unconscious, 106
valuing process, 124

Summary

- The psychodynamic perspective holds that much of our behavior is not the result of conscious choice but is driven by unconscious, internal forces, which often reflect our childhood experiences and family relationships.
- Sigmund Freud's theory of psychoanalysis laid the foundation for the psychodynamic perspective. The key concept in Freud's theory is the depth hypothesis, the idea that almost all mental activity takes place outside conscious awareness. The unconscious contains material that has been actively forgotten, or repressed.
- Freud held that psychology cannot limit itself to observations but must use interpretation to probe beneath manifest (surface) reasoning to identify latent (unconscious) motivations. The goal of psychoanalysis, in Freud's words, is "to make the unconscious conscious."
- Freud later proposed the structural hypothesis, which divides the mind into three forces—the id, ego, and superego.

  Present from birth, the id consists of primitive biological drives, the most powerful of which are sex and aggression. The id operates on the pleasure principle, ignoring reason, reality, and morality.

  The ego develops later and operates on the reality principle, seeking ways to gratify the id that are both safe and effective.

  The superego, which develops last, represents the moral standards of society and parents that the child internalizes. Rigid and uncompromising, the superego demands perfection. The ego's task is to satisfy the id without provoking the superego.
- The id, ego, and superego coexist in a state of dynamic tension, which may explode at any time. Anxiety results when the ego senses danger. Most anxiety is not experienced consciously but is held in check by defense mechanisms. Though often adaptive, overuse of defense mechanisms may interfere with thought processes and everyday functioning.
- Freud viewed personality as the product of childhood psychosexual development, from the oral and anal stages to the phallic, latency, and genital stages. At each stage, the child is forced to resolve conflicts between his or her biological urges and social restraints. Under- or overgratification at any stage may create anxiety and lead to maladaptive adult behavior.
- Freud believed that both normal and abnormal behavior result from interactions among the id, ego, and

superego. A healthy adult has the ego strength to balance conflicting demands by the id and the superego.

When the ego experiences too much conflict, it is weakened. This produces rigid behavior patterns, called neuroses. In extreme cases, the ego collapses and adaptive functioning ceases, a condition known as psychosis.

- Freud's theories were extended and modified by a number of other thinkers. Post-Freudian theorists tended to put less emphasis on the id and more on the ego; to focus less on sexual drives, or libido, and more on personal fulfillment and social relationships; and to pay less attention to childhood traumas and more to present circumstances and ongoing development.
- Among the most influential post-Freudian theorists are Harry Stack Sullivan, who focused on interpersonal relationships; Karen Horney, for whom basic anxiety caused by weak parent-child attachment led to interpersonal neurotic trends; Heinz Hartmann, whose ego psychology created a bridge between psychoanalytic theory and cognitive psychology, and Erik Erikson, who saw the development of ego identity as the product of lifelong psychosocial development.
- One of the most influential schools in contemporary psychodynamic psychology is object relations theory (in which "objects" are the people to whom an individual is emotionally attached). One influential object relations theorist, Margaret Mahler, studied the processes of individuation, whereby children achieve psychological separation from their mothers. Heinz Kohut developed self psychology and identified narcissistic personality disorder. The attachment perspective of John Bowlby has generated intense interest across disciplines and has led to research on adult attachment as well as infant attachment.
- All psychodynamic therapy is based to some extent on Freudian psychoanalytic theory. In psychoanalysis, the client talks, and the analyst interprets possible connections with unconscious material. Most therapists today speak directly to the client much more than Freud would have considered appropriate. Still, the one-to-one therapist-client consultation Freud pioneered underlies almost every form of psychotherapy.
- The psychodynamic perspective has been criticized for lack of experimental support, dependence on inference, unrepresentative sampling, cultural biases (especially relating to gender differences), and a negative portrait of human nature.

  But psychodynamic theory played a major role in demystifying abnormal behavior by exposing the irrationality of everyday life and showing that normal and abnormal behavior are not so much distinct categories as points on a continuum. Psychodynamic theory has also had an enormous impact on Western culture by calling attention to the inner world of dreams and fantasies.
- Humanistic-existential psychology is both an outgrowth of and a reaction to psychodynamic theory. Humanistic and existential thinkers reject the determinism of psychodynamic theory and the passivity this implies. Rather they emphasize the human capacity for growth, freedom to choose one's fate, and responsibility for one's decisions.
- Humanistic psychology sees people as basically good, rational, and social beings. Human beings are distinguished from other animals by their drive toward self-actualization, the fulfillment of one's capacities. Abnormal behavior occurs when this drive is blocked, either because of incongruence between a person's behavior and his or her true self (Carl Rogers' theory) or because of a failure to satisfy basic needs (Abraham Maslow's theory).

  Humanistic psychologists hold that psychotherapy should aim not only to help people with damaged psyches but also to help people who are functioning adequately to lead richer lives.
- Existential psychology focuses on alienation, or feelings of meaninglessness, and on the struggle to live authentically, by one's own principles and values. It stresses the importance of the present and future as opposed to the past.
- The humanistic-existential perspective has not had the impact of the psychodynamic approach. Rather, its influence is seen in the greater emphasis on empathy with patients and clients and a concern with personal growth rather than mere adjustment.
- The interpersonal perspective, delineated by Harry Stack Sullivan and other theorists, places special emphasis on the importance of relationships for psychological adjustment. The guiding principle behind the interpersonal therapy approach is that psychological problems hinge to a major extent on problems in a person's relationships with others.

CHAPTER 6

Behavior Genetics
- Clinical Genetic Studies
- Molecular Genetic Studies

The Central Nervous System
- Neurons
- Neurotransmitters
- The Anatomy of the Brain
- Measuring Brain Activity and Structure
- Lateralization: Effects on Language and Emotion

The Peripheral Nervous System: Somatic and Autonomic
- The Somatic Nervous System
- The Autonomic Nervous System

The Endocrine System

Evaluating the Neuroscience Perspective
- Integrating the Neuroscience and Psychological Perspectives

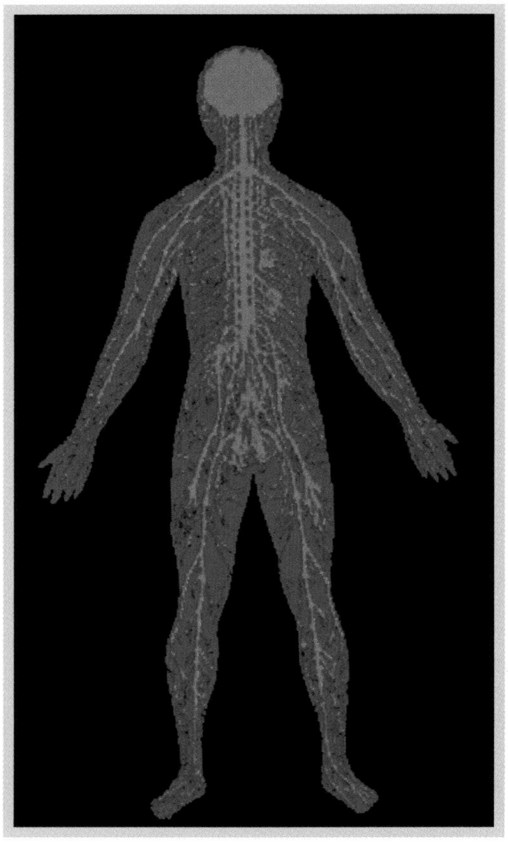

The Neuroscience Perspective

In this chapter we focus on the neuroscience perspective, which holds that the causes of abnormal behavior lie in the functioning of the brain and other systems of the body. The neuroscience perspective is the oldest view of abnormal behavior, yet it is continually being revised as science reveals more about both mind and body.

Long before recorded history, people associated abnormal behavior with things going on inside the head. But the brain does not permit easy access; therefore, theories about the neurological bases of abnormal behavior remained for centuries in the realm of speculation. Today such theories are being built with concrete evidence. With the help of advanced technology, researchers can now flip a switch, see a moving picture of a living brain as it is functioning, and search such pictures for blood clots, tumors, and other possible causes of behavioral problems. The brain, then, is no longer the dark territory that it used to be. The same is true of other biological functions that affect our thoughts and emotions. Perhaps the greatest source of optimism and excitement in abnormal psychology in the past 40 years has been the tremendous advance in the study of the biological bases of behavior.

The neuroscience perspective focuses on the interaction between behavior and organic functions. It is not a single, general theory but, rather, a collection of specific theories about specific pathologies. Most of these theories will be dealt with in the chapters that discuss the disorders in question. Our purpose here is to lay the groundwork by describing the kinds of biological mechanisms—the genes, the nervous system, the endocrine system—now being investigated by neuroscientists and by giving some picture of their research methods.

Fundamental to the **neuroscience perspective** is the issue of the relationship between the physical and psychological aspects of our functioning—the so-called **mind-body problem.** Though most of us tend to regard our minds as things apart from our bodies, the two are really aspects of a single, complex entity. What the mind experiences affects the body. A stressful job can contribute to hypertension; a death in the family can alter the survivors' immune systems, making them illness-prone. Conversely, alterations in body chemistry can have massive effects on emotion and behavior. Physical and mental functioning cannot realistically be considered apart from each other.

It has long been recognized that certain abnormal behavior patterns are caused by organic factors. Two chapters of this book—Chapter 15, "Neuropsychological Disorders," and Chapter 17, "Mental Retardation and Autism"—are devoted largely to such patterns. But in recent years researchers have come increasingly to suspect—indeed, to show—that organic factors are involved in disorders *not* traditionally considered organic, such as anxiety and depression. The reverse is also true: Researchers are discovering more and more ways in which what used to be regarded as purely organic illness is, in fact, related to psychological stress—a matter that is the subject of Chapter 9, "Psychological Stress and Physical Disorders." It is to the biological factors involved in this new research that we now turn.

Behavior Genetics

Every cell in the human body contains a mass of threadlike structures known as **chromosomes.** Coded on the chromosomes are all the instructions, inherited from the parents at the moment of conception, as to what proteins the body should produce. The proteins in turn determine what the body will become: brown-eyed or blue-eyed, tall or short, male or female. The individual units in which this information is carried are called **genes.** There are more than 2,000 genes on a single chromosome. In some cases, a given trait is controlled by a single gene. But the vast majority of human traits are **polygenic,** the products of the interaction of many genes.

It has long been known that genetic inheritance influences not only physical traits, such as eye color, but also behavior. What is not known is the extent to which genes control behavior. This is the famous nature-nurture question, and it is as unresolved in abnormal psychology as it is in any other branch of psychology. Researchers in **behavior genetics,** as this subfield is called, have methods of determining whether a behavioral abnormality is subject to genetic influence. But establishing the degree of genetic influence is a much thornier matter. As we just saw, most traits are controlled by the subtle interaction of many genes—and affected, furthermore, by other factors in the body chemistry, as well as by experience. Thus, the relationship of genes to traits is not a single link but a vast net of influences.

Because of these complexities, it is only in the past four decades that researchers have begun to make any genuine progress in relating genetics to behavior disturbances (Plomin, DeFries, McClearn, et al., 2001). To date, genetic defects have been shown to be directly responsible for a few forms of abnormality—for example, Down syndrome, a form of mental retardation. But such clear-cut cases of direct genetic causation are apparently rare. Instead, most genetically influenced disorders seem to fit what is called the **diathesis-stress model.** According to this model, certain genes or gene combinations produce a **diathesis,** or constitutional predisposition, to a disorder. If this diathesis is then combined with certain kinds of environmental stress, abnormal behavior will result. Studies within the past 40 years indicate that, just as a tendency to develop diabetes, heart disease, and certain types of cancer can be genetically transmitted, so can a predisposition to certain behavioral disturbances.

Clinical Genetic Studies

To understand the genetic evidence, one must understand the methods by which it is obtained. Every human being is born with a unique **genotype**—that is, a highly individual combination of genes representing the biological inheritance from the parents. This genotype interacts with the person's environment to determine the **phenotype**—that is, the person's equally unique combination of observable characteristics. The entire purpose of behavior genetics is to discover to what extent different behavioral disorders are due to genetic inheritance rather than environmental influence.

However, a complication in separating the effects of genes and environment is that genes and environment may be correlated or associated with one another. **Genotype-environment correlation** refers to the tendency for individuals' genetic predispositions for a trait or disorder to be associated with environmental experiences that also influence the trait or disorder (Rhee, Feigon, Bar, et al., 2001; Rowe & Jacobson, 1999). Reactive genotype-environment correlation occurs when individuals elicit certain reactions from others in their environment based in part on their genetically influenced traits; for example, a person's unattractive appearance (which is partially genetically determined) may elicit rejection from others. Active genotype-environment correlation occurs when people choose environments that are consistent with their genetically influenced traits. An example would be a child with a high IQ (which is partly genetically determined) who chooses to read a lot, thereby exposing herself to a more intellectually stimulating environment (Rhee, Feigon, Bar, et al., 2001; Rowe & Jacobson, 1999). To address the problem of genotype-environment correlation, behavior geneticists rely on complex statistical techniques and increasingly sophisticated research designs.

There are three types of clinical genetic studies: family studies, twin studies, and adoption studies.

Family Studies Family studies are based on our knowledge that different types of family relationships involve different degrees of genetic similarity. All children receive half their genes from one parent and half from the other. Thus, parents and children are 50 percent identical genetically. On average, any two siblings have approximately 50 percent of their genes in common. Aunts and uncles, one step further removed, are approximately 25 percent identical genetically to a given niece or nephew. And first cousins, yet another step removed, have approximately 12.5 percent of their genes in common.

With these percentages in mind, the genetic researcher puts together a sample of families containing one diagnosed case, referred to as the index case, or proband case, of the disorder in question. Then the researcher studies the other members of each family—grandparents, parents, children, grandchildren, siblings, aunts and uncles, cousins—to determine what percentage of persons in each of these relationship groups merits the same diagnosis as the index case. When all the families have been examined in this way, the percentages for each relationship group are averaged, so the researcher ends up with an average percentage of siblings sharing the index case's disorder, an average percentage of aunts and uncles bearing the index case's disorder, and so on. If it should turn out that these percentages roughly parallel the percentages of shared genes—if, for example, siblings prove approximately twice as likely as aunts and uncles to share the index case's disorder—then this would strongly suggest that predisposition to the disorder in question might be transmitted genetically. If you turn ahead to Figure 14.1 (page 408), you will see a graph summarizing family studies of schizophrenia. The figures clearly suggest that the more closely one is related to a person with schizophrenia, the more likely one is to develop schizophrenia.

Such evidence, however, only suggests—it does not prove—genetic transmission. While a person has more genes in common with siblings than with aunts and uncles, he or she also has much more of the environment in common with siblings (same parents, same schools) than with aunts and uncles. Though recent research suggests that shared environment is not the primary cause of similarity between family members (Plomin, DeFries, McClearn, et al., 2001; Rhee, Feigon, Bar, et al., 2001), it is still potentially a confounding factor in family studies.

Twin Studies The genes-versus-environment confusion is less troublesome in twin studies. Here the basic technique is to compare monozygotic and dizygotic twins. **Monozygotic (MZ) twins,** also called identical twins, develop from a single fertilized egg and therefore have exactly the same genotype. They are always of the same sex, have the same eye color,

Family studies are an important avenue of investigation into the genetic aspects of psychological disorder. Such research explores the extent to which the shared genes of parents, children, cousins, and other relatives affect the likelihood that any one member of a family will develop a disorder.

Twin studies have revealed the concordance rate of various disorders in both MZ (identical) and DZ (fraternal) twins. Even when identical twins do not grow up in the same household, they are likely to have a great deal in common. These twins, separated at birth and reunited at age 31, had both become firefighters. Unfortunately, some twins also share a greater vulnerability to psychological disorders such as schizophrenia.

share the same blood type, and so on. In contrast, **dizygotic (DZ) twins,** also called fraternal twins, develop from two eggs fertilized by two different sperm. Therefore, DZ twins, like any pair of siblings, have only approximately 50 percent of their genes in common. As with ordinary siblings, one may be female and the other male, one blue-eyed and one brown-eyed, and so forth. Thus, while monozygotic twins are as likely as dizygotic twins to share the same environment, they have approximately twice as many genes in common.

From this configuration, one can guess the research design. The researcher assembles one group of index cases, each of whom is an MZ twin, and a second group of index cases, each of whom is a DZ twin. All the co-twins (the twins of the index cases) are then examined to determine how many of them are **concordant**—that is, share the same disorder—with their index twin. If the researcher should discover that the concordance rate for the MZ twins is considerably greater than that for the DZ twins, then this would be substantial evidence that predisposition to the disorder is genetically transmitted. And that, in fact, is what has been discovered in the case of both schizophrenia and bipolar (manic-depressive) disorders: a concordance rate three to five times higher for MZ twins than for DZ twins. Even more than the family studies, this is strong evidence for a hereditary factor in those disorders. At the same time, twin studies also provide good evidence for environmental causation. In the behavioral disorders for which genes have been shown to increase risk, they have not been found, on average, to account for more than half the difference between those with "genetic loading" and those without. Therefore, the environment is obviously an important influence as well (Plomin, DeFries, McClearn, et al., 2001).

Twin studies are beautifully simple in design but not in practice, the chief problem being that MZ twins are very rare. It is no easy task to assemble an adequate sample of MZ twins who have paranoid schizophrenia. Furthermore, the question of environmental influence cannot be eliminated altogether from twin studies, since MZ twins, so similar physically and always of the same sex, may be reared more alike than DZ twins and, therefore, may have more similar environments.

Adoption Studies Adoption studies attempt to make a decisive separation between genetic and environmental influence. As we have seen, as long as two relatives share the same environment—live under the same roof, pet the same dog, fight the same family fights—the fact that they share the same behavioral disorder cannot be attributed with certainty to genetic influence. But if through adoption the environmental tie were broken, then any significant similarities in

Research Highlights: The Minnesota Study of Twins Reared Apart

One of the most extensive studies of twins reared apart began in 1979 at the University of Minnesota. Since that time, the Minnesota researchers have studied more than 100 sets of monozygotic and dizygotic twins from across the United States and around the world. The twins were all separated early in life, reared apart in their formative years, and reunited as adults. The researchers located the twin pairs through such means as adoption officials, friends and relatives of the twins, and the twins themselves, many of whom volunteered for the project, hoping to be reunited with a separated twin.

The idea behind the project is to collect information about the medical and social histories of each twin, assess each twin's current medical and psychological states, and then compare any differences or similarities within each twin pair. During a week at the research center, each participant undergoes intensive medical and psychological assessment, including a psychophysiological test battery, individual ability testing, measurement of special mental abilities, personality inventories, psychomotor assessment, a life stress interview, a life history interview, a twin relationship survey, a test of emotional responsiveness, and measurement of interests, values, and expressive style—answering more than 15,000 questions in the process (Bouchard & Pedersen, 1999). In addition, the researchers study the twins' rearing environments.

This study has so far yielded two unmistakable conclusions: Genetic factors account for a large part of behavioral variability, and being reared in the same environment has only a negligible effect on the development of similar psychological traits (Bouchard, Lykken, McGue, et al., 1990; Bouchard & Pedersen, 1999). Of all the traits tested, IQ shows the highest correlation between monozygotic twins reared apart: a heritability factor of about .70. But other psychological traits, such as personality variables, social attitudes, and interests, have also shown strong correlations. (DiLalla, Carey, Gottesman, et al., 1996). The researchers have also evaluated the degree of heritability for alcohol and drug abuse and antisocial behavior. Initial results have found a genetic component for drug abuse and for both child and adult antisocial behavior but not for alcohol abuse (Grove, Eckert, Heston, et al., 1990).

In sum, the study of twins at the Minnesota Center has found that correlations for monozygotic twins reared apart are about the same as those for monozygotic twins reared together. According to Bouchard and his associates, "Being reared by the same parents in the same physical environment does not, on average, make siblings more alike as adults than they would have been if reared separately in adoptive homes" (Bouchard, Lykken, McGue, et al., 1990, p. 227).

The twin studies, however, do not discount environment altogether. That is because people with the same genotype tend to seek out or be exposed to the same type of environment. What each of us finds a congenial environment is influenced by our genetic individuality. The learning experiences of an energetic toddler will differ from those of a passive toddler. An outgoing child will elicit different reactions from people than will a shy child. These varying experiences will certainly have an effect on psychological variability, but it is important to remember that many of these experiences are self-selected, a process directed by our genetic predispositions. (Rhee, Feigon, Bar et al., 2001). Bouchard has shown that monozygotic twins reared apart tend to select very similar environments, and, to the extent that these experiences have an impact on their behavior, there is an interaction between heredity and environment. The old nature-versus-nurture argument should probably give way to a new understanding of nature *via* nurture.

Source: Based on Bouchard, Lykken, McGue, et al., 1990, and Bouchard & Pedersen, 1999.

behavioral history should be entirely the result of the genetic tie. For example, if infants who were born of severely disturbed mothers and adopted into other families at birth developed that same disturbance at approximately the same rate as infants born of *and* raised by mothers suffering from that disorder, then the disorder must, to a large extent, be in the genes. Likewise, if a pair of MZ twins who were separated at birth and raised in different homes still showed a substantially higher concordance rate for a given disorder than did DZ twins raised together or separately, then this would constitute the firmest possible evidence for genetic transmission. (See the box above for a large-scale study of separated twins, though this research focused on personality in general.)

It is just such mother-child pairs and twin pairs that are the object of adoption studies. The adopted-twin studies are the less important of the two, because the samples are so small. (If it is difficult to assemble a group of MZ twins, all of whom have paranoid schizophrenia, imagine the difficulty of putting together a group of MZ twins, all of whom have paranoid schizophrenia *and* have been raised apart from their co-twins.) The mother-child adoption studies are somewhat easier to do, since a severely disturbed mother is likely to give up her child for adoption. Several such studies have been done, and, as we shall see, they now constitute our best evidence for the genetic transmission of a tendency toward bipolar disorder (Chapter 10) and schizophrenia (Chapter 14). Current knowledge in behavioral genetics suggests that most complex behavioral traits, such as mental disorders, are caused by many genes combining with environmental experiences, each with small effects, rather than by single genes with large effects (Plomin & Crabbe, 2000).

Molecular Genetic Studies

Whereas clinical genetic studies aim to determine the extent of genetic inheritance in behavioral disorders, molecular genetic studies attempt to identify exactly which genes are involved. We know that genes located close to one another on a chromosome tend to be "linked," or inherited together. In linkage analysis, therefore, researchers use a **genetic marker,** a gene with a known location on the human chromosome set, as a clue to the location of a gene controlling a disorder. For example, if people who are colorblind—a trait whose controlling gene has been located—were unusually susceptible to bipolar disorder, we could assume that a gene related to bipolar disorder was located near the "color-blind" gene on the same chromosome.

Newer linkage studies involve studying pairs of siblings, both of whom have the same disorder. If a gene that contributes to the disorder is linked to (near) a genetic marker, then the siblings will be more alike on the marker than will siblings who don't share the disorder in common (Plomin & Crabbe, 2000). Linkage studies are now being actively pursued for schizophrenia, bipolar disorder, alcoholism, and panic disorder (Dunner, 1997; Plomin & Crabbe, 2000). Another molecular genetic strategy is to target specific genes for deletion, called **knockouts,** because the gene is "knocked out," or deleted. This method, used most commonly in mice, is designed to learn what a particular gene does, rather than where it is located, by observing what effects on behavior the gene's deletion causes. Knockouts of various genes have been shown to affect learning, aggression, alcohol preference, and sensitivity to many drugs (Plomin & Crabbe, 2000; Waddington, Clifford, McNamara, et al., 2000).

The Central Nervous System

If behavioral abnormalities do result from some form of biological malfunction, then the likely place to look for such malfunction is the nervous system. The **nervous system** is a vast electrochemical conducting network that extends from the brain through the rest of the body. Its function is to transmit information, in the form of electrochemical impulses, among various cells throughout the body.

The nervous system has many divisions (see Figure 6.1), but its headquarters is the **central nervous system (CNS),** consisting of the brain and spinal cord. Of all the parts of the nervous system, the CNS is the one primarily responsible for the storage and transmission of information.

Logically, when there is a problem in the CNS, there is a problem in behavior. As we shall see in Chapter 15, any damage to the brain, whether from injury or disease, can cause a massive change in the personality. Recent research, however, has concentrated more on subtle chemical changes that may be implicated in psychopathology.

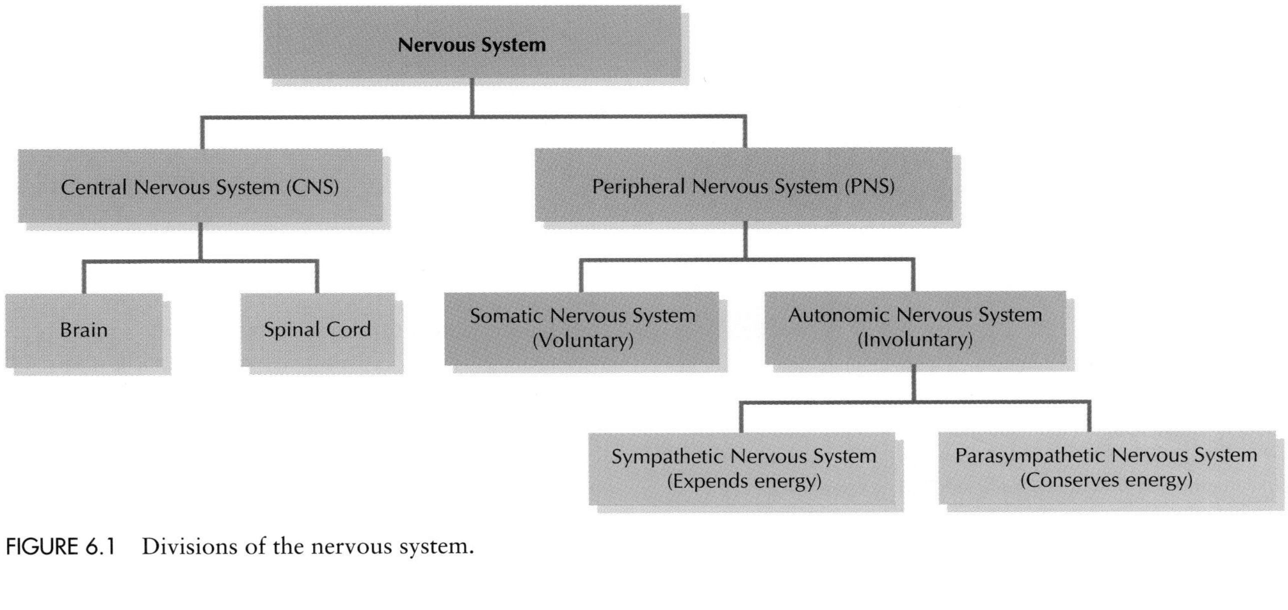

FIGURE 6.1 Divisions of the nervous system.

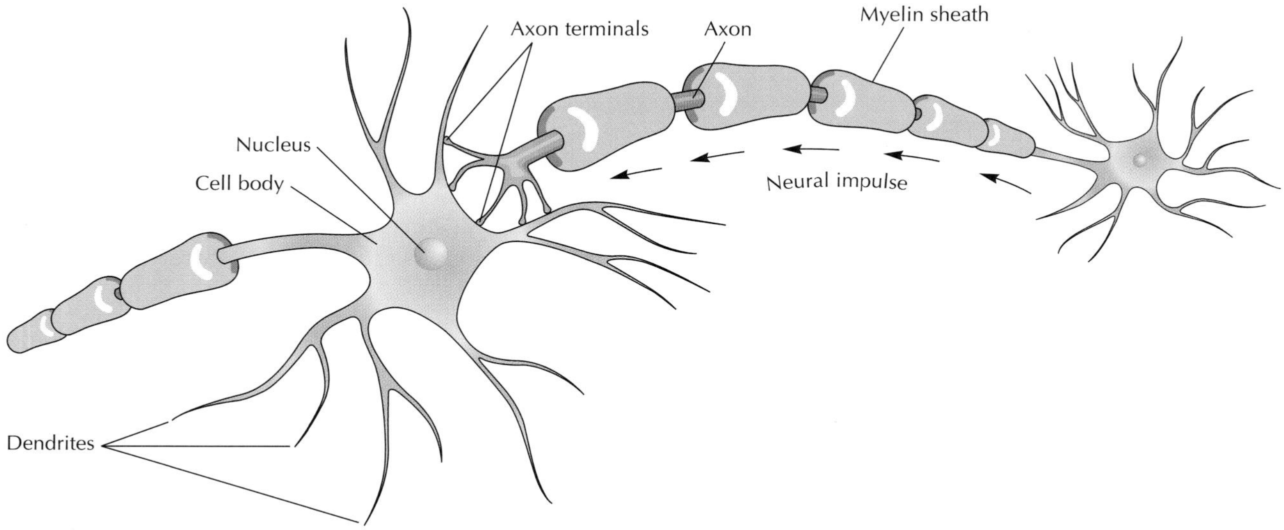

FIGURE 6.2 The structure of this motor neuron is typical of many neurons. The dendrites, short fibers branching out from the cell body, receive impulses from other neurons and transmit them along the axon to the axon terminals. Impulses cross the gap at the end of each axon terminal, moving on to the next group of dendrites. In many neurons, a myelin sheath wrapped around the axon speeds the transmission of the impulses.

Neurons

Like every other part of the body, the nervous system is made up of cells specifically adapted for its functions. Nerve cells, called **neurons,** have the following characteristic structural features (Feldman, Meyer, & Quenzer, 1997) (see Figure 6.2):

1. The *cell body,* which contains the nucleus. The chemical reactions that take place in the cell body provide the energy and the chemicals needed for the transmission of impulses.

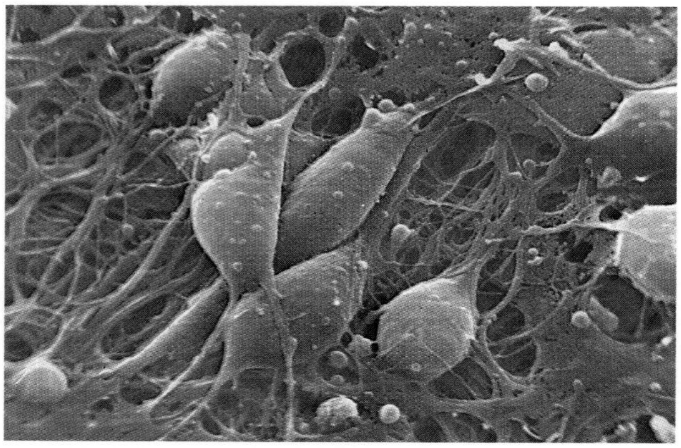

This is a false-color scanning electron micrograph (SEM) of neurons from the cerebral cortex. It clearly shows the large central cell body of each neuron, with a single axon extending from one end, and one or more smaller dendrites from the other.

2. The *dendrites,* short fibers branching out from the cell body. In most neurons, it is the dendrites that receive impulses from other neurons.
3. The *axon,* a long fiber stretching outward from the cell body. This is the passageway through which impulses are transmitted along the neuron on their way to other neurons or to the muscles and glands.
4. The *axon terminals,* the axon's branchlike endings, each with a buttonlike structure at its tip. It is through these buttons at the ends of the axon terminals that the impulse is transmitted to the next neuron.
5. In some neurons, a *myelin sheath,* which is made up of fatty cells wrapped around the axon in segments. The myelin sheath speeds neural transmission by insulating the axon from other cells, just as traffic on an interstate is sped along by limiting the access of other roadways.

The typical pathway is as follows. Through its dendrites, a neuron receives an impulse from a neighboring neuron. (The number of neighboring neurons may range from one to several thousand.) The neuron then passes that impulse along its axon to the axon terminals. At the terminal, the impulse must leap a small gap, called the **synapse,** between the terminal button and the dendrite of the neuron that is to receive the impulse. This leap is accomplished by a chemical known as a **neurotransmitter.** If a sufficient amount of neurotransmitter crosses the synapse, the receiving neuron will "fire"—that is, send on the impulse.

Firing is an all-or-nothing response: If enough neurotransmitter is received, the neuron fires; if not, it doesn't. This is important, because changing the amount of neurotransmitter available in the synapse, even by a little bit, may determine whether the receiving neuron fires or not. In fact, most psychoactive drugs do exactly this: They affect the amount of neural activity by altering the amount of neurotransmitter in the synapse.

It is also important to note that not all impulses stimulate the nerve to fire. Some may inhibit transmission; that is, the impulse makes the receiving neuron *less* likely to fire. In a typical case, a receiving neuron is stimulated by both excitatory and inhibitory impulses. It will then tally the excitatory and inhibitory input and will or will not fire.

Thus, the information that our nervous system receives, and the way in which it will be acted on, is regulated by synaptic transmission. Synaptic transmission, in turn, is determined by the action of neurotransmitters. It is, thus, no surprise that the neurotransmitters have been a major focus of biological research in abnormal psychology.

Neurons: Seeing How They Work

This MindMAP video gives a dynamic illustration of how neurons communicate with one another, enabling us to think and act. What do you think about the idea that behavior can be explained in terms of the firing or non-firing of impulses in the brain?

Neurotransmitters

In the cell body, amino acids from the protein we eat are converted into neurotransmitters, which are then stored in the axon terminals in small sacs called *synaptic vesicles* (Figure 6.3). When an impulse reaches the axon terminal, the neurotransmitter is released into the synapse, where it floods the gap and makes contact with special proteins called **postsynaptic receptors** on the surface of the receiving neuron. Neurotransmitter molecules fit into the postsynaptic receptors like a key into a lock, and this reaction causes a change in voltage in the receiving neuron, which will then transmit the impulse to adjacent neurons. The neurotransmitter may then be reincorporated into the axon terminal through a process called **reuptake,** or remain circulating in the synapse.

Receptors for neurotransmitters can change over time. If too much neurotransmitter is being released into the synapse, the postsynaptic receptors, to compensate, will decrease in number or become less sensitive to the neurotransmitter—a process called **down-regulation.** Or the opposite may occur: If the presynaptic neuron is not releasing enough neurotransmitter to carry the impulse, the postsynaptic receptors will undergo **up-regulation,** increasing in number or sensitivity. Neuroscience researchers are now exploring the possibility that some behavioral disorders are due in part to faulty up- or down-regulation. Several drug treatments for those disorders are thought to work by restoring smooth regulation (Feldman, Meyer, & Quenzer, 1997; Hamblin, 1997).

Scientists have been aware of the existence of neurotransmitters only since the 1920s, and the study of their relation to psychological disorders is more recent still, beginning in the 1950s. This is now one of the most exciting areas of neuroscience research in abnormal psychology. It is not yet known how many kinds of neurotransmitters exist in the human body—probably more than 50. The ones that seem to have important roles in psychopathology are the following (Feldman, Meyer, & Quenzer, 1997; Stahl, 1996):

1. *Acetylcholine.* The first neurotransmitter discovered, acetylcholine is involved in transmitting nerve impulses to the muscles throughout the body. In the central nervous system, it may also be involved in attentional processes, in sleep disorders, and in Alzheimer's disease (Blokland, 1996; Feldman, Meyer, & Quenzer, 1997).
2. *Dopamine.* This substance seems to be crucially involved in the regulation of motor behavior and in reward-related activities. Certain frequently abused drugs, such as stimulants, act on the dopamine system. Disturbed dopamine activity is thought to be related to Parkinson's disease and schizophrenia (Carlsson, Waters, Waters, et al., 2000).
3. *Enkephalins.* These substances seem able to act upon the opiate receptors in the brain (the parts that are affected by opium or related drugs). As such, they may be the body's "natural drugs" (Feldman, Meyer, & Quenzer, 1997).

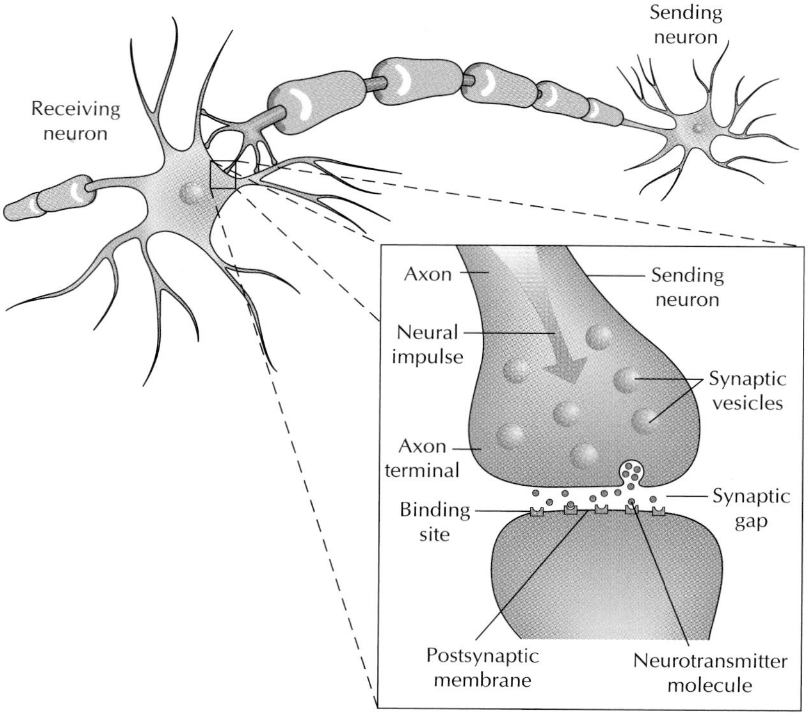

FIGURE 6.3 Neurotransmitters manufactured in the cell body are stored in synaptic vesicles in the axon terminals. An electrochemical impulse passing through the sending neuron causes the neurotransmitter to be released into the synaptic gap, where it bonds with receptors on the receiving neuron to transmit the impulse. Following transmission, some neurotransmitter molecules are returned to the synaptic vesicles in the sending neuron (reuptake). The rest circulate in the extracellular environment.

4. *GABA (gamma-amino-butyric acid).* GABA is a neurotransmitter that works almost exclusively in the brain, inhibiting neurons from firing. Tranquilizing drugs that inhibit anxiety work by increasing the activity of GABA (Feldman, Meyer, & Quenzer, 1997).
5. *Norepinephrine (NE).* In the autonomic nervous system, this substance is involved in producing "fight or flight" responses, such as increased heart rate and blood pressure. In the central nervous system, norepinephrine activates alertness to danger and may be involved in panic disorder and depression (Delgado & Moreno, 2000).
6. *Serotonin.* This neurotransmitter has an important role in constraint. Imbalances in serotonin and norepinephrine may be involved in severe depression, as well as in a number of other disorders, including anxiety disorders, obsessive-compulsive disorder, eating disorders, aggression, suicide, schizophrenia, and alcoholism (Dubovsky & Thomas, 1995; Feldman, Meyer, & Quenzer, 1997).

Drug Treatment Research on neurotransmitters is intimately linked with **psychopharmacology,** the study of the drug treatment of psychological disorders. Not all psychoactive, or behavior-affecting, drugs target the neurotransmitters, but many do, attempting to correct neurotransmitter imbalances at any one of several stages. If the goal is to increase the action of a neurotransmitter, drugs may be used to increase the level of the neurotransmitter in the synapse—for example, by slowing down its reuptake. If the goal is to suppress the action of a neurotransmitter, drugs may be used to attach to the postsynaptic receptors in place of the neurotransmitters, thus blocking them. Or drugs may be used to influence neurotransmitters via up- or down-regulation. But these are very delicate manipulations, still in the experimental stages. Indeed, in some cases researchers still do not know whether the neurotransmitter in question needs to be enhanced or suppressed.

Drugs are now the most common form of treatment for psychological disorders. In some cases, they are very effective, but they often have unwanted side effects. They also raise the question of whether the drug is merely treating the symptom, without addressing the cause. There are five main categories of drugs used in the treatment of abnormal behavior (see Table 6.1): antianxiety drugs, sedative-hypnotic drugs, antipsychotic drugs, antidepressant drugs, and antimanic/mood-stabilizer drugs. We will discuss these medications in the chapters on the relevant disorders.

TABLE 6.1 Major Psychotherapeutic Drugs

CATEGORY	CHEMICAL STRUCTURE OR PSYCHOPHARMACOLOGIC ACTION	GENERIC NAME	TRADE NAME
Antipsychotic drugs (also called major tranquilizers or neuroleptics)	Phenothiazines		
	Aliphatic	Chlorpromazine	Thorazine
	Piperidine	Thioridazine	Mellaril
	Piperazine	Trifluoperazine	Stelazine
		Fluphenazine	Prolixin
	Thioxanthenes		
	Aliphatic	Chlorprothixene	Taractan
	Piperazine	Thiothixene	Navane
	Butyrophenones	Haloperidol	Haldol
	Dibenzoxazepines	Loxapine	Loxitane
	Benzisoxazoles	Risperidone	Risperdal
	Dibenzodiazepines	Olanzapine	Zyprexa
		Clozapine	Clozaril
Antidepressant drugs	Tricyclic antidepressants (TCAs)	Amitriptyline	Elavil
	Tertiary amines	Imipramine	Tofranil
		Clomipramine	Anafranil
		Doxepin	Sinequan
	Secondary amines	Desipramine	Norpramin
		Nortriptyline	Pamelor
		Protriptyline	Vivactil
	Monoamine oxidase (MAO) inhibitors	Phenelzine	Nardil
		Tranylcypromine	Parnate
	Selective serotonin reuptake inhibitors (SSRIs)	Fluoxetine	Prozac
		Sertraline	Zoloft
		Paroxetine	Paxil
		Fluvoxamine	Luvox
		Citalopram	Celexa
	Others	Bupropion	Wellbutrin
		Venlafaxine	Effexor
		Mirtazapine	Remeron
		Nefazodone	Serzone
Antimanic/mood-stabilizer drugs		Lithium carbonate	Eskalith or Lithobid
		Carbamazepine	Tegretol
		Divalproex	Depakote
Antianxiety drugs (also called minor tranquilizers)	Benzodiazepines	Chlordiazepoxide	Librium
		Diazepam	Valium
		Chlorazepate	Tranxene
		Oxazepam	Serax
		Lorazepam	Ativan
		Alprazolam	Xanax
		Clonazepam	Klonopin
	Azaspirodecanediones	Buspirone	BuSpar
Sedative-hypnotic drugs	Benzodiazepines	Triazolam	Halcion
		Temazepam	Restoril
		Flurazepam	Dalmane
	Imidazopyridines	Zolpidem	Ambien

The Anatomy of the Brain

While behavior may be affected by chemical reactions at the finest level of brain activity, we also know that many behavioral abnormalities are related to the gross structure of the brain. Therefore, a knowledge of the anatomy of the brain is essential to an understanding of psychopathology.

The outermost part of the brain is an intricate, convoluted layer of "gray matter" called the **cerebral cortex** (see Figures 6.4 and 6.5). The external surface of the cerebral cortex has many sulci (fissures) and gyri (ridges between sulci), which are "landmarks" in the structure of the brain. A major sulcus called the longitudinal fissure divides the brain along the midline into two hemispheres, the right and left brain, connected by the **corpus callosum,** a band of nerve fibers. Each hemisphere is further divided into four lobes. The *central sulcus* (or fissure of Rolando) divides the cortex into the **frontal lobe** and the receptive

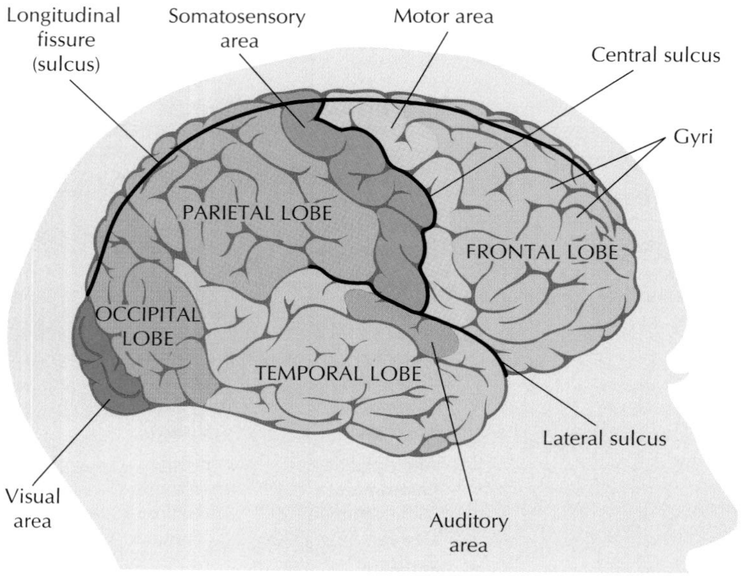

FIGURE 6.4 The four lobes of the cortex and the major fissures that separate them.

cortex, made up of the **parietal, temporal,** and **occipital lobes.** Another major fissure, the *lateral sulcus* (or fissure of Sylvius), runs along the side of each hemisphere, separating the temporal lobe from the frontal and parietal lobes.

The functions of these different lobes have been the subject of much debate. The frontal lobes are a particular enigma, but it appears that they are related essentially to language ability, to the regulation of fine voluntary movements, and to higher cognitive functions such as judgment, planning, the ordering of stimuli, and the sorting out of information. In addition, the frontal lobes serve as a comparator organ—that is, they somehow allow us to look at our behavior and evaluate its appropriateness by seeing how it is perceived by others (Feldman, Meyer, & Quenzer, 1997). This enables us to change our behavior when feedback suggests the need. The frontal lobes also serve to overcome psychological inertia (that is, they help tell us when to start and stop an action). Knowing the proper time to stop or change course is crucial to socially appropriate behavior. Finally, the frontal lobes, because they have two-way connections between the perception-processing centers and the emotion-processing centers, are key to the integration of emotion and cognition (LeDoux, 2000), which in turn is critical to mental health. Many mental disorders—depression, for example—involve a disruption of that relationship (Davidson, Lewis, Alloy, et al., 2002).

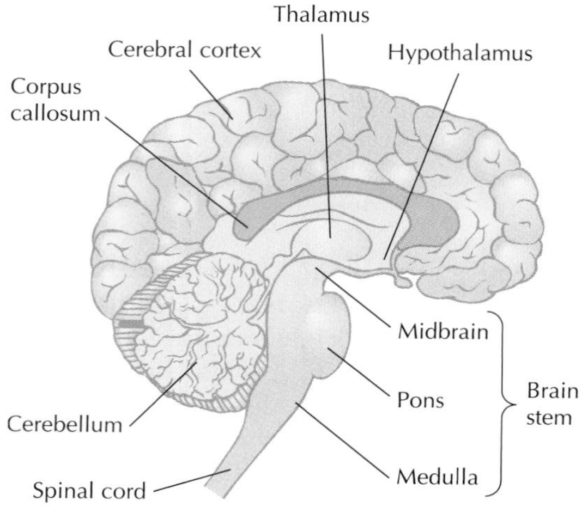

FIGURE 6.5 A cross section of the brain showing its major structural features.

The temporal lobes control auditory perception and some part of visual perception and may be involved in schizophrenia. Furthermore, they clearly have some role in memory, for damage to the temporal lobes generally involves memory loss. The parietal lobes are the center of intersensory integration (e.g., the ability to visualize a cow upon hearing a "moo") and of motor and sensory-somatic functions. Damage to the parietal lobes frequently results in spatial disorientation and in loss of control over gross-motor behavior (e.g., walking). Finally, the occipital lobes appear to control visual discrimination and visual memory. Although the four lobes have been described separately, in fact they are intricately connected to one another, so the functions of each are affected by the functions of the others (Feldman, Meyer, & Quenzer, 1997).

A cross section of the brain reveals other important structural features (see Figure 6.6). Particularly important in emotional functioning are the hypothalamus

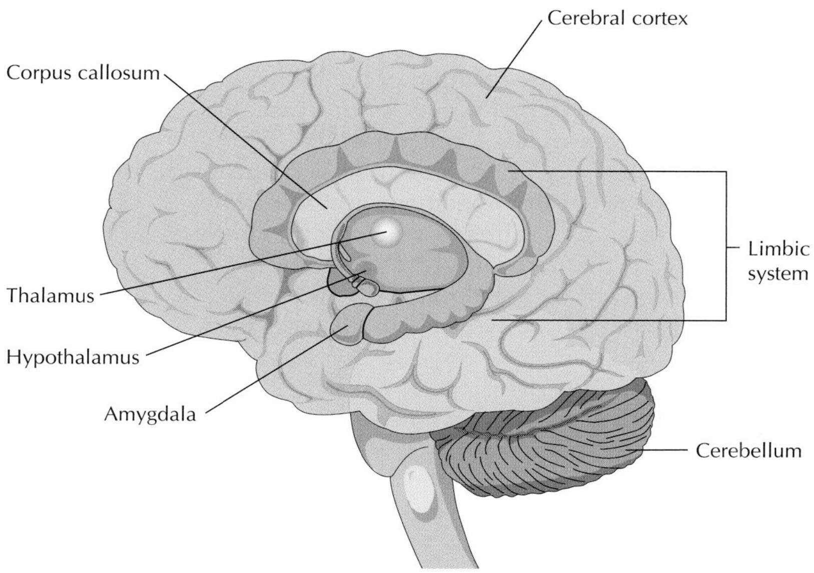

FIGURE 6.6 The limbic structures and hypothalamus. The word *limbic* comes from the Latin word for "border." *Limbus,* and the limbic structures, including the amygdala and the hippocampus, form a kind of dividing line between the cerebral cortex above and the midbrain and cerebellum below.

and the limbic structures. The *hypothalamus* controls hunger, thirst, and sexual desire; regulates body temperature; and is involved in states of emotional arousal. The *limbic structures,* interacting with the hypothalamus, control behaviors such as mating, fighting, and experiencing pleasure. The *amygdala,* one of the limbic structures, is involved in emotional responses, both positive (such as romantic attraction) and negative (such as "fight or flight" and fear reactions) (Aggleton & Young, 2000; LeDoux, 2000). The *hippocampus,* another limbic structure, operates on memory as well as emotion, which may help to explain why we remember emotionally charged experiences more clearly than neutral ones.

Buried in the middle of the brain is the *thalamus,* which relays input from the peripheral nervous system to other brain structures, including the frontal lobe and the limbic structures. Scientists have recently discovered direct connections between the thalamus and the amygdala, which may help to account for "automatic" emotional reactions such as phobias (LeDoux, 2000). Other brain structures include the *basal ganglia,* which are involved in carrying out planned, programmed behaviors; the *cerebellum,* which is involved in posture, physical balance, and fine-motor coordination; the *pons,* a relay station connecting the cerebellum with other areas of the brain and with the spinal cord; and the *medulla,* which regulates such vital functions as heartbeat, breathing, and blood pressure. The *brain stem* includes the pons, the medulla, and the *reticular activating system,* which extends through the center of the brain stem and regulates sleep and arousal. Within the brain are *ventricles,* cavities filled with cerebrospinal fluid.

Several of these brain structures are now the focus of intense study by neuroscience researchers in abnormal psychology. Schizophrenia has been associated with abnormalities of size in various parts of the brain: enlarged ventricles and smaller frontal lobes, temporal lobes, cerebrums, and craniums (skulls) (Pearlson & Marsh, 1999). Temporal-lobe malfunction may be responsible for the memory loss seen in Alzheimer's disease (Herndel & Salmon, 2001). The appetite-control function of the hypothalamus is being investigated in relation to obesity and bulimia. Basal ganglia abnormalities have been linked to conditions involving ritualistic behavior, such as obsessive-compulsive disorder (Leocani, Locatelli, Bellodi, et al., 2001). Damage to the limbic structures may lead to emotional problems and personality disturbance. These theories will be discussed in later chapters.

Measuring Brain Activity and Structure

For years, much of what was known about the relationship between structure and function in the brain was inferred from the behavior of brain-damaged patients. It was found, for example, that patients with damaged parietal lobes often could no longer walk; therefore, it was concluded that the parietal lobes had some control over gross-motor behavior. Or, on rare occasions, the functioning of the brain could be observed and tested in the course of brain surgery. Today, however, there are techniques that allow researchers to see inside the brain without surgically invading it.

A test that has been used for decades is electroencephalography (EEG), which we discussed in Chapter 2. EEG can be used to measure general brain activity, such as sleep patterns in people with insomnia, or to detect brain abnormalities, such as epilepsy. It can also give a picture of the brain's responses to specific external events. In this case, the test is called **event-related potentials,** or **ERPs.** ERPs measure changes in brain activity as a consequence of specific sensory, cognitive, or motor stimuli. People with schizophrenia consistently show EEGs or ERPs that are different from those of normal controls (Harris, Bahramali, Slewa, et al., 2001). EEGs and ERPs can also help predict which hyperactive children will respond to stimulant medication (Chabot, di Michele, Prichep, et al., 2001) and which depressed patients will respond to antidepressant medication (Bruder, Stewart, Tenke, et al., 2001).

In recent years, however, neuroscientists have invented a number of extremely sophisticated techniques that produce an actual image of the brain, like a photograph. One such technique is **positron emission tomography (PET).** In a PET scan, radioactive molecules are injected into the bloodstream. Then a computerized scanner tracks the molecules on a screen as they are metabolized by the brain (Buckner & Logan, 2001). Differences in metabolism in different parts of the brain show up as color contrasts on the screen, and these can point to brain damage—for example, from a stroke. They can also indicate which parts of the brain are active as a person performs a task or engages in behavior and, therefore, which parts of the brain are involved in that behavior (Shulman, 2001). Finally, PET scans can show whether patients with a known disorder are improving after drug treatment (Brody, Saxena, Stoessel, et al., 2001). A related technique, **single photon emission computer tomography (SPECT),** has also been used to measure blood flow and glucose metabolism in the brain.

While PET, like EEG, measures brain activity, two other techniques, **computerized tomography (CT)** and **magnetic resonance imaging (MRI),** focus on brain structure. CT passes X rays through cross sections of the brain, measuring the density of tissue within each cross section. In patients with memory loss or language disorders, this can reveal tumors or lesions (tissue damage) that may be the root of the problem. In MRI, the most recently developed technology, the subject is enclosed in a magnetic field, which causes the hydrogen atoms in the brain to shift their positions. Then smaller magnetic fields are used and the atoms return to their original positions, leaving electromagnetic tracks, which, read by the computer, produce an image of the brain tissue. MRI, thus, works at a subatomic level (Scheele, Maravilla, & Dager, 1997). Because it works with such minute particles, MRI yields very precise images, like photographic negatives. A recently developed variation, **functional MRI (fMRI),** measures the magnetic action of blood oxygen and thus—like PET but, again, far more precisely—produces images of brain activity (Shulman, 2001; Buckner & Logan, 2001).

Each of these techniques has its strengths and weaknesses. EEG and ERPs, because they measure electrical activity, are far more precise at specifying the timing of brain activity. Indeed, they can record events in the brain within milliseconds of neuron firing. They are also inexpensive and completely noninvasive, with no radioactive tracers (PET), no X rays (CT), no powerful magnetic fields (MRI). CT, PET, and MRI are also safe, but more expensive and more invasive, and they give less information about the timing of brain functions. Their great virtue is

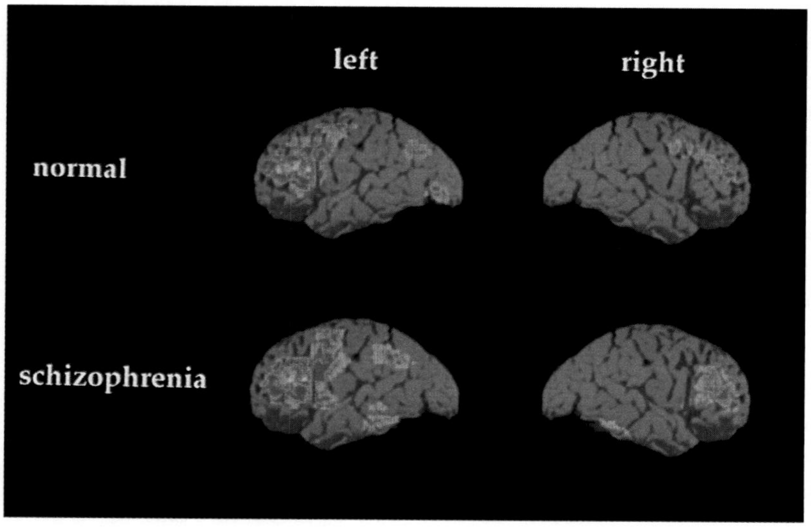

Positron emission tomography (PET) scans provide color images of the brain's activity. Shown here are images of the brain of a normal adult (top) and the brain of a schizophrenic patient (bottom) while each was speaking. Notice the greater activity in the left and right frontal lobes of the schizophrenic patient.

their ability to reveal brain structure and, in the case of PET and fMRI, the location of brain activity (Buckner & Logan, 2001). The choice of technique usually depends on the purposes of the test—what the testers are trying to find—and, to a large extent, on the patient's financial resources.

Neuroscientists are now using these technologies to test hypotheses about various psychological disorders—schizophrenia, for example. As previously mentioned, schizophrenia has been linked to abnormalities in the size of various parts of the brain: enlarged ventricles, smaller frontal lobes, and so on. These findings, which will be discussed in Chapter 14, are largely the product of CT, PET, and MRI scans (Pearlson & Marsh, 1999; Taber, Lewis, & Hurley, 2001).

Psychosurgery The new neuroimaging technologies have also led to advances in **psychosurgery,** surgery aimed at reducing abnormal behavior. Early forms of psychosurgery, such as the prefrontal lobotomy (Chapter 1), were often harmful. In recent years, however, researchers have developed more refined psychosurgical techniques—techniques that destroy less brain tissue and therefore produce fewer and milder side effects (Hurley, Black, Stip, et al., 2000; Weingarten & Cummings, 2001). One procedure, called *cingulotomy,* involves inserting an electrode into the cingulate gyrus, a ridge of brain tissue lying above the corpus callosum. The electrode is then heated, creating a small lesion. The principle here is to disrupt pathways leading from the emotion centers of the thalamus and hypothalamus to the frontal lobe and thus to reduce the expression of emotion. Cingulotomy has proved effective for severe obsessive-compulsive patients who have not responded to other treatments (Jenike, 1998; Turner, Beidel, Stanley, et al., 2001). In another procedure, called *stereotactic subcaudate tractotomy,* a small, localized area of the brain is destroyed by radioactive particles inserted through small ceramic rods. The site varies with the nature of the disturbance. For depressed patients, it is the frontal lobe; for aggressive patients, it is the amygdala, a structure in the lower part of the brain.

Psychosurgery has been found to be effective with severe depression—and with anorexia nervosa, an eating disorder of self-starvation (Morgan & Crisp, 2000). Nevertheless, it is still extremely controversial, and, even in its newer, more conservative forms, it is used only when other treatments have failed. Its defenders claim that the benefits are substantial and the side effects relatively mild. Other observers doubt both claims and feel that the public should be very wary of such radical and irreversible treatments.

Lateralization: Effects on Language and Emotion

One aspect of brain functioning that researchers are studying is **lateralization,** the differences between the right and left hemispheres of the brain. Though the two hemispheres appear similar, they have pronounced differences in structure and function. To begin with, neuron connections between the brain and the peripheral nervous system are crossed, so each hemisphere controls the opposite side of the body. This lateralization is most pronounced in right-handed males, but it is also seen in females and in left-handed males.

In the past, it was popular to assign neat "function" labels to the two sides of the brain. The left brain handled language; the right brain, visual-spatial skills. The left brain was "logical"; the right brain, "emotional." Today we know that these generalizations do not hold. Complex cognitive processes such as language and emotion require interplay among various parts of the brain, on both sides. Nevertheless,

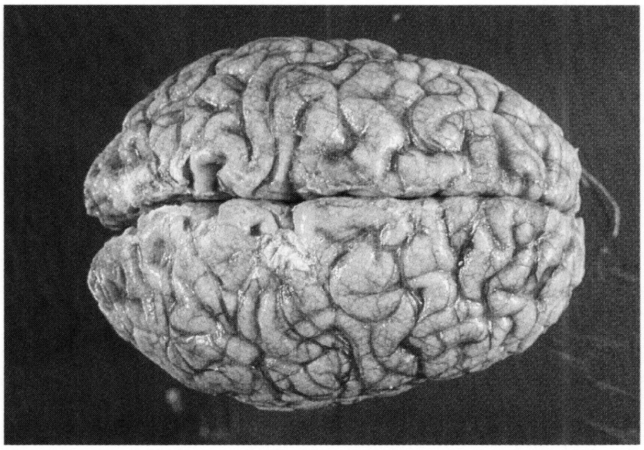

The two hemispheres of the brain, while symmetrical in appearance, do not divide so neatly when it comes to various brain functions. Strict lateralization is limited to just a few brain processes.

different aspects of these processes do seem to be localized on the left or right.

In the case of language, the left brain has long been recognized as the center of language production (Provins, 1997). Recently, however, areas in the right hemisphere have been found to affect "pragmatic" aspects of language, such as the understanding of context and the use of metaphors and humor (Hough, 1990; Knecht, Deppe, Draeger, et al., 2000).

As for emotion, many studies have shown that the perception of emotion is a right-hemisphere activity (Kolb & Taylor, 2000). Indeed, it seems to be controlled by the area where the right temporal lobe meets the right parietal lobe. But this does not mean that emotion in general is headquartered in the right brain. Actually, it now appears that different emotions may be controlled by the right *and* left hemispheres. One EEG finding is that people with a history of depression tend to have reduced electrical activity in the left-hemisphere emotion centers, whereas those in a manic state tend to have increased EEG activity in the left-hemisphere frontal cortex (Davidson, 2000; Harmon-Jones, Abramson, Sigelman, et al., 2002). As we shall see in Chapter 10, researchers now believe that some people are biologically predisposed to depression and mania. Possibly, the predisposition involves relative deactivation or activation of mechanisms in the left brain.

The Peripheral Nervous System: Somatic and Autonomic

While the central nervous system is the high command of the body's information network, the **peripheral nervous system,** a network of nerve fibers leading from the CNS to all parts of the body, is what carries out the commands. Look back at Figure 6.1. The peripheral nervous system has two branches: somatic and autonomic.

The Somatic Nervous System

The **somatic nervous system** senses and acts on the external world. The somatic nervous system relays to the brain information picked up through the sense organs, and it transmits the brain's messages to the skeletal muscles, which move the body. The actions mediated by the somatic nervous system are actions that we think of as voluntary: picking up a telephone, crossing a street, tying one's shoes.

The Autonomic Nervous System

The second branch of the peripheral nervous system, the autonomic nervous system, is the branch that is of special interest to abnormal psychology. While the somatic nervous system activates the skeletal muscles, the **autonomic nervous system (ANS)** controls the smooth muscles, the glands, and the internal organs. Thus, while the somatic division directs our more purposeful responses to environmental stimuli, such as crossing a street when the light turns green, the autonomic division mediates our more automatic responses, such as increased heart rate if we come close to being run over as we cross the street. Because the functions of the ANS tend to be automatic, it used to be known as the "involuntary" nervous system. And, though we now know that many autonomic functions can be brought under voluntary control, it is still true that this function—the regulation of heartbeat, respiration, blood pressure, pupil dilation, bladder contraction, perspiration, salivation, adrenaline secretion, and gastric-acid production, to name only a few—is generally carried out without our thinking about it.

The role of the ANS is to adjust the internal workings of the body to the demands of the environment (Feldman, Meyer, & Quenzer, 1997). But the ANS can become overstimulated in response to extreme environmental demands. For example, under conditions of chronic stress at work or severe anxiety, the ANS may continually produce secretion of gastric acid, leading eventually to the development of stomach ulcers. Like the central and the peripheral nervous systems, the ANS is subdivided into two branches—the sympathetic division and the parasympathetic division—which are structurally and functionally distinct (Figure 6.7).

The Sympathetic Division The **sympathetic division,** consisting of the nerve fibers that emanate from the middle of the spinal cord, mobilizes the body to meet emergencies. To return to the example of crossing the street, if you were to see a car speeding toward you, you would automatically experience a sudden increase in sympathetic activity, which in turn produces a number of physiological changes. The heart beats faster and pumps out more blood with each beat. The blood vessels near the skin and those that lead to the gastrointestinal tract constrict, increasing blood pressure and slowing digestion. At the same time, the blood vessels serving the large muscles—the muscles that will be needed for action—dilate, so they receive more blood. The pupils of the eyes also dilate, making vision more acute. Adrenaline is pumped into the blood, and this in turn releases blood sugar from the liver so that it can be used by the muscles. Breathing becomes faster and deeper so as to take in more oxygen. All these changes prepare the body for quick action. Of course, sympathetic arousal is not always so intense, but, regardless of its intensity, the result is an adjustment of internal

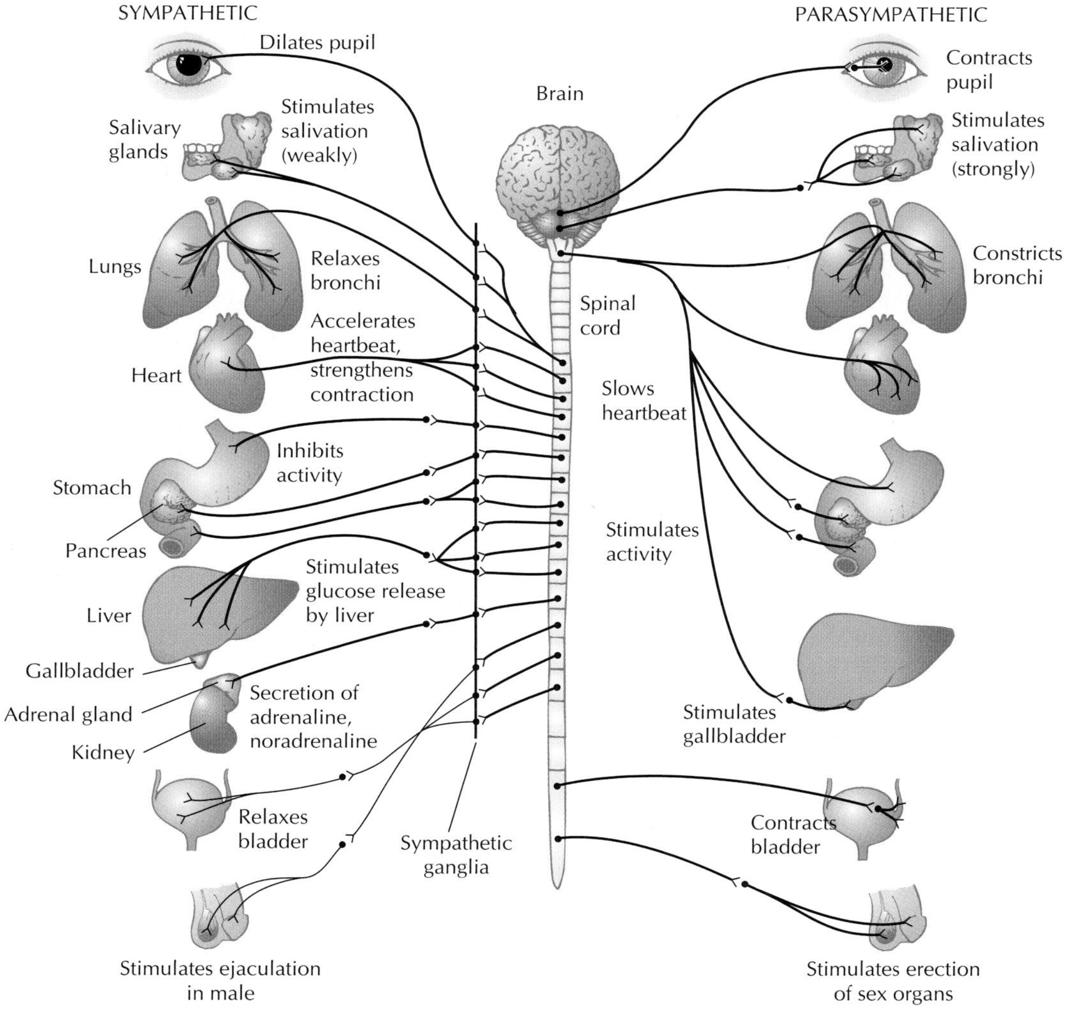

FIGURE 6.7 The sympathetic and parasympathetic branches of the autonomic nervous system (ANS) consist of nerve fibers emerging from the spinal cord.

conditions so that the organism can make maximum use of whatever energy it has stored within it (Feldman, Meyer, & Quenzer, 1997).

The Parasympathetic Division The **parasympathetic division,** which consists of nerve fibers emerging from the top and bottom of the spinal cord (Figure 6.7), is essentially opposite in function to the sympathetic division. While the latter generally gears up the body to use its energy, the parasympathetic division slows down metabolism and regulates the organs in such a way that they can do the work of rebuilding their energy supply. Thus, while sympathetic activity increases heart rate, parasympathetic activity decreases it; while sympathetic activity inhibits digestion, parasympathetic activity promotes it; and so on. The relationship between the two systems is complex, however, and sometimes they work together rather than in opposition (Feldman, Meyer, & Quenzer, 1997). For example, the orienting response—when an infant instinctively turns toward its mother—involves a slowing of heart rate (parasympathetic activity) in combination with pupil dilation and increased sweating (sympathetic activity).

Because of its connection to arousal, the ANS is critically important in regard to stress-related disorders such as headaches, hypertension, and insomnia. As we shall see in Chapter 9 an important theory in the study of these disorders is that something has gone wrong in the regulation of the cycle connecting the brain to the ANS to the organ in question as they operate together in response to the environment.

The Endocrine System

Closely integrated with the central nervous system is the **endocrine system,** which is responsible for the production of **hormones,** chemical messengers that are released into the bloodstream by the endocrine glands and that affect sexual functioning, appetite, sleep, physical growth and development, the availability of energy, and emotional responses. For example, chronically low levels of thyroid activity result in anxiety-like symptoms, such as tension and irritability, and depression-like symptoms—fatigue, apathy, and so forth (Berlin, Payan, Corruble, et al., 1999; Joffe & Sokolov, 1999).

The headquarters of the endocrine system is the hypothalamus, which, as we saw, lies at the center of the brain. Just below the hypothalamus is the pituitary gland, called the "master gland" because it regulates hormone secretion by the other glands of the body.

Hormones may be involved in certain highly specific psychological disorders. One is major depression. Many studies suggest that, in depressed people, hypothalamus dysfunction leads to oversecretion of a chemical called corticotropin-releasing factor (CRF), which in turn leads to overactivation of the pituitary and adrenal glands (Holsboer, 2001). At the same time, animal research indicates that prenatal stress may result in chronically elevated CRF levels in adult life, thus creating a predisposition to depression (Weinstock, 2000). Hormone imbalances have also been implicated in bipolar disorder, eating disorders, and stress-related disorders.

Evaluating the Neuroscience Perspective

The neuroscience perspective is intuitively appealing. If the causes of abnormal behavior are understood as even partly organic, this would help to relieve the stigma that still attaches to psychopathology. And, if psychopathology is biologically caused, then it might be biologically cured, through treatments quicker and less expensive than psychological therapy. But the greatest argument in favor of this perspective is simply its record of achievement. In the past few decades, neuroscience researchers have made immense strides in understanding the relationship between physiological systems and psychological disorders. Such breakthroughs *have* led to the development of some effective drugs and to the invention of remarkable diagnostic tools such as CT, PET, and MRI. These, in turn, have provided the foundation for further discoveries.

But we must not embrace this approach uncritically. For example, it cannot be assumed that, if a psychological disorder is linked to biochemical abnormalities, such abnormalities are the cause of the disorder. They might be the result of the disorder. (Or both might be due to a third, unknown factor.) Similarly, we cannot infer the cause of a disorder from an effective treatment for it. Aspirin may relieve headaches, but that does not mean that headaches are caused by a lack of aspirin. Finally, not all biological treatments are successful. From medieval bleeding to modern psychosurgery, the history of abnormal psychology provides numerous examples of widely accepted biological treatments that later turned out to be ineffective or even dangerous. With these facts in mind, neuroscience researchers are careful to acknowledge the limitations and risks of any biological treatment.

Neuroscience research in abnormal psychology also raises ethical questions. In the case of disorders that are linked to genes, such as schizophrenia, should we attempt to "repair" the defective genes if and when technology makes this possible? In the meantime, should we prohibit people with these disorders from having children? Can we even require that they be cautioned about the risk of passing on the disorder (Duster, 1999)?

Another ethical problem has to do with symptom reduction and its consequences. Since the 1950s, for example, drugs have been available that control schizophrenia. While they do not cure the disorder, they eliminate its most dramatic symptoms, with the result that thousands of mental patients have been released from hospitals. But what have they been released to? Many of them end up on the street. Have drugs been used as a "quick fix," enabling us to put off the challenge of developing long-term community care for psychotic patients?

But it is not the fault of the neuroscience perspective if its discoveries raise ethical problems. Einstein's theory of relativity also raised ethical problems, in the form of nuclear arms. It is up to societies to solve these problems. As for hasty conclusions about biological causation, it is rarely the researchers who make one-cause claims. As we saw, they tend to espouse the diathesis-stress model, acknowledging both biological and environmental causes. In recent years, the prestige of this model has been greatly boosted by the evidence for brain plasticity, the brain's capacity to shape itself in response to external events. Before, we knew that the environment worked together with brain chemistry to mold behavior. Now we know that the environment can actually alter brain chemistry—even brain structure (Nemeroff, 1996; Sapolsky, 1996). Given this kind of interaction, it is no longer possible

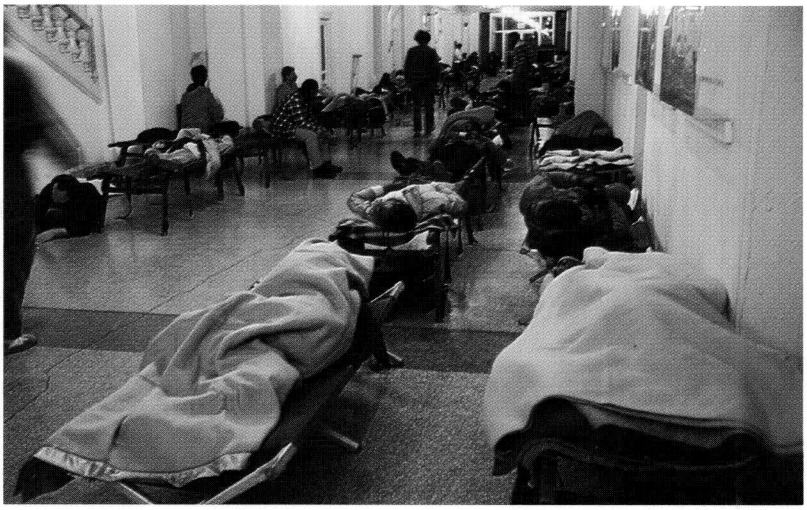

One of the unforeseen consequences of advances in neuroscience research has raised ethical questions: The release of patients from mental hospitals with prescriptions for the drugs they need but without provisions for adequate follow-up care meant that many of these discharged patients would end up living on the streets and sleeping in public shelters.

to consider biogenic and psychogenic causation as an either-or proposition. As a result, one may argue with this or that biological finding, but the neuroscience perspective itself cannot be dismissed.

Integrating the Neuroscience and Psychological Perspectives

Given the evidence that the environment can alter brain functioning and structure, there has been increasing emphasis in recent years on integrating the neuroscience perspective with other psychological perspectives. Advances in the correlation of brain structures with processes such as learning, memory, and motivation offer promising new avenues of study when combined with other psychological approaches. Here are two examples: one that integrates the neuroscience and psychodynamic perspectives and one that integrates the neuroscience and cognitive-behavioral approaches.

Neuroscience/Psychodynamic Integration The influence of psychoanalysis has been waning since the middle of the twentieth century. Psychoanalysis has not developed objective methods for testing its theories, while neuroscience has unearthed progressively more detailed pictures of the physiological workings of the mind (Kandel, 1999). A closer relationship between the psychodynamic and neuroscience perspectives could reenergize psychoanalytic thinking and form a new foundation for testing psychoanalytic ideas about how the mind works (Kandel, 1999).

For example, the idea that we are unaware of much of our mental life—that is, that much of what we think, dream, and perceive is unconscious—is central to the psychodynamic perspective. What can neuroscience teach us about unconscious mental processes? Neuroscientists speak of two types of long-term memory: declarative and procedural. Declarative, or explicit, memory is the conscious memory of people, places, and things. Procedural, or implicit, memory encompasses those perceptual and motor skills that are abundantly evident in our everyday performance and yet are out of our awareness. Procedural memory is a biological example of unconscious mental process. Neuroscience has shown that the processes of procedural memory involve several brain structures: The recognition of recently encountered stimuli involves the sensory cortices; the acquisition of cued feeling states involves the amygdala; new motor habit formation involves the neostriatum; learning and coordinating new motor behavior involves the cerebellum (Kandel, 1999). Procedural memory is quite similar to Freud's notion of the unconscious part of the ego that is concerned with habits and perceptual and motor skills, which are not accessible to consciousness even though they are not repressed. Psychoanalysts believe that most advances in psychoanalytic therapy sessions are in the domain of unconscious procedural knowledge and behavior.

A second central feature of psychoanalysis is its emphasis on the important role of early childhood experience, particularly the attachment relationship between mother and child, in the development of psychopathology later on. The development of internal representations of the attachment relationship occurs during early critical periods of life. During the first two to three years of life, when the infant's attachment to its mother is particularly crucial, the infant relies primarily on procedural memory systems (declarative memory develops later). Neuroscience researchers have shown that early separations from the mother lead to changes in hormonal responses to stress as well as increased gene expression for hypothalamus-mediated hormone responses to stress in the brain (Levine et al., 1967; Nemeroff, 1996; Plotsky & Meaney, 1993). Moreover, the adverse effects of early separation on hormonal responses cause atrophy of parts of the hippocampus, which in turn leads to deficits in memory of the sort seen in posttraumatic stress disorder and depression. Thus, early adverse environmental experiences that affect mother-child attachment may produce actual functional and structural changes in the brain that affect vulnerability to stress in adulthood.

Neuroscience/Cognitive-Behavioral Integration A growing number of theorists have suggested that integrating the neuroscience and cognitive-behavioral perspectives might improve psychologists' understanding of some forms of psychopathology, such as depression and mania (Abramson, Alloy, Hankin, et al., 2002; Fowles, 2001; Johnson, Sandrow, Meyer, et al., 2000). Behavioral psychologists (e.g., Gray, 1994), neuroscientists interested in emotion (e.g., Davidson, 1994), personality theorists (e.g., Cloninger, 1987), and psychopathology researchers (e.g., Fowles, 2001) have focused on two motivational systems fundamental to the regulation of behavior. One of these, the behavioral approach system, or behavioral activation system (BAS) (Gray, 1994; Fowles, 2001), regulates approach behavior to attain rewards and goals; the other, the behavioral inhibition system, or BIS (Gray, 1994; Fowles, 2001), regulates inhibition of behavior and withdrawal in response to threat and punishment.

The BAS is activated by cues in the environment that signal that reward or escape from punishment is possible (e.g., the presence of an attractive goal) or by internal thoughts of reward (e.g., expectations of goal attainment). Such activation of the BAS leads the person to begin to move toward goals and is associated with cognitions of self-efficacy and hope and the emotions of happiness and elation. In contrast, the BIS is activated by environmental cues that signal punishment (e.g., failure) or cognitions of punishment (e.g., thoughts of failure or loss). Activation of the BIS by these cues causes the person to inhibit behavior and is associated with cognitions of hopelessness and emotions of anxiety and depression. The BAS and BIS are reciprocally related, such that greater activity in one leads to less activity in the other. Moreover, recent evidence has provided information on the neural circuitry underlying these two motivational systems. Relatively greater activation of the left frontal cortex as measured by EEG appears to be a neurobiological index of BAS activity, whereas relatively greater activation of the right frontal cortex on EEG is associated with BIS activity (Harmon-Jones & Allen, 1997; Sutton & Davidson, 1997).

Based on these motivational systems, several theorists (e.g., Abramson & Alloy, 2002; Fowles, 2001; Johnson, Sandrow, Meyer, et al., 2000) have suggested that hyperactivation of the BAS in response to BAS-relevant events in the environment (e.g., goal attainment and striving) leads to symptoms of mania such as euphoria, excessive self-confidence, high energy, and decreased need for sleep. Such BAS hyperactivation and mania should also be associated with greater left than right frontal cortical activity on EEG. In contrast, hypoactivation of the BAS and overactivation of the BIS in response to BIS-relevant stressors (e.g., insurmountable failures and losses) leads to symptoms of anxiety and depression such as fear and sadness, helplessness, decreased energy, and motor retardation. BIS hyperactivation and depression should be associated with greater right than left frontal cortical activity on EEG. Currently, researchers are actively testing this neuro-cognitive-behavioral integrative perspective for understanding mania and depression (Abramson & Alloy, 2002).

Key Terms

autonomic nervous system (ANS), 144
behavior genetics, 131
central nervous system (CNS), 135
cerebral cortex, 139
chromosomes, 131
computerized tomography (CT), 142
concordant, 133
corpus callosum, 139
diathesis, 131
diathesis-stress model, 131
dizygotic (DZ) twins, 133
down-regulation, 137
endocrine system, 146
event-related potentials, 142
frontal lobe, 139
functional MRI (fMRI), 142
genes, 131
genetic marker, 135
genotype, 131
genotype-environment correlation, 131
hormones, 146
knockouts, 135
lateralization, 143
magnetic resonance imaging (MRI), 142
mind-body problem, 131
monozygotic (MZ) twins, 132
nervous system, 135
neurons, 136
neuroscience perspective, 131
neurotransmitter, 137
occipital lobe, 140
parasympathetic division, 145
parietal lobe, 140
peripheral nervous system, 144
phenotype, 131
polygenic, 131
positron emission tomography (PET), 142
postsynaptic receptors, 137
psychopharmacology, 138
psychosurgery, 143
reuptake, 137
single photon emission computer tomography, 142
somatic nervous system, 144
sympathetic division, 144
synapse, 136
temporal lobe, 140
up-regulation, 137

Summary

- The neuroscience perspective focuses on the interaction between people's physical and psychological functioning. The mind and body are two aspects of a single complex entity. Psychological stress and physical illness often influence each other.
- Behavior genetics is a subfield of psychology that attempts to determine the degree to which specific psychological disorders are genetically inherited. Only a few psychological disorders have a clear-cut genetic cause, but many disorders, including schizophrenia, apparently result from the interaction of environmental stressors and an inherited predisposition to the disorder. A person's observable characteristics, or phenotype, are the product of experience combined with his or her genotype, or genetic endowment. Through family, twin, and adoption studies, behavior geneticists try to assess heritability.
- The central nervous system (CNS), consisting of the brain and spinal cord, controls behavior by processing, transmitting, and storing information. Neurotransmitters mediate the transmission of impulses across the synapse between two neurons, or nerve cells. Drugs intended to alleviate a disorder by increasing the action of a given neurotransmitter may do so by slowing down its reuptake into the neurons' axon terminals, where it is made. A neurotransmitter's action may be suppressed by using a drug to attach to receptors on the neurons in the neurotransmitter's place.
- Drugs are now the most common of the biological treatments for abnormal behavior. The five main categories are antianxiety drugs, sedative-hypnotic drugs, antipsychotic drugs, antidepressant drugs, and antimanic/mood-stabilizer drugs.
- A major focus of neuroscience research in abnormal psychology has been brain anatomy. The external surface of the cerebral cortex shows many fissures (sulci) and ridges (gyri). The longitudinal fissure divides the brain along the midline into two hemispheres, each containing four lobes with differentiated functions. Regulatory structures include the hypothalamus, limbic structures, thalamus, basal ganglia, cerebellum, and brain stem, a structure containing the pons, medulla, and reticular activating system. Psychological disorders have been traced to dysfunctions in many of these structures.
- Research on the relationship between brain anatomy and psychological functioning has been greatly aided by electroencephalography (EEG), positron emission tomography (PET), computerized tomography (CT), and magnetic resonance imaging (MRI).
- Psychosurgery is brain surgery performed for the purpose of reducing abnormal behavior when no organic brain disorders are present. Prefrontal lobotomy is rarely performed today. Less destructive techniques are cingulotomy and stereotactic subcaudate tractotomy. Psychosurgery is controversial and is used only when other treatments have failed.
- Lateralization is the localization of functions in one hemisphere of the brain. Only a few, very limited functions are completely lateralized. Complex cognitive processes, such as language and emotion, involve interplay among parts of the brain in both hemispheres, although aspects of these processes are apparently lateralized. For example, in most people, the left hemisphere seems to control language production; the right hemisphere seems to be specialized for the subtle interpretation of language.
- The peripheral nervous system consists of the somatic nervous system and the autonomic nervous system (ANS). The somatic nervous system activates skeletal muscles and controls purposeful behavior. The autonomic nervous system activates smooth muscles, glands, and internal organs and controls such automatic responses as heart rate, respiration, and the release of adrenaline. The ANS adjusts the body to changing environmental demands through its sympathetic and parasympathetic branches. Sympathetic arousal prepares us for quick action in emergencies—for example, increasing heart rate, respiration, and blood sugar. The parasympathetic division slows metabolism and helps to restore the system to equilibrium. The ANS is associated with such stress-related disorders as hypertension and insomnia.
- The endocrine system influences emotional states, sexual functioning, energy availability, and physical growth and development by releasing hormones into the bloodstream from the hypothalamus, pituitary gland, and other endocrine glands. Glandular dysfunction may be involved in certain psychological disorders.
- The neuroscience perspective presents problems of both causality and ethics. Finding that a genetic predisposition or chemical imbalance accompanies a given disorder does not mean that the organic factor is the only or even the principal cause of the disorder. Ethical concerns involve genetic engineering and the sometimes negative consequences of symptom reduction without adequate follow-up care. Neuroscientists have made great strides in developing diagnostic tools and discovering effective drug treatments for some disorders. Even for these disorders, however, researchers favor the diathesis-stress model, which studies the combined influences of environmental stress and biochemical factors.
- In recent years there has been increased emphasis on integrating the neuroscience perspectives with other psychological perspectives. Promising new avenues of study include one that integrates the neuroscience and psychodynamic approaches and one that integrates the neuroscience and cognitive-behavioral approach.

CHAPTER

7

Anxiety Disorder Syndromes

- Phobias
- Generalized Anxiety Disorder
- Obsessive-Compulsive Disorder
- Posttraumatic Stress Disorder
- Panic Disorder

Anxiety Disorders: Theory and Therapy

- The Cognitive Perspective: Overestimation of Threat
- The Behavioral Perspective: Learning To Be Anxious
- The Psychodynamic Perspective: Neurosis
- The Neuroscience Perspective: Biochemistry and Medicine

Anxiety Disorders

A young medical student clutches her chest, feeling a sensation of tightness that makes it harder to breathe and worrying that it could indicate she has a heart condition. For the past few weeks, a sense of dread has possessed her, an unsettling feeling of foreboding that something is about to happen and that she is utterly unprepared to deal with it. She has been a nervous person for much of her life, and her dreadful imaginings have lately begun to make her fear that there is danger in every direction, from personal problems to health problems to conflicts with her medical supervisors. Today, in the middle of a meeting with several other medical students, she begins to feel dizzy. Muscle pains shoot through her arms and legs, and she feels as if someone is standing on her chest—she is not getting enough air. She abruptly leaves the meeting, afraid that she will begin to shake, worried the others will notice and wonder if she is losing her sanity.

At the heart of this young woman's problem are multiple symptoms of anxiety (related to the emotion of fear) that affect many areas of functioning. Anxiety is part and parcel of human life, as common an emotional state as one can identify. All people experience anxiety, although not usually to the extent described above. Anxiety is a theme in literature, in modern art, and in the writings of philosophers struggling with existential questions. As Rollo May said (1950), "one runs athwart the problem of anxiety at almost every turn." Anxiety originates in the fear response, the "fight or flight" reaction that probably evolved in the human species as a reaction to clear threats to well-being (Lang, Bradley, & Cuthbert, 1998; Nesse, 1998).

Although they are both closely entwined with the emotion of fear, it is useful to distinguish between anxiety and panic. Anxiety and panic both begin with some feeling of fear, but they differ strikingly in the way that they unfold (Zinbarg, 1998). **Anxiety** is a feeling of dread and gnawing apprehension about vague or unrealized threats and hardships that exist sometime in the future but are not a clear, immediate danger to well-being. Anxiety begins with an initial "low-throttle" fear response that is redirected into worry, vigilance for signs of threat, and a chronic feeling of edginess.

In a **panic attack,** by contrast, a "full-throttle" activation of the fear system erupts intensely and suddenly and mobilizes a person to take flight. A person having a panic attack has symptoms such as heart palpitations and shortness of breath and feels impelled by a sense of emergency conditions to make a last desperate bid to escape catastrophic harm. Although the physical symptoms of anxiety (e.g., chronic tension) can be distinguished from panic symptoms (e.g., heart palpitations) (Brown, Marten, & Barlow, 1995; Joiner, Steer, Beck, et al., 1999), people can sometimes have both reactions. Indeed, the presence of one state can increase the risk of the other.

In this chapter, we will focus on the **anxiety disorders,** characterized either by manifest anxiety or by self-defeating behavior patterns aimed at warding off anxiety. Until 1980, the anxiety disorders were grouped with the somatoform and dissociative disorders (Chapter 8) under the single diagnostic heading of *neurosis*. This term was coined in the eighteenth century by a Scottish physician, William Cullen, to describe a general affliction of the nervous system that produced "nervous" behavior. Throughout the nineteenth century, people who were "sane" but nevertheless engaged in rigid and self-defeating behaviors were labeled neurotic and were thought to be the victims of some unidentified neurological dysfunction. Then, beginning around the start of the twentieth century, this biogenic view was gradually replaced by Freud's psychogenic view. To Freud, neurosis was due not to organic causes but, rather, to anxiety. As repressed memories and desires threatened to break through into the conscious mind, anxiety occurred as a danger signal to the ego. Neurotic behavior was either the expression of that anxiety or a defense against it.

The early editions of the *DSM* implicitly endorsed Freud's view by gathering all the so-called neurotic disorders into a single, anxiety-based category. Many people objected to this kind of classification, however. The diagnostic manual, as they pointed out, was meant to be used by mental health professionals of all theoretical persuasions; therefore, using a term that implied psychodynamic interpretation was inappropriate. In response to these criticisms, *DSM-III* (1980) eliminated the "neurosis" heading and broke up the "neurotic disorders" into separate categories, based on the behavior patterns they involved—a practice that has survived into *DSM-IV-TR*. Nevertheless, the term *neurosis* is still widely used in psychodynamic writings. And mental health professionals of many persuasions continue to use it to indicate that the anxiety disorders, unlike schizophrenia, say, do not destroy reality contact. People with anxiety disorders may misinterpret or overreact to certain stimuli related to their psychological problems, but in general they see the same world as the rest of us. And in most cases they still go about their daily routines, carrying on fairly reasonable conversations, engaging in relationships with other people, and so on. They may cope inefficiently or poorly, but they cope.

Although the anxiety disorders may not be crippling, they still represent the most common psychological disorder in the United States, with approximately 30 to 40 percent of the population developing anxiety disorders at some point in their lives (Shepherd, Cooper, Brown, et al., 1996). Anxiety disorders cost billions of dollars, making them the most expensive of all mental health problems (Rovner, 1993). They can significantly impair occupational, social, and family functioning (Mogotsi, Kaminer, & Stein, 2000), and they can lead to other severe disorders, such as depression and alcoholism (Burke, Burke, & Rae, 1994). They may also lead to physical disorders, such as heart disease (Boscarino & Chang, 2001).

In this chapter, we will describe the various syndromes that fall under the heading of anxiety disorders. Then we will examine the theoretical perspectives on the anxiety disorders, together with the corresponding therapies.

Anxiety Disorder Syndromes

Although anxiety can be experienced in a variety of ways, there are three basic patterns. Phobias, acute stress disorder, and posttraumatic stress disorder involve a fear aroused by an identifiable object or situation. By contrast, in panic disorder and generalized anxiety disorder, the anxiety is unfocused; either it seems to descend out of the blue, unconnected to any specific stimulus (panic disorder), or it is with the person continually (generalized anxiety disorder). Finally, in obsessive-compulsive disorder, anxiety occurs if the person does *not* engage in a thought or behavior that otherwise serves no purpose and, in fact, may be unpleasant and embarrassing.

Phobias

A **phobia** has two components: (1) an intense and persistent fear of an object or a situation that, as the person realizes, actually poses no real threat and (2) avoidance of the phobic stimulus. In some cases, the phobic stimulus is something that seems utterly harmless. Often, however, the stimulus carries a slight suggestion of danger—for example, it might be something that a child fears, such as dogs, insects, snakes, or high places. Nonphobic people may also avoid these things. Many of us, for example, distinctly prefer not to step out onto a fire escape and would never touch a snake, no matter how harmless. The difference between these reactions and a phobic reaction is, first, one of severity. While the normal person may feel apprehension at the sight of a snake, the snake-phobic person shows intense anxiety—escalated heart rate, sweating, and so forth—and may have a panic attack. Second, because of the severity of the anxiety response, phobic people, unlike others, must design their lives so that they avoid the thing they fear. Phobias are divided into two types: specific phobia, or fear of circumscribed objects or situations; and social phobia, or fear of social embarrassment.

Specific Phobia **Specific phobia** is a fear, without apparent justification, of a particular object or situation. The more frequently seen types of specific phobia are **acrophobia,** fear of heights; **claustrophobia,** fear of enclosed places (e.g., elevators, subways); phobias of body injury (e.g., blood, injections); and animal phobias, particularly for dogs, snakes, mice, and insects. The most common are the animal phobias (Cox & Taylor, 1999), but many people with these phobias do not seek help, for they can manage, without much difficulty, to avoid the animal in question. People with cases of body injury phobia are particularly impaired by their fears of dentists, hospitals, and injections, because these can erect obstacles to necessary or even life-saving health care (Kendler, Myers, Prescott, et al., 2001). In general, the degree of impairment in phobia cases depends on the degree to which the phobic stimulus is a usual factor in the person's normal round of activities. Dog-phobic people are in a bad position, for dogs are a common sight. Fear of air travel might be more debilitating to a business executive than to a stay-at-home parent. In other cases, the phobic stimulus is so rare a factor in the person's environment that it has little or no effect on daily activities. For example, a city dweller with a phobia for snakes need only avoid going to the zoo.

Many ordinary people have irrational fears of certain things or situations, such as snakes, heights, or public speaking, but do not have a clinical phobia (Kendler, Myers, Prescott, et al., 2001). To be diagnosed as phobic, their fears must have a substantial objective impact on their lives or behavior (e.g., causing them to avoid important situations). Specific phobias can have significant negative impact on the quality of life (Kendler, Myers, Prescott, et al., 2001).

A commuter with claustrophobia would need to avoid this crowded subway car. Without an alternative method of transportation to work, he or she would need to seek treatment or find another job close to home.

❖ Groups at Risk

Specific phobias often begin in childhood—the mean age at onset is between 11 and 17 (Boyd, Rae, Thompson, et al., 1990)—and they are common, affecting up to 11 percent of the general population. African Americans and Latinos are at higher risk than other American ethnic groups, and women are twice as susceptible as men (Magee, Eaton, Wittchen, et al., 1996).

Social Phobia People suffering from **social phobia** experience acute nervousness, fear, and embarrassment when dealing with other people. Social phobics avoid performing certain actions in front of others, for fear of embarrassing or humiliating themselves. The most common object of social phobia is public speaking, including simply carrying on conversations with others (Kendler, Myers, Prescott, et al., 2001; Roth, Fresco, & Heimberg, in press). Social phobics may also fear dating, using crowded public restrooms and even writing in front of other people.

Such fears can be severely handicapping; many social phobics go to great lengths to avoid performing certain actions in front of others, for fear that they will blush or their hands will shake and others will notice their anxiety and judge them unfavorably

(Gerlach, Wilhelm, Gruber, et al., 2001; Roth, Fresco, & Heimberg, in press). Social phobia thus erodes self-confidence: To have to plan one's life in order to avoid encountering a stranger in the lavatory is humiliating. More importantly, social phobia restricts people's choices, forcing them into narrow channels of behavior. Thus, it may interfere seriously with work and relationships (Mogotsi, Kaminer, & Stein, 2000; Stein & Kean, 2000), as the following case study shows:

> The patient was a 28-year-old man who first showed signs of social phobia at the age of 15. He was shy and introverted and had few friends. He avoided contact with his peers and took seven years to complete the normal curriculum in the university, primarily because of his avoidance of tests, especially oral examinations. His social relationships were largely superficial; he avoided them, because of his high level of anxiety. He experienced somatic symptoms—blushing, trembling, sweating, dry mouth, palpitations—whenever he was in social situations or in contact with persons in authority. After he graduated from the university with a degree in engineering, he completely avoided all social interaction outside his family, including friends of his brother. Because of his fear of scrutiny, he had worked for only six months as an engineer and was reluctant to seek further employment. (Bobes, 1999)

As this example shows, social phobia can produce relatively severe impairment by affecting employment as well as social life (Mogotsi, Kaminer, & Stein, 2000; Stein & Kean, 2000). Thus, social phobia is associated with greater financial dependence and unemployment and lower income than in the general population. The disorder can also increase the risk that individuals will develop other psychiatric disorders (Magee, Eaton, Wittchen, et al., 1996). No genetic studies have been conducted of people with social phobias, but researchers have identified what seem to be high-risk parenting styles. Parents who are overprotective without being emotionally supportive; parents who are overconcerned with dress, grooming, and manners; and parents who discourage children from socializing, thus preventing them from learning social skills and mastering social fears—these three patterns are frequently reported by those with social phobia (Bruch & Heimberg, 1994).

Without treatment, social phobia is a chronic, lifelong condition with little hope of improvement or recovery (Fresco & Heimberg, 2001; Reich, Goldenberg, Vasile, et al., 1994). Individuals with social phobias are more likely to have a unipolar mood disorder (in which there is significant clinical depression but no personal or family history of manic symptoms) than individuals without the phobia, and they are more than twice as likely to meet the criteria for alcohol abuse or dependence (Magee, Eaton, Wittchen, et al., 1996). People with social phobia are also more likely to consider suicide than persons without social phobia (Fresco & Heimberg, 2001).

In many cases, people with social phobia seem to have been shy or introverted as children; such childhood shyness seems to be more strongly associated with social anxiety than other types of anxiety symptoms (Mick & Telch, 1998).

❖ Groups at Risk

Social phobia is the most common form of anxiety disorder and the third most common psychiatric disorder. Some 13.3 percent of the population suffers from social phobia at some time in their lives, and almost 8 percent of the population suffer from the disorder in any given year (Kessler, McGonagle, Zhao, et al., 1994). Women are more likely to have social anxiety disorder (with a lifetime prevalence rate of 15.5 percent versus 11.1 percent in men), but men are more likely to seek treatment (Weinstock, 1999). In a study that raises intriguing questions about risk factors, researchers looking at two groups of people with social phobia found that one group reported difficulties with anger, hostility, and mistrustfulness, while the other reported difficulties with unassertiveness, exploitability, and overly submissive behavior (Kachin, Newman, & Pincus, 2001).

Social phobias usually begin in early adolescence, the developmental stage at which children become acutely aware of how they are impressing others and thus become prone to embarrassment. The less a person's income or education, the greater the risk of both specific and social phobias (Magee, Eaton, Wittchen, et al., 1996), which makes sense; the poor have reason to fear.

Generalized Anxiety Disorder

As the name suggests, the main feature of **generalized anxiety disorder** is a chronic state of diffuse anxiety. *DSM-IV-TR* defines the syndrome as excessive and uncontrollable worry, over a period of at least six months, about several life circumstances. Of course, many normal people worry at times about such things as family, money, work, and health. The pathological worry of people with generalized anxiety disorder is very different in important respects because it is excessive, difficult to terminate, and uncontrollable. Essentially, people with generalized anxiety disorder become worriers who often seem the very picture of misery, as they are continually expecting the worst and waiting for something dreadful to happen, either to themselves or to the people they care about. Their psychological condition spills over into their cognitive and physiological functioning, and they feel restless, snappy, and irritable; have difficulty concentrating; tire easily; and typically suffer from chronic muscle tension and insomnia (Thayer, Friedman, & Borkovec, 1996).

Generalized anxiety disorder can disrupt both social and occupational functioning (Bell, 1995). In fact, recent studies suggest that generalized anxiety disorder often has disabling effects that are as serious as, if not more serious than, those of lung disease, drug addiction, and major depression (Kessler, in press). The worry and anxiety can also worsen and exacerbate coexisting health conditions (Bell, 1995), as well as lead to demoralization and depression and other anxiety disorders. Recent research suggests that generalized anxiety disorder leads to more lost workdays than any other chronic disorder, including depression, panic disorder, ulcers, lung disease, and drug addiction (Kessler, in press). Generalized anxiety disorder often has its onset in the teenage years, and occasionally in childhood; and only about a third of lifetime sufferers experience spontaneous recovery without treatment (Wittchen & Hoyer, 2001). Many patients seek help in medical settings, but most of these are unlikely to openly complain of anxiety symptoms and usually present with somatic and sleeping problems (Wittchen & Hoyer, 2001).

❖ Groups at Risk

Recent studies indicate that approximately 5 percent of the U.S. population and 5 percent of the world population suffer from generalized anxiety disorder at some point in their lives (Kessler, in press). Other research indicates that in any given year, about 2 to 3 percent of the population has the disorder (Wittchen & Hoyer, 2001). It is twice as common in women as in men (Kessler, McGonagle, Zhao, et al., 1994), and this differ-ence is even greater in older age groups (Carter, Wittchen, Pfister, et al., 2001; Kessler, McGonagle, Zhao, et al., 1994). The disorder becomes increasingly prevalent among people who are older than 35 (Wittchen & Hoyer, 2001). People who are separated, divorced, or widowed are also at higher risk (Wittchen & Hoyer, 2001), as are homosexuals (Fergusson, Horwood, & Beautrais, 1999), the unemployed, and housewives (Wittchen & Hoyer, 2001).

Obsessive-Compulsive Disorder

Obsessive-Compulsive Disorder: A Case of Paperwork, Clothing Tags, and Zippers

View the video on obsessive-compulsive disorder on the MindMAP CD to learn how this disorder interferes with the normal functioning of two friends. After watching the video, consider whether OCD might be learned from other people.

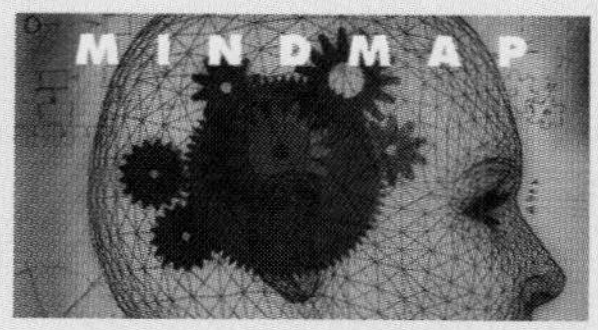

An **obsession** is a thought or image that keeps intruding into a person's consciousness. The person finds the thought distressing and inappropriate and tries to suppress it, but still it returns. For example, an individual might have persistent fearful thoughts about coming into contact with dirt or contamination or about hurting someone else. A **compulsion** is an action that a person feels compelled to repeat again and again, in a rigid, stereotypical fashion, though he or she has no conscious desire to do so. People suffering from either obsessions or compulsions—or, as is usually the case, from both—are said to have **obsessive-compulsive disorder (OCD)**.

Mild obsessive-compulsive symptoms are common in the general population (Gibbs, 1996), as many people can attest. A song may keep playing in our heads; our minds may return again and again to the question of whether we fed the cat before going to work. But these thoughts pass, and we go on about our business. Pathological obsessions, on the other hand, do not pass; though the person tries to suppress them, they recur day after day. The most common obsessions revolve around aggressive impulses and fears of contamination, as well as concerns about the need for symmetry and order (Summerfeldt, Antony, Downie, et al., 1997). For example, a person might fold sheets repeatedly, with diminishing returns, to ensure that they are perfectly folded. Other obsessions are related to hoarding or saving possessions, religious transgression, and sexual themes.

Compulsions, though they may be as irrational and disruptive as obsessions, tend to have more neutral content. For example, the most common compulsions are cleaning rituals and checking rituals (Khanna & Mukherjee, 1992; Rachman &

Focus On... Animal Hoarding and Obsessive-Compulsive Disorder

One unusual behavior that has been associated with obsessive-compulsive disorder (OCD) is hoarding, in which people acquire and keep large quantities of possessions that appear to be useless or of limited value (Frost & Gross, 1993). Hoarders accumulate so many stacks of newspapers and magazines, or old phonograph records and books, or items found on the streets and in the alleys, that their living spaces become virtually unusable. Often, the hoarded possessions spill over into hoarders' yards, so that neighbors complain about unsightly collections of car parts or unsanitary piles of trash.

A peculiar variant of such behavior is the hoarding of animals. Frost (2000) describes the case of a Los Angeles woman who was arrested on charges of animal cruelty after more than 600 animals were found in her home, some of them dead, others so ill they had to be euthanized. The woman insisted that the animals were well cared for and that her home was clean, despite clear evidence (such as animal feces and urine accumulated in the living areas) to the contrary. She refused to give the animals up voluntarily because she was afraid they would be put to death.

Animals hoarders, sometimes called collectors, like this woman in Los Angeles are in a state of denial. They do not see the filth in their homes, and they cannot see that their animals are sick, dying, or already dead. An animal hoarder is identified not by the number of pets kept but by how the animals and their owner live. A person with 20 dogs who keeps them in healthy, sanitary conditions is not considered a hoarder. But a person with 20 dogs who keeps them in overcrowded, unsanitary conditions; who fails to act on the deteriorating condition of the animals; and who fails to recognize the negative impact of the animal collecting on his or her own health is considered an animal hoarder (Patronek, 1999).

Animal hoarding, which exists in all communities, is a poorly understood phenomenon. Even with inanimate forms of hoarding, such as of old appliances, which have received modest attention in the mental health literature, there is no consensus about the exact nature of this behavior or predisposing conditions. Although there is not enough evidence or research at this time to classify hoarding as a mental illness, the behavior has many similarities with OCD (Frost, 2000).

Animal hoarders appear to feel an overwhelming sense of responsibility for preventing imagined harm to animals, and they engage in unrealistic steps to fulfill this responsibility. OCD patients experience this same sense of excessive responsibility for preventing harm and engage in unrealistic ritualization to prevent it (Frost, 2000). Similarities are also seen between people who hoard animals and those who hoard objects—for example, people who can't bring themselves to throw away trash—which suggests that an OCD model may be useful. People who hoard possessions frequently identify their possessions as part of themselves, so when they lose a possession, it often leads to a great sense of loss.

Others see parallels with an addiction model (Patronek, 1999), including a preoccupation with animals (the addiction), denial, excuses for the behavior, isolation from society, claims of persecution, and neglect of personal and environmental conditions (Lockwood, 1994). Another possible model for animal hoarding is an attachment model, in which the individual suffers from early deprivation of parental attachment and cannot establish close relationships in adulthood (Frost, 2000).

To date, no research has addressed strategies for resolving cases of animal hoarding, despite its seriousness and the attention it gets in the news media. Until models for this behavior are established and tested, our understanding of the problem will be limited (Frost, 2000).

The cleaning rituals that often characterize obsessive-compulsive disorder go far beyond the requirements of ordinary hygiene. People who need to wash their hands dozens of times a day are severely restricted in their actions.

Hodgson, 1980). Simply checking that the oven has been turned off is not itself bizarre. However, a person with a checking ritual compulsion is compelled, again and again, to interrupt his activities and go make sure he has turned off the oven. People who perform cleaning rituals are forced, with equal frequency, to stop whatever they are doing and go through some hygiene procedure, such as hand washing. Other compulsive rituals involve ordering or arranging, counting, or hoarding.

Typically, a patient with OCD has multiple types of obsessions and often multiple rituals (Rasmussen & Tsuang, 1986). Most people's obsessions and rituals are related. For example, individuals with contamination obsessions usually have cleaning rituals, and those with aggressive obsessions tend to have checking rituals (Rasmussen & Tsuang, 1986; Antony, Downie, & Swinson, 1998).

Obsessive-compulsive disorder is the world's tenth leading cause of disability, according to the World Health Organization (WHO, 1996). It is associated with unemployment, marital separation or divorce, and impaired social functioning (Hollander, Stein, Kwon, et al., 1997; Mogotsi, Kaminer, & Stein, 2000). A high percentage of people with OCD, especially men, never marry (Steketee & Pruyn, 1998). Obsessive-compulsive disorder can have very negative effects on family life. Patients with severe contamination fears have been known to barricade themselves in their living room, refusing to allow entry to anyone, including family members, because of their fears (Van Noppen, Steketee, & Plato, 1997). Similarly, extreme perfectionist concerns with order or symmetry (such as how dishes ought to be placed in the dishwasher) can be a source of marital conflict.

It was once believed that only patients with OCD had odd intrusive thoughts and compulsive rituals. Now, after decades of study, it is clear that mild symptoms are found widely in the population. In fact, more than 80 percent of the population admit to having odd, intrusive thoughts at times (Rachman & de Silva, 1978; Salkovskis & Harrison, 1984), and their concerns—about contamination or the possibility of committing aggressive acts—are much the same as those of people with OCD. Similarly, more than half of normal individuals admit that they engage in compulsive rituals (Muris, Merckelback, & Clavin, 1997), not in essence unlike the compulsive rituals of clinical patients.

Based on this evidence, the main differences between normal persons and patients seem to be a matter of degree and not content. Intrusive thoughts and compulsive rituals are found throughout the population, but they tend to be more frequent, more intense, and more distressing in OCD patients.

Although the general population reports mild symptoms of OCD, it is important not to use the terminology of the disorder in misleading ways. We often hear people casually speaking about someone as "obsessed" with a girlfriend, a hobby, or a sport. These are not true obsessions, however, because the thoughts don't feel intrusive or forced on the person. Likewise, we hear people speak of "compulsive gamblers" or "compulsive eaters." These activities are not true compulsions. By definition, a compulsion is engaged in not as an end in itself but as a means of relieving the distress attendant upon *not* engaging in it. "Compulsive eaters" and "compulsive gamblers," while they may be pained by the consequences of these excesses, nevertheless pursue eating and gambling as ends in themselves.

Nevertheless, several psychological problems may be related to or overlap with OCD. Like depression, obsessive-compulsive symptoms respond to certain antidepressant drugs, including clomipramine (Anafranil) and selective serotonin reuptake inhibitors (SSRIs). Obsessive-compulsive patients sometimes show depression reactions—guilt, dejection, feelings of helplessness—as strongly as they show anxiety (Gibbs, 1996). Several other disorders show less overlap but may be related on a broader spectrum of syndromes related to obsessive-compulsive disorder. For example, compulsive lottery ticket gamblers show symptoms of OCD (Frost, Meager, & Riskind, 2001). Other disorders such as Tourette's syndrome (involuntary movements and verbalizations), trichotillomania (hair pulling), and impulse control disorders (which involve patterns of impulsive behavior, such as kleptomania, the theft of objects not needed for personal use or monetary value) may also relate broadly to obsessive-compulsive disorder (Black, 1998), although this is still a point of controversy. The following case study of a man with OCD illustrates the distress such a problem can cause:

> Gary was a 26-year-old Caucasian carpenter who sought treatment for "terrible thoughts" about "perverse" sexual images that he "could not shake off." These thoughts, which occurred nearly constantly throughout the day, were tormenting images of incest with his family members, particularly his mother. Gary realized that these intrusive thoughts were senseless and excessive, and he suffered extreme feelings of shame because of them. He tried to suppress his thoughts with numerous rituals, such as tensing all his muscles or walking in a certain way. His greatest fear was that he would become aroused by his sexual thoughts about his mother, and he developed extensive avoidance behaviors. At first, he only avoided his mother, but in time he avoided all women and any activity that might be enjoyable to him and therefore arousing. Gary reported that if he had an intrusive thought while doing something pleasurable, that activity would be ruined for him; he therefore avoided all activities during which he had ever had an intrusive thought. Gary also described contamination fears and cleaning rituals, reporting that he avoided public restrooms and spent over 90 minutes a day washing his hands; but these contamination fears were not nearly as troubling to him as the sexual obsessions and related compulsions. He was convinced that his intrusive thoughts meant he was a bad person, and that he would never have peace of mind as long as he had these intrusive thoughts. (Wilhelm, 2000, p. 247)

❖ Groups at Risk

Although some recent estimates suggest that OCD may affect 2 to 3 percent of the population worldwide (Weissman, Bland, Canino, et al., 1997), other studies indicate that this rate is too high and the true prevalence is still unknown (Antony, Downie, & Swinson, 1998). Some findings suggest that African Americans are more at risk for OCD than many other groups (Valleni-Basile, Garrison, Waller, et al., 1996), but other studies do not support this conclusion (Antony, Downie, & Swinson, 1998).

Men and women are equally at risk (Yonkers & Gurguis, 1995), though there is a curious sex differential in the nature of compulsions: Young, single men are more likely to have checking rituals, whereas married women are more likely to have cleaning rituals (Khanna & Mukherjee, 1992; Sturgis, 1993). Obsessive-compulsive disorder also tends to begin earlier in males than in females (Antony et al., 1998). Obsessive-compulsive disorder usually appears in late adolescence or early adulthood; the median age of onset is 23 (Burke, Burke, Regier, et al., 1990). Instances of childhood onset are relatively rare, but they are often associated with greater severity (Lensi, Cassano, Correddu, et al., 1996; Rasmussen & Tsuang, 1986), particularly in males. Negative life events and past psychological problems (Valleni-Basile, Garrison, Waller, et al., 1996)—including miscarriage in women (Geller, Klier, & Neugebauer, 2001) and a history of depression or substance abuse (Douglass, Moffitt, Terrie, et al., 1995)—also increase the risk of an initial or recurrent episode of OCD.

Posttraumatic Stress Disorder

PTSD and Returning From Vietnam: Innocence Lost

This MindMAP video on PTSD provides an emotionally powerful presentation of one man's struggle with PTSD. The video presents a Vietnam veteran who talks about his painful experiences, and of his ultimate loss of innocence, having served in the war and finding himself returning to a society that was indifferent to his suffering. If he had been treated as a hero when he returned from Vietnam, would his adjustment have been different? How?

Posttraumatic stress disorder (PTSD) is a severe psychological reaction, lasting at least one month and involving intense feelings of fear, helplessness, or horror, to intensely traumatic events—events involving actual or threatened death or serious injury to oneself or others. Such events include assault, rape, natural disasters such as earthquakes and floods, accidents such as airplane crashes and fires, and terrorist attacks (see the box on page 160). The *DSM-IV-TR* distinguishes two forms of posttraumatic stress disorder. In the acute form, the disorder lasts just a month or so and then fades away. The more severe, chronic form may last for years and even decades. Predictably, most of our knowledge of PTSD comes from war survivors—people who survived Nazi concentration camps, the bombing of Hiroshima, or the daily agonies of combat during war.

Posttraumatic stress disorder differs from other anxiety disorders in that the source of stress is an external event of an overwhelmingly painful nature, so the person's reaction, though it may resemble other anxiety disorders, seems to some degree understandable. Nevertheless, it is extremely debilitating. The person may go on for weeks, months, or years reexperiencing the traumatic event, either in painful recollection or in nightmares. In some cases, stimuli reminiscent of the traumatic event may cause the victim of PTSD to return psychologically to the scene of the disaster and to replay it all over again in his or her mind. Consequently, victims of PTSD usually take pains to avoid being reminded of the trauma. At the same time, they seem to numb themselves emotionally to their present surroundings. They may find it difficult, for example, to respond to affection—a source of great pain to families of returning soldiers—or to interest themselves in things that they once cared for. Typically, they may also show symptoms of heightened arousal, such as insomnia, irritability, and exaggerated startle responses. Some survivors of the September 11, 2001, terrorist attack on the World Trade Center reported experiencing the whole configuration of symptoms: replaying images of the Twin Towers falling over and over again; feeling numbed and shocked; and jumping at abrupt noises. Beyond the basic symptoms, other common reactions include distressing feelings of survivor guilt (about surviving when other people did not) and anger or shame.

Ironically, the more a person tries to avoid physical and emotional reminders of trauma, the more likely she is to have "rebound effects" with a paradoxical increase in flashbacks and intrusive memories. A major study by Taylor, Kuch, Koch, et al. (1998) of motor vehicle accident victims and Bosnian peacekeepers who were exposed to trauma suggests that intrusive memories, flashback symptoms, and physical avoidance of reminders of trauma may all reflect a victim's attempts to avoid being reminded. Many unfortunate victims with posttraumatic stress disorder may also suffer from repeated episodes of trauma that arise from exposure to multiple and different devastating traumas; for example, they may

It is not uncommon for survivors of life-threatening disasters, such as the terrorist attack on the World Trade Center in New York City, to experience symptoms of PTSD. For the rescue workers and others who labored for months to clear the World Trade Center site and identify human remains, the daily reminders of the event have made psychological recovery especially difficult.

"doubly suffer" from both a violent crime and a later automobile accident. The tragic effect is that the typical victim of posttraumatic stress disorder has a chronic disorder that may last for more than 2 decades (Breslau, Kessler, Chilcoat, et al., 1998; Kessler, 2000), as the following case shows:

> Ms. B is a 36-year-old European-American female who reported that she was sexually assaulted from ages 4–8 by a cousin and at age 12 by an uncle. At age 33 she was raped and beaten by a stranger. She presented with symptoms of PTSD including nightmares, flashbacks of the most recent rapist's voice, avoiding thoughts and reminders of the most recent rape, loss of interest in activities, feeling distant and cut off from others, feeling numb, having difficulty sleeping, difficulty concentrating, being irritable, and being easily startled. She reported having approximately one panic attack a week since the most recent rape 3 years ago. Her panic attacks were often triggered by conditioned cues related to the most recent rape, but some attacks also appeared out of the blue and at night while she was sleeping. (Falsetti & Resnick, 2000)

Symptoms of PTSD generally appear shortly after the trauma. In some cases, however, there is an "incubation period." For days or even months after the event, the person is symptom-free; then, inexplicably, the traumatic reaction begins to surface. In many cases, symptoms clear up by themselves within about 6 months, but some linger for years. A study of 1,098 Dutch veterans who had fought in the Resistance against the Nazis in World War II discovered that, 50 years after the end of the war, 25 to 50 percent of these people were still suffering from PTSD; only 4 percent showed no symptoms at all (Op den Velde, Hovens, Aarts, et al., 1996).

The ultimate burden of PTSD to the individual and to society is enormous. Victims of PTSD have a higher risk of developing a variety of secondary disorders, including mood disorders (such as depression or mania), anxiety disorders, and substance abuse disorders (Kessler, 2000). They are also more likely than other people to suffer from difficulties such as failure in high school and college, teenage pregnancy, marital instability, and unemployment and to have interpersonal relationship problems (Kessler, 2000). Moreover, there is evidence of a direct link between PTSD and the risk of heart disease. Boscarino and Chang (2001) recently found that the rate of serious heart disease among Vietnam veterans who had PTSD was nearly double that of other veterans who had faced similar trauma but had not developed the disorder.

Reaction to Combat Since World War I, traumatic reactions to combat have been known by a succession of names: "shell shock," "combat fatigue," "combat neurosis," and now "posttraumatic stress disorder." Some soldiers become depressed and curl up in their bunks, unable to move. Others experience anxiety, which escalates to panic attacks. What-

More than other American conflicts, the Vietnam War is associated with lingering cases of posttraumatic stress disorder. Public acknowledgments of the courage of those who served, such as this memorial wall in New York City, were belated attempts to ease the veterans' return to civilian life.

ever the response, the precipitating circumstance is usually the same: a close escape from death, often with the added horror of seeing one's companions killed. Such traumas are usually preceded by months or years of accumulated stress: fear, sleep deprivation, cold, heat, and numerous brushes with death. Many soldiers seem to succumb not so much to a single trauma as to this constant piling up of stress. Indeed, many show no effects until they have returned to civilian life and are suddenly surprised by nightmares, flashbacks, and nervous tremors. Their symptoms may be a problem not just for them but for their families as well. Research on Vietnam veterans has shown that those with PTSD are more likely to show hostility and aggression toward their partners or families (Chemtob, Hamada, Roitblat, et al., 1994).

Civilian Catastrophes Disaster is not confined to wartime. There are civilian catastrophes as well. Victims of a plane or car crash, an earthquake, or a violent crime are also subject to posttraumatic stress disorder (Brewin, Andrews, & Valentine, 2000; Ehlers, Mayou, & Bryant, 1998; Feeney & Foa, in press; Resnick, Kilpatrick, Dansky, et al., 1993; Taylor & Koch, 1995). Some civilian catastrophes, such as terror attacks, may

Victims of natural catastrophes like the tornados and flood that devastated Deshler, Nebraska in 2003 are at risk for PTSD.

Focus On... Terrorism from the Skies: Communal Posttraumatic Stress

On September 11, 2001, Americans were horrified by the news that terrorists had attacked the World Trade Center in New York City and the Pentagon in Washington, D.C. Eyewitnesses in downtown New York City told of looking up to see flames billowing from both towers of the World Trade Center, debris splintering into the air like confetti, people on fire leaping from high floors to certain death, as they themselves ran for their lives through clouds of dense smoke.

Like any trauma, a terrorist attack can shatter a person's assumption that the world is, basically, safe and controllable; conversely, such an event can strengthen one's belief that the world is an unpredictable, dangerous place where disaster can strike without warning. Feelings accompanying traumatic shock can include the sudden, frightening awareness of our own personal vulnerability as well as that of our loved ones. In the case of the September 11 attacks, the communal traumatic reaction for Americans included the abrupt realization of the vulnerability of their society itself and of their cherished social values.

Communal traumas can be extremely debilitating, even for people who were not at the disaster scene themselves and who did not directly suffer the loss of loved ones or personal injury. In the modern information age, people everywhere can witness the most shocking and horrific scenes of tragedy and destruction in their own living rooms. To the extent that they can identify with the victims, individuals far from the scene of the trauma can be powerfully affected by the images supplied by television, the Internet, newspapers, and magazines. Their feelings may be milder by degree than those of the people who actually fled from the attacks that day, but media viewers on September 11 experienced the same feelings of helplessness, vulnerability, numbness, and impending doom felt by the survivors. In polls 2 weeks after the attacks, 7 out of 10 Americans reported problems sleeping, and 3 out of 10 reported depression. These and other reported symptoms of numbness, nightmares and flashbacks and feelings of powerlessness and fear are all manifestations of a communal posttraumatic response to a cataclysmic event.

fall in the gray area between combat-related and civilian catastrophes, for they involve the same sense of deliberately caused, widespread loss of life as combat traumas. Whatever the differences in the traumatic event, the general symptoms of PTSD are similar.

❖ Groups at Risk

Posttraumatic stress disorder is not rare. Nearly 9 percent of the general population will develop the reaction over their lifetimes (Breslau, Davis, Andreski, et al., 1991; Feeney & Foa, in press). However, not all people are disabled by traumatic experiences; the same event that causes PTSD in some people may cause short-lived reactions in others. For example, even though nearly 70 percent of the U.S. population is exposed to at least one traumatic experience during their lifetimes, only a fraction of those people ever develop PTSD (Solomon & Davidson, 1997).

It is natural for people to experience numerous symptoms of PTSD, such as shock or numbing, shortly after the occurrence of a trauma. These symptoms normally tend to undergo a natural reduction over the course of time (Riggs, Rothbaum, & Foa, 1995; Rothbaum, Foa, Riggs, et al., 1992). Many soldiers go through grueling combat experiences and emerge with nothing more than a few bad dreams. What determines the severity of the response?

The likelihood of PTSD depends in part on the nature of the trauma (see Table 7.1). Posttraumatic stress disorder has been found to occur in up to 65 percent of female victims of sexual assault (Resnick, Kilpatrick, Dansky, et al., 1993; Rothbaum, Foa, Riggs, et al., 1992), up to 40 percent of people surviving serious motor vehicle accidents (Taylor & Koch, 1995), and 15 percent of Vietnam combat veterans (Kulka et al., 1990).

The risk of developing PTSD increases with the number of traumatic events; some individuals have suffered from multiple exposures to trauma, such as an initial, precipitating violent crime and a later car accident. A victim's personal characteristics also play a role. For example, younger age at time of trauma, lack

TABLE 7.1 Factors Affecting the Likelihood of Posttraumatic Stress Disorder

FEATURES OF THE TRAUMA	FEATURES OF THE PERSON	FEATURES OF THE POSTTRAUMA ENVIRONMENT
Intensity of exposure to trauma	Pretrauma psychological adjustment	Availability and quality of social support
Duration of exposure to trauma	Family history of psychopathology	Additional major stressors
Extent of threat posed by trauma	Cognitive and coping styles	
Nature of trauma: caused by humans or natural disaster	Feelings of guilt	

of education, and female gender increase a person's risk of disorder (Brewin, Andrews, & Valentine, 2000). Women are twice as likely as men to develop PTSD (Kessler, Sonnega, Bromet, et al., 1995), but this seems to depend on the trauma type (Brewin, Andrews, & Valentine, 2000). Stein, Walker, and Forde (2000) found that women were at increased risk for PTSD after a violent assault, such as a mugging or a rape. Their risk was the same as men's following other types of trauma, such as surviving a major fire or witnessing injury to others. In a careful reanalysis of earlier studies, Brewin, Andrews, and Valentine (2000) found that gender and age at the time of trauma predicted PTSD in just some populations or settings but not in others.

The reanalysis of earlier studies of risk factors by Brewin and colleagues confirmed that the severity of the trauma and of the perceived threat are strong predictors of the future risk of PTSD. Their study also confirmed the negative effects of inadequate social support and of exposure to additional stresses during or after the trauma. Brewin's group showed that risk factors operating during or after the trauma had a somewhat stronger effect on the development of PTSD than pretrauma factors, such as a history of child abuse, a past psychiatric history, or related indicators of personal psychological strength. Even so, these indicators of pretrauma adjustment were important predictors of risk.

How people cope with trauma—whether they blame themselves for the event or for their response to the event—seems to be a factor in their chance of developing PTSD. Emotional reactions such as prolonged shame, anger, or survivor guilt also increase the risk for developing posttraumatic stress disorder (Andrews, Brewin, Rose, et al., 2000; Ehlers, Mayou, & Bryant, 1998).

Finally, the onset of an acute stress disorder, which persists for less than a month and then improves, is a predictor of later PTSD, as not all individuals with acute stress maintain their improvement (Bryant & Harvey, 1998; Classen, Koopman, Hales, et al., 1998; Harvey & Bryant, 1998).

Problems in the Classification of Posttraumatic Stress Disorder There are a number of questions about posttraumatic stress disorder as a diagnostic category (Davidson & Foa, 1991). To begin with, *DSM-IV-TR* defines the disorder as a response to an event that involves "actual or threatened death or serious injury, or a threat to the physical integrity of oneself or others." But studies have found that more usual events, such as a miscarriage or the discovery of a spouse's affair, can also precipitate the symptoms of posttraumatic stress disorder (Helzer, Robins, & McEvoy, 1987). Currently, severe reactions to these more ordinary traumas are classified separately as adjustment disorders. But it is possible that they, too, should be called posttraumatic stress disorders.

A second problem with this diagnosis is that *most* victims of severe trauma show symptoms associated with posttraumatic stress disorder. Even if, in most people, the symptoms do not last for the month required to earn the diagnosis of posttraumatic stress disorder, we are still left with the question of whether a response that is almost universal should be designated as a psychological disorder (Solomon, Laor, & McFarlane, 1996).

A final problem with this diagnostic category is whether it should be grouped with the anxiety disorders. There are grounds for doing so. Not only is anxiety one of the foremost symptoms of posttraumatic stress disorder, but the disorder also shares additional symptoms, such as fear-based avoidance, with the other anxiety syndromes (Davidson & Foa, 1991; Rothbaum, Foa, Murdock, et al., 1990). Furthermore, first-degree relatives of posttraumatic patients show a high rate of anxiety disorders (Davidson, Smith, & Kudler, 1989). But there is also an argument for placing posttraumatic stress disorder among the dissociative disorders (Chapter 8), for the defining characteristic of that group—the dissociation, or splitting off, of a part of experience or personality—is also seen in the "psychic numbing" and other denial symptoms of posttraumatic stress disorder patients. According to some researchers, however, posttraumatic stress disorder should not be classified with either the anxiety or the dissociative disorders. They argue that, because posttraumatic stress disorder is defined in large measure by its precipitating event, the trauma, it should be placed in a separate category of stress-related disorders (Davidson & Foa, 1991). But this may not be a good solution, either, for many forms of psychopathology—depression, dissociative disorders, and borderline personality disorder, to name a few—seem to be precipitated by trauma (McGorry, 1995).

Panic Disorder

We have already seen the general features of anxiety, in the example that began this chapter. In a panic attack, an intense fear or full-blown alarm reaction begins suddenly and seemingly "out of the blue" and soon mounts at full throttle to an almost unbearable level. The person sweats, feels dizzy, trembles, and gasps for breath. The pulse quickens and the heart pounds. Nausea, chest pains, choking, feelings of numbness, and hot flashes or chills are also common. To people in the grip of such an attack, the world may suddenly seem unreal (derealization), or they may seem unreal to themselves (depersonalization). Above all, they have a sense of inescapable doom—that they are about to lose control, go crazy, or die. Indeed, patients are often first recognized as having panic disorder when they turn up in hospital emergency rooms claiming, despite evidence of good health, that they are dying of a heart attack (Katerndahl, 1996). Such catastrophic thoughts are central to panic disorder and help to distinguish it from other anxiety disorders (Noyes, Woodman, Garvey, et al., 1992). A panic attack is usually a brief, episodic event that develops and peaks within 10 minutes, though it may seem to the victim to last for hours. When it subsides, the person feels exhausted, as if he or she has survived a traumatic experience. Between attacks, the person may worry constantly about having another attack.

Virtually anyone who is exposed to what he or she perceives to be a life-threatening emergency (whether or not the perceptions are accurate) can have a panic attack. In uncued, or unexpected, attacks, the attack seems to come out of nowhere, unconnected to any specific stimulus. In cued attacks, the attack occurs in response to a situational trigger, such as a near automobile accident or a phobic public speaking situation. This distinction is used in differential diagnosis, for although panic attacks may occur in all the anxiety disorders, cued attacks are more characteristic of phobias, while uncued attacks are by definition present in panic disorder. According to *DSM-IV-TR*, a person has **panic disorder** when he or she has had recurrent, uncued panic attacks, followed by psychological or behavioral problems—that is, persistent fear of future attacks, worry about the implications or consequences of the attacks, or significant changes in behavior as a result of the attacks.

However, while uncued attacks are required for the diagnosis of panic disorder, panic disorder patients still report more cued than uncued attacks (Garssen, DeBeurs, Buikhuisen, et al., 1996). Even their uncued attacks, moreover, may involve precipitating events—subtle changes, such as physical exertion, that cause some alteration in body chemistry (Craske, 1991). Nonetheless, self-reports of uncued attacks are important, for they help to account for the victims' catastrophic feelings and their sense of going out of control. People with panic disorder cannot go anywhere—to work, to the movies, to the supermarket—without fearing that they may have an attack in front of everyone, and with help nowhere in sight.

Given panic disorder patients' fears of panic attacks, it is not surprising that the disorder can drastically reduce the quality of life. A study by Candilis and colleagues found that people with panic disorder had many more reported physical and mental health problems than the general population (Candilis, McLean, Otto, et al., 1999).

Sanderson and Rego (2000) described the case of a man with panic disorder:

> RL was a 40-year-old Caucasian man who complained of panic attacks and agoraphobia. He was single and lived alone in New York City, his home town. He reported an unremarkable childhood, though he remembered himself as having been an "anxious kid." RL's first panic attack occurred at age 23. He reported that he experienced several panic attacks and continuous anxiety while on vacation in Miami and began to fear that he would "go crazy and end up in a psychiatric hospital," so he quickly returned home to New York. The attacks began to occur more frequently, and RL developed moderate agoraphobia, avoiding trains, elevators, crowded places, social situations, and traveling outside a 20-mile radius from home. (p. 238)

Agoraphobia: The Fear of Losing Control in Public Places

The MindMAP video on agoraphobia features a 24-year-old woman who has been dealing with this disorder for eight years. Women are much more likely than men to develop agoraphobia (Bekker, 1996). What might some possible explanations for this difference be?

Because of their fear of having a panic attack in front of others, with no one to help them, some people with panic disorder stop going anywhere—a complication of panic disorder called agoraphobia. Literally, **agoraphobia** means "fear of the marketplace." Actually, what the person with agoraphobia fears is being in any situation from which escape might be difficult, and in which help would be unavailable, in the event of panic symptoms. Agoraphobia is often preceded by a phase of panic attacks, the first of which is likely to have occurred outside the home. (Only 10.6 percent of first attacks occur at home [Shulman, Cox, Swinson, et al., 1994].) Eventually, the person becomes so afraid of having an attack, especially in a public place, that he or she begins to stay closer and closer to home. For example, some individuals become afraid to leave the house for fear of losing control of their bowels in public. Some people with agoraphobia refuse to leave home unless someone goes with them; some are able to leave home to go to places in which they feel safe; others refuse to leave home at all. The most common fears that impair people with agoraphobia are being in crowds (Kendler, et al., 2001).

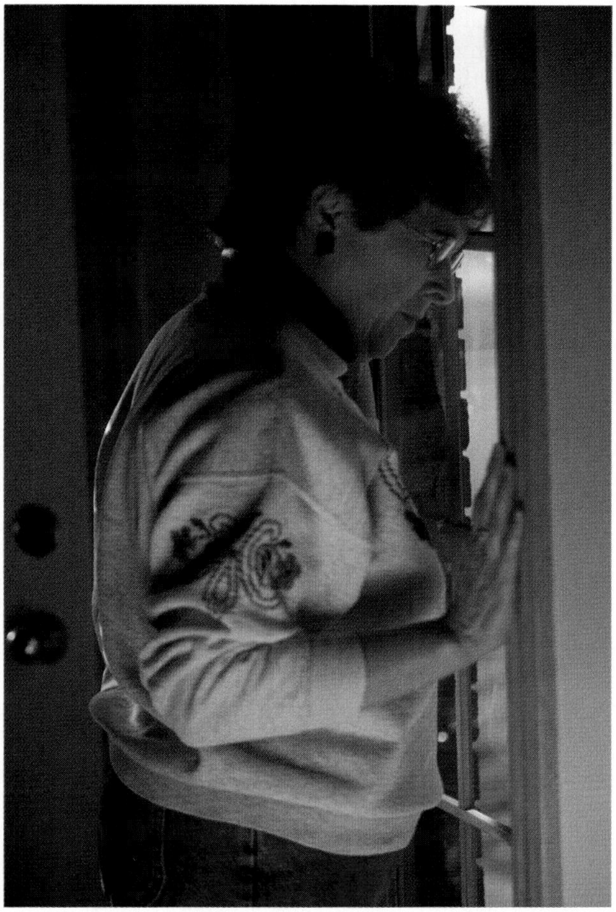

Agoraphobia can become so severe that the person does not dare to venture outside the home for months—sometimes even years—at a time.

Because so many people with panic disorder also suffer from agoraphobia, *DSM-IV-TR* lists agoraphobia as a complication of panic disorder. But the manual also classifies agoraphobia as a disorder in its own right, for many people with agoraphobia—indeed, two thirds, according to one estimate—have no history of panic disorder (Eaton & Keyl, 1990). So while panic attacks often lead to agoraphobia, they are by no means a prerequisite.

❖ Groups at Risk

Panic disorder is a common anxiety disorder, affecting about 3.5 percent of Americans during their lifetimes; agoraphobia is more common, with a prevalence of 5.3 percent (Eaton, Kessler, Wittchen, et al., 1994; Kessler, McGonagle, Zhao, et al., 1994). A cross-national study by Weissman, Bland, Canino, et al. (1997) found that cultural factors may influence risk: Lifetime rates for panic disorder are only 0.4 percent in Taiwan, where rates for most psychiatric disorders are low. In Puerto Rico and other Caribbean cultures, "ataques de nervios" (panic attacks) frequently include shouting and weeping, whereas in equatorial Africa, people with panic attacks may report sensations of worms crawling in their heads (Kirmayer, Young, & Hayton, 1995). In the United States, African Americans tend to report different panic attack symptoms than European Americans do—reporting more intense levels of numbing or tingling in their extremities, as well as greater fear of dying or losing their sanity than European Americans (Smith, Friedman, & Nevid, 1999).

The mean age of first onset of panic disorder is usually in early to middle adulthood (Weissman, Bland, Canino, et al., 1997), often in the mid-twenties, and it rarely begins before puberty (McNally, 2001), although panic attacks are reported in adolescents. Only in the elderly is panic disorder uncommon, and onset in old age is very rare (Flint, Cook, & Rabins, 1996). In addition to age, gender and marital status are key factors in vulnerability. In their cross-national study, Weissman, Bland, Canino, et al. (1997) found that women had higher rates of panic disorder than men in all countries. Women are also more likely than men to develop panic with agoraphobia, and about three quarters of agoraphobia patients are women (Bekker, 1996). In addition, women are more likely than men to suffer a recurrence of panic symptoms after remission of panic (Yonkers, Zlotnick, Allsworth, et al., 1998; Bekker, 1996). Finally, people who are separated or divorced are at greater risk for both panic disorder and agoraphobia (Wittchen & Essau, 1993). In addition, cross-national findings show that an initial panic disorder is a risk factor for the development of agoraphobia as well as major depression (Weissman, Bland, Canino, et al., 1997).

Anxiety Disorders: Theory and Therapy

In Chapters 4 through 6, we presented a general overview of the various perspectives on psychological disturbance. Now we will see how adherents of these perspectives interpret and treat the anxiety disorders. We will begin with the cognitive-behavioral perspective, because it is the dominant and most extensively investigated theoretical approach to anxiety disorders, and it offers the most empirically validated form of psychotherapy (Chambliss & Ollendick, 2000). Then we will look at the behavioral, psychodynamic, and neuroscience approaches to anxiety disorders.

The Cognitive Perspective: Overestimation of Threat

As soon as there is life there is danger.
—Ralph Waldo Emerson

As we have seen, cognitive processes play a role in the development of anxiety disorders. To cognitive theorists, that role is central. Cognitive theorists propose that the basic problem for anxiety disorder patients is that they overestimate danger and rely inflexibly on self-defeating ways to deal with their fears (Beck & Clark, 1997; Riskind & Williams, in press). It is not just the sheer level of objective danger in a situation that determines how anxious people feel, but also their subjective appraisals of danger.

There is no doubt that a fear-inducing perception of potential danger is sometimes adaptive—such as when one is trying to cross a busy intersection in heavy traffic. In fact, a cognitive bias for threatening stimuli may have an evolutionary benefit. A study by Oehman, Flykt, and Esteves (2001) suggests that pictures of threatening stimuli that were relevant to the long-ago survival of early humans—such as a snake in the grass—are more likely to capture our attention quickly than pictures of threats that were not relevant to human evolutionary history, such as guns. They found this rapid capture of attention was especially the case with people who are fearful of such stimuli. Riskind and colleagues found that individuals who were cognitively vulnerable to anxiety showed a selective bias to remember threatening words or images (e.g., of automobile accidents) rather than neutral or positive material, even when they were currently not feeling anxious (Riskind, Williams, Gessner, et al., 2000). This "looming maladaptive style" led them to overestimate the extent to which risk was intensifying.

Childhood events, including faulty attachment relationships, seem to lead individuals to develop cognitive vulnerabilities to anxiety disorders and other psychological problems (Reinecke & Rogers, 2001; Roberts, Gotlib, & Kassel, 1996; Solomon, Ginzburg, Miklulincer, et al., 1998). Recent research suggests that insecure and avoidant adult attachment styles are related to a cognitive vulnerability to anxiety, as well as to measures of anxiety, general well-being, and general health (such as the number of times that participants had seen a doctor over a six-month period) (Williams & Riskind, in press).

Theorists presume that each type of anxiety disorder has distinct cognitive content. Some anxiety disorders largely center on the overestimation of outside threats (such as spiders or social rejection), while others primarily center on the overestimation of inside threats (such as the fear of "going insane" or having a heart attack), but all disorders may involve both sorts of threat to some degree.

Phobias

Specific Phobia According to the cognitive view, individuals with specific phobia overestimate the dangers presented by particular objects or situations. For example, people who are phobic of spiders or insects tend to have many distorted beliefs related to their fear of harm from the phobic stimuli (Thorpe & Salkovskis, 1997). Moreover, they may be unaware of some of these beliefs because they are automatic as well as largely unverbalized (Teachman, Gregg, & Woody, 2001). People with phobias also exaggerate the extent to which a threat is intensifying. For example, an individual with a spider phobia overestimates the speed with which spiders are approaching (Riskind & Williams, in press; Riskind, Moore, & Bowley, 1995).

Social Phobia Socially anxious people tend to overestimate the threat of public embarrassment, criticism, or scrutiny (Clark & Wells, 1995; Rapee & Heimberg, 1997; Roth, Fresco, & Heimberg, in press). They seem to focus on their own distorted images of how others see them (e.g., as stupid or unattractive), which sets off a cycle of avoidance or other faulty "safety behaviors" (see Figure 7.1). As is the case with other types of avoidance behaviors, these safety behaviors perpetuate social phobias, because they prevent the distorted images and beliefs from being disproven and corrected (Clark & Wells, 1995; Wells & Clark, 1997).

Generalized Anxiety Disorder For cognitive theorists, individuals with generalized anxiety disorder perceive and interpret the world through biased mental filters. Their thinking is dominated by the exaggerated cognitive structures they have developed for thinking about their vulnerability to threats (Beck & Clark, 1997; Riskind & Williams, in press; Thayer, Friedman, Borkovec, et al., 2000). Thus the sense of danger such people feel is finely tuned, making them excessively vigilant for signs of threat and giving them a continual feeling that they are "walking on pins and needles." Generalized anxiety disorder patients experience a stream of fear-inducing and threatening automatic thoughts that serve as triggers for maladaptive worry. The threatening automatic thoughts involve multiple sources of concern, threat overestimation, and catastrophizing (for example, thinking up exaggerated disasters that could threaten their physical and financial health).

Although people with generalized anxiety disorder experience a world full of threats, they cannot find a sense of safety simply by physically avoiding specific stimuli. Instead, they tend to handle the fear caused by their ongoing threatening thoughts by engaging in lengthy cycles of unproductive worry (Borkovec, Ray, & Stoeber, 1998). Such worry cycles are continuous and almost impossible for the worrier to terminate. They make it difficult for people with generalized anxiety to concentrate on other matters—but do little to solve their problems. Added to all this, people with generalized anxiety disorder often make their problems

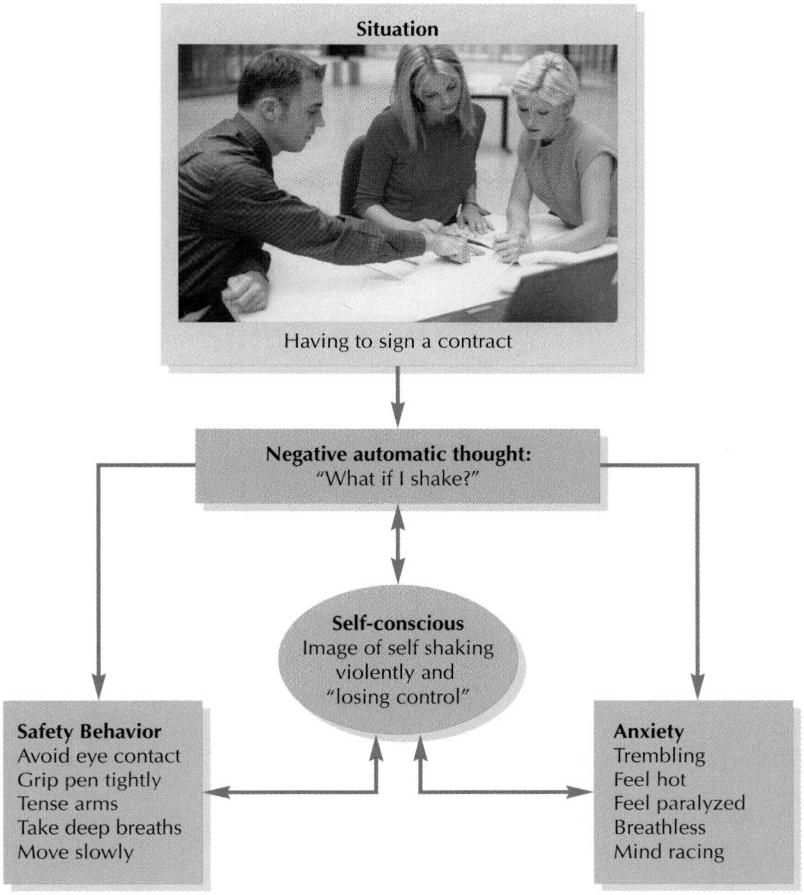

FIGURE 7.1 Social phobia can result in a cycle of avoidance or safety behaviors. As shown here, these behaviors perpetuate the problem by preventing the person from learning that others do not see her in the negative way she thinks they do.

even worse by "worrying about their own worry," a type of worry that Wells (1999) calls "metaworry."

Paradoxically, maladaptive worry seems to help patients avoid full-fledged fear reactions in several ways. Worrying can give sufferers a false feeling that they are doing something about their problems, which fosters an illusory sense of control (Borkovec, Ray, & Stoeber, 1998). Engaging in worry might also help to change the fear into chronic tension, which is more bearable than an acute panic attack. Worry usually involves an active form of predominantly verbal thoughts (an activity of the left hemisphere of the brain), which seems to decrease the vivid mental images of threat (a right-hemisphere activity) that can induce intense, full-throttle fear (Borkovec & Inz, 1990).

But chronic worry hinders people with generalized anxiety disorder from overcoming their feelings of fright and fear. By worrying, they are engaging in verbal thinking that focuses on the *least* fear-producing part of the threatening stimuli or worry triggers. However, it seems necessary to focus on the most fear-producing parts of threatening stimuli, such as vivid mental images of catastrophe and feelings of hurt, to learn to be less frightened or fearful, a process psychologists call desensitization (Mohlman & Zimbarg, 2000).

Panic Disorder As cognitive theorists point out, in the course of a day, virtually all of us at some moment probably experience odd sensations—such as having our heart beat fast, or feeling short of breath or hot and dizzy (Clark, 1988; 1993; Schmidt & Woolaway-Bickel, in press). If a person interprets such sensations catastrophically—for example, as a signal that he or she is about to pass out or have a heart attack—panic can result. The misinterpretation of normal bodily sensations as frightful harbingers of imminent catastrophe triggers a full-throttle alarm that mobilizes the person for flight or desperate action.

Most experts do not believe that panic attacks come out of the blue. Often, an attack is found to have been preceded by an event that altered the sufferer's physiological state in some way—for example, exercising, having sexual relations, drinking caffeinated beverages, being watched by a new boss, or even getting up quickly from a seated position. Most of us, when we do these things, experience some internal adjustments—our heart skips a beat, our

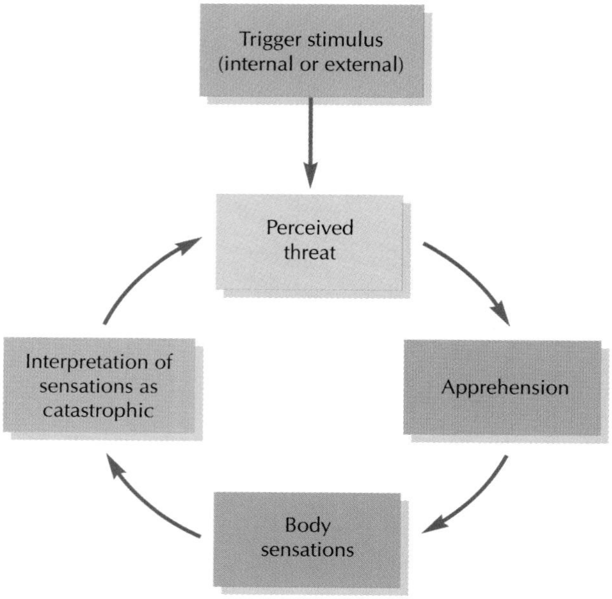

FIGURE 7.2 A cognitive model of a panic attack. According to this model, misperceptions of physical sensations intensify the sensations and lead to a panic attack.

breathing becomes momentarily labored—but we ignore these sensations. Panic disorder patients do not ignore them; in fact, they often scan themselves for any "odd" sensations (Ehlers & Breuer, 1996; Schmidt, Lerew, & Trakowski, 1997), an activity that seems to paradoxically increase their risk of having uncued, spontaneous panic attacks. There is also evidence that people with panic disorder interpret these sensations as dangerous, and this misperception aggravates the sensations. As the sensations become more extreme, so does the interpretation, eventually escalating to the conviction of impending doom that characterizes a panic attack (Clark, 1993).

Sometimes, a history—having had a panic attack in the past or a relative who died of a heart attack—may lead individuals to develop a learned trait called anxiety sensitivity (Schmidt & Woolaway-Bickel, in press; Stewart, Taylor, Jang, et al., 2000), a feeling of fear and discomfort from physical sensations of anxiety. This trait itself seems to predict the risk of future panic attacks (Schmidt & Woolaway-Bickel, in press).

The cognitive model helps to explain the fact that panic attacks can be induced under laboratory conditions, with results closely resembling those of natural attacks. They can be induced in many different ways: by pharmacological agents such as sodium lactate (a metabolic by-product of stress and fatigue) and caffeine; by breathing-related procedures such as exercise, hyperventilation, and carbon dioxide inhalation; and by behavioral procedures such as relaxation exercises or confrontation with a phobic stimulus. The panic-provoking agent that has been studied most extensively is sodium lactate, which produces panic attacks in 70 to 80 percent of individuals with panic disorder, compared with 0 to 10 percent of normal controls (Nutt & Lawson, 1992). No single biological mechanism can account for the effects of all these panic-provoking agents, but the cognitive model can. Figure 7.2 shows how interaction between physical sensations and one's interpretation of them could result in spontaneous panic attacks.

Cognitive factors also help to explain how a person with panic attacks will develop agoraphobia. Panic disorder victims who believe that their attacks will be beyond their ability to cope are most likely to become agoraphobic (Clum & Knowles, 1991).

Obsessive-Compulsive Disorder Most people, at one time or another, report experiencing unwanted intrusive thoughts, such as wanting to strike someone, or of being contaminated by filthy substances or germs, but few of us consider such odd, unwanted thoughts to be reflective of our personal worth. A person who judges himself as unworthy for having unwanted, intrusive thoughts, who sees himself as "bad," "mad," or potentially dangerous, can come to suffer from OCD. As a result of dysfunctional interpretations of their intrusive thoughts (e.g., "I must be going crazy"), individuals with OCD experience intense distress about intrusive thoughts and use dysfunctional ways of dealing with their thoughts (e.g., trying to stop the thoughts), which both increases their distress about having the thoughts as well as the persistence of the thoughts (Rachman, 1997; Salkovskis & Kirk, 1997). In fact, trying to prevent thoughts can paradoxically increase their occurrence (Wegner, Erber,

Focus On... A Panic Attack

The progression of a typical panic attack:

1. A man is sitting in a meeting at work.
2. He notices that his heart has begun to beat faster (physical symptom).
3. He assumes these palpitations are the early signs of a panic attack and that he will soon lose control and begin to yell. Everyone in the room will think he's crazy (catastrophic thought)!
4. He becomes even more anxious and worried about losing control in front of his colleagues, and he begins to perspire heavily (escalation of physical symptoms).
5. He excuses himself from the meeting (escape and avoidance).

Source: Sanderson & Rego, 2000.

& Zanakos, 1993). As an illustration, try to stop yourself from thinking about "white bears" for four minutes and see what happens!

Individuals with OCD suffer from a barrage of thoughts they regard as repugnant or even dangerous. Individuals who develop OCD are often perfectionists who have an exaggerated sense of responsibility for stopping the intrusive thoughts (Obsessive Compulsive Cognitions Working Group, 1997; Rachman, Shafran, & Riskind, in press).

Posttraumatic Stress Disorder Cognitive theorists note that most people are exposed to at least one traumatic experience in their lifetime, but only a relative few of them develop posttraumatic stress disorder (Solomon & Davidson, 1997). These theorists suggest that exposure to trauma can shatter people's core assumptions about the meaning of life and about their own safety in the world (Janoff-Bulman & Frantz, 1997)—and abruptly force people to realize that they are vulnerable to personal annihilation or bodily damage or the loss of loved ones.

In most cases, people rebuild these assumptions of safety and meaning and recover. But for the minority who develop PTSD, this recovery does not occur. Such individuals form—or have already developed—a vulnerability based on negative core assumptions, such as the belief that the world is unpredictably dangerous and that they are helpless or even incompetent to deal with these unpredictable dangers (Foa & Rothbaum, 1998). This ominous crystallization of negative assumptions may explain why people who have already suffered from earlier traumatic experiences are particularly impaired and find it more difficult to successfully recover from new traumas (Foa, Ehlers, Clark, et al., 1999; Solomon, Iancu, & Tyano, 1997; Warda & Bryant, 1998).

Individuals are more likely to form negative assumptions about their own incompetence to deal with a negative world if they blame themselves for the traumas (Foa, Ehlers, Clark, et al., 1999; Delanty, Heberman, Craig, et al., 1997; Mikulincer & Solomon, 1988), and suffering multiple traumas can increase self-blame. These individuals are also more likely to form negative assumptions if they (wrongly) view normal aspects of trauma reactions (e.g., experiencing trauma-related intrusive thoughts and images, emotional numbing, or strong emotions) as signs that they are personally incompetent or have grave psychological problems (Ehlers & Clark, 2000; Steil & Ehlers, 2000). Engaging in faulty defensive behaviors such as active thought suppression or denial may also hinder the recovery process (Feeney & Foa, in press; Harvey & Bryant, 1998; Shipherd & Beck, 1999).

Cognitive Treatment of Anxiety Disorders Cognitive (or cognitive-behavioral) therapy is the prevalent treatment for the anxiety disorders. One of the largest studies yet of social phobia found that cognitive therapy was essentially equal to drug therapy with Nardil (an MAO inhibitor) at 12 weeks, with approximately 75 percent of both groups responding to treatment (Liebowitz, Heimberg, Schneier, et al., 1999). However, cognitive therapy produced more durable improvement a year later, with only 17 percent of the cognitively treated patients experiencing a relapse, as compared to about 50 percent of the drug-treated patients (Liebowitz, Heimberg, Schneier, et al., 1999). Other effective cognitive-behavioral treatments include social skills training (teaching basic skills for social interaction, which makes such interaction more pleasant) and relaxation strategies (Fresco & Heimberg, 2001).

Likewise, cognitive therapy was identified, by a distinguished group of psychiatrists and psychologists, as the only empirically validated psychological treatment for generalized anxiety disorder (Ballenger, Davidson, Lecrubier, et al., 2001). Cognitive therapy for panic disorder—which involves helping patients to identify alternative, noncatastrophic interpretations of physical sensations to combat their overestimation of threat—has proved highly successful in more than 10 controlled studies (Sanderson & Rego, 2000). In many of these studies, between 75 and 95 percent of the

Prevention — Cognitive-Behavioral Intervention to Prevent Anxiety Disorders

Recent studies have found that cognitive-behavioral prevention programs are useful in reducing the risk of anxiety disorders. As we saw in Chapter 4 (Seligman, Schulman, DeRubeis, et al., 1999), Seligman and colleagues found that a brief and inexpensive cognitive-behavioral program had preventive effects in university students at risk for depression. The program had preventive effects for anxiety, as well: After three years, participants had significantly fewer episodes of generalized anxiety disorder than the control group.

Other studies have examined the effect of early-intervention programs on children. In the Queensland Early Intervention and Prevention of Anxiety Project, a group of Australian researchers (Dadds, Spence, Holland, et al., 1997, 1999) created a brief school-based cognitive-behavioral program based on a plan known as FEAR, in which children develop their own plans for graduated exposure to fear stimuli (Kendall & Treadwell, 1996). The FEAR plan includes training in relaxation, positive self-talk, taking actions to face up to fear stimuli, and self-reward for these efforts.

All of the 128 children participating in the program showed anxiety symptoms or mild anxiety disorders, but none had yet been referred for mental health treatment. The early-intervention program led to a 20 percent improvement in the rates of anxiety disorder at a 2-year follow-up, as compared to the rates for children in a control group who did not receive early intervention. The strongest benefits of the program were found for children with the mildest anxiety problems, leading researchers to conclude that children with more severe pretreatment anxiety disorders may need longer treatment. These promising findings indicate that relatively brief and inexpensive cognitive-behavioral interventions can have preventive effects on the development of some forms of anxiety disorder.

panic disorder patients became free of panic attacks after just 3 months of cognitive therapy, and these improvements have been maintained at 1- and 2-year follow-ups (Clark, 1991; Sanderson & Rego, 2000). Moreover, compared with drug treatments, cognitive therapy appears to increase the successful maintenance of improvements and decrease the likelihood of relapse (Clark, 1991; Barlow, Gorman, Shear, et al., 2000; Sanderson & Rego, 2000). Recent studies suggest that cognitive therapy is also effective for obsessive-compulsive disorder (Abramowitz, 1996; Freeston, Ladouceur, Gagnon, et al., 1997) and posttraumatic stress disorder (Falsetti & Resnick, 2000). However, whether cognitive therapy is a more cost-effective approach for the latter two disorders than simpler, easy-to-provide behavioral strategies has yet to be shown.

The cognitive approach to anxiety does have its critics. A recent analysis (Beck & Perkins, 2001) of results from both clinical and nonclinical studies found that on questionnaire measures the overestimation of danger seems as common in depression as in anxiety. This finding could partly reflect the overlap between anxiety and depression, which share many features in common. However, while depressed individuals may overestimate danger because of their pessimism and hopelessness, recent research suggests that they don't overestimate the extent to which danger comprises rapidly rising risk or looming vulnerability. The overestimation of risk rapidly moving to its dreaded end, as assessed by the looming maladaptive style, is specific to anxiety and anxiety disorder symptoms and does not apply to depression (Riskind, Williams, Gessner, et al., 2000; Riskind & Williams, in press).

Another criticism of the cognitive approach is that emotional processes may be activated by lower brain centers (e.g., the amygdala) prior to the influence of higher-level cognitive processes (LeDoux, 1993). Thus, some fear reactions may not be mediated by higher-level cognitive processes.

The Behavioral Perspective: Learning To Be Anxious

Behaviorists emphasize observable conditions for anxiety reactions and their context. Behavioral therapy for anxiety disorders focuses on helping people overcome anxiety by confronting the feared stimulus.

How We Learn Anxiety One traditional behavioral theory of anxiety disorders is that they are engendered through avoidance learning (Mowrer, 1948). This theory, discussed briefly in Chapter 4, involves a two-stage process:

Stage 1: A neutral stimulus is paired with an aversive stimulus; thus, through respondent conditioning, the neutral stimulus becomes anxiety-arousing.

Stage 2: The person avoids the conditioned stimulus (CS), and because this avoidance results in relief from anxiety (i.e., negative reinforcement), the avoidance response, via operant conditioning, becomes habitual.

Imagine, for example, a man who periodically gets drunk and beats his young daughter. Soon the signs of the father's drinking (CS) will become paired in the child's mind with the pain of the beating (unconditioned stimulus, or UCS), and she will experience anxiety (conditioned response, or CR) at the first sign that her father has been drinking. Eventually, this anxiety may generalize to the father as a whole, drunk or sober, in which case he himself becomes the CS. Therefore, she avoids him, and every time she does so, her anxiety is relieved, thus reinforcing the avoidance responses. In time, the anxiety may generalize further—for example, to men in general. Again she responds with avoidance, and again avoidance produces negative reinforcement in the form of anxiety relief. Ultimately, this process may leave her, as an adult, with serious social problems.

In the view of many behaviorists, the disorders that we have discussed in this chapter are variations on avoidance-reinforced anxiety. In specific phobias, an essentially harmless object becomes aversive through respondent conditioning (e.g., a childhood experience of being scratched by a cat), and then avoidance is learned through negative reinforcement. In obsessive-compulsive disorder, the anxious person has found that some action, such as hand washing, reduces his or her anxiety; the action thus becomes a form of avoidance, strengthened, once again, through negative reinforcement. In panic disorder, an aversive state becomes conditioned to internal physiological sensations (Bouton, Mineka, & Barlow, 2001; Wolpe & Rowan, 1988); agoraphobia, which, as we have seen, often develops as a way of avoiding a panic attack in public, is thus the product of stage 2. The agoraphobia starts with a panic attack–conditioning episode and, as the avoidance becomes increasingly widened, agoraphobia crystallizes. In PTSD, the psychological distress and heightened arousal that patients show in response to reminders of the trauma are the products of respondent conditioning, and their psychic numbing and amnesia for the event are the avoidance strategy.

This two-stage avoidance learning theory has been buttressed by a number of studies (Rachman, 1990). However, it has at least four problems. First, while some anxiety patients do report traumatic conditioning experiences (Merckelbach, de Jong, Muris, et al., 1996), others do not. Many patients with phobias, for example, cannot remember any formative encounter with the object of their phobia. Second, traditional learning theory is hard put to explain why only very select, nonrandom types of stimuli typically become phobic objects. Guns, knives, and electrical outlets, for example, should be at least as likely as animals, heights, and enclosed spaces to be associated with traumatic conditioning experiences, yet the former are rare as phobic objects, while the latter are common. Why? Seligman (1971) proposed that, via natural selection, human beings may be "prepared" to fear certain stimuli that would have been threatening to our evolutionary ancestors—for example, as snakes would have been but as electrical outlets would not. This ingenious theory has been supported by some experimental evidence, though it is contradicted by other evidence (Davey, 1995; Tomarken, Sutton, & Mineka, 1995).

However, researchers have found evidence of multiple pathways to fear (Rachman, 1991). Although classical conditioning through direct traumatic conditioning is one of the most common pathways, people are capable of learning phobic fears simply through a process of observational learning. Thus a person can learn to fear dogs simply through vicarious experience, such as seeing how someone else fears dogs. People can also acquire fears by reading magazines, hearing stories, or even by having vivid nightmares. Finally, there is evidence that classical conditioning is far more likely to produce conditioned fear for some stimuli (e.g., spiders or snakes) than others (Rachman, 1991). Thus it appears that frightful encounters with various objects or situations are neither necessary nor sufficient to create a phobia.

A fourth and very serious problem with the avoidance-learning theory is that it focuses entirely on concrete stimuli and observable responses without concern for the *thoughts* that may be involved in anxiety. Many studies indicate that such an explanation is insufficient (Rachman, 1991). A stimulus does not have to be experienced directly in order to arouse anxiety. As noted, people can acquire anxiety responses vicariously, by watching others react with pain to a given stimulus. For instance, children of spider-phobic parents are more likely than children of controls to show fear when viewing a film with spiders in it (Unnewehr, Schneider, Margraf, et al., 1996). Even monkeys can learn to be afraid just by watching other monkeys respond with fear to an unfamiliar object (Cook, Mineka, Wolkenstein, et al., 1985). In humans, not even observation is required to feel fear. In a high-crime neighborhood, it's not necessary to have seen someone mugged in that part of town to feel fear. One need only have heard that the neighborhood is dangerous.

Unlearning Anxiety For the anxiety disorders, behavioral therapists have developed a set of techniques for reducing anxiety by confronting the feared stimulus. In Chapter 4, we described **systematic desensitization** (Wolpe, 1973), in which the client draws up a hierarchy of fears and then imagines them, one by one, while in a state of deep muscle relaxation. Alternatively, the client might approach the feared stimulus *in vivo,* or in the flesh, also while in a state of relaxation.

Systematic desensitization works well with specific phobias, but eventually behavioral therapists found that the relaxation-training component is often unnecessary. Clients can be helped simply through **exposure,** or confrontation (sudden or gradual) with the feared stimulus. Exposure therapy includes several techniques designed to help anxious individuals to confront feared stimuli that they are motivated to avoid, such as objects, situations, memories, and images (Foa, 2000). For example, exposure treatment for posttraumatic stress disorder would include both imaginal and *in vivo* exposure. Imaginal exposure involves having the person engage in repeated emotional description of the traumatic memory or images of the frightening situation. *In vivo* exposure might involve confronting an individual with injection phobia with pictures of hypodermic needles.

When exposure is imagined rather than *in vivo,* it often takes the form of **flooding,** in which the person is confronted with the feared stimulus for prolonged periods of time. Exposure therapy is the most empirically supported psychological treatment for PTSD (Foa, 2000) and is an important part of cognitive-behavioral treatment for phobias and other anxiety disorders.

Recently, there has been much interest in an approach called Eye Movement Desensitization and Reprocessing (EMDR) therapy for anxiety disorders, but an exposure component may account for most of the benefit of EMDR (Foa, 2000; Lohr, Lilienfeld, Tolin, et al., 1999). In EMDR therapy, clients are instructed to move their eyes from side to side while they visualize disturbing events. However, recent evidence suggests that nothing special is contributed by the saccadic, or side-to-side, eye movement in EMDR; the therapy's success can be largely accounted for by the desensitizing effects of visualizing disturbing events—that is, by exposure.

The Psychodynamic Perspective: Neurosis

In the psychodynamic view, the anxiety disorders, or neuroses, stem from unconscious processes and inner conflict. Often, according to psychodynamic theorists, the cause of one's anxiety can be traced to early childhood.

The Roots of Neurosis As we saw in Chapter 5, Freud viewed anxiety as stemming not just from an external danger but also from threatened breakdowns in the ego's struggle to satisfy the id without violating the demands of reality and the superego. This push and counterpush goes on all the time in normal lives and usually works well enough so that anxiety over the id impulse is never experienced consciously. In some cases, however, the anxiety is so intense that it *is* experienced consciously, with debilitating results. Alternatively, it is kept at bay only through the use of extremely rigid defense mechanisms. It is these situations that, according to psychodynamic theory, constitute neurotic behavior.

In cases where there is pervasive—what Freud called "free-floating"—anxiety, there is no elaborate defense, and what we see is generalized anxiety disorder. The cause is repressed, but the anxiety leaks through. In a panic attack, the cause—that is, the id impulse—moves closer to the boundaries of the conscious mind, resulting in an urgent buildup of anxiety. In phobia, the ego defends against the anxiety by displacing it. For example, a male child who is experiencing castration anxiety might displace it—and disguise it from himself—by developing a fear of animals (such as horses or dogs).

Psychodynamic thinkers may interpret obsessive-compulsive disorder in a number of ways, depending on the nature of the symptoms. In the case of a man obsessed with the fear that he will kill his wife in her sleep, psychodynamic theory would suggest that the unconscious aggressive impulse has, in fact, made its way into the conscious mind. On the other hand, cleanliness rituals and obsessions with germs would be interpreted as a reaction formation against wishes surviving from childhood, and especially from the anal stage: the desire to soil, to play with feces, and to be generally messy.

A recent psychodynamic explanation of the anxiety disorders comes from Bowlby's attachment theory. As we saw in Chapter 5, Bowlby claimed that disturbances in the parent-child bond could leave the child in a state of "anxious attachment" marked by dependency and insecurity. Proponents of this theory have suggested that such children grow up vulnerable to anxiety disorders, especially panic disorder and agoraphobia. Retrospective studies of panic disorder patients do show that these people are disproportionately likely to have childhood histories marked by separation anxiety, parental loss, or inadequate parenting in general (Shear, 1996; Silove, Manicavasagar, Curtis, et al., 1996).

Treating Neurosis The goal of psychodynamic therapy for the anxiety disorders, as for most disorders, is to expose and neutralize the material that the ego is defending against, so that the ego will be free to focus on more useful tasks, such as building one's career or relationships. In Chapter 5, we outlined the basic techniques that psychoanalysis traditionally used to achieve this goal. Treatment was intense and often lasted for many years; a patient would lie on a couch, with the analyst seated out of sight, and analysis focused heavily on the past. In recent decades, psychodynamic therapists have moved toward briefer, face-to-face therapies, directed more at the present than at the past and aimed at specific symptoms (Crits-Christoph, 1992).

Psychodynamic concepts have inspired new kinds of cognitive-behavioral treatments. For example,

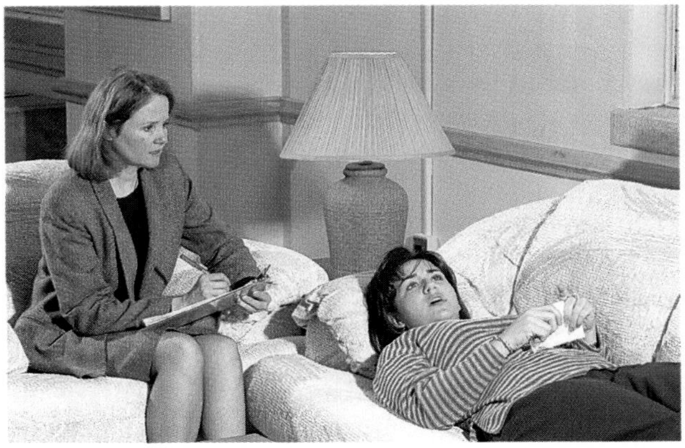

In traditional psychoanalysis, the client lies on a couch and the therapist sits out of his or her view (left). In the past few decades, however, psychodynamic therapists have shifted to face-to-face encounters with their clients (right).

Shear and her colleagues (Shear, Pilkonis, Clotre, et al., 1994; Shear & Barlow, 1998; Shear & Weiner, 1997) have experimented with an "emotion-focused" treatment (now called EFT) for panic disorder. In EFT, panic is seen as being related either to a feeling of being trapped (the result of being overprotected by others) or to a fear of being unable to get needed help (the result of being abandoned by others). People with panic disorder, it is thought, tend to avoid pinpointing these feelings. The object of emotion-focused therapy is to get the patient to identify and confront them and to understand how they might trigger panic attacks.

The Neuroscience Perspective: Biochemistry and Medicine

Genetics Research Recent research has explored the contributions of genetic factors to anxiety disorders. One study of the genetic epidemiology of irrational fears and phobias found evidence that genetic risk factors play a moderate role in the etiology of phobias and their associated irrational fears (Kendler, Myers, Prescott, et al., 2001). The role of genetic factors is probably similar in men and women, with one exception. In women, there appears to be a much larger genetic influence for agoraphobia than for animal phobias, whereas for men the situation is reversed. Overall, the study found evidence for three common influences on phobias. One was a common genetic factor, and two factors were environmental, reflecting the effects of shared and unique environments in twin pairs. Thus certain individual environmental experiences seem to increase risk nonspecifically for all phobic subtypes, whereas others were phobia-subtype specific in their impact. A study of the first-degree relatives of people with phobia found them to be three to four times more likely to have phobias than first-degree relatives of normal controls (Fyer, Mannuzza, Chapman, et al., 1995). For social phobia, the evidence is sketchier, though there are indications that the disorder runs in families (Fyer, Mannuzza, Chapman, et al., 1995).

Among all of the anxiety disorders, panic disorder has been the one most studied from a genetic standpoint (Finn & Smoller, 2001) and the one that seems most likely to have a genetic basis (Crowe, 1991). Panic disorder seems to run in families, and twin studies indicate that genes contribute to a liability to the disorder (Kendler, Neale, Kessler, et al., 1992b; Skre, Onstad, Torgersen, et al., 1993). In one study with female twins, Kendler and his colleagues found evidence that genes accounted for nearly 40 percent of the variance in liability to panic disorder and agoraphobia (Kendler, Neale, Kessler, et al., 1992b). However, the specific genes involved, and their location, remains unknown (Finn & Smoller, 2001).

For the other anxiety disorders, the genetic evidence is weaker but still significant. A recent twin study showed that genes accounted for a modest 15 to 20 percent of the variance in liability to generalized anxiety disorder (Hettema, Prescott, and Kendler, 2001). A well-controlled family study of adult obsessive-compulsive patients found that the rate of OCD in their first-degree relatives was about 10 percent, as opposed to about 2 percent in the relatives of controls (Pauls, Alsobrook, Goodman, et al., 1995).

Posttraumatic stress disorder also seems to involve some genetic predisposition, if only toward psychological disturbance in general. Recent twin studies indicate that genes specific to PTSD account for 14 to 20 percent of the variance in liability to developing the disorder (Chantarujikapong, Scherrer, Xian, et al., 2001; Xian, Chantarujikapong, Scherrer, Xian, et al., 2000).

If anxiety disorders are in some part inherited, *what* exactly is inherited? Probably a liability, or vulnerability, toward "nervousness" or "neuroticism" in general, rather than toward a specific syndrome, is inherited (Eysenck, 1967; Chantarujikapong, Scherrer, Xian, et al., 2001; Xian, Chantarujikapong, & Scherrer, 2000). Possibly this vulnerability is produced by an overly responsive autonomic nervous system (Eysenck, 1967) or an attentional bias for threat (Oehman, Flykt, & Esteves, 2001). Or it may be what is called behavioral inhibition, a childhood tendency to withdraw from unfamiliar situations (Biederman, Hirshfeld-Becker, Rosenbaumm, et al., 2001a, 2001b; Kagan, 1989; Rosenbaum, Biederman, Pollack, et al., 1994). Behavioral inhibition may be particularly related to social anxiety (Biederman et al., 2001a, 2001b).

Whatever the basis for genetic vulnerability turns out to be, however, keep in mind that the vulnerability is only a predisposition for anxiety to occur under appropriate conditions (e.g., conditioning, trauma). For example, Norwegian twin studies have shown a 31 percent concordance rate between MZ twins for panic disorder (Torgersen, 1983). This rate is high, but it still means that more than two thirds of the MZ twins, people with exactly the same genetic endowment, were not concordant. These figures are consistent with what we would expect from a diathesis, or vulnerability-stress, framework.

The Role of Neurotransmitters Research on the biochemical basis of anxiety disorders has implicated abnormalities in a number of neurotransmitter systems (Nutt, 2000, 2001). These include the GABA/benzodiazepine system, the norepinephrine sympathetic nervous system, and the serotonin system.

GABA/Benzodiazepine System For years, it was known that under many circumstances, anxiety could be relieved by drugs, such as Valium, that belong to a group of chemicals called the **benzodiazepines.** But how the benzodiazepines actually affect the brain's chemistry remained a mystery until 1977. Then it was discovered that the benzodiazepines attach to certain receptors on the neurons of the brain. This finding suggests that the brain may have a natural chemical, similar to the benzodiazepines, that regulates certain forms of anxiety. It follows that abnormalities in the level of this chemical—too high or too low—may underlie some anxiety disorders.

Whatever the chemical process in question, it involves a neurotransmitter called GABA (gamma-aminobutyric acid), for it is GABA that is activated by the benzodiazepines (Costa & Guidotti, 1985; Nutt, 2001). GABA is an inhibitory neurotransmitter; that is, once it is activated, it turns *off* the affected neurons. Presumably, this is the chemical basis of the benzodiazepine's ability to control some forms of anxiety: They signal GABA to shut off a certain measure of neural activity, including the activity of neurons that use norepinephrine and serotonin for neurotransmission.

It is doubtful, however, that a shortfall in the inhibitory action of GABA underlies all anxiety conditions, nor is stimulation of GABA the only way in which the benzodiazepines operate. Certain types of anxiety, those experienced as generalized tension, are more responsive to the benzodiazepines than are other anxiety conditions, such as panic disorder, which are more responsive to another class of drugs, the antidepressants. (See Table 6.1 on page 139 for the classification of psychotherapeutic drugs.) This finding suggests that the chemical basis of panic disorder is probably different from that of generalized anxiety—a conclusion already suggested by the genetic evidence (Johnson & Lydiard, 1995).

The GABA system seems to play a role in forms of anxiety disorder that involve that experience of generalized tension, particularly generalized anxiety disorder (Nutt, 2001). Abnormalities in the interaction between the GABA system and the glutomate system (a neurotransmitter system involved in memory and learning) also seem to contribute to posttraumatic stress disorder, particularly to the encoding of memory (Nutt, 2000).

Norepinephrine System The norepinephrine system is involved in the control of breathing, blood pressure, and heart rate. It releases the neurotransmitter norepinephrine and is implicated in panic disorder, intense alarm reactions, and a variety of anxiety disorders. For example, research suggests that chronic overactivity of norepinephrine in the brain may result in reduced sensitivity to its effects in individuals with generalized anxiety disorders (Nutt, 2001). Norepinephrine is also believed to be involved in panic disorder as well as depression (Nutt & Lawson, 1992). Supersensitivity to stimulation by norepinephrine may occur in posttraumatic stress disorder (Nutt, 2000). It is important to consider that there are links between panic disorder and depression, which both respond to antidepressant drugs that enhance norepinephrine and serotonin transmission (Nutt & Lawson, 1992).

Serotonin System The neurotransmitter serotonin is particularly distributed in brain regions associated with anxiety. According to Deakin (1998), serotonin controls a number of different neuronal pathways

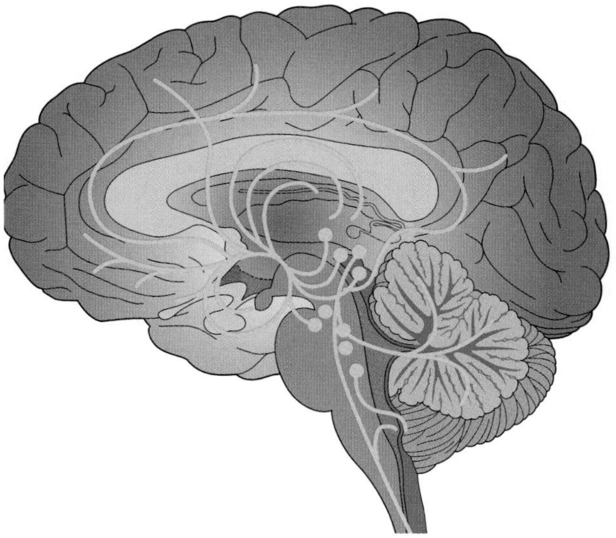

FIGURE 7.3 Serotonergic pathways. Each neurotransmitter functions in specific pathways in the brain. This map shows the serotonergic pathways.

(see Figure 7.3). These serotonergic pathways have different links to different forms of anxiety. In Deakin's view, one pathway is involved in the anticipatory anxiety—and avoidance of threats not yet present—that is central to generalized anxiety disorder. A second, separate serotonergic pathway may be involved in panic responses to immediate aversive stimuli, such as pain or suffocation. Others suggest that the serotonin dysfunction implicated in panic involves abnormalities in serotonin, although it is unclear whether an excess or a deficit is to blame (Nutt, 2001).

Serotonergic abnormalities are also believed to be involved in several anxiety disorders, including posttraumatic stress disorder (Nutt, 2000), obsessive-compulsive disorder (Pigott, 1996), and perhaps social phobia (Tancer, 1993).

Neurotransmitters in Specific Anxiety Disorders

One hypothesis for the biochemistry of panic disorder posits that panic attacks are triggered by increased neurological firing in a section of the brain stem known as the locus ceruleus, a major norepinephrine center (Gorman, Liebowitz, Fyer, et al., 1989). However, these findings have been challenged. Researchers in the laboratory have now provoked panic attacks with a wide range of stimuli, not all of which are clearly connected to the brain stem, let alone to the locus ceruleus.

A competing biochemical theory of panic disorder is the suffocation false alarm hypothesis (Klein, 1996a). A monitor in the central nervous system signals impending suffocation in response to elevated levels of carbon dioxide and brain lactate. According to the suffocation false alarm hypothesis, some people's suffocation monitors are hypersensitive and produce false alarms, which then produce panic attacks. Yet this explanation for panic disorder is not supported by recent studies (Schmidt, Telch, & Jaimez, 1996; Taylor, Woody, Koch, et al., 1996), such as the finding by Taylor and his colleagues that "suffocation" panickers (who report severe shortness of breath) respond just as well to cognitive therapy as "nonsuffocation" panickers (who don't have shortness of breath).

Biochemical studies have led to a growing consensus that obsessive-compulsive disorder is connected to serotonin abnormalities, for drugs that prevent the reuptake of serotonin by presynaptic neurons do relieve the symptoms of this disorder (Dolberg, Iancu, Sasson, et al., 1996; Pigott, 1996). At the same time, some dysfunction of the frontal lobe of the brain may also be involved, for PET scans of the brains of OCD patients in the process of glucose metabolism show abnormalities. Pursuing another line of research, scientists have turned up a number of connections between OCD and movement disorders thought to be caused by abnormalities in the basal ganglia, a region of the brain involved with movement. One such movement disorder is Tourette's syndrome, which produces tics—involuntary movements and verbalizations. People with Tourette's syndrome show a disproportionately high rate of OCD, as do their relatives; conversely, OCD patients and their relatives are disproportionately likely to have tics (Pauls, Alsobrook, Goodman, et al., 1995).

At this point, little is known about the biology of social phobia, but serotonin abnormalities may be involved (Tancer, 1993). Drugs that help relieve social phobia include those, such as Prozac and the benzodiazepines, that enhance serotonin reuptake (Prozac), or that work by blocking the inhibitory effect of GABA on serotonergic neurons (benzodiazepines) (Jefferson, 1996).

Even the anxiety disorder with the greatest environmental component has been probed for biochemical underpinnings (Nutt, 2000). We know that hormones and neurotransmitters are involved in memory processes, and they may therefore be responsible for the intrusive memories that haunt people with PTSD (Pitman, 1989). The trauma may overstimulate stress-responsive hormones and neurotransmitters, with the result that the memory of the trauma becomes so strongly stamped in one's mind that it cannot fade. This hypothesis is consistent with the recent findings that victims of PTSD tend to show hormone abnormalities associated with an exaggerated response to stress (Yehuda, Levengood, Schmeidler, et al., 1996).

Whatever the specific biochemical processes involved in the anxiety disorders, recent findings have given new impetus to research on neurotransmitters. And knowledge of a connection between neurotransmitters and anxiety states has fueled interest in the possible role of drugs in treating these disorders.

Drug Treatment It is likely that the effects of various drugs involve multiple mechanisms that mirror the complex neurotransmitter systems and interactions (Shelton & Brown, 2001). The two categories of drugs used to treat anxiety disorders are minor tranquilizers and antidepressants.

Minor Tranquilizers Among the **minor tranquilizers,** or drugs taken to reduce anxiety, the most popular are the benzodiazepines—particularly Valium (diazepam), Xanax (alprazolam), Ativan (lorazepam), and Tranxene (chlorazepate)—and they are very popular, indeed. In 1989, American pharmacies filled over 52 million prescriptions for the antianxiety benzodiazepines (Shader, Greenblatt, & Balter, 1991); that is one prescription for one out of every five men, women, and children in the United States. For a number of years, Valium was the most widely prescribed drug in the world. This wide use of antianxiety medications is often assumed to be a plague of modern life. As it happens, the percentage of people using drugs to control anxiety and insomnia has remained relatively stable over the past hundred years. The drugs themselves have changed—whereas people in the 1990s used benzodiazepines, people in the 1890s used bromides and opium-based compounds—but the use of drugs for these purposes was as widespread in the late nineteenth century as it is now (Woods, Katz, & Winger, 1987). In most cases, antianxiety drugs are prescribed by family doctors for people who are not in psychological treatment but are simply going through a hard time in their lives. Indeed, half the users of such drugs are people who are medically ill; the drug is prescribed to control the patient's emotional reactions to the illness (Maxmen & Ward, 1995). Antianxiety drugs are also widely used in conjunction with psychological treatment, particularly for the anxiety disorders.

Benzodiazepines are CNS depressants; they slow down the workings of the central nervous system, and, in doing so, they can create disturbing side effects. A common problem is daytime sedation in the form of fatigue, drowsiness, and impaired motor coordination (Maxmen & Ward, 1995). (Benzodiazepines are often implicated in falls in the elderly and in automobile and industrial accidents.) These drugs may also interfere with memory, particularly for events that occur after taking the drug. Finally, benzodiazepines may aggravate physical disorders involving breathing, such as congestive heart failure and sleep apnea, a disorder in which breathing repeatedly stops for 10 seconds or more during the night (Chapter 9). All these side effects are dose-dependent: The higher the dose, the greater the likelihood of problems (Maxmen & Ward, 1995). (Therefore, physicians try to prescribe the lowest effective dose.) The risk of side effects is also multiplied if benzodiazepines are taken in combination with other central nervous system depressants, especially alcohol. When combined with alcohol, benzodiazepines have a synergistic effect: Each multiplies the other's power, placing the person at risk for an overdose.

Apart from side effects, a major drawback of benzodiazepines is the difficulty of **withdrawal,** or termination of the drug. When a benzodiazepine is taken in large doses, termination is often followed by *rebound:* The symptoms return with redoubled force. Thus, the person is likely to start taking the drug again in order to suppress the now-magnified symptoms (Maxmen & Ward, 1995). This has been a problem with Xanax. Xanax is very effective in the treatment of panic attacks (Shader & Greenblatt, 1993), but when it is withdrawn, up to 90 percent of patients relapse, many of them experiencing worse panic attacks than they had before (Michelson & Marchione, 1991).

The difficulty of withdrawal is related to whether a drug is short-acting or long-acting—that is, how quickly it is absorbed into the bloodstream and how long it stays there. Long-acting benzodiazepines, such as Valium and Tranxene, tend to accumulate in the body over time, so that, the longer the person takes the drug, the higher the dose he or she is getting. By contrast, short-acting benzodiazepines, such as Xanax and Ativan, are usually eliminated from the system in less than eight hours. As a result, going "cold turkey" with a short-acting benzodiazepine is more likely to result in rebound and other withdrawal symptoms (Rickels, Schweizer, Case, et al., 1990). The long-acting benzodiazepines, however abruptly terminated, naturally eliminate themselves from the system bit by bit, with less disturbing effects.

However, even with long-acting benzodiazepines and a therapeutically tapered withdrawal, discontinuing these drugs is very hard for long-time users—people who have taken the drug daily for over a year. In a study of 63 benzodiazepine-dependent patients going through a gradual termination, only 63 percent of those on long-acting drugs—and worse, only 58 percent of those on short-acting drugs—were able to achieve a drug-free state (Schweizer, Rickels, Case, et al., 1990). For panic disorder patients, the figures are even less encouraging. In one study, only one fourth of the panic disorder patients who had participated in a gradual benzodiazepine withdrawal program were drug-free at a 3-month follow-up, though when the patients received cognitive-behavioral therapy in conjunction with the drug taper, their success rate tripled (Otto, Pollack, Sachs, et al., 1993). Here, then, is an example of a promising way to combine antianxiety medication with psychotherapy. Because Xanax works so quickly, it may be used for a brief period of time, with cognitive-behavioral therapy instituted as a longer-term solution while the drugs are withdrawn.

Because of the problems with benzodiazepines, physicians have tried treating anxiety disorders with other drugs. One alternative is BuSpar (buspirone), a recently introduced nonbenzodiazepine. BuSpar does not interact with alcohol and seems to be more selective in its effects on anxiety, though it is ineffective with panic disorder and only sometimes effective for generalized anxiety (Maxmen & Ward, 1995). But the major alternative to the benzodiazepines has been antidepressants.

A recent study by the Harvard/Brown Anxiety Disorders Research Program (Salzman, Goldenberg, Bruce, et al., 2001) found evidence of a shift in pharmacologic treatment of anxiety disorders between 1989 and 1996. First, the number of anxiety disorder patients who received medication increased slightly, from nearly 33 percent in 1989 to 63 percent in 1996. Researchers also discovered a decrease in benzodiazepine treatment and an increase in antidepressant treatment for generalized anxiety disorder patients who did not also have additional depression or anxiety disorders.

Antidepressant Drugs **Antidepressant drugs,** as the name indicates, are used to elevate mood in depressed patients. However, because antidepressants are often effective for panic disorder and obsessive-compulsive disorder (Rosenbaum & Gelenberg, 1991), we will begin our discussion of them in this chapter. The first important class of antidepressants to gain a wide following were the **MAO inhibitors,** including phenelzine (Nardil) and tranylcypromine (Parnate). The name of this class of drugs was based on the belief that they interfered with the action of the enzyme monoamine oxidase (MAO), which in turn degrades certain neurotransmitters, including norepinephrine and serotonin, in the nervous system. The MAO inhibitors are often quite effective in treating anxiety disorders. However, these drugs can also have adverse effects on the brain, the liver, and the cardiovascular system and, when combined with certain other drugs or foods—especially foods prepared by fermentation (e.g., beer, wine, some varieties of cheese)—can result in severe illness and even death. Because of these risks, the MAO inhibitors are recommended as the first medication to use with anxiety disorders only when they are clearly more successful than other medications. One such case is social phobia, for which Nardil seems to be the most effective drug.

For other anxiety disorders, the MAO inhibitors have proved less useful than another class of antidepressants, the **tricyclics,** so named for their three-ringed molecular structure. Commonly used tricyclics are Tofranil (imipramine), Elavil (amitriptyline), Sinequan (doxepin), and Anafranil (clomipramine). Tricyclics have proved quite effective with panic disorder, and Anafranil has been used with some success in treating OCD. However, the tricyclics can have unpleasant side effects: blurred vision, dry mouth, constipation, weight gain, drowsiness, and jitteriness. As many as 40 percent of anxiety-disorder patients cannot tolerate the tricyclics (Kunovac & Stahl, 1995).

The tricyclics are gradually being displaced by a newer class of antidepressants, the **selective serotonin reuptake inhibitors,** or **SSRIs.** Like the tricyclics, the SSRIs work by blocking neurotransmitter reuptake, but they zero in on only one neurotransmitter, serotonin (hence, their name). For reasons that are not well understood, this makes the

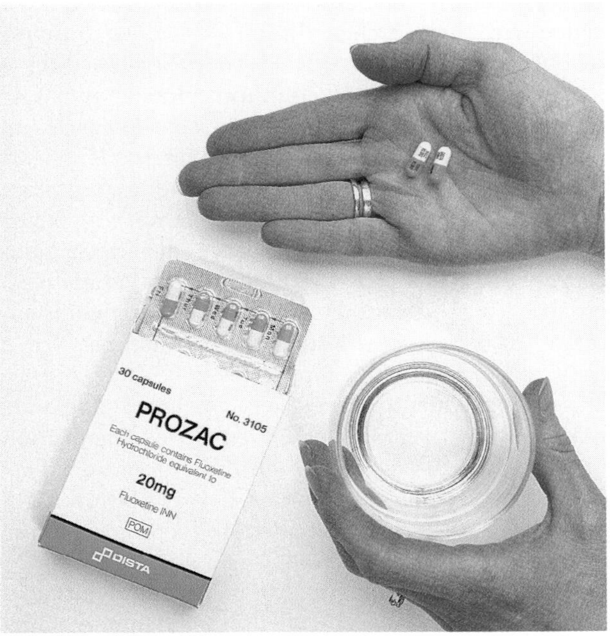

SSRIs such as Prozac, long used to treat depression, are now frequently prescribed in the treatment of anxiety disorders as well.

SSRIs effective for many patients who have abandoned other antidepressants because of the side effects. There are several SSRIs on the market—Paxil (paroxetine) and Zoloft (sertraline) are two of the newer ones—but the best known, because it was the first, is Prozac (fluoxetine). Introduced in 1987, it soon became (and remains) America's most widely prescribed antidepressant.

Just as the SSRIs have replaced the tricyclics as the drug of choice for depression, they have now become the physician's favorite in the treatment of most anxiety disorders. Sixty percent of the physicians surveyed now start an anxiety-disorder patient with an SSRI rather than with Xanax, Nardil, or Tofranil (Lydiard, Brawman, & Ballenger, 1996). Because the SSRIs are still relatively new, there has been less research on them than on the other antidepressants, but early reports indicate that they work very well with panic disorder and are helpful with social phobia too (Lydiard, Brawman, & Ballenger, 1996). They have also shown some promise in the treatment of OCD, though at this point the tricyclic Anafranil seems to be more effective (Greist, Jefferson, Koback, et al., 1995). For posttraumatic stress disorder, a recent study suggests that the drug sertraline, like other SSRIs, works well in treating many symptoms (Davidson, Rothbaum, van der Kolk, et al., 2001).

SSRIs, too, can have side effects. Prozac, for example, often causes headache, upset stomach, jitteriness, and sexual dysfunction. But these problems are generally easier for patients to tolerate than the side effects, such as weight gain and blurred vision, associated with the tricyclics. Jitteriness—which amounts to one of the symptoms of the anxiety the drug is meant to treat—is not common enough as a side effect to preclude using this antidepressant as an antianxiety drug; a way to avoid jitteriness is to start the patient at a low dose and then gradually increase the dose to the therapeutic level (the dose at which the drug relieves symptoms). Other side effects associated with the SSRIs are often mild or short-lived. None of the medications prescribed for anxiety is curative. At best, the drug suppresses symptoms. When the drug is removed, there is likely to be rapid relapse. Consequently, many experts have concluded that, unless patients want to remain on medication for the rest of their lives, they should consider psychotherapy, either alone or in combination with drugs, for psychotherapy *is* aimed at getting rid of the disorder permanently.

The most common criticism of antianxiety drugs is not that they don't work well enough but that, by working as well as they do, they may invite people to avoid solving their problems. As Freud pointed out, anxiety is a *signal*. By taking antianxiety drugs, we suppress the signal, but we do not solve the problem. Indeed, the problem may become more serious as a result of our ignoring it. Taking antianxiety drugs, then, is like turning off a fire alarm because we can't stand the noise. Again, the solution seems to be psychotherapy, preferably in combination with drugs. The drugs, it is hoped, will relieve the symptoms to the point that patients can actually concentrate on the therapy. The therapy will then teach them new skills and help them to solve problems so that they can live their lives without anxiety.

For panic disorder, cognitive-behavioral therapy seems to have an 80 percent cure rate, a result at least as impressive as that of any medication, and the gains are maintained after the treatment is completed, which is not the case with any drug therapy. Some investigators have wondered if there is any advantage to combining drug and cognitive-behavioral treatment; that is, does the combination of cognitive therapy and drug treatment produce better results than cognitive-behavioral therapy alone? Current research suggests that any benefits gained from combining drug treatment, such as antidepressant or antianxiety drugs, with cognitive-behavior therapy, seem to be temporary; cognitive-behavioral therapy has better long-term outcomes in reducing panic after treatment has stopped (Schmidt, 1999).

For the other anxiety disorders, the prospects for combined treatments are less clear. Obsessive-compulsive disorder, as we saw, is hard to treat, though both Anafranil and exposure techniques have had some success. This suggests that the best treatment would use both, but results from a study of such a treatment seem to favor behavioral therapy alone, without the drug (Foa & Liebowitz, 1995). For specific phobias and generalized anxiety disorder, cognitive-behavioral therapy remains the treatment of choice, while for social phobia, cognitive-behavioral therapy and Nardil seem to work equally well. The effectiveness of drug/psychotherapy treatments for these disorders, and for posttraumatic stress disorder, remains an unexplored question.

As a final caveat, there is some reason to be concerned about the concept of combining drugs and psychotherapy, however promising the preliminary results. As psychologists have discovered, learning is state-dependent (Ho, Richard, & Chute, 1978; Overton, 1984). What we learn in a given biological or psychological state does not fully generalize to other states. Thus, if, while taking antianxiety medication, we acquire new skills for dealing with stress, these skills will not necessarily survive the withdrawal of the medication.

Key Terms

acrophobia, 152
agoraphobia, 162
antidepressant drugs, 175
anxiety, 151
anxiety disorders, 151
benzodiazepines, 172
claustrophobia, 152
compulsion, 154
exposure, 170
flooding, 170
generalized anxiety disorder, 153
MAO inhibitors, 175
minor tranquilizers, 174
obsession, 154
obsessive-compulsive disorder, 154
panic attack, 151
panic disorder, 162
phobia, 152
posttraumatic stress disorder (PTSD), 157
selective serotonin reuptake inhibitors (SSRIs), 175
social phobia, 152
specific phobia, 152
systematic desensitization, 169
tricyclics, 175
withdrawal, 174

Summary

- Anxiety disorders are characterized by either manifest anxiety or self-defeating behavior problems aimed at warding it off. Anxiety is a feeling of apprehension about vague or unrealized threats. It is a "low-throttle" emotional state characterized by chronic edginess, worrisome thoughts, and vigilance for signs of threat.
- In a panic attack, a "full-throttle" alarm reaction erupts suddenly and mobilizes a person to take flight. Physical sensations such as dizziness, trembling, and shortness of breath give rise to a feeling of impending catastrophe, such as total loss of control or death. Panic disorder can lead to agoraphobia, a fear of leaving the safety of home.
- A person with a phobia intensely fears some object or situation and persistently tries to avoid that stimulus. People with a specific phobia react to a particular object (such as a spider) or situation (such as an enclosed space). Social phobia, which is essentially a fear of the disapproval of others, is aroused by a social situation (such as public speaking or conversation with others) that the person with a phobia perceives as carrying a risk of embarrassment or humiliation.
- The main feature of generalized anxiety disorder is a chronic state of excessive and uncontrollable worry. Like panic disorder, generalized anxiety disorder tends to follow stressful life events. It is much more common among women than among men.
- People suffering from obsessive-compulsive disorder are bothered by recurring, often disturbing thoughts (obsessions) and/or stereotyped actions (compulsions) that they seem unable to control. Many normal people have intrusive thoughts and compulsions, but they are more frequent, more intense, and more distressing in those suffering from obsessive-compulsive disorder.
- Posttraumatic stress disorder is a severe reaction, involving intense fear, helplessness, or horror, to traumatic events that pose mortal danger, such as natural disaster, assault, and combat. Victims typically reexperience the event for long periods of time, show diminished responsiveness to their surroundings, develop physical symptoms, and may suffer from depression, anxiety, irritability, and guilt. When the disorder is of short duration—a few days to a few weeks—it is classified as acute stress disorder.
- Cognitive theorists believe that people with anxiety disorders overestimate danger and rely on maladaptive ways of handling their fears, such as physical avoidance, protracted worry, or thought suppression. Cognitive therapy aims to correct these dysfunctional thinking and coping problems. The cognitive-behavioral approach is the dominant psychological perspective in current treatment and research.
- Behaviorists attribute anxiety disorders to faulty learning, not unconscious conflicts. In the process of learning to avoid anxiety, people may also learn to associate a neutral stimulus with the anxiety-producing stimulus and then be conditioned to habitually avoid that stimulus. Behavioral therapy is directed at removing the symptoms of a disorder through such techniques as systematic desensitization and exposure.
- Psychodynamic theorists view the anxiety disorders as neuroses resulting from unconscious conflicts between id impulses and ego actions. The individual experiences conscious anxiety over these conflicts or keeps the anxiety at bay through rigid defense mechanisms. Treatment has traditionally focused on uncovering what the ego is trying to suppress.
- The neuroscience perspective seeks genetic and biochemical links to anxiety. Some anxiety disorders, especially panic disorder, appear to have a genetic component. Recent evidence also suggests that brain chemistry and neurotransmitters influence some forms of anxiety.
- Antianxiety drugs, or minor tranquilizers, such as the benzodiazepines Valium, Xanax, Ativan, and Tranxene, are used to treat symptoms of many of the anxiety disorders. They are also used to relieve stress related to illness and medical treatment. Side effects of these drugs include daytime sedation, interference with memory, and aggravation of respiratory disorders. These drugs also act synergistically with alcohol and may produce a rebound effect upon withdrawal.

- Antidepressant drugs, those used to elevate mood in depressed patients, are often effective in treating panic disorder, obsessive-compulsive disorder, and social phobia. Among these are the MAO inhibitors (Nardil, Parnate) and the tricyclics (Tofranil, Elavil, Anafranil, Sinequan). These drugs are also associated with a number of side effects. The tricyclics are being replaced by SSRIs, especially Prozac, the most widely prescribed antidepressant in the United States.
- No antianxiety medication is curative. Drugs can only suppress the symptoms of an anxiety disorder, and only for as long as they are being taken. It is widely accepted that some form of psychotherapy is needed to eliminate the anxiety permanently.
- A combination of drugs and psychotherapy is often advantageous in treating anxiety disorders. The major drawback is that people who are under medication when they learn skills for dealing with stress may not retain those skills after withdrawal of the medication.

CHAPTER

8

Dissociative and Somatoform Disorders

Dissociative Disorders
- Dissociative Amnesia
- Dissociative Fugue
- Dissociative Identity Disorder
- Depersonalization Disorder

Dissociative Disorders: Theory and Therapy
- The Psychodynamic Perspective: Defense Against Anxiety
- The Behavioral and Sociocultural Perspectives: Dissociation as a Social Role
- The Cognitive Perspective: Memory Dysfunction
- The Neuroscience Perspective: Brain Dysfunction

Somatoform Disorders
- Body Dysmorphic Disorder
- Hypochondriasis
- Somatization Disorder
- Pain Disorder
- Conversion Disorder

Somatoform Disorders: Theory and Therapy
- The Psychodynamic Perspective: Defense Against Anxiety
- The Behavioral and Sociocultural Perspectives: The Sick Role
- The Cognitive Perspective: Misinterpreting Bodily Sensations
- The Neuroscience Perspective: Brain Dysfunction

A well-dressed woman in her early thirties was brought to the hospital by the police after she was found wandering on an interstate highway. She had no identification with her. She spoke coherently but slowly and was apparently traumatized, but not psychotic. On the ward she seldom spoke, and she ate only when she was coaxed. When asked who she was, she would stare into space or shrug her shoulders with a gesture of despair. She was given the temporary name of Jane Doe, and, after four weeks of futile attempts to establish her identity, she was moved to a ward for chronic patients.

Jane was taken to the psychologist's office every day, but she barely responded to him, and she could not be hypnotized, because she would not close her eyes or concentrate on the procedure. Eventually the psychologist tried progressive relaxation, to which Jane responded well. After each relaxation session, the psychologist would pick up his office telephone and pretend to call a friend or relative. Then he would give Jane the phone and suggest that she make a call, but she always said that she didn't remember anyone's number. Finally, one day, after Jane had achieved a state of deep relaxation, the psychologist gave her the phone again and asked her just to punch in numbers at random. She did so, and after a while she was consistently punching the same area code and phone number, though she never waited for the ring. But the psychologist wrote down the number, and, taking the phone from Jane, he called it himself and gave the phone back to Jane, whereupon she got to speak to her mother in Detroit, 400 miles away. As it turned out, Jane was a highly skilled engineer who had wandered away from her home in Boston on the day when the movers came to move her household to another state, where she was supposed to be relocating. Jane's family arrived to pick her up the next day. (Adapted from Lyon, 1985.)

DB was a 33-year-old man who had a clerical job and lived with his parents. Seven years earlier, during military training, he had been hit in the right eye by a rifle butt. Thereafter he claimed that he was blind in that eye, though medical examinations indicated that the eye was functioning normally.

To find out whether DB was in fact receiving no information through his right eye, he was given a test during which his left eye was completely covered. The test involved a machine that emitted a buzz. The machine had three switches, only one of which could turn off the buzz, and with each trial the controlling switch changed at random. DB's hands were placed on the machine, and he was told that on each trial he was to try to turn off the buzz. What he was not told was that the machine also had a visual component: a screen showing three triangles, one of which was always pointed in a direction different from the other two. On each trial the controlling switch was the one under the twisted triangle. So the machine gave its user the right answer—if the user could see.

DB had 21 sessions with the machine. Four of those were control sessions: The screen was turned off, so that there were no visual cues. On these control sessions, DB pulled the right switch 39 percent of the time, roughly what one would expect by chance. But in the 17 experimental sessions, when the screen was on, he pulled the right switch 74 percent of the time—far greater than a chance percentage. Furthermore, when the visual cue was present, he took twice as long to pull the switch, indicating that he was processing information. DB's "blind" eye was clearly seeing, and he was reclassified as having a psychological, not a physical, disorder. (Adapted from Bryant & McConkey, 1989.)

According to current psychiatric terminology, these two cases represent different disorders. Jane Doe has dissociative amnesia with fugue, one of the dissociative disorders, which are disturbances of higher cognitive functions such as memory or identity. DB, on the other hand, has a conversion disorder, which is one of the somatoform disorders, characterized by physical complaints or disabilities for which there is no apparent organic cause.

Despite their different labels, conversion disorder and the dissociative disorders have much in common (Spitzer, Spelsberg, Grabe, et al., 1999; Kihlstrom, 2001). First, both mimic actual neurological disorders—amnesia in the case of Jane Doe, blindness in the case of DB. Second, in both cases, the problem is not a neurological disability but a disruption of conscious awareness. Jane Doe knew her mother's telephone number, and DB could see with his right eye. In each case, the ability affected behavior, but neither Jane Doe nor DB was consciously aware of that ability.

Because of these similarities, conversion disorder and the dissociative disorders were grouped together for a long time in a broad category called "hysterical neurosis," **hysteria** being a psychogenic disorder that mimics a biogenic disorder. But when the *DSM* abandoned the concepts of neurosis and hysteria in 1980, the dissociative disorders and conversion disorder became separated. The dissociative disorders now include only disturbances of higher cognitive functions. Conversion disorder, because it affects not cognitive functions but sensory functions (as in blindness) or motor functions (as in paralysis), has been moved into the category of somatoform disorders, psychological disorders that take somatic, or physical, form. But, in view of their shared features and their historical connection (Kihlstrom, 2001), the present chapter will consider these two categories, and their theories and treatments, together.

Dissociative Disorders

As the name indicates, the **dissociative disorders** involve the dissociation, or splitting apart, of components of the personality that are normally integrated. As a result, some psychological function—identity, memory, perception of oneself or the environment—is screened out of consciousness. Many people, especially children and adolescents, have dissociative experiences—feelings of "strangeness," brief spells of memory loss or identity confusion—in the course of normal life (Rauschenberger & Lynn, 1995; Kihlstrom, 2001). In some measure, dissociation is an adaptive skill. For example, when we drive a car while having a conversation, what we attend to is the conversation, all the while screening out the psychological and motor functions involved in driving the car. However, if we have to attend to these functions—if, for example, the road suddenly becomes dangerous—we can do so. What was screened out can be called back. In the dissociative disorders, the screened-out function cannot be called back voluntarily. Furthermore, it is a critical function, such as our memory of past events or of who we are.

The dissociative disorders occur without any demonstrable damage to the brain. Indeed, pathological dissociation may not have much of a genetic component (Waller & Ross, 1997). Instead, as we shall see, they have their origin in severe psychological stress and develop as a way of coping with that stress (Gershuny & Thayer, 1999). In this regard, they are like posttraumatic stress disorder and acute stress disorder (Chapter 7), which often include dissociative symptoms and which may accompany dissociative disorders (Morgan, Hazlett, Wang, et al., 2001). We will discuss four syndromes: dissociative amnesia, dissociative fugue, dissociative identity disorder, and depersonalization disorder.

Dissociative Amnesia

Amnesia, the partial or total forgetting of past experiences, may be caused by a blow to the head or by any one of a number of brain disorders. Some amnesias, however, occur without any apparent neurologic cause, as a response to psychological stress. In addition to medical tests for brain pathology, there are several ways of distinguishing between organic and **dissociative amnesia** (Sackeim & Devanand, 1991; Sivec & Lynn, 1995; Kihlstrom, 2001). First, dissociative amnesia is almost always *anterograde,* blotting out a period of time after the precipitating stress, whereas organic amnesia, particularly from a head injury, is usually *retrograde,* erasing a period of time prior to the precipitating event. Second, dissociative amnesia is often selective; the "blank" period tends to include events that most people would want to forget—either a trauma or perhaps an unacceptable action such as an extramarital affair. Third, people with dissociative amnesia are often much less disturbed over their condition than are those around them—an indifference that suggests relief from conflict. Fourth, most people with dissociative amnesia remain well oriented to time and place and have little problem learning new information, whereas organic amnesias typically involve some disorientation and difficulty with new learning. Finally, because the events forgotten in dissociative amnesia are simply screened out of consciousness rather than lost altogether (as is the case in organic amnesia), they can often be recovered under hypnosis or with the aid of sodium amytal, a barbiturate, or lorazepam, a benzodiazepine (Kihlstrom, 2001).

Patterns of Memory Loss There are five broad patterns of dissociative amnesia. First and most common is *localized amnesia,* in which all events occurring during a circumscribed period of time are blocked out. For example, a man who has survived a fire in which the rest of his family have died might have no memory of anything that happened from the time of the fire until three days later. Second is *selective amnesia,* in which the person makes "spot" erasures, forgetting only certain events that occurred during a circumscribed period of time. In the just described example, the man might recall the fire engines coming and the ambulance taking him to the hospital but forget seeing his children carried out of the house or identifying their bodies the next day. Third is *generalized amnesia,* in which, as in the case of Jane Doe, the person forgets his or her entire life. Though this is the kind of amnesia that tends to turn up in novels and movies, it is actually rare. A fourth pattern, also rare, is *continuous amnesia,* in which the person forgets all events that occur after a specific period up to the present, including events that occur *after* the onset of amnesia. For example, if the amnesia begins on Monday, the person does not know on Wednesday what he or she did on Tuesday, let alone prior events. Finally, in

Dissociative amnesia is a popular plot device for Hollywood movies. In this scene from Alfred Hitchcock's classic, Spellbound *(1945), the psychiatrist, played by Ingrid Bergman, tries to help the patient (Gregory Peck) recover his memory.*

systematized amnesia, the person forgets only certain categories of information (e.g., all information about his or her family); other memories remain intact. While some patterns are more common than others, amnesia in general is rare. However, its incidence tends to spiral among victims of war and natural disasters. Indeed, many of the reported cases of amnesia have been soldiers in World War I and World War II (Loewenstein, 1996).

As noted, dissociative amnesias may involve no disorientation. The exceptions are generalized and continuous amnesia, in which all or much of the person's past is blocked out. Patients with these forms of amnesia do not know who or where they are, do not recognize family or friends, and cannot tell you their name, address, or anything else about themselves. In other words, their **episodic memory,** or memory of personal experience, is lost. Typically, however, their **semantic memory,** or general knowledge, is spared. For instance, a patient who cannot identify a picture of his wife is still able to identify a picture of John Kennedy (Kopelman, Christensen, Puffett, et al., 1994). **Procedural memory,** or memory for skills, is also usually intact. Amnesia victims can read and write, add and subtract.

In most cases, though, even episodic memory is only partially erased. **Explicit memories,** memories we are aware of, may be gone, but often the person shows evidence of having **implicit memories,** memories that he or she cannot call into conscious awareness but that still affect behavior (Kihlstrom, 2001). At the beginning of this chapter, we saw an example of this: Jane Doe's dialing the telephone number of the mother she didn't remember she had. Under the influence of implicit memory, many amnesia victims show strong reactions to things that recall the initiating trauma. In one reported case, the patient, a rape victim, had no conscious memory of the rape but clearly had unconscious knowledge of it. When shown a TAT card that depicted a person attacking another person from behind, he became extremely upset. Then he left the testing session to go to his room, where he attempted suicide (Kaszniak, Nussbaum, Berren, et al., 1988).

When dissociative amnesia occurs in novels and movies, it appears suddenly and dramatically, as the only symptom; it also disappears suddenly, with the person gratefully resuming his or her former life. This, apparently, is not the usual pattern. Many amnesias do remit suddenly, without treatment—others become chronic—but, even when they remit, they tend to recur. In a recent survey of 25 patients, almost half had had more than 1 episode of amnesia. Furthermore, their memory loss was accompanied by a wide range of other symptoms—above all, depression, headaches, and sexual dysfunction (typically, decreased sexual desire). Indeed, in most cases, the amnesia was discovered only on questioning; the presenting complaint was usually depression. As for what precipitated the first amnesic episode, this was retrospective evidence, which is always questionable—especially, in people with memory disorders—but 60 percent named childhood sexual abuse; 24 percent, marital trouble; 16 percent, a suicide attempt; 16 percent, disavowed sexual behavior such as adultery or promiscuity (Coons & Milstein, 1992; Kihlstrom, 2001). Studies have also indicated that during amnesia, patients show smaller brain event-related potentials (ERPs), but when they recover from the amnesia, their ERPs return to normal (Fukuzako, Fukuzaki, Fukuzako, et al., 1999).

Amnesia and Crime Amnesia has created difficulties for the legal system (Porter, Birt, Yuille, et al., 2001). Crime victims who cannot consciously recall the crime are unable to offer what would be valuable testimony in court. A worse problem is that people accused of crimes often do not remember the event. Between 10 and 70 percent of people charged with or convicted of homicide claim to have no memory of the crime (Porter, Birt, Yuille, et al., 2001). In such cases, alcohol or other drugs are often involved, so some of these amnesias may be drug-induced "blackouts." Many may be faked. But others are probably true dissociative amnesias, responses to the extreme emotional arousal surrounding the crime. Whatever the source, defendants claiming amnesia may be judged incapable of assisting in their own defense, in which case they may be judged incompetent to stand trial. If they are tried, they may qualify for the insanity defense, on the grounds that they committed the crime in an altered state of consciousness, in which they did not know what they were doing or that it was wrong (Porter, Birt, Yuille, et al., 2001). Such was the case in the 1993 trial of Lorena Bobbitt, who claimed to have no memory of cutting off her husband's penis and who was acquitted on the grounds of temporary insanity. For other legal problems posed by the dissociative disorders, see the box on the next page.

Dissociative Fugue

A condition related to amnesia is **dissociative fugue,** in which the person not only forgets all or most of his or her past but also takes a sudden, unexpected trip away from home. We saw an example of this in the

Focus On... Dissociative Identity Disorder and the Law: Who Committed the Crime?

In 1977, a man named William Stanley Milligan was arrested for the rape of three women in Columbus, Ohio. Two of the women positively identified him as the Ohio State University "campus rapist," and fingerprints found at the scene of one of the crimes matched his. It seemed to be an open-and-shut case. Not until Milligan twice tried to commit suicide in jail while awaiting trial did it occur to his lawyers that he might need psychiatric help.

The report of the examining psychologists and psychiatrists profoundly altered the nature of the case. At the time of the trial, they had identified at least 10 different personality states somehow coexisting within Milligan. These included the host, or core personality state, Billy; Arthur, an emotionless Englishman, who dominated the other personality states; Ragen, a Yugoslavian known as the protector of women and children and the "keeper of hate"; Allen, an 18-year-old manipulator and con artist; Tommy, a 16-year-old antisocial personality, who was also a landscape painter and escape artist; Danny, 14, a timid painter of still lifes; 8-year-old David, who "absorbed" the pain and suffering of the others; Christene, a 3-year-old English girl; Christopher, her troubled 13-year-old brother; and Adalane, 19, an introverted lesbian.

Milligan was eventually found not guilty by reason of insanity—the first case of dissociative identity disorder to be acquitted of a major crime under that plea. Accordingly, he was sent to a mental hospital near Columbus, where he was placed under the care of David Caul, a psychiatrist who had experience in treating dissociative identity disorder.

Caul soon discovered more identities, including 13 "undesirables." (Arthur called them this because they rebelled against his control.) One of the undesirables was the Teacher—the fusion of all 23 identities. Described as "Billy all in one piece," the Teacher had total recall of the events in Milligan's life. In his sessions with Caul, Milligan's identities fused more and more into 1 competent person. Soon he was allowed unattended trips into town and weekend furloughs. These privileges, however, provoked anger from the people of Columbus, who still feared Milligan's potential for violent behavior.

Under the glare of unfavorable publicity and open public hostility, Milligan's identities once again split apart. Aggressive identities came to the fore, causing Milligan to be sent to a maximum-security institution. Eventually, after years of treatment, his identities seemed to fuse, and he was released. He established a child-abuse prevention agency, worked as a farmer, and developed a career as an artist (Kihlstrom, Tataryn, & Hoyt, 1993).

Even though several experienced psychiatrists testified that Milligan had dissociative identity disorder, traceable to traumatic abuse suffered in childhood at the hands of his stepfather, many professionals and laypeople alike still suspect that Billy Milligan was faking. This disorder typically arouses such skepticism, sometimes justifiably.

In another case soon after Milligan's, Kenneth Bianchi, a man accused of a number of rape-murders in the Los Angeles area, claimed in an insanity defense that the crimes he was accused of were committed by one of his personality states, Steve Walker. The defense was undermined, however, by evidence that Bianchi was faking. (His alter egos were not consistent, for example.) He was convicted of multiple counts of murder.

In another twist, a Wisconsin man named Mark Peterson was accused of sexual assault by a dissociative identity disorder patient who said that only one of her personality states gave consent. (Another watched the event and another went to the police.) Peterson was eventually convicted under a law that makes it equivalent to rape to have sexual intercourse with a mental patient (Noonan, 2000).

These cases raise fascinating and difficult questions. Should a person be held responsible for crimes committed by a subordinate personality state? Is a person the victim of a crime if one identity gives consent? The legal system has not yet come to a firm decision. But at present the courts generally consider people with dissociative identity disorder responsible for crimes committed by one identity if that identity knew right from wrong at the time of the crime (Noonan, 2000; Porter, Birt, Yuille, et al., 2001).

case of Jane Doe. Fugue, then, is a sort of traveling amnesia, but it is more elaborate than amnesia. While people with amnesia, in their confusion, may wander about aimlessly, fugue patients are purposeful in their actions. Furthermore, while amnesia patients may also forget their identity, many fugue patients go one step further and manufacture a new one.

The length and elaborateness of fugues vary considerably. Some people may go no farther than the next town, spend the day in a movie house, check into a hotel under an assumed name, and recover by morning. Such modest adventures are the usual pattern. In rare cases, however, patients travel to foreign countries, assume a new identity, fabricate a detailed past, and pursue an altogether new life for months or even years. During the fugue, they appear fairly normal to observers. Finally, however, they "wake up," often after a jolting reminder of their former life or, as it appears in some cases, simply when they once again feel psychologically safe (Riether & Stoudemire, 1988). Fugue usually remits suddenly, and when fugue victims wake up, they are completely amnesic for the events that occurred during the fugue. The last thing they may remember is leaving home one morning. This second-stage amnesia is what usually brings fugue victims to professional attention. They seek therapy only once the fugue ends, partly because they want to find out what they did during the fugue.

Like amnesia, fugue is generally rare but is more common in wartime and after natural disasters (Coons, 1999). Again, like amnesia, it tends to occur after a severe psychological trauma and—as the term (derived from the Latin word for "flight") suggests—seems to function as an escape from psychological stress. The following case shows both the precipitating trauma and the escape motivation. It also offers a good example of implicit memory:

Bernice L., a middle-aged homemaker, had been raised in a stern, loveless, and extremely religious home. She grew up shy and anxious, but, when she went away to college, she began to bloom a little. This was largely the work of her roommate, a vivacious girl by the name of Rose P. who introduced Bernice to her friends, encouraged her to develop her talent for the piano, and in general drew her out. In their junior year, however, their friendship suffered a crisis. Rose became engaged to a young man with whom Bernice also promptly fell in love. When the man married Rose, Bernice lapsed into a severe depression. She returned home, but, at her parents' insistence, she eventually went back to school.

Upon graduation, Bernice married a young clergyman to whom she felt little attraction but of whom her parents approved. They had 2 children and eventually settled in a small town not unlike her childhood home. Bernice had few satisfactions in life other than her children and her happy memories of her first 2 years in college. Then, when she was 37 years old, her younger child, a musically talented boy, died. The next day she disappeared, and for 4 years she could not be found.

Later, with the help of a therapist, Bernice recalled some of the events of those 4 years. Totally amnesic for her past life, she had returned to her old college town. There, under the name of Rose P., she began giving piano lessons, and within 2 years she became assistant director of the local conservatory of music. She made a few friends, but she never spoke of her life, for it was still a complete blank to her. Then one day she was recognized by a woman who had known both her and Rose P. during college. Bernice's husband, now a minister in Chicago, was located, and reluctantly she returned to him.

In therapy, Bernice's amnesia was finally dispelled. She resumed her old identity; readjusted to her husband, who proved patient and sympathetic; and settled down to life in Chicago. (Adapted from Masserman, 1961, pp. 35–37.)

Dissociative Identity Disorder

Dissociative Identity Disorder: One Knows Martial Arts, the Other One Writes Death Notes to Me

In the MindMAP video on Personality with Dissociative and Borderline Features, one man recounts his unusual experience with alternative identities, including one that writes ominous notes to him. As this patient discovered, a diagnosis of DID is not in and of itself sufficient to absolve one from legal accountability if the personality charged with committing a crime knew right from wrong when the crime was committed. After seeing this account, consider whether or not you agree and why.

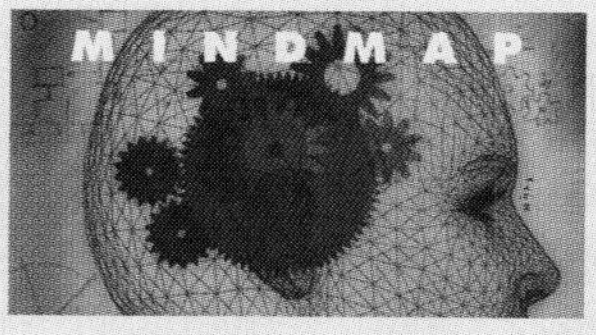

Perhaps the most bizarre of the dissociative disorders is **dissociative identity disorder (DID)**, formerly known as *multiple personality disorder.* In this pattern, the personality breaks up into 2 or more distinct identities or personality states, each well integrated and well developed, which then take turns controlling the person's behavior. (Sometimes called "split personality," dissociative identity disorder should not be confused with schizophrenia, which is an altogether different syndrome. See Chapter 14.) Amnesia is part of the pattern. At least 1 of the identities is amnesic for the experiences of the other or others (Dorahy, 2001). The first case of DID to receive extensive professional attention—the case of Miss Beauchamp, who may have had as many as 17 identities—was reported by Morton Prince in 1905. Ever since, this disorder has held a certain fascination for the public, as shown by the immense popularity of Thigpen and Cleckley's *The Three Faces of Eve* (1957), both book and movie, and by the best-seller *Sybil* (Schreiber, 1974), about a girl with 16 personality states.

In DID, a distinction is usually made between the **host**, the personality state corresponding to who the person was before the onset of the disorder, and the **alters**, the later-developing identities. There are many different configurations of host and alters (Putnam, 1997). In the simplest pattern, called *alternating personality,* 2 identities take turns controlling behavior, each having amnesia for the thoughts and actions of the other. In a slightly more complex pattern, the alter knows about the host, but

The film The Three Faces of Eve *depicts a woman with dissociative identity disorder.*

the host doesn't know about the alter (Dorahy, 2001). While the host is directing the person's behavior, the alter, fully aware of the thoughts and actions of the host, continues to operate covertly and to make its presence felt now and then. In such cases, the alter is said to be **coconscious** (Prince, 1905) with the host. When the coconscious alter finally surfaces, it can discuss in detail the interesting problems of the host. Meanwhile, the host only gradually becomes aware of the existence of the alter, usually by encountering the evidence of his or her activities. In one case (Osgood, Luria, Jeans, et al., 1976), the host, "Gina," first learned of the existence of her alter, "Mary Sunshine," when she began waking up in the morning to find cups with leftover hot chocolate in the kitchen sink. Gina did not drink hot chocolate. But even this is an atypically simple pattern. Most DID patients have far more than 1 alter—surveys have found an average of 13 per patient (Putnam, 1997; Putnam, Guroff, Silberman, et al., 1986)—and the host and alters often have complex patterns of coconsciousness. One identity may know about another, but not about a third; that third identity may be in league with a fourth and a fifth, but not with the sixth and seventh; and so on.

The pattern of an initially ignorant host and coconscious alters is illustrated in the following recent case of a Puerto Rican woman:

Madeline, 28 years old, was the host. She reported that she had virtually no autobiographic memory from her twelfth through eighteenth years, a period of time in which she had been repeatedly raped by a cousin, Andres. Madeline also had no memory of ever having been abused. Because her husband, Alfredo, had been physically and verbally abusive to her, she had separated from him and was now living with her 3-year-old daughter and a boyfriend.

Madeline had made two suicide attempts by taking pills; on the second attempt, she also cut one wrist deeply enough to require eight stitches. On both occasions she did not retain any memories of either taking the pills or cutting herself. In fact, although her last hospitalization had lasted 18 days, she remembered almost nothing about it.

Madeline, her parents, and her boyfriend described the long-standing presence of the following symptoms:

1. Constant and deep headaches, especially during blackouts or when some of her identities manifested themselves.
2. Demeaning voices inside her head calling her names, especially "whore," and telling her to kill herself.
3. Dramatic and rapid changes in mood: She could speak and behave like a man who was aggressive toward Madeline, and in a moment she could be very fearful and sad.
4. Frequent depersonalizations—that is, experiencing herself as if she were in a fog—completely unable to take charge of her own actions, even to stop herself from hurting herself or others.
5. Constant amnesia and blackouts that often lasted 4 to 5 hours.
6. Her parents and boyfriend had sometimes spoken with different identities, especially the aggressive ones. The changes in Madeline's personality at those times were dramatic.

During the first clinical interview, one of Madeline's alter identities, "Flor," appeared spontaneously. Flor's personality was the opposite of Madeline's: She described Madeline as "stupid" and "too good" and said she fell in love too easily; Flor described herself as tough and said she enjoyed impersonal sex. It was Flor who told the therapist about Madeline's abuse by her cousin. Madeline had 10 additional identities besides Flor, including Fredo (a nickname for Alfredo, the name of Madeline's estranged husband) and Andres, who revealed themselves in Madeline's diary entries. The alter Andres was clearly an internal representation of the cousin who had raped Madeline from the ages of 9 to 18. Andres and Fredo were both hostile and aggressive identities who said they wanted to "kill" Madeline. The following message they wrote in Madeline's diary demonstrates the "internal homicides" (when one identity tries to kill another) that can occur in DID patients: "Nobody loves you because you were born a woman. . . . We failed with the pills and with the knife last time. But, we aren't to fail the third time. . . ."

The two other primary identities were Deline (a nickname for Madeline), who had many of the memories of the sexual abuse, and Diana, whose angry personality represented the rage toward male figures that Madeline could not express. Only these 5 alters were in real control much of the time; the other 6 were fragments or very weak.

Eventually, through intensive work with her dissociative selves, which included writing diary entries to her alters (who usually wrote back right away), Madeline was able to understand her alters as internal representations of the past and to recognize that it was time they stop repeating the abuse she had suffered from others. As she came to understand her shattered selves, Madeline began to develop stronger internal defenses and became more assertive and self-sufficient. "Many times in my past I wished that another person would *feel* for me," she wrote. "But now I recognize that life is not so bad. At times it is hurtful, but one can still survive." (Adapted from Martinez-Taboas & Rodriguez-Cay, 1997.)

Types of Personalities As with Madeline, many cases of DID involve identities that are polar opposites: one conformist, reserved, "nice" personality and one rebellious, aggressive, "naughty" personality. In surveys of dissociative identity patients by two teams of researchers, at least 50 percent of the patients reported drug abuse by an alternate identity; 20 percent claimed that an alternate identity had been involved in a sexual assault on another person; and 29 percent reported that one of their alternates was homicidal (Putnam, Guroff, Silberman, et al., 1986; Ross, Miller, Reagor, et al., 1990). Dissociative identity patients may do violence to themselves when one identity tries to kill another. Such "internal homicide" attempts were reported by more than half the people in the previously mentioned surveys and can be seen in Madeline's case.

But "good versus bad" is not the only pattern. As with Madeline, one identity encapsulates a traumatic memory, while another reflects a former abuser. In other cases, the personality states may divide up the emotional life, one dealing with anger, another handling sadness, and so on. Often the personality states specialize in different areas of functioning, one for family relations, one for sex life, one for work, others for specific skills. And these patterns may overlap. For example, a personality state that embodies the memory of an abusive father may also be the only one who can solve complex mathematical problems (Loewenstein & Ross, 1992). Most patients, like Madeline—85 percent in the Putnam survey—have at least one personality state who is a child, and more than half of Putnam's subjects had at least one personality state of the opposite sex. The younger the patient was when the first alter appeared, the more subordinates he or she is likely to have.

Childhood Abuse In the Putnam survey, only 3 out of 100 patients did not report some significant trauma in childhood. The most common was sexual abuse, reported by 83 percent of the patients; in 68 percent of the patients, this sexual abuse involved incest. (See the box on page 187 on prevention of child abuse.) Three fourths of the patients also claimed to have suffered repeated physical abuse in childhood, and almost half reported having witnessed a violent death, usually of a parent or sibling, during their early years (Putnam, Guroff, Silberman, et al., 1986). The Putnam findings have been roughly duplicated by other studies (Loewenstein, 1994; Kisïel & Lyons, 2001).

These nearly unanimous testimonies of abuse suggest that dissociative identity disorder may be a stratagem that terrified children use to distance themselves from the realities of their lives (Atchison & McFarlane, 1994). In support of this view, most patients report that the disorder began in childhood, at a time of severe trauma. (In the Putnam survey, 89 percent reported onset before the age of 12.) It should be kept in mind, however, that most of the evidence of childhood abuse is based on retrospective surveys of the patients or their therapists. Some experts (Frankel, 1990; Kihlstrom, 2001; Piper, 1997) are concerned that claims of abuse may be biased by current theories of DID. (Because some experts have hypothesized that the cause is childhood abuse, the therapist seeks, and the patient finds, memories of childhood abuse.) More important, there have been no prospective studies examining the outcomes of children who have been abused. Thus, we do not know whether abused children are more likely to develop DID than are nonabused children (Kihlstrom, 2001). Finally, we do not know whether the incidence or severity of childhood abuse is any greater for DID than for other psychological disorders, such as depression or borderline personality disorder (Chapter 11), for which childhood abuse has also been reported to be common (Lilienfeld, Lynn, Kirsch, et al., 1999). The recall of childhood abuse is itself a highly controversial issue. (See the box on pages 190–191.)

Even if a connection between childhood abuse and DID becomes more firmly established in the future, researchers will still be left with the task of identifying the mechanism by which one leads to the other. Many children are abused. Why do only some of them—the minority of them—develop multiple identities? Certain studies (Butler, Duran, Jasiukaitis, et al., 1996; Waldo & Merritt, 2000) have found that people with dissociative identity disorder are easier to

Prevention Educating Children About Child Abuse

Child abuse, including child sexual abuse, has received much attention in the past two decades. Although the taboo nature of the subject makes it difficult to gather reliable estimates, research suggests that the number of victims is not small: Rind, Tromovitch, and Bauserman (1998) note that 27 percent of women and 14 percent of men have reported being sexually victimized in childhood, and other studies suggest a similarly high prevalence (MacMillan, Fleming, Trocme, et al., 1997; Finkelhor, 1994).

A reported history of child abuse and, especially, sexual abuse has been associated with many of the dissociative and somatoform disorders discussed in this chapter, although the association needs to be demonstrated definitively through prospective studies. Therefore, to the extent that a history of child abuse is associated with these disorders, preventing child abuse may reduce the likelihood that they will develop at a later time.

Child abuse prevention programs have been widely implemented in schools in recent years. Most preventive interventions are designed to help preschool and elementary school children recognize potentially abusive situations, teach them strategies for resisting sexual abuse, and encourage them to disclose any abuse to a trusted adult (Wurtele & Miller-Perrin, 1992). Quebec's ESPACE program, described by Hebert and colleagues (2001), is typical. Using role playing, guided discussions, and modeling, the ESPACE program seeks to enhance children's awareness of their personal rights and to teach them basic prevention concepts and skills, such as saying no or yelling. Role play is an especially important part of effective prevention education, because it gives children an opportunity to see how it feels to say no in a difficult situation. Practicing these skills makes it more likely that children can really use them if they ever need to.

The results of many studies suggest that children who participate in child abuse prevention programs similar to the ESPACE program tend to score approximately one standard deviation higher than control group children on knowledge and skills gains (Davis & Gidycz, 2000). Programs that use physically active participation (such as role playing) and make use of behavioral skills training such as modeling, rehearsal, and reinforcement produce better effects on knowledge and skills than those that do not (Davis & Gidycz, 2000; MacIntyre & Carr, 2000). Programs that spread the training across more sessions also have better results (Davis & Gidycz, 2000), as do multisystem programs that target parents or teachers as well as children (MacIntyre & Carr, 2000).

It is important to note that although these prevention programs show promise in terms of increasing children's knowledge of potentially abusive situations and their skills for coping with such situations, no studies have yet examined whether these programs do actually decrease the prevalence of child abuse. Future research will need to monitor the effects of such programs on child abuse rates.

hypnotize and in general are more suggestible or more fantasy-prone than either the general population or other psychiatric patients. Thus, it is possible that hypnotic susceptibility or something related to it, such as proneness to fantasy or the ability to focus attention narrowly, may make some people vulnerable to subdividing their identities under stress (Waldo & Merritt, 2000; Butler, Duran, Jasiukaitis, et al., 1996).

Problems in Diagnosis While dissociative identity disorder was once considered very rare, it is now reported much more frequently. Indeed, the number of reported cases of DID in the world jumped from 79 as of 1980 to about 6,000 in 1986 (Elzinga, van Dyck, & Spinhoven, 1998). And the vast majority of cases have been reported in North America, where public interest in this disorder—aroused by books, movies, and magazine articles on cases such as Eve, Sybil, and Billy Milligan (see the box on page 183)—seems to run highest. Such circumstances, together with the fact that therapists have often used hypnosis or other suggestive questioning in getting DID patients to switch from one identity to another, raise the possibility that the power of suggestion may be influencing some patients to convert severe but common disorders into more interesting "multiple personalities" (Piper, 1997; Powell & Gee, 1999). Some experts (e.g., Feldman & Feldman, 1998) believe that DID is more a fad than a legitimate syndrome.

Alternatively, the rise in the numbers of reported cases may reflect better recognition of the syndrome (Gleaves, 1996). DID patients suffer a wide variety of symptoms besides alternating identities. Depression, suicidal behavior, insomnia, amnesia, sexual dysfunction, and panic attacks were all reported by more than half the people in the Putnam and Ross surveys. Many patients also hear voices, the voices of their other identities (Boon & Draijer, 1993). When such patients first come before a diagnostician, they report all these symptoms, and, if the diagnostician is unfamiliar with or skeptical about dissociative identity disorder, the patient may easily be diagnosed as suffering from some other disorder, such as schizophrenia or depression (Loewenstein, 1994). Indeed, in the Putnam and Ross surveys, an average of seven years passed between the time the patients first contacted a mental health professional about symptoms related to dissociative identity disorder and the time when that diagnosis was applied.

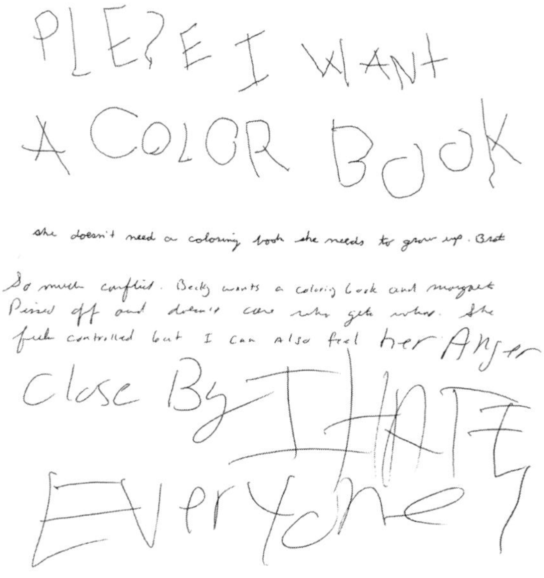
PLE?E I WANT
A COLOR BOOK
she doesn't need a coloring book she needs to grow up. Brat
So much conflict. Becky wants a coloring book and margaret
Pissed off and doesn't care who gets what. She
feels controlled but I can also feel her Anger
Close By
I HATE
Everyone

The same person—a dissociative identity disorder patient—produced these dramatically different handwriting samples under the influence of different identities.

Other trends also have contributed to the rise in the number of DID diagnoses (Gleaves, 1996). One is the increased awareness and reporting of childhood sexual abuse, which, as we saw, is often thought to be a cause of DID. Another is the interest in posttraumatic stress disorder—and, consequently, in trauma syndromes in general—that grew out of the Vietnam War. Finally, in the 1970s and 1980s, there was a growth in the field of cognitive psychology and, therefore, in such DID-related matters as memory and consciousness. All these factors helped to legitimize the disorder. In 1980, DID was first included as a distinct syndrome in the *DSM;* once it was listed, of course, it began to be more frequently diagnosed.

In recent years, even firm defenders of the DID diagnosis have become more concerned about false cases. For example, Ross (1997) now estimates that a quarter of the DID cases in the dissociative disorders unit that he directs are either faked or **iatrogenic** (induced by therapy). That the central feature of DID, the presentation of multiple identities, is usually not observable before treatment and that this essential feature becomes florid during treatment are major reasons why some critics have argued that DID is, at least in part, induced by therapy (Spanos, 1996; Lilienfeld, Lynn, Kirsch, et al., 1999). Indeed, a recent survey of board-certified American psychiatrists found little consensus regarding the diagnostic status and scientific validity of DID (Pope, Oliva, Hudson, et al., 1999).

In a discussion of courtroom cases, Coons (1991) lists a number of criteria by which false cases might be distinguished from the true. Patients whose subpersonalities change over relatively short periods of time; patients who manifest subpersonalities only under hypnosis; patients whose personality switches are not accompanied by the usual signs (headache, altered appearance); patients who do not show the multiple symptomatology (depression, panic attacks, etc.) typical of dissociative identity disorder—in these cases, according to Coons, the diagnostician should strongly consider the possibility of **malingering,** the conscious faking of symptoms in order to avoid responsibility. Further, cases in which patients do not show objective evidence—on psychophysiological measures (e.g., galvanic skin responses, event-related potentials [see Chapter 6])—of amnesia for information learned by their alters may also provide evidence of malingering (Allen & Iacono, 2001). The cause of the DID diagnosis has not been helped by a number of highly publicized lawsuits recently brought against therapists by patients whom they treated for DID. In 1997, a patient, Patricia Burgus, received a settlement of $10.6 million from the Chicago hospital and doctors under whose care she came to believe that she had 300 identities (Belluck, 1997).

In defense of the syndrome, a number of experts have reported that the physiology of DID patients—brain waves, PET scans, pain sensitivity, and skin conductance—may vary significantly depending on which personality state is in charge (Atchison & McFarlane, 1994; Allen & Iacono, 2001). The different identities of a single patient may also score very differently on standardized personality tests. These findings, however, do not rule out iatrogenesis. If a patient has been induced in therapy to develop several identities, those identities, encapsulating different emotions and cognitions, may well score differently on such tests (Merskey, 1995; Lilienfeld, Lynn, Kirsch, et al., 1999).

Depersonalization Disorder

Like fugue and dissociative identity disorder, **depersonalization disorder** involves a disruption of personal identity. Here, though, the disruption occurs without amnesia. The central feature of this syndrome is **depersonalization,** a sense of strangeness or unreality in oneself. People with depersonalization disorder feel as though they have become cut off from themselves and are viewing themselves from the outside or that they are functioning like robots or living in a dream. The sense of strangeness usually extends to the body. Patients may feel as though their extremities have grown or shrunk, as though their bodies are operating mechanically, as though they are dead, or as though they are imprisoned inside the body of somebody else.

These feelings of strangeness in the self are often accompanied by **derealization**, a feeling of strangeness about the world: Other people, like oneself, seem robotic, dead, or somehow unreal, like actors in a play. People experiencing depersonalization or derealization may also have episodes of *déjà vu* (French for "already seen"), the sense of having been in a place or situation before, when one knows that this is not the case. Or they may have the opposite experience, *jamais vu* (French for "never seen"), the sense, when one is in a familiar place or situation, of never having encountered it before. In the view of cognitive psychology, depersonalization and derealization constitute a failure of recognition memory. The person is unable to match current experience with past experience, as might happen on entering a familiar room that has been redecorated (Kihlstrom, 2001). Depersonalization often involves reduced emotional responsiveness, a loss of interest in others and the world in general. Often it also involves deficits in attention, short-term memory, and spatial reasoning (Guralnik, Schmeidler, & Simeon, 2000) as well as reduced physiological responsiveness (Griffin, Resick, & Mechanic, 1997)—reduced heart rate and skin conductance. People afflicted with depersonalization do not lose touch with reality. They know that their perceptions of strangeness are wrong. Nevertheless, the perceptions are frightening. The person may feel that he or she is going insane. A possible neuroanatomical basis for these strange perceptions has been reported recently. PET scans have shown abnormalities in the visual, auditory, and somatosensory association areas of the posterior cortex (Simeon, Guralnik, Hazlett, et at., 2000). Also, like the other dissociative disorders, depersonalization has been linked with childhood trauma, particularly emotional abuse (Simeon, Guralnik, Schmeidler, et al., 2001).

Depersonalization can occur briefly in the course of normal life. When people wake up from sleep, when they have had a bad scare, or when they are very tired or practicing meditation, they may have a brief spell of depersonalization. Depersonalization also occurs as a component of other psychological disorders, particularly anxiety disorders, depression, and schizophrenia, and it is a common symptom of the other dissociative disorders (Simeon & Hollander, 1993). Finally, depersonalization often occurs after "near-death experiences," in which people are rescued at the last moment from drowning or other accidents. Some research indicates that the experience of depersonalization *during* a traumatic event is adaptive—that it decreases the risk of depression and anxiety after the event (Shilony & Grossman, 1993). Possibly, the sense that this is happening in a dream or to someone else protects the person from suffering the full impact of the trauma. At the same time, other evidence (Griffin, Resick, & Mechanic, 1997; Gershuny & Thayer, 1999) suggests that people who develop pronounced feelings of depersonalization *after* a trauma are more likely to succumb to a full-blown posttraumatic stress disorder (Chapter 7).

A brief spell of depersonalization connected with a trauma does not, however, constitute depersonalization disorder. The diagnosis is made only when depersonalization (with or without a trauma) is severe and persistent enough to disrupt the person's life, as in the following case:

> Mr. B was a 37-year-old married professional man who had suffered from depersonalization disorder since age 10. He vividly recalled its acute onset on a day when he was playing football: he was tackled by another boy and suddenly felt that his body had disappeared. The depersonalization was initially episodic but became continuous by age 14. He described it as "not being in this world . . . I am disconnected from my body. It is as if my body is not there." The depersonalization was lessened when he was alone and almost disappeared in his wife's presence. All social settings made it much worse. He met criteria for schizoid personality disorder. As a child he had suffered marked emotional neglect. His parents fed and clothed him but never expressed emotion; he recalled hardly ever being touched or kissed. It is of interest that his sense of detachment only involved his body and not other aspects of the self (Simeon, Gross, Guralnik, et al., 1997, pp. 1109–1110).

The onset of depersonalization disorder may be either sudden, as in this case, or gradual. The condition is usually chronic.

❖ Groups at Risk for Dissociative Disorders

The prevalence of dissociative identity disorder, like most other aspects of that disorder, is a topic of controversy and awaits careful research. Some experts estimate prevalence to be less than 1 percent (Rifkin, Ghisalbert, Dimatou, et al., 1998). DID is anywhere from 5 to 9 times more common in women than in men (Putnam & Loewenstein, 2000), and, according to the research, most of these women are already deeply troubled. The Putnam group's survey found that at the time of diagnosis, almost 90 percent of its sample was suffering from depression, and more than half had histories of substance abuse and suicide

Research Highlights

Recovered Memory of Childhood Abuse: A Modern Dilemma

In 1990, a jury in Redwood City, California, convicted a man, George Franklin, of murdering a child some 20 years earlier—a verdict based on Franklin's daughter's claim that she had suddenly remembered witnessing the crime. This was only the most sensational of hundreds of recent cases of so-called recovered memory—memories of childhood abuse, particularly sexual abuse, that according to the rememberers were repressed and then eventually returned to consciousness. A number of people have sued their remembered abusers, and won. At the same time, recovery specialists, therapists expert in excavating such memories, have published best-selling books, claiming that many people with psychological problems are suffering from buried memories of abuse.

Recovered memory has generated huge public interest, stimulated by magazine articles and television talk shows. This fascination, in turn, has prompted a wave of skepticism. According to some observers, many recovered memories of abuse are nothing more than the product of suggestion—and hypnosis—by irresponsible therapists and exposure to talk shows and self-help books (Heaton & Wilson, 1998). Such skepticism, however, is mild compared with the outrage of parents who say they have been wrongly accused. Some are fighting back in court, not just against their children but also against the therapists in whose offices these alleged memories have surfaced. Patients, too, are suing their therapists. In one case, former patient Patricia Burgus claimed that she was induced in therapy to produce false memories of being sexually abused, of abusing her own two sons, and of having belonged to a satanic cult whose activities included cannibalism. Burgus received a settlement of $10.6 million (Belluck, 1997). In 1995, the conviction of George Franklin was reversed, largely because of questions raised about the validity of his daughter's recovered memory.

How can false memories be distinguished from true ones? This question has prompted a flurry of research, which so far has established a few principles. First, it is apparently possible to forget and then remember a childhood trauma. In one study, researchers asked a random national sample of 724 adults whether they had experienced some form of trauma and, if so, whether they had ever forgotten this. Almost three quarters said they had undergone a trauma. (The most common were assault, rape, or sexual molestation; natural disasters or car accidents; and the witnessing of assault or murder.) Almost a third of this group said that, at some point in their lives, they had forgotten all or part of the trauma (Elliott, 1997).

That study, however, relied on self-report. Another researcher, L. M. Williams (1994), began her study with records of documented abuse. Using a hospital's files on 206 girls, ages 10 months to 12 years, who had received medical treatment following verified sexual abuse in the early 1970s, Williams tracked down as many of those girls, now women, as she could and asked them if they would participate in a survey about women treated at that hospital. More than half consented, and in the course of a 3-hour interview, they were asked about many things. But, when the question of childhood sexual abuse was put to them, 38 percent did not report the incident for which the hospital records showed they had been treated. Perhaps they were simply withholding this information, out of a sense of privacy. Probably not, says Williams, for two thirds of these nonreporters told the interviewer about *other* episodes of childhood abuse. Of those who did report the documented abuse, 16 percent said there had been a time in the past when they did not remember it (Williams, 1995).

Thus, apparently people can forget true episodes of abuse. And, according to other recent research, they can also have false memories of abuse. Recent research has found that women with recovered memories of abuse are prone to greater false recognition of material they've never seen before than women with continuous memories of abuse or no abuse history (Clancy, Schacter, McNally, et al., 2000). This study suggests, but does not prove, that women with recovered memories of abuse may have a tendency to falsely remember events that they didn't experience. False memories of abuse seem to hinge on what is called *source amnesia*. In storing a memory, the brain distributes it among various areas—the sounds of the memory in one part, the sight of it in another part, and so on. Information as to the *source* of a memory, when and where the thing happened—in life, in a movie, in a story told to the person—seems to be stored primarily in the frontal cortex, and this information is more fragile than other parts of memory. People often remember things but forget the source. For example, they may recognize a man's face but not recall where they know him from. Or they misidentify the source. (For example, they claim to remember an event from childhood when in fact they have only been told about it.)

Eileen Franklin Lipsker testified about her recovered memory of having seen her father sexually abuse and murder her playmate 20 years before, when she was 8 years old. Her testimony resulted in her father's conviction, which was later reversed.

According to some researchers, source amnesia is what happens in many cases of recovered memory. The rememberers are not inventing the memory; they are simply misattributing it—to their own lives (Schacter, 1999). Where, then, does it come from?

One possibility is the media: the talk shows, magazine articles, and books mentioned earlier. An item of special interest to researchers is Ellen Bass and Laura Davis' *The Courage to Heal*. This 1988 book, which has no doubt given needed comfort to numerous survivors of childhood abuse, may also have confused many other people. One of its main premises is that a great number of people are victims of incest but don't realize they were abused. For readers who are in doubt, the book offers a list of things they might recall, ranging from the relatively harmless, such as being held in a way that made them uneasy, to the clearly criminal, such as rape. Then readers are told, "If you are unable to remember any specific instances like the ones mentioned above but still feel that something abusive happened to you, it probably did" (p. 21). Abuse can also be deduced from psychological symptoms, the authors claim, and they list as symptoms depression, self-destructive thoughts, low self-esteem, and sexual dysfunction, problems experienced by many people, including the children of irreproachable parents. *The Courage to Heal* has been repeatedly implicated in disputed memories of abuse.

Another possible source of suggestion is therapists. Psychologist Elizabeth Loftus reported a case in which a man, whose daughter claimed to have recovered memories of his molesting her, hired a private investigator to go to the daughter's therapist. The investigator pretended that she was seeking psychological help; her complaint was nightmares and insomnia. By the fourth session, the therapist had declared the investigator a probable incest survivor, a diagnosis she said was "confirmed on the basis of the 'classic symptoms' of body memory and sleep disorders." Although the investigator "insisted that she had no memory of such events, the therapist assured her that this was often the case" (Loftus, 1993, p. 530). The therapist recommended that she read *The Courage to Heal*.

The fact that therapists specializing in recovered memory often unearth such memories through hypnosis and hypnotic age regression (telling the patient, under hypnosis, that he or she is now a child) only increases people's concerns about such therapy, for the research on memories obtained through hypnosis seriously questions their accuracy (Destun & Kuiper, 1996; Powell & Gee, 1999). Under hypnosis, for example, people have remembered being abducted by aliens (Gordon, 1991).

But can the memory of a traumatic event actually be planted in a person's brain? According to several recent studies, the answer is yes (Porter, Yuille, & Lehman, 1999). In one experiment (Loftus, Feldman, & Dashiell, 1995), the researchers were reluctant to instill a memory of sexual abuse, so they chose instead the widespread childhood fear of getting lost in a store. One 14-year-old subject, Chris, was told by his older brother, Jim, that their mother had lost Chris in a shopping mall when he was 5. Jim told Chris the story briefly, with few details. Then, for several days afterward, Chris was questioned about the episode, and he began to recover the memory. On the second day, he recalled how he felt when he was lost; on the fourth day, he reported what his mother had said to him when she found him. Within a few weeks, he remembered a great deal more:

> I was with you guys for a second and then I think I went over to look at the toy store, the Kay-bee toy and uh, we got lost and I was looking around and I thought, "Uh-oh. I'm in trouble now." . . . I thought I was never going to see my family again. I was really scared you know. And then this old man, I think he was wearing a blue flannel, came up to me . . . he was kind of old. He was kind of bald on top . . . he had like a ring of gray hair . . . and he had glasses. (Loftus, 1993, p. 532)

When Chris was finally debriefed, he was incredulous. By that time, he remembered the episode very well.

But being lost is not the same as being molested. As noted, the researchers in this case did not feel it was safe to implant a memory of abuse, but such an experiment took place informally in the widely publicized case of Paul Ingram. Ingram, a county sheriff in Olympia, Washington, was arrested in 1988 after his 2 daughters, ages 18 and 22, claimed to have retrieved memories of being abused by him. Ingram was at first bewildered by the accusations, but gradually he claimed that he remembered episodes in which he had assaulted the girls. Soon the accusations escalated. One daughter, who had read books on satanic ritual abuse and had seen satanic abuse survivors on *Geraldo*, then remembered that Ingram had forced her to take part in satanic rituals—she estimated that she had attended 850 such events—in which babies were chopped up. Under prodding by police investigators, Ingram remembered the satanic rituals too.

Social psychologist Richard Ofshe, an authority on cults and mind control, was brought in by the prosecution to question Ingram. To determine how suggestible Ingram was, Ofshe told him a lie: that 1 of his daughters and 1 of his sons were now claiming that he had forced them to have sex with each other. As before, Ingram seemed puzzled at first, but, by his third meeting with Ofshe, he proudly produced a 3-page confession, describing how he had watched the 2 children have sex and including numerous details of their intercourse. Ofshe eventually concluded that all of Ingram's memories of the abuse he had inflicted were fantasies, the product of suggestion by the investigators questioning him. Ingram concluded the same thing— too late to retract his guilty plea. He was convicted of rape and sentenced to 20 years in prison (Wright, 1994).

No one involved in the recovered-memory controversy denies that children are sexually abused (including many whose memories of abuse require no recovery). Nor, in the face of the studies cited above, would most experts claim that all recovered memories of abuse are false. Clearly, some that are called true are false, with terrible consequences for the accused, and some that are called false are true, with the equally traumatic consequences for the accusers. What would be possible, however, is a commitment on the part of therapists to seek out confirming physical evidence. Such evidence can help separate false charges from the true (Porter, Birt, Yuille, et al., 2001; Allen & Iacono, 2001).

attempts (Putnam, Guroff, Silberman, et al., 1986). Although, as noted, its victims say that DID begins in childhood—and some child cases have been identified (Peterson & Putnam, 1994)—DID tends not to be diagnosed until the patient is in his or her twenties or thirties. The symptoms generally look the same across cultures (Atchison & McFarlane, 1994; Sar, Yargic, & Tutkun, 1996), but not across age groups. Children, it seems, are less likely to have clear-cut identities, but very likely to show amnesia and trancelike states. Without the identities, they may fail to be diagnosed with DID and yet still be at high risk. A new diagnostic category—"dissociative disorder of childhood," stressing amnesia and trance, together with abrupt shifts in behavior—has been proposed to cover this condition (Peterson & Putnam, 1994).

As for depersonalization disorder, specialists agree that it is rare. Like DID and other dissociative disorders, it seems to be more common in women than in men (Simeon, Gross, Guralnik, et al., 1997). The condition is seen worldwide, but in some cultures it is not regarded as a disorder but as a legitimate trance or spirit possession (Castillo, 1997b). In contrast, dissociative fugue, though also rare, may be more common in men than women (Coons, 1999).

Dissociative Disorders: Theory and Therapy

Most theories of the dissociative disorders begin with the assumption that dissociation is a way in which people escape from situations that are beyond their coping powers. As for how the process occurs, and how the resulting disorders should be treated, these questions receive different answers. The psychodynamic, behavioral, and sociocultural perspectives have been the most influential. However, as new discoveries are made about the psychological and brain processes that underlie memory, the cognitive and neuroscience perspectives are likely to become increasingly important.

The Psychodynamic Perspective: Defense Against Anxiety

It was in the late nineteenth century that the dissociative disorders were first extensively studied. A pioneer in this research was French psychologist Pierre Janet (1929), who originated the idea of mental dissociation. Under certain circumstances, Janet claimed, one or more divisions of mental functioning could become split off from the others and operate outside conscious awareness. Janet called this phenomenon *désagrégation,* which was translated into English as "dissociation." Janet and others considered the dissociative disorders a subdivision of hysteria. But it was left to Janet's contemporary, Sigmund Freud, to enunciate a cause of dissociation in the theory of hysteria that was to become the basis for his entire theory of the mind.

Dissociation as Defense Freud, as we have seen, believed that many basic human wishes were in direct conflict with either reality or the superego and that the result of this conflict was painful anxiety. To protect the mind against the anxiety, the ego repressed the wish and mounted defenses against it. The dissociative disorders—indeed, all the neuroses—were simply extreme and maladaptive defenses. Dissociative amnesia, for example, is regarded by Freudian theorists as a simple case of repression. Fugue and dissociative identity disorder are more complicated, in that the person also acts out the repressed wish directly or symbolically—the fugue patient goes off and has adventures, the person with dissociative identity disorder becomes a different, "forbidden" self—while the ego maintains amnesia for the episode, thus protecting the mind against the strictures of the superego.

This theory has on its side the observation that dissociative disorders do appear to operate in such a way as to grant wishes that the person could not otherwise satisfy (as illustrated in the case history of Bernice). There is also some research support for the anxiety-relief hypothesis. One recent study found that dissociative patients experience less intrapsychic conflict than alcoholic patients (Alpher, 1996). But, with its strict division between conscious and unconscious, the Freudian model does not seem to offer an adequate explanation of dissociative identity disorder, in which the "forbidden" self does not, in fact, remain unconscious but, instead, seizes the consciousness. Several writers (Brenner, 1996; Kluft, 1992; Pica, 1999) have put forth more complex theories of DID in line with current psychodynamic and developmental thinking. Kluft's hypothesis is that this condition develops when a child with a special capacity to dissociate—that is, to focus intensely on one thing and disengage from trauma—is exposed to overwhelming stress. Imagine, for example, a young girl who has an imaginary companion (as many DID patients report having had [Sanders, 1992]). If she were sexually abused and no adult were available to minister to her distress, she might expand the imaginary companion to contain the abuse experience, thus walling it off from herself. (This would help to account for the frequent reports of child subordinates in multiple personality.) Indeed, according to Pica (1999), only traumatized children who have imaginary companions have the capacity to develop DID. The girl in our example might also develop a third, punitive identity, based on the abuser, as a refraction of her guilt feelings, as well as a protector identity, in answer to her need for protection. Over time, this constellation could be expanded to contain and enclose other upsetting experiences. The subpersonalities might remain dormant for years, but the stress of later traumas could cause them to emerge as overt, alternating identities, symptoms of dissociative identity disorder. A recent study contradicts Kluft's hypothesis, finding that women with repressed or recovered memories of childhood sexual abuse were no more likely to forget or dissociate trauma-related words than women with no abuse history (McNally, Clancy, & Schacter, 2001).

Treating Dissociation Psychodynamic therapy is the most common treatment for the dissociative disorders. When trauma is involved, or thought to be involved, the treatment generally proceeds in three stages. Stage 1 involves settling the patient down: establishing an atmosphere of trust and helping the patient to gain some mastery over the dissociative symptoms. Then, in stage 2, the traumatic memory is recovered and grieved over. Stage 3 is devoted to the reintegration of the traumatic memory, so that the patient no longer has to use dissociation to wall it off (Herman, 1992; Kluft, 1999).

Exposing the repressed memory may be no easy task, however. After all, the whole thrust of the dissociative disorders is to protect that material from exposure. In amnesia, fugue, and DID, the traditional method of bringing forth the lost material has been hypnosis. (Barbiturates and benzodiazepines may achieve the same effect.) Under hypnosis, fugue and amnesia patients often reveal the events covered by the amnesia, and people with DID bring forth subordinate identities. Indeed, some cases of dissociative identity disorder are *discovered* through hypnosis. A disadvantage of hypnosis is that in some cases it seems to bring on or exacerbate dissociative symptoms (Destun & Kuiper, 1996; Powell & Gee, 1999). But, because it also uncovers dissociated material, some treatments for dissociative identity disorder still rely on this method (Kluft, 1999). Another concern is that the memory retrieval may be retraumatizing—particularly when it takes the form of **abreaction,** or the intense reexperiencing of the event—and unnecessarily prolonged, plunging the patient again and again into a state of emotional crisis. Some therapists now avoid abreactions (Ross, 1997). Kluft (1999) has proposed a technique called fractionated abreaction, in which the memory is retrieved only gradually, in small parts, while the therapist encourages mastery and discourages surrender to emotion.

Although hypnosis is an effective method for bringing forth dissociated material, it has drawbacks. In some cases it creates or aggravates dissociative symptoms. In others, the memory retrieval brought on by hypnosis may retraumatize the client.

Therapeutic outcome studies (Coons, 1986; Kluft, 1988) indicate that this may be a long process. As we pointed out earlier, fugue tends to remit without treatment, and dissociative amnesia may also. Hence, the usual goal of therapy in these disorders is to recover and integrate the lost material so that the patient doesn't suffer a relapse. But DID is far more stubborn. The more identities, the more difficult it is to integrate them into a single personality (Kluft, 1999); and when integration is achieved, it can crumble in the face of stress or if, as sometimes happens, another, previously undetected identity surfaces. A recent 2-year follow-up of patients treated for DID found that they showed marked improvement in a wide variety of symptoms, including dissociative symptoms (Ellason & Ross, 1997). Those who had achieved integration were significantly more improved, but they appear to be a minority. By 1 count, only 38 of the 153 patients who began treatment for DID achieved a stable integration of their identities (Piper, 1994b).

The Behavioral and Sociocultural Perspectives: Dissociation as a Social Role

Learning to Dissociate The behaviorists have conceptualized the dissociative disorders as a form of learned coping response, with the production of symptoms in order to obtain rewards or relief from stress. According to the behaviorists, the dissociative disorders, like many other psychological disorders, are the result of a person's adopting a social role that is reinforced by its consequences (Seltzer, 1994). In amnesia, fugue, and dissociative identity disorder, the rewarding consequence is protection from stressful events. Fugue, for example, gets its victims away from situations painful to them, and amnesia for the fugue protects them from painful consequences of their actions during the fugue. Note the similarity between this interpretation and the psychodynamic view: In both cases, the focus is on motivation, and the motivation is escape. The difference is that in the psychodynamic view the process is unconscious, whereas in the behavioral view dissociative behavior is maintained by reinforcement, like any other behavior.

Like the behaviorists, sociocultural theorists see dissociative symptoms as the product of social reinforcement. In a theory put forth by Spanos (1996), for example, dissociative identity disorder is a strategy that people use to evoke sympathy and escape responsibility for certain of their actions. Those actions, they say, were performed by some other, nonresponsible part of themselves. According to Spanos, this process is aided by hypnosis: Patients learn the "hypnotic role" and in that role produce the kind of behavior that the clinician hypnotizing them seems to want. Once they produce it, the clinician validates it with an expert diagnosis, and that diagnosis results in a number of possible rewards: relief from distress, an ability to control others, permission for misbehavior, and even, in some cases, avoidance of criminal proceedings. The clinician is rewarded, too, by attention: He or she has uncovered another case of this celebrated disorder. Thus, having created the disorder, both therapist and patient come to believe in its existence, for they have good reason to do so.

To test this hypothesis, Spanos and his colleagues designed an experiment based on the case of Kenneth Bianchi, the so-called Hillside Strangler, who raped and murdered several women in the Los Angeles area during the early 1980s. (See the box on page 183.) Upon arrest, Bianchi claimed he was innocent, and he was sent for a psychiatric evaluation, during which he supposedly showed evidence of dissociative identity disorder. What happened was as follows. First, Bianchi was hypnotized. Then the clinician described the situation to him as one in which another, hidden "part" of him might emerge. Bianchi was given an easy way to signal the arrival of that part. The clinician said to him:

> I've talked a bit to Ken, but I think that perhaps there might be another part of Ken that I haven't talked to. And I would like to communicate with that other part. And I would like that other part to come to talk to me . . . And when you're here, lift the left hand off the chair to signal to me that you are here. Would you please come, Part, so I can talk to you . . . Part, would you come and lift Ken's hand to indicate to me that you are here . . . Would you talk to me, Part, by saying "I'm here"?
>
> (*Schwarz, 1981, pp. 142–143*)

Kenneth Bianchi, the "Hillside Strangler," made an unsuccessful attempt to prove that he was not guilty by reason of insanity, in the form of dissociative identity disorder.

Bianchi answered yes and then had the following exchange with the clinician (B = Bianchi; C = clinician):

C: Part, are you the same as Ken or are you different in any way?
B: I'm not him.
C: You're not him. Who are you? Do you have a name?
B: I'm not Ken.
C: You're not him? Okay. Who are you? Tell me about yourself. Do you have a name I can call you by?
B: Steve. You can call me Steve.

(*Schwarz, 1981, pp. 139–140*)

"Steve" went on to say that, with the help of a cousin, he had murdered a number of women and that Ken knew nothing either about him (Steve) or about the murders. When he was released from his hypnotic state, Bianchi was "amnesic" for all that

Steve had said. He then pleaded not guilty by reason of insanity, the insanity being dissociative identity disorder. (The defense failed.)

What Spanos and his colleagues did was to subject a number of college students to variations on the procedure Bianchi went through. The students were instructed to play the role of accused murderers, and they were divided among three experimental conditions. In the Bianchi condition, the participants were hypnotized and then put through an interview taken almost verbatim from the Bianchi interview. In a second, hidden-part condition, the participants were also hypnotized, after which they were told that under hypnosis people often reveal a hidden part of themselves. However, in contrast to the Bianchi condition, that hidden part was not directly addressed, nor was it asked whether it was different from the participant. In the third, control condition, the participants were not hypnotized, and they were given only vague information about hidden parts of the self.

After these experimental conditions were set up, all the participants were questioned about whether they had a second identity. They were also asked about the murders. In the Bianchi condition, 81 percent of the participants came up with second identities that had different names from themselves, and in the majority of cases this second identity admitted guilt for the murders. In the hidden-part condition, only 31 percent revealed second identities with new names, though, here again, the majority of second identities confessed to the murders. In the control condition, only 13 percent confessed to the murders, and no one produced a new identity with a different name.

Thus, it appears that, when the situation demands, people who are given appropriate cues can manufacture a subordinate identity and will shift blame onto it. Furthermore, in keeping with Spanos' theory, the students who produced a second identity in some measure knew how to design it skillfully. In a second session, when these "multiple-personality" participants were given the same personality test twice, one time for each identity, their new alter identities tested very differently from their host identities (Spanos, Weekes, & Bertrand, 1985). Recall that this finding of differences between alters on personality tests has been put forth as support for the genuineness of DID. But apparently such differences can also be manufactured.

According to Spanos and others (Lilienfeld, Lynn, Kirsch, et al., 1999), these findings suggest that most cases of dissociative identity disorder are strategic enactments. Many of these patients are highly imaginative people, with rich fantasy lives. And recent evidence suggests that fantasizers score high on measures of dissociation (McNally, Clancy, Schacter, et al., 2000; Waldo & Merritt, 2000). Moreover, DID patients are very susceptible to suggestion and hypnosis. If such people were placed in difficult circumstances from which "multiple personality" would help them escape and if, under hypnosis or even without hypnosis, an admired authority figure (the therapist) were to give them the suggestion that they might have a subordinate identity and were to tell them how such a personality state could be expressed, they could, in fact, develop one and come to believe in it. On the other hand, critics of Spanos' theory note that just because individuals can enact an alter identity does not mean that all cases of DID are strategic enactments.

Nonreinforcement According to behavioral and sociocultural theory, the way to treat dissociative symptoms is to stop reinforcing them (Spanos, 1996). In a case of dissociative identity disorder, for example, therapists, friends, and family members would express no interest in the alters. At the same time, they would expect the patient to take responsibility for actions supposedly produced by the alters. Using such an approach with a woman who reported alters, Kohlenberg (1973) found that the alters' behaviors became less frequent when they were not reinforced. The therapist may also help patients deal with emotions that they are presumably pushing off onto alters. In one case, a passive patient, L, had a very aggressive alter, "Toni." Once L was given assertiveness training and taught how to express anger, Toni disappeared (Price & Hess, 1979).

The Cognitive Perspective: Memory Dysfunction

Cognitive theorists view the dissociative syndromes as fundamentally disorders of memory (Dorahy, 2001). In each case, what has been dissociated is all or part of the patient's autobiography. As we have seen, the patient's skills (procedural memory) and general knowledge (semantic memory) are usually intact. What is impaired is the patient's episodic memory, or record of personal experience. As we have also seen, it is only partially impaired. Patients may still show evidence that they have implicit memory of their past. What they don't have is explicit memory for the dissociated material, the ability to retrieve it into consciousness.

Retrieval Failure What causes this selective impairment of explicit episodic memory? Two cognitive theories have been proposed. One has to do with what is

Sirhan Sirhan gave dramatic evidence of state-dependent memory. In his normal waking state, he said he did not remember having killed Senator Robert F. Kennedy, but in an agitated state under hypnosis he remembered and even reenacted the murder.

called **state-dependent memory.** A number of studies have shown that people have an easier time recalling an event if they are in the same mood state as the one they were in when the event occurred (Putnam, 1997; Bower, 1994). Hence, memories established in an extreme emotional state—for example, the kind of severe traumatic reaction that is thought to set off dissociative amnesia and fugue—may be lost simply because they are linked to a mood that is not likely to recur. A dramatic case of state-dependent memory is that of Sirhan Sirhan, the man convicted of killing Robert F. Kennedy. In the waking state, Sirhan claimed amnesia for the crime, but under hypnosis his mood became more and more agitated, as it had been during the crime, and in this state he not only recalled the murder but reenacted parts of it (Bower, 1992).

Such a mechanism may also help to explain dissociative identity disorder. Typically, the different identities are characterized by different mood states. Therefore, state dependency may lead one identity to have amnesia for the experiences of another. By the same token, situations that produce strong emotion may cause a shift from one identity to a different identity, one with moods and memories consistent with that emotion. For example, if a quiet-tempered patient is made angry, this may cause a sudden shift to a hostile subordinate identity, for that is the identity that can process and express the anger (Bower, 1994; Dorahy, 2001).

A second cognitive theory of dissociation has to do with reconstructive memory. According to this model, a person will recognize a given mental representation as an actual memory of his or her past experience to the extent that enough of the features associated with the past experience (e.g., perceptual features, context, emotion at the time) can be retrieved and associated with each other. Under some circumstances, not all the features of a past experience will be simultaneously activated in the brain (particularly since the brain stores these features in different locations; see the Research Highlights box on "Recovered Memory of Childhood Abuse," pages 190–191), and so the person will not recognize the representation as a memory from his or her own past. The **source-monitoring deficit theory** proposes that DID patients do not retrieve a sufficient number or a proper configuration of features that would allow them to identify past experiences as memories. When there are state or mood differences between a DID patient's alters from the time the memory was encoded to the time the person tries to retrieve it, the strategic search processes will differ between alters, and the memory will not be retrieved.

Improving Memory Retrieval To date, there has been little work on cognitive therapy for dissociative disorders. Nevertheless, many therapists use cognitive techniques in treating patients with dissociative disorders (Brand, 2001). For example, in the case of Jane Doe at the beginning of this chapter, the therapist appealed to her implicit memory when he asked her to punch in telephone numbers at random. Other patients have been asked to state the first name that comes to mind or to say which of a list of cities rings a bell, the hope being that the name or city will be the patient's own, arising from implicit memory. State dependency has also been used by therapists in efforts to reinstate strong emotions in their patients, first under hypnosis and then in the waking state, and spring the lock on state-dependent memories. This technique was applied in the case of Sirhan Sirhan.

Some treatments for DID, such as tactical-integration therapy, combine cognitive-behavioral and psychodynamic approaches (Fine, 1999). In this therapy, the first stage of treatment focuses on the cognitive distortions and dysfunctional beliefs arising from past traumas among the various alters. These trauma-based cognitive biases are challenged with typical cognitive techniques, such as hypothesis testing and reattribution training. The second stage is more psychodynamic and involves fractionated abreaction and mastery of emotion.

The Neuroscience Perspective: Brain Dysfunction

The dissociative disorders, as we have pointed out, involve psychiatric symptoms that look like the product of neurological disease but are thought instead to be the result of psychological processes. Are they? According to neuroscience researchers, some so-called dissociative disorders may be neurological disorders after all. According to one theory (Sivec & Lynn, 1995), the dissociative syndromes may be a by-product of undiagnosed epilepsy (Chapter 15). Epileptic-type seizures have been associated with dissociative identity disorder ever since the disorder was first described (Charcot & Marie, 1892). Conversely, some victims of epilepsy have reported dissociative experiences such as blackouts, fugues, depersonalization, déjà vu, and feelings of demonic possession following seizures. This theory may apply to certain dissociative conditions, but it is unlikely to explain DID, in which the symptoms are far more elaborate than the dissociative experiences reported by epileptic patients. Furthermore, as we saw, DID is far more common in women, whereas epilepsy is more frequently diagnosed in men.

A second hypothesis has to do with the hippocampus (Chapter 6), a part of the limbic system. Recent evidence suggests that memories are divided among different parts of the brain, according to the sensory modality through which they were acquired. For example, visual information is stored in the occipital cortex, and tactile information in the sensory cortex. When a memory needs to be retrieved, it is apparently the hippocampus that brings the memory elements back together and integrates them. But stress can derail this process. In autopsies of monkeys and in MRI scans of human beings, it has been shown that stress can lead to structural changes in the hippocampus, including the atrophy of cells. Stress can also trigger the release of neurotransmitters that are highly concentrated in the hippocampus—a process that is thought to interfere with the encoding and retrieval of memories. Thus, if dissociative disorders originate in stress and if the stress is chronic—as would be the case, for example, with long-term child abuse—this might alter the functioning of the hippocampus to the point where it could no longer unite memory elements. The result would be amnesia or, in DID, the isolation of different memories in different states of consciousness (Bremner, Krystal, Charney, et al., 1996; Bremner, Krystal, Southwick, et al., 1995). In support of this hypothesis, it has been found that electrical stimulation of the hippocampus and nearby regions of the brain produces symptoms that resemble dissociation.

Finally, it has been suggested that, at least in depersonalization disorder, there may be some abnormality in serotonin functioning. Patients with depersonalization disorder tend to have migraine headaches (Chapter 9), and serotonin has been implicated in migraines. Second, episodes of depersonalization can be brought on by marijuana, and marijuana intoxication is also thought to involve an alteration in serotonin levels. It has also been shown that drugs that lower serotonin levels can induce depersonalization, while selective serotonin reuptake inhibitors (SSRIs), which increase serotonin levels, have been found to relieve depersonalization disorder in some patients (Simeon, Stein, & Hollander, 1995).

It should be kept in mind that none of these hypotheses rule out psychological causation. What neuroscience researchers are speculating about is the neurological processes underlying dissociative states. Such processes, in their view, could be activated by psychological stress as well as by neurological disease or injury (Sackeim & Devanand, 1991).

Drug Treatment Little in the way of biological treatment has been developed for the dissociative disorders. The barbiturate sodium amytal or the benzodiazepine lorazepam can be used as alternatives to hypnosis to aid in the recovery of memories, although the reliability of such memories is no better than with hypnosis. As noted, SSRIs such as Prozac (Chapter 7) have helped in some cases of depersonalization disorder, although their usefulness for this condition has never been evaluated in controlled studies (Simeon, Stein, & Hollander, 1995). As researchers gain more knowledge about stress-induced changes in memory function, it is hoped that they will be able to develop medications for the dissociative disorders.

Somatoform Disorders

The primary feature of the **somatoform disorders** is that, as the name suggests, psychological conflicts take on a somatic, or physical, form. Some patients complain of physical discomfort—stomach pains, breathing problems, and so forth. Others show an actual loss or impairment of normal physiological function: Suddenly they can no longer see, swallow, or move their right leg. In either case, there is no neurological evidence to explain the symptom, while there *is* evidence (or at least a strong suspicion) that the symptom is linked to psychological factors. Although the somatoform symptom has no neurological basis, some individuals with somatoform disorders may also have objective signs that are part of a comorbid medical condition (*DSM-IV-TR,* American Psychiatric Association, 2000). We will discuss five syndromes: body dysmorphic disorder, hypochondriasis, somatization disorder, pain disorder, and conversion disorder.

Body Dysmorphic Disorder

Many of us are preoccupied with our appearance. We worry that we are too fat or too thin, that we have too little hair or hair in the wrong places, that our nose is too big, that our ears are too prominent, and so on. Such concerns are normal, particularly during adolescence. Some people, however, are so distressed over how they look that they can no longer function normally. Such people are said to have **body dysmorphic disorder,** defined as preoccupation with an imagined or a grossly exaggerated defect in appearance.

Most people with this condition complain of facial flaws, such as the quality of the skin or the shape of the nose. Another common complaint is thinning hair. But any part of the body, or several parts at once, may be the focus of the concern. In one type of body dysmorphic disorder, called muscle dysmorphia, much more common in men than women, the patient is preoccupied with his small musculature and is often associated with excessive weight lifting and anabolic steroid use (Olivardia, Pope, & Hudson, 2000; Pope, Phillips, & Olivardia, 2000). People with body dysmorphic disorder are not usually delusional (though they may eventually become so). If confronted, they usually concede that they are exaggerating. Possibly, their preoccupation with minor flaws in their appearance is related to a visual attention bias. One neuropsychological study found that patients with body dysmorphic disorder overfocused on irrelevant and minor stimuli (Deckersbach, Savage, Phillips, et al., 2000). Nevertheless, they suffer great unhappiness. They may spend 3 to 8 hours a day looking in mirrors and trying to correct the defect—recombing the hair, picking the skin. In one reported case, a woman picked at her neck so much that she exposed her carotid artery, requiring emergency surgery (O'Sullivan, Phillips, Keuthen, et al., 1999). People with this disorder may try to camouflage the imagined defect—for example, by growing a beard to cover "scars." Some resort to plastic surgery, which, however, rarely satisfies them and often makes their appearance concerns worse (Veale, 2000). Many of them repeatedly seek reassurance. (Again, this does not reassure.) To avoid being seen, they may drop out of school, quit their jobs, avoid dating, and become housebound (Phillips, 2001). In severe cases, the person may contemplate or even attempt suicide (Phillips, 2001), as in the following case:

A person with body dysmorphic disorder may spend hours in front of a mirror every day, trying to fix an imagined or highly exaggerated flaw in appearance.

Ms. A was an attractive 27-year-old woman whose chief complaint was "I look deformed." Since early childhood she had been convinced that she was ugly; her mother reported that Ms. A had "constantly been in the mirror" since she was a toddler. She was excessively preoccupied with her "crooked" ears, "ugly" eyes, "broken out" skin, "huge" nose, and "bushy" facial hair. Ms. A thought about her looks every waking hour, she said, and spent 5 hours a day checking herself in the mirror. She repeatedly compared herself with others and compulsively sought reassurance about her looks from her son and her boyfriend. She covered her face with her hand, applied and reapplied makeup for hours, washed her face excessively, and picked at her facial hair. As a result of her appearance obsessions, Ms. A avoided friends and social interactions. She had first dropped out of high school and then college. She felt chronically suicidal and had tried to kill herself twice because, she stated, "I'm too ugly to go on living."

The onset of body dysmorphic disorder is usually gradual and may begin with someone making a negative comment on the person's appearance. A history of having been teased as a child, of having once had a disfiguring condition (e.g., severe acne), or of being unloved by parents may place people at risk for the disorder (Cororve & Gleaves, 2001; Phillips, 2001). The media, with their emphasis on physical beauty, probably also contribute to the development of this condition (Phillips, 1996a). Unless it is treated, body dysmorphic disorder tends to be chronic.

Not surprisingly, the disorder is associated with social phobia; it is also associated with depression—four out of five patients have experienced major depression—and it can sometimes be treated with antidepressant drugs (Phillips, 2001; Cororve & Gleaves, 2001). Another related syndrome is obsessive-compulsive disorder, which turns up in the histories of almost a third of body dysmorphic patients. It is possible that body dysmorphic disorder is a form of obsessive-compulsive disorder. Both conditions involve obsessional thinking as well as compulsive behaviors (e.g., mirror checking); both involve a preoccupation with perfection and symmetry; both tend to appear in adolescence and to be chronic; both show similar neuropsychological deficits; both may respond to the same drugs, such as Prozac; in some cases, both occur in the same families (Cororve & Gleaves, 2001; Phillips, 2001). But there are also important differences between the two syndromes. The most obvious is the content of the preoccupations: body dysmorphic patients are focused on their appearance, while obsessive-compulsive patients are usually concerned with danger or contamination. Also, body dysmorphic patients generally show lower self-esteem, greater shame, and more concern over rejection by others than do patients with obsessive-compulsive disorder (Phillips, Nierenberg, Brendel, et al., 1996; Rosen & Ramirez, 1998).

Hypochondriasis

The primary feature of **hypochondriasis** is a gnawing fear of disease—a fear maintained by constant misinterpretation of physical signs and sensations as abnormal. People with hypochondriasis have no real physical disability; what they have is a conviction that a disability is about to appear. Hence, they spend each day watching for the first signs, and they soon find them. One day the heart will skip a beat, or the body will register a new pain. This is then interpreted

Molière's comedy The Imaginary Invalid *was written in the seventeenth century, a time when hypochondriasis was widely regarded as a common, inevitable disease of civilization.*

as the onset of the disease. Often, when they appear at the doctor's office, individuals with hypochondriasis have already diagnosed their condition, for they are usually avid readers of articles on health in popular magazines. And, when the medical examination reveals that they are perfectly healthy, they are typically incredulous. Soon they are back in the doctor's office with reports of further symptoms, or they may simply change doctors. Some go through several doctors a year. Others resort to miracle cures or try to cure themselves, either with strenuous health regimens or with pills, of which they typically have large collections (Fallon & Feinstein, 2001). *DSM-IV-TR* notes that because individuals with hypochondriasis have a history of multiple complaints without a clear physical basis, they may receive cursory examinations, and the presence of a medical condition might be missed.

It should be emphasized that people with hypochondriasis do not fake their symptoms. They truly feel the pains they report; they are convinced that their records of their heart irregularities are accurate (although research has found that people with hypochondriasis are no more accurate than controls in detecting their own heartbeats [Barsky, Brener, Coeytaux, et al., 1995]). Insofar as they cannot be reassured by the medical evidence, their fears are irrational. However, these fears do not have the bizarre quality of the disease delusions experienced by those with psychosis who report that their feet are about to fall off or that their brains are shriveling. Hypochondriac patients tend to confine their anxieties to more ordinary syndromes, such as heart disease or cancer. Hypochondriac fears are also different from obsessive-compulsive fears of contamination and disease. Obsessive-compulsive patients know that their fears are groundless, and they try to resist them. Hypochondriac patients find their fears quite reasonable and don't see why others question them (Barsky, 1992a). Although the nature of the fears is different, hypochondriasis also has much in common with obsessive-compulsive disorder because it involves intrusive obsessions about feared diseases and compulsive urges to seek reassurance (Fallon, Quereshi, Laje, et al., 2000).

Several developmental factors may predispose a person to hypochondriasis. Hypochondriac patients are more likely than others to have suffered, or to have had a family member who suffered, a true physical disease, thus making their fears, however unfounded, at least understandable (Barsky, Wool, Barnett, et al., 1994; Robbins & Kirmayer, 1996). And, if the sick person in their past was a parent, their symptoms often resemble the parent's (Kellner, 1985). There is also some evidence that people who had overprotective mothers are more likely to develop hypochondriasis (Baker & Merskey, 1982; Parker & Lipscombe, 1980). Finally, many hypochondriac patients have histories of childhood physical or sexual abuse (Barsky, Wool, Barnett, et al., 1994; Salmon & Calderbank, 1996). Thus, prevention of child abuse may ultimately be helpful in lessening the likelihood of development of hypochondriasis (see box on page 187).

Somatization Disorder

A third somatoform pattern is **somatization disorder,** characterized by numerous and recurrent physical complaints that begin by age 30, that persist for several years, and that cause the person to seek medical treatment but cannot be explained medically. Somatization disorder resembles hypochondriasis in that it involves symptoms with no demonstrable physical cause, although there may be comorbid physical illness, yet the disorders differ in the focus of the patient's distress. What motivates the person with hypochondriasis is the fear of disease, usually a specific disease; the symptoms are troubling not so much in themselves but because they indicate the presence of that disease. In contrast, what bothers the victim of somatization disorder is actually the "symptoms" themselves. There is also a difference in the patients' approaches to the symptoms. Whereas hypochondriac patients may try to be scientific, measuring their blood pressure several times a day and carefully reporting the results, victims of somatization disorder usually describe their symptoms in a vague, dramatic, and exaggerated fashion (Iezzi, Duckworth & Adams, 2001). Finally, the two disorders differ in the number of complaints. Hypochondriac patients often fear a particular disease; therefore, their complaints tend to be limited. In somatization disorder, on the other hand, the complaints are many and varied (Iezzi, Duckworth, & Adams, 2001). Indeed, *DSM-IV-TR* requires that the patient present at least four pain symptoms, two gastrointestinal symptoms, one sexual symptom, and one symptom that mimics neurological disorder, such as blindness, dizziness, or seizures, before this diagnosis can be made. Like hypochondriac patients, somatization patients tend to engage in "doctor shopping," going from physician to physician in search of the one who will finally diagnose their ailments (Holder-Perkins & Wise, 2001).

Though the complaints for which they are diagnosed are not physically based, somatization patients may develop actual physical disorders as a result of unnecessary hospitalization, surgery, and medication (Holder-Perkins & Wise, 2001). In fact, they are major users of health care (Iezzi, Duckworth, & Adams, 2001).

Like hypochondriasis, somatization disorder is often accompanied by depression and anxiety (Gureje, Simon, Üstün, et al., 1997). In other respects, somatization patients resemble patients with dissociative disorders. They, too, are highly hypnotizable (Bliss, 1984), and, like dissociative identity patients, they tend to report histories of physical and sexual abuse (Iezzi, Duckworth, & Adams, 2001; Holder-Perkins & Wise, 2001).

Pain Disorder

Many people experience pain on a daily basis. For example, 10 to 15 percent of adults in the United States have some form of work disability as a result of back pain alone (American Psychiatric Association, 1994). In some cases, however, even when an organic disorder is present, the pain seems to be more severe or persistent than can be explained by medical causes, and psychological factors are assumed to play a role as well. Such cases are diagnosed as **pain disorder.** In support of the psychogenic explanation, pain disorder patients tend to have psychiatric symptoms. A sample of 40 chronic pain patients had higher somatization, depression, anxiety, and obsession scores than a normal comparison group (Monsen & Havik, 2001).

Of course, the psychological problems of these patients may be the result of rather than—or certainly in addition to—the cause of their pain, but there are indications that the pain has a psychological basis. For one thing, the patients' descriptions of their pain tend to differ from those of patients whose pain is thought to be primarily organic. They have a harder time localizing the pain; they have more sites of pain; they tend to describe it in emotional terms (e.g., "frightening") rather than sensory terms (e.g., "burning"); and they are less likely to specify changes in the pain—for example, that it is worse at night or when they are walking (Streltzer, Eliashopf, Kline, et al., 2000). Finally, they tend to see the pain as their disorder, rather than as a symptom of a disorder (Adler, Zamboni, Hofer, et al., 1997). The fear of pain leads them to avoid physical and social activities which, in turn, maintains the pain and related behaviors (Asmundson, Norton, & Norton, 1999). Pain is also maintained by biases to recall pain-related stimuli (Pincus & Morley, 2001). Like hypochondriac patients, many pain disorder patients have what seems to be a predisposing family history, such as parents who suffer from chronic pain or who were overconcerned with their children's health (Scharff, 1997).

Conversion Disorder

In hypochondriasis and somatization disorder, patients have fear of or complaints about illness or disability. In **conversion disorder,** patients experience an actual disability: The loss or impairment of a motor or sensory function, although, again, there is no neurological pathology that would explain the disability. Conversion symptoms vary considerably, but among the most common are blindness, deafness, paralysis, and anesthesia (loss of sensation)—often partial but sometimes total (Iezzi, Duckworth, & Adams, 2001). Also common are conversion symptoms that mimic physical illnesses, such as epilepsy or cancer (Bowman & Markand, 1996), though the choice of symptoms varies with the culture. For example, some men in non-Western cultures show *couvade,* a condition in which they experience pains similar to their wives' labor pains during childbirth (Iezzi & Adams, 1993). Like the "symptoms" involved in hypochondriasis and somatization disorder, conversion symptoms are not supported by the medical evidence, but neither are they faked. They are involuntary responses, independent of the person's conscious control. At the same time, they contradict the medical facts. Upon examination, for example, the eyes are found to be perfectly free from defect or damage, yet the person is unable to see.

Conversion disorder, formerly known as hysteria, has played a central role in the history of psychology. As we saw in Chapter 1, it was named and described by Hippocrates, who believed that it was confined to women, particularly childless women. In Hippocrates' view, hysteria was caused by the wanderings of a uterus that was not being put to its proper use. Idle and frustrated, the uterus traveled around inside the body, creating havoc in various organ systems. The Greek word for uterus is *hystera,* hence the term *hysteria.*

In the nineteenth century, hysteria served as the focal point for debate between psychogenic and biogenic theory. It was the cure of this disorder through hypnosis that laid the foundation for Freud's theory of the unconscious. Interestingly, Freud's explanation of hysteria stressed the same factor as Hippocrates': sexual conflict. Today, many psychologists reject the sexual interpretation, but it is generally agreed that conversion disorders are the result of *some* psychological conflict (Vierderman, 1995). According to this view, the conversion symptom serves two important psychological purposes. First, it blocks the person's awareness of internal conflict; this is called the **primary gain.** In addition, it confers the nonconscious **secondary gain** of excusing the person from responsibilities and attracting sympathy and attention (Maldonado & Spiegel, 2001).

One reason psychologists tend to accept the conflict-resolution hypothesis is that many conversion patients (about one third) seem completely unperturbed by their symptoms—a response known as **la belle indifférence,** or "beautiful indifference." Whereas most people would react with horror to the discovery that they were suddenly half-blind or could no longer walk, "indifferent" conversion patients are undismayed. Typically, they are eager to discuss their symptoms and describe them in the most vivid terms, but they do not seem eager to part with them. This paradoxical reaction, like the equanimity of people suffering from dissociative amnesia, has been interpreted by psychodynamic theorists as a sign of relief once the newfound disability supplies a defense against unconscious conflicts and thereby reduces anxiety.

Conversion disorders represent something of a philosophical paradox. On the one hand, the patient's body appears to be in good health. Biologically, conversion patients *can* do whatever it is they say they can't do. And often they can be made to do it, either by trickery or under hypnosis or drugs such as sodium amytal or lorazepam. Further evidence for their lack of neurological pathology is that the symptoms are often selective. Conversion "epileptics," for example, seldom injure themselves or lose bladder control during attacks, as true epileptic patients do. Likewise, in conversion blindness, patients rarely bump into things (Maldonado & Spiegel, 2001). Furthermore, victims of conversion blindness, when given visual discrimination tests, often perform either much better, like DB at the beginning of the chapter, or much worse than if they had answered merely at random—a result indicating that they *are* receiving visual input (Kihlstrom, Barnhardt, & Tataryn, 1991). In short, all evidence points to the conclusion that the patient's body is capable of functioning properly. On the other hand, conversion patients, by definition, are *not* consciously refusing to use parts of their bodies. The response is involuntary.

This situation is something like the memory problem in dissociative disorders. Just as dissociative patients lose explicit memory but retain implicit memory, so conversion patients lose explicit perception but still show implicit perception. As in the case of DB, these patients show clear evidence that their supposedly disabled organs are, in fact, operating normally, but they are not aware of those operations. The organ's functioning has been dissociated, as it were, from the patient's conscious awareness (Kihlstrom, Barnhardt, & Tataryn, 1991).

The following case illustrates la belle indifférence, together with other features of conversion disorder:

> Mr. Sione is a 50-year-old minister from Western Samoa. He is quite famous there as a biblical scholar and leader in the religious community. Over a period of several months he began experiencing weakness in his legs to the point where he was unable to walk. He was excused from some of his duties at the high school where he teaches. He continued to give lectures but did not have to mete out corporal punishment to students, which is a common form of punishment in Samoa. He previously had been given the task of paddling students because the principal knew that he would be fair and not as harsh as some other teachers. . . .
>
> In Hawaii, he underwent some neurologic tests without any pathological findings. His neurologist told him he could walk and attempted to lead him about the room. At this point, Mr. Sione collapsed on the floor, unable to support his own weight. A psychiatrist was called to consult. Further history revealed two prior episodes of leg weakness. Once as a teenager he had fallen out of a tree and spent several weeks in bed. He recalled this time fondly, saying that he had never received so much attention from his family, since he was from a large family and often felt ignored. . . .
>
> While in Hawaii for the medical evaluation, he seemed to be having a great time. His wife, with whom he had a good relationship, had come with him. When not undergoing tests, she would help him get around the hospital. The psychiatrist noted that he avidly watched violent television shows. As they discussed this topic over a couple of sessions, it became clear that he was fascinated by violence but at the same time he found it quite repugnant. He began to talk about the conflict he experienced in Samoa over being the teacher who was supposed to physically punish students. He felt this was against his religious training, even though it was culturally accepted. He also worried that he might secretly enjoy the punishment that he inflicted and felt aghast at this possibility. As his stay in Hawaii neared an end, the psychiatrist said he was allowed to return to work, in a wheelchair if necessary, but under no circumstances would he be permitted to mete out corporal punishment to students. He accepted this prohibition. He was able to walk onto the departing airplane that week and was able to return to teaching (Chaplin, 1997, pp. 60–70).

In this instance, the conflict-resolution function is obvious. In the words of the writer who presented the case, Steven L. Chaplin, "the conversion symptom afforded [Mr. Sione] the opportunity to solve a difficult psychological dilemma. When the consulting psychiatrist was able to offer an alternative solution, the need for the disabling symptoms was resolved" (1997, p. 80).

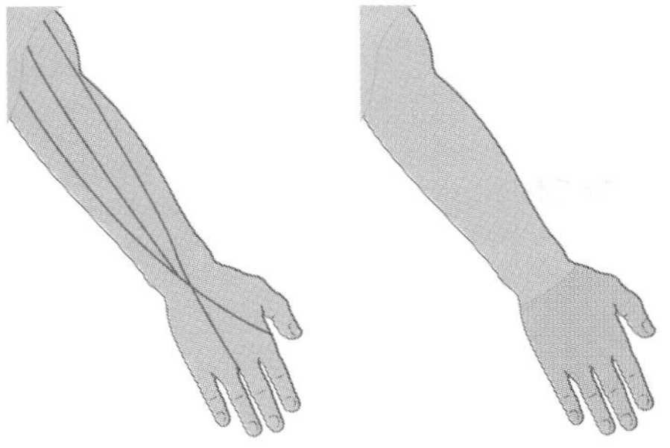

FIGURE 8.1 A patient with glove anesthesia—that is, numbness in the whole hand, ending at the wrist—will be suspected of having conversion disorder. The skin areas served by nerves in the arm are shown in (a). Glove anesthesia, shown in (b), cannot result from damage to these nerves.

Conversion, Malingering, or Organic Disorder? With conversion disorder, differential diagnosis is both important and tricky. First, malingering must be ruled out, which is often hard to do. However, malingerers are usually cautious and defensive when questioned about their symptoms, because they are afraid of being caught in a lie. Conversion patients, on the other hand, are typically candid and, as we noted, sometimes talk eagerly and at length about their disabilities. Furthermore, precisely *because* they are unaware that their organs are functioning normally, conversion patients sometimes innocently reveal this. Most malingerers, for example, would not be foolish enough to claim blindness and then catch a ball thrown in their direction, but a conversion patient might do this (Kihlstrom, Barnhardt, & Tataryn, 1991).

Second and more difficult is the task of ruling out an actual neurological disorder. In some cases, the symptoms constitute "neurological nonsense," as Charcot put it—that is, they directly contradict what we know about the nervous system. For example, in *glove anesthesia*, patients report that the entire hand is numb, from the tips of the fingers to a clear cutoff point at the wrist (see Figure 8.1)—in other words, the area covered by a short glove—whereas, if they were suffering from a true neurological impairment, the area of numbness would run in a narrow stripe from the lower arm through one or two of the fingers (Maldonado & Spiegel, 2001).

These, however, are the easier cases. In others, the symptoms are uncannily similar to those of true neurological disorders. Nevertheless, there may still be certain signs that suggest conversion disorder. (Note the similarity between these criteria and those for distinguishing dissociative from organic amnesia.) These signs include the following:

1. *Rapid appearance of symptoms, especially after psychological trauma.* Neurological disorders tend to surface more gradually.
2. *La belle indifférence.* Neurological patients are more likely to be upset over their symptoms.
3. *Selective symptoms.* If "paralyzed" legs move during sleep, the paralysis is presumably not neurological.

These criteria, in addition to specialized medical tests, are usually the basis for the diagnosis of conversion disorder. However, they are not foolproof—a fact that research has made embarrassingly clear. In a study involving 30 patients, 80 percent were eventually found to have a diagnosable medical disorder as the underlying cause of symptoms originally diagnosed as conversion (Gould, Miller, Goldberg, et al., 1986). Clearly, a substantial proportion of conversion disorders are, in fact, neurological disorders in their early stages, when they are hardest to detect (Iezzi, Duckworth, & Adams, 2001). Fortunately, the rate of misdiagnosis may be decreasing (Maldonado & Spiegel, 2001). In a recent 4-year follow-up study, Kent, Tomasson, and Coryell (1995) reported that only 13 percent of conversion patients were initially misdiagnosed and really had a disease.

Conversion disorder is usually described as rare. It is possible, however, that what is rare is merely the diagnosis of conversion disorder. Conversion patients, after all, believe they have a medical problem. Therefore, they go to physicians, not to psychotherapists. As we have noted, differential diagnosis is tricky. Furthermore, many physicians may associate conversion disorder with the more bizarre symptoms of late-nineteenth-century hysteria—glove anesthesia, inability to swallow, paralysis—thus allowing the more ordinary conversion symptoms that tend to turn up today, such as back trouble or blurred vision, to slip by unnoticed. In short, it seems likely that, while many "conversion disorders" are actually neurological, many conditions diagnosed as neurological are actually conversion disorders (Maldonado & Spiegel, 2001).

❖ Groups at Risk for Somatoform Disorders

Body dysmorphic disorder is common in certain medical settings. In one study, 12 percent of dermatology patients had body dysmorphic disorder (Phillips, Dufresne, Wilkel, et al., 2000), and rates of 6 to 15 percent have been reported among people seeking cosmetic surgery (Phillips, 2001). In the general population, prevalence estimates range from about 1 to 13 percent (Phillips, 2001). Nonetheless, body dysmorphic disorder often goes unrecognized because sufferers are ashamed of their symptoms and thus loathe to report them (Phillips, 2001). Most patients are unmarried, and the average age of onset is 16 (Phillips & Diaz, 1997), with some childhood cases occurring as well. The disorder seems to be equally common in males and females (Phillips & Diaz, 1997), and this is also true of hypochondriasis. African American adolescents were found to have a lower rate of body dysmorphic disorder than European American, Asian, and Latino adolescents (Mayville, Katz, Gipson, et al., 1999).

By contrast, somatization disorder is seen far more often in women than in men (Martin, 1995; Kroenke & Spitzer, 1998), but does not differ across ethnic groups (Iezzi, Duckworth, & Adams, 2001). This condition is reasonably common, occurring in an estimated 2.8 percent of people contacting health centers worldwide (Gureje, Simon, Üstün, et al., 1997), but researchers have found that, apart from aches and pains, which are universal, the symptoms reported vary from culture to culture. In a recent study, sexual and menstrual symptoms figured in somatization disorder only in the West; complaints of body odor only in Japan; body heat and coldness only in Nigeria; and kidney weakness only in China (Janca, Isaac, Bennett, et al., 1995). Full-scale somatization disorder occurs more frequently among less-educated people (Ford, 1995; Holder-Perkins & Wise, 2001) in which the verbal expression of emotional distress is frowned upon (Iezzi, Duckworth, & Adams, 2001); however, it is equally prevalent worldwide (Gureje, Simon, Üstün, et al., 1997; Kirmayer & Young, 1998).

Because its diagnosis is so problematic, conversion disorder's prevalence is open to question, but one estimate is that 5 to 14 percent of all consultations in a general medical setting are for conversion symptoms (Iezzi, Duckworth, & Adams, 2001). In many, but not all, cultures the disorder is much more common in women than in men (Maldonado & Spiegel, 2001). As with somatization disorder, there is also a socioeconomic risk factor. The poorer, the less educated, and the less psychologically sophisticated a community, the greater the prevalence of conversion disorder. Rural rather than urban populations also tend to produce conversion cases (Chaplin, 1997; Maldonado & Spiegel, 2001). Not surprisingly, patients in such communities tend to report more bizarre symptoms, whereas more sophisticated patients generally report symptoms that resemble true organic diseases (Iezzi, Duckworth, & Adams, 2001). Conversion disorder usually begins in adolescence or early adulthood (Maldonado & Spiegel, 2001). With conversion disorder, as with other somatoform disorders—and the dissociative disorders—a history of childhood trauma seems to increase vulnerability (Bowman & Markand, 1996).

Somatoform Disorders: Theory and Therapy

Although historically, the psychodynamic perspective contributed the most to the understanding of somatoform disorders, currently, the behavioral and cognitive perspectives have produced the most effective treatments.

The Psychodynamic Perspective: Defense Against Anxiety

Somatizing as Conflict Resolution As we saw in Chapter 1, Freud and Josef Breuer found that, if hysterical patients could be induced under hypnosis to talk uninhibitedly about their childhoods and their present problems, their symptoms subsided somewhat. Out of this treatment, Freud independently evolved his theory of the conservation of energy, which stated that strong emotions that were not expressed would lead to somatic symptoms. The distressing memories that Freud's patients revealed to him were often of childhood seduction. In the beginning, Freud assumed that these seductions had actually occurred. Later, he came to believe that they were usually fantasies generated during the Oedipal period. Real or imagined, however, the episodes seemed to be reawakened in the mind by the sexual feelings accompanying puberty. The result was anxiety, leading in turn to repression of the memory, leading in turn to physical symptoms, which both expressed the wish and prevented its fulfillment. But sexual feelings were not the only cause; hostility, too, could lead to hysteria. A hysterical paralysis, for instance, could be a defense against the expression of violent feelings. (Recall the case of Mr. Sione.) In Freud's opinion, the effectiveness of this mechanism in blocking both the impulse and the person's awareness of the impulse accounted for *la belle indifférence*. The symptoms relieved the anxiety; therefore, the person was not in a hurry to get rid of them.

In the psychoanalytic view, hypochondriasis, somatization disorder, and body dysmorphic disorder are also defenses against the anxiety produced by unacceptable wishes. Hypochondriac patients, Freud reasoned, were people who, deterred by the superego from directing sexual energy onto external objects, redirected it onto themselves. Eventually, this self-directed sexual energy overflowed, transforming itself into physical symptoms. Other psychoanalytic thinkers have blamed hostility rather than sexual desire. In one theory (Brown & Vaillant, 1981), people with hypochondriasis are angry over having been unloved or hurt. Rather than express their grievances, they displace them onto the body, imagining *it* to be hurt. Similar conflict-resolution theories have been offered for somatization disorder and body dysmorphic disorder (Kellner, 1990; Phillips, 1996a). In all of the somatoform disorders, psychodynamic theorists also see a strong element of regression. Beset by anxiety, the person regresses to the state of a sick child, in which he or she unconsciously hopes to receive attention, babying, and relief from responsibilities—in other words, secondary gains. The primary gain is the relief of anxiety.

This conflict-resolution model of somatoform disorders is an old and famous theory, intuitively appealing (Viederman, 1995). But, as usual with psychodynamic theories, it is hard to test. Furthermore, there is some evidence against it. For example, as noted earlier, only about one third of conversion patients seem to show la belle indifférence. That leaves two thirds who are often very alarmed over their sudden disabilities. Studies show that hypochondriasis and somatization disorder also tend to involve high levels of expressed anxiety (Gureje, Simon, Üstün, et al., 1997; Noyes, Kathol, Fisher, et al., 1994). If the function of the somatoform disorders is to relieve psychological suffering, they do not seem to be doing a good job—a fact that casts some doubt on the psychodynamic interpretation.

Uncovering Conflict Psychodynamic treatment for the somatoform disorders involves roughly the same "talking cure" that led to Freud's theory of these syndromes. As usual in psychodynamic therapy, the patient is induced to release the repression, thus bringing into consciousness the forbidden thoughts and memories. Presumably, the somatic symptoms will then subside, and the ego's energy, formerly tied up in maintaining the symptoms, will be free to pursue more constructive ends.

There is no evidence, however, that this psychodynamic approach is any more effective than other therapies for somatoform disorders. In general, the somatoform disorders are not particularly responsive to treatment, nor do they generally improve without treatment. One study found that, on a 4-year follow-up, 63 percent of the conversion patients and 92 percent of the somatization patients still merited those diagnoses (Kent, Tomasson, & Coryell, 1995). It may be that the best treatment for somatization patients is simply low-level medical care: brief physical examinations, supportive talks. This does not cure the disorder, but it helps to prevent patients from seeking more invasive cures, thus harming themselves with unnecessary surgery or drugs (Maldonado & Spiegel, 2001). Supportive group therapy may also be of use. One study found that somatization patients who attended 8 group therapy sessions reported better physical and mental health on a 1-year follow-up than did patients who received standard medical care (Kashner, Rost, Cohen, et al., 1995).

The Behavioral and Sociocultural Perspectives: The Sick Role

Illness is not just a biological dysfunction. It also has social components (Mechanic, 1962). People who are ill are justified in adopting the "sick role." They can stay home from work or school; they are relieved of their normal duties; others are expected to be sympathetic and attentive to them. According to behavioral and sociocultural theorists, somatoform disorders are inappropriate adoptions of the sick role (Pilowsky, 1994).

Learning to Adopt the Sick Role The sick role also involves sacrifices: loss of power, loss of pleasurable activities. Why would people want to give up these things for long? The behaviorists say that their learning histories have probably made the rewards of the sick role more reinforcing than the rewards of illness-free life. According to Ullmann and Krasner (1975), two conditions increase the chances that a healthy person will adopt the sick role. First, the person must have had some experience with the role, either directly, by being ill, or indirectly, by having the sick role modeled. Many people with somatoform disorders meet this condition. Hypochondriasis, somatization, and conversion patients are all likely to have had early personal or family histories of physical illness or somatic symptoms (Iezzi, Duckworth, &

Did Elizabeth Barrett Browning (1806–1861) suffer from a somatoform disorder? Behavioral and sociocultural theorists might say that she adopted the "sick role." Following a minor accident at the age of 15, she spent 25 years as an invalid, cared for at home by her family. She experienced a rapid and nearly total recovery when she married fellow-poet Robert Browning.

Adams, 2001; Robbins & Kirmayer, 1996). The second condition, according to Ullmann and Krasner, is that the adoption of the sick role must be reinforced. This, too, has been found to be the case with somatoform patients. Many have childhood histories of receiving attention and sympathy during illness—recall the case of Mr. Sione on page 202—and research suggests that this operant-conditioning process predisposes them to adopt the sick role as a coping style in adult life (Iezzi, Duckworth, & Adams, 2001; Holder-Perkins & Wise, 2001). Respondent conditioning may also play a part. The autonomic nervous system, which controls breathing, heart rate, and numerous other bodily functions (Chapter 6), is subject to conditioning, so, if anxiety is paired, for example, with minor heartbeat irregularities, as it may be in an illness-preoccupied household, then anxiety can come to *trigger* that symptom, which in turn will cause further anxiety, then further symptoms—in other words, the beginning of hypochondriasis (Kellner, 1985).

Sociocultural theorists also regard somatoform disorders as a case of role adoption, but they focus less on the family than on larger cultural forces. In the sociocultural view, the likelihood of people's using the sick role as a coping style depends on their culture's attitudes toward unexplained somatic symptoms. If this theory is correct, then rates of somatoform disorder should vary from culture to culture. However, the evidence is mixed. Some studies have found that somatization and conversion disorder are more prevalent in non-Western cultures and in less-industrialized cultures—India, China, Nigeria, Libya, Mexico—cultures in which the expression of emotional distress in psychological terms is less accepted, more stigmatized (Raguram, Weiss, Channabasavanna, et al., 1996). Other studies indicate that somatization is a common problem across all cultures (Gureje, Simon, Üstün, et al., 1997; Kirmayer & Young, 1998). In the United States, as we saw, conversion and somatization disorder are more common in rural communities and in lower socioeconomic groups, in which, again, psychological expressions of emotional problems may be frowned on. Thus, people in these communities and groups may be encouraged to somaticize unhappiness rather than psychologize it (Goldberg & Bridges, 1988).

Treatment by Nonreinforcement As with dissociative disorders, the behavioral treatment of somatoform disorders is usually two-pronged. First, the therapist withdraws reinforcement for illness behavior. Second, the therapist tries to build up the patient's coping skills, a lack of which is presumably part of the reason for resorting to the sick role. One short-term treatment for 17 people with hypochondriasis and illness phobia (disabling fear of illness) emphasized the withdrawal of reinforcement, particularly the negative reinforcement (via anxiety relief) that the patients obtained through reassurance seeking. When they sought reassurance from the therapist, they were given none, and their families were instructed to give them none. In a 5-year follow-up, about half the patients located were symptom-free (Warwick & Marks, 1988). In a more recent comparison of behavioral stress-management therapy with cognitive-behavioral therapy and a waiting-list control group, both the stress-management and cognitive-behavioral treatments were more effective than the no-treatment control in reducing hypochondriasis (Clark, Salkovskis, Hackmann, et al., 1998). The stress-management therapy consisted of relaxation training, education about alternative explanations for somatic symptoms, and behavioral techniques to reduce worrying. In addition, behavioral therapies, like those used for obsessive-compulsive disorder, involving prolonged and repeated exposure to anxiety-provoking somatic sensations and response-prevention of body checking and reassurance seeking (see Chapter 7) have also proved effective for hypochondriasis, as effective as cognitive therapy (Visser & Bouman, 2001). Similar exposure and response prevention treatments have been effective for body dysmorphic disorder as well (McKay, 1999).

As for building coping skills, behavioral treatments often include social-skills training, in which patients are taught how to deal effectively with other people, and assertiveness training, which teaches patients how to show strength—how to make requests, how to refuse requests, how to show anger when necessary. For many people, the sick role may be a way of making demands on others, and of evading their demands, without taking responsibility for such actions. ("Because I am sick, you have to do things for me and I don't have to do things for you.") Behaviorists try to teach people how to manage social give-and-take without such blackmail.

In treating conversion disorders, the therapist often tries to provide a face-saving mechanism so that patients can give up the illness without having to face the accusation that they were never ill to begin with. This mechanism may be a placebo drug or physical therapy. In any case, the placebo is there to provide a socially acceptable reason for the cure; the cure, meanwhile, is effected through a change in reinforcement (Maldonado & Spiegel, 2001). This was the case with Mr. Sione, who was prohibited by his doctor from inflicting corporal punishment on his students, the very thing that probably brought on his symptoms.

For chronic pain disorder, behavioral therapists have used such techniques as relaxation and contingency management to decrease pain medication, to reduce verbal reports of pain, to discourage "sick" behaviors, and to increase activity levels. Recent evidence suggests that such treatment is quite effective, especially when combined with cognitive restructuring (Wilson & Gil, 1996).

The Cognitive Perspective: Misinterpreting Bodily Sensations

Overattention to the Body Recall the cognitive interpretation of panic disorder (Chapter 7): it is essentially a problem of misinterpretation. The cognitive view of hypochondriasis and somatization disorder is roughly the same. According to several theorists, people with these disorders have a cognitive style predisposing them to exaggerate normal bodily sensations and catastrophize over minor symptoms. Given these tendencies, they misinterpret minor physiological changes as major health problems (Barsky, 1992b; Warwick, 1995). When, for example, these patients are under stress and experience indigestion, they say, "I may have undetected stomach cancer" rather than "I am nervous." In support of this idea, it has been shown that people with hypochondriasis focus more attention on bodily sensations, catastrophize more readily about symptoms, hold more false beliefs about disease, and fear aging and death more than do nonhypochondriac psychiatric patients or normal controls (Haenen, de Jong, Schmidt, et al., 2000). Moreover individuals with hypochondriasis show more of a threat-confirming reasoning bias, tending to seek information that suggests threat, when dealing with ambiguous health-related situations than do normal controls (Smeets, de Jong, & Mayer, 2000). Patients who tended to amplify bodily sensations, attribute common symptoms to disease, and somaticize their distress, all at the same time, were less likely to be in remission from their hypochondriasis at a 4-year follow-up than patients who didn't exhibit these cognitive/perceptual biases (Barsky, Bailey, Fama, et al., 2000). Likewise, body dysmorphic patients selectively attend to minor physical flaws and catastrophize about how these will cause them to be rejected (Phillips, 1996a; Veale, Gournay, Dryden, et al., 1996). Such cognitive biases lead them to mirror checking, reassurance seeking, and avoidance of social situations with rejection potential, all of which increase their misery.

It has also been found that somatizers, or people with a high rate of medically unexplainable somatic complaints, have correspondingly high rates of negative affect: pessimism, self-blame, general unhappiness (Pennebaker & Watson, 1991). If this negative affect were combined with difficulty in expressing emotion, a trait that apparently runs high in somatization disorder patients (Taylor, Boday, & Parker, 1997), then the person would be all the more likely to redirect distress onto the body—an explanation consistent with Freud's.

Treatment: Challenging Faulty Beliefs Recent reports show that hypochondriac patients can be helped by a combination of cognitive therapy (revising thinking habits) and behavioral therapy (change in reinforcement). Salkovskis and Warwick (1986), for example, have described their treatment of a man who, because he had developed a harmless rash, was convinced that he had leukemia. He inspected the rash constantly, spent hours reading medical textbooks, and discussed his problem incessantly with his family. He eventually became suicidal and was hospitalized. The therapists got the patient to agree that his condition had one of two explanations: (1) he was suffering from a deadly illness, not yet diagnosed, or

A person with hypochondriasis might spend hours every day reading about suspected illnesses in medical textbooks. Cognitive therapies can relieve the anxieties of people with hypochondriasis by helping them to reattribute their bodily sensations to harmless causes rather than deadly diseases.

(2) he had a problem with anxiety. In view of the strong evidence for the second hypothesis, the therapists persuaded the patient to test it by altering the conditions that might be maintaining his anxiety. This meant that he would stop reading medical books, stop checking the rash, and stop seeking reassurance. The hospital staff, the family doctor, and the family were also instructed to stop giving reassurance. His hypochondriacal anxieties swiftly declined. Controlled clinical trials based on these cognitive-behavioral techniques demonstrated significant improvement among hypochondriac patients (Warwick, Clark, Cobb, et al., 1996; Clark, Salkovskis, Hackmann, et al., 1998). Other cognitive therapists have reported success with hypochondriac patients by teaching them to distract themselves from bodily sensations and to reattribute such sensations to benign causes rather than fatal diseases (Barsky, 1996).

Cognitive-behavioral therapies have also proved effective for pain disorder (Wilson & Gil, 1996), somatization disorder (McLead & Budd, 1997), and body dysmorphic disorder. In the latter case, for example, patients are confronted with their presumed physical flaws and are prevented from seeking reassurance—the behavioral technique of exposure. Meanwhile, they undergo cognitive restructuring, in which they are taught how to challenge faulty assumptions (e.g., "I must look perfect in order to be loved") and how to redirect their attention away from their appearance (Cororve & Gleaves, 2001). Finally, a cognitive-behavioral group treatment for somatization disorder involving stress management, relaxation training, and cognitive restructuring was more effective than a waiting-list control in reducing somatic preoccupation, hypochondriasis, and medication usage (Lidbeck, 1997).

The Neuroscience Perspective: Brain Dysfunction

Genetic Studies We have already discussed the fact that people with somatoform disorders tend to have family histories of somatic complaints. Is it possible that this is the product not of learning but of genes? Guze and his colleagues have conducted several family studies of somatization disorder, with intriguing results. First, it appears that, among the first-degree relatives of patients with somatization disorder, the women show an increased frequency of somatization disorder, while the men show an increased frequency not of somatization disorder but of antisocial personality disorder, a personality pattern characterized by chronic indifference to the rights of others (Chapter 11) (Holder-Perkins & Wise, 2001). Furthermore, somatization disorder and antisocial personality are seen together in the same person much more frequently than we would expect by chance. These findings have led to the hypothesis that somatization disorder and antisocial personality disorder may be the product of similar genetic endowment and that what determines whether a person with this endowment will develop somatization disorder or an antisocial personality is his or her sex (Guze, Cloninger, Martin, et al., 1986; Lilienfeld, 1992).

Of course, the basis of these family patterns need not be genetic. It could be environmental. To document the genetic factor more clearly, twin and adoption studies are needed. One twin study (Torgersen, 1986), conducted in Norway, found that the MZ twins had a higher concordance rate for somatoform disorders than the DZ twins. The sample was small, however, and there was reason to believe that the MZ twins shared not only more similar genotypes but also more similar environments than did the DZ twins. In an adoption study conducted in Sweden, the researchers tracked down the medical and criminal histories of the biological and adoptive parents of 859 women with somatization disorder. The results seemed to show not 1 but 2 patterns, depending on whether the woman was a high-frequency somatizer (frequent somatic complaints, but few kinds of complaints) or a diversiform somatizer (less frequent complaints, but of a more diverse nature). The biological fathers of the high-frequency somatizers showed disproportionately high rates of alcoholism; the biological fathers of the diversiform somatizers showed disproportionately high rates of violent crime (Bohman, Cloninger, von Knorring, et al., 1984; Cloninger, Sigvardsson, von Knorring et al., 1984). These findings, though preliminary, support the suggestion that there is a genetic factor in somatization disorder and that the factor is somehow linked to antisocial behavior (Lilienfeld, 1992).

Brain Dysfunction and Somatoform Disorders The essential mystery of conversion disorder—that, while the body is functioning normally, the conscious mind does not know this—has been the subject of some neuroscience research. Tests of brain waves in people with conversion anesthesias, blindness, and deafness clearly indicate that these patients' brains are receiving normal sensory input from their "disabled" organs. If you prick the finger of a person with glove anesthesia, this message does arrive in the cerebral cortex, as it is supposed to. Likewise, electrical stimulation of the movement centers of the brain does produce normal movement in patients with conversion paralysis. In other words, there seems to be no blockage of the neural pathways between the brain and the peripheral organs. Why, then, can't conversion patients consciously feel sensations or initiate movement?

Presumably the problem lies in the processing of sensory signals in the cerebral cortex, for it is that processing that would bring the signal into conscious awareness. Conversion patients seem to have suppressed some stage of cerebral processing (Marsden, 1986). In support of this hypothesis, several studies of conversion patients with loss of sensory function have revealed high levels of inhibitory (transmission-suppressing) action in the cerebral cortex in response to sensory stimuli (Hernandez-Peon, Chavez-Ibarra, & Aguilar-Figueroa, 1963; Levy & Mushin, 1973). Such a slowdown in processing might be caused by a shock to the brain. Some evidence indicates that hypoxia (oxygen deprivation) and hypoglycemia (low blood sugar) can bring on conversion symptoms (Eames, 1992). Moreover, whatever the processing problem is, it may be mimicked under hypnosis. One functional imaging study found that the areas of the brain activated by paralysis induced by hypnosis were similar to those activated by paralysis in conversion disorder (Oakley, 1999; Halligan, Athwal, Oakley, et al., 2000).

Another interesting finding has to do with lateralization, the difference between the right and left hemispheres of the brain (Chapter 6). In a study of 61 patients with somatoform disorders (as well as anxiety and depressive disorders), somatic symptoms and pain occurred more often on the left side of the body (Min & Lee, 1997). Because the left side of the body is controlled by the right side of the brain, this suggests that somatoform disorders may stem from dysfunction in the right cerebral hemisphere, a possibility that has been supported by other neurological studies (Flor-Henry, Fromm-Auch, Tapper, et al., 1981; James, Singer, Zurynski, et al., 1987).

In body dysmorphic disorder, it is possible that there is some abnormality in serotonin functioning. The evidence for this is still sketchy. Basically, it consists of the finding that drugs that decrease serotonin transmission exacerbate body dysmorphic symptoms, while drugs that increase such transmission relieve symptoms (Phillips, 1996b). At the same time, it must be reemphasized that the discovery of a neurological basis for a psychological disorder does not rule out a psychological basis. If the neurons of body dysmorphic patients are not processing serotonin properly, or if the brains of conversion patients are inhibiting sensory input, this may be for psychological reasons.

Drug Treatment Like the biological findings, biological treatments for somatoform disorders are scarce and preliminary. Antidepressant drugs seem to help some patients. Several studies suggest that body dysmorphic patients improve markedly when given SSRIs such as Prozac or Zoloft and show greater improvement with SSRIs than with norepinephrine reuptake inhibitors (Hollander, Allen, Kwon, et al., 1999), but these findings need to be followed by controlled studies comparing SSRI treatment with placebo treatment (Phillips, 2001). SSRIs may be effective with hypochondriasis patients as well (Fallon & Feinstein, 2001). For pain disorder, tricyclic antidepressants (Chapter 7) have been found to decrease subjective ratings of pain, but their long-term effectiveness has not yet been established (Wilson & Gil, 1996).

Key Terms

abreaction, 193
alters, 184
amnesia, 181
body dysmorphic disorder, 198
coconscious, 185
conversion disorder, 201
depersonalization, 188
depersonalization disorder, 188
derealization, 189
dissociative amnesia, 181
dissociative disorders, 180
dissociative fugue, 182
dissociative identity disorder (DID), 184
episodic memory, 182
explicit memories, 182
host, 184
hypochondriasis, 199
hysteria, 180
iatrogenic, 188
implicit memories, 182
la belle indifférence, 202
malingering, 188
pain disorder, 201
primary gain, 201
procedural memory, 182
secondary gain, 201
semantic memory, 182
somatization disorder, 200
somatoform disorders, 197
source-monitoring deficit theory, 196
state-dependent memory, 196

Summary

- Dissociative disorders occur when stress causes components of the personality, which are normally integrated, to split apart, or dissociate. As a result, a critical psychological function is screened out of consciousness. These disorders disturb only the higher cognitive functions, not sensory or motor functions.
- In dissociative amnesia, psychological stress screens out the memory function. The loss of memory typically applies to a period of time *after* the precipitating stressful event, is selective, does not reduce the amnesic patient's ability to learn new things, is not disorienting or disturbing to the amnesic patient, and is recoverable.

- A related condition is dissociative fugue, in which a person not only forgets all or some of the past but also takes a sudden, unexpected trip and often assumes a new identity.
- In dissociative identity disorder (DID), formerly known as multiple personality disorder, a person develops two or more distinct identities or personality states that take turns controlling the person's behavior. At least one of the identities is amnesic of the other(s). In some cases, the various identities display significant physiological differences.
- Depersonalization disorder involves a persistent sense of strangeness or unreality about one's identity. The person may feel like a robot or an actor in a dream. Such feelings are often accompanied by derealization, a sense of strangeness about the world and other people. Those suffering with this disorder recognize the strangeness of their feelings and may fear they are going insane.
- Gender is a risk factor in DID and depersonalization disorder, which are more common in women than men. Some cultures view depersonalization disorder as a legitimate, trancelike state and not as a disorder.
- In the psychodynamic view, dissociative disorders are extreme and maladaptive defenses against the anxiety produced by repressed wishes. Psychodynamic therapy—the most common treatment for these disorders—aims at identifying the repressed material and reintegrating it into the personality.
- Both behaviorists and socioculturalists hold that a person adopts the symptoms of a dissociative disorder in order to get the reward of protection or relief from stress. These theorists believe that reinforcement maintains the dissociative behavior. Accordingly, the way to treat dissociative symptoms is to stop reinforcing them.
- Cognitive theorists view these disorders as impairments of episodic memory, or one's record of personal experience. Cognitive therapy uses various cognitive techniques to trigger and release memories.
- Some neuroscience researchers hypothesize that the dissociative disorders are a by-product of undiagnosed epilepsy. Others suggest involvement of the hippocampus or changes in levels of serotonin. Biological therapies are undeveloped.
- The primary feature of the somatoform disorders is that psychological conflicts take on a somatic, or physical, form.
- A person with body dysmorphic disorder is so preoccupied with an imagined or a grossly exaggerated defect in appearance that he or she cannot function normally. This syndrome is associated with obsessive-compulsive disorder and depression.
- In hypochondriasis, a person maintains a chronic fear of disease by misinterpreting physical signs and sensations as abnormal. Hypochondriac patients do not fake their symptoms; they are genuinely convinced they are ill.
- In somatization disorder, a person has physical complaints that begin by age 30, persist for several years, and cannot be medically explained. The complaints are many, varied, and dramatic and are not focused on a particular disease, as in hypochondriasis.
- For people with pain disorder, the pain seems more severe or persistent than can be explained by medical causes. Patients have difficulty localizing the pain, describe it in emotional rather than sensory terms, and often do not specify changes in the pain.
- In conversion disorder, an actual disability, such as blindness or paralysis, exists with no medical basis. The condition is produced involuntarily, but it is generally agreed that conversion disorders provide relief for an internal conflict.
- The risk factors for somatoform disorders include gender, education level, and socioeconomic status. Body dysmorphic disorder and hypochondriasis are equally common in men and women, but somatization and conversion disorders are more prevalent in women. The symptoms of somatization disorder vary across cultures.
- From the psychodynamic perspective, the somatoform disorders are defenses against the anxiety caused by unacceptable wishes. All contain a strong element of regression, or return to a childlike state, that will elicit care from others. Therapy aims at uncovering what is repressed and resolving the conflicts the repression is creating.
- Behavioral and sociocultural theorists believe the somatoform disorders represent inappropriate adoptions of the "sick role" in order to reap its rewards (attention, relief from responsibility, etc.). Treatment calls for not reinforcing illness behavior and for developing the patient's coping skills.
- Cognitive theorists attribute the somatoform disorders to a cognitive style that exaggerates normal bodily sensations and makes catastrophic interpretations of minor symptoms. Cognitive therapy calls on patients to challenge their faulty beliefs and cease seeking reassurance from others, who would give negative reinforcement to their claims.
- Neuroscience researchers have found evidence for a genetic role in somatization disorder and some evidence of brain dysfunction in conversion disorder. However, biological treatments are scarce.

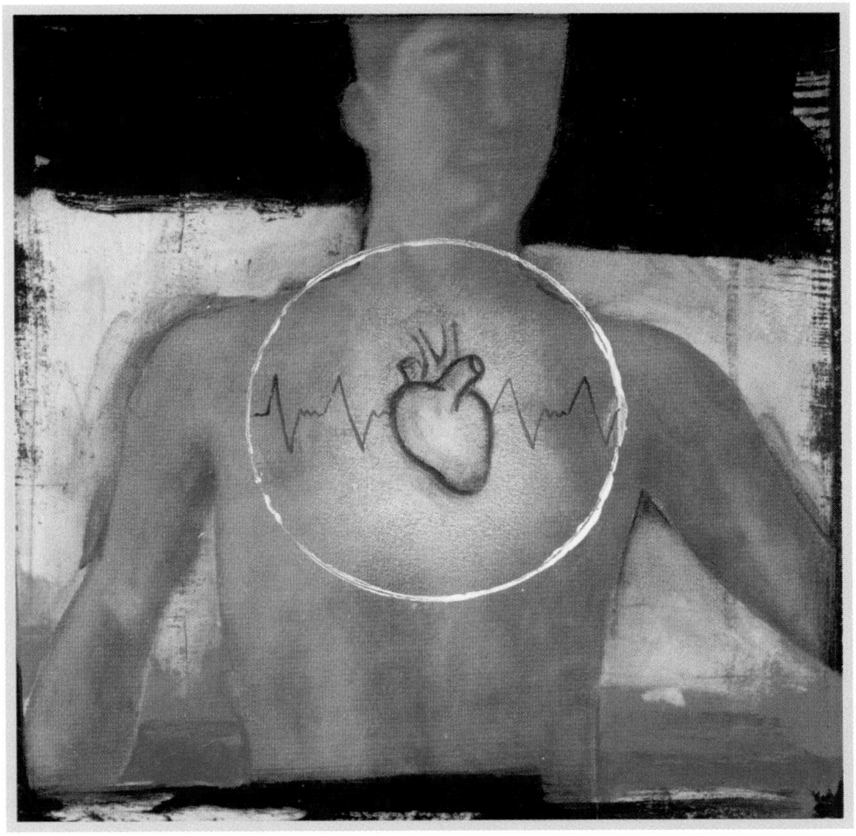

CHAPTER 9

Mind and Body

Stress

- Defining Stress
- What Determines Responses to Stress?

How Stress Influences Illness

- Changes in Physiological Functioning
- Changes in High-Risk Behavior

Psychological Factors and Physical Disorders

- Coronary Heart Disease
- Hypertension
- Cancer
- AIDS
- Headache
- Obesity
- Sleep Disorders

Stress and Illness: Theory and Therapy

- The Behavioral Perspective: Learning and Unlearning Responses to Stress
- The Cognitive Perspective
- The Psychodynamic Perspective
- The Interpersonal Perspective
- The Sociocultural Perspective
- The Neuroscience Perspective

Stress and Physical Disorders

Our bodies function as a delicately balanced system. When we are resting, restorative processes are at work; when we need to prepare ourselves for action, the body ensures that the necessary systems are at "full alert." In a normal range of physiological and psychological fluctuations, these mechanisms work efficiently to maintain our health. But what happens when this balance is upset—when normal self-regulating fluctuations become abnormal states? What effect does psychological stress have on physical health? How might our mental state affect the progression of a physical illness, such as cancer? Are certain personality types at greater risk for certain physical disorders? Increasingly, clinicians and researchers have been striving to delineate the complex interactions of mind and body as they relate to health and illness, with the ultimate goal of identifying important risk factors and generating psychological techniques to improve health. As scientific methodology in the domain of psychology has evolved, and as the bewildering intricacy of the human body has slowly been unveiled through advances in medical technology, researchers have become progressively more sophisticated in their explorations of this mind-body relationship.

In one experiment, Sheldon Cohen and his colleagues asked 420 volunteers to fill out questionnaires about the amount of stress they had been coping with during the preceding year. Then 394 of the subjects were given nose drops containing cold viruses, and the remaining 26 were given placebo drops. They were quarantined and watched, to see who caught colds. Some of the experimental subjects came down with colds, while others did not. That was to be expected—people's immune responses differ. What was not expected, however, was how clearly these people's immune responses reflected the psychological pressures they had been under. The more stress a subject had reported on the pretest questionnaire, the more likely he or she was to catch the cold (Cohen, Tyrrell, & Smith, 1991).

This was a watershed study. For years psychology had acknowledged the existence of **psychophysiological disorders** (also called *psychosomatic disorders*)—that is, illnesses influenced by emotional factors. But it was generally believed that there were only a few such illnesses. These conditions, including asthma, ulcer, hypertension, and migraine headaches, were listed in the *DSM* as "psychophysiological disorders," the assumption being that all other illnesses were purely organic. Increasingly, this assumption came under attack, as evidence accumulated that widely diverse medical conditions were affected, if not caused, by psychological factors. Accordingly, in the 1980s, *DSM-III* dropped the list of psychophysiological disorders in favor of a comprehensive category—"psychological factors affecting physical condition"—that could be applied to any illness. Still, the importance of such factors was bitterly contested. In June 1985, the *New England Journal of Medicine* published an editorial dismissing most reports of psychological influence on physical health as "anecdotal." "It is time to acknowledge that our belief in disease as a direct reflection of mental state is largely folklore," the editorial concluded (quoted in Kiecolt-Glaser & Glaser, 1991). Particularly in the case of cancer and infectious diseases such as colds, theories of psychological influence were viewed with great skepticism. Then, four years after the *New England Journal of Medicine* editorial, a competing journal published the results of a carefully controlled study showing that breast cancer patients who were given supportive group therapy in addition to their medical care survived almost twice as long, after the beginning of treatment, as those not receiving group therapy (Spiegel, Bloom, Kraemer, et al., 1989). (See the discussion on page 227.) Two years after that, the Cohen group's findings about stress and the common cold were published—in the *New England Journal of Medicine.* More recently, a review of more than 85 studies designed to test the physiological effects of psychological interventions found evidence that such interventions can often directly influence the immune system (Miller & Cohen, 2001). Today there are very few experts who still doubt that the workings of the mind influence the health of the body. In the words of *DSM-IV-TR,* "Psychological . . . factors play a potential role in the presentation or treatment of almost every general medical condition," including eating disorders, high-risk behaviors, and compliance with medical recommendations (American Psychiatric Association, 2000, p. 732*).

The conceptualization of the role of psychological factors in physical illness has not only broadened in recent years but also become far more complex. Researchers now recognize that, even if an illness is caused by a purely physical factor, the illness in turn *causes* emotional stress. Surveys have found that about 20 percent of people in the hospital, for whatever illness, have a diagnosable depressive syndrome (Rodin & Voshort, 1986). These emotional factors in turn affect the course of the illness—how serious it will become and whether and how quickly the patient will recover. Other data have shown that depression in cardiac patients is a significant risk factor for predicting subsequent heart attack death (Lesperance, Frasure-Smith, Talajic, & Bourassa, 2002) and that reducing stress can improve the prognosis for patients with heart disease (Cossette, Frasure-Smith, Lesperance, 2001). In sum, many professionals are coming to believe that physical illness can no longer be studied apart from psychological factors.

This more *holistic,* or unified, concept of body and mind has led to the development of a new research discipline, **health psychology** (also called *behavioral medicine*). Three major historical trends have met in health psychology. The first is the trend toward holistic thinking: the recognition that our way of living and state of mind affect our physical well-being. Researchers studying the economic and health burdens of the use of alcohol, tobacco, and other addictive drugs estimate that these substances account for 25 percent of all deaths in the United States annually (McGinnis & Foege, 1999). The second is the recognition that psychological and lifestyle factors can be used to prevent, as well as treat, illness. The third is the discovery that certain treatments pioneered by behavioral psychology, such as biofeedback and relaxation training, can relieve stress-related physical ailments.

In this chapter, we first review the history of the concept of mind versus body. Then we discuss psychological stress: how it is defined and how it influences illness, particularly via the immune and cardiovascular systems. Finally, we examine the interaction of mind and body in certain illnesses, and we describe the current psychological perspectives on the nature of that interaction.

Mind and Body

What is the relationship between the mind and the body? This question—the **mind-body problem**—has been under debate for centuries. Logically, it would seem that mind and body are essentially the same thing. Mind, after all, is simply an abstract term for the workings of the brain. And the brain not only is part of the body but also is directly connected by nerves to all other parts of the body. Therefore, whatever is going on "mentally" inside a person is also going on physically, and vice versa. Most of the time, however, we are unaware of the activity going on in our brains. We are conscious only of the effects of that activity—effects that we think of as "mental," not physical. This is undoubtedly one reason we tend to regard the mind as something apart from the body (Schwartz, 1978).

Whatever the reason, prevailing Western opinion for centuries has been that mind and body are separate entities—interrelated, perhaps, but still independent. This dualism of mind and body is often said to have originated with Greek philosopher Plato, in the fifth century B.C.E., but it undoubtedly reaches much further back, to prehistoric peoples' efforts to explain death. In death, they observed, the body remained, yet it was no longer alive. Something, then, must have departed from it. That something—the mind, soul, or spirit—was clearly separate from the body.

Incorporated into the Jewish and Christian religions, mind-body dualism was handed down from ancient times to the Middle Ages and the Renaissance. In the early seventeenth century, French philosopher René Descartes described mind and body as altogether independent entities—the mind spiritual, the body physical. Descartes' influential theories, together with the discoveries of Galileo and Sir Isaac Newton, laid the foundation of modern scientific rationalism. In this view, nature was a vast, self-powered machine. To explain its operations, one need not—indeed, should not—resort to philosophical or religious concepts. Nature could be explained only by reference to its internal parts—that is, only through empirical evidence, things that could be observed and measured.

Of course, there were many illnesses whose empirical causes were not known. Might they involve factors that could not be observed? In the late nineteenth century, with the discovery by Louis Pasteur and others that germs caused disease, such questions were largely answered. The causes of illness were indeed observable; all we needed were better microscopes. Some exceptions were still recognized. Over the years, physicians repeatedly noted a connection between certain disorders, such as high blood pressure and psychological tension, so the list of psychophysiological disorders was drawn up. They were the exceptions, though. Organic causation was the rule.

Only in the past half century has this assumption been called into serious question. In the 1960s, it was discovered that physiological functions such as

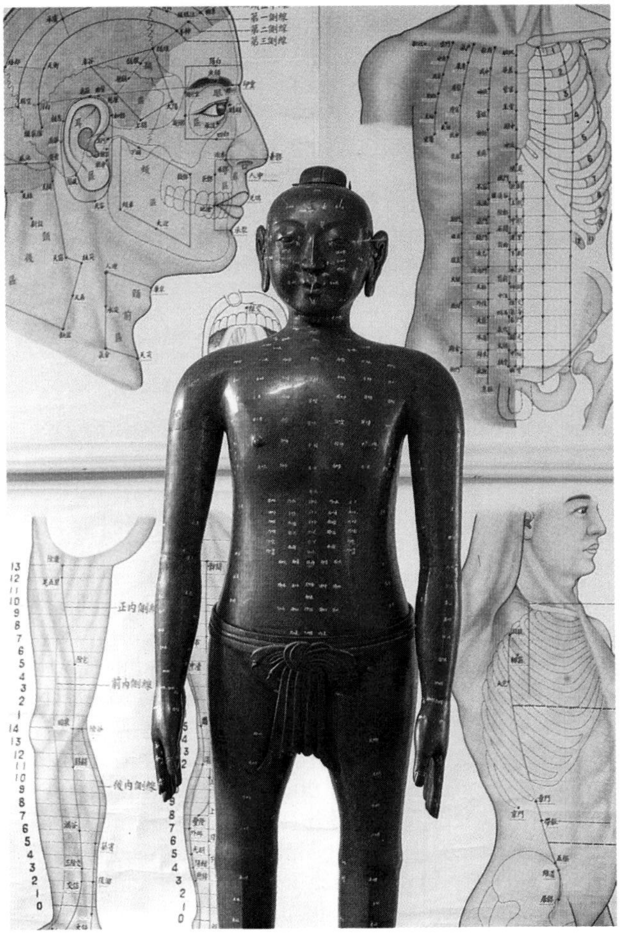

While Western philosophy and medicine separated the mind from the body, Eastern cultures, such as the Chinese, have always joined them. This Sung Dynasty (tenth through thirteenth centuries) bronze statue was used to teach acupuncture, a pain-relieving technique based on the connections between the brain and the rest of the nervous system.

blood pressure and heart rate, which were once considered completely involuntary (i.e., the province of the body, not of the mind), could be influenced voluntarily using biofeedback techniques (Barrows & Jacob, 2002). And, if the mind could affect the beating of the heart and the dilation of blood vessels, why could it not also affect such processes as the growth of cancer cells? The remainder of this story was told at the beginning of the chapter. As recent research has demonstrated, psychological factors *can* affect the growth of cancer cells, as well as cardiovascular and many other disease processes, down to the common cold. The course of all illnesses is now thought to be potentially influenced by psychological factors. Kept apart for centuries, mind and body are increasingly considered one.

In this chapter, we will take the position that mind and body are, in fact, one. What people experience as a mental event, such as sadness, is also a physical event, whether they realize it or not. Likewise, physical events, such as the firing of neurons in the brain, trigger mental events. It is not so much that the one causes the other as that they cannot, in truth, be separated. As one researcher explained, the words *psychological* and *physical* refer not to different phenomena but to different ways of talking about the same phenomenon (Graham, 1967, p. 52).

Stress

Defining Stress

The term **stress** is frequently used in many different ways. Some writers, such as W. B. Cannon (1936), define it as a stimulus: Stress consists of environmental demands that lead to physical responses. This definition has been adopted by many later researchers and has generated a number of studies on how various life events, such as divorce or losing a job, affect people. An interesting question in this line of research has to do with positive life events. According to some researchers, not just divorce but also marriage, not just losing a job but also taking one, can be stressful enough to tax one's health (Holmes & Rahe, 1967). Other researchers have pointed to the usefulness of minor positive events such as gossiping with friends or getting a good night's sleep as buffers against stress (Lazarus, Kanner, & Folkman, 1980).

A second definition holds that stress is a *response*. On the basis of extensive research, Hans Selye (1956, 1974) described a **general adaptation syndrome,** which divides the body's reaction into three successive stages: (1) alarm and mobilization—a state of rapid, general arousal in which the body's defenses are mobilized; (2) resistance—the state of optimal biological adaptation to environmental demands; and (3) exhaustion and disintegration—a stage reached when the body loses its ability to cope with prolonged demands.

Finally, some cognitive theorists define stress not as stimulus or response but as the interaction between the stimulus and the person's appraisal of it, a process that determines the person's response (Lazarus & Folkman, 1984). This theory will be discussed later, under the cognitive perspective.

What Determines Responses to Stress?

Regardless of whether stress is a response, a stimulus, or an appraisal of a stimulus, the fact remains that different people experience stress differently. Why do some people cope well with stress and others fall ill? And why do some people fall ill with migraines whereas others develop high blood pressure or backaches?

Stimulus Specificity One of the earliest indications that people's responses to stress are keyed to the type of stress involved came from a rather bizarre experiment (Wolf & Wolff, 1947). In 1947, a patient named Tom, who had experienced severe gastrointestinal damage, underwent surgery, and with his permission the surgeon installed a plastic window over his stomach so that its internal workings could be observed. In subsequent sessions with Tom, the investigators found that his flow of gastric juices decreased when he was exposed to anxiety-producing stimuli and increased when he was exposed to anger-producing stimuli. This experiment showed that gastric activity was related to emotional states, as researchers had long suspected. It also established the principle of **stimulus specificity**—that different kinds of stress produce different kinds of physiological response. This principle has since been confirmed by other investigators. Different emotions—fear, anger, disgust, sadness, happiness—have been shown to have significantly different effects, not only on gastric activity but also on heart rate, blood pressure, muscle tension, respiration rate, and other physiological functions (Schwartz, Weinberger, & Singer, 1981). Researchers have pinpointed subtler distinctions as well. Apparently, the physiological reaction differs, depending on whether we are anticipating a stressful event or actually undergoing it, as students may verify in the case of final exams. It also differs according to whether the stress is short term or long term (Weiner, 1994). Finally, the reactions in question are extraordinarily complex. It is not just a matter of changes in heart rate or breathing. Different stressors produce whole, distinctive patterns of physiological response, involving not just autonomic activity but also different facial expressions, brain-wave changes, and hormone secretions (Weiner, 1994).

Individual Response Specificity Physiological responses to stress depend not only on the kind of stress, but also on the person responding. Whether as a result of genes or learning (probably both), people appear to have characteristic patterns of physiological response, which carry over from one type of stress to another—a phenomenon called **individual response specificity.** The first hint of this fact came in an experiment in which a group of people with a history of cardiovascular complaints (e.g., high blood pressure) and a group of people with a history of muscular complaints (e.g., backache) were both exposed to the same painful stimulus. Though the stressor was the same, the cardiovascular group responded with greater changes in heart rate than did the muscular group, while the muscular group showed greater changes in muscle tension than did the cardiovascular group (Malmo & Shagass, 1949). What this suggested—and it has since been confirmed—is that, in responding to stress, people tend to favor one physiological system.

It also appears that some people respond more intensely to stress in general. In an intriguing experiment, it was found that whether or not a 10-month-old baby would cry when its mother left the room could be predicted from the baby's EEG brain-wave pattern recorded when the mother was in the room. Infants whose EEGs showed hemispheric asymmetry, or more activity on one side of the brain—in this case, more activity in the right frontal area than in the left—were the most likely to cry when their mothers exited (Davidson & Fox, 1989). This same pattern of asymmetry has also been observed in shy 3-year-olds and in depressed adults (Davidson, 1992). Possibly, it reflects an innate hypersensitivity to stress.

Stimulus Versus Individual Response There is an apparent contradiction between individual response specificity and stimulus specificity. If people have characteristic patterns of response that carry over from stressor to stressor, how can patterns of response vary with changes in the stressor? This seems improbable only if we think of physiological response to stress as a simple process. But, as we saw, it is an extremely complex process, and many variables influence the final response. The two variables we are considering—the person and the stressor—operate simultaneously (Engel, 1960; Engel & Bickford, 1961). As described, the flow of gastric juices tends to increase with anger and decrease with anxiety; here we see stimulus specificity. The degree of increase and decrease, however, is subject to individual response specificity; that is, "gastric reactors" may show extreme increases and decreases; "cardiac reactors," on the other hand, may show only mild gastric changes, concentrating instead on heart-rate changes. And if, as the hemispheric asymmetry research suggests, some people are generally heavy reactors to stress, then this factor, too, would influence the response.

Acute Versus Chronic Stress Though it generally has a negative connotation, stress itself is not a "bad" thing. In his entertaining book *Why Zebras Don't Get Ulcers,* Robert Sapolsky (1998) reminds us that the sort of stresses our bodies are designed for are short-lived. In evolutionary terms, such physiological reactions to acute stressors are in some way adaptive and increase our chances of survival. The normal response to stress involves activation of the sympathetic nervous system to "rev up" our cardiovascular, muscular, and endocrine systems to protect ourselves from bodily harm. It has been suggested that such acute responses to stress also temporarily boost immune functioning (Dhabhar, 2002). Imagine an animal in the wild, either surviving an aggressive fight or barely escaping the attack of a predator. It's likely some damage may occur—a bite or scratch, or worse. Having made it through this ordeal, what terrible irony to then succumb to bacterial infection through the open wound. But, with a surge in immune system functioning, our bodies are better adapted to survive such stressful encounters.

If such acute responses to stress are perfectly healthy, then why does stress have such negative connotations today? Problems seem to arise when stress is relentless, when the stressor is not short-lived. Acute stress may last a few minutes or hours. Stress becomes chronic when it persists for many hours a day for weeks or even months. According to Selye (1979), an individual who experiences chronic stress and consequently remains in a high state of physiological arousal lacks sufficient resources to also deal with everyday events: The individual may become irritable and be more vulnerable to illness. Eventually, resistance becomes impossible and the individual reaches the final stage of the general adaptation syndrome—*exhaustion.* The body's reserves are depleted, and disease or even death may result. The differential effect of acute versus chronic stress has received increased attention recently, particularly in relation to changes in the immune system.

How Stress Influences Illness

Over the years, research has established a connection between stress and illness. The study discussed at the opening of this chapter—the Cohen group's investigation of colds—is a good example, and it has been built upon by later researchers. For example, the Cohen group found that levels of stress predicted not only who developed cold symptoms but also who became infected (as revealed by levels of antibodies in the blood), whether or not they developed symptoms (Cohen, Tyrrell, & Smith, 1991). Later, another research group (Stone, Bovberg, Neale, et al., 1992) found much the same thing. They exposed 17 subjects to a cold virus, and all 17 became infected, but only 12 went on to show cold symptoms. As in the Cohen study, the subjects had filled out stress questionnaires, and the questionnaires revealed that those who came down with the colds were those who

Research Highlights: Minor Stresses and Illnesses

In exploring the links between psychological stress and physical illness, researchers have tended to concentrate on the impact that major stressors have on the human body. Divorce, a death in the family, the loss of a job, a move to a distant city—these and other major life events cause tremendous stress and put a person at increased risk of becoming ill (Holmes & Rahe, 1967; Selye, 1976). Happy occasions—getting married, receiving a promotion, going on vacation—may also cause stress, but they are much less likely to result in illness.

More recently, researchers have begun to look into the role that less dramatic events play in the stress-disease connection. Surprisingly, the daily hassles of life—getting caught in traffic jams, waiting in lines, losing the car keys—may be more stressful than major unpleasant events (Lazarus, 1980). In fact, continual mild stress has been found to be a better predictor of declines in physical health—and of depression and anxiety—than major life events (DeLongis, Coyne, Dakof, et al., 1982).

Other studies have shown that stress affects the body's defenses against herpesviruses. Unlike most other common viruses, which the immune system actually eliminates from the body, herpesviruses, once they enter the system, remain there for life. Most of the time, they are inactive, but they may flare up now and then, producing cold sores, genital herpes, mononucleosis, or other illnesses, depending on which herpesvirus is involved. In medical students who have been infected with herpesviruses, immune activity against the virus has been shown to drop during final exams and then to rise again during summer vacation (Glaser, Pearson, Bonneau, et al., 1993).

Stress apparently affects not only one's defenses against already present herpesviruses but also one's risk of being infected in the first place. In one experiment, a group of West Point cadets was tracked for four years after they entered the academy. None of these students had been infected with the Epstein-Barr virus, which causes mononucleosis, before going to West Point. But in the course of the four years a number of them became infected. Those who did—and those who spent longest in the infirmary—tended to be the ones who, on an earlier test, had shown three risk factors for stress: high motivation for a military career, poor grades, and fathers who were "overachievers" (Kiecolt-Glaser & Glaser, 1991). We now know that psychological stress and high levels of negative affect can reduce the effectiveness of vaccinations (Marsland, Cohen, Rabin, et al. 2001).

had experienced the greatest number of "major life events," both positive and negative, in the preceding year. Thus, if, as we have so often been told, colds strike when we are "run-down," there is more to this than staying up late. Even positive changes in our lives can run us down.

A more dramatic example has to do with sudden cardiac death (SCD), a form of heart attack that kills 450,000 people per year in the United States (Centers for Disease Control and Prevention, 2002). Seventy percent of people who die of SCD are found to have an underlying heart disease, but only about one third show evidence of the coronary occlusion (blockage in the arteries of the heart) that causes most heart attacks. Rather, SCD is primarily an electrical accident that occurs when the heart's large, steady contractions give way to rapid, irregular contractions known as fibrillations. Vulnerability to SCD seems to be associated with long-term psychological stress (Kamarck & Jennings, 1991). Furthermore, in about 20 percent of cases, SCD is connected to an experience of great emotion, such as sudden surprise, anger, grief, or even happiness (Lane & Jennings, 1995). Other kinds of heart disease are also associated with stress (Kamarck, Eranen, Jennings, et al., 2000). Heart patients often show constriction of the coronary arteries and reduced blood flow during acute stress; these effects can also be produced by laboratory stressors such as having to solve difficult arithmetic problems or give a speech about one's personal life, as well as during exercise and by naturalistic stressors (Sheps, McMahon, Becker, et al., 2002). Conversely, some people who are especially reactive to stress seem to be at high risk for heart disease (Krantz & McCeney, 2002)—a subject that we will come to later in this chapter.

Stress and illness are clearly related, but what mediates the relationship? How are thought and emotion translated into physical breakdown?

Changes in Physiological Functioning

Stress and the Autonomic Nervous System What are the physiological changes associated with stress? To attempt an answer, we must look again at the autonomic nervous system (ANS). As we saw in Chapter 6, the ANS controls the smooth muscles, the glands, and the internal organs, regulating a wide variety of functions—among them heartbeat, respiration, blood pressure, bladder contraction, perspiration, salivation, cholesterol release, adrenaline secretion, and gastric acid production—to allow the body to cope with the ebb and flow of environmental demands. In general, the sympathetic division mobilizes the body to meet such demands by speeding up heart rate, constricting the blood vessels near the skin (thereby raising blood pressure), increasing adrenaline flow, and so forth. And, in general, the parasympathetic division reverses these processes, returning the body to a resting state so that it can rebuild the energy supply depleted by sympathetic activity (see Figure 6.7).

Several decades ago, W. B. Cannon (1936) proposed that stress resulted in a massive activation of the entire sympathetic division: increased heart rate and blood pressure, fast breathing, heavy adrenaline flow, dilated pupils, inhibited salivation and digestion. Regardless of the nature of the stress or of the person, the physiological response, according to Cannon, was the same generalized sympathetic arousal. That hypothesis has been confirmed in broad outline.

Imagine walking down a deserted street at night. Suddenly, you notice someone standing in the shadows of a doorway right next to you—and the person moves toward you. At this point, it's likely that your body will react to this perceived threat: Your heartbeat and breathing rate will increase, your muscles will tense, adrenaline will be released, and you will become incredibly focused on the event at hand. Cannon termed this primitive response, seen in all animals, the fight-or-flight reaction, a highly adaptive response designed to prepare the organism to fight for its life or run away. During this response, controlled by the ANS, generally speaking, the sympathetic system is aroused and the parasympathetic system suppressed.

Changes in the Immune System In the studies of colds, as we saw, not all the people who were exposed to the virus became infected, and not all the people who became infected developed symptoms—in both cases, only those who had been under greater stress were infected and developed symptoms. Clearly, the factor mediating this connection was the **immune system**, the body's system of defense against infectious disease and cancer. We are constantly exposed to microorganisms, most of which pose no threat to us—indeed, a number of them are even useful. Among these microorganisms, however, certain bacteria, viruses, parasites, and the like, can be harmful or even deadly. If these agents enter the body through the skin or through the digestive, respiratory, genital, or urinary systems, it is the job of the immune system to protect us by distinguishing between self and nonself and then eliminating nonself.

The immune system is a complicated and highly orchestrated system, silently coordinating attacks on invading antigens through chemical messengers. Certain immune cells appear to be highly specialized; others are far more adaptive. In this way, our immune system protects us from newly evolved strains of viruses and bacteria, even creating "memory cells" that circulate for years after an infection and rapidly

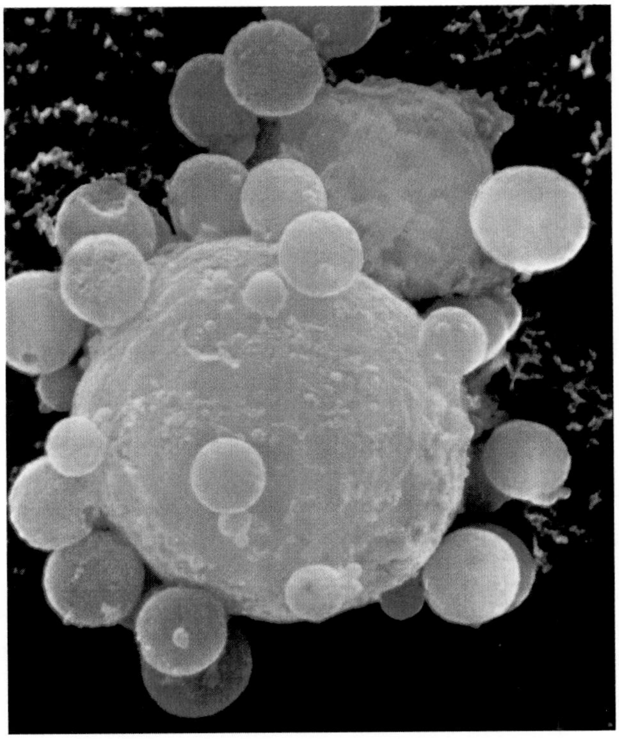

Scanning electron micrograph of T-cell lymphocytes attacking a cancer cell.

recognize and respond to an old foe should it dare to show its face again.

The primary agents of the immune system are small white blood cells, called lymphocytes, that patrol the body, identifying foreign substances, called antigens, and either attacking them or producing special proteins called antibodies to launch the attack. In either case, the first stage of attack occurs when the immune particle attaches itself to the foreign particle, which it can do only if its chemical structure fits that of the invader.

Scientists have not yet completed their inventory of the immune system, but this research has accelerated rapidly in the past 20 years. One reason is the AIDS epidemic. The AIDS virus kills its victims by destroying immune cells, thus leaving the body undefended against illness. Obviously, if we knew more about the immune system, we might find a cure for AIDS. Another stimulus to research on immune functions has been the effort to save lives through organ transplants. A major frustration in organ transplant surgery is that the immune system often perceives the new organ as nonself and rejects it. Again, with more detailed knowledge of the immune system, we would be in a better position to control this response. Finally, a critical factor in the intensifying research on immune functions has been the research on stress and illness. The study of the immune system as a link between stress and illness has evolved into a subspecialty of health medicine called **psychoneuroimmunology, or PNI.**

In most PNI research, immune responses are studied by means of blood samples or mucosal secretions such as saliva. One method of assessing immune functioning is to take a blood sample from an individual, isolate the white blood cells, and expose these cells to mitogens, compounds that mimic the action of antigens in the body. Upon encountering mitogens, healthy white blood cells will begin multiplying and secreting attack compounds. Less healthy white blood cells will do this less efficiently. Thus, by recording the number and activity of white blood cells in people who are under stress and then comparing those results with white-blood-cell action in the same people when they are under less stress or in control subjects, researchers can draw conclusions about the relationship between stress and immune function.

In this research, then, immune function is the dependent variable, stress the independent variable. PNI research has focused on three broad categories of stressors: naturalistic major events, naturalistic minor events, and laboratory stressors.

Naturalistic Major Events Needless to say, the major real-life events that are most likely to produce stress—divorce, a death in the family—cannot be arranged for experimental purposes, nor, in most cases, can they be studied prospectively; they are too infrequent and unpredictable. But, by assembling and studying subjects after the event, researchers have been able to establish that major life stresses do, indeed, penetrate to the immune system.

One of the earliest studies to demonstrate this principle involved 26 people whose spouses had recently died. The subjects' blood was tested 2 weeks after the death of the spouse and then again 6 weeks after the death. On the second trial, the responsiveness of these people's white blood cells to mitogens was significantly lower than that of the controls (Bartrop, Luckhurst, Lazarus, et al., 1977). Most of us have heard of people dying of a "broken heart" after the death of a loved one, and this phenomenon has been documented by research (Lynch, 1977). Possibly one of the avenues by which the heart is broken is the immune system.

For many of the subjects in the study just cited, the spouse's death was sudden. What is the immune response to the long-term stress of watching a family member die slowly? A major health problem in the United States today is Alzheimer's disease, an organic brain disorder that strikes the elderly and causes dementia, a progressive breakdown of mental functioning involving memory loss, agitation, and irrational behavior (Chapter 15). There is no cure for Alzheimer's; in most cases, neither is there a speedy end. Patients may survive for 20 years. Many are placed in nursing homes, but some are cared for by their families, a situation that is often extremely stressful for the caregivers. Day by day, they watch the personality of a spouse, father, or mother disintegrate. This process has been described by caregivers as a "living bereavement," and, like ordinary bereavement, it taxes the immune system, as one study showed. Janice Kiecolt-Glaser and her colleagues studied a group of 69 men and women who had been taking care of a spouse with Alzheimer's dementia for an average of 5 years. During the yearlong interval between the beginning of the study and the follow-up, the caregivers, compared with controls, showed decreases in 3 different measures of cellular immunity. They were also ill for more days with respiratory infections (Kiecolt-Glaser, Dura, Speicher, et al., 1991). This study provided the first good evidence that chronic stress led to chronically depleted immune function. More recently, researchers have examined the effects of

Caring for a spouse with Alzheimer's disease can be extremely stressful. Witnessing a loved one turning into a virtual stranger over time, a process called "living bereavement," has been shown to weaken the immune system in the same way that ordinary bereavement does.

bereavement among the caregivers of people with HIV and AIDS. Studies have shown that bereavement can have negative health effects, in part because of increases in health-damaging behaviors among the caregivers (Mayne, Acree, Chesney, et al., 1998) and in part because of mood and cognitive coping strategies (Billings, Folkman, Acree, et al., 2000). Researchers have also shown that spiritual beliefs can moderate the effects of bereavement (Richards, Acree, & Folkman, 1999). (See the box on page 240.)

Naturalistic Minor Events Interesting as these studies are, they have limited bearing on the question of how the immune system responds to ordinary, daily stress: traffic jams, family arguments, bounced checks. Until recently, these naturalistic minor events were rarely studied by PNI researchers. (Indeed, human beings were rarely studied by PNI researchers. Most experiments involved rodents.) Then, in 1982, Kiecolt- Glaser and her co-workers began looking at the immune responses of Ohio State University medical students during final examinations. The students' blood was tested periodically throughout the academic year, including the tense three-day final-exam period. On every measure of response studied—the numbers of different kinds of immune cells, the cells' activity, their secretions—immune functioning decreased during the exam period. On one measure, the production of chemicals that activate the so-called natural-killer (NK) cells, which fight tumors and viruses, immune activity dropped by as much as 90 percent during the exam period. In a later study, the medical students' blood showed increased levels of the stress-response hormones adrenaline and noradrenaline during both waking and sleeping hours over the course of the exam period. It is possible that these hormone changes were responsible in part for the immune-function changes (Glaser, Pearson, Bonneau, et al., 1993; Kiecolt-Glaser & Glaser, 1991). For more on the link between minor stress and illness, see the box on page 216.

Laboratory Stressors When researchers study real-life stressors, there are many factors they can't control. Perhaps some third variable was affecting the immune functions of the Alzheimer's patients' caregivers. Out of respect for such possibilities, experimenters studying real-life stress have to be cautious in drawing cause-and-effect conclusions. By using laboratory stressors, on the other hand, researchers can control conditions in such a way as to eliminate confounding variables. They can also observe the response to stress *as it occurs* and thus study its internal dynamics.

In an interesting study, 30 subjects were given 2 challenging and stressful tasks to perform. One was an arithmetic problem. Starting with a 4-digit number (e.g., 4,269), the subjects had to subtract 13 repeatedly in their heads and announce the results ("4,256, 4,243, 4,230, . . ."). All the while, an experimenter urged them to work faster. The second task was the so-called Stroop color-word test (Stroop, 1935), in which the subjects were shown, on a video monitor, the names of colors appearing in a different color. (For example, the word *blue* might appear printed in red.) Subjects were asked to ignore the word on the screen and just report the color that the word was printed in—a difficult task made even harder by the fact that each presentation was accompanied by a taped voice naming various colors randomly connected to the one on the screen. The subjects in the PNI experiment worked at these tasks for 20 minutes, after which blood samples were taken. The samples showed significantly reduced immune functioning, compared with that of the controls, who did not perform the tasks. An hour later, blood was taken again, and again it showed depleted immune activity. Thus, immune responses to stress are not necessarily brief, transient effects (Stone, Valdimarsdottir, Katkin, et al., 1993).

For all its advantages, laboratory research has the disadvantage that its conditions are not those of ordinary life. The Stroop color-word test is not among the trials that most people endure in their daily existence. However, some studies come close to duplicating important sources of real-life stress. In one study, a model of marital conflict was tested (Kiecolt-Glaser & Glaser, 1991). Ninety recently married couples were admitted to a hospital research unit for 24 hours. The couples were asked to discuss topics of conflict and try to resolve them during a 30-minute session. The session was videotaped, and blood samples were taken several times in the course of it. (The couples had been outfitted with catheters.) The videotapes were later rated on various measures—negative behavior, positive behavior, problem-solving behavior, avoidant behavior—by independent raters, and these results were compared with the results of immune-function tests on the blood samples. What the researchers found, in general, was that the more negative behavior, such as arguing or accusing, a subject showed, the more likely he or she was to show reduced immune functioning. Interestingly, immune changes were not found to be related to positive, problem-solving, or avoidant behaviors, only to negative behaviors. Another curious finding was that women were more likely than men to show negative immune changes. As in the stress-task experiment, the immune effects were not transient. They were still present 24 hours after the taped session (Kiecolt-Glaser, Malarkey, Chee, et al., 1993).

Feedback Loops Stress produces direct physiological effects, and those effects have other effects. The body's functions—digestion, respiration, circulation—are not single-component operations. They are systems of many parts, each of which sends the others **feedback,** or information about regulating the system. Especially important in theories of stress and illness is **negative feedback,** in which the turning *on* of one component in a system leads to the turning *off* of another component. According to Gary Schwartz's (1977) disregulation model, stress-related illness occurs when there is a disruption in the negative-feedback cycle. Consider the case of blood pressure. In response to threats in the environment, the brain causes the arteries to constrict. In doing so, it depends on the baroreceptors, pressure-sensitive cells surrounding the arteries, to signal when blood pressure is running too high. But various circumstances, such as chronic stress or genetic predisposition, may blunt the responsiveness of the baroreceptors and cause them to fail to provide this crucial negative feedback. When that happens, a regulated system becomes a disregulated system, and the result is illness—in this case, chronically high blood pressure.

Another influential theory, developed by Herbert Weiner (1994), concerns the oscillations, or rhythmic back-and-forth cycles, of the various systems in the body. Such oscillating cycles control almost all bodily functions. Breathing, blood pressure, heartbeat, temperature, digestion, menstruation, sleep, the production of hormones, neurotransmitters, immune cells—all go up and down on a number of time scales, whether second by second, day by day, or month by month. These cycles, too, are controlled by negative feedback. Indeed, that is what keeps them oscillating: Turning on in one cycle leads to turning off in another, and vice versa. (For example, the turning off of sleep results in the turning on of stomach contractions, so we want breakfast.) According to Weiner, stress may throw a system out of rhythm, in which case the other systems are also affected. After the disruption, the system may find a new rhythm, or it may become chronically irregular. In either case, the result may be a disease process. For example, people who work late shifts suffer chronic disruptions of their sleep cycle. On workdays they wake up in the afternoon; on days off, if they want to see their families and friends, they wake up in the morning. This irregularity apparently takes its toll, and not just on sleep. Long-term night-shift workers have more gastrointestinal problems and more illness than people who work day shifts (Rutenfranz, Haider, & Koller, 1985; Knutsson & Boggild, 2000).

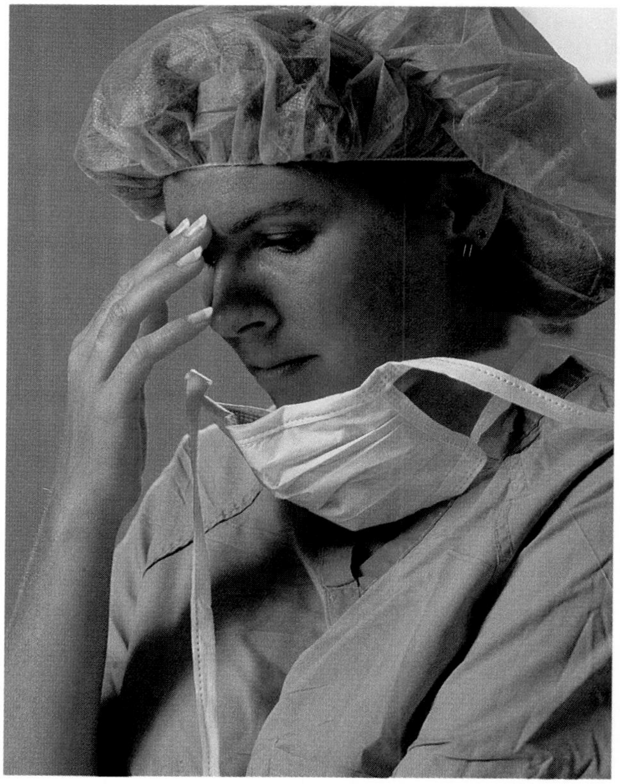

Medical interns once epitomized the kind of chronic irregularities in work schedule—many hours on duty alternating with a few hours off—that can result in stress-related illness. Now that such fatigue has been shown to interfere with patient care, many teaching hospitals are scheduling shorter and more regular shifts for their interns.

Schwartz's model, then, focuses more on the failure of a single component, which then disregulates the system as a whole. Weiner's model concentrates from the beginning on the system—on the whole body as a finely tuned network of oscillating systems, all vulnerable to stress.

Changes in High-Risk Behavior

Schwartz's and Weiner's theories are models—comprehensive, abstract descriptions. On a more concrete level, stress may contribute to illness by causing people to behave in a way that puts them at risk for illness. For example, people with adult-onset diabetes can usually maintain their health by taking medication and following a special diet. As studies (Brantley & Garrett, 1993) have shown, however, diabetics who are under stress are likely to stray from their diets and forget their pills, with the result that they may fall ill.

Stress can also interfere with preventive measures against disease. In a study of women who engaged in self-initiated exercise, the subjects exercised fewer days, skipped planned exercise sessions, reported lower levels of confidence in meeting their exercise goals, and were less satisfied with their exercise sessions during periods of high stress (Stetson, Rahn, Dubbert, et al., 1997). Ironically, 70 percent of the women reported that they used exercise to manage stress. But, in order to see the chain leading from stress to high-risk behavior to illness, it is hardly necessary to look to this kind of study. As anyone knows, stress may lead to smoking, drug use, sleep loss, overeating, and undereating, and any of these will increase the risk of illness (Sinha, 2001).

Stress may also encourage its victims to report illness. People whose lives are going smoothly tend to overlook health problems; people who are under pressure are more likely to call the doctor. This is one reason for the association between stress and illness—which is not to say that such reports of illness are exaggerated. On the contrary, this connection illustrates one of the few beneficial effects of stress: It causes people who are at risk to seek help earlier, with the possibility that they may receive needed treatment or learn to change their behavior—for example, by eating more healthfully or starting an exercise regimen.

Psychological Factors and Physical Disorders

As we saw, psychological factors can affect many physical disorders. We will discuss only a few conditions in which the influence of mental processes has been of special concern to researchers and clinicians, beginning with coronary heart disease and high blood pressure, which have been linked strongly to psychological factors. The evidence on the relationship between stress and cancer, AIDS, and other conditions covered in this section is progressively less conclusive.

Coronary Heart Disease

The heart is a specialized muscular tissue fed by major arteries, which supply it with oxygen and nutrients. Those arteries can become occluded, or blocked, by atherosclerosis—the formation of fatty deposits on the inside walls of the arteries. The deposits build up over the years, causing the formation of scar tissue and calcium deposits that restrict the passage of blood, sometimes leading to a heart attack. Sometimes, a blood clot (thrombus) suddenly blocks a coronary artery at a point already narrowed by atherosclerosis, cutting off the blood supply to part of the heart (ischemia) and causing a myocardial infarction, or heart attack. In some people, the heart's electrical impulses become disorganized, and blood circulation ceases, causing sudden cardiac death.

Coronary heart disease, brought about by atherosclerosis and manifested as either heart attack or sudden cardiac death, is usually made evident when the heart's oxygen demands exceed the available supply. Transient reductions in the oxygen supply due to exercise or stress can cause angina pectoris, or chest pain; more enduring reductions can cause permanent damage via a myocardial infarction, which results in the death of a portion of the heart muscle. But, in individuals who have not yet been diagnosed with coronary artery disease, routine testing can often identify the disease before a major event. Electrocardiograms administered while a subject exercises can reveal "silent" ischemia, most often due to undiagnosed atherosclerosis.

Coronary heart disease is the number one cause of death in the United States and other industrialized countries of the West. Although the underlying pathogenic process, coronary atherosclerosis, begins early in life, the expression of the disease—heart attack or sudden cardiac death—often occurs in mid- to late adulthood. The development, expression, and course of the disease represents a complex interplay of biological, psychological, and social factors. Traditional risk factors for coronary heart disease include a family history of the disease, increasing age, sex (males are more at risk than females), high blood levels of cholesterol, high blood pressure, cigarette smoking, obesity, physical inactivity, and diabetes mellitus. Research indicates that stress and some personality traits are also risk factors for coronary heart disease. Day-to-day lifestyle, including diet, exercise, and stress level, has an important impact on the progression of the disease (Kromhout, Menotti, Kesteloot, et al., 2002; Morris, 2001), as the following case history suggests:

> Mr. Smith, a fifty-year-old auto worker, was 20 percent overweight, smoked, ate the typical American diet (high in animal fat and low in fruits, vegetables, and fiber), and lived a sedentary lifestyle. The primary wage earner of his family, he had two children in college. Recently his company had decided to downsize, threatening Mr. Smith's job. For the next month, he had experienced episodic tightness in his chest, primarily when he exerted himself and after meals. He attributed the tightness to indigestion.
>
> One Friday in January, Mr. Smith received a pink slip. The next week there was a big snowfall. After a large breakfast, during which he argued with his wife about how he was spending his time,

Mr. Smith decided to shovel the driveway. Experiencing tightness in his chest, he attributed it to indigestion and continued to work. But within a few minutes, the feeling had become more oppressive, expanding into a pain that radiated down his left arm. Overwhelmed, Mr. Smith fell to his knees, clutching his chest, and passed out. His wife, who had been watching from the window, called 911 immediately. At the emergency room, physicians diagnosed a myocardial infarction ("heart attack") and admitted him for diagnostic tests. After returning home, Mr. Smith began a cardiac rehabilitation program that included exercise, diet modification, and advice on smoking cessation and stress management.

Over the next six months, Mr. Smith stopped smoking, lost more than ten pounds, and found a new job. Though he no longer experiences chest pain, he worries about having another heart attack. He practices the relaxation techniques he learned through a stress management class regularly. He also is learning cognitive strategies for managing his anger and fear. While maintaining his new eating habits and exercise regimen is a struggle, Mr. Smith is getting a great deal of support from his wife and children, who have modified their own diets to match his "heart healthy" diet. (J. Haythornthwaite, Johns Hopkins University, personal files)

Since the 1960s, the death rate from heart attacks has declined steadily, as has the apparent number of initial acute myocardial infarctions (heart attacks). Improved emergency services as well as earlier detection of underlying cardiovascular disease may have contributed to the reduced death rate. More important, some major risk factors have declined, including dietary intake of animal fat and cholesterol and cigarette smoking. The detection and management of high blood pressure have also improved.

Research on nonhuman primates has demonstrated the link between social environment/status and atherosclerosis (Kaplan & Manuck, 1999; Manuck, Marsland, Kaplan, et al., 1995). In socially dominant males, a moderately high-risk diet combined with an unstable social environment produced twice the amount of coronary atherosclerosis as is normal; that is, the stress of retaining a dominant social status in a constantly changing social environment contributed to the disease. Later work demonstrated that activation of the sympathetic nervous system (SNS) contributed to atherosclerosis. Dominant males placed in an unstable social environment and given a medication that blocked specific SNS activity did not develop increased atherosclerosis, suggesting that the medication protected the heart by reducing the physiological response to stress. In a similar unstable social environment, unmedicated dominant males exhibited large increases in heart rate during social encounters. In these studies, researchers found sex differences in the impact of social status on the development of atherosclerosis. Subordinate female animals showed greater atherosclerosis, regardless of the stability of their social environment (Kaplan, Manuck, Anthony, & Clarkson, 2002). Overall, these studies demonstrate the potential effects of social stress in facilitating the development of coronary artery disease.

In humans, researchers have used a variety of epidemiological methods to examine the relationship between social and occupational stress and the development and progression of coronary heart disease (Krantz & McCeney, 2002). In a large, prospective study done over a 6-year period. Karasek and colleagues (1981) found that the Swedish men who described their work as psychologically demanding and scored low on a scale measuring latitude in decision making were at increased risk of developing symptoms of coronary heart disease and eventually dying from it. Men whose jobs were characterized by low intellectual demands were also at increased risk. These findings were independent of age, educational level, smoking, and obesity (Karasek, Baker, Marxer, et al., 1981). Shiftworkers, who experience social and behavioral problems as well as changes in their sleep patterns, also have increased risk of cardiovascular disease (Knutsson & Boggild, 2000). Other studies suggest that a demanding work environment is not as important as low control in predicting increased risk of coronary heart disease (Bosma, Marmot, Hemingway, et al., 1997). These findings suggest that giving employees more variety in their work, and more input into decisions about their work, may decrease their risk of coronary heart disease.

Large cardiovascular, neuroendocrine, and cholesterol responses have been observed in response to both laboratory stressors (for example, the mental arithmetic and Stroop color-word tests described on page 219) and naturalistic stressors (for example, public speaking and driving in traffic). These acute cardiac responses, which are referred to as cardiovascular reactivity, have long been thought to contribute to the development and expression of coronary heart disease (Krantz & Manuck, 1984). The most compelling support comes from the primate experiments on social environment and social dominance just described. However, some recent studies have provided more direct support in humans. For example, in one laboratory study using procedures similar to the ones used for the Stroop color-word tests, researchers found that there is a decrease in fat metabolism during stress, suggesting that diet may interact

People whose jobs are repetitive and unchallenging have been shown to be at an increased risk of developing coronary heart disease. This risk can be decreased by introducing variety into the work and by offering them a greater role in making decisions about their work.

with stress to influence risk for heart disease (Stoney, West, Hughes, et al., 2002). Another recent study discovered that healthy men with large anticipatory blood pressure responses to exercise had enlargement of the left ventricle (an important risk factor for mortality) (Kamarck, Eranen, Jennings, et al., 2000). A previous study of the same group showed that large cardiovascular change during stress was associated with atherosclerosis (Kamarck, Everson, Kaplan, et al., 1997). Even more compelling evidence comes from a study of cardiac patients, which showed that those with ischemia (reduced blood flow to the heart) during stress were more likely to die within 5 years after stress testing (Sheps, McMahon, Becker, et al., 2002).

In the book *Type A Behavior and Your Heart* (1974), Friedman and Rosenman advanced the thesis that coronary heart disease, along with other cardiovascular disorders, tends to strike a specific kind of personality, which the authors called **Type A.** Type A people are aggressive achievers. They talk, walk, and eat rapidly and are highly impatient. They fidget in frustration if kept waiting at an elevator or a traffic light. They finish other people's sentences for them. They pride themselves on getting things done in less time than other people, and they measure their own performance by rigorous standards. In short, they keep themselves under heavy pressure—pressure that eventually takes a toll on their cardiovascular systems.

In an impressive longitudinal study, 2,249 male executives between the ages of 39 and 59 were evaluated and followed for 9 years (Rosenman, Brand, Jenkins, et al., 1975). Approximately half were identified as Type A and the other half as Type B (the more relaxed, patient executive). Of the 257 men who had heart attacks during the 9 years, 178 were Type A, while only 79 were Type B—a striking 2:1 differential. Soon, however, conflicting findings began to appear. In a study of heart-attack survivors, the Type As actually lived longer than the Type Bs (Ragland & Brand, 1988). Other studies have also indicated that workaholic Type As are not in as much danger as was once thought. There seems to be no correlation between heart disease and the impatient struggle to accomplish ever more work. There is, however, a correlation between heart disease (with depression) and certain specific traits of the Type A personality such as high levels of anger, hostility, and aggression (Booth-Kewley & Friedman, 1987). More recent research has focused on the possibility that hostility is the pathogenic component of the Type A pattern. Research has confirmed the link between heart disease and hostile or negative beliefs and attitudes toward others, including cynicism, distrust, and denigration (Matthews, 1988; Miller, Smith, Turner, et al., 1996).

Numerous studies have demonstrated correlations between hostility and the severity of coronary heart disease; some have demonstrated a relationship between hostility, the development of coronary heart disease, and premature mortality (Miller, Smith, Turner, et al., 1996). Hostility is thought to contribute to the development of heart disease through frequent, intense episodes of physiological arousal. A number of laboratory studies support this notion: Individuals who score high on measures of hostility show larger-than-normal cardiovascular, lipid, and neuroendocrine responses to a wide variety of stressful situations, particularly those that involve interpersonal challenges (Davis, Matthews, & McGrath, 2000; Suarez & Harralson, 1999).

Cardiovascular reactivity has also been implicated in the expression of coronary heart disease. For example, in one study, individuals suffering from stress-induced myocardial ischemia were found to be more than twice as likely as others to experience a cardiac event, including death, bypass surgery, and angioplasty, over the next 2 years (Jiang, Babyak, Krantz, et al., 1996). In another study, subjects wore an ambulatory ECG monitor and kept diaries for 48 hours, noting feelings of happiness, sadness, tension, and frustration. After adjustment for physical activity and time of day—factors known to affect myocardial functioning—investigators showed that emotional distress in the form of tension, frustration, or sadness increased the risk of transient myocardial ischemia by a factor of 2 (Guilette, Blumenthal, Babyak, et al., 1997). Finally, individuals who report large fluctuations in tension have more cardiovascular reactivity (Carels, Blumenthal, & Sherwood, 2000) and more cardiac ischemia during laboratory and real-life stress (Carels, Sherwood, Babyak, et al., 1999).

Anger has been shown to be particularly stressful for patients with cardiovascular disease. In one study, patients were asked to recall an event that had recently evoked their anger. Recalling the event reduced the functioning of their hearts more than did exercising, giving a brief speech, or performing mental arithmetic (Ironson, Taylor, Boltwood, et al., 1992). In a more recent study of survivors of myocardial infarction, investigators found that episodes of intense anger can actually trigger a heart attack (Mittleman, Maclure, Sherwood, et al., 1995).

Hypertension

Of all the physical disorders commonly associated with psychological stress, chronically high blood pressure, known as **hypertension**, is the most common and the most dangerous. An estimated 15 percent of the population of the United States suffers from this cardiovascular disorder, which in turn predisposes them to other deadly cardiovascular disorders, heart attack and stroke (MacMahon, Peto, Cutter, et al., 1990). Untreated hypertensives have an average life expectancy of between 50 and 60 years, compared with 71 years for the population at large.

We saw earlier how hypertension illustrates the principle of disregulation (Schwartz, 1977): Breakdown in one component leads to breakdown in the system as a whole. The function of the cardiovascular system, consisting of the heart and the peripheral blood vessels, is to pump blood through the body, carrying nutrients where they are needed and carrying wastes where they can be disposed of. Every heartbeat represents a contraction of the heart; with each contraction, blood is pushed out of the heart and through the blood vessels. At the same time, the blood vessels are contracting and dilating in response to internal and external stimuli. The blood pressure—that is, the pressure that blood exerts on the walls of the blood vessels—is a function of several variables, but one of the most important, at least in hypertension, seems to be the degree of constriction in the blood vessels (Forsyth, 1974). When a normal person's blood pressure rises too high, the baroreceptors convey this information to the brain; in response to this negative feedback, the brain then relaxes the constricted vessel walls. In hypertensives, however, the regulatory mechanism fails to work, with the result that the blood vessels remain chronically constricted and, hence, the blood pressure chronically high.

Why does this happen? In a small percentage of cases, 10 to 15 percent, hypertension is linked to an identifiable organic cause, usually kidney dysfunction (Shapiro & Goldstein, 1982). In the remaining cases, known as **essential hypertension,** there is no known organic cause. Many different factors have been suggested.

One factor in the development of essential hypertension is environment. It may be that some essential hypertensives live in environments that are particularly rich in the kinds of stressors that increase blood pressure. For example, more modern and economically advantaged cultures have individuals with higher blood pressure (Dressler, 1999). Long-term exposure to stressful occupations has been linked to hypertension, while long-term exposure to low-stress environments has been associated with an absence of the age-associated increase in blood pressure typically observed in Western societies. For instance, air traffic controllers working in high-volume control centers were found to have significantly higher rates of hypertension than members of a control group who performed other jobs in the same work environment (Cobb & Rose, 1973). Those working overtime also have higher blood pressure (Epstein, 1977). And, over the course of 20 years, Italian nuns living in a cloistered community did not show the expected age-related increase in blood pressure that was found in a control group of women (Timio, Verdecchia, Venanzi, et al., 1988).

In light of these findings, it is interesting to note that essential hypertension is twice as common among African Americans as it is among European Americans. While this disparity may be a function of genes, diet, or other factors, one might also hypothesize that African Americans as a group are exposed to greater stress than European Americans (Anderson, 1989; Jackson, Treiber, Turner, et al., 1999). A study

Even for young people, the stress of living in a dangerous, drug-ridden neighborhood such as New York City's South Bronx raises the risk for developing essential hypertension.

of African Americans in Detroit found that those living in high-stress areas—neighborhoods with lower income, higher unemployment, higher divorce rate, higher crime rate—had higher blood pressure than those living in low-stress areas (Harburg, 1978).

Essential hypertension may also be due in part to individual response specificity. In other words, genes or experience may have programmed the brain to respond to different kinds of stress with increases in blood pressure. Recent research has focused on subjects assumed to be at risk for hypertension, including people with at least one hypertensive parent and people who had mildly elevated blood pressure in childhood or early adulthood. When confronted with demanding behavioral and cognitive tasks, such people do experience greater cardiovascular reactions than people without a family history of hypertension (Fredrikson & Matthews, 1990). Moreover, healthy individuals with a family history of hypertension and large physiological responses to stress have higher blood pressure later in life (Light, Girdler, Sherwood, et al., 1999). Research suggests that elevated blood pressure and hypertension may be related to the way in which individuals express affect, particularly its inhibition, as well as to defensiveness and high levels of negative affect, such as anger (Gross & Levenson, 1997). Defensiveness appears to be the strongest predictor of blood pressure (Jorgensen, Johnson, Kolodziej, et al., 1996).

Because high blood pressure produces no symptoms until late stages of the disease, many hypertensives are unaware of their condition, with the result that it may go untreated for years. Furthermore, those who are aware that they have hypertension are often unaware that circumstances in their family lives or work environments may be aggravating it. Like the baroreceptors mentioned earlier, they have adapted to the stress and no longer see it as stressful. Often, it takes a crisis—a situation in which blood pressure and environmental pressures simultaneously increase dramatically—before such patients will take seriously the connection between their blood pressure and their way of life and consider changing the latter. In many cases, family and work circumstances are not all that need changing. A number of behavioral factors—above all, smoking, obesity, and high salt intake—have been shown to aggravate hypertension. Obese people are three times more likely to be hypertensive than people who are not overweight (Van Italli, 1985). As for smoking, it apparently combines synergistically with hypertension to create a high risk of coronary heart disease (Kannel & Higgins, 1990).

Cancer

Cancer is one of the greatest challenges that the human body has ever posed to medical science. Cancer is the second leading cause of death in the United States, exceeded only by cardiovascular disease. As such, it accounts for almost one quarter of all deaths (American Cancer Society, 2003). According to the Centers for Disease Control (2003a), more than 17 million new cases of cancer have been diagnosed since 1990, with an expected diagnosis of roughly 1.3 million new cases in 2003. Although prior research had shown a bleak picture of ever-increasing cancer deaths, new data suggest that the incidence rate (the number of cases of cancer that are diagnosed) has stabilized and the mortality rate (the number of deaths from cancer) may actually be decreasing overall (Edwards, Howe, Ries, et al., 2002). However, even with these encouraging results, the mere fact that the risk of cancer increases with age and that more people are living longer appears to be shifting the balance of cancer rates. Based on the U.S. Census Bureau population projections for the next five decades, it is expected that the *number* of cancer patients will double from 1.3 million to 2.6 million persons between 2000 and 2050.

The term *cancer* really refers to a collection of related diseases in which abnormal body cells multiply and spread uncontrollably, forming a tissue mass known as a tumor. There are various classifications of cancer, the most common of which are the carcinomas, including breast, prostate, colon, lung, and skin cancers. Because of the variation in cancer sites and cancer types, developing an overall understanding of the role of psychological factors in cancer formation and cancer progression has been particularly challenging.

For a long time, it was believed that whatever physical disorders might be associated with stress, cancer was not one of them. Now, the role of psychological factors in this disease is at the center of an ongoing controversy. Early animal studies demonstrated the powerful effects of stress in the formation of cancerous tumors. In one study, Sklar and Anisman (1979) implanted tumor cells in rats and then divided the rats into three groups. One group received electric shocks that they could escape by pressing a bar. The second group received inescapable shocks, and the third group, no shocks. The experimenters found that the tumors grew more quickly in the rats given inescapable shocks than in either of the other groups. In a later study, with much the same design, the cancer cells were implanted in smaller doses, so that the animals' immune systems could conceivably combat them. The results were quite striking: The rats given the inescapable shocks were only half as likely to reject the cancer and were twice as likely to die of it as the escapable-shock and no-shock groups (Visintainer, Volpicelli, & Seligman, 1982). More recent research has supported the notion of increased tumor growth as a result of prolonged stress (Palermo-Neto, Massoco, & de Souza, 2003).

There is little doubt that cancer is affected by both genetic and environmental factors. Women are at a higher risk for breast cancer if there is a family history of the disease, and environmental factors such as tobacco use and sun exposure increase the risk of developing specific cancers. Research into the psychological aspects of developing cancer has focused on three main areas: (1) whether there is a cancer-prone personality type, (2) whether negative life events and stresses lead to cancer, and (3) whether psychological factors can have an impact on cancer development and progression.

Various researchers have argued that having a certain personality type may play a factor in both the development and subsequent progression of cancer. Generally, researchers have attempted to demonstrate this link by administering questionnaires to both patients with cancer and individuals without cancer, then looking for psychological variables that distinguish them. One of the most popular ideas is that someone who represses emotions is at greater risk. Indeed, Lydia Temoshok (Temoshok, Heller, Sagebiel, et al., 1985) conceived of a Type C, cancer-prone personality who "is cooperative, unassertive, patient, who suppresses negative emotions (particularly anger), and who accepts/complies with external authorities." She describes this personality type as "the polar opposite of the Type A behavior pattern which has been demonstrated to be predictive of coronary heart disease" (Temoshok, p. 141). Others have suggested that hopelessness in response to stress is predictive of cancer development (Grossarth-Maticek, Eysenck, Pfeifer, et al., 1997). However, a recent review of this area (Dalton, Boesen, Ross, et al., 2002) reported inconsistencies in the results of such investigations, perhaps due to the intrinsic difficulty in viewing cancer as one thing. Future research will undoubtedly be aimed at delineating the potential associations between personality and the various forms of cancer.

Perhaps it is best that *who you are* doesn't impact your risk of cancer; personality traits can be difficult to change. But how does *what happens to you* influence the development of cancer? Researchers have attempted to address this issue by examining the relationship of life events, particularly negative life events such as the loss of a spouse, to cancer development. The general concept is that such events are likely to suppress healthy immune functioning, which, in turn, may increase the risk of cancer. A few studies have supported this notion, showing that women with severe life events and difficulties are at greater risk for recurrence of breast cancer after remission (Ramirez, Craig, Watson, et al., 1989) and are more likely to be diagnosed with breast cancer following biopsy of breast tissue (Chen, David, Nunnerley, et al., 1995). Once again, however, recent research has failed to demonstrate such relationships (Protheroe, Turvey, Horgan, et al., 1999). Some believe this is a positive finding for cancer patients; as one commentator put it: "Recriminations over real or imagined life stress may be counterproductive for individuals with cancer and their families" (McGee, 1999).

In 1989, one of the most influential papers on the psychological aspects of cancer was published in the journal *Lancet* (Spiegel, Bloom, Kraemer, et al., 1989), In this study, patients with breast cancer that had spread to other parts of the body were randomly assigned to one of two groups. One group received supportive-expressive group therapy in addition to standard medical treatment, while a control group of cancer patients received no such intervention. Ten years later, the results were clear: Those patients involved in group therapy lived an average of 18 months longer than patients in the no-intervention group. Breast cancer is the most frequently diagnosed form of cancer in women and remains the second most deadly form of cancer among women after lung/bronchial cancer, with an estimated 40,200 deaths from breast cancer expected in 2003 alone (American Cancer Society, 2003). Breast cancer brings with it not only the physical reality, but also the psychological impact of diagnosis. Not surprisingly, women in the early stages of breast cancer have strong fears about being sick, the risks of treatment, not seeing their children grow up, and having their life cut short (Spencer, Lehman, Wynings, et al., 1999). Thus, Spiegel's findings generated great excitement: Finally there was evidence for psychological factors in cancer, and here was proof of mind-over-body. The therapy sessions addressed various matters. The women were taught by the group leaders how to control pain through self-hypnosis; they were also advised on how to communicate with their families and how to be assertive with their doctors. But the main function of the group was to give the women a chance to express their feelings and support one another. They discussed their family problems, their physical distress as a result of chemotherapy and radiation, and their fear of dying. Eventually, they developed strong bonds. They visited one another in the hospital, wrote poems together, and even, at one point, moved their meeting to the home of a dying member. As we saw, these women were found, on follow-up, to have survived twice as long as controls after the beginning of treatment. What kept them alive? The experimenters speculated that the advice and sympathy the subjects received may have influenced them to follow health regimens better—eat, exercise, take medication—and thus live longer. But in the experimenters' opinion a major factor was simply social support. It is a well-established fact that married cancer patients survive longer than unmarried cancer patients (Goodwin, Hunt, Key, et al., 1987; Kravdal, 2001), but even families, out of worry and grief, may be of limited psychological use to a dying member. The women in this study had each other, and apparently that helped them to fight breast cancer.

Soon after Spiegel's landmark study, other encouraging reports bolstered the notion of social support. In one such study, patients with malignant melanoma (a form of skin cancer) were assigned to either a control group that received medical treatment only or to a condition in which they received group therapy along with their medical treatment. The therapy group attended 6 sessions that focused on education, stress management, coping skills, and psychological support. Recontacted 5 to 6 years later, the groups showed widely different health records. Twice as many of the controls had had a recurrence of malignant melanoma, and 3 times as many of the controls had died (Fawzy, Fawzy, Hyun, et al., 1993). How such treatments exert their effect is still unknown. Taken as a group, Fawzy's patients demonstrated increases in certain immune cells at the 6-month mark following intervention but, on an individual basis, such changes did not seem to correlate with survival.

The findings from these studies was certainly encouraging, but before long, other studies muddied the waters. Research published in the *New England Journal of Medicine* (Goodwin, et al., 2001) found no intervention effect on survival time for women whose breast cancer had spread. The experimenters in this study used the same supportive-expressive group therapy as Spiegel's study, led by experienced therapists who had been trained in the technique (the original researcher, David Spiegel, even attended their training workshops). There was also a debate as to the importance of Spiegel's original results. A comparison of survival time for patients who received group therapy with survival time for cancer patients from the same geographical area (but not included in the original study) showed no significant difference (Fox, 1998). What it showed, however, was that patients in the control group survived significantly less time than cancer patients who were never involved in the study!

The issue remains unresolved: Currently, the findings seem to be evenly divided. Recently, David Spiegel noted that failures to replicate his original findings may partly be explained by evolving societal attitudes toward cancer (Spiegel, 2001). Cancer used to be one of those topics, like sex, that was rarely openly talked about. Today, cancer patients are far more likely to have candid discussions about the disease or to be a part of some support group. Thus, in more recent studies, control groups who did not receive specific interventions may nonetheless be receiving some form of ongoing support through their own actions. Thus, differences between the groups may not be quite so obvious.

Although no definitive conclusions can be drawn about the impact of social support on survival time, it certainly does not demonstrate any negative effects. In light of this, and because studies have more consistently shown psychological benefit (e.g., reductions in distress and pain) as a result of such interventions, it seems reasonable to continue to prescribe group therapy for cancer patients. Thus, although the question of quantity of life still remains to be resolved, it appears that quality of life can certainly be improved. As Spiegel (2001) states, "Curing cancer may not be a question of mind over matter, but mind does matter" (p. 1768).*

AIDS

Acquired immune deficiency syndrome, or **AIDS,** was first identified in 1981. It is caused by the **human immunodeficiency virus (HIV),** which is spread via the blood, semen, vaginal secretions, or breast milk of an infected person, either during unprotected sex, through a shared hypodermic needle, from a contaminated blood transfusion, or (in the case of a newborn whose mother is infected) in the womb. Once the virus becomes active, it attacks the immune system, leaving the person open to various infections, including Kaposi's sarcoma, a form of cancer that is rare in the general population. HIV can remain dormant for a long time before becoming active. Some people are said to have harbored HIV for 20 years before developing symptoms.

Between 800,000 and 900,000 Americans are estimated to be HIV-positive (Centers for Disease Control, 2003b), but this figure may be unrealistically low, for many people have not yet been tested. Indeed, the largest risk group, heterosexual men and women having unprotected sex with multiple partners, has a testing rate of only 35 percent (Berrios, Hearst, Coates, et al., 1993).

HIV progresses through four stages of infection. The first stage may involve minor symptoms, such as mild illness, sore throat, or fever, as the virus spreads throughout the body. After this, symptoms may disappear, though most people will suffer a weakening of their immune system, particularly CD4 cells (T cells), which serve as a major indicator of the progression of HIV. As CD4 cells continue to drop, people enter a third stage of HIV where they begin to experience opportunistic infections and may experience symptoms such as night sweats and weight loss. As CD4 cells drop to a level below 200 per cubic milliliter of blood, almost all natural immunity is lost, and the individual is diagnosed with AIDS.

As of December 2000, almost 775,000 Americans had been diagnosed with AIDS, including almost 9,000 children aged 12 or younger. By that same year, over 448,000 people in the United States had died from AIDS (Centers for Disease control, 2003b). Additionally, the greatest danger of AIDS lies outside the United States; 95 percent of all AIDS deaths have occurred in developing regions, such as Africa. The progression of AIDS is not the same for all people; both the time from HIV infection to AIDS and the time from diagnosis of AIDS to death vary considerably among individuals. A number of factors are believed to determine this differential rate, including genetics, age (older people progress to AIDS more quickly), and the particular strain of HIV virus. Of particular interest to health psychologists is the influence of behaviors, personality, stress, and social support on the progression of HIV.

Psychologists have slowly been uncovering certain individual differences that may predict AIDS progression. Among homosexual men with HIV, three studies to date have shown an association between the rate of HIV disease progression and whether these men conceal their homosexuality. In the latest study investigating this effect, Philip Ullrich (Ullrich, Lutgendorf, & Stapleton, 2003) asked 73 HIV-positive gay or bisexual men to rate themselves in relation to other gay men and indicate whether they were "definitely in the closet, in the closet most of the time, half in and out, out of the closet most of the time or completely out of the closet." As with prior research, concealment of their homosexual identity was associated with lower CD4 cell counts, one of the primary biological markers of HIV progression. Research with HIV-positive women has shown that more frequent use of emotional inhibition words during interviews, such as "restrain," "avoid," "suppress," is associated with lower CD4 counts (Eisenberger, Kemeny, & Wyatt, 2003), which fits nicely with research demonstrating higher CD4 counts in women who use positive emotional expression in their written essays about life after HIV diagnosis (O'Cleirigh, Ironson, Antoni, et al., 2003).

There is a well-documented pattern of sleep-pattern disturbances in individuals with HIV and AIDS, which may be one of the important mechanisms through which psychological distress compromises the immune system (Cruess, Douglas, Petitto, et al., 2003). Researchers have shown that simple behavioral programs to reduce caffeine consumption can have dramatic positive effects on sleep for people with HIV, with associated improvements in patients' ratings of well-being and even in their health (Dreher, 2003).

*A branch of the National Cancer Institute is currently spearheading a scientific initiative known as the Biological Mechanisms of Psychosocial Effects on Disease (BiMPED). The objective of BiMPED is to evaluate current knowledge in psychoneuroimmunology and related fields and investigate the applicability of the research findings to the control of cancer.

Early treatment for HIV began in 1987 with the introduction of an antiretroviral agent known as AZT. More recent combination therapies have proved increasingly effective in delaying AIDS and death, particularly the newer reverse transcriptase inhibitors referred to as highly active antiretroviral therapy (HAART). However, increased confidence in the availability of such AIDS treatments may have negatively influenced risk behaviors associated with HIV transmission, such as unprotected anal sex. Some HIV-positive individuals appear to be more willing to engage in risky sexual behaviors because they now perceive HIV to be a less serious health threat (Vanable, Ostrow, & McKirnan, 2003).

Psychologists have tried to identify effective techniques for discouraging high-risk behaviors associated with HIV infection; and for those already infected, research has focused on what factors might predict whether people stick to prescribed treatment programs such as HAART. In relation to the first line of attack, a number of cognitive-behavioral skills-training programs have been designed to discourage unsafe sex. Typically, these programs include several components: instructions about safe and unsafe sex, assertiveness training (to enable people to say no to unsafe sex), problem-solving training (to teach people to anticipate and avoid risk factors such as alcohol or drug use), and reinforcement of behavior change. Such programs, so far aimed primarily at homosexual men (Kelly & Murphy, 1992) and sexually active teenagers (Rotheram-Borus, Koopman, & Haignere, 1991), have reported good results.

It should come as no surprise that the stress associated with HIV is higher for those with lower income and poor relationships and that the level of stress increases as HIV progresses (Riley & Fava, 2003). What is perhaps surprising is that at the highest level of stress, found once HIV has progressed to AIDS, individuals infrequently use stress-management techniques to deal with their stress. However, within the context of HIV, adopting such practices may be particularly challenging. In view of the evidence that psychological stress affects the immune system, we might assume that stress would speed the course of AIDS, a disease centered in the immune system. The findings are contradictory, however. Some studies have found no relationship between stress and the progress of HIV infection (Kessler, Foster, Joseph, et al., 1991; Rabkin, Williams, Remien, et al., 1991), while others have shown severe life stress to be a predictor of early disease development, increasing the odds of HIV progression fourfold (Evans, Leserman, Perkins, et al., 1997). In HIV-positive men with a negative attitude about their health, exposure to an AIDS-related death was associated with increased risk of HIV-related symptoms such as night sweats and chronic diarrhea (Reed, Kemeny, Taylor, & Visscher, 1999), and in men diagnosed with AIDS the same factors were associated with shorter survival (Reed, Kemeny, Taylor, et al., 1994). Additional research has shown more vigorous immune responses in HIV-positive men with more active coping styles (Goodkin, Blaney, Feasler, et al., 1992). One possible explanation for inconsistent findings in the relationship between stress and HIV progression may be the wide variability of stress measures administered and the fact that the sort of stressors faced by people with HIV, such as social

The Aliveness Project in Minneapolis helps AIDS patients reduce stress, in an effort to relieve some of their symptoms.

isolation, multiple bereavements, and rejection, are rarely addressed in generic stress scales. A recently designed scale, tailored to the demands faced by HIV-positive individuals, may prove invaluable in generating more uniform results (Pakenham & Rinaldis, 2002).

In addition to refinements in research methodology, investigators are turning to animal models to examine cause-and-effect relationships between stress and HIV. Research with humans relies on looking for associations between naturally occurring levels of stress and subsequent HIV progression. With animal models, researchers are able to infect rhesus macaques with the simian immunodeficiency virus (SIV—a "monkey version" of HIV) and then stress the monkeys with housing relocations and social isolation. Such social stressors have been shown to result in decreased survival (Capitano & Lerche, 1998). Such research strengthens the notion of psychological factors in HIV/AIDS progression and validates the ongoing search for viable psychological interventions. Some results are particularly encouraging; for example, one recent study demonstrated enhanced immune function of HIV-positive men after a stress-management intervention (Antoni, Cruess, Klimas, et al., 2002).

Headache

Stress has long been implicated in chronic headaches, including the very severe form known as **migraine headache.** Migraines differ from ordinary headaches—often called **muscle-contraction headaches,** or tension headaches—in that they are usually localized on one side of the head and are far more intense. A migraine attack further differs from a tension headache in that it is sometimes preceded by an aura, or spell of perceptual distortion, often involving strange visual sensations such as flashing lights or blind spots. Finally, in migraine, unlike tension headaches, head pain is typically accompanied by other symptoms: physical (nausea, vomiting), cognitive (confusion), and affective (depression, irritability). Intolerance to light and sound are also common. Migraine attacks range from bearable discomfort to complete immobilization. They may last from several hours to several days and may occur as frequently as every day or as infrequently as once every few months.

In recent years, theories of migraine have shown a dramatic shift from psychological to biogenic causation. For the past half century, migraine was thought to be the product of a stress-induced cardiovascular process involving the constriction and dilation of the blood vessels in the head (Wolff, 1948). As for the psychological causes behind this cardiovascular quirk, there were various theories, ranging from descriptions of a "migraine personality" to speculations about female emotional instability. (Migraine is twice as common in women as in men.)

Recently, however, these theories have been essentially scrapped, together with the idea that migraine is a cardiovascular disorder. According to newer findings (Raskin, Hosobuchi, & Lamb, 1987), migraine is a neurological disorder involving a dysfunction in the operation of the neurotransmitter serotonin. A number of signs pointed researchers in this direction. For one thing, the most effective drugs for migraine are all connected to serotonin, whereas they are not directly connected to blood-vessel function. Furthermore, serotonin and its chemical counterpart, norepinephrine, are both linked to depression and sleep disturbances, which in turn are linked to migraine and are commonly seen in families with a susceptibility to migraine. The connection between migraine and serotonin was also signaled by a curious accidental experiment. Fifteen people with no history of migraine, but with intractable back pain, were given electrode implants in their brains as a treatment for their back problems. All of them developed severe migraine. According to Raskin and colleagues (1987), the site of the electrode implantation was near the region of the brain where serotonin is most active.

No one knows as yet the precise nature of the presumed serotonin dysfunction. Perhaps, in migraine sufferers, the body simply produces too little serotonin. Or perhaps the available serotonin is destroyed too quickly by enzymes as it crosses the synapses between the nerve cells. Another possibility is that the receptors responsible for taking up serotonin are not accepting enough of it. In any case, the serotonin hypothesis has unleashed a great flurry of research, and more refined hypotheses are expected shortly.

If effective drugs are developed, they will be welcome, for migraine is a common disorder, afflicting approximately 18 million people in the United States alone. The fact that two thirds of these people are women—and that their attacks tend to appear in adolescence and disappear after menopause—suggests that hormonal changes associated with the menstrual cycle are also involved in migraine. And underlying all these organic factors is presumably some measure of genetic causation, for as many as 90 percent of migraine sufferers have a family history of the disorder.

None of this means that stress is not involved in migraine. Many different stimuli—bright lights, red wine, changes in atmospheric pressure—can precipitate a migraine, but one of the most common triggers is minor stress (Brantley & Jones, 1993; Hadson,

Thompson, and al-Azzawi, 2000). In one study, it was found that the best predictor of migraines was stress one to three days prior to the headache. For muscle-contraction headaches, the best predictor was stress on the same day (Mosley, Penizen, Johnson, et al., 1991). What the serotonin research suggests is simply that migraine is one of many physical disorders involving both organic and environmental causes.

Obesity

Eating behavior, like most other bodily functions, is regulated by feedback loops. In highly simplified terms, the sequence is as follows. When the body is in need of nourishment, it sends hunger signals to the brain. Then, as we eat, other internal signals alert the brain that the body is satiated, at which point we put down our forks. This is the normal regulatory cycle. It, too, can succumb to disregulation, however. The feedback may fail to reach the brain, or the brain may receive the feedback but still respond inappropriately. In either case, the cycle is thrown off, and the person either fails to eat when the stomach signals hunger or goes on eating when the stomach signals satiety.

The first of these two patterns of disregulation—chronic failure to eat, to the point of extreme malnutrition—is known as anorexia nervosa. Because it normally begins in adolescence, we will discuss it under childhood and adolescent disorders (Chapter 16). We turn our attention now to the second and far more familiar pattern, obesity.

Obesity is a socially defined condition. Strictly speaking, the term refers to an excessive amount of fat on the body, but every culture has its own idea of what is excessive. What would have been regarded as a healthy adult in the nineteenth century would now be called a fat person; conversely, to nineteenth-century eyes, the thinness of today's fashion models would seem grotesque. Our society, actually, is caught in a curious paradox. Perhaps in no other culture has thinness been so highly prized, and obesity so prevalent. Researchers estimate that 61 percent of adults and 13 percent of children and adolescents in the United States are overweight, and the rate of obesity in the last 20 years has doubled among adults. The prevalence of obesity increases with age and is highest among lower socioeconomic groups.

Obesity is not good for the body. It increases the likelihood of digestive disease, cardiovascular disease, adult-onset diabetes, and cancer (Brantley & Garrett, 1993; Bray, 1984). But does this make an "abnormal" condition? It certainly does not by the statistical-rarity criterion, as we have just seen.

The line that separates obesity from normal weight varies across cultures and centuries. More than a few of today's Americans wish they could have lived in seventeenth-century Europe, when Rubens' voluptuous nudes represented the ideal of female beauty. (Men have had their turn in other ages—in the early decades of the last century, for example, when a protruding abdomen was a sign of a man's success and prosperity.)

However, it might be defined as such according to the norm-violation criterion, the norm being thinness. Above all, the abnormality of obesity would be related to the personal-discomfort criterion. In many sectors of our society, obesity is viewed as "a state verging on crime" (Rodin, 1977). As a result, the obese suffer not only the consequences of their socially defined unattractiveness—ranging from a mild sense of inferiority to extreme social and sexual maladjustment—but shame and discrimination as well (Puhl & Brownell, 2001). This is personal discomfort, indeed, and it pushes many people into therapy.

What causes obesity? In part, the reasons are directly physiological. Excess weight is not necessarily due to excessive eating. Many obese people eat moderately and still remain fat, while many thin people can "eat anything" and still stay thin—an injustice of which overweight people often complain. Factors that influence body weight include genetic differences, such as the resting metabolic rate and number of fat cells, and behavioral differences, such as caloric intake, eating habits, and activity level (Brownell, 1999). And, while activity level can be altered by exercise programs, metabolic rate is in large measure genetically determined. Furthermore, once a person becomes overweight, the added pounds *further* lower the metabolic rate (meaning that once the weight is gained, fewer calories are needed to keep it on than were needed to put it on). To make matters worse, dieting also tends to lower the metabolic rate, with the result, ruefully noted by many dieters, that one can count calories religiously and still not lose weight (Rodin, 1981). In sum, certain bodies are apparently born to carry more fat than others.

However, obesity is due not to physiology alone but to an interaction of physiological and psychological factors. A recent study suggests that hormonal (cortisol) responses to stress may lead to greater "central fat," or fat deposits in the middle torso. This may be particularly important because central fat is a risk factor for disease (Epel, McEwen, Seeman, et al., 2000). A number of studies indicate that obese people are far more responsive than others to any food-relevant stimulus: the taste of food (Nisbett, 1968), the sight and smell of food (Rodin, 1981; Schachter, 1971), the clock indicating that it is mealtime (Schachter & Gross, 1968), and, presumably, television commercials and magazine advertisements. Other experiments suggest that overweight people may also have a problem with the transmission of feedback from the stomach to the brain. When normal people are asked how hungry they are, their answers correlate strongly with the frequency of their stomach contractions. When overweight people are put to the same test, the correlation is much weaker (Stunkard & Koch, 1964).

It is hard to say, however, whether the disregulation observed in these experiments was actually due to obesity. Most overweight people are dieters, and whatever disregulation they show may be the result not of excess weight but of dieting. Several experiments have found that obese people who are not dieters do not show overresponsiveness to food cues (Herman & Mack, 1975; Ruderman & Wilson, 1979). On the other hand, overresponsiveness and many of the other peculiarities said to characterize the eating behavior of the obese *are* found in people who are of normal weight but are chronic dieters (Klajner, Herman, Polivy, et al., 1981). There is now solid evidence that chronic dieting may lead to disregulation. People who, whether or not they are overweight, have been kept from their normal eating pattern are more likely to engage in binge eating (Wardle, 1980), are more likely to eat in response to stress (Cools, Schotte, & McNally, 1992; Heatherton, Herman, & Polivy, 1991), and are more likely to go on eating once they have violated the dietary restraint (Ruderman, 1986)—facts that will sound familiar to anyone who has been on a diet. This disregulation may eventually lead to the chronic pattern of binge eating known as bulimia (Polivy & Herman, 1985). Bulimia will be discussed, with anorexia, in Chapter 16.

Such findings, together with the physiological evidence previously described, have caused many weight-reduction programs to shift their emphasis from dieting to exercise. Exercise presumably does not interfere with the regulatory cycle that controls eating. On the other hand, it does burn up calories, suppress the appetite, and increase the metabolic rate, so, even when one is not exercising, calories are being burned faster. But exercise alone may not be enough. Recent research indicates that the most effective weight-reduction programs focus on several components—typically dietary changes, problem solving, and peer support as well as exercise—and extend over a long period, such as a year. As for the maintenance of weight loss, those who go on exercising are the most likely to keep the pounds off (Craighead & Agras, 1991).

In addition to advocating weight reduction for the obese, many experts feel that what our society needs is a broader definition of physical attractiveness, so that beauty is not confined to the thinnest end of the spectrum of human body types. Many moderately heavy people have nothing wrong with them, either physically or psychologically. On the other hand, it is possible that dieting has acquired an undeservedly bad name in recent years. "The 1990s are taking shape as an antidieting decade," weight expert Kelly Brownell has written (1993, p. 339). Popular magazines regularly publish articles critical of weight consciousness, and antidieting books are appearing. A statistic often cited in such writings is that 95 percent of all diets fail. That figure, however, is over 30 years old (Stunkard & McLaren-Hume, cited in Brownell, 1993) and was derived from people in university-based treatment programs—people who were heavier, showed more psychological disorders, and were more likely to be binge eaters than overweight people in general (Brownell, 1993). In fact, it is not at all clear how successful most diets are; research is badly needed on this question. In the meantime, it appears that the perils of dieting have been exaggerated. According to one review (French & Jeffrey, 1994), dieting is not usually associated with nutritional deficiencies, adverse physiological reactions, severe psychological reactions, or the development of eating disorders. Such problems can arise, but ordinarily they don't.

Sleep Disorders

Common sleep disorders include insomnia, circadian rhythm disorders, nightmares, night terrors, and sleepwalking. The last three tend to afflict children; therefore, they will be discussed under childhood disorders in Chapter 16.

Insomnia Although **insomnia,** the chronic inability to sleep, can be a symptom of other disorders, such as depression, for an extremely large number of people, sleeplessness is the sole complaint, one that causes severe physical and psychological distress. Insomnia is the most prevalent sleep disorder in the United States and in most industrialized countries; over a lifetime, up to 40 percent of the population experiences transient insomnia. Women are at higher risk than men, and older people are at considerably higher risk than younger people.

There are three broad patterns of insomnia. Some people take an extremely long time to fall asleep; others fall asleep easily but awaken repeatedly during the night; others fall asleep easily but wake up much too early in the morning (e.g., 3 or 4 A.M.) and are unable to fall asleep again. At some point in our lives, each of us has probably experienced one of these difficulties. The term *insomnia* is applied only if the problem persists and the person's daily functioning is clearly disturbed—by fatigue, irritability, inability to concentrate, and so forth—as a result.

Sleep disturbance is almost always a source of concern for the person experiencing it, and this concern leads to what is called anticipatory anxiety. The minute the person gets into bed, or even while undressing, he or she begins to worry: Will I be able to sleep? Will it be like last night? And, since worry of any kind impedes sleep, the person probably *will* have another night like last night. Hence, insomnia is a classic example of the vicious cycle.

Dreaming and Rapid Eye Movement (REM): Does Dreaming Help Us Sleep?

The MindMAP video "REM Sleep" examines dreams and how dreaming may help us maintain good sleep. What other functions do you think dreaming has for us? Why? Do you think dreaming is always useful or helpful? Why or why not?

Insomnia can stem from many factors, including drugs, alcohol, caffeine, nicotine, stress and anxiety, physical illness, psychological disturbance, inactivity, poor sleep environment, and poor sleep habits (Bootzin & Perlis, 1992). It may also be a subjective matter in part. Many insomniacs underestimate the amount of sleep they get, at least as measured by instruments such as EEGs. When the gap between reported and measured sleep is extreme, this condition is called sleep-state misperception. Some cases of sleep-state misperception seem to be due to an inability to distinguish between sleep states and going-to-sleep states. People who go on thinking, during sleep, about problems that were on their minds during the day are likely to believe that they weren't sleeping but were still in that twilight stage between waking and sleep (Engle-Friedman, Baker, & Bootzin, 1985). Actually, what insomnia experts call sleep, based on EEG brain-wave patterns, is simply an operational definition. People who are "asleep" by EEG criteria often, if you wake them up, say that they are awake. Still, this happens far more often with insomniacs than with good sleepers (Borkovec, Lane & VanOot, 1981). And by measures other than the EEG, some of these insomniacs *are* awake. In one experiment, a group of insomniacs "slept" (by EEG criteria) while, every four or five minutes, a voice on a tape, speaking at normal volume, said a letter of the alphabet. If awakened and asked to repeat the last letter spoken, some of the subjects were able to give the right answer (Engle-Friedman, Baker, & Bootzin, 1985). Such evidence suggests that, at least for some insomniacs, the critical problem may be hypervigilance; that is, they are less able than the rest of us to turn off the sounds of the night while asleep.

Until recently, the most widely used hypnotics, or sleeping pills—Dalmane (flurazepam), Halcion (triazolam), and Restoril (temazepam)—were benzodiazepines, which cause numerous problems: daytime sedation, memory loss, a synergistic effect with alcohol, and a high rebound rate upon withdrawal (Maxmen & Ward, 1995). All the benzodiazepine hypnotics have the disadvantage of altering the "architecture" of sleep—our passage through the various stages of sleep in the course of the night. In particular, they all suppress REM sleep, with the result, in some cases, that the patient experiences REM rebound—restless sleep, nightmares—when he or she tries to go to bed without taking the drug. And, in most cases, withdrawal from the drug means a return to insomnia (Maxmen & Ward, 1995).

Because of these drawbacks, and because benzodiazepines are often diverted onto the illegal drug market, efforts have been made to stem their use. Some drugs have been removed from the market.

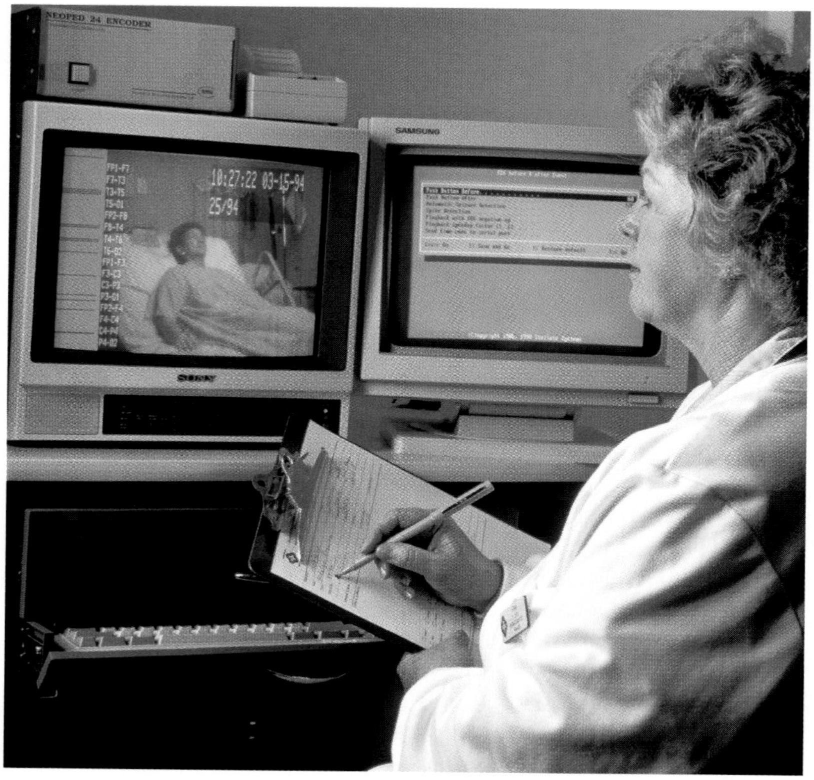

Sleep researchers use brain-wave patterns produced by an EEG from participants in a sleep laboratory to determine when an individual is asleep. Sometimes participants who are awakened when their EEG indicates they were asleep will say they were awake. Insomniacs might be hypervigilant sleepers, while good sleepers may be better able to tune out environmental stimuli.

(Halcion's side effects and rebound potential have caused it to be banned in Britain.) In other cases, laws have been changed to make these drugs harder to prescribe. But while the number of benzodiazepine prescriptions has diminished, the number of prescriptions for barbiturates, which are generally more dangerous, has increased (Shader, Greenblatt, & Balter, 1991). Apparently, when people cannot sleep, they turn to drugs, though behavioral therapy has proven to be more effective than medication for severe insomnia.

An encouraging recent development has been the introduction of Ambien (zolpidem), a hypnotic that is not a benzodiazepine. Ambien is short-acting and is absorbed very quickly. Therefore, it is useful primarily for sleep-onset disorders. Most crucial, however, is the fact that it has far fewer side effects than the benzodiazepines. It does not have a synergistic effect with alcohol; it does not alter the architecture of sleep; it does not produce rebound or severe withdrawal. As a result, it is now very popular. In 1994, less than a year after its approval by the FDA, Ambien became the most frequently prescribed hypnotic in the United States.

Most sleep-inducing drugs are ineffective when used over a long period, and many of them have undesirable side effects. Hence, there is a great need for treatments that can compete with drugs. A number of psychological treatments for insomnia have been tested and compared (Bootzin & Perils, 1992; Lacks & Morin, 1992; Murtagh & Greenwood, 1995). Behavioral therapy includes relaxation and biofeedback strategies to alleviate stress and physiological arousal and to reduce anticipatory anxiety. Cognitive-behavioral treatments include changing dysfunctional cognitions and expectations about sleep; changing sleep habits (such as maintaining a regular bedtime); and altering the environment to enhance healthy sleeping patterns. All of these strategies are generally effective and can improve both the quality and the amount of sleep achieved.

Circadian Rhythm Disorders **Circadian rhythm disorders** occur when people try to sleep at times that are inconsistent with circadian rhythms, the cycles dictated by their "biological clocks." Sometimes the disorder is due to work shifts. We noted earlier that many late-shift workers try, on their days off, to wake up at the same time as their friends and families, thus derailing their sleep cycles. Other workers' cycles are disturbed by rotating shifts. In both cases, the result is often reduced sleep, drowsiness on the job, and health problems (Knutsson & Boggild, 2000). But circadian rhythm disorders are not limited to shift workers. Many people, for no external reason, fall asleep earlier or later than seems to them normal or desirable. They get a good night's sleep, but not when they want to. Age is often a factor in this pattern. Many young people lie awake at 2 A.M., while old people fall asleep after dinner and then wake up at 3 A.M. Such problems, which can be very distressing, are sometimes treated by chronotherapy, which involves moving bedtime later and later in regular increments. For example, a night person who regularly goes to sleep at 3 A.M. is told to put off going to sleep until 6 A.M., then the next day until 9 A.M., and so on, until, by moving bedtime around the clock, he or she reaches the desired bedtime. Once the target bedtime is reached, however, it must be adhered to strictly, for there is a tendency to drift back to the former pattern (Czeisler, Richardson, Coleman, et al., 1981). Another therapy that appears promising for circadian rhythm disorders is light treatment. To move bedtime earlier, the person is exposed to bright light in the morning; to move bedtime later, lights are used in the evening. This treatment is still new, but it has been shown to help shift workers, jet-lag sufferers, night people, and elderly people suffering from early-morning waking (Bootzin, Manber, Perlis, et al., 1993; Czeisler, Kronauer, Allen, et al., 1989).

❖ Groups at Risk

Gender Although, in the United States, coronary heart disease is the leading cause of death for both men and women, the risk is higher for men than for similarly aged women. In fact, coronary heart disease is delayed about 10 years in women, relative to men. In animal studies, the male primates that were fed an atherogenic diet (a diet high in saturated fat and cholesterol) developed coronary heart disease in greater numbers than did the females on the same diet (Kaplan, Adams, Clarkson, et al., 1984). Although the rates of coronary heart disease vary widely throughout Westernized countries, every industrialized nation in the world reports a gender difference in the incidence of the disease. Two primary hypotheses have been proposed to explain these differences (Matthews, 1989). One is that reproductive hormones, particularly estrogen, exert a protective effect on lipids, blood pressure, and other biological risk factors in females. There is moderate support for this hypothesis. Women whose ovaries have been surgically removed generally show higher rates of coronary heart disease, compared with those of control groups. Postmenopausal women also show higher rates of coronary heart disease than premenopausal women. Stoney and colleagues confirmed the effect of hormones in a study of premenopausal women scheduled for hysterectomies (Stoney, Owens, Guzick, et al., 1997). The women were tested in a stress protocol prior to surgery. They agreed to be tested again 3 months after surgery and agreed (in consultation with their physicians) to forgo hormone replacement therapy prior to being retested. During surgery, some of the women had their ovaries removed and thus became immediately postmenopausal. The other women underwent hysterectomies only; their ovaries remained intact. Prior to surgery, both groups of women had the same physiological stress responses. However, after surgery, the women whose ovaries had been removed—who no longer had circulating levels of estrogen—had larger physiological stress responses than did the women whose ovaries had not been removed.

The second hypothesis is that men more frequently engage in potentially health-damaging behaviors, including smoking and drinking alcohol. But epidemiological studies suggest that the differential rates of coronary heart disease among men and women are not attributable to the effects of these behavioral risk factors. Matthews (1989) has proposed a more complicated, interactive model in which men and women differ in their experience of stressors (in their number, frequency, and type), as well as in their cardiovascular, neuroendocrine, and metabolic responses to stressors. Over time, the complex interplay of these differences produces different rates and, perhaps, different patterns of coronary heart disease in the two genders. There is some support for this model. In laboratory studies of married couples solving problems, the women's cardiovascular responses were found to be associated with their husbands' expressions of hostility rather than with their own hostility, while the men's cardiovascular responsivity was more associated with their own hostility (Smith & Brown, 1991). Researchers have shown that men generally have larger magnitude cardiovascular and neuroendocrine stress responses than do women (Stoney, Davis, & Matthews, 1987; McCubbin, Helfer, Switzer, et al., 2002), even when they report experiencing the same amount of stress. McCubbin and colleagues (2002) found that postmenopausal women with cardiovascular risk factors (such as a positive family history of coronary heart disease or elevated blood pressure at rest) have larger physiological stress responses than men with the same risk factors, but that these responses are reduced with hormone replacement therapy.

Ethnicity As a group, African Americans experience higher infant mortality rates, a shorter life expectancy, and higher rates of death from homicide, cancer, stroke, diabetes, and liver disease than do European Americans. Blacks have higher rates of hypertension than whites and, consequently, higher rates of morbidity and mortality from coronary heart disease, stroke, and renal disease. Finally, African Americans have higher rates of obesity than European Americans (Kumanyika, 1987), as well as higher blood pressure—a difference that applies to both men and women.

Ethnicity influences socioeconomic status in the United States: African Americans have significantly lower socioeconomic status than European Americans on all measures (Anderson & Armstead, 1995). As is noted in the following section, socioeconomic status is an important predictor of health. At almost all levels, African Americans show higher mortality and morbidity rates than European Americans, a disparity that is particularly striking at the low end of the socioeconomic scale (Anderson & Armstead, 1995).

Perceptions of stress vary somewhat across cultures, and events that are considered stressful to Americans may not have the same effect in other cultures, and vice versa. Unger and colleagues found that Chinese students are more susceptible to stress from school-related concerns, such as bad grades, than American students and that this stress is associated with increased smoking and alcohol use among Chinese adolescents (Unger, Li, Johnson, et al., 2001). Stoney and associates report different patterns of physiological stress responses among Asian Indian and European American men and women (Stoney, Hughes, Kuntz, et al.), while Bishop and Robinson (2000) describe similar differences between Chinese and Indian men.

Socioeconomic Status Socioeconomic status (SES)—education, income, and employment level—has long been identified as a factor in determining health. Individuals of low SES show poorer health and greater risk of early death than those of high SES. While health behaviors—smoking, diet, exercise, and obesity—differ according to SES, they do not fully account for the disparity between groups, nor do documented differences in access to and quality of medical care (Adler, Boyce, Chesney, et al., 1993). Some data suggest that the association between SES and health may be a function of the greater emotional impact of stressful life events on individuals of lower SES, compared with those of higher status (Anderson & Armstead, 1995; Ewart & Suchday, 2002). In particular, the chronic stress of living in poverty may induce chronic physiologic reactivity, ultimately leading to greater incidence of disease (Gump, Matthews, & Räikkönen, 1999).

The relationship between SES and coronary heart disease is independent of other traditional risk factors and appears to affect the development and progression of coronary heart disease (Pickering, 1999). Though coronary heart disease rates have been declining in recent years, epidemiological studies suggest that the declines may be specific to high socioeconomic groups. Low SES is associated with other risk factors for coronary heart disease, including smoking, obesity, elevated cholesterol levels, and hypertension. But those factors do not fully account for the consistently negative relationship observed between SES and coronary heart disease (Cooper, 2001). Recent data suggest that differences in the psychological aspects of the work environment, particularly low control over decision making and low skill requirements, may account for the inverse relationship between SES and coronary heart disease (Marmot, Bosma, Hemingway, et al., 1997). Another study suggests that SES may interact with personality and other variables to influence risk for cardiovascular disease (Grewen, Girdler, West, et al., 2000).

Finally, a few studies of survival and recovery from acute cardiac events suggest an association between SES and survival. For example, in one study, social class was inversely associated with functional improvement in the year following an acute myocardial infarction (Ickovics, Viscoli, & Horwitz, 1997). The effects of social class were found to be independent of the subjects' medical history, age, race, mental state, and life stress, as well as the severity of their heart attacks. Similar findings have been observed in patients who underwent cardiac diagnostic tests: Over a 5-year period, lower socioeconomic status was associated with increased risk for death from coronary heart disease (Williams, Barefoot, Califf, et al., 1992).

Stress and Illness: Theory and Therapy

The Behavioral Perspective: Learning and Unlearning Responses to Stress

Respondent Versus Operant Conditioning For years it was generally accepted that autonomic responses were involuntary. Therefore, if conditioning were involved in the disregulation of these responses, it would have to be respondent conditioning, for operant conditioning requires that the organism be capable of voluntarily modifying responses in order to obtain rewards or avoid punishments. We now know that respondent conditioning can have a powerful effect on physiological responses. A problem with cancer patients, for example, is that in response to chemotherapy they develop conditioned nausea and immune dysfunction. In a study of 20 women receiving chemotherapy for ovarian cancer, the women were tested first at home and then at the hospital. Even though the hospital tests were done before the chemotherapy, the women still showed an increase in nausea and a decrease in immune activity—clearly a conditioned response and one that does not aid in recovery (Bovjberg, Redd, Maier, et al., 1990).

Until about 30 years ago, such respondent behaviors were all that behaviorists could point to as an explanation for stress-related illness, and they were not a very comprehensive explanation. Then, in the 1960s, Neal Miller performed a series of breakthrough experiments with rats that showed heart rate, blood pressure, and urine formation could be modified through operant conditioning (Miller, 1969). One rat was even taught to dilate the blood vessels in one ear and, at the same time, constrict the blood vessels in the other ear in response to a cue (Di Cara & Miller, 1968). This latter finding generated great excitement, and others quickly tried to replicate the result. Unfortunately, no one—not even Miller himself—could show the same visceral response, and Miller finally conceded defeat (Dworkin & Miller, 1986).

In spite of some failures, Miller's basic discovery paved the way for future research and the application of conditioning principles to health and illness. His findings helped to explain how learning could operate in the development of physical disorders: If the disorder had any rewarding consequences, then these consequences might be maintaining the disorder through operant conditioning. What's more, whether or not voluntary control was involved in the development of the disorder, it could be enlisted to relieve the disorder.

Biofeedback, Relaxation, Meditation, and Exercise

Since these early experiments, scientists have learned that the physiological responses underlying many physical disorders can be partially controlled if patients are first trained to recognize these responses in their bodies—to know what it "feels like" when their heart rate or blood pressure, for example, goes up and down. Given this information, the patient can then make it go up and down. This training is known as **biofeedback training.** Migraine patients, for example, are hooked up to a machine that gives them feedback on temperature and blood flow in their hands. (Whatever the implications of the serotonin hypothesis, many migraine patients obtain relief when blood flows away from the head toward the periphery [Blanchard & Andrasik, 1985].) The patients, in other words, are given immediate feedback on their bodily functioning; and then, through a process we do not yet understand, they begin to exert control over this functioning—a control that it is hoped will extend beyond the biofeedback laboratory, into their daily lives. Indeed, biofeedback has proved quite helpful with headaches (McGrath, 1999), other pain conditions (Gentz, 2001; Edwards, Sudhakar, Scales, et al., 2000), and even insomnia (Morin, Jauri, Spielman, et al., 1999).

Another technique that behaviorists have used extensively in stress-relief programs is **relaxation training.** Perhaps the most popular of the several procedures for inducing deep muscle relaxation is *progressive relaxation,* developed by Edmund Jacobson (1938). In this technique, the client, going from muscle group to muscle group within the body, is instructed to contract the muscles, to hold them that way for about 10 seconds, and then to release them, thus achieving a state of relaxation. The object is to teach the person, first, how to distinguish between tension and relaxation and, second, how to achieve the latter. With practice in this technique, many people can relax their bodies as soon as they feel themselves going tense—a great aid in combating stress. Relaxation training has been used for years, successfully, in treating a wide variety of conditions—depression, anxiety disorders, insomnia—that involve stress. Researchers have found that it can also stimulate immune functioning (Reid, Drummond, & MacKinnon, 2001) and decrease cholesterol levels (Orth-Gomer, Eriksson, Moser, et al., 1994). Several researchers described the positive effect of transcendental meditation on stress responses, as well as on risk for disease (Schneider, Nidich, & Salerno, 2001; Castillo-Richmond, Schneider, Alexander, et al., 2000; Calderon, Schneider, Alexander, et al., 1999). Particularly among African Americans, transcendental meditation has been shown to reduce perceived stress levels, incidence of major cardiovascular disease risk factors, and even atherosclerosis.

Finally, exercise can relieve stress, as was shown in studies with men who were HIV-positive. LaPierre and colleagues found convincing evidence that exercise provides not only stress reduction benefits among HIV-positive individuals, but also enhances CD4 cell counts (LaPierre, Klimas, Fletcher, et al., 1997). Another study of both HIV-positive and HIV-negative individuals found that exercise decreases death rates due to AIDS, is associated with slower progression from infection to full-blown AIDS, and is associated with an increase in CD4 cell counts (Mustafa, Sy, Macera, et al., 1999).

Research has shown that exercise can reduce stress and bolster the immune system.

The Cognitive Perspective

Predictability and Control With stress, as with anxiety, the cognitive theorists have pointed out that there is more to the process than simply stimulus and response. Two cognitive variables that seem to be particularly important in stress reactions are the person's ability to predict the stressful stimulus and his or her sense of perceived control over the stimulus. As research has shown, predictable stimuli are less stressful than unpredictable stimuli. This principle was borne out during the London blitz of World War II. Londoners, who were bombed regularly and frequently, experienced very few serious stress reactions, whereas people in the countryside, who were bombed far less frequently but unpredictably, often responded with severe anxiety (Vernon, 1941).

Even more important than predictability, however, seems to be the sense of control. Remember the rats that were implanted with cancer cells. Remarkably, the rats that were able to control the shock were as likely to reject the cancer as those that received no shock (Visintainer, Volpicelli, & Seligman, 1982). This study's applicability to humans has been shown experimentally. The point is not just that by coping we can actually solve the problems that create stress; coping also affects our physiological responses to stress. Researchers have found that decreased catecholamine levels, which are associated with depression, were also associated with subjective judgments of inability to cope and that, as people's sense of their coping ability increased, so did their catecholamine level (Bandura, Taylor, & Williams, 1985). One example of perceived control is high self-efficacy, a person's own sense of competence to cope with a stressor. Several investigations have demonstrated that low self-efficacy is related to higher physiological stress responses (Hilmert, Christenfeld, & Kulik, 2002; Gerin, Litt, Deich, et al., 1995). Coping also affects the immune system. Poor coping suppresses immune responses, good coping enhances them (Kiecolt-Glaser, Fisher, Ogrocki, et al., 1987). Thus effective coping not only keeps people healthy but probably also helps them get better once they fall ill (Rodin & Salovey, 1989).

In all cases, however, according to cognitive researchers, coping is connected to cognitive processes and is determined by cognitive styles. This interaction is the focus of the model of stress developed by Richard Lazarus and his research group (Folkman, Lazarus, Dunkel-Schetter, et al., 1986; Lazarus & Folkman, 1984; Park, Folman, & Bostrum, 2001). The model describes stress not as something in the person or something in the environment but as a dynamic, mutually reciprocal, bidirectional relationship between the two, involving six basic factors. One is the environmental event itself. Another is the primary appraisal of that event, in which the person decides whether he or she has anything at stake in the event. The event may be irrelevant (the person has no stake in the event), benign-positive (a good stake), or stressful (a potentially bad stake). A third factor in Lazarus' model is secondary appraisal; having decided that there is something at stake, the person determines whether he or she can influence the situation. The fourth factor is coping, which may be either problem-focused (taking action to change the situation) or emotion-focused (e.g., seeking social support). Coping and appraisal are linked in a constant back-and-forth dynamic: The person appraises, copes, appraises the feedback, copes again, and so on. The fifth factor involves the outcomes of coping. These may be physiological (ANS arousal, immune system activation), behavioral (changes in high-risk behaviors), and cognitive (changed goals or beliefs). Finally, the sixth factor consists of health outcomes, such as illness or, if one copes effectively, prevention, illness reporting, and/or recovery. Conceptually, the value of this model is its interactive nature, but it also has a practical benefit: Because it is broken down into multiple factors, with multiple reappraisals, it offers second and third chances for improved coping.

Stress-Management Intervention Cognitive principles have been put into practice in so-called stress-management programs (Meichenbaum & Jaremko, 1983). The goal of such programs is to pinpoint the cognitive and environmental sources of the patient's stress and then to build up the skills that he or she needs in order to cope with those stressors. If the person complains of being pushed around by others, for example, assertiveness training can help him or her avoid being pushed around. Likewise, people who feel overwhelmed by demands on their time may be given help with time management. Most patients are also instructed in muscle relaxation, either through the contracting-and-relaxing technique or through meditation. The newer psychological treatments for people with serious illnesses often involve such training. Stress management was part of the Fawzy team's group therapy for malignant melanoma patients, for example (Fawzy, Fawzy, Hyun, et al., 1993). In the workplace, stress-management programs have been shown to reduce illness and doctors' visits (Rahe, Taylor, Tolles, et al., 2002).

Stress-management programs have been used with Type A personalities and people with high hostility, teaching them how to cope with anger and stress more effectively. In one such program, for example, a group of cardiac patients exhibiting high hostility were randomized into either a cognitive-behavioral hostility treatment program or an information-only control group. After 8 weeks of treatment, those in cognitive-behavioral therapy were less hostile and more likely to verbalize their anger constructively; blood pressure was also significantly reduced (Davidson, MacGregor, Stuhr, et al., 1999).

The addition of stress management and psychosocial intervention to routine cardiac rehabilitation programs has been shown to reduce patients' psychological distress (depression and anxiety) and to lower their heart rate, blood pressure, and cholesterol levels (Linden, Stossel, & Maurice, 1996). Over a 2-year period, cardiac patients who received psychosocial intervention along with routine cardiac rehabilitation showed a lower death rate and a 46 percent reduction in nonfatal cardiac events. This analysis of many studies suggests that such interventions are quite powerful, despite wide variability in length and type of treatment and in the person delivering it.

Cognitive-behavioral stress-management intervention has also been provided to gay men awaiting the results of their HIV tests (Antoni, Baggett, Ironson, et al., 1991). The program included relaxation training, cognitive restructuring, assertiveness training, and health education; a group of control subjects received no intervention. Psychological distress and immune functioning were assessed after 5 weeks of treatment, before notification of the test results, and again 2 weeks after notification. In the control group, the HIV-positive individuals showed twice the level of depression as the HIV-positive individuals in the stress-management program. Although the HIV-positive men in the control group showed no change in their immune function following notification, the HIV-positive men in the intervention program actually improved their immune function. The individuals who practiced relaxation more frequently showed the greatest improvement in their immune function.

The Psychodynamic Perspective

Psychological Inhibition Psychodynamic theorists, as we have seen, regard most behavior as symptomatic of buried emotional content. Thus, it comes as no surprise that the psychodynamic school was the first to recognize that psychological difficulties might contribute significantly to physical illness. Traditionally, psychodynamic theorists have referred to stress-related physical disorders as *organ neuroses.* As the term suggests, psychodynamic theory regards these disorders as caused by the same mechanisms—repression, anxiety, defense—that cause the anxiety, somatoform, and dissociative disorders. Accordingly, they would be treated by the same therapy: excavation of the repressed material, catharsis, the working out of better defenses. Where a serious physical illness is involved, however, a psychodynamic therapist would also insist on the patient's receiving medical treatment at the same time.

Psychodynamic theorists regard family interactions as central to stress-related physical disorders, as they are to all other psychological disorders. And they may be correct, for these disorders tend to run in families. Migraine and hypertension are more common in families of people with these disorders than in the population at large, though this might be a function of shared genes rather than, or as well as, shared emotional distress.

Inhibition of the expression of emotion has long been thought to contribute to the development of many "psychosomatic" diseases, including cancer and hypertension. Recent work has extended this concept to psychological inhibition, or the inhibition of emotional, social, and behavioral impulses. In a study of gay men, Steve Cole and colleagues (1996) found that, over a 5-year period, the men who did not reveal their homosexuality were at increased risk of developing infectious diseases and cancer. The rate of disease incidence increased in proportion to the degree to which the individuals concealed their homosexuality (Cole, Kemeny, Taylor, et al., 1996). These effects were found to be independent of other factors, including demographic variables, depression, other negative affect, and the tendency to inhibit emotions. In another study, the same group of investigators found that, in HIV-positive gay men who concealed their homosexuality, the infection progressed faster than in those who did not conceal their sexual orientation.

Prevention: The Role of Spirituality in Health and Well-Being

Until recently, medical science drew a sharp distinction between mental disease and physical disease. This distinction was an important way to maintain objectivity in medical research, and indeed the advancement of medical science has been remarkable during the modern period in which this view held sway. However, research (as well as common sense) now tells us that the mind and the body must be unified in some way. Time and again, simple observations show that the health of the mind affects the health of the body and that the health of the body affects the health of the mind. And today, just as the body and the mind have been increasingly united in medical treatment, there is also a growing recognition—as well as empirical evidence—that spirituality and religious beliefs play a role in health and illness.

Medicine and religion have a long history of linkage: Think of the shamans of the earliest civilizations, who treated illnesses with rituals and prayers to the gods. In fact, it is only in recent decades that the split between the physical and the spiritual has been made and that illnesses have been treated entirely by physicians, without reliance on spiritual leaders (although some religions do promote healing through prayer and faith alone). Today, however, with research indicating a relation between spirituality and health, almost half of medical schools in the United States offer courses on how to incorporate spirituality into medical practice.

Studies have shown how the connection between religious beliefs and wellness might be made, including the stress reduction that may occur with spirituality (Thoreson & Harris, 2001). Researchers found that people who score higher on measures of religiosity—counted as church attendance, spiritual beliefs, and religious activities such as prayer and scripture study—usually have less depression and anxiety, better coping abilities, and increased social support compared with people who are less religious (Steffen, Hinderliter, Blumenthal, et al., 2001). Evidence also exists to show a relationship between spirituality and health outcomes in people who are HIV-positive. Ironson and colleagues (2001) studied several religious factors—sense of peace, faith in God, religious behavior, and the feeling of compassion for others—and found that each factor is significantly related to longer survival in people living with AIDS compared with an HIV-positive control group. These factors are also strongly correlated with less distress, more hope, healthy behaviors, and lower cortisol levels. In addition, Ironson and colleagues found that longer survival is significantly related to the frequency of prayer (positively) and a judgmental attitude (negatively).

Other—controversial—research by Harris and colleagues describes an investigation of the effects of prayer on the health of cardiac patients (Harris, Gowda, Kolb, et al., 1999). In the experiment, a group of new patients in the coronary care unit (CCU) were randomized to receive remote, intercessory prayers (prayers from strangers on their behalf) or not. The patients' first names were given to a team of outside incessors who prayed for them daily for 4 weeks. Patients were unaware that they were being prayed for, and the intercessors did not know and never met the patients. The medical course from hospital admission to discharge was summarized in a CCU course score showing that the patients who had received intercessory

The Value of Catharsis A psychodynamic principle that has been confirmed by health psychology research is the value of emotional catharsis to physical health. Researchers have found that writing about personal experiences in an emotional way for as little as 15 or 20 minutes over the course of 3 days brings about improvements in mental and physical health (Pennebaker & Seagal, 1999; Smyth, Stone, Hurewitz, et al., 1999). In one early experiment, 50 undergraduates at Southern Methodist University were asked to keep journals for 20 minutes a day for 4 days. Half the students agreed to write about personal or traumatic events, and some of the entries they produced were quite painful: accounts of homesickness, family quarrels, family violence. The other half of the students were asked to write on trivial topics, which were assigned each day. (On one day, they were asked to describe the shoes they were wearing, on another, to tell about a party they had recently attended.) At the beginning of the experiment, there were no differences in immune function between the groups, but there were by the end. The immune cells of the traumatic-journal students were more active than those of the trivial-journal students, and these differences had an impact on health. Six weeks after the journal keeping, the experimenters checked the students' health center records for the period before and after the journal assignment. Compared with the trivial-journal students, the traumatic-journal students showed a significant drop in clinic visits after the experiment (Pennebaker, Kiecolt-Glaser, & Glaser, 1988).

These results have been supported by experiments with other groups of students (Pennebaker & Francis, 1996; Cameron & Nicholls, 1998) and with patients with asthma or rheumatoid arthritis, who showed improvement after keeping "stressful" journals (Smyth, Stone, Hurewitz, et al., 1999). For many people, expressing emotion is a healthy activity. According to James Pennebaker (1993), the originator of this research, what is most crucial is the expression of *negative* emotion. This was confirmed by the Fawzy prayer had lower CCU scores. The researchers concluded that prayer may be an effective adjunct to standard medical care.

Prayers for the sick have been a common response to the illness of loved ones since the beginning of time (Harris, Gowda, Kolb, et al., 1999). And, in fact, people who believe in God and who pray during illness have been reported to have better health outcomes than people who do not (Oxman, Freeman, & Manheimer, 1995; Koenig, George, Hays, et al., 1998). Some research shows that such things as positive beliefs, the comfort and strength gained from religion, and meditation and prayer can contribute to healing and a sense of well-being (Thoresen, 1999).

Although there is significant disagreement about the extent to which spirituality and religiousness should be incorporated into medical and psychological practice and about the mechanisms linking spirituality, religious beliefs, and prayer with health and illness, it is clear that these factors may strongly influence perceptions of stress. Improving one's spiritual health may not cure an illness, but it may help a person feel better, cope with illness or death, and prevent some health problems.

Research suggests that spirituality and religion can have a positive effect on health and well-being.

group's malignant melanoma study. In that experiment, the group-therapy patients who showed the best outcomes in terms of recurrence and survival were those who had expressed the most emotional distress before beginning the therapy (Fawzy, Fawzy, Hyun, et al., 1993).

The Interpersonal Perspective

Several theorists claim that a major source of physical illness is the stress imposed by modern industrial societies. One such stress is the disruption of marriage and the family. The number of single-person households in the United States has multiplied many times in the past century. And, according to an impressive array of findings, people living alone, if they have no regular social support, are depriving themselves of potent protection against illness. As we saw earlier, married cancer patients survive longer than the unmarried, and there is good evidence that social support also helps people combat many other illnesses, as well as injuries (Cohen, Doyle, Skoner, et al., 1997; House, Landis, & Umberson, 1988; Hamrick, Cohen, & Rodriguez, 2002). There is also strong evidence that people without social support are more prone to disease. Among the leading causes of premature death in our society are heart disease, cancer, stroke, cirrhosis of the liver, hypertension, and pneumonia. For each of these disorders, without exception, premature death rates are significantly higher in the unmarried than in the married. In the case of coronary heart disease, our society's major killer, the death rate, depending on age group, is 2 to 5 times higher among the unmarried (Lynch, 1977). While the lack of an intimate relationship may predispose people to disease, the *loss* of such a relationship may be an even greater health hazard. In a study of 400 cancer patients, 72 percent had suffered the loss of an important personal relationship within 8 years prior to the diagnosis of cancer, compared with 10 percent of a control group for a comparable period (LeShan, 1966).

Analyses of data collected in a 70-year longitudinal study concluded in 1991 confirmed that individuals who remain married live longer than those who experience divorce or separation—but not longer than those who never marry (Tucker, Friedman, Wingard, et al., 1996). The impact of a marital breakup was evident, despite the number of years the subjects had been married. The researchers concluded that marital breakup was a stressful event that had long-term health risks, risks not entirely reduced by remarriage. But the apparent protective effects of marriage may be due partially to selection factors, which account for the stability of a marriage. The subjects who exhibited low conscientiousness in childhood or who had witnessed their parents' divorce were less likely to remain married, and more likely to die sooner, than the others. Finally, simply being married may not be enough to help keep stress levels down. The quality of the marriage seems to count as well: Broadwell and Light (1999) queried married men and women about their perceived level of support in the family and tested them for cardiovascular stress responses. They found that the people with higher levels of perceived support showed smaller physiological stress response, as well as better marital relations, than those who described low levels of support. The effect was more prominent for husbands, less so for wives.

The Sociocultural Perspective

In addition to the breakup of the family, other broad changes in our society appear to be affecting the susceptibility of certain groups to particular illnesses. For example, ulcers were once 4 times as prevalent among men as among women. This ratio has now been reduced to about 2:1, presumably because more women are now doing the same work as men and therefore are exposed to the same stressors. As this change in the workplace continues, it is possible that the sex differential for ulcers will disappear altogether. Likewise, if the fact that African Americans are twice as likely as European Americans to develop hypertension is due to the stresses of being a disadvantaged minority rather than to genes (or to a salt-heavy diet, another possibility), this ratio, too, may be equalized as opportunities are equalized.

The Neuroscience Perspective

Genetic Predisposition As we have seen, stress-related physical disorders tend to run in families—a fact that suggests genetic risk. This is true of migraine and hypertension. As we saw earlier, people with at least one hypertensive parent show greater cardiovascular reactions to stress than do people without a family history of hypertension. This evidence is supported by twin studies, which have found exaggerated reactivity to be more commonly shared between MZ twins than between DZ twins or siblings (Rose & Chesney, 1986). Because we know from longitudinal studies that people with heightened cardiovascular reactivity are at risk for hypertension (Light, Girdler, Sherwood, et al., 1999), early identification and treatment of stress-reactive people should help to prevent this disorder. The cardiovascular reactivity hypothesis may also help in early intervention. Type A personalities tend to breed Type As (Plomin & Rende, 1991), so it is possible to identify and help them before they develop the heart problems to which some of them are clearly predisposed.

PNI and Interactive Theories Apart from genetic risk, the major concern of recent biological research has been a matter that we have already discussed at length in this chapter: the immune system. The PNI findings, combined with interactive models such as those of Schwartz, Weiner, and Lazarus, have basically overturned our conceptualization of stress and illness. In other chapters of this book, there may be close ties between the various perspectives, but in this chapter the division into perspectives indicates nothing more than slight differences of focus. No one in the field claims that there is one cause, or even one kind of

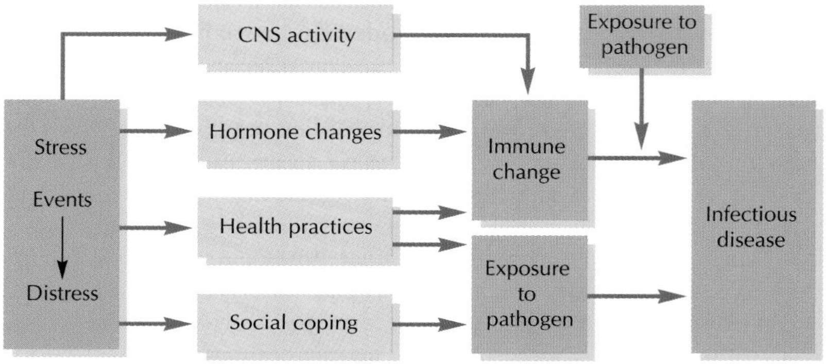

FIGURE 9.1 Model for the relationship between stress and the onset of infectious disease. (Adapted from Cohen & Williamson, 1991, p. 8.)

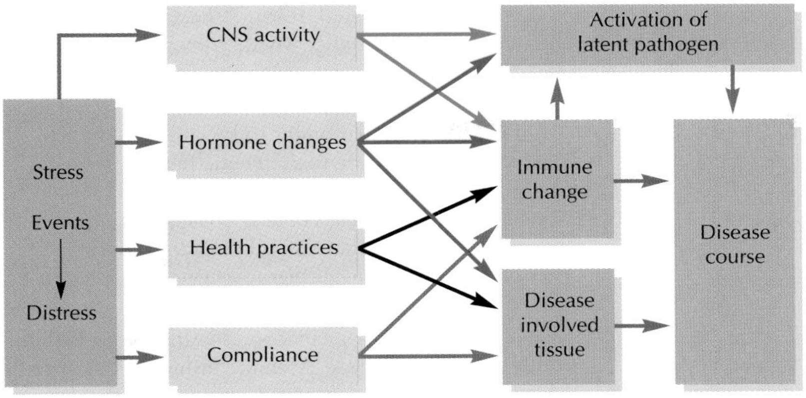

FIGURE 9.2 Model linking stress to the reactivation of latent pathogens and to the severity of the ongoing disease. (Adapted from Cohen & Williamson, 1991, p. 8.)

cause. The subject itself—stress and illness—is interactive, and the most promising theories are all cat's cradles of intersecting causes. Consider Figures 9.1 and 9.2, which were adapted from the work of Sheldon Cohen (of the cold research) and Gail Williamson. Figure 9.1 shows the relationship between stress and the onset of infectious disease. Figure 9.2 shows the relationship between stress and the reactivation of latent pathogens (disease-causing agents), such as HIV or a herpesvirus. For purposes of clarity, feedback loops are not indicated; but even in this simplified form, what the figures show are highly intricate systems, including physical, behavioral, and emotional causes. Researchers on stress and illness face a complicated problem, but by accepting this fact, they have begun producing very exciting findings.

Key Terms

acquired immune deficiency syndrome (AIDS), 228
biofeedback training, 237
circadian rhythm disorders, 234
coronary heart disease, 221
essential hypertension, 224
feedback, 220
general adaptation syndrome, 214
health psychology, 212
human immunodeficiency virus (HIV), 228
hypertension, 224
immune system, 217
individual response specificity, 214
insomnia, 233
migraine headache, 230
mind-body problem, 212
muscle-contraction headaches, 230
negative feedback, 220
obesity, 231
psychoneuroimmunology (PNI), 218
psychophysiological disorders, 212
relaxation training, 237
stimulus specificity, 214
stress, 214
Type A, 223

Summary

- The mind-body problem—the relationship between mental and physical processes—has been debated for centuries. Until recently, science has drawn a sharp line between physical and psychological disorders. Stress-related illnesses were regarded as exceptions to the rule. However, recent research has demonstrated that a person's state of mind influences diseases ranging from the common cold to cancer. Health psychology takes the holistic view that mind and body are one and that the course of *any* illness can be influenced by psychological factors.
- Stress can be defined in terms of the stimulus, the person's response, or the person's appraisal of the stimulus. The physiological reaction to stress depends on the type of stress, the person's characteristic mode of responding to stress, and his or her general level of reactivity.
- Researchers who study the physiological changes associated with emotion focus on the autonomic nervous system (ANS), which mobilizes the body to meet environmental challenges and then (usually) reverses these processes to permit the body to build energy resources.
- Some of the most interesting research comes from the subfield of psychoneuroimmunology (PNI). The immune system defends the body against "invaders" by circulating a large and varied number of small white blood cells, called lymphocytes, that identify foreign bodies and either attack them directly or produce antibodies to do so. When the immune system is not functioning properly, health is compromised.
- PNI research has shown that immune functioning may decline after major events, whether sudden shock (the death of a spouse) or chronic stress (caring for a spouse

with Alzheimer's); minor events (such as final exams); and laboratory stressors (frustrating test, induced marital conflict).

- Researchers who study coronary heart disease, hypertension, cancer, AIDS, headaches, obesity, and sleep disorders have paid special attention to the role of psychological factors.
- Coronary heart disease, the number one cause of death in the United States, is influenced by a complex interplay of biological, psychological, and social factors, including family history of the disease, lifestyle, and stress level. Hypertension, or chronic high blood pressure, has been linked to anger and hostility, occupational stress, and family history.
- Cancer is a collection of related diseases in which abnormal body cells multiply and spread uncontrollably to form a tissue mass known as a tumor. For a long time, it was believed that cancer was not associated with stress. Now evidence indicates that psychological factors play a role in this disease. Early animal studies demonstrated the powerful effects of stress in the formation of cancerous tumors, and recent research suggests that prolonged stress increases tumor growth. Several studies have found that cancer patients who participate in group therapy, as well as receive medical treatment, live longer than controls, perhaps because they are better able to overcome feelings of hopelessness. Aside from the effects of stress on cancer, there is little doubt that cancer is affected by environmental factors, such as tobacco use and sun exposure, and by genetics.
- AIDS (acquired immune deficiency syndrome) is caused by the human immunodeficiency virus (HIV), which is spread via direct contact with bodily fluid from an infected person. Inconsistent findings regarding the relationship between stress and HIV progression may be due to the wide variability of stress measures administered and to the fact that the sort of stressors faced by people with HIV, such as social isolation, multiple bereavements, and rejection, are rarely addressed in generic stress scales. A well-documented pattern of sleep disturbances in individuals with HIV and AIDS may be one of the important mechanisms through which stress compromises the immune system; behavioral programs to reduce caffeine consumption can have a positive effect on sleep and feelings of well-being for people with HIV. Psychologists have also tried to identify effective techniques for discouraging high-risk behaviors associated with HIV infection; and for those already infected, research has focused on what factors might predict whether people will stick to prescribed drug treatment programs.
- Migraine headache, once thought to arise from psychological causes, is now thought to be largely biogenic. Obesity is influenced by both genetic factors, such as metabolic rate, and behavioral factors such as eating habits and activity level. There is no single explanation of sleep disorders (insomnia and circadian rhythm problems), but behavioral therapies often are the most effective treatment.
- Gender, ethnicity, and socioeconomic status put certain groups at risk for disease. Men are at higher risk for coronary heart disease than are women. African Americans are at higher risk than European Americans for a wide range of diseases, from hypertension and heart disease to diabetes. And people of low SES are particularly prone to coronary heart disease.
- The behaviorist perspective emphasizes the role of respondent and operant conditioning in the disregulation of ANS responses. Behavioral therapists treat many disorders with biofeedback, relaxation training, meditation, and exercise, which can stimulate the immune system.
- The cognitive perspective emphasizes the person's ability to predict stressful events and his or her sense of control. Lazarus' dynamic model identifies six factors in coping with stress, from the event to the health outcome. Stress-management programs help people to pinpoint the stage at which they experience stress and to develop appropriate coping skills.
- Psychodynamic theorists emphasize the role of unconscious conflicts; the goal of psychodynamic therapy is catharsis. Research shows that catharsis, in "traumatic" journals or group therapy, can boost immune function and aid recovery, even from cancer.
- Interpersonal theorists emphasize the role of the family in supporting health. Couples who remain married for life, for instance, live longer than those who separate or divorce.
- The sociocultural perspective focuses on the role of social change—especially family breakdown and women's entry into the workforce—in stress-related physical disorders.
- The neuroscience perspective emphasizes the role of heredity and, increasingly, the immune system in stress and illness. It highlights complex patterns of interaction among psychological and biological factors.

CHAPTER 10

Mood Disorders

Depressive and Manic Episodes
- Major Depressive Episode
- Manic Episode

Mood Disorder Syndromes
- Major Depressive Disorder
- Bipolar Disorder
- Dysthymic Disorder and Cyclothymic Disorder
- Dimensions of Mood Disorder
- Comorbidity: Mixed Anxiety-Depression

Suicide
- The Prevalence of Suicide
- Myths About Suicide
- Suicide Prediction
- Suicide Prevention

Mood Disorders: Theory and Therapy
- The Behavioral and Interpersonal Perspectives
- The Cognitive Perspective
- The Psychodynamic Perspective
- The Sociocultural Perspective
- The Neuroscience Perspective

Paula Stansky was a 57-year-old woman, widow and mother of four children, who was hospitalized . . . because, according to her children, she was refusing to eat and take care of herself.

The patient . . . was described as a usually cheerful, friendly woman who took meticulous care of her home. . . . About two months prior to her hospitalization, however, her younger children reported a change in their mother's usual disposition, for no apparent reason. She appeared more easily fatigued, not as cheerful, and lackadaisical about her housework. Over the course of the next few weeks, she stopped going to church and canceled her usual weekly bingo outing with neighborhood women. As the house became increasingly neglected and their mother began to spend more time sleeping or rocking in her favorite chair, apparently preoccupied, the younger children called their married brother and sister for advice. . . .

When her son, in response to the telephone call, arrived at her house, Ms. Stansky denied that anything was wrong. She claimed to be only tired, "possibly the flu." For the ensuing week, her children tried to "cheer her up," but with no success. After several days had gone by without her taking a bath, changing her clothes, or eating any food, her children put her in the car and drove her to the hospital. . . .

On admission, Ms. Stansky was mostly mute, answering virtually no questions except correctly identifying the hospital and the day of the week. She cried periodically throughout the interview, but only shook her head back and forth when asked if she could tell the interviewer what she was feeling or thinking about. She was agitated, frequently wringing her hands, rolling her head toward the ceiling, and rocking in her chair. . . . Her children indicated that during the past week she had been waking up at 3 A.M., unable to fall back to sleep. She also seemed to them to have lost considerable weight. (Spitzer, Skodol, Gibbon, et al., 1983, p. 118)

Many of us go through occasional periods of dejection, where life seems gray and nothing seems worth doing. Some of us have also known the opposite state, a mood of excitement and recklessness in which we become feverishly active and think we can accomplish anything. In other words, **depression** and **mania,** in mild and temporary forms, are part of ordinary existence. In some cases, however, such mood swings become so prolonged and extreme that the person's life is seriously disrupted. These conditions are known as the **mood disorders,** or *affective disorders, affect* meaning "emotion."

The mood disorders have been recognized and written about since the beginning of the history of medicine. Hippocrates described both depression and mania in detail in the fourth century B.C.E. As early as the first century C.E., the Greek physician Aretaeus observed that manic and depressive behaviors sometimes occurred in the same person and seemed to stem from a single disorder. In the early nineteenth century, Philippe Pinel (1801/1967), the reformer of Parisian mental hospitals (Chapter 1), wrote a compelling account of depression, using Roman emperor Tiberius and French king Louis XI as illustrations. Depression has also been vividly described by some of its more famous victims. In one of his recurring episodes of depression, Abraham Lincoln wrote, "If what I feel were equally distributed to the whole human family, there would not be one cheerful face on earth."

Abraham Lincoln, whom many historians consider to be the greatest U.S. president, was subject to recurring bouts of severe depression.

Though they have been scrutinized for centuries, the mood disorders still remain something of a mystery. What is known about them is outlined in the first section of this chapter. In the second section, we turn our attention to suicide, which is often the result of depression. Finally, we describe the theory and treatment of mood disorders according to various perspectives.

Depressive and Manic Episodes

One of the most striking features of the mood disorders is their episodic quality. Within a few weeks, or sometimes within a few days, a person who has been functioning normally is plunged into despair or is scaling the heights of mania. Once the episode has run its course, the person may return to normal or near-normal functioning, though he or she is likely to have further episodes of mood disturbance. The nature of the episode (whether depressive or manic), its severity, and its duration determine the diagnosis and often the treatment—matters we will discuss. For now, let us examine the typical features of severe depressive and manic episodes.

Major Depressive Episode

In some cases, a psychological trauma plunges a person into a **major depressive episode** overnight, but usually the onset of depression is gradual, occurring over a period of several weeks or several months. The episode itself typically lasts several months and then ends, as it began, gradually (Coryell, Akiskal, Leon, et al., 1994).

The person entering a depressive episode undergoes profound changes in most areas of his or her life—in not just mood but also motivation, thinking, and physical and motor functioning. The following are the characteristic features of the major depressive episode, as described by *DSM-IV-TR:*

1. *Depressed mood.* Almost all severely depressed adults report some degree of unhappiness, ranging from a mild melancholy to total hopelessness. Mildly or moderately depressed people may have crying spells; severely depressed patients often say they feel like crying but cannot. Deeply depressed people see no way that they or anyone else can help them—a type of thinking that has been called the **helplessness-hopelessness syndrome.**

2. *Loss of pleasure or interest in usual activities.* Aside from depressed mood, the most common characteristic of a major depressive episode is loss of pleasure and, therefore, lack of interest in one's accustomed activities. This loss of pleasure, known as **anhedonia,** is generally far-reaching. Whatever the person once liked to do—in the case history at the beginning of the chapter, for example, keep house, play bingo, go to church—no longer seems worth doing. Even emotional responses to pleasant stimuli are diminished (Sloan, Strauss, & Wisner, 2001). Severely depressed patients may experience a complete "paralysis of the will"—an inability even to get out of bed in the morning.
3. *Disturbance of appetite.* Most depressed people have poor appetite and lose weight. A minority, however, react by eating more and putting on weight. Whatever the weight change, whether loss or gain, that same change tends to recur with each depressive episode (Kendler, Eaves, Walters, et al., 1996).
4. *Sleep disturbance.* Insomnia is an extremely common feature of depression. Waking up too early and then being unable to get back to sleep is the most characteristic pattern, but depressed people may also have trouble falling asleep initially, or they may awaken repeatedly throughout the night. As with eating, however, sleep may increase rather than decrease, with the patient sleeping 15 hours a day or more. Depressed individuals who sleep to excess are usually the same ones who eat to excess (Kendler, Eaves, Walters, et al., 1996).
5. *Psychomotor retardation or agitation.* Depression can usually be "read" immediately in the person's motor behavior and physical bearing. In the most common pattern, **retarded depression,** the patient seems overcome by fatigue. Posture is stooped, movement is slow and deliberate, gestures are kept to a minimum, and speech is low and halting, with long pauses before answering. In severe cases, individuals may fall into a mute stupor. Some evidence suggests that the symptom of psychomotor retardation is related to low presynaptic dopamine levels (Paillere Martinot, Bragulat, et al., 2001). More rarely, the symptoms take the opposite form, **agitated depression,** marked by incessant activity and restlessness—hand wringing, pacing, and moaning.
6. *Loss of energy.* The depressed person's reduced motivation is usually accompanied by a sharply reduced energy level. Without having done anything, he or she may feel exhausted all the time.
7. *Feelings of worthlessness and guilt.* Typically, depressed people see themselves as deficient in whatever attributes they value most: intelligence, beauty, popularity, health. Their frequent complaints about loss—whether of love, material goods, money, or prestige—may also reflect their sense of personal inadequacy. Such feelings of worthlessness are often accompanied by a profound sense of guilt. Depressed individuals seem to search the environment for evidence of problems they have created. If a child has trouble with schoolwork or the car has a flat tire, it is their fault.
8. *Difficulties in thinking.* In depression, mental processes, like physical processes, are usually slowed down. Depressed people tend to be indecisive, and they often report difficulties in thinking, concentrating, and remembering. The harder a mental task, the more difficulty they have (Hartlage, Alloy, Vázquez, et al., 1993).
9. *Recurrent thoughts of death or suicide.* Not surprisingly, many depressed people have recurrent thoughts of death and suicide. Often, they say that they (and everyone else) would be better off if they were dead.

Manic Episode

The typical **manic episode** begins rather suddenly, over the course of a few days, and is usually shorter than a depressive episode. A manic episode may last from several days to several months and then usually ends as abruptly as it began. *DSM-IV-TR* describes the prominent features as follows:

1. *Elevated, expansive, or irritable mood.* The mood change is the essential, "diagnostic" feature of a manic episode. Typically, manic people feel wonderful, see the world as an excellent place, and have limitless enthusiasm for whatever they are doing or plan to do. This expansiveness is usually mixed with irritability. Manic individuals often see other people as slow, doltish spoilsports and can become quite hostile, especially if someone tries to interfere with their behavior. In some cases, irritability is the manic person's dominant mood, with euphoria either intermittent or simply absent.
2. *Inflated self-esteem.* People with mania tend to see themselves as extremely attractive,

important, and powerful people, capable of great achievements in fields for which they may, in fact, have no aptitude whatsoever. They may begin composing symphonies, designing nuclear weapons, or calling the White House with advice on how to run the country.

3. *Sleeplessness.* The manic episode is almost always marked by a decreased need for sleep. Manic individuals may sleep only 2 or 3 hours a night and yet have twice as much energy as those around them.
4. *Talkativeness.* People with mania tend to talk loudly, rapidly, and constantly. Their speech is often full of puns, irrelevant details, and jokes that they alone find funny.
5. *Flight of ideas.* Manic individuals often have racing thoughts. This is one reason they speak so rapidly—to keep up with the flow of their ideas. Manic speech also tends to shift abruptly from one topic to the next.
6. *Distractibility.* Manic individuals are easily distracted. While doing or discussing one thing, they notice something else in the environment and abruptly turn their attention to that instead. They also show deficits on tasks that require sustained attention (Clark, Inversen, & Goodwin, 2001).
7. *Hyperactivity.* The expansive mood is usually accompanied by restlessness and increased goal-directed activity—physical, social, occupational, and often sexual.
8. *Reckless behavior.* The euphoria and grandiose self-image of manic people often lead them into impulsive actions: buying sprees, reckless driving, careless business investments, sexual indiscretions, and so forth. They are typically indifferent to the needs of others and think nothing of yelling in restaurants, calling friends in the middle of the night, or spending the family savings on a new Porsche.

The following is a clear-cut case of a manic episode:

Terrence O'Reilly, a single 39-year-old transit authority clerk, was brought to the hospital in May, 1973, by the police after his increasingly hyperactive and bizarre behavior and nonstop talking alarmed his family. He loudly proclaimed that he was not in need of treatment, and threatened legal action against the hospital and police.

The family reported that a month prior to admission Mr. O'Reilly took a leave of absence from his civil service job, purchased a large number of cuckoo clocks and then an expensive car which he planned to use as a mobile showroom for his wares, anticipating that he would make a great deal of money.

He proceeded to "tear around town" buying and selling the clocks and other merchandise, and when he was not out, he was continuously on the phone making "deals." He rarely slept and, uncharacteristically, spent every evening in neighborhood bars drinking heavily and, according to him, "wheeling and dealing." Two weeks before admission his mother died suddenly of a heart attack. He cried for two days, but then his mood began to soar again. At the time of admission he was $3000 in debt and had driven his family to exhaustion. . . . He said, however, that he felt "on top of the world." (Spitzer, Skodol, Gibbon, et al., 1983, p. 115)

For a condition to be diagnosed as a manic episode, it must have lasted at least a week (or less, if hospitalization is required) and must have seriously interfered with the person's functioning. A briefer and less severe manic condition is called a **hypomanic episode.** Sometimes, patients meet the diagnostic criteria for both manic episode and major depressive episode simultaneously. (For example, they show manic grandiosity and hyperactivity, yet weep and threaten suicide.) This combined pattern is called a **mixed episode** and is not uncommon (Dilsaver, Chen, Shoaib, et al., 1999). Whichever type of manic episode a person has, purely euphoric or mixed, subsequent episodes tend to be of the same kind (Woods, Money, & Baker, 2001).

Mood Disorder Syndromes

Major Depressive Disorder

People who undergo one or more major depressive episodes, with no intervening periods of mania, are said to have **major depressive disorder.** This disorder is one of the United States' greatest mental health problems: Its prevalence during any given month is close to 4 percent of men and 6 percent of women. The lifetime risk—that is, the percentage of Americans who will experience major depression at some point in their lives—varies, but is about 17 percent (Ustun, 2001). Depression is second only to schizophrenia in frequency of admissions to American mental hospitals (Olfson & Mechanic, 1996). As for the nonhospitalized, private physicians report that depression leads to more office visits than any other medical problem except hypertension (IMS Health Canada, 2001), and those patients are more debilitated—lose more workdays, spend more time in bed—than patients with many chronic medical conditions, such as diabetes or heart disease (Druss, Rosenheck, & Sledge, 2000; Wells & Sherbourne, 1999). Further, although there are several effective treatments for depression, most people with major depression do not receive adequate treatment (Young, Klap, Sherbourne, et al., 2001). As grave as the situation is, it is getting worse. Each successive generation born since World War II has shown higher rates of depression (Burke, Burke, Rae, et al., 1991; Klerman, 1988). Major depression is now the fourth leading cause of disability and premature death worldwide (Murray & Lopez, 1996). According to some experts, we are in an "age of depression."

Course In about 80 percent of all cases of major depression, the first episode is not the last (Judd, 1997). The more previous episodes a person has had, the younger the person was when the first episode struck, the fact of being a woman, the more painful events recently endured, the less supportive the family has been, and the more negative cognitions the individual has, the greater the likelihood of recurrence (Belsher & Costello, 1988; Lewinsohn, Rohde, Seeley, et al., 2000; Mueller, Leon, Keller, et al., 1999). Over a lifetime, the median number of episodes per patient is 4, with a median duration of 4½ months per episode (Judd, 1997; Solomon, Keller, Leon, et al., 1997).

The course of recurrent depression varies considerably. For some people, the episodes come in clusters. For others, they are separated by years of normal functioning. As for the quality of the normal functioning, that also varies. Some people also return to their **premorbid adjustment**—that is, their level of functioning prior to the onset of the disorder. As for the others, even 10 years after a major depressive episode, people still showed serious impairment in job status, income, marital adjustment, social relationships, and recreational activities (Judd, Akiskal, Zeller, et al., 2000). Depression also affects the immune system, leaving its victims more susceptible to illness and death (Schleifer, Keller, Bartlett, et al., 1996; Penninx, Geerlings, Deeg, et al., 1999), and increases the risk of cardiac death by 2 to 3 times (Penninx, Beekman, Honig, et al., 2001). All of these effects make it difficult for people coming out of a depressive episode to resume their former lives. Indeed, some research indicates that the symptoms and behaviors characteristic of a depressive episode actually generate stressful life events, which in turn can maintain the depression and produce a cycle of chronic stress and impairment (Daley, Hammen, Burge, et al., 1997; Joiner, 2000). Thus, people snap back, but many of them do not snap back entirely, just as scar tissue is not the same as the original tissue. Not surprisingly, the longer a depressive episode lasts, the less likely it is that the person will fully recover (Keller, Lavori, Mueller, et al., 1992).

❖ Groups at Risk for Depression

Certain groups within the population are more susceptible than others to major depression. The rate for European Americans is higher than for African Americans and Mexican Americans (Zhang & Snowden, 1999; Oquendo, Ellis, Greenwald, et al., 2001); it is higher for separated and divorced people than for married people (Blazer, Kessler, McGonagle, et al., 1994; Harlow, Cohen, Otto, et al., 1999) and for women than for men. Indeed, the risk for women is two times higher than for men (Nolen-Hoeksema, 2001)—a fact that investigators have tried to explain with theories ranging from hormonal differences to the changing social role of women. One promising theory has to do with differences in the way men and women respond to depressed moods. According to Susan Nolen-Hoeksema (1991, 2001), women, when they are "down," tend to ruminate on this, focusing on the depression, wondering why it is happening and what it will lead to. Men take the opposite tack: They try to distract themselves. Because the evidence indicates that rumination exacerbates and prolongs depression, whereas distraction relieves it, women are likely to have longer and more serious depressions (Nolen-Hoeksema, 2001). For a more comprehensive theory of the female disadvantage with regard to depression, see the box on page 250.

Women are about twice as likely as men to experience depression. A possible explanation for this difference in prevalence is that women tend to analyze their depression, whereas men are more likely to try to distract themselves from it.

Research Highlights
Gender Differences in Depression

Women are about twice as likely as men to develop a serious depression, but, curiously, the same is not true of boys and girls. Prior to age 14 or 15, the two genders are at equal risk (Hankin & Abramson, 2001; Nolen-Hoeksema, 2001). (If anything, boys show a slightly higher risk.) What happens to girls in adolescence to make them so much more prone to depression?

To answer that question, several researchers (Cyranowski, Frank, Young, et al., 2000; Hankin & Abramson, 2001; Nolen-Hoeksema, 2001; Kendler, Gardner, Neale, et al., 2001) have proposed integrative models. According to these models, girls already carry a heavier load of risk factors for depression from childhood, but it is not until those factors are activated by the special challenges of adolescence that they crystallize into a greater vulnerability to depression. In defense of this theory, the researchers list a number of characteristics associated with depression: genetic risk, a negative attributional style, a tendency to ruminate on depression, helplessness, need for affiliation, and biological reactivity to stress. Though all these characteristics correlate with depression in both males and females, girls show them to a greater extent than boys long before adolescence.

Then, in adolescence, new risk factors arise, and it is the combination of these with the prior risks that tips the balance. One new risk, for example, is that the number of stressful life events experienced rises at puberty for both boys and girls, but more so for girls (Hankin & Abramson, 2001; Rudolph & Hammen, 1999). A second risk is shame about one's body. Research has shown that boys value the physical changes associated with puberty more than girls do (Harter, 1999; Kostanski & Gullone, 1998). Boys like their newly muscled shoulders; girls, on the other hand, tend to be distressed by the gain in body fat, and they often find menstruation embarrassing. Such "body dissatisfaction" is associated with depression (Hankin & Abramson, 2001; Wichstrom, 1999). So is sexual abuse and rape, another puberty-connected risk factor that is far more common for girls than for boys. It is estimated that girls aged 14 to 15 have a higher risk of being raped than any other age or sex group (Weiss, Longhurst, & Mazure, 1999).

Also, it is in adolescence that girls begin to confront most directly the restricted role carved out for them by their society. Many adopt the role quickly. Youngsters of both genders show less interest in school as they pass from sixth to seventh grade, but girls show a sharper drop in academic ambition (Nolen-Hoeksema, 2001). By the time they enter college, women are sorting themselves into less lucrative, less competitive fields.

Apparently, girls who accept the narrowed role prescribed for women are at higher risk for depression (Nolen-Hoeksema, 2001). Girls who defy such role expectations are *also* more prone to depression (Nolen-Hoeksema & Girgus, 1994)—no doubt a reflection of the widespread disapproval of assertive women. In addition, girls' greater need for affiliation (close interpersonal relationships, intimacy), already present before puberty, intensifies after puberty (Cyranowski, Frank, Young, et al., 2000). When this combines with the greater exposure to stressful life events in girls after puberty, particularly interpersonal events that threaten relationships with friends and romantic partners, adolescent girls are more likely to become depressed.

If they encountered the challenges of adolescence with no disadvantage, girls might weather them well enough. But, because they are already characterized by a higher load of biological, cognitive, and interpersonal risk factors, they are less likely to cope well. And so, according to these recent models, women may develop the patterns that will make them, from then on, twice as vulnerable to depression as men.

As for age, it was once thought that the middle-aged and the elderly were the high-risk groups. But recent research indicates that growing old does not increase one's susceptibility to depression (Roberts, Kaplan, Shema, et al., 1997). If anything, it is the young who are at risk. The rates of depression begin to surge in mid-adolescence (Hankin, Abramson, Moffitt, et al., 1998; Wichstrom, 1999), and the peak age at onset for major depression is now 15 to 19 years for women and 25 to 29 years for men (Burke, Burke, Regier, et al., 1990), though the disorder may strike at any age, even in infancy. Moreover, onset of major depression before puberty is associated with higher rates of major depression, bipolar disorder, and substance use disorder as well as poor school, work, and social functioning as adults (Geller, Zimerman, Williams, et al., 2001; Weissman, Wolk, Wickramaratne, et al., 1999).

The symptom picture differs somewhat, depending on age group (Harrington, 1993; Kessler, Avenevoli, & Merikangas, 2001). In depressed infants, the most striking and alarming sign is failure to eat. In older children, depression may manifest itself primarily as apathy and inactivity. Alternatively, it may take the form of separation anxiety, in which the child clings frantically to parents, refuses to leave them long enough to go to school, and is haunted by fears of death (or of the parents' deaths). In adolescents, the most prominent symptoms are sulkiness, negativism, low self-esteem, withdrawal, complaints of not being understood, and perhaps antisocial behavior and drug abuse (Kessler, Avenevoli, & Merikangas, 2001; Goodyer, 1992)—in other words, an exaggeration of normal adolescent problems. (See Chapter 16 for further discussion of depression in childhood.) In the elderly, lack of pleasure and motivation, expressions of hopelessness, and psychomotor retardation or agitation are common signs, as are delusions and hallucinations (Brodaty, Peters, Boyce, et al., 1991). The neurobiological correlates of depression also differ across age groups. Depressed children and adolescents don't show elevated cortisol levels or respond to tricyclic antidepressants as depressed adults do (Kaufman, Martin, King, et al., 2001).

Bipolar Disorder

Whereas major depression is confined to depressive episodes, **bipolar disorder,** as the name suggests, involves both manic and depressive phases. In the usual case, bipolar disorder first appears in late adolescence in the form of a manic episode. Subsequent episodes may occur in any of a variety of patterns. The initial manic episode may be followed by a normal period, then by a depressed episode, than a normal period, and so forth. Or one episode may be followed immediately by its opposite, with normal intervals occurring only between such manic-depression pairs (Rehm, Wagner, & Ivens-Lyndal, 2001). In a less common pattern, called the *rapid-cycling type,* the person (usually a woman) switches back and forth between depressive and manic or mixed episodes over a long period, with little or no "normal" functioning between (Leibenluft, 2000). This pattern, which tends to have a poor prognosis (Leibenluft, 2000), turns up in about one fourth of bipolar patients in response to antidepressant medication (Suppes, Dennehy, & Gibbons, 2000).

The occurrence of manic episodes is not all that differentiates bipolar disorder from major depression (see Table 10.1). The two syndromes differ in many important respects (Rehm, Wagner, & Ivens-Tyndal, 2001). First, bipolar disorder is much less common than major depression, affecting an estimated 0.8 to 1.6 percent of the adult population

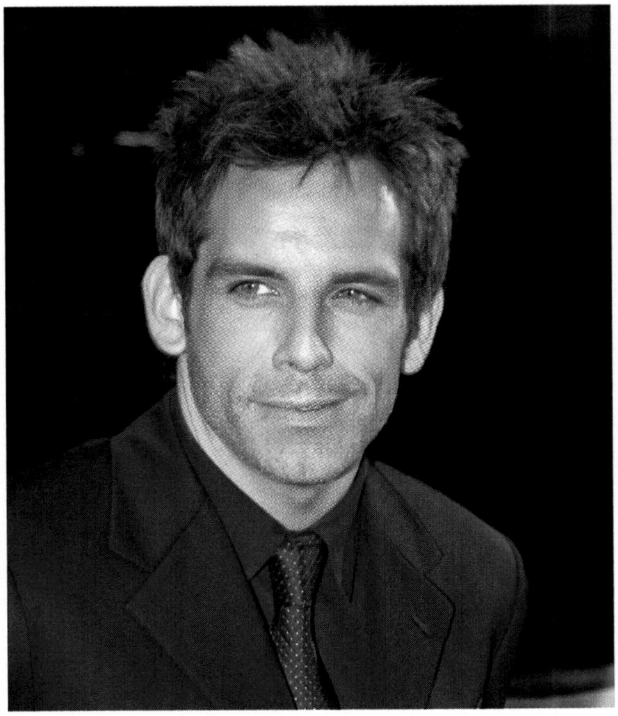

Actor Ben Stiller talks openly about his experience with bipolar disorder.

(Kessler, McGonagle, Zhao, et al., 1994). Second, the two disorders show different demographic profiles. Unlike major depression, bipolar disorder occurs in the two sexes with approximately equal frequency, and bipolar disorder is more prevalent among higher socioeconomic groups. Third, age of onset is later for bipolar disorder than for unipolar depression. Fourth, while people who are married or have intimate relationships are less prone to major depression, they have no advantage with respect to bipolar disorder. Fifth, people with major depression tend to have histories of low self-esteem, dependency, and

TABLE 10.1 Differences Between Major Depression and Bipolar Disorder

	MAJOR DEPRESSION	BIPOLAR DISORDER
Prevalence	About 17% of population	1–2% of population
Sex ratio	2:1 (Women:Men)	1:1
Age of onset	Earlier	Later
Marital status	Less common in married people	Marriage provides no protection
Personality features	Low self-esteem, dependency, and obsessional thinking	Hyperactivity and ADHD
Depressive episodes	Less likely to involve pervasive slowing	More likely to involve pervasive slowing
Course	Episodes longer and less frequent	Episodes briefer and more frequent
Prognosis	Less impairment and better outcome	Greater impairment and worse outcome
Genetics	Weaker genetic component	Stronger genetic component

obsessional thinking, whereas people with bipolar disorder are more likely to have a history of hyperactivity or ADHD (Winokur, Coryell, Endicott, et al., 1993; Sachs, Baldassano, Truman, et al., 2000). Sixth, the depressive episodes in bipolar disorder are more likely to involve a pervasive slowing down—psychomotor retardation, excess sleep, weight/appetite increase—than are those in major depression (Benazzi, 2000, 2001). Seventh, the two disorders differ in their course. Episodes in bipolar disorder are generally briefer and more frequent than are those in major depression (Cusin, Serretti, Lattuada, et al., 2000). Eighth, the two conditions differ in prognosis. In general, bipolar disorder creates greater impairment and has a worse long-term outcome (Gitlin, Swendsen, Heller, et al., 1995; Suppes, Dennehy, & Gibbons, 2000). Finally, bipolar disorder is more likely to run in families. On the basis of these clues, many researchers think that the two disorders, similar as they may appear, spring from different causes.

We may, however, be looking at more than two disorders. Some patients have a manic or mixed episode—or a series of such episodes—with no subsequent depressive episode. Such cases, though they involve only one "pole," are nevertheless classified as bipolar disorder, because, apart from the absence of depressive episodes, they resemble the classic bipolar disorder. (Some researchers suspect that they are simply cases of insufficient follow-up.) Alternatively, some patients have both depressive and manic phases but in the latter are hypomanic rather than fully manic. In recognition of these two patterns—and the need to assemble research groups to test whether they are different disorders—*DSM-IV-TR* has divided bipolar disorder into two types. In *bipolar I disorder,* the person has had at least one manic (or mixed) episode and usually, but not necessarily, at least one major depressive episode as well. In *bipolar II disorder,* the person has had at least one major depressive episode and at least one hypomanic episode but has never met the diagnostic criteria for manic or mixed episode.

The following is a case of bipolar I disorder, involving both full-blown manic and depressive episodes:

> At 17 [Mrs. M. had] suffered from a depression that rendered her unable to work for several months. . . . At 33, shortly before the birth of her first child, the patient was greatly depressed. For a period of four days she appeared in coma. About a month after the birth of the baby she "became excited" and . . . signed a year's lease on an apartment, bought furniture, and became heavily involved in debt. Shortly thereafter, Mrs. M. became depressed and returned to the hospital in which she had previously been a patient. After several months she recovered and . . . remained well for approximately two years.
>
> She then became overactive and exuberant in spirits and visited her friends, to whom she outlined her plans for reestablishing different forms of lucrative business. She purchased many clothes, bought furniture, pawned her rings, and wrote checks without funds. She was returned to a hospital. Gradually her manic symptoms subsided, and after four months she was discharged. For a period thereafter she was mildly depressed. In a little less than a year Mrs. M. again became overactive. . . . Contrary to her usual habits, she swore frequently and loudly, created a disturbance in a club to which she did not belong, and instituted divorce proceedings. On the day prior to her second admission to the hospital she purchased 57 hats.
>
> During the past 18 years this patient has been admitted and dismissed from the hospital on many occasions. At times, with the onset of a depressed period, she has returned to the hospital seeking admission. At such times she complained that her "brain just won't work." She would say, "I have no energy, am unable to do my housework. I have let my family down; I am living from day to day. There is no one to blame but myself." During one of her manic periods, she sent the following telegram to a physician of whom she had become much enamored: "To: You; Street and No.: Everywhere; Place: the remains at peace! We did our best, but God's will be done! I am so very sorry for all of us. To brave it through thus far. Yes, Darling—from Hello Handsome. Handsome is as Handsome does, thinks, lives and breathes. It takes clear air. Brother of Mine, in a girl's hour of need. All my love to the Best Inspiration one ever had." (Kolb, 1982, pp. 376–377)

Dysthymic Disorder and Cyclothymic Disorder

Many people are chronically depressed or chronically pass through depressed and expansive periods, but their condition is not severe enough to merit the diagnosis of major depressive disorder or bipolar disorder. Such patterns, if they last for two years or more, are classified as dysthymic disorder and cyclothymic disorder, respectively.

Dysthymic disorder involves a mild, persistent depression. Dysthymic individuals are typically morose, pessimistic, introverted, overconscientious, and incapable of fun (Akiskal & Cassano, 1997). In addition, they often show the low energy level, low self-esteem, suicidal ideation, and disturbances of eating, sleeping, and thinking that are associated with major depression, but their functioning is worse (Klein,

Schwartz, Rose, et al., 2000). The syndrome is about half as common as major depressive disorder.

Dysthymic Disorder: Seeing the Tunnel, But No Light at the End

The MindMAP video "Dysthymia" illustrates some of the negative thoughts and feelings found among individuals with dysthymic disorder. Under what conditions might the experiences of these thoughts and feelings be quite normal, and under what conditions be quite odd? Why?

Cyclothymic disorder, like dysthymic disorder, is chronic. For years, the person never goes longer than a few months without a phase of hypomanic or depressive behavior. Because the pattern is mild and persistent, as in dysthymia, it becomes a way of life. In their hypomanic periods, which they come to depend on, cyclothymics work long hours without fatigue—indeed, with their mental powers newly sharpened—before lapsing back into a normal or depressed state. It has been suggested that cyclothymia and bipolar disorder are especially common in creative people and help them get their work done (Jamison, 1992; Post, 1994). (See the box on page 254.) However, more recent evidence suggests that hypomanic symptoms specifically may be associated with enhanced creativity and dysthymia may be linked to reduced creativity (Schuldberg, 1999; Shapiro, 2001; Shapiro & Weisberg, 1999).

Both dysthymia and cyclothymia have a slow, insidious onset in adolescence and may persist for a lifetime. In this sense, they are like the personality disorders, the subject of Chapter 11. Far closer, however, is the link with the major mood disorders. Like people with major depressive disorder or bipolar disorder, dysthymic and cyclothymic individuals have relatives with higher-than-normal rates of mood disorders (Alloy & Abramson, 2000). In addition, dysthymia and cyclothymia show the same gender distribution as their graver counterparts. Dysthymic disorder, like major depression, is one and a half to three times more common in women, whereas in cyclothymic disorder, as in bipolar disorder, the genders are at equal risk (Kessler, McGonagle, Zhao, et al., 1994). Finally, patients with dysthymia and cyclothymia tend to show the same neurophysiological abnormalities and the same reactions to antidepressant drugs as people with major depressive disorder and bipolar disorder (Akiskal, Judd, Lemmi, et al., 1997; Alloy & Abramson, 2000). About 77 percent of people with dysthymia go on to develop major depressive disorder (Klein, Schwartz, Rose, et al., 2000), and 15 to 50 percent of people with cyclothymia eventually show bipolar disorder.

Dimensions of Mood Disorder

In addition to the important distinction between bipolar disorder and depressive disorder, there are certain dimensions, or points of differentiation, that researchers and clinicians have found useful in classifying mood disorders. We shall discuss three dimensions: psychotic-neurotic, endogenous-reactive, and early-late onset.

Psychotic Versus Nonpsychotic As we saw in Chapter 7, historically, psychological disorders were described, in terms of severity, as either psychotic or neurotic—a distinction that hinges on the matter of reality contact. Neurotics do not lose their ability to interact with their environment in a reasonably efficient manner. Psychotics do, partly because their thinking processes are often disturbed by **hallucinations,** or false sensory perceptions, and **delusions,** or false beliefs. However, since the term "neurotic" was dropped from *DSM-III* in 1980, the psychotic-neurotic distinction is now discussed as a psychotic-nonpsychotic differentiation and is often applied to depression. In psychotic depression, hallucinations, delusions, and extreme withdrawal are usually congruent with the depressed mood—such as delusions of persecution due to some personal inadequacy. Manic episodes can also have psychotic features. Mrs. M.'s letter to her doctor (page 252) qualifies as evidence of psychotic-level thought disturbance. However, many cases of major depression and bipolar disorder—and, by definition, all cases of dysthymia and cyclothymia—remain at the nonpsychotic level.

Are nonpsychotic- and psychotic-level mood disorders two different entities altogether? The traditional position is that they are. For example, Kraepelin (Chapter 1), in his original classification system, listed all incapacitating mood disorders under the heading "manic-depressive psychosis," which he considered an organic illness distinct from nonpsychotic-level mood disturbances. Many theorists still hold to this position, and there is some evidence to support it. Psychotic depressed people tend to differ from nonpsychotic depressed individuals not just in reality contact but also in psychomotor symptoms, cognitive deficits, biological signs, family history, and response to

The "mad genius" is an ancient idea, but recently it has been restated by Kay Redfield Jamison, a professor of psychiatry at Johns Hopkins School of Medicine. In her 1992 book, *Touched With Fire: Manic-Depressive Illness and the Artistic Temperament,* Jamison argues that artists show an unusually high rate of mood disorder and that this is part of what makes them creative. To assemble her evidence, Jamison studied the lives of a large group of British and Irish poets born between 1705 and 1805. Her conclusion was that they were 30 times more likely to have suffered manic-depressive illness, 20 times more likely to have been committed to an asylum, and 5 times more likely to have killed themselves than were members of the general population. Jamison studied not just poets but artists in many media: Baudelaire, Blake, Byron, Coleridge, Dickinson, Shelley, Tennyson, Whitman, Balzac, Conrad, Dickens, Zola, Handel, Berlioz, Schumann, Tchaikovsky, Michelangelo, van Gogh, Gauguin. All these, Jamison believes, probably suffered from serious mood disorders.

Neither is the evidence confined to past centuries. Jamison provides a list of major American poets of the twentieth century: Hart Crane, Theodore Roethke, Delmore Schwartz, John Berryman, Randall Jarrell, Robert Lowell, Anne Sexton, and Sylvia Plath. Of these, five won the Pulitzer prize, and five committed suicide. All eight were treated for depression, and all but one were treated for mania. Many of Jamison's creative manic-depressives also had family histories of mood disorder. Lord Byron, who once described his brain as "a whirling gulf of fantasy and flame," had a great-uncle known as "Mad Lord Byron" and a father known as "Mad Jack Byron." His mother had violent mood swings; his maternal grandfather, a depressive, committed suicide.

Together with these sad histories, Jamison describes the creative benefits of mania. For one thing, it instills confidence. It also allows its victims to work uninterruptedly for long hours. But, above all, the euphoria, the hyperintense perceptions, the feeling of bursting inspiration that accompanies mania provide rich material for art. Novelist Virginia Woolf wrote, "As an experience madness is terrific . . . and in its lava I still find most of the things I write about." Composer Hugo Wolf described his blood as "changed into streams of fire."

Some observers find Jamison's conclusions more romantic than scientific, particularly insofar as they involve "diagnosing the dead" on the basis of the anecdotal evidence of biographies. There were no *DSM* criteria in the nineteenth century, let alone before; consequently, it is hard to know whether the eccentricities of people such as "Mad Jack Byron" constitute the same condition that we call bipolar disorder. Also, famous artists' lives have been very heavily scrutinized, and this may lead to distortion. Schoolteachers and bus drivers may also feel, now and then, that their brains are licked with fire, but, because they are not artists, they are less likely to interest the public in this fact. Partly because of the "mad genius" stereotype—and because mad geniuses make lively reading—artists' biographers tend to stress the extravagant and the pathological.

However, Jamison's findings have been supported in some measure by studies of living people. Richards and her colleagues found that bipolar and cyclothymic patients and their normal first-degree relatives scored significantly higher on creativity than did either normal controls or people with psychiatric diagnoses other than mood disorder. An interesting aspect of this study was that the research team used a much broader and more "normal" definition of creativity than other researchers have used. The subjects who were involved in social and political causes, who showed a special flair for business, who worked at hobbies—they, too, got points for creativity. The researchers concluded that the most creative people were not those with or without bipolar disorder but those in between, the cyclothymics and the even milder, "subclinical" moody types, together with the normal first-degree relatives of people with pronounced mood disorders (Richards, Kinney, Lunde, et al., 1988).

Novelist Virginia Woolf (1882–1941) struggled with what was probably bipolar disorder throughout her adult life. She finally drowned herself. Peter Ilyich Tchaikovsky (1840–1893), one of the most popular and influential Russian composers of the nineteenth century, suffered severe depressions.

various treatments (Coryell, 1996; Belanoff, Kalehzan, Sund, et al., 2001). They are also more likely to later develop manic or hypomanic episodes and thus convert to bipolar disorder (Goldberg, Harrow, & Whiteside, 2001).

Other theorists argue that the distinction between nonpsychotic and psychotic depression is quantitative rather than qualitative. This theory, known as the **continuity hypothesis,** rests on the idea that depression appears, above all, to be an exaggerated form of everyday sadness (Ruscio & Ruscio, 2000; Solomon, Haaga, & Arrow, 2001). According to the proponents of the continuity hypothesis, psychotic depression, nonpsychotic depression, dysthymia, and normal "blues" are simply different points on a single continuum. The findings that people with low-level mood disorders—not just dysthymia and cyclothymia but also people with "subsyndromal" symptoms (symptoms not severe enough to merit diagnosis)—are at risk for more severe depression and have relatives with higher rates of mood disorder lends some support to the continuity hypothesis (Angst & Merikangus, 1997; Lewinsohn, Solomon, Seeley, et al., 2000).

Endogenous Versus Reactive Many proponents of the continuity hypothesis believe that all mood disorders are largely psychogenic. Those who hold to the Kraepelin tradition, on the other hand, generally believe that only the milder forms are psychogenic. They regard the psychotic forms as biogenic.

Basic to the latter point of view is a second dimension of mood disorder: the endogenous-versus-reactive dimension. Originally, the terms *endogenous* and *reactive* were intended to indicate whether or not a depression was preceded by a precipitating event, such as a death in the family or the loss of a job. Those linked to such an event were called **reactive;** those not linked were called **endogenous** (literally, "born from within"). According to adherents of Kraepelin's position, nonpsychotic depressions were generally reactive and therefore psychogenic, while psychotic depressions were generally endogenous and therefore biogenic (Rehm, Wagner, & Ivens-Tyndal, 2001).

As it turns out, however, the distinction is not so easily made. The research indicates that *most* depressive episodes, including those in bipolar patients, are preceded by stressful life events (Alloy, Reilly-Harrington, Fresco, et al., in press; Johnson & Kizer, 2002), and such stressful events are a major cause of depressive episodes (Kendler, Karkowski, & Prescott, 1999). In many cases, there is a precipitating event for a first episode but not for later episodes (Brown, Harris, & Hepworth, 1994; Lewinsohn, Allen, Seeley, et al., 1999). As a result of these confusions, the terms *endogenous* and *reactive,* despite their dictionary meanings, are now generally used not to indicate the absence or presence of precipitating events but to describe different patterns of symptoms (Rehm, Wagner, & Ivens-Tyndal, 2001). Patients who show pronounced anhedonia together with the more vegetative, or physical, symptoms (e.g., early-morning waking, weight loss, psychomotor changes) and who describe their depression as different in quality from what they would feel after the death of a loved one are classified as endogenous, or, in *DSM-IV-TR's* terminology, as having "melancholic features." Those whose disturbance is primarily emotional or cognitive are called reactive, or without melancholic features. Of these symptoms, psychomotor disturbance is the best at discriminating melancholic from nonmelancholic depression (Parker, Roy, Hadzi-Pavlovic, et al., 2000).

The endogenous-reactive distinction made on the basis of symptoms does seem to describe a genuine difference. Endogenous patients differ from reactive patients in their sleep patterns. They are also more likely than reactive patients to show the biological abnormalities that we will describe later in this chapter and to respond to biological treatments, such as electroconvulsive ("shock") therapy (Rush & Weissenburger, 1994). Accordingly, some researchers still suspect that endogenous cases are more biogenic, but this has not been established, and there is some evidence to the contrary. For example, if endogenous depression were more biochemically based, then we would expect endogenous patients to have greater family histories of depression than do reactive patients, but numerous studies have shown that they do not (Rush & Weissenburger, 1994). Researchers are still investigating this question intensively, and it is partly to help them assemble research groups that the *DSM* requires diagnosticians to specify whether or not a depression has melancholic features.

When depression is preceded by a clearly precipitating event, that event is usually an uncontrollable loss—being laid off from work, losing one's home—and particularly, an interpersonal loss (Cronkite & Moos, 1995; Kendler, Karkowski, & Prescott, 1999). "Exit events"—death, separation, divorce, a child's leaving home—rank high among stressors associated with the onset of depression (Paykel & Cooper, 1992; Monroe, Rohde, Seeley, et al., 1999). By the same token, if a person has a close relationship, and therefore someone to confide in, he or she is less likely to succumb to depression in the face of stressful life events (Panzarella, Alloy, & Whitehouse, 2003). The same principles hold for people recovering from depression. Stress, particularly stress connected with exit

Having the comfort and support of a family member can help a person avoid the onset or relapse of depression that is associated with uncontrollable losses such as death.

events and other losses, is associated with relapses, while positive life events and social support, particularly in the form of a confidant, is associated with quicker recovery, even in the face of stress (Oldehinkel, Ormel, & Neeleman, 2000; Lara, Leader, & Klein, 1997).

Interestingly, recent theory and evidence suggests that stressful life events may be more important in precipitating first onsets than recurrences of major depression. For example, Post's (1992) "kindling" model suggests that certain neurobiological changes occur with each episode of depression such that episodes become more autonomous. As a consequence, stressors are hypothesized to be less likely to precipitate recurrences than first onsets of depression. Consistent with the kindling model, most studies have found that stressful events are less involved in precipitating recurrences than first onsets of depression (Kendler, Thornton, & Gardner, 2000; Lewinsohn, Allen, Seeley, et al., 1999), although one study suggested that an individual's age may be more important than his or her number of prior episodes in determining the role of stressful events in precipitating depression (Hlastala, Frank, Kowalski, et al., 2000).

Early Versus Late Onset In the past few years, evidence has been steadily accumulating that age at onset is an important dimension of mood disorder. The earlier the onset of the disorder, the more likely it is that the person's relatives have, or have had, mood disorders (Klein, Schatzberg, McCullough, et al., 1999). Some of the findings are quite remarkable. In a study of children of people with major depression, when the parent's age at onset was under 20, the lifetime risk of major depression in the child was almost twice as great as the risk when the parent's age at onset was over 30 (Weissman, Warner, Wickramaratne, et al., 1988). Early-onset patients are also more likely to have children and other relatives who are alcoholic (Kupfer, Frank, Carpenter, et al., 1989).

Early onset affects not just the relatives but also the person with the early onset. In a study of dysthymic patients, 94 percent of the early-onset group graduated to major depression, compared with 55 percent of the late-onset group—again, about a 2:1 ratio (Klein, Taylor, Dickstein, et al., 1988). Likewise, in a study of people with chronic major depression, the early-onset patients were more likely to have recurrent major depressive episodes, personality disorders, substance use disorders, and hospitalization (Klein, Schatzberg, McCullough, et al., 1999).

In general, then, the earlier the onset, the harder the road, both for the person and for the rest of the family. These findings may suggest that early-onset patients have a higher "genetic loading" for mood disorder. Alternatively, the higher rates of depression in the relatives of early-onset patients could be due to environmental effects. Relatives of early-onset cases have lived with a depressed person for a longer period of time. In particular, children of an early-onset depressed parent have had greater opportunity to learn depressive behaviors from the parent.

Comorbidity: Mixed Anxiety-Depression

One important trend in the study of depression is the increasing evidence of the **comorbidity,** or co-occurrence, of depressive and anxiety disorders (Pini, Cassano, Simonini, et al., 1997). Indeed, two thirds of depressed patients have a concurrent anxiety disorder and three quarters have had an anxiety disorder in their lifetime (Zimmerman, McDermut, & Mattia, 2000). Bipolar disorder also shows high comorbidity with anxiety disorders (Johnson, Cohen, & Brook, 2000; Suppes, Dennehy, & Gibbons, 2000). The symptomatologies of anxiety and depression show considerable overlap. Both include weeping, irritability, worry, fatigue, insomnia, low self-esteem, dependency, poor concentration, and feelings of helplessness (Alloy, Kelly, Mineka, et al., 1990). People in these two diagnostic groups also tend to respond to the same antidepressant drugs (Fyer, Liebowitz, & Klein, 1990), share similar endocrine abnormalities (Heninger, 1990), and have family histories of both anxiety and depressive disorders (Merikangus, 1990; Weissman, 1990). These findings have reignited an old debate over whether depression and anxiety are, in fact, two distinct entities or whether they are somewhat different manifestations of the same underlying disorder. One theory with considerable support, called the tripartite model, suggests that depression and anxiety each have unique features as well as a common underlying component. Both disorders are characterized by high negative affect (distress). However, depression is unique in also being characterized by low positive affect (low joy, engagement, etc.), whereas anxiety is unique in also being characterized by high autonomic nervous system arousal (Mineka, Watson, & Clark, 1988).

The comorbidity findings have also led to a proposal that a new category, mixed anxiety-depression, be included in the *DSM*. This would make the *DSM* consistent with the World Health Organization's *ICD-10,* which has such a category. More important, it would provide a diagnostic label for people who have mixed symptoms of anxiety and depression but who do not meet the *DSM-IV-TR* criteria for either disorder alone. Such people may be at risk for more severe mood and anxiety disorders, especially if they are not given appropriate treatment (Stein, Kirk, Prabhu, et al., 1995; Zinbarg, Barlow, Liebowitz, et al., 1994). Having no diagnostic label for them makes appropriate treatment less likely. However, mixed anxiety-depression that doesn't meet criteria for a diagnosis of either depression or anxiety may be infrequent and have few characteristic risk factors (Wittchen, Schuster, & Lieb, 2001).

Suicide

People take their lives for many reasons, but a very common reason is depression and bipolar disorder. People with major depression are at 11 times greater risk of making a suicide attempt, whereas those who also have had a manic episode are at almost 30 times greater risk for making a suicide attempt than people without a mood disorder (Kessler, Borges, & Walters, 1999). Among people who commit suicide, an estimated 55 percent were depressed before the fatal attempt (Isacsson & Rich, 1997).

The Prevalence of Suicide

Accurate statistics on the prevalence of suicide are difficult to obtain, because many people who commit suicide prefer to make their deaths look accidental. It has been estimated that at least 15 percent of all fatal automobile accidents are actually suicides, for example (Finch, Smith, & Pokorny, 1970). In 1998, the last year for which statistics are available, there were just over 30,000 suicides reported in the United States (National Center for Injury Prevention and Control, 2000). In the general population of the United States, it has been estimated that 4.6 percent attempt suicide and 13.5 percent have thought about committing suicide (Kessler, Borges, & Walters, 1999). Many statisticians and public health experts would consider these figures far too low (Madge & Harvey, 1999). As Figure 10.1 shows, other countries have far higher rates—Hungary's is almost four times that of the United States—and recent studies suggest that the worldwide rate is increasing (Harrison, 1997). But even at 30,000 per year, suicide is the ninth most common cause of death in this country.

❖ Groups at Risk for Suicide

Certain demographic variables are strongly correlated with suicide. Twice as many single people as married people kill themselves—widowed and divorced people, in particular, are at higher risk—and childless women are more likely to commit suicide than are those with children (Brockington, 2001; Kessler, Borges, & Walters, 1999). In general, the likelihood of a person's committing suicide increases as a function of age, especially for men (see Figure 10.2). Three times as many women as men attempt suicide, but four times as many men as women succeed in killing themselves (Peters & Murphy, 1998). The fact that men choose more lethal methods, such as shooting themselves, is one of the reasons more

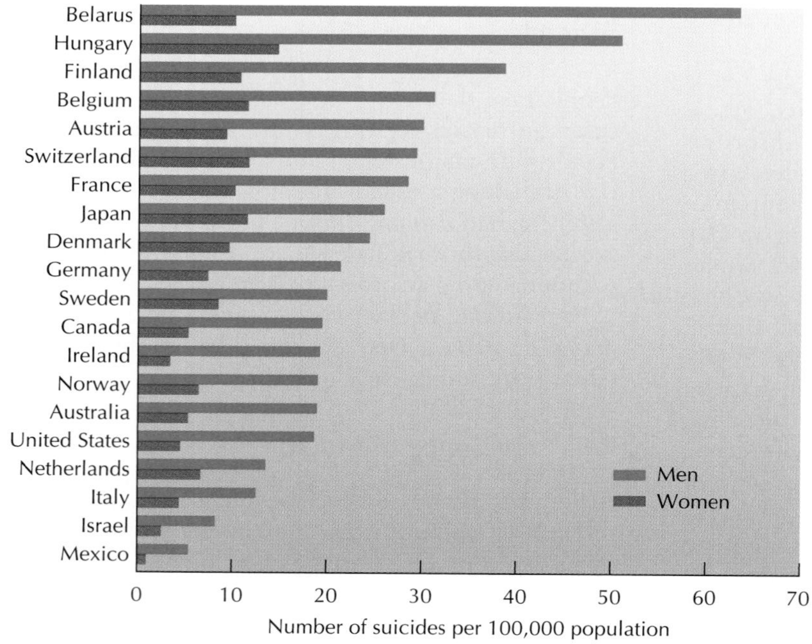

FIGURE 10.1 Age-adjusted suicide rates per 100,000 population for people aged 15 to 74, as of 1998 or most recent date available. (Based on World Health Organization statistics, 2000)

men die (Sachs-Ericsson, 2000). (Only in China and India do women commit suicide more frequently than men—a fact that may be related to the low status of women in those societies [Brockington, 2001].) Apart from depressed people, drug abusers are at higher risk (Shaffer, Gould, Fisher, et al., 1996), as are people with a history of childhood physical or sexual abuse (Wagner, 1997; Brockington, 2001).

According to a demographic summary put together by Shneidman and Farberow in 1970, the *modal suicide attempter* (i.e., the person who most commonly attempts suicide and survives) is a native-born European American woman, a homemaker in her twenties or thirties, who attempts to kill herself by swallowing barbiturates and gives as her reason either marital difficulties or depression. In contrast, the *modal suicide committer* (i.e., the person who succeeds in taking his or her own life) is a native-born European American man in his forties or older who, for reasons of ill health, depression, or marital difficulties, commits suicide by shooting or hanging himself or by poisoning himself with carbon monoxide (see Figures 10.3 and 10.4).

These generalizations still hold (Kessler, Borges, & Walters, 1999), but there have been some recent shifts

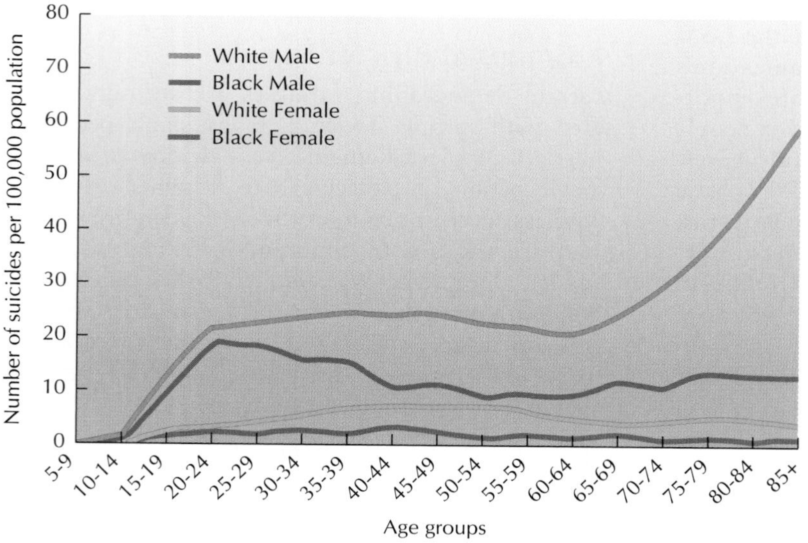

FIGURE 10.2 U.S. suicide rates by age, gender, and ethnic group in 1999. (National Institute of Mental Health, 2002)

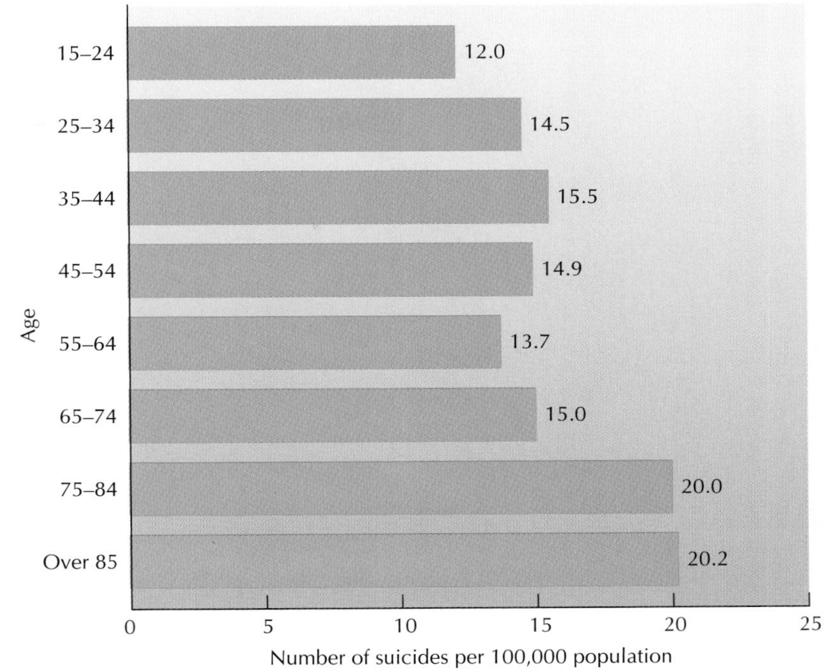

FIGURE 10.3 U.S. suicide rates by age. The largest number of suicides occurs in people over 85 years of age; in this group, there are 20.2 deaths per 100,000 of population. (Peters & Murphy, 1998)

in suicide-related variables, particularly regarding age. Suicide rates among men aged 15 to 34 have increased in the past few decades (Silverman, 1997). Older men are still more likely than younger men to kill themselves, but the gap is narrowing. The ethnic picture is also changing. Though European American men are still at higher risk than African American men (Kessler, Borges, & Walters, 1999), suicide among African American men is on the rise (Joe & Kaplan, 2001; Silverman, 1997).

Teenage Suicide Of special concern among groups at risk are teenagers, whose suicide rate has risen 200 percent since 1960. In 2000, suicide became the third leading cause of death among 15- to 24-year-olds (National Center for Health Statistics, 2000). As many as 15 percent of high school students have made at least one suicide attempt (King, 1997; Centers for Disease Control, 2001). Teenage girls are especially at risk for suicide attempts (Lewinsohn, Rohde, Seeley, et al., 2001). For many of their elders, this is hard to understand. How can people who "have their whole lives ahead of them" want to take those lives?

In some measure, the answer probably lies in the special circumstances of adolescence, the fact that, while teenagers may be exposed to situations as stressful as those facing adults, they lack the resources—emotional self-control, problem-solving capacity, mobility, money—that adults can marshal in order to find relief (Reynolds & Mazza, 1994). At the same time, teenagers today seem to have more cause for distress. Depression and substance abuse, two powerful risk factors for suicide, are both on the rise among adolescents (Gould & Kramer, 2001).

FIGURE 10.4 U.S. suicide rates by ethnicity and gender. Suicide occurs most frequently among white males, least frequently among African American females. (Peters & Murphy, 1998)

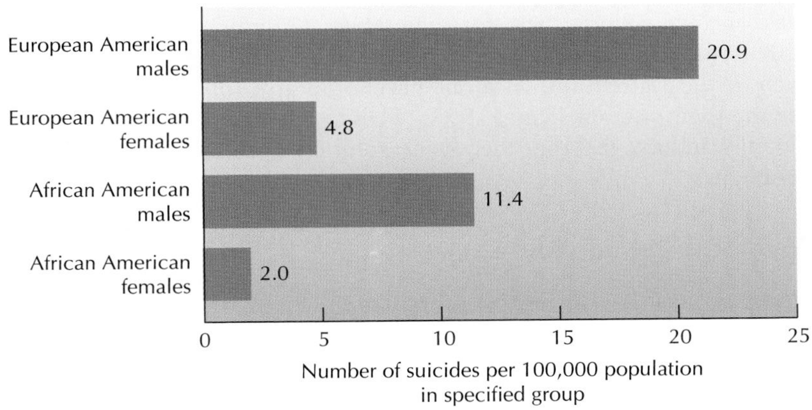

Teenage suicide has reached epidemic proportions in the United States. The episode shown here ended well, with the guard talking the young woman back into the building.

Apparently, another major risk factor for adolescent suicide is trouble within the family (Wagner, 1997). One "psychological autopsy" compared 120 teenage suicide victims with 147 controls matched for age, gender, and ethnic group. Compared with the controls, the suicide victims scored higher on several risk factors: depression, substance abuse, school problems, and social isolation. But another important difference between the two groups was the level of disturbance within the families. The suicide victims' families had suffered more suicides; they also showed poorer parent-child communications (Gould, Fisher, Parides, et al., 1996; Shaffer, Gould, Fisher, et al., 1996). Other studies found that, compared with the families of controls, the families of adolescent suicide attempters showed more conflict, more childhood sexual abuse, and poorer parental care (Gould & Kramer, 2001).

Thus, the problems of suicidal teenagers are often rooted in their families' problems. But, for the teenagers, the difficulties are multiplied: They are still dependent on their families for love and support that may not be forthcoming, and many are too young to seek out professional help for themselves. Only one fifth of the teenagers who attempt suicide receive even medical attention, let alone psychotherapy, following their attempt (King, 1997). These young people may, indeed, feel that there is no solution to their problems.

Myths About Suicide

Common as it is, suicide is still surrounded by an aura of mystery and by a number of popular misconceptions (Segal, 2000). One of the most unfortunate myths about suicide is that people who threaten to kill themselves will not carry out the threat—that only the "silent type" will pull it off. This is not true. In a study of 71 completed suicides, more than half the victims had clearly communicated their suicidal intent within 3 months before the fatal act (Isometsä, Henriksson, Aro, et al., 1994). When people threaten suicide, they should be taken seriously (Segal, 2000).

Another myth is that people who attempt suicide and fail are not serious about ending their lives—they are just looking for sympathy (Segal, 2000). On the contrary, about 40 percent of all suicides have made a previous attempt or threat (Maris, 1992), and the more prior attempts, the greater the likelihood of a completed suicide (Goldstein, Black, Nasrallah, et al., 1991).

People's emotional reactions to suicide—fear, horror, curiosity, incomprehension—have given it the status of "unmentionable" in the minds of many, a taboo that is strengthened by the Judeo-Christian prohibition against taking one's own life. Hence, a third myth about suicide is that one should never speak of it to people who are depressed. According to this notion, questioning depressed people about suicidal thoughts will either put the idea into their heads or, if it is already there, give it greater force. In opposition to this belief, most clinicians agree that encouraging patients to talk about suicidal wishes helps them to overcome such wishes (Segal, 2000).

Suicide Prediction

When someone commits suicide, family and friends are often astonished—which shows how often they are oblivious to the signs. As we just saw, most suicidal people clearly communicate their intent. For example, they may say, "I don't want to go on living" or "I know I'm a burden to everyone." But even those who don't announce their plans usually give signals (Shneidman, 1992). Some withdraw into an almost contemplative state. Others act as if they were going on a long trip. Others give away their most valued possessions. Sometimes the expression of suicidal intent is less direct, however clear in retrospect. For example, a depressed patient leaving the hospital on a weekend pass may say, "I want to thank you for trying so hard to help me." Failure to pick up such signs may be due in part to the fact that depressed people who commit suicide tend to do so as they are coming out of their depression. It is not clear whether they seem less depressed because they have made the decision to commit suicide or whether, being less depressed, they at last have the energy to act upon their suicidal wishes.

Predictably, suicide is often directly related to stress (Gould & Kramer, 2001). There is some evidence that the nature of the stress may vary over the life cycle. One study found that interpersonal conflicts, rejections, and separations most often precede suicide in younger people, whereas economic problems are more critical in middle age, illness in old age (Rich, Warsradt, Nemiroff, et al., 1991). Like the onset of depression, suicide attempts are frequently preceded by "exit" events.

Cognitive variables may be among the most useful predictors of who will attempt suicide. Not surprisingly, the cognitive variable most frequently associated with serious suicidal intent is hopelessness (Abramson, Alloy, Hogan, et al., 2000). In a 10-year follow-up study of hospitalized patients who expressed suicidal thoughts, hopelessness turned out to be the best single predictor of who would eventually kill themselves (Beck, Steer, Kovacs, et al., 1985), and this has proved true with outpatients and adolescents as well (Beck, Brown, Berchick, et al., 1990; Shaffer, Gould, Fisher, et al., 1996). Violent behavior also predicts completed suicide. A recent comparison of 753 victims of suicide with 2,115 accident victims found that the suicides were more likely to have exhibited violent behavior in the prior year (Conner, Cox, Duberstein, et al., 2001). From accounts of people who survived suicide attempts, together with research on those who died, suicide expert Edwin Shneidman (1992) put together a "suicidal scenario," a summary of elements that are usually present in the decision to take one's own life:

Severe stress and feelings of hopelessness drive some people to attempt suicide. This desperate man seized a gun and threatened suicide from the back seat of a police car. He later surrendered.

1. A sense of unbearable psychological *pain,* which is directly related to thwarted psychological *needs*
2. Traumatizing *self-denigration*—a self-image that will not include tolerating intense psychological pain
3. A marked *constriction* of the mind and an unrealistic narrowing of life's actions
4. A sense of *isolation*—a feeling of desertion and the loss of support of significant others
5. An overwhelmingly desperate feeling of *hopelessness*—a sense that nothing effective can be done
6. A conscious decision that *egression*—leaving, exiting, or stopping life—is the *only* (or at least the best possible) solution to the problem of unbearable pain (pp. 51–52)

As this summary shows, many people who commit suicide imagine that it is the only way out of an unbearably painful situation—a conviction that is often clear in the notes they leave. In a study comparing real suicide notes with simulated notes written by a well-matched control group, Shneidman and Farberow (1970) found that the writers of the genuine notes expressed significantly more suffering than the control group. Suicidal anguish is evidently hard to feign. Interestingly, though, the genuine suicide notes also contained a greater number of neutral statements—lists of things to be done after the suicide has taken place, and so forth. Both the ring of authentic hopelessness and the neutral content are illustrated in the following two genuine suicide notes:

Barbara,

I'm sorry. I love you bunches. Would you please do a couple of things for me. Don't tell the kids what I did. When Theresa gets a little older, if she wants to cut her hair please let her. Don't make her wear it long just because you like it that way. Ask your Mom what kind and how much clothes the kids need and then buy double what she says. I love you and the kids very much please try and remember that. I'm just not any good for you. I never learned how to tell you no. You will be much better off without me. Just try and find someone who will love Theresa and Donny.

Love Bunches—Charlie

P. S. Donny is down at Linda's
Put Donny in a nursery school

Dear Steve:

I have been steadily getting worse in spite of everything and did not want to be a burden the rest of my life.

All my love,
Dad

My brown suit is the only one that fits me.

Not all suicides feel unqualified despair, however. According to statistics from a national survey (Kessler, Borges, & Walters, 1999), only about 39 percent of people who attempt suicide are truly determined to die. Another 13 percent fall into what the researchers call the "to be or not to be" group—those who are ambivalent about dying. Finally, about 47 percent of suicide attempters do not really wish to die but, instead, are trying, through the gesture of a suicide attempt, to communicate the intensity of their suffering to family and friends. Regarding the last two groups, it bears repeating that their mixed feelings do not mean that they are not in danger. As we saw, many of those who are not determined this time will be more determined next time (King, 1997). Indeed, believing that one is a burden to one's family may make a person more determined to die. In a recent study comparing the suicide notes of people who attempted suicide with those of people who successfully completed suicide, Joiner and colleagues found that the expressed belief that one was a burden to family members distinguished the completed from the attempted suicide and also predicted use of more lethal methods, such as gunshot or hanging rather than overdose or cutting (Joiner, Pettit, Walker, et al., 2002).

Suicide Prevention

As we just pointed out, most people who attempt suicide do not absolutely wish to die. It was on the basis of this finding, together with the fact that suicide attempters are often reacting to crises in their lives, that the first telephone hotlines for potential suicides were established in the late 1950s. Hotline staffers, often volunteers, try to "tune in" to the caller's distress while presenting arguments against suicide and telling the caller where he or she can go for professional help. Another preventive effort, this one aimed specifically at the newly high-risk adolescent population, involves school-based programs. Here, teachers, parents, and the teenagers themselves are given workshops in which they are informed of the "warning signs" of suicide and are told how and to where to refer someone who seems to be in danger.

Unfortunately, neither of these efforts has been especially successful. Communities with suicide hotlines appear to have lower suicide rates only for one group—young white women, the most frequent hotline users—and, even for them, the decrease is slight (Gould & Kramer, 2001). As for the school-based programs, they seem to be minimally effective in changing attitudes and coping behavior, particularly in boys (Gould & Kramer, 2001), who are less likely than girls to turn to the kind of social and professional support that such workshops recommend (Gould & Kramer, 2001). It is probable, furthermore, that school-based programs are not reaching their target population. The adolescents most at risk for suicide—delinquents, substance abusers, runaways, incarcerated teenagers—are the ones least likely to be in school, let alone paying close attention to a suicide-prevention workshop. Other suicide-prevention efforts are designed to reduce the risk factors for suicide, such as gun availability, substance abuse, and depression (see the box on page 270). These efforts have been more successful (Gould & Kramer, 2001).

Mood Disorders: Theory and Therapy

Because depression is far more common than mania, most theories of mood disorder have concentrated on depression and suicide, and the therapies focus on depression. However, some theoretical perspectives have addressed bipolar disorder as well, and we will discuss these in turn. Among the theoretical approaches to mood disorders, the behavioral/interpersonal, cognitive, and neuroscience perspectives have had the greatest influence on understanding the causes of and generating treatments for mood disorders. Thus, we will present these three perspectives in greater detail than the psychodynamic and sociocultural models.

The Behavioral and Interpersonal Perspectives

Although the behavioral and interpersonal perspectives on depression and suicide include a collection of theories, we will discuss the two major approaches, one focusing on external reinforcers and the other on interpersonal processes.

Extinction Many behaviorists regard depression as the result of extinction (Ferster, 1973; Lewinsohn, 1974; Jacobson, Martell, & Dimidjian, 2001). That is, once behaviors are no longer rewarded, people cease to perform them. They become inactive and withdrawn—in short, depressed.

What causes the reduction in reinforcement? Lewinsohn (1974) has pointed out that the amount of positive reinforcement a person receives depends on three broad factors: (1) the number and range of stimuli that are reinforcing to that person; (2) the availability of such reinforcers in the environment; and (3) the person's skill in obtaining reinforcement. Sudden changes in a person's environment may affect any one of these factors. A new and reluctant retiree, for example, may find that the world outside the office holds few things that are truly reinforcing. Or a man whose wife has recently died may find that, whereas he had the social skills to make a success of marriage, he is at a loss in the dating situation. In their new circumstances, these people simply do not know how to obtain reinforcement; therefore, they withdraw into themselves.

A number of studies have produced results consistent with the extinction hypothesis. For example, one objection to this hypothesis has been the widely held assumption that depressed people are immune to reinforcement; it is not that they lack sources of pleasure but, rather, that they have lost the ability to experience pleasure. However, even severely depressed people show an elevation of mood if they become more active and thus make contact with reinforcing experiences (Jacobson, Martell, & Dimidjian, 2001). Depressed people also lack skill in obtaining reinforcement, as Lewinsohn suggested. Depressed people are much less adept than nondepressed people at interacting with others (Segrin & Abramson, 1994; Joiner, 2000). They are also less skillful at coping with the impediments to reinforcement. Not surprisingly, this is all the more true of suicide attempters. When a group of teenagers, hospitalized after a suicide attempt, was compared with a group of distressed but nonsuicidal teenagers, the suicidal subjects were far more likely to use social isolation as their way of coping with problems (Spirito, Overholser, & Stark, 1989). Suicidal adolescents are also likely to avoid problems, to see them inaccurately, and to respond to them in a more emotional fashion (Sadowski & Kelley, 1993). Of course, poor coping and avoidance of problems mean that these people are less likely to get help.

Aversive Social Behavior Some research has found that depressed individuals are more likely than nondepressed individuals to elicit negative reactions from people with whom they interact (Coyne, 1990; Joiner, 2000), and this finding has formed the basis of interpersonal theories of depression. According to one theory, people who are depressed have an aversive behavioral style in which, by constantly seeking reassurance, they try to force "caring" behavior from people who, they feel, no longer care enough. Instead of love, however, what depressed people are likely to get from their put-upon families and friends is shallow reassurance of the "now, now" variety or, worse, rejection, which simply aggravates their depression (Coyne, 1976; Joiner, Metalsky, Katz, et al., 1999). Morever, their depression may be contagious, especially if they engage in reassurance seeking, leading family and friends to also become more depressed (Joiner & Katz, 1999). Depression, then, is a cry for help, but one that rarely works. An alternative interpersonal theory is that people with depression actually seek out rejection, for this is more familiar and predictable to them than positive feedback (Giesler,

Josephs, & Swann, 1996). In response, they are rejected, and this deepens their depression (Joiner, 1995).

In support of these interpersonal hypotheses, some studies have found that rejecting responses from friends and family do tend to maintain or exacerbate depression (Joiner, 1995; Swann, Wenzlaff, Krull, et al., 1992). For example, depressed and bipolar patients whose spouses or parents were critical toward them were more likely to suffer a relapse in the next nine months than were those with more accepting families (Butzlaff & Hooley, 1998). Moreover, excessive reassurance seeking predicts later depressive symptoms (Joiner, Metalsky, Katz, et al., 1999). For example, Joiner and Schmidt (1998) found that Air Force cadets who engaged in high reassurance seeking showed subsequent increases in depressive symptoms during basic training. Whether or not aversive social behavior predates the depression, though, depressed individuals' interpersonal skills probably help to maintain their depression.

Increasing Reinforcement and Social Skills In keeping with the extinction theory of depression, behaviorists developed a treatment designed to get depressed people to become more active and thus expose themselves to reinforcing experiences. Jacobson, Martell, and Dimidjian (2001) describe behavioral activation (BA) therapy as a way to break the vicious cycle that can develop between a person's depressed mood, decreased activity and increased withdrawal, and worsened depression. Dispelling the notion that a depressed person's mood must change before his or her behavior can change, behavioral activation therapists have found that engaging in planned, positive activities elevates depressed individuals' moods and helps them reengage in their lives. Patient and therapist work together to identify positively reinforcing behaviors—specific activities the patient believes would be most helpful to him or her. Patients then must engage in these activities according to a schedule, whether or not they feel like it. If the behavior helps patients function better in spite of their mood, or improves their mood, they are encouraged to continue to perform the activity. By completing increasingly difficult tasks, patients gradually begin to fully participate in those activities most likely to encourage further activity and improve their mood.

Another important thrust in the behavioral treatment of depression has been **social-skills training.** As we have seen, depressed people are not popular with others—a problem that social-skills training aims to remedy directly by teaching basic techniques for engaging in satisfying social interactions. Patients are shown how to initiate a conversation, how to keep eye contact, how to make small talk, how to end a conversation—in other words, the nuts and bolts of socializing. Such behaviors are often modeled for patients, after which they are practiced through role playing. The therapist, for example, might pretend to be a guest at a party with whom the patient must open a conversation.

Most behavioral treatments for depression are multifaceted, using the techniques previously described, together with others. For example, Lewinsohn and his colleagues have put together a treatment that includes self-monitoring of mood and activities, instruction in positive coping self-statements, and training in a variety of areas—coping skills, social skills, parenting skills, time management—with the aim of decreasing unpleasant experiences and increasing pleasant experiences (Lewinsohn & Gotlib, 1995). Similar multifaceted programs have been used with suicidal patients.

In evaluating the effectiveness of any treatment (behavioral or otherwise) for depression, one must keep in mind that 85 percent of depressed people recover from an episode within a year, even with no treatment. Furthermore, drug studies indicate that 20 to 40 percent of outpatient depressed patients recover in 2 to 4 months, even if all they receive is a placebo. Thus, it is relatively easy to design a therapy that ends with a substantial rate of recovery. There is going to be substantial recovery, anyway.

Because, as we will see, there are effective antidepressant drugs that are much less expensive than psychotherapy, the latter has to outperform these drugs (and placebos) in order to justify its use. However, because none of the drugs actually *cures* depression—that is, prevents relapses as well as lifts current mood—psychotherapy could prove its usefulness by showing that it does prevent recurrence. Initial findings from studies of BA therapy show that it is effective in both reducing acute depression and preventing relapse over a 2-year period (Jacobson, Dobson, Truax, et al., 1996; Gortner, Gollan, Dobson, et al., 1998).

The Cognitive Perspective

As we saw earlier, depression involves a number of changes: emotional, motivational, cognitive, and physical. Cognitive theorists hold that the critical variable is the cognitive change. In all cognitive formulations, it is the way people *think* about themselves, the world, and the future that gives rise to the other factors involved in depression.

Helplessness and Hopelessness In a cognitive-learning model of depression, Martin Seligman (1975) has suggested that depression may be understood as analogous to the phenomenon of **learned helplessness.** This phenomenon was first demonstrated with laboratory dogs. After exposing a number of dogs to inescapable electric shocks, Seligman and his colleagues found that when the same dogs were later subjected to escapable shocks, they either did not initiate escape responses or were slow and inept at escaping. The investigators concluded that during the first phase of the experiment, when the shocks were inescapable, the dogs had learned that the shock was *uncontrollable*—a lesson they continued to act upon even in the second phase of the experiment, when it was possible to escape the shocks (Maier, Seligman, & Solomon, 1969; Peterson, Maier, & Seligman, 1993).

After further research on learned helplessness in animals and humans, Seligman noted that this phenomenon closely resembled depression. He therefore proposed that depression, like learned helplessness, was a reaction to inescapable or seemingly inescapable stressors, which undermined adaptive responses by teaching the person that he or she lacked control over reinforcement. This formulation is consistent with the finding that when there is a clear, precipitating event for a depression, it is often an uncontrollable loss. Learned helplessness also fits with certain neuroscience findings. For example, exposure to uncontrollable (versus controllable) stress results in neurobiological changes consistent with depression (Minor & Saade, 1997), and depressed patients who see themselves as helpless tend to show higher levels of MHPG, a product of norepinephrine metabolism (Samson, Mirin, Hauser, et al., 1992). As we will see, norepinephrine abnormalities are often found in depressed people. In addition, PET scans of people doing unsolvable problems—which tend to produce learned helplessness—show that learned helplessness is associated with increased brain activity in the limbic system. The limbic system is also implicated in the processing of negative emotions such as depression (Schneider, Gur, Alavi, et al., 1996).

Note the difference between the learned helplessness theory and extinction theory. In extinction theory, the crucial factor is an objective environmental condition, a lack of positive reinforcement; in learned helplessness theory, the crucial factor is a subjective cognitive process, the *expectation* of lack of control over reinforcement.

When it was originally formulated, the learned helplessness model had certain weaknesses. As Seligman and his colleagues pointed out, the model explained the passivity characteristic of depression but did not explain the equally characteristic sadness, guilt, and suicidal thoughts. Neither did it account for the fact that different cases of depression vary considerably in intensity and duration. To fill these gaps, Abramson, Metalsky, and Alloy (1989) adapted the model from a helplessness to a hopelessness theory. According to their view, depression depends not just on the belief that there is a lack of control over reinforcement (a *helplessness expectancy*) but also on the belief that negative events will persist or recur (a *negative outcome expectancy*). When a person holds these two expectations—that bad things will happen and that there is nothing one can do about it—he or she becomes hopeless, and it is this hopelessness that is the immediate cause of the depression (Abramson, Metalsky, & Alloy, 1989).

But what is the source of the expectations of helplessness and negative outcomes? According to the researchers, these expectations stem from the *attributions* and *inferences* people make regarding stressful life events—that is, the perceived causes and consequences of such events. People who see negative life events as due to causes that are (1) permanent rather than temporary, (2) generalized over many areas of their life rather than specific to one area of their functioning, and (3) internal, or part of their personalities, rather than external, or part of the environment, are at greatest risk for developing hopelessness and, in turn, severe and persistent depression. Likewise, people who infer that stressful events will have negative consequences for themselves are more likely to become hopeless and depressed. In fact, Abramson, Metalsky, and Alloy have proposed that "hopelessness depression" constitutes a distinct subtype of depression, with its own set of causes (negative inferential styles combined with stress), symptoms (passivity, sadness, suicidal tendencies, low self-esteem), and appropriate treatments. This theory also applies to suicide. Hopelessness is the best single predictor of suicide—even better than depression (Glanz, Haas, & Sweeney, 1995; Abramson, Alloy, Hogan, et al., 2000).

In the past decade, the revised hopelessness theory has been extensively tested with mostly positive results. It has been found that depressed individuals are more likely than controls to explain negative events by means of the kind of attributions listed in the previous paragraph (Joiner & Wagner, 1995; Sweeney, Anderson, & Bailey, 1986) and to exhibit expectations of low control or helplessness (Weisz, Southam-Gerow, & McCarthy, 2001). Moreover, inferential style can help predict who, in a given sample, has been depressed in the past (Alloy, Abramson, Hogan, et al., 2000), who will be depressed or suicidal in the future (Abramson, Alloy, Hogan, et al., 1998; Alloy, Abramson, Whitehouse, et al., 1999; 2003), and who, having recovered from depression, will relapse

(Ilardi, Craighead, & Evans, 1997; Alloy, Abramson, Whitehouse, et al., 1999; 2003). It also predicts the duration of major depressive episodes (McMahon, Alloy, & Abramson, 2003) and who, in a group of depressed people, will recover when exposed to positive events (Needles & Abramson, 1990). Other studies have shown that the reason a combination of stress and negative inferential style predicts depression is that this combination predicts hopelessness. It is hopelessness that, in turn, predicts depression (Alloy & Clements, 1998; Metalsky, Joiner, Hardin, et al., 1993). Finally, people who show this combination also exhibit many of the symptoms said to be part of the hopelessness-depression subtype (Alloy, Just, & Panzarella, 1997; Alloy & Clements, 1998), and these symptoms hang together to form a distinct dimension of depression (Joiner, Steer, Abramson, et al., 2001). At the same time there is conflicting evidence. For example, some researchers have found that the stress-plus-negative-attributions combination did not necessarily lead to depression (Cole & Turner, 1993; Lewinsohn, Joiner, & Rohde, 2001). To summarize, most of the evidence argues that inferential style and hopelessness play a role in predicting risk for depression. What is not clear is whether they actually help *cause* the depression.

Given the evidence that a negative inferential style does act as a vulnerability factor for depression, it becomes important to uncover the developmental origins of this cognitive vulnerability. Recent findings suggest that both social learning factors and a childhood history of maltreatment may contribute to the development of cognitive vulnerability to depression. Individuals whose parents had negative cognitive styles, provided negative inferential feedback about the causes and consequences of stressful events in the individual's life (e.g., told their child, "you weren't invited to that party because you're unpopular, and now you'll be seen as a social outcast at school"), and whose parenting was low in warmth and affection are more likely to have negative cognitive styles as adults (Alloy, Abramson, Tashman, et al., 2001; Garber & Flynn, 2001; Ingram & Ritter, 2000). In addition, people with childhood histories of emotional abuse from either parents or nonrelatives (peers, teachers, etc.) are also more likely to have negative cognitive styles as adults (Gibb, Abramson, & Alloy, in press; Gibb, Alloy, Abramson, et al., 2001). Thus, a history of negative emotional feedback and abuse may help lead to the development of later cognitive vulnerability to depression. However, prospective studies beginning in childhood are needed to truly test this hypothesis.

Negative Self-Schema A second major cognitive theory of depression, Aaron Beck's negative self-schema model, evolved from his findings that the hallucinations, delusions, and dreams of depressed patients often contain themes of self-punishment, loss, and deprivation. According to Beck, this negative bias—the tendency to see oneself as a "loser"—is the fundamental cause of depression. If a person, because of childhood experiences, develops a cognitive "schema" in which the self, the world, and the future are viewed in a negative light, that person is then predisposed to depression. Stress can easily activate the negative schema, and the consequent negative perceptions merely strengthen the schema (Beck, 1987; Clark, Beck, & Alford, 1999).

Recent research supports Beck's claim that depressed individuals have unusually negative self-schemas (Dozois & Dobson, 2001; Williams, Watts, MacLeod, et al., 1997) and that these schemas can be activated by negative cues. In one interesting study, depressed and normal participants performed an emotional Stroop task: They were shown positive and negative self-descriptive adjectives and were asked to name the color of ink the adjectives were printed in. When the participants were exposed to a series of negative self-statements (e.g., "I often feel judged") before performing the Stroop test, the depressed subjects were significantly slower at naming the ink colors for the negative adjectives on the Stroop task (Segal, Gemar, Truchon, et al., 1995). Presumably, their negative self-schemas were primed in the first stage and then, on the Stroop task, went into action. Negative self-schemas can also be activated by sad mood in people who have recovered from depression (Ingram, Miranda, & Siegel, 1998; Gemar, Segal, Sagrati, et al., 2001), and such reactivated negative schemas predict later relapse and recurrence of depression (Segal, Gemar, & Williams, 1999).

Other studies indicate that people at high risk for depression either because they have negative cognitive styles, a past history of major depression, or parents who are depressed selectively attend to and remember more negative than positive information about themselves (Alloy, Abramson, Murray, et al., 1997; Ingram & Ritter, 2000; Taylor & Ingram, 1999). Still other research suggests that depressed individuals may have two distinct negative self-schemas, one centered on dependency, the other on self-criticism (Nietzel & Harris, 1990). For those with dependency self-schemas, stressful social events—in other words, situations in which their dependency would be most keenly felt—lead to depression. For those with self-criticism schemas, failure should trigger depression. Researchers testing this hypothesis have found that it may not work to predict onsets of major depression (Mazure, Bruce, Maciejewski, et al., 2000) and that in predicting symptoms of depression, it works better for dependency self-schemas and social events than for self-criticism schemas and failure (Coyne & Whiffen, 1995).

An interesting finding is that, while people with depression may be more pessimistic than the rest of us, their pessimism is sometimes more realistic than our optimism. Lewinsohn and his colleagues put a group of depressed outpatients and two control groups through a series of social interactions and then asked the participants (1) how positively or negatively they reacted to the others and (2) how positively or negatively they thought the others reacted to them. As it turned out, the depressed individuals' evaluations of the impression they had made were more accurate than those of the other two groups, both of whom thought they had made more positive impressions than they actually had (Lewinsohn, Mischel, Chaplin, et al., 1980). To quote the report of another Lewinsohn research team, "To feel good about ourselves we may have to judge ourselves more kindly than we are judged" (Lewinsohn, Sullivan, & Grosscup, 1980, p. 212).

We may also have to judge ourselves more capable than we are. Alloy and Abramson (1979) found that depressed people, in doing an experimental task, were far more accurate in judging how much control they had than were nondepressed participants, who tended to overestimate their control when they were doing well and to underestimate it when they were doing poorly. Thus, in certain respects it may be that normal people, not depressed people, are cognitively biased—and that such bias is essential for psychological health (Alloy & Abramson, 1988; Haaga & Beck, 1995). Research supports this view. Alloy and Clements (1992), for example, tested a group for bias in judging personal control. They found that the individuals who had been inaccurately optimistic about their personal control when they were first tested were less likely than more realistic participants to become depressed a month later in the face of stress. Another study suggests that both realistic and unrealistically negative self-perceptions predict later depressive symptoms in children (Hoffman, Cole, Martin, et al., 2000).

Although most research on the cognitive theories of depression (both Beck's theory and the hopelessness theory) has focused on unipolar depression, recent findings suggest that cognitive models may be applicable to bipolar disorder as well. Individuals with bipolar disorders exhibit cognitive styles and self-schemas as negative as those with unipolar depression (Alloy, Reilly-Harrington, Fresco, et al., 1999; Lyon, Startup, & Bentall, 1999; Scott, Stanton, Garland, et al., 2000). Moreover, negative cognitive styles and self-schema information processing combine with stressful life events to predict subsequent increases in manic as well as depressive symptoms among people with bipolar disorder (Reilly-Harrington, Alloy, Fresco, et al., 1999).

While these studies strongly suggest that cognitive variables play an important role in depression, it is by no means clear that the role is causal (Haaga, Dyck, & Ernst, 1991). However, as we have seen before, a factor need not be causal in order to be useful in treatment.

Cognitive Retraining Aaron Beck and his coworkers have developed a multifaceted therapy that includes behavioral assignments, modification of dysfunctional thinking, and attempts to change schemas. The alteration of schemas is considered most important and, according to Beck's theory, will inoculate the patient against future depressions. First, however, the therapist attacks the present depression, through "behavioral activation"—that is, getting the patients to get out and engage in pleasurable activities (see the discussion on page 264)—and by teaching them ways of testing dysfunctional thinking. On a form (Figure 10.5), patients are asked to record their negative thoughts, together with the events that preceded them. Then they are to counter such thoughts with rational responses and record the outcome (Young, Beck, & Weinberger, 1993). An example of countering negative thoughts with more rational responses can be seen in the case of Irene, who felt stupid for not knowing the answer to one of the therapist's questions. In the extended excerpt below, the therapist helped Irene set up an experiment to test the thought, "I look dumb":

> T: OK, now let's just do an experiment and see if you yourself can respond to the automatic thought and let's see what happens to your feeling. See if responding rationally makes you feel worse or makes you feel better.
>
> I: OK.
>
> T: OK, why didn't I answer that question right? I look dumb. What is the rational answer to that? A realistic answer?
>
> I: Why didn't I answer that question? Because I thought for a second that was what I was supposed to say, and then when I heard the question over again, then I realized that was not what I heard. I didn't hear the question right, that's why I didn't answer it right.
>
> T: OK, so that is the fact situation. And so is the fact situation that you look dumb or you just didn't hear the question right?

DATE	**SITUATION** Describe: 1. Actual event leading to unpleasant emotion, or 2. Stream of thoughts, daydream, or recollection, leading to unpleasant emotion.	**EMOTION(S)** 1. Specify sad/ anxious/ angry, etc. 2. Rate degree of emotion, 1–100.	**AUTOMATIC THOUGHT(S)** 1. Write automatic thought(s) that preceded emotion(s). 2. Rate belief in automatic thought(s), 0–100%.	**RATIONAL RESPONSE** 1. Write rational response to automatic thought(s). 2. Rate belief in rational response, 0–100%.	**OUTCOME** 1. Rerate belief in automatic thought, 0–100%. 2. Specify and rate subsequent emotions, 1–100.

Explanation: When you experience an unpleasant emotion, note the situation that seemed to stimulate the emotion. (If the emotion occurred while you were thinking, daydreaming, etc., please note this.) Then note the automatic thought associated with the emotion. Record the degree to which you believe this thought: 0% = not at all; 100% = completely. In rating degree of emotion: 1 = a trace; 100 = the most intense possible.

FIGURE 10.5 Form for "daily record of dysfunctional thoughts," as used in the cognitive treatment developed by Beck and his co-workers. (Young, Beck, & Weinberger, 1993, p. 250)

I: I didn't hear the question right.

T: Or is it possible that I didn't say the question in such a way that it was clear.

I: Possible.

T: Very possible. I'm not perfect, so it's very possible that I didn't express the question properly.

I: But instead of saying you made a mistake, I would still say I made a mistake.

T: We'll have to watch the video and see. Whichever. Does it mean if I didn't express the question, if I made a mistake, does it make me dumb?

I: No.

T: And if you made the mistake, does it make you dumb?

I: No, not really.

T: But you felt dumb?

I: But I did, yeah.

T: Do you feel dumb still?

I: No.

A refinement of cognitive retraining is *reattribution training,* which aims to correct negative attributional styles (Beck, Rush, Shaw, et al., 1979). In this approach, patients are taught to explain their difficulties to themselves in more constructive ways ("It wasn't my fault—it was the circumstances, " "It's not my whole personality that's wrong—it's just my way of reacting to strangers") and to seek out information consistent with these more hopeful attributions. A similar approach has been used with suicidal patients. Beck and his colleagues see this as a way of correcting negative bias. As the research cited previously suggests, it may also be a way of instilling positive bias. In any case, it seems to combat hopelessness.

In some encouraging evaluations, cognitive therapies have been shown to be at least as effective as drug therapy and perhaps superior to drugs at 1-year follow-up (Blackburn & Moorhead, 2000; Hollon, Shelton, & Davis, 1993). A combination of cognitive-behavioral therapy and drugs may have a slight advantage when compared with either treatment by itself (Hollon, DeRubeis, Evans, et al., 1992; Kupfer & Frank, 2001). Some experts interpret the evidence as indicating that cognitive-behavioral therapy, unlike drug therapy, has a relapse-prevention effect (Evans, Hollon, DeRubeis, et al., 1992), but there is considerable debate about this (Jacobson & Hollon, 1996; Klein, 1996b). More recent studies have supported a relapse and recurrence prevention effect for cognitive-behavioral therapy (Jarrett, Kraft, Doyle, et al., 2001; Paykel, Scott, Teasdale, et al., 1999). There is also some question as to whether cognitive-behavioral therapy works as well as drugs for severely depressed patients (DeRubeis, Gelfand, Tang, et al., 1999; Blackburn & Moorhead, 2000).

Furthermore, there is controversy about the mechanisms by which cognitive-behavioral therapy produces change. For example, there is evidence that cognitive-behavioral therapy produces changes both in negative cognitions, as it is hypothesized to work, as well as in abnormal biological processes (Blackburn & Moorhead, 2000). So whether it works through the proposed cognitive mechanism or by changing biological processes is unclear. Also, as noted, Beck's treatment is multifaceted, including behavioral activation together with cognitive tasks. A recent study by Jacobson and his colleagues found that the behavioral activation component of cognitive-behavioral therapy worked as well as the entire treatment package, both at alleviating depression and at preventing relapse (Gortner, Gollan, Dobson, et al., 1998; Jacobson, Dobson, Truax, et al., 1996). Thus, it could be that cognitive-behavioral therapy is just as effective without its cognitive components. Regardless of how it works, cognitive-behavioral therapy does indeed work. Thus, recent efforts have extended this approach to the prevention of depression in children and adolescents (see the box on the Penn Optimism Project, page 270). Cognitive-behavioral therapy has also been extended to the treatment of patients with bipolar disorder as an adjunct to mood-stabilizing medications (Basco, 2000; Newman, Leahy, Beck, et al., 2002). And recent findings suggest that it is promising in improving bipolar patients' medication compliance, symptoms, and interpersonal functioning (Newman, Leahy, Beck, et al., 2002; Scott, Garland, & Moorhead, 2001).

The Psychodynamic Perspective

Reactivated Loss The first serious challenge to Kraepelin's biogenic theory of mood disorder came from Freud and other early psychoanalytic theorists, who argued that depression was not a symptom of organic dysfunction but a massive defense mounted by the ego against intrapsychic conflict. In his now-classic paper "Mourning and Melancholia" (1917/1957), Freud described depression as a response to loss (real or symbolic), but one in which the person's sorrow and rage in the face of that loss remain unconscious, thus weakening the ego. This formulation was actually an elaboration of a theory put forth by one of Freud's students, Karl Abraham (1911/1948, 1916/1948). Abraham had suggested that depression arises when one loses a love object toward whom one had ambivalent, positive and negative, feelings. In the face of the love object's desertion, the negative feelings turn to intense anger. At the same time, the positive feelings give rise to guilt, a feeling that one failed to behave properly toward the now-lost love object. Because of this guilt—and because of early memories in which the primary love object was symbolically "eaten up, " or incorporated, by the infant—the grieving person turns his or her anger inward rather than outward, thus producing the self-hatred and despair that we call depression. In the case of suicide, the person is actually trying to kill the incorporated love object. "Anger in" has escalated to "murder in."

While "anger in" still figures importantly in traditional psychoanalytic discussions of depression and suicide, modern theorists have expanded and revised this early position. There are now many psychodynamic theories of depression, yet they share a certain number of core assumptions (Bemporad, 1988; Blatt & Homann, 1992). First, it is generally believed that depression is rooted in a very early defect, often the loss or threatened loss of a parent (Bowlby, 1973). Second, the primal wound is reactivated by a recent blow, such as a divorce or job loss. Whatever the precipitating event, the person is plunged back into the infantile trauma. Third, a major consequence of this regression is a sense of helplessness and hopelessness—a reflec-tion of what was the infant's actual powerlessness in the face of harm. Feeling incapable of controlling his or her world, the depressed person simply withdraws from it. Fourth, many theorists, while perhaps no longer regarding anger as the hub of depression, feel that ambivalence toward introjected objects (i.e., love objects who have been "taken in" to the self) is fundamental to the depressed person's emotional quandary. Fifth, it is widely agreed that loss of self-esteem is a primary feature of depression. Otto Fenichel (1945) described depressed people as "love addicts," trying continually to compensate for their own depleted self-worth by seeking comfort and reassurance from others. This leads to the sixth common psychodynamic assumption about depression: that it has a functional role. It is not just something that people feel but something that they *use,* particularly in the form of dependency, in their relationships with others.

Like most psychodynamic theories, these assumptions are not fully open to empirical validation, but two claims have been tested. First, a high level of dependency on others does appear to characterize some depressed persons (Bornstein, 1992), and these highly dependent people are more likely to become depressed

Prevention The Penn Optimism Project

If you are more than 18 years old and have not experienced an episode of depression, you have passed one of the important periods of risk for this disorder. A recent longitudinal study of more than 600 people from birth to age 21 (Hankin, Abramson, Moffitt, et al., 1998) revealed that almost 25 percent of the girls and 10 percent of the boys experienced a clinically significant case of depression by the age of 21. As seen in Figure 10.6, the greatest increase in cases occurred during the period from 15 to 18 years of age. Prior to age 15, only about 1 percent of the boys and 4 percent of the girls had experienced a serious case of depression. These findings suggest that, if we are to prevent the majority of adolescent cases of depression, the time to intervene would be prior to age 15. Intervention for girls would be especially important, because of their dramatically greater incidence at this time.

Effective prevention programs for adolescent depression are just being developed. In a very promising effort known as the Penn Optimism Project, researchers at the University of Pennsylvania (Gillham, Reivich, Jaycox, et at., 1995; Gillham & Reivich, 1999) reported some success in preventing the incidence of depressive symptoms in a group of 69 fifth- and sixth-grade children from a Philadelphia suburban school district. The children were selected because they were above the average in their school on a screening test for childhood depression. A comparison group of 49 children from a different school but with similar screening scores was formed to assess the natural increase in depressive symptoms that were expected to occur in the absence of intervention. Both groups were assessed shortly before the intervention, shortly after the intervention, and at 6-month intervals for a 2-year period.

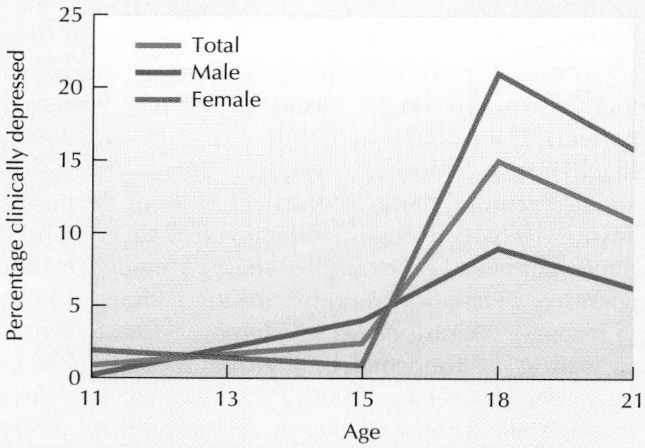

FIGURE 10.6 Development of new cases of clinical depression by age and gender. (Hankin, Abramson, Moffitt, et al., 1998)

The intervention took place in small groups (of about 10 children) with a professional leader who conducted exercises and training sessions that lasted about 1½ hours. The sessions occurred once a week for 12 weeks. One component of the training was based on cognitive therapy for depression. Children were taught to reconsider negative beliefs about themselves and to think about more realistic and constructive beliefs. They were also taught to identify pessimistic (stable, general) attributions for their successes and failures and to replace them with more optimistic (unstable, specific) attributions. Another component of the training centered on problem-solving skills that would enable the children to cope more effectively with stressful events, such as conflicts with parents and peers. Training exercises were also conducted to give the children practice in solving problems and in role-playing effective coping behaviors.

The results of the program were quite impressive. After 1 year of follow-up,

when they experience social rejections (Coyne & Whiffen, 1995; Spasojevic & Alloy, 2002). Second, research has examined the role of parental loss, though the results are mixed. There is evidence for the link. Women who have lost their mothers in childhood through either death or separation are apparently more likely to succumb to depression (Harris, Brown, & Bifulco, 1990), and depressed patients who have suffered a serious childhood loss, particularly separation from a parent, are more likely to attempt suicide (Bron, Strack, & Rudolph, 1991). But many researchers now believe that the crucial risk factor, at least for depression is not so much parental loss as poor parenting (Kendler, Neale, Kessler, et al., 1992a; Lara & Klein, 1999). Recent research has focused especially on a parenting pattern called *affectionless control*—that is, too much protectiveness combined with too little real warmth and care. This pattern may leave children feeling chronically helpless and overdependent. As adults, when they encounter stress, they are more vulnerable to depression because they feel helpless (Alloy, Abramson, Tashman, et al., 2001; Garber & Flynn, 2001).

The recent focus on poor parenting in the histories of depressed individuals is consistent with a more modern psychoanalytic theory, **attachment theory** (Cassidy & Shaver, 1999). According to attachment theory, people who had close, caring bonds with a caregiver while growing up are more apt to develop an adaptive interpersonal style of relating to others, called a "secure" attachment style. In contrast, people exposed to punitive or inconsistent parenting are likely to develop a more maladaptive interpersonal style, described as an "insecure" attachment style. Such insecure attachment has been found to be associated with problems in later interactions with the children in the prevention group began to report less severe symptoms of depression than the children in the comparison group. As seen in Figure 10.7, only about 7 percent of the children in the prevention group reported high levels of depressive symptoms at the 12-month follow-up, while nearly 30 percent of the control group did. This pattern continued through the second year of follow-up. It was also encouraging that the beneficial effects of the program occurred for children who had very few symptoms at the outset of the program as well as for children who had already begun to show symptoms of childhood depression when the program began. In either case, one would expect symptoms of depression to increase, but it was primarily the untreated group that showed the developmentally predicted increases. Unfortunately, the beneficial effects of the intervention on depressive symptoms faded after 2 years, although more positive attributional styles appeared to be a lasting effect of the intervention (Gillham & Reivich, 1999). However, another team of researchers found that a cognitive-behavioral prevention program reduced the likelihood of major depressive episodes in children of depressed parents (Clarke, Hornbrook, Lynch, et al., 2001).

The children in this program had not yet entered the critical 15- to 18-year age period of risk at the time of the 2-year follow-up. Future research will also be needed to determine how well the program works with children from different socioeconomic backgrounds and whether it is equally successful for boys and girls. However, this initial research suggests that it will be possible to prevent early onset of depression by providing children with cognitive and social skills that can be used to cope with stress and other risk factors for depression.

A similar cognitive-behavioral program has been developed for college students considered at risk for depression because they exhibit negative attributional styles. Those who received the preventive intervention had fewer moderate (but not severe) depressive episodes and showed greater improvement in their attributional styles, sense of hopelessness, and dysfunctional attitudes than the control group (Seligman, Schulman, DeRubeis, et al., 1999).

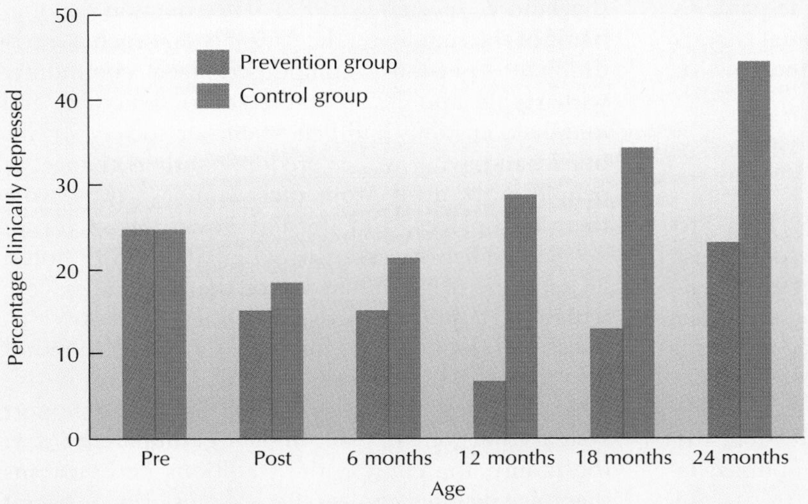

FIGURE 10.7 Depressive symptoms in children. (Gillham, Jaycox, & Seligman, 1995)

significant others and with depression (Safford, Alloy, Crossfield, et al., in press).

Repairing the Loss In Chapter 7, we described the basic psychodynamic treatment for the "neuroses." Such treatment is used for nonpsychotic depression as well. Through free association, dream analysis, and analysis of resistance and transference, the therapist tries to uncover the childhood roots of the current depression and to explore the patient's ambivalent feelings toward the lost object, both primal and current.

As we have noted, however, today's psychodynamic therapists tend to be more directive than their predecessors, as well as more concerned with the patient's present circumstances than with the past. Hence, many therapists focus less on childhood trauma than on the current cause of the depression and on how the patient uses the depression in his or her dealings with others. This pragmatism is even more pronounced in short-term therapy. Klerman and his co-workers have devised a treatment, based on the work of Harry Stack Sullivan (Chapter 5), called **interpersonal psychotherapy,** or **IPT.** In this 12- to 16-session therapy, therapist and patient first identify the core problem. The four most common core problems are assumed to be grief, interpersonal disputes (e.g., a failing marriage), role transition (e.g., retirement), and lack of social skills. Once the problem is identified, however, therapist and patient do not spend time on interpretation or analysis. Instead, they attack the problem directly through discussion of possible solutions and strategies for carrying out those solutions (Klerman, Weissman, Rounsaville, et al., 1984). Recent studies indicate that IPT does prevent relapses in formerly depressed patients who have discontinued drug treatment (Frank, Kupfer, Perel, et al., 1990). It also appears to be effective in helping people who are depressed (Mufson, Weissman, Moreau, et al., 1999). Although IPT has not been subjected to as many studies as cognitive therapy for depression, it seems to work just as well, at least in the short run (Shea, Elkin, Imber, et al., 1992). For severely depressed patients, it may be even more effective than cognitive treatments (Elkin, Shea, Watkins, et al., 1989).

Psychodynamic treatment of the suicidal patient tends to follow the same lines as treatment for depression, but with special emphasis on emotional support. With potential suicides, therapists are careful to avoid doing or saying anything that could be viewed as rejection. In their analysis of the patient's behavior, they are likely to interpret suicidal threats as an appeal for love, whether from the therapist or from others.

The Sociocultural Perspective

Society and Depression One of the first scholars to study suicide scientifically was French sociologist Émile Durkheim, writing in the late nineteenth century (1897/1951). Durkheim saw suicide as an act that occurred within a society and, in some measure, under the control of that society. Today, it is widely recognized that socioeconomic factors affect suicide rates. In 1932, at the height of the Depression, the suicide rate in the United States almost doubled in one year. During the recession of the 1970s, it rose again (Wekstein, 1979).

An even more dramatic indicator of social determinants of hopelessness is the rise in rates of depression in the past century. The first clear evidence of this phenomenon came from a study conducted in the mid-1980s (Robins, Helzer, Weissman, et al., 1984). The researchers surveyed 9,500 people randomly selected from urban and rural areas to see how many had had an episode of serious depression in their lives. In the 20- to 25-year-old group, 5 to 6 percent had at least 1 episode; in the 25- to 44-year-old group, the rate was higher: 8 to 9 percent. That made sense—the longer you have lived, the greater your chance of having experienced depression. But what were the researchers to make of the fact that the 70-year-olds in the survey showed a rate of only 1 percent? The people who had lived the *longest* had the least experience of depression. These results were essentially duplicated by a study of close relatives of depressed patients (Klerman, Lavori, Rice, et al., 1985). Even among people at risk for depression, the young adults were 6 times as likely as the over-65 group to have had a depressive episode, and these findings, too, have been confirmed (Blazer, Kessler, McGonagle, et al., 1994; Lewinsohn, Rohde, Seeley, et al., 1993). The conclusion is that the prevalence of depression in the United States has increased steadily and the age of onset has dropped precipitously in the past hundred years.

Why? Presumably, social change has something to do with it. We know, for example, that rates of depression tend to be lower in highly traditional social groups. Depression does not seem to exist, for instance, in a New Guinea tribe called the Kaluli (Scheiffelin, 1984). And, among the Amish living in Pennsylvania, the incidence of major depression is one fifth to one tenth the rate of depression among people living in Baltimore, only 100 miles away (Egeland & Hostetter, 1983). The common denominator of the Kaluli and the Amish is that each is a traditional, tight-knit, nonindustrialized community with stable families, a stable social structure, and long-held customs and beliefs. In our society, on the other hand, what we see predominantly is change, as people move away from their families, away from their birthplaces, and up and down the socioeconomic ladder. As Martin Seligman (1988) notes, "The modern individual is not the peasant of yore with a fixed future yawning ahead. He (and now she, effectively doubling the market) is a battleground of decisions and preferences" (p. 91). What this means is that young people today cannot rely on the support systems that were in place in their grandparents' day: the family, the church, the traditions and customs that once dictated choices. People must rely on themselves, and, if the answer is not there, apparently, a sense of helplessness sets in, greatly increasing the risk of depression. (For sociocultural factors that may contribute to women's increased vulnerability to depression, see the box on page 250.)

Changing the Society As we saw earlier, there have been some attempts—hotlines, school programs—at preventing suicide on the social level, but they have not been especially effective. A recent review of such programs suggests that efforts might be better spent attacking the social problems most closely associated with suicide: delinquency, truancy, substance abuse, teen pregnancy, and family distress (Gould & Kramer, 2001). Several researchers have also called for stricter gun-control laws (Gould & Kramer, 2001) and for educating journalists about the possible imitative effects of suicide coverage. There is some evidence, though mixed, that highly publicized suicides may negatively inspire others, particularly young people who share characteristics such as age, gender, and ethnicity, with the celebrity suicide (Velting & Gould, 1997). In 1977, for example, there was a significant increase in suicide by gunshot in Los Angeles County during the week following comedian Freddie Prinze's suicide by gunshot (Berman, 1988).

The Neuroscience Perspective

Genetic Research Family studies have shown that first-degree relatives of people with major mood disorders are much more likely than other people to develop these disorders. For major depression, their risk is almost 3 times higher, and for bipolar disorder it is fully 10 times higher, than that of the general population (Goodwin & Jamison, 1990; Sullivan, Neale, & Kendler, 2000). As we have seen, the family risk for both conditions is even greater when the index case had an early onset. Although unipolar patients are found among the relatives of bipolar patients, the reverse seldom occurs (Winokur, Coryell, Keller, et al., 1995)—further support for the theory that the two syndromes spring from different causes. Finally, suicide also runs in families, even when the association with depression is controlled (Mitchell, Mitchell, & Berk, 2000).

As we know, it is difficult in family studies to separate environmental from genetic influence. However, twin studies also support the role of genetic inheritance in the mood disorders and suicide. In a review of genetic research on mood disorders in twins, M. G. Allen (1976) found that the concordance rate for bipolar disorder was 72 percent among monozygotic twins, as compared with 14 percent among dizygotic twins. A review by Sullivan, Neale, and Kendler (2000) found that the concordance rate for unipolar disorder was around 43 percent among monozygotic twins, as compared with around 28 percent among dizygotic twins. Moreover, the genetic contribution to major depression is similar for men and women (Sullivan, Neale, & Kendler, 2000). The difference between the bipolar and unipolar concordance rates among monozygotic twins (72 percent versus 43 percent) suggests that genetic factors are more important in bipolar disorder than in depression. But more recent twin studies indicate that genes play a crucial role in major depression as well. According to this research, about 37 percent of the difference in depression rates between MZ and DZ twins is attributable solely to genes. The rest of the difference, the results indicated, is due to individual-specific environment—in other words, life events specific to each member of the twin pair—and not at all to shared environmental factors such as social class, parental child-rearing practices, or early parental loss (Sullivan, Neale, & Kendler, 2000). Even more current research suggests that the way genes increase risk for major depression is by increasing the person's sensitivity to stressful life events (Kendler, Kessler, Walters, et al., 1995).

But the most impressive evidence for the heritability of mood disorders comes from adoption studies. In a study of the biological and adoptive parents of bipolar adoptees as compared with the biological and adoptive parents of normal adoptees, Mendlewicz and Rainer (1977) found a 31 percent prevalence of mood disorders in the biological parents of the bipolar adoptees, as opposed to 2 percent in the biological parents of the normal adoptees—a striking difference. A more recent study (Wender, Kety, Rosenthal, et al., 1986), this time of the biological and adoptive parents, siblings, and half-siblings of adoptees with a broad range of mood disorders, found that the prevalence of unipolar depression was 8 times greater—and the suicide rate *15* times greater—in the biological relatives of the mood disorder cases than in the biological relatives of the normal adoptees. These two studies constitute firm support for a genetic component in both bipolar and unipolar mood disorder (Sullivan, Neale, & Kendler, 2000).

An important new direction in the genetic study of mood disorders is linkage and association analyses (Chapter 6). In an intriguing linkage-analysis study, blood samples were taken from every person in an 81-member Amish clan. Then, for each participant, the researchers isolated the DNA molecule and searched the molecule for evidence of a characteristic that tended to be inherited with bipolar disorder. They found what appeared to be the characteristic on chromosome 11. Furthermore, when they compared the chromosomes of the 19 family members diagnosed as suffering from psychiatric disorders (primarily bipolar disorder) with those of the 62 members considered psychiatrically well, they consistently found a difference at chromosome 11 (Egeland, Gerhard, Pauls, et al., 1987).

Unfortunately, other studies have had mixed results. Some have failed to show linkage between bipolar disorder and markers on chromosome 11 (Gill, McKeon, & Humphries, 1988; Hodgkinson, Sherrington, Gurling, et al., 1987). Other newer studies of bipolar disorder using association analysis have found evidence of abnormalities of the serotonin transporter protein gene on chromosome 17 (Mundo, Walker, Cate, et al., 2001) and the monoamine oxidase A gene on the X chromosome (Preisig, Bellivier, Fenton, et al., 2000) although these findings have not been obtained in all studies either. Both of these genes play a role in serotonin transmission, which has been strongly associated with mood disorders (see the section "Neurotransmitter Imbalance," page 278). Rather than viewing the discrepant results across studies as a negation of the genetic findings, many scientists see

Research among the Amish links a chromosomal characteristic and bipolar disorder. Such studies can shed light on the heritability of mood disorders.

them as an indication that bipolar disorder is not a single disease but a group of related diseases, with a variety of genetic (and environmental) causes that await identification. In the 1990s, the National Institutes of Health sponsored a project to map the entire human chromosome set, the Human Genome Project, most of which remained unexplored. This project is basically complete, and we may see the emergence of genes that are consistently linked to bipolar disorder.

Neurophysiological Research Given that organic factors are implicated in the mood disorders, the next question is, *what* organic factors? According to neurophysiological researchers, the problem may have to do with biological rhythms. As we have seen, sleep disturbance is one of the most common symptoms of depression. Depressed people also consistently show abnormalities in their progress through the various stages of sleep and in their sleep efficiency (Benca, Obermeyer, Thisted, et al., 1992; Emslie, Armitage, Weinberg, et al., 2001), possibly as a result of overarousal (Ho, Gillin, Buchsbaum, et al., 1996). One such abnormality is shortened rapid eye movement (REM) latency—that is, in depression the time between the onset of sleep and the onset of REM sleep, the stage of sleep in which dreams occur, is unusually short. And this characteristic may indicate a biological vulnerability to depression, for depressed individuals who have shortened REM latency (1) are more likely to have the endogenous symptom pattern and to respond to antidepressant drugs, but not to psychotherapy, (2) tend to go on showing shortened REM latency, even after the depressive episode has passed, (3) are likely to have first-degree relatives who also have shortened REM latency, and (4) are more likely to relapse (Buysse & Kupfer, 1993; Giles, Kupfer, Rush, et al., 1998).

These sleep disturbances, together with the hormonal abnormalities associated with depression, suggest that in depression the "biological clock" has somehow gone out of order—a hypothesis that Ehlers and her colleagues have combined with the findings on loss and depression to produce an integrated biopsychosocial theory. According to this theory, our lives are filled with social *zeitgebers* (literally, "time givers"): personal relationships, jobs, and other responsibilities and routines that help to activate and regulate our biological rhythms. Having someone with whom you sleep, for example, helps to enforce your sleep rhythms. When he or she goes to bed, so do you. Consequently, when an important social zeitgeber is removed from a person's life—when a spouse dies, for example—the removal may not only produce an important loss but also may disrupt the survivor's circadian rhythms, or biological cycles, leading to a range of consequences (sleep disturbance, eating disturbance, mood disturbance, hormonal imbalance) that we call depression (Ehlers, Frank, & Kupfer, 1988; Frank, Swartz, & Kupfer, 2000). In keeping with this

The Social Rhythm Metric (SRM)
MacArthur Foundation Mental Health Research Network I
Please fill this out at the end of the day

Respondent #: Day of Week: Date:

ACTIVITY	TIME	AM or PM	S	M	T	W	T	F	S
			PEOPLE 0 = Alone 1 = Others just present 2 = Others actively involved 3 = Others very stimulating						
			DAY OF WEEK						
TAKE AN AFTERNOON NAP	Earlier								
	Exact earlier time								
	2:00								
	2:15								
	2:30								
	2:45						0		
mid-point of your normal range →	3:00	PM						0	0
	3:15								
	3:30								
	3:45		0						
	4:00								
	Later								
	Exact later time								
	Check if did not do			✓	✓	✓			
HAVE DINNER	Earlier								
	Exact earlier time								
	5:30								
	5:45								
	6:00								
	6:15								
mid-point of your normal range →	6:30	PM			2		2	2	
	6:45			1		2			
	7:00								
	7:15								
	7:30		0						
	Later								3
	Exact later time								9:00
	Check if did not do								

FIGURE 10.8 Sample page from the Social Rhythm Metric.

Frank, E., Swartz, H. A., & Kupfer, D. J. (2000). Interpersonal and social rhythm therapy: Managing the chaos of bipolar disorder. *Biological Psychiatry, 48*, 598.

disrupted-rhythm theory, some evidence suggests that depriving a depressed patient of sleep, particularly of REM sleep, may have a therapeutic effect (Liebenluft & Wehr, 1992; Orth, Shelton, Nicholson, et al., 2001). Moreover, in bipolar individuals, sleep reduction can precipitate mania (Leibenluft, Albert, Rosenthal, et al., 1996). Thus, the social zeitgebers theory has been extended to bipolar disorder as well. People with bipolar disorders are thought to be especially vulnerable to psychosocial stressors that disrupt social rhythms and, thus, circadian rhythms. Consistent with this model, recent studies found that stressful life events that disrupt social rhythms are associated with the onset of manic, but not depressed, episodes in bipolar individuals (Malkoff-Schwartz, Frank, Anderson, et al., 2000). This theory has led to a treatment for bipolar disorder that extends interpersonal therapy for depression (see pages 271–272) to include behavioral strategies for regularizing daily social rhythms and sleep-wake cycles. This new therapy, called interpersonal and social rhythm therapy (IPSRT), adds monitoring of daily social rhythms (see Figure 10.8) and strategies for regularizing these rhythms to standard IPT (Frank, Swarz, & Kupfer, 2000). Preliminary evidence suggests that IPSRT may be an effective adjunctive treatment along with medication for patients with bipolar disorder (Frank, Swarz, & Kupfer, 2000).

One form of depression that may be closely related to the body's biological rhythms is **seasonal affective disorder, or SAD.** Beginning with Hippocrates, physicians over the centuries have noted that many depressions come on in winter. In the late nineteenth century, surgeon and Arctic explorer Frederick Cook made the connection between this phenomenon and light exposure. In the Eskimos, and also in the members of his expeditionary team, Cook observed a depressed mood, together with fatigue and decreased sexual desire, during the long, dark Arctic winter. Recently, this seasonal depression, which includes not only increased sleeping but also increased eating and

Sometimes the treatment for a troubling disorder is as blessedly simple as a few extra hours of sunshine each day. Many people with the aptly named SAD, or seasonal affective disorder, benefit from sitting in front of an ultraviolet light box for a prescribed amount of time during the short days of winter.

a craving for carbohydrates, has been added to the *DSM*. Many people experience it in a mild degree. In order for the diagnosis of SAD to be made, however, the patient must meet the criteria for major depressive episode; remission as well as onset must be keyed to the seasons; and the pattern must have lasted for at least 2 years. There is a summer version of SAD that may be more frequent in Asians (Han, Wang, Du, et al., 2000), but the winter version is much more common in the West. As Cook suspected, the latter seems to be tied to the much shorter photoperiod, or period of daylight, during the winter (Young, Meaden, Fogg, et al., 1997) and the resulting increase in the duration of secretion of the hormone, melatonin, at night, in SAD patients (Wehr, Duncan, Sher, et al., 2001). Women are at far higher risk—60 to 90 percent of patients are female—and so are the young. The average age of onset is 23 (Oren & Rosenthal, 1992). Recent studies suggest that the disorder has a genetic component (Jang, Lam, Livesley, et al., 1997).

The most promising current theory of SAD is that it is caused by a lag in circadian rhythms; thus, during the day, the person experiences the kind of physical slowdown he or she should be undergoing at night (Teicher, Glod, Magnus, et al., 1997; Nurnberger, Adkins, Debomoy, et al., 2000). About three quarters of SAD patients improve when given the same kind of light therapy that is used for circadian rhythm sleep disorders (Chapter 9): exposure to bright artificial light for several hours a day (Oren & Rosenthal, 1992). In some cases, light therapy, if it is applied at the first sign of symptoms, can actually prevent a full-blown episode (Meesters, Jansen, Beersma, et al., 1993). If this circadian rhythm theory is correct, then light therapy should work best if it is applied in the morning, because extra morning light advances circadian rhythms, whereas extra evening light does not. Several studies support this prediction (e.g., Lewy, Bauer, Cutler, et al., 1998; Terman, Terman, Lo, et al., 2001), although not all do (Lee, Blashko, Janzen, et al., 1997). Moreover, consistent with the circadian rhythm theory, Terman and colleagues found that the greater the circadian rhythm advance produced by morning light, the greater the improvement in depression symptoms (Terman, Terman, Lo, et al., 2001).

Neuroimaging Research Recent CT and MRI studies suggest that mood disorders involve abnormalities in brain structure. People with mood disorders tend to show enlargement of the ventricles and the sulci (the spaces between brain tissues). They also show reduced volume in the frontal lobe, the hippocampus, and the basal ganglia, all of which are brain regions thought to be involved in mood regulation (Baumann & Bogerts, 2001; Bremner, Narayan, Anderson, et al., 2000). In addition, the reduced volume of the prefrontal cortex is associated with the attentional difficulties of manic patients (Sax, Strakowksi, Zimmerman, et al., 1999), whereas reduced activation of the prefrontal cortex seen in PET studies may be associated with the poor judgment seen in manic patients (Blumberg, Stern, Ricketts, et al., 1999). Moreover, recent studies using PET scans have found that sadness is associated with reciprocal increases in activation of limbic areas and decreases in activation of frontal cortical areas, whereas recovery from depression is associated with the opposite pattern of activation of limbic and frontal cortical areas (Mayberg, Liotti, Brannan, et al., 1999). Treatment of the depression is associated with normalization of metabolism in these brain regions (Brody, Saxena, Stoessel, et al., 2001).

Biochemical Research At present, perhaps the most vital area of research on mood disorders is biochemistry. There are two major biochemical theories.

Hormone Imbalance One biochemical theory is that depression is due to a malfunction of the hypothalamus, a portion of the brain known to regulate mood. Because the hypothalamus affects not only mood but also many other functions that are typically disrupted in the course of a depression, such as appetite and sexual interest, some researchers (e.g., Holsboer, 1995) suggest that the hypothalamus may be the key to depressive disorders. If so, the abnormality may have to do with the control of hormone production. The hypothalamus regulates the pituitary gland, and both the hypothalamus and the pituitary control the production of hormones by the gonads and the adrenal and thyroid glands. There is substantial evidence of some irregularity in this process in depressed people. In the first place, depressed individuals often show abnormally low thyroid hormone levels (Sullivan, Hatterer, Herbert, et al., 1999). Second, people with abnormal hormone activity often show depression as a side effect. Third, CT scans show that many depressed people have enlarged pituitary and adrenal glands (Nemeroff, Krishnan, Reed, et al., 1992). Fourth, postmortem studies of the brains of depressed patients show abnormalities in the neurons of the hypothalamus (Purba, Hoogendijk, Hofman, et al., 1996). Fifth, low levels of some thyroid hormones predict recurrences of major depressive episodes (Joffe & Marriott, 2000). But perhaps the best evidence is that depression can sometimes be effectively treated by altering hormone levels. In certain cases, for example, induced changes in thyroid output have aided in recovery from depression; in others, administering thyroid hormones has sped up depressed patients' response to antidepressant medications (Altshuler, Bauer, Frye, et al., 2001).

Hormone imbalances appear to be particularly characteristic of endogenous and psychotic depressions. Indeed, such imbalances can be used to help differentiate between endogenous and reactive cases, and between psychotic and nonpsychotic cases, via a technique called the **dexamethasone suppression test (DST).** Dexamethasone is a drug that in normal people suppresses the secretion of the hormone cortisol for at least 24 hours. However, endogenously and psychotically depressed patients, who seem to secrete abnormally high levels of cortisol, manage to resist the drug's effect as long as they are in the depressive episode (Nelson & Davis, 1997; Posener, DeBattista, Williams, et al., 2000). This is the basis for the DST. Depressed patients are give dexamethasone, and then their blood is tested at regular intervals for cortisol. The nonsuppressors—those whose cortisol levels return to high levels within 24 hours despite the drug—are classed as endogenous or psychotic. Since the DST was developed, researchers have discovered other interesting things about nonsuppressors. They tend not to respond to psychotherapy (or placebos); they tend to show nonsuppression in later depressive episodes as well; continuing to show nonsuppression after treatment predicts relapse (Zobel, Yassouridis, Frieboes, et al., 1999). All these facts support the notion that DST nonsuppression is a marker of a more endogenous and psychotic depression (Posener, DeBattista, Williams, et al., 2000; Thase, Dube, Bowle, et al., 1996). Nonsuppression also seems to be tied to social and childhood history. Among humans, there is evidence that childhood stress, including childhood sexual abuse, is associated with excessive cortisol levels in adulthood (Weiss, Longhurst, & Mazure, 1999). Among baboons, DST nonsuppressors are likely to be isolated, socially subordinate individuals. It is possible that the high stress associated with low social rank causes the nonsuppression (Sapolsky, Alberts, & Altmann, 1997). On the other hand, nonsuppression may be linked to behaviors that create a social disadvantage.

An important finding in the research on hormone imbalances is that such imbalances occur both in major depression and in depressive episodes of bipolar disorder. Genetic research, as we noted, suggests that major depression and bipolar disorder are two distinct syndromes, with different causes. For this reason, it seems unlikely that the hormonal abnormalities common to both syndromes constitute a *primary* cause. (A good possibility is that they are caused by the neurotransmitter imbalances that we will discuss next [Lambert, Johansson, Agren, et al.,

2000].) Neither does the stubborn cortisol production of the DST nonsuppressors seem to be a primary cause of depression, for DST nonsuppression is also seen in many other disorders, including schizophrenia, obsessive-compulsive disorder, eating disorders, and alcoholism (Thase, Frank, & Kupfer, 1985). At the same time, the fact that hormones can sometimes relieve depression suggests that in certain, perhaps atypical, cases, hormone imbalance may play a causal role.

Neurotransmitter Imbalance The second important theory of biochemical research has to do with the neurotransmitters norepinephrine and serotonin. According to the **catecholamine hypothesis,*** increased levels of norepinephrine produce mania, while decreased levels produce depression (Schildkraut, 1965; Delgado & Moreno, 2000). The only way to test this hypothesis directly would be to analyze brain-tissue samples of manic and depressed patients to determine whether their norepinephrine levels are, in fact, abnormally high and low, respectively. Because this cannot be done without damage to the brain, we have to rely on indirect evidence. That evidence consists of findings that drugs and other treatments that relieve depression or produce mania increase the level of norepinephrine in the brain, while drugs that produce depression or alleviate mania reduce the level of norepinephrine in the brain (Berman, Narasimhan, Miller, et al., 1999; Delgado & Moreno, 2000).

This research is spurred by the hope that the action of the drugs will tell us something about the process by which mood disorders develop in the first place. As we saw in Chapter 6, when an impulse travels down a neuron and reaches its end, this neuron, the presynaptic neuron, releases the neurotransmitter into the synapse that lies between it and the next, or postsynaptic neuron. The neurotransmitter bonds with the receptors of the postsynaptic neuron, thereby transmitting the impulse. Some of the neurotransmitter is taken back up into the presynaptic neuron—a process called reuptake. (Review Figure 6.3, page 138.)

The tricyclics, a class of drugs widely used for depression, generally work by blocking the reuptake of norepinephrine (and serotonin) by the presynaptic neuron. Superficially, this suggests that depression may be due to too-rapid reuptake or to inadequate secretion. However, the picture is probably more complicated than that. First of all, recent research indicates that if depressed people have a problem with norepinephrine function, it has to do not with the presynaptic receptors, which appear to operate normally, but with the postsynaptic receptors, which appear to be undersensitive to norepinephrine (Berman, Narasimhan, Miller, et al., 1999; Lambert, Johansson, Agren, et al., 2000). Interestingly, in bipolar patients the opposite may be true. Recent findings from a PET study suggest that bipolar patients show abnormalities in their presynaptic catecholamine receptors (Zubieta, Haguelet, Ohi, et al., 2000). Second, some newer, and effective, tricyclics do not work by blocking reuptake; they increase norepinephrine levels by more subtle means. The fact that tricyclics generally take 2 weeks to start relieving symptoms suggests that their success has to do not with immediate effects, such as blocking reuptake, but with long-term effects—specifically, the enhancement of proteins that affect the atrophy or growth of the neurons (Duman, Heninger, & Nestler, 1997).

As the research suggests, neither does the system have to do with norepinephrine alone. Serotonin is

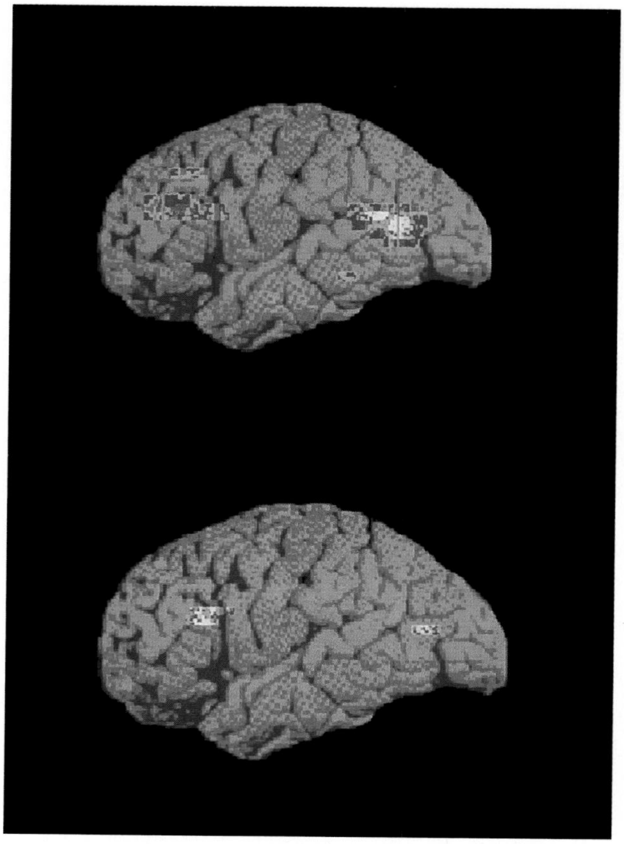

These PET scans compare the brain of a depressed person (top) with the brain of a person whose depression has been treated (bottom). Regions shown in red and yellow depict areas of low brain activity in the depressed individual. The healthy brain treated for depression shows that metabolic activity and blood flow has resumed in the affected areas.

*This theory is so-called because norepinephrine belongs to a group of structurally similar molecules called the *catecholamines*.

probably involved as well. It has been shown, for example, that L-tryptophan, an amino acid that increases serotonin levels, is an effective treatment for *both* mania and depression. Furthermore, when recovered depressed patients—and recovered SAD patients—are put through a procedure that depletes their tryptophan levels, their depressive symptoms return (Bremner, Innis, Salomon, et al., 1997; Delgado & Moreno, 2000). Another connected finding is that children who have major depression, together with children whose parents have the disorder, show abnormalities in their response to drugs that enhance serotonin (Birmaher, Kaufman, Brent, et al., 1997). Finally, PET scans and postmortem studies show that the brains of depressed patients have a reduced responsiveness to serotonin and fewer serotonin receptors (Mann, Huang, Underwood, et al., 2000; Yatham, Liddle, Shiah, et al., 2000). Thus, serotonin is probably involved, together with norepinephrine, in the mood disorders.

Serotonin has been implicated in suicide as well. As we saw in the discussion of adoption studies, the biological relatives of adoptees with mood disorders appear to be 15 times more likely to commit suicide than the biological relatives of control adoptees. This argues very strongly for an inheritable risk for suicide, even apart from depression. It has been proposed that a decreased flow of serotonin from the brain stem to the frontal cortex may be associated with suicide, independent of depression—indeed, with impulsive, aggressive behavior as well. In support of this hypothesis, tests of the cerebrospinal fluid of suicide attempters, particularly those who have chosen violent methods, have found evidence of abnormally low serotonin activity (Mann, McBride, Brown, et al., 1992). In addition, postmortem analyses of suicides have found subnormal amounts of serotonin and impaired serotonin receptors in the brain stem and frontal cortex (Arango & Underwood, 1997; Meyer, Kapur, Houle, et al., 1999). Should this hypothesis gain further support, it is possible that in the future we will have special drug therapies for people who attempt suicide.

A newer biochemical theory of depression is that depressive episodes, especially those triggered by stress, are caused by the atrophy, or death, of certain neurons in the hippocampus (Chapter 6), a region of the brain involved in emotion, learning, and memory as well as in the regulation of sleep, appetite, and cortisol function. According to this hypothesis, antidepressant drugs reverse this atrophy by increasing the expression of a gene, the so-called *brain-derived neurotrophic factor,* that promotes neuron growth (Duman, Heninger, & Nestler, 1997).

A Summary of Biochemical Findings It seems indisputable that norepinephrine, serotonin, and hormone abnormalities are all involved in the mood disorders, and the most compelling current theories differ only in the emphasis they give to each of these three factors. What is most likely is that mood disorders are due to a complex interaction of genetic, neurophysiological, biochemical, developmental, cognitive, and situational variables (Kendler, Kessler, Neale, et al., 1993; Ackenheil, 2001).

Whatever the neuroscience perspective ultimately contributes to uncovering the cause of mood disorders, it has already contributed heavily to their treatment—a matter to which we now turn.

Antidepressant Medication The most common therapy for depressed patients, whether or not they are receiving other kinds of therapy, is drugs. The three major classes of **antidepressant medication**—the **MAO inhibitors,** the **tricyclics,** and the **selective serotonin reuptake inhibitors (SSRIs)**—have already been described in Chapter 7, in relation to the anxiety disorders, and the most commonly used drugs within those classes were listed in Table 6.1 on page 139. All three classes seem to work by improving functioning of the neurotransmitters that we have just discussed, the MAO inhibitors by interfering with an enzyme (MAO) that degrades norepinephrine and serotonin, the tricyclics by blocking the reuptake of norepinephrine and serotonin, the SSRIs by blocking the reuptake of serotonin alone.

The prescription of these drugs is a matter of balancing symptom relief against side effects. As we saw in Chapter 7, the MAO inhibitors have the most troubling side effects, but for certain types of depression—especially "atypical depression," characterized by excessive sleeping and/or eating—they tend to work better than other antidepressants (McGrath, Stewart, Janal, et al., 2000). The tricyclics can also have unpleasant side effects. Another disadvantage with the tricyclics is that they do not begin to take effect for about 2 weeks—which, for a severely depressed person, is a long time to wait (Nierenberg, Farabaugh, Alpert, et al., 2000). Finally, it is relatively easy to overdose on tricyclics, and this makes them dangerous to prescribe for suicidal patients. Still, the tricyclics have proved successful with 50 to 60 percent of depressed outpatients. Interestingly, though, men respond to the tricyclics better than women (Kornstein, Schatzberg, Thase, et al., 2000). Although it is estimated that 30 percent of these patients would have improved in that time period anyway, the response rate was still better than with placebos (Quitkin, Rabkin, Gerald, et al., 2000).

In the past decade, however, most of the excitement in drug treatment for depression has been over the SSRIs, which have gradually displaced most other antidepressants. The SSRI that has received the most attention is Prozac (fluoxetine). Introduced in 1987, by 1993 it had been prescribed for more than 10 million people in the United States (Barondes, 1994), and it continued to lead all other antidepressants in U.S. sales in 2000 (Schatzberg, 2000). As with other SSRIs, Prozac can take 2 weeks to work (Nierenberg, Farabaugh, Alpert, et al., 2000) and have side effects, primarily headache, upset stomach, and sexual dysfunction (Rosen, Lane, Menza, et al., 1999). Furthermore, in a small number of cases, it seems to produce anxiety and insomnia. Also, there have been reports that Prozac increases the risk of suicide; however, a recent study of 643 depressed patients treated with Prozac did not support this claim (Leon, Keller, Warshaw, et al., 1999). Finally, determining the correct dose is a delicate procedure. Prozac's half-life, the amount of time it stays in the system, is very long: 7 days (Agency for Health Care Policy and Research, 1993). Therefore, patients who take the drug daily are gradually increasing its level in the bloodstream, a process that can lead to overdose. Unfortunately, the symptoms of Prozac overdose resemble the symptoms of depression, so there is a danger, when the signs of overdose appear, that the patient will increase the dose, thinking that what is needed is simply more of the drug (Cain, 1992).

Because of these complications, Prozac has probably peaked in popularity. Physicians are now switching to SSRIs with short half-lives, particularly Paxil (paroxetine) and Zoloft (sertraline). It seems that Paxil and Zoloft not only reduce the risk of overdose but are less likely to produce anxiety and insomnia. They also work better for women than men (Kornstein, Schatzberg, Thase, et al., 2000). However, there is still controversy over how well the SSRIs work at all. Some researchers have analyzed large data sets from clinical trials of SSRIs and have suggested that they may not be much more effective than placebos (Kirsch & Saperstein, 1998; Kirsch, Moore, Scoboria, et al., 2002). Other authors have criticized these analyses and argued that the SSRIs have superior efficacy over placebos (Klein, 1998; Hollon, DeRubeis, Shelton, et al., 2002; Thase, 2002). The SSRIs approved for use in the United States are at least as effective as the tricyclics in combating depression. Moreover, continued use of either tricyclics or SSRIs reduces risk for recurrence of depression (Kupfer & Frank, 2001). In general, the major advantage of the SSRIs over other antidepressants is that they act more quickly and have somewhat fewer side effects.

Two newer antidepressants are Effexor (venlafaxine) and Serzone (nefazodone). Effexor is like a tricyclic, but without the unpleasant side effects. (Its side effects are closer to those of the SSRIs.) Although it has been under investigation for only a short time, it may turn out to be the drug of choice for severe depressions; it has already been shown to outperform SSRIs in two studies with hospitalized patients (Thase & Kupfer, 1996). Serzone has a unique biochemical structure, but it effectively increases available norepinephrine and serotonin, just like the tricyclics. It, too, has the same side-effect profile as the SSRIs, with one important exception: no sexual dysfunction. Preliminary research suggests that Serzone may be just as effective as the other antidepressants (Thase & Kupfer, 1996).

A substantial minority of patients do not respond to the first antidepressant given to them. Ordinarily, they are then switched to another. It appears that, on average, 40 percent of patients not responding to a tricyclic respond to an SSRI, and vice versa. In cases in which both tricyclics and SSRIs have failed, an MAO inhibitor or Wellbutrin (bupropion), another new antidepressant, may work. For many years, the use of Wellbutrin was delayed because, in a small number of cases, it caused seizures. However, careful regulation of dosage can minimize this risk, and Wellbutrin has few other side effects and seems to work quite well (Thase & Kupfer, 1996).

All these antidepressants are effective not only with major depressive episodes but also with chronic major depression (episodes lasting more than 2 years), dysthymia, and "double depression," in which major depression is superimposed on dysthymia (Hellerstein, Kocsis, Chapman, et al., 2000; Thase, Fava, Halbreich, et al., 1996). They are also helpful for people with chronic low-grade depression. Such people, however, are the ones least likely to be given antidepressants, because psychiatrists and family doctors tend to assume that these long-lasting depressions are best treated by psychotherapy. (Alternatively, such patients, if they show any anxiety—which they usually do—are given antianxiety drugs, for physicians seem to pay more attention to anxiety symptoms than to depression.) Nevertheless, many victims of chronic depression can get immediate relief from antidepressants. Ideally, most of them should probably have psychotherapy as well, in the hope of preventing relapse and to deal with the problems created in their lives by the depression (see the box on page 281).

Antimanic Medication While there are many competing drugs in the antidepressant market, the field of **antimanic medication** is dominated by one medication, **lithium.** Lithium is administered as lithium carbonate, a natural mineral salt (Schou, 1997). This simple salt is capable of ending swiftly and effectively about 70 percent of all manic episodes. In

Focus On... Drug Therapy Versus Psychotherapy

The recent successes of psychopharmacology have created a sometimes bitter controversy within the field of psychological treatment. Certain advocates of drug therapy speak as if drugs were on their way to making behavioral and insight therapies obsolete. In the words of psychiatrist Paul Wender, one day "every disease is going to be [seen as] a chemical or an electrical disease" (quoted in Gelman, 1990, p. 42). Indeed, some experts believe that personality itself may come to be seen as a biological phenomenon. As Peter Kramer (1993) puts it, "When one pill at breakfast makes you a new person, . . . it is difficult to resist the suggestion, the visceral certainty, that who people are is largely biologically determined" (p. 18).

To many psychotherapists—people who have spent their careers treating psychological disturbance as part of the deepest problems of living—such statements seem naïve and presumptuous. An editorial in the *Journal of the American Psychoanalytic Association* called attention to the dangers of "the recent and forceful biologization of everything from cigar smoking to love (a deficiency of phenylalanine treatable by chocolate in the absence of the loved person)" (Shapiro, 1989). Some experts also fear that psychotherapists may be becoming like internists, "managing" depression, for example, the way internists manage hypertension, by prescribing drugs and monitoring their effects, while the root cause of the depression goes unexplored. As noted earlier, to suppress symptoms is not necessarily the wisest course. By definition, symptoms are symptoms *of* something.

On the side of the drug-therapy advocates, it must be said that the root cause of some depressions may, in fact, be biochemical—that biochemical imbalance is what the symptoms are signaling and what the drugs are correcting. Furthermore, as we have seen, in some cases they correct it very efficiently. Drug treatment for certain disorders is now so widely regarded as effective that *not* to prescribe drugs for these disorders can be viewed as malpractice. (In a celebrated case, a doctor suffering from bipolar disorder sued a Maryland hospital for treating his illness with psychotherapy rather than drugs. The case was settled out of court.)

Does drug therapy, in fact, work better than psychotherapy? Most of the research on this question has to do with depression. One large-scale review of outcome studies concluded that both biological and psychological therapies are effective treatments for depression, though the most effective treatment is a combination of the two (Kupfer & Frank, 2001; Thase, Greenhouse, Frank, et al., 1997). The Agency for Health Care Policy and Research (1993) conducted a review of the literature on the treatment of depression and came to four conclusions. First, about half of depressed outpatients show marked improvement from medication. Second, the most appropriate patients for medication are those who have the most severe symptoms, plus recurrent episodes and family histories of depression. Third, psychotherapy—particularly cognitive, behavioral, and interpersonal—is effective for mild to moderate depression. Fourth, combined treatment should be considered for more severe depressions and for those who have not improved with psychotherapy or drug therapy alone.

While these recommendations have been criticized for overstating the effectiveness of medication, in a sense they are nothing new, for they repeat a long-held principle: that the treatment of choice depends on severity. Ever since the introduction of the phenothiazines in the 1950s, it has been widely believed that, in general, the most severely disturbed patients needed drugs, while the less severely disturbed needed psychotherapy. It should be added, however, that this principle is now being challenged. Recent researchers (e.g., DeRubeis, Gelfand, Tang, et al., 1999) have found that the most severe depressions are as likely to yield to cognitive therapy as to drug therapy. As for the idea that the least severe depressions are those that require psychotherapy, much of the controversy surrounding Prozac has to do with Prozac's challenge to that point. Sensitivity to criticism, low self-esteem, fear of rejection: These mild, nagging problems, which have for so long been thought the province of psychotherapy, not drugs, are exactly what Prozac seems to relieve—a fact that is causing "a rethinking of fundamental assumptions in psychiatry" (Barondes, 1994, p. 1102).

One preliminary finding is that drug therapy, when it is discontinued, is more likely than psychotherapy to be followed by relapse (Kupfer & Frank, 2001). In a study of medication versus cognitive therapy for depression, it was found that the two worked equally well during the acute phase of the depression but that, once the treatment ended, the patients in the medication group were more likely to have subsequent depression (Hollon, Shelton, & Loosen, 1991). This result, however, was not replicated by a later, large-scale study, which found roughly equal relapse rates for all treatment conditions (Shea, Elkin, Imber, et al., 1992).

It may be that the wave of the future is combined treatment (Kupfer & Frank, 2001). Even if there is a clear biochemical abnormality, and one that can be corrected biochemically, the patient is still left with the damage that has been done to his or her life by the disorder. People who have been depressed on and off for years often have wrecked marriages, strained family relations, and few friends. While the drug may help to relieve the symptoms of the disorder, psychotherapy may be needed to repair the results of the disorder.

Furthermore, a psychological disorder is never just biochemical. All behavior is multidetermined. Drug therapy and psychotherapy are two different ways of approaching mental events. With gradual adjustments, the two therapies may be able to work together. While the defenders of psychotherapy often feel called upon to protect psychology against the incursions of biology, Freud, who was certainly a defender of psychotherapy, repeatedly predicted that this treatment would ultimately be served by biological research. "Let the biologists go as far as they can," he said, "and let us go as far as we can—one day the two will meet" (quoted in Gelman, 1990, p. 42).

approximately 40 percent of cases, lithium also terminates depressive episodes in bipolar patients. When bipolar depressive episodes are unresponsive to lithium, physicians usually prescribe either Wellbutrin or an SSRI, because they do not make patients sleepy, and unimpaired alertness seems to speed recovery in bipolar patients.

Currently, the great virtue of lithium is preventive: When taken regularly, in a maintenance dose, it is generally effective in eliminating or at least in diminishing mood swings in bipolar disorder (Schou, 1997; Baldessarini, & Tondo, 2000). Lithium appears to work by modulating the expression of a variety of genes that change the signaling of many neurotransmitter systems in the brain (Lenox & Hahn, 2000). It is not easy, however, to determine what the maintenance dose is, because for most patients the effective dose is close to the toxic dose, which can cause convulsions, delirium, and in rare cases death. An overdose is generally preceded by clear warning signs, such as nausea, alerting the patient to discontinue the drug. Still, because of its potential dangers, patients who take lithium must have regular blood tests to monitor the level of the drug in their systems. Another problem with lithium is that, when people have taken it for more than 2 years, stopping it often results in a new depressive or manic episode and increased risk or suicide (Baldessarini, Tondo, & Viguera, 1999). Because of these risks, researchers have been trying to develop other drugs for mania. An anticonvulsant, Tegretol (carbamazepine), has been found to be effective for about a third of manic patients (Small, Klapper, Milstein, et al., 1991). And Depakote (valproate) has also been shown to be an effective mood stabilizer for bipolar patients (Sachs, Prinz, Kahn, et al., 2000).

Thus far, we have discussed only acute treatment response, the ability of these medications to relieve a current episode of mania or depression. Most psychiatrists now feel that, after an acute phase, there should be a "continuation" phase, in which the patients are maintained for 6 months to a year on the medication that helps them. Continuation therapy results in a 30 to 40 percent lower risk of relapse during the period in which the drug is continued. Usually, if a patient has responded positively to antidepressants and has remained free of depression through the continuation phase, he or she is assumed to have recovered from the episode that led to the treatment (Thase & Kupfer, 1996).

Electroconvulsive Therapy For reasons that are not completely understood, electric shock, when applied to the brain under controlled circumstances, seems to help relieve severe depression. This type of treatment, known as **electroconvulsive therapy (ECT),** involves administering to the patient a shock of approximately 70 to 130 volts, thus inducing a convulsion similar to an epileptic seizure. Typically, therapy involves about 9 or 10 such treatments, spaced over a period of several weeks, though the total may be much lower or higher.

This technique was first discovered in the 1930s (Bini, 1938). Since that time, it has become clear that,

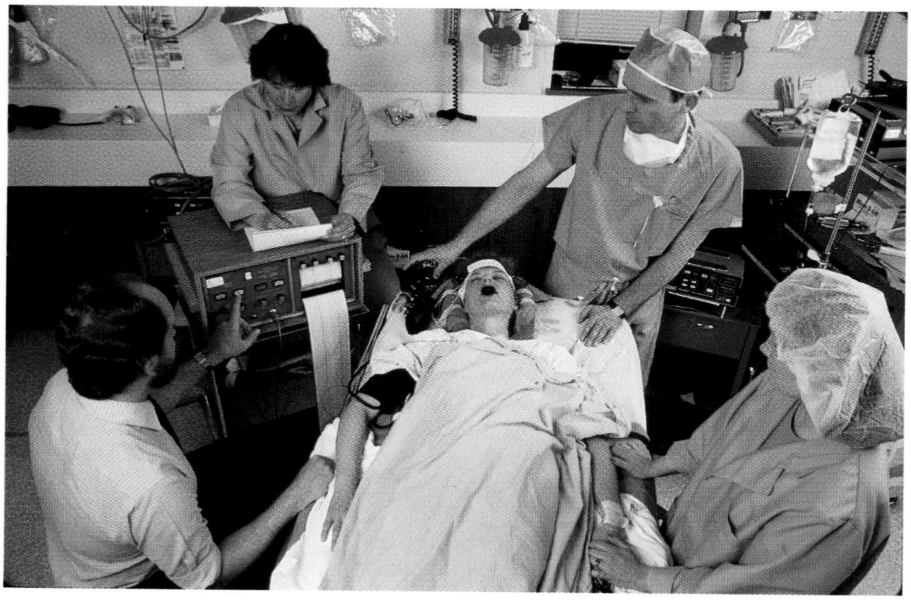

Electroconvulsive therapy is a controversial treatment with potentially serious side effects, but it has been shown to help many severely depressed people.

like antidepressants, the shock affects the levels of norepinephrine and serotonin in the brain, but theories as to its exact mode of operation are as various and incomplete as those regarding the antidepressants (Mann & Kapur, 1994). At present, all we know is that electric shock apparently *does* work, and quite well, for many seriously depressed patients (Bailine, Rifkin, Kayne, et al., 2000; Cohen, Taieb, Flament, et al., 2000).

Like other biological treatments, ECT has its complications. The most common side effect is memory dysfunction, both anterograde (the capacity to learn new material) and retrograde (the capacity to recall material learned before the treatment). Research indicates that, in the great majority of cases, anterograde memory gradually improves after treatment (Hay & Hay, 1990). As for retrograde memory, there is generally a marked loss 1 week after treatment, with nearly complete recovery within 7 months after treatment. Long-term follow-ups (3.5 years after ECT) suggest few permanent memory deficits (Cohen, Taieb, Flament, et al., 2000). In many cases, however, some subtle memory losses, particularly for events occurring within the year preceding hospitalization, persist beyond 7 months (Lisanby, Maddux, Prudic, et al., 2000). Memory loss is greater for impersonal events (world affairs) than for autobiographical (personal) events (Lisanby, Maddux, Prudic, et al., 2000). The probability of memory dysfunction is less if ECT is confined to only one hemisphere of the brain (Sackeim, Prudic, Devanand, et al., 2000), the one having less to do with language functions—as we saw in Chapter 6, this is usually the right hemisphere—and this approach has proved as effective as bilateral shock (Sackeim, Prudic, Devanand, et al., 2000). Memory loss is also lessened if ECT is applied to the frontal lobes rather than the temporal lobes, which is an equally effective approach (Bailine, Rifkin, Kayne, et al., 2000).

Another problem with ECT is that, although the treatment is painless (the patient is anesthetized before the shock is administered), many patients are very frightened of it. And, in some cases, ward personnel have made use of this fear, again for "patient management," telling patients that, if they don't cooperate, they will have to be recommended for an ECT series.

These problems have made ECT a controversial issue over the years. Defenders of ECT point out that many studies have found it highly effective—more effective, in fact, than antidepressants (Mann & Kapur, 1994; Cohen, Taieb, Flament, et al., 2000). Furthermore, unlike antidepressants, it works relatively quickly—an important advantage with suicidally depressed patients. On the other hand, ECT has vociferous critics, who consider it yet another form of psychiatric assault on mental patients. In support of this view, the voters of Berkeley, California, in 1982 passed a referendum making the administration of ECT a misdemeanor punishable by a fine of up to $500 and 6 months in jail. While the courts later reversed the ban, the fact that the voters passed it indicates the strength of opposition to this treatment.

Though the controversy over ECT is not settled, it has had its impact on practice. State legislatures have established legal safeguards against the abuse of ECT, and in general the technique is being used less frequently than it was in the 1960s and 1970s. At the same time, a 1990 report of the American Psychiatric Association concluded that ECT *was* an effective treatment for serious depressions and should be used, particularly in cases in which other treatments, such as psychotherapy and antidepressant medication, have failed.

In the past decade, an experimental treatment for depression has been developed that uses powerful magnetic fields to alter brain activity. Transcranial magnetic stimulation (TMS) involves placing an electromagnetic coil on the scalp (George, Lisanby, & Sackeim, 1999). When a high-intensity current is rapidly turned on and off in the coil, it produces a powerful, brief magnetic field that induces electrical current in neurons, causing neural depolarization—the same effect produced by ECT. Unlike ECT, however, where the skull acts as a massive resistor, magnetic fields are not deflected by intervening tissue; TMS can therefore be more focal than electrical stimulation (George, Lisanby, & Sackeim, 1999). Unlike ECT, as well, TMS is usually performed in outpatient settings without anesthesia. Patients usually notice no adverse effects other than the occasional mild headache and discomfort at the site of the stimulation (George, Lisanby, & Sackeim, 1999).

As with imaging and other studies that link depression to prefrontal dysfunction, the effects of TMS differ according to where on the prefrontal cortex it is administered. When administered over the left prefrontal region in normal volunteers, TMS causes increased sadness; over the right prefrontal cortex, its effect is increased happiness (Klein, Kreinin, Chistyakov, et al., 1999). Initial studies of patients with major depression have shown that TMS leads to reductions in depressive symptoms. Klein and colleagues found that 49 percent of patients with major depression who received TMS had a reduction of 50 percent or more on at least one of their depression scales, while only 25 percent of patients in the control group met this criterion (Klein, Kreinin, Chistyakov, et al., 1999).

TMS is a promising new area of research, though more needs to be learned about its long-term effects. Safety concerns cited by George, Lisanby, and Sackheim (1999) include headaches and short-term hearing loss; more critically, repetitive TMS has resulted in seizures in a very few cases. TMS has also been shown to disrupt cognition during the procedure itself, though these effects have not been demonstrated beyond the period of stimulation.

Key Terms

agitated depression, 247
anhedonia, 247
antidepressant medication, 279
antimanic medication, 280
attachment theory, 270
bipolar disorder, 251
catecholamine hypothesis, 278
comorbidity, 257
continuity hypothesis, 255
cyclothymic disorder, 253
delusions, 253
depression, 246
dexamethasone suppression test (DST), 277
dysthymic disorder, 252
electroconvulsive therapy (ECT), 282
endogenous, 255
hallucinations, 253
helplessness-hopelessness syndrome, 246
hypomanic episode, 248
interpersonal psychotherapy (IPT), 271
learned helplessness, 265
lithium, 280
major depressive disorder, 248
major depressive episode, 246
mania, 246
manic episode, 247
MAO inhibitors, 279
mixed episode, 248
mood disorders, 246
premorbid adjustment, 249
reactive, 255
retarded depression, 247
seasonal affective disorder (SAD), 275
selective serotonin reuptake inhibitors (SSRIs), 279
social-skills training, 264
tricyclics, 279

Summary

- People who suffer from the major mood disorders—disorders of affect, or emotions—experience exaggerations of the same kinds of highs and lows all human beings experience. Mood disorders are episodic: The depressive or manic episode often begins suddenly, runs its course, and may or may not recur. Thinking, feeling, motivation, and physiological functioning are all affected.
- A major depressive episode is characterized by depressed mood (the helplessness-hopelessness syndrome), loss of pleasure in usual activities, disturbance of appetite and sleep, psychomotor retardation or agitation, loss of energy, feelings of worthlessness and guilt, difficulty remembering or thinking clearly, and recurrent thoughts of death or suicide.
- A major manic episode is characterized by an elated, expansive, or irritable mood combined with inflated self-esteem, sleeplessness, talkativeness, flight of ideas, distractibility, hyperactivity, and reckless behavior.
- Major depressive disorder is one of the most common mental health problems in the United States. It affects women more often than men, European Americans more than African Americans, and separated and divorced people more than married people. People with bipolar disorder experience mixed or alternating manic and depressive episodes. Many others suffer from dysthymic disorder (milder but chronic depression) or cyclothymic disorder (recurrent depressive and hypomanic episodes). Demographic, family, and individual case patterns suggest that different mood disorders may have different etiologies.
- Mood disorders differ along several dimensions, including psychotic versus nonpsychotic; endogenous (from within) versus reactive (a response to loss); and early versus late onset. Evidence of comorbidity, especially mixed anxiety-depression, is increasing.
- People suffering from depression are at high risk for suicide. Single people are more likely than married people to kill themselves. Although more women than men attempt suicide in most countries, more men succeed in killing themselves. Teenagers are at risk for suicide due to a complex set of factors, including family problems. People who threaten to commit suicide often attempt to do so; people who attempt suicide, but fail, often try again. Encouraging people to talk about suicidal thoughts often helps them overcome these wishes. Among factors that predict suicide, hopelessness—the belief that there is no other escape from psychological pain—stands out. Suicide hotlines and school-based prevention programs often do not appeal to the people who need them most.
- There are two prominent behaviorist perspectives on depression and suicide. According to one view, the extinction hypothesis, depression results from a loss of reinforcement, often exacerbated by a lack of skill in seeking interpersonal rewards. According to a second view, depressed people elicit negative responses by demanding too much reinforcement in inappropriate ways. However, which comes first, depression or aversive behavior, is debatable. Behavioral therapies focus on increasing self-reinforcement and on teaching social and other skills.

- The cognitive perspective also has two main theories of depression and suicide. One focuses on learned helplessness (the belief that one cannot control or avoid aversive events) combined with hopelessness (the feeling that negative events will continue and even increase). Hopelessness, in particular, is a predictor of suicide. A second cognitive theory traces depression and suicide to negative schemas, or images, of the self, the world, and the future. But, again, whether these feelings are a cause of depression is debatable. Cognitive therapists seek to correct negative thoughts and attributions by such methods as cognitive training and reattribution training.
- Psychodynamic theorists, beginning with Freud, trace depression to an early trauma that is reactivated by a recent loss, bringing back infantile feelings of powerlessness. Some see depressed people as "love addicts" who attempt to compensate for their low self-esteem by seeking reassurance from others. But dependency on a loved one can turn to anger and guilt. According to this view, suicidal people are attempting to destroy another person whom they have incorporated into their own psyches. Empirical studies lend some support to the association of depression with dependency and with early loss of a parent or poor parenting. Psychodynamic treatment of depression aims not only to unearth the early trauma but also to examine how the patient uses depression in dealing with others. A short-term therapy that uses this approach is interpersonal therapy.
- The sociocultural perspective attempts to explain historical changes and cross-cultural differences in the rates of depression and suicide. One view is that rapid social change, one of the defining characteristics of modern life, deprives people of necessary social supports.
- The neuroscience perspective holds that, whatever the contribution of early or current emotional and/or social stress, mood disorders are at least partly organic. Some neuroscientists study families, twins, and adopted children and their biological and adoptive parents to discover the degree to which mood disorders are inherited. There is strong evidence that vulnerability to mood disorders and suicide runs in families. Some neuroscientists look at seasonal fluctuations in mood. Some examine CT, MRI, and PET scans for abnormalities in structures or regions thought to be involved in mood regulation. And some focus on biochemistry, especially hormonal imbalances and the neurotransmitters norepinephrine and serotonin. Today the most common treatment of major depression is the use of antidepressant medication (MAO inhibitors, tricyclics, and selective serotonin reuptake inhibitors [SSRIs]). Many depressed patients receive antidepressants in addition to another kind of therapy. Lithium, a natural mineral, is the dominant medication for treating bipolar depressive and manic episodes. Electroconvulsive therapy is a controversial treatment for severe depression. It works relatively quickly, compared to antidepressants, but critics note its side effects, such as a negative effect on memory.

CHAPTER

11

Odd/Eccentric Personality Disorders

Paranoid Personality Disorder

Schizotypal Personality Disorder

Schizoid Personality Disorder

Dramatic/Emotional Personality Disorders

Antisocial Personality Disorder

Borderline Personality Disorder

Histrionic Personality Disorder

Narcissistic Personality Disorder

Anxious/Fearful Personality Disorders

Avoidant Personality Disorder

Dependent Personality Disorder

Obsessive-Compulsive Personality Disorder

Personality Disorders: Theory and Therapy

The Psychodynamic Perspective

The Behavioral Perspective

The Cognitive Perspective

The Sociocultural Perspective

The Neuroscience Perspective

Personality Disorders

Ms. C, a 36-year-old woman, was referred to the day hospital Borderline Personality Disorders Treatment Program after her fourth hospitalization for depression and suicidality. Ms. C had not known her father. She was raised by her mother, who had a multiple-substance dependence. Her relationship with her mother was described as negligent and distant. She had two brothers. The oldest brother abused her sexually for 3 years after she was 13 years old. The abuse ended when he was drafted into the army. She denied any feelings of anger or bitterness toward him and in fact described substantial feelings of fondness and affection. He died while serving in Vietnam.

She obtained good to excellent grades in school but had a history of indiscriminate sexual behavior, substance abuse, and bulimia nervosa. Her first treatment was at the age of 19 years. She became significantly depressed when she discov-ered that her fiancé was sexually involved with her best friend. Her hospitalization was precipitated by the ingestion of a lethal amount of drugs. After this hospitalization, she began to mutilate herself by scratching or cutting her arms with broken plates, dinner knives, or metal. The self-mutilation was usually precipitated by episodes of severe loneliness and feelings of emptiness.

She had an active social life and a large network of friends. However, her relationships were unstable. She could be quite supportive, engaging, and personable but would overreact to common conflicts, disagreements, and difficulties. She would feel intensely hurt, depressed, angry, or enraged and hope that her friends would relieve her pain through some gesture. However, they typically felt frustrated, annoyed, or overwhelmed by the intensity of her affect and her reactions.

Her sexual relationships were even more problematical. She quickly developed intense feelings of attraction, involvement, and dependency. However, she soon experienced her lovers as disappointing and neglectful. Indeed many were neglectful, unempathic, or abusive, but all of them found the intensity of the inevitable conflicts and her anger to be intolerable (Widiger & Sanderson, 1997, p. 1304).

Many of the psychological disorders that we have discussed so far arise like physical disorders in the sense that their sufferers, having once been "well," find themselves "ill," and in a specific way. They can no longer look at a dog without fear; they can no longer find reason to be happy. By contrast, the personality disorders are conditions that have generally been with the person for many years and have to do not so much with a specific problem, such as dog phobia or depression, as with the entire personality. *DSM-IV-TR* defines **personality disorder** as "an enduring pattern of inner experience and behavior that deviates markedly from the expectations of the individual's culture, is pervasive and inflexible, has an onset in adolescence or early adulthood, is stable over time, and leads to distress or impairment" (American Psychiatric Association, 2000, p. 685).* This disorder, then, has to do with stable traits. To quote *DSM-IV-TR* again, "*Personality traits* are enduring patterns of perceiving, relating to, and thinking about the environment and oneself that are exhibited in a wide range of social and personal contexts. Only when personality traits are inflexible and maladaptive and cause significant functional impairment or subjective distress do they constitute Personality Disorders" (American Psychiatric Association, 2000, p. 686). Because personality disorders are so generalized and of such long standing, people with these disorders may not see their condition as a problem that can be treated; it is just who they *are*. Typically, they are very unhappy, though in some cases they may give less pain to themselves than to those who have to deal with them—their families, co-workers, and so forth.

Some experts propose that people with personality disorders be classed not by diagnostic categories but by dimensional ratings (Chapter 2). In other words, people would be rated on such things as dominance versus submission or novelty seeking versus novelty avoiding. Ms. C, for example, would be identified not as having borderline personality disorder but simply as having a high score on aspects of antagonism and neuroticism, plus other ratings that might be relevant to her problem. (Costa & Widiger, 1994). Some researchers have attempted to view such dimensional ratings in terms of a basic set of 5 personality traits (Costa & McCrae, 1990, 1995; Trull, Widiger, Useda, et al., 1998). In this "5-Factor" model of personality, most differences between people occur in 5 domains: (1) neuroticism (or negative emotions) as opposed to emotional stability, (2) extraversion (or sociability) as opposed to introversion, (3) conscientiousness (or self-control), (4) agreeableness as opposed to antagonism to others, and (5) openness as opposed to closedness to experience. Studies have shown that extreme scores on these 5 factors are strongly related to personality disorders (Costa, McCae, & Siegler, 1999; Trull, Widiger, Useda, et al., 1998).

The burden that personality disorders place on individuals and society is evident in their undesirable effects on psychological adjustment, impulse-control disorders (see box on page 300), and the risk of mood and anxiety disorders. A recent study by Johnson and colleagues found that adolescents with personality disorders were more than twice as likely as adolescents who were free of personality disorders to suffer from problems such as suicidality, anxiety, mood, and substance use disorders during early adulthood (Johnson, Cohen, Skodol, et al., 1999). This negative long-term influence of personality disorders was found regardless of any other disorders the children had during adolescence. Patients with personality disorders have far more extensive histories of psychiatric treatment, including outpatient and inpatient treatment, and psychopharmacologic treatment, than patients with major depressive disorder (Bender, Dolan, Skodol, et al., 2001).

DSM-IV-TR lists 10 personality disorders. The diagnostic manual organizes them into 3 "clusters": odd/eccentric personality disorders, dramatic/emotional personality disorders, and anxious/fearful personality disorders (see Figure 11.1).

Odd/Eccentric Personality Disorders

People with *odd/eccentric personality disorders* have some traits in common with victims of schizophrenia and delusional disorder (Chapter 14), though they do not show the decisive break in reality contact that characterizes those very grave conditions.

Paranoid Personality Disorder

The defining characteristic of **paranoid personality disorder** is suspiciousness. We all feel suspicious in certain situations and with certain people, often for good reasons. However, paranoid personalities feel suspicious in almost all situations and with almost all people, usually

*Reprinted with permission from the *Diagnostic and Statistical Manual of Mental Disorders,* Fourth Edition, Text Revision.

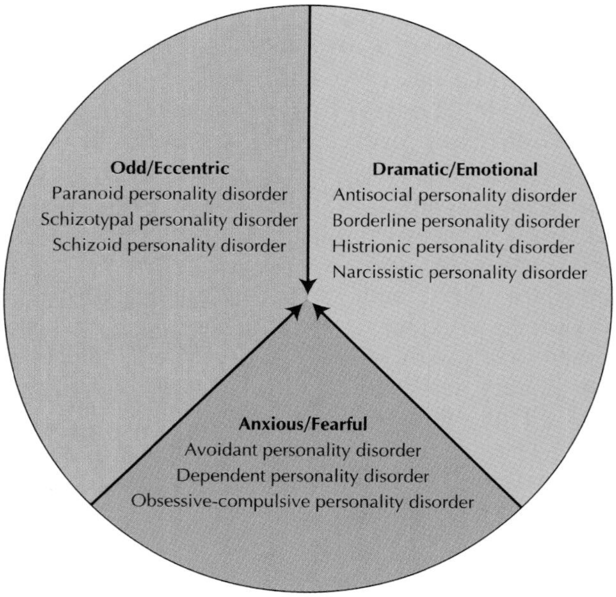

FIGURE 11.1 Clusters of personality disorders.

Someone who is continually suspicious that people engaged in casual conversation are plotting against him or her exhibits a key characteristic of paranoid personality disorder.

without good reason. And, when they are confronted with evidence that their mistrust is unfounded, they typically begin to mistrust the person who brought them the evidence: "So he's against me too!"

Such an attitude, of course, involves an impairment in cognitive functioning. Paranoid personalities are constantly scanning the environment for evidence to support their suspicions—and constantly finding such evidence. If two people are talking together near the coffee machine, or if the mail is late, or if the neighbors are blaring music at midnight, this is taken as evidence of personal hostility.

This suspiciousness has equally drastic effects on emotional adjustment, for it stands in the way of love and friendship. Paranoid personalities typically have few friends. They may have an "ally," usually someone in a subordinate position, but eventually they begin distrusting that person, too, and look for another ally—a process that repeats itself. Some paranoid personalities become very isolated; others join fringe political groups. Their work record is often spotty. They tend to be hypercritical, stubborn, and controlling, and they often become embroiled in hostile disputes, which may escalate to lawsuits. With all these interpersonal problems, however, paranoid personalities rarely turn up in psychotherapists' offices, for they see their difficulties as coming from without rather than within. For this reason, it is difficult to estimate the prevalence of this disorder.

Despite similarities in name and in the defining trait of suspiciousness, paranoid personality disorder should not be confused with paranoid schizophrenia or delusional disorder, which are psychoses—that is, severely disabling disorders, involving loss of reality contact. Paranoid personality disorder is not as disabling. For example, patients with paranoid personality disorder do not hear voices or experience the other auditory hallucinations that are common in people with schizophrenia. It should be added, however, that researchers have found paranoid personality disorder to be significantly more common among the biological relatives of individuals with schizophrenia than in the population at large (Nigg & Goldsmith, 1994). Yet the links remain less than fully clear, and research also indicates that paranoid personality disorder is more frequent among the relatives of individuals with unipolar depression than in relatives of people with schizophrenia (Maier, Lichteran, Minges, et al., 1994).

Schizotypal Personality Disorder

The person with **schizotypal personality disorder** manifests odd speech, behavior, thinking, and/or perception, but the oddity is not enough for a diagnosis of schizophrenia. For example, speech may ramble, but never to the point of actual incoherence, as is often the case with people with schizophrenia. Or the person may report recurrent illusions, such as feeling as if a dead parent were in the room—a situation different from that of a person with schizophrenia, who is more likely to report that the dead parent *is* in the room. Schizotypal personalities may also show magical thinking, claiming that they can predict the future, read the thoughts of others, and so on. Like paranoid personalities, they may become involved with fringe groups—astrology enthusiasts, self-proclaimed alien-abduction survivors—and isolated from anyone who does not share this interest. Often, such people also have childhood histories of having been teased and excluded because of their peculiar behaviors, as in the following case:

Ms. G is a 60-year-old woman who has never been married and lives by herself with 13 cats. Ms. G's appearance is strange, and her behavior is obviously eccentric. Although she has an endearing quality and is likable, anyone who sees her immediately senses that she is "different." Ms. G dresses in a crazy quilt of colors in an eclectic style that favors the 1920s. She has never been able to work, but she lived on an inheritance from her parents until she was in her 40s and since then has been supported by disability payments and welfare. Ms. G was raised in a devout Roman Catholic home and believes that she is destined to receive a visitation from the Virgin Mary, as the children at Lourdes did. She is constantly on the lookout for messages or clues that she believes will reveal to her when and where the visitation will occur. For example, she carefully reviews the most ordinary statements made by individuals (e.g., the checker at the grocery store or the clerk at the post office) to see whether their words have hidden and deeper meanings. Ms. G experiences almost constant feelings of depersonalization and derealization: She says she feels as if she is not connected to herself and as if she is a character in a movie. She is fascinated by the subject of out-of-body experiences and describes frequent episodes of astral travel. Her apartment is filled with signs and refuse she has collected over the years. Despite her odd beliefs, Ms. G is not delusional and is able to acknowledge that she may be mistaken in her beliefs. She often feels that other people are talking about her when she leaves the apartment but acknowledges that this may be because of the unusual way she dresses. For this reason and because she is extremely stilted and shy in social situations, Ms. G generally goes out only at night to avoid talking to others or meeting them in the elevator. She sneaks in and out of her apartment surreptitiously and does her shopping at the 24-hour store at 3 A.M. when hardly anyone is there.

Ms. G had a maternal uncle who was schizophrenic. She has been very shy and retiring since she was a child and says that she was always "odd" and never fit in with her brothers or sisters or fellow students. Although her siblings have suggested at various times over the years that Ms. G seek some sort of psychiatric treatment, she has refused. Ms. G is brought in for evaluation at this time because she was picked up by the police after she took a figure of the Virgin Mary from a religious supply store without paying for it, claiming that she was meant to have it. When the policeman insisted that Ms. G must return the statue, she became argumentative, irritable, and threatened to strike him. At this point she was handcuffed and brought to the emergency room.

Ms. G has four brothers and two sisters. To varying degrees, they have tried to remain in contact with her over the years. She has rejected most of their overtures, however, and is irritated at each one of them for different reasons. She says she feels more comfortable alone. Although in earlier years she used to be invited to family gatherings for holidays, her brothers and sisters have long since abandoned their attempts to get her to participate in these social occasions. For the past 15 years she has lived in almost complete isolation, except for an occasional phone call from one of her brothers or sisters. Her siblings have arranged for her to receive disability and welfare payments, however, and also provide her with hand-me-down clothes (Frances & Ross, 1996, pp. 288–289).

Schizotypal personality disorder was added to the *DSM* in 1980 as part of an effort to improve the reliability of the diagnosis of schizophrenia and to study its relation (if any) to other conditions. In schizophrenia, diagnostic lines are often hard to draw. In the "classic" case, the person appears decidedly odd in many respects: speech, thought, perception, emotion, social behavior, motor behavior, and so on. However, many cases are not classic ones. For example, the person may seem only marginally odd in a number of respects or very odd in only one respect, social withdrawal. These two patterns, classified in the past as subtypes of schizophrenia, are now labeled as personality disorders: schizotypal personality disorder and schizoid personality disorder, respectively.

Schizoid Personality Disorder

The defining characteristic of **schizoid personality disorder** is a severely restricted range of emotions that is most notably associated with social detachment. Schizoid personalities appear to have little or no interest in relationships: They are often distant from their families, they rarely marry, and they have no close friends. In the contacts they do have with others, they seem not to experience the emotions that are part of ordinary social life: warmth, pleasure, disappointment, hurt. They also seem to take little pleasure in solitary activities. In the most severe cases, the ability to experience positive emotional experiences such as joy, happiness, gaiety, and pleasure is completely lacking. (The absence of pleasurable emotions is known as *anhedonia*.) If questioned, schizoids may claim that they have friends, but these usually turn out to be superficial acquaintances. They may try to make a friend, but the effort will founder on their inability to show the expected warmth and emotional investment. In fact, with their social detachment, solitary behavior, and insensitivity to others, individuals with schizoid personality disorder may resemble individuals with autism. Some studies suggest a genetic link between the two disorders, although the nature of the link remains to be clarified (Wolf, 2000; Wolf & McGuire, 1995).

Because of their self-absorption, schizoid personalities may appear absentminded—"out of it," so to speak. However, they do not show the unusual thoughts, behaviors, or speech patterns seen in the schizotypal personality. And, unlike schizotypal personalities, they may be quite successful in their work if it requires little social contact.

A further distinction between the schizoid and schizotypal personality disorders is susceptibility to schizophrenia. Researchers have found schizotypal disorder to be significantly more common among the biological relatives of people with schizophrenia than among the population at large (Maier et al., 1994; Nicolson & Rapoport, 2001), indicating a possible genetic relationship. Furthermore, schizotypal personality disorder tends to respond to the same medications as schizophrenia (Schulz, Schulz, & Wilson, 1988), a finding which suggests a biological relationship between the two disorders. Thus, schizotypal personalities may be at risk, genetically or otherwise, for schizophrenia, but this is apparently not as likely with schizoid personalities (Nigg & Goldsmith, 1994). Watson (2001) found possible links between schizotypal disorder and measures of dissociation, with evidence that they share a common domain of unusual cognitions and perceptions.

Finally, some aspects of schizotypal disorder seem related to abnormalities in the language areas of the brain (Shihabuddin, Buchbaum, Hazlett, et al., 2001).

Dramatic/Emotional Personality Disorders

People with *dramatic/emotional personality disorders* tend to be attention-seeking, demanding, and erratic in their behavior. This category includes antisocial, borderline, histrionic, and narcissistic personality disorders.

Antisocial Personality Disorder

The defining trait of **antisocial personality disorder (APD)** is a predatory attitude toward other people—a chronic indifference to and violation of the rights of one's fellow human beings. Antisocial personality disorder is by no means an unusual phenomenon. It affects about 1 percent of females and 4 to 6 percent of males among the general population, according to *DSM-IV-TR* and epidemiological research (Cloninger, Bayone, & Przybeck, 1997; Kessler, McGonagle, Zhao, et al., 1994; Robins, Tipp, & Przybeck, 1991). Furthermore, because antisocial behavior often involves criminal behavior, this disorder raises the whole issue of the relationship between abnormal behavior and crime. For these reasons—and because it is the most reliably diagnosed of the personality syndromes—we will discuss this disorder at greater length than the others.

Characteristics of the Antisocial Personality *DSM-IV-TR'* s list of criteria for the diagnosis of antisocial personality disorder can be summarized as five basic points:

1. *A history of illegal or socially disapproved activity beginning before age 15 and continuing into adulthood.* Usually a pattern of antisocial behavior is evident in puberty in the form of truancy, delinquency, theft, vandalism, lying, drug abuse, running away from home, and/or chronic misbehavior in school. In adulthood, prostitution, pimping, drug dealing, and other crimes may be added to the list.
2. *Failure to show constancy and responsibility in work, sexual relationships, parenthood, or financial obligations.* People with antisocial personalities lack steadiness and a sense of obligation. They tend to walk out on jobs, spouses, children, and creditors.
3. *Irritability and aggressiveness.* People with antisocial personalities are easily riled, and they express their anger not just in street brawls but also often in abuse of mates and children.
4. *Reckless and impulsive behavior.* Unlike "normal" criminals, people with antisocial personalities rarely engage in planning. Instead, they tend to operate in an aimless, thrill-seeking fashion, traveling from town to town with no goal in mind, falling into bed with anyone available, and stealing a pack of cigarettes or a car, depending on what seems easiest and most gratifying at the moment.
5. *Disregard for the truth.* People with antisocial personalities lie frequently and easily. Cleckley (1976) offered the following example:

> In a letter to his wife, at last seeking divorce and in another city, one patient set down dignified, fair appraisals of the situation and referred to sensible plans he had outlined for her security. He then added that specified insurance policies and annu-

> ities providing for the three children (including their tuition at college) had been mailed under separate cover and would, if she had not already received them, soon be in her hands. He had not taken even the first step to obtain insurance or to make any other provision, and, once he had made these statements in his letter, he apparently gave the matter no further thought. (p. 342)

As is usually the case with the *DSM* criteria, only some, not all, of these characteristics need be present in order for the case to be diagnosed as antisocial personality disorder. However, a history of antisocial behavior during both adolescence and adulthood must be present. Also, in keeping with the policies of the diagnostic manual, this list confines itself to verifiable behaviors.

Antisocial Behavior and Psychopathy The question of the relationship between psychological disturbance and **antisocial behavior,** behavior that violates the rights of others, forms an interesting chapter in the history of psychology. Until about 200 years ago, criminals were generally treated as criminals, with little thought as to their psychological well-being. In 1835, an English psychiatrist, J. C. Prichard, identified a condition that he called "moral insanity," which he described as "a form of mental derangement in which the intellectual functions appear to have sustained little or no injury, while the . . . moral or active principles of the mind are strangely perverted or depraved" (Preu, 1944, p. 923). In the late nineteenth century, such people came to be called "psychopaths," and, in keeping with the biogenic thinking of the period, it was assumed that their problem was a hereditary defect. Then, with the rise of sociology in the twentieth century, researchers began, instead, to stress the influence of social conditions. Accordingly, "psychopaths" were relabeled "sociopaths" (Birnbaum, 1914), the implication being that the problem lay not in the person but in the person's relationship to society.

Thus, while its causes were still being disputed, antisocial behavior was absorbed into abnormal psychology. There were no longer any criminals, just disturbed people. Yet many criminals seem to commit their crimes for simple and relatively understandable reasons—to supplement their incomes, to punish someone who has done them wrong, and so forth. Should these people also be regarded as psychologically disturbed? In early editions of the *DSM*, there was some hedging on this point. *DSM* swung from one direction to the other but has now settled in the middle. Some people who engage in antisocial behavior are psychologically "normal," and others are not. However, has the *DSM* actually succeeded in clearly distinguishing between normal criminals and people with APD? In the research conducted to determine the criteria for APD in *DSM-IV-TR,* 70 percent of those in prison met *DSM-IIIR* criteria for APD (Widiger, Cadoret, Hare, et al., 1996). Like *DSM-III-R, DSM-IV-TR* bases the diagnosis of APD largely on behavior that is common among criminals and fails to include the interpersonal and emotional characteristics traditionally associated with psychopathy. When such *psychopathic* characteristics as a lack of empathy, an inflated sense of one's self-importance, and a glib, superficial interpersonal style were included in diagnostic considerations, only 28 percent of the prison inmates qualified as psychopaths (Widiger, Cadoret, Hare, et al., 1996). This suggests that the diagnosis of APD has moved *closer* to reliably identifying criminals, but further from the classic notion of psychopathy (Hare, 1996; Zagon, 1995).

Despite the omission of psychopathic characteristics from *DSM-IV* and *DSM-IV-TR,* many experts have held on to the term *psychopathy* for a subgroup of people diagnosed with APD to emphasize the more subjective portraits that they consider part and parcel of some of the antisocial personalities. For example, Cleckley, who treated psychopaths for many years, devoted an entire book, *The Mask of Sanity* (1976), to a description of this disorder and did not distinguish between APD and psychopathy. (His conceptualization, updated and expanded by Hare and his colleagues, formed the basis, in part, for *DSM-IV*'s debate about whether to include psychopathy as a subgroup of those with APD [Hare, 1993; Hart & Hare, 1997; Widiger, Cadoret, Hare, et al., 1996]). According to Cleckley, psychopaths differ from normal people, including "normal"criminals, not only in their actions but also in their emotions, motivations, and thought processes. First, their misdeeds are not just impulsive but almost unmotivated—or, rather, not motivated by any understandable purpose. Their behavior, therefore, often has a perverse or an irrational quality. Cleckley (1976) cites the case of a teenager whose exploits included "defecation into the stringed intricacies of the school piano, the removal from his uncle's automobile of a carburetor for which he got 75 cents, and the selling of his father's overcoat to a passing buyer of scrap materials" (p. 65). This lack of purposefulness, Cleckley claims, is what makes most psychopaths unsuccessful criminals. However, as Lykken (1995) notes, some psychopaths are "successful" and do not end up getting caught and going to prison. He suggests that successful psychopaths have higher IQs, come from relatively privileged backgrounds, and exhibit the superficial charm and ability to "con" that is often associated with psychopathy (see the box on page 292 for a discussion of successful and unsuccessful psychopaths).

Research Highlights: Are There Two Types of Psychopath—Successful and Unsuccessful?

While earlier research has primarily studied "unsuccessful" psychopaths, those who have been caught by the legal system and put into jails or psychiatric facilities, recent studies have suggested a whole new way of thinking about psychopaths. It may be that while most psychopaths are unsuccessful criminals, as Cleckley claims, others have characteristics that help them avoid detection.

Ishikawa and colleagues compared "successful" psychopaths, who have eluded conviction, with psychopaths who have been convicted by the legal system (Ishikawa, Raine, Lenz, et al., 2001). They found that successful psychopaths are more sensitive to risky situations and better able to recognize contextual cues (Newman, 1998) that, if missed, might get them into trouble. Successful psychopaths also show a stress-induced rise in heart rate, another response that may help them avoid capture.

By contrast, unsuccessful psychopaths show a striking lack of fear in the face of aversive, punishing events (Herperts, Werth, Lukas, et al., 2001; Schmitt & Newman, 1999) and have trouble recognizing faces that express fear, as compared to faces that express happiness, surprise, disgust, or anger (Mitchell & Blair, 2000). These characteristics may make their behavior more reckless and render these psychopaths more vulnerable to being caught.

Mitchell and Blair (2000) suggest that these emotional features of psychopathy are explained by a deficit in the functioning of the amygdala. Other researchers report that the vast majority of the limbic system appears to be underactivated in psychopathy during emotional processing (Kiehl, Smith, Hare, et al., 2001). It may be that "successful" psychopaths do not have these deficits, but more research remains to be done.

Second, according to Cleckley, psychopaths have only the shallowest emotions. Through lack of love, lack of loyalty, and, above all, lack of empathy—an inability to imagine what might be the feelings of the child they have left alone all day in an empty house or the friend whose credit cards they have stolen—they are able to ignore what most people would regard as obligations. Neither do they feel anxiety or remorse over such actions, for they are as deficient in guilt as they are in other basic emotions. Zax and Stricker (1963) report the case of a boy who killed a neighborhood child by shooting her in the head:

> He spoke of the incident . . . in a nonchalant, unfeeling way, and was very suave and unnaturally composed in explaining why he was on the ward. He said, "I was showing her the gun. I didn't know it was loaded. She turned her head and it got her in the temple. I told the police that I was very sorry. You're to find out if there is anything mentally wrong with me. I thought I'd have to go to reform school." (p. 240)

Courtesy of C. Scott Moss.

A hostile, sociopathic patient made this doodle of a bloody knife being plunged into a female breast. On a subsequent occasion, only the face within the circle was shown to the patient, and he identified it as his mother's.

A third aspect of Cleckley's portrait is poor judgment and failure to learn from experience. Psychopaths, he argues, do not make the connection between their actions and the consequences of those actions. Or, as later theorists (Newman, 1997) have refined the concept, antisocial personalities (and psychopaths) are bad at **passive avoidance learning,** learning to stop making a response that results in punishment. Once punished for an action, normal people learn either not to repeat the action or to repeat it in such a way that they will not be caught. In contrast, people with antisocial personalities may repeat an offense again and again, and in the same manner, even though they have been punished for doing so. Barratt and colleagues theorize that antisocial personalities have information-processing problems that make it hard for them to switch their attention from cues for reward to cues for punishment (Barratt, Sanford, Kent, et al., 1997). This cognitive defect appears to be reflected in other ways as well. For example, psychopaths' communication behavior is less logically organized than that of nonpsychopaths (Brinkley,

Bernstein, & Newman, 1999). Researchers have found that these cognitive deficits are specific to conditions in the left hemisphere of the brain (Bernstein, Newman, Wallace, et al., 2000).

Finally, according to Cleckley, most psychopaths are able to maintain a pleasant and convincing exterior. Because of their lack of anxiety and guilt, they can lie, cheat, and steal with remarkable poise, as in the following case:

A 28-year-old man began serving a two-year sentence for armed robbery. Although psychological tests revealed some psychotic thinking, his behavior was calm and controlled. He was thought to be faking the psychotic symptoms. However, he began to cause trouble and become very aggressive shortly thereafter. He flooded the entire unit of the prison, spat on staff members, and threw fecal matter and urine at other inmates.

He was then transferred to a maximum security prison and put in solitary confinement. But even though he had neither clothes nor bed to sleep on, he continued to cause trouble. For example, he managed to strip his cell of its surface and make himself a knife out of these materials, just a day after a session with the ward psychiatrist, when he had seemed remorseful, controlled, and contrite. He blamed the guards for his violent behavior, rather than himself. In the past, he had a documented record of repeatedly trying to act "crazy" and get transferred to a psychiatric unit, from where he would ultimately escape. He managed to convince all mental health professionals that he had psychiatric problems, although no one could describe exactly what they were. Yet these "problems" kept him from being severely punished for his aggression.

Finally, the weary staff transferred the man to a forensic psychiatric unit. The workers making the transfer wore riot gear as they held him, tranquilized him with a benzodiazepine, put him in a straightjacket, and took him away.

From that time on, the 28-year-old thief was cooperative. He took his antipsychotic medication, and showed dramatic improvement in his social functioning. He was later transferred to a more comfortable facility specializing in the long-term care of criminals who were chronic mental patients. Previously, a very similar sequence of actions had gotten him paroled. Would it happen again? (Conacher & Fleming, 1996).

A psychoanalyst might interpret this case as evidence that many psychopaths have underlying psychoses and, if properly treated, can be managed if not rehabilitated. On the other hand, this inmate made a much better life for himself by behaving as if he were crazy and was reinforced for doing so, again and again. At one time or another, many psychopaths display psychotic behavior even though they may not be truly psychotic.

The debate about whether someone is clinically antisocial, simply a criminal, or a psychopath is by no means settled. There is considerable overlap and not always perfect agreement about whether an individual best fits one category rather than another. Hart and Hare (1989) reported findings that are representative of those in the literature. They found that 50 percent of the men sentenced to a psychiatric unit within a prison met *DSM-III* criteria for APD, while only 13 percent met the criteria for psychopathy, based on Hare's widely used Psychopathy Checklist (Hare, 1993). In addition to the largely behavioral criteria used to identify APD, Hare and his colleagues require that psychopaths have additional qualities such as a lack of empathy, a glib and superficial demeanor, and a distorted sense of their own self-importance that makes them seem arrogant.

The decision to confine the diagnosis in *DSM-IV* and *DSM-IV-TR* to APD and not include the extra criteria necessary for a diagnosis of psychopathy was based in large part on research conducted by Widiger and others (Widiger, Cadoret, Hare, et al., 1996). However, the results of that research were far from conclusive, and the ultimate decision to ignore the term *psychopathy* in *DSM-IV* and *DSM-IV-TR* seems to have been motivated primarily by the desire to maximize the likelihood of a reliable diagnosis by clinicians (Widiger, Cadoret, Hare, et al., 1996). There is good reason to believe that a subgroup of antisocial people are psychopaths, and it could still prove to be important to separate them from those with APD but no psychopathy (Hare, 1996; Zagon, 1995).

Finally, we should not overlook the overlap between APD and substance abuse (Strain, 1995). At least 50 percent of people meeting the criteria for substance abuse also have antisocial personalities. The question of which is primary—the antisocial behavior or the drug use—may have important implications for etiology, as well as for treatment. To what extent do people with antisocial personalities drink and use drugs to acquire the reinforcers associated with them? To what extent do drug abusers "look" antisocial simply because of their substance abuse? These are important but as yet unanswered questions.

Borderline Personality Disorder

Borderline personality disorder was illustrated in the case history that opened this chapter. First proposed by psychodynamic theorists (e.g., O. F. Kernberg,

The first serial killer in recorded history was Gilles de Rais, a fifteenth-century French nobleman who was convicted of murdering more than 800 children. He pleasured himself by mutilating them and then having sex with their bodies after they were dead.

Gilles de Rais and other serial killers, such as Jack the Ripper, the Boston Strangler, and Jeffrey Dahmer, have both horrified and fascinated us for centuries. FBI experts claim to be able to profile serial killers, and more serial killers seem to be emerging each year, but they are still too few in number for systematic research (DeHart & Mahoney, 1994). Nevertheless, serial killing is probably more common than most people think (Holmes & DeBurger, 1985). Law enforcement officials believe that many unsolved and apparently motiveless murders—perhaps 20 percent of all homicides—were committed by serial killers. It is possible that, in the past 15 years, as the murder rate has doubled, the number of serial killers has tripled. At least 5,000 people per year are killed by serial killers. There are probably between 30 and 100 serial killers at large in the United States today.

Catching serial killers poses major problems, in part because some move from place to place. In the 1970s, Ted Bundy drifted from Washington to Utah and then to Colorado, where he managed to escape from prison. After that, he passed through Chicago, East Lansing, and Louisville, before finally being arrested and executed in Tallahassee. Bundy may have killed more than 300 women during his sojourns. About the same time, John Wayne Gacy managed to maintain the façade of a respectable businessman in Chicago, while killing as many as 33 people, most of them children, and burying them in various places in his house.

Most serial killers are white males 25 to 34 years of age. Like many perpetrators of violence, most serial killers were abused as children and, as adults, are dependent on drugs and alcohol. They tend to be charming, charismatic, intelligent, and psychopathic; they tend to choose one type of victim, one that is vulnerable and easy to control. Typically, they use deceit to gain access to their victims. The killings generally are elaborately planned, and the weapons chosen—knives, fists, and so on—bring the murderers into close physical contact with their victims.

Most serial killers are sexual sadists (Drukteinis, 1992; Warren, Hazelwood, & Dietz, 1996). They are aroused by controlling and degrading their victims in painful sexual acts and torture. Interestingly, as serial killers repeat their crimes, their killings become less calculated and elaborate, and their acts seem more and more driven by desperation and boredom.

People with antisocial personality disorder generally commit violence as a way of getting something they want—sex, drugs, money, and so on, but some psychopaths commit violence for the sake of violence—simply for the joy of killing. Why? What can possibly motivate such horrifying behavior? Robert Hale (1994) theorizes that the victims of serial killers remind them of people who humiliated them in early life. The Dutch psychiatrist Willem H. J. Martens (2002) argues that psychopathic killers suffer emotionally for a number of reasons. Like healthy people, Martens writes, many psychopaths love their spouse, children, parents, and pets. But unlike healthy people, they have difficulty loving and trusting the rest of the world. Yet psychopaths desire very much to be loved and cherished. This human longing frequently remains unfulfilled, however, and most psychopaths lack social networks or close personal bonds with others. Their lives are often full of misery, characterized by a disordered family life, parental substance abuse and other antisocial behavior, bad relationships, separation and divorce, and bad neighborhoods (Martens, 2002).

Psychopathic killers do not necessarily see their behavior as wrong. In fact, they often view themselves as victims. Gacy, for instance, considered himself the real victim: He had been cheated out of his childhood, he believed, and after his crimes came to light, he felt that the media portrayed him in an unfairly negative way (Baumeister, 1997).

Psychopaths believe that the world is working against them, and as their suffering increases, so does their criminal behavior. Palermo and Martens (in press) describe the cases of two psychopaths, the notorious serial killers Jeffrey Dahmer and Dennis Nilsen. Both men said that they did not enjoy the act of killing: They killed simply for the company. Neither man had any friends; their only social life was an occasional encounter in a gay bar. Dahmer said that he ate parts of his victims' bodies in order to keep them with him, inside his body. Nilsen reported that he was more comfortable with dead bodies than with living people because, he said, the dead could not abandon him. Nilsen wrote poetry and spoke tenderly to the bodies of the men he killed, keeping them beside him as long as he could. Both men described their loneliness and social isolation as unimaginably painful. Eventually, each man became convinced that he deserved to get back at the cruel world for the misery he felt over its rejection, and he turned to sadism and murder.

Social isolation and emotional suffering preceded unspeakable violence in these two psychopaths. Significantly, researchers have found a relationship between the kind of sadness and loneliness Dahmer and Nilsen reported and the degree of expressed violence, recklessness, and impulsivity in other psychopaths as well (Martens, 1999; Palermo & Martens, in press). Psychopaths are at risk of targeting their aggression toward themselves as much as others. They may feel that *all* lives are worthless, including their own (Martens, 1997; Palermo & Martens, in press).

Psychopathic killers are notorious for the sick pleasure and feelings of power they derive from their hideous offences. Often overlooked, however, is the hidden suffering of the disorder. It is essential that clinicians working with psychopaths recognize their feelings of victimization, loneliness, and emotional pain, because this suffering may constitute a recognizable risk factor for violent, criminal behavior.

1975)—and still questioned by some other theorists (e.g., Siever & Davis, 1991)—this category has received a great deal of attention in recent years (Clarkin, Marziali, & Monroe-Blum, 1991; Gunderson & Phillips, 1991). Morey (1991) describes the disorder as a syndrome involving four core elements:

1. *Difficulties in establishing a secure self-identity.* Borderline personalities have an unstable sense of self and are therefore heavily dependent on their relationships with others in order to achieve a sense of identity, of selfhood. Hence, they have a hard time being alone and tend to be devastated when a close relationship comes to an end. The character played by Glenn Close in the movie *Fatal Attraction* resembles borderline personality and, in particular, exemplifies this catastrophic response to the end of a relationship.
2. *Distrust.* As dependent as they are on other people, borderline personalities are also suspicious of those people and expect to be abandoned or victimized by them. Given their difficult behavior, they may well be (Kroll, 1988). This combination of dependence and mistrust creates a profound ambivalence in the borderline personality's feelings for others. A friend who is idolized one moment may be attacked the next.
3. *Impulsive and self-destructive behavior.* Borderline personalities are typically impulsive and unpredictable in their actions. When they cut loose, they often engage in self-destructive behavior such as drug abuse, reckless driving, fighting, and promiscuity. They are also given to making manipulative suicide threats.
4. *Difficulty in controlling anger and other emotions.* This is a very prominent feature of borderline personalities. They exist in a state of perpetual emotional crisis, the primary emotions being grief and anger.

Glenn Close's character in the movie Fatal Attraction *provides an example of borderline personality disorder.*

Borderline Personality Disorder: "Do You Want Me to Slash My Wrist Again?!"

The MindMAP video "Borderline Personality Disorder" illustrates some of the core elements of borderline personality disorder. Can you identify some of these core elements in the video? What are they?

Many theorists have asked whether borderline personality is a form of depression. Many borderline patients meet the diagnostic criteria for depression, and they are at greater risk for recurrent episodes of major depression (Lewinsohn, Rohde, Seeley, et al., 2000). There is also some evidence, though not conclusive, that mood disorders may be more prevalent in the families of borderline personalities (Gunderson & Elliot, 1985). Yet evidence exists that the depression in borderline patients is qualitatively distinct from depression in other patients (Rogers, Widiger, & Krupp, 1995). Rogers and colleagues found that depression in borderline personality disorder was particularly linked to feelings of extreme self-condemnation, feelings of emptiness, and fears of abandonment. These feelings differ from the ones reported by other patients with depression.

Recent research reveals that depression is not the only form of emotional disturbance in borderline personality. In fact, anxiety disorders are almost as common among borderline patients as depression disorders, and anxiety disorders distinguish borderline patients from other personality disorder patients better than depression disorders do (Zanarini, Frankenburg, Dubo, et al., 1998).

Some researchers have wondered whether borderline personality could be a form of chronic posttraumatic stress disorder (Zanarini, Frankenburg, Dubo, et al., 1998). Many borderline patients report childhood histories of severe physical and sexual abuse (Heffernan & Cloitre, 2000). However, the overlap between borderline patients and PTSD is far from universal (Zanarini, Frankenburg, Dubo, et al., 1998), and most indications are that the two are separate disorders (Heffernan & Cloitre, 2000).

An outstanding characteristic of borderline personality disorder is its highly negative effect on adjustment. Borderline personality increases the risk of suicide (Davis, Gunderson, & Myers, 1999), substance abuse and impulse-control disorders (Trull, Sher, Minks-Brown, et al., 2000; Zanarini, Frankenburg, Dubo, et al., 1998), self-mutilation and self-destructive activities (Trull, Sher, Minks-Brown, et al., 2000), unstable relationships (Gunderson, 1996), severe anger problems, mood and anxiety disorders (Zanarini, Frankenburg, Dubo, et al., 1998), and other difficulties. Bender and colleagues found that patients with borderline personality received greater amounts of every type of psychosocial treatment, except self-help groups, and were also more likely to have used antianxiety, antidepressant, and mood stabilizer medications (Bender, Dolan, Skodol, et al., 2001). Borderline patients were more likely to receive antipsychotic medications than were any other personality disorder patients except for schizotypal personality. Persons with borderline personality may be especially tolerant of feelings of aloneness, perhaps because they lack stable attachment relationships with other people and suffer from such strong fears of abandonment (Gunderson, 1996). Substance abuse disorders are far more common among males than females with borderline personality disorder, whereas eating disorders are far more common among females than males with the disorder (Zanarini, Frankenburg, Dubo, et al., 1998). There is some overlap between borderline personality disorder and dissociative identity disorder (Putnam, 1989). It has been suggested that many people said to have dissociative identity disorder are actually misdiagnosed borderline patients.

Among patient populations, borderline is one of the most frequently diagnosed personality disorders, and it is said to be especially hard to treat, for the borderline patient's intense ambivalence is, of course, redirected onto the therapist.

Histrionic Personality Disorder

The essential feature of **histrionic personality disorder** is self-dramatization—the exaggerated display of emotion. Such emotional displays are often clearly manipulative, aimed at attracting attention and sympathy. Histrionic personalities "faint" at the sight of blood, dominate an entire dinner party with the tale of their recent faith healing, are so "overcome" with emotion during a sad movie that they have to be taken home immediately (thus spoiling their companions' evening), threaten suicide if a lover's interest cools, and so forth. To themselves, they seem sensitive; to others, after the first impression has worn off, they usually seem shallow and insincere.

Their interpersonal relationships, then, are usually fragile. Initially, upon meeting a new person, they seem warm and affectionate. Once the friendship is established, however, they become oppressively demanding, needing their friends to come right over if they are having an emotional crisis, wondering why no one called them after a traumatic visit to the dentist, and generally taking without giving. They are typically flirtatious and sexually provocative, but their characteristic self-absorption prevents them from establishing any lasting sexual bond.

Bornstein (1999) recently examined the link between histrionic personality disorder and physical attractiveness in male and female college students. Strikingly, Bornstein found that women with histrionic personality disorder were, on average, more physically attractive than other women, both those with other personality disorders and those with no personality disorders. Bornstein further examined how physical attractiveness and adjustment were related among the women with histrionic personality disorder. He found that the women with the disorder who were the most physically attractive had better social support networks but also had far more problems in social adjustment. He concluded that there may be occasions when attractiveness can hinder the development of maturity. The most attractive women with histrionic personality disorder exhibited more negative behaviors in important relationships—such as engaging in threats or extreme emotional displays—and used less mature defense mechanisms.

Histrionic personality disorder seems, at times, like a portrait of women as drawn by a misogynist: vain, shallow, self-dramatizing, immature, overdependent, and selfish. Most reports indicate that at least two thirds of people diagnosed with the disorder are women (Corbitt & Widiger, 1995).

Narcissistic Personality Disorder

The personality syndrome most commonly diagnosed in a number of psychoanalytic centers has been the so-called narcissistic personality (Millon & Davis, 1996). The essential feature of **narcissistic personality disorder** is a grandiose sense of self-importance, often combined with periodic feelings of inferiority (Kernberg, 1975; Kohut, 1966). Narcissistic personalities brag of their talents and achievements, predict great successes for themselves—a Pulitzer prize, a meteoric rise through the company ranks—and expect from others the sort of attention and adulation due to one so gifted. However, this apparent self-love is often accompanied by a very fragile self-esteem, causing the person to "check" constantly on how he or she is regarded by others and to react to criticism with rage or despair (Gramzow & Tangney, 1992). (Alternatively, in keeping with their sense of self-importance. narcissistic personalities may respond to personal defeats with nonchalance.)

Narcissistic personalities are poorly equipped for friendship or love. They characteristically demand a great deal from others—affection, sympathy, favors—yet they give little in return and tend to show a striking lack of empathy. If a friend calls to say that he has had an automobile accident and cannot go to the party that night, the narcissistic personality is likely to be more concerned over the missed party than over the friend's well-being. Narcissistic personalities are also given to exploitation, choosing friends on the basis of what they can get from them. Their feelings about such friends tend to alternate between opposite poles of idealization and contempt, often depending on how flattering the friend has been lately. Not surprisingly, in view of these facts, narcissistic personalities tend to have long histories of erratic interpersonal relationships, and it is usually failures in this area that bring them into therapy.

The term narcissistic personality disorder *comes from the ancient Greek legend of Narcissus, a handsome boy who fell in love with his own reflection in a pool of water. In the painting shown here, François LeMoyne depicts Narcissus admiring himself.*

Given that people with narcissistic personalities are self-centered to the extreme, what kind of romantic relationships do they tend to have? Campbell (1999) compared the romantic partners preferred by narcissists and non-narcissists. As could be expected, narcissists displayed a preference for romantic partners who were highly admiring and positive toward them and showed significantly less attraction to highly caring partners. It appears to be more important to the narcissistic person to have a partner who is openly admiring than one who is openly caring.

Narcissistic personality disorder resembles histrionic personality disorder. Some theorists have even suggested that they are simply the masculine (narcissistic) and feminine (histrionic) versions of a common underlying trait. (As histrionic personality disorder is diagnosed more frequently in women, narcissistic personality disorder is found more frequently in men.) The two types are distinguishable, however, in the nature of their attention seeking. What the narcissistic personality wants is admiration; what the histrionic personality wants above all is concern. Consequently, while histrionic personalities sometimes make dramatic shows of helplessness—tears, desperate phone calls, suicide threats—the narcissistic personality would be too proud to display such vulnerability (Widiger & Sanderson, 1997).

Narcissistic personality also shares conspicuous similarities with antisocial personality disorder, which raises the question of whether the two should be separate categories. The presence of a grandiose self-image and tendencies toward interpersonal exploitation, the principal features of narcissistic personality, are known to be risk factors for juvenile delinquency (Calhoun, Glaser, Stefurak, et al., 2001), which predicts later development of antisocial personality (*DSM-IV-TR*). But even so, there are important areas of difference between narcissistic personality and antisocial personality disorder (Gunderson &

Ronningstam, 2001). The inclination toward grandiosity, to exaggerating one's uniqueness and superior talents, seems to be particularly characteristic of individuals with narcissistic personality disorder.

A number of articles and books have been written about narcissistic personality disorder from two opposite perspectives: the psychoanalytic and social learning points of view. Psychoanalytic theory suggests that such personalities are compensating for inadequate affection and approval from their parents in early childhood (Kernberg, 1975; Kohut, 1972). The social learning perspective (Millon & Davis, 1996) sees this disorder as created by parents who have inflated views of their children's talents and therefore have unrealistic expectations.

Anxious/Fearful Personality Disorders

As the name indicates, the *anxious/fearful personality disorders* all involve nervousness and worry. They differ in the object of the worry and in the behaviors used to cope with it.

Avoidant Personality Disorder

Like schizoid personality disorder, **avoidant personality disorder** is marked by social withdrawal. However, the avoidant personality withdraws not out of inability to experience interpersonal warmth or closeness but out of fear of rejection. This category, derived from a theoretical model of personality developed by Millon (1981), has as its essential feature a hypersensitivity to any possibility of rejection, disapproval, humiliation, or shame. For most of us, making new friends is somewhat difficult; for avoidant personalities, it is supremely difficult, because, though they want to be loved and accepted, they expect not to be. Therefore, they tend to avoid relationships unless they are reassured again and again of the other's uncritical affection. Even then, they remain watchful for any hint of disapproval. Not surprisingly, avoidant personalities generally have low self-esteem. They typically feel depressed and angry at themselves for their social failure. On the other hand, like schizoid personalities, they may be successful professionally if the profession does not require social skills. Indeed, their work may serve as a refuge from loneliness.

Avoidant personality disorder is difficult to differentiate from social phobia, and many patients receive both diagnoses (Widiger, 2001). The strong, possibly genetic link between the two disorders is suggested by research on familial rates of the disorders. When an individual has either one of the disorders, the person's biological relatives are 2 to 3 times more likely than others in the general population to have one of the disorders as well (Tillfors, Furmark, Ekselius, et al., 2001). The distinction between the two is normally made on the grounds of how pervasive and chronic the person's condition is. While people with social phobia may recall having been shy as children, avoidant personalities typically report extreme timidity and withdrawal as far back as they can remember. While social phobics' fears are often restricted to specific situations (e.g., public speaking), so that they have some relief, avoidant personality disorder is more engulfing, affecting almost every day of the person's life (Widiger, Mangine, Corbitt, et al., 1995), as can be seen in the following case of a 43-year-old man:

Fear of rejection leads people with avoidant personality disorder to withdraw from social relationships and situations.

> Timid and easily daunted, [Mr. X] avoids new experiences in order to avoid feeling inadequate, embarrassed, or even slightly uncomfortable. He would like to date. Through his work with the Library Association

he has contact with many single women (perhaps with similar problems) who would probably be most delighted by an invitation; but he lacks the courage to ask someone out. He would be terrified if the woman said yes, and humiliated if she said no. . . .

Mr. X's professional life is also in a rut. He would advance to a more stimulating and responsible position at a university library if he were more productive, but for 10 years he has worked and reworked his master's thesis for eventual publication in book form. Each time he has written a "final draft" the fears about exposing his work prevent his moving the project forward, and he decides to make one more revision. Even if the thesis were published, he realizes that he might be once again passed over for a promotion because his supervisors have openly stated that he lacks the air of authority to supervise others. Mr. X does not deny their assessment. . . .

[According to Mr. X's family, he was] a timid, easily startled baby from birth and, unlike his siblings, was upset by any minor changes in the nursery or dietary routine. He had difficulty adjusting to babysitters, playgroups, and kindergarten. Whereas many of the first graders were more excited than frightened about entering school, Mr. X cried piteously each morning his mother left him with the teacher. . . .

Later in grade school, Mr. X was regarded as an outsider and was teased by the other boys for being a "scaredycat." To relieve the loneliness, Mr. X would usually be able to find a close friend—sometimes a boy, sometimes a girl—who was also outside the "in groups" and who also felt frightened. Along with this capacity to always find at least one close friend, Mr. X's other saving grace has been his ability to perform research by doggedly pursuing every small reference until a given subject has been thoroughly mastered. Because of this ability, he was an exceptionally fine graduate student and was encouraged to go on for a doctorate degree. He declined on the grounds that doctoral candidates were too competitive (i.e., intimidating) and that he would be comfortable living at a level that was more relaxed. He now realizes that in seeking comfort he has found boredom and loneliness (Perry, Frances, & Clarkin, 1990, pp. 324–326).

Dependent Personality Disorder

The defining characteristic of **dependent personality disorder,** as the name indicates, is dependence on others (Bornstein, 1993). Fearful or incapable of making their own decisions, dependent personalities turn over to one or two others—for example, a spouse or parent—the responsibility for deciding what work they will do, where they will go on vacation, how they will handle the children, what people they will associate with, even what they will wear. Underlying this self-effacement is a fear of abandonment. For most of us, waiting for a friend who is late is an inconvenience or annoyance. For the dependent personality, it is an emotional catastrophe: the long-dreaded sign that the friend no longer cares. Because of the fear of abandonment, the dependent personality, often a woman, tolerates her husband's infidelities, drunkenness, even physical abusiveness for fear that, should she protest, he will leave her. This passivity breeds a vicious cycle. The more the dependent personality lets others control and abuse her, the more helpless she feels, and these feelings in turn further discourage her from taking any self-respecting action.

While dependent personalities share with borderlines an intense fear of abandonment, the two disorders are otherwise distinct, and borderline personality disorder is far more disabling. Dependent personalities do not generally engage in the reckless or self-mutilating behavior characteristic of borderline personalities. Furthermore, dependent personalities may find peace in a stable relationship if the other person can tolerate their submissiveness. (Some spouses apparently find it attractive.) By contrast, the borderline personality's distress is not relieved by a relationship. Indeed, it may become worse when the person is involved with someone and discovers that the feelings of emptiness remain (Gunderson, 1984, 1996).

The following history illustrates the basic features of dependent personality:

Matthew is a 34-year-old single man who lives with his mother and works as an accountant. He seeks treatment because he is very unhappy after having just broken up with his girlfriend. His mother had disapproved of his marriage plans, ostensibly because the woman was of a different religion. Matthew felt trapped and forced to choose between his mother and his girlfriend, and since "blood is thicker than water," he had decided not to go against his mother's wishes. Nonetheless, he is angry at himself and at her and believes that she will never let him marry. . . .

Matthew works at a job several grades below what his education and talent would permit. On several occasions he has turned down promotions. . . . He has two very close friends, whom he has had since early childhood. He has lunch with one of them every single workday and feels lost if his friend is sick and misses a day.

Matthew is the youngest of four children and the only boy. He was "babied and spoiled" by his mother and elder sisters. He had considerable separation anxiety as a child—difficulty falling asleep unless his

Personality disorders are pervasive, penetrating all areas of the sufferers' lives. But other disorders involve patterns of impulsive behavior in just one aspect of life and do not seem to be part of other major syndromes. *DSM-IV* calls these patterns the **impulse-control disorders,** their essential feature being the failure to resist impulses to act in a way harmful to oneself or others. The disorders included in this category, together with the behavior involved, are *intermittent explosive disorder* (destructiveness), *kleptomania* (theft of objects not needed for personal use or monetary value), *pyromania* (setting fires for pleasure or tension relief), *trichotillomania* (compulsively pulling out one's own hair), and *pathological gambling* (also called compulsive gambling). For the first three, prevalence, where it is known, is low. (Kleptomania, for example, seems to occur in only about 5 percent of identified shoplifters.) Pathological gambling and trichotillomania are more common and deserve discussion.

Estimates of the number of compulsive gamblers in the United States range from 2 to 3 percent of the population (DeCaria, Hollander, Grossman, et al., 1996), or 6 to 8.5 million people. Pathological gamblers are likely to be male, unmarried, and European American, and they seem to share certain personality characteristics: below-average education and a tendency to become restless and bored when not gambling (Zuckerman, 1999). Compulsive gamblers often have additional psychological problems, including mood and alcohol or other substance use disorders (Flory, Lyman, Milich, et al., 2000). Among men, gambling usually begins in adolescence, and some become hooked from virtually their first bet (Lesieur & Rosenthal, 1991). Environmental influences play a role. Lester (1994) found significant correlations between the ease of access to or number of legal gaming opportunities (e.g., casinos, slot machines, sports betting) in different states with the number of chapters of Gamblers Anonymous in those states. However, the ease of access to other kinds of gambling, such as bingo or most forms of lotteries, was unrelated to the number of chapters of Gamblers Anonymous in the states, suggesting that these forms of gambling are not as closely related to compulsive gambling.

Like other addictive disorders, pathological gambling seems to develop in stages with predictable crises. In some cases, a "big win" sets off a gambling compulsion. The winning phase gives way to the second phase, losing. The gamblers begin betting compulsively and "chasing," or betting more and more to get back the money they lost. Betting poorly and heavily, they fall deeply into debt. Having run through their income and savings, they begin borrowing, buoyed by the irrational belief that they will soon win and repay the debt.

Most compulsive gamblers report that the initial experience of borrowing is not depressing, but as debts mount, so do personal consequences. Like alcohol-dependent people who hide bottles around the house, pathological gamblers often try to conceal their losses from their families. At the same time, they may manipulate family and friends to pay off pressing debts. Divorce, imprisonment, and job loss become increasing threats. Although they may find getting "bailed out" by family members exhilarating at first, this eventually gives way to desperation and mood disorder (Flory, Lyman, Milich, et al., 2000). Many compulsive gamblers recover in self-help groups such as Gamblers Anonymous, but mental health professionals have taken little interest in the problem—so people who suffer from this ruinous disorder often do not get the help they need. More research is needed on compulsive gambling, because some researchers do not believe that compulsive gambling is a disorder in the same way that trichotillomania is.

Unlike pathological gambling, trichotillomania shares many characteristics with obsessive-compulsive disorder (discussed in Chapter 7) and can even be treated with similar drugs. Most trichotillomanics pull out the hairs on their heads—in severe cases, this can produce large bald spots—but they may also pull at their eyebrows, eyelashes, pubic hair, and facial hair. Like people with compulsions, trichotillomanics recognize their behavior is senseless, try to resist it, eventually succumb, and—once they succumb—obtain tension relief until the urge strikes again. There is also some evidence for a biological connection between the two syndromes. For example, first-degree relatives of trichotillomanics are at increased risk for obsessive-compulsive disorder. Furthermore, trichotillomania, like obsessive-compulsive disorder, responds to certain antidepressant drugs—those that block serotonin reuptake—and not to other antidepressants.

On the other hand, there are significant differences between the two disorders. Trichotillomania is more common in women than in men, a pattern not seen in obsessive-compulsive disorder. A greater proportion of male hair-pullers seem to have comorbid tics, or involuntary facial movements, compared to female hair-pullers (du Toit, van Kradenburg, Niehaus, et al., 2001). In one study, nearly 3.5 percent of college women reported symptoms of trichotillomania, more than double the rate for college men (Christenson, Pyle, & Mitchell, 1991). Also, trichotillomanics, unlike people with obsessive-compulsive disorder, do not seem to experience clear obsessions before engaging in their compulsive behavior (Jaspers, 1996; Mansueto, Stemberger, Thomas, et al., 1997). Instead of dispelling frightening thoughts, they gain pleasure, gratification, or relief when they give in to their impulses. However, the relief is temporary. Like compulsive gamblers, trichotillomanics must live with the results of their behavior long after the impulse has passed and the harm has been done.

mother stayed in the room, mild school refusal, and unbearable homesickness when he occasionally tried "sleepovers." . . . He has lived at home his whole life except for one year of college, from which he returned because of homesickness (Spitzer, Gibbon, Skodol, et al., 1994, pp. 179–180).

Although the maladaptive side of dependent personality traits has long received attention by clinicians and researchers, Bornstein (1998) has suggested that dependency is often a normal and expected part of human experience and adjustment. He points out that dependent traits do not always represent a flaw, and that a "mature" form of dependency helps individuals form positive ties to others who can provide them with genuine help or assistance and helps increase their own willingness to give help and support to others in return.

Recent research indicates that there is a relationship between dependent personality disorder and the 5-Factor model of personality. Bornstein and Cecero (2000) reanalyzed a number of studies and found strong evidence that dependent personality is related to elevated levels of neuroticism (negative emotions) and agreeableness (lack of antagonistic behavior). Conversely, dependent personality is related to lower levels of extraversion (sociability), openness to experience, and conscientiousness.

Obsessive-Compulsive Personality Disorder

The defining characteristic of **obsessive-compulsive personality disorder** is excessive preoccupation with orderliness, perfectionism, and control. Obsessive-compulsive personalities are so taken up with the mechanics of efficiency—organizing, following rules, making lists and schedules—that they cease to be efficient, for they never get anything important done. In addition, they are generally stiff and formal in their dealings with others and find it hard to take genuine pleasure in anything. For example, they may spend weeks or months planning a family vacation, deciding what the family will see and where they will eat and sleep each day and night, and then derive no enjoyment from the vacation itself. Typically, they spoil it for the others as well by refusing to deviate from the itinerary, worrying that the restaurant will give away their table, and so forth.

This personality disorder should not be confused with obsessive-compulsive disorder, which, as we say in Chapter 7, is one of the anxiety syndromes. Though a superficial similarity—the shared emphasis on rituals and propriety—has led to their having similar names, the two conditions are quite different. In the personality disorder, compulsiveness is not confined to a single sequence of bizarre behaviors, such as constant hand washing, but is milder and more pervasive, affecting many aspects of life. Furthermore, while obsessive-compulsive disorder is not common, obsessive-compulsive personality disorder is fairly common (more so in men than in women). People suffering from obsessive-compulsive disorder generally do not also show obsessive-compulsive personality disorder.

People with obsessive-compulsive personality disorder tend to be "workaholics," but they may have trouble at work when their perfectionism prevents them from making decisions and meeting deadlines. On the other hand, there are some jobs in which perfectionism is an asset. Many obsessive-compulsive personalities are quite successful in their careers and have sacrificed their personal lives to that end. Typically, they seek treatment only after their condition has left them with a series of divorces, a depression due to loneliness, or a physical disorder resulting from years of stress.

People with obsessive-compulsive personality disorder spend their days vigorously resisting any sudden change in plans. By contrast, sufferers of *impulse-control disorders* regularly disrupt their own lives when they experience urges to perform destructive behaviors and act on them. These disorders do not belong to the personality disorders or any other group of major syndromes (see the box on page 300).

❖ Groups at Risk

Comorbidity Table 11.1 gives the estimated prevalence rates for the personality disorders within the community at large and within clinical settings—that is, among people being treated for psychological disorders. As the table shows, personality disorders are rare in the general population but at times very common—in the case of histrionic personality disorder, 10 times more common—in clinical populations.

Thus, one group at risk for personality disorders is people in psychological treatment, not necessarily for a personality disorder. Most people with personality disorders do not seek help for that condition. It has been with them since childhood; it feels normal, if not comfortable. In any case, it seems unsolvable. What brings them into treatment is usually a more specific problem, perhaps a sexual disorder or marital conflict, and it is only in treatment that the personality disorder is identified. Borderline

TABLE 11.1 Estimated Prevalence Rates and Gender Differences for Personality Disorders

PERSONALITY DISORDER	PREVALENCE		GENDER COMPARISON
	Community	Clinical	
Paranoid	0.0–4.5%	2–20%	M, F
Schizotypal	0.0–5.6%	2–5%	M, F
Schizoid	0.0–4.1%	2–5%	M, F
Borderline	0.0–4.6%	8–15%	F, M
Histrionic	0.3–4.5%	10–15%	F, M
Narcissistic	0.0–5.3%	2–16%	M, F
Antisocial			
Avoidant	0.0–5.2%	5–25%	M, F
Dependent	0.0–10.3%	5–30%	F, M
Obsessive-compulsive	0.0–9.3%	3–10%	M, F

Adapted from American Psychiatric Association (2000); Widiger & Sanderson (1997); Torgersen, Kringlen, & Cramer (2001).

personalities tend to turn up in substance abuse, eating disorder, and mood disorder clinics; avoidant personalities in anxiety disorder clinics; dependent personalities in mood disorder clinics and marriage counseling. While the condition for which the treatment was sought—the anxiety disorder or mood disorder—is listed as the Axis I diagnosis (see Chapter 2) and the personality disorder as the Axis II diagnosis, in fact, it is the personality disorder that has predisposed the person to the Axis I condition. In the usual case, it also makes that condition much more severe.

A large community study by Torgersen, Kringlen, and Cramer (2001) found that the most common personality disorders are avoidant, schizoid, and paranoid personality disorders. Personality disorders are not equally prevalent in all parts of the population, but seem to be more frequent among the lower socioeconomic classes in cities, particularly in the central areas of cities. They also tend to be more frequent among single or divorced individuals. It remains unclear whether the personality disorders are an antecedent cause or an end result of the low socioeconomic and single status of such individuals.

Recent studies vividly show that mistreatment of children increases their risk of developing personality disorders (Johnson, Cohen, Brown, et al., 1999). Physical and sexual abuse during childhood increases the frequency with which children develop personality disorders—particularly borderline personality—during adolescence or early adulthood (Heffernan & Cloitre, 2000). Childhood verbal abuse can also be quite hurtful. One study found that individuals who had experienced maternal verbal abuse during childhood were more than three times as likely to have borderline, narcissistic, obsessive-compulsive, and paranoid personalities during adolescence and early adulthood (Johnson, Cohen, Smailes, et al., 2001).

The Dispute Over Gender Bias Another risk factor in the diagnosis of personality disorders is gender. Look again at Table 11.1. For 5 of the personality disorders listed, men are at higher risk; for 3, women are at higher risk. Some of the differentials are extreme. Women account for three quarters of diagnosed borderlines (Widiger & Trull, 1993) and for two thirds of diagnosed histrionic personalities (Corbitt & Widiger, 1995). They are also at greater risk for dependent personality disorder. None of these female risk factors is greater than the male risk factor for antisocial personality disorder, in which men outnumber women 3 to 1; however, because of the nature of the power imbalance in our society, the female-heavy categories are the ones that have drawn the most attention. In no other area of abnormal psychology has the question of diagnostic bias against women been debated as bitterly as in the personality disorders.

Some researchers have suggested that the different diagnostic rates for men and women are produced in part by a gender bias in the assessment procedures. Lindsay, Sankis, and Widiger (2000) found that items from three commonly used personality disorder self-report measures contained gender biases. Even though each gender scores differently on these items, which would bias the overall scores, the items did not turn out to measure personality dysfunction. In effect, some of the items were related to gender but not to personality dysfunction. It is also possible that diagnosticians do view men and women differently. If so, this may be an extension of the fact that men and women behave differently. Personality disorders are maladaptive exaggerations of personality traits that, when not exaggerated, are normal and useful: modesty in dependent personality, self-assertion in narcissistic personality, and so on. We know that, whether because of nature or nurture, men and women, as groups, differ in such traits (Feingold, 1994). Despite manifold exceptions, women in general are more tender, more emotional, and more empathic than men. Men, in general, are more assertive, more confident, and more tough-minded than women. Therefore, it is no surprise that personality disorders involving emotionalism (histrionic, borderline) are more frequently diagnosed in women and that those involving self-importance (narcissistic) or callousness (antisocial) are more common in men. As anthropologists have pointed out, every culture has its own "idiom of distress"—a range of symptoms from which members of that culture choose when they are in psychological trouble. Viewed metaphorically as two cultures, the two genders are employing their unique idioms of distress.

However, the fact remains that those idioms are related to social injustices. It is partly because women are more emotional that they have historically been given less power and freedom than men. Thus, one can argue that, by focusing on gender-specific traits in defining personality disorders, the psychiatric establishment is perpetuating injustice and opposing the liberation of both genders from confining roles.

The authors of the diagnostic manual have not been indifferent to this argument. In *DSM-IV*, the criterion for histrionic personality disorder was changed from "overly concerned with physical attractiveness" to "consistently uses physical appearance to draw attention to self" (American Psychiatric Association, 1994, p. 658), in response to complaints that the earlier criterion involved a female-related characteristic and therefore raised the possibility that women might be overdiagnosed with histrionic personality disorder. And to encourage nonbiased application of the criterion, the manual gave not just a female example but also a male one: "A man with this disorder may dress and behave in a manner often identified as 'macho' and may seek to be the center of attention by bragging about athletic skills" (American Psychiatric Association, 1994, p. 656).

It is unlikely, however, that such a revision will equalize the distribution of the histrionic personality disorder diagnosis. And there remains the problem of whether it is possible to create "gender-blind" criteria for disorders related to gender stereotypes. As noted, those stereotypes have had their effect. In general, men and women do specialize in those traits. It is questionable whether the diagnostic manual should be based on a hypothetical future in which that is not the case, rather than reflecting present-day reality. In the meantime, however, *DSM-IV-TR* strongly cautions against the overapplication of the personality disorder diagnoses to one gender.

Cultural Bias Some of the same questions apply to the diagnosis of personality disorder in various ethnic subgroups. What seems normal behavior to a young Latino male may seem macho to a non-Latino diagnostician. What a Japanese American woman sees as normal wifely submissiveness may look like dependent personality disorder to someone of a different ethnicity. Cultural variations can also make a difference in the expression of personality disorder traits (Cooke & Michie, 1999). For example, antisocial traits may be more common in cultures where individual male competitiveness is emphasized, while dependent traits might be more common in cultures where collective social cooperation is favored. However, recent evidence suggests that conceptions and measures of personality disorder in the *DSM-IV-TR* do have validity in other cultures. Yang and colleagues demonstrated that *DSM-IV* personality disorders are cross-culturally generalizable to Chinese psychiatric populations (Yang, McCrae, Costa, et al., 2000).

Part of the definition of personality disorder in *DSM-IV-TR* is that the behavior in question "deviates markedly from the expectations of the individual's culture" (American Psychiatric Association, 2000, p. 685), but how well do diagnosticians know the patient's culture, and how thoroughly can they suppress the values of their own culture? On the other hand, as was pointed out in Chapter 2, there is also the danger that diagnosticians bending over backwards to respect the patient's supposed cultural values will fail to treat a serious disorder. Such problems are far from solved, but the fact that *DSM-IV-TR* now warns diagnosticians about them is already a mark of progress.

Personality Disorders: Theory and Therapy

The Psychodynamic Perspective

Character Disorders Psychodynamic theorists interpret personality disorders, which they call character disorders, as stemming from disturbances in the parent-child relationship. The more severe syndromes, such as borderline personality, are thought to originate in the early, pre-Oedipal relationship between infant and mother (or other caretaker), and particularly in what Mahler called the *separation-individuation* process (Chapter 5), in which children learn to separate from their mothers and regard themselves, and others, as individuals persons. A troubled separation-individuation could lead to a poorly defined sense of self, a central problem in borderline personality or narcissistic personality.

Whatever the root of the problem, the final result, as in all psychological disorders according to the psychodynamic view, is a weakened ego and therefore poor adaptive functioning. Psychodynamic theorists see people with character disorders as falling somewhere between neurotics and psychotics in terms of ego strength. (In other words, they function better than psychotics and worse than neurotics.) In all the character disorders, normal "coping" behavior, the province of the ego, has broken down, to some extent, and has been replaced by erratic, distorted, or deviant behavior. The borderline personality falls apart in times of stress; the dependent personality is constantly ceding decisions to others. These breakdowns in coping behavior affect the broad range of ego functions—perception, memory, language, learning. Obsessive-compulsive personalities shift all mental energy into planning; paranoid personalities shift all energy into perception, scanning the environment for signs of who is against them.

Narcissistic personality disorder has been the subject of intense study and controversy in psychodynamic circles. Otto Kernberg (1975), along with *DSM-IV-TR,* sees the basic pattern as a combination of grandiosity and feelings of inferiority, with the inferiority being primary; the grandiosity is merely a defense against childhood feelings of rage and inferiority. Heinz Kohut (1966, 1972, 1977), on the other hand, sees the grandiosity as primary—the expression of a "narcissistic libido" that, for various reasons, has evaded the neutralizing efforts of the ego. When the narcissistic personality shows rage and wounded self-esteem, these are reactions to blows to the grandiose self-image.

A prominent theme of current object-relations theory is that the self-image is the product of the child's introjection, or incorporation, of the parents' attitudes, particularly their attitudes toward the child. Parents who give their children unconditional love instill in them strong self-esteem. Parents who have ambivalent feelings toward their children and treat them inconsistently create in them ambivalent, conflicted self-images. This mechanism has been invoked as an explanation for narcissistic personality disorder (Gabbard, 1994; Kohut, 1977). Children who are generally ignored by their parents but who are flooded with praise and attention when they do something the parents are proud of are likely to grow up hungry for attention and convinced that they can win it only through success. But the need is never satisfied, for it never heals the original wound of the parents' indifference—hence the relentless attention seeking of the narcissistic personality.

Psychotherapy for Personality Disorders Because people with personality disorders are often not distressed by their behavior, they tend not to seek treatment. When they do end up in a therapist's office, it is often not on their own initiative but rather because they have been induced into marriage counseling or family therapy on the basis of a spouse's complaints or a child's emotional problems. In such situations, they are generally resistant to treatment. And, even when they do experience sufficient unhappiness to enter treatment on their own, they tend to see the problem as external to them rather than internal—an attitude that bodes ill for insight-oriented therapy.

Psychodynamic therapists often take a more directive, more parental approach with personality-disorder patients than with other patients. Waldinger and Gunderson (1987) list a number of basic tenets common to the psychodynamic treatment of borderline personality: The therapist is more active, more likely to block acting-out behavior, more focused on the present than on the past, and more concerned with connecting feelings and actions than is the case in the usual insight therapy.

However, psychodynamic therapists still look to insight as the mechanism of change. As the patient with personality disorder begins deploying his or her characteristic patterns of behavior in the therapy hour, the therapist gently and empathically points out the distortions in the pattern and asks the patient what, in his or her childhood experience, might have created such a need for admiration (narcissistic personality disorder), fear of rejection (avoidant), devotion to perfectionism (obsessive-compulsive), or need for nurturance (dependent). As with much psychodynamic therapy, this may be a slow process.

Recent research indicates that psychoanalytically oriented partial hospitalization is superior to standard psychiatric treatment for borderline personality disorder (Bateman & Fonagy, 2001). Treatment included both individual and group psychoanalytic psychotherapy for a maximum of 18 months. Patients who completed this psychoanalytically oriented program not only made substantial gains, but they also maintained

Prevention Childhood Intervention To Prevent Personality Disorders

Because personality disorders are so costly both to the individual and to society, researchers have begun to study the preventative effects of early childhood interventions. Reynolds and colleagues evaluated the long-term effectiveness of an early childhood intervention, the Chicago Child-Parent Center (CPC), a large-scale, federally funded program of education, family, and health services for urban low-income children ages 3 through 9 (Reynolds, Temple, Robertson, et al., 2001).

Compared to a control group in a preschool program, the 3- and 4-year-olds who participated in the CPC program for 1 or 2 years had a higher rate of high school graduation (49.7 percent vs. 38.5 percent), more years of completed education (10.6 vs. 10.2), and lower rates of juvenile arrest (16.9 percent vs. 25.1 percent), violent arrest (9 percent vs. 15.3 percent), and school dropout (46.7 vs. 55.0 percent). The program's encouraging results indicate that such interventions can help antisocial personality disorder and perhaps other disorders as well.

A study by Webster-Stratton and Hammond (1997) compared the effects of child and parent training interventions. Approximately 100 families of children ages 4 through 8 with early-onset conduct problems were randomly assigned to either a parent training group (PT), a child training group (CT), a combined child and parent training group (CT + PT), or a waiting-list control group (CON). Parents in the PT group attended weekly 2-hour meetings with 10 to 12 other parents and a therapist. Over 24 months, the PT group watched 17 videotaped programs on parenting and interpersonal skills. The children in the CT group watched a videotape of more than 100 vignettes showing children in a variety of settings, including at home, in the classroom, and on the playground. The children also played with life-sized puppets, including several dinosaurs who had interpersonal problems. The vignettes and puppet play targeted the common difficulties of children with conduct problems, such as a lack of social skills and of techniques for resolving conflict, loneliness, an inability to understand another person's point of view, and school problems.

Post-treatment results were very positive: Although the combined child and parent training group showed the greatest improvement over a year's time, all three intervention programs resulted in significant benefits for the children. Children who received CT training, either alone or with PT training, showed significant, immediate improvements in problem solving and conflict management skills, as assessed by interactions with best friends. These treatment gains were maintained, in all cases, over a year's time, and other issues, such as conduct problems at home, were significantly reduced.

the gains and showed continued improvement in their social and interpersonal functioning over an additional 18-month follow-up period.

The Behavioral Perspective

Many behaviorists, as we saw, object to the very concept of personality disorder, because it implies fixed personality traits. However, as pointed out in a review of behavioral work in this area (Turkat & Levin, 1984), the personality disorders can be usefully addressed by behaviorists if the diagnostic terms are understood as "descriptors of classes of behavior that have been learned and can be changed"(p. 497). This position is actually not so different from the behaviorists' approach to other, less trait-bound disorders. As for how these "classes of behavior" are learned, the behaviorists point, as usual, to eliciting stimuli and reinforcing consequences.

Skills Acquisition, Modeling, and Reinforcement In a study of borderline personality, Marsha Linehan (1987) claims that many borderline patients come from families that show "invalidating syndrome," "the tendency to invalidate affective experiences and to oversimplify the ease of solving life's problems" (p. 264). These are families that expect children to be cheerful and to understand that, if they fail, it is their fault. Such parents do not coddle. As a result, the child is never able to obtain sympathy for minor upsets. The only thing that gets such parents' attention is a major emotional display, so that is what the child learns to produce. Furthermore, because these parents do not address minor sorrows, their children never learn the emotional skills that other children do when they take their problems to their parents: how to calm themselves down, how to comfort themselves. Such children, Linehan argues, may logically grow to show the kind of constant and uncontrollable emotional turbulence we call borderline personality.

In addition to skills acquisition—or failure of skills acquisition—reinforcement and modeling may also play a role in the development of personality disorders. For example, dependent personality disorder might result from a childhood in which assertiveness was repeatedly punished, histrionic personality disorder from parental indulgence of temper tantrums, and obsessive-compulsive personality disorder from consistent rewards for neatness, rule following, and other "goody-goody" behaviors (Millon & Davis, 1996). In other cases, parental modeling of the behaviors in question might be as important as rewards and punishments.

New Learning In handling personality disorders, behaviorists have operated on the assumption that, because most of these disorders can be seen as inappropriate social behavior, what the patients need is social-skills training. Avoidant and dependent personalities can apparently benefit greatly from social-skills and assertiveness training (Stone, 1993). Histrionic patients, too, have been given social-skills training, with special attention to interacting with the other sex, because most of them complain of troubled romances (Kass, Silver, & Abrams, 1972). Behavioral techniques have also been used to teach empathic behavior to histrionic patients (Woolson & Swanson, 1972).

With borderline patients, Linehan (1993) has used a more comprehensive treatment, which she calls **dialectical behavior therapy.** Dialectical behavior therapy combines social-skills training with coaching in how to regulate emotions and tolerate distress. For example, patients are taught the Zen technique of *mindfulness* as a form of relaxation. In mindfulness, one begins by trying to listen only to one's breathing. If negative thoughts intrude (as usually happens with borderline personalities), patients are told not to criticize themselves for this but simply to accept the negative thoughts and return to their breathing. This technique is useful not only in teaching patients how to relax when in the grip of negative feelings—a major achievement for borderline patients—but also in instilling in them an acceptance of life's disappointments. Hence the "dialectical" nature of this therapy: One takes a step back, into acceptance of pain, in order to take a step forward, out of pain. A number of studies support the efficacy of dialectical behavior therapy for borderline personality (Bohus, Haaf, Stiglmayr, et al., 2001; Linehan, Schmidt, Demeff, et al., 2000). Bohus and colleagues evaluated a 3-month impatient treatment program for chronically suicidal borderline patients and found significant improvements in depression, anxiety, dissociation, global distress, and suicidality.

The behavioral perspective on personality disorders emphasizes positive parent-child interaction, such as reinforcement as shown here. If a parent does not address minor joys and sorrows, the child may establish inappropriate patterns of behavior.

The Cognitive Perspective

Faulty Schemas and Information Processing Cognitive theory holds that our thoughts, emotions, and behavior are organized by underlying schemas, structures of information that we have in our minds about various domains of life (Chapter 4). In keeping with this assumption, cognitive theorists interpret the personality disorders as the product of distortions or exaggerations in the schemas. Because faulty schemas are "structuralized," or woven into a person's normal cognitive processes (Beck, Freeman, Pretzer, et al., 1990), the person does not recognize them as faulty. On the contrary, the distortions generate perceptions, and even situations, that confirm the schemas. They may also help someone to survive in a job or marriage, which in turn would increase his or her investment in the schemas.

Consider, for example, obsessive-compulsive personality. For people who fit this label, a central belief of the self-schema may be "I am basically overwhelmed, so I need strict systems and rules in order to function." This belief, in turn, generates the view that others, who do not show the same system-bound behavior, are incompetent or irresponsible, and their incompetence makes the obsessive-compulsive personality even more insistent on rules.

Other common beliefs of the obsessive-compulsive personality are "I have to drive myself and others relentlessly" and "Everything must be done perfectly."

"See—It's not impossible for an obsessive-compulsive person to get a responsible job."

When, life being what it is, things are not done perfectly, the obsessive-compulsive personality's response is guilt over his or her own failures and anger over others' derelictions. This produces a constant state of tension, stifling pleasure, affection, and spontaneity. Thus, the final result is emotional distress and ineffective behavior, both traceable to the faulty beliefs.

According to cognitive theorists, such beliefs are acquired through learning—often through modeling—and may be a response to developmental conditions. (Perfectionistic parents, for example, could breed a child's obsessive-compulsive personality.) What distinguishes the beliefs peculiar to personality disorder, however, is not just their dysfunctional character—for many of us hold unhelpful beliefs—but their rigid character. In the cognitive view, schemas normally exist on a continuum from compelling to noncompelling. Many of us, for example, have schemas about nutrition that are on the relaxed end of the scale, whereas our schemas about child rearing are likely to be much more compelling—that is, based on firmly held beliefs. In personality-disorder patients, most schemas are pushed to the compelling end of the range. The beliefs are rigid and admit no exceptions.

Cognitive theories have also contributed to our understanding of personality disorders by focusing on social information processing and attribution styles (Dodge & Schwartz, 1997). Dodge and Schwartz describe an antisocial child who has just had paint spilled on him by a classmate. The boy looks at the child who spilled the paint to see whether it was done on purpose, relying on nonverbal cues. The antisocial boy might falsely conclude that the other child spilled the paint intentionally, a conclusion called the "hostile attributional bias." The boy's goal might then become to get even, and he might decide to spill paint on the schoolmate. Such deficiencies in social information processing and the hostile attributional bias have been associated with antisocial behavior, and we can guess they may also be related to paranoid personality.

Altering Schemas Because the schema is seen as the root of the problem, the goal of cognitive therapy is to induce the patient to alter the schema. In the case of personality disorders, in which habits are old and deeply ingrained, cognitive therapists generally do not try to tear down the schema altogether. Rather, they opt for the more realistic goal of getting the patient to modify, reinterpret, or camouflage the schema (Beck, Freeman, Pretzer, et al., 1900; Freeman, 1989; Freeman & Leaf, 1989).

With obsessive-compulsive personality, for example, modifying the schema might mean inducing the patient to confine his or her perfectionism to the job and not let it spill over into the home, where the patient might be destroying family harmony over such matters as the proper way to make a bed or load a dishwasher. Reinterpreting a schema means putting it to more functional use. Thus, the therapist might guide an obsessive-compulsive personality into a line of work in which perfectionism would be appropriate and less of a nuisance to others. Finally, "schematic camouflage" involves teaching patients socially acceptable behaviors that they can use simply to ease their way in situations in which their habitual rigidity is likely to cause them difficulties. For instance, if they must always have their steak done exactly medium rare when they go to a restaurant, the therapist can teach them, through social-skills training, how to be very specific in ordering and how to complain effectively if the order comes back wrong.

Although there are relatively few treatment studies of cognitive therapy for personality disorders, a variety of case studies and other evidence suggest that cognitive therapy shows promise for treating personality disorders (Arntz, 1999; Davidson & Tyrer, 1996).

The Sociocultural Perspective

While other theorists look to the individual psyche for the explanation of the personality disorders, sociocultural theorists feel that these conditions are the products of large-scale social processes—processes that ensure the advantage of certain social groups and the disadvantage of others. Accordingly, they argue that psychologists should devote their efforts to changing the society rather than trying to change its victims (Holland, 1978).

An illustration is the feminist critique of dependent personality disorder (Brown, 1992). According to this view, to diagnose a psychological disorder in women who are clinging and submissive is to blame the victim. It is the society that has created this condition in women, by denying them the power a person needs in order not to be submissive. Giving therapy to women for this condition is like treating a contaminated food system by giving antibiotics to the people who get sick from it. Until the contamination in the system is addressed, it will go on poisoning people.

The Neuroscience Perspective

As we have seen, the swing of the pendulum in the early twentieth century toward seeing human behavior as the product of environmental influence in some measure was reversed in the twentieth century. With the rise of neuroscience research, we are returning, with empirical finding, to the pre-twentieth-century belief that much of human behavior is biologically based. In the last decade, for example, neurobiological explanations have become available for many of the traits of psychopathy. Impulsivity, recklessness/irresponsibility, hostility, and aggressiveness may be determined by abnormal levels of neurochemicals (Martens, 2002), and other features of psychopathy, such as sensation seeking and the incapacity to learn from experience, might be linked to cortical underarousal (Martens, 2002, 1997; Raine, 1997). The problem of underarousal often goes back to childhood: When Raine, Venables, and Mednick (1997) examined 3-year-old children to see whether their heart rates would predict subsequent antisocial behavior, they found that aggressive 11-year-olds had had lower resting heart rates at age 3 than the nonaggressive 11-year-olds. Many psychopaths can thus be seen, to an extent, as the victims of neurobiological abnormalities. Research has shown that between 31 and 58 percent of people with antisocial personality disorder show some EEG abnormality, including an increased activation in the left hemisphere of the frontal lobe. Antisocial personality may be partly the product of cortical immaturity, a delayed development of the cerebral cortex, the topmost layer of the brain and seat of most of its "higher" learning. This immaturity may affect the psychopath's capacity for fear.

Genes and Personality Research from twin studies indicates that personality characteristics (Tellegen, Lykken, Bouchard, et al., 1988), including individual differences in the traits known as the 5 factors (McCrae, Jang, Livesly, et al., 2001), have a sizeable genetic component. Tellegen and associates concluded that only 50 percent of measured personality difference among their subjects was due to environmental difference. The rest they attributed to genetic influence.

If genetic factors are so powerful in forming the normal personality, presumably they are also involved in personality disorder (Livesley, 2001; Niggs & Goldsmith, 1994). Researchers studying personality disorders in childhood have found that the genetic component of schizotypal and dependent personality disorders is particularly high (with a heritability coefficient of .81), while it is somewhat lower for paranoid personality disorder (a coefficient of .50) (Coolidge, Thede, & Jang, 2001). An important line of research on this question has to do with the relationship of personality disorders to Axis I disorders that have a genetic component. Some researchers (Siever & Davis, 1991) have proposed that the personality disorders are just characterological versions of Axis I disorders—that avoidant personality, for example, is a form of social phobia, schizotypal personality is a variant of schizophrenia, borderline personality is a version of mood disorder, and so on. This argument is supported by the family studies cited earlier. As we saw, schizotypal personality disorder and schizophrenia tend to run together in families, as do borderline personality disorder and depression.

Studies have shown that personality disorders, as well as personality traits, are largely genetically determined.

Drug Treatment Another finding suggestive of a connection between the personality disorders and Axis I conditions is that personality disorders can sometimes be alleviated by the drugs used for their Axis I counterparts. Schizotypal patients have been helped by low doses of phenothiazines, the class of drugs most often used for schizophrenia (Siever, 1992). Borderline and avoidant personalities often respond to antidepressants (Coccaro, 1993). Some personality disorders have no drug treatment as yet, but that may change.

Drugs and Diagnosis These treatment links, together with the family studies, have raised questions about the diagnostic system. Should personality disorder patients be reclassified as having the corresponding Axis I disorder? As we pointed out, the distinction between personality disorders and Axis I conditions such as the anxiety and mood disorders is usually made on the grounds that a personality disorder is more chronic and pervasive. The person has had the disorder for most of his or her life, and it affects nearly every aspect of the individual's functioning. But, if a chronic and pervasive avoidant personality disorder clears up in response to the drugs used in treating social phobia, why shouldn't we regard it as a chronic and pervasive social phobia? In the words of the man who chaired the *DSM-IV* work group on anxiety disorders,"One may have to rethink what the personality disorder concept means in an instance where six weeks of phenelzine [Nardil] therapy begins to reverse long-standing interpersonal hypersensitivity"(Liebowitz, 1992, p. 251).

But the fact that two disorders respond to the same drug does not indicate that they are the same disorder. Aspirin relieves both colds and menstrual cramps, but that doesn't mean that a cold is a form of menstrual cramps. It means that aspirin treats a symptom common to both, pain. As for avoidant personality disorder's responsiveness to Nardil, Nardil is an antidepressant. If we were going to revise the classification system according to the results of drug treatment, we would have to reclassify avoidant personality disorder—and social phobia—as a form of depression.

Key Terms

antisocial behavior, 291
antisocial personality disorder (APD), 290
avoidant personality disorder, 298
borderline personality disorder, 293
dependent personality disorder, 299
dialectical behavior therapy, 306
histrionic personality disorder, 296
impulse-control disorder, 300
narcissistic personality disorder, 297
obsessive-compulsive personality disorder, 301
paranoid personality disorder, 287
passive avoidance learning, 292
personality disorder, 287
schizoid personality disorder, 289
schizotypal personality disorder, 288

Summary

- A personality disorder is a long-standing, pervasive, rigid pattern of thought, feeling, and behavior that impedes functioning and causes unhappiness for the person and, usually, the people around him or her.
- *DSM-IV-TR* lists 10 personality disorders, which it informally groups into "clusters": odd/eccentric (paranoid, schizotypal, and schizoid personality disorders); dramatic/emotional (antisocial, borderline, histrionic, and narcissistic personality disorders); and anxious/fearful (avoidant, dependent, and obsessive-compulsive personality disorders). Antisocial personality disorder is of broad social and clinical interest and is a subject of much study apart from other personality disorders.
- The odd/eccentric personality disorders in some ways resemble schizophrenia and delusional disorder but are not accompanied by the severe disability and loss of reality contact associated with those conditions. Paranoid personality disorder is marked by suspicion of people in almost all situations. In schizotypal personality disorder, the person's speech, behavior, thinking, and/or perceptions are disturbed. In schizoid personality disorder, eccentricity is confined to social withdrawal: Schizoid individuals seem unable to form attachments, and they often seem unable to experience positive emotions, such as joy or happiness, in any situation.
- The dramatic/emotional personality disorders are characterized by attention-seeking, demanding, and erratic behavior; people with these disorders tend to experience failure in interpersonal relationships because of their difficult behavior. The defining trait of antisocial personality disorder is a predatory attitude toward other people, marked by failure to show constancy and responsibility, irritability and aggressiveness, reckless and impulsive behavior, and a disregard for the truth. Elements of borderline personality disorder include problems in forming a secure self-identity, distrust, impulsive or self-destructive behavior, and difficulty in controlling anger and other emotions. The dominant feature of histrionic personality disorder is self-dramatization, often clearly intended to attract attention and sympathy. Narcissistic personality disorder is characterized by exaggerated self-importance, often combined with fragile self-esteem.
- The anxious/fearful personality disorders involve worry in various forms and behaviors for coping with it. The essential feature of avoidant personality disorder is hypersensitivity to the possibility of rejection, humiliation, or shame; the result is a recoil from others and, typically, loneliness and regret. Dependent personality disorder is characterized by excessive dependence on others, to the point of submissiveness; it is built on a fear of abandonment. Obsessive-compulsive personality disorder is defined by excessive preoccupation with orderliness, perfectionism, and control, at the cost of real effectiveness and of spontaneity in interpersonal relationships.
- A group that is perhaps most at risk for personality disorders is people in psychological treatment. Personality disorders are not usually the disturbances for which people seek or are admitted for treatment, but their very high incidence in clinical populations suggests that they are what predispose patients to their Axis I conditions—such as anxiety disorders, mood disorders, and substance abuse.
- Gender is a risk factor in most of the personality disorders. Men are at greater risk than women for many of the personality disorders and are at far greater risk for antisocial personality disorder. Women are at far greater risk for borderline and histrionic personality disorders and at greater risk for dependent personality disorder. The disorders that more often affect women receive undue attention, and arguments over the existence of gender bias are more intense in the area of the personality disorders than in any other area of psychological diagnosis.
- Diagnosis of personality disorders across ethnic and cultural boundaries is also a sensitive matter. Behavioral traits that are taken for granted in one ethnic group may seem maladaptive to diagnosticians from another group or from the majority culture; professionals who are overly concerned with respecting a patient's cultural values may fail to treat a serious disorder.
- Psychodynamic theorists trace personality disorders, which they call character disorders, to disturbances in the early parent-child relationship, leading to a weak ego; in terms of ego strength, they consider people with character disorders to fall between neurotics and psychotics. In all the character disorders, normal coping behavior, governed by the ego, breaks down and is replaced by erratic, distorted, or deviant behavior.
- Insight-oriented therapy, a slow process under the best of circumstances, may seem to hold little promise for treatment of personality disorders. People with the disorders do not often seek treatment of their own initiative; rather, they may be induced into counseling because of marital or family problems and tend to see the problem as something external to themselves. Nevertheless, psychodynamic therapists will regard the insight approach as the road to change.
- Behavioral theorists generally reject the concept of personality disorders because it implies the existence of stable personality traits—an assumption they do not endorse. They regard the disorders as types of behavior that have been learned and thus can be changed; they focus on the maladaptive modeling and reinforcement and the lack of skills acquisition that led to the behaviors. Social-skills training is a major part of behavior therapy for the personality disorders.

- The cognitive perspective holds that personality disorders are products of distortions or exaggerations in the schemas that structure the information in our minds. The faulty beliefs are rigid and admit no exceptions. Cognitive therapy is directed at modifying faulty schemas, reinterpreting the schemas, or camouflaging them.
- Sociocultural theorists emphasize the role of large-scale social processes as background for the personality disorders—processes that create advantage and disadvantage for different groups. Sociocultural theorists argue that psychologists should strive to change society instead of trying to change its victims.
- The neuroscience perspective focuses on genetic and physiological factors that may contribute to personality disorders. The neuroscience position is supported by research that links specific personality disorders with some of the more typical Axis I disorders that are known to have a genetic component. Some successes in drug treatment have tended to support these findings: Both schizotypal patients and schizophrenics have been helped by phenothiazines, and borderline personalities are sometimes helped by antidepressants. However, response to the same medication is far from proof that two disorders are variants of the same condition.

CHAPTER

12

The Difference Between Dependence and Abuse

Alcohol Dependence

The Social Cost of Alcohol Problems

The Personal Cost of Alcohol Dependence

The Development of Alcohol Dependence

Treatment of Alcohol Dependence

Nicotine Dependence

The Antismoking Movement

Legal Remedies

Nicotine Dependence: Theory and Therapy

Other Psychoactive Drugs

Depressants

Stimulants

Hallucinogens

Marijuana and Hashish

Substance Dependence: Theory and Therapy

The Psychodynamic Perspective

The Behavioral Perspective

The Interpersonal Perspective

The Cognitive Perspective

The Neuroscience Perspective

The Sociocultural Perspective

The Nature of Substance Dependence and Abuse

A 30-year-old white female lost custody of her twin girls, aged 2, who were born with fetal alcohol syndrome, a pattern of physical and mental impairment, but regained custody after treatment. She had started drinking when she was 15 years old and taking methamphetamines when she was 16. By the time she was 21, she drank alcohol daily and had a severe alcoholism habit. She explained that her alcohol intake increased during her pregnancy, when she would drink two cases of beer a day. She said that she felt nauseous during the pregnancy and "would hardly eat anything" and would "drink beer all day long to try to numb the pain." After her doctor advised her to cut down her drinking, she got down to two or three six-packs daily when she was 7 months pregnant. Shortly after, a sonogram showed that her twins had stopped growing, and the doctor had to deliver the twin girls by C-section. Their birth weights were 2 pounds, 11 ounces, and 2 pounds, 12 ounces, and they were diagnosed with fetal alcohol syndrome. The twins were taken from their mother's custody due to her alcohol abuse during pregnancy; at one point, one of the twins wasn't expected to live because of heart problems due to the syndrome. Besides alcohol addiction, the woman had a record of 17 felony charges. (Adapted from Miller, 1995.)

To many people, the very word *drug* has connotations of danger, yet most Americans use some form of **psychoactive drug**—that is, a drug that alters one's psychological state—either occasionally or regularly. Most confine themselves to legal drugs such as alcohol, nicotine, and caffeine, which, precisely because they *are* legal, tend not to be looked upon as drugs. However, as can be seen in the preceding case history, legal drugs can damage people as severely as illegal drugs.

Psychoactive substances do not invariably cause harm. When they are prescribed by physicians, they can be very helpful. In many societies, and in subcultures of our own society, they are an integral part of social and religious ritual. Neither is occasional recreational use, in small doses, necessarily the road to destruction. Certain drugs are an important source of harmless pleasure, as anyone knows who has ever enjoyed a beer at a ball game. It is when drug use becomes habitual and when it begins to erode the person's normal functioning—work, studies, relationships with others—that it is redefined as "abuse." As functioning continues to decline, and as use of and recovery from the drug come to occupy a major portion of the person's life, "abuse" is redefined as "dependence."

In the past few decades, drugs have become a major focus of social concern, as evidenced by the recent proliferation of alcohol- and drug-treatment centers, educational programs aimed at the prevention of abuse, and efforts to mandate urine testing for holders of high-responsibility jobs (and even for teenagers in after-school programs) in order to detect drug users. Substance use disorders place staggering costs on individuals and society, destroying families and careers as well as productivity and health. In 1992, the most recent year for which there is adequate information available, substance use disorders cost our society $246 billion (NIDH, 2002). A poll by the Princeton Research Associates (Illegal drugs, 2002) indicated that 74 percent of Americans believe the country is losing the drug war. Recent concerns have focused on the drug Ecstasy (MDMA), which increased in use among teenagers between 1997 and 1999 by 69 percent (Strote, Lee, & Wechsler, 2002), though some researchers found a decrease in 2001 (Johnson, O'Malley, & Blackman, 2001). In fact, however, although "club drugs" like Ecstasy and street drugs like crack cocaine are the targets of public antidrug campaigns, alcohol has always been America's number one drug problem. And social alarm, though it may ultimately contribute to prevention, may have so far done more harm than good, creating a "war on drugs" whose major effect has merely been to put poor, young drug users in jail. Meanwhile, those who control the illegal drug trade tend to go free, and effective treatments for drug abusers have only begun to be developed.

In this chapter, we first describe the common features of drug dependence. Then we discuss alcohol and nicotine, the most easily available and most widely abused drugs in our society. Finally, we examine other varieties of drugs: depressants, stimulants, hallucinogens, and marijuana. Theories as to the cause and treatment of abuse are also covered.

Though our chapter will go drug by drug, it is important to keep in mind that in many cases drugs are not used individually. Indeed, the majority of people who abuse one drug abuse other drugs (Tsuang, Lyons, Meyer, et al., 1998), such as cocaine, marijuana, and crack cocaine, which greatly increases the likelihood of automobile crashes, violent behavior, harm to mental and physical health, and sexual risk taking (Greenwood, White, Page-Shafter, et al., 2001). Nearly two thirds (64 percent) of alcoholics have lifetime diagnoses of joint alcohol and drug dependence/abuse (Staines, Magura, Foot, et al., 2001). As a result, the current trend in drug-treatment centers is to deal with patients as people who seek *a* drug experience—any alteration in their state of consciousness—rather than to worry over whether they are abusing alcohol, heroin, or another drug.

The Difference Between Dependence and Abuse

The discussion of drug abuse is hampered by the fact that neither the society nor the mental health profession has yet agreed on a clear and consistent terminology. For years it was customary to distinguish physiological and psychological need. Drug use that had altered the body's chemistry to the point where its "normal" state was the drugged state, so that the body required the drug in order to feel normal, was called **addiction.** By contrast, the psychological dimension of drug abuse—the abuser's growing tendency to center his or her life on the drug—was called *psychological dependence.* These definitions, however, were not accepted by all professionals. (Indeed, recent editions of the *DSM* reserve the term *dependence* specifically for conditions that involve addiction.) Furthermore, as methods for detecting "withdrawal symptoms" became more precise, researchers discovered that all psychoactive drugs had both physiological and psychological effects. The two could not be separated.

In response to these confusions, *DSM-IV-TR,* like *DSM-III* and *DSM-IV,* placed both the physical and psychological manifestations of pathological drug use under two diagnostic categories: substance dependence and substance abuse. Both problems are defined in terms of behavioral criteria. In other words, the problem lies not in the drug but in the way a person uses the drug. By itself, the fact that a person takes a drug—whether legal or not—does not necessarily indicate dependence or abuse. The drug may or may not be physiologically addictive. Substance use becomes abuse or dependence when the pattern of use begins causing problems in the person's life.

A person qualifies for the diagnosis of **substance dependence** when he or she meets any 3 of the following 7 criteria, which reflect compulsive use of drugs and loss of control:

1. *Preoccupation with the drug.* A great deal of time is spent in activities necessary to obtain the substance (e.g., theft), in taking the substance (e.g., chain smoking), or in recovering from its effects.
2. *Unintentional overuse.* Problem users begin to find repeatedly that they have taken more of the drug than they intended.
3. *Tolerance.* As noted, habitual drug use alters body chemistry. The body adjusts to the drug, so that the usual dose no longer produces the desired effect—a phenomenon called **tolerance.** (Some alcohol abusers, for example, can drink a quart of whiskey a day without seeming intoxicated.) As tolerance develops, the person requires larger and larger amounts of the drug in order to achieve the desired biochemical change.
4. *Withdrawal.* With prolonged use, the body eventually *requires* the drug in order to maintain stability. If the drug level is decreased, the person undergoes **withdrawal,** psychological and physical disruptions ranging from mild anxiety and tremors to acute psychosis and, in extreme cases, death. Consequently, the person often takes the drug in order to avoid or relieve withdrawal symptoms.
5. *Persistent desire or efforts to control drug use.* Many drug-dependent people repeatedly quit and repeatedly relapse. Drug dependence is a chronic disorder.
6. *The abandonment of important social, occupational, or recreational activities for the sake of drug use.* Many of life's major functions—work, friendship, marriage, child rearing—conflict with heavy drug use and may be given up as a result.
7. *Continued drug use despite serious drug-related problems.* Many people go on smoking despite emphysema or taking narcotics despite a long record of drug-related arrests. This is no longer recreational use.

In tolerance—one of the major criteria for substance dependence—a person requires more of the drug to achieve the same biochemical change.

Substance abuse is essentially a pattern of maladaptive drug use that has not progressed to full-blown dependence. But the difference between substance dependence and substance abuse is not just a simple matter of degree. Research has shown that there is far more to substance dependence than using a lot of drugs (Leshner, 1999; Kalivas, 2003). It seems that once individuals develop a substance dependence, long-term changes may occur in their brain metabolism. According to *DSM-IV-TR,* a person qualifies for the diagnosis of substance abuse if he or she shows any one of the following characteristics, which reflect adverse consequences of use:

1. Recurrent, drug-related failure to fulfill major role obligations (e.g., absenteeism from school or work, neglect of children)
2. Recurrent drug use in physically dangerous situations (e.g., drunk driving)
3. Drug-related legal problems (e.g., arrests for disorderly conduct)
4. Continued drug use despite social or interpersonal problems (e.g., marital quarrels) caused by the effects of the drug

Alcohol Dependence

For thousands of years, alcohol has been the traditional "high" of Western culture. And, unlike most of the other drugs we discuss in this chapter, it can be purchased legally in all but a few parts of the United States. For both of these reasons, alcohol is the most widely used of all the psychoactive drugs. A recent national survey revealed that approximately 1 in 4 children younger than 18 years is exposed to alcohol abuse or dependence in the family (Grant, 2001). In

Some of the social costs of alcohol abuse are beyond measurement. Five passengers died and more than 100 were injured when the driver of this New York City subway train drove it off the tracks in 1991. It was later determined that he had been intoxicated.

1995, 52 percent of Americans aged 12 or older used alcohol. About 16 percent engaged in "binge drinking," meaning that they took 5 or more drinks on the same occasion within a month. And about 6 percent were "heavy drinkers," defined as people who had 5 or more drinks on the same occasion on at least 5 different days in the past month (Substance Abuse and Health Services Administration, 1996).

The Social Cost of Alcohol Problems

It is impossible to determine exactly how much damage is done to society at large as a result of alcohol dependence and abuse. Easier to measure is the amount of money it costs. In 1998 alcohol-related problems cost the American economy approximately $185 billion in lost productivity, medical expenses, and other costs (National Institute on Alcohol Abuse and Alcoholism, 2000). The health-care costs for alcohol dependence constitute social costs as well as economic costs, because those funds could have been used for many other needed social services had they not had to be spent to treat the consequences of alcohol dependence.

Alcohol-related motor vehicle accidents alone cost $45 billion annually (National Highway Traffic Safety Administration, 2001). The effects of alcohol on the nervous system—and, consequently, on the drinker's behavior—are directly proportionate to the amount of alcohol in the bloodstream. This latter factor is called the **blood alcohol level,** which is expressed in terms of the amount of alcohol in relation to a specific volume of blood. Table 12.1 on page 316 indicates the approximate relationship between alcohol intake and blood alcohol level. Note that there is a gender difference. Women have less body fluid (but more fat) per pound of body weight. Therefore, if a 150-pound woman and a 150-pound man have 5 drinks apiece, she will have a higher blood alcohol level than he and, consequently, will be more intoxicated.

Under federal law, a person with a blood alcohol level of 0.08 percent is considered to be intoxicated. As Table 12.2 on page 316 indicates, a driver with a blood alcohol level of 0.10 percent is less cautious, less alert, and slower to react than a nondrinking driver. As the blood alcohol level rises, so does the level of impairment. A nighttime driver who has had several drinks is also laboring under a severe visual handicap; it has been shown that visual recovery from glare slows down as blood alcohol level increases (Sekuler & MacArthur, 1977).

Research has shown that the vast majority of men killed in car accidents were drunk at the time. Of these, 73 percent were chronically heavy drinkers, and most had a history of DUI convictions and license suspensions (Kennedy, Isaac, & Graham, 1996). Other studies have clearly documented a relationship between a bad driving record and alcohol abuse, which in turn increases the risk of injury (Voas, Holder, & Gurenewald, 1997). One emergency room survey of people surviving car accidents found that 68 percent were drunk at the time of the accident (Voas, Holder, & Gurenewald, 1997). Those with previous arrests, hospital admissions, criminal records, and histories of drug abuse were much more likely to be drunk at the time of the accident.

Even if alcohol abusers don't drive, they can still cause serious damage. Alcohol consumption is implicated in the full panoply of social problems. It increases the risk of suicide and of a variety of accidents that can

TABLE 12.1 Relationships Among Gender, Weight, Oral Alcohol Consumption, and Blood Alcohol Level

ABSOLUTE ALCOHOL (OUNCES)	BEVERAGE INTAKE*	BLOOD ALCOHOL LEVELS (MG/100ML)					
		Female (100 lb)	Male (100 lb)	Female (150 lb)	Male (150 lb)	Female (200 lb)	Male (200 lb)
0.5	1 oz spirits† 1 glass wine 1 can beer	0.045	0.037	0.03	0.025	0.022	0.019
1	2 oz spirits 2 glasses wine 2 cans beer	0.09	0.075	0.06	0.05	0.045	0.037
2	4 oz spirits 4 glasses wine 4 cans beer	0.18	0.15	0.12	0.10	0.09	0.07
3	6 oz spirits 6 glasses wine 6 cans beer	0.27	0.22	0.18	0.15	0.13	0.11
4	8 oz spirits 8 glasses wine 8 cans beer	0.36	0.30	0.24	0.20	0.18	0.15
5	10 oz spirits 10 glasses wine 10 cans beer	0.45	0.37	0.30	0.25	0.22	0.18

*In one hour.
†100-proof spirits.
Source: Ray & Ksir, 1993, p. 194.

cause death (Lunetta, Penttilae, & Sarna, 2001), including motor vehicle accidents (Abel-Aty & Abdelwahab, 2000), boating accidents (Smith, Keyl, Hadley, et al., 2001), and drownings (Bell, Amoroso, Yore, et al., 2001). Extremely high blood alcohol levels can trigger a state of mental confusion called intoxication delirium (*DSM-IV-TR*), which heightens the risk of accidents by creating disorientation and reduced mental clarity and by disrupting memory and attention to the environment. Alcohol consumption is significantly related to violent crime (Friedman, Glassman, & Terras, 2001; McClelland & Teplin, 2001) and sexual assault, including rape; violence against intimate partners (Merrill, Thomsen, Gold, et al., 2001; Ullman & Brecklin, 2000); stalking (Willson, McFarlane, Malecha, et al., 2000); and child molestation (Aromacki & Lindman, 2001). Impaired judgment also increases the likelihood of sexual risk taking, a particular problem in teenagers (Bonomo, Coffey, Wolfe, et al., 2001), with the possible consequences of pregnancy and sexually transmitted diseases, including AIDS.

TABLE 12.2 Blood Alcohol Level: Physiological and Psychological Effects

BLOOD ALCOHOL LEVEL (%)	EFFECT
0.05	Lowered alertness; usually good feeling; release of inhibitions; impaired judgment
0.10	Less caution; impaired motor function
0.15	Large, consistent increases in reaction time
0.20	Marked depression in sensory and motor capability, decidedly intoxicated
0.25	Severe motor disturbance, staggering; sensory perceptions greatly impaired
0.30	Stuporous, but conscious—no comprehension of world around them
0.35	Equivalent to surgical anesthesia
0.40	Probable lethal dose

The Personal Cost of Alcohol Dependence

The Immediate Effects of Alcohol Pharmacologically, alcohol is classified as a depressant. It slows down and interferes with the transmission of electrical impulses in the higher brain centers, areas that control, organize, and inhibit some of our complex mental processes. This release from control helps people to relax, to stop worrying about what other people think of them, and to have a good time. For similar reasons, alcohol is also consumed by people to ease feelings of depression, but its consumption can actually worsen depression over time.

Initially alcohol may have a stimulating effect rather than a depressing one. With a drink or two, people often become more talkative, more active. By the time the blood alcohol level reaches 0.03 to 0.06 percent, two types of effects occur. First, mood and social behavior change. Some people become depressed and remorseful; others become amorous or belligerent. The second effect is that judgment is impaired. Amorous types begin making wanton remarks to strangers, belligerent types start fights, and so forth. As the blood alcohol level continues to rise, the depressant effect of alcohol becomes more obvious. People slow down, stumble, and slur their words. Their judgment is further impaired, and they tend to engage in even more reckless behavior. "Depressive" drunks, for example, may begin loudly confessing their sins and failures.

For a long time, it was believed that the "bad" behaviors associated with drinking, particularly sexual indiscretion and belligerence, resulted directly from the physiological effect of alcohol on the brain. Presumably, alcohol impeded the brain's inhibition functions, and the "real person" came out. To quote the old Latin saying, "*In vino veritas*"—"In wine, truth." But experiments in which the behavior of people who have drunk alcohol is compared with the behavior of people who merely think they have drunk alcohol suggest that the disinhibiting effect has as much to do with the predictions made by the drinkers (and others) about how the alcohol is going to affect them. These predictions are often expressed as expectancies, which in turn reflect learned beliefs about what alcohol does to people. Increased sexual arousal, in particular, seems to be less a product of alcohol's chemical effects than of the drinker's expectancy that alcohol enhances sexual performance (Hull & Bond, 1986; George & Stoner, 2000), though the alcohol has its effects on some aspects of sexual response too. Positive expectancies about how alcohol makes one feel also account for some of the relationship between excitement seeking and drinking (Finn, Sharkansky, Brandt, et al., 2001). But aggressive behavior seems due less to the drinker's belief that alcohol unleashes aggressive behavior (Bushman, 1993; Giancola & Zeichner, 1997) than to alcohol's chemical effects, including its effects on loss of self-control and executive functions (cognitive activities of planning, decision making, etc.).

The Long-Term Effects of Alcohol Abuse Because it can relieve tension, alcohol is often resorted to as a means of coping with, or at least enduring, life's problems. The ironic result is that alcohol abusers end up with more problems than they had before and fewer resources for dealing with them. Hence, they drink more. Hence, they have more problems—a classic vicious cycle. In the process, their mental acuteness is lost; memory, judgment, and the power to concentrate are all diminished. As their capabilities are eroded, so is their self-esteem. They neglect and alienate their friends. Often unable to work, alcohol abusers typically feel guilty toward their families, but at the same time they may take out their problems on the family. Child abuse, for example, is often connected with alcohol abuse. Alcohol also impairs sexual functioning and is one of the leading causes of impotence. Whether as cause or result of their drinking, alcohol abusers also have very high rates of other psychiatric disorders, especially antisocial personality disorder, depression, and anxiety disorders (Finn, Sharkansky, Viken, et al., 1997; Prescott, Aggen, & Kendler, 2000; Roy, DeJong, Lamparski, et al., 1991). Alcohol abuse and dependence can broadly impair an individual's mental, emotional, and social abilities. One study found that recently detoxified alcoholics were far less able to recognize the emotions—such as happiness, anger, disgust, or fear—expressed in a series of photos of people's faces than were nonalcoholic controls (Kornreich, Blairy, Phillippot, et al., 2001). Moreover, some deficits in recognizing emotions, such as overestimating the intensity of anger, were still present in some alcoholics even after long-term abstinence.

As serious as the psychological consequences are the physiological effects. Habitual overuse of alcohol can cause stomach ulcers, hypertension, heart failure, cancer, and brain damage. Shrinkage in the volume of the frontal lobe, an apparently natural correlate of aging, is rapidly accelerated by heavy alcohol use, even among people who are not alcohol-dependent (Kubota, Nakazaki, Hirai, et al., 2001), and may bring on an earlier onset of dementia, a wide-ranging loss of mental capacity sometimes found in the elderly (Thomas & Rockwood, 2001). Recent hints suggest that DNA damage caused by alcoholism is implicated in the brain shrinkage (Brooks, 2000). Binge drinking (such as having 10 drinks a day), even for a few days, produces lasting damage to the brain (Crews, Brown, Hoplight, et al., 2001). Another common consequence is cirrhosis of the liver, which is now the ninth leading cause of death in the United States (Debakey, Stinson, Grant, et al., 1996). In addition, alcohol dependence often entails malnutrition. Alcohol is high in calories, which provide energy, but it is devoid of any known nutrient. Because alcohol-dependent people typically eat little and unselectively, their protein and vitamin intake tends to be dangerously insufficient. In extreme cases, they may develop Korsakoff's psychosis (Chapter 15), a severe memory disorder thought to be caused by vitamin B deficiency.

Pictured here (from left to right) are a healthy liver, a liver that is fatty from alcohol disease, and a liver that is cirrhotic with alcohol disease.

An infrequent but terrifying complication of chronic alcohol dependence is *delirium tremens*—literally meaning "trembling delirium" and better known as the DTs. This severe reaction is actually a withdrawal symptom, occurring when the blood alcohol level drops suddenly. Deprived of their needed dosage, patients with the DTs tremble furiously, perspire heavily, become disoriented, and suffer nightmarish delusions. This condition usually lasts for 3 to 6 days, after which the patient may vow never to take another drink—a vow that in many cases is broken shortly after discharge from the treatment center.

In short, alcohol abuse damages health. Death rates are much higher for alcohol abusers than for nonabusers—2 to 4 times higher in the case of men, 3 to 7 times higher in the case of women (Edwards, 1989). The higher death rates for women reflect a difference in the way women and men metabolize alcohol. Women also tend to begin drinking heavily at an older age, when their organ systems are more vulnerable (Schuckit, 1995).

The Development of Alcohol Dependence

There is considerable variability in how people become alcohol-dependent, but some common patterns have been noted. While certain people develop abusive drinking patterns quite rapidly, most go through a long period of social drinking, during which they gradually increase the quantity and frequency of their drinking and come to rely on the mood-altering effects of alcohol. As consumption increases, many people begin to experience blackouts, periods in which they are drinking heavily and seem to be carrying on in a fairly normal fashion, but of which they have no memory the following day. In social situations, the alcohol user may also begin sneaking drinks (e.g., stopping at the bar on the way to the men's room) in order to keep ahead of the others without letting them know. Another serious danger sign is morning drinking, to get oneself "going."

Whatever the pattern, most people headed for alcohol dependence eventually find that they have trouble stopping themselves once they start drinking and that, as a result, they are drunk at least 2 or 3 times a week. Some abusers, however, remain spree drinkers, staying sober for long periods but then, often in response to stress, going on "benders," binges lasting several days. Jellinek (1946), who described many of these patterns, claimed that the total itinerary, from the beginning of heavy drinking to complete defeat by alcohol, took 12 to 18 years, but for many people the route is shorter. According to Jellinek, individuals in the early stages of alcoholism drink to calm their nerves, but they come to require increased quantities of alcohol to get this relief. As they start to lose control over their drinking, they may miss meals (because they are drinking) and deceive others about the quantities they have consumed. The middle stage of alcoholism is characterized by an increasing preoccupation with drinking and loss of interest in other activities; financial problems and trouble at work may also be evident. Drinkers in the late stage of alcoholism face severely deteriorated family relationships and an impaired ability to work. Without treatment, alcoholics face wrecked lives and premature death, The course of alcohol dependence has interesting parallels with the course of another devastating behavioral disorder, compulsive gambling (see the box on impulse-control disorders on page 300).

❖ Groups at Risk for Alcohol Abuse and Dependence

Different social groups have different patterns of alcohol consumption. Interestingly, people with higher incomes are more likely to use alcohol. So are people with more education. If you have a college degree, chances are (68 percent) that you drink; if you have less than a high school education, chances are that you don't (42 percent). On the other hand, less-educated Americans are almost twice as likely to drink to excess (Substance Abuse and Mental Health Services Administration, 1996), so the distinction between use and abuse is an important one.

Exposure to major negative life events, such as getting divorced or being the victim of a crime, is another risk factor for alcohol abuse (San Jose, van Oers, van de Mheen, et al., 2000). Alcohol use increased in New York City following the September 11, 2001, terrorist attack on the World Trade Center, suggesting that alcohol is one way people deal with the sudden recognition of vulnerability that major traumas cause. Chronic stressors such as protracted unemployment or marital difficulties can also be risk factors (Claussen, 1999; San Jose, van Oers, van de Mheen, et al., 2000). The higher levels of chronic stress to which bisexuals, gays, and lesbians are often exposed likely explains, at least in part, why gay and bisexual men and lesbians are at greater risk for alcohol and drug abuse (Greenwood, White, Page-Shafer, et al., 2001; Jaffe, Clance, Nichols, et al., 2001). Greenwood and colleagues found that young gay and bisexual men who reported frequent visits to gay bars and multiple sex partners also reported more alcohol abuse and concurrent use of alcohol and other drugs. Such alcohol use, as noted, can lead to sexual risk taking. Other important risk factors have to do with gender, ethnic origin, religion, and age.

Gender In every way, men are more involved with alcohol than women are. About 60 percent of American men, as opposed to 45 percent of women, use alcohol, and about 32 percent of men, as opposed to 11 percent of women, use it to excess (Substance Abuse and Mental Health Services Administration, 1995). There are also marked differences between the genders in patterns of use and abuse. First, women usually begin drinking later in their lives, experience their first intoxication later, develop dependence later, and go to facilities with shorter histories of drinking problems than do men. Women are more likely than men to cite a stressful event as precipitating the problem, and they are more likely than men to have a problem-drinking spouse or lover. Alcohol-dependent women are much more likely than their male counterparts to drink alone, but, when women do drink with someone else, it is likely to be a person close to them. Conversely, men are more likely than women to drink in public places and with strangers. Women also drink large amounts less often, do less bender and morning drinking, and have shorter drinking bouts. Finally, women more frequently combine alcohol with other substances—tranquilizers, barbiturates, amphetamines, hypnotics, antidepressants, and nonprescription drugs (Gomberg, 1997).

It is not clear whether these divergent drinking patterns have to do more with the social role differences or with biological differences between men and women. In favor of the first hypothesis, it should be added that, although the rate of alcohol abuse among women still lags far behind the rate for men, it has risen steadily in recent years—a fact that some experts attribute to the increase in the number of women taking on high-pressure jobs formerly reserved for men. Other writers, however, argue that what has risen is not the number of women with drinking problems but the number of women seeking help for alcohol abuse, rather than drinking in secret (Weisner & Schmidt, 1992).

Ethnicity and Religion European Americans have a higher rate of alcohol use (56 percent) than either Latinos (45 percent) or African Americans (41 percent) (Substance Abuse and Mental Health Services Administration, 1996). Evidence suggests that these ethnic differences reflect differences in perception: Researchers have discovered that European Americans are less likely than African Americans or Latinos to perceive risks for alcohol abuse (Ma & Shive, 2000). As for patterns of abuse, however, the picture becomes more complicated. The U.S. Department of Health and Human Services (1991) has reported that European American teenagers and young adults are more likely to have alcohol-related problems than are Blacks their age. But, between ages 30 and 39, rates of alcohol abuse for African American men rise rapidly, surpassing rates for European American men. Interestingly, as African American males' incomes rise, their rates of alcohol abuse fall; the reverse is true for European American men. As for women, African American women are far more likely to abstain from alcohol than are European American women. The fact that income and gender override skin color suggests that the differences between European Americans and African Americans are the result of different social conditions, not inherited genetic differences.

There are additional ethnic patterns. Men of Irish extraction are more at risk than men of Italian extraction. Latino men are particularly likely to engage in periodic binge drinking and heavy alcohol use (Ma & Shive, 2000). Most Latino women either abstain or drink infrequently. A study by Caetano and

Regular attendance at religious services, regardless of religious affiliation, seems to correlate highly with alcohol abstinence. However, the percentage of abstainers versus abusers varies from one religious group to another.

Rasperry (2000) suggests the impact of sociocultural conditions on ethnic differences: Within the Latino community, Mexicans who were born in Mexico exhibit far fewer drinking problems than Mexican Americans who were born in the United States. Native American men have the highest rate of alcohol abuse of all American ethnic groups (U.S. Department of Health and Human Services, 1991). Alcohol is implicated in 40 percent of all Native American deaths, including accidents, liver disease, homicide, and suicide. Almost all crimes for which Native Americans are jailed or imprisoned are alcohol-related (Yetman, 1994). One study found a 70.4 percent lifetime prevalence of alcoholism among Navajo Indian males and females (McCloskey, Quintero, Russell, et al., 1999).

Another cultural correlate of alcohol abuse is religious affiliation. One religious group that seems particularly resistant to alcohol problems is, predictably, conservative Protestants, who have a notably high percentage of alcohol abstainers and a notably low percentage of heavy drinkers. There are also few alcohol abusers among Orthodox Jews, who drink wine but in controlled and primarily religious settings (Goodwin & Gabrielli, 1997; Snyder, 1958). Catholic, Reform Jewish, and liberal Protestant groups all contain a fairly high proportion of alcohol users, with the Catholics leading the other groups in the percentage of heavy drinkers. In all religious groups, it appears that attendance at religious services correlates highly with abstinence.

Age Rates of general alcohol use in the United States have remained stable in recent years, but not, it seems, within age groups. Researchers have recently shown that alcohol and tobacco use peaks among young adults and declines in older age groups (Anthony & Echeagaray-Wagner, 2001). Older adults appear to drink less; young people, more (see Figure 12.1). America's children start drinking at a younger age, drink more often, and get drunk more often than most adults realize. By sixth grade, significant numbers of young people have at least tried alcohol, and the proportion of young drinkers increases with each grade. In one survey, 70 percent of high school seniors said they had tried alcohol, and 50 percent had used alcohol during the previous 30 days. Of those who had drunk recently, more than 60 percent had become intoxicated (Hansen, 1993). The age at which heavy drinking begins is a major risk factor. People who begin drinking at a younger age are more likely than others to report drunk driving and alcohol-related motor vehicle accidents (Hingson, Heeren, Levenson, et al., 2002).

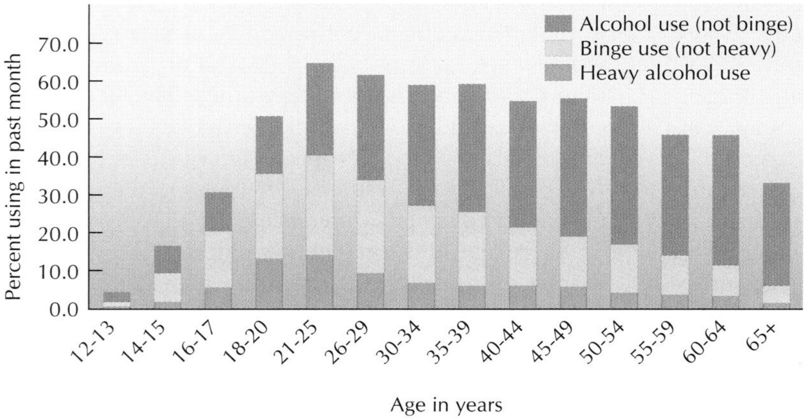

FIGURE 12.1 Frequency of alcohol use among different age groups. Binge drinking and heavy alcohol use is much more common among young adults than among older ones.

Bon Scott (alcohol), died at age 33

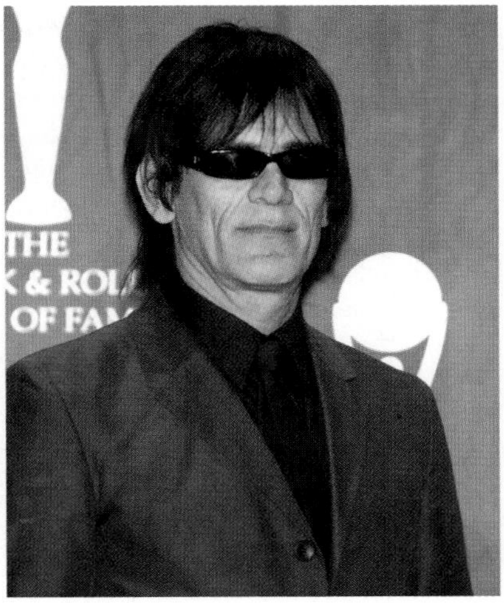

Dee Dee Ramone (heroin overdose), died at age 50

John Belushi (drug overdose), died at age 34

Janis Joplin (heroin overdose), died at age 27

Sid Vicious (heroin overdose), died at age 21

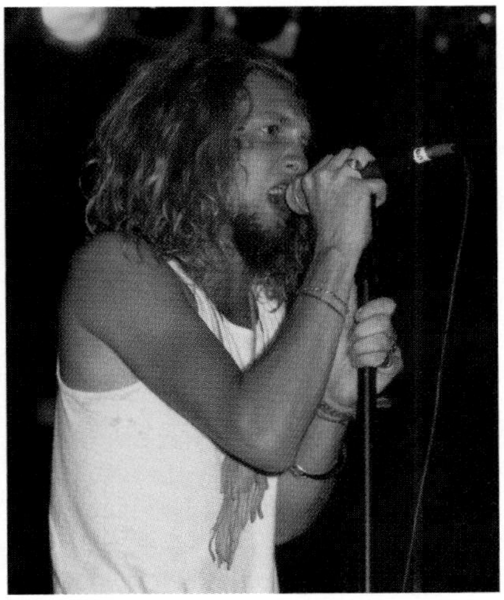

Layne Staley (heroin and cocaine), died at age 34

Substance dependence is a problem for people in most professions, but in popular music it can be said to be a tradition, or a plague. Various explanations have been put forward: Musicians keep late hours; they work in nightclubs, where alcohol and nicotine are all around them (and other drugs are often available as well); many of them grew up poor, and the poor are at greater risk for substance dependence. The habit is more likely to destroy talent than to nourish it. The musicians pictured here all had their careers shortened by substance dependence. Their average age at death was 33.

The proportion of young people who drink regularly and heavily climbs during college. A 1994 survey found that almost half of all college students go in for binge drinking (see the box on page 322). Why, when adults are drinking less, are students drinking more? One answer is advertising—billboards and commercials proclaiming "It's Miller time" or "The night belongs to Michelob." These images and slogans are so much a part of our environment that we hardly think about them—which makes their impact more insidious. Most of the ads, especially those for beer, associate alcohol use with success and happiness. They do not show young drinkers throwing up at the dormitory or crashing their cars into telephone poles. They show them going on dates, wearing smart clothes, and looking vivacious, sexy, and athletic.

However, advertising is not the only factor. Parents often loudly condemn the use of illegal drugs but send a mixed message about alcohol abuse. "Don't drink and drive" can easily be interpreted to mean "It's okay to get drunk, but don't drive." The message from peers is typically less mixed—indeed, decidedly pro-abuse—and, according to research (Hansen, 1993), such attitudes are the primary risk factor for alcohol use.

Focus On... Binge Drinking on Campus

National Public Radio reporter David Baron, researching a story about drinking among college students, went to a student party in Boston. Introduced to a freshman named Brian, Baron asked him how much he had had to drink. "Five or six pints of Guinness and then two or three beers, so far," Brian answered. "Are you expecting to have more?" Baron asked. "Yes, uh-huh," Brian replied.

In a nationwide survey of almost 18,000 college students, Henry Wechsler and colleagues of Harvard School of Public Health found that half the males and 40 percent of the females engaged in "binge drinking," defined as having 5 drinks in a row for men, 4 for women (Wechsler, Dowdall, Davenport, et al., 1995). The vast majority of these students saw nothing wrong with their behavior. Indeed, less than 1 percent felt they had an alcohol problem, yet the binge drinkers were far more likely than their sober classmates to have been injured, to have gotten in trouble with the police, and to have missed classes because of alcohol. They were also 7 times more likely to have had unprotected sex, 10 times more likely to have driven after drinking, and 11 times more likely to have fallen behind in their schoolwork than nonbingers. Clearly, they had a problem, whether they thought so or not.

Beer busts on campus, and their destructive effects, are nothing new. The major revelation of the Wechsler survey was the degree to which campus alcohol abuse imposes hardships on *nonabusers,* the students who are trying to study while the party is going on. The survey found that at heavy-drinking schools nondrinkers and moderate drinkers were 2 to 3 times more likely to report physical assault, sexual harassment, destruction of their property, and interruption of their sleep and studies by drinkers. On some campuses, students reported that Thursday through Sunday the dormitory halls were loud with drunks, the bathrooms unusable. Female students claimed that they woke up Sunday after Sunday to find a strange man in their roommate's bed. (Often, the man was strange to the roommate too.) To deal with such problems, certain colleges have now set up "substance-free" dorms. Others have stepped up controls on campus parties, banning kegs and sending out roving patrols of campus police to check on underage drinkers.

Why do some students engage in binge drinking? Studies have shown that binge drinking is associated with difficulties in making the transition from being a family member to being an independent adult. Other researchers have found that young people who had conduct problems in high school are more likely to be binge drinkers in college, especially if they are male and join fraternities. Another critical factor, it seems, is the person's attitude toward drinking (Baer, Kivlahan, & Marlatt, 1995). Hansen (1993) evaluated 12 risk factors for alcohol use among young people: low self-esteem, poor coping skills, and the like. As it turned out, the factor that had the highest correlation with alcohol use was normative beliefs, specifically the belief "that alcohol use and abuse is prevalent and acceptable among young people" (Hansen, 1993, p. 57). In the past, programs to discourage high school students from abusing alcohol have tried *affective approaches:* stress management, confidence building, and other strategies for fostering emotional strength. Today, such programs are shifting to *social-influence approaches,* which place greater emphasis on changing attitudes and building resistance to peer pressure (Hansen, 1993).

That peer attitudes influence drinking is clear from the wide variations the Wechsler survey found in drinking patterns among different student bodies. It was the small residential colleges and large universities of the northeastern and north-central states that had the highest rates of binge drinking. The large regional or research universities in the South and West had lower rates. Women's colleges and African American colleges also had fewer binge drinkers. These variations seem to indicate that the school subculture can encourage or discourage alcohol abuse, which in turn suggests that nonabusers might start trying to make their voices heard. Many people, and probably most young people, do not wish to be killjoys. But, just as nonsmokers have begun objecting to secondary smoke, victims of the secondary effects of alcohol abuse should probably begin speaking out.

Treatment of Alcohol Dependence

The treatment of alcohol dependence begins with **detoxification**—that is, getting the alcohol out of the person's system and seeing him or her through the withdrawal symptoms. Detoxification can be done at home, under outpatient care, though it is often undertaken in the hospital. The patient is usually given a tranquilizer, such as Serax (oxazepam), for about a week to prevent the seizures that can sometimes follow a "cold-turkey" termination of chronically high alcohol consumption. At the same time, large amounts of vitamins and liquids are administered daily to counter nutritional deficiency and dehydration.

Through this process, the toxic effects of alcohol are eliminated from the system and the body is returned to a near-normal state. That, however, is only a prelude to the behavioral changes that are the major goal of alcohol rehabilitation—the effort to turn a person with a disrupted social, family, and professional life into an integrated, self-sustaining, coping member of society. This is no easy task. Because rehabilitation touches so many aspects of the alcohol-dependent person's life, the better-designed alcohol rehabilitation treatments are multimodal, combining many strategies.

Every day, more than 700,000 people in this country receive treatment for alcoholism (National Institute on Alcohol Abuse and Alcoholism, 2001). How well does it work? Miller, Walters, & Bennett (2001) recently examined how effective alcoholism treatment is in the United States. Combining the findings from seven large multisite studies, these researchers concluded that during the first year after treatment, about 1 in 4 clients remained completely abstinent; the remainder of the clients abstained for 3 days out of 4 and reduced their average alcohol consumption by 87 percent.

Recovering from Alcohol and Drug Dependence: Giving Up Best Friends

The MindMAP video "Alcohol Addiction" illustrates a woman's successful 20-year battle with alcohol and drug dependence after having entered a detoxification program. Do you think detoxification is enough to cure alcohol dependence? Why or why not? How might dependence on one substance lead to dependence on other substances?

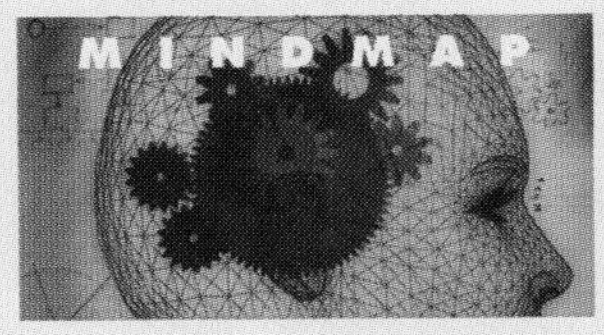

Multimodal Treatments Virtually all treatments for alcoholism are now multimodal, addressing physical, psychological, and social problems simultaneously. In the best multimodal programs, patients are provided with occupational therapy, to help them learn or relearn job skills; relaxation training, to teach them how to reduce tension without alcohol; group and individual therapy, to help them learn something about themselves and to show them how to relate to others without drinking; family and marital therapy, to resolve the problems at home that may have contributed to and/or resulted from their drinking; and job counseling, to get them back to work. These various forms of treatment are given concurrently, and most, if not all, patients participate in them daily. That, however, is the ideal scenario. In practice, most alcohol treatments, inpatient or outpatient, consist of group therapy twice a week plus educational films and Alcoholics Anonymous meetings.

Sometimes hospital treatment programs supply an additional deterrent to drinking, in the form of a drug called Antabuse. Antabuse (disulfiram) is a chemical that interferes with the normal metabolic processing of alcohol for about two days after the medication is taken. When the Antabuse taker drinks alcohol, a toxic by-product of alcohol metabolism, acetaldehyde, accumulates in the bloodstream, causing flushing, increased heart rate, and intense nausea. Antabuse treatment is based on the assumption that it will help alcoholics to avoid impulsive drinking (Moss, 1999), because if they want to take a drink without becoming violently ill, they must stop taking the Antabuse at least two days in advance. The drug thereby provides support for the patient's willpower. However, the support is artificial. Once out of the hospital, many alcoholics simply stop taking the drug. Moreover, it is not clear that Antabuse is particularly effective for those who go on taking it. A review and analysis of data from multiple studies showed that Antabuse-treated groups demonstrated modest evidence of drinking less frequently than placebo groups—but showed no evidence of greater abstinence (Garbutt, West, Carey, et al., 1999). Some alcoholics keep drinking despite the Antabuse and the vomiting or nausea it induces (Kalat, 2001).

Alcoholics Anonymous and Other Self-Help Groups
One part of most successful rehabilitation programs is support groups. Ex-patients may attend one or more meetings a week for 3 to 6 months, or they may continue indefinitely. This continued contact reminds people recovering from alcohol dependency that they need not battle their problem alone—that help is available. Follow-up meetings give them the opportunity to continue working on their problems and to learn additional interpersonal coping skills.

The most widely known of these regular meeting programs is Alcoholics Anonymous, better known as AA. The AA program started in the mid-1930s and has since spread around the world. AA operates on two basic tenets: (1) once an alcoholic, always an alcoholic and (2) an alcoholic can never go back to "normal" drinking. AA sees alcoholism as a lifelong problem; to combat it, the alcoholic must abstain from drink. For help in this difficult task, AA offers not just regular meetings, at which members come together, usually several times a week, to air their problems, but also a sponsor system. New members are assigned a sponsor from among the regular members. If the new member has an overpowering urge to drink, he or she can call the sponsor, who will then give support over the phone or even stay with the new member until the crisis passes. Sponsors also help new members to begin the so-called Twelve Steps to recovery, which, while spiritual in focus, involve some very practical measures, such as self-examination, admission of fault, and the making of amends.

AA appears to have an extremely high dropout rate. Less than 10 percent of people who go to an AA meeting continue in treatment, become abstinent,

Support groups such as this teen group can be helpful to recovering substance abusers by reminding them that they are not alone.

and stay abstinent for a year (Tonigan, Toscova, & Miller, 1996). However, for those who stay with AA, the program does seem to work. In one study that followed 100 patients 1 month and then 6 months after treatment, those who continued to go to meetings drank significantly less (Tonigan, Toscova, & Miller, 1996). Not surprisingly, those who were most confident, most highly motivated, and most active in their coping methods were more likely both to continue with AA and to benefit from the program (Morgenstern, Labouvie, McCrady, et al., 1997). Still, given the high dropout rates and the poor quality of much of the research on AA, it would be something of an overstatement to say that the program is effective (Tonigan, Toscova, & Miller, 1996).

Other self-help groups, such as SMART Recovery (for Self-Management and Recovery Training), take a different approach. SMART Recovery differs from AA because it teaches self-reliance, rather than reliance on a higher power, and because it views addiction as a complex maladaptive behavior rather than as a disease. In line with an emphasis on self-reliance, it encourages individuals not to use labels such as "alcoholic" or "addict" (About SMART Recovery, 2003).

Outpatient and Brief Treatments The past two decades have seen a tremendous growth in residential care for people who are alcohol-dependent. There are units in the Veterans Administration hospitals and in the psychiatric and general hospitals. In addition, the United States now has more than 400 private residential treatment facilities (Moore, 1985), some of them, such as the Betty Ford Center, highly visible. It is questionable, however, whether alcohol-dependents need to be hospitalized round the clock. Outpatient and day-hospital programs have also been expanding in recent years, and several studies have found no difference in relapse rates between outpatient and inpatient programs—a fact that seems to hold regardless of whether the choice between inpatient and outpatient was made by the patient or by random assignment (McKay, Alterman, McLellan, et al., 1995). Partly because of such findings and also because inpatient care costs 5 to 10 times more than outpatient care (Alterman, O'Brien, McLellan, et al., 1994), most insurance programs are now reluctant to pay for full hospitalization except when the patient has clear medical or psychiatric problems beyond alcohol dependence.

At the same time, the trend throughout the psychotherapy field toward brief treatments has also hit alcohol rehabilitation. One of the resulting treatments—which, according to its developers, can work in as few as four sessions—is **motivational interviewing** (Miller & Rollnick, 2002). As its name suggests, motivational interviewing is a question-and-answer method aimed at increasing the patient's motivation to change. Ambivalence is the norm among substance-dependent people: They want to live drug-free, and they don't. Motivational interviewing tries to shift them toward wanting to, so that they become ready to give up the drug. The style of interviewing follows five principles: (1) Show compassion for the patients; (2) help them see the ways in which their lives are not going well; (3) avoid arguing with them; (4) for the time being, let them hold on to whatever mechanisms they are using to avoid changing, whether rationalizations ("I can't stop drinking until I meet a woman") or distortions of reality ("I don't really have a drinking problem); (5) help them develop confidence that they can change. Most of these principles are achieved through the therapist's asking questions. Here is a sample dialogue:

Therapist: How many beers would you like to be drinking per day?

Client: One at most.

Therapist: How many beers do you think you're now drinking per day?

Client: Two.

Therapist: For the next week, keep track. It may be useful to us later.

A week later, the therapist asks about the assignment:

Therapist: What did you find out?

Client: I'm drinking more than I want to be.

Therapist: How much?

FRAMES is the acronym used by motivational interviewers to describe the treatment process: Feedback, Responsibility, Advise, Menu (of alternative strategies for changing drinking), Empathy, and Self-efficacy. The therapist provides feedback in a nonconfrontational, reflective manner and lets the client guide the direction and speed of change.

Cognitive-Behavioral Treatment and Relapse Prevention A very important recent trend in alcohol rehabilitation is **relapse prevention.** Most alcoholics who stop drinking, even for years, do eventually slip and take a drink again at some point. The goal of relapse prevention is to lessen the likelihood of such "slips" and, when they happen, to prevent them from turning into full-scale relapses.

The relapse prevention movement was given its greatest boost from the cognitive-behavioral model generated by Marlatt and his colleagues (Marlatt & Gordon, 1985; Parks, Anderson, & Marlatt, 2001). This was the first and most influential cognitive-behavioral approach to substance abuse (it will be discussed more fully later in the chapter). It can lead a clinician in a variety of directions; thus, the relapse prevention (RP) model has spawned numerous treatment programs for a variety of addictions. The RP model can be used in conjunction with other models of treatment. It is not just a set of techniques but also a theory of relapse. The model states that the risk for relapse begins with a high-risk situation: any threatening circumstance that makes the former addict afraid of losing control, therefore being at risk for drinking. An example might be a recovered alcoholic who unexpectedly runs into his ex-wife at a party where alcohol is served. Anything that produces unpleasant feelings, social pressure, or conflict with another person can trigger the risk for relapse. The high-risk situation generates a variety of internal reactions, according to the model. Patients with good coping skills end up feeling confident that they can refrain from relapsing, despite the high-risk situation. This confidence helps protect them from relapsing. In contrast, those without good coping skills are less confident in their abilities to resist the temptation. Instead, they look to the drug to lead them out of the troubled waters of risk. Once they slip and have a drink, they experience an "abstinence violation effect" (AVE). Having acted in a way that directly contradicts their commitment to abstinence, they feel guilty, out of control, and thus continue to drink. RP techniques suggested by Marlatt and Gordon include identifying in advance and later avoiding high-risk situations, analyzing the chain of thoughts leading to alcohol use in high-risk situations; making constructive lifestyle changes, such as choosing friends who do not drink; and learning that "one drink does not make a drunk." In other words, just because you have slipped does not mean you are doomed to relapse.

How effective are treatment programs based on the RP model? Although results have not been consistent, relapse prevention treatments do appear to make relapses rarer and milder (Carroll, 1996). In the few studies that have compared relapse prevention treatments with AA, the absolute success rates seem to be about the same (Ouimette, Finney, & Moos, 1997).

Matching Recall the finding, described earlier, that certain kinds of individuals—those with more confidence, higher motivation, and more active ways of coping—tend to do best in AA. Most experts agree that alcoholics are a heterogeneous group. Hence, it would seem, treatment would be more likely to work if, by **matching,** they could be directed to the program that best fit their characteristics. For example, some experts have argued that treatment should be tailored to a person's readiness to change (Annis, Schober, & Kelly, 1996). When motivation is low, a treatment aimed at that problem, such as motivational interviewing, might be the answer, whereas people already committed to changing should be channeled into more demanding programs. Other characteristics that have been proposed as a basis for matching are demographic variables (e.g., age, gender, ethnic group), intelligence, severity of abuse, presence or absence of other psychological disorders, and strength of social network (whether the patient has supportive family or friends).

Among experts in substance dependence, the belief in matching is strong, but not until recently was that belief tested, in Project MATCH, the most ambitious and expensive treatment outcome study ever conducted in the field of alcohol rehabilitation. In this experiment, large groups of alcoholics in different cities were randomly assigned to three different treatments: motivational interviewing, a program modeled on AA, and a cognitive-behavioral treatment based on relapse prevention. Then they were followed for a year to see how well the treatment worked. Meanwhile, on the basis of 10 characteristics often targeted in matching, a number of predictions were made: for example, that the least motivated patients would do best in motivational interviewing; that patients with the least psychopathology were expected to benefit more from AA; and that motivational interviewing (MI) was expected to be inferior for patients with severe alcohol problems. In all, there were 16 predictions, and almost none of them were borne out. All the treatments were somewhat effective and about equally effective, but not according to any principles of matching (Project MATCH Research Group, 1997).

Do the results of Project MATCH prove that the matching hypothesis is utterly unfounded? Not necessarily, but they do raise doubts about this widely cherished belief. The study also shows once again that alcohol dependence is very hard to treat. Follow-up studies indicate that, of those who enter treatment, inpatient or outpatient, only about 30 percent stop drinking permanently. The others resume some level of drinking and require ongoing care. We are not even close to identifying truly effective therapies for alcohol-dependent people, let alone discovering which therapy works best for whom.

Nicotine Dependence

One out of every four American adults is a smoker (Schmitz, Schneider, & Jarvik, 1997). Fewer people smoke than drink, but a much higher proportion of smokers become dependent. As a result, nicotine dependence is the most common form of drug dependence in the United States. However, discussions of psychoactive drugs often give little if any attention to nicotine, for, of all the psychoactive drugs, it is the least destructive *psychologically.* Yet nicotine does have negative psychological effects, and withdrawal from nicotine can lead to depression and anxiety. The disorder nicotine dependence, as defined by *DSM-IV-TR,* refers primarily to those who want to stop smoking but cannot.

Tobacco contains nicotine, which has apparently paradoxical effects on the central nervous system. On the one hand, it stimulates the system by elevating the blood pressure and increasing the heart rate. At the same time, it has a calming effect. This effect is not just psychological—the product of the pleasure of indulging a habit. Animal studies have shown that injections of nicotine reduce aggression. In any case, nicotine does not seem to impair mental functioning. What it impairs is the smoker's health.

The Antismoking Movement

In a famous *Surgeon General's Report* (U.S. Public Health Service, 1964), the public received compelling evidence that smoking is a major health hazard. Current research shows that, each year, more than 400,000 Americans die prematurely from tobacco-induced diseases, including lung cancer (136,000 deaths), coronary heart disease (115,000 deaths), and chronic obstructive lung disease, such as emphysema (60,000). Smoking has killed more Americans than all wars and all automobile accidents in the country's history (Schmitz, Schneider, & Jarvik, 1997).

Tobacco users are not the only ones who are harmed by smoking. In 1992, the Environmental Protection Agency reported that each year secondhand smoke causes 3,000 deaths from lung cancer, contributes to respiratory infections in babies (7,500 to 15,000 of whom require hospitalization), and triggers new cases of asthma in 8,000 to 26,000 young children (Cowley, 1992a). However, congressional hearings held in the spring of 1994 revealed that tobacco companies not only suppressed research that showed smoking to be a health hazard but also halted research designed to isolate the addictive ingredients in cigarettes. Critics claim that the companies have deliberately raised the level of nicotine in their products to make them even more addicting. Tobacco company executives counter that the reason is to enhance taste (Hilts, 1994).

These findings have resulted in legislation banning cigarette advertisements from radio and television and requiring that each pack of cigarettes sold in this country carry an advertisement of its own potentially lethal effects. In recent years, there has been a marked increase in antismoking legislation. Smoking is banned in most movie theaters, stores, and office buildings, as well as on public transportation systems and in many restaurants.

The tobacco companies have vigorously opposed antismoking legislation. At the congressional hearings in 1994, the top executives of America's seven largest tobacco companies all testified that they did not believe cigarettes were addictive. But all said they would rather their own children did not smoke!

Nevertheless, the antismoking message has gotten through. The proportion of adult Americans who smoke dropped from 45 percent in 1954 to 25 percent in 1997. People who still use tobacco smoke fewer cigarettes than before (Schmitz, Schneider, & Jarvik, 1997; see Figure 12.2). And, while many people are quitting, fewer are starting: The percentage of high school seniors who smoke daily dropped from 27 percent in 1975 to 19 percent in 1993 (Johnston, O'Malley, & Bachman, 2000). Some, however, have

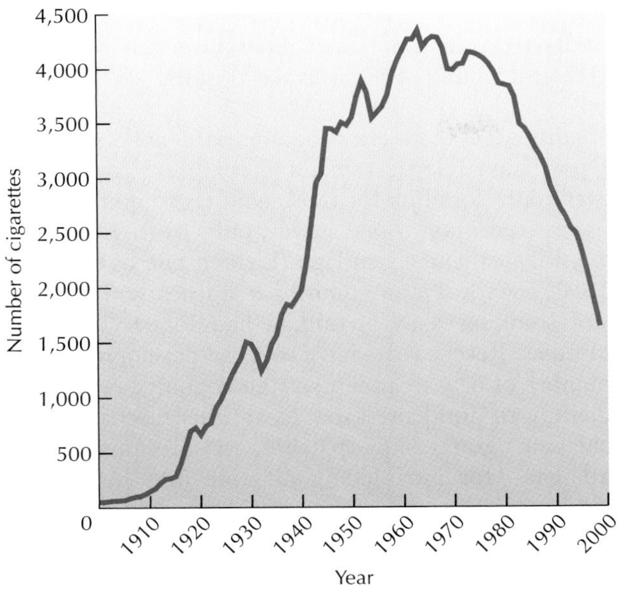

FIGURE 12.2 Cigarette consumption, per capita, in the United States, 1900–1999.

taken up smokeless tobacco (chewing tobacco and snuff) instead. According to one survey, 9 percent of male high school seniors used smokeless tobacco during a sample 30-day period in 1993 (Johnston, O'-Malley, & Bachman, 1994). Many adolescents apparently believe that smokeless tobacco is safe, which is not the case. While it is not associated with lung cancer, it is associated with throat and mouth cancer.

Legal Remedies

In the past few years, both the public and the government have begun pressuring the tobacco industry at unprecedented rates. The federal government has brought lawsuits; in many states, the tobacco companies have been hit by class action suits as well. Antismoking advocates and public policy makers have formed advisory committees to guide such litigation.

An initial far-reaching and controversial outcome of this campaign was an agreement reached between the federal government and the tobacco companies in early 1997. An industry that until recently has not even conceded that smoking is bad for one's health agreed to pay $368 billion for public health benefits—the largest legal settlement ever paid by a private industry. The federal government was also given some power to regulate the tobacco industry in the future.

In 1999, the attorneys general of 46 states and 5 territories signed a $206 billion agreement with tobacco companies, the "Master Settlement," to settle Medicaid lawsuits. In that same year, the U.S. Department of Justice sued the tobacco industry for the recovery of billions of dollars spent on smoking-related health care, and accused cigarette makers of a "coordinated campaign of fraud and deceit." Tobacco billboards came down and were temporarily replaced by pro-health messages paid for by the tobacco industry as part of the Master Settlement. However, in 2000 a judge struck down the portion of the lawsuit that dealt with recovering Medicare expenses for ill smokers. The federal racketeering suit regarding the coordinated campaign of fraud and deceit was allowed to proceed.

Many public health advocates feel that the tobacco industry got off too lightly. As they point out, $368 billion may sound like a lot of money, but it is not nearly enough to reimburse Medicare, Medicaid, the Veterans Administration, and other health programs for the money they have spent, and are spending, on smoking-related illnesses. Indeed, when spread over 25 years—the amount of time the tobacco companies have to make these payments—the sum represents less than 15 cents per dollar for the $100 billion per year of medical costs due to smoking.

Nevertheless, the tobacco settlements represent large amounts that will do some good. (Part of the funds will be used to provide health coverage for uninsured children.) And, with these dramatic settlements, the fact that nicotine is a dangerous drug, one that requires government regulation, was put squarely before the public.

However, fighting smoking still remains an urgent public health problem. Of special importance is the need to prevent teenagers from taking up tobacco. (Tax increases raising the price of a pack of cigarettes by a dollar or two would help greatly.) Such efforts are bound to be opposed. Many states depend on tobacco for their economic stability; in those states, a political candidate who is not willing to fight tobacco regulation cannot get elected. The tobacco industry is also powerful enough to influence government officials from nontobacco states. Despite the funds they have received, many states have also failed up to now to adequately fund tobacco prevention and smoking cessation programs. Thus, this will be a long struggle.

Nicotine Dependence: Theory and Therapy

Learning or Addiction? Why tobacco should have such a firm hold over so many people is not at all clear. Behavioral theorists see it as a learned habit maintained by a number of reinforcers—the stimulant effects of nicotine, the pleasure associated with inhaling and exhaling smoke, the experience of tension reduction in social situations, the enhanced image of oneself as "sophisticated," or perhaps all of these, the primary reinforcer varying from smoker to smoker (O'Leary & Wilson, 1975). However, these reinforcers seem rather weak to maintain such a dangerous habit.

Is smoking, then, a physiological addiction? For years, some experts doubted this. For one thing, there was no evidence of tolerance; many people go on smoking a pack a day for decades. And the withdrawal symptoms experienced by those who stop smoking—irritability, anxiety, restlessness, difficulty in concentrating, decreased heart rate, craving for nicotine, overeating (White, 1991)—seem mild compared with those of addictions such as alcohol.

In the early 1980s, however, Stanley Schachter presented impressive evidence in support of the addiction hypothesis. In a number of studies, Schachter and his colleagues found that smoking does not calm smokers or markedly elevate their mood, nor does it improve their performance over that of nonsmokers. On the other hand, *not* smoking, or an insufficient nicotine level in the bloodstream, causes smokers to perform considerably worse than nonsmokers. Schachter concluded that smokers get nothing out of smoking other than avoidance of the disruptive effect of withdrawal and that it is for this reason—avoidance of withdrawal—that they smoke (Schachter, 1982).

In support of this conclusion, Schachter and his coworkers have good evidence that smokers regulate their nicotine levels in order to ensure that withdrawal symptoms do not occur. In one experiment, smokers increased their cigarette consumption when low-nicotine cigarettes were substituted for their regular, high-nicotine brands. In another experiment, a group of smokers was given vitamin C, which lowers the nicotine level in the bloodstream. (Vitamin C acidifies the urine and so increases the rate at which nicotine is excreted.) Once again, the subjects compensated by smoking more. Schachter suggests that this mechanism may explain why people smoke more when they are under stress. Stress, like vitamin C, acidifies the urine. Thus, smokers under stress would have to increase their nicotine intake in order to maintain their usual nicotine level and thereby fend off withdrawal.

Some evidence suggests that nicotine operates on regions of the brain involved in addiction to stimulant drugs such as cocaine or methamphetamine (Stein, Prankiewicz, Hanch, et al., 1998). Although the reinforcing actions of nicotine are far milder and more subtle than cocaine, nicotine, like cocaine, releases dopamine in the mesolimbic system, the emotion center of the brain (Stahl, 1996). The release of dopamine in these neurons helps to elevate mood, decrease appetite, and enhance cognition or mental efficiency. Nicotine's impact on dopamine could explain why it is so habit-forming. The release of dopamine creates a sense of reward and pleasure, but its decreased production when nicotine is not produced creates a feeling of noxious discomfort.

Treatment Treatment programs for smokers tend to report high relapse rates, and relapse is apparently even more common for those who try to quit on their own: According to one survey, only 10 to 20 percent are still abstinent a year later (Lichtenstein & Glasgow, 1992). Mark Twain summed it up neatly. He could stop smoking easily, he said; he had done so hundreds of times. Recent years have seen the development of a number of new treatments, from cognitive-behavioral therapy to antidepressants to various mechanisms—chewing gum, skin patches, nasal sprays, and inhalers—for introducing nicotine into the bloodstream without tobacco use. These methods have proved moderately successful. One study, for example, found a 26 percent success rate with nicotine chewing gum at 6-month follow-up, as opposed to 19 percent without the gum (Fortmann & Killen, 1995).

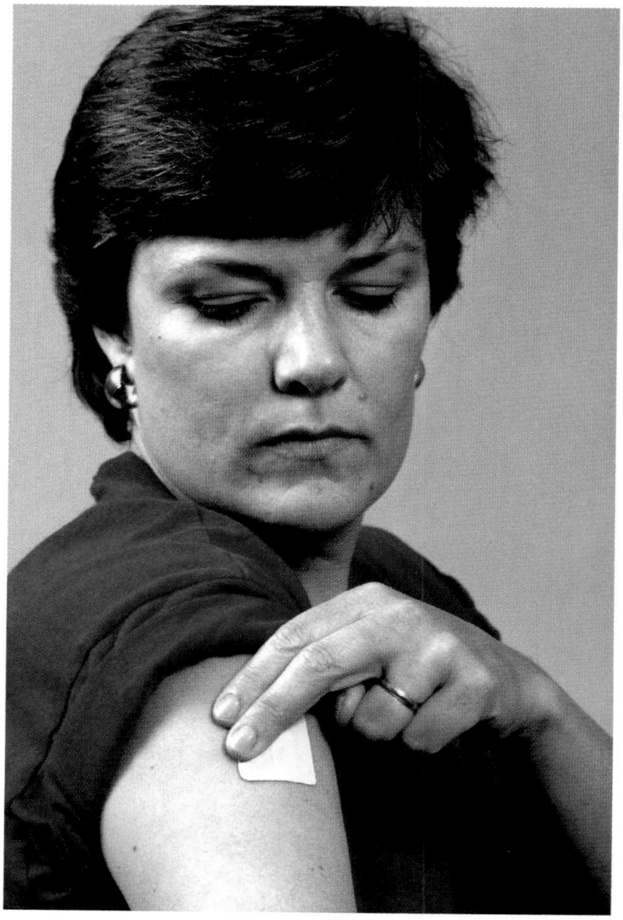

Nicotine-replacement mechanisms such as the patch have proved moderately successful in helping smokers to quit.

Why are some people able to break the habit and others not? Research suggests that a number of factors—motivational, cognitive, social—predict who, having quit smoking, will remain abstinent. Not surprisingly, the higher the person's motivation, the less likely a relapse (Marlatt, Curry, & Gordon, 1988; Parks, Anderson, & Marlatt, 2001), and it makes a difference whether the motivation is intrinsic (the person truly wants to stop smoking) or extrinsic (the person would happily go on smoking but accedes to family pressure). Intrinsic motivation works better than extrinsic motivation (Curry, Wagner, & Grothaus, 1990). Two cognitive factors that predict continued abstinence are self-efficacy (Garcia, Schmitz, & Doerfler, 1990)—whether the person believes that he or she can actually succeed—and the use of coping mechanisms. Those who struggle actively with the desire to smoke—by talking to themselves, by calling up thoughts of emphysema and lung cancer, by substituting exercise or gum chewing—are most likely to conquer it (Bliss, Garvey, Heinold, et al., 1989). Another psychological factor that may affect nicotine dependence is depression. One study found that more than 50 percent of smokers who made repeated unsuccessful attempts to quit met the diagnostic criteria for major depressive disorder (Glassman, 1993). This is one reason antidepressants are now being tried as a smoking-cessation aid.

In an effort to study the relapse process more closely, Shiffman and his colleagues developed little computers that could be connected to the palm of the hand so that people who had quit smoking could record their temptations and the results on the spot (Shiffman, Paty, Gnys, et al., 1996). Using this methodology, the researchers discovered a number of predictors of the ability to resist temptation. We have already discussed one: cognitive coping strategies. People who struggle with themselves mentally are more likely to win. Another factor that influences the likelihood of relapse is mood. Bad moods weaken resistance. But the most powerful predictor of relapse is the environment—whether the person is in a place where cigarettes are available, where smoking is allowed, and where there are other people smoking. Thus, those who manage to quit don't seem to be different types from those who fail. They are simply the ones who are exposed to more high-risk situations.

Other studies, too, have pointed to the power of the environment. Cigarettes are one of the most heavily advertised consumer products on the market. In 1996, tobacco companies paid New York advertising agencies $500 million to promote smoking in the United States alone. Often their ads are targeted at the groups that are the most likely to smoke and the least likely to quit—women, African Americans, Latinos, young people, and the international market (Barry, 1991). Although it is difficult to prove cause and effect, the data suggest that advertising pays off. For example, smoking rates have declined more sharply for men than for women—not because fewer women quit smoking but because more teenage girls and young women have taken up the habit (Firoe, Novotny, Pierce, et al., 1989). The fact that women are less likely than men to participate in sports, more likely than men to want to lose weight, and more inclined to view cigarettes as relaxing all contribute to this trend (Waldron, Lye, & Brandon, 1991). Tobacco companies capitalize on "femininity" by featuring sexy young women in their ads and naming their cigarettes "thins," "lights," and "slims." But advertising also can be used to "sell" quitting. Smoking rates dropped twice as fast in California as in the nation as a whole after that state launched a media antismoking campaign (Cowley, 1992b).

The smoker's immediate environment also has an impact. People whose spouses and friends smoke are more likely to relapse than people who travel in smoke-free circles (Morgan, Ashenberg, & Fisher, 1988). Would-be quitters benefit more from spouses who exhibit positive behaviors such as compliments and praise rather than negative behaviors such as nagging (Cohen & Lichtenstein, 1990). The good news is that about 45 percent of smokers are eventually able to stop permanently (American Psychiatric Association 2000), but they often try multiple times before they succeed.

Other Psychoactive Drugs

For the person in search of a potent psychoactive drug other than alcohol, a wide variety of drugs—depressants, stimulants, hallucinogens—can be equally destructive if they are used habitually. Most of these drugs are nothing new. Opium has been easing people's pain for almost 9,000 years. And until recently many of these drugs were sold legally, over the counter, in the United States. In the nineteenth century, countless self-respecting women thought nothing of taking laudanum, a form of opium, to help them sleep. During the Civil War, morphine was commonly administered as a cure for dysentery and other ailments, with the result that many soldiers returned from the war as morphine addicts. One hundred years ago, the major ingredient in the best-selling cough syrups was a recently discovered miracle drug called heroin.

Eventually, however, controls began to be imposed. In 1914, Congress passed the Harrison Act, making the nonmedical use of the opiates illegal. Marijuana was made illegal in some states in 1937, and other states followed. Most of the drugs that we will discuss in the

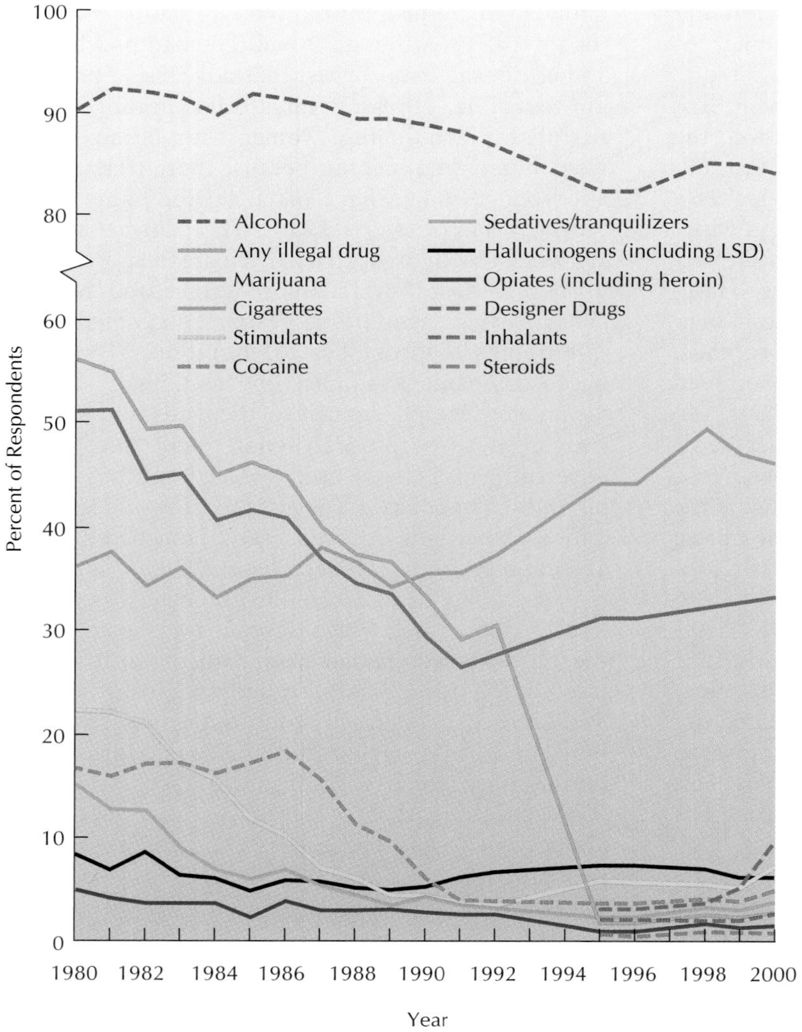

FIGURE 12.3 Trends in drug use among college students. Drug use declined during the 1980s but began to rise again around 1990. In contrast, alcohol and cigarette use remained fairly constant throughout this period.

remainder of this chapter cannot be legally purchased for recreational purposes. They must be obtained either from a doctor or from illegal sources. Many people do obtain them, however. Figure 12.3 illustrates trends in drug use among college students. Prevalence rates for most drugs declined during the 1980s but began to increase again starting around 1990. In contrast, the use of legal drugs (alcohol and cigarettes) has remained fairly constant throughout this period.

Depressants

As we have seen in the case of alcohol, a **depressant** is a drug that acts on the central nervous system to reduce pain, tension, and anxiety; to relax and disinhibit; and to slow intellectual and motor reactivity. Along with alcohol, the major depressants are opiates, sedatives, and tranquilizers. All have a number of important effects in common: Tolerance develops; withdrawal symptoms occur; and high dosages depress the functioning of vital systems, such as respiration, and thus may result in death.

Opiates The **opiates** are drugs that induce relaxation and reverie and provide relief from anxiety and pain. Included in this group are opium, the derivatives of opium, and chemically synthesized drugs that imitate certain effects of opium.

The grandfather of the opiates is **opium,** a chemically active substance derived from the opium poppy. Early in the nineteenth century, scientists succeeded in isolating one of the most powerful ingredients in opium. This new opiate, which they called **morphine** (after the Greek god of dreams, Morpheus), was soon widely used as an *analgesic,* or pain reliever. As the years passed, however, it became clear that morphine was dangerously addictive. Thus, scientists went back to work, trying to find a pain reliever that would not cause addiction. In 1875, this research culminated in the discovery, by Heinrich Dreser (who also discovered aspirin), that a minor chemical change could transform morphine into a new miracle drug, **heroin,** much stronger than morphine and presumably nonaddictive—an assumption that turned out to be cruelly mistaken.

The final entry in our list of opiates is **methadone,** a synthetic chemical developed by the Germans during World War II, when they were cut off from their opium supply. Methadone differs from other opiates in 3 important ways. First, it is effective when taken orally, so injection is not necessary. Second, it is longer-acting. Heroin, for example, takes effect immediately and is active for only 2 to 6 hours. Methadone, by contrast, takes effect slowly—likewise, its effects taper off slowly—and it is active for 24 to 36 hours. Third, because of its slow onset and offset, methadone satisfies the craving for opiates without producing an equivalent euphoria, or high. For this reason, it is now used as a replacement drug in the treatment of heroin addicts.

Our discussion will focus on heroin, which is the most widely abused opiate in the United States. Through the early 1970s, heroin use increased each year. In 1972–1973, there were 500,000 to 600,000 opiate abusers in the United States, most of them on heroin. Since then, the percentage of heroin users in the country seems to have remained constant.

Heroin is normally taken by injection, either directly beneath the skin (skin-popping) or into a vein (mainlining). The immediate positive effects of mainlining heroin are twofold. First is the rush, lasting 5 to 15 minutes. As one addict described it, "Imagine that every cell in your body has a tongue and they are all licking honey" (Ray, 1983). The second effect is a simple state of satisfaction, euphoria, and well-being, in which all positive drives seem to be gratified and all negative feelings—guilt, tension, anxiety—disappear completely. As noted, this artificial paradise lasts only 2 to 6 hours, after which the heroin addict needs another injection.

Such are the positive effects. The negative effects are even more impressive. In the first place, not all people have the "honey-licking" experience. All users respond initially with nausea, and for some, this response outweighs the euphoric effects. Second, if heroin use becomes regular, both withdrawal symptoms and tolerance develop. As with alcohol and nicotine, people dependent on heroin must continue dosing themselves in order to avoid withdrawal symptoms, and as in alcoholism, this eventually requires larger and more frequent doses.

Third, should withdrawal take place, it can be a terrible experience. Withdrawal symptoms begin about 4 to 6 hours after the injection and vary in intensity according to the dosage regularly used. The first sign of withdrawal is anxiety. Then comes a period of physical wretchedness, something like a bad case of flu, which lasts 1 to 5 days. The symptoms generally include watering eyes, a runny nose, yawning, hot and cold flashes, tingling sensations, increased respiration and heart rate, profuse sweating, diarrhea and vomiting, headache, stomach cramps, aches and pains in other parts of the body, and possibly delirium and hallucinations as well—all this combined with an intense craving for the drug. In hospital settings, however, withdrawal symptoms are far less dramatic, for they are relieved by other drugs.

Most people believe that repeated exposure to opiates automatically leads to long-term addiction. An alternative view is that drug use represents a means of

Heroin is highly addictive, but addiction to it may depend on the person's situation. Most soldiers who abused the drug in Vietnam gave it up once that extremely stressful experience was behind them.

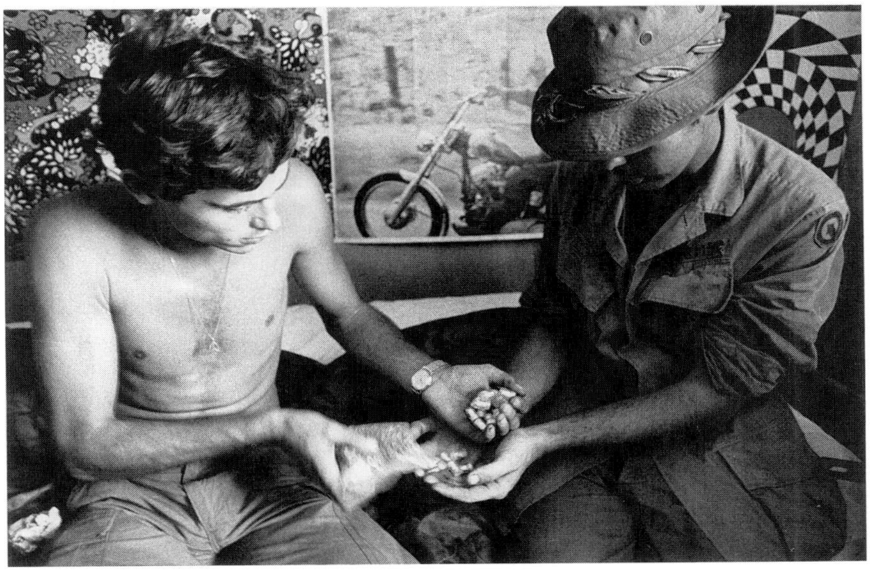

adapting to major stresses in one's life; if these stresses are temporary, the addiction is also likely to be (Alexander & Hadaway, 1982). For instance, many soldiers became dependent on heroin while serving in Vietnam, but few of them continued the habit once they returned home (Bourne, 1974). Similarly, most people who are given opiates in the hospital do not become addicted after they have left the hospital (Melzack, 1988; San Jose, van Oers, van de Mheen, et al., 2000).

Barbiturates The **barbiturates**, including Nembutal (pentobarbital) and Seconal (secobarbital), are a group of powerful *sedative,* or calming, drugs whose major effects are to alleviate tension and bring about relaxation and sleep. These drugs are legally prescribed by some physicians as sleeping pills. They are sold illegally on the street as "downers" to provide an alcohol-like experience without the alcohol taste, breath, or expense.

An alarming fact about barbiturates is the dramatic and rapid increase in tolerance associated with their use. In addicts, this quick increase in tolerance can mean that they are ingesting 100 times the dose that would kill a person who does not use the drugs. This rapid development of tolerance increases the harmful physical effects of the drug and mortality risks associated with barbiturate withdrawal (Schuckit, 1995).

Barbiturates have long been the drug of choice for suicide attempts. An overdose first induces sleep and then stops respiration. Furthermore, the overdose need not be made up solely of barbiturates. Both barbiturates and alcohol are depressants, so their combined impact is multiplied over the sum of their separate effects in what is called a **synergistic effect.** If a barbiturate is taken with alcohol, the effect is 4 times as great as that of either of the drugs taken alone (Combs, Hales, & Williams, 1980). The person who combines the two drugs runs the risk, intentionally or unintentionally, of becoming a suicide-overdose statistic. This was the cause of the well-publicized deaths of Judy Garland and Marilyn Monroe. Today, partly because of their danger, barbiturates are less widely prescribed, but, as noted, they are still sold illegally and continue to be implicated in many suicides.

The use of barbiturates by the young is generally recreational and sporadic. Among older people, barbiturate use typically begins as a way of relieving insomnia. As we shall see, however, barbiturates, along with other depressants, tend over time to aggravate rather than relieve sleeping problems. Thus, the person takes more and more of the drug and eventually becomes addicted.

In their effects, which generally last from 3 to 6 hours, barbiturates are similar to alcohol. Like alcohol, they disinhibit, induce relaxation and mild euphoria, and impair judgment, speech, and motor coordination. Like alcohol-dependent people, some barbiturate addicts exhibit an unsteady gait, slurred speech, diminished intellectual functioning, and confusion, but mostly do so when they are intoxicated with barbiturates. Again like alcohol, the barbiturates, though they are technically depressants, often have a stimulating effect, especially if they are taken with the expectation of having fun rather than of getting sleep (Wesson & Smith, 1971). Indeed, one of the major concerns of those who study barbiturates is the relationship between aggression and Seconal, a favored barbiturate of the young. For most people, however, the stimulating effect is only an early phase of barbiturate intoxication and wears off within a half hour. A final area of similarity between barbiturates and alcohol is withdrawal. Withdrawal from barbiturate addiction is much more unpleasant and dangerous than withdrawal from alcohol dependence. Without medical supervision, either can result in death.

Tranquilizers and Nonbarbiturate Sedatives Within the past decade, the dangers associated with barbiturates have led to their widespread replacement, as a prescription sleeping medication, by such nonbarbiturate sedatives as Dalmane and Halcion. At the same time, **tranquilizers** such as Tranxene (chlorazepate) and Valium (diazepam), which have long been used in the treatment of anxiety disorders and stress-related physical disorders, are also prescribed for insomnia.

All these drugs have essentially the same problems as the barbiturates. They are habit-forming and they have serious side effects, including drowsiness, breathing difficulties, and impaired motor and intellectual functioning. The elderly are particularly vulnerable to the dangers of tranquilizers and nonbarbiturate sedatives, for they are more likely to have disorders the drugs can aggravate—respiratory disorders and kidney and liver ailments (Institute of Medicine, 1991). Taken in high doses over a long period, these drugs can also create symptoms very close to those of major depression. Finally, like barbiturates, tranquilizers and nonbarbiturate sedatives have a synergistic effect in combination with other depressants, though the risk of accidental suicide is not as great.

As with barbiturates, dependence on nonbarbiturate sedatives often begins with a sleeping problem. The person takes the drug and initially obtains some relief. After about 2 weeks of continuous use, however, tolerance develops, and the usual dose no longer produces a good night's sleep. However, at this point many people go on taking the drug. First, by this time their difficulties in sleeping may not only have returned but may also be worse than before. Prolonged drug use often creates what is called *drug-induced insomnia,* a pattern of fitful and disrupted slumber, without any deep sleep. Faced with this new problem, many users reason that, if they needed pills before in order to sleep, now they really need them. Second, these drugs suppress rapid eye movement (REM) sleep, the stage of sleep in which dreams occur. If, following a week or more of drug-induced sleep, users try to sleep without the medication, they are likely to experience a REM rebound—a night of restless dreaming, nightmares, and extremely fitful sleep—after which they may go back to the drug simply to avoid a repetition of such a miserable night. (Dalmane is the only one of these drugs that suppresses REM sleep but does not produce a REM rebound, because it stays in the bloodstream for more than 24 hours. As a result of its prolonged effect, however, it produces daytime hangover and sedation effects.)

Thus, although the drug soon loses its effectiveness against the original sleeping problem, the usual solution is not to abandon the drug but to take more of it. Once the person increases the dose to about 2 to 3 times the normal sleep-inducing dose, addiction begins to develop. From that point on, the drug becomes a way of life.

Tranquilizers, of course, are taken not just for insomnia but for generalized anxiety (Chapter 7)—anxiety that is often the result of high-pressure jobs and an overstressful environment. Possibly for this reason, minor tranquilizers are among the most commonly prescribed drugs in this country, with more than 70 percent of the prescriptions written not by psychiatrists but by family doctors (Clinthorne, Cisin, Balter, et al., 1986). While many people who take tranquilizers develop no problems, they may suffer side effects and many do become dependent.

Stimulants

The **stimulants** are a class of drugs whose major effect, as the name indicates, is to provide energy, alertness, and feelings of confidence. We have already discussed one widely used stimulant, nicotine. Another is the caffeine that we take in with our coffee, tea, and cola drinks. Far more powerful are the amphetamines, which can be obtained only by prescription or "on the street," and cocaine, which must be bought illegally.

Amphetamines The **amphetamines** are a group of highly addictive synthetic stimulants—the most common are Benzedrine (amphetamine), Dexedrine (dextroamphetamine), and Methedrine (methamphetamine)—which reduce feelings of boredom or weariness. Suddenly users find themselves alert, confident, full of energy, and generally ready to take on the world. The amphetamines depress appetite—hence their use by people with weight problems. When taken in small doses for brief periods, they improve motor coordination—hence their use by professional athletes. And they inhibit sleepiness—hence their use by college students preparing for exams. Contrary to campus wisdom, however, they do not improve complex intellectual functioning (Tinklenberg, 1971). The amphetamine user may experience a number of physical effects, including elevated blood pressure, racing heartbeat, fever, headache, tremor, and nausea. Psychologically, the user may feel restless, irritable, hostile, confused, anxious, or, briefly euphoric (Kaplan & Sadock, 1991).

According to the 2000 National Household Survey on Drug Abuse, an estimated 8.8 million people (4 percent of the population) have tried methamphetamines (National Institute on Drug Abuse, 2000). As long as they are taken irregularly and in low doses, amphetamines do not appear to pose any behavioral or psychological problems. As with most other psychoactive drugs, the problems arise from high doses and habitual use. Once use becomes habitual, tolerance develops, and higher doses become necessary. At the far end of the amphetamine-abuse spectrum are the "speed freaks," people who inject liquid amphetamine into their veins for periods of 3 to 4 days, during which they neither eat nor sleep but remain intensely active and euphoric to the point of mania. This heightened activity level can easily lead to paranoid and violent behavior.

Amphetamines are clearly neurotoxic. Indeed, amphetamine abuse causes more damage to the brain than heroin, cocaine, or alcohol abuse (Volkow, Chang, Wang et al., 2001). Negative changes are evident even 1 year after quitting the drug, in impaired functioning on motor tasks and in cognitive tasks of attention and memory. Over time, the abuse of amphetamines inhibits the production of dopamine; with extended abuse, the body is left chronically low in dopamine. Amphetamines also appear to produce changes (e.g., pressure on cerebral spinal fluid) that reflect brain inflammation, and these are greater than those seen for heroin, alcohol, or cocaine. According to Volkow and her colleagues, these changes put users at risk for neurodegenerative diseases such as Parkinson's, a movement disorder that is caused by a loss of dopamine in the brain (Volkow, Chang, Wang, et al., 2001).

Of special importance to the student of abnormal psychology is the resemblance between the effects of amphetamine abuse and the symptoms of paranoid schizophrenia (Chapter 14). Under the influence of heavy doses of amphetamines, people may express the same delusions of persecution seen in the person with paranoid schizophrenia (Bell, 1973; Snyder, 1979). This amphetamine psychosis, the closest artificially induced counterpart to a "natural" psychosis, appears to be unrelated to any personality predispositions and is thus assumed to be the direct result of the drug. Accordingly, research is now in progress with both animals and human beings to determine whether paranoid schizophrenia may be caused by the same chemical changes that amphetamines induce in the brain.

Cocaine Unlike the synthetic amphetamines, **cocaine** is a natural stimulant; it is the active ingredient in the coca plant. An "in" drug in the 1920s, cocaine again became very fashionable in the 1970s. Its popularity peaked in the mid-1980s at 5.8 million users and then declined to 1.3 million users in the United States by 1995 (preliminary estimates, National Institute on Drug Abuse, 1997). In its classic form, cocaine is sold as a powder, which may be injected but is usually snorted—that is, inhaled into the nostrils, where it is absorbed into the bloodstream through the mucous membranes. The rush produced by a snort of cocaine takes effect in about 8 minutes and lasts about 20 minutes. A more elaborate procedure is freebasing, in which the powder is heated with ether or some other agent—a process that "frees" its base, or active ingredients—and is then smoked. This method carries the psychoactive ingredients to the brain more quickly and thereby delivers a more rapid high than snorting or even injection.

Until recently, cocaine was quite expensive; consequently, its regular users tended to be middle- and upper-class white-collar workers and executives. (It was also favored by entertainment celebrities, whose glamour attached itself to the drug.) But, with the development of the variant form called **crack cocaine,** this drug is now within the buying power of people on weekly allowances. Crack is a form of freebased cocaine that is sold in small chunks, or "rocks," which are smoked in a pipe. Because it is freebased, crack is exceptionally powerful, producing in seconds an intense rush (stronger than that of regular cocaine), which wears off within 20 minutes.

Cocaine intoxication is characterized by excitement, intense euphoria, impaired judgment, irritability, agitation, and impulsive sexual behavior. Physically, the user's blood pressure and heart rate increase. If a high dose is taken, seizures and cardiac arrest may result. Some people develop transient periods of paranoia from cocaine use, and those who do may be at higher risk of developing psychosis in the future (Satel & Edell, 1991).

As with amphetamines, tolerance develops with regular use of cocaine, and prolonged heavy use is followed by severe withdrawal symptoms. In a study of 14 binge users, Gawin and Kleber (1986) charted the withdrawal symptoms in 3 distinct phases (Figure 12.4). The first phase, known to cocaine users as the crash, begins horribly. Within a half hour of the final cocaine dose, the person experiences a mounting depression and agitation combined with an intense crav-

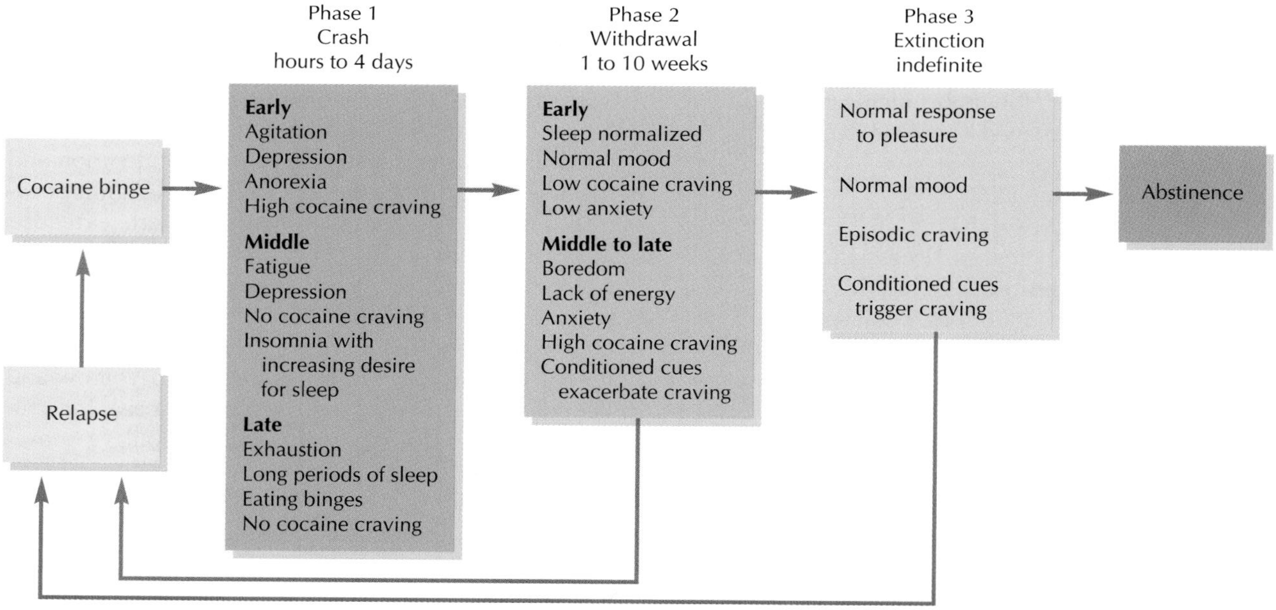

FIGURE 12.4 The three phases of cocaine withdrawal. As the symptom lists show, the craving for cocaine disappears in phase 1, only to reappear in phase 2 and then dissipate very gradually. The arrows at the bottom indicate the likelihood of relapse: strong in phase 2, moderate in phase 3. (Gawin & Kleber, 1986)

ing for the drug. These feelings then change to fatigue and an overwhelming sleepiness, which last several days. In the second, or withdrawal phase, the person returns to deceptively normal functioning, which then gives way to a fluctuating state of boredom and listlessness, mixed with anxiety. At this point, strong cocaine cravings return, and the person may begin another binge. If not, the withdrawal phase passes in 1 to 10 weeks. It is followed by phase 3, extinction, in which the person regains normal functioning, though with occasional cocaine cravings, usually in response to some conditioned stimulus, such as seeing old cocaine-using friends. Such episodic cravings may recur indefinitely.

Hallucinogens

The **hallucinogens** are a class of drugs that act on the central nervous system in such a way as to cause distortions in sensory perception—hence their name, which means "hallucination producers." Unlike stimulants, which increase arousal, or depressants, which reduce it, hallucinogens achieve their effect without substantial changes in level of arousal. Tolerance develops rapidly to most hallucinogens, but there is no evidence that they are physiologically addictive. More than 1 in 10 people in the United States have tried some form of hallucinogen at some time in their lives (APA, 2000). There are many hallucinogens, including mescaline, psilocybin, PCP, and, best known of all, LSD. Despite this variety, rarely can any hallucinogen other than LSD or PCP be bought on the street. However, on the Internet, potential users can learn in rich detail how to obtain and use numerous drugs with unknown hazards (Halpern & Farrison, 2001). Some Internet sites describe how to cultivate and harvest cactus plants that contain mescaline and other plants that contain lysergic acid, reminding readers that cultivating such plants is legal so long as no steps are taken to ingest the drugs.

LSD Albert Hoffman, a Swiss chemist, first synthesized **LSD (lysergic acid diethylamide)** in 1938. Five years later, after working one morning with this new chemical, he had an interesting experience:

> Last Friday . . . I was forced to stop my work in the laboratory . . . and to go home, as I was seized by a peculiar restlessness associated with the sensation of mild dizziness. On arriving home, I lay down and sank into a kind of drunkenness which was not unpleasant and which was characterized by extreme activity of imagination. As I lay in a dazed condition with my eyes closed (I experienced daylight as disagreeably bright) there surged upon me an uninterrupted stream of fantastic images of extraordinary plasticity and vividness and accompanied by an intense, kaleidoscope-like play of colours. This condition gradually passed off after about two hours. (Hoffman, 1971, p. 23)

Hoffman guessed that this experience might have been due to his having ingested some of the new chemical on which he was working, so he purposely swallowed a small amount of LSD and found that he had guessed correctly.

LSD and the other hallucinogens seem to work by interfering with the processing of information in the nervous system. That is their attraction and their danger. They can produce a kaleidoscope of colors and images. They can give the user a new way of seeing things. For example, they can produce changes in body image and alterations in time and space perception (Kaplan & Sadock, 1991). And they may open up new states of awareness, allowing the user to find out things about the self that were never imagined before. These are potentially attractive benefits. The problem arises with people who are unable to process or accept the new kinds of perceptions induced by hallucinogens. The person whose grasp on reality is not firm, who derives great support from the stability of the surrounding world, or who has emotional problems may suffer negative effects, possibly for years, from any of the hallucinogens.

Artist Ralph Steadman produced this image to represent what it feels like to take LSD, an experience he says he had only once.

The hallucinogens are most harmful when they produce a "bad trip," in which the user becomes terrified and disorganized in response to distorted perceptions. Such an experience is not quickly forgotten. For some people, the drug-induced disruption of their relationship with reality is so severe that they require long-term therapeutic assistance (Frosch, Robbins, & Stern, 1965). Also, a small percentage of regular LSD users suffer flashbacks—spontaneous recurrences, when not under the drug, of hallucinations and perceptual distortions that occurred under the drug—a phenomenon that may disrupt their functioning. Flashbacks and other disruptions of visual processing can recur for as long as 8 years after LSD use (Abraham, 1983; Abraham & Wolf, 1988). They are more likely to occur when the former LSD user is under stress, fatigued, or ill (Kaplan & Sadock, 1991).

PCP and "MDMA" **PCP (phencyclidine),** or angel dust, is a hallucinogen that surfaced in the 1970s and was widely used because it was cheap, easily available, and often mixed with (or misrepresented as) other substances. The drug soon acquired a bad reputation. For one thing, overdoses were common and extremely toxic. In one large mental health facility in Washington, DC, PCP poisoning accounted for one third of inpatient admissions between 1974 and 1977, outstripping even alcoholism (Luisada, 1977). A more serious risk was PCP's behavioral toxicity, the tendency of users to harm themselves—through burns, falls, drowning, automobile accidents—and to endanger others as a result of the paranoia and perceptual distortions produced by the drug. These problems discouraged many users, and PCP consumption has declined steadily since the late 1970s. In its place has come **MDMA,** more commonly known as Ecstasy. In the past two decades the use of Ecstasy has surged, especially at late-night dance clubs (Klitzman, Pope, & Hudson, 2000). Ecstasy has a strong association with high-risk sexual behaviors (Klitzman, Pope, & Hudson, 2000), possibly because users tend to be sensation seekers or because their judgment is impaired by the use of the drug. Regular Ecstasy users are also more likely to suffer mental health problems such as paranoia, panic attacks, and depression; prolonged use can result in long-term impairment in memory (Fox, McLean, Turner, et al., 2002; Kopelman, Reed, Marsden, et al., 2001).

Marijuana and Hashish

Marijuana and **hashish** are often classified as hallucinogens, yet they deserve separate treatment. In the first place, their effects are considerably milder than those of the hallucinogens previously described. For this reason, they are often referred to as "minor hallucinogens," while LSD, PCP, mescaline, and the others are called "major hallucinogens." Second, they are the only drugs classified both as hallucinogens and sedatives/depressives, as they have a depressant effect on the nervous system. Third, although the major hallucinogens may be widely used, the use of marijuana and hashish is far more common. More than 1 of every 2 Americans between the ages of 18 and 25 has tried marijuana (National Institute on Drug Abuse, 1989), and many, having tried it, have become frequent users. Marijuana use among the young increased dramatically in the 1970s, peaked in 1979 and 1980, and has been declining slowly since then, though it is still America's most popular illegal drug (U.S. Department of Health & Human Services, 1997). (Figure 12.5 shows the percentages of eighth, tenth, and twelfth graders who tried marijuana.)

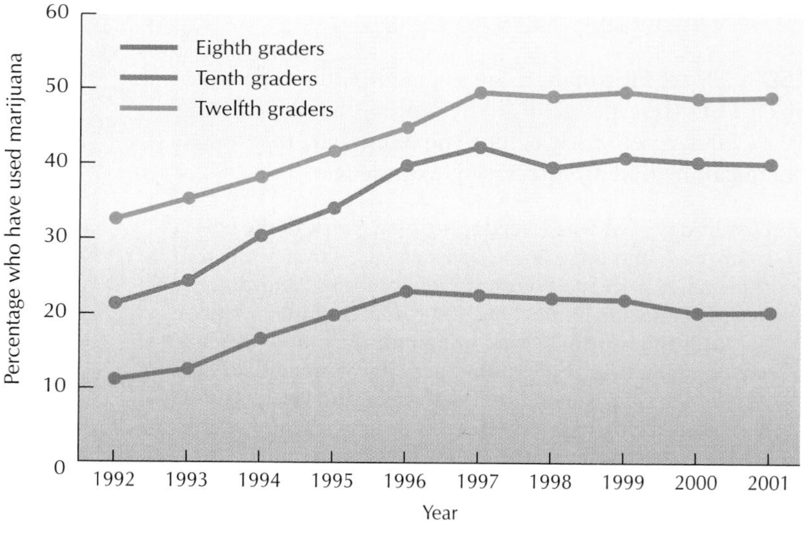

FIGURE 12.5 Marijuana is the most widely used illegal drug among students in the eighth, tenth, and twelfth grades. Note that although marijuana use increased steadily in the 1990s, by the end of the decade it stabilized. (National Institute on Drug Abuse)

Marijuana and hashish are both derived from cannabis, a hemp plant that grows, cultivated and wild, in many countries, including the United States. Marijuana consists of the dried and crushed leaves of cannabis. Though it is usually rolled into a cigarette, or "joint," and smoked, it can also be eaten. Hashish, derived from the resin rather than the leaves of cannabis, is five or six times stronger than marijuana. Like marijuana, it can be eaten, but it is usually smoked in a specially designed pipe.

In both forms, the active ingredient is the same: THC (delta 9, tetrahydrocannabinol), which most researchers agree is not physiologically addictive. THC has 2 consistent physiological effects. The first is an accelerated heart rate. As the dose increases, so does the heart rate, which may go up to 140 to 150 beats per minute. The second change is a reddening of the whites of the eyes. Both effects disappear as the drug wears off.

The behavioral effects of marijuana have been studied in a variety of situations. The impact of a mild marijuana high on simple behaviors is either nil or minimal. The person can easily turn on the television, dial a phone number, make a pot of coffee, and so forth. However, as the complexity of the task increases, as speed of response becomes more important, and as a more accurate sense of time and distance is required, the impairment of ability from a single-joint marijuana high becomes more apparent. It has been clearly established that driving under the influence of marijuana is dangerous (Liguori & Gatto, 1998).

The major reason for using marijuana and hashish is the psychological effects, which have been summarized by Tinklenberg (1974):

> Initial effects of cannabis at low doses usually include euphoria, heightening of subjective sensory experiences, alterations in time sense, and the induction of a relaxed, laissez-faire passivity. With moderate doses, these effects are intensified with impaired immediate memory function, disturbed thought patterns, lapses of attention, and a subjective feeling of unfamiliarity. (p. 4)

It should be noted that the latter group of reactions is generally not at all disturbing. The individual simply feels "spaced out"—a not unpleasant experience for most people under relaxed conditions. Many marijuana users report being totally absorbed in their drug experience while it is happening. During these episodes of total involvement, the person's perceptual, imaginative, and cognitive resources are completely engaged (Fabian & Fishkin, 1981).

There is also a negative side to marijuana: It can heighten unpleasant experiences. The drug may intensify an already frightened or depressed mood until the person experiences acute anxiety. This is most likely to happen to an inexperienced user who takes a large dose and is unprepared for its effect (Grinspoon, 1977). At high levels of THC intake, the effects and the dangers are similar to those of LSD. Some people experience sensory distortions, depersonalization, and changes in body image—all of which can result in a panic reaction and a fear of "going crazy." At this point, intervention by a professional or a trained lay therapist becomes necessary, and short-term psychotherapy may eventually be required. These severe reactions to the use of THC are the exception, however, not the rule, and they generally occur only at the higher dose levels.

Is Marijuana Dangerous? Much less clear than the short-term effects of high doses of THC use are the long-term effects of low doses. Can regular use of marijuana or hashish cause psychological or physiological damage? This question has polarized scientists (Grinspoon & Bakalar, 1997), who see four areas of specific concern.

Although marijuana is considered a "minor hallucinogen," the long-term effects of prolonged, heavy use of THC are potentially hazardous, especially to a smoker's respiratory system.

The first has to do with the effect of prolonged heavy marijuana use on blood levels of the male sex hormone, testosterone. There seems to be general agreement that regular marijuana use (about nine joints a week) for 6 or more months results in a reduction of the testosterone level in the blood (Grinspoon & Bakalar, 1997). The degree of testosterone reduction is directly related to the amount of marijuana smoked. But even the 40 percent reduction in testosterone reported in the original study of this problem (Kolodny, Masters, Kolodner, et al., 1974) does not seem to be enough to impair significantly the sexual activity of males with established patterns of sexual activity. Nevertheless, variations in sex-hormone level have a greater impact on the sexual activity of men who have not yet stabilized their patterns of sexual behavior. Therefore, it is possible, though it has not been proved, that heavy, chronic marijuana use by young, sexually inactive men could result in impaired sexual functioning.

The second question is whether marijuana use suppresses immune reactions, the body's mechanisms for fighting off the invasion of foreign substances such as germs. The evidence is fairly solid that chronic marijuana smoking does impair the functioning of one part of the immune system (Cohen, 1986; Nahas, Suten, Harvey, et al., 1999). However, this impairment has yet to show any recognizable clinical effect. Therefore, as with the testosterone problem, the significance of the immune response effect is unclear.

A third concern is the effect of marijuana smoke on the lungs. Because marijuana smoke contains about 50 percent more carcinogenic hydrocarbon than does tobacco smoke and because laboratory exposure of human lung cells to marijuana smoke produces changes that are characteristic of early cancer, researchers are concerned that heavy, prolonged marijuana use could lead to lung cancer and other respiratory problems (Ray & Ksir, 1993).

A fourth problem centers on the psychological effect of chronic marijuana use. Some professionals feel strongly that prolonged use of marijuana eventually results in impaired judgment, diminished memory, negative moods, apathy, and—as with the more potent drugs—a focusing of one's existence on the drug experience. Related to this thinking is the argument that those who begin by smoking marijuana will go on to more dangerous drugs, such as heroin. Although a comparison of the figures on frequency of marijuana use and narcotics shows that very few marijuana smokers make the transition to narcotics, some research exists to support the claim that marijuana use leads to the use of hallucinogens. Wilcox, Wagner, and Anthony (2002) studied teenage marijuana smokers and reported that by age 21, almost half of them have been offered the chance to try a hallucinogen (LSD, mescaline, mixed stimulant-hallucinogens, or PCP), compared to just 1 in 16 teenagers who have never smoked marijuana. And, within a year after being offered the chance, two thirds of the marijuana smokers do try a hallucinogen, compared to just 1 in 6 of the teenagers who have never smoked marijuana (Wilcox, Wagner, & Anthony, 2002). As for general deficits that may result from prolonged use, the first study of long-term use among Americans found no cognitive effects after more than 7 years of extremely heavy use (Schaeffer, Andrysiak, & Ungerleider, 1981). Intellectual functioning among these 10 adults was above average and virtually identical with that shown in tests they had taken 15 to 20 years previously. There *is* evidence that *amotivational syndrome*—apathy, loss of ambition, difficulty in concentrating—does exist among marijuana smokers, but there is some indication that it may be primarily an accentuation of preexisting behavior patterns (Maugh, 1982). Finally, some research suggests that marijuana can induce psychosis and exacerbate schizophrenia, at least among individuals who are predisposed to that disorder (Boutros & Bowers, 1996; Hollister, 1998), although rigorous studies are sparse.

In sum, the issues are clear, but the answers are not. Testosterone levels go down, but sexual activity may not. One immune response is suppressed, but there is no observable effect. The personality may be affected, but the evidence is incomplete. The only thing that we know for sure about long-term marijuana smoking is that it increases the likelihood of respiratory ailments.

Marijuana as a Medical Treatment There is compelling evidence that marijuana is useful in treating certain medical disorders (Voth & Schwartz, 1997). Particularly in cancer patients undergoing chemotherapy, it seems to decrease nausea and increase appetite, thus speeding recovery as well as relieving suffering. It has also been reported to help glaucoma and AIDS patients. As a result, ballot initiatives in some states have made marijuana available by medical prescription for certain disorders. The public seems to be in favor of allowing physicians to weigh the potential risks and benefits and to advise their patients accordingly. However, some government officials are concerned that the medical use of marijuana is merely a first step toward the eventual legalization of all drugs. Testifying before Congress in June 1999, a spokesman for the Drug Enforcement Administration in the U.S. Department of Justice expressed a fear that medical use of marijuana will encourage young people to perceive

Anabolic steroids have stalked the fringe of sports for 40 years, mostly in the shadows, illuminated for seconds by the sudden spotlight of breaking news:

- Chinese female swimmers test positive in 1994.
- NFL guard attempts suicide after flunking drug test in 1991.
- Canadian sprinter Ben Johnson is stripped of Olympic medal and world record in 1988.
- American baseball player Mark McGwire admits to using an over-the-counter steroid to help build up his muscles during the 1998 season, in which he broke baseball's home run record.

Time moves on, and as once-celebrated names disappear from the media, steroids move back into the shadows, where as many as a million Americans take them every day, swallowing them and injecting them into their muscles. The majority of users are not elite athletes; they have moved on to more sophisticated drugs, harder to detect. The new converts to anabolic steroids are construction workers, cops, and lawyers, adding muscle to look good, and teenagers, bulking up to earn a spot on the team. Adolescent steroid users are most likely to be male, to participate in strength-related sports, and to use other drugs as well as steroids. Prevalence rates range from 4 to 12 percent for male adolescents and 0.5 to 2 percent for female adolescents (Bahrke, Yesalis, & Brower, 1998).

Vanity and glory were not the drugs' intent. Anabolic-androgenic steroids are a synthetic version of testosterone, the male hormone that occurs naturally in the body. Developed in the 1930s in Germany, they were used to help patients with wasting disorders to rebuild their bodies. Today their legitimate use is limited: They are prescribed primarily as androgens in treating men whose testes, through accident or disease, have lost the ability to produce testosterone.

Use of steroids by athletes was first confirmed when the success of Soviet weight lifters at the 1954 Vienna championships was traced to steroids. Within 10 years, they were widely used in all strength areas of sports.

The governing agencies of various sports first moved against steroids, mostly on the basis that they afforded an unfair advantage; they were banned in collegiate and Olympic competition in the mid-1970s. By 1991, Congress had declared steroids a controlled substance, making illicit use and trafficking federal offenses.

The drugs' value was widely accepted within sports. They added lean muscle mass to athletes in training and helped them work harder and require less recovery time. But their worth outside sports has been debated; many medical and government officials insisted that their impact was psychological. The debate hurt the establishment's credibility. Doctors and drug officials insisted that gains from steroids were limited, while Ben Johnson pumped up on steroids and ran the 100 at the Olympics in a time still unmatched 15 years later.

That credibility suffered even further with official claims of the drugs' risks. In women, certain effects of taking high levels of male hormone were predictable: acne, deepening voice, and proliferation of facial and body hair. Men may experience the paradoxical side effects of enlarged breasts and high-pitched voice. But doctors warned of heart attacks, strokes, and severe liver and kidney damage. While in varying degrees many of these were linked to steroid abuse, they were rare enough that few users knew anyone suffering serious side effects.

The problem has been that little solid research exists on the hazards of long-time, high-dose steroid use, and none is anticipated soon: No medical ethics board would risk a controlled study administering 100 times the therapeutic dose of steroids, the amount taken by many athletes.

While the best available knowledge contends that steroids are not killers, no one suggests they are safe. "You've got to look at the history of hormones and the ever-present possibility of delayed, adverse effects," says Gary Wadler, a trustee of the American College of Sports Medicine and clinical associate professor at Cornell University Medical College. "I have great concerns for what we're going to see 10 to 15 years down the road." Wadler draws comparisons with DES, a synthetic female hormone that had been used to stabilize pregnancies in women who had had repeated miscarriages; a generation later, their daughters showed increased rates of vaginal cancer. High-dose use of the corticosteroid cortisone put patients at risk for hip fractures 15 years later.

Other adverse effects of steroid abuse are reduction of HDL cholesterol (the beneficial kind) and increased total cholesterol, testicular shrinkage, decreased spermatogenesis, reduced testosterone production, benign and malignant liver tumors, liver chemistry abnormalities, alterations in tendons, and dependency syndrome, as well as the risk (from sharing needles) of AIDS and hepatitis. Among teenage users, premature closure of the growth plates in the long bones has been proved.

This last effect is particularly disturbing in light of the expansion of steroid use from elite athletes to teenagers. Boys using steroids to swell their muscles may also be stunting their growth. According to Charles Yesalis, professor of health policy and administration and sports science at Penn State University, "Between 250,000 and 500,000 adolescents in the country have used or are currently using steroids," and 38.3 percent of them began by age 15.

Add to all the other risks a wide range of possible behavioral changes, including increased sleeplessness, restlessness, and mood disturbances such as irritability, aggressiveness, euphoria or depression, and even thoughts of suicide (Porcerelli & Sandler, 1998; Rashid, 2000). "Maybe one person of 20 will be very susceptible to these side effects," says Harrison Pope (Pope & Katz, 1990), who has studied the effects of anabolic steroids. "In rare cases, people on steroids have become homicidal, committed murder." The phenomenon occurs just often enough that it has its own name, "roid rage." Its existence, according to Pope and his research partner, David L. Katz, means that these drugs pose "a greater-than-expected public health problem, both for users and for society at large."

marijuana use as harmless, when in fact, he said, it combines the worst risks of alcohol and tobacco: the intoxicating effects of alcohol and the long-term lung damage of tobacco. Nevertheless, Great Britain and Canada have recently liberalized their laws on possession of marijuana, and the question of liberalizing such possession is being put on the ballot in the United States in such states as Nevada. It is ironic that, while morphine, an addictive drug with a potential for lethal overdose, can be prescribed for medical patients, such patients are not allowed to use marijuana, whose only established risk is the possibility of respiratory illness after years of regular use.

❖ Groups at Risk for Abuse of Illegal Drugs

As we will discuss in the section on the sociocultural perspective, abuse and dependence on illegal substances are highly related to ethnicity, class, education level, gender, and socioeconomic status. African American and Latino men who are poor, relatively uneducated, and either under- or unemployed are at particularly high risk.

In addition to these sociocultural factors, medically ill patients, patients with coexisting mental disorders (such as adolescents with mood or anxiety disorders [Burke, Burke, & Rae, 1994]), and those afflicted with chronic pain are also at greater risk for drug abuse than others (Beeder & Millman, 1997; Novick, Haverkos, & Teller, 1997; Portenoy & Payne, 1997). Patients with both physical and mental illnesses often medicate themselves with illegal substances in order to heal their physical or psychic pain, whereas chronic pain patients often get hooked on the high more than the pain relief provided by controlled prescription painkillers.

The use of anabolic steroids continues to plague the sports world as athletes from the elite to the amateur take the drug to bulk up or boost their performance (see the box on page 339).

Substance Dependence: Theory and Therapy

In our discussions of alcohol and nicotine, we have already described a number of theories and treatments that pinpoint those drugs. But research findings strongly suggest that certain principles apply to substance dependence in general, regardless of the substance (McLellan, Alterman, Metzger, et al., 1994). Therefore, this section will focus on the overall problem of drug dependence.

The Psychodynamic Perspective

Current psychodynamic thinking about substance dependence stresses the *homeostatic* function of drugs—that is, their ability to restore equilibrium in the face of painful emotions (Brehm & Khantzian, 1997).

Drugs and Conflict For adolescents suffering anxiety over having to take on new, adult roles, drugs can ease adaptation in the short run, especially if an adolescent lacks good role models and adequate coping skills. The choice of drug depends in part on the defense the adolescent is trying to bolster. For those with low self-esteem, amphetamines can provide feelings of power. For those frightened by social interactions, heroin can ease social withdrawal.

Related to this interpretation is the idea of substance abuse as self-medication—for example, in the case of Vietnam veterans who abuse heroin or barbiturates. According to current psychodynamic thinking, the establishment of self-care—the ability to control and calm one's emotions—is a crucial task of early childhood, and it is dependent on adequate nurturing. If parents are cold and underprotective, the child will have no caring skills to internalize and thus will grow up susceptible to the artificial calming effects of drugs.

Oral Needs and Dependency Psychoanalytic theorists have also held that frustrated oral needs, perhaps the result of erratic breast-feeding in infancy, could produce a so-called oral fixation that manifests itself in addictive behaviors, such as drug abuse or overeating. More than 200 years ago, and more than a century before Freud developed his theory about the oral stage of development (see Chapter 5), British physician Thomas Trotter proposed that early weaning could elevate the risk of alcohol dependency later in life. Trotter's hypothesis disappeared from sight until recent research seemed to confirm his suggestion. Goodwin and colleagues conducted a 30-year high-risk follow-up study of the antecedents in alcoholism in 200 babies delivered at a Danish hospital (Goodwin, Gabrietti, Penick, et al., 1999). Of the 27 men who were diagnosed as alcohol-dependent at age 30, nearly half (48 percent) came from the group of babies who were weaned from the breast before the age of 3 weeks, while just 19 percent of the 173 non-alcohol-dependent men came from the early-weaning group (Goodwin, Gabrietti, Penick, et al., 1999).

Acquiring Self-Care Psychodynamic therapy for substance-dependent people aims at remedying self-care skills. For example, in a brief supportive-expressive therapy developed by Luborsky (1984), cocaine abusers are given psychodynamic interpretations to bring up the painful emotions that the drugs are suppressing; then they are given supportive suggestions to show them how to deal with those emotions. The goals are to build up patients' intrapsychic strength and to improve their relationships with the other people in their lives. Currently, this approach is being evaluated in comparison with several other treatment strategies (Crits-Christoph, Siqueland, Blaine, et al., 1997; Siqueland, Crits-Christoph, Gallop, et al., 2002)—a rare attempt to validate psychodynamic therapy for substance dependence. But psychodynamic treatment is not widely used in drug rehabilitation, partly because there have been so few efforts to demonstrate its effectiveness.

The Behavioral Perspective

Psychological and Biochemical Rewards Traditionally, behaviorists have viewed alcohol dependence as a powerful habit maintained by many antecedent cues and consequent reinforcers. Several suggestions have been offered as to what the primary reinforcer might be: social approval, ability to engage in relaxed social behavior, avoidance of physiological withdrawal symptoms, or reduction of psychological tension. For years, tension reduction was considered a prime suspect. According to this view, all of us have our share of troubles—anxiety, self-doubt, depression, guilt, annoyance. In the process of trying to reduce our psychological discomfort, some of us take a drink; and if this works, then alcohol use becomes associated with the alleviation of psychological pain and is likely to be repeated. Eventually, of course, excessive drinking may itself create further psychological distress, especially guilt, which in turn will be alleviated by more drinking. Thus, the vicious cycle begins. This theory has also been applied to drug dependence in general.

The tension-reduction hypothesis has received some support from animal research. In a classic study (Conger, 1951), laboratory rats were given an electric shock whenever they came near their food dishes. As a result, the rats showed hesitation, vacillation, and other signs of inner conflict when they approached their food, yet when they were injected with alcohol, they went up to their food dishes with no signs of conflict. Other animal studies, however, have not consistently supported the tension-reduction hypothesis.

Today, behavioral theories of alcohol dependence are generally based not so much on negative reinforcement, the reduction of unpleasant states, as on positive reinforcement, the creation of pleasant states. As we will see, neuroscience researchers have discovered that one of alcohol's effects on the central nervous system is to release the neurotransmitters dopamine and norepinephrine, together with endorphins, the body's natural opiates. In a combination of learning theory and biochemical theory typical of contemporary psychology, many behaviorists now believe that these chemical rewards are the prime reinforcers of excessive drinking, though tension reduction and other kinds of maladaptive coping are thought to be involved as well.

Learning Not to Abuse Drugs One major behavioral strategy for substance dependence relies on aversion conditioning: For example, alcohol is paired with an unpleasant stimulus, usually electric shock or induced nausea. One effective version of aversion conditioning involves pairing an emetic, a drug that makes a person feel nauseated and vomit, with the ingestion of the abused drug (Owen, 2001). Another strategy, known as covert sensitization, involves asking the patient to imagine nausea and vomiting in vivid detail as a result of taking the abused drug (Cautela, 2000).

The problem with these treatments is that, while they suppress the behavior, they do nothing to alter the conditions that elicit and maintain it. Whatever the rewards of excessive drinking, compensation for poor coping skills is probably involved as well. Under the influence of drugs, coping skills deteriorate further, while stresses (e.g., unemployment, marital conflict) increase. The object of most current behavioral programs is to remedy this broad adjustment problem, usually through a combination of cognitive and behavioral techniques. The alcoholism is still addressed directly. Patients are taught to identify cues and situations that lead to drug taking, and through role playing and practicing, they are taught alternative responses. But they are also taught new ways of dealing with life: how to solve problems and, by training in relaxation and social skills, how to cope with stress. Such programs have helped many people to stop abusing drugs, but they are not superior to other treatments (including other cognitive-behavioral treatments) that we will discuss shortly (Sobell, Toneatto, & Sobell, 1990).

In Chapter 4, we discussed dialectical behavior therapy (DBT), an approach to treating borderline personality disorder (Chapter 11) and suicidal behavior. DBT incorporates acceptance strategies adopted from Zen teachings with cognitive-behavioral strategies. DBT has proven to be a useful treatment for many difficult disorders, and there is evidence that it is also useful in treating drug dependence. Linehan and colleagues showed that

DBT led to a significant reduction in substance abuse in suicidal, drug-dependent women with borderline personality disorders (Linehan, Schmidt, Dimeff, et al., 1999).

We also mentioned in Chapter 4 the innovative work of Higgins and his colleagues in applying reinforcement theory to the treatment of cocaine abusers (Higgins, Delaney, Budney, et al., 1991; Higgins & Abbott, 2001). In the contingency management program these researchers set up, patients were given regular urine tests to determine whether they were cocaine-free. After each test that they passed, they received points worth 15 cents each. The points were then converted into vouchers that the patients could use to buy what they wanted in various neighborhood stores participating in the program. Each time they passed a test, the number of points increased. (Conversely, patients who failed the urine test not only got no points but, on their next test, dropped down to the original rate of points-per-test-passed and had to work their way back up again.) Meanwhile, for 3 months the patients also had weekly therapy in which they were given counseling on employment and family relations, advice on finding recreational activities that were not drug-related, and help in identifying and avoiding high-risk situations. Finally, if friends or family were available, they were informed of the test results and instructed to reward test passing with reinforcements that were planned beforehand.

This carefully designed program had mixed results. On the one hand, only a minority of the participants remained drug-free throughout the 3 months. On the other hand, the group did better than a comparison group in an AA-like program. Further research has consistently shown that the vouchers played a significant role in keeping patients in the program. Thus, material rewards, plus what the researchers called community reinforcement—the participation of the friends, families, and stores—did seem to work for some people, though it is not known how long such gains last. Perhaps this approach gives cocaine abusers a good start, after which they need other kinds of support to prevent relapse.

The Interpersonal Perspective

Whether as cause or result, substance dependence is very often associated with problems in the family. Therefore, some experts have suggested that couple or family therapy might be a good way to treat both problems. If domestic relations are repaired, maybe the former drug abuser will be less likely to relapse.

Behavioral Couple Therapy Behavioral couple therapy, either alone or in combination with individual counseling, has been used for many years as a treatment for alcohol dependence. There is some evidence that this approach reduces drinking, and there is very good evidence that it reduces problems in the relationship (O'Farrell & Fals-Stewart, 2000; Rotunda, Alter, & O'Farrell, 2001).

One such problem may be domestic violence. Almost three quarters of wife-beaters meet the criteria for alcohol dependence, and many are drunk when they attack (Brookoff, O'Brien, Cook, et al., 1997). It appears that behavioral couple therapy can substantially reduce such violence. In a study of male alcoholics, the men's rates of domestic violence were significantly higher than in the general population during the year before treatment. After behavioral couple therapy, the violence decreased markedly, and this reduction was directly related to reductions in drinking. In general, the patients who stopped beating were the

Nearly three quarters of male wife-beaters meet the criteria for alcohol dependence, and many are drunk when the abuse occurs. Behavioral couple therapy has been shown to reduce domestic violence substantially.

ones who stopped drinking (O'Farrell, Van Hutton, & Murphy, 1999).

Behavioral couple therapy has also been tried with other kinds of drug abusers. In one study, illegal-drug abusers who were receiving individual therapy were randomly assigned to either receive or not receive behavioral couple therapy as well. Then all these men were evaluated after the therapy and reevaluated at regular intervals for a year. Compared with the couples where only the drug-abusing husband received therapy, those for which the couple therapy was added showed greater improvements in marital happiness and fewer days of separation. In addition, the men in the couple-therapy group used fewer drugs, reported longer periods of abstinence, were less often arrested, and spent less time in the hospital. Unfortunately, as is so often the case in drug treatment, the gains began to diminish during the follow-up period (Fals-Stewart, Birchler, & O'Farrell, 1996).

Family Therapy Interestingly, 60 to 80 percent of drug-dependent people, and especially those who are under 35, either live with their parents or contact a parent at least once a day. Almost all drug-dependent people are in touch with a parent at least once a week. This is true not only in the United States but also in Puerto Rico, England, Italy, and Thailand. What it suggests is that family therapy makes sense for drug abusers. On one hand, the family may be willing to help in the abuser's treatment. On the other hand, it may be the family that needs treating. It often turns out that the parents are also drug-dependent (Stanton & Shadish, 1997).

Family therapy seems especially promising in the case of teenagers. A good example is the home-based, multi-system treatment that Henggeler and his associates have developed for substance-abusing delinquents and other difficult adolescents. In this treatment, the therapists basically collaborate with the family, but it is not just the family that is drawn in. All the institutions surrounding the adolescent—school, work, peers, community—are viewed as interconnected systems influencing the family and, therefore, the adolescent's problem. Thus all are used, as in the following instance:

> Frank, 15 years old, was an alcoholic and a delinquent. He often stayed out all night with his friends, drinking and committing robberies. This was not an abnormal pattern in his neighborhood. The community had a thriving criminal subculture, and that is what was available by way of recreation for local teenagers. Frank's mother was single, socially isolated, devoid of parenting skills, and depressed. She felt powerless to control the boy. Still, she placed great value on education (she had finished high school), and she was pained over Frank's indifference to school. The therapists assumed that, if the boy was to stop misbehaving, the mother had to take a stronger hand. After treating her depression with medication and cognitive therapy, they gave her lessons in effective parenting. Her church, her extended family, and her neighbors were all engaged to provide her with social support. Gradually, the mother began setting curfews for Frank and rewarding him for good behavior. She got him involved in various community activities, and the boy set vocational goals for himself. Thus, a new context, prosocial rather than antisocial, was created for him. Both his delinquency and his alcohol abuse stopped. (Adapted from Henggeler, Pickrel, Brondino, et al., 1996.)

The Cognitive Perspective

Thinking About Drugs As we saw earlier, people's expectations about the effects of alcohol play a role in whether they will use and abuse alcohol (Goldman, Brown, & Christiansen, 1987). Through modeling—the example of parents, peers, and people on television and in movies—children develop *alcohol expectancies,* beliefs about the effects of alcohol consumption. These expectancies congeal into a schema that, later, when the opportunity to drink arises, will determine how the person will use alcohol and how he or she will act under its influence. According to research, the major positive expectancies that people hold about alcohol are that it transforms experiences in a positive way, that it enhances social and physical pleasure, that it enhances sexual performance, that it increases power and aggressiveness, that it facilitates social assertiveness, and that it reduces tension (Brown, Goldman, Inn, et al., 1980). People also hold certain negative expectancies about alcohol—specifically, that it impairs performance and encourages irresponsibility (Rohsenow, 1983)—but, for many people who have problems with alcohol, the positive expectancies outweigh the negative, so they drink, often to excess.

In support of this view, it has been shown that young adolescents' expectations about alcohol do significantly predict whether they will begin drinking, even when other known predictors—age, religious observance, parental drinking patterns—are controlled (Goldman, Brown, & Christiansen, 1987). Such expectations also predict whether they will go on to problem drinking (Christiansen, Smith, Roehling, et al., 1989; Stacy, Newcomb, & Bentler, 1991). It has been shown, in addition, that heavier drinkers have stronger positive expectancies about alcohol than do light drinkers (Brown, Goldman, & Christiansen, 1985). But while expectancy theory is persuasive on the subject of why people *begin* to drink, it is not as good at explaining why some of them go on to become alcohol-dependent. In the words of one researcher, "Expected consequences may play a greater part in influencing a teenager's first drink than in influencing an alcoholic's millionth drink" (Leigh, 1989, p. 370). By the millionth drink it is the rare person who would still be nursing hopes of good times and enhanced sexual power.

Expectancies seem to be a more complicated issue than was once thought. It matters whether suppressing the urge to drink inhibits expectancies or enhances them (Palfai, Monti, Colby, et al., 1997)—for example, making the next drink seem even *more* likely to produce fun. Another factor is memory: how well the person makes the connection between drinking cues and outcome expectancies (Stacy, 1997). Finally, temperament has an effect on how one responds to expectancies. If the expectancy is of having a new thrill, the response will depend on whether the person is a novelty-seeker or a harm-avoider (Galen, Henderson, & Whitman, 1997).

Research has shown that areas of stress created by drug abuse are most likely to undermine abstinence. For instance, if drug abuse jeopardizes a person's job, stress at work is most likely to lead to a relapse.

Cognitive-Behavioral Therapy Cognitive therapy was added to behavioral therapy for substance abuse in the 1980s because improvements from behavioral therapy alone were usually temporary. It wasn't so hard to get people to give up drugs for a few weeks or a few months; the problem was to make the change last. Estimated relapse rates ranged from 50 to 90 percent (Brownell, 1986). As we saw in our discussion of alcohol rehabilitation, Marlatt and his colleagues (Marlatt & Gordon, 1985), in their relapse prevention model, placed great emphasis on the *abstinence violation effect,* whereby former drinkers who suffer a lapse say to themselves, "Well, I had a drink—I might as well get drunk." According to Marlatt and his group, such people have been indoctrinated by the disease or loss of control concept of drinking: Once you have a drink, you have to get drunk. Needless to say, such a view provides a handy excuse for a relapse. Most cognitive theory and therapy for substance dependence in the past decade has been aimed at countering the abstinence violation effect. Slips are now seen as *part* of the recovery. (Some therapists even guide their patients through planned slips.) The goal is to control the cognitive responses to the slip so that it does not initiate a relapse.

Researchers are now beginning to identify specific factors that lead to relapse. These fall into three categories: individual (intrapersonal), environmental (situational), and physiological. In the first category, negative emotional states such as stress, anger, depression, and anxiety are among the strongest determinants of relapse, accounting for an estimated 30 percent of relapses across the substance-dependence disorders (Cummings, Gordon, & Marlatt, 1980). Interestingly, the relationship between stress and relapse seems to be reciprocal (Brown, Patterson, Grant, et al., 1995). Areas of stress created by the drug problem are most likely to sabotage abstinence. (For example, if drugs have put your job at risk, problems on the job are most likely to send you back to drugs.) Finally, it should come as no surprise that "psychosocial vulnerability"—poor coping skills, lack of social support, perceived inability to resist temptation—place people at higher risk for relapse (Brown, Patterson, Grant, et al., 1995).

On the basis of findings such as these, McAuliffe (1990) developed a program to help substance-dependent people head off negative emotional states by refining their coping skills. In McAuliffe's study, 168 recovering heroin addicts were randomly assigned either to the usual aftercare treatment or to a specially designed relapse-prevention program involving 2 weekly meetings—1 led by a professional counselor, 1 by a recovering addict—for 6 months. In the meetings, the experimental subjects were taught strategies for dealing with former drug-using companions, with drug offers, and with job and family problems. They were also taught how to make new friends and develop drug-free recreational activities, as well as how to respond to slips. At a 1-year follow-up, the subjects in the relapse-prevention program were significantly more likely to be completely abstinent or suffering only rare slips than were those who had only the traditional aftercare.

In addition to negative emotional states, motivation and commitment are key factors in the prediction of relapse (Hall, Havassy, & Wasserman, 1990). Bolstering motivation and assessing motivation—does the person really want to quit using the drug, or has the boss delivered an ultimatum?—should become part of relapse-prevention programs in the future (Hall, Havassy, & Wasserman, 1991).

Apart from individual factors, environmental contingencies figure heavily in relapse risk. Possibly the key environmental factor is social support, its presence or absence. Relapses are often precipitated by interpersonal conflict—for example, family quarrels. Conversely, the recovering substance abuser can be greatly helped by encouragement from family, friends, and co-workers. Another source of social support is self-help groups such as Alcoholics Anonymous and Narcotics Anonymous, which offer the kind of understanding that only fellow sufferers can extend. At the same time, these groups teach their members how to cope with environmental contingencies. For example, two notorious predictors of lapses and relapses are exposure to the drug and social pressure from users (Shiffman, 1982). Alcoholics Anonymous and other self-help groups offer members advice on how to avoid or control such cues. This kind of contingency management can greatly increase a person's chances of remaining drug-free.

As for physiological factors, withdrawal cravings can lead swiftly to a slip, especially if they are combined with risk-laden individual and environmental factors. People who are angry or depressed, or who are spending the evening with old drinking buddies, will have a far harder time withstanding physiological pressures to return to the drug. In addition, it may be true that a lapse places the would-be abstainer on a slippery slope. Research with animals suggests that the ingestion of small amounts of drugs creates a priming effect, activating conditioned physiological responses that lead to further drug consumption (Carroll & Comer, 1996). Another area of interest for physiological researchers has been the substitution of new, benign addictions, such as physical exercise.

When a truly effective treatment is found, it will probably combine all these factors: intrapersonal, situational, and physiological. In the meantime, cognitive-behavioral treatment based on relapse prevention does continue to show promise. Maude-Griffin, and colleagues compared the efficacy of cognitive-behavioral therapy with an AA-type 12-step program in a 12-week treatment for cocaine abuse (Maude-Griffin, Hohenstein, Humfleet, et al., 1998). They found that the cognitively treated participants were significantly more likely to achieve abstinence than participants in the 12-step program. At the same time, some evidence suggested that the 12-step program was more effective for certain patients. Regarding other kinds of drug-dependency problems, Copeland and colleagues found that a relatively brief (6 sessions or less) cognitive-behavioral treatment was effective in treating adults for marijuana use (Copeland, Swift, Roffman, et al., 2001).

The Neuroscience Perspective

Genetic Studies Most of the genetic research on substance abuse has focused on alcohol, and most of the findings suggest that some people inherit a predisposition to problems with this drug. One type of evidence comes from cross-cultural studies. It has been reported, for example, that the Japanese, Koreans, and Chinese respond with obvious facial flushing and clear signs of intoxication after drinking amounts of alcohol that have no detectable effect on European Americans (Harada, Agarwal, Goedde, et al., 1982). Researchers have documented the association of such ethnic differences with a genetic variation that is common in northeastern Asian populations but quite rare among non-Asians (Goedde, Agarwal, Fritze, et al., 1992). This inherited mutant gene, for the ALDH2 allele, seems to confer genetic protection against developing alcohol dependence.

There is strong evidence that genetic factors play a role in the development of alcoholism (Cadoret, Troughton, O'Gorman, et al., 1986; Goodwin, Schulsinger, Hermansen, et al., 1973). Cadoret and colleagues examined alcohol and drug problems in children who were adopted as infants and found that children whose biological parents had alcohol or drug problems were more likely to develop alcoholism and addictions to drugs other than alcohol as adults.

According to an influential formulation proposed by Cloninger and his co-workers, a susceptibility to alcoholism is inherited, but in two different ways (Devor, Abell, Hoffman, et al., 1994; Cloninger, 1987; Cloninger, Bohman, & Sigvardsson, 1981). What these researchers call Type 1 susceptibility affects both men and women and follows the diathesis-stress model; that is, in order for the genetic susceptibility to lead to actual alcohol dependence, there must be environmental stress—above all, the stresses associated with low socioeconomic status. Type 2 susceptibility is far more heritable—it seems to be independent of environmental influences—and is passed from father to son. In Type 2, it is very rare for either the mothers of alcohol-dependent sons or the daughters of alcohol-dependent fathers to be dependent themselves, whereas the heritability from father to son is about 90 percent. The two types also differ in their age at onset—Type 2 generally beginning in adolescence, Type 1 in adulthood—and they differ dramatically in severity. Type 1 is rarely associated with criminal behavior; these drinkers tend to be dependent, quiet-living people. By contrast, Type 2 alcohol-dependent men are impulsive and aggressive, prone to brawling, reckless driving, and other criminal behavior. They also seem to be significantly more prone to depression and suicide (Buydens-Branchey, Branchey, & Noumair, 1989). Thus it seems likely that there is more than one genetic factor involved in drinking problems and that at least one is sex-linked.

Twin studies have provided strong evidence of a genetic influence on alcoholism. Research has found that there is a 55 percent concordance rate for alcohol dependence in MZ twins, while for DZ same-sex twins the concordance is 28 percent (Kaprio, Koskenvuo, Langinvainio, et al., 1987; True, Xian, Scherrer, et al., 1999). Some studies suggest that genetic influences are just as important for the development of alcoholism in women as in men (Heath, Slutzke, & Madden, 1997; Heath, Bucholz, Madden, et al., 1997), while others find stronger genetic effects for men (McGue, Pickens, & Svikis, 1992), but this may well depend on the type of alcoholism.

Environmental factors also play an important role in alcoholism. Goodwin and his co-workers conducted a revealing study with a group of male adoptees (Goodwin, Schulsinger, Hermansen, et al., 1973). Each of the men in the index group had been separated in infancy from his biological parents, one of whom had been hospitalized at least once for alcohol dependence. Many more of the index children grew up to have drinking problems and to seek psychiatric treatment than did a matched group of adoptees whose biological parents were not alcohol-dependent. However, the rate of drinking problems among the men with an alcoholic parent was less than would be expected if their drinking pattern were due solely to genetic factors.

As in other mental disorders, the development of a disorder is more likely when genes are combined with precipitating life events. The importance of gene-environment interaction in alcohol use was strikingly demonstrated in a recent Finnish twin study (Dick, Rose, Kaprio, et al., 2001). Dick and her co-workers discovered that in addition to the substantial effect of genes on the risk for alcohol use, the social environment also has an influence on the magnitude of that risk. For example, living in a place where there was a larger proportion of young adults and more social mobility seems to particularly increase the effects of the genetic risk factors for alcohol use. Another study of twins and substance abuse found that a common vulnerability, influenced by both genetic and environmental factors, contributes to the development of drug abuse (Tsuang, Bar, Harley, et al., 2001).

Studies have shown how genetic and environmental factors interact in the development of alcohol dependence. A person's initiation to drinking to the point of intoxication, or to drinking at all, is primarily influenced by environmental factors, such as peer pressure or parental modeling (Rose, 1998). Once alcohol use begins, differences in consumption patterns are strongly influenced by genetic factors (Heath, 1995). The influence of genes increases as experience with alcohol grows (Rose, 1998). This implies that genes, such as the ALDH2 allele, affect certain aspects of drinking, such as sensitivity to alcohol, and that this difference becomes increasingly relevant after increased drinking experience (Wall, Shea, Chan, et al., 2001). Indeed, researchers have found that individuals with a history of familial alcoholism are less likely than others to transition out of heavy drinking during the college years to more moderate drinking after college (Jackson, Sher, Gotham, et al., 2001).

ALDH2 is the candidate gene with the strongest association with alcohol dependence to date (Chen, Lu, Peng, et al., 1999; Wall, Shea, Chan, et al., 2001). How does the ALDH2 gene exert its effect, and how does this explain the finding that north Asians are about half as likely as non-Asians to develop alcohol dependence problems (Goedde, Agarwal, Fritze, et al., 1992; Tue & Israel, 1995)? In the normal course of metabolizing alcohol in the liver, the alcohol is converted in a transitional phase to a poisonous substance, acetaldehyde, and then converted to acetic acid, which the body can use as a source of calories (Kalat, 2001). North Asians who have the mutant allele for ALDH2 metabolize the acetaldehyde more slowly, causing it to build up, and the toxic reaction to this build-up can cause facial flushing, nausea, headaches, stomach pains, and signs of intoxication. Perhaps these unpleasant reactions discourage many north Asians from abusing alcohol. For example, researchers have found that Asian college students who possess this allele were less likely to be regular drinkers or to have engaged in binge-drinking episodes (Wall, Shea, Chan, et al., 2001). It is as if individuals with the mutant allele are endowed with a natural form of Antabuse, which reduces the likelihood they will develop alcohol dependence.

Besides having fewer of these unpleasant physiological reactions to alcohol (e.g., nausea, vomiting, headaches), individuals who are prone to developing alcohol dependence have other, more positive reactions to alcohol as well. The sons of alcoholics experience more relief from tension and stress than others do after drinking alcohol (Levenson, Oyama, & Meek, 1987; Schuckit, Tsuang, Anthenelli, et al., 1996). They also report feeling less intoxicated after a moderate amount of alcohol and show fewer symptoms of intoxication such as body sway or loss of balance (Schuckit, Tsuang, Anthenelli, et al., 1996). These findings point to the probable importance of differences in metabolic reactions to alcohol in the development of dependence problems. Other research suggests that individuals who are high risk for alcoholism may possess greater hyperexcitability of the central nervous system, reflected in a deficit in neural inhibition (Zhang, Cohen, Porjesz, et al., 2001). Such a deficit conceivably intensifies stress or makes it harder for at-risk individuals to naturally reduce stress. Dependence on alcohol may partly reflect such individuals' attempts to self-medicate themselves so as to reduce the excessive excitation of their nervous system.

It is likely that other genes are also important, but they have been subject to less investigation than the ALDH2 allele. One such set of genetic factors involves personality differences related to impulsivity and thrill seeking. Recently, Slutske and colleagues studied more than 3,000 adult twins, both male and female, from the Australian Twin Registry. They discovered that genetic influences on a personality variable related to impulsivity, or what the researchers refer to as "behavioral undercontrol," accounted for almost 40 percent of the genetic variation in alcohol dependence (Slutske, Heath, Madden, et al., 2002). These and other results suggest that genetic factors account for a substantial portion of the common genetic risk for alcoholic dependence and conduct disorder in men and women (Slutske & Madden, 1997), as well as the common risk for alcohol dependence and pathological gambling (Slutzke, Eisen, True, et al., 2000).

It appears that social and environmental factors determine the initial exposure and initiation to drinking, but once alcohol use is begun, genetic factors such as the ALDH2 allele can create a specific vulnerability for the progression of drug use to end in alcoholism. Other genes also probably contribute to defects in neural inhibition, leading to hyperexcitability of the central nervous system. These genes may influence both the unpleasant reaction to alcohol, as well as its effect in reducing tension and stress.

Biochemical Studies Research has amply demonstrated that the ingestion of commonly abused drugs influences the neurotransmitters that affect a person's sense of well-being, pleasure, comfort, and alertness. Because such drugs provide the brain with external sources of neurotransmitters, the brain ceases to produce the neurotransmitters in a normal way (Goldstein, 1994). Accordingly, the person becomes increasingly dependent on the drugs, setting the stage for an addictive process and withdrawal symptoms. This grim development can affect a variety of neurotransmitters. The system influenced depends on the type of drug.

Endorphins In the early 1970s, scientists discovered that nerve cells in the brain have opiate receptors, sites to which opiates such as heroin and morphine attach themselves. The fit between the opiates and the receptors is so perfect that researchers suspected the brain must produce a natural substance that the receptors were intended to fit. This suspicion led in 1975 to the discovery of enkephalins, brain chemicals that are similar to morphine and that do, indeed, fit the opiate receptors (Goldstein, 1976). Several of these substances have been given the name **endorphins**, meaning "morphine within."

The "runner's high" is produced by the release of endorphins—natural brain chemicals that cause feelings of pleasure—in response to exertion. Morphine and other opiates produce the same biochemical reaction.

Endorphins may account for a number of mind-body phenomena that have puzzled scientists for many years. For one thing, they may underlie our natural control of pain and our natural experience of pleasure. It has long been known that stimulation of certain parts of the brain can produce pleasure and help control intractable pain. The stimulation seems to cause the brain to produce more endorphins. (If acupuncture controls pain—a point that is still being debated—it may do so via the same mechanism.) Endorphins may also be the mechanism by which placebo drugs can relieve pain. Possibly the person's learning history—the linking of pain-relieving drugs with endorphin production—creates a conditioned response whereby simply being told that a drug will relieve pain releases the endorphins that will do the job.

More to the point of this chapter, endorphins may also explain physiological dependence on drugs. It is possible that when external opiates are taken, the brain ceases to produce internal opiates, or endorphins. The person thus becomes entirely dependent on external opiates for the relief of pain and the achievement of pleasure. Withdrawal symptoms, accordingly, occur during the time between the cessation of external opiate consumption and the resumption of internal opiate production.

Recently, scientists have discovered that the opiate receptor sites can be occupied by substances that prevent both opiates and endorphins from attaching themselves to the receptors. One such opiate antagonist is naltrexone, which has been used under the brand name Revia in the treatment of opiate addiction. When a person on Revia takes an opiate, the opiate has no effect—it neither produces a rush nor reduces withdrawal symptoms. The hope is that the repeated experience of taking an opiate without any effect will eventually break the addiction.

Dopamine A second important theory has to do with the neurotransmitter dopamine. According to this theory, most of the abused drugs, including alcohol, amphetamines, cocaine, and opiates, work by increasing dopamine activity in the brain, releasing it from parts of the brain thought to be responsible for both the urge to fill basic biological needs and the feeling of pleasure when these needs have been fulfilled (Franken, 2002; Ungless, Whistler, Malenka, et al., 2001). This increased dopamine production is what creates the drug's positive effects (euphoria, stimulation) and thus, by reinforcement, the risk of addiction. Animal research has provided some support for this theory. Rats that have been trained to administer opiates, alcohol, and amphetamines to themselves stop using these drugs if they are given a chemical that blocks the synthesis of dopamine. Presumably, once dopamine production is turned off, the drugs are no longer reinforcing. Such dopamine-suppressing chemicals can also block the stimulant effects of alcohol and amphetamines in human beings (Wise, 1988). Other support for the theory comes from recent findings that the same dopamine system and brain circuitry may be central to the reinforcing effects of rewards or pleasures. While eating chocolate, people who identify themselves as "chocoholics" show a pattern of brain activation in this common dopamine/reward circuitry similar to that of cocaine addicts when they take cocaine (Small, Zatorre, Dagher, et al., 2001). If the implications of this research prove to be correct—that is, if a variety of addictive drugs all turn out to deliver their rewarding effects via dopamine—then one drug may satisfy the urge for a different drug. If so, people who have conquered an addiction to one drug, such as heroin, might be at risk for relapse from even occasional use of any other dopamine-mediated drug, such as alcohol, cocaine, or even caffeine.

The effects of certain drugs on neurotransmitters may particularly elevate the risk of developing cravings. Researchers found that a single exposure to cocaine produced a weeklong surge in brain activity in the region related to addiction (Ungless, Whistler, Malenka, et al., 2001), priming the brain to a state of addiction by doubling the responsiveness of dopamine neurons.

Beyond Dopamine: Genes, Serotonin, and Cognitive Processes Over the past few years, the study of biochemical processes has moved beyond the bounds of the dopamine system and even of neurotransmitters. Research suggests that the effect of drugs on the sense of reward and reinforcement, and on dopamine production, is only part of the story (Kalivas, 2001). Dopamine helps to account for the immediate, short-term influence of drugs on mood, but it does not fully explain why people develop dependence and chronic drug abuse. According to some researchers, apart from the acute effects of drugs on feelings of euphoria or pleasure, long-term changes in the brain play a role in chronic substance dependence (Kalivas, 2003; Volkow, Chang, Wang, et al., 2001). Substance abuse over time can harm the activities of the frontal cortex, which regulates such functions as decision making, planning, memory, and response inhibition. The result of chronic drug use is that individuals lower these crucial self-regulation abilities, making addiction and relapse more likely. People who are less able to make wise decisions about the use of drugs are more likely to fall into a pattern of long-term drug dependence.

The neurotransmitter serotonin seems to play two roles in substance dependence (Heinz, Mann, Weinberger, et al., 2001). First, researchers have found that the stress of early social isolation (such as early separation from a mother or peers) may contribute to serotonin dysfunction and predispose individuals to aggressive behavior and impulsive drinking later in life. Serotonin deficits may drive individuals to self-medicate by drinking alcohol to calm themselves. Second, over time individuals with serotonin deficits may develop a dependence on alcohol that sets the stage for further problems. The long-term abuse of alcohol can disturb the serotonergic system in different ways that induce depression and increase the risk of relapse, which makes it difficult for the substance abuser to quit the drugs. These researchers, as well as Cloninger (1987), suggest that serotonin dysfunction may correspond to the Type 2 alcoholism that involves early onset and more severe drinking problems, as well as aggressive behavior and criminality.

Finally, it also appears that combinations of neurotransmitters may become unbalanced in the causes and development of alcoholism. Dopamine, serotonin, and others, including GABA, probably interact in the origins of alcohol dependence.

Drug Treatment for Drug Dependence Several medications are now being prescribed to reduce cravings and other withdrawal symptoms in people coming off drug dependence. One of the most widely studied is Revia, which is being used not just for opiate dependence but also for alcoholism. In one experiment in which a group of alcoholics who had been through detoxification were randomly assigned either to Revia or to a placebo, the Revia group reported fewer cravings and lower relapse rates (O'Brien, Volpicelli, & Volpicelli, 1996). Unfortunately, some people seem not to respond to Revia, and many people fail to take the pills (Volpicelli, Rhines, Rhines, et al., 1997). Two other drugs, buspirone and acamprosate are also being tried in alcohol rehabilitation, and they, too, show some promise. But none of these drugs is a panacea, and all have to be combined with one of the psychosocial treatments, such as cognitive-behavioral therapy or AA.

A more familiar drug is methadone, which is at the center of many drug rehabilitation programs. As we saw earlier, methadone is a synthetic opiate; and like other opiates, it is highly addictive. It does not produce the extreme euphoria of heroin, but it does satisfy the craving for heroin and prevent withdrawal symptoms. In short, what methadone maintenance programs do, at best, is switch people from dependence on heroin, in the form of three to four injections daily (with the attendant risk of AIDS), to dependence on methadone, in the form of one oral dose per day. This relieves them of their "doped" behavioral symptoms and of the need to steal in order to finance their habit.

Methadone maintenance programs have had substantial success, particularly in terms of controlling the public health and public safety problems associated with drug abuse—notably AIDS and crime. At the same time, methadone does not prevent its takers from becoming dependent on alcohol, barbiturates, or other drugs. Furthermore, methadone maintenance programs do not have a good track record in keeping patients off heroin once the methadone is discontinued (Woody, McLellan, Luborsky, et al., 1995).

A recent study in Sweden of heroin addicts treated with the drug buprenorfin in combination with cognitive-behavioral group therapy achieved encouraging results (Swedish Research Council, 2002). Buprenorfin blocks the expected "high" of heroin by blocking opiate receptors in the brain, thereby reducing the craving for heroin. If the patient relapses to heroin abuse as a matter of habit, the opiate receptors will still be blocked and the expected high will not occur. The study found that fully 75 percent of addicts given this treatment combination were still in the treatment program after a year, as opposed to none of the addicts who were given placebos along with group therapy. The patients who stayed in the program showed signficant improvement in social functioning as well as a dramatic reduction in or cessation of drug abuse.

The Sociocultural Perspective

All the treatments for substance abuse that we have examined so far target the individual abuser and his or her immediate environment, and none of them is notably effective. Perhaps no form of psychotherapy is strong enough to combat a problem that has so much to do with political systems and cultural practices.

Drugs and Poverty As we discussed in the section on groups at risk for abuse of illegal drugs, drug dependence in the United States has been gradually shaped by a legacy of racism and poverty. Together, these two forces have created a breeding ground for illegal drugs, the ghetto. Even though illegal drug use has declined overall since the 1970s, and though people of all ethnicities and classes abuse drugs, African American and Latino communities have been disproportionately victimized by drug abuse. In turn, drug abuse has ravaged those communities.

The forces that stabilize drug use have accelerated. At all levels of government, there have been cuts in programs aimed at the well-being of the inner cities.

SESS
STARTING EARLY STARTING SMART
Key Principles in Providing Integrated Behavioral Health Services for Young Children and Their Families:
The *Starting Early Starting Smart* Experience

If you were designing an early-intervention program for substance abuse, what age group would you target? Eighteen- to 21-year-olds, because that is the legal drinking age? High school students, because many of them experiment with drugs? Junior high school ages, because that is when many students try drugs or alcohol for the first time? Interventions at any of these ages might be considered early, but the Federal Substance Abuse and Mental Health Services Administration (SAMHSA) is targeting children from birth to age 7, because even children of these young ages can show risk factors for future substance abuse. The program is "Starting Early Starting Smart"(SESS), designed by SAMHSA in collaboration with a private foundation, the Casey Family Programs.

SESS is a major study of integrated behavioral health services to children and families impacted by the environment, substance abuse problems, and mental disorders. Currently operational at 12 centers nationwide, the SESS system centers on children from birth to age 7, in order to focus services that support the family. The programs are located in primary-care settings (such as hospital maternity wards and pediatric clinics) and in child-care centers (such as Head Start programs). SESS centers are in urban, suburban, and rural settings, and participants come from diverse ethnic backgrounds and personal circumstances. Most are members of racial minorities; about 60 percent have finished high school; 50 percent are single parents; 14 percent are unemployed; 30 percent lack health insurance. Poor transportation resources, language barriers, uncertain legal status, multiple-job pressure, and low income are also common circumstances.

While the study continues to analyze site, service, and program characteristics in relation to short-term and long-term outcomes, preliminary reports are promising. The early findings demonstrate that SESS programs improve access to substance abuse programs among parents, improve appropriate parental discipline and positive reinforcement practices, strengthen mother-and-baby interaction during feedings in infancy, and strengthen social-emotional development of SESS children, based on pre/ post teacher reports.

The SESS program was created with the belief that single-service solutions, offering just one narrow kind of treatment, are not effective. By contrast, the SESS program offers access to a range of family and parenting services, mental health services, substance abuse services, and child development services. For example, services include individual and group therapy, behavioral- management techniques, and social-skills training. The SESS program also establishes and maintains relationships with other agencies to assist families broadly. An important key of the SESS approach is to identify the personal strengths of caregivers and their families, not just the needs of families.

The SESS approach involves coordinating the different kinds of services and programs available in local communities, and improving access to them (Figure 12.6). For instance, the SESS program can ask preschool teachers to identify and respond to the particular developmental needs of different children, a simple act of advocacy that SESS parents might not be ready to do. The SESS program is rooted in the idea that improving parenting skills increases the general well-being of the family, thus creating a supportive and nurturing bond that is the best preventative against problems in life such as substance abuse. The hope is that success in childhood increases the chances for success in school and society. While providing services in settings that are familiar to children and families, SESS is identifying best practices for improving developmental outcomes for at-risk children, while empowering families as meaningful participants.

Source: Casey Family Programs and the U.S. Department of Health and Human Services (2001).

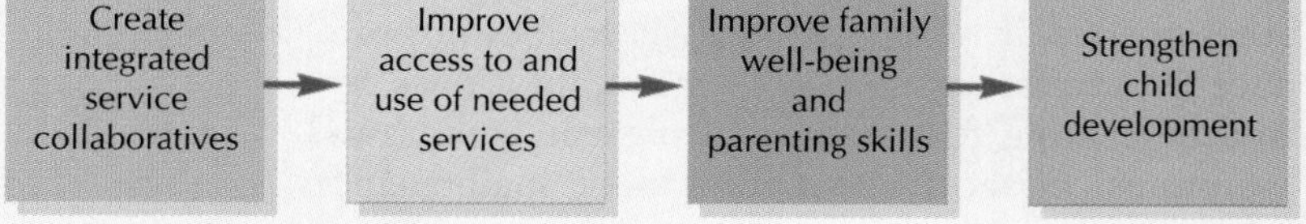

FIGURE 12.6 The purposes of SESS.

Meanwhile, American corporations—and, consequently, jobs—have continued leaving the cities for greener pastures in the suburbs or in Third World countries. The result has been a dramatic decline in the standard of living among the poor in American cities. Crack cocaine stymies both drug rehabilitation and the criminal justice system. None of the attempted solutions to the crack problem, or to the heroin epidemic surrounding it, seem in any way sufficient. There is not enough money and not enough hope, either among drug users or in the society at large.

When drugs are available and opportunities for drug-free personal fulfillment are not, drugs will be used. What is there to lose? In an environment where the legal paths to financial success are virtually nonexistent, how surprising is it that drug dealing is a high-status profession in the inner city? Until racism and poverty are confronted and dealt with, any treatment discussed in this chapter has to be viewed as little more than a side issue. Given the mood of the American public, what can mental health professionals do to curb drug dependence?

Making matters more complicated is the spread of AIDS. Injecting drugs intravenously is a primary way of contracting the AIDS virus, and female IV users may not only contract the virus but also pass it on to a child during pregnancy. Finally, as we have stated, there is an inevitable correlation between drugs and crime. Heroin and cocaine addicts must come up with a substantial amount of money every day to support their habits. They are generally unemployable; therefore unless they are independently wealthy, they must steal. Addicts are responsible for millions of dollars worth of property crimes annually. As many as 20 percent of inmates in federal prisons committed their offenses in order to obtain drugs. More than 5 percent of the murders committed in this country are directly related to the sale of narcotics.

Harm Reduction Assuming that the United States and other Western countries continue to be more concerned with balanced budgets than with poverty and racism, what is left as a solution at the policy level? One answer is *harm reduction,* a set of interventions that concentrates not on ending drug dependence but on controlling the harm that drug dependence does to the society at large. First introduced in the Netherlands in the 1980s, harm-reduction policies attempt to integrate drug abusers into the larger society and to distinguish between use and abuse. Harm reduction began when it was first discovered that HIV was often transmitted through the sharing of needles for drug injection. We might prefer that HIV-infected people not use drugs, but if they do, we would prefer that they not spread this deadly disease in the process—hence the beginning of needle-exchange programs, whereby heroin addicts trade in their contaminated needles for clean ones. Harm-reduction advocates also want to reduce the criminal activity that results from drug abuse. One proposal is to legalize drugs and dispense them to addicts under medical supervision and at nominal cost. Such a system was tried in Great Britain during the 1970s and 1980s. Opponents of this approach claim that it simply encourages addiction, and the apparent increase in the number of British addicts during the 1980s seemed to support this argument. It was because of this increase that the British system was abandoned. However, defenders of legalization claim that it is the only reasonable way to prevent addicts from doing as much harm to society as they do to themselves.

Despite some successes reported in Holland, Australia, and Switzerland, harm-reduction policies have

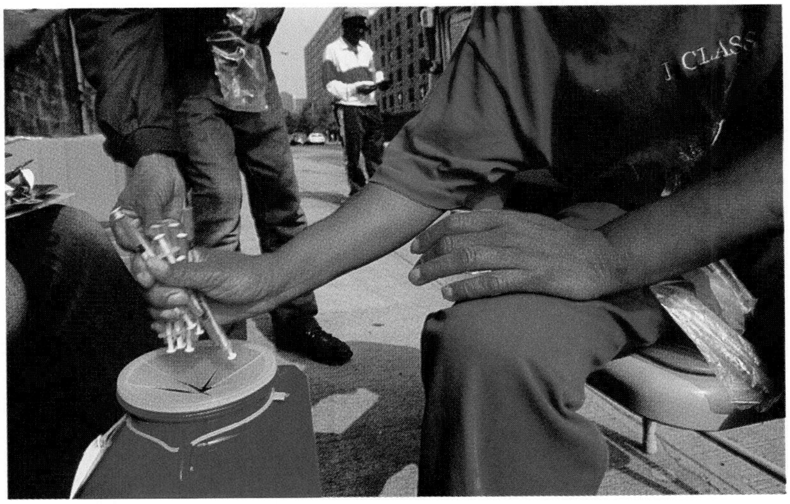

Needle-exchange programs, which allow heroin users to trade in their used needles for clean ones to help reduce the spread of HIV, are an example of harm reduction. Rather than ending drug use, harm reduction policies attempt to control the damage that drug use does to society at large.

been slow to catch on in the United States. As regards drugs, American politicians seem wedded to a philosophy of zero tolerance. Needle-exchange programs offer a good example. Contaminated needles spread about one third of all new AIDS cases nationwide. Drug use accounts for two thirds of new cases of HIV among women, and more than half of those among children, who, as noted, contract it from their mothers in the womb. More than 60 cities now have needle-exchange programs, and the American Medical Association and other groups have called for the legalization of needle exchange. In 2000, the U.S. Surgeon General issued a report that called on Congress to lift the ban on federal funding of needle-exchange programs. The report was based on extensive evidence that needle-exchange programs do not promote the spread of HIV, but rather seem to help limit its spread. Nonetheless, Congress, as well as many state and local governments, continues to place administrative barriers to these programs and has yet to approve the use of federal funds.

While harm reduction has gained little support, some efforts are being put into the *prevention* of drug abuse. Drug education is now common in the schools and the workplace. Television commercials show movie stars and sports heroes warning teenagers against drugs, and advertisements in buses and subways tell people who already have drug problems where they can go for help, what number they can call, before they become defeated. Such efforts probably do some good, but the most obvious way to prevent drug abuse is to end poverty.

Key Terms

addiction, 313
amphetamines, 333
barbiturates, 332
blood alcohol level, 315
cocaine, 334
crack cocaine, 334
depressant, 330
detoxification, 322
endorphins, 347
hallucinogens, 335
hashish, 336
heroin, 331
LSD (lysergic acid diethylamide), 335
marijuana, 336
matching, 325
MDMA ("Ecstasy"), 336
methadone, 331
morphine, 330
motivational interviewing, 324
opiates, 330
opium, 330
PCP (phencyclidine), 336
psychoactive drug, 312
relapse prevention, 325
stimulants, 333
substance abuse, 314
substance dependence, 314
synergistic effect, 332
tolerance, 314
tranquilizers, 332
withdrawal, 314

Summary

- Psychoactive drugs are substances people use to alter their psychological state. *DSM-IV-TR* defines two categories of pathological drug use—substance dependence and substance abuse—on the basis of problems a drug is causing in a person's life. Either diagnosis depends on behavioral criteria rather than on whether the drug is dangerous or illegal.
- A diagnosis of substance dependence requires that a person meet three of the following criteria: preoccupation with the drug; unintentional overuse; tolerance (progressively larger doses are needed to achieve the same effect); withdrawal symptoms when the drug is not used; persistent efforts to control use, followed by relapse; abandonment of important social, occupational, or recreational activities that interfere with drug use; and continued use despite serious drug-related problems.
- A diagnosis of substance abuse requires that a person meet one of four criteria: recurrent, drug-related failure to meet social role obligations; recurrent use in dangerous situations (e.g., drunk driving); drug-related legal problems; continued use despite social or interpersonal problems.
- Alcohol, legal and sanctioned by custom, is one of the most widely abused drugs. The social and personal costs of its abuse are enormous. A depressant, alcohol interferes with the higher brain centers, which control behavior. After one or two drinks, a person may become talkative and active; as blood alcohol level rises after more drinks, there are changes in mood and behavior, and very high levels lead to stupor, unconsciousness, and, ultimately, death. Whether a person becomes amorous, aggressive, or sad when drinking heavily depends largely on the individual's expectancy of the effect of drink. Long-term overuse can cause heart disease, cirrhosis of the liver, and brain damage; withdrawal may cause DTs (delirium tremens), a severe reaction characterized by trembling, delusions, and disorientation. Other results of long-term abuse include loss of self-esteem, inability to work, family violence, and depression and other psychiatric disorders.
- Most alcohol-dependent persons develop their abuse patterns over a long period, during which they gradually rely more and more on the mood-altering effects of alcohol and continually increase their drinking.

- Alcohol use and abuse patterns and the relationship between them vary in American society according to social class, gender, skin color, ethnicity, religion, and age. Rates of drinking to excess are increased among less-educated Americans. Use and abuse are higher among men than among women. Relative rates of drinking between Whites and Blacks also vary by age and gender. Black women are less likely to drink than White women, and White teenagers are more likely to abuse alcohol than are Black teenagers; however, alcohol-abuse rates are higher for Black men in their thirties than for White men the same age. Native American men are particularly at risk. Rates of drinking have been decreasing among older people but rising among young people.
- Treatment of alcohol dependence begins with detoxification: getting the person free of alcohol and through the withdrawal symptoms. Further rehabilitation requires significant behavior changes. An ideal treatment would be multimodal, combining occupational therapy, relaxation training, individual and group psychotherapy, job training, and support groups such as Alcoholics Anonymous (AA). In practice, most clients mainly attend group therapy and AA meetings.
- Motivational interviewing, a form of short-term psychotherapy, is a question-and-answer method aimed at getting substance-dependent persons to overcome ambivalence toward living drug-free. Relapse prevention based on a cognitive-behavioral approach has gained importance: Patients learn to recognize and avoid situations that could put them at risk of relapse, to cope with the unavoidable high-risk situations, and to prevent slips from becoming relapses.
- Cure rates for all forms of alcohol treatment are low. Highly motivated patients with good coping methods benefit from AA, but only small numbers of those who begin going to AA stay abstinent for a year. Relapse prevention treatment also has a low success rate. Matching clients to therapies—motivational interviewing, AA, relapse prevention-based cognitive-behavioral treatment—according to their readiness to change has also been disappointing.
- Although fewer people now smoke than drink, a higher number of smokers become dependent. Nicotine is a drug that both stimulates and calms users. Smoking leads to premature deaths from heart disease, lung cancer, and other respiratory disorders—not only in smokers but also in the people (especially children) around them. Health warnings, social pressure, and legislation banning smoking in public places have led a significant number of smokers to quit, but advertising targeted at vulnerable groups encourages others to start.
- The cause of nicotine dependence is unclear. Behavior theorists proposed that smoking is a learned habit reinforced by pleasurable sensations and associations. Stanley Schachter and colleagues found evidence that the only benefit smokers receive from nicotine is avoiding the mainly psychological withdrawal symptoms that result from quitting smoking.
- Relapse rates are high among those quitting smoking. Factors affecting relapse rate include the motivational, the cognitive (whether one believes one can quit), and the social (whether cigarettes are available and whether spouses and friends are smokers). Depression was also found to be common among smokers who had repeatedly attempted to quit and failed. Methods of helping people quit now include cognitive-behavioral therapy, antidepressants, and nicotine replacement mechanisms such as patches; nicotine replacement has a moderate advantage.
- Other psychoactive drugs fall into three main categories: depressants, stimulants, and hallucinogens. Most of these drugs can be obtained only by prescription or illegally. The depressants include opiates (e.g., morphine and heroin), which induce relaxation, euphoria, and usually addiction; barbiturates (e.g., Nembutal and Seconal), which induce sleep but, combined with alcohol, may cause death; and tranquilizers (e.g., Valium), which reduce anxiety but may lead to dependence. While most of these drugs have medical uses, all can be abused. Overuse of depressants leads to tolerance; withdrawal is extremely uncomfortable and often dangerous.
- The stimulants increase energy, alertness, and feelings of confidence. This category includes amphetamines (e.g., Benzedrine and Dexedrine), which in high doses may lead to induced psychosis; cocaine (and crack cocaine), which produces a rapid but short-lived "high"; and caffeine. Regular or heavy use of amphetamines or cocaine leads to tolerance, addiction, and withdrawal symptoms upon quitting.
- The hallucinogens cause distortions in sensory perception. While LSD may induce "bad trips" and "flashbacks," it does not appear to be addictive. PCP is a behavioral toxin that often induces risky and/or violent behavior. While usually classified as hallucinogens, marijuana and hashish are milder, producing euphoria, heightened sensory experiences, and a relaxed, timeless state. They can also heighten negative feelings and experiences and can impair activities (such as driving) that require quick and accurate judgments. Research on the effects of marijuana on testosterone and sexual activity, the immune system, and personality has not produced consistent findings, but smoking marijuana does increase the incidence of respiratory ailments. Marijuana is not known to be addictive; severe responses are rare except at high dose levels.
- Marijuana may be effective in relieving the suffering of persons undergoing chemotherapy and may have some use in treating AIDS and glaucoma patients. However, its use as a prescription drug remains illegal in most states.
- Rates of dependence on and abuse of illegal drugs vary with ethnicity, class, gender, and educational and socioeconomic status; underemployed or relatively uneducated African American and Latino men are a particularly high-risk group. Also at greater than average risk for drug abuse are those who take medication:

people with medical illnesses and mental disorders or with chronic pain.

- Current psychodynamic thinking about substance abuse in general focuses on drug use as a way to establish self-care, or the ability to control and calm one's emotions—normally, a capability acquired in early childhood. Psychodynamic therapy for drug rehabilitation thus aims at building up patients' intrapsychic strength; its effectiveness has not been widely demonstrated.
- Traditional behavior theories emphasized tension reduction (negative reinforcement) as a cause of alcohol abuse; a vicious cycle ensues when an individual learns that taking a drink relieves psychological discomfort and then more drinking leads to more discomfort. More recent theories emphasize pleasure seeking (positive reinforcement), the reinforcer being natural substances in the central nervous system released as a result of alcohol consumption. The theories have been applied to substance abuse in general. Behavior therapies for substance abuse teach patients to recognize cues that lead to drug taking and to develop alternative means of solving problems and coping with stress.
- Therapies associated with the interpersonal perspective—behavioral couple therapy and family therapy—are especially applicable to substance dependence because of the damage drug use does to families. Behavioral couple therapy has shown results in both reduced drug use and improved marital happiness, but relapse remains a problem. Family therapy has been found promising for teenaged drug users.
- Cognitive theorists focus on alcohol expectancies—the ideas people develop early in life, by watching the example of others, about their future alcohol-use patterns and their likely response to alcohol. People with excessive positive expectancies may be at greater risk for excessive drinking. Cognitive therapy has recently focused on countering the abstinence violation effect: the sense of failure after a lapse in abstinence, which creates vulnerability to relapse. It is expected that a truly effective relapse-prevention method will address intrapersonal factors (handling stress and anxiety), situational factors (presence or absence of social support), and physiological factors (resisting cravings).
- Neuroscience studies suggest that genetic factors might predispose individuals to alcohol dependence. There may be a particular type of inherited susceptibility that affects males only.
- Brain chemistry plays a special role in drug dependence. One theory holds that use of opiates decreases the production of endorphins, the brain's natural opiates, and thus creates a craving for external opiates; another holds that opiates and other addictive drugs increase the brain's production of dopamine, causing a surge of pleasure that the user seeks again.
- Medication can reduce withdrawal symptoms from some drugs, as well as relapse rates. Revia, combined with psychosocial treatments, has been effective in treating people coming off dependence on alcohol and opiates, and buspirone shows promise in alcohol rehabilitation. Methadone, a synthetic opiate that blocks cravings for heroin but doesn't produce the doped behavioral symptoms, has been very successful in keeping users off heroin for the duration of its use.
- The sociocultural perspective stresses the political and social causes of drug abuse (such as racism, poverty, and lack of opportunity) and suggests that solutions must go beyond treating individual users. Although public budget reductions and migration of jobs from cities have undercut efforts to relieve the causes of drug abuse, harm-reduction policies could still control the damage that drug dependence does to society. An example is needle-exchange programs for heroin users to lessen the spread of HIV; the programs are illegal in most states.

CHAPTER

13

Sexual Dysfunctions, Paraphilias, and Gender Identity Disorders

Classifying Sexual Behavior

Sexual Dysfunctions
- Forms of Sexual Dysfunction
- Diagnosing Sexual Dysfunction

Sexual Dysfunction: Theory and Therapy
- The Psychodynamic Perspective
- The Behavioral and Cognitive Perspectives
- Multifaceted Treatment
- The Neuroscience Perspective

Paraphilias
- Fetishism
- Transvestism
- Exhibitionism
- Voyeurism
- Sadism and Masochism
- Frotteurism
- Pedophilia
- Rape

Paraphilias: Theory and Therapy
- The Psychodynamic Perspective
- The Behavioral Perspective
- The Cognitive Perspective
- The Neuroscience Perspective
- Treatment Efficacy

Gender Identity Disorders
- Patterns of Gender Identity Disorder
- The Psychodynamic Perspective
- The Behavioral Perspective
- The Neuroscience Perspective
- Gender Reassignment

Mr. and Ms. Albert are an attractive, gregarious couple, married for 15 years, who present in the midst of a crisis over their sexual problems. Mr. Albert, a successful restaurateur, is 38. Ms. Albert . . . is 35. She reports that throughout their marriage she has been extremely frustrated because sex has "always been hopeless for us." . . .

The difficulty is the husband's rapid ejaculation. Whenever any lovemaking is attempted, Mr. Albert becomes anxious, moves quickly toward intercourse, and reaches orgasm either immediately upon entering his wife's vagina or within one or two strokes. He then feels humiliated, recognizes his wife's dissatisfaction, and they both lapse into silent suffering. . . .

Mr. Albert has always been a perfectionist, priding himself on his ability to succeed at anything he sets his mind to. . . . His inability to control his ejaculation is a source of intense shame, and he finds himself unable to talk to his wife about his sexual "failures." Ms. Albert is highly sexual, easily aroused by foreplay, but has always felt that intercourse is the only "acceptable" way to reach orgasm. Intercourse with her husband has always been unsatisfying, and she holds him completely responsible for her sexual frustration. . . .

In other areas of their marriage, including rearing of their two children, managing the family restaurant, and socializing with friends, the Alberts are highly compatible. Despite these strong points, however, they are near separation because of . . . their mutual sexual disappointment. (Spitzer, Gibbon, Skodol, et al., 1994, pp. 266–267)

While human sexual tastes are extremely broad, life in society places limits on them. To begin with, people must cope with the needs of their sexual partners. Rapid ejaculation may be satisfactory for some men but not for the women they are having sex with, as the case illustrates. Some sexual patterns, such as child molesting, are designated as crimes. A number of other sexual behaviors (e.g., cross-dressing), while they involve no harm to others, nevertheless transgress social norms and are therefore considered psychological disorders—in the eyes of many people, shameful disorders. There are very few categories of abnormal behavior to which society attaches as much stigma as sexual disorders.

The disorders that we will cover in this chapter are grouped according to the aspect of sexuality that they interfere with:

1. *Sexual dysfunction:* disruption of the sexual response cycle or pain during intercourse
2. *Paraphilias:* sexual desires or behaviors involving unusual sources of gratification
3. *Gender identity disorders:* dissatisfaction with one's own biological sex and a desire to change to the opposite sex

Before discussing sexual behaviors, however, we must first look at our sexual norms and the extent to which they actually reflect our sexual makeup and behavior.

Classifying Sexual Behavior

Compared with other cultures, Western culture has been sexually repressive. For example, while the ancient Greeks not only tolerated but actually glorified homosexuality, the Judeo-Christian tradition that supplanted Greco-Roman civilization has, for the most part, condemned same-sex relationships. Today, church doctrine on sexual morality has relaxed somewhat. Nevertheless, most present-day denominations still place restrictions on sexual activities that circumvent or replace *coitus,* or penile-vaginal intercourse, within the context of marriage.

Western sexual mores are derived not only from religious dogma but also from the writings of experts on mental health and *sexology,* the scientific study of sexuality. Some writings were notably open-minded. Magnus Hirschfeld, a German sexologist of the late nineteenth and early twentieth centuries, argued that homosexuality was a normal form of sexual orientation and that the rights of homosexuals should be protected. Other experts were far more restrictive, however. One of the most influential early psychiatric works on sex, Richard von Krafft-Ebing's *Psychopathia Sexualis* (1886/1965a) condemned masturbation as a psychologically dangerous practice. In his opinion, masturbation halted the development of normal erotic instincts and thus led to homosexuality. Krafft-Ebing regarded homosexuality as a form of psychopathology. In his view, and in Freud's, the only genuinely healthy, mature, and normal sexual outlet was coitus. Succeeding generations of psychologists and psychiatrists concurred. In *DSM-II,* published in 1968, people whose sexual interests were "directed primarily toward objects other than people of the opposite sex [or] toward sexual acts not usually associated with coitus" were classified as suffering from sexual disorders.

The definition of sexual normality has always varied between cultures and across time. In ancient Greece, for example, male homosexuality was considered a normal adjunct to heterosexual marriage.

However, there is little to indicate that human beings are programmed biologically to confine their sexual gratification to coitus. On the contrary, while the sex drive itself is inborn, the direction that it will take is partly a result of socialization. While Western culture considers the female breast an erotic object, many societies consider it sexually neutral. While homosexuality is generally frowned on in our society, in other societies it is not only accepted but actually institutionalized as the proper sexual outlet for adolescent boys (Herdt & Stoller, 1990).

As for freedom of sexual expression, an instructive contrast is provided by two small villages, one in Polynesia and one on an island off the coast of Ireland. In the Irish village of Inis Beag, a researcher (Messenger, 1971) who interviewed the inhabitants over 19 months found that they had no apparent knowledge of tongue kissing, oral-genital contact, premarital coitus, or extramarital coitus. The idea of a man putting his mouth on the woman's breast, or the woman stimulating the man's penis with her hand, was also unheard of. Intercourse was considered a health risk and was achieved quickly, without removing underwear. Female orgasm was apparently unknown. By contrast, in the same year another researcher (Marshall, 1971) reported that, on the Polynesian island of Mangaia, copulation was "a principal concern of the Mangaian of either sex" (p. 116). Mangaians began full-scale sexual activity at about 13 years, after receiving detailed and enthusiastic instruction from their elders. Sexual technique and sexual anatomy were objects of connoisseurship: "The average Mangaian youth has fully as detailed a knowledge . . . of the gross anatomy of the penis and vagina as does a European physician" (Marshall, 1971, p. 110). For males, the average rate of orgasm at age 18 was 3 per night, 7 nights a week; at age 28, 2 per night, 5 to 6 nights a week. Women had a higher rate, since the male's goal in intercourse was to bring the woman to orgasm several times before he himself reached climax. All Mangaian women were orgasmic. When told that many European and American women do not experience orgasm, Mangaians typically asked whether this did not impair their health. In short, the definition of what is sexually normal and abnormal in Mangaia was almost the opposite of that in Inis Beag. These two cultures are extremes—perhaps the most sexually permissive and the most sexually repressive societies known to Western research. But they illustrate a crucial point: Human sexual behavior, viewed across cultures, is extremely variable.

Within a culture, attitudes toward sexuality may change over time. Our own society is far more open about sex today than it was just a few decades ago, for example. Even in less tolerant times, however, sexual behavior does not necessarily conform to declared standards of sexual morality or normality. The famous Kinsey reports (Kinsey, Pomeroy, & Martin, 1948; Kinsey, Pomeroy, Martin, et al., 1953) revealed that many Americans had engaged in culturally prohibited sexual activities. More than 90 percent of the males Kinsey interviewed had masturbated; over 80 percent of the men and 50 percent of the women in his samples had participated in premarital sex; and oral sex was not a rare occurrence. In the 1940s and 1950s, when the Kinsey reports were published, these findings were shocking to many people. Today, they would be considered unremarkable.

In its early editions, the *DSM* listed homosexuality as a sexual disorder, along with pedophilia, fetishism, sadism, and so forth. Then in 1973 the board of trustees of the American Psychiatric Association voted to drop homosexuality per se from the list. The trustees' report described homosexuality as "a normal form of sexual life" (American Psychiatric Association, 1974). Still, the *DSM* retained a category called "ego-dystonic homosexuality disorder" for individuals who *themselves* rejected their homosexuality and wanted to become exclusively heterosexual. Many psychologists, together with gay rights groups, objected to this category as well. In their view, homosexuals who rejected their sexual orientation did so because they had internalized negative stereotypes—stereotypes reinforced by psychiatric labeling, even in the milder form of "ego-dystonic homosexuality disorder." At the same time, more and more research

Gay rights groups have worked to maintain homosexuality as a "normal form of sexual life." Research finds no justification for considering homosexuality as a pathological pattern.

was accumulating to show that there was no justification for regarding homosexuality as a pathological pattern. As these studies showed, homosexuals are no more prone to psychopathology than are matched groups of heterosexuals (Hooker, 1957; Paul, Gonsiorek, & Hotvedt, 1982; Saghir & Robins, 1969; Saghir, Robins, & Walbran, 1969). Moreover, there is no typical homosexual personality; homosexuals, both male and female, differ as much from one another in personality as do heterosexuals (Hooker, 1957; Wilson, 1984). In response to such findings—together with the fact that ego-dystonic homosexuality was rarely diagnosed, anyway—the APA in 1986 voted to drop homosexuality from the *DSM* altogether. Today, in *DSM-IV-TR*'s listing of sexual disorders, there remains a residual category, "sexual disorder not otherwise specified" (p. 582), to cover problems not included in other categories, and one of the examples given is "persistent and marked distress about sexual orientation," but otherwise the manual makes no reference to homosexuality.

Nevertheless, the catalog of psychiatrically recognized sexual disorders remains long. The remainder of this chapter is devoted to these conditions.

Sexual Dysfunctions

In the past three decades, our society has seen two major upheavals in sexual attitudes. First came the "sexual revolution" of the 1960s and 1970s, with a new openness about sex and a new interest in sexual satisfaction—giving it and getting it. Sex manuals became best sellers. Movies and television began showing explicit sex scenes. Popular magazines, even "family" publications such as *Reader's Digest,* began running articles on how to improve your love life.

In the 1980s, the fervor died down somewhat. In part, this was probably just the passing of a trend. (It is also possible that the trend was more in the media than in the population—see the box on the next page.) But a crucial factor was the rapidly spreading AIDS epidemic. Casual sex lost its allure. Many people sought, instead, to settle down with one partner. Others opted for abstinence (Ingrassia & Beck, 1994). But, for those having sex, the emphasis was on safe sex, with sports and entertainment stars, not to speak of school health services, broadcasting the message.

The campaign for safe sex has not quelled the interest in good sex, however. Though more people are now confining their sex lives to a single relationship, the lesson of the 1960s has not been forgotten: Today's young and middle-aged adults, particularly the women, have far higher expectations for sexual satisfaction than their parents did. This change has had many beneficial effects. It has eased the flow of information about sex, has increased sexual communication between partners, and has dispelled anxiety over harmless sexual practices. At the same time, however, it has ushered in new forms of anxiety. Many sexually normal people now worry about the adequacy of their sexual performance. The concern with gratification has also resulted in psychology's devoting considerable attention to sexual dysfunctions, disorders that prevent satisfactory sex.

Forms of Sexual Dysfunction

Sexual dysfunctions are disorders involving either a disruption of the sexual response cycle or pain during intercourse. The contemporary study of sexual dysfunction began, appropriately, in the 1960s, with the work of William Masters and Virginia Johnson at the Reproductive Biology Foundation in St. Louis. When Masters and Johnson began their research, studies of sexuality were rare, and clinicians who dealt with sexual problems were rarer still. However, since the publication of Masters and Johnson's *Human Sexual Response* (1966) and *Human Sexual Inadequacy* (1970), the number of researchers, therapists, and journals specializing in sexuality has grown enormously. One result has been a more sophisticated understanding of sexual dysfunctions. In the past, any lack of sexual interest or arousal in males was called "impotence." Similarly, the pejorative label "frigidity" was applied to almost every female sexual complaint. Today psychologists recognize a variety of specific difficulties. In *DSM-IV-TR,* most of the sexual dysfunctions are grouped according to the phase in the sexual response cycle in which they occur.

Sexual Desire Disorders The first phase of the sexual response cycle is the *desire* phase, or interest in having sex. Masters and Johnson paid little attention to sexual desire, because it could not be measured physiologically, but more recent researchers have focused on this elusive problem (Rosen & Leiblum, 1990). The two disorders of the desire phase are basically two degrees of negativity toward sex.

Hypoactive Sexual Desire Disorder People with **hypoactive sexual desire disorder** are generally uninterested not only in sexual activity but even in sexual fantasy. What constitutes low desire, however, has to be decided within the context of age, gender, and cultural norms. The most common biological factors in hypoactive desire are pain, illness, and reduced testosterone, the hormone that controls sexual interest in both sexes. It is the most common sexual dysfunction

Focus On... Sex in America: Myths and Reality

From what Americans see in the movies, on television, and, above all, in advertising, a person might easily conclude that everyone else in the country has a vigorous, varied, even exotic sex life and that he or she is the only one home alone on Saturday night. But the findings of the so-called Sex in America survey (Laumann, Gagnon, Michael, et al., 1994), studying a sample of more than 3,500 Americans aged 18 to 59, should offer comfort. The central finding of this study was that Americans are far more conservative sexually than has been thought.

Of those surveyed, only 56 percent of the men and 29 percent of the women had had more than 4 sexual partners since age 18. (One fifth of the men and almost one third of the women reported having had only 1 sexual partner since age 18.) Over a lifetime, the typical American male seems to have had 6 partners; the typical female, 2. And however many partners they have had, most of them are faithful to the one they marry. Nearly 75 percent of the married men and 85 percent of the married women said they had never had sex outside their marriage.

Not only do most Americans have limited sexual histories; they also have less sex than might have been guessed. In terms of frequency, the population breaks down, roughly, into thirds. About one third reported having sex twice a week or more often; another third, a few times a month; another third, a few times a year or not at all. And the people doing it most often (and most frequently reaching orgasm when they do it) were the married. Almost 40 percent of the married people, compared with 25 percent of the unmarried, said they had sex at least twice a week. Swinging singles were the exception, not the rule.

According to the survey, homosexuality, too, is less prevalent than is often claimed. Only 7.1 percent of the men and 3.8 percent of the women reported that they had ever had sex with someone of their own sex. (Only 2.7 percent of the men and 1.3 percent of the women said they had done so within the past year.) Masturbation was also less common than one might imagine. Only 63 percent of men and 42 percent of women said they had masturbated within the past year, and, curiously, the people who masturbated the most were not those who were deprived of other outlets. On the contrary, they were the ones who were also having the most partnered sex.

Another finding was that American tastes in sex acts are far from kinky. In a list of 14 acts, the one most often rated as appealing by the women (78 percent) and the men (83 percent) was coitus. Next in line, in a near-tie for both the men and women, were watching one's partner undress and receiving oral stimulation. Finally, the age at which Americans lose their virginity has dropped in the past few decades, but not by much: 6 months. For Americans born in the decade 1933–1942, the average age of deflowering was about 18. For those born 20 to 30 years later, it was about $17\frac{1}{2}$.

While the survey exploded many popular notions, it confirmed others:

- Men are more likely than women to have sex on the mind. Among the respondents, 54 percent of the men but only 19 percent of the woman said they thought about sex every day.
- There is such a thing as a pickup establishment. People who meet in bars are far more likely to end up in bed together before the month is out than people who meet at school, at work, or even at a private party.
- There was a free-love boom in the 1960s. The percentage of people who reported having had more than 20 sexual partners was significantly higher for the generation that came of age in the 1960s.
- The AIDS crisis has caused people to be more careful. Of those who reported having had five or more sexual partners within the past year, three quarters said they had changed their sexual behavior by having fewer partners, getting an HIV test, or using condoms more scrupulously.
- With aging, women have a harder time finding a sexual partner than men. By age 50, 22 percent of the women, as compared with 8 percent of the men, had no sexual partner. The good news is that women—and men—who have no sexual partners think less about sex and often report that they are happy and fulfilled without it.

The survey also revealed interesting differences between ethnic and religious groups. For example, age at first intercourse varies along ethnic lines. Half of African American males have lost their virginity by age 15, half of Latino males by about $16\frac{1}{2}$, half of African American females by about 17, and half of White and Latina females by about 18.

The methodology of the Sex in America survey has been highly praised. Unlike the Kinsey studies, which, conducted in less candid times, often had to rely on special groups, such as college fraternities, in order to find people willing to talk about their sex lives, this was a truly random sample, highly representative of the general population. And almost 80 percent of those contacted—in other words, not just the sexually talkative (therefore, presumably, the sexually active)—agreed to participate. Nevertheless, any self-report survey is limited by what people choose to report, and obviously a survey of sexual behavior has greater problems in this regard. According to one of the researchers, Stuart Michaels, the subject on which distortion was most likely was homosexual behavior: "There is probably a lot more homosexual activity going on than we could get people to talk about." (Quoted in Elmer-DeWitt, 1994.)

in women (Beck, 1995) and may be secondary to physiological factors such as hormone deficiencies, menopausal changes, or medical interventions (Berman, Berman, Werbin, et al., 1999). As for psychological factors, these may include depression, stress, ambivalence about sex, and conflict in the relationship. Not surprisingly, low desire is often accompanied by disorders of other response phases, especially arousal disorder in women and erectile disorder in men. In the Sex in America survey (see the box on page 359), one third of the women and one sixth of the men reported a persistent lack of interest in sex in the past year. This is now the most common complaint of couples seeking treatment for sexual dysfunction, and, about half the time, the low-desire member is a man. For most therapists, hypoactive desire is the most difficult sexual dysfunction to treat, especially in men.

Sexual Aversion Disorder The person with **sexual aversion disorder** is not just uninterested in sex but also disgusted or frightened by it and, therefore, actively avoids it. This problem is far more common in women than in men and is often the result of sexual trauma, such as rape or childhood sexual abuse (Berman, Berman, Werbin, et al., 1999), though it may also follow a period of dyspareunia, or pain during sex. About one fourth of people with sexual aversion disorder also have panic disorder (Chapter 7).

Sexual Arousal Disorders During *arousal,* the second phase of the response cycle, feelings of sexual pleasure are accompanied by muscular tension and vascular engorgement, or increased blood flow. In men, this creates an erection. In women, the genitals swell and the walls of the vagina secrete lubricant. Disruptions of this phase take two forms, one male and one female.

Female Sexual Arousal Disorder The presence of **female sexual arousal disorder** is best indicated by insufficient vaginal lubrication. In the Sex in America study, about one fifth of the women surveyed reported a problem with lubrication during the preceding year (Laumann, Gagnon, Michael, et al., 1994). Although the disorder can be caused by psychological factors, including emotional distress, a history of sexual trauma, and lack of trust in one's partner, it can also be the result of medical and physical problems such as surgery or hormonal deficiencies.

Male Erectile Disorder Until recently, **male erectile disorder,** formerly known as *impotence,* was the one form of sexual dysfunction most often brought to the therapist's office; therefore, it was the one that received the most attention. It is a devastating problem for tens of millions of American men, and it costs almost half a billion dollars a year in inpatient urological care (National Hospital Discharge Survey, 1985). Over the years, there have been heated debates as to whether its causes are physical or psychological. In fact, most erection problems seem to have multiple causes (Buvat, Buvat-Herbaut, Lemaire, et al., 1990). Age may be a contributing factor. In the general population, about 10 percent of men report serious problems with erections, but in the over-50 population the prevalence rises to 20 percent (Laumann, Gagnon, Michael, et al., 1994). High blood pressure, high cholesterol levels, diabetes, smoking, and heart disease are all associated with erectile disorder (Berman, Berman, Werbin, et al., 1999). So are various medications, together with most forms of substance abuse. (Alcoholism is often accompanied by erectile disorder.) The range of psychological causes is equally broad: performance anxiety, stress, depression, underlying paraphilia, avoidance of intimacy, sexual inexperience, and unresolved anger toward one's sexual partner. Of these, the most common cause is performance anxiety, though that problem is normally enmeshed in others, as in the following case:

Abe and Layla were an Egyptian couple in their mid-thirties who had been married for 10 years. They presented with an erection problem that had developed when they had moved to the United States several years before. In the initial evaluation, Layla reported that she had never enjoyed sex but that she had never told Abe about this because she felt that she should not expect to enjoy sex. She had been raised in a strict Muslim household and had never been taught about sex or discussed it with anyone. Once she arrived in the United States, however, she began to learn more about sex, mainly from women's magazines and from talking with her new American friends. She understood that sex could be very different from what she had experienced and that it could be exciting for her as well. Abe, too, began to see that sex could be different than the quick, passionless encounters they had had, but this realization made him feel inadequate sexually. He imagined that American men were much better lovers than he. He was also worried about his wife's growing frustration with their sexual relationship. His self-doubt quickly developed into performance anxiety, and he began to lose his erection during sex. Sex therapy helped the couple to develop a new approach to sex, which allowed them to focus more on giving and pleasure and less on performance. (Adapted from Carroll, Northwestern University Medical School, composite and altered clinical case histories.)

Focus On... What Is Normal Sexual Response in a Woman?

One of the most common complaints women bring to sex therapists is a socially defined dysfunction: They reach orgasm not through intercourse but only through manual or oral stimulation of the clitoris or only when intercourse is combined with manual stimulation. The designation of this pattern as somehow less than normal is due in part to our society's moral strictures against masturbation; intercourse may be normal, but "touching" yourself (or being touched) is not. It is also reflected in an old Freudian distinction between "clitoral" and "vaginal" orgasms. According to Freud, only the woman who has "vaginal" orgasms is sexually normal and psychologically mature.

Many sex researchers feel that this definition of sexual normality is absurd. (It is also male-centered: Because men reach orgasm through intercourse, women should.) All orgasms, no matter how they are achieved, constitute the same physical process, and there is no evidence that women who require direct stimulation to achieve orgasm are any less healthy or mature than those who do not. Women who reach orgasm during intercourse receive indirect stimulation of the clitoris: Their partner's pubis (the bony structure behind the penis) rubs against their genitals, and penile thrusting pulls the clitoral hood back and forth. Many, possibly most, women require the more intense, *direct* stimulation of the clitoris, but the physiological mechanism of the orgasm is identical in both instances.

To say that direct clitoral stimulation is less healthy or less normal than indirect stimulation is, in the words of psychologist Joseph LoPiccolo (1977), "to draw almost mystical distinctions between the male pubis and the male hand" (p. 1239). Thus, according to LoPiccolo,

> A woman who can have coital orgasm if she receives concurrent manual stimulation of her clitoris does not have secondary orgasmic dysfunction; she is normal. Similarly, a woman who regularly has orgasm during manual or oral stimulation . . . and who enjoys intercourse even though orgasm does not occur during coitus, is a candidate for reassurance about her normality rather than for sex therapy. (p. 1239)

As Helen Singer Kaplan (1974) pointed out, female sexual response, like most human traits, is extremely variable. Women reach orgasm from erotic fantasy alone, from brief foreplay, from coitus, from manual or oral stimulation of the clitoris without coitus, from coitus combined with manual stimulation, or from intense stimulation such as that provided by a vibrator. About 10 percent of women never experience orgasm, and, although they may justifiably seek professional help if they are distressed by this, any pattern of response can serve as the foundation for a happy sexual relationship. Of course, women who are dissatisfied with their response pattern should seek sex therapy, for the pattern may well be changeable. But those who are satisfied sexually yet worry that they do not fit some definition of "normal" should save their money. There is no single normal pattern.

Men who have never been able to achieve or maintain an erection during intercourse are said to have *primary erectile dysfunction.* Those who are having trouble currently but who have a past history of successful erections in intercourse are said to have *secondary erectile dysfunction.* Successful treatment is more likely for the second form.

Orgasmic Disorders Once a critical threshold of sexual stimulation has been achieved, the person enters the third phase of the sexual response cycle, *orgasm.* In both men and women, orgasm is manifested by a muscular contraction of the genitals and the internal sex organs at 0.8-second intervals. In men, this is accompanied by an ejaculation of semen from the penis. Either sex may fail to reach orgasm, though men are more likely to complain of reaching it too soon.

Female Orgasmic Disorder When a woman has trouble reaching orgasm, she is said to have **female orgasmic disorder.** This problem has received a great deal of attention over the years, though some of the concern may have been due to an insistence on "vaginal orgasm." (See the box above.) Whatever the definition, a persistent problem in achieving orgasm was reported by almost one fourth of the women in the Sex in America survey (Laumann, Gagnon, Michael, et al., 1994). Common causes include other sexual problems (especially sexual arousal disorder), inadequate sexual stimulation, and anxiety about sex or sexual performance, body image, or the relationship with the partner. However, an increasingly frequent cause is the use of antidepressant drugs, particularly SSRIs such as Prozac, Zoloft, and Paxil. As with men, high blood pressure, high cholesterol levels, diabetes, heart disease, and smoking are associated with sexual dysfunction in women (Berman, Berman, Werbin, et al., 1999).

Male Orgasmic Disorder Male inability to reach orgasm, or **male orgasmic disorder** (also known as retarded ejaculation), is less common, reported by only 8 percent of men (Laumann, Gagnon, Michael, et al., 1994); therefore, it has been less studied. This condition, too, may be caused by antidepressant drugs, though it appears that some men just have a constitutionally high threshold for orgasm. Another common cause is an inability to "let go" with a sexual partner. Many men who cannot achieve orgasm with a partner can do so by masturbating.

Premature Ejaculation Far more common—indeed, the most common male sexual complaint, reported by almost one third of men (Laumann, Gagnon, Michael, et al., 1994)—is the opposite problem, **premature ejaculation,** in which the man reaches orgasm before, on, or shortly after penetration. A recent study found that 90 percent of men with this disorder ejaculate within 1 minute of penetration, with 80 percent ejaculating within 30 seconds (Waldinger, Hengeveld, Zwinderman, et al., 1998). Traditionally, premature ejaculation has been regarded as due to psychological factors, but recent research suggests that there may be biological causes as well (Metz, Pryor, Nesvacil, et al., 1997).

Sexual Pain Disorders Two forms of sexual dysfunction, dyspareunia and vaginismus, do not fit into the response-cycle typology.

Dyspareunia Pain during sexual activity, or **dyspareunia,** was reported by 14 percent of the women—but only 3 percent of the men—in the Sex in America survey (Laumann, Gagnon, Michael, et al., 1994). Such pain is usually due to gynecological or urological problems, but it may also be a conditioned response to sexual trauma; and there is increasing evidence that it is often psychological in origin (Binik, Bergeron, & Khalife, 2000; Graziottin, 2001).

Vaginismus An exclusively female problem is **vaginismus,** in which the muscles surrounding the outer part of the vagina contract involuntarily when attempts are made to insert the penis. This makes intercourse either impossible or painfully difficult. Like sexual arousal disorder or dyspareunia, with which it often overlaps (Graziottin, 2001), vaginismus often turns out to be a consequence of sexual trauma (Segraves & Althof, 1998), as in the following case:

Joan, 34 years old, presented with a complaint of being unable to undergo a pelvic examination because of anxiety. It soon came out that she had an additional problem. She was in a serious relationship with a man to whom she felt close, but, whenever they attempted intercourse, they were prevented by vaginismus. She felt little sexual pleasure and avoided sexual contact as much as possible.

Joan reported that when she was 10 years old her stepfather had rubbed her breasts and genitals and had inserted his finger into her vagina on a number of occasions. In high school she had avoided relationships with boys. In college, feeling peer pressure to be sexually active, she had had several bad sexual experiences, including an occasion of date rape during a party. After college, she had had a series of short-term relationships, which she had invariably ended when the man approached sex.

In therapy, she had a difficult time discussing her sexual history. She felt that it was wrong to talk about sex. She also said that she felt "dirty," and she imagined that she had a sexually transmitted disease, though there was no evidence of this. Treatment first focused on getting her to feel safe enough to discuss her past abuse. She reported that she had always felt that she was to blame for this, because she hadn't struggled. Therapy revealed that she had long mistrusted men and expected that they would eventually hurt her. As treatment progressed, she was able to develop a more emotionally intimate and pleasurable sexual relationship with her boyfriend. (Adapted from Carroll, Northwestern University Medical School, composite and altered clinical case histories.)

Diagnosing Sexual Dysfunction

In categorizing sexual problems, the *DSM-IV-TR* distinguishes between **lifelong dysfunction** (one that has existed, without relief, since the person's earliest sexual experiences) and **acquired dysfunction** (a dysfunction that develops after at least one period of normal functioning). In the case of Abe and Layla, for example, Abe had an acquired erectile disorder. It also distinguishes between **generalized dysfunction,** a dysfunction that is present in all sexual situations at the time of diagnosis, and **situational dysfunction,** which, as the term indicates, is one that occurs only in certain situations or with certain partners. For example, a woman with a generalized orgasmic disorder never experiences orgasm, while a woman with a situational orgasmic disorder may reach orgasm when masturbating alone but not while having sex with a partner. (But review the box on the preceding page for problems in defining situational orgasmic disorder in women.)

It is very important to note that, according to *DSM-IV-TR,* no sexual dysfunction can be diagnosed without evidence that the person's condition "causes marked distress or interpersonal difficulty." In other words, if a person has no interest in sex or no arousal or no orgasm—or even vaginismus—and this does not cause unhappiness or disrupt a relationship, then the person does not have a sexual dysfunction. Furthermore, the term *sexual dysfunction* applies only to problems that persist over time. Occasional episodes of "sexual failure" are normal. When a person is tired, sick, upset, intoxicated, or simply distracted, sexual responsiveness may be dulled. Neither should the label of sexual dysfunction be applied to the common occurrence of premature ejaculation, fleeting erections, or missing orgasms in young people who have not yet established a regular pattern of sexual activity and are so concerned with "doing it right" that they cannot fully enjoy sex. The myths that sex comes naturally and that a couple should be able to achieve mutual ecstasy under any and all conditions are frequent causes of sexual problems. Therapy often reveals that one episode of failure leads to another simply because the first episode created so much anxiety that sexual responsiveness is impaired on the next occasion. The second failure aggravates the anxiety, further undermining sexual performance, and so on, until a regular pattern of sexual failure is established. Furthermore, such anxiety is communicable: Sexual anxiety is often found in both members of a couple. Vaginismus and lifelong erectile disorder, or premature ejaculation and female orgasmic disorder, are often seen together in couples.

❖ Groups at Risk for Sexual Dysfunction

As Tables 13.1 and 13.2 show, the more education and money a person has, the less likely he or she is to suffer from a sexual dysfunction, as from other major problems. However, there are exceptions within this rule. For example, the rich are somewhat more likely than the middle class to report sexual problems, but the poor are far more likely than either group. Tables 13.1 and 13.2 also reveal striking ethnic differences. In general, African American people—and, according to other studies, African American men in particular—are at higher risk for sexual dysfunction than the population as a whole, though the situation varies within the dysfunction. Asian Americans, for example, are almost twice as likely as African Americans to have problems reaching orgasm.

Prevalence also varies with gender. As can be seen in Figure 13.1, women greatly outnumber men in disorders involving pain during sex, inability to achieve orgasm, and lack of interest, pleasure, or arousal. On the other hand, men are more likely to feel anxiety about sex—probably because the "performance" pressures on them are greater—and they are almost three times more likely to complain of climaxing too early. As noted, premature ejaculation is the most common male sexual complaint. (As we will see, it is also one of the most treatable sexual complaints.)

Overall, sexual dysfunction is more prevalent in women (43 percent) than in men (31 percent) (Laumann, Paik, & Rosen, 1999). It is most likely among men and women in poor physical and emotional health (Laumann, Paik, & Rosen, 1999).

TABLE 13.1 Frequency of Sexual Dysfunction in Men by Education, Ethnicity, and Income

STATUS	SEXUAL DYSFUNCTION						
	Pain During Sex	Sex Not Pleasurable	Unable to Orgasm	Lack of Interest in Sex	Anxiety About Performance	Climax Too Early	Unable to Keep an Erection
Education							
Less than high school	4.6	14.7	12.7	22.3	23.2	36.0	15.4
High school graduate	4.1	5.7	8.2	13.2	17.3	32.5	9.5
Some college	2.1	8.9	7.9	15.7	17.8	24.4	10.2
Finished college	2.2	6.6	6.5	15.7	10.9	25.8	9.1
Advanced degree	1.7	5.2	6.8	13.3	14.5	24.1	9.3
Overall	3.0	8.0	8.3	15.7	16.9	28.5	10.4
Ethnicity							
European American	3.0	7.0	7.4	14.7	16.8	27.7	9.9
African American	3.3	15.2	9.9	20.0	23.7	33.8	14.5
Latino	2.0	8.2	10.9	16.7	7.1	25.0	8.9
Asian/Pacific Islander	0.0	6.3	18.8	14.7	15.6	31.3	9.4
Overall	3.0	8.1	8.2	15.7	17.0	28.5	10.4
Income							
Poor	5.5	15.3	15.9	25.4	20.5	29.7	14.0
Middle	2.8	6.0	7.2	13.0	15.3	28.0	9.1
Rich	1.9	9.1	6.1	15.0	14.2	30.3	11.3
Overall	2.9	7.5	7.9	14.6	15.6	28.6	10.0

Source: Adapted from Laumann, Gagnon, Michael, et al., 1994, p. 370.

TABLE 13.2 Frequency of Sexual Dysfunction in Women by Education, Ethnicity, and Income

STATUS	SEXUAL DYSFUNCTION						
	Pain During Sex	Sex Not Pleasurable	Unable to Orgasm	Lack of Interest in Sex	Anxiety About Performance	Climax Too Early	Trouble Lubricating
Education							
Less than high school	16.1	25.8	30.0	43.2	16.2	17.4	14.0
High school graduate	16.8	22.2	28.0	35.4	11.8	11.7	19.5
Some college	14.5	20.5	22.4	32.0	10.4	9.3	19.2
Finished college	9.6	18.4	19.1	27.9	8.3	6.2	19.3
Advanced degree	9.3	16.5	13.3	23.4	13.3	4.1	23.7
Overall	14.3	21.2	24.0	33.4	11.5	10.3	18.8
Ethnicity							
European American	14.7	19.7	23.2	30.9	10.5	7.5	20.7
African American	12.5	30.0	29.2	44.5	14.5	20.4	13.0
Latino	13.6	19.8	20.3	34.6	11.7	18.4	12.0
Overall	14.4	21.2	24.1	33.4	11.5	10.3	18.8
Income							
Poor	16.2	23.3	27.4	39.7	20.0	18.2	13.9
Middle	14.5	21.5	23.6	32.0	10.2	10.6	19.0
Rich	11.4	17.3	20.8	27.5	11.7	4.4	23.7
Overall	14.3	21.1	23.8	32.5	12.0	10.8	18.9

Source: Adapted from Laumann, Gagnon, Michael, et al., 1994, p. 371.

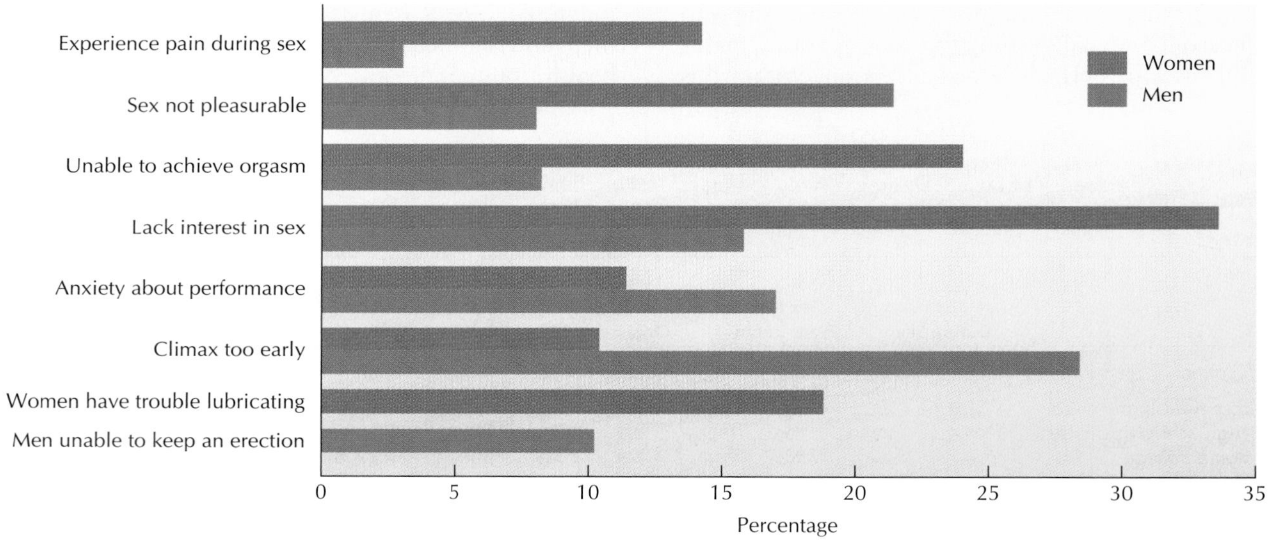

FIGURE 13.1 Sexual dysfunction by gender. (Adapted from Laumann, Gagnon, Michael, et al., 1994, p. 369.)

Sexual Dysfunction: Theory and Therapy

The Psychodynamic Perspective

As we saw in Chapter 5, Freud claimed that mature genital sexuality was the product of successful resolution of the Oedipus complex. Accordingly, classical psychodynamic theory tends to attribute sexual dysfunction to unresolved Oedipal conflicts. This line of thinking can be seen in the interpretation of impotence offered by Otto Fenichel (1945) in the following excerpt:

> Impotence is based on a persistence of an unconscious sensual attachment to the mother. Superficially no sexual attachment is completely attractive because the partner is never the mother; in a deeper layer, every sexual

> attachment has to be inhibited, because every partner represents the mother. (p. 170)

Similarly, psychoanalytic formulations of female orgasmic disorder tend to stress the role of continued penis envy.

More current psychodynamic approaches to sexual disorders have focused instead on disturbances in object relations as underlying most sexual dysfunctions (Scharff & Scharff, 1991).

Psychodynamic therapy for sexual dysfunction follows the same principles as psychodynamic treatment in general: uncovering the conflict and working through it, primarily via analysis of defenses. While there is no evidence from controlled studies that such an approach actually relieves sexual dysfunction, for many years it was the only form of treatment that was generally available. Certain authorities who took other approaches (Ellis, 1962; Wolpe, 1958) argued that sexual dysfunction, instead of being analyzed as a symptom of underlying conflict, should be attacked directly, by altering either the behavior in question or the attitudes surrounding it. But this was a minority view. Then in 1970 came the publication of Masters and Johnson's *Human Sexual Inadequacy,* outlining a systematic, short-term approach to direct symptomatic treatment. This approach, described in the next section, revolutionized sex therapy.

The Behavioral and Cognitive Perspectives

Learned Anxiety and the Spectator Role Behavioral theories of sexual dysfunction have focused consistently on the role of early respondent conditioning, in which sexual feelings are paired with shame, disgust, fear of discovery, and especially anxiety over possible failure, all of which then proceed to block sexual responsiveness (Kaplan, 1974; Wolpe, 1969). This is also the position of Masters and Johnson, though they do not associate themselves with behaviorism or with any other theoretical school. According to Masters and Johnson (1970), any one of a number of painful experiences can cause a person to worry that he or she will be unable to perform adequately—will not achieve erection, will reach orgasm too quickly or not quickly enough, or whatever. As a result of this anxiety, the worried partner assumes what Masters and Johnson call the **spectator role;** that is, instead of simply relaxing and experiencing pleasure, the person is constantly watching and judging his or her performance. And, with cruel irony, the performance is almost inevitably a failure, because the person's tense and critical attitude blunts his or her responsiveness to sexual stimuli.

As for the factors that first trigger performance anxiety and lead to the adoption of the spectator role, Masters and Johnson (1970) point to several possibilities: religious and sociocultural taboos on sexual feelings, particularly for women; disturbance in the marriage; parental dominance of one partner; overuse of alcohol; and, finally, early psychosexual trauma, which can range from molestation and rape to ordinary humiliation, such as the following:

> During the patient's first sexual episode the prostitute took the unsuspecting virginal male to a vacant field and suggested they have intercourse while she leaned against a stone fence. Since he had no concept of female anatomy, of where to insert the penis, he failed miserably in this sexually demanding opportunity. His graphic memory of the incident is of running away from a laughing woman.
>
> The second prostitute provided a condom and demanded its use. He had no concept of how to use the condom. While the prostitute was demonstrating the technique, he ejaculated. He dressed and again fled the scene in confusion. (p. 177)

If sexual dysfunction stems from faulty learning, so that sexual arousal comes to be associated with anxiety, then presumably it may be curable through new learning that gradually breaks down and eliminates this association. This idea is the basis of Masters and Johnson's treatment strategy and of most current behavioral sex therapies.

Assessment Crucial to direct treatment is proper assessment, for that is how the therapist finds out what factors are lurking behind the sexual problem. In assessment, every effort is made to include both members of the sexual relationship, in order to take into account all the biological, psychological, interpersonal, and cultural factors impinging on the case. After a description of the problem has been developed, the therapist typically explores with the couple their "sexual script" (Gagnon, Rosen, & Leiblum, 1982): who does what to whom, sexually and what thoughts, emotions, and sensations each associates with sex. The therapist also tries to tap into social norms and cultural mores that influence the couple's behavior. A full formulation of the sexual problem also includes a detailed history of how each member developed his or her sexuality, including learned attitudes, patterns of sexual arousal, and any episodes of sexual trauma.

Direct Symptomatic Treatment In the treatment itself, the couple is retrained to experience sexual excitement without performance pressure.* Training

*When the person seeking therapy does not have a partner, or when the partner is unwilling, Masters and Johnson, together with other therapists, have sometimes provided surrogate partners. However, this practice is controversial. Indeed, it has been called prostitution. Furthermore, in the case of unwilling partners, the relationship is unlikely to benefit from what the willing partner learned with a surrogate. It is rarely used these days.

Sensate focus exercises are designed to help partners rediscover their natural sexual responses and provide feedback to each other.

usually takes the form of *sensate focus exercises.* During the period devoted to these exercises, the partners observe a ban on sexual intercourse. Instead, they simply devote a certain amount of time to gentle stroking and caressing in the nude, according to instructions given by the therapist. Very gradually, the allowed sexual play is increased, but always without performance demands.

The purpose of sensate focus exercises is not only to allow the partners to rediscover their natural sexual responses without anxiety but also to improve their communication. In the course of the exercises, each provides the other with feedback—what feels good, what doesn't feel good. The sharing of such information, aside from its crucial value in allowing the partners to satisfy each other, also deepens their trust in each other, which may have been sorely damaged by years of unhappy sex. After a period of sensate focus exercises, the couple is given more specific exercises, aimed directly at the disorder in question.

For premature ejaculation, many therapists prescribe the so-called start-stop technique (Semans, 1956). In this procedure, the woman stimulates the man's penis until the man feels ready to ejaculate, at which point he signals her to stop. Once the need to ejaculate subsides, she stimulates him again, until he once again signals her to stop. Once the need to ejaculate subsides, she stimulates him again, until he once again signals her to stop. Repeated many times, this technique gradually increases the amount of stimulation required to trigger the ejaculation response, so that eventually the man can maintain an erection for a longer time. The "squeeze" technique, in which the woman squeezes the shaft of the man's penis when he feels close to ejaculation, has a similar effect.

With erectile disorder, the therapist, to eliminate anxiety, may actually tell the patient to try *not* to have an erection while he and his partner are going through their sensate focus exercises. This technique of forbidding the behavior that the patient is trying to accomplish is called *paradoxical instruction.*

Instructed not to have an erection, the patient may find himself sufficiently free of anxiety that he begins to respond to the sexual stimuli and, thus, has the prohibited erection. Once this happens, the therapist permits the couple, in very gradual stages, to proceed further and further toward intercourse, always with the warning that the techniques work best if the man can prevent himself from having an erection. In the end, intravaginal ejaculation is allowed only after it has already occurred because the man could not stop himself (LoPiccolo & Lobitz, 1973).

The most effective treatment for lifelong orgasmic dysfunction in women (Heiman, 2002; LoPiccolo & Stock, 1986) begins with education on female sexual anatomy and self-exploration exercises designed to increase body awareness. Then the woman is taught techniques of self-stimulation, perhaps with the aid of an electric vibrator and/or erotic pictures and books. This approach is based on the belief that masturbation enables a woman to identify the signs of sexual excitation, to discover which techniques excite her, and to anticipate pleasure in sex. When she has achieved orgasm alone, the therapist recommends sensate exercises with her partner, gradually incorporating the "orgasm triggers" she used alone. She may be encouraged to use a vibrator while her partner is present and to engage in the fantasies that arouse her when she is masturbating. Teaching her partner what stimulates her is an essential element of this program. Treatment of women with situational orgasmic disorder is similar. For women with sexual aversion disorder, these procedures are often combined with systematic desensitization. As with male sexual problems, the goal is to remove the pressure to perform and to encourage, instead, the simple experience of pleasure.

Because anxiety is common in most patients with sexual disorders, relaxation techniques and other antianxiety interventions are often useful. One such technique uses frequent and increasingly intense endorphin-producing exercises (Hernandez-Serrano, 2001), which can enhance arousal by reducing anxiety and stimulating positive mood states.

Cognitive Psychology and Direct Treatment Masters and Johnson popularized the concept of direct treatment of sexual dysfunction: attacking the symptom itself, without extensive exploration of its psychic roots. At the same time, their concern is not just with the couple's sexual behavior but also with the partners' thoughts about sex—and about each other. Throughout this therapy, the emphasis is on the *couple*. During the assessment phase, the therapist explores the beliefs and experiences that may have led to the present dysfunction. Shame-ridden memories are discussed with comforting matter-of-factness; repressive attitudes are challenged outright; the person is encouraged to appreciate his or her sexuality. Resentments and fears that may have blocked communication are aired. As with the sensate focus exercises, the aim here is not just to increase the flow of information but also to restore a sense of trusting collaboration between the partners.

Following Masters and Johnson's lead, cognitive psychologists have further explored the mental processes underlying sexual response—for example, the development of attitudes that can block arousal. Wincze (1989) cites the case, not an unusual one, of a man who learned when he was young the difference between "good girls" and "bad girls." He knew that his wife was a "good girl," a respectable woman, but her desire for sex confused and inhibited him because it was "bad-girl" behavior. This man also believed that in order to approach his wife sexually he needed to be fully aroused; it did not occur to him that arousal might develop in the *course* of sexual intimacy. Between these two beliefs, this man and his wife, both in their thirties, had had intercourse only once in the seven months before they sought treatment (at the wife's urging).

Cognitive therapists have also developed treatments that aim directly at attitudes and beliefs hostile to sex. For women, common interferences include negative attitudes toward the body ("Does he think I'm fat?") and worries about the propriety of sexual expression ("If I act too eager, he won't respect me"). But thoughts need not be antisexual in order to interfere with sex. Worries about work or children can also block sexual responsiveness. Often, cognitive therapists urge patients to allow sexual stimuli into their lives—for example, by reading erotic literature or giving some time each day to sexual thoughts. Such techniques are not confined to strictly cognitive therapy. Almost all sex therapists try to attack negative cognitions. Conversely, cognitive therapy is often combined with other approaches, particularly behavioral "direct treatment."

Weisberg and co-workers (Weisberg, Brown, Wincze, et al., 2001) studied the role of causal attributions in the sexual response of normally functioning men. Participants viewed sexually explicit films and were then told, falsely, that their erectile response had been relatively small. Some of the men were given an internal reason for their supposedly low response (they had problematic thoughts about sex); others were given an external reason (the films were not erotic enough). Unlike the men in the first group, who blamed their own thoughts for their lack of erectile response, the men who blamed their lack of arousal on the poor quality of the films had greater erectile response and subjective arousal while watching another erotic film. The researchers concluded that when a man has an erectile difficulty or other sexual problem, the cause to which the difficulty is attributed plays an important role in future sexual functioning.

Multifaceted Treatment

Some sex researchers are dissatisfied with the theory that sexual dysfunction is caused by faulty learning. As they point out, millions of sexually untroubled people have been exposed to learning of this sort. Many people, perhaps most, were taught that sex was dirty. For many people, the first attempt at intercourse was painful and embarrassing. (Indeed, for many people, the attempt failed.) And many people have unhappy marriages—yet their sexual functioning remains stubbornly normal. Obviously, the cause of sexual dysfunction involves more than bad experiences and repressive attitudes. Consequently, some sex therapists, while using the kind of direct treatment outlined in this section, combine it with an exploration of intrapsychic or relationship factors that may be causing sexual dysfunction, or at least helping to maintain it.

Kaplan: Remote Causes The sex therapists who came after Masters and Johnson tended to probe psychological factors more systematically and more deeply. Helen Singer Kaplan (1974), for example, combined the psychodynamic approach with behavioral techniques. She argued that sexual dysfunction was probably due to a combination of immediate and remote causes. *Immediate causes* are factors such as performance anxiety, overconcern about pleasing one's partner, poor technique, lack of communication between partners, and marital conflict—the sort of causes on which Masters and Johnson concentrated. Such factors, Kaplan claimed, are potent stressors, but in most cases they are not enough to undermine sexual functioning unless they are combined with (or based on) *remote causes* of sexual dysfunction: intrapsychic conflicts that predispose the person to anxiety over sexual expression. These conflicts are essentially the same as those the psychodynamic theorists blame for sexual dysfunction: infantile needs, deep-seated guilt, and—above all—unresolved Oedipal struggles.

Helen Singer Kaplan, a noted sex therapist, devised a multifaceted treatment for sexual dysfunction that she called psychosexual therapy.

On the basis of this theory, Kaplan (1974, 1979) devised a combined "direct" and psychodynamic treatment that she called psychosexual therapy. She agreed with other direct therapists that behavior should be the primary focus of treatment and that unconscious conflicts, even when they are obvious to the therapist, should be bypassed as long as the patient is responding to the direct treatment. But, in some instances, she argued, the remote causes prevent the patient from responding to therapy. In such cases, Kaplan felt, brief insight therapy is called for. Furthermore, in many instances the direct therapy itself brings to the surface psychological problems that the patient has been blocking through avoidance of normal sexual functioning. Indeed, it is extremely common for patients to progress well in direct therapy until they are just on the edge of reaching their goal, at which point they seem to experience a flood of anxiety and begin to resist treatment. Kaplan interpreted this response as a last-ditch attempt to maintain psychological defenses against whatever conflict has been blocking sexual responsiveness. And she claimed that at this point psychodynamic exploration of the patient's conflict was necessary before direct therapy could be resumed.

Interpersonal Theory: The Function of the Dysfunction A central principle of Masters and Johnson's treatment was that the patient was the *couple:* To solve the sexual problem, the therapist had to address the psychological conflicts between the partners. Other therapists confront the psychological components of sexual dysfunction via interpersonal theory, the analysis of relationships as systems of interlocking needs (Chapter 5). According to this approach, sexual dysfunction, distressing though it may be to the couple, usually has an important function in the couple's total relationship—that is, it serves psychological purposes for both partners (Heiman, LoPiccolo, & LoPiccolo, 1981). Consider, for example, low sexual desire on the part of the man, a problem that is turning up more and more frequently in sex therapy (Kaplan, 1974; Schover & LoPiccolo, 1982; Spector & Carey, 1990). Low sexual desire often has a number of causes. If the relationship in question involves conflicts over power and control, with the woman tending to dominate, then the man's lack of interest in sex may be his way of preserving some area of control for himself. At the same time, the woman, though she may complain of the man's sexual indifference, may also be deriving benefits from it. By seeing him as weak, for example, she maintains power in the relationship.

According to interpersonal theorists, such secret payoffs underlie many cases of sexual dysfunction and must be dealt with if the problem is to be relieved. The therapist generally addresses the "function of dysfunction" from the beginning of treatment, asking patients to describe the benefits they derive from the problem, warning them that they may feel considerable fear when the problem begins to lessen; analyzing this fear, once it appears, as the product of a shaken system; and helping them to devise a better system. Such analysis, like Kaplan's, is combined with direct treatment.

Results of Cognitive-Behavioral Direct Treatment Though success rates for cognitive-behavioral direct treatment have rarely matched the outcomes claimed by Masters and Johnson (1970) in their early work, they are still good (Hawton, 1992; Heiman, 1997). For female arousal and orgasmic disorder, self-stimulation exercises have been very successful, especially in the case of lifelong rather than acquired dysfunctions. For vaginismus, a gradual program of relaxation and dilation of the vagina, either by fingers or by dilators, is effective in 75 to 100 percent of cases. For male erectile disorder, the basic cognitive-behavioral techniques—sensate focus exercises, relaxation, and systematic desensitization—work with about two thirds of patients (Hawton, 1992; Wylie, 1997). For premature ejaculation, the stop-start technique is helpful in about three quarters of cases. There have been no controlled outcome studies of treatment of low desire in either men or women. Low desire in men seems especially difficult to alter; some men may simply have a constitutionally low level of sexual interest. However, treatment of this dysfunction is still in its early stages, and it is unlikely that any one therapy will be best for the majority of patients, male or female, because the range of factors underlying the problem is so broad. Recently, cognitive therapists have developed treatment programs that have several components, such as helping patients to overcome denial and minimization of their behavior, enhancing empathy for patients, providing intimacy training, changing distorted attitudes and beliefs, changing inappropriate fantasies, and developing relapse-prevention plans (Caballo, 1998).

Outcome studies have addressed the treatment setup as well. While Masters and Johnson (1970) popularized the idea of an intensive, live-in, two-week program, with the couple receiving counseling from two co-therapists, one male and one female, later research has not supported these requirements. It appears that once-a-week sessions, in the couple's home city, are sufficient; that one therapist works as well as two; and that no matching of patient and therapist by gender is necessary. (On the other hand, Masters and Johnson's insistence on having both members of the couple in therapy has been strongly supported.) Research has also shown that group therapy is useful with certain dysfunctions, notably female orgasmic disorder and male erectile disorder. Instructional books are helpful, too. Finally, in keeping with systems theory, it does seem that combining relationship therapy with direct treatment is very beneficial (Hawton, 1992; Heiman & Meston, 1997).

The Neuroscience Perspective

In 1970, Masters and Johnson asserted that 95 percent of erectile failures were psychological, not physiological or organic, in origin. Today researchers are not so sure (LoPiccolo, 1992; Hernandez-Serrano, 2001). In some cases, organic causes are known. Erectile disorder may be the result of diabetes, heart disease, kidney disease, or alcoholism. A variety of medical treatments—renal dialysis, tranquilizers, antidepressants, medications for hypertension—can also interfere with erection. Long-term use of oral contraceptives can reduce the female sex drive. Female dyspareunia may be caused by vaginal infections, ovarian cysts, or lacerations or scar tissue resulting from childbirth (Sarrel, 1977). Other organic factors—hormonal deficiencies, neurological impairment, neurotransmitter imbalances—are suspected contributors to sexual dysfunction.

In the 1970s and early 1980s, many sex researchers concentrated on developing diagnostic tools for differentiating between psychological and organic sexual dysfunction. They invented devices for measuring vasocongestion in the genital region; they devised tests of the sensory threshold in the genital area. Research on *nocturnal penile tumescence* (NPT) attracted a good deal of attention. Men have erections during rapid-eye-movement (REM) sleep, the stage of sleep associated with dreams. NPT research is based on the assumption that, if a man has erections while he is asleep but not during sexual encounters, his problem is primarily psychological in origin.

Today, however, researchers are questioning the very concept of differentiating the organic from the psychological cases (LoPiccolo, 1992). Rather, they believe that many, if not most, cases of sexual dysfunction involve *both* psychological and physiological factors. A mild organic impairment—perhaps one that cannot be detected by current techniques, or one not yet known to be associated with sexual functioning—may make a person vulnerable to sexual dysfunction. But whether that person actually experiences sexual difficulties may depend on psychological factors, learning, and/or sexual technique. This would help to explain, for example, why some people who have been taught that sex is sinful or who had humiliating early experiences with sex function normally, while others do not. Research and clinical experience have shown that some cases of sexual dysfunction are purely psychological, some primarily organic, and many others the result of interacting organic and psychological factors.

Over the past decade, considerable progress has been made in developing biological treatments, particularly for erectile disorder. One technique involves the man's injecting a vascular dilation agent (papaverine) into his penis when he wants an erection. The penis becomes erect within 30 minutes of the injection and remains erect for 1 to 4 hours. Many men have reported satisfaction with this method (Iribarren, 1999), but there is some question about its long-term use, because a substantial number of patients develop nodules on their penises as a side effect. Researchers are now experimenting with a variation on this technique: inserting the vasodilator, in pellet form, into the urethra, where it is absorbed into the tissue of the penis. A third treatment involves taking (by mouth) a drug called yohimbine, which has long had a reputation as an aphrodisiac. Yohimbine stimulates the secretion of norepinephrine and thereby increases the firing rate of nerve cells in the brain. Therefore, it is possible that the drug corrects neurotransmission problems that are causing the erectile disorder. Research by Mann and his colleagues suggests that yohimbine has a stronger effect on erectile dysfunction that does not have a biological basis. But further research is necessary to resolve this issue (Mann,

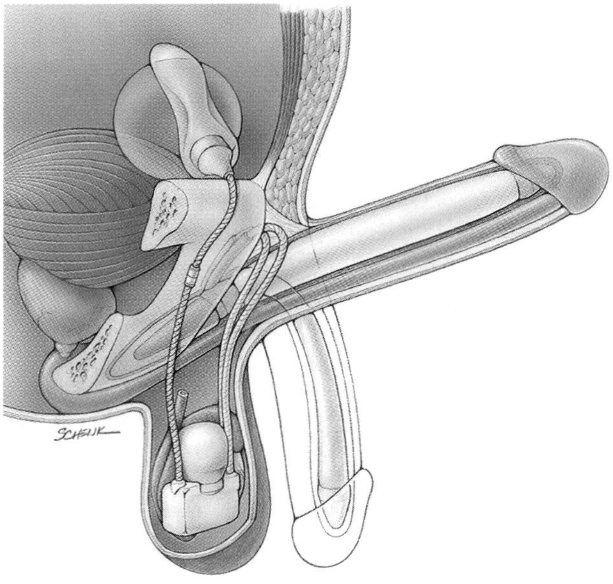

Here is how one type of penile prosthesis (the Ambicor Penile Prosthesis) works.

Klingler, Noe, et al., 1996). In women, yohimbine seems to help increase sexual arousal (Hernandez-Serrano, 2001).

For men who do not benefit from medications or sex therapy, penile prostheses have proven to be reliable and safe, with few complications (Levine, Estrad, & Morgenthaler, 2001). They are used for nonreversible, organically based erectile dysfunctions (Hernandez-Serrano, 2001). In one type, a semirigid rod is surgically inserted into the penis. This makes the penis permanently stiff enough for intercourse. At the same time, the rod is bendable enough for the penis to look normal under clothing. In another type of prosthesis, a water-filled bag is surgically inserted into the abdomen and connected by tubes to inflatable cylinders that are inserted into the penis. When the man wants an erection, he pumps the bag, causing the water to flow into the penile cylinders and thus engorge the penis. Follow-ups on penile prosthesis recipients (Steege, Stout, & Culley, 1986; Tiefer, Pedersen, & Melman, 1988) indicate that most of them, if they had to do it over again, would choose the prosthesis, primarily for the repair of their self-esteem, but that their sexual satisfaction was still not equal to what they enjoyed before they developed erection problems.

The newest medical treatment for erectile disorder is via oral medications such as sildenifil (Viagra) and apomorphine, which seem to help in some cases regardless of whether the erection problem is due to organic or psychological factors. These drugs act peripherally—that is, in the tissue of the penis itself—to trigger relaxation of the smooth muscle of the penis, which results in vascular enlargement and produces an erection. In drug trials, nearly 75 percent of men taking Viagra got erections within 60 minutes of swallowing the pill, double the rate of response in a control group taking a placebo (Goldstein, Lue, Padma-Nathan, et al., 1998). Because of Viagra's side effects, which include facial flush, headache, and dizziness, many patients with erectile dysfunction prefer to use a penile prosthesis, despite the drug's greater comfort and ease of use (Jain, Rademaker, & McVary, 2000). Testosterone supplementation is another recent treatment that has shown promise for some men with erectile dysfunction (Jain, Rademaker, & McVary, 2000).

Some evidence suggests that Viagra works in women to restore lost libido (sex drive and arousability) caused by the use of the SSRI antidepressants (Hernandez-Serrano, 2001). Hormone therapy, such as estrogen-replacement therapy, given to women during menopause also seems to enhance sexual drive and to decrease discomfort during intercourse (Hernandez-Serrano, 2001). Finally, some women with orgasmic dysfunction find that nonprescription topical solutions, such as Viacreme or Viagel, increase sensitivity and assist in reaching orgasm, probably by increasing blood flow to the clitoris.

Another recent advance in medical treatment is the use of SSRI antidepressants for premature ejaculation. As noted, many people taking SSRIs for depression develop delayed orgasm as a side effect. By the same token, these drugs help control premature orgasm (Assalian & Margolese, 1996).

A major trend in today's sex therapy is the integration of physical and psychological treatment. For example, even in cases of erectile disorder in which there is clearly an organic cause, treatment with injections works better if the psychological aspects of the problem are also addressed, and if the couple are helped to incorporate the injection process into their "sexual script." For almost everyone, sex is a tender matter, and even the most purely organic problem has psychological consequences—embarrassment, nervousness—that cannot be addressed by purely organic treatments.

Paraphilias

Our definition of normal sexual behavior is much broader than it was prior to the sexual revolution of the late twentieth century. Premarital sex, oral sex, homosexuality—behaviors that were spoken of in whispers, if at all, 50 years ago—are now discussed casually by many people. This does not

Most paraphilic behaviors occur in mild form in daily life. For example, this billboard caters to mild voyeurism.

mean, however, that all barriers have fallen. According to *DSM-IV-TR*—and, it is safe to assume, according to most members of our society—normal sexuality still consists of a nondestructive interplay between consenting adults.

A number of recognized sexual patterns deviate from this standard. These patterns are called **paraphilias** (from the Greek *para,* meaning "beside" or "amiss," and *philia,* meaning "love"). We shall discuss the following:

1. **Fetishism:** reliance on inanimate objects or on a body part (to the exclusion of the person as a whole) for sexual gratification
2. **Transvestism:** sexual gratification through dressing in the clothes of the opposite sex
3. **Exhibitionism:** sexual gratification through display of one's genitals to an involuntary observer
4. **Voyeurism:** sexual gratification through clandestine observation of other people's sexual activities or sexual anatomy
5. **Sadism:** sexual gratification through infliction of pain and/or humiliation on others
6. **Masochism:** sexual gratification through pain and/or humiliation inflicted on oneself
7. **Frotteurism:** sexual gratification through touching and rubbing against a nonconsenting person
8. **Pedophilia:** child molesting—that is, sexual gratification, on the part of the adult, through sexual contact with prepubescent children
9. **Rape:** sexual intercourse with a nonconsenting partner

Some paraphilias—most importantly, child molesters and rapists—are defined by the law as *sexual offenders:* Their acts are grounds for criminal prosecution.

At the same time, a distinction must be made between paraphilias that involve harm to others and those that are essentially victimless, such as fetishism and transvestism. Other paraphilias fall between the two poles: They may or may not cause harm, depending on the circumstances.

It is important to note that most of these behaviors occur in mild, playful, or sublimated forms in what we call everyday life. Sexually explicit movies, videos, websites, and television programs—magazine and billboard advertisements, too—cater to what might be called normal voyeurism. The Internet provides an outlet not only for normal voyeuristic pursuits but also for paraphilic behavior that our society considers abnormal (Kim & Bailey, 1997). It is only when the unusual object choice becomes the central focus and *sine qua non* of the person's arousal and gratification that the pattern is generally deemed abnormal by the society and by diagnosticians. Similarly, many people have fantasies involving sexual aggression, but it is only when these impulses are acted upon that they are labeled pathological.

Fetishism

Fetishism is a good example of a spectrum disorder, one that exists on a continuum ranging from normal to abnormal, with many variations in between. It is not unusual, of course, for people to concentrate sexual interest on a particular attribute of the opposite sex. Certain women consider the male buttocks to be particularly important, while many men are fascinated by large breasts. Other men prefer as sexual partners women who are stylishly dressed, and the sight of a pair of underpants held together with a safety pin can leave them discouraged sexually. In general, however, such people, despite their preferences, do not disregard the rest of the person and can respond to conventional sexual stimuli.

Further along the continuum, we can place the following case, reported by von Krafft-Ebing (1886/1965a):

> A lady told Dr. Gemy that in the bridal night and in the night following her husband contented himself with kissing her, and running his fingers through the wealth of her tresses. He then fell asleep. In the third night Mr. X produced an immense wig, with enormously long hair, and begged his wife to put it on. As soon as she had done so, he richly compensated her for his neglected marital duties. In the morning he showed again extreme tenderness, whilst he caressed the wig. When Mrs. X removed the wig she lost at once all charm for her husband. Mrs. X recognized this as a hobby, and readily yielded to the wishes of her husband, whom she loved dearly, and whose libido depended on the wearing of the wig. It was remarkable, however, that a wig had the desired effect only for a fortnight or three weeks at a time. It had to be made of thick, long hair, no matter of what colour. The result of this marriage was, after five years, two children, and a collection of seventy-two wigs. (pp. 157–158)

Mr. X's "hobby" still falls in the middle of the continuum, for, once the wig was present, he was interested in intercourse with his wife. In most cases of fetishism that come to the attention of diagnosticians, sexual absorption in a single body part—a pattern known as *partialism*—or, more commonly, fascination with an inanimate object—has totally crowded out any interest in normal sexual interplay with another human being. Much of the person's life is occupied with collecting new examples of his favored object.

Most fetishes are closely associated with the human body. Common choices are fur, women's stockings, women's shoes, women's gloves, and especially women's underpants. More exotic fetishes have also been reported. Bergler (1947) cited the case of a man whose major source of sexual gratification was the sight of well-formed automobile exhaust pipes. The fetishist's sexual activity, typically, consists of fondling, kissing, and smelling the fetish and masturbating in the process.

Transvestism

Transvestism is similar to fetishism—indeed, *DSM-IV-TR* calls it "transvestic fetishism"—in that it involves a fascination with inanimate objects. But transvestites go one step further and actually put on their fetish, which is the clothing of the opposite sex. Once cross-dressed, transvestites typically masturbate privately or have heterosexual intercourse, though they may also enjoy appearing publicly in their costumes.

Transvestites usually do not come into conflict with the law, and in recent years social attitudes toward transvestism have eased somewhat. Indeed, nightclubs featuring transvestite performers have become increasingly popular. Partly as a result of this social tolerance, there has been little psychological investigation of transvestism. As a group, transvestites appear to be no more prone to psychological disturbance than the population at large (Bentler & Prince, 1970; Bentler, Shearman, & Prince, 1970), although about half of all cross-dressers seek counseling (Docter & Prince, 1997) for problems in their marriages. A recent study by Reynolds and Caron (2000) examined the effect of cross-dressing on transvestites' intimate relationships. The researchers found that most of the men (aged 31–79) had identified themselves as cross-dressers for decades, had developed an entire feminine identity with a name, and regularly appeared in public cross-dressed. Most of the men were married, and many wives were accepting of their husbands' behavior, though they worried what other people would think if they found out about it. Wives who do not learn about the cross-dressing until years into the marriage feel angry and betrayed. But some women tolerate their husbands' transvestism and incorporate it into the sexual relationship, as in the following case:

> Curtis is a 29-year-old married contractor who has a secret. When he goes to work each morning he wears a pair of women's panties. He began cross-dressing as a young boy when he would sneak into his older sister's room and put on her panties or bra. Eventually, he stole some women's underwear from the girls' locker room at school. He wore the panties while he masturbated. When Curtis left home and went to college he began wearing women's panties under his clothes every day and continued to use them to masturbate.
>
> He dated infrequently in college until he met Sally. She was kind and he enjoyed being with her. Curtis had his first sexual experience with a woman when he and Sally had sex one night during his junior year. As their relationship progressed, Curtis felt he

could no longer hide his secret from her. One night he told Sally that he wore women's panties under his clothes. She seemed confused about why he needed to wear the panties, but was not very upset about the fact that he wore them. Tentatively, Curtis asked her if she would be willing to let him wear the panties while they were having sex. Sally nodded, and said, "I guess so, if that makes you happy." A year later they were married. During the first few years of their marriage Curtis continued to wear panties during sex. His wife periodically went shopping and brought home new panties for him as the old ones wore out. (Fauman, 1994, p. 295)

Transvestism is thought to be relatively rare, but the reported rarity may be due to lack of public exposure or public alarm. Many transvestites lead quiet, conventional lives, cross-dressing only in their bedrooms and never appearing on talk shows or in therapists' offices. Thus, the pattern may be more common than is assumed.

Transvestism is often confused with other forms of cross-dressing. There are two primary reasons a man will dress in women's clothing: first, for sexual pleasure and, second, for the purpose of assuming a female role. It is men in the first category who are transvestites. (However, many transvestites, as they grow older, come to associate cross-dressing more with a sense of calm and well-being than with sexual arousal.) Men in the second category, who are dressing as women not for sexual arousal but to take on the role of a woman, are not transvestites. This group includes "drag queens," who are almost always homosexual men who simply enjoy playing with the female role, and female impersonators, who assume female roles as part of a performance.

Transvestites are also sometimes confused with transsexuals, or people with gender identity disorder. As we will see, such confusion is justified by the facts. There appears to be a continuum between pure transvestism (sexual arousal associated with the fetish of cross-dressing) and transsexualism (the desire to change one's gender). While most transvestites are content, outside the sexual setting, with being men, others experience a persistent desire to become female, and some go on to seek sex reassignment surgery.

Another related phenomenon is **autogynephilia,** from the Greek *auto-* (self), *gyne-* (woman), and *philia* (love). In this pattern, the man depends for sexual arousal on the fantasy of being a woman (Blanchard, 1989). When asked which of three images—a nude male, a nude female, or himself as a woman—is most exciting sexually, the autogynephilic chooses the third. Some of these men label themselves as homosexual and say that they enjoy fantasies of making love to a man, but, when the fantasy is explored, it usually becomes clear that the other man in the fantasy is mainly a prop. The primary sexual stimulus is the image of the self as a woman. Autogynephilia probably underlies many cases of transvestism; that is, the man probably cross-dresses in order to support the fantasy of being a woman.

Exhibitionism

Exhibitionism and voyeurism are the two sex offenses most often reported to the police. They are usually treated harshly by the courts, on the assumption that, if treated leniently, the offender will graduate to more serious sex crimes. Studies of sex offenders indicate that more than 10 percent of child

Cross-dressing is seen in transvestites, in transsexuals, and also in homosexual "drag queens."

molesters and 8 percent of rapists began as exhibitionists (Abel, Rouleau, & Cunningham-Rathner, 1984). But most exhibitionists are not dangerous; they do not attempt to have sexual contact with their victims.

Exhibitionism usually has its onset in the midteens or early twenties (Murphy, 1997). The typical exhibitionist is a young man, sexually inhibited and unhappily married (Blair & Lanyon, 1981; Mohr, Turner, & Jerry, 1964). Experiencing an irresistible impulse to exhibit himself, he usually goes to a public place, such as a park, a movie theater, or a department store, or simply walks down a city street and upon sighting the appropriate victim—typically, a young woman, though sometimes a young girl—shows her his penis. The penis is usually, but not always, erect. The exhibitionist's gratification is derived from the woman's response, which is generally shock, fear, and revulsion, although exhibitionists also enjoy victims who show excitement. Observing the reaction, the exhibitionist experiences intense arousal, at which point he may ejaculate spontaneously or masturbate to ejaculation. Usually, however, he goes home and then masturbates while fantasizing about the event. (In some instances, the episode is not followed by ejaculation; the exhibitionist merely obtains psychic relief.) Although an encounter with an exhibitionist may involve no physical harm, it can be very upsetting for an adult and traumatic for a child.

In some cases, exhibitionism occurs as a symptom of a more pervasive disturbance, such as schizophrenia, epilepsy, senile brain deterioration, or mental retardation, or, more rarely, as preliminary stalking behavior in serial killers. Early studies suggested that most exhibitionists turn out to be simply shy, submissive, immature men who have uncommonly puritanical attitudes about sex (Witzig, 1968), particularly about masturbation, and feelings of social and sexual inferiority (Blair & Lanyon, 1981). But recent research raises doubts about these findings and suggests there is little evidence of any specific personality pattern, such as shyness or unassertiveness, or even any unusually disordered family background, in exhibitionists (Murphy, 1997). It has been suggested that exhibitionists display their genitals for shock value, perhaps in an effort to convince themselves of their masculine prowess (Blane & Roth, 1967; Christoffel, 1956), all the while arranging the circumstances so that the victim is unlikely to respond positively and thus make sexual demands on them. In the rare instance in which the victim shows indifference or scorn rather than the expected shock and dismay, the exhibitionist is generally cheated of sexual gratification. Indeed, it has been suggested that the best cure for exhibitionism would be to educate the public not to respond to it.

Voyeurism

An element of voyeurism, as of exhibitionism, is usually involved in normal sexual activity. In recent years, sexually oriented magazines and videos have provided more or less acceptable outlets for those who derive pleasure from looking. The traditional definition of voyeurism distinguished true voyeurs—or Peeping Toms, as they are sometimes called—as people for whom the pleasure of looking interferes with normal sexual interplay with another person. Actually, voyeurism often occurs alongside normal sexual interplay. Thus, a realistic definition of voyeurism must take into account social sanctions against violating the privacy of others. In practice, then, a voyeur obtains gratification from watching strangers, in violation of their sexual privacy. This usually means watching women who are undressing or couples engaged in sex play. The risk involved in watching strangers may be a desirable adjunct to the voyeur's pleasure. The danger of being discovered, perched on the fire escape or balcony, adds to the sexual thrill of the peeping, which usually leads to masturbation. The disorder usually has its onset before age 15 and can last a person's lifetime (Kaplan & Krueger, 1997). In some individuals, voyeuristic fantasies and urges are experienced episodically, usually during stressful times. In others, voyeurism is the only form of sexual activity.

Like exhibitionism, voyeurism in some cases seems to provide a substitute gratification and a reassurance of power for otherwise sexually anxious and inhibited males. Voyeurs are often withdrawn both socially and sexually, with little in their developmental histories to support the learning of more appropriate interpersonal skills. Again, like exhibitionists, most voyeurs are harmless, but not all: 10 to 20 percent of them go on to rape the women they peep at.

Sadism and Masochism

There appears to be an element of aggression in even the most "natural" sexual activity. Human beings, like most other mammals, sometimes bite and scratch during intercourse, and aggressive sexual fantasies—of raping or of being raped—are common (Masters & Johnson, 1966). Conversely, a sexual element often underlies aggression. Both men and women have reported becoming sexually excited at boxing matches and football games or while watching fires or executions—a

Jeffrey Dahmer (center) was one of the most notorious multiple murderers in U.S. history. His killings were sex-related, centering on sadistic abuse of and necrophilic sex with young men whom he abducted and drugged.

fact that has led some theorists to propose that our society's preoccupation with violence may be sexually motivated.

In sadism and masochism, however, the element of physical and/or psychological cruelty—inflicting and being subjected to it, respectively—assumes a central role in sexual functioning. Both disorders are named for literary figures who publicized the sexual pleasures of cruelty. The term *sadism* is taken from the name of the Marquis de Sade (1740–1814), whose novels include numerous scenes featuring the torture of women for erotic purposes. Masochism is named for an Austrian novelist, Leopold von Sacher-Masoch (1836–1895), whose male characters tended to swoon with ecstasy when physically abused by women.

Individual patterns of sadism turn up primarily in men. The degree of cruelty may range from sticking a woman with a pin to gruesome acts of mutilation, numerous examples of which can be found in von Krafft-Ebing's *Psychopathia Sexualis* (1886/1965a). Between these two extremes are sadists who bind, whip, bite, and cut their victims. For some, the mere sight of blood or the victim's cries of pain are sufficient to trigger ejaculation; for others, the act of cruelty merely intensifies arousal, which eventually leads to rape. Similarly, the masochist may need to suffer only a mild pain, such as spanking or verbal abuse, or may choose to be chained and whipped. And, like the sadist, he or she may reach orgasm through the experience of pain alone, or the abuse stage may serve simply as foreplay, leading eventually to intercourse. Often, sadists and masochists fantasize specific scenarios and express a desire for more intense encounters than they currently have (Sandnabba & Niklas, 1999). Masochists without sadistic partners usually have to resort to prostitutes, some of whom specialize in abusing clients. Sadists without partners may prey on prostitutes or other unwary women.

In many cases, however, sadists and masochists do have complementary partners, with whom they share a **sadomasochistic** relationship. In some of these pairings, one partner is always the sadist, the other always the masochist. Alternatively, both partners may enjoy both sadism and masochism, in which case they switch between the two. According to a survey of male readers of a sadomasochistically oriented magazine (Moser & Levitt, 1987), most sadists and masochists are heterosexual, well educated, reasonably affluent, given to switching between sadism and masochism, and undisturbed by their specialized tastes. A recent study of men in two sadomasochistic clubs in Finland revealed that although the men seemed to have difficulties finding partners or forming permanent relationships, they had positive views of their sexual behavior (Sandnabba & Niklas, 1999). Some sadists and masochists are homosexuals; in fact, there is a substantial so-called S-and-M segment within the homosexual subculture. To serve sadomasochists, many underground newspapers carry advertisements by sadists and masochists seeking partners and stating their special requirements. Likewise, in many large American cities there are sex shops that specialize in selling sadomasochistic equipment.

In sadism and masochism, the line between normal and abnormal may be hard to draw. According to Baumeister and Butler (1997), sexual masochism does not necessarily indicate deeper problems, nor does it generally involve pathological self-destructive wishes for injury or punishment. Just as with the sexual dysfunctions, *DSM-IV-TR* requires evidence of distress or interpersonal difficulty, so with all the paraphilias one of the diagnostic criteria is that the person's sexual pattern has caused "clinically significant distress or impairment in social, occupational, or other important areas of functioning." By this standard, mutually consenting S-and-M partners who are satisfied with their sexual pattern and who show no disturbance in other aspects of their lives are not candidates for diagnosis, though most people would probably consider their behavior to be abnormal.

Frotteurism

According to *DSM-IV-TR,* a frotteur (from the French word *frotter,* "to rub") is a person who obtains gratification by touching or rubbing against a nonconsenting person. Frotteurs usually operate in crowded places, such as buses or subways, where they are more likely to escape notice and arrest. Typically, the frotteur touches the person's breasts or genitals or rubs his own genitals against a person's thighs or buttocks. Part of the excitement for the frotteurist, as with most sexual offenders, is the sense of power over the unsuspecting victim that the act produces. Some have suggested that frotteurism is a form of sexual assault, acted out by an ineffectual rapist (Horley, 2001).

Pedophilia

Children, by definition, lack the knowledge and experience to consent to sexual relations. Thus, pedophilia (from the Greek, meaning "love of children") involves a violation of the rights of the child, who may suffer serious psychological harm as a result. The pedophile may (in order of increasing rarity) covertly or overtly masturbate while caressing the child, stroke the child's genitals, masturbate between the child's thighs, have the child stimulate him or her manually or orally, or attempt intercourse. The pedophile may entice a group of children to participate in sexual activities and pose for pornographic pictures, using peer pressure to maintain secrecy (Burgess, Groth, & McCausland, 1981). Some pedophiles look for jobs or volunteer positions that involve extensive contact with children (Abel, Lawry, Karlstrom, et al., 1994).

More than 300,000 cases of child sexual abuse are estimated to occur in the United States every year. Most victims are young girls (77 percent) aged 9.2 years (Marshall, 1997). Although cases of female sexual abuse of children do turn up, they are rare: Most pedophiles are male (Finkelhor, 1984). The stereotype of the child molester includes a number of myths, however. First, the typical pedophile is not a "dirty old man" who lives on the margins of society. In most cases, he is an otherwise law-abiding citizen who may escape detection precisely because he does not appear disreputable. Although ranging in age from the teens to the seventies, most pedophiles are in their twenties, thirties, or forties. Many are also married or divorced, with children of their own. Second, most child molestation is not committed by strangers lurking about the schoolyard. The offender is usually acquainted with the victim and his or her family; indeed, many are related to the victim (Conte & Berliner, 1981). Third, child molestation usually does not entail physical violence. Rather, the offender uses his authority as an adult to persuade the child to acquiesce (Finkelhor, 1979). Fourth, child molestation usually is not an isolated event but consists of repeated incidents with the same child. The molestation may begin when the child is quite young and recur over 5 or 10 years before it is discovered or broken off (Finkelhor, 1980). A final interesting point about pedophilia is that it is usually accompanied by other paraphilias. In a survey of over 500 paraphiliacs, most of them pedophiles, half the respondents reported engaging in 4 or more paraphilias (Abel, Becker, Cunningham-Rathner, et al., 1988).

Several researchers feel that a distinction should be made between situational and preference molesters (Howells, 1981; Karpman, 1954). *Situational molesters* are people with more or less normal, heterosexual histories who most of the time prefer adult sexual partners. Their child molesting is impulsive—it is usually a response to stress—and they may view it with disgust. Incest offenders are usually of this type, rather than true pedophiles. By contrast, *preference molesters,* people who actually prefer children as sexual partners, are generally not married, prefer male children, and do not view their behavior as abnormal. For these people, child molesting is a regular sexual outlet. Their contacts with children are planned, not impulsive or precipitated by stress. Whether or not they are preference molesters, pedophiles who specialize in male children have a much higher rate of recidivism, or repeat offenses (American Psychiatric Association, 2000). In the survey mentioned earlier (Abel, Becker, Cunningham-Rathner, et al., 1988), the pedophiles who preferred boys averaged about 150 victims; those who preferred girls averaged about 20 victims.

The causes of pedophilia seem to vary (Finkelhor & Araji, 1986). Sometimes it is associated with arrested psychological development: Experiencing himself as a child, with childish emotional needs, the pedophile is most comfortable relating to children. Other pedophiles may be so isolated socially or so timid that they are unable to establish adult heterosexual relationships and turn to children as substitutes. Many pedophiles appear to lack intimacy in their relationships and describe themselves as lonely (Garlick, Marshall, & Thornton, 1996). In still other cases, an early experience of arousal with other children may become fixed in the person's mind. Finally, because about half of pedophiles were themselves molested as children (Dhawan & Marshall, 1996), some may be trying to restore feelings of control by reenacting their histories, with the roles reversed.

Children usually do not report their victimization immediately; they are afraid their parents will blame them. Molestation is generally discovered when an adult becomes suspicious, when the child tells an adult other than his or her parent, or when a physician sees signs of sexual abuse (Finkelhor, 1980). But children tell adults about their problem in indirect ways (Browne & Finkelhor, 1986). Most studies of child victims report varying degrees and combinations of sleep and eating disorders, fears and phobias, difficulties at school, and inappropriate sexual behavior. The effects do not go away when the abuse stops. Adults who were sexually exploited as children frequently exhibit depression, dissociative disorders, self-destructive behavior, feelings of being isolated and stigmatized, and distrust of others. Tragically, women who were sexually abused as children are more likely than other women to be physically abused by their husbands or other partners as adults (Finkelhor, 1984; Herman, 1981).

Some types of child abuse seem to do more psychological harm than others. A review of empirical research found that the negative psychological impact of abuse was worse if it occurred at an early age, if it continued over a long period of time, if there was a close relationship to the perpetrator, and if the abuse was severe or violent (Kendall-Tuckett, Williams, & Finkelhor, 1993). On the basis of clinical experience, Groth (1978) argued that, if the abuse continues over a period of time, if it involves violence or penetration, or if the molester is closely related to the child, the risk of severe trauma is that much greater. According to MacFarlane (1978), any collusion or suggestion of collusion on the part of the child increases the risk. If the child cooperates to some degree, if he or she is older and aware of the taboo violation, or if the child's disclosure is met by parental anger or accusation, the psychological damage will be worse.

Incest, or sexual relations between family members, has been prohibited, in varying degrees, by virtually all human societies throughout their known histories. Explanations of this universal taboo range from the argument that it encourages families to establish wider social contacts to the contention, supported by scientific studies, that inbreeding fosters genetic defects in offspring.

Despite the taboo, incest does occur. Alfred Kinsey (Kinsey, Pomeroy, & Martin, 1948; Kinsey, Pomeroy, Martin, et al., 1953) reported that only 3 percent of his sample had had incestuous relations. More recent studies indicate that the rate of incest in the general population is much higher: 7 to 17 percent (Finkelhor, 1994; Greenwald & Leitenberg, 1989; Hunt, 1979).

One study (Russell, 1986) concluded that father-daughter incest is "the supreme betrayal": More than twice as many victims of fathers reported being extremely upset and suffering severe long-term effects as victims of all other incest perpetrators combined. Other researchers (Kendall-Tuckett, Williams, & Finkelhor, 1993) have also found that abuse by a father or stepfather is more damaging than any other form of abuse. What kind of man would assault his daughter? One who is promiscuous and unselective in his sexual partners? Research suggests not. Cavallin (1966) reports that the typical incestuous father confines his extramarital sexual contacts to his daughter, or perhaps to several daughters, beginning with the eldest. Far from being indiscriminately amoral, such fathers tend to be highly moralistic and devoutly attached to fundamentalist religious doctrines (Gebhard, Gagnon, Pomeroy, et al., 1965). Father-daughter incest tends to occur in connection with a troubled marriage. The man may abuse his wife (as well as his children) and then turn to the daughter sexually when the wife rejects his advances. The wife may pretend not to notice because she is afraid of her husband's violence. She is often isolated from other family members due to chronic illness or infirmity. In many cases, the victim assumes the caretaking role in the family, even acting as a surrogate wife. Some mothers blame their daughters for threatening to break up the family (Herman, 1981).

Not surprisingly, the impact on the daughter can be profound. The long-term effects reported by incest victims are similar to those of nonincestuous child molestation: lowered self-esteem, self-blame, and self-hatred; a tendency to be vengeful or passive; emotional coldness and lack of responsiveness; negative feelings about physical closeness; and the belief that other people would think ill of them if the incest were known. Incest victims are also at higher risk for a range of psychological disorders, especially depression, anxiety, suicidality, and substance abuse (Kendall-Tuckett, Williams, & Finkelhor, 1993; Russell, 1986).

Rape

Rape, or sexual intercourse with a nonconsenting partner, is a common crime. An estimated 12 million adult women in the United States report experiencing rape in their lifetimes (Monnier, Resnick, Kilpatrick, et al., 2002), but most rapes are not reported to the authorities (Koss, 1996). Victims are particularly likely to hesitate to report a rape to authorities when it is committed by an acquaintance (date rape), perhaps because they are more likely to blame themselves for the rape or to fear being seen by others as responsible for the rape (Finkelson & Oswalt, 1995). In a 1998 survey of 81,247 ninth- and twelfth-graders, 9 percent of girls reported experiencing and 6 percent of boys reported perpetrating an act that met the legal definition of rape (which includes attempted rape and date rape) (Ackard & Neumark-Sztainer, 2002).

In dealing with rape, we are faced with the question of why a man who presumably could find a willing sex partner, even if a prostitute, would violently force himself on an unwilling woman. There seem to be several answers to this question. Some men apparently resort to rape because they cannot find—or feel they cannot find—a willing sex partner. Like the typical voyeur and exhibitionist, this type of rapist is described as a timid, submissive male lacking in empathy who has grave doubts about his masculinity and is so fearful of rejection that he cannot seek sexual gratification through more acceptable channels (Janssen, 1995; Marshall & Hambley, 1996; Marshall, Hudson, Jones, et al., 1995; Ward, Hudson, & Marshall, 1996). Other rapists have clearly antisocial personalities—they simply seize whatever they want and are indifferent to the pain they inflict on others. In still other cases, the element of force may be a necessary prerequisite of sexual arousal for them, much as cruelty is for the sadist. In some instances, however, the rapist's motivation appears to be more aggressive than sexual (Malamuth, Linz, Heavey, et al., 1995; Marshall & Hambley, 1996). A significant proportion of rapists were victims of child abuse (Haapasalo J. & Kankkkonen, 1997; Hall & Barongan, 1997); for them, hurting and humiliating women is a form of revenge or "identification with the aggressor." But many rapists are no different psychologically from other men. They have adequate sexual relationships and show no pattern of abnormality on tests of psychological functioning (Polaschek, Ward, & Hudson, 1997).

This last finding suggests that many rapes are the result not of psychological disorders but of our cultural emphasis on sex and violence. To some extent, men in our culture are socialized to become sexual predators. A comparison of college undergraduates who admitted that they had forced a date to have intercourse and undergraduates who had never done so found that the former were "sexually very active, successful, and aspiring"; they believed that rape was justified under certain circumstances (if they thought the woman was "loose," a "pickup," or a "tease"); they said their best friends would "definitely approve" of coercive tactics with certain women; and they felt considerable pressure from their peers to engage in sexual exploits (Hall & Barongan, 1997).

With rape, as with pedophilia and incest, psychology must concern itself not only with the perpetrator but also with the victim. The psychological damage suffered by rape victims is enormous. Rape victims are at risk for a number of psychological disorders—above all, sexual dysfunctions and posttraumatic stress disorder (see Chapter 7). In a study by Resnick, Monnier, Seals et al, (2002), more than 90 percent of the female rape victims reported fears of contracting HIV. At the same time, many women who report rape find that the search for justice leads to humiliation. Until recently, the laws in many states were designed to protect men from false accusations of rape, not to protect victims of rape. New York State, for example, required that there be a witness to the crime. (Needless to say, there rarely is.) The vast majority of rape cases reported to the police do not go to trial, either because identification of the rapist is uncertain or the evidence is insufficient. Thus, not only is justice not done, but the woman is left open to retaliation. If the case does go to court, the woman may feel that she, not the rapist, is on trial. Her way of dressing, her sexual history, her "reputation" may all be subject to skeptical scrutiny. If, to save her life, she submitted to the rape without a struggle, this may be used against her. Thus, the trial may be as traumatic as the rape.

Fortunately, these injustices are now receiving some attention. Counseling centers have been set up for rape victims. Police officers are being given special training for handling rape cases. (Some police departments have set up "rape squads" staffed with female officers.) And state laws dealing with rape are being revised. For example, many states no longer require a witness and do not permit the victim's sexual history (even with the defendant) to be brought into evidence unless it relates directly to the alleged crime.

❖ Groups at Risk for Paraphilias

According to *DSM-IV-TR,* most of the paraphilias are all but exclusively male aberrations. The only exception is masochism, but even there the male-female

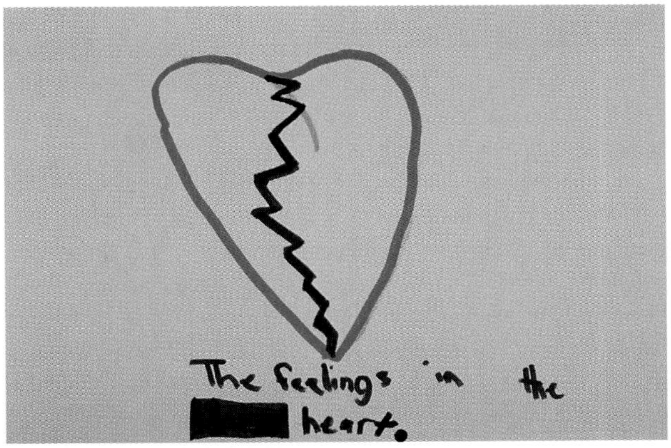

Art therapy helps children express difficult feelings. Children who were molested drew these pictures.

ratio is 20 to 1. Some writers believe this is because female sexuality is repressed in the process of socialization, with the result that most women never develop truly normal or truly abnormal forms of sexual expression. It should be added, however, that data on the prevalence of the paraphilias generally come from arrest records, and women are much less likely than men to be arrested, or even reported, for unconventional sexual behavior. (Should a woman choose to undress regularly in front of a window, neighbors may disapprove, but they are unlikely to call the police.) Still, these facts do not account for the vastly greater numbers of male paraphiliacs. There seems to be a true difference between the sexes in this respect. Sociobiologists (e.g., Wilson, 1987) have proposed that natural selection breeds into males an instinctive desire to inseminate as many partners as possible and that this instinct makes men more responsive to a greater variety of sexual stimuli. Other researchers have suggested that the difference between the sexes in risk for paraphilias may be due to male-female differences in brain structure (Flor-Henry, 1987). If so, this might help to explain the early onset of most paraphilias. Half of paraphilic adults report that their pattern developed before age 18 (Abel, Osborn, Anthony, et al., 1992).

Paraphilias: Theory and Therapy

The Psychodynamic Perspective

Oedipal Fixation According to Freudian theory, paraphilias represent a continuation into adulthood of the diffuse sexual preoccupations of the child. In Freud's words, young children are "polymorphously perverse"—that is, their sexual pleasure has many sources: sucking, rubbing, defecating, displaying themselves, peeping at others. Furthermore, according to Freud, children are capable of any number of defensive maneuvers in attempting to deal with the castration anxiety and penis envy endemic to the Oedipal period. Thus, psychodynamic theorists generally consider paraphilias to be the result of fixation at a pregenital stage. In general, with paraphilias as with sexual dysfunctions, it is the Oedipal stage, with its attendant castration anxiety, that is considered the major source of trouble.

In keeping with this theory, transvestism has been interpreted as a denial of the mother's presumed castration. Dressed in the clothes of a woman but still equipped with a penis underneath, the transvestite can unconsciously convince himself that his mother did not suffer castration after all and that, therefore, he need not fear the same fate for himself (Nielson, 1960). Similarly, Fenichel (1945) viewed sadism as an attempt, through cruelty and aggression, to take the part of the castrator rather than that of the castrated and thus to relieve anxiety. Indeed, castration anxiety is often seen as paramount in any paraphilia case that involves the avoidance of coitus.

Other psychodynamic interpretations of paraphilias have stressed the person's inability to disentangle and control his or her basic id impulses. Thus, sadism has been explained as a continuation of the child's confusion of sexual and aggressive impulses. Similarly, masochism may be seen as a redirection onto the self of aggressive impulses originally aimed at a powerful, threatening figure.

Group and Individual Therapy In individual psychotherapy or psychoanalysis, the treatment of paraphilia follows the usual procedure of uncovering the conflict and working through it. A variation on this technique—group therapy—has been used as a substitute for imprisonment in the cases of some rapists, pedophiles, and other criminal offenders. The group technique has the advantage of placing the troubled person in a situation where he can take comfort from the knowledge that he is not the only one—a reassurance that can hasten his confrontation of his problem. In addition, group therapy saves costs.

Although successful treatment of paraphilias through group therapy, individual psychotherapy, and psychoanalysis has been reported (e.g., Cohen & Seghorn, 1969), such cases are the exceptions. Psychodynamic therapy for sex offenders has been found to be largely ineffective (Knopp, 1976). Such patients may have committed hundreds of offenses before they enter treatment, and, when they do begin therapy, it is nearly always because they have been required to by the courts. Their motivation to stay out of jail, hence their motivation to lie to the therapist—to claim that they are responding to treatment, thinking normal sexual thoughts, engaging in normal sexual acts—is often high. But their motivation to change may be very low. Having convinced a therapist (and perhaps themselves) that they are cured, they often slip back into their old patterns.

The Behavioral Perspective

Conditioning The simplest behavioral interpretation of sexual deviations is that the deviation results from a respondent-conditioning process in which early sexual experiences, particularly masturbation, are paired with an unconventional stimulus, which then becomes the discriminative stimulus for arousal. For example, if a child experiences sexual arousal in connection with the help of a furry toy or a pair of women's underpants, this may lead to fetishism.

In the case of sadism and masochism, behavioral theorists have noted that sex, aggression, and the experience of pain all involve strong emotional and physiological arousal. Hence, it has been proposed that the sadist and the masochist are simply persons who never learned to discriminate among the various types of arousal. Another learning theory of masochism is that the child may have been cuddled and loved by his parents only after being punished, with the result that physical affection and punishment became paired. More recent behavioral theories of the paraphilias tend to stress cognitive factors as well as, or in preference to, direct conditioning. Albert Bandura (1986), for example, has argued that parents may knowingly or unknowingly model unconventional sexual behavior.

Unlearning Deviant Patterns New programs for the treatment of sex offenders take the complex nature of sexual behavior into account. A multifaceted approach combines elements of traditional psychotherapy with specific techniques for dealing with sexual issues. The goal is to change the patient's sexual arousal patterns, beliefs, and behavior (Abel, Osborn, Anthony, et al., 1992; Hudson, Marshall, Ward, et al., 1995).

Treatment begins with steps to bring deviant sexual behavior under temporary control. A man who drinks to reduce his inhibitions may be required to join Alcoholics Anonymous; a child molester is required to abandon any job or recreational activities that bring him into contact with children; an incestuous father may be required to move out of his home temporarily.

Behavioral techniques are then used to eliminate deviant arousal. One such technique is called *stimulus satiation.* Suppose the patient is an exhibitionist who preys on young girls. He is asked to collect pictures of girls that arouse in him an urge to expose himself and to arrange them in order from the least to the most exciting. He is also told to collect "normal" sexual materials, such as erotic pictures from *Playboy.* Then he is instructed to take these materials home and masturbate while looking at the normal stimuli and to record his fantasies verbally with a tape recorder. Two minutes after he has ejaculated (or after 10 minutes if he does not), he must switch to the deviant stimuli, begin masturbating again, no matter how uninterested he is, and continue for 55 minutes. However, if he should become aroused again during this time, he switches his attention back to the normal pictures of adult women and ejaculates again while focused on normal sex. Therefore, he focuses on deviant stimuli only while he is not aroused and is not feeling any physical pleasure. The patient is required to repeat this procedure 3 times a week for at least a month, moving from the stimuli that excite him least to those that stimulate him the most. His tapes are analyzed carefully. If his fantasies with normal stimuli are confined to such exhibitionist acts as looking at an adult woman and being looked at by her, he is encouraged to imagine physical contact with her. After 10 to 15 sessions, most sex offenders find the deviant stimuli boring or even aversive (LoPiccolo, 1985).

Stimulus satiation may be combined with other procedures. In *covert sensitization,* the patient is taught to indulge in a deviant fantasy until he is aroused and then to imagine the worst possible consequences—his wife finds him engaged in sex play with a child, he is arrested in front of his neighbors, the arrest makes headlines, his son attempts suicide, and so on (Barlow, 1993). In *shame aversion therapy,* the patient is required to rehearse his paraphilic behavior—to exhibit himself or, if he is a transvestite, to dress in women's clothing—in the therapist's office, while the therapist and the patient's wife observe and comment. (This technique is so distressing that it is used only when other techniques seem to fail.)

However, deviant sexual behavior, once suppressed, is not automatically replaced by normal behavior. The final task of behavior therapy is to build an appropriate sexual orientation. Sex offenders often lack basic social and sexual skills. Treatment of unmarried offenders includes training in making conversation, maintaining eye contact, using empathy skills, listening, asking for a date, and making socially acceptable sexual advances. Married sex offenders often report that their sexual relationships with their wives are good or adequate, but further probing usually reveals that sex is infrequent and stereotyped, lacking in playful, erotic activities. The partners are taught to do sensate exercises, to communicate their desires, and to explore new sexual experiences. Weekly therapy for at least a year is recommended for most sex offenders. Follow-up sessions every two weeks or once a month should continue for another year or year and a half. Thereafter, the patient should be reassessed every six months for three to five years.

Even this refined, intensive, long-term therapy does not guarantee a cure, however. Recently, behavioral therapy for sex offenders has placed less emphasis on a comprehensive (and often elusive) cure than on simple relapse prevention—that is, teaching people how to prevent themselves from committing the offense again. Relapse prevention involves training patients to avoid situations that place them at risk, showing them how to interrupt thought chains that lead to the offense and persuading them that having the impulse to commit the offense does not mean they must commit it—they can exert voluntary control through behavioral strategies. Reports on such programs indicate that they are successful in preventing relapses both in pedophiles and in rapists (Furby, Weinrott, & Blackshaw, 1989; Marshall & Pithers, 1994; Pithers & Cumming, 1989).

The Cognitive Perspective

Learning Deviant Attitudes As noted in the section on sexual dysfunction, the cognitive perspective holds that, while we are born with a sex drive, the way that drive is expressed depends on the attitudes we develop in childhood. A great deal of childhood sexual experimentation crosses normal boundaries. Children peep and display themselves, for example. If such behavior is reinforced—if, for example, a young boy's exhibiting himself to a girl is met with a reaction of pleasure or curiosity—this will foster attitudes ("Girls like this," "I can get attention this way") that lead to its adult repetition.

One attitude common to sex offenders is a tendency to objectify their victims, regarding them simply as potential sources of gratification rather than as human beings with feelings of their own (Abel, Gore, Holland, et al., 1989). Such beliefs are widespread in our society. According to cognitive theory, if they are combined with other predisposing factors—uncorrected childhood norm violation, lack of parental modeling of normative sexual values, poor self-esteem, poor social skills, and poor understanding of sexuality—they may well lead to sexual deviation (Malamuth, Heavey, & Linz, 1993; Ward, Hudson, Johnston, et al., 1997).

Combating Deviant Beliefs The cognitive treatment for paraphilias is essentially the same as that for sexual dysfunction: The procedure is to identify the deviation-supporting beliefs, challenge them, and replace them with more adaptive beliefs (Murphy, 1990). As usual, this cognitive restructuring is typically combined with behavior therapy, just as behavior therapy and most psychological therapies now incorporate cognitive techniques.

A mental process to which cognitive therapists have recently given great attention is objectification of the victim, for, as long as sex offenders think in that way, they are likely to repeat the offense. (And at least in the case of pedophiles, the more they repeat the offense, the greater the degree of objectification [Abel, Gore, Holland, et al., 1989]—a vicious cycle.) Many programs for sex offenders now include victim awareness or victim empathy training, in which offenders are confronted with the emotional damage done to sex-offense victims. In one program, sex offenders are asked to imagine what one of their victims was thinking during the assault (Wincze, 1989). They may also be assigned to read books, listen to audiotapes, and view videotapes in which victims of child molesting describe their experience of the episode and its psychological consequences. The attackers often respond to these descriptions with great surprise, saying such things as, "I didn't think it would hurt her [a six-year-old]; she had already been abused by someone else" (Hildebran & Pithers, 1989). Another technique is role reversal: The therapist takes the role of the offender, while the offender takes the role of an authority figure and argues against the sexually aggressive belief system (Abel, Osborn, Anthony, et al., 1992).

The Neuroscience Perspective

Because sexual arousal is controlled in part by the central nervous system, it is possible that paraphilias are related to dysfunction in neurotransmitters.

Prevention Pedophilia and Child Sexual Molestation

Recent disclosures that members of the clergy have been guilty of child sexual molestation focused attention on this crime, which can have long-lasting, harmful effects on its victims. Most sexual molestation of children is committed by people with pedophilia, although occasionally people with other disorders, such as dementia, molest children. The earlier persons with pedophilia can be identified and treated, the more children can be protected. Researchers have therefore turned to the issue of prevention, an urgent priority in view of the nature of the crime.

In a recent major study of child molestation, Abel and Harlow (2001) examined more than 16,000 people in Georgia, including nearly 4,000 men who admitted to being child molesters. Nearly half (47 percent) of the admitted child molesters reported having been sexually abused themselves as children. Surprisingly, more than 70 percent of the men who molest boys consider themselves heterosexual. Most are either married or living with an adult female partner or are widowed or divorced. Thus, sexual molestation of boys by men does not typically reflect a homosexual orientation. Of the pedophiles who primarily molest boys, 53 percent also molest girls; 21 percent of the pedophiles who primarily molest girls also molest boys. More than 60 percent of people with pedophilia have other paraphilias, primarily voyeurism and exhibitionism.

The study found that pedophilia starts early, usually in the early teenage years. Teens may meet all of the diagnostic criteria for pedophilia before they have ever touched a child sexually. Furthermore, teenagers who are evaluated at this early stage and given effective treatment have an excellent chance of controlling their pedophilia and never becoming child molesters.

Several risk factors for pedophilia have been identified. Abel and Harlow recommend psychological screening of the following groups of people for possible pedophilia:

- Teenagers and adults who are concerned that they may have a sexual interest in children
- Teenagers and adults who report child-centered sexual fantasies for more than 6 months
- Children who sexually interact with children 5 or more years younger than themselves
- Children who have been sexually molested
- Exhibitionists, such as flashers, and voyeurs, or peepers
- Any child, teenager, or adult accused of sexually molesting a younger child

A variety of interventions are being developed that can help to treat people with pedophilia or prevent high-risk individuals who show signs of pedophilia from developing the full disorder. Behavioral techniques, such as aversive conditioning, are promising, but the data are limited on whether they are useful prevention techniques or prevent long-term relapse. Parents and communities may also be reluctant to employ such techniques, particularly where there is uncertainty about whether a teenager actually has the disorder. Certainly, parents may be reluctant to view their children as child molesters "in the making."

Cognitive-behavioral techniques show promise, particularly in light of findings that pedophiles show signs of cognitive bias. Abel and Harlow found that 15 percent of self-acknowledged child molesters claimed that the child had initiated the act; fully 50 percent reported that the act was by mutual consent.

One treatment of pedophilia and other paraphilias involves the prescription of SSRIs, antidepressant drugs that affect serotonin levels. Studies in laboratory animals suggest that increasing brain serotonin leads to decreased sex drive, and indeed the SSRIs have proven effective in reducing activity in some pedophiles. However, the unpleasant side effects of pharmacological approaches lead to high dropout rates (Barbaree & Seto, 1997).

Ethical and legal issues complicate early-intervention prevention efforts that involve screening children against their own, or their parents', will. Some parents and communities may be reluctant to allow their children to participate in such screening. This understandable reluctance must be overcome in developing early-prevention interventions for pedophilia and the other paraphilias as well.

Researchers have found evidence that paraphilias are accompanied by alterations in serotonin metabolism and in catecholaminergic turnover (Maes, 2001; Maes, De Vos, Van Hunsel, et al., 2001). Whatever the role of neurotransmitters in causation, however, there is no question (other than the ethical one) that biology can be used in the treatment of sexual deviation. In various European countries, both castration and brain surgery have been used with dangerous sex offenders (usually rapists and pedophiles), this treatment usually being offered as an alternative to imprisonment (Abel, Osborn, Anthony, et al., 1992). Such treatments don't offer guarantees, however; for example, from 10 to 30 percent of men who have been castrated are still capable of intercourse and ejaculation up to a decade later (Grubin & Mason, 1997). Another route is the use of antiandrogen drugs, which decrease the level of testosterone, a hormone essential to sexual functioning. Antiandrogen treatment is now widely used with chronic offenders in Europe and the United States, and it does seem to decrease arousal and thereby reduce recidivism (Bradford, 1990; Bradford & Pawlak, 1993). In a study of 3 chronic pedophiles, 1 of whom had averaged 1 offense weekly for 40 years, all were able to control their behavior after antiandrogen treatment combined with psychotherapy (Wincze, Bansal, & Malamud, 1986). Antidepressants have also proved effective in treating paraphilias, particularly in cases involving shame and depression (Kafka & Pretky, 1992).

To assess arousal in such studies and to detect deviant (usually pedophile) attraction in men who have been arrested on sex-offense charges but deny any deviant pattern, a technique called *penile plethysmography* is often used. In penile plethysmography, an apparatus attached to the penis measures erection while the subject is exposed to the presumed erotic stimulus via slides, films, or audiotapes ("You are baby-sitting your neighbors' little girl for the evening" [Freund & Blanchard, 1989; Freund & Watson, 1991]). This technique seems to have some validity, though it is not foolproof (McConaghy, 1989). Many men are able to suppress deviant arousal in the laboratory, while others are sufficiently traumatized by being arrested on a sex charge that they temporarily lose their arousal capacity. Furthermore, the invasive nature and high cost of laboratory techniques makes them impractical for other purposes, such as screening job applicants. Researchers have developed a noninvasive test, involving self-report and a few simple physiological measures, to screen people applying for positions that involve close contact with children (Abel, Lawry, Karlstrom, et al., 1994).

Treatment Efficacy

Some researchers ask whether a pedophile or exhibitionist can or even would want to change his or her sexual patterns (Laws & O'Donohue, 1997), any more than an ordinary person without paraphilias would want to change. Theoreticians who believe that individuals with sexual deviations are generally incurable assert that the goal in therapy should be to help them abstain from acting on their paraphilias. Even so, therapy is complicated by the fact that people with paraphilias frequently undermine their treatment by failing to report information fully and honestly. Clients also often have much to gain by exaggerating their improvements in treatment. They are not often highly self-motivated to seek treatment, nor to cooperate with treatments required by the court system. Complicating these difficulties, people with paraphilias frequently have other problems, such as substance abuse problems, marital difficulties, personality disorders, difficulties with anger control, and anxiety and depression.

Because of such concerns, over the past few years the trend has been to emphasize treatment of adolescent sexual offenders. Many paraphilias first appear during adolescence, and an emphasis on early treatment may increase the chances of successful treatment or at least partial cure. Such early intervention may also help to reduce the harm that sex offenders can cause to others and to themselves. Even here, however, there are difficulties, particularly because the adolescent patient is legally a minor, and parents or the community may have concerns about using treatments that rely on explicit sexual materials.

Gender Identity Disorders

The **gender identity disorders (GID)** are a group of patterns characterized by a central dilemma, that of having a gender identity, or sense of gender, opposite to one's biological sex. GID is defined by two features, **gender dysphoria** (unhappiness with one's own gender) and a desire to change to the other gender. GID is apparently quite rare. Some European studies indicate that it occurs in only 1 out of 30,000 men and 1 out of 100,000 women (American Psychiatric Association, 2000).

The phenomenon of gender-crossing has been known since ancient times (Bullough & Bullough, 1993). A famous story in Greek and Roman mythology is that of the wise man, Tiresias, who was changed by a god from a man to a woman as a punishment for killing two snakes that were copulating. (As a result of his double experience, he was called in to settle a dispute among the gods as to which gender had more pleasure in lovemaking. When he said women had more pleasure, Hera, the queen of the gods, became angry and blinded him.) History offers many examples of people who at times took the role of the opposite sex, including at least one Roman emperor, the first governor general of New York, and the first surgeon general of the United States. The historical record also shows that, as a rule, men presented themselves as women mainly for sexual purposes, while women have crossed gender primarily to gain the power and freedom of men. Some cultures (not including our own) have made broad allowances for this. In many native North American societies, for example, there was an institutionalized role, the berdache, for men who dressed and acted as women.

Harry Benjamin (1964), an endocrinologist, coined the term **transsexual** to refer to people seeking to change their gender by means of hormones or surgery. In the 1960s, a large number of people began to request gender-reassignment surgery, and many physicians were willing to perform this. Today, the enthusiasm over gender reassignment has waned, but around the world there are still programs that offer psychological and medical help to transsexuals. While in past decades many clinicians treating GID regarded it as akin to borderline personality disorder or even

Israeli singer Yaron Cohen became Dana International following gender reassignment surgery in the 1990s.

psychosis, recent research indicates that most GID patients do not manifest any other psychological disorder. When given personality tests—the MMPI, for example—they do not show significantly more abnormal profiles than the general population (Cole, O'Boyle, Emory, et al., 1997).

Patterns of Gender Identity Disorder

Among adults with GID, there are three basic patterns, each with its characteristic history:

1. *Homosexual male-to-female transsexuals* are usually girlish from childhood. As they grow, they are attracted to men as sex partners. They do not find cross-dressing sexually exciting. They have tried to live as homosexuals but are not satisfied, because they want men to be attracted to them as *women.*
2. *Homosexual female-to-male transsexuals* show essentially the same pattern, with the genders reversed: boyish behavior in childhood, attraction to women (though they may date boys in adolescence), no sexual excitement from cross-dressing, adult effort to live as a lesbian, and dissatisfaction due to wanting to be loved as a man.
3. *Heterosexual male-to-female transsexuals* have a different history. Typically, they do not show feminine behavior as children. (Indeed, they are often hyper-masculine.) They are sexually attracted to women, but, from adolescence on, they are more aroused by transvestism and by imagining themselves as women (autogynephilia). They have tried to live as heterosexuals and are often married, but they are dissatisfied.

Gender Identity Disorder: When David Became Angela

The MindMAP video "Changing Genders" presents the story of a family man seeking to change his gender. How do you think other members in the family will adjust to the change in gender? Why?

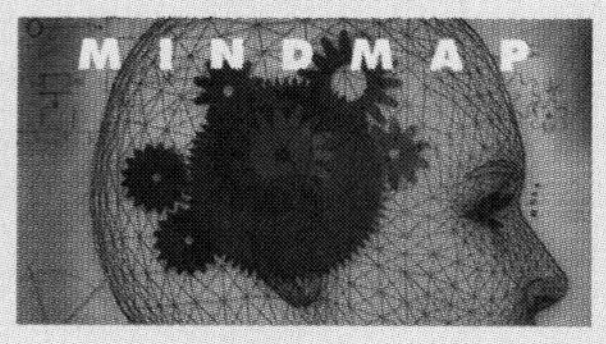

GID is categorized as either "of childhood and adolescence" or "of adulthood." The childhood version is far more common. At some point in childhood, about 1 percent of boys and 3 percent of girls express a desire to be of the opposite gender (Zucker & Bradley, 1995). Interestingly, very few of these children grow up to be transsexual adults. In a major study by Green and his colleagues, 66 boys who were taken to a mental health clinic because they said they wanted to be girls were followed up through late adolescence of adulthood. Three quarters of them developed into homosexuals or bisexuals. Only 1 became an adult transsexual (Green, 1987). Clearly, most children with gender dysphoria resolve their gender dilemma before adulthood.

The Psychodynamic Perspective

After their change in gender identity, some seek sexual relations with men, while others prefer women and live as lesbians. Psychodynamic theorists have usually attributed GID to a disturbance in the parent-infant bond. In the case of males, this is said to be an overlong, symbiotic relationship with the mother, thus creating a female identity in the infant. Female GID, on the other hand, is thought to be due to the mother's physical or emotional absence, with the result that the girl identifies with her father instead. There has been some controversy over whether the disorder is due to an intrapsychic conflict and whether, therefore, it can be treated by the usual psychoanalytic route of conflict resolution. Stoller (1975) has argued that the "blissful symbiosis" with the opposite-sex parent is part of the core identity—in other words, not based on conflict and not open to change. Meyer (1979), on the other hand, sees GID as the result of a serious developmental failure—indeed, a condition akin to psychosis—and believes that psychoanalysis is the appropriate treatment.

The Behavioral Perspective

Behavioral theorists interpret GID as the result of a long, subtle process in which the child's gender-role behavior is shaped toward the opposite gender by an important caretaker. The treatment that follows from such a theory is to stop reinforcement for cross-gender behavior and increase reinforcement for gender-appropriate behavior. Four decades ago, John Money and his colleagues proposed a different but related theory, based on the imprinting of birds by their caretakers. In this model, GID is the result of an imprinted gender fixation on the opposite-sex parent, occurring during a critical developmental period and then stamped in through reinforcement (Money, Hampson, & Hampson, 1957).

The Neuroscience Perspective

Researchers in neuroscience have also turned their attention to GID (Hoenig, 1985). One hypothesis attributes the disorder to hormone imbalance. Research has shown that both male and female rats can be reprogrammed to show the sexual behavior of the opposite gender if they are given the hormones that control sexual arousal in the opposite gender (Beach, 1975). This research is hard to apply to human beings, however, because one cannot know the gender identity of a rat. Furthermore, tests on GID patients have not turned up evidence of hormone abnormalities. Other neuroscience researchers have suggested that GID may be related to a difference in the brain. Several studies have found that transsexuals are likely to show EEG abnormalities, especially in temporal-lobe functioning. Temporal lesions have been associated with paraphilias, and it is possible that they are involved in GID as well.

Gender Reassignment

Because the problem in GID is a discrepancy between gender identity and physical gender, one solution is to change the identity to fit the body. A number of psychodynamic and behavioral therapists have tried this, in keeping with the theories previously outlined, but there is no empirical evidence for the effectiveness of such treatment.

The alternative is to change the body to fit the gender identity, a process called **gender reassignment** that has developed over the past 30 years. The Harry Benjamin International Gender Dysphoria Association (HBIGDA, 1990), a group devoted to studying and treating GID, recently published a set of standards of care that probably represents the ideal scenario. After a detailed evaluation by a mental health professional trained and experienced in the treatment of GID, patients are given at least 3 months of psychotherapy to help them understand what their options are and decide what they actually want. If they still choose gender reassignment, they are given hormone treatment to initiate physical changes. Next comes the most critical phase, the so-called real-life test. In this phase, patients must live completely in the desired gender, dressing, working, and presenting themselves in that role for a minimum of a year, the goal being to make the person understand, before any irreversible changes are made, what it means to occupy that role. Psychotherapy and hormone treatment are continued during this period. For male-to-female patients, the hormones (estrogen) typically result in decreased beard growth, changes in fat distribution, breast development, and voice changes. For female-to-male transsexuals, the hormone (testosterone) produces facial-hair growth, a deepening of the voice, muscle development, breast reduction, and enlargement of the clitoris.

After a year in the real-life test, the person may proceed to surgery. In male-to-female surgery, the testicles are removed, together with the body of the penis, and the skin of the genitals is inverted to create a neo-vagina. The surgeon can also fashion an approximation of external sex organs: labia and a clitoris. In addition, the patient may be given breast implants, and the trachea may be shaved to raise the pitch of the voice. For female-to-male transsexuals, the genital surgery, involving the creation of a neo-phallus, is much more difficult, but in many cases it has been possible to build a penis almost indistinguishable from one produced by nature. Female-to-male patients may also have hysterectomies and breast-reduction surgery.

The outcome of such surgery has been the subject of more than 70 empirical studies (Carroll, 1997). The single most consistent finding is that gender reassignment produces an improvement or a satisfactory outcome in between two thirds and nine tenths of patients (Abramowitz, 1986; Green & Fleming, 1990). The areas in which patients report the most improvement are self-satisfaction, interpersonal relationships, and psychological health. They report less improvement in their work life, and the impact on their sexual functioning is still unclear. Nevertheless, these are encouraging results.

There have also been some casualties, people who regretted the surgery or afterwards had serious psychological breakdowns. (There have been suicides, too.) The rate of poor outcomes seems to be about 8 percent (Abramowitz, 1986). It is rarely clear, however, whether a poor outcome is due to the gender reassignment or to preexisting problems in the person's life. If poor outcome is defined simply as regretting the surgery, this seems to occur in less than 1 percent of female-to-male and less than 2 percent of male-to-female transsexuals.

Outcome is influenced by a number of factors, notably the nature of the therapy. Research has found that the longer the patient is kept in the real-life test phase and the more realistic his or her expectations, the better the result (Botzer & Vehrs, 1997). In addition, some categories of patients are likely to have more positive results. Female-to-male reassignment seems to yield more satisfaction than male-to-female; and, in the male-to-female group, those who began as homosexuals have better results than those who were heterosexual. Not surprisingly, the person's prior psychological health is also a predictor of success. Patients with a history of serious psychological disturbance are not likely to be fully cured by gender reassignment (Abramowitz, 1986; Bodlund & Kullgren, 1995; Botzer & Vehrs, 1997; Green & Fleming, 1990). Satisfaction is also more likely for those who have family and social support, as in the following case:

Joe was a 45-year-old steelworker when he presented with a request for gender-reassignment surgery. He was married and had two young children. He lived in a blue-collar community, in which he was well known and where he served as president of the local softball league. He reported that at the age of 7 he had begun to cross-dress in his older sister's clothes several times per week. This was not sexually exciting to him at the time—he simply enjoyed it—but, when he reached puberty, he began to masturbate while cross-dressed, usually fantasizing about himself as a woman. He was attracted to girls of his own age and began to date. After high school, he tried to rid himself of his urge to cross-dress and went into the army in order to make himself "more of a man." He stopped cross-dressing for several years, but the autogynephilic fantasies remained. After discharge from the service, he had several relationships with women and eventually met his future wife, Barbara.

After several months of dating, Joe told Barbara of his cross-dressing urges. She was concerned but supportive. They had a satisfying sexual relationship in the beginning. After they married, he continued to cross-dress in secret. On several occasions, he threw out his women's wardrobe and stopped cross-dressing. Over time, however, his unhappiness with being male increased. He became overweight and made no attempt to stay healthy. The sexual excitement of cross-dressing decreased, but he felt a strong urge to go out in public as female. He became very depressed.

Joe stated that he wanted gender-reassignment surgery as soon as possible. After a careful evaluation, he was given psychotherapy focusing on his gender dysphoria and possible resolutions to it. In therapy, he considered the options of trying to rid himself of his cross-dressing, living as a male and cross-dressing occasionally, or making the transition to female. Part of his therapy included his wife, who said she would support whatever decision he made. Eventually, he decided on gender reassignment. At this point, he started taking female hormones and prepared to make the transition to living as female. He began to "come out" to his family and friends. The most difficult times for him were when his friends shunned him for his decision to change. His children were included in family sessions in order to help them understand the changes their father was going through.

On Memorial Day, Joe "came out" to the softball league as Josephine. She was re-elected as president of the league, though she had to move from the men's league to the co-ed league. After two years of therapy and one year of taking hormones and living as a woman, she was re-evaluated for appropriateness for surgery. By this time, she had developed breasts and had gone through extensive electrolysis. She had lost 70 pounds and had given up smoking in order to look and feel better. She had legally changed her name and gender on all her identification. She and her wife had divorced but maintained joint custody of their children. She continued to act as a parent to their children, who now called her "Aunt Joey." Her genital surgery went well and there were no major complications. One year after surgery, on a follow-up evaluation, Josephine admitted that there had been some difficult times, especially with other people's negative reactions. Also, she had not yet been able to form a satisfying relationship with a man. She stated, however, that she was much happier living as a woman than she had been as a man and was very glad to have been able to accomplish her "dream." (Adapted from Carroll, Northwestern University Medical School, composite and altered clinical case histories.)

Just as our understanding of homosexuality has changed in the past few decades, so has our view of GID. What was once seen by clinicians as a serious mental disorder is now regarded as a variant of gender experience. Today, for most professionals working with GID, the task is simply to help patients decide on their own resolution to their gender dilemma.

Key Terms

acquired dysfunction, 362
autogynephilia, 373
dyspareunia, 362
exhibitionism, 371
female orgasmic disorder, 361
female sexual arousal disorder, 360
fetishism, 371
frotteurism, 371
gender dysphoria, 383
gender identity disorders (GID), 383
gender reassignment, 385
generalized dysfunction, 362
hypoactive sexual desire disorder, 358
incest, 377
lifelong dysfunction, 362
male erectile disorder, 360
male orgasmic disorder, 361
masochism, 371
paraphilias, 371
pedophilia, 371
premature ejaculation, 362
rape, 371
sadism, 371
sadomasochistic, 375
sexual aversion disorder, 360
sexual dysfunctions, 358
situational dysfunction, 362
spectator role, 365
transsexual, 383
transvestism, 371
vaginismus, 362
voyeurism, 371

Summary

- Sexual disorders are among the most stigmatized behaviors in society. Western culture generally regards heterosexual relations as the only acceptable form of sexual activity and tends to view all other forms as abnormal. However, views of sexual activity vary greatly among different cultures and can change within a society over time.
- Sexual dysfunctions are disorders that, over a long period of time, disrupt the sexual response cycle or cause pain during intercourse. They are grouped according to the phase of the sexual response cycle in which they occur: hypoactive sexual desire disorder and sexual aversion disorder (desire phase); female sexual arousal disorder and male erectile disorder (arousal phase); and orgasmic disorder and premature ejaculation (orgasm phase). Other disorders, which don't disrupt a specific part of the cycle, include dyspareunia and vaginismus (sexual pain disorders). Studies have shown that several types of sexual dysfunction are common.
- The risk factors for sexual dysfunction include gender, ethnicity, education, and socioeconomic status. However, differences in reporting sexual problems have complicated these findings. Generally, women are more likely than men to suffer from disorders of sexual pain and arousal. Premature ejaculation is the most common male sexual complaint.
- The psychodynamic perspective links sexual dysfunction to an unresolved Oedipal conflict among males and to penis envy among females. Though psychodynamic approaches were not proven effective, for many years they were the only treatment widely available.
- Masters and Johnson believe that sexual dysfunction results from performance anxiety, which causes the worried partner to become more of a spectator than a participant. Their work in the 1970s revolutionized the sex therapies, especially behavioral ones.
- Research has shown that behavioral and cognitive therapies are quite effective. The behavioral theory maintains that, if sexual dysfunction results from learned anxiety, then the problem can be cured through new learning. Direct symptomatic treatments, especially sensate focus exercises, are used to treat sexual dysfunctions through the behavioral method. Cognitive psychologists focus on attitudes and thoughts about sex that can block arousal.
- Some therapists use a multifaceted approach, combining direct treatment with an exploration of attitudes or problems in the relationship. Interpersonal therapy focuses on relationship therapy as part of the treatment of sexual dysfunction.
- Researchers believe that sexual dysfunction may result from a combination of organic and psychological factors. New biological therapies have been developed, especially for male erectile disorders, over the past decade. A significant trend in sex therapy is the integration of biological and psychological factors.
- In the paraphilias, the person is aroused by something other than what is usually considered a normal sexual object or activity. Males are much more likely than females to develop a paraphilia.
- In fetishism, inanimate objects or a body part is used for sexual gratification, generally replacing all interest in normal sexual activity.
- Transvestites seek sexual gratification by wearing clothing of the opposite sex, often at home. Most are heterosexual, but transvestism often leads to marital problems if discovered by the spouse.
- Exhibitionists display their genitals to an involuntary observer. Exhibitionists receive gratification from the observer's response—often shock or fear.
- Voyeurism is the observation of other people's sexual activity or anatomy, unbeknownst to the subject. Voyeurs receive sexual gratification from the thrill of watching or the danger of being discovered.
- Sadism and masochism—inflicting pain on others and subjecting oneself to pain, respectively—are sometimes difficult to classify as paraphilias, because in a consenting sadomasochistic couple there is generally no social or occupational distress or impairment.

- In frotteurism, a person obtains sexual gratification by touching or rubbing against a nonconsenting person. Frotteurs tend to be adolescents or young adults.
- Pedophiles are adults who seek sexual gratification through sexual contact with children. Though pedophiles rarely cause physical harm to children, they can create severe emotional distress in their victims. Pedophilia has several causes, including arrested psychological development, social isolation, and childhood sexual abuse. Unfortunately, children rarely tell their parents that they have been abused.
- Rape, or sexual intercourse with a nonconsenting partner, is a common crime. Some men apparently resort to rape because they cannot find—or feel they cannot find—a willing sex partner. Other rapists have antisocial personalities. In still other cases, the element of force may be a necessary prerequisite for sexual arousal. A significant proportion of rapists were victims of child abuse. But many rapists are no different psychologically from "normal" men. Thus, many rapes are the result not of psychological disorders but of our cultural emphasis on sex and violence.
- Incest, sexual relations between family members, is a crime, not a psychological disorder, but it can have severe mental effects on the victim. Incest is most common between father and daughter, and the effects on the victim include low self-esteem, depression, anxiety, substance abuse, and difficulties in sexual adjustment as adults.
- The psychodynamic perspective maintains that paraphilias result from Oedipal fixation and the associated castration anxiety. Psychodynamic therapy has not been shown to be effective.
- Behavioral therapists believe that paraphilias are caused by respondent conditioning and the modeling of unconventional sexual behavior. Therapy involves removing the abnormal stimulus from the patient and then using a technique such as stimulus satiation, covert sensitization, or shame aversion therapy. Behavioral therapy for paraphilias has demonstrated moderate success.
- The cognitive perspective links paraphilias to attitudes developed in childhood. Offenders often objectify their victims. Therapy concentrates on identifying the deviation-supporting beliefs and replacing them. Therapists also try to increase the attacker's empathy for the victim.
- Neurological research on the causes of paraphilias has been inconclusive. However, biological treatments, including antiandrogen drugs, seem to be effective.
- Gender identity disorders are a group of patterns defined by unhappiness with one's own gender and a desire to change to the other gender. A person with gender identity disorder believes that he or she was born as the wrong biological gender.
- Psychodynamic theorists attribute gender identity disorder to a disturbance in the parent-infant bond and view psychoanalysis as the treatment. Behavioral theorists see it as the result of an influential caretaker shaping a child's gender-role behavior and work on stopping the reinforcements. Biological researchers have looked for EEG abnormalities. Therapies based on changing the person's identity to fit the body have generally been ineffective.
- People with gender identity disorders who seek to change their gender are known as transsexuals. Some transsexuals elect to undergo gender-reassignment surgery, which involves a long period of therapy, hormonal treatment, a period of living as the desired gender, and then genital surgery. Gender reassignment improves self-satisfaction, relationships, and psychological health in over two thirds of transsexuals. The nature of the therapy, the person's mental health history, and the amount of social support influence the level of success.

CHAPTER

14

Schizophrenia and Delusional Disorder

Schizophrenia
- The Prevalence of Schizophrenia
- The History of the Diagnostic Category
- The Symptoms of Schizophrenia
- The Course of Schizophrenia
- The Subtypes of Schizophrenia
- The Dimensions of Schizophrenia

Delusional Disorder
- The Symptoms of Delusional Disorder

Problems in the Study of Schizophrenia

Schizophrenia: Theory and Therapy
- The Neuroscience Perspective
- The Cognitive Perspective
- The Interpersonal Perspective
- The Behavioral Perspective
- The Sociocultural Perspective
- Unitary Theories: Diathesis and Stress

The widow, aged thirty-five, . . . gives full information about her life in answer to our questions, knows where she is, can tell the date and the year, and gives proof of satisfactory school knowledge. . . . For many years she has heard voices, which insult her and cast suspicion on her chastity. They mention a number of names she knows, and tell her she will be stripped and abused. The voices are very distinct, and, in her opinion, they must be carried by a telescope or a machine from her home. Her thoughts are dictated to her; she is obliged to think them, and hears them repeated after her. She is interrupted in her work, and has all kinds of uncomfortable sensations in her body, to which something is "done." In particular, her "mother parts" are turned inside out, and people send a pain through her back, lay ice-water on her heart, squeeze her neck, injure her spine, and violate her. . . .

The patient makes these extraordinary complaints without showing much emotion. She cries a little, but then describes her morbid experiences again with secret satisfaction and even with an erotic bias. She demands her discharge, but is easily consoled, and does not trouble at all about her position and her future. Her use of numerous strained and hardly intelligible phrases is very striking. She is ill-treated "flail-wise," "utterance-wise," "terror-wise"; she is "a picture of misery in angel's form," and "a defrauded mamma and housewife of sense of order." They have "altered her form of emotion." She is "persecuted by a secret insect from the District Office. . . ." Her former history shows that she has been ill for nearly ten years. (Kraepelin, 1904/1968, p. 157)

This case, from Emil Kraepelin's *Lectures on Clinical Psychiatry* (Chapter 1) describes a woman he called "the widow." The "widow" offers a good illustration of psychosis. As we have noted previously, the **psychoses** are a class of psychological disorders in which reality contact—the capacity to perceive, process, and respond to environmental stimuli in an adaptive manner—is radically impaired, with the result that the person cannot meet the ordinary demands of life. The psychoses, then, are the most severe of all the psychological disorders. Most of the conditions that we have discussed in earlier chapters allow for some measure of adaptive functioning. An acute psychotic episode does not. For this reason—and because the behavior of people with psychoses is disturbing to others—people with psychoses are often hospitalized.

There are three main groups of psychoses:

1. *The mood disorders,* characterized, as their name indicates, primarily by disturbances of *mood* (but remember that not all mood disorders are psychotic)
2. *Schizophrenia,* considered to be primarily a disturbance of *thought*
3. *Delusional disorder,* in which the essential, and possibly the only, abnormality is a limited system of *delusions*

Mood disorders have already been described in Chapter 10. The present chapter will focus on the two other main types of psychosis, schizophrenia and delusional disorder, with special emphasis on the former, as it is far more common. First we will describe these disorders. Then we will discuss theories and treatment.

Schizophrenia

Schizophrenia is the label given to a group of psychoses in which deterioration of functioning is marked by severe distortion of thought, perception, and mood; by bizarre behavior; and by social withdrawal.

The Prevalence of Schizophrenia

Between 1 and 2 percent of people in the United States have had or will have a schizophrenic episode (Kendler, Gallagher, Abelson, et al., 1996). In other countries, the rates are similar (Jablensky, 2000; Lin & Lin, 2001). However, recent evidence suggests that the rates of new cases of schizophrenia may be declining (Suvisaari, Haukka, Tanskanen, et al., 1999). At present, there are about a million people with schizophrenia in the country. Such people occupy about half the beds in U.S. mental hospitals (Kaplan & Sadock, 1991). Many other people with schizophrenia have been released from the hospital—either to smaller facilities or simply into the community. (It has been estimated that as many as one third of homeless people have schizophrenia [American Psychiatric Association, 1997].) But about half of those discharged for the first time return to the mental hospital within two years (Kaplan & Sadock, 1991). The estimated cost of schizophrenia to our society is about $19 billion in health care alone (American Psychiatric Association, 1997). Clearly, this disorder constitutes an enormous public health problem.

The History of the Diagnostic Category

Although schizophrenia has probably been with us for thousands of years, it was not described as a distinct disorder until 1896, when Emil Kraepelin proposed that there were three major types of psychosis: manic-depressive psychosis, paranoia, and **dementia praecox,** a syndrome marked by delusions, hallucinations, attention problems, and bizarre motor behavior. Kraepelin believed that dementia praecox normally began in adolescence and led to irreversible mental breakdown—hence his term for the disorder, which is Latin for "premature mental deterioration."

While Kraepelin's description of the disorder has lasted, the name he gave it was soon replaced. In 1911, Swiss psychiatrist Eugen Bleuler, a highly influential teacher and writer, pointed out that dementia praecox was actually a poor description. In the first place, the disorder was not necessarily premature; many patients did not develop symptoms until well into their adult years. Second, most patients did not proceed to complete mental deterioration. Some remained the same year after year; others improved; others improved and relapsed. Bleuler (1911/1950), therefore, proposed a new term, *schizophrenia,* meaning "split mind" (from the Greek *schiz-*, or "divide," and *phren,* or "mind"). Actually, Bleuler's term also poses problems, because many people mistake it to mean multiple personality, or dissociative identity disorder (Chapter 8), which is an entirely different condition. What Bleuler was referring to was not a splitting of the personality into two or more personalities but, rather, a split among different psychic functions within a single personality. In the mind of the person with schizophrenia, emotion, perception, and cognition cease to operate as an integral whole. Emotions may split off from perception, perception from reality. As Bleuler put it, "The personality loses its unity" (p. 9). A former schizophrenic patient quoted by Mendel (1976) described the experience more concretely: "The integrating mental picture in my personality was taken away and smashed to bits, leaving me like agitated hamburger distributed infinitely throughout the universe" (p. 8).

The Symptoms of Schizophrenia

DSM-IV-TR lists five characteristic symptoms of schizophrenia: delusions, hallucinations, disorganized speech, disorganized or catatonic behavior, and "negative symptoms," meaning a reduction or loss of normal functions such as language and goal-directed behavior. If a person has shown 2 or more of those signs for at least a month and has been noticeably disturbed for at least 6 months, the diagnosis is schizophrenia.

In cases in which the episode has lasted for less than a month, the diagnosis is *brief psychotic disorder.* When it has lasted more than a month but less than 6 months, the diagnosis is *schizophreniform disorder.* Only when the episode exceeds the 6-month cutoff line is the diagnosis of schizophrenia made.

For the sake of discussion, we will break down the symptoms of schizophrenia into separate categories. Keep in mind, however, that in reality they are not separate, for they influence one another. If a person's thought processes are derailed, this affects mood; if mood is disturbed, this affects behavior. And, while all people with schizophrenia display some of these symptoms some of the time, no one displays all of them all of the time. Indeed, some people diagnosed with schizophrenia often behave quite normally.

Disorders of Thought and Language

> I'm a doctor, you know. . . . I don't have a diploma, but I'm a doctor. I'm glad to be a mental patient, because it taught me how to be humble. I use Cover Girl creamy natural makeup. Oral Roberts has been here to visit me. . . . This place is where *Mad* magazine is published. The Nixons make Noxon metal polish. When I was a little girl, I used to sit and tell stories to myself. When I was older, I turned off the sound on the TV set and made up dialogue to go with the shows I watched. . . . I'm a week pregnant. I have schizophrenia—cancer of the nerves. My body is overcrowded with nerves. This is going to win me the Nobel Prize for medicine. I don't consider myself schizophrenic anymore. There's no such thing as schizophrenia, there's only mental telepathy. . . . I'm in the Pentecostal Church, but I'm thinking of changing my religion. I have a dog at home. I love instant oatmeal. When you have Jesus, you don't need a diet. Mick Jagger wants to marry me. I want to get out the revolving door. With Jesus Christ, anything is possible. I used to hit my mother. It was the hyperactivity from all the cookies I ate. (Quoted in S. Sheehan, 1982, pp. 72–73.)

This is a transcript of a woman with schizophrenia's attempt at conversation in a hospital ward. The disordered language of people with schizophrenia, with its odd associations and rapid changes of subject, is presumably a clue to their disordered thought processes. Some experts on schizophrenia have tried to distinguish between disturbances of thought and disturbances of language, but such distinctions are possible only at a theoretical level. Language is the expression of thought. Conversely, our primary clue to thought is language. Therefore, we will consider the two functions together. First, we will discuss disturbances in the *content* of schizophrenic thought, known as delusions, and then we will discuss abnormalities in the *form* schizophrenic thought takes.

Delusions **Delusions,** or firmly held beliefs that have no basis in reality, may accompany a variety of psychological conditions—mania, depression, organic syndromes, drug overdose—but they are extremely common in schizophrenia (Maher, 2001), affecting three quarters or more of hospitalized schizophrenic patients (Maher, 2001).

Most schizophrenic patients do not seem to realize that other people find their delusional beliefs implausible (McGuire, Junginger, Adams, et al., 2001). Neither will they abandon their delusions in the face of contradictory evidence—a point that was vividly demonstrated some years ago by psychologist Milton Rokeach. In 1959, Rokeach had three men, each of whom claimed to be Jesus Christ, transferred to the same ward of a hospital in Ypsilanti, Michigan. For two years, the "three Christs" lived together, sleeping in adjacent beds, sharing the same table in the dining hall, and working together in the hospital laundry room while Rokeach observed them. His purpose was "to explore the processes by which their delusional systems of belief and their behavior might change if they were confronted with the ultimate contradiction conceivable for human beings: more than one person claiming the same identity" (Rokeach, 1964, p. 3). In other words, would any of them figure out that all three of them couldn't be Jesus? The following is an excerpt from one of their first encounters:

> "Well, I know your psychology," Clyde said, "and you are a knick-knacker, and in your Catholic church in North Bradley and in your education, and I know all of

it—the whole thing. I know exactly what this fellow does. In my credit like I do from up above, that's the way it works."

"As I was stating before I was interrupted," Leon went on, "it so happens that I was the first human spirit to be created with a glorified body before time existed."

"Ah, well, he is just simply a creature, that's all," Joseph put in. "Man created by me when I created the world—nothing else."

—Did you create Clyde, too? Rokeach asked.

"Uh-huh. Him and a good many others."

At this, Clyde laughed. (Rokeach, 1964, pp. 10–11)

After two years of daily contact, each of the three men still firmly believed that he alone was Jesus Christ.

Most delusions fall into certain patterns:

1. *Delusions of persecution:* the belief that one is being plotted against, spied upon, threatened, or otherwise mistreated, particularly by a conspiracy.
2. *Delusions of control* (also called *delusions of influence):* the belief that other people, forces, or perhaps extraterrestrial beings are controlling one's thoughts, feelings, and actions, often by means of electronic devices that send signals directly to the brain.
3. *Delusions of reference:* the belief that one is being referred to by things or events that, in fact, have nothing to do with one. For example, people with schizophrenia may think that their lives are being depicted on television or in news stories.
4. *Delusions of grandeur:* the belief that one is an extremely famous and powerful person. Such delusions may crystallize into a stable delusional identity, with the person claiming, for example, that he or she is Joan of Arc, or, as with Rokeach's patients, Jesus Christ.
5. *Delusions of sin and guilt:* the belief that one has committed "the unpardonable sin" or has inflicted great harm on others. Schizophrenic patients may claim, for example, that they have killed their children.
6. *Hypochondriacal delusions:* the unfounded belief that one is suffering from a hideous physical disease. The hypochondriacal delusions of people with schizophrenia differ from the fears seen in hypochondriasis (Chapter 8) in that they refer not to recognized diseases but to bizarre afflictions. While patients with hypochondriasis may complain of brain tumors, for instance, people with schizophrenia claim that their brains are full of mold or are being carried away in pieces.
7. *Nihilistic delusions:* the belief that one or others or the whole world has ceased to exist. The patient may claim, for example, that he or she is a spirit returned from the dead.

Finally, many individuals with schizophrenia complain that their thoughts are being tampered with in some way. Such delusions, related to delusions of control, include

1. *Thought broadcasting:* the belief that one's thoughts are being broadcast to the outside world, so that everyone can hear them
2. *Thought insertion:* the belief that other people are inserting thoughts, especially obscene thoughts, into one's head
3. *Thought withdrawal:* the belief that other people are removing thoughts from one's head

These particular delusions seem to be highly specific to schizophrenia (Frith & Dolan, 2000)—in any case, they are not seen in people with psychotic mood disorders (Junginger, Barker, & Coe, 1992)—and they may represent an effort by individuals with schizophrenia to explain to themselves the mental chaos that this disorder entails. Many schizophrenic patients, for example, experience what is called *blocking:* In the middle of talking about something, they suddenly fall silent, with no memory of what they were talking about. Such an experience is as disturbing to a person with schizophrenia as it would be to anyone else, and one way to explain it is to say that someone is stealing the thoughts out of one's head. Some researchers believe that many schizophrenic delusions represent "normal" explanations for abnormal experiences (Maher, 2001).

Consistent with this view are studies showing that people with delusions are just as good at reasoning and logic problems as normal people and that normal individuals can be induced to show delusions under conditions in which they had strange perceptual experiences (Maher, 2001). Some recent evidence suggests that the basis for delusions may be an inability to integrate current perceptions with prior knowledge stored in memory, a process involving the right prefrontal cortex (Frith & Dolan, 2000).

Loosening of Associations As we saw earlier, it was for the quality of psychological "splitting"—a disconnection between different ideas or different mental functions—that Bleuler named the disorder schizophrenia. One of the clearest demonstrations of this splitting is the rambling, disjointed quality of the language produced by schizophrenic patients, particularly the younger ones (Kerns & Berenbaum, 2002).

Vaslav Nijinsky (1889–1950), the great Polish-Russian ballet dancer, is shown here on the left, a few years before he was diagnosed with schizophrenia. The drawing of staring eyes was done by Nijinsky while he was in an asylum. Nijinsky suffered from chronic schizophrenia for the last 30 years of his life.

Normal speech tends to follow a single train of thought, with logical connections between ideas. By contrast, schizophrenic speech often shows a **loosening of associations.** Ideas jump from one track to another, with the result that the person wanders further and further away from the topic. When the problem is severe, speech may become completely incoherent. Moreover, some of the disorganized language problems run in families (DeLisi, 2001).

We do not know exactly what mental processes cause this confusion in speech, but it becomes worse when schizophrenic patients are discussing negative topics (Barbridge & Barch, 2002). It is likely that the problem lies in the mind's way of dealing with associations. In communicating with one another, people make many mental associations, both to the statements of those they are speaking to and to their own statements. Before speaking, however, they "edit" these associations, selecting the ones that are most relevant to the topic and discarding the others. In the schizophrenic patient's mind, this process seems to break down, so that the speaker follows his or her own private train of associations, without editing for relevance or inhibiting irrelevant associations (Docherty & Gottesman, 2000; Titone, Levy, & Holzman, 2000). These difficulties in editing for relevance, in turn, may be related to more fundamental problems in attention and short-term memory (Docherty & Gordiner, 1999). Loose associations will result if one cannot remember one's recent output long enough to complete the sentence effectively.

This does not mean that people with schizophrenia cannot give a straight answer to a direct question. They can make very common primary associations to a given stimulus about as easily as normal people. It is the more subtle secondary associations that many schizophrenic patients cannot make without becoming confused and incoherent. This phenomenon was illustrated in an experiment conducted by Cohen and his colleagues. A group of normal subjects and a group of schizophrenic patients were shown two colored disks and were asked to describe one of the colors in such a way that a listener who was also looking at those two colors could pick out the one being described. When the colors were quite dissimilar, the people with schizophrenia did about as well as the normal subjects. For example, when one color was red and the other a purple-blue, they described the second one as purple or blue. In the next stage of the experiment, however, the two colors were quite similar, requiring that the speaker make subtle associations in order to describe the difference between the two. Faced with this task, the normal speakers managed to refine their associations in such a way as to indicate which color they meant. The speakers with schizophrenia, on the other hand, began reeling off associations that, while quite vivid, failed to convey the appropriate information:

Normal
Speaker 2: My God, this is hard. They are both about the same, except that this one might be a little redder.

Normal
Speaker 3: They both are either the color of canned salmon or clay. This one here is the pinker one.

Schizophrenic
Speaker 2: This is a stupid color of a shit ass bowl of salmon. Mix it with mayonnaise. Then it gets tasty. Leave it alone and puke all over the fuckin' place. Puke fish.

Schizophrenic
Speaker 3: Makeup. Pancake makeup. You put it on your face and they think guys run after you. Wait a second! I don't put it on my face and guys don't run after me. Girls put it on them.

(Cohen, Nachmani, & Rosenberg, 1974, p. 11)

What is it that pushes people with schizophrenia off the track? Some experts believe that, once schizophrenic patients make a given association, they cannot let go of it, as normal people can, and search for a more appropriate association. They get "stuck" on the first association, and the remainder of the response is "chained" off that first association, without any concern for relevance to the topic at hand (Titone, Holzman, & Levy, 2002). In other words, schizophrenic patients are at the mercy of their associative processes. In the examples just given, for instance, both of the schizophrenic speakers made a first association—one to salmon, one to pancake makeup—but then, instead of refining it in order to explain the difference between the two colors, they went off on trains of private associations to that first thought. (The same sort of loose associations show up in milder form in the biological relatives and monozygotic twins of schizophrenic patients [Kinney, Holzman, Jacobsen, et al., 1997; Docherty & Gottesman, 2000].) This characteristic seems to be related to another peculiarity of schizophrenic thinking, a difficulty in grasping context (Cohen, Barch, Carter, et al., 1999). Recent EEG studies have found that when people with schizophrenia have sentences read to them, they often show abnormal, event-related potentials when they get to the last word of the sentence. What this suggests is that they do not understand the context well enough to process the last word (Nestor, Kimble, O'Donnell, et al., 1997). As with the color-association test, it seems that people with schizophrenia have trouble "seeing the forest for the trees." Moreover, the difficulty in using context appears to be related to reduced activity of the prefrontal cortex (Barch, Carter, Braver, et al., 2001).

Poverty of Content The result of loosened associations is that schizophrenic language may convey very little. Though the person may use many words, all grammatically correct, he or she communicates poorly. This **poverty of content** can be seen in the following excerpt from a letter by a schizophrenic patient:

Dear Mother,

I am writing on paper. The pen which I am using is from a factory called "Perry & Co." This factory is in England. I assume this. Behind the name of Perry Co. the city of London is inscribed; but not the city. The city of London is in England. I know this from my school days. Then, I always liked geography. My last teacher in that subject was Professor August A. He was a man with black eyes. I also like black eyes. There are also blue and gray eyes and other sorts, too. I have heard it said that snakes have green eyes. All people have eyes. There are some, too, who are blind. These blind people are led about by a boy. It must be terrible not to be able to see. There are people who can't see and, in addition can't hear. I know some who hear too much. One can hear too much. (Quoted in Bleuler, 1911/1950, p. 17.)

Bleuler, who first published this letter, points out that the only common denominator of the ideas expressed in it is that they are all present in the patient's awareness: London—geography lesson—geography teacher—his black eyes—gray eyes—green snake eyes—human eyes—blind people—deaf people—and so on. The letter says much, and all very properly, but it conveys little, for it lacks any unifying principle beyond the irresistible linkage of associations.

Neologisms As we pointed out earlier, the confused speech of people with schizophrenia is generally interpreted as the product of confused thinking. However, some researchers have suggested that certain peculiarities of schizophrenic language may result not from radical thought disturbances but simply from an inability to retrieve commonly agreed-upon verbal symbols. That is, what individuals with schizophrenia have to say may be reasonable enough; they just can't find the right words with which to say it (DeLisi, 2001; Barch & Berenbaum, 1996).

This hypothesis might account for the rare appearance in schizophrenic speech of words and phrases not found in even the most comprehensive dictionary. These usages, called **neologisms** (literally "new words"), are sometimes formed by combining parts of two or more regular words. Or the neologism may involve the use of common words in a new way (Willerman & Cohen, 1990). In either case, what is interesting about neologisms is that, while they are sometimes unintelligible, at other times they manage to communicate ideas quite vividly, as can be seen in the following transcript (possible intended meanings are indicated in brackets):

TH.: Sally, you're not eating supper tonight. What's the problem?

PT.: No, I had belly bad luck and brutal and outrageous. [I have stomach problems, and I don't feel good.] I gave all the work money. [I paid tokens for my meal.] Here, I work. Well, the difference is I work five days and when the word was [when I am told to work] but I had escapingly [I got out of some work]. I done it for Jones. He planned it and had me work and helped me work and all and had all the money. He's a tie-father [a relative]. Besides generation ties and generation hangages [relationships between family generations—the way generations hang together] . . . he gave love a lot. I fit in them generations since old-fashion time [since long ago]. I was raised in packs [with other people] . . . certain times I was, since I was in littlehood [since I was a little girl] . . . she said she concerned a Sally-twin [my twin sister]. She blamed a few people with minor words [she scolded people], but she done goodship [good things]. I've had to suffer so much. I done it United States long.

TH.: Sally, is there anything else you want to tell me before you go?

PT.: Well, I expect there's a lot of things, but I would know what they were, especially the unkind crimery [the bad things]. (Hagen, Florida State University, clinical files)

Clanging Another oddity sometimes found in the speech of schizophrenic patients (and of manic patients as well) is **clanging,** the pairing of words that have no relation to one another beyond the fact that they rhyme or sound alike. Clanging may be related to the associational problem just discussed. In this case, however, the basis for the associations is sound rather than sense. Hence, clanging speech is often closer to nonsense verse than to rational communication.

The following is a transcript of a conversation between a therapist and a schizophrenic patient who was particularly adept at clanging. (About half of all his daily speech was rhymed.) As the transcript shows, clanging often involves neologisms:

TH.: How are things going today, Ernest?

PT.: Okay for a flump.

TH.: What is a flump?

PT.: A flump is a gump.

TH.: That doesn't make any sense.

PT.: Well, when you go to the next planet from the planet beyond the planet that landed on the danded and planded on the standed.

TH.: Wait a minute. I didn't follow any of that.

PT.: Well, when we was first bit on the slit on the rit and the man on the ran or the pan on the ban and the sand on the man and the pan on the ban on the can on the man on the fan on the pan. [All spoken very rhythmically, beginning slowly and building up to such a rapid pace that the words could no longer be understood.]

TH.: What's all that hitting your head for . . . and waving your arms?

PT.: That's to keep the boogers from eatin' the woogers. (Hagen, Florida State University, clinical files)

Word Salad In some cases, schizophrenic language seems to show a complete breakdown of the associational process, so it becomes impossible for the listener to trace any links between successive words and phrases. This extreme situation is illustrated in the following statement, made by the same patient whose clanging was previously quoted:

It's all over for a squab true tray and there ain't no music, there ain't no nothing besides my mother and my father who stand alone upon the Island of Capri where there is no ice, there is no nothing but changers, changers, changers. That comes like in first and last names, so that thing does. Well, it's my suitcase, sir. I've got to travel all the time to keep my energy alive. (Hagen, Florida State University, clinical files)

Appropriately, this type of speech, in which words and phrases are combined in what appears to be a completely disorganized fashion, is referred to as **word salad.** Unlike neologisms, word salad suggests no effort to communicate. Neither does it appear to reflect a train of tangential association. Neither are the words even connected on the basis of sound, as in clanging. Word salad, then, is the ultimate in schizophrenic splitting. Nothing is related to anything else.

Disorders of Perception

My eyes became markedly oversensitive to light. Ordinary colors appeared to be much too bright, and sunlight appeared dazzling in intensity. When this happened, ordinary reading became impossible, and print seemed excessively black.

Objects appeared to be far away and flat. If I spoke to anyone, the person in question looked to me like a cutout picture without any relief. (Benioff, 1995, p. 88)

Many schizophrenic patients, like the one quoted here, report changes in perception, including visual illusions, disturbingly acute hearing, inability to focus attention, difficulty in identifying people, and difficulty in understanding what other people are saying. People with schizophrenia have also reported changes in smell, complaining that their own body odor is more pronounced and more unpleasant, that other people smell stronger, and that objects have peculiar smells (Kaplan & Sadock, 1991). Among the many perceptual oddities involved in schizophrenia, two are of special concern: the breakdown of selective attention and the experience of hallucinations.

Breakdown of Selective Attention Normal people exercise selective attention without thinking about it; that is, they decide what they want to focus on in the environment and then concentrate on that, with the result that sensory data from the thing they are interested in register forcibly in the mind, while extraneous data (the sound of the air conditioner in the classroom, the earrings on the student in the front row) are confined to the edge of consciousness. People with schizophrenia, however, seem unable to engage in this normal selection process (Lussier & Stip, 2001)—a fact that was noted by Kraepelin and Bleuler. Today, a century later, many researchers feel that the breakdown of selective attention underlies most of the other symptoms of schizophrenia. McGhie and Chapman (1961), two major proponents of this theory, ask us to imagine what would happen if the mind ceased to exercise selective attention:

> Consciousness would be flooded with an undifferentiated mass of incoming sensory data, transmitted from the environment via the sense organs. To this involuntary tide of impressions there would be added the diverse internal images, and their associations, which would no longer be coordinated with incoming information. Perception would revert to the passive and involuntary assimilative process of early childhood, and, if the incoming flood were to carry on unchecked, it would gradually sweep away the stable constructs of a former reality. (p. 105)

In consequence, the person would see an altered world, make odd associations, produce bizarre speech, experience inappropriate emotions—and, it is easy to imagine, work out strange beliefs and strange behavior patterns as a defense against the sensory overload. The result would be what we call schizophrenia. One patient of McGhie and Chapman (1961) testified to his attention problems in simple and poignant terms:

My thoughts get all jumbled up. I start thinking or talking about something but I never get there. Instead I wander off in the wrong direction and get caught up with all sorts of different things that may be connected with the things I want to say but in a way I can't explain. People listening to me get more lost than I do. (p. 108)

Hallucinations Added to the perceptual problems of people with schizophrenia is the fact that many of them perceive things that are not there. Such perceptions, occurring in the absence of any appropriate external stimulus, are called **hallucinations.** Auditory hallucinations are apparently the most common, occurring in 70 percent of schizophrenic patients (Cleghorn, Franco, Szechtman, et al., 1992), and certain types of auditory hallucinations are especially characteristic of schizophrenia, notably the experience of hearing two or more voices conversing with one another or of hearing voices that keep a running commentary on the patient's thoughts or behavior or say derogatory things about the patient (Nayani & David, 1996). After auditory hallucinations, visual hallucinations are the most frequent, followed by hallucinations of the other senses (Ludwig,

Jane H., a schizophrenic patient with auditory hallucinations, painted this picture while in an art therapy program. Particularly striking are the rather sinister eyes of the central figure, together with the many hands surrounding him.

1986). While some schizophrenic patients recognize that their hallucinations are not real—that the voices are only in their heads—others are not sure (Frith, 1996; Brebion, Amador, David, et al., 2000), and a fair percentage, presumably the more severely psychotic, are convinced that their hallucinations are perceptions of real events.

People with schizophrenia, then, have not only a perceptual problem but also a reality-monitoring problem, and this in turn may be related to their difficulties in exercising selective attention. Their inability to screen out irrelevant stimuli may make it hard for them to tell the difference between self-generated and externally generated sounds and thus to distinguish between real voices and imaginary ones (Brebion, Amador, David, et al., 2000; Johns, Rossell, Frith, et al., 2001). On the other hand, some voices "in the head" may be more than imaginary: They may be the patient's own voice, speaking subvocally—that is, with activation of the larynx but with no audible sound. PET scans of schizophrenic patients taken while the subjects were having auditory hallucinations have shown a pattern of activity in the language regions of the brain that is similar to the activity seen in the brains of normal subjects speaking in and listening to their own voices (Woodruff, Wright, Bullmore, et al., 1997).

Disorders of Mood While schizophrenia is considered to be primarily a disturbance of thought, it often involves disturbances of mood as well. However, schizophrenic mood abnormalities have little in common with the psychotic mood disorders. As we saw in Chapter 10, the mood disorders involve either deep depression or manic elation, or an alternation between the two. Some other patients have either a manic or a major depressive episode while also showing the symptoms of schizophrenia. This intermediate syndrome is called **schizoaffective disorder** and has an intermediate prognosis; that is, schizoaffective patients fare somewhat better than schizophrenic patients, on the average, and somewhat worse than mood disorder patients (Davidson & McGlashan, 1997). However, in schizophrenia, there are generally two patterns of mood disorders.

One is a reduced emotional responsiveness, known either as **blunted affect** (when the patient shows little emotion) or **flat affect** (when the patient shows no emotion). In either case, this reduction of emotion is often accompanied by **anhedonia,** a reduced experience of pleasure that is often stable over the course of schizophrenic illness (Herbener & Harrow, 2002). The second major pattern of schizophrenic mood disturbance is **inappropriate affect,** the expression of emotions unsuitable to the situation. For example, the patient may giggle while relating a painful memory or show anger when given a present. Usually, however, the inappropriateness is subtler. A number of studies have shown that people with schizophrenia tend to use the same gestures, show the same facial expression, and gaze at the listener in the same way regardless of whether the emotion they are describing is happy, sad, or angry (Limpert & Amador, 2001). Furthermore, in all these situations, their gestures, facial expression, and gaze tend to be similar to those that nonschizophrenic people use when describing something happy (Knight & Roff, 1985). Thus, here again, the problem for schizophrenic patients seems to be one of differentiation. This is true even for those with blunted affect. Recent research suggests that such patients have difficulty in expressing and perceiving different emotions but not in feeling them (Berenbaum & Oltmanns, 1992; Kring & Neale, 1996; Penn, Combs, Ritchie, et al., 2000).

Disorders of Motor Behavior The following portrait of a schizophrenic ward shows a mix of behaviors that might be observed daily in hundreds of schizophrenic wards throughout the country:

> In the day room Lou stands hour after hour, never saying a word, just rubbing the palm of his hand around and around the top of his head. Jerry spends his day rubbing his hand against his stomach and running around a post at the same time. Helen paces back and forth, her head down, mumbling about enemies who are coming to get her, while Vic grimaces and giggles over in the corner. Virginia stands in the center of the day room, vigorously slapping her hand against her dress, making a rhythmical smacking sound, which, because of its tireless repetition, goes unnoticed. Nick tears up magazines, puts bits of paper in his mouth, and then spits them out, while Bill sits immobile for hours, staring at the floor. Betty masturbates quietly on the couch, while Paul follows one of the young nurse's aides on her room check, hoping to get a chance to see up her dress as she leans over to smooth a bed. Geraldine is reading her Bible; Lillian is watching television; and Frank is hard at work, scrubbing the floor. (Adapted from Hagen, Florida State University, clinical files.)

In some cases, such as the last three in this example, schizophrenic motor behavior appears perfectly normal. In other cases, such as those of Betty and Paul, it is merely inappropriate to the setting. However, certain repetitive motor behaviors, such as the head rubbing, dress smacking, and paper tearing in the quoted case, are clearly abnormal. The act of engaging in purposeless behaviors repetitively over long periods of time is called **stereotypy.**

Schizophrenic patients sometimes show frenetically high levels of motor activity, running about, thrashing their arms, upsetting furniture, and generally expending a good deal of energy. Much more common, however, is the opposite: inactivity. In the extreme case, schizophrenic patients may lapse into a *catatonic stupor,* remaining mute and immobile for days on end.

Social Withdrawal As we shall see, an early sign of schizophrenia is emotional detachment—a lack of attention to or interest in the goings-on of the external world. Preoccupied with their own thoughts, people with schizophrenia gradually withdraw from involvement with the environment. Above all, they withdraw from involvement with other people. One study of male adolescents, aged 18 to 20, found that four social factors during childhood and adolescence—having fewer than 2 friends, preferring to socialize in small groups, feeling more sensitive than others, and not having a steady girlfriend—predicted the 195 men who later developed schizophrenia (Malmberg, Lewis, David, et al., 1998). Note that, in spite of the wide range of behaviors taking place on the ward described in the case study, there is one behavior that is strikingly absent: social interaction. Rarely do schizophrenic patients engage in small talk. Often they act as if others do not exist.

This may be due in part to their social handicaps. They are less adept than normal individuals at picking up interpersonal cues—that is, at understanding what the other person is feeling or trying to do (Penn, Combs, & Mohamed, 2001). Many of them also have problems with gaze discrimination: They think other people are looking directly at them when this is not the case (Rosse, Kendrick, Wyatt, et al., 1994). Given these problems, it is no surprise that they recoil

Social withdrawal is one of the leading symptoms of schizophrenia.

from social interaction. And, schizophrenic individuals' poor social skills are a major contributor to their stigmatization by others (Penn, Kohlmaier, & Corrigan, 2000).

The social withdrawal of schizophrenic patients is related to their attention problems as well (Green, 1996; Ohno, Ikebuchi, Henomatsu, et al., 2000). The mental havoc that presumably results from the attention deficit would make communication very difficult, and, as we have seen, people with schizophrenia communicate poorly. Knowing that they are unlikely to make themselves understood—and knowing, furthermore, that people may treat them very curtly—schizophrenic patients may choose to focus on anything rather than other people.

The Course of Schizophrenia

Schizophrenia, like some other disorders, seems to follow a regular course, or progression of stages, through time. The course of the disorder has traditionally been divided into three phases: the prodromal phase, the active phase, and the residual phase.

The Prodromal Phase In some cases, the onset of schizophrenia is very sudden. In a matter of days, a reasonably well-adjusted person is transformed into a hallucinating psychotic. In other cases, functioning deteriorates gradually for years before any clearly psychotic symptoms appear. This slow downhill slide is known as the **prodromal phase.** The earlier the prodromal phase begins, the worse the prognosis (Häfne, Löffler, Maurer, et al., 1999).

During the prodromal phase, incipient schizophrenic patients generally become withdrawn and socially isolated. Often, they cease to care about their appearance or hygiene, forgetting to bathe, sleeping in their clothes, and so on. Performance in school or at work begins to deteriorate; the person shows up late, if at all, and seems careless and inattentive. Disturbances of thought and language begin to become evident. At the same time, emotions begin to seem shallow and inappropriate. Eventually, family and friends note a change in the person (Gaebel, Janner, Frommann, et al., 2000). Sometimes, however, the disorder proceeds so gradually that it is not remarked upon until the person begins acting very bizarrely—dressing in odd ways, collecting trash, talking to invisible companions. By this time, the active phase has begun.

The Active Phase In the **active phase,** the patient begins showing prominent psychotic symptoms—hallucinations, delusions, disorganized speech, severe withdrawal, and so forth. The symptoms outlined earlier in this chapter describe the active phase of schizophrenia. As we noted, however, no one patient is likely to show all those symptoms.

The Residual Phase Just as onset may occur almost overnight, so may recovery. Ordinarily, however, what recovery there is is gradual. In most patients, the active phase is followed by a **residual phase,** in which behavior is similar to that of the prodromal phase. Blunted or flat affect is especially common in this period. Speech may still ramble, hygiene may still be poor, and, while outright hallucinations and delusions may have dissipated, the person may continue to have unusual perceptual experiences and odd ideas, claiming, for example, to be able to tell the future or to have other special powers. In consequence, holding down a job is still difficult for most schizophrenic patients in the residual phase (Mueser, Salyers, & Mueser, 2001).

In some cases, the residual phase ends with a return to perfectly normal functioning, or "complete remission," as it is known in the psychiatric vocabulary. This is not the usual outcome, however. Many patients remain impaired to some degree, and many go on to have further psychotic (i.e., active-phase) episodes, with increasingly impaired functioning between episodes. Several long-term follow-up studies have found that approximately 22 percent of schizophrenic patients remained schizophrenic chronically, 28 percent fully remitted after one or more psychotic episodes, and 50 percent alternated between the residual phase and recurrences of the active phase (Ram, Bromet, Eaton, et al., 1992; Wiersma, Nienhuis, Slooff, et al., 1998). Discontinuing antipsychotic medications has been found to increase the risk of relapse almost fivefold (Robinson, Woerner, Alvir, et al., 1999). Other recent long-term studies have produced similar findings (Davidson & McGlashan, 1997; Jablensky, 2000). As one might expect, relapses tend to be triggered by stressful life events (Norman & Malla, 1993a, 1993b).

Another sad truth revealed by longitudinal studies is that people with schizophrenia tend to die about 10 years younger than other people (Jeste, Gladsjo, Lindamer, et al., 1996) and that their suicide rate is very high. Between 20 and 42 percent of schizophrenic patients attempt suicide, and 10 to 15 percent succeed. Suicide is more likely for those who are under age 35 and more suspicious and delusional and, not surprisingly, for those who are more aware that they are ill (Amador, Friedman, Kasapis, et al., 1996; Fenton, McGlashan, Victor, et al., 1997; Abed, Vaidya, & Baker, 2000). People with schizophrenia are also disproportionately the victims of crime and, in the case of women, of physical and sexual abuse (Bellack, Gearon, & Blanchard, 2000).

The Subtypes of Schizophrenia

Ever since the days of Kraepelin and Eugen Bleuler, schizophrenia has been divided into subtypes, based on behavior. Patients were described not merely as having schizophrenia but as having catatonic schizophrenia, paranoid schizophrenia, and so forth. These subtypes are often problematic for the diagnostician (Sanislow & Carson 2001). If, upon intake, a schizophrenic patient claims that he is a famous person pursued by enemies, he will probably be classified with paranoid schizophrenia. But if two weeks later he no longer speaks of enemies but will not move from his chair, should he be reclassified as having catatonic schizophrenia?

Despite the difficulties, subtype diagnoses may ultimately be of value. As we saw in Chapter 2, the process of sorting patients into restrictive diagnostic groups is essential to research. Though at present we do not know whether different patterns of schizophrenic behavior issue from different causes and call for different treatments, we can never find out unless we study groups of patients with similar behavior patterns. And this means sorting them into subtypes.

DSM-IV-TR lists five subtypes. One of these, the "undifferentiated" type, is a miscellaneous category, used for patients who do not fit into any of the other categories or who fit into more than one. Such patients are common. Another category, the "residual" type, is for patients who have passed beyond the active phase. This leaves three categories that actually describe active-phase symptomatology: disorganized, catatonic, and paranoid schizophrenia.

(Top) This painting was done by a young man in the early stages of schizophrenia. The sad, partially faceless woman alone in the desert suggests loss of identity and loss of meaning. (Bottom) Another schizophrenia patient made this painting of the earth being split apart by lightning—perhaps the person's effort to picture his own, internal disintegration.

Disorganized Schizophrenia Of all the varieties of the psychologically disturbed, the patient with disorganized schizophrenia is the one who best fits the popular stereotype of a "crazy" person. Three symptoms are especially characteristic of **disorganized schizophrenia.** First is a pronounced incoherence of speech; it is the disorganized schizophrenic patient who is most likely to produce neologisms, clang associations, and word salad. Second is mood disturbance. Some people with disorganized schizophrenia have flat affect; others act silly—giggle, make faces, and so on. The third key symptom is disorganized behavior, or lack of goal orientation—for example, a refusal to bathe or dress. Though these three signs may define the subtype, most disorganized schizophrenic patients run the gamut of schizophrenic symptomatology. Their motor behavior is strikingly odd. They may also experience hallucinations and delusions, though these are often confused and fragmentary, unlike the more coherent imaginings of the paranoid schizophrenic patient. Furthermore, most people with disorganized schizophrenia are severely withdrawn, utterly caught up in their own private worlds, and at times almost impervious to whatever is happening around them.

The onset of disorganized schizophrenia is usually gradual and tends to occur at a relatively early age (Fenton & McGlashan, 1991). The distinguishing mark of the onset—withdrawal into a realm of bizarre and childlike fantasies—is illustrated in the following case of a professional golfer:

> John joined the Army [when he was in his teens]. In boot camp he would sit for hours in a garage where jeeps and other motor vehicles were kept and talk to the cars. He would "dance" and act out animated soliloquies. He was sent to the base psychiatrist who tested his urine for illicit substances. His drug tests were all negative and John

was given a discharge "for the convenience of the government." . . .

John returned to the town where his parents had now retired. He got a job at the local golf course. Within months of his employment there, he came to believe that an older woman who ran a concessions stand was "spying" on him and was telling co-workers that John was having sex with an underage high school girl working at the pro shop for the summer. . . . He was noted by co-workers and golfers alike to be "strange," to smile and grimace inappropriately, and occasionally to make no sense when he spoke. A greens keeper made the comment that he always avoided John because "he just goes on and on, and I don't know what he is talking about; he tells jokes that aren't funny, but he nearly breaks a rib laughing. I just have to get away from the guy."

John came to the attention of the authorities when he threatened to hit the older woman with a golf club. [He was hospitalized and later released.] . . .

Three years later, the pope came to San Francisco and John decided that he wanted an audience with him. Church officials told John that this was not possible. . . . [He then decided that] the pope was the Antichrist. John believed that he should warn the faithful that the pope was an impostor, and he concocted a scheme of lying down in front of the pontiff's motorcade and stopping traffic. . . .

The police arrested John before he could get within three-hundred yards of the pope's motorcade. They transferred him to a psychiatric facility. . . .

During this second hospitalization, John had a marked thought disorder with some loose associations, some neologisms, and tangential phraseology: "The Pope is the Vicar of Christ, and since Vicary Street is near the highway, I felt that roads had something to do with it . . . you know, the macadam as in Adam and the Sistine Chapel and that picture of the trans-fingeration," he said. (Booth, 1995, pp. 166–169)

Catatonic Schizophrenia Once a common disorder but now quite rare (Morrison, 1991), **catatonic schizophrenia** has as its distinguishing feature a marked disturbance in motor behavior. Sometimes this disturbance takes the form of **catatonic stupor,** or complete immobility, usually accompanied by *mutism,* the cessation of speech; the patient may remain in this condition for weeks. Some catatonic patients assume extremely bizarre postures during their stupors. They may also show *waxy flexibility,* a condition in which their limbs, like those of a rubber doll, can be "arranged" by another person and remain in whatever position they are placed. However, catatonia is not limited to decreases in motor activity. Many cata-

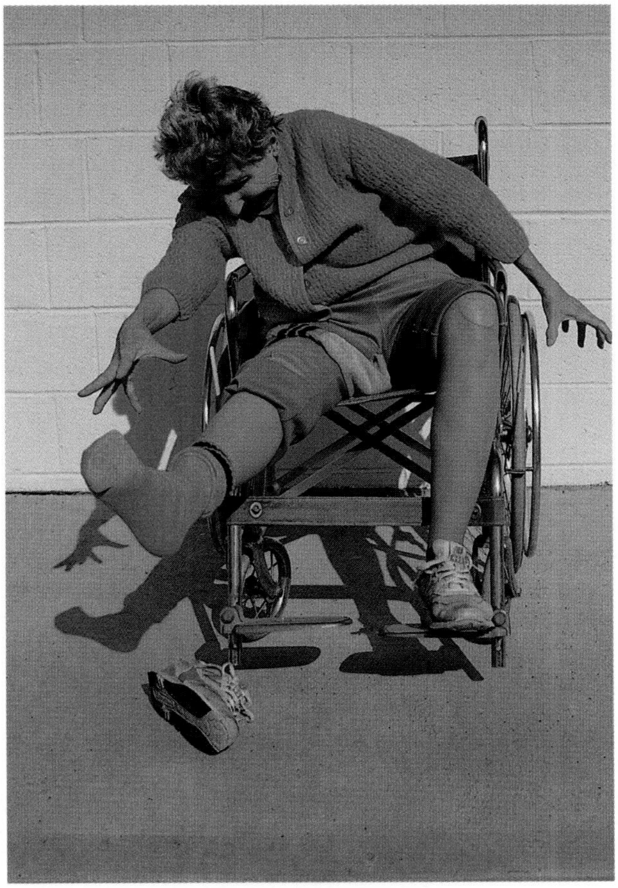

The woman pictured here exhibits catatonic rigidity, the stiff and bizarre postures assumed by patients with catatonic schizophrenia.

tonic patients alternate between periods of immobility and periods of frenzied motor activity, which may include violent behavior. In either form, catatonic schizophrenia often involves medical emergencies. When excited, patients may injure themselves or others; when stuporous, they must be prevented from starving.

Though catatonic immobility suggests passivity, it may in fact be quite "active." To hold for hours the bizarre postures that catatonic patients often assume requires an extraordinary expenditure of energy. Furthermore, while some patients assume waxy flexibility, others strenuously resist any effort on the part of others to move their limbs—a feature known as *catatonic rigidity.* Similarly, though catatonia seems to suggest extreme withdrawal, it is clear that many patients are well aware of what is going on around them. Some show **echolalia,** parroting what is said by others; some show *echopraxia,* imitating the movements of others. Finally, in many patients one sees what is called *catatonic negativism;* that is, they not only refuse to do what is requested of them but consistently do just the opposite, indicating that they understand very well the nature of the requests.

The following case of a 22-year-old mathematics student illustrates the odd motor behavior of catatonic patients, together with their potential for violence:

> Anna was brought to the psychiatric hospital by the police for an emergency admission after she had attacked a child. She had walked up to a 9-year-old girl at a bus stop and tried to strangle her. Some passersby fortunately intervened, restraining Anna, and called the police. At first she fought violently and tried to get at the child, but then suddenly she became motionless and rigid as a statue, with one arm stretched out toward the child and a wild stare on her face. When the police arrived, it was difficult to get her into the car, because she would not move and resisted attempts to move her. She almost had to be carried to the police car and forced into it. . . .
>
> When she was brought to the ward, she remained standing just inside the entrance and resisted invitations to go further. She refused to have anything to eat and would not go to the examination room. She remained standing rigid, with her right arm stretched out in front of her, staring at her hand. She did not answer questions or respond in any way to the ward assistants. After several hours she finally had to be taken to her room and put in bed with the use of mild force. She lay in bed in the position where she had been placed, staring at the ceiling. . . . The next morning Anna was found standing rigid again, this time behind the door. She had urinated on the floor in the corner of the room. . . .
>
> Anna's sister turned up and informed the physician that the family had been concerned about Anna for some time. For the last 2–3 months she had seemed reclusive and odd, with recurrent episodes of muteness and staring that lasted for several minutes. Several times she made peculiar statements that "children are trying to destroy mathematics" or "rational figures have a hard time." She stopped going to the university and stayed in her room, leaving it only for a walk in the evening. (Üstün, Bertelsen, Dilling, et al., 1996)

Paranoid Schizophrenia The defining characteristics of **paranoid schizophrenia** are delusions and/or hallucinations of a relatively consistent nature, often related to the themes of persecution and grandeur. The delusions can range from a jumble of vague suspicions to an exquisitely worked-out system of imagined conspiracies. In either case, they are often accompanied by hallucinations—especially auditory hallucinations—supporting the delusional belief. When, in the classic case, the theme is persecution, it is often combined with the theme of grandeur. Paranoid delusions are associated with an attributional style in which others are blamed for negative events (Bentall, Corcoran, Howard, et al., 2001).

Paranoid schizophrenia is far more common than either the disorganized or the catatonic type. A 1974 survey of more than 8,000 hospitalized schizophrenic patients found that close to half were diagnosed as paranoid (Guggenheim & Babigian, 1974). Paranoid schizophrenic patients are also, in the main, more "normal" than other schizophrenic patients. They may perform well on cognitive tests (Strauss, 1993). They have superior perception of genuine emotional expressions (Davis & Gibson, 2000). They have better records of premorbid adjustment, are more likely to be married, have a later onset, and show better long-term outcomes than do other kinds of schizophrenic patients (Fenton & McGlashan, 1991; Kendler, McGuire, Gruenberg, et al., 1994; Sanislow & Carson, 2001).

Though the active phase of paranoid schizophrenia usually does not appear until after age 25, it is typically preceded by years of fear and suspicion, leading to tense and fragile interpersonal relationships. The onset and development of paranoid schizophrenia are illustrated in the following case of a man hospitalized at the age of 36. He had begun expressing paranoid ideas about 10 years earlier:

> Most of the content related to his girlfriend, beginning with plausible claims that she was being unfaithful to him. The paranoid ideation soon evolved to include totally unfounded accusations of her having a sexual relationship with one of his brothers. Within a few weeks, the allegations had progressed to include more bizarre claims, such as the belief that his girlfriend was having sex with dogs and farm animals and that she had been setting fires all over town. . . .
>
> Over the next few years, . . . he would seclude himself in his room for days at a time, with multiple locks on his bedroom door, and his parents reported that he would frequently talk aloud in his room. He slept with a gun under his bed and a knife by his side. Such periods would often last several weeks at a time. These would be intermixed with periods of relative calm. . . .
>
> [When he was finally hospitalized, he explained what he was afraid of.] He was convinced that his enemies had been coming into his house at night and raping him while he slept. He said that this had been occurring off and on over the previous several months and probably longer and that this was the

reason for the elaborate locks on his bedroom door and the weapons under his bed. While in the hospital, he slept more during the day than at night, which he admitted was because of his ongoing concerns about being sexually assaulted while sleeping at night. Although he continued to deny frank hallucinations, he ultimately described having "dog ears" and explained that this enabled him to hear conversations that were going on far in the distance. He also admitted to concerns that his audio equipment had been tampered with in such a way that "the wrong lyrics come out of the music." Finally, he had entertained the idea that some sort of an electrical device had been placed in his body that allowed his enemies to hear everything he said, but he was not convinced this was true. (Flaum & Schultz, 1996, pp. 812–813)

The Dimensions of Schizophrenia

The subtypes we have just discussed are a classic way of looking at schizophrenia, but research has yet to prove that they are valid groupings—that is, that the schizophrenias they delineate are, in fact, different disorders, springing from different causes, requiring different treatments, and so forth. Accordingly, researchers have looked for other ways in which to organize information about schizophrenia. Today, discussions of this disorder are generally framed not according to subtypes but in terms of dimensions. Like spatial dimensions (width, length), *dimensions* of schizophrenia are measures of continuous variation and are thus less exclusive than subtypes. With dimensions, patients are never "in" or "out"; they fall somewhere on the dimension. In practice, however, dimensions, too, tend to sort patients into groups. It is possible that their advantage over subtypes is simply that the groups they yield have so far proved more meaningful. The three that have received the most attention are the process-reactive dimension, the positive-negative symptoms dimension, and the paranoid-nonparanoid dimension.

Process-Reactive, or Good-Poor Premorbid As we noted, there is considerable variation in the onset of schizophrenia. Some patients go through an extended prodromal phase. Others go from normal functioning to full-blown psychosis almost overnight. This dimension of variation has traditionally been known as the **process-reactive dimension**. The cases in which onset is gradual are called *process schizophrenia*. Those in which onset is sudden and apparently precipitated by a traumatic event are called *reactive schizophrenia*.

This dimension has a long history, beginning with Kraepelin and Eugen Bleuler. These two theorists believed that the onset of the psychoses was a clue to their cause. The biogenic psychoses, because they were the result of an abnormal physiological *process*, would presumably have a gradual onset. By contrast, the psychogenic psychoses, because they were *reactions* to traumatic experiences, would appear suddenly, hence the terms *process* and *reactive*. Today, many researchers view the process-reactive dimension more as a continuum than as a dichotomy. Indeed, some now prefer to speak not of a process-reactive dimension but of a **good-poor premorbid dimension**—that is, in terms of how well the patient was functioning before the onset of the active phase. Actually, the good-poor premorbid dimension is basically the same as the process-reactive dimension, minus the causal implications. To describe onset is to describe premorbid adjustment, and vice versa.

Although there is some disagreement over the usefulness of the process-reactive dimension, there is general agreement as to what the terms describe. The process (or poor-premorbid) case typically involves a long history of inadequate social, sexual, and occupational adjustment. People with process schizophrenia typically did not belong to a group of friends in school, did not date regularly during adolescence, did not continue their education after high school, never held a job for longer than two years, and never married (Sanislow & Carson, 2001). Furthermore, there appears to have been no precipitating event—no sudden stressor such as a divorce or a job change—immediately preceding the active phase. Rather, the history usually reveals a gradual eclipse of thoughts, interests, emotions, and activities, until the person becomes so withdrawn that he or she is hospitalized.

In contrast, histories of people with reactive (or good-premorbid) schizophrenia are apparently normal. The patient fit in at home and at school, had friends, dated, and got along well in general. The onset of the schizophrenic symptoms usually occurs after a clearly precipitating event and is sudden and spectacular, often involving hallucinations and delusions. Such patients also tend to show extreme panic and confusion, for they are as horrified as everyone else over what has happened to them (Sanislow & Carson, 2001).

Premorbid adjustment has been useful in predicting which patients will recover and which will not (Lay, Blanz, Hartmann, et al., 2000; Wiersma, Nienhuis, Slooff, et al., 1998). Individuals with poor-premorbid schizophrenia are more likely to have long hospitalizations—and, when discharged, to require rehospitalization—than are good-premorbid patients (Robinson, Woerner, Alvir, et al., 1999).

TABLE 14.1 Summary of Differences Between Positive-Symptom (Type I) and Negative-Symptom (Type II) Schizophrenia

	POSITIVE (TYPE I) SCHIZOPHRENIA	NEGATIVE (TYPE II) SCHIZOPHRENIA
Symptoms	Delusions Hallucinations Incoherence Bizarre behavior	Poverty of speech Flat affect Social withdrawal Apathy
Premorbid adjustment	Good	Poor
Onset	Tends to be later	Tends to be earlier
Prognosis	Relatively good	Poor
Structural brain abnormalities	Absent	May be present
Drug response	Good	Poor
Gender distribution	More likely to be women	More likely to be men

Positive-Negative Symptoms Of all the dimensions of schizophrenia, the one that has attracted the most research attention in recent years—and, therefore, the one that will be most important in our discussion of the possible causes of schizophrenia—is the **positive-negative symptoms dimension. Positive symptoms,** characterized by the presence of something that is normally absent, include hallucinations, delusions, bizarre or disorganized behavior, and positive thought disorder such as incoherence. **Negative symptoms,** characterized by the absence of something that is normally present, include poverty of speech, flat affect, withdrawal, apathy, and attentional impairment (Bellack, Gearon, & Blanchard, 2000). The positive-negative symptoms dimension seems to parallel the good-poor premorbid dimension. Patients with negative symptoms are more likely to have had poor premorbid adjustment. And, like poor-premorbid patients, they tend to have an earlier onset (Castle & Murray, 1993) and a worse prognosis (Tek, Kirkpatrick, & Buchanan, 2001). Indeed, they are the ones most likely to have an unremitting course—that is, never to recover. Positive and negative symptoms also seem to be associated with different kinds of cognitive problems. Patients with negative symptoms do worse on tests involving the processing of visual stimuli. Patients with positive symptoms do worse on tests that require the processing of auditory stimuli, especially language (Buchanan, Strauss, Breier, et al., 1997).

These findings have led to increased speculation that there may be two biologically distinct types of schizophrenia, of which the one with negative symptoms is more like Kraepelin's original dementia praecox. Some researchers (Crow, 1989; Lenzenweger, Dworkin, & Wethington, 1989) have distinguished two such types (see Table 14.1). **Type I schizophrenia** is characterized by positive symptoms and tends to respond to medication. **Type II schizophrenia** is characterized by negative symptoms (and associated with greater structural abnormalities in the brain) (Sanfilipo, Lafargue, Rusenek, et al., 2000), and according to some research does not respond as well to typical antipsychotic medication (Earnst & Kring, 1997). Also supporting the idea that positive and negative symptoms may have distinct causes is the finding that positive and negative symptoms in schizophrenia predict corresponding symptoms in nonpsychotic schizotypal relatives (Fanous, Gardner, Walsh, et al., 2001). As we will see, the two types also seem to fit differently into the dopamine hypothesis, the leading biochemical theory of schizophrenia.

However, these two categories are not as tidy as they sound. Often, a typical Type I characteristic will turn up in an otherwise Type II patient. Some schizophrenic patients show positive and negative symptoms at the same time. Others initially show negative symptoms and then develop positive symptoms, or the reverse. In the latter case, the negative symptoms may be secondary—that is, they may develop as a *response* to the primary symptoms: Under the pressure of frightening hallucinations (positive symptom), the patient withdraws socially, speaks little, and assumes a flat affect (negative symptoms). But it is very hard to determine whether negative symptoms are primary or secondary (Sanislow & Carson, 2001). To add to the complexity, some researchers now feel that there may be another important dimension, a disorganized-nondisorganized dimension, on which patients do not necessarily line up neatly into Type I and Type II (Toomey, Kremen, Simpson, et al., 1997 Loftus, DeLisi, & Crow, 1998). One approach to resolving some of the inconsistencies of the positive-negative symptoms distinction has been to further distinguish between **deficit symptoms,** those negative symptoms that are primary and endure across prodromal, active, and residual phases of schizophrenia; and nondeficit symptoms, transient negative symptoms that are secondary to depression or medication side effects (Kirkpatrick, Buchanan, Ross, et al., 2001). Deficit symptoms seem to be more strongly associated with neuropsychological and brain abnormalities than nondeficit symptoms (Galderisi, Maj, Mucci, et al., 2002; Kirkpatrick, Buchanan, Ross, et al., 2001).

Paranoid-Nonparanoid On the **paranoid-nonparanoid dimension,** the criterion of classification is the presence (paranoid) or absence (nonparanoid) of delusions of persecution and/or grandeur. Some studies have found the paranoid-nonparanoid dimension to be related to the process-reactive dimension (Fenton & McGlashan, 1991). As we saw, paranoid schizophrenia tends to have better premorbid adjustment, later onset, and better outcomes. It also resembles reactive schizophrenia in that its victims are more intact intellectually. Thus, the paranoid-nonparanoid dimensions, like the process-reactive, the good-poor premorbid, and the positive-negative symptoms, has had prognostic value and may aid in the development of theories as to the causes of schizophrenia (Sanislow & Carson, 2001).

❖ Groups at Risk for Schizophrenia

Although schizophrenia occurs in all cultures, symptoms differ depending on the culture. While people with paranoid schizophrenia in industrial societies may fear the police, their African counterparts are more likely to think they are pursued by a sorcerer (Takeshita, 1997). Also, prognosis differs among cultures, with schizophrenia patients faring better in less-industrialized societies (Jablensky, 2000; Lin & Lin, 2001). The emphasis on competition and self-reliance in industrial societies makes them a hard place for a recovering schizophrenic patient. Developing countries, with their stable social structures and their emphasis on family and interdependence, seem to offer a better halfway house (Takeshita, 1997; Lin & Lin, 2001).

Within industrialized societies, there are certain known risk factors. Schizophrenia is more likely to be found in people of lower IQ and in people who are unemployed and unmarried; it is also more likely to be diagnosed in city-dwellers (Pedersen & Mortensen, 2001; van Os, Hanssen, Bijl, et al., 2001). In the United States, African Americans have a higher rate of schizophrenia than European Americans, though it is not known whether this is due to actual differences or to diagnostic bias (Strakowski, Flaum, Amador, et al., 1996).

Age, too, is involved in risk. Schizophrenia normally strikes in adolescence or early adulthood, and the timing of onset is related to outcome. Early-onset cases, particularly those beginning in adolescence, have a worse prognosis (Lay, Blanz, Hartmann, et al., 2000). For men, the median age of onset is mid-twenties; for women, late twenties (Haas & Sweeney, 1992; Jablensky, 2000). Some researchers believe that the female sex hormone, estrogen, delays onset in women (Kulkarni, 1997).

Gender affects more than onset; it also determines vulnerability. Men are one and a half times more likely than women to develop schizophrenia (Iacono & Beiser, 1992a, 1992b). The genders also express the disorder differently (Goldstein & Lewine, 2000). Males with schizophrenia are more likely to be withdrawn and to exhibit negative symptoms; women are more likely to have affective and positive symptoms (Castle & Murray, 1993; Gur, Petty, Turetsky, et al., 1996). In addition, men tend to have poorer premorbid adjustment, poorer response to medication, and worse prognosis (Doering, Müller, Köpcke, et al., 1998; Bellack, Gearon, & Blanchard, 2000). Finally, men with schizophrenia are less likely than women to have a family history of schizophrenia (Goldstein, Faraone, Chen, et al., 1990) but are more likely to have had birth complications and to show brain abnormalities (Nopoulos, Flaum, & Andreason, 1997), and the brain abnormalities they show are different from those typically seen in women with schizophrenia (Goldstein, Seidman, O'Brien, et al., 2002). These findings suggest that men and women may be differentially at risk for different types of schizophrenia, with men more susceptible to process, poor-premorbid, Type II schizophrenia and women more susceptible to reactive, good-premorbid, Type I schizophrenia.

Delusional Disorder

The Symptoms of Delusional Disorder

Sarah P., 15 years old, was taken to a therapist because she kept running away from home, but apart from her disappearances she seemed a well-adjusted teenager. The therapist, trying to forge a bond with Sarah's father, asked him about his work. He replied that he had recently left a job of 18 years because of conflict with the union leadership:

> The conflict had been so severe, he reported, that union officials were still persecuting him. In fact, he whispered, they had implanted a minute radio receiver in his head through which they transmitted all manner of disgusting

> messages to him. Specifically, these messages told him to sexually molest various women, including his daughter.
>
> Mr. P. became increasingly agitated as he spoke. The union had surrounded him with agents that tempted him. For example, a secretary at work persistently leaned over the filing cabinet in a way that suggested he was supposed to rape her. He, however, was onto their game and had resisted all of their efforts to get him to engage in these despicable behaviors. They had targeted him years ago, but he had been strong enough to ignore their behavior and to continue to work until he was able to get a new job at the same rate of pay. After all, he had a family to support.

The therapist later discussed the father's delusions with the mother. She said that she knew all about them:

> She had long since stopped trying to talk him out of them, since her experience had been that he had only gotten more agitated when they discussed it. It was better, she had discovered, to gently change the subject after sympathizing with how difficult the situation must be for him. She reported that he had never behaved inappropriately, had never missed work, had never even spoken about his odd ideas to anyone other than to herself as far as she knew.

The therapist, with the wife's help, tried to persuade the father to take some antipsychotic medication. He refused. However, since Sarah's running away was no doubt connected to her father's state of mind, an arrangement was made for her to move in with her mother's sister. (Adapted from Bernheim, 1997, pp. 132–134.)

Mr. P.'s major symptom, a system of delusions, is something that we have already discussed under the heading of paranoid schizophrenia. In paranoid schizophrenia, however, the delusional system is simply one item in a cluster of abnormalities, all of which may function independently of one another. In **delusional disorder,** on the other hand, the delusional system is the fundamental abnormality. Indeed, in some cases, the delusional system is the *only* abnormality; in all other respects, the person seems quite normal. Other patients may show some disturbances of mood, but only as a consequence of the delusional system. (For example, they may explode in anger at complete strangers, but only because they suspect those strangers of spying on them, flirting with their spouses, or whatever.) In other words, it is assumed that, if there were no delusions, there would be no abnormality. Furthermore, whatever other symptoms the person shows, they do not include the characteristic symptoms of schizophrenia, such as loosening of associations, incoherence, or thought broadcasting. Finally, in this disorder the delusions are generally less bizarre than those of paranoid schizophrenia. As with Mr. P., the person may claim to be pursued by enemies, but not by enemies from outer space.

As for the content of the delusions, *DSM-IV-TR* lists five categories. The classic and most common type, just seen in the case of Mr. P., is the *persecutory type,* involving the belief that one is being threatened or maltreated by others. In the *grandiose type,* as the name indicates, the person believes that he or she is endowed with extraordinary power or knowledge. In the *jealous type,* the delusion is that one's sexual partner is being unfaithful. In the *erotomanic type,* the person believes that someone of high status—the president of the company or of the United States—is in love with him or her. Finally, the *somatic type* involves the false conviction that one is suffering from a physical abnormality or disorder.

❖ Groups at Risk for Delusional Disorder

Delusional disorder differs from schizophrenia in striking more women than men and in having a later onset, between ages 25 and 45 (Manschreck, 1992), although the somatic type has an earlier age of onset than the persecutory type (Yamada, Nakajima, & Noguchi, 1998). It is also far less common. For schizophrenia, as we saw, the lifetime risk is 1 to 2 percent; for delusional disorder, it is 0.3 percent (Evans, Paulsen, Harris, et al., 1996). It is possible, of course, that many more cases exist. We have all probably encountered a few candidates for this diagnostic label: ignored geniuses, self-styled prophets, radio talk show callers who have a detailed scheme for solving the world's problems. Because such people tend to have relatively good contact with reality, apart from their isolated delusional systems, many of them remain within the community and never see a therapist. Those who present themselves for treatment often do so not of their own volition but at the insistence of others.

Problems in the Study of Schizophrenia

So far, we have described schizophrenia and related psychoses, but we have not touched upon the cause or treatment of schizophrenia. Those topics will occupy the remainder of this chapter. First, however, it must be pointed out that schizophrenia involves special problems for researchers. In no other area of research is there greater danger of having one's research confounded by a third variable. Most of the schizophrenic patients available for research purposes are (1) hospitalized and (2) taking antipsychotic drugs. Consequently, any interesting differences that turn up between these subjects and nonhospitalized, nonmedicated controls may well be a function not of schizophrenia but of the medication or of the overcrowding, poor diet, difficult sleeping conditions, lack of exercise, and lack of privacy that are routine conditions of hospitalization (Blanchard & Neale, 1992). This problem is often addressed by studying patients just after their first psychotic break, before they have received antipsychotic medication or experienced lengthy hospitalization.

A graver problem is that researchers do not agree on what actually constitutes schizophrenia—what the primary pathology is. Consider the analogy of a leg fracture. The fracture produces pain, a bent leg, and a limp. But, of these three symptoms, only the first two are primary—direct results of the broken bone. The limp is a secondary symptom, a strategy that the person adopts in order to cope with the primary symptom of pain. Likewise, in schizophrenia, there is little doubt that, among the recognized symptoms of the disorder, some are primary and others merely reactions to the primary symptoms. But which is which? Is social withdrawal the primary pathology, as some theorists believe, or do schizophrenic patients withdraw simply because their thought disorders make it difficult for them to communicate with others? Are delusions a primary symptom, or are they, as suggested earlier, merely the schizophrenic person's way of explaining the chaos of his or her thoughts? Answering these questions is crucial to research on schizophrenia. Until we know what the basic disorder is, we stand little chance of discovering its cause.

Another vexing problem for schizophrenia researchers is finding what are called **differential deficits,** deficits specific to the disorder in question (as opposed to other disorders) and presumably central to it. Because schizophrenia has many debilitating symptoms, people with schizophrenia have problems with many different kinds of tasks, but such problems do not necessarily tell us about schizophrenia in particular (Chapman & Chapman, 1973; Knight & Silverstein, 2001; Strauss, 2001). For example, if a researcher were to give a group of schizophrenic patients a driving test, they would probably not do as well as controls, but that does not mean that bad driving is causally related to schizophrenia. In order to show a differential deficit in schizophrenia, research must be able to show that, on two carefully constructed tasks, differing only in subtle ways, schizophrenic patients perform poorly on one and not on the other. Such findings are often very hard to produce, but the question of which deficits represent the core of schizophrenia cannot really be addressed without them.

Schizophrenia: Theory and Therapy

No one in the field of schizophrenia research believes that the disorder stems from a single cause. Clearly, it has multiple sources, and one of them is already known. It is well established that genetic factors are partially, but not wholly, responsible for the development of schizophrenia. Consequently, most researchers have adopted a **diathesis-stress model** (Chapter 6), which states that schizophrenia is due to the combination of a genetically inherited *diathesis,* or predisposition, and environmental *stress*. The various perspectives use this model in accordance with their specialties, some focusing on the diathesis, others on the stress, but always keeping other factors in mind as well.

The Neuroscience Perspective

One of the most exciting areas of abnormal psychology today is neuroscience research in schizophrenia. For years, neuroscientists concentrated primarily on the schizophrenic diathesis: first establishing its existence and then trying to discover what it actually consists of in biological terms. Today they are also investigating biological stressors that might activate that diathesis. A vast amount of work remains to be done, but the evidence accumulated so far has revolutionized our understanding of this disorder.

Genetic Studies The idea that schizophrenia might be passed from parent to child goes back at least as far as the eighteenth century. By the late nineteenth century, when biogenic theories were popular, the genetic hypothesis was endorsed by Kraepelin, Eugen Bleuler, and many other experts on schizophrenia. But it was not until about 30 years ago that researchers were able to design studies sophisticated enough to test the hypothesis scientifically. The evidence produced by these studies is extremely persuasive. The studies leading up to this conclusion are family, twin, and adoptive studies.

Family Studies The earliest studies of the genetics of schizophrenia were family studies. Their findings,

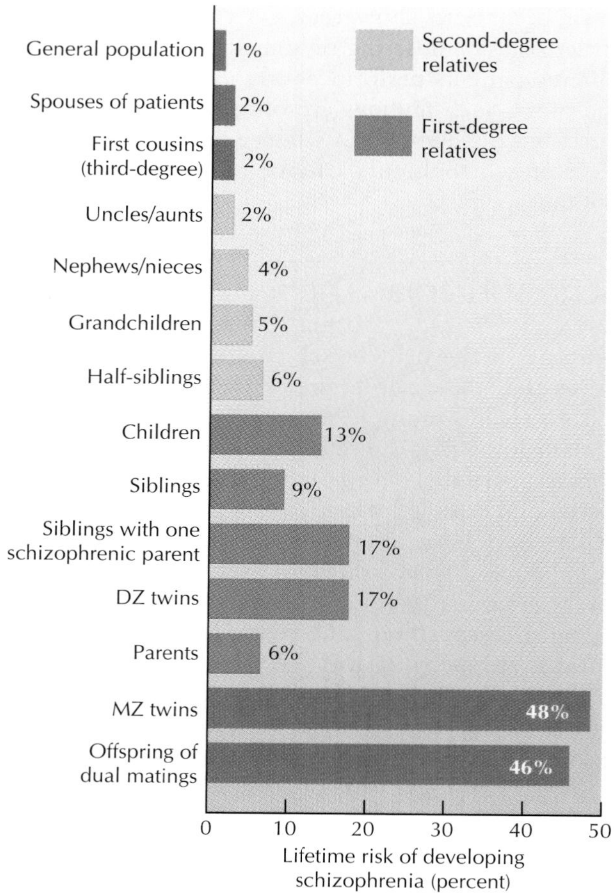

FIGURE 14.1 Lifetime risk of developing schizophrenia for the relatives of people with schizophrenia. The kinds of relatives are listed at the left. The children of a person with schizophrenia have a 13 percent risk; the siblings of a person with schizophrenia, a 9 percent risk; and so on. These figures are averages of statistics compiled by family and twin studies in Europe between 1920 and 1987. (Gottesman, 1991)

together with those of more recent research, clearly indicate that, the more closely one is related to a person with schizophrenia, the more likely one is to develop schizophrenia. Figure 14.1 shows the data published by Gottesman in 1991. As may be seen from this graph, children of one parent with schizophrenia have a 13 percent chance, and children of two parents with schizophrenia ("offspring of dual matings") have a 46 percent chance of developing schizophrenia, as compared with a prevalence of 1 to 2 percent in the general population—a striking differential. According to a recent review of family studies, a person with a first-degree relative with schizophrenia is almost 10 times likelier to develop schizophrenia than a person with no schizophrenia in the immediate family (Kendler & Diehl, 1993; Schneider & Deldin, 2001).

Beautiful Minds: An Interview with John Nash and Son, Part 1

The MindMAP video "Beautiful Minds: An Interview with John Nash and Son" presents clips based on an interview with John Nash, Jr., the winner of the 1994 Nobel Prize in Economics, and one of his sons, Johnny Nash. Both father and son are brilliant mathematicians, and both suffer from schizophrenia. Does this prove that schizophrenia is a genetically transmitted disorder? Do you think there is a link between creativity and schizophrenia? Why or why not?

However, as we have seen in previous chapters, any psychological similarity among family members may be due to shared environment rather than shared genes. For more precision in controlling the environmental factor, we must turn to twin and adoption studies.

Twin Studies In twin studies conducted since 1960, the average concordance rate for schizophrenia in MZ twins is approximately 46 percent, three times greater than the 14 percent average concordance rate for DZ twins (Gottesman, 1996). As more recent studies have improved in research methodology, the concordance rates for both MZ and DZ twins have dropped, but proportionately. The MZ-DZ concordance ratios still lie between 3:1 and 5:1. Moreover, the MZ-DZ concordance difference tends to be

These quadruplets, the Genain sisters, were studied intensively for genetic causes of schizophrenia. All four had the disorder, with a wide range of severity.

greater when the index twin has more severe symptoms (Sweeney, Haas, & Nimgaonkar, 2000). It also varies with the nature of the index twin's symptoms. When the index twin has prominent negative symptoms, the MZ-DZ concordance difference is greater than when the index twin has prominent positive symptoms (Dworkin & Lenzenweger, 1984). This finding supports the validity of the Type I–Type II distinction and the belief that Type II has a stronger genetic component.

Such data must be considered strong evidence for the genetic hypothesis. However, as we saw, twin studies, too, are subject to objections. To begin with, the researcher is dealing with a small sample. (There are not that many MZ twins with schizophrenia in the world.) Second, as we saw, some researchers feel that MZ twins share not only a more similar genotype but also a more similar environment than DZ twins, in that the MZ twins are always the same sex, tend to be dressed alike, and so forth. Hence, it is possible that here, too, the differential may be due to environment as well as genes.

Indeed, even if MZ twins are separated at birth and reared apart, they still share the same *intrauterine* environment. Given the recent evidence that some kind of prenatal damage—injury, exposure to a virus—may contribute to schizophrenia, the high concordance rates for MZ twins may be due to a shared intrauterine environment as well as to shared genes (Sanislow & Carson, 2001). One study found that the concordance rates for the MZ twins who shared the same placenta was almost double the concordance rate for the MZ twins who had separate placentas (Davis & Phelps, 1995). That is a striking finding, and good evidence that an intrauterine factor is involved in schizophrenia.

In an effort to distinguish between genes and environment, several researchers have studied the offspring of MZ twins who are discordant for schizophrenia (Gottesman & Bertelsen, 1989; Kringlen & Cramer, 1989). The logic of these studies has to do with the fact that because MZ twins are genetically identical, they must transmit to their children the same genetic risk for schizophrenia, regardless of whether they themselves have schizophrenia. Thus, all the cousins have the same genetic risk. They do not all grow up under the same conditions, however. The children of the twin with schizophrenia have the experience of being raised by a schizophrenic parent; the children of the other twin do not. Therefore, if both twins' children develop schizophrenia at approximately the same rate, this is very strong evidence for genetic transmission.

That is what these studies have found. In one study (Gottesman & Bertelsen, 1989), the risk for schizophrenia and schizophrenia-like disorders in the children of the twin with schizophrenia was 16.8 percent; in the children of the nonschizophrenic twin, it was 17.4 percent. As might be expected, the differential was far greater in the children of the discordant DZ twins, who had only half their genes in common. Using the same research design, the researchers found that the children of the DZ twins with schizophrenia were at a 17.4 percent risk; the children of their nonschizophrenic co-twins were at a 2.1 percent risk.

Again, this is good evidence for genetic transmission, and, again, there is a problem with it: The samples were very small. As noted, MZ twins with schizophrenia are rare. But these twin studies are backed up by another kind of research with far larger samples: adoption studies.

Adoption Studies As we have seen, the subjects of adoption studies are children who were adopted away from their biological families in infancy and thus have the genetic endowment of one family and the environmental history of another. If such a study could show that children who were born to mothers with schizophrenia but were adopted in infancy by psychologically normal families still developed schizophrenia at approximately the same rate as the children who were born of one parent with schizophrenia and were not adopted away, then again this would be very strong evidence for the genetic hypothesis.

Such studies have been done, and such were the findings. In a pioneering study, Heston (1966) located 47 adoptees who had been born to hospitalized mothers with schizophrenia. He also gathered a matched control group of 50 adoptees whose mothers did not have schizophrenia. From a large variety of sources—mostly firsthand interviews—information was gathered on all these subjects. A file was then compiled on each subject, all identifying information was removed, and diagnoses were made by several independent psychiatrists. The results were that schizophrenia was found only in the children of mothers who had schizophrenia. The rate for schizophrenia among this group was 16.6 percent, very close to the 13 percent figure for children who were born of a parent with schizophrenia and not adopted away.

Another study that has produced immensely influential findings was begun in 1963 in Denmark by David Rosenthal and his colleagues (Rosenthal, Wender, Kety, et al., 1968). Through various central registries that have been maintained by the Danish government for about 50 years, the investigators identified 5,500 adoptees and 10,000 of their 11,000 biological parents. Then they identified all of the biological parents, called the *index parents,* who had at some time been admitted to a psychiatric hospital with a diagnosis of either schizophrenia or affective psychosis. The 76 adopted-away children of these parents *(index children)* were then matched with a control group of adopted children whose biological parents had no history of psychiatric hospitalization. Eventually, 19 percent of the index children versus 10 percent of the control children were diagnosed as having definite or possible schizophrenia (Gottesman & Shields, 1982). Perhaps of greater interest is the finding that 28 percent of the index children, compared with 10 percent of the control children, showed schizophrenic characteristics (Lowing, Mirsky, & Pereira, 1983).

Using the same Danish records, the same investigators (Kety, 1988; Kety, Rosenthal, Wender, et al., 1968, 1975) did another study with a different design. In the same group of 5,500 adoptees from Copenhagen, 33 were identified as having psychiatric histories that warranted a diagnosis of schizophrenia. A matched control group of nonschizophrenic adoptees was selected from the same records. Then 463 biological and adoptive parents, siblings, and half-siblings were identified for both the index and control groups, and these relatives were interviewed to determine whether they had ever suffered from schizophrenia. As it turned out, the rate of schizophrenia in the biological relatives of the index cases was about double (21.4 percent) that in the biological relatives of the control cases (10.9 percent), whereas the rates of schizophrenia in the adoptive relatives of the index and control cases were about the same (5.4 versus 7.7 percent). Thus, adopted children who later developed schizophrenia are much more likely to have biological, rather than adoptive, relatives with schizophrenia. This finding, since confirmed (Kety, Wender, Jacobsen, et al., 1994), is persuasive evidence that there is a genetic component to schizophrenia.

Mode of Transmission If there is a genetic component, where does the genetic abnormality lie? One viewpoint is that one or a few major genes are responsible for transmitting the risk, and some initial studies did succeed in linking schizophrenia to specific genes. But later studies have failed to support such connections (Kendler & Diehl, 1993; Conklin & Iacono, 2002). Consequently, many researchers now suspect that schizophrenia is caused not by one gene but by a variety of genetic subtypes and that what they produce is not one disorder but a range of similar disorders that, for want of evidence, are grouped into a single category (Kendler & Walsh, 1995). Researchers are now trying to identify genetic markers, or simpler related traits, for these subtypes (Tsuang, Stone, & Faraone, 2001). (See the box on page 411.)

Another view is that schizophrenia is the product not just of many genes but of their combination with environmental factors. Genetic and environmental disadvantages combine until a certain threshold is reached. Beyond that threshold, the person develops schizophrenia (Tsuang, 2000). There is evidence for this view. For example, an adoption study that is still in progress (Tienari, Wynne, Moring, et al., 1994; Wahlberg, Wynne, Oja, et al., 1997) has found that its adoptees' risk for schizophrenia correlates not only with the psychiatric history of their biological parents but also with the psychological functioning of their *adoptive* families. Not surprisingly, the latter correlation is strongest when the adoptee is the child of a mother with schizophrenia and therefore genetically at risk. Specifically, it was children with both schizophrenic biological mothers *and* adoptive mothers who showed communication deviance who were most likely to show schizophrenic thought disorder themselves (Wahlberg, Wynne, Oja, et al., 1997). Thus, this study, while supporting the role of genes, connects it back to the diathesis-stress model.

A third possibility is that new genetic mutations that contribute to schizophrenia regularly occur in the population. In humans, like other mammals, the male of the species introduces the vast majority of new mutations into the gene pool. This is because human male sperm cells are constantly dividing throughout life, providing repeated opportunities for mutations to occur whereas female eggs are finished dividing at birth. Based on this, Malaspina and colleagues predicted that greater paternal age at the time of their offspring's conception would be associated with higher rates of schizophrenia in those offspring (Malaspina, Harlap, Fennig, et al., 2001). And, this is precisely what they found. In a birth cohort of 87,907 individuals born in Jerusalem from 1964 to 1976, the risk of schizophrenia increased monotonically with every 5 years of their fathers' advancing age, relative to offspring with fathers younger than age 25. In contrast, mothers' age at conception was not related to the likelihood of schizophrenia in their offspring. These findings suggest that new genetic mutations may contribute to risk for schizophrenia.

Genetic High-Risk Studies A vast number of studies have been conducted with children who have been born to parents with schizophrenia and who have shown at least some symptoms of schizophrenia. These studies have revealed a wealth of information, but they are almost always contaminated by

Focus On... Eye Tracking as a Marker for Schizophrenia

For researchers trying to locate the genetic bases of schizophrenia, a major problem is that the symptoms of this disorder are all complex behaviors, controlled by many genes, not to mention environmental influence. Social withdrawal, attention problems, odd perceptions—these experiences are quite removed from the protein-coding functions of any single gene. To study the genetics of schizophrenia via family tendencies toward such symptoms is, in the words of one researcher, "like studying the genetics of color blindness through familial tendencies to run traffic lights" (Cromwell, 1993).

A more profitable approach is to try to find in the schizophrenic population an unusual trait that may have a simpler and more direct link with genes. Such a trait, called a *genetic marker,* may be much less disabling than the main symptoms of schizophrenia—indeed, it may be utterly benign—but it could lead researchers to the genes that produce the disabling symptoms.

One of the hypothesized genetic markers for schizophrenia is an abnormality in what is called *smooth-pursuit eye tracking.* Most people can follow a moving object with their eyes in a smooth, continuous line while keeping their heads still. (Try this. Move your finger like a pendulum and track it with your eyes while keeping your head in a fixed position.) Many schizophrenic patients, however, cannot do this. Their eyes travel not in a smooth line but in a saccadic, or jerking, pattern (Levy, Holzman, Matthysse, et al., 1993; Schneider & Deldin, 2001)—a characteristic that is probably related to a specific neurological abnormality.

Schizophrenic patients with deviant eye tracking have other things in common as well. Compared with schizophrenic patients who show normal eye tracking, they are more likely to have negative symptoms—flat affect, poverty of speech, anhedonia. They do not perform as well on tasks controlled by the frontal lobes of the brain (Clementz, McDowell, & Zisook, 1994; Ross, Thaker, Buchanan, et al., 1996). They are more likely to have relatives with poor eye tracking, and those relatives tend to show schizophrenic-like traits, such as odd social behavior (Keefe, Silverman, Mohs, et al., 1997; Karuami, Saoud, d'Amato, et al., 2001) and subtle dysfunction of the frontal cortices (O'Driscoll, Benkelfat, Florencio, et al., 1999). Finally, schizophrenia patients with poor eye tracking are less likely to recover (Katsanis, Iacono, & Beiser, 1996).

Interestingly, people with schizotypal personality disorder (Chapter 11) are also unusually prone to deviant eye tracking, as are their relatives (Siever, Friedman, Moskowitz, et al., 1994). This is an important finding. As we will see, children who have a genetic risk for schizophrenia but do not develop the disorder often show schizotypal personality disorder.

What all this evidence suggests is that there is a specific subgroup of schizophrenic patients with a similar genetic abnormality, or pattern of abnormalities. It seems likely that the defect involves one major gene, a recessive gene, together with a number of less potent genes that can aggravate or mitigate the effect of the major gene (Iacono & Grove, 1993). So far, however, researchers have been unsuccessful in identifying or locating any of the genes responsible for the poor eye tracking (Schneider & Deldin, 2001).

methodological problems. If, for example, you wanted to identify significant events in the background of a child who is now showing schizophrenic symptoms, your theoretical notions might well bias your attention toward certain details of the child's history. Furthermore, if you interview people who have known the child—parents, grandparents, and so forth—their recollection will be influenced by what they know of the child's present condition. Retrospective information is always questionable.

The solution would be to conduct a *prospective* study—a longitudinal study (Chapter 3)—testing and interviewing a large, random sample of children at regular intervals over a period of time. Then, when some of these children developed schizophrenia, you would already have on file a reliable record of their physiological, psychological, and social histories and could begin searching for correlations. There is one problem with such a project, however. As we have seen, only 1 to 2 percent of the general population develops schizophrenia. Hence, in order to end up with a reliable sample of schizophrenic participants you would have to include thousands of children in your study, making it prohibitively expensive and time-consuming.

In the early 1960s, Mednick and Schulsinger made a breakthrough in schizophrenia research by devising a longitudinal project that would resolve most of the problems just outlined (Mednick, 1970). Recognizing the impossibility of studying a random sample of normal children, the investigators turned to the **genetic high-risk design** (Chapter 3); that is, they chose as their sample 200 children who, by virtue of being born to mothers with schizophrenia, were already genetically vulnerable to schizophrenia. As we have seen, such children stand about a 13 percent chance of developing the disorder. Thus, the investigators could predict that the number of eventual schizophrenic offspring in their high-risk group would be large enough to permit meaningful comparisons with low-risk control children—children not born of mothers with schizophrenia.

Mednick (1971) lists the following advantages of this research design over that of previous studies:

1. The children have not yet experienced the confounding effects of the schizophrenic life, such as hospitalization and drugs.
2. No one—teacher, relative, child, or researcher—knows who will develop schizophrenia, which eliminates much bias from testing and diagnosis.
3. The information is current; the researchers do not have to depend on anyone's recollection.
4. There are two built-in groups of controls for the children who become ill: the high-risk subjects who stay well and the low-risk subjects. (p. 80)

By 1989, the children in the project had reached a mean age of 42 and were therefore past the major risk period for the onset of schizophrenia. (Remember that onset tends to occur in adolescence or early adulthood.) In the high-risk group, 16 percent had developed schizophrenia—approximately the expected figure—and another 26.5 percent had developed a *schizophrenic-spectrum* disorder—that is, a disorder related to schizophrenia. (In most cases, it was schizotypal personality disorder—see Chapter 11.) In the low-risk group, by contrast, only 2 percent had developed schizophrenia, and only 6 percent had developed a schizophrenic-spectrum disorder (Parnas, Cannon, Jacobsen, et al., 1993). The researchers (e.g., Olin & Mednick, 1996) list the factors that separate the high-risk children who developed schizophrenia from the high-risk and low-risk children who remained normal:

1. *Home life.* Their home lives were less stable, they had less satisfactory relationships with their parents, and their mothers were more likely to be irresponsible and antisocial.
2. *Early separation and institutionalization.* They were more likely to be separated from their mothers in the first year of life, and they spent more time in institutions.
3. *School problems and criminal behavior.* They had behavior problems. The males were more domineering, aggressive, and unmanageable in school, and they were more likely (as were their mothers) to have arrest records. The females were more likely to be lonely, passive, nervous, and sensitive to criticism.
4. *Attention problems.* They showed less ANS habituation to the environment—that is, they had more difficulty "tuning out" incidental stimuli.
5. *Birth complications.* They were more likely to have experienced complications before or during birth, and those who had such complications were more likely to show brain atrophy.

This project has inspired many similar projects, and there is now intense activity in genetic high-risk research. Between the Mednick group and other research teams, the findings in this list have been confirmed and extended (Hans, Marcus, Nuechterlein, et al., 1999; Cornblatt & Obuchowski, 1997). A number of researchers have found a history of attention problems—for example, an inability to screen out repetitive stimuli, such as the ticking of a clock—in high-risk children who eventually develop schizophrenia (Hollister, Mednick, Brennan, et al., 1994). High-risk children also showed lower IQ and poorer learning and memory than low-risk controls (Byrne, Hodges, Grant, et al., 1999). Neurological tests and studies of home movies suggest that these children may also show poor motor coordination and negative facial expressions (Walker, Grimes, Davis, et al., 1993). There is further evidence that these children's mothers are more disturbed—they developed schizophrenia at an earlier age, were more likely to have been hospitalized during the child's early years, were more prone to childbirth-related psychosis, and had more unstable relationships with men (Olin & Mednick, 1996). Finally, both the Mednick group and other groups have accumulated further evidence that prenatal or birth trauma is an important dividing line between high-risk children who develop schizophrenia and high-risk children who don't (Cannon, Rosso, Bearden, et al., 1999; Buka, Tsuang, Tofrey, et al., 2001).

What do all these findings amount to? First, they support the role of genetic inheritance. Second, the high rate of attention problems constitutes further support for the idea that attention deficits are a primary symptom of schizophrenia. Finally, and perhaps most important, the results of the high-risk studies offer suggestions as to the kinds of stress that may be especially likely to convert a schizophrenic diathesis into schizophrenia. Disrupted home lives, disabled mothers, institutionalization—these misfortunes may be the product of the genetic defect, but they also produce massive stress. As for prenatal and birth trauma, this is now a major concern to researchers trying to pinpoint the environmental pressures that may tip the balance in high-risk children.

Behavioral High-Risk Studies A second type of high-risk study uses the **behavioral high-risk design** (Chapter 3), which selects high-risk people not on the basis of genetics but on the basis of behavioral traits that are thought to be associated with the disorder in question. Using this design with schizophrenia has the advantage of yielding a more representative sample of people who will develop schizophrenia. (Only about 5 to 10 percent of schizophrenic patients have a parent with schizophrenia. The genetic high-risk studies thus represent only a small portion of the schizophrenic population.) Loren and Jean Chapman and their colleagues have used the behavioral high-risk design to screen a large number of college students for those prone to perceptual abnormalities and magical thinking (Allen, Chapman, Chapman, et al., 1987; Chapman & Chapman, 1985). Their screening mechanism is a test called the Perceptual Aberration–Magical Ideation Scale, or Per-Mag Scale, in which the participants respond true or false to such statements as 'Sometimes I've had the feeling that I am united with an object near me" and "The hand motions that strangers make seem to influence me at times." Perceptual abnormalities and magical thinking seem to have a genetic basis (Grove, Lebow, Clementz, et al., 1991) and often turn up in the early histories of people diagnosed with schizophrenia. The Chapmans' goal is to discover whether this link holds up prospectively as well as retrospectively, and their method is to track the psychiatric progress of people who score high on the Per-Mag Scale.

They have already produced interesting findings. In a 10-year follow-up, 10 of their 182 high-risk subjects had developed a full-blown psychosis, as compared with only 2 of their 153 low-risk subjects (Chapman, Chapman, Kwapil, et al., 1994). But, for firmer results, we must await later follow-ups. The Chapmans' participants are now only about 35 years old and are therefore still at risk for a first-time psychotic episode.

One potential problem with the Per-Mag Scale is that the people it selects are at risk not just for schizophrenia but for other psychoses as well. Still, researchers have been able to relate the cognitive idiosyncrasies measured by the scale to a wide range of schizophrenic characteristics. Compared with low Per-Mag scorers, high Per-Mag scorers show more hallucinations, delusions, and social withdrawal, more thought disorder and communication deviance, and more attention problems and perceptual biases (Coleman, Levy, Lenzenweger, et al., 1996; Lenzenweger, 2001; Luh & Gooding, 1999). They also have more first-degree relatives who have been treated for schizophrenia (Lenzenweger & Loranger, 1989).

Brain Imaging Studies As we saw in Chapter 6, the study of the brain has been revolutionized in recent years by the development of new brain imaging technologies: PET, which measures brain functioning, and CT and MRI, which measure brain structure. Through these methods, researchers have been able to identify certain characteristic abnormalities in the brains of people with schizophrenia. To begin with, CT and MRI scans have shown that in chronic schizophrenia, brain size is smaller than normal (Ward, Friedman, Wise, et al., 1996). And this reduced brain size is found in both the schizophrenic and nonschizophrenic members of discordant MZ twin pairs, suggesting a genetic contribution to reduced brain growth (Baare, van Oel, Hulshoff Pol, et al., 2001). In addition, they have demonstrated that the brain ventricles of people with chronic schizophrenia—the cavities containing the cerebrospinal fluid—tend to be enlarged (Brennan & Walker, 2001) and that this particular sign is related to cognitive impairment, poor response to drug treatment, poor premorbid adjustment, and more negative than positive symptoms (Schultz, Nopoulos, & Andreasen, 2001) as well as with birth complications, such as fetal hypoxia (too little oxygen) (Cannon, Van Erp, Rosso, et al., 2002). It is also more likely to be found in males with schizophrenia than in females (Flaum, Arndt, & Andreasen, 1990). These findings have been supported by postmortem analyses of schizophrenic brains (Heckers, 1997). As noted, chronic patients tend to show enlarged ventricles. Therefore, it is possible that this abnormality is not so much a cause of schizophrenia as a result of the disorder—or a result of the cumulative effects of antipsychotic drugs. Consistent with this view, repeated assessments of brain structure have shown increasing abnormalities over time (DeLisi, 1999; Mathalon, Sullivan, Lim, et al., 2001). On the other hand, recent studies have reported similar abnormalities in patients with a first episode of schizophrenia (Cecil, Lenkinski, Gur, et al., 1999; Velakoulis, Pantelis, McGorry, et al., 1999).

If ventricles are enlarged, this suggests that the brain structures lying near those ventricles may also be affected. Brain imaging studies, together with postmortem studies, have found abnormalities in three specific systems: the frontal cortex, the temporal lobe–limbic structures, and the basal ganglia or cerebellum (Cannon, 1998; Hulshoff Pol, Schnack, Mandl, et al., 2001; Gur, Cowell, Latshaw, et al., 2000; Gur, Turetsky, Cowell, et al, 2000). And these abnormalities also show up in the relatives of schizophrenic patients, suggesting that they may have a genetic basis (Lawrie, Whalley, Abukmeil, et al., 2001).

Several PET scan studies have found that, when schizophrenic patients are given metabolism tests while they are performing cognitive tasks requiring the selective-attention and other problem-solving abilities of the frontal lobe, many of them show abnormally low frontal-lobe activity (Carter, Mintun, Nichols, et al., 1997; Artiges, Martinot, Verdys, et al, 2000). Furthermore, their frontal cortices seem to

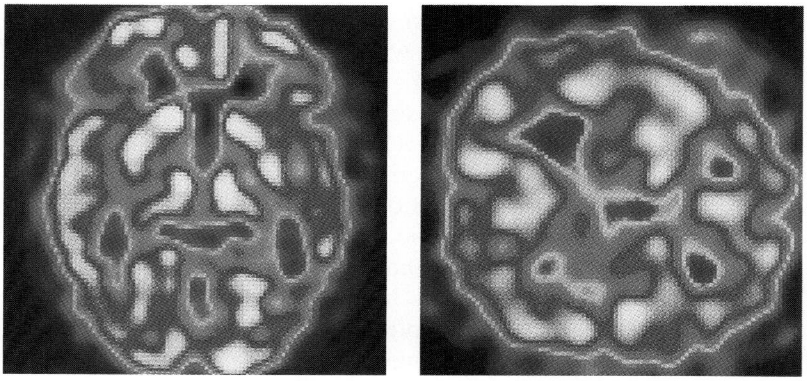

The PET scan at left shows brain activity in a normal person; the image at right shows the temporal lobe of a hallucinating schizophrenic patient. Normal brain metabolic activity produces a roughly symmetrical pattern in the yellow areas of the left and right cerebral hemispheres. In contrast, the visual areas (in yellow) of the schizophrenic patient are more active, possibly as a result of the hallucinations.

have fewer synapses, making neural transmission more difficult (Glantz & Lewis, 1997; McGlashan & Hoffman, 2000). These patients tend to be those with negative symptoms. By contrast, patients with positive symptoms often show abnormalities in the temporal lobes or limbic structures (Marsh, Harris, Lim, et al., 1997), and these temporal lobe abnormalities are present in first-episode schizophrenia patients (McCarley, Salisbury, Hirayasu, et al., 2002). Indeed, MRI studies suggest that auditory hallucinations are associated with activation in the temporal lobes, the thalamus, and the hippocampus (Shergill, Brammer, Williams, et al., 2000). Thus, positive symptoms and negative symptoms seem to stem from different parts of the brain—further evidence for the Type I–Type II theory. But, as usual, the picture is not simple. Both positive-symptom and negative-symptom patients show abnormalities in the basal ganglia (Siegel, Buchsbaum, Bunney, et al., 1993). Furthermore, some patients show abnormalities in the connections among all three of the brain systems in question. This may explain why so many patients have both positive and negative symptoms (Andreason, 1999; Pierri, Volk, Auh, et al., 2001; Kubicki, Westin, Maier, et al., 2002).

Prenatal Brain Injury The histories of people with schizophrenia show an abnormally high rate of birth complications (Jones & Cannon, 1998; Schneider & Deldin, 2001), and as we saw, high-risk children who develop schizophrenia are likelier than those who don't to have suffered a prenatal or birth complication. Could this be a stressor that, at least for some people, helps to convert the genetic diathesis into schizophrenia? Several lines of evidence point to such a conclusion.

One involves MRI and postmortem studies. The structure of the normal human brain is asymmetrical—a feature that develops in the second trimester (fourth through sixth months) of pregnancy. During that period, the frontal and temporal lobes become larger on the right than on the left, and other regions grow larger on the left than on the right. But in MRI and postmortem studies, many schizophrenic patients do not show this normal asymmetry, particularly in the language and association areas of the brain (Barta, Pearlson, Brill, et al., 1997; Sommer, Aleman, Ramsey, et al., 2001). They are also less likely to be right-handed, another indicator of reduced cerebral lateralization. This suggests that their brains may have suffered trauma during the second trimester.

Another line of evidence comes from studies of prenatal stress and risk for schizophrenia. Several studies have found that individuals who were in utero when their mothers were exposed to severe stress, such as a military invasion, a catastrophic tornado, or the death of their husbands, were significantly more likely to develop schizophrenia as adults than were individuals not in utero at the time of their mothers' exposure to these stressors (Kinney, 2001).

There are other hints of early prenatal brain damage. Damage to fetal brain tissue leads to a tissue-repair response called gliosis, but this response occurs only in the third trimester, not before. Thus, when the brain shows structural abnormalities *without* evidence of gliosis, such changes must have occurred before the third trimester. And that is what postmortem examinations of schizophrenic patients have shown: structural changes without gliosis (Brennan & Walker, 2001). Minor physical anomalies (MPAs) of the head and face (e.g., asymmetric ears, stippled palate) also originate during fetal development and are considered indirect markers of compromised brain development. MPAs occur at an elevated rate in individuals with schizophrenia (Brennan & Walker, 2001; McGrath, El-Saadi, Grim, et al., 2002) and suggest that such individuals suffered prenatal injuries.

Other postmortem studies point specifically to the second trimester. During that period, neurons in the developing brain migrate from the walls of the ventricles to a temporary structure called the subplate in order, eventually, to form the association areas of the cerebral cortex. Those areas are responsible for the ability to make appropriate associations between

Research Highlights — Is Schizophrenia an Infectious Disease? The Viral Hypothesis

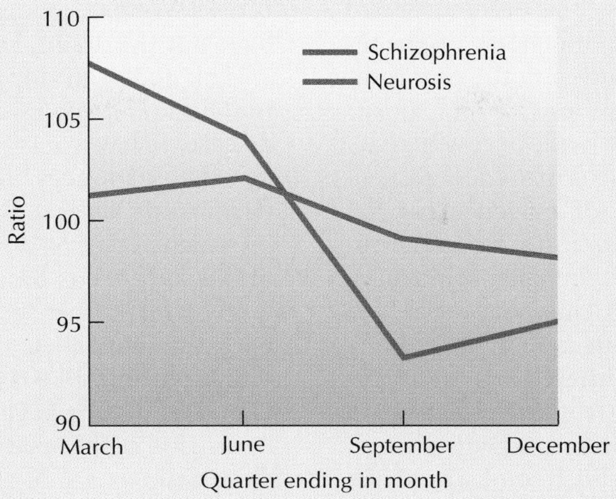

FIGURE 14.2 Schizophrenia and winter births: ratio of observed to expected numbers of births by quarter of the year for patients with a diagnosis of schizophrenia and neurosis (characterized by negative emotions) and born between the years 1921 and 1960. A ratio of 100 means that the expected number of births occurred during that quarter. (Adapted from Hare, Belusu, & Adelstein, 1979.)

Is schizophrenia caused, in part, by infection? Certainly not in the way that the common cold is, or the virus would have been discovered long ago. Yet certain research findings raise the possibility that to some degree, in some people, schizophrenia is due to viral infection.

First put forth by Torrey and Peterson in 1976, the *viral hypothesis* states that, if infection is involved in schizophrenia, it cannot be the sole cause. It must interact with other causes, probably genetic abnormalities. Furthermore, such a virus could not be fast-acting, like the viruses that cause measles and chicken pox. It would have to be one of the "slow" viruses, which can remain latent within the body for years before any symptoms appear (Kirch, 1993). Slow viruses are known to be involved in other mental disorders, such as Jakob-Creutzfeldt disease, which involves progressive mental deterioration.

What is the evidence for the viral hypothesis? One well-established finding (Torrey, Miller, Rawlings, et al., 1997; Mortensen, Pedersen, Westergaard, et al., 1999) is that people with schizophrenia are significantly more likely than other people—including people who exhibit a level of neuroticism (negative emotions; see Chapter 11)—to have been born in the winter (see Figure 14.2). Many viral infections show a peak incidence in the spring and winter months, so it is possible that the higher rate of schizophrenia in people who were winter babies is due to the fact that they were more likely to have been exposed to a virus in the late prenatal period (winter) or shortly after birth (spring).

Further support for the viral hypothesis comes from research on the relationship between schizophrenia and epidemics. One large-scale study followed up people who were exposed prenatally to the influenza epidemic that swept Helsinki, Finland, in 1957. As it turned out, those who were exposed in the second trimester were significantly more likely to have developed schizophrenia than either those who were not exposed or those who were exposed in the first or third trimester (Mednick, Machon, Huttunen, et al., 1988). Another study found that individuals conceived during the peak of the Nazi-imposed Dutch famine of 1945 were more likely to show brain anomalies and to develop schizophrenia as adults (Hoek, Brown, & Susser, 1998). In another study, mothers of schizophrenic patients were asked about infections during their schizophrenic child's gestation. The women reported more infections (especially influenza) during the second trimester than during the first and third combined (Wright, Takei, Rifkin, et al., 1995). Also, CT scans of the brains of schizophrenic patients have found an association between enlarged ventricles and exposure to influenza during the second trimester (Takei, Lewis, Jones, et al., 1996). Note how these findings link up with the suggestions of second-trimester brain damage that have been produced by other studies. Further research on the relationship between schizophrenia and epidemics has shown conflicting results, however. Many studies have found a correlation (Venables, 1996), but some have not (Battle, Martin, Dorfman, et al., 1999).

All the evidence for the viral hypothesis is circumstantial. If a virus is involved in schizophrenia, it has yet to be identified. Nevertheless, it is possible that for some people this is the stressor, or one of the stressors, that interacts with genetic vulnerability to produce schizophrenic symptoms.

---

things, a function that is radically disrupted in schizophrenia. And postmortem examination of the brains of schizophrenic patients has shown evidence of some disruption in the neural migration that forms the association areas—a problem that could have occurred only in the second trimester (Akbarian, Kim, Potkin, et al., 1996; McClure & Weinberger, 2001).

Finally, twin studies have also found signs of problems during the second trimester. MZ twins have nearly identical fingerprints, with only minor variations. In MZ twins who are discordant for schizophrenia, however, fingerprint differences are greater than in normal MZ twins (Davis & Bracha, 1996). These twins, then, are abnormally different from each other in two ways: fingerprints and mental functioning. Fingerprints are established during the second trimester, so, if both abnormalities were caused by the same prenatal disturbance, which is logical, that disturbance must have happened during the second trimester. (One theory about the nature of the prenatal disturbance is examined in the box above.)

Biochemical Research: The Dopamine Hypothesis

A biochemical abnormality has long been suspected of causing schizophrenia. The biochemical theory that has attracted the most attention in the past three decades is the **dopamine hypothesis,** which posits that schizophrenia is associated with excess activity in the parts of the brain that use dopamine as a neurotransmitter. The major line of evidence for the dopamine hypothesis comes from research on the antipsychotic drugs, particularly the phenothiazines, which we will discuss later in this chapter. These drugs have been dramatically effective in controlling schizophrenic symptoms. An interesting finding is that the antipsychotic drugs are most effective on symptoms such as thought disorder and withdrawal, are moderately effective on hallucinations, and are ineffective on neurotic symptoms such as anxiety (Tamminga, 1997). In other words, these drugs seem to act on fundamental schizophrenic symptoms; therefore, many researchers feel that their chemical activity should provide a clue to the chemical activities underlying schizophrenia. The drugs work by blocking the brain's receptor sites for dopamine—that is, they reduce the activity of the parts of the brain that use dopamine to transmit neural impulses (Schneider & Deldin, 2001), hence the dopamine hypothesis: Schizophrenia is connected to excess dopamine activity.

Another piece of evidence involves the stimulants amphetamine and methylphenidate, both of which are known to increase dopamine activity in the brain. As we saw in Chapter 12, amphetamines can produce psychotic states similar to schizophrenia, and so can methylphenidate. Furthermore, when these drugs are given to schizophrenic patients, the patients' symptomatology becomes more dramatic (Faustman, 1995), and PET scans show that too much dopamine is released from their basal ganglia (Carlsson, 2001). Here, then, we see another connection between schizophrenia and increased levels of dopamine activity. A third piece of evidence comes from PET studies that show increased dopamine function in response to administration of dopa, a precursor of dopamine, in schizophrenic patients compared to controls (Carlsson, 2001). A final link has been provided by postmortem examinations. A number of postmortem studies have found increased brain dopamine and an increased number of dopamine receptors in the limbic structures of deceased schizophrenic patients (Seeman & Kapur, 2001). Many of these patients, however, had been taking antipsychotic medication, and that may have caused the increase. PET scans of the brains of living schizophrenia patients who have not been taking antipsychotic drugs have produced inconsistent results. Some have shown an increased number of dopamine receptors in the limbic structures (Wong, Gjedde, Wagner, et al., 1986); some have not (Karlsson, Farde, Halldin, et al., 2002).

This focus on dopamine has suggested a conceptual link between schizophrenia and Parkinson's disease (Chapter 15), a neuropsychological disorder that produces uncontrollable bodily tremors. Parkinson's disease is known to be caused, in part, by a deficiency of dopamine in certain parts of the brain, and drugs that increase dopamine levels are quite effective in reducing tremors in Parkinson's patients. However, these drugs can also produce schizophrenia-like symptoms (Tamminga, 1997). Conversely, antipsychotic drugs often produce a Parkinson's-like movement disorder called **tardive dyskinesia** as a side effect.

Thus, many lines of evidence converge to support the dopamine hypothesis. It is mostly indirect evidence, however. Other than the postmortem data and the PET scan findings, both of which have been challenged, there is no direct evidence that people with schizophrenia do, in fact, experience dopamine abnormalities (Lieberman & Koreen, 1993). And, if they do, there are probably different patterns of abnormality (Davis, Kahn, Ko, et al., 1991). It is only patients with Type I schizophrenia, those with positive symptoms, who seem to have excess dopamine activity in the limbic system (Goldsmith, Shapiro, & Joyce, 1997; Carlsson, 2001). According to some studies, Type II schizophrenia is related to dopamine *underactivity* in the frontal lobe (Meador-Woodruff, Haroutunian, Powchik, et al., 1997). Moreover, the dopamine underactivity in the frontal lobe may lead to the dopamine overactivity in the limbic structures (Moore, West, & Grace, 1999).

At the same time, there is some evidence *against* the dopamine hypothesis (Davis, Kahn, Ko, et al., 1991). For example, when schizophrenia patients are first given antipsychotic drugs, their response (if they respond) is gradual, building over a period of about six weeks, yet it takes only a few hours for the drugs to block dopamine receptors in the brain. If schizophrenia were merely the result of activity in these neural tracts, the patients' improvement would also come within a few hours (Sanislow & Carson, 2001). Furthermore, clozapine, a medication that works on many patients who do not respond to other antipsychotic drugs, has only a weak effect on dopamine receptors. Its primary action is to block serotonin receptors (Nordström, Farde, Nyberg, et al., 1995). Recent evidence from postmortem studies and PET scans of living schizophrenic patients not on antipsychotic drugs show an increased number of serotonin receptors in the medial temporal cortex (Tauscher, Kapur, Verhoeff , et al., 2002). Many experts now believe that it is not dopamine alone but an interaction between dopamine and serotonin activity that underlies schizophrenic symptoms (Kapur & Remington, 1996). Meanwhile, new studies suggest that yet another neurotransmitter system, the glutamate system, is also involved (Volk, Austin, Pierri, et al., 2000; Umbricht, Schmid, Koller, et al., 2000). It seems likely that the biological explanation of schizophrenia, if it is ever arrived at, will be a highly complex one, involving a combination of biochemical imbalances—and different combinations both for different types of schizophrenia and for different phases of any single case of schizophrenia.

Chemotherapy As their name indicates, the **antipsychotic drugs** (also called *neuroleptics*) are used to relieve symptoms of psychosis: confusion, withdrawal, hallucinations, delusions, and so on. The most widely used group of antipsychotic drugs has been the **phenothiazines,** including Stelazine, Prolixin, Mellaril, and, above all, Thorazine (chlorpromazine). In general, antipsychotic drugs are quite effective at reducing schizophrenic symptoms (Lehman & Steinwachs, 1998). As a result, they have radically altered the conditions under which individuals with schizophrenia live. Patients who would have been in straitjackets 30 years ago are now free to roam hospital grounds. And many patients are sufficiently calm and functional to be released altogether, though they must go on taking the medication.

At the same time, these drugs have had an enormous impact on schizophrenia research. It was the effort to find out how the phenothiazines worked that led biochemical researchers to the dopamine hypothesis. Today, research on new, nonphenothiazine antipsychotics is leading to refinements of that hypothesis. These newer drugs often work better than phenothiazines for Type II, negative-symptom patients, the group most likely to show the brain abnormalities previously discussed. In other words, the dopamine-blocking phenothiazines are good at correcting positive symptoms, such as hallucinations and delusions, but are less good at relieving negative symptoms. This has led to a new hypothesis (Lingjaerde, 1994)—actually, it is a revival of an old hypothesis, put forth by Eugen Bleuler—that positive symptoms are secondary and the negative symptoms primary, that schizophrenic reality-distortions (e.g., hallucinations) are a consequence of information-processing problems, presumably originating in abnormal brain development.

While antipsychotic drugs have revolutionized the theory and treatment of schizophrenia, they are not without problems. First, a substantial proportion of the population with schizophrenia, 20 to 40 percent, get little or no relief from them (Tamminga, 1997). Second, long-term use of phenothiazines can have serious side effects. In producing calm, these drugs can also produce apathy, reducing the patient to a "zombie"-like state. They can also cause constipation, blurred vision, dry mouth, muscle rigidity, and tremors. But the gravest side effect is tardive dyskinesia, a muscle disorder causing uncontrollable grimacing and lip-smacking. The prevalence of tardive dyskinesia in schizophrenic patients maintained on antipsychotic drugs is estimated at 20 to 30 percent (Gelenberg, 1991). Unlike other side effects, tardive dyskinesia cannot be relieved by other drugs, and it does not disappear when the antipsychotic medication is discontinued. Such problems often discourage patients from taking their antipsychotic medication, in which case they may soon be back in the hospital (Frances, Docherty, & Kahn, 1996).

These complications have sent researchers back to the laboratory to develop other antipsychotic medications. One recently marketed drug is Clozaril (clozapine), which seems to help patients unresponsive to phenothiazines, while posing a far lower risk of tardive dyskinesia. Unfortunately, Clozaril poses a slight risk of something else—agranulocytosis, a potentially fatal blood disease—which means that patients taking the drug have to have their blood monitored weekly (Lehman & Steinwachs, 1998). Another new drug, Risperdal (risperidone), is biochemically similar to Clozaril; therefore, like Clozaril, it carries only a slight risk for tardive dyskinesia, but it poses no risk of blood disease. On the other hand, both Clozaril and Risperdal can adversely affect glucose regulation (Newcomer, Haupt, Fucetola, et al., 2002), and the antipsychotic drugs may increase the risk of sudden cardiac death (Ray, Meredith, Thapa, et al., 2001). Compared with the phenothiazines, both Clozaril and Risperdal are apparently as effective in reducing positive symptoms, but their great virtue is that they seem to be more effective in alleviating cognitive impairments (Bilder, Goldman, Valavka, et al., 2002) and negative symptoms, such as apathy, anhedonia, and blunted affect, although not all studies find effectiveness with negative symptoms (Kane, Marder, Schooler, et al., 2001). Many people believe that these newer drugs and their offshoots will eventually replace the phenothiazines as first-line medications for schizophrenia (Green, Marshall, Wirshing, et al., 1997).

Still, there is a limit to what any medication can accomplish when there are defects in brain development. Patients who are released from the hospital under the calming influence of antipsychotic drugs usually make only a marginal adjustment to life on the outside. Once outside, they often stop taking the

Schizophrenic illness usually emerges in late adolescence or early adulthood, disrupting the life of the afflicted person, and having an impact on education, choice of occupation, and development of social skills (Wahlberg & Wynne, 2001). The costs of treatment and lost productivity place a huge burden on family caregivers and the community at large. Consequently, the prevention of schizophrenia is an important public health goal.

Preventing schizophrenia requires being able to predict the illness, so that clinicians can identify individuals at risk and in need of early treatment. With this in mind, research has gradually focused on the schizophrenic prodrome, the stage of the illness that begins with the first changes in behavior and lasts until the onset of psychosis.

Increased interest in the prodrome has been driven by three factors (Cornblatt, 2001). First, long-term studies of individuals considered high risk for developing schizophrenia—children and other immediate relatives of people with schizophrenia—seem to reveal abnormalities long before the emergence of psychosis. These studies suggest that schizophrenia is a developmental disorder of the brain and that it may be possible to identify risk factors and predictors of the illness early. Second, clinical results seem to show that the earlier schizophrenia is treated pharmacologically, the more effective the medication appears to be—thus, treating the disease before onset might be even more effective. These two developments are converging with a third—the availability of new antipsychotic medications with less severe side effects than those used traditionally—to direct research to the prodrome as an opportunity for preventative intervention (Cornblatt, 2001).

Barbara Cornblatt and her colleagues (in press) describe a program on the cutting edge of this prodrome research, the Hillside Recognition and Prevention Program (RAPP) based in Long Island, New York. RAPP, a clinical treatment program for prodromal adolescents ages 14 to 22, is currently conducting two independent studies: a genetic project focusing on at-risk siblings and a clinical study trying to assess adolescents who display what are thought to be prodromal symptoms of schizophrenia. A major goal of these studies is to determine how predictive the prodromal symptoms really are.

Numerous studies have established that genetic relatedness is a risk factor for schizophrenia. In the modern neurodevelopmental model of schizophrenia, a genetic component is thought to initiate structural, functional, or biochemical abnormalities in the brain. These abnormalities, in turn, cause predictors or "biomarkers" to appear in behavioral testing or screening of individuals. For instance, deficits in certain cognitive functions, such as attention deficit measured at age 12, seem to be biomarkers for schizophrenia.

However, genetic risk is merely a population statistic and by itself does not predict that a person will eventually develop schizophrenia; only about 10 percent of persons considered to be at high risk genetically actually develop the disease. Genetic risk combined with positive biomarkers is a somewhat better indicator, resulting in about 80 percent accuracy; but medicating all of these people, including the 20 percent who will never actually develop the disorder, in a preventative program is not feasible or ethical, even with the improved antipsychotic drugs available today. Furthermore, most people who develop schizophrenia are not recognized as having any particular risk factors in advance. Therefore, the primary prevention of schizophrenia still requires an accurate method for detecting the disease before it happens.

In an effort to improve the methods and accuracy of detection before onset of psychosis, RAPP has focused on the

drugs, in which case they may have to be readmitted. Thus, although antipsychotic drugs have definitely reduced the number of chronically hospitalized patients, it has been argued that they have merely replaced long-term hospitalization with "revolving door" admission. This, however, is not the fault of the medication—no one ever claimed that the antipsychotic drugs *cured* schizophrenia—but, rather, society's failure to provide community services for released patients. Research underway, however, suggests that early use of medication may prevent relapse or even the initial onset of schizophrenia in individuals at risk (see the box above).

The Cognitive Perspective

While neuroscience researchers concern themselves with both the diathesis and the stressor components of the diathesis-stress model, most cognitive theorists focus exclusively on the diathesis. As we know, a prominent symptom of schizophrenia is attention dysfunction. Remember the words of the patient quoted earlier: "My thoughts get all jumbled up. I start thinking or talking about something but I never get there." Since the time of Kraepelin and Eugen Bleuler, many researchers have suspected that this attention problem is the primary pathology in schizophrenia, with the other symptoms developing as results of the attention problem. And that, in brief, is the position of today's cognitive researchers. Cognitive theorists do not claim that attention deficits are the root cause of schizophrenia. In their view, the cause is biological. What they do claim, however, is that the psychological function most impaired by the biological abnormality is attention and that the attention problem, in turn, creates a predisposition to schizophrenia by making it hard for the person to cope with environmental stress time period just before onset, the schizophrenic prodrome. In contrast to genetic risk studies, prodromal research focuses on clinical indicators characteristic of the prepsychotic time period. Although the prodrome typically lasts about a year, it can last from weeks to years. In the past, prodromal research has relied upon patients' and family members' recollections of signs and symptoms after the fact. However, symptoms that seem significant in retrospect may not actually prove to be predictive. The RAPP research hopes to establish prospective, rather than retrospective, criteria that health practitioners could use to detect warning signs before psychosis.

Preliminarily, RAPP assessments use two lists of negative and positive symptoms to screen adolescent patients (Cornblatt, 2001). The first list consists of symptoms considered nonspecific to schizophrenia, including depressed mood, social withdrawal, deterioration in functioning, impairment in personal hygiene, reduced concentration, reduced motivation, sleep disturbance, anxiety, and suspiciousness. The second list includes more attenuated symptoms associated with schizophrenia: peculiar behavior; inappropriate affect; vague, over-elaborate speech; odd beliefs or magical thinking; and unusual perceptual experiences.

The RAPP studies discovered a common pattern of early negative symptoms: sharp increase in social withdrawal, emerging school difficulties, odd behaviors, and suspiciousness. These findings seem to confirm the hypothesis that the illness begins with a premorbid period during which only subtle deficits may be noticeable, followed by an early prodromal phase of relatively mild negative symptoms, followed by later prodromal phases when positive symptoms emerge. Left untreated, these symptoms will intensify, leading to psychosis and eventually schizophrenia.

Other researchers have had interesting results with prevention programs based on identifying prodromes. Herz, Lamberti, Mintz, et al. (2000) found that a program for preventing relapse in people with schizophrenia was effective in detecting prodromal symptoms of relapse early. Crisis therapy and increasing the use of antipsychotic medication when prodromal symptoms were detected were both effective in reducing relapse and rehospitalization rates. These researchers concluded that the greatly reduced rate of relapse outweighed the risk of a small number of false-positive reports.

In another study, Falloon, Kydd, Coverdale, et al. (1996) evaluated a primary prevention program aimed at the prepsychotic phase. The program was built around the collaboration of local, general health practitioners who were trained to screen and detect prodromal signs. When further evaluation indicated it was necessary, a mental health professional set up a home-based program of low-dose medication and follow-up. Over a 4-year period, the annual incidence of schizophrenia in the program area decreased tenfold, strongly suggesting that an early intervention program simply as part of general health care might be effective. The study noted a high rate of false-positive referrals to the mental health team, however.

The best prevention program would be one implemented before the onset of psychosis. However, the majority of persons who are considered to be at risk do not in the end develop fullblown schizophrenia. False positive identifications of schizophrenia can seriously stigmatize people and have long-term effects on their lives. Because statistics alone cannot predict who will actually develop schizophrenia, active research on the conditions for identifying persons who could benefit from preventive interventions will continue. Procedures for defining the prodrome are very new, and in many ways, the prodrome remains as mysterious as schizophrenia itself.

(Rosenfarb, Nuechterlein, Goldstein, et al., 2000). Imagine, for example, a family with a highly charged, negative emotional atmosphere or a family in which the parents tend to give confusing messages. (As we will see, these are two circumstances that, according to interpersonal theorists, may contribute to schizophrenia.) A child with normal cognitive skills would probably be able to navigate the emotional perils of such a family, but a child with difficulty in focusing attention or working memory (and, hence, difficulty in solving problems) might well respond by becoming overaroused and disorganized—a condition that over time could develop into psychosis (Rosenfarb, Nuechterlein, Goldstein, et al., 2000).

The goal of cognitive research in schizophrenia has been to determine the exact nature of the attention problems of schizophrenic patients and to relate these problems to other features of the disorder. Researchers have identified two distinct patterns, overattention and underattention.

Overattention We have already described the breakdown in selective attention that is seen in many people with schizophrenia. These patients "overattend" to the stimuli in their environment; they cannot focus on one thing and screen out the others. This phenomenon appears to be related to Type I, positive-symptom schizophrenia (e.g., Cornblatt, Lenzenweger, Dworkin, et al., 1985); and, according to current cognitive theory, the positive symptoms of Type I patients—hallucinations, delusions, incoherent speech—are the product of their overattention (Perry & Braff, 1994; Perry, Geyer, & Braff, 1999). The reason these patients are confused and disorganized is that their information-processing functions are overburdened, and their nervous system overaroused, by stimuli that they cannot screen out (Dawson, Nuechterlein, & Schell, 1992). The reason

To test the poor-selective-attention hypothesis, researchers had a series of stories, several of them including distractions, read to participants with schizophrenia and mania, as well as to normal subjects, fitted with headphones. As the hypothesis predicted, the subjects with schizophrenia did worse than the manic and normal subjects in recounting the stories only when the distraction was introduced.

their speech is full of irrelevant associations is that, unlike normal people, they cannot filter out such associations (Docherty & Gottesman, 2000). Auditory hallucinations, according to this theory, are explainable as traces of real sounds that the patient hears but cannot eliminate from consciousness, and delusions arise as the patient's effort to account for these and other bizarre perceptions (Maher, 2001).

Many studies have documented the poor selective attention and consequent distractibility of schizophrenic patients (Braff, 1993). In one experiment (Wielgus & Harvey, 1998), subjects with schizophrenia and mania, along with normal subjects, were fitted with headphones. Eight successive stories were read to them in one ear by a male voice. During four of the stories, however, a distraction was introduced: At the same time that the subjects heard the story from the male voice in one ear, they were told a different story by a female voice in the other ear. The subjects' task was to repeat back word-for-word the story that was being told to them by the male voice. As the poor-selective-attention hypothesis predicts, the schizophrenic patients did worse than the other subjects only when the distraction was introduced. The problem uncovered by this experiment is a good example of a differential deficit.

The inability of people with schizophrenia to filter out irrelevant stimuli has been documented in neurophysiological tests as well. In one experiment, schizophrenic patients and normal controls had their brain waves (event-related potentials, or ERPs) measured in response to presentations of closely paired auditory stimuli. When normal people hear pairs of sounds close together, they inhibit their ERPs to the second sound, indicative of rapid habituation to the sound. However, many schizophrenic patients cannot do this and show ERPs to the second sound as large as to the first (Clementz, Geyer, & Braff, 1998). Moreover, those schizophrenic patients who are unable to inhibit their ERPs to the second of a pair of stimuli also show poor selective attention and distractibility (Erwin, Turetsky, Moberg, et al., 1998).

Finally, it has also been shown that, when an experiment is set up in such a way that picking up interfering stimuli *improves* performance, people with schizophrenia outperform nonschizophrenics (Peters, Pickering, Kent, et al., 2000; Barch & Carter, 1998). Here again is a differential deficit, and a remarkable one. When schizophrenic patients do better on a task than normal people, we are presumably tapping into something fundamental to schizophrenia (Braff, 1993).

As noted, this particular attention problem, the inability to screen out distractions, has been found to correlate with Type I, positive-symptom schizophrenia but not with Type II, negative-symptom schizophrenia (Cornblatt, Lenzenweger, Dworkin, et al., 1985; Wielgus & Harvey, 1988). The connection with Type I schizophrenia has also been demonstrated on a biochemical level. Type I, as we just saw, seems to be related to overactivity of dopamine transmission in subcortical areas of the brain. Following this lead, Swerdlow and his colleagues injected rats with dopamine in subcortical areas of the brain, thus creating the kind of dopamine overactivity that is presumed to underlie Type I schizophrenia. The rats responded by showing the kind of selective-attention problems seen in Type I schizophrenia. Furthermore, the attention problems of both Type I schizophrenia and dopamine-injected rats can be decreased by antipsychotic drugs that decrease dopamine activity (Swerdlow, Braff, Taaid, et al., 1994; Daskalakis, Christensen, Chen, et al., 2002).

Underattention Whereas people with Type I schizophrenia seem to be overattentive, those with Type II schizophrenia appear to be underattentive to external stimuli. This fact has been repeatedly demonstrated in studies of the *orienting response,* a pattern of physiological changes (involving galvanic skin response, blood pressure, pupil dilation, heart rate, and brain waves) that is thought to indicate that the brain has allocated its central attentional resources to the perception and processing of a stimulus. In a review of such experiments, Bernstein (1987) found that 40 to 50 percent of people with schizophrenia, when presented with a stimulus of moderate intensity, failed to show a normal orienting response and more recent studies have confirmed this finding (Olbrich, Kirsch, Pfeiffer, et al., 2001), although the orienting response becomes more normal when the schizophrenia symptoms remit. Schizophrenic patients also tend to show abnormally low-magnitude brain waves in response to unexpected sounds—another indication of underattention (Catts, Shelley, Ward, et al., 1995).

Another kind of study that has been used to measure underattention employs what is called the *backward-masking paradigm*. The subject is shown a visual stimulus, the so-called target stimulus, quickly or indistinctly. Then, after an interval, this is followed by a "masking stimulus," such as a picture of a grid. When the masking stimulus comes right after the target stimulus, it "masks" the target stimulus: The subject does not register recognition of the target stimulus. But, as the time interval between the presentation of the target stimulus and the masking stimulus is increased, the subject becomes more and more likely to remember the target stimulus. For many schizophrenic patients, however, the interval between the two has to be stretched far longer than for normal subjects before the target stimulus registers on the consciousness (Saccuzzo, Cadenhead, & Braff, 1996). In other words, these schizophrenic patients seem to have deficient perception of and responsiveness to environmental stimuli. Recent research indicates that people with schizophrenia also have other "working memory" deficits, making it hard for them to hold information in their minds long enough to process it (Granholm, Morris, Sarkin, et al., 1997). According to cognitive theorists, such underattention leads to negative symptoms such as flat affect and social withdrawal (Braff, 1993). This conclusion is quite logical. If a person's perception of the environment is dulled, he or she may become apathetic and withdrawn.

In keeping with this hypothesis, both deficient orienting responses and poor performance on backward-masking tasks have been found to correlate with negative symptoms such as blunted affect, withdrawal, and motor retardation, as well as with other factors in the Type II profile, such as poor premorbid adjustment and poor prognosis (Slaghuis & Curran, 1999). They do not correlate with positive symptoms, however. Indeed, the orienting responses of people with positive-symptom schizophrenia are more likely to be abnormally high than abnormally low. Of course, these findings give further support to the Type I versus Type II hypothesis. There do, in fact, seem to be at least two distinct schizophrenic patterns, one marked by overattention and one by underattention.

Vulnerability If cognitive theorists are correct in claiming that biologically based attention problems create a vulnerability to schizophrenia, then these abnormalities should be present not just in active-phase schizophrenia but also in remitted (recovered) schizophrenia, in biological relatives, and in people designated as being at risk for schizophrenia (Maher & Deldin, 2001). They are. As we saw in our discussion of Mednick's high-risk children, one of the five characteristics separating those who developed schizophrenia from those who didn't was a history of selective-attention problems. Likewise, remitted schizophrenic patients, relatives of schizophrenic patients, discordant MZ twins of schizophrenic patients, children of schizophrenic parents, and people thought to be at risk for schizophrenia by virtue of showing schizophrenic-like personality features all show significantly high rates of selective-attention dysfunction (Maher & Deldin, 2001; Finkelstein, Cannon, Gut, et al., 1997; Pardo, Kresevich, Vogler, et al., 2000). Many remitted schizophrenic patients and high-risk people also show lowered orienting responses (Hazlett, Dawson, Filion, et al., 1997). For more solid confirmation of the attention-dysfunction hypothesis, we must await the outcomes of further longitudinal studies of high-risk children. But it seems clear already that, if "preschizophrenic" people are to be treated, attention deficits are a logical target.

Cognitive Therapy Cognitive therapy for schizophrenic patients is still in early stages. There are two basic approaches, one addressing the processes of schizophrenic thought, the other addressing its content.

The "process" approach, called *cognitive rehabilitation,* uses techniques borrowed from rehabilitation therapy for brain-injured people, such as stroke patients. The idea is to give patients tasks calling upon defective cognitive skills—memory, attention, social perception—and to build up those skills by means of instruction, training, prompting, and even monetary rewards. In one program, for example, patients were given tests that involved sorting objects into categories, to improve attention and conceptual understanding. To build social perception, they were shown slides of people engaged in various activities and were asked to make judgments about what the people were doing and what the emotional tone of the slides were: friendly, unfriendly, and so on. Studies have shown that this approach, combined with other techniques, does improve cognitive functioning and reduce symptoms (Spaulding, Reed, Sullivan, et al., 1999; Wyes & van der Gaag, 2001).

The other cognitive approach is aimed directly at schizophrenic hallucinations and delusions. Using basically the same techniques as cognitive therapy for nonpsychotic patients, the therapist leads the patient into a questioning of the thought. (Are those voices really coming from the outside? Is there actually a conspiracy against the patient?) For example, one patient who was hearing voices saying that she was going to be killed was asked to wear heavy, industrial earmuffs; if she could still hear the voices, then she had to consider the possibility that the voices were coming from her own mind (Chadwick, Lowe, Horne, et al., 1994). Then the therapist suggests alternative explanations. Typically, such therapy also includes teaching the patient coping devices for dealing with the unwelcome thoughts—for example, listening to music to drown out "voices" (Tarrier, Harwood, Yusopoff, et al., 1990). Recent evidence from randomized controlled clinical trials suggests that such cognitive therapy is effective in reducing positive and negative symptoms of schizophrenia and may reduce risk of relapse as well (Garety, Fowler, & Kuipers, 2000; Rector & Beck, 2001).

These therapies have come up against a number of problems. Whatever gains are made may not generalize to other areas of cognition, let alone to mood or behavior. Furthermore, on follow-up, the gains may be lost (Penn & Mueser, 1996). Still, both the "process" and "content" approaches remain promising and need to be further evaluated.

The Interpersonal Perspective

The environmental stresses contributing to the development of schizophrenia may be biological—for example, prenatal brain injury—but it is likely that social factors are involved as well. Such environmental stressors have been the focus of the theories of schizophrenia coming from the other psychological perspectives.

The major concern has been trouble in the family. If, in Mednick's high-risk studies, one factor separating the high-risk children who developed schizophrenia from those who didn't was attention problems, another was an unstable family life. In that group, family disruption was probably due in part to genetic factors. The mothers of the high-risk children all had a history of schizophrenia, which does not bode well for parent-child interactions. But, according to family and interpersonal theorists, psychological tensions in the home may also be a stress factor in schizophrenia, and not just for the children of mothers with schizophrenia.

Expressed Emotion A hostile atmosphere seems to permeate the homes of many children who develop schizophrenia. Earlier researchers often focused on the personality traits of the family members, notably the mother. Today, researchers are more interested in what the people in the family say to one another—something that is more easily measured. In a number of studies (e.g., Weardon, Tarrier, Barrowclough, et al., 2000), families of hospitalized schizophrenic patients have been rated on **expressed emotion (EE)** toward the patient. In these studies, the EE rating was based on two factors—the level of criticism and the level of emotional overinvolvement—in the remarks made by a key relative (e.g., the father, the mother, the spouse) in an interview regarding the patient shortly after his or her admission. For example, the sister of a 36-year-old schizophrenic patient remarked:

> To me [schizophrenia] is a totally selfish illness. . . . Rachel could, if she really wanted to, pull herself out of it. But it's as though she wants to . . . go into hospital. . . . I feel that she should care enough about other people to keep herself well . . . because it worries my father, it worries my family, it worries my brother, and it worries me. To me that is enough to try to keep yourself well. (Brewin, MacCarthy, Duda, et al., 1991, p. 552)

Nine to 12 months after a group of high-EE patients were discharged, they were followed up to see who had relapsed. Interestingly, of all the factors on which the patients varied, the family EE was the best single predictor of relapse: Patients who lived with high-EE relatives were 3 to 4 times more likely to have been rehospitalized than patients who lived with low-EE relatives (Linszen, Dingemans, Nugter, et al., 1997; Miklowitz, Goldstein, Doane, et al., 1989). Thus, EE seems to influence relapse risk. In turn, EE is influenced by family members' attributions regarding the patient's condition. Logically, high-EE relatives tend to be those, like the woman quoted earlier, who hold the patient responsible for his or her condition (Lopez, Nelson, Snyder, et al., 1999; Weisman, Nuechterlein, Goldstein, et al., 2000).

Some studies (e.g., Parker, Johnston, & Hayward, 1988) have failed to confirm the link between schizophrenia and high family EE. Still, many EE studies do suggest that a negative and emotionally charged family atmosphere may be related to both the onset and the course of schizophrenia. Indeed, high family EE is associated with competition for verbal control during conversations between family members and the schizophrenic patient (Wuerker, Haas, & Bellack, 2001). Other researchers feel that EE should be considered not as a contributor to the development of schizophrenia but specifically as a contributor to relapse—as a measure of the environmental stress that the remitted schizophrenic patient is exposed to when he or she returns home. In support of this idea, it has been

The film A Beautiful Mind *is based on the life of the genius mathematician John Nash (left), who suffers from schizophrenia. At right is a scene from the movie, starring Russell Crowe as Nash.*

shown that people with schizophrenia show higher autonomic arousal in the presence of high-EE relatives than in the presence of low-EE relatives (Tarrier, Barrowclough, Porceddu, et al., 1988). In addition, they recall fewer nonstressful and more stressful memories about high-EE than low-EE parents (Cutting & Docherty, 2000). Finally, schizophrenia patients with poor performance on a test of sustained attention show more psychotic thinking during family interactions when exposed to high criticism from relatives than when exposed to low criticism from relatives (Rosenfarb, Nuechterlein, Goldstein, et al., 2000).

Communication Deviance Some experts feel that the heart of the interpersonal disturbance lies in the matter of communications between parent and child. In a classic theory put forth in the 1950s, Bateson and his co-workers proposed that schizophrenia might be the product of *double-bind communication,* a kind of no-win interchange, illustrated in the following account:

> A young man who had fairly well recovered from an acute schizophrenic episode was visited in the hospital by his mother. He was glad to see her and impulsively put his arm around her shoulders, whereupon she stiffened. He withdrew his arm and she asked, "Don't you love me any more?" He then blushed, and she said, "Dear, you must not be so easily embarrassed and afraid of your feelings." The patient was able to stay with her only a few minutes more and following her departure he assaulted an aide. (Bateson, Jackson, Haley, et al., 1956, p. 251)

The double-bind situation, then, is one in which the mother gives the child mutually contradictory messages (e.g., both rejection and affection in the case just cited), meanwhile implicitly forbidding the child to point out the contradiction. Whichever message the child acts upon, he or she is the loser. Bateson and his colleagues proposed that the type of mother most likely to engage in double-bind communication was one who found closeness with her child intolerable but who also found it intolerable to admit this to herself. Thus, she would push the child away, but, when the child withdrew, she would accuse the child of not loving her.

This theory, while less discussed today, helped to generate a line of more empirical research, and the research has indeed shown that families of schizophrenic patients tend to have unusual communication patterns (Wahlberg, Wynne, Keskitalo, et al., 2001). Their verbal exchanges are variously described as blurred, muddled, vague, fragmented, and incomplete (Velligan, Mahurin, Eckert, et al., 1997). Here, for example, is a recorded exchange between a schizophrenic woman and her parents:

> Daughter: (complainingly) Nobody will listen to me. Everybody is trying to still me.
>
> Mother: Nobody wants to kill you.
>
> Father: If you're going to associate with intellectual people, you're going to have to remember that still is a noun and not a verb.
>
> *(Wynne & Singer, 1963, p. 195)*

According to the diathesis-stress model, a healthy family environment may prevent the onset of schizophrenia in a person with a genetic predisposition to the disorder.

Many current studies describe this phenomenon in terms of **communication deviance (CD)**, measured according to the number of deviant or idiosyncratic responses on a test such as the TAT or Rorschach. In one study, CD in parents proved a good predictor of whether their adolescent children would be diagnosed with schizophrenia 15 years later (Goldstein, 1987). The findings (Miklowitz, Strachan, Goldstein, et al., 1986; Wahlberg, Wynne, Keskitalo, et al., 2001) that communication deviance seems to correlate with expressed emotion—relatives that are high-EE are also high-CD—and is stable in adulthood have given added impetus to this line of research.

These findings can be interpreted in a number of different ways, however. Given that schizophrenia in the child correlates with deviant communications in the family, there may still be no causal relationship between the two factors, for both may be the result of a third variable, such as a shared genetic defect (Miklowitz, Velligan, Goldstein, et al., 1991) or shared attention problems (Velligan, Mahurin, Eckert, et al., 1997). Furthermore, even if there is a causal relationship between the two, we are faced with the chicken-and-egg problem: While disturbed family communications—and a negative emotional climate—may have fostered the child's disorder, it is equally possible that the child's disorder has fostered the high levels of CD and EE (Sanislow & Carson, 2001). That the families of schizophrenic patients tend to express painful emotions is no surprise. Indeed, in the case of EE, most researchers today view the correlation with schizophrenia simply as a broad, interactive process, with the patient's symptoms causing the family to feel and vent negative emotions, which in turn exacerbate the patient's symptoms, thus creating a vicious cycle (Weardon, Tarrier, Barrowclough, et al., 2000).

There is one further problem in evaluating the EE and CD findings. If the family setting is of major importance in the development of schizophrenia, why does one child in the family develop schizophrenia while another turns out normally? It may be that the one who develops schizophrenia is more vulnerable biologically to the emotional stress of a hostile family environment. But we do not know whether this is the case.

Despite these difficulties, most experts have not discarded the idea that the family may figure in the development of schizophrenia—only the claim that the family *alone* can engender the disorder. Again, the emphasis today is on diathesis and stress, and family hostility is still high on the list of stressors that could help to determine whether a schizophrenic diathesis is translated into schizophrenia.

Treatment for Families The findings regarding EE and CD have prompted the development of treatments for the families of schizophrenic patients. In one study, researchers spent several weeks with the families of 18 schizophrenic patients, studying the family members' difficulties in dealing with the patient and with each other. Then the families were taught a step-by-step method of working out problems, from planning a dinner menu to coping with major crises. The families were also briefed on schizophrenia, so that they would be less alarmed and distressed by the patient's symptoms. At a 9-month follow-up, only 1 patient from the 18 experimental-group families had relapsed, compared with 8 patients from 18 families in which the patient had received only individual treatment. These results held through a 2-year follow-up as well, so the gains seem to last (Falloon, Boyd, McGill, et al., 1985). In another study, high-EE families were counseled in how to make their interactions with the patient calmer and less negative. A year later, only 20 percent of the patients from these families had relapsed, compared with 41 percent of the patients from high-EE families that had received no treatment (Hogarty, Anderson, Reiss, et al., 1986). A recent review of 18 controlled trials of family therapy shows that it resulted in greater improvement than standard care on reducing relapse, symptoms, and social and vocational functioning (Huxley, Rendall, & Sederer, 2000). Family therapy was even more effective for patients in underdeveloped countries than those in Western industrialized countries (Lauriello, Bustillo, & Keith, 1999).

Another line of research has addressed the question of whether therapy for the family can reduce the patient's need for medication. In one study, the subjects, all of whom had just been released from the hospital after an acute psychotic episode, were divided into three medication conditions: continued high dose, continued low dose, or dose varying according to symptoms. Then, in each group, the families were given either "applied family management"—the intensive problem-solving approach previously described—or a "family placebo," in which the therapist held monthly meetings with the family but made no attempt to teach them relapse-prevention skills. The result was that the low-dose and adjusted-dose patients showed higher relapse rates regardless of which type of therapy their families received (Schooler, Keith, Severe, et al., 1997). Many studies have shown that family therapy does lower the risk of relapse, but at this point it seems that no one form is more effective than others (Huxley, Rendall, & Sederer, 2000). On the other hand, early reports show that intensive problem-solving therapy applied to groups of families meeting together, as opposed to single families, may be superior to the other approaches (McFarlane, Lukens, Link, et al., 1995).

The Behavioral Perspective

Learned Nonresponsiveness The behaviorists have offered environmental theories of schizophrenia. According to Ullmann and Krasner (1975), for example, people with schizophrenia, because of a disturbed family life or other environmental misfortunes, have not learned to respond to the social stimuli to which most of us respond. As a result, they cease to attend to these stimuli and begin taking their behavioral cues from other, idiosyncratically chosen stimuli. In consequence, they tend to become objects of disciplinary action and social rejection, leading to feelings of alienation and to the belief that others are out to "get" them. Hence, their behavior becomes even more bizarre. And if, as may happen, they are rewarded for bizarre responses—through attention, sympathy, or release from responsibilities—such responses are likely to become habitual.

There is some support for this hypothesis. It has been shown, for example, that, like the learned behaviors of normal people, the "crazy" behaviors of people with schizophrenia are sometimes produced in situations where they will lead to rewards. But this does not prove that those behaviors originated through reinforcement. Today, in view of the neuroscience findings, most behaviorists use learning theory not to explain the development of schizophrenia—they, too, tend to believe that it develops in part from biological causes—but to reduce schizophrenic symptoms.

Relearning Normal Behavior Whatever the cause of schizophrenic behavior, it may be that mental health settings encourage such behavior by reinforcing "craziness" and not reinforcing adaptive responses. If so, then reversing that reinforcement pattern should lead to improvement. Historically, this has been one goal of behavioral treatment of schizophrenia.

Direct Reinforcement Early behavioral treatments were straightforward applications of the principles of operant conditioning: They attempted to change behavior by changing the consequences of behavior. Let us look at a specific case:

> Mr. C.'s most obnoxious behaviors were: urinating and defecating on the floor, shouting, swearing, name-calling, begging cigarettes, demanding other things, striking at other patients. It . . . seemed evident that Mr. C.'s inappropriate conduct usually was followed by some kind of staff attention. Two procedures for eliminating Mr. C.'s disruptive behavior were [implemented]. 1. Social attention should no longer be given following inappropriate behavior. 2. Social attention and cigarettes . . . would be the consequence of socially acceptable behavior. (Sushinsky, 1970, p. 24)

Modest though it was, this treatment program proved effective. In two weeks, Mr. C.'s "obnoxious" behaviors disappeared. Furthermore, he began striking up conversations and participating in rehabilitation therapy.

In exchange for keeping his room neat, grooming, or performing other specified behaviors, the schizophrenia patient (right) is receiving tokens as reinforcers. The patient then trades the tokens for specific priviledges.

Procedures that involve the giving or withholding of the tangible reinforcers are surrounded by a number of ethical and legal questions (Chapter 18). There is no question, however, that such procedures can change behavior. Researchers have succeeded in instituting or increasing speech in mute and near-mute patients through the use of such simple reinforcers as fruit, chocolate, and magazines (Thomson, Fraser, & McDougall, 1974).

The Token Economy Some hospitals have extended operant-conditioning procedures to entire wards, using a system called the token economy. In a **token economy** patients are given tokens, points, or some other kind of generalized conditioned reinforcer in exchange for performing certain target behaviors, such as personal grooming, cleaning their rooms, or doing academic or vocational-training tasks. The patients can then exchange the tokens for any number of backup reinforcers, such as snacks, coffee, new clothes, or special privileges. The procedure is very much like that which operates outside the hospital: We earn money by performing specified tasks and then exchange this money for the privileges and goods that we want. Token economies have proved very useful in helping patients—even the most dysfunctional "chronic" patients—improve their behavior to the point where they can be released from the hospital (Paul & Lentz, 1977).

Social-Skills Training Many operant-conditioning programs have been aimed largely at improving patients' behavior *within* the hospital. Today, with the greater emphasis on release, attention has shifted to helping patients learn skills that will enable them to live on the outside—making friends, holding down a job, and the like. Foremost among such treatments is social-skills training.

As we have seen, most schizophrenic patients are socially inept. They withdraw and speak little, or else they speak a lot, but about bizarre things. **Social-skills training** aims to alleviate this problem by teaching patients conversation skills, eye contact, appropriate physical gestures, smiling, improved speech intonation—in general, characteristics that make a person attractive to others (Mueser, 1998; Smith, Bellack, & Liberman, 1996). Such training is usually done in groups and is highly structured. A crucial component is role-playing, in which patients, under the therapist's supervision, practice their new skills. Typically, the patients are also given homework assignments and complete them with an assigned "buddy."

How effective is social-skills training? One study (Lieberman, Wallace, Blackwell, et al., 1998) compared social-skills training with an alternative treatment, occupational therapy. The patients in the social-skills program worked with a problem-solving model on how to receive, process, and give interpersonal communications. The occupational therapy patients spent as many hours in treatment as the social-skills patients, but their time was devoted to job-training and interviewing skills. Both groups showed significant improvement in schizophrenic symptoms. Not surprisingly, the social-skills group showed better social skills and independent living skills. In addition, the gains were maintained at an 18-month follow-up. Research now suggests that some patients who receive social-skills training do retain the skills and make a better adjustment in the community than those who have not had social-skills training (Huxley, Rendall, & Sederer, 2000).

The Sociocultural Perspective

None of the treatments described thus far actually cures schizophrenia. Medication, family therapy, social-skills training—at best, they prevent relapse and help the patient to make some adjustment within the community. But in most cases schizophrenia is a recurring disorder. Released patients require many kinds of assistance, ideally from many kinds of professionals. Short of a cure for schizophrenia, what is most needed in this field is long-term, multifaceted support programs within the community.

One such program was part of a study that took place in Madison, Wisconsin (Test & Stein, 1978). Patients seeking psychiatric hospitalization were randomly assigned either to brief hospitalization (the median stay was 17 days), with typical aftercare, or to a community treatment service not involving hospitalization. In the latter service, the staff helped the patients find an acceptable community residence if staying at home was not feasible, and they showed them how to find jobs or places in sheltered workshops if they were unemployed. They also created an individually tailored treatment program for each patient, based on an assessment of what coping skills that particular patient was lacking. Treatment took place *in vivo*—that is, in the patients' homes, places of work, and neighborhood haunts. For 14 months, the staff maintained daily contact with the patients, calling them, dropping by, offering suggestions, and in general actively helping them make their way in the community. At the end of the 14-month experimental period and again upon follow-up $1\frac{1}{2}$ years later, the community treatment patients showed better adjustment (e.g., fewer days unemployed) than the hospitalized patients. Upon 2-year follow-up, however, the advantage of the community treatment program began to lessen. This finding suggests that community treatment must maintain active involvement with patients long after their crises have passed.

This program gave rise to an approach called *assertive community treatment,* or *ACT,* that is now being tried in a number of cities in the United States and Great Britain. In ACT, the released patient is contacted frequently and can draw on the services of a wide range of professionals—not just mental health workers—all based in the community, where they are readily available. A recent analysis of the existing research concluded that ACT programs reduce symptoms, improve social functioning, and facilitate independent living (Scott & Dixon, 1995; Lauriello, Bustillo, & Keith, 1999). They may also reduce the overall cost of caring for schizophrenic patients—that was part of their goal—but this is not yet clear.

Another recently developed community-based treatment is *personal therapy,* a one-on-one case-management treatment designed to fit the special emotional circumstances of schizophrenic patients. Personal therapy focuses on control of emotions, the goal being to avoid the kind of emotional escalation that leads to relapse. But the teaching of emotional control is carefully spaced over three stages in order not to burden patients with tasks for which they are not ready. During one stage, for example, patients are taught "internal coping," a strategy for identifying internal signs of upcoming stress. Only later are they taught how to meet the stress. A crucial aspect of personal therapy is that it is long term, lasting from around the time of discharge for about three years.

The preliminary outcomes of personal therapy are promising. While relapse rates depend on whether patients are living with a family or on their own, the treatment does seem to result in less interpersonal anxiety and improved social relationships. These effects increase through the three-year treatment period, whereas the effects of most other treatments peak at one year and then decline as the patient starts to relapse (Hogarty, Greenwald, Ulrich, et al., 1997; Hogarty, Kornblith, Greenwald, et al., 1997). If these results hold up, we may have to acknowledge that a brief treatment model, or any model that provides limited services in deference to managed care, simply doesn't fit the needs of someone with a severe, recurring disorder such as schizophrenia.

Unitary Theories: Diathesis and Stress

For a time, the breakthroughs in genetic research on schizophrenia seemed to cast doubt on environmental theories altogether. But, while the genetic findings seem unchallengeable, they are obviously not the whole story. As Seymour Kety (1970), one of the foremost genetic researchers, has pointed out, schizophrenia cannot be entirely controlled by genes, for, if it were, the concordance rate for MZ twins would be 100 percent. Not only is it not 100 percent but, as we saw, it is only 46 percent. Likewise, while having a first-degree relative with schizophrenia increases one's risk of developing the disorder, it is by no means a necessary condition: 81 percent of people with schizophrenia have no schizophrenic parent or sibling (Gottesman, 1991).

Such are the findings that have led today's researchers to look for *both* genetic and environmental causes—in other words, to adopt the diathesis-stress model. But many questions remain. If there is a genetically inherited diathesis, what, exactly, is the genetic defect? And what is its primary expression? That is, what are the psychological functions that it directly impairs? Finally, what are the stresses most likely to convert such a diathesis into schizophrenia? In an extensive review of the research, Mirsky and Duncan (1986) list the prime suspects: (1) feelings of clumsiness and a sense of being "different" as a result of attention deficits; (2) increased dependence on parents as a result of being impaired; (3) poor academic performance and poor coping skills, again as a result of the basic organic impairment; (4) stressful family interactions, including high expressed emotion; (5) communication deviance in the family, leading to difficulty in communicating with people outside the family and, hence, to increased isolation; and (6) frequent hospitalization of a parent or other family members. In view of later research, prenatal brain injury should probably be added to this list.

A number of studies (e.g. Norman & Malla, 1993a, 1993b) have shown that schizophrenic relapses tend to be preceded by an increase in stressful life events, and patients with psychosis have been found to show greater emotional reactivity to daily life events than do normal controls (Myin-Germeys, van Os, Schwartz, et al., 2001). These events look more like triggering events than like fundamental causes, but what is interesting is that the researchers now not only acknowledge diathesis-stress interaction but also try to examine it. We have looked at other such studies in this chapter—notably, Mednick's high-risk studies. Another example is the Davis and Bracha group's study of fingerprints in MZ twins discordant for schizophrenia; here the hypothesized cause is both environmental (prenatal brain injury) and genetic. The diathesis-stress model has also led researchers to ask what happens to people who inherit a genetic vulnerability to schizophrenia but do not develop schizophrenia. Some studies indicate that in such cases the genetic diathesis is often expressed as schizotypal personality disorder. As we noted, this syndrome was commonly seen in those of Mednick's high-risk children who did not develop schizophrenia.

The recent breakthroughs in the study of schizophrenia have been very exciting, yet each new discovery has made the disorder seem more complicated. If the causes had proved to be wholly genetic or wholly environmental, research would have been far easier. But, framed as a diathesis-stress interaction—and one that probably involves many different kinds of genetic diathesis, together with many kinds of stress—the disorder poses a highly intricate problem, one that will occupy researchers for many years to come.

Key Terms

active phase, 399
anhedonia, 397
antipsychotic drugs, 417
behavioral high-risk design, 412
blunted affect, 397
catatonic schizophrenia, 401
catatonic stupor, 401
clanging, 395
communication deviance (CD), 424
deficit symptoms, 404
delusional disorder, 406
delusions, 391
dementia praecox, 390
diathesis-stress model, 407
differential deficits, 407
disorganized schizophrenia, 400
dopamine hypothesis, 416
echolalia, 401
expressed emotion (EE), 422
flat affect, 397
genetic high-risk design, 411
good-poor premorbid dimension, 403
hallucinations, 396
inappropriate affect, 397
loosening of associations, 393
negative symptoms, 404
neologisms, 395
paranoid-nonparanoid dimension, 405
paranoid schizophrenia, 402
phenothiazines, 417
positive-negative symptoms dimension, 404
positive symptoms, 404
poverty of content, 394
process-reactive dimension, 403
prodromal phase, 399
psychoses, 390
residual phase, 399
schizoaffective disorder, 397
schizophrenia, 390
social-skills training, 426
stereotypy, 398
tardive dyskinesia, 416
token economy, 426
Type I schizophrenia, 404
Type II schizophrenia, 404
word salad, 396

Summary

- Schizophrenia is the label given to a group of relatively common psychoses characterized by severe distortion of thought, bizarre behavior, and social withdrawal.
- *DSM-IV-TR* identifies five characteristic symptoms of schizophrenia: delusions, hallucinations, disorganized speech, disorganized or catatonic behavior, and negative symptoms (a reduction in or loss of normal language and other functions). To be diagnosed with schizophrenia, a person must have shown 2 or more of these disturbances for at least a month and must

have been functioning abnormally for at least 6 months.

- Disorders of thought and language include delusions and loosening of associations between concepts. Loosening of associations results in language marked by poverty of content, neologisms, clanging, and word salad.
- Disorders of perception produce a breakdown of selective attention, which some experts believe constitutes the basic pathology in schizophrenia. Hallucinations are often another perceptual problem for schizophrenic patients.
- Disorders of mood in schizophrenia may take two forms. One is blunted or flat affect (reduced or absent emotional responsiveness). The other form is inappropriate affect (emotional expression unsuited to the situation).
- Schizophrenic patients may display a wide variety of disorders of motor behavior. The behaviors range from merely inappropriate to bizarre.
- Social withdrawal is an early sign of schizophrenia. This condition is exacerbated by difficulty in maintaining appropriate interpersonal behavior.
- Schizophrenia follows a fairly regular course, involving three stages: (1) the prodromal phase, marked by a gradual social withdrawal and deterioration of functioning; (2) the active phase, marked by overt signs of psychosis; and (3) the residual phase, in which gross psychotic symptoms recede, but functioning remains impaired. Some patients experience a complete remission, but most remain impaired to a greater or lesser degree.
- Schizophrenia may be classified into subtypes according to symptomatology. The three main subtypes are (1) disorganized schizophrenia, characterized by incoherent speech, mood disturbance (either flat affect or extreme silliness), and disorganized behavior; (2) catatonic schizophrenia, characterized by extremes of motor behavior (i.e., immobility or hyperactivity); and (3) paranoid schizophrenia, characterized by delusions and/or hallucinations of persecution and grandeur.
- Today, classification of schizophrenia by symptomatology is considered less valid than classification along certain dimensions—an approach that allows for continuous variation in, rather than the mere presence or absence of, symptoms.
- One dimension is the process-reactive dimension, in which cases with a gradual onset (process, or poor-premorbid) are distinguished from those with a rapid onset precipitated by a traumatic event (reactive, or good-premorbid).
- The positive-negative symptoms dimension distinguishes those with new and abnormal behaviors (positive symptoms), such as hallucinations, delusions, and bizarre behaviors, from those with abnormal "nonbehaviors" (negative symptoms), such as withdrawal, flat affect, and poverty of speech. This dimension is now the focus of considerable research, because its two patterns may represent two biologically distinct disorders: Type I schizophrenia (positive symptoms) and Type II schizophrenia (negative symptoms).
- A third dimension is the paranoid-nonparanoid dimension. This dimension indicates the presence or absence of paranoid delusions.
- The symptoms of and prognosis for schizophrenia differ across cultures. Recovery is easier in developing countries, which maintain a stronger emphasis on social interdependence and family support. In industrialized societies, schizophrenia is more likely to strike males, people of lower IQ, and unemployed or unmarried people. It first appears in adolescence or early adulthood.
- Delusional disorder, another category of psychosis, resembles paranoid schizophrenia in that the most prominent symptom is a system of delusions. In delusional disorder, however, the delusions are the fundamental abnormality, from which any other abnormalities emanate, and in many cases they are the patient's only symptom. Furthermore, if the patient does have other symptoms, they do not include the characteristic symptoms of schizophrenia (e.g., loosening of associations and incoherence). The delusions are more plausible and less bizarre than those found in paranoid schizophrenia.
- Delusional disorder also differs from schizophrenia in prevalence and onset. It is far less common, it strikes more women than men, and it has a later onset.
- Scientists have encountered several obstacles in trying to understand the causes of schizophrenia. Researchers don't agree on the primary pathology. The difficulty of discriminating between primary symptoms and secondary symptoms adds to the problem of diagnosis. The hospitalization and medication most schizophrenic patients receive could actually produce some of the unique features of schizophrenia. The difficulty in discovering differential deficits for schizophrenia further complicates research.
- The neuroscience perspective has convincingly indicated that genetic factors contribute to the development of schizophrenia. Genetic studies on schizophrenia in families, twins, and adopted children have produced very strong evidence for a genetic component of schizophrenia. Scientists have used deviant eye tracking, a trait unique to some people with schizophrenia, as a marker when trying to find a genetic cause of schizophrenia.
- Brain scans of schizophrenia sufferers have shown several abnormalities. These irregularities may be a result of the medication schizophrenic patients receive, but it is believed that they are a cause of the disease, as the findings also appear in people with first-episode schizophrenia.
- Another possible cause of the disorder is prenatal brain injury, specifically in the second trimester, when the brain undergoes important developmental stages.This theory is supported by studies showing that babies exposed to illnesses in their second trimester are more likely to develop schizophrenia than are babies exposed

in their first or third trimester or those not exposed to an illness prenatally.

- The dopamine hypothesis, a theory based on biochemical research states that schizophrenia is related to excess dopamine activity in the brain. The theory has been disputed by some researchers, and it is probable that a biological cause for the disorder will involve not one but many biochemical imbalances. Antipsychotic drugs are quite effective at reducing the symptoms of schizophrenia.
- Cognitive theorists believe that the primary problem in schizophrenia is a biologically based attention deficit, with other symptoms developing as a result of this problem. It is believed that Type I schizophrenia is related to overattention, the inability to screen out irrelevant stimuli. Type II schizophrenic patients, however, appear to be underattentive to external stimuli, as seen in their abnormal orienting responses. In support of these theories, researchers have found attention deficits in people with active and remitted schizophrenia, in their relatives, and in high-risk preschizophrenics. Cognitive therapy is designed to rehabilitate deficient cognitive skills and to reduce hallucinations and delusions.
- Interpersonal theorists propose that psychological tensions in the home may be a stress factor in causing schizophrenia. Studies on expressed emotion (based on levels of criticism and emotional overinvolvement) of close relatives of schizophrenic patients have shown that a negative and highly emotional family atmosphere may lead to the onset of, or a recurrence of, schizophrenia. Communication deviance in parents has proved a good predictor of schizophrenia in adolescents. Family therapists emphasize the need to work with the families of patients to prevent recurrences of the disorder.
- The behavioral perspective sees people with schizophrenia as those who do not respond to normal social stimuli due to environmental factors. Behaviorists feel that schizophrenic patients may continue their abnormal behaviors if they are rewarded for them; therefore, treatment aims at changing the behaviors by reversing the reinforcement. Patients are rewarded only for normal behaviors. Behavioral treatments include direct reinforcement, token economies, and social-skills training.
- Sociocultural theorists promote long-term, multifaceted support for released patients, to complement the relapse prevention function addressed by the other therapies. Assertive community treatment programs enable patients to draw on the services of a wide range of professionals in the community. Personal therapy provides one-to-one case-management treatment.
- Although there are many different perspectives on the causes and treatment of schizophrenia, most researchers now recognize that environmental and genetic factors interact in the causation of schizophrenia. Hence, many adopt the diathesis-stress model, which states that a predisposition to schizophrenia is inherited but that the disorder must be triggered by environmental stresses, such as poor coping skills and high expressed emotion and communication deviance within the family.

CHAPTER

15

Problems in Diagnosis
- Identifying an Acquired Brain Disorder
- Specifying the Type of Disorder
- Specifying the Site of the Damage

Types of Acquired Brain Disorders
- Cerebral Infection
- Traumatic Brain Injury
- Cerebrovascular Accidents: Strokes
- Brain Tumors
- Degenerative Disorders
- Nutritional Deficiency
- Endocrine Disorders
- Toxic Disorders

The Epilepsies
- Causes of Epilepsy
- Types of Seizures
- Psychological Factors in Epilepsy
- Treatment of Epilepsy

Neuropsychological Disorders

Mrs. L., a 76-year-old widow and former secretary, lived alone in a small midwestern town. Though her two daughters and one son lived in other parts of the country, they spoke with her on the telephone and visited her regularly. Over the last two years they had noticed increasing anxiety and depression in their mother, as well as some change in her thinking and memory. Mrs. L.'s face had become rather unexpressive, and she shuffled when she walked. At first her children interpreted these changes as the result of old age. However, as their mother became more and more sad, they became concerned.

Finally they took her to a psychiatrist, who noted her recent weight loss and difficulty sleeping. He placed Mrs. L. on the antidepressant medication Prozac, which brought a mild improvement in her mood. Because of her shuffling gait, the psychiatrist referred her to a neurologist, who observed a "masked" facial expression and decreased arm swing. Concluding that they were symptoms of Parkinson's disease, he ordered an MRI scan of Mrs. L.'s head, which revealed a small tumor in the meninges overlying her brain. The neurologist judged the tumor to be largely incidental, however.

Approximately two months later, Mrs. L. developed a stomach virus, with vomiting and diarrhea. Shortly after that she began telling her children that she had been seeing them in her home, lying dead on the living room floor. At first she tried to talk to the images, but receiving no response, she gradually gave up. She later reported feeling mildly agitated that the images were not responding to her, though she did seem to understand that they could not be real. The family contacted the psychiatrist, who interpreted the images as mood-congruent hallucinations associated with depression. He increased Mrs. L.'s antidepressant medication and added an antipsychotic drug, Olanzepine.

Over the next three weeks Mrs. L.'s ability to care for herself deteriorated rapidly, and she became uncommunicative. One of her daughters returned home to help her dress, eat, and bathe. Again the family contacted the psychiatrist, who recommended that Mrs. L. be hospitalized. Because Mrs. L. had not responded to medication, soon after hospitalization she was considered for electroshock therapy (ECT). But first she was referred for neuropsychological testing, which revealed serious impairments of her visual perception. Mrs. L. could not copy even simple geometric figures, and her ability to learn and retain new information was impaired, as was her ability to focus and sustain her attention.

A neurologist was asked to reevaluate the possibility that the small tumor in Mrs. L.'s meninges could be contributing to her visual hallucinations, which had not ceased. While he felt that the tumor was only incidental, he noted that her hallucinations, disturbance of visual perception, decline in memory, poor attention and concentration, and Parkinson's-like symptoms could indicate a variant of Alzheimer's disease, possibly Lewy body disease. Because such patients are particularly sensitive to antipsychotic medications, the neurologist and neuropsychologist encouraged the psychiatrist to discontinue the Olanzepine. Mrs. L. was placed on a medication called Aricept, which is used to treat Alzheimer's disease. Within days Mrs. L.'s hallucinations ceased. She was discharged to a nursing home, where her initiative and ability to care for herself began to improve. Three weeks later she left the nursing home to return to her family's care. (Smith, The Mayo Clinic, personal files)

Most of the disorders that we have discussed in this book so far are thought to be either partly or largely psychological, the result of the person's relations to his or her experience and environment. By contrast, the **acquired brain disorders,** as their name tells us, are by definition biological. They are directly traceable to the destruction of brain tissue or to biochemical imbalances in the brain, and they have a major effect on cognitive processes such as memory. This is not to say that these disorders are "purely" biological. The form such syndromes take depends in part on psychosocial factors—above all, what sort of personality the person has and what his or her living situation is. Likewise, the treatment of acquired brain disorders (also known as neuropsychological disorders) is psychological as well as medical. Rehabilitation programs typically involve not just physicians but also psychologists, social workers, occupational therapists, physical therapists, and speech therapists.

Acquired brain disorders constitute a major health problem. At present they account for one fourth of all first admissions to mental hospitals in the United States. In this chapter, we first examine the difficulties of diagnosing acquired brain disorders. Then we discuss the symptoms and the known causes of the major syndromes.

Problems in Diagnosis

There are four major problems in the diagnosis of an acquired brain disorder: (1) deciding whether the syndrome is in fact an acquired brain disorder or disease or simply a psychological disorder; (2) if it is a brain disorder or disease, determining the cause of the pathology; (3) if the damage is localized (i.e., restricted to a specific area of the brain), determining the location; and (4) deciding how psychosocial factors influence the disorder's symptoms and whether medical treatment or psychological therapy can modify them. None of these decisions is a simple matter.

Identifying an Acquired Brain Disorder

The symptoms of acquired brain disorders closely resemble those of psychological disorders. Disorientation, impaired intellectual functioning, and inappropriate affect are well-recognized symptoms of both schizophrenia and brain disorder, for example. Diagnosis in such cases may not be easy, at least initially. Furthermore, the symptoms of a brain disorder may be complicated by emotional disturbances developing *in response* to the impairment. Look again at the opening case. When the onset of a brain disorder or disease is gradual, secondary emotional problems may be present long before the person gets to the hospital. When people find themselves taking the wrong bus, calling the wrong phone numbers, or making embarrassing mistakes on the job, they tend to become anxious and depressed, so, by the time they see a diagnostician, they may have *both* a brain disorder and a psychological disorder.

Before the development of modern diagnostic techniques such as magnetic resonance imaging, or MRI (Chapter 6), it was exceedingly difficult to differentiate between brain disorders and psychological disorders. Often it was not until the autopsy that a patient whose symptoms had been curiously resistant to several years of psychotherapy was found to have a brain tumor (Patton & Sheppard, 1956; Waggoner & Bagchi, 1954). Such was the case with composer George Gershwin. Young and seemingly healthy, Gershwin one day lost consciousness momentarily while conducting a concert of his works. In the months that followed, he began to act peculiarly. He was irritable and restless, and he had terrible headaches. At the urging

Before MRI and other sophisticated diagnostic techniques became available, brain disorders were even harder to diagnose than they are now. George Gershwin (1898–1937), composer of such classics as An American in Paris *and* Porgy and Bess, *was thought to be mentally ill when he began behaving strangely. Exploratory surgery revealed a fatal brain tumor.*

of his family, he entered a hospital for a complete physical examination and was declared "a perfect specimen of health" (Ewen, 1956, p. 298). He then began daily treatment with a psychotherapist, who decided that what Gershwin needed was rest and seclusion. The rest seemed to help, for about a month. Then Gershwin collapsed and went into a coma. He was rushed to a hospital, where exploratory surgery located an inoperable brain tumor. Gershwin died that same day, at the age of 38.

The reverse mistake—diagnosing a psychological problem as a brain disorder—also occurs, especially with elderly patients. Physicians may diagnose dementia (an acquired brain disorder) when in fact the person is suffering from depression brought on by the loss of a spouse, health problems, money problems, or any of the many difficulties faced by older people (Gurland, Dean, Craw, et al., 1980).

The differential diagnosis of brain disorder and psychological disturbances is crucial. Many brain disorders can be treated, but only if they are recognized for what they are. Misdiagnosis can be fatal. Sound practice calls for a diagnostician to rule out brain disorder or disease before concluding that a disorder is psychological in origin. Diagnosticians can draw on a number of resources: direct observation of the patient, a detailed history of the onset and progress of the symptoms, interviews with the patient's family and physician. In addition, diagnosticians usually put the patient through a series of tests: neurological tests to assess reflexes, which may be faulty if there is damage to the nervous system; EEGs, brain CT scans and MRI, and chemical analyses of cerebrospinal fluids; and, finally, neuropsychological tests, such as the Halstead-Reitan Battery and others that are specifically designed to detect impairment. Newer technologies such as PET (positron emission tomography) scans and SPECT (single positron emission computed tomography) scans offer even better detection of brain pathology and are fast becoming the primary means of diagnosis (D'Esposito, 2000). These tests are discussed in Chapters 2 and 6.

Specifying the Type of Disorder

If a man appears in an emergency room with a revolver in his hand and a bullet hole in his head, the physician on duty will have little difficulty determining the source, to say nothing of the presence, of brain damage. In most cases, however, it is even more difficult to specify the source of the impairment—tumor, poisoning, infection, stroke, whatever—than to distinguish between psychological disorders and acquired brain disorders. Yet the accurate identification of a brain disorder or disease is essential, because treatment is based on this decision. A physician does not wish to treat for a brain tumor, only to discover that the patient actually has hyperthyroidism.

Several possible sources of confusion can make diagnosis difficult. In the first place, the symptoms of the various brain disorders overlap considerably. If it is determined that a patient's amnesia is due to a brain disorder or disease, this condition could still be caused by a number of pathologies, each requiring different treatment. Second, just as different disorders may produce the same symptoms, so the same disorder may produce widely different symptoms, depending on the area of the brain involved. A brain tumor may cause a speech disorder in one patient, double vision in another, emotional lability in a third. Furthermore, the source of the brain disorder is only one of the many factors determining the patient's behavioral responses to the disease. The patient's age, general physical condition, prior intellectual achievements, premorbid personality, emotional stability, and social situation—as well as the nature, location, and extent of the brain damage—affect the symptoms. A patient who is rigid and pessimistic, uninsured, or alone in the world may respond to unwelcome symptoms with panic or total dejection. On the other hand, a patient who has money, family, and a resilient disposition may show a surprisingly moderate response, even to a severe impairment. From this bewildering array of variables, the diagnostician must ferret out the single primary variable: the source of the brain disorder.

There is one final problem in determining the source of acquired brain injuries. As with so many of the psychological disorders, there are many brain injuries about which very little is known. Unfortunately, the better-understood syndromes are often the rarest, while many of the most common injuries remain baffling.

Delirium Delirium differs from other acquired brain disorders in that it remits quickly, leaving most patients unharmed. It is very dramatic, however. **Delirium** is a transient, global disorder of cognition and attention. Delirious patients are profoundly confused. Their thinking is disorganized, even dreamlike. In about half of all cases, hallucinations and delusions (usually of persecution) are present, and, when they are, patients may harm themselves or others as they attempt to escape or fight the imagined enemy. Some patients are hyperalert, others lethargic and drowsy, and these disturbances extend to the sleep cycle. Patients are often drowsy during the day and awake and agitated at night. Emotional lability is common, running the gamut from apathy to the extremes of fear and rage. The onset of delirium is sudden, and its severity fluctuates during the course of the day. (Most patients are worse at night.) In the typical case, the delirium passes within a month, recovery is complete, and the patient is partially or totally amnesiac for the whole episode.

Delirium is caused by a widespread disruption of cerebral metabolism and neurotransmission. It is a common condition in older people, and, when it strikes the elderly, the cause is often intoxication from medication, even ordinary medication in prescribed doses. (Older people may respond to drugs very differently than the young.) Another common cause is surgery. Surgery produces delirium in 10 to 15 percent of older patients (Seymour, 1986), and certain kinds of surgery pose a far greater risk. (Heart surgery provokes delirium in 24 to 32 percent of older patients.) Other causes are withdrawal from alcohol or other drugs, head injury, sleep loss, malnutrition, and psychological stress, such as the death of a spouse, relocation to a nursing home, or sensory deprivation.

A final common cause is physical illness, such as heart attack or pneumonia, of which delirium is often the main presenting symptom in the elderly. To quote one expert, "Acute confusion [delirium] is a far more common herald of the onset of physical illness in an older person than are, for example, fever, pain, or tachycardia" (Hodkinson, 1976). For this reason, it is very important that the delirium not be misdiagnosed. It is often mistaken for dementia, particularly in patients who already have dementia. (As with other acquired brain disorders, these two can coexist in the same patient.) But, if delirium is not recognized as such, the possibility of underlying physical illness is ignored, perhaps with fatal results. The treatment of delirium is the removal of its cause—withdrawal of the intoxicating medication or treatment of the underlying physical illness, for example. Patients who are agitated may also be given sedatives (Lipowsky, 1989).

Specific Cognitive Impairments Acquired brain disorder can produce specific impairments in a variety of cognitive areas. The most common signs of acquired brain disorder are the following:

1. *Impairment of attention and arousal.* The person may be easily distracted by sounds and sights in the environment or have difficulty focusing on an activity or conversation. He or she may have slower thinking speed and, consequently, require more time to make decisions or have trouble keeping up with conversations.
2. *Impairment of language function.* The person may have difficulty speaking coherently, understanding the speech of others, reading, and the like.
3. *Impairment of learning and memory.* The person may experience difficulty learning and retaining new information. He or she may also forget events of the distant past or, more typically, of the very recent past—an impairment called **amnesia.** To fill in the gaps in memory, the person may invent stories.
4. *Impairment of visual-perceptual function.* The person may be unable to recognize everyday objects for what they are—name them, use them correctly, or draw them.
5. *Impairment of motor skills.* The person may suddenly become paralyzed, unable to move an arm or a leg or to produce speech. Or he or she may lose the ability to coordinate movements or manipulate objects correctly, a disorder called **apraxia.** A person with apraxia cannot perform a well-learned movement, such as brushing his hair, when asked to do so, though he brushes his hair spontaneously each morning. Patients

with apraxia may try to write with a pair of scissors or light a match by striking the wrong end (Hécaen & Albert, 1978).

6. *Impairment of executive function, or the ability to plan, initiate, sequence, monitor, and stop complex behaviors.* The person may make inappropriate decisions—to drive unsafely, to give money away to strangers, or to walk out of the house in pajamas. He or she may move quickly and inappropriately from apathy to hostility or from laughing to weeping.
7. *Impairment of higher-order intellectual function.* The person may have difficulty performing mental tasks that draw on general knowledge, such as numerical calculation, or have trouble with deductive reasoning.

Impairments of language function, termed **aphasia,** are common. The diagnosis of aphasia depends on fluency of speech, comprehension, and the ability to repeat phrases and sentences (Cummings, 1985). Patients with *fluent aphasia* produce streams of incoherent speech. Syllables are reversed, word order is jumbled, and so on. Patients with *nonfluent aphasia* have difficulty initiating speech and respond to questions with one-word answers, short phrases, and long pauses. Aphasia patients also differ in their ability to understand speech (ranging from good to poor) and their ability to repeat speech correctly (also ranging from good to poor).

When the patient is aphasic, the diagnostician can usually say with some precision where it is that the brain is damaged. In most people, language is controlled largely by the left hemisphere (Chapter 6). Aphasia is caused by damage to this hemisphere. Fluent aphasia is produced by injury closer to the rear of this hemisphere, nonfluent aphasia by injury closer to the front of the hemisphere. When damage is limited to the left frontal lobe, comprehension is usually preserved. When damage extends to the regions behind the frontal lobe, comprehension is impaired.

Impairments of the ability to recognize familiar objects are called **agnosia.** Agnosia usually occurs in one sensory domain, so that a person who is unable to recognize an object by sight will be able to recognize the object by touch or smell. In his book *The Man Who Mistook His Wife for a Hat and Other Clinical Tales* (1985), Oliver Sacks described the case of Dr. P., a professor of music, who had developed visual agnosia. Dr. P. often failed to recognize his students' faces, yet when they spoke, he knew immediately who they were. At the same time, he saw faces that didn't exist: He patted the tops of fire hydrants as if they were the heads of children. An ophthalmologist examined Dr. P. and, finding nothing wrong with his eyes, recommended that he see Sacks, a neurologist. Sacks found Dr. P. "a man of great cultivation and charm, who talked well and fluently, with imagination and humor" (p. 8). Gradually, however, it became clear that there was something seriously wrong with him. He was able to see but not to make sense of his perceptions. He could identify a cube, a dodecahedron, and other complex geometric forms, but, when Sacks handed him a rose, he was baffled:

> "About six inches in length," he commented. "A convoluted red form with a linear green attachment."
>
> "Yes," I [Sacks] said encouragingly, "but what do you think it *is*, Dr. P.?"
>
> "Not easy to say." He seemed perplexed. . . .
>
> "Smell it," I suggested, and he again looked somewhat puzzled, as if I'd asked him to smell a higher symmetry. (p. 12)

When Sacks handed him a glove, he was again bewildered:

> "A continuous surface," he announced at last, "infolded on itself. It appears to have"—he hesitated—"five outpouchings, if this is the word." (p. 13)

On one occasion, as he was preparing to leave Sacks' office, Dr. P. reached for his wife's head and tried to lift it off, mistaking his wife for a hat. Interestingly, although Dr. P.'s visual sense was totally impaired, his musical sense remained intact. He was able to function in everyday life by composing eating songs, dressing songs, and bathing songs, which guided his actions. Dr. P.'s symptoms were due to brain damage in the visual-processing region of the brain.

Dr. P. was an unusual patient in that his symptoms were so isolated and specific. Most patients show a combination of disabilities. Thus, it is the rare case in which the diagnostician can accurately specify one spot, and one spot alone, in which the damage has occurred. Nevertheless, an educated guess must be made as to the site or sites.

Dementia *DSM-IV-TR* describes **dementia** as the impairment of at least two cognitive functions, resulting in a decline from a higher level of performance that compromises a person's occupational or social functioning. Some dementias are caused by infectious diseases, such as syphilis or AIDS (see pages 437–438). Others are degenerative—that is, caused by progressive physical deterioration. Degenerative dementia is described in more detail later in this chapter.

In diagnosing an acquired brain disorder such as dementia, the clinician classifies it according to its cause—trauma, infection, poisoning, or whatever.

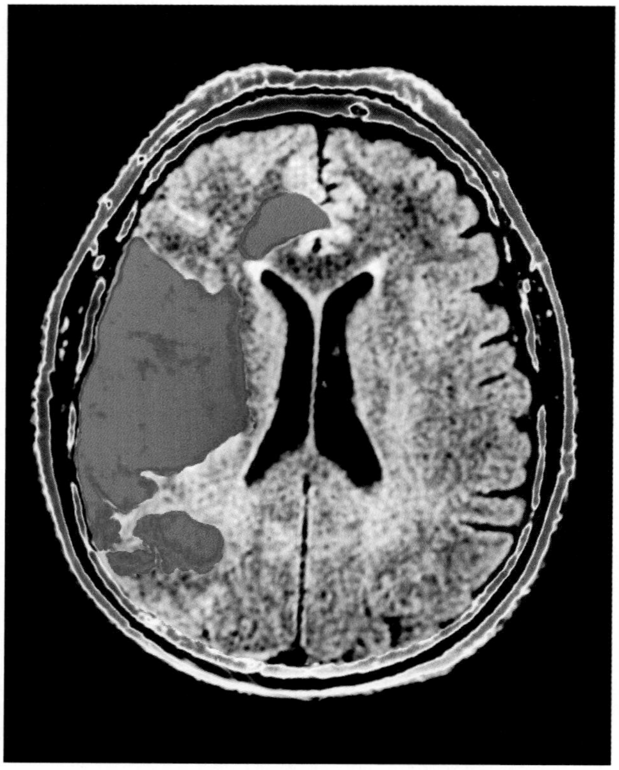

Computerized scans can help pinpoint the site of brain damage.

The one exception to this classification system is epilepsy, which, because its cause is in some cases unknown, is classified by its symptomatology. This chapter will follow the same organizational plan.

Specifying the Site of the Damage

We mentioned earlier the matter of determining the location of the brain damage. This is the third important problem in diagnosis. In the case of some brain disorders, such as the degenerative disorders, the problem may not apply, for the damage is usually diffused throughout the brain. But, with many other disorders, such as "strokes" and brain tumors, damage may be restricted to one specific area, leaving the rest of the brain relatively unaffected. When this is the case, it is essential to determine the site of the injury, for treatment depends on this information. Obviously, a surgeon who is about to operate on a brain tumor needs to know where the tumor is. Such knowledge also guides rehabilitation. Therapists who know where the damage is can retrain patients to use the damaged parts or can teach them to compensate by developing undamaged parts.

Physiological measures such as the EEG can sometimes give vague hints as to the location of the brain damage. The patient's symptoms and history provide further hints. As we saw in Chapter 6, certain areas of the brain are known to control certain behaviors. Using this knowledge, a neurologist may be able to determine the location of the damage on the basis of how the patient is acting and how he or she performs on neuropsychological tests.

Today, CT, PET, SPECT, and MRI are the primary methods of pinpointing the site of brain damage (Bigler, Yeo, & Turkheimer, 1989; Jernigan, 1990; Pykett, 1982; Theodore, 1988a, 1988b). While fMRI has been of immense use in research, its clinical use is still being established (Chen & Chen, 2002). See Chapter 6 for a description of the detailed information these tests can provide and Chapter 2 for an explanation of their use in diagnosis.

Types of Acquired Brain Disorders

Cerebral Infection

Neuropsychological disorders can result from infections that damage and destroy the neural tissue of the brain. Cerebral infections can be caused by bacteria, viruses, protozoa, or fungi. There are three major categories of brain infection: cerebral abscess, encephalitis, and meningitis. After reviewing these categories of brain infections, we will briefly discuss four specific infections: neurosyphilis, human immunodeficiency virus (HIV), mad cow disease, and Lyme disease.

Cerebral Abscess A **cerebral abscess,** like an abscess in any other part of the body, is an infection that becomes encapsulated by connective tissue. Because it cannot drain and heal like an infection on the outside of the body, it simply continues to grow inside the body. Brain abscesses usually occur when an infection in another part of the body travels to the brain or when a foreign object such as a piece of shrapnel enters the brain, introducing germs. With improved measures for preventing infection after injury, cerebral abscesses have become rare.

Encephalitis **Encephalitis** is a generic term meaning an inflammation of the brain. It is caused by the direct infection of the brain by viral, bacterial, parasitic, or fungal agents. A large number of organisms are known to cause encephalitis. One form, *epidemic encephalitis,* also known as sleeping sickness, was widespread following World War I. Its most striking symptoms are profound lethargy and prolonged periods of sleep, often for days or even weeks at a time. In their periods of wakefulness, however, patients might become extremely hyperactive, irritable, and then breathless and unable to sleep. Other symptoms include convulsive seizures and delirium—a state of excitement and disorientation marked by incoherent speech, restless activity, and often hallucinations. Epidemic encephalitis often leads to death. In those who survive—and especially in children, who are more susceptible—the disease often leaves an altered personality, in many cases a sociopathic personality.

The virus responsible for epidemic encephalitis, while still active in certain areas of Asia and Africa, is now virtually unknown in Europe and North America. However, there remain scores of viruses that can cause encephalitis. Typically transmitted by such animals as mosquitoes, ticks, and horses, these viruses produce many of the same symptoms as epidemic encephalitis—lethargy, irritability, seizures—and often lead to death or, in those who survive, brain damage. In 1999, an outbreak of West Nile virus encephalitis in the northeastern United States resulted in at least seven deaths.

Meningitis Another type of cerebral infection is **meningitis**, an acute inflammation of the *meninges*, the membranous covering of the brain and spinal cord. It is caused by a bacterial infection that is introduced to the brain directly as a result of an injury that penetrates the brain, thereby causing an open head wound; through an infection elsewhere in the body; or via the bloodstream. Among the symptoms usually observed in meningitis are drowsiness, fever, headache, stiff neck, confusion, irritability, inability to concentrate, memory defects, and sensory impairments. In milder cases, the primary infection may be effectively eliminated, but residual effects such as motor and sensory impairments and, in infants, mental retardation are not uncommon.

Neurosyphilis **Neurosyphilis**, the deterioration of brain tissue as a result of syphilis, was once far more common than any of the forms of encephalitis. It was not until the late nineteenth century that the degenerative disorder called **general paresis** was finally linked to syphilis. Throughout the previous centuries, syphilis had raged unchecked through Europe, taking a huge toll in infant mortality, blindness, madness, and death. Among its more famous victims were Henry VIII and most of his many wives, and probably Christopher Columbus.

With the development of such early detection procedures as the Wasserman test and with the advent of penicillin, the incidence of syphilis decreased dramatically in the late 1940s and the 1950s. Today, general paresis accounts for less than 1 percent of all first admissions to mental hospitals in the United States.

HIV Infection Neuropsychological difficulties develop in 30 to 50 percent of individuals with HIV infection. While these usually take the form of mild cognitive changes, a small percentage of infected individuals develop serious cognitive impairment, referred to as *HIV dementia*. Often, HIV dementia appears in the late stages of the disease (Marcotte, Grant, Atkinson, et al., 2001), but it may also occur as an early symptom, as in the following case (McArthur, Hoover, Bacellar, et al., 1993):

> Ted is a 32-year-old man who is a talented artist. He has been Human Immunodeficiency Virus (HIV) positive for 8 years. Two of his close friends have died during the last year from active AIDS. Ted has had AIDS-related complex (ARC) with weight loss, fever, night sweats, fatigue, depression, and generalized lymphadenopathy for 2 years without other serious medical problems. Six months ago he developed [pneumonia], which was treated successfully.
>
> Three months ago his lover, Randy, noted that Ted was becoming forgetful and had difficulty concentrating on his artwork. Gradually, his memory impairment worsened and he began to have problems painting. He described the problem to Randy, "I can't seem to make the brush go where I want it to go. My hands don't work right." Ted complained of a constant headache and depression. He became increasingly confused and finally, in frustration, stopped trying to paint. The diagnosis is Dementia Due to HIV Disease. (Fauman, 1994, p. 63)

The early symptoms of HIV dementia sometimes go unnoticed or are mistaken for other problems, physiological or psychological. In many cases, cognitive changes are the first sign of acquired immunodeficiency syndrome, or AIDS. At first patients may seem forgetful, apathetic, withdrawn, and either depressed or anxious or both. Later, they become confused, disoriented, and uncoordinated. In the final stages, the patient may go blind, have seizures, become mute, and lapse into a coma (Holland & Tross, 1985).

The HIV virus tends to invade the central nervous system early in the illness. In one study of patients in the early stages of AIDS, the virus was found in the cerebrospinal fluid of about half the subjects (McArthur, Cohen, Seines, et al., 1989; Sonnerborg, Ehrnst, Bergdahl, et al., 1988). But, while the HIV virus will attack the brain itself, HIV dementia is often caused by other infectious agents, because the body's weakened immune system allows a multitude of pathogens to gain a foothold. The damage done to the brain seems to be diffuse rather than confined to a single area. Over months or years, the dementia usually grows progressively worse. Medications to reverse or delay neuropsychological impairments associated with HIV infection have received a great deal of attention in recent years. Several drugs have shown some benefit, although the research is ongoing (Marcotte, Grant, Atkinson, et al., 2001).

Mad Cow Disease **Mad cow disease** is one of several fatal infectious diseases, called *spongiform encephalopathies,* that attack the brain in both animals and humans. Over the past decade, the disease has hit herds of cattle in Great Britain and may have spread to some consumers who ate the contaminated beef. In human beings, this type of encephalopathy is called Creutzfeldt-Jakob disease. While recent cases of Creutzfeldt-Jakob in Great Britain may be linked to mad cow disease, in most cases the source of the infection cannot be identified (Brown, 1997).

In the past, Creutzfeldt-Jakob disease afflicted mostly the middle-aged, but recently it has been seen in much younger people, with an average age of 27. The first signs of infection are memory loss or confusion, sometimes accompanied by behavioral change or difficulty walking. As the disease progresses, visual perception and motor skills deteriorate rapidly, and the patient falls into dementia. Death occurs about 4 months after the onset of the illness.

Autopsies of these patients have revealed widespread degeneration of brain tissue. Plaques composed of prions, or protein deposits, have encrusted or replaced what were once normal neurons. Though further research remains to be done, scientists strongly suspect that the prion is the cause of the infection.

The form of Creutzfeldt-Jakob disease that is linked to mad cow disease has an incubation period of 10 to 15 years. The disease is comparatively rare, given the widespread consumption of beef in Great Britain. Why it has affected relatively few British citizens is still a mystery to researchers, as is the relatively young age of most of its victims (Brown, 1997).

U.S. government agencies have taken several preventive measures to keep mad cow disease from arising in this country, including banning the importation of cattle, goats, and sheep from Great Britain and other countries where mad cow disease has been found; inspecting cattle suspected of having the disease and destroying the infected cattle or, in some cases, the entire herd; and regulating against the inclusion of animal remnants in animals' feed. To date, there has been no evidence of mad cow disease in the United States (Enserink, 2001).

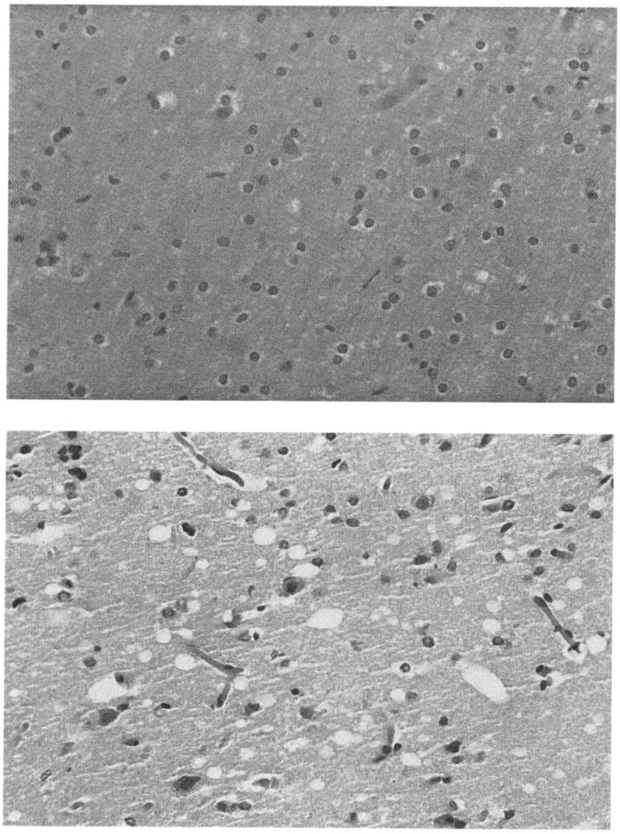

(Top) A normal human brain. (Bottom) The brain of a patient with Creutzfeldt-Jakob disease. Note the spongelike, or spongiform, characteristics of the brain tissue.

Lyme Disease **Lyme disease** is the most common tickborne disease in the United States, with more than 15,000 cases reported each year (Steere, 2001). The disorder appears primarily in the northeastern United States; in the Midwest in Wisconsin and Minnesota; and on the West Coast in northern California and Oregon. Ticks acquire the disease by feeding on infected animal hosts, such as deer, and then spread it to humans. Usually, Lyme disease begins as a slowly expanding, ringlike rash at the site of the tick bite. The lesion is frequently accompanied by mild flulike symptoms, such as low-grade fever, fatigue, and headache. Over the next few weeks, the infection may spread to the central nervous system, heart, and joints. When Lyme disease does affect the central nervous system, in about 15 percent of untreated patients (Steere, 2001), it can lead to encephalitis or meningitis. Victims may experience a variety of cognitive difficulties, such as poor memory or slowed thinking, and psychological symptoms such as anxiety and mood disturbance.

Only about 1 percent of individuals who are bitten by an infected tick develop Lyme disease; transmission can usually be avoided by checking for and removing ticks at the end of every day spent outdoors in infested areas. Other preventive measures include avoiding tick-infested areas, wearing protective clothing, and using insect repellants. A vaccine was approved for Lyme disease in 1998, though it is not 100 percent effective and should never be the main preventive measure. Lyme disease can be treated with antibiotics, but despite treatment with either oral or intravenous antibiotics, a small percentage of patients in the United States continue to suffer from persistent joint inflammation, neurocognitive difficulties, and/or fatigue for months or even years after therapy (Steere, 2001). This disabling syndrome is sometimes called "chronic Lyme disease."

❖ Groups at Risk

Often, the source of cerebral infection is unknown. Encephalitis can be caused by many common illnesses, including measles, mumps, and influenza. People who are infected with the Epstein-Barr or herpes simplex virus can also develop encephalitis. In the case of herpes encephalitis, risk factors that place persons at risk for herpes infection also place them at greater risk for encephalitis. Similarly, groups at risk for HIV infection are at greater risk than the general population for developing dementia.

Another common source of infection is organisms that are transmitted through insect and rodent bites. For example, California and western equine encephalitis are mosquito-borne, while Rocky Mountain spotted fever is carried by a tick. Though all three of these diseases are prevalent throughout the United States, other types of encephalitis are found only in specific regions. For example, valley fever, which is transmitted by rodents, occurs mainly in the Southwest; St. Louis encephalitis is generally found in the southern states. Thus, people who live in those regions—especially those who spend considerable time outdoors—are at greater risk than are those who live in other regions.

Treatment of Cerebral Infections The treatment of brain injuries caused by infection depends on the type of infection. Most bacterial infections are treatable with antibiotics. Cerebral fungal infections are also treatable, if they are identified correctly. Viral infections are more challenging to treat. Steroids can sometimes help the body to fight off a viral infection, and strong drugs such as Acyclovir may help to control infections such as herpes encephalitis. But some infections, such as Creutzfeldt-Jakob disease, the variant of mad cow disease, are largely untreatable (Ashe, Rosen, McArthur, et al., 1993).

Some researchers believe that, in the early stages, the course of an HIV infection of the central nervous system may be reversible (Grant & Martin, 1994). For this reason, they emphasize the importance of both proper diagnosis and timely drug therapy. Certainly, any secondary infections that may contribute to HIV dementia can and should be eliminated.

Traumatic Brain Injury

More common than cerebral infection is **traumatic brain injury,** or injury to the brain as a result of jarring, bruising, or cutting. In the United States, 1.5 to 2 million people sustain a traumatic brain injury each year, making it the leading cause of disability and death in children and young adults (NIH Consensus Development Panel on Rehabilitation of Persons with Traumatic Brain Injury, 1999).

A traumatic brain injury can have huge consequences. The more serious cases lapse into a persistent vegetative state or develop epilepsy. The majority of traumatic brain injuries are classified as mild. But a small percentage of individuals who sustain a mild traumatic brain injury suffer long-term disability. Common symptoms following a mild traumatic brain injury include fatigue, sleep disturbances, poor attention and concentration, slowed reactions, emotional ups and downs, and social and moral failures such as selfishness and callousness (Gronwall, Wrightson, & Waddell, 1990). In general, traumatic brain injury survivors constitute a very troubled population, and a hidden one. They do not look disabled, and partly for that reason they often receive little understanding, let alone adequate treatment. But many of them are unable to live normal lives. Many victims of traumatic brain injury have trouble sustaining marriages and friendships, and a substantial number of adults with traumatic brain injuries are unable to work. In one study, only 37 percent of individuals with a severe traumatic brain injury were employed two years later, whereas 64 percent of individuals with a moderate traumatic brain injury were employed (Dikman, Temkin, Machamer, et al., 1994). Many of those individuals who are able to work do so in settings less demanding than those they had worked in prior to the injury.

Traumatic brain injury is subdivided into three categories: concussion, contusion, and penetrating head injury.

Concussion In the case of a **concussion,** the blow to the head jars the brain, momentarily disrupting its functioning (see Figure 15.1). The usual result is a temporary loss of consciousness, often lasting for only a few seconds or minutes, after which the person

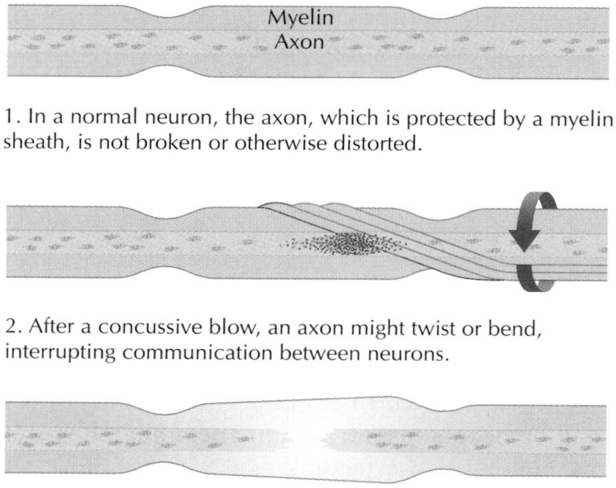

1. In a normal neuron, the axon, which is protected by a myelin sheath, is not broken or otherwise distorted.

2. After a concussive blow, an axon might twist or bend, interrupting communication between neurons.

3. If a concussion is severe enough, the axon swells and disintegrates. Less severely damaged axons return to normal.

FIGURE 15.1 Anatomy of a concussion.

is typically unable to remember the events immediately preceding the injury. A familiar instance of concussion is a knockout in a boxing match. Concussions occur frequently, too, during football games.

In general, the longer the person remains unconscious after the blow, the more severe the posttraumatic symptoms and the less likely it is that the victim will recover completely. In addition to experiencing headaches and dizziness, the person may display apathy, depression, irritability, and various cognitive problems (poor memory, poor concentration). In less severe cases, these symptoms disappear within the span of a few days to a few months, but in some cases, aftereffects may still be experienced months or even years later.

Contusion In a **contusion,** the trauma is severe enough that the brain is not just jarred; it is actually bruised. The person typically lapses into a coma for several hours or even days and afterward may suffer convulsions and/or temporary speech loss. On awakening from the coma, contusion victims may fall into a state of disorientation called **acute confusional state,** in which they may experience hallucinations, delusions, agitation, and a host of cognitive difficulties. This state is also known as delirium, which we discussed earlier. These symptoms generally disappear within a week or so, but a very severe contusion or repeated contusions can result in permanent emotional instability and intellectual impairment. Again, the length of the period of unconsciousness is useful in predicting the severity and duration of the posttraumatic symptoms.

The effects of repeated head injuries, such as those suffered by boxers, can result in cumulative damage. The effects can be manifested years later, in *dementia pugilistica* (better known as the punch-drunk syndrome), which involves memory lapses, loss of coordination, dizziness, tremors, and other physical and psychological impairments. One study of a small sample of former prizefighters found that 87 percent exhibited abnormalities on at least two of four measures (Casson, Seigel, Sham, et al., 1984). Researchers have also found structural changes in the brains of former boxers, including abnormalities similar to those found in Alzheimer's disease (Lampert & Hardman, 1984). Indeed, head injury may be a risk factor for Alzheimer's disease (Jellinger, Paulus, Wrocklage, et al., 2001).

Penetrating Head Injury In a **penetrating head injury,** a foreign object, such as a bullet or a piece of metal, enters the skull and directly ruptures and destroys brain tissue. Penetrating head injuries may result in less severe impairment than a severe concussion, though their effects depend on the site of the damage. Penetrating injuries to certain areas of the brain result in death or extreme disability, while damage to other areas may have relatively minor consequences. Periodically, the newspapers report a case in which a person who has been shot in the head simply waits for the external wounds to heal and then resumes normal functioning, going about his or her daily business with a bullet or two lodged in the brain. Such cases are rare, however. Normally, a penetrating injury results in physical and cognitive impairment, whether major or minor.

The following classic case, reported in 1868, illustrates the subtle, variable, and unpredictable effects of a penetrating head injury (see also Figure 15.2):

Phineas P. Gage, age 25 and strong and healthy, was the popular foreman of a railroad excavation crew. While he was working at a site, an explosion drove a tamping iron into the left side of his face and up through his skull. Thrown onto his back by the force of the blast and by the entry of the rod, Gage convulsed, but he quickly regained speech and was placed in a cart, in which he rode in a sitting position for three quarters of a mile to his hotel. He got out of the cart by himself and walked up a long flight of stairs to his room. Although bleeding profusely, he remained conscious during the doctor's ministrations. Soon afterward he appeared completely recovered physically, but his personality had undergone a radical change. The equilibrium between his intellectual faculties and his instincts seemed to have been destroyed. He was now inconsiderate, impatient, and

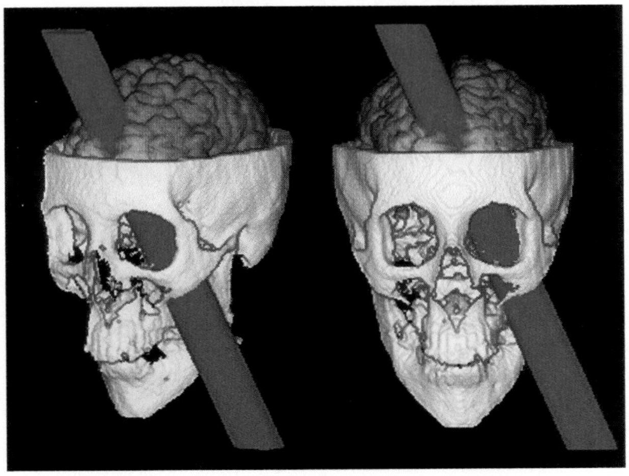

FIGURE 15.2 Phineas Gage's brain injury. Modern neuroimaging techniques have helped to identify the precise location of damage to Phineas Gage's brain.

obstinate, and yet at the same time capricious and vacillating. He also began indulging in the grossest profanity. The change in temperament was so extreme that his employers had to replace him. To his friends he was simply "no longer Gage." (Adapted from Harlow, 1868, pp. 330–332, 339–340.)

❖ Groups at Risk

According to the National Institutes of Health (1999), traumatic brain injury results principally from motor vehicle accidents, falls, acts of violence, and sports injuries. It is more than twice as likely to occur in males as in females, with the highest-risk age group 15- to 24-year-olds. Children and the elderly are also at risk, usually through falls. Indeed, falls are the second most common cause of head injury.

The most common cause of traumatic brain injury, accounting for more than half of all serious head injuries, is automobile and motorcycle accidents (see p. 442, "Preventing Traumatic Brain Injuries"). Many of these injuries could be prevented through the use of seat belts, air bags, infant and child car seats, and helmets. Traumatic brain injury could also be reduced if people would not drive after drinking. Alcohol is reported to be associated with half of all traumatic brain injuries, either in the person causing the injury or in the person with the injury, or both. Studies have shown that a large proportion of traumatic brain injury victims had evidence of psychoactive substance use around the time of their accident (Taylor, Kreutzer, & Demm, 2003). In addition to playing a causal role in the injury, substance abuse may ensue or get worse after the traumatic brain injury, as a result of emotional or cognitive changes brought on by the trauma (Corrigan, 1995).

Violence-related incidents account for approximately 20 percent of traumatic brain injuries, including shaken-baby syndrome, which results specifically in brain trauma and spinal cord injury. Finally, sports- and recreation-related injuries account for 3 percent of people hospitalized with traumatic brain injury, though the actual incidence rate of sports-related brain injury is much higher (NIH Consensus Development Panel, 1999).

Treatment of Traumatic Brain Injury For many patients, head injuries can be devastating: They face the arduous task of relearning how to walk, talk, or dress. For others, the deficits are more subtle. Often, the frontal lobes are involved; these patients may lose control over their emotions or their ability to behave in a socially appropriate manner. Depending on the severity of the injury, then, rehabilitation of head injury can range from intensive inpatient treatment, including coma management and residential rehabilitation, to periodic outpatient treatment (Malec & Basford, 1996).

Rehabilitative treatments following traumatic brain injury include restorative training focused on improving a specific cognitive function, such as exercises designed to improve attention, and compensatory training, focused on developing methods to "compensate" for the specific cognitive impairment. A person with memory impairment may be trained in using a notebook to record information, for example. As many as 50 percent of people with traumatic brain injury may develop mood disorders, anxiety disorders, apathy, psychosis, and behavioral disorders (Rao & Lyketsos, 2002). In some cases, these may be an exacerbation of previous disturbance. Psychotherapy is important in helping people with traumatic brain injuries to adjust to changes in their overall functioning, as well as to treat the depression and anxiety that may be associated with the injury; medications are also used to treat associated emotional and behavioral disturbance (NIH Consensus Development Panel, 1999). Cholinesterase inhibitors, which are used as a treatment for dementia, may also hold promise for treatment of traumatic brain injury (Griffin, van Reekum, & Masanic, 2003).

Cerebrovascular Accidents: Strokes

A third category of brain disorder includes the disorders due to a **cerebrovascular accident (CVA)**—better known as a **stroke**—in which blockage or breaking of the blood vessels in the brain results in injury to

Prevention Preventing Traumatic Brain Injuries

Traumatic brain injury (TBI) is one disorder for which simple preventive measures—measures that anyone can take—do make a difference. If bike riders and motorcyclists, rollerbladers and hockey players, all wore protective helmets, the incidence of TBI would fall dramatically: Researchers found that almost half of fatalities and nearly a fifth of head injuries following bicycle accidents could have been avoided if the riders had been wearing helmets (Schulman, Sacks, & Provenzano, 2002).

Numerous studies support the conclusion that helmets and other protective devices save brains. In Canada, Benson, Rose, and Meeuwisse (2002) studied 642 interleague university hockey players over a season to discover the impact of face shield use on concussion, one of the most dangerous sports injuries. Half the young men in the study wore full face shields; the others wore half shields, or visors, for every practice and game. Results demonstrated that the players who wore only half shields missed significantly more practices and games per concussion than players wearing full face shields. In addition, players who wore half face shields and no mouthguards at the time of concussion missed more playing time than players who wore half shields and mouthguards. Players who were wearing full face shields and mouthguards at the time of concussion lost no playing time at all compared with 1.8 sessions lost per concussion for players in full shields but no mouthguards. Clearly, concussion severity may be reduced by the use of a full face shield; a mouthguard helps even more.

The study of bicycle accidents by Schulman, Sacks, and Provenzano (2002) estimated that if all bikers wore helmets, more than 100,000 traumatic brain injuries would be avoided yearly. Another study by the National Highway Traffic Safety Administration (1998) showed that injured motorcyclists who were not wearing helmets at the time of their accident were 3 times as likely to suffer a brain injury as were helmeted injured motorcyclists (Vaca & Berns, 2001)

Despite the fact that these findings have been available to American legislators for years, many states continue to limit or even repeal the universal helmet laws that once were mandated for all motorcyclists. In Florida, where efforts to reenact helmet laws have met with stiff opposition, researchers studied the impact of a repealed motorcycle helmet law on brain injury admissions (Hotz, Cohn, Popkin, et al., 2002). They found that the repeal of the law led to a significant decrease in helmet use and a simultaneous increase in the number and severity of brain injuries admitted to one trauma center.

The NIH estimates the annual cost of acute care and rehabilitation in the United States for new cases of TBI at $9 to $10 billion, with the average lifetime cost of care for a person with severe TBI ranging from $600,000 to $1,875,000. Because TBI may result in lifelong impairment of physical, cognitive, and psychosocial functioning, it is a disorder of major public health significance (NIH Consensus, Statement, 1998). The good news is that TBI is in a great many cases a preventable tragedy. Given the devastation it causes, both personal and public, and the absence of a cure, prevention is of paramount importance.

brain tissue. CVAs are common—indeed, they are the third leading cause of death in the United States. In many cases, the occurrence of the CVA is marked by *stroke syndrome,* the acute onset of specific disabilities involving the central nervous system. The person wakes up from a nap or sits down to dinner, and suddenly he or she can no longer speak, understand speech, move the right side of the body, or perform another function. In some cases, the stroke victim dies immediately or within days. In other cases, the victim not only lives but also does not show stroke syndrome. Many people have what are called "silent strokes," small CVAs that occur in less critical regions of the brain and that have a less noticeable effect on behavior, though the person may find that certain functions, such as memory, are gradually eroded. CVAs are found in 25 percent of routine autopsies, and many of these are silent strokes. There are two broad categories of CVAs: infarction and hemorrhage.

Infarction In **infarction,** the supply of blood to the brain is somehow cut off, resulting in the death of brain tissue fed by that source. The two most common causes of infarction are embolism and thrombosis. In an **embolism,** a ball of something such as fat, air, or clotted blood breaks off from the side of a blood vessel or in some other way enters the bloodstream and floats upward until it reaches a blood vessel too narrow to let it pass. At that point, it blocks the vessel, cutting off the blood flow. In a **thrombosis,** fatty material coating the inside of a blood vessel gradually builds up until it blocks the flow of blood in that vessel. Predictably, these two different causes produce different kinds of onset. When a CVA results from an embolism, onset is usually sudden, with dramatic symptoms: The person may collapse, suffer seizures, become paralyzed. In thrombosis, the onset may be more gradual.

Hemorrhage The other major category of CVA is cerebral **hemorrhage,** in which a blood vessel in the brain ruptures, causing blood to spill out into the brain tissue. When the hemorrhage occurs inside the brain, it is usually traceable to hypertension. A sudden increase in blood pressure—such as is associated with cocaine abuse—can also contribute to a hemorrhage.

When a hemorrhage occurs in the space around the brain, it is usually due to an aneurysm, or bulge in the wall of the blood vessel. Many such hemorrhages can be traced back to congenital aneurysms, in which, the patient was born with a weakened artery wall, which ballooned and eventually ruptured with age. Aneurysms may be as small as a pea or as large as a plum. They are common—they turn up in 2 percent of autopsied adults (Merritt, 1967)—and, if they do not lead to hemorrhage, they may produce no symptoms whatsoever.

The Effects of a Stroke The aftereffects of a stroke depend on the nature of the stroke—infarction or hemorrhage, embolism or thrombosis, hemorrhage within or around the brain—together with the extent of the damage and, above all, the location of the damage. The most common effects are aphasia, agnosia, apraxia, and paralysis, usually of one limb or one half of the body (because a stroke occurs in one brain hemisphere). Of all forms of stroke, the most common is infarction due to thrombosis, usually in the left-middle cerebral artery. Because the left hemisphere of the brain regulates language, aphasia is a very common effect of stroke. And, because most people are right-handed, and the left side of the brain controls the right side of the body, many stroke patients suffer motor impairments in their dominant hand or leg.

These disabilities (whether they result from CVAs or from any other organic brain disorder) are usually accompanied by some degree of emotional disturbance, partly the result of injury and partly a psychological response to the new impairment. Depression is the most common reaction, seen in 40 percent of patients (Robinson, 1997). Another common reaction is emotional lability: The patient may pass from laughing to weeping in an instant. The response depends greatly on the premorbid personality. People with compulsive tendencies are generally intolerant of any reduction in their abilities and therefore may become very depressed after a stroke. Likewise, suspicious natures are exacerbated by the sudden helplessness that accompanies a stroke. Such people may develop paranoid symptoms, accusing others of making fun of them, of stealing their belongings, and so forth. The symptomatology, then, is the result not just of a specific disorder in a specific part of the brain but also of this disorder's interaction with specific personality features.

Half of first-stroke patients die within 5 years, usually from another stroke (Terént, 1993). This is a harsh statistic, but in fact it represents a medical victory. Stroke survival rates have almost doubled since the 1940s (Whisnant, 1993), and they are still improving. In patients who survive, some of the behavioral symptoms may disappear spontaneously, while others can be remedied through rehabilitation. And, as the disability is remedied, so in most cases is the attendant emotional disturbance. Some CVA patients recover completely, but most continue to labor under some form of impairment for the rest of their lives. In general, the younger the patient and the smaller the area of brain damage, the better the chance of recovery.

A therapist works with a patient to improve motor functions impaired by a stroke.

❖ Groups at Risk

The clearest risk factor for CVAs is age. Between the ages of 60 and 80, the risk increases almost eightfold. In people over 75, the rate of first stroke is almost 20 times that of the general population (Terént, 1993). That is because the incidence of physical conditions that weaken the blood vessels—above all, hypertension, heart disease, and atherosclerosis, or thickening of the walls of the blood vessels—increases with age.

Another risk factor is gender. Men are more vulnerable than women by a ratio of 1.3 to 1 (Kurtzke, 1980). The women's advantage is due in part to the fact that estrogen seems to protect against atherosclerosis, but even after menopause, when estrogen levels fall, women are still somewhat less susceptible to strokes. Other higher-risk groups are diabetics, people with a family history of strokes, and African Americans, who bear twice the stroke risk of most other ethnic groups (Singleton & Johnson, 1993).

Those are the uncontrollable risk factors. In addition, there are several other conditions that make people vulnerable to this disorder. High cholesterol and obesity increase stroke risk; smoking almost doubles it; hypertension increases it from two to five times (Boysen, 1993). All these factors can be controlled.

Treatment of Stroke Fearing heart attack, most people tend to seek medical attention quickly when they experience chest pain. However, people often ignore the first signs of stroke. A tingling or weakness on one side of the body, a drooping face, difficulty understanding or expressing oneself—all may be signs of a stroke. The importance of seeking treatment at the first appearance of such symptoms cannot be overemphasized. Medications have been developed that can limit the effects of a stroke, if they are administered in a timely manner (Albers, 1997).

Brain Tumors

Brain tumors are classified as either metastatic or primary. **Metastatic brain tumors** originate in a different part of the body and then metastasize, or spread, to the brain. Usually, they develop from cancer of the lung, breast, stomach, or kidney and travel to the brain through the blood vessels. By contrast, **primary brain tumors,** as their name suggests, originate in the brain. Some primary tumors are *intracerebral*—that is, they grow inside the brain tissue. Others are *extracerebral,* growing outside the brain but inside the skull, often in the meninges. Intracranial tumors are more frequently seen in adults; extracranial tumors, in children. Brain tumors in general are common. Every year about 20,000 new primary brain tumors are diagnosed, and another 20,000 people are diagnosed as having metastatic brain tumors (Segal, 1991).

Although the actual cause of tumors has not yet been determined, their clinical course is clear. For some reason, a few cells begin to grow at an abnormally rapid rate, destroying the surrounding healthy brain tissue and resulting in a wide variety of psychological symptoms. In most cases, the first signs are subtle and insidious—headaches, seizures, visual problems, neglect of personal hygiene, indifference to previously valued activities, and failures of judgment and foresight. With the progressive destruction of brain tissue, the patient eventually develops at least one of the more obvious symptoms: abnormal reflexes; blunting of affect; disorientation in regard to time, place, and/or person; poor memory and concentration; double vision; and jerky motor coordination. The kind and severity of symptoms are directly related to the location of the tumor in the brain: The functions controlled by that section are probably impaired earlier and more severely than other functions. However, as the tumor grows, pressing against other sections, their functioning too is affected.

Any tumor that continues to grow, untreated, in the brain will eventually cause extreme physical distress (splitting headaches, vomiting, seizures), along with personality changes that may reach psychotic proportions. Some patients develop this so-called acquired sociopathy suddenly, after an illness (Eslinger & Damasio, 1985; Barrash, Tranel, & Anderson, 2000). Just before death, the patient may become overtly psychotic and, finally, lapse into a coma.

❖ Groups at Risk

Not much is known about risk factors for brain tumors. About all that can be said is that some types of cancer, such as lung cancer, metastasize to the brain; a significant risk factor for lung cancer, of course, is smoking.

Treatment of Brain Tumors Several types of tumors can be removed surgically, and in many cases they are. However, because the surgery itself can cause additional brain damage, the physician may choose to avoid it. Surgeons are especially reluctant to operate on the language areas and on the major motor areas. In such cases, radiation treatment may be used, though this too can destroy brain tissue. In other cases, surgery, chemotherapy, and radiation are used in combination, both to remove the growth and to prevent future growths.

Degenerative Disorders

Degenerative disorders are syndromes characterized by a general deterioration of intellectual, emotional, and motor functioning as a result of progressive pathological change in the brain. As usual with organic brain disorders, symptoms vary, depending on the site of the damage (Cummings & Benson, 1992). Disorders caused by deterioration of the cerebral cortex produce memory disturbances, impaired comprehension, naming difficulties, and environmental disorientation. Until the late stages of the disease, gait, posture, muscle tone, and reflexes are usually unimpaired. Alzheimer's disease is such a disorder. In disorders caused by deterioration of the subcortical regions of the brain (below the cerebral cortex), the usual symptoms are slowed thinking, difficulty in solving problems, mood disturbances, and motor disturbances. Huntington's chorea and Parkinson's disease are disorders of this type. Still other disorders are caused by vascular disease that affects both the cortical and subcortical regions of the brain. These disorders are characterized by abrupt onset, stepwise deterioration—that is, deterioration in a series of downward plateaus—and focal symptoms, such as aphasia. Vascular dementia is an example of this last category.

Is Severe Cognitive Deterioration Inevitable with Advancing Age? Not for Some

The MindMAP video "Cognitive Functioning in Centenarians" presents a 100-year old man whose cognitive abilities are as good as those of most young adults. Why do you think some older adults and centenarians show little cognitive deterioration or decline? What conditions do you think help foster and maintain high cognitive functioning in aging adults? Why?

Aging and Dementia Psychologists used to think that **dementia,** or severe mental deterioration, was a final stage of aging that would occur in everyone who lived long enough. Today, we know that dementia is the result of degenerative brain disorders that affect only a small minority of the aged. Approximately 4 to 7 percent of people over 65 have definite signs of dementia. Prevalence rises with age, however: Among people over 85, about 30 percent show dementia (Johansson & Zarit, 1991; Kokmen, Beard, Offord, et al., 1989). Fortunately, even at such advanced ages, most people have little or no evidence of degenerative brain disorder—no pronounced loss of memory, impaired reasoning, or impaired judgment.

Almost all old people experience some psychological changes simply as a function of aging. Although the precise biological processes are still not clear, it seems that all behavior mediated by the central nervous system slows down as the body ages. Old people in general experience a slowing of motor reactions, a reduced capacity to process complex information, and decreased efficiency in memory and in the learning of new material. These changes are part of the normal process of aging; they are no more pathological than wrinkles or gray hair. By contrast, the degenerative diseases known collectively as dementias are pathological; they are the direct result of a severe organic deterioration of the brain. Dementias account for more hospital admissions and for more inpatient hospital days than any other psychiatric disorder among elderly people (Cummings & Benson, 1992). The most common dementias are Alzheimer's disease, Lewy body disease, and frontotemporal dementia.

The diagnosis of these syndromes is a complicated matter. A host of treatable problems, including other illnesses, reactions to medication, and depression, can mimic the symptoms of dementia. Furthermore, Alzheimer's disease is sometimes difficult to distinguish from other dementias. The courses of these disorders do differ: For instance, vascular dementia involves a stepwise deterioration, whereas in Alzheimer's the deterioration is smooth and gradual. But, usually, when the patient comes for diagnosis, most of the course is in the future, and there is considerable overlap between symptoms. As yet, there is no sure medical test for Alzheimer's disease; the disorder cannot be diagnosed conclusively until postmortem examination. To make matters worse, many dementia patients have *both* Alzheimer's and Lewy body disease or vascular dementia. A final source of confusion is one mentioned earlier: The symptoms in any case of acquired brain disorder have everything to do with the patient's premorbid personality and psychosocial history, the availability of outside supports, and any number of other intangible factors. This is particularly true of the elderly. Two patients with the same disorder may behave quite differently.

Alzheimer's Disease The most common form of dementia, and one of the most tragic, is **Alzheimer's disease.** Autopsies of patients with this disorder reveal both neurofibrillary tangles (twisted and distorted nerve fibers) and senile plaques (microscopic lesions in the neurons). Alzheimer's can occur as early as age 40, but its prevalence increases with age. It is estimated that, in the United States, 4 to 5 percent of people over age 65, and 20 percent over 85, suffer from Alzheimer's (Johansson & Zarit, 1995).

The primary symptoms of Alzheimer's disease are cognitive deficits—particularly, loss of memory for recent events. An Alzheimer's patient may be able to tell you the names of all the people in the office where

Former president Ronald Reagan suffers from Alzheimer's disease, the most common form of dementia.

she worked 50 years ago, and all their children's names, but not what she ate for breakfast that morning. As the disease worsens, there is loss of memory for distant events as well. The characteristic early signs of the disease are irritability and failure of concentration and memory, with mild difficulty in recalling names and words. Patients may also have problems with perception and spatial orientation.

The cognitive deficits of Alzheimer's patients create major difficulties for them and their families. Usually, complex behaviors such as playing poker or balancing the checkbook are disrupted first, but eventually simple, daily behaviors such as bathing and dressing also degenerate. Patients may also do things that are disturbing or simply stressful to their caregivers. They may ask the same question over and over; they may confuse night and day. Some forget that they have turned on the bath water or have lit the stove; some wander off and get lost; some become violent. As they weaken physically, they are likely to become bedridden. At this point, they may have little awareness of their surroundings. The rate of progression of the disease is highly variable. In some people, severe impairment and death occur between 3 and 5 years after onset, while other patients live 15 years or more after onset.

Gene research indicates that the disorder is controlled in part by genes, but in a complex way, involving not just one genetic abnormality but several (Hardy, 1993). The normal human cell contains 23 pairs of chromosomes, each of which has been numbered and partially "mapped" as to which genes it contains. The first breakthroughs in genetic research on Alzheimer's had to do with chromosome 21. It is a well-documented fact that almost all people with Down syndrome (Chapter 17), a disorder caused by the addition of a copy of chromosome 21, develop Alzheimer's disease if they live past age 40 (Zigman, Schupf, Zigman, et al., 1992). Thus, Alzheimer's researchers were alerted to the possible involvement of chromosome 21, and their interest was further piqued by the discovery that the production of amyloid, the substance at the core of the senile plaques found in the brains of Alzheimer's patients, is controlled by genes on chromosome 21 (Goldgaber, Lerman, McBride, et al., 1987). Finally, in 1987, researchers at Massachusetts General Hospital announced that they had found abnormalities on chromosome 21 in four families with a long history—145 cases—of Alzheimer's disease (Tanzi, Gusella, Watkins, et al., 1987).

However, efforts to replicate those findings were only partly successful. Today, while it is accepted that chromosome 21 may be involved in some cases of Alzheimer's, interest has shifted to two other chromosomes: chromosome 14, which is associated with early-onset (before age 60) cases, and chromosome 19, which is implicated in many late-onset cases. But this is not the end of the story. The Germans of the Volga region and their American descendants, who have a strong inherited pattern of Alzheimer's, do not seem to show abnormalities at any of the identified sites on chromosomes 21, 14, or 19, so other chromosomes are probably involved as well. Indeed, chromosomes 12 and 1 have been linked to Alzheimer's disease (Pericek-Vance, Bass, Yamaoka, et al., 1997).

To account for this heterogeneity, researchers have proposed the so-called amyloid-cascade hypothesis (Hardy, 1993). According to this hypothesis, the key element in the onset of Alzheimer's disease is the buildup of toxic levels of one kind of amyloid, beta amyloid, in the brain, but this buildup can be caused by the breakdown of any one of several regulatory mechanisms, each controlled by a different gene. Researchers have discovered, for example, that beta-amyloid accumulations (and a high risk for Alzheimer's) are linked to variations in a protein, ApoE (apolipoprotein E), that is controlled by genes on chromosome 19 (Corder, Saunders, Strittmatter, et al., 1993). That protein, however, is only one element in the long chain of reactions that, according to the cascade theory, constitutes the brain's processing of beta amyloid. Thus, ApoE is one link that can break, in which case the fault lies on chromosome 19. But other links, controlled by other genes, may also break.

Thus, Alzheimer's is one of those disorders, like schizophrenia, for which researchers have identified multiple contributing factors but no single cause. And, as with schizophrenia, many researchers feel that in any given case the causes probably are multiple. Gatz and her colleagues, for example, have proposed a "threshold model" for Alzheimer's, whereby genetic risk together with any combination of other risk factors—head injury, exposure to toxic substances, alcohol abuse, poor nutrition, even lack of mental stimulation—gradually brings the person closer to a threshold beyond which symptoms begin to appear (Gatz, Lowe, Berg, et al., 1994).

Lewy Body Disease Today, Alzheimer's disease is a relatively well-known cause of dementia in the elderly. But another, less-well-known disorder, Lewy body disease, is the second most common degenerative brain disease. Lewy body disease affects an estimated 15 to 25 percent of elderly patients who suffer from dementia (McKeith, Galasko, Kosaka, et al., 1996). The disorder gets its name from the presence of microscopic rounded structures called *Lewy bodies* in neurons throughout the brain. Composed mostly of altered neurofilaments, Lewy bodies also contain a protein called ubiquitin, whose function is to break down abnormal cellular proteins (Kalra, Bergeron, & Lang, 1996).

Because the presence of Lewy bodies is usually confirmed only by autopsy, clinicians must rely on an analysis of the patient's symptoms to diagnose the disease. The task is complicated by the fact that, in some cases, the symptoms of Lewy body disease are similar to those of Alzheimer's. Indeed, the same plaques and tangled neurons associated with Alzheimer's are found in the brains of about 50 percent of those with Lewy body disease. Furthermore, in many cases, Lewy body disease is followed by Parkinson's disease. Lewy body disease may be linked genetically to both Alzheimer's and Parkinson's (Kalra, Bergeron, & Lang, 1996). Given the overlapping symptoms, the classification of the disorder is still a matter of controversy; some researchers consider Lewy body disease to be a variant of Alzheimer's or Parkinson's, while others do not (Cercy & Bylsma, 1997).

Perhaps the most distinguishing symptom of Lewy body disease is the day-to-day fluctuations in the patient's mental state. Hallucinations, confusion, agitation, and delusions come and go, often in a matter of minutes. Unexplained falls and transient clouding or loss of consciousness are also distinctive. (These symptoms do not fit well with *DSM-IV-TR* criteria, which require the exclusion of delirium before a diagnosis of dementia is made.) Like Alzheimer's, Lewy body disease occurs most often in the elderly. All cases eventually progress to dementia, and most involve memory impairment followed by symptoms of Parkinson's disease, particularly rigidity (Kalra, Bergeron, & Lang, 1996).

Vascular Dementia As we saw earlier, an infarction is a kind of stroke in which blood flow in the brain becomes blocked, resulting in damage to the area of the brain fed by the blood vessels in question. (The damaged area is called an *infarct.*) **Vascular dementia** is the cumulative effect of a number of small strokes of this kind, eventually impairing many of the brain's faculties. The physical signs of vascular dementia are blackouts, heart problems, kidney failure, hypertension, and retinal sclerosis (a scarring of the retina of the eye). Common psychological symptoms are language and memory defects, emotional lability, and depression. Psychosis may also develop, typically with delusions of persecution. As noted, some of these symptoms overlap those of Alzheimer's, making diagnosis difficult.

Alzheimer's disease, Lewy body disease, and vascular dementia all affect mainly the elderly. The degenerative disorders to which we now turn—frontotemporal dementia, Huntington's chorea, and Parkinson's disease—afflict the middle-aged or, in the case of Huntington's, young adults.

Frontotemporal Dementia **Frontotemporal dementia** is the result of progressive deterioration of the frontal and temporal lobes of the brain. The disorder usually occurs between ages 45 and 65 and accounts for approximately 20 percent of middle-age-onset degenerative dementias (Snowden, Bathgate, Varma, et al., 2001). The illness shows equal incidence in men and women; the average duration is 8 years, with a range of 2 to 20 years (Snowden, Neary, & Mann, 2002). Frontotemporal dementia accounts for about 70 percent of the three syndromes associated with degeneration of the frontal and temporal lobes. The others are *semantic dementia,* in which the ability to understand the meaning of words, faces, smells, tastes, and tactile stimuli is progressively lost, and *progressive nonfluent aphasia,* which is characterized by language impairment, including struggles with speech and word retrieval.

The overriding feature of frontotemporal dementia is a profound change in behavior. People with frontotemporal dementia become disinhibited, easily distracted, socially inappropriate, and engage in purposeless overactivity. They may show an increased talkativeness and sexuality and make tactless or offensive comments. Some patients, on the other hand, may become inactive and apathetic. Other features include emotional blunting and loss of empathy; overeating, especially of sweets; a decline in personal hygiene; and repetitive behaviors such as foot tapping or humming. Patients are unaware of the changes in their behavior and indifferent when others confront them about the changes. Because of the marked behavioral changes in people with frontotemporal dementia, differentiating this syndrome from psychological disorders may be difficult (Snowden, Neary, & Mann, 2002; Neary, Snowden, Gustafson, et al., 1998).

Like Alzheimer's disease, frontotemporal dementia is probably caused by many factors, but a family history of the disorder is present in just under half of the cases (Snowden, Neary, & Mann, 2002; Pasquier & Delacourte, 1998). Genetic studies have linked chromosomes 17, 9, and 3 to some cases of frontotemporal dementia. A mutation of the tau gene is also found in some cases (Lovestone, Anderton, Betts, et al., 2001).

Huntington's Chorea **Huntington's chorea** is one of the very few neurological disorders definitely known to be transmitted genetically. It is passed on by a dominant gene from either parent to both male and female children. Forty to 70 cases of Huntington's chorea occur in every 1 million people (Cummings & Benson, 1992).

The primary site of the damage that causes Huntington's chorea is the basal ganglia, clusters of nerve-cell bodies located deep within the cerebral hemispheres and responsible primarily for posture, muscle tonus, and motor coordination. However, the first signs of the disease are not so much motor impairments as vague behavioral and emotional changes. In the typical case, the person becomes slovenly and rude, and his or her moods become unpredictable and inconsistent, running the gamut from obstinacy, passivity, and depression to inexplicable euphoria. Intellectual functions, particularly memory and judgment, are also disrupted. As the disease progresses, delusions, hallucinations, and suicidal tendencies commonly appear (Boll, Heaton, & Reitan, 1974).

In addition to developing these psychological problems, the patient eventually begins to show the characteristic motor symptoms—an involuntary, spasmodic jerking of the limbs—to which the term *chorea* (from the Greek *choreia,* meaning "dance") refers. This sign appears to indicate irreversible brain damage (James, Mefford, & Kimbell, 1969). From then on, patients show increasingly bizarre behavior. They may spit, bark out words (often obscenities) explosively, walk with a jerky or shuffling gait, and smack their tongues and lips involuntarily. Eventually, they lose control of bodily functions altogether. Death is the inevitable result, occurring, on average, 14 years after onset.

Parkinson's Disease First described in 1871 by James Parkinson (who suffered from it), **Parkinson's disease** also involves damage to the basal ganglia, particularly the region known as the substantia nigra. The cause of this condition is unknown,

Boxer Muhammad Ali (left) and actor Michael J. Fox (right) both suffer from Parkinson's disease and are outspoken advocates for research on its causes and treatment.

although it has been attributed to a variety of factors, including heredity, encephalitis, viruses, toxins, deficient brain metabolism, and head trauma. The illness occurs most frequently in people between the ages of 50 and 70.

The primary symptom of Parkinson's is tremor, a rhythmic jerking of arms, hands, jaws, and/or head. The tremors are usually present during rest periods but tend to diminish or cease when the patient is sleeping. Another highly characteristic sign of Parkinson's is an expressionless, masklike countenance, probably due to difficulties initiating movement and slowed motor responses. Parkinson's patients also tend to walk, when they *can* walk, with a distinctive slow, stiff gait, usually accompanied by a slight crouch.

Approximately 40 to 60 percent of Parkinson's disease patients also experience psychological disturbances. These include problems with memory, learning, judgment, and concentration, as well as apathy and social withdrawal. As many as half of Parkinson's patients also develop dementia. In more severe cases, there may be highly systematized delusions and severe depression, including suicidal tendencies. However, it is difficult to determine whether these symptoms are due directly to the brain pathology or simply to patients' distress over their physical helplessness.

❖ Groups at Risk

We have seen that the incidence of dementia increases with age. Because women live longer than men, many more women than men will experience dementia. However, at any given age, the percentage of men and women who will develop dementia is the same (Kokmen, Beard, O'Brien, et al., 1993).

Both age and gender are related to the type of dementia an individual is likely to develop. Patients with pure Lewy body disease (uncomplicated by symptoms of Alzheimer's) tend to be identified at a younger age than those with Alzheimer's, many of them before they develop dementia. Patients with mixed symptoms of Lewy body and Alzheimer's tend to be older, and most are demented when they are first seen (Cercy & Bylsma, 1997). Though women as a group live longer than men, men are twice as likely as women to develop Lewy body disease (Kalra, Bergeron, & Lang, 1996). In one retrospective study, most of the subjects diagnosed with Lewy body disease at autopsy were male, while most of those diagnosed with Alzheimer's were female (Klatka, Louis, & Schiffer, 1996).

Research also suggests that educational level may affect either the incidence or rate of diagnosis of Alzheimer's disease. Several studies have suggested a connection between the disease and limited education, perhaps because education can affect performance on the diagnostic tests administered to patients to detect cognitive impairment. In a follow-up study of nearly 600 subjects of 60 years of age or older, researchers found that the risk of dementia was higher among subjects of low educational level and/or low lifetime occupational achievement. The risk was highest among subjects with both a low educational level and low lifetime achievement (Stern, Gurland, Tatemichi, et al., 1994). Researchers were unsure whether these factors merely increased the likelihood of diagnosis or they somehow contributed to the onset of the disease.

Vascular dementia occurs in about 3 percent of people over 65 (Cummings, 1987). An estimated 53 percent of stroke patients also go on to develop vascular dementia. The major risk factor for the disorder is high blood pressure. Eighty percent of vascular dementia patients have a history of hypertension; for this reason, African Americans are probably at greater risk for vascular dementia than are other ethnic groups. Other risk factors are diabetes, obesity, and smoking.

Huntington's chorea is a genetic disorder, and the defective gene has been identified. There is now a test that can identify carriers, and it may eventually be possible, through genetic engineering, to treat them before symptoms develop. Frontotemporal dementia does have a familial element, and genetic studies have linked several different genes to this disorder. However, research is ongoing.

Treatment of Degenerative Disorders It is known that in Alzheimer's disease the production of the neurotransmitter acetylcholine is disrupted. Therefore, presumably, the symptoms might be relieved if levels of acetylcholine could be raised. Following this reasoning, researchers developed a drug, tacrine—its brand name is Cognex—that blocks acetylcholine reuptake. The first drug specifically approved for treating Alzheimer's patients, Cognex went on the market in the early 1990s amid a great blast of publicity. The results were disappointing, however. Only 20 to 30 percent of patients on Cognex showed any benefits. Furthermore, the benefits were modest and, in some cases, transient (Farlow, Gracon, Hershey, et al., 1992), while the side effects, including liver problems, were serious.

Since then, several other drugs that block acetylcholine reuptake have been approved for use in Alzheimer's disease. The most commonly used medication today is Aricept, which research has found to delay the functional decline in patients with Alzheimer's disease by an average of 4 months (Grundman &

Focus On... Caregivers: The Hidden Victims of Dementia

Caring for a patient with dementia can be brutally taxing. What follows is the record of a typical day in the life of a young woman living with her husband, her 7-year-old son, and her grandmother, a dementia patient:

> The caregiver's day began at 5 A.M. when she got up and did light housekeeping chores. At 6, she prepared breakfast for her husband, and they had breakfast together. At 6:30, she woke her son up and began helping him get ready for school. From that time until 8, she either did chores or was with her son. At 8, she began the bathwater for her grandmother. Her grandmother got up at 8:15 and she assisted her with her bath and then with dressing. At 8:45, she fixed breakfast for her grandmother and gave her medications. After breakfast, her grandmother sat in a rocker and watched television until about 10:15. During this time, she talked to an ornamental Santa Claus (it was a few days before Christmas), calling it by her great-grandson's name. The caregiver did not intervene and was not disturbed by this behavior. She was cleaning in the kitchen during this time. From 10:15 to 12, the caregiver did housekeeping chores and the patient followed her around. She asked repeatedly to go out and see Fred (her deceased husband). The caregiver made excuses why they could not go out, which satisfied the patient. She also gave the patient a snack during this period. At noon, the patient laid down on the couch and rested. The caregiver then did some laundry. Her grandmother called to her a few times during this period, and she would then go to her to tuck her in again.

The afternoon and evening followed the same pattern, except that the woman was now looking after her son as well as her grandmother and handling friction between the two. At one point,

> the patient became agitated because of the noise her great-grandson was making while playing, and she hit him on the head with a newspaper. The caregiver intervened, but the patient denied doing anything.

Finally, by 10:30 P.M., the woman got both the son and the grandmother into bed:

> From 11:10 to 11:20, the caregiver had a cup of tea and watched television. At 11:20, her husband came home, and she fixed him supper. They talked until 12:10 A.M. and then went to bed. At 2:00 A.M., her grandmother called for assistance to go to the bathroom, and then had difficulty going back to sleep. To calm her, the caregiver talked with her about Christmases they had spent together in the past when the caregiver was a child. At 2:30, they both went back to bed, and the caregiver slept until 5 A.M. (Zarit, 1992, pp. 3–5)

As noted, many dementia patients, such as those with Alzheimer's, may live for 15 years or more after the onset of symptoms. Almost everyone agrees that the best situation for such patients is to remain with their families when possible, but this places a huge burden on the family. Even if patients are not agitated, as they often are, they still require constant supervision, and many of them sleep so little that they need close to 24-hour care.

In consequence, the family members suffer considerable stress (Gatz, Bengston, & Blum, 1990) and not just in the caregiving situation. They may have to give up their leisure activities and social lives; indeed, they may have to quit their jobs. (The woman in this case did.) Or, if they go on working, they must struggle to divide their time between the requirements of the job and those of the patient, while their spare minutes are often spent arguing over the phone with other relatives over what should be done with the patient. Such a situation can lead to what researchers have called an "erosion of the self-concept" (Pearlin, Mullan, Semple, et al., 1990). The caregiver feels that he or she no longer has a self; it has been parceled out for use by others. Predictably, Alzheimer's caregivers are at higher-than-average risk for psychological disorders (Zarit, 1994). They also show lowered immune responses and are therefore more susceptible to physical disorders (Kiecolt-Glaser, Dura, Speicher, et al., 1991).

How can the caregivers be cared for? As soon as possible after the diagnosis of a degenerative brain disorder, the family members should meet with the professional who can advise them. This may be a psychologist, a social worker, or a representative of the Alzheimer's Association or another, similar organization. Such a professional can tell them what to expect as the disease progresses, teach them simple behavior-management techniques for coping with agitation, and direct them to services that can give them relief, such as adult day care and overnight respite care. (In the latter, the patient stays for short periods in a hospital or nursing home. This can free the family to take a vacation.) Legal and financial counseling is usually critical, so that families can plan how to manage the expense of caring for a dementia patient. And, if there is conflict among the family members, as there typically is in this stressful situation, they can be referred for family counseling, which is often very effective for relatives of dementia patients (Mittelman, Ferris, Steinberg, et al., 1993; Whitlatch, Zarit, & von Eye, 1991).

Finally, caregivers can join a support group. Support groups have been found to be very helpful to people with a wide range of problems—cancer patients, drug abusers, families of drug abusers, and so on. They can also be useful to families of dementia patients, providing them with tips, fellowship, and the kind of understanding that can come only from people in the same situation.

Comprehensive counseling and support benefit patients as well as their caregivers. In a recent study of more than 200 Alzheimer's patients and their caregivers, researchers found that, in families that received such services, caregivers were able to care for patients at home (rather than placing them in a nursing home) almost a year longer than were caregivers in a control group. Caregivers who belonged to the group that received counseling and support were only about two thirds as likely as those in the control group to place their spouses in a nursing home (Mittelman, Ferris, Shulman, et al., 1996).

Thal, 2000). Moreover, Aricept does not have an adverse effect on liver function (Rogers, Friedhoff, Apter, et al., 1996).

Another treatment that shows promise is a daily dose of 2,000 IU of vitamin E. In a 2-year study of more than 300 subjects, vitamin E slowed the progression of Alzheimer's disease among subjects with moderately severe impairment. Patients who took the vitamin lived longer, were institutionalized later, and retained the ability to perform basic activities longer than those who took a placebo (Sano, Ernesto, Thomas, et al., 1997). Anti-inflammatory drugs have shown some benefit, but there appear to be significant long-term side effects associated with their use. Research on estrogen replacement therapy in older women has not been promising (Bullock, 2002). Other classes of drugs are under investigation, including muscarinic agonists and nicotinic drugs; the latter has had some promising early findings.

At present, then, there is no cure and little treatment for Alzheimer's disease. Behavior therapy techniques may suppress some symptoms. Tranquilizers may also be useful, though in some patients they make the symptoms worse. The most common treatment is custodial care, often in a nursing home. Still, many patients are able to remain at home with their families, especially if the families can rely on professional support services. The development of such services (see the box on caregivers on the previous page) is one of the most hopeful avenues in the treatment of degenerative brain diseases.

Like Alzheimer's disease, Lewy body disease and frontotemporal dementias are still not curable. However, there has been progress in treating the symptoms. Rivastigmine, which blocks acetylcholine reuptake, has been found to reduce the psychiatric symptoms, such as delusions, apathy, agitation, and hallucinations of Lewy body disease (McKeith, 2002). In individuals with frontotemporal dementia, the selective serotonin reuptake inhibitors have reduced disinhibited and compulsive, stereotypical behaviors (Snowden, Neary, & Mann, 2002).

We have seen that high blood pressure, diabetes, obesity, and smoking are risk factors for vascular dementia. Better control of these problems may help in the prevention of vascular dementia, but, as with the other degenerative disorders, there is no cure. Once the damage has occurred, decline is irreversible.

Parkinson's is unusual among degenerative disorders in that it can be treated with some success. The substantia nigra is involved in dopamine synthesis, so, when this area degenerates in the course of Parkinson's, the patient's dopamine levels drop. Drugs that increase the amount of dopamine can in most cases control the tremor and other motor symptoms for several years, though they cannot cure the disease. Unfortunately, the beneficial effects of these medications decline with long-term use.

Nutritional Deficiency

Malnutrition—or, specifically, insufficient intake of one or more essential vitamins—can result in neurological damage and, consequently, in psychological disturbances. Two common syndromes in less industrialized nations are beriberi, due to thiamine deficiency, and pellagra, due to niacin deficiency, but improvements in diet have largely eliminated these conditions from the American population. More commonly seen in this country is Korsakoff's psychosis.

Korsakoff's psychosis is considered irreversible. Alcoholics are the most common victims because of their notoriously bad diets. It is generally agreed that the primary pathology in this disorder is due to a deficiency of vitamin B_1, or thiamine (Brion, 1969; Redlich & Freedman, 1966).

There are two classic behavioral signs of Korsakoff's psychosis, anterograde amnesia and confabulation. *Anterograde amnesia* is the inability to incorporate new memories, and *confabulation* is the tendency to fill in memory gaps with invented stories. In response to questioning, for example, patients may placidly offer a nonsensical account of why they are in the hospital, if indeed they admit that the place is a hospital. Such patients usually seem calm and affable, while their total unawareness of the fantastic quality of their stories reveals a psychotic impairment of judgment. This impairment gradually spreads to other aspects of psychological functioning. In addition to having these memory deficits, many alcoholics experience a more generalized intellectual decline. Like the degenerative diseases previously discussed, chronic alcoholism can lead to deficits in most cognitive abilities (Cummings & Benson, 1992).

Endocrine Disorders

The **endocrine glands** are responsible for the production of hormones. When released into the bloodstream, the hormones affect various bodily mechanisms, such as sexual functions, physical growth and development, and the availability of energy. Disturbances in the endocrine system, and particularly in the thyroid and adrenal glands, can give rise to a variety of psychological disorders.

Thyroid Syndromes Overactivity of the thyroid gland—a condition called *hyperthyroidism*, or *Graves' disease*—involves an excessive secretion of the hormone thyroxin, which gives rise to a variety of physical and psychological difficulties. Psychological symptoms accompanying the disorder may include severe apprehension and agitation, easy fatigability, excessive motor activity, sweating, and other symptoms suggestive of anxiety. Former president George Bush and his wife, Barbara, both suffer from Graves' disease.

Opposite to hyperthyroidism in both cause and effect is *hypothyroidism,* sometimes referred to as *myxedema,* in which underactivity of the thyroid gland results in deficient production of thyroxin. Hypothyroidism may be due to iodine deficiency, a problem that has become much less common in the United States since the advent of iodized table salt. People suffering from hypothyroidism are frequently sluggish, have difficulties with memory and concentration, and appear to be lethargic and depressed.

Adrenal Syndromes Chronic underactivity of the cortex, or outer layer, of the adrenal glands gives rise to *Addison's disease,* which involves both physical and psychological changes. Some patients just seem moderately depressed; others experience debilitating extremes of depression, anxiety, and irritability. Appropriate medication can relieve the symptoms of even a severe case of Addison's disease, restoring the person to normal functioning.

When the adrenal cortex is excessively active, several disorders may arise, one of which is *Cushing's syndrome.* This relatively rare disorder usually affects young women. Like the other endocrine disorders, Cushing's syndrome involves both physical symptoms—in this case, obesity and muscle weakness—and psychological difficulties, especially extreme emotional lability, with fluctuations in mood ranging from total indifference to violent hostility.

Toxic Disorders

Various plants, gases, drugs, and metals, when ingested or absorbed through the skin, can have a toxic, or poisonous, effect on the brain. Depending on the person, the substance, and the amount ingested, the results of such toxic poisoning range from temporary physical, cognitive, and emotional distress to psychosis and death.

Lead An especially tragic form of toxic brain disorder is lead poisoning. The excessive ingestion of lead may cause a condition called **lead encephalopathy,** in which fluid accumulates in the brain, causing extreme pressure. Early symptoms include abdominal pains, constipation, facial pallor, and sometimes convulsions and bizarre behaviors such as hair pulling. In severe cases, the symptoms may be similar to those of psychosis, including hallucinations. The most common victims of lead poisoning are children, who may incur cognitive and behavioral impairments as a result of exposure to high levels of lead.

Children who eat lead-based paint chips may fall victim to lead poisoning and suffer from neuropsychological difficulties as a result.

Consumer advocacy groups have identified a number of sources of lead contamination, including old, lead-lined water pipes, lead-based paint on children's toys and furniture, old plaster walls, candles with lead-core wicks, certain electric tea kettles that release lead from soft solder joints when heated, pottery glazes from which foods that contain acetic acid (e.g., grape juice) can leach lead, exhaust from automobiles that burn leaded gasoline, and industrial pollution. As can be seen from this list, the issue of metal poisoning often involves a conflict between the needs of industry and the needs of the person.

Other Heavy-Metal Toxins The "industry versus the individual" conflict also crops up in two of the more common varieties of heavy-metal poisoning, mercury and manganese poisoning. Victims of these toxic disorders are usually those whose jobs bring them into close daily contact with mercury and manganese. However, other victims are simply unwitting citizens whose food or air has been contaminated by industrial wastes containing metallic toxins. One notorious source of such poisoning is fish taken from waters polluted by mercury wastes from nearby factories. In Japan, thousands of people have been permanently paralyzed and brain-damaged as a result of eating mercury-contaminated fish.

Early signs of brain damage due to mercury poisoning are memory loss, irritability, and difficulty in concentration. As the disease progresses, the individual typically develops tunnel vision (i.e., loss of peripheral vision), faulty motor coordination, and difficulty in speaking and hearing. In extreme cases, these symptoms lead to paralysis, coma, and death. Manganese poisoning is manifested in motor and speech impairments, restlessness, and emotional instability. Some experts believe that the personality changes that accompany both types of poisoning are often simply pathological exaggerations of the individual's premorbid personality traits.

Psychoactive Drugs As we saw in Chapter 12, abuse of psychoactive drugs such as alcohol, opiates, and amphetamines can cause severe psychological disturbances. Other drugs have also been implicated in brain damage. The inhalation of aerosol gases and the fumes of certain glues, for example, is a popular source of a "high" among adolescents. Unfortunately, the toxins in these gases and fumes tend to accumulate in the users' vital organs and can cause permanent damage, not only to the liver and kidneys but also to the brain, resulting in neuropsychological deterioration and, in extreme cases, death.

Carbon Monoxide Carbon monoxide, an odorless, tasteless, and invisible gas usually inhaled with automobile exhaust fumes, combines with the hemoglobin in the blood in such a way as to prevent the blood from absorbing oxygen. The usual result of this process is a swift and rather painless death, which makes carbon monoxide inhalation a favored means of suicide. Patients who survive, however, suffer a number of neuropsychological consequences, typically including apathy, confusion, and memory defects. While these symptoms may clear up within two years, some patients suffer permanent damage (Kolb, 1982).

The Epilepsies

Approximately 0.6 percent of Americans suffer from the disease called epilepsy (Sander, 2003). **Epilepsy** is a broad term covering a range of disorders. In all of them, however, the primary symptom is recurrent seizures caused by a disruption of the electrical and physiological activity of the brain cells. This abnormal activity, which can usually be documented by electroencephalography, or EEG, in turn disrupts the functions controlled by the affected part of the brain.

Causes of Epilepsy

Any condition that interferes with the brain's functioning, altering brain-wave patterns, can cause epilepsy. This may happen at any time in life, beginning with prenatal life. People with severe seizures often have a history of trauma or anoxia (oxygen deprivation) at birth. But the most common cause is head injury (Meinardi & Pachlatko, 1991). This linkage is probably due in part to the fact that most cases of epilepsy have their onset during childhood or adolescence—a period in which, as noted earlier, there is a high risk for head injury. When epilepsy begins in middle age, a more likely cause is brain tumor; when it strikes in older age, it is often due to one of the cerebral vascular diseases that older people are prone to, such as stroke or cerebral arteriosclerosis (Wyllie, 2001).

Cases such as these, in which the origin of the seizures can be identified, are known as **symptomatic epilepsy.** More common in the general population (Meinardi & Pachlatko, 1991), however, is **idiopathic epilepsy,** epilepsy in which the origin of the seizures is unknown. In many idiopathic cases, there is a family history of seizures, so genetic factors are probably involved (Anderson & Hauser, 1991).

Types of Seizures

There are two basic categories of seizures. The first is **partial seizures,** which originate in one part of the brain rather than in the brain as a whole. In a **simple partial seizure,** cognitive functioning remains intact. The person may experience sensory changes, such as stomach trouble or a strange smell, and/or motor symptoms on one side of the body. (For example, the fingers on one hand may start twitching.) Some people also report minor psychological changes, such as hearing a tune repeat itself again and again in their heads. But even in the midst of the seizure the person can still speak, understand speech, and think straight.

By contrast, a **complex partial seizure,** the most common form of seizure (Annegers, 1993), interrupts cognitive functioning. Such attacks are often preceded by an *aura,* or warning, which the person may be able to describe only in vague terms (e.g., "a funny feeling"). Then, as the seizure begins, the person can no longer engage in purposeful activity and does not respond normally. What he or she does instead is highly variable. Some patients seem to fall into a stupor; others engage in automatisms, repetitive, purposeless movements such as fumbling with their clothes; others have been known to break into a run. But, whatever the activity, the person is not thinking normally; neither can he or she speak coherently. Complex partial seizures usually last more than 10 seconds, often for several minutes. They are sometimes called "temporal-lobe seizures" because they tend to arise in the temporal lobe, but they can originate in other parts of the brain as well.

While partial seizures begin and often remain in only one part of the brain, **generalized seizures,** the second major category of epileptic seizures, either involve the entire brain at the outset (primary generalized seizures) or soon spread from one part of the whole brain (secondary generalized seizures). Among the primary type are **absence seizures,** previously called *petit mal* ("little illness"). These attacks are usually seen in children rather than in adults. Absence seizures come without warning and typically last only a few seconds. During that period, children with these seizures seem to absent themselves from their surroundings. Their faces may take on a "spaced-out" look; they stop moving and speaking; if spoken to, they cannot respond. Then, as abruptly as it started, the seizure ends, whereupon some children are confused, while others, unaware of what has happened, simply resume whatever they were doing before.

Tonic-clonic seizures, found in both children and adults, are another type of generalized seizure. Sometimes heralded by an aura, these attacks typically begin with a tonic, or rigid, extension of the arms and legs. This is followed by a clonic, or jerking, movement throughout the body. The jerking gradually diminishes until the attack ends, at which point the person usually feels confused and sleepy. People can bang their heads or otherwise harm themselves during a tonic-clonic seizure, so hard objects should be moved out of the way, if possible. The only other way bystanders can help people having such seizures is to move them onto their sides, so that if they vomit, the vomit will not back up into the air passages. (Contrary to popular wisdom, one should not put anything into their mouths to prevent them from swallowing their tongues; people cannot swallow their tongues.) Once known as *grand mal* ("great illness") seizures, tonic-clonic seizures are the most dramatic form of epileptic attack, and they are what most people think of when they think of epilepsy, though they are not the most common type.

Seizures starting in one part of the brain may spread to other parts. A simple partial seizure may develop into a complex partial seizure; a complex partial seizure, into a generalized tonic-clonic attack. In the latter case, the attack may look very much like a primary tonic-clonic seizure, but it is important for diagnosticians to distinguish between them, because each requires a different kind of drug.

Psychological Factors in Epilepsy

It is not just during seizures that the epilepsy disrupts the brain's functioning. Even between seizures, irregular brain waves often persist, interfering with concentration and learning. The most common complaint of people with epilepsy is that they have poor memories. This is due to the fact that most epilepsies involve the temporal lobes and related structures, and these are the areas of the brain most related to memory. Patients with temporal-lobe epilepsy often manifest depression, anxiety, and social limitations, as well as impaired memory (Helmstaedter, 2001). By contrast, patients with frontal-lobe epilepsy demonstrate cognitive impairment, hyperactivity, and obsessive and addictive behaviors (Helmstaedter, 2001). Despite these difficulties, however, many patients perform quite well in life, and some show great achievements. Julius Caesar, Fyodor Dostoyevsky, and Vincent van Gogh all reportedly suffered from epilepsy.

It was once thought that there was such a thing as an "epileptic personality." But, in view of the fact that people with epilepsy have widely different kinds

Fyodor Dostoyevsky, a Russian novelist, suffered from tonic-clonic seizures, as does the hero of his novel The Idiot, *Prince Myshkin.*

of seizures, beginning at different ages and occurring with different frequencies, there is little reason to believe that they would have similar personality traits. In any case, there are no data to support such a claim. However, people with epilepsy do share problems that other people do not face. Consider the following firsthand account of a tonic-clonic attack by writer Margiad Evans:

> The food was on the table, the oil-stove lit. I picked up the coffee percolator to fill it. Just as I reached the sink and was standing in the doorway, I found I could not move, could not remember what I wanted to do. It seemed a long time that I stood there (actually perhaps a few seconds) saying to myself, "This is nothing. It will be all right in a moment and I shall remember *all the rest*." Then I felt my head beginning to jerk backwards and my face to grimace. Then the percolator fell from my hand into the sink. But still some dogged part of me kept saying, "All this is really controllable." I was still conscious and felt violent gestures and spasms were shooting all over me, even till I felt my knees give and I fell down on the concrete floor. As I went, it shot through me, the astonishment: "As bad as this then?"
>
> The next thing I remember was the B__s' kitchen and Betty B__ . . . giving me tea and talking to me in the tone mothers use to little children coming out of nightmares. (Quoted in Kaplan, 1964, pp. 346–347.)

Such an experience, even if the person has had it many times, is nonetheless unsettling and damaging to self-esteem. Therefore, it is no surprise that people with epilepsy are more prone to anxiety and depression than is the general population (Dodrill, 1992; Beghi, Spagnoli, Airoldi, et al., 2002).

❖ Groups at Risk

As has been noted, groups that are at risk for other acquired brain disorders, particularly head injury, tumor, and stroke, are at higher risk for epilepsy than is the general population. These types of risk have to do with age—a relatively young age for head injury, a relatively advanced age for stroke—as well as gender (men are at higher risk for stroke than are women) and the presence of certain medical conditions, such as hypertension. (Daoud, Batieha, Bashtawi, et al., 2003; Fountain, 2000; Jallon, 2002).

There is some evidence that gender may also affect the outcome of surgical treatment of epilepsy. In a study of 118 epileptic patients, researchers found that the women experienced a significant improvement in verbal memory after a lobectomy, while the men experienced a significant decline (Trenerry, Jack, Cascino, et al., 1995). In a similar study, researchers found that the women, but not the men, experienced a decline in visual memory following a lobectomy (Trenerry, Jack, Cascino, et al., 1996). These differences in the outcome of surgery appeared to be related to differences in the volume of the hippocampus in the men and women, as determined by MRI.

Treatment of Epilepsy

Most people with diagnosed seizure disorders take antiepileptic drugs, most commonly Depakote, Dilantin, Tegretol, or phenobarbital. If used as prescribed, these drugs suppress seizures in about 80 percent of patients (Richens & Perucca, 1993). Many patients also report side effects—notably, slowed movements and a general feeling of being "drugged down." Antiepileptic medication is designed to alter the functioning of the nervous system so as to prevent seizures; if it also affects other behaviors, such as fully normal motor responses, that is not surprising. But side effects can often be reduced if the medication is taken correctly (Dodrill, 1993).

When drugs are not successful in controlling the seizures, surgery may be recommended (Jutila, Immonen, Mervaala, et al., 2002; Shaefi & Harkness, 2003; Meador, 2002). The most common type of surgery involves the removal of the focal epileptic area, the area where the attacks are known to originate. But this type of surgery can be done only when the area is focal: known and limited. (Thus, the seizures must be partial rather than generalized.) Furthermore, the focal area must be one that can be removed without major damage to the person's mental faculties. Epilepsy surgery is becoming more common, but it is still performed on no more than perhaps one out of a hundred patients. Of these, 40 to 80 percent are seizure-free after surgery (Engel, Van Ness, Rasmussen, et al., 1993), and many report dramatic improvements in their lives as a result.

Key Terms

absence seizures, 454
acquired brain disorders, 432
acute confusional state, 440
agnosia, 435
Alzheimer's disease, 445
amnesia, 434
aphasia, 435
apraxia, 434
brain tumors, 444
cerebral abscess, 436
cerebrovascular accident (CVA), 441
complex partial seizure, 453
concussion, 440
contusion, 440
degenerative disorders, 444

delirium, 434
dementia, 435, 445
embolism, 442
encephalitis, 436
endocrine glands, 451
epilepsy, 453
frontotemporal dementia, 447
general paresis, 437
generalized seizures, 454
hemorrhage, 442
Huntington's chorea, 448
idiopathic epilepsy, 453
infarction, 442
Korsakoff's psychosis, 451
lead encephalopathy, 452
Lewy body disease, 447
Lyme disease, 438
mad cow disease, 438
meningitis, 437
metastatic brain tumors, 444
neurosyphilis, 437
Parkinson's disease, 448
partial seizures, 453
penetrating head injury, 440
primary brain tumors, 444
simple partial seizure, 453
stroke, 441
symptomatic epilepsy, 453
thrombosis, 442
tonic-clonic seizures, 454
traumatic brain injury, 439
vascular dementia, 447

Summary

- Unlike most disorders discussed in this book, which have largely psychological causes, acquired brain disorders are directly caused by destruction of brain tissue or by biochemical imbalances in the brain. There are four main problems in diagnosing acquired brain disorders: (1) is the disorder, in fact, an acquired brain disorder? (2) if so, what caused the disorder? (3) what part of the brain is damaged? And (4) how are psychosocial factors influencing the symptoms, and can they be modified?
- There are seven major symptoms of acquired brain disorder: impairments of attention and arousal, language function, learning and memory, visual-perceptual function, motor skills, executive function, and higher-order intellectual function. The similarity of many of these symptoms to those of certain psychological disorders makes a correct diagnosis very difficult.
- There are three general types of acquired brain disorder: delirium, specific cognitive impairments, and dementia. Delirium is a transient, global disorder of cognition and attention that is often caused by physical illness. Besides confusion and disorganization, it may include hallucinations and delusions. Most patients recover from delirium within a month. The second general type of injury, specific cognitive impairment, is focal—that is, restricted to a certain aspect of behavior. For instance, amnesia is an impairment of memory, usually of the very recent past. Other specific cognitive impairments include aphasia (impairment of the language function), apraxia (impairment of the ability to coordinate movements or manipulate objects), and agnosia (impairment of the ability to recognize familiar objects). The third general type of brain disorder, dementia, involves the lasting impairment of at least two cognitive functions, which causes a compromising decline in a person's occupational or social functioning. Some dementias are caused by infections, others by progressive physical deterioration.
- Acquired brain disorders are usually classified by their cause. Cerebral infection, traumatic brain injury, stroke, tumors, degenerative disorders, nutritional deficiency, endocrine disorders, and toxic disorders are the major causes of brain disorder.
- There are three main forms of cerebral infection: abscess, encephalitis, and meningitis. In a cerebral abscess, an infection becomes encapsulated within the brain. Encephalitis is an inflammation of the brain. Meningitis is an inflammation of the meninges, the covering of the brain and spinal cord. Recently, HIV dementia, a cerebral infection that can be caused by either the HIV virus or a secondary infection, has reached epidemic proportions, while neurosyphilis, which can now be prevented by antibiotics, has become rare. Mad cow disease is a cerebral infection whose cause has not yet been determined. Lyme disease is a cerebral infection spread to humans by ticks, who pick up the bacteria from infected animals.
- Traumatic brain injury, physical injury to brain tissue, is the leading cause of disability and death in young adults; children and the elderly are also at risk, mainly due to falls. There are several forms of traumatic brain injury: concussion, contusion, and penetrating head injury. In a concussion, a blow to the head jars the brain, often causing a brief loss of consciousness. A contusion is a bruise on the brain tissue, generally resulting in a coma of several hours or days. In a penetrating head injury, a foreign object enters and destroys brain tissue. Consequences vary, depending on the location of the damage.
- Cerebrovascular accidents (CVAs), or strokes, result from a blockage or the breaking of a blood vessel in the brain. The two main types of strokes are infarction and hemorrhage. In an infarction, the brain's blood supply is cut off due to a thrombosis or an embolism. A hemorrhage occurs when a blood vessel in the brain ruptures. The effects of a stroke depend on the location and extent of the damage to the brain. Risk of a stroke increases with age, because of the increased prevalence of conditions that weaken blood vessels.
- There are two types of brain tumors: metastatic tumors, which originate elsewhere in the body and spread to the brain, and primary tumors, which originate in the brain. Some primary tumors are intracerebral—that is, they grow inside the brain—while others are extracerebral, or located outside the brain, often in the meninges. Little is known about the risk factors for brain tumor, other than that smoking is a risk factor for metastatic brain tumors.
- Degenerative disorders are characterized by a general deterioration of intellectual, emotional, and motor

functioning. Symptoms vary, depending on the site of the damage. The degenerative disorders include Alzheimer's disease, Lewy body disease, and vascular dementia, all of which affect mainly the elderly, as well as Huntington's chorea, frontotemporal dementia, and Parkinson's disease, which more often strike in middle age. While all elderly people experience normal psychological changes as a function of aging, only a small percentage of the aged suffer from dementia.

- Alzheimer's disease is characterized by a loss of memory for recent events, and eventually for long-past events. It can be definitively diagnosed at autopsy by the presence of senile plaques and neurofibrillary tangles in the brain. Lewy body disease, which in the early stages often involves delirium, is quite similar to Alzheimer's in the later stages. It can be diagnosed at autopsy by the presence of rounded structures, called Lewy bodies, in the brain. Alzheimer's disease, which affects more women than men, and Lewy body disease, which affects more men than women, may be genetically related. Vascular dementia, whose symptoms closely resemble those of Alzheimer's and Lewy body disease, is the cumulative effect of a number of small strokes. It is particularly common in people with high blood pressure.
- Frontotemporal dementia is a dementing illness caused by progressive deterioration of the frontal and temporal lobes. Its chief characteristic is a profound change in behavior. Huntington's chorea is a genetically transmitted degenerative disease involving damage to the brain's basal ganglia. The disease begins with mood changes and progresses to paralysis and death. Parkinson's disease, also resulting from damage to the basal ganglia, is characterized by tremors and slowed motor responses. Treatment with drugs can control symptoms but cannot cure the disease.
- Malnutrition, specifically vitamin deficiency, can lead to neurological damage. Patients with Korsakoff's psychosis, a disease commonly associated with alcoholism, suffer from memory deficits.
- Disturbances in the endocrine system can produce many psychological problems. Thyroid syndromes, resulting from a malfunctioning thyroid gland, include hyperthyroidism and hypothyroidism. Abnormalities in the adrenal glands may give rise to Addison's disease and Cushing's syndrome.
- Toxic substances absorbed into the body may cause brain damage, with results ranging from temporary emotional distress to death. Toxic disorders almost always produce delirium. Lead and other heavy metals, some psychoactive drugs, and carbon monoxide all are toxic agents that may cause brain damage.
- The epilepsies are characterized by sudden seizures caused by a disruption of activity in brain cells. While in some cases the cause of epilepsy can be determined (usually a head injury or brain tumor), generally the origin of the seizures is unknown. There are two broad types of seizures: partial seizures, which start in only a portion of the brain, and generalized seizures, which involve the entire brain. The most common form, a complex partial seizure, interrupts cognitive functioning for up to several minutes. Between seizures, epileptics often complain of poor memories. Though the disease can interfere with concentration and learning, many epileptics are treated with drugs that suppress seizures. If the drug treatment is unsuccessful, surgery can sometimes be performed to control the seizures.

CHAPTER

16

Issues in Child Psychopathology
- Prevalence
- Classification and Diagnosis
- Long-Term Consequences

Disruptive Behavior Disorders
- Attention Deficit Hyperactivity Disorder
- Conduct Disorder

Disorders of Emotional Distress
- Anxiety Disorders
- Childhood Depression

Eating Disorders
- Anorexia Nervosa
- Bulimia Nervosa
- Childhood Obesity

Elimination Disorders
- Enuresis
- Encopresis

Childhood Sleep Disorders
- Insomnia
- Nightmares and Night Terrors
- Sleepwalking

Learning and Communication Disorders
- Learning Disorders
- Communication Disorders

Disorders of Childhood and Adolescence: Theory and Therapy
- The Behavioral Perspective
- The Cognitive Perspective
- The Interpersonal Perspective
- The Sociocultural Perspective
- The Psychodynamic Perspective
- The Neuroscience Perspective

Disorders of Childhood and Adolescence

Michael was a 12-year-old boy referred to an outpatient clinic for recent problems attending school as well as related concerns. He was referred by his school guidance counselor and his parents because he had missed about 60% of school days during the first semester. In addition, he often refused to complete his homework, was sullen and withdrawn, and had begun to fight with his parents.

Michael's home situation was tense and full of turmoil. He was the middle of three children whose parents worked full-time. Because Michael was skipping school, one or both of his parents was forced to miss work to supervise him. In addition, there was a lot of verbal fighting in the house as Michael's parents tried to figure out what was going on, and as Michael himself just wanted to be left alone. During the clinic interview, Michael reported that he didn't like school and felt anxious and upset when he was there. He wanted to be educated at home. Michael's parents, however, emphasized the fact that their son was increasingly noncompliant toward their commands and had even gotten into four physical fights recently with his siblings and kids in the neighborhood.

A developmental history revealed that Michael had had problems attending school the year before, but his parents were tolerant of the misbehavior because it occurred toward the end of the academic year. This year, however, Michael had entered a new middle school and felt overwhelmed by the various classes, teachers, homework assignments, and crowds. He started skipping certain classes and then began to stay home altogether. A medical examination revealed no physical problems, although Michael complained often of headaches and stomachaches. (Kearney, University of Nevada–Las Vegas, personal files)

The mental disorders of childhood and adolescence include a wide range of problems. Often, these problems represent some change in a normal developmental process or a failure to pass a developmental milestone on time. For example, bed-wetting is considered normal at ages 2 to 4, but if the behavior persists into the elementary school years, it is considered a problem. Similarly, most children develop the capacity to speak to others; those who cannot or will not often qualify for a mental disorder. Still other disorders in childhood and adolescence are simply mental disorders that normally have their onset prior to adulthood (e.g., anorexia nervosa) or that afflict children as well as adults (e.g., depression).

Historically, children and adolescents with mental disorders were viewed much the same as adults, even receiving the same treatments that adults received. Today we recognize that childhood, adolescence, and adulthood are very different stages of life. Rapid changes in development during childhood mean that mental disorders during this stage must be assessed and treated differently than in adulthood. Think, for example, of two adults who are depressed and who are 10 years apart in age (e.g., 25 and 35 years old). In many cases, treatment for depression can be quite similar for these two adults. Imagine, though, two youths who are depressed and who are 10 years apart in age (e.g., 7 and 17 years old). Their assessment and treatment will have to be dramatically different, because the adolescent likely has better cognitive development and will be better able to understand and modify his or her emotions and thoughts.

Rapid changes in development during childhood also mean that things can go off track in a hurry. Deviations in language, social skill, emotional regulation, or impulse control, for example, can quickly lead to behavior problems. The field of developmental psychopathology has grown in recent years to identify which pathways most often lead to certain behavior problems. Children are often evaluated over time to see what variables led to certain outcomes. For example, a child with a fussy, difficult temperament may coerce her parents into giving her what she wants. Over time, parental indulgence may lead to a situation where noncompliance and more serious behavior problems are inadvertently rewarded, and the child eventually becomes delinquent in adolescence.

Developmental psychopathologists are interested in defining normal and abnormal behavior, identifying which pathways lead to these behaviors, and discovering how to prevent or treat early problems before they progress to more serious ones. These professionals look at early risk (genetics, temperament), family (parenting style, divorce), social (peers, support), and other factors to piece together a picture of why children develop behavior problems. Assessments for children focus on many different internal and external factors, involve multiple sources of information, and are linked to immediate treatment recommendations.

In this chapter, we begin with general issues in childhood and adolescent psychopathology. Then we turn to the individual disorders. Finally, we examine the various theories and treatments of these disorders.

Issues in Child Psychopathology

Prevalence

It is estimated that 1 out of every 5 children and adolescents has a moderate or severe psychological disorder (Brandenburg, Friedman, & Silver, 1990; McDermott & Weiss, 1995). When do the troubles begin? Are problems likely to surface at some ages rather than others? Surveys of mental health clinics show that admission rates begin to increase gradually at age 6 or 7—a fact that is probably related to school entry. Problems that can be ignored or endured at home may not be tolerated in the classroom, and teachers, in general, are more prone than parents to conclude that a child needs treatment. Furthermore, starting school or switching to a new school, as in the example that began this chapter, may itself be stressful enough to create or aggravate psychological problems. Until adolescence, psychological disturbance in general is more common in boys than in girls (Zahn-Waxler, 1993). In adolescence, however, the girls dominate certain categories, as we will see.

Classification and Diagnosis

In *DSM-IV-TR,* disorders of childhood and adolescence, like adult disorders, are classified by syndromes, with the hope that this will help to relate individual cases to other, similar cases. An alternative classification method involves statistically grouping together the preadult problems that tend to occur together in the same children or the same age groups. This is called the *empirical method,* because it was developed by asking parents, teachers, and clinicians to fill out checklists describing the types of problems experienced by children at different ages.

Empirical studies indicate that there are four major categories of childhood and adolescent disorders (Achenbach, 1991):

1. *Disruptive behavior disorders,* involving impulsive, aggressive, and other kinds of "acting-out" behaviors
2. *Disorders of emotional distress,* in which the main problem is mental suffering, usually in the form of anxiety or depression

The diagnosis of a childhood psychological disorder depends not only on the kind of behavior involved but also on the age of the child. An occasional outburst of aggression is normal in young children, but by adolescence such behavior may well be a sign of psychological disturbance.

3. *Habit disorders,* disruptions of daily physical habits such as eating, sleeping, and elimination
4. *Learning and communication disorders,* involving difficulties with such skills as reading, writing, and speaking

The empirical method may be consistent with *DSM-IV-TR,* Indeed, most of the *DSM-IV-TR* diagnostic categories can be grouped under these four headings. Clinicians who treat children are wary of diagnostic labels, however. First, as we noted, children change rapidly. Second, they may not fit neatly into any one category. As was shown in the opening case of Michael, a child may have both a disruptive behavior disorder (fighting with siblings and neighbors) and an emotional stress disorder (repeatedly feeling anxious and upset at school). Likewise, many children who are overanxious also have sleeping problems, many children who are depressed are also disruptive, and so on.

Long-Term Consequences

People who treat disturbed youngsters hope that by doing so they are not only relieving a childhood disorder but also heading off an adult disorder. But do childhood disorders actually predict adult disorders? If so, by treating the one, can we prevent the other?

The answer to the first question depends on what kind of predictability we are looking for. The clearest, and rarest, instance of predictability is *stability,* in which a childhood disorder simply persists into adulthood in the same or a similar form. One childhood problem that tends to remain stable is antisocial behavior. Antisocial behavior in adolescence is often followed by antisocial personality disorder in adulthood. Kratzer and Hodgins (1997), who studied adolescents with conduct disorder over a 16-year period, found that 64 percent of boys and 17 percent of girls committed a crime during the follow-up period.

Another type of predictability is *continuity of developmental adaptation.* In this case, the childhood problem handicaps later development not by persisting in the same form but by setting the child on a skewed developmental path, which then leads to other, later disorders that may bear little resemblance to the original one. For example, infants who develop avoidant or resistant relationships with their parents are prone to become highly oppositional at age 2 and highly disruptive at age 3 or 4. In turn, disruptive behavior during the transition into the school years (ages 5 to 7) places a child at risk for more extreme behavioral problems and for learning disorders. In such a case, we cannot say that the learning disorder represents a continuation of the infant avoidance, but it does seem that the early problem may have established a maladaptive pattern of development, with the form of maladaptiveness changing over time.

A third kind of predictability has to do with an early disorder's creating *reactivity to particular stressors.* For example, a young child who becomes depressed upon losing a parent is not necessarily on the road to adult depression. Still, this early loss may make the person more reactive to later, similar losses (e.g., divorce) and thus render him or her more vulnerable to adult depression. In general, childhood disorders of emotional distress, such as depression or anxiety, tend to clear up. However, these disorders may predict other problems later in life if they arrest emotional development, increase reactivity to stress, or involve poor peer relations (Goodyer, Herbert, Tamplin, et al., 1997; La Greca & Fetter, 1995). Thus, if we consider the three kinds of predictability together, the answer to our earlier question is yes, some childhood disorders do predict adult disorders, though often indirectly.

As for the second question—whether treatment can prevent childhood disorders from leading to adult disorders—the answer remains unclear. Clearly, treatment helps in the short term. Outcome studies have found psychotherapy to be about as successful with children as with adults (Weisz, Donenberg, Han, et al., 1995), though it tends to be more helpful for girls and for those with problems other than social maladjustment. Children who receive psychosocial treatment, especially cognitive and behavior therapy, tend to do better than children who receive no therapy. Indeed, many children respond well to treatment, which suggests that treating them will help to prevent some adult disorders.

Disruptive Behavior Disorders

The **disruptive behavior disorders** are characterized by poorly controlled, impulsive, acting-out behavior in situations where self-control is expected. The ability to control one's behavior depends on a number of skills developed over time. No one expects hungry infants to show restraint—to wait patiently and refrain from crying. During the toddler and preschool years, however, expectations are raised. Children of this age are asked to learn to inhibit behavior on command ("Don't touch that electric outlet!") and to moderate their behavior in consideration of other people's feelings ("Don't take her toy—play with this one"). Such learning is slow and involves many lapses in the form of disobedience, aggression, and temper tantrums. Nevertheless, it proceeds. By the time they enter school, most children have developed the self-control skills necessary for compliant and organized behavior in the classroom and for responsive, nonaggressive interactions with peers. Those who have not developed these skills, who continue to be disruptive, impulsive, and aggressive, are at high risk for school adjustment difficulties, learning problems, and peer rejection. Among the disruptive behavior disorders listed by *DSM-IV-TR,* the two most important are attention deficit hyperactivity disorder and conduct disorder.

Attention Deficit Hyperactivity Disorder

Dennis, an eight-year-old boy, was referred for treatment by his school psychologist. According to his teachers, he was uncooperative and disruptive in the classroom. He grabbed his classmates' pens and rifled through their desks. He talked incessantly, except when he was asked a question; then he would not answer. He fidgeted and squirmed constantly. He often got into fights with his classmates and had few friends. He seemed comfortable only with younger children.

These reports from school were seconded by Dennis' parents, who said that he was chronically disobedient and always in motion. He climbed on the furniture and, if reprimanded, did not seem to remember the prohibition a minute later. He was also very distractible, they said. He could never concentrate long enough to finish a chore or complete a homework assignment. (Eisen, Fairleigh Dickinson University, 1997, personal files)

In every elementary school, there are children who cannot sit still, cannot finish a task, cannot wait their turn, cannot focus their attention for longer than a minute or two. A few decades ago, researchers began to suspect that this pattern, characterized primarily by excess motor activity and short attention span, might be due to brain damage. It was known, for example, that certain kinds of brain infection produced restless motor activity. Furthermore, many children who manifested this pattern also showed "soft," or ambiguous, neurological signs that could suggest brain damage, and a small percentage of them showed definite signs of neurological impairment. On this evidence, the pattern was labeled "minimal brain dysfunction." Still, no one could say exactly what the dysfunction was. Furthermore, there was (and still is) a strong trend away from labeling disorders according to cause when that cause has not been definitely established. In time, therefore, the syndrome was given a new name, *hyperactivity,* which had to do with its symptoms rather than its presumed cause. Eventually, however, those who studied the disorder came to feel that the short attention span was as fundamental a symptom as the hyperactivity. Accordingly, the syndrome is now called **attention deficit hyperactivity disorder,** or **ADHD.**

Between 3 and 5 percent of elementary school children are said to have ADHD (Barkley, 1998), with boys outnumbering girls by about 3.4 to 1. Thus, it is a common diagnosis. It is also a controversial one. Some experts believe that it is too readily applied to children whom parents and teachers find difficult to control (McArdle, O'Brien, & Kolvin, 1995).

The symptoms of ADHD greatly impair a child's ability to function effectively in life situations. Children with ADHD, for example, are likely to have poor academic performance, adaptive functioning,

A child with ADHD (attention deficit hyperactivity disorder) lives in a state of incessant, purposeless activity and finds it almost impossible to concentrate.

social relationships, rule-governed behavior, health, and sleep patterns (Barkley, 1998). The disorder's most salient features are incessant restlessness and an extremely poor attention span, leading in turn to impulsive and disorganized behavior. These handicaps affect almost every area of the child's functioning. Even the most trivial human accomplishments—setting a table, playing a card game—depend on the ability to set goals, plan ahead, organize one's behavior, and postpone gratification. It is this ability that is most strikingly absent in a child with ADHD. Thus, the characteristic motor behavior of these children is often distinguished less by its excessiveness than by its haphazard quality. Most children are more physically active than adults—according to ratings by their parents and teachers, one quarter to one half of children and adolescents are restless and fidgety—but their getting up and down and running back and forth are usually directed toward a goal (McArdle, O'Brien, & Kolvin, 1995). By contrast, the incessant activity of children with ADHD seems purposeless and disorganized. Furthermore, a normal child can, if motivated, sit still and concentrate; a child with ADHD finds this almost impossible to do.

This inability to focus and sustain attention has a ruinous effect on academic progress. Children with ADHD have great difficulty following instructions and finishing tasks. Often, they cannot even remember what they set out to do. Consequently, no matter how intelligent they are, they tend to have severe learning problems. They are also extremely disruptive in the classroom, making incessant demands for attention. (Typically, it is not until such children enter school that their problem is recognized. What parents can put up with, a teacher with 25 pupils and a lesson plan to complete usually cannot.) By adolescence, 25 to 35 percent of children with ADHD have received some form of special education.

Children with ADHD also show poor social adjustment. They disrupt games, get into fights, refuse to play fair, and throw temper tantrums. Such behavior does not make them popular. Of course, it also strains the parent-child relationship. ADHD takes its toll on self-care, trustworthiness, and independence (Stein, Szumowski, Blondis, et al., 1995)—all the areas that the child is supposed to be mastering in order to become a social being.

Not all children with ADHD have all these symptoms. In some, the problem is much more one of inattention than hyperactivity; in others, the opposite. Accordingly, *DSM-IV-TR* divides the syndrome into three subtypes: the *predominantly inattentive type,* the *predominantly hyperactive/impulsive type,* and the *combined type.* Most children with ADHD are the combined type—that is, they have the full range of symptoms. Some studies (Barkley, DuPaul, & McMurray, 1990; Biederman, Newcorn, & Sprich, 1991) have shown that children of the combined type are more likely than those of the other two types to have problems with other children, to engage in antisocial behavior, and to be placed in special education classes. Children with ADHD also differ in the constancy of their symptoms. In some, the problem behaviors occur only at home or only at school, while the child shows adequate adjustment in the other setting. These children with situational ADHD generally have less serious difficulties and a better prognosis than do children with pervasive ADHD, who show their symptoms in all settings.

As for general prognosis, about 80 percent of children continue to show significant ADHD symptoms into adolescence (Biederman, Faraone, Milberger, et al., 1996), and perhaps as many as 42 percent still show the symptoms as adults (Fischer, 1997). In adolescence, ADHD may branch out into the pattern of antisocial behavior known as conduct disorder (see the next section). According to teacher rating scales, 85 percent of children with conduct disorder also meet the criteria for ADHD (Pelham, Gnagy, Greenslade, et al., 1992). As for later adjustment, a study of young men who had had ADHD in childhood showed that, compared with controls, they had significantly higher rates of conduct or antisocial personality disorders (27 versus 8 percent), drug-use disorders (16 versus 3 percent), and full ADHD syndrome (31 versus 3 percent). Cognitive problems such as poor concentration tend to persist into adolescence, with predictable academic results: poor grades, expulsion, early withdrawal from school (Weiss & Hechtman, 1993). It is not yet clear whether cognitive disabilities continue into adulthood, but the adult lives of children with ADHD are marked by their poor academic records (Barkley, 1998).

Attention Deficit Hyperactivity Disorder: Bouncing Words and Loud Noises

The MindMAP video "Attention Deficit Hyperactivity Disorder" illustrates some of the symptoms of attention deficit hyperactivity disorder (ADHD). Can you identify some of these symptoms in the video? What are they? Which subtype of ADHD seems most consistent with the symptoms presented? Why?

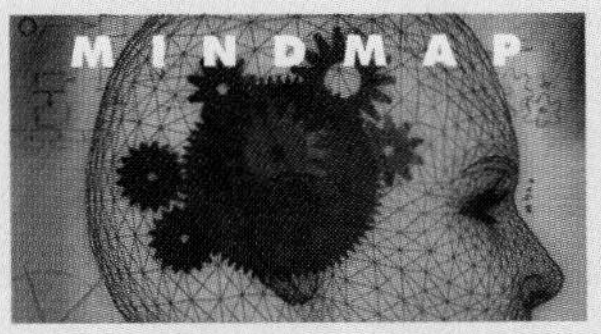

Conduct Disorder

Derek, 15 years old, was referred to treatment by his school counselor and by a juvenile detention officer. He had a history of shoplifting and vandalism (throwing rocks at windows, breaking into cars). He hung out with his friends day and night. He frequently smoked marijuana. He was sexually promiscuous. At school, where he showed up infrequently, he was withdrawn and contributed little. He rarely did any homework and was failing all his courses.

Derek's parents were divorced, and his mother, who had remarried and was living out of state, had little contact with him. He lived with his father, who reported that Derek could not be trusted: he lied constantly and, when confronted, felt no remorse.

Before going into treatment, Derek had been placed on six-month probation by the juvenile court. He was also on the verge of being expelled from school. (Adapted from Kearney, 2002.)

Some children seem indifferent to the rights of others. Rather than yield to anyone else, they argue, threaten, cheat, and steal. They may also go in for reckless behavior—setting fires, jumping off roofs—and for gratuitously cruel behavior. As they grow older, they graduate to the violation of major social norms. They are no longer just throwing blocks; they are committing assault and rape. At this point, usually in adolescence or preadolescence, they are given the diagnosis of **conduct disorder.**

The *DSM-IV-TR* criteria for this diagnosis are grouped under 4 categories: aggression against people or animals (bullying, fighting, mugging, committing rape), destruction of property (vandalism, fire setting), deceitfulness or theft (lying, shoplifting, breaking and entering), and other serious violations of rules (being absent from school, running away from home). If a person is under 18, has committed any 3 of these infractions (in any category) in the past year, and shows poor adjustment at home or at school, he or she qualifies for the diagnosis of conduct disorder.

Family factors are thought to strongly contribute to the development of conduct disorder. A particularly salient model was developed by Patterson and colleagues (Patterson, Reid, & Dishion, 1992), who found that many children are disruptive in order to coerce their parents into giving them what they want. In a positive reinforcement trap, for example, a child is noncompliant or disruptive until a parent bribes the child to act otherwise, thus rewarding the misbehavior. In a negative reinforcement trap, a child is so noncompliant or disruptive following a parent's command that the parent eventually gives up, also rewarding the misbehavior. Over time, this coercive behavior on the child's part worsens and may lead to conduct disorder.

Like ADHD, conduct disorder is one of the most common syndromes of childhood and adolescence, with an estimated prevalence of 4 to 16 percent in the under 18 population (Cohen, Cohen, Kasen, et al., 1993). And, as with ADHD, boys outnumber girls by a ratio of anywhere from 4 to 1 to 12 to 1 (Zoccolillo, 1993). In addition to gender, age of onset seems to be important in conduct disorder. Indeed, *DSM-IV-TR* requires that diagnosticians specify whether a given case falls into the *childhood-onset type* (at least 1 symptom prior to age 10) or the *adolescent-onset type* (no symptoms before age 10). People of the childhood-onset type are usually male; they are more likely to be physically aggressive; they tend to have few, if any, friends. They are also more likely to graduate from conduct disorder to adult antisocial personality disorder. Teenagers with adolescent-onset conduct disorders are less aggressive, generally have friends—indeed, they may be valued gang members—and are less likely to become antisocial personalities as adults. (See the box on the next page.) The prognostic value of age of onset has been confirmed by research (Fergusson, Horwood, & Lynskey, 1995; Tolan & Thomas, 1995). One study, for example, tested a group of adults who had had pronounced conduct disorders as children to see if they met the criteria for antisocial personality disorder. The subjects who did meet the criteria constituted 48 percent of those whose symptoms began after age 12, 53 percent of those whose symptoms appeared between 6 and 12, and 71 percent of those whose symptoms surfaced before age 6 (Robins, 1991). But the children with conduct disorders who do not develop antisocial personality disorder are still more likely to become "ordinary" criminals. Some studies (e.g., Kratzer & Hodgins, 1997; Zoccolillo & Rogers, 1991) have found that 50 to 70 percent of juvenile offenders are arrested again as adults. Some children and adolescents with conduct disorder have been found to have problematic cognitive and attributional processes. In particular, these youths have attention problems, a tendency to see others' motivations as hostile, an inability to foresee all of the consequences of their aggressive behavior, and poor social problem-solving skills (Dodge, Lochman, Harnish, et al., 1997). However, these patterns may be less applicable to girls (Crick & Dodge, 1996).

Whatever their future prospects, children with conduct disorders are cause for grave social concern. Whether in gangs or on their own, these children commit serious crimes. Over 50 percent of those arrested in the United States in 1995 for violent crimes were under 18 (U.S. Bureau of the Census, 1997). Even more alarming is the fact that the rate of violent crime by juveniles increased by almost 50 percent between 1980 and 1995 (U.S. Bureau of the Census, 1997)—a rise that was probably due, however, not just to antisocial tendencies but also to the increased availability of firearms.

Attention deficit hyperactivity and conduct disorder are the child disorders most likely to lead to problems in adulthood. This may be due to symptoms in the disorders (e.g., poor concentration, interpersonal violence) that persist over time and lead to occupational and social problems in adulthood. Or, this may be due to the fact that many youth with conduct disorders and ADHD come from disorganized and unhappy families. However, the poor prognosis for the disruptive behavior disorders is also certainly due in part to the process described earlier: continuity of developmental adaptation. The behaviors involved in ADHD and conduct disorders cause immense disruptions in the lives of the children who have these disorders, damaging their academic performance, their social lives, and their relationships with their families—in other words, all the critical areas of a child's existence. It is not easy to recover from such setbacks.

❖ Groups at Risk for Disruptive Behavior Disorders

Far and away the strongest risk factor for the disruptive behavior disorders is gender (Robins, 1991). As we saw, boys outnumber girls 3.4 to 1 in ADHD; in conduct disorder, the differential is even greater. The genders also express conduct disorders differently. In boys, the most common symptoms are fighting, stealing, committing vandalism, and having school problems. In girls, the predominant behaviors are lying, being truant, running away from home, shoplifting, using drugs, and engaging in prostitution. But the most striking difference is that boys are more prone to physical aggression.

Like so many other gender issues, these findings have been the subject of recent debate. Why are girls less prone than boys to antisocial behavior? One possibility is that the difference is, to some extent, an artifact of reporting. Boys are more likely to be suspected of antisocial acts and therefore more likely to get caught (Zahn-Waxler, 1993). Also, the crimes in which girls specialize, such as shoplifting, are taken less seriously than those in which boys specialize—notably, assault. Another argument is that boys, more than girls, are socialized to be antisocial. In some measure, conduct disorder is just a pathological exaggeration of the behaviors—boldness, fearlessness, the ability to take action—for which boys, and not girls, have been traditionally rewarded in our society. Also, because boys are more likely than girls to be physically punished (Lytton & Romney, 1991), they

Focus On... Antisocial Adolescents: Are There Two Types?

Most criminal offenders are teenagers. A graph that plots crime rate against age would produce a curve that rises sharply from age 11, peaks at 17, and declines fairly steeply in the twenties. This pattern does not represent just a few adolescents who commit many offenses. Rather, it represents a tenfold increase in the number of young criminals. Arrest statistics do not even begin to tell the story of how prevalent delinquency is in adolescence. Using self-reports of deviant behavior, researchers have found that antisocial behavior appears to be a normal part of teenage life (Elliott, Ageton, Huizinga, et al., 1983). A study of more than 1,000 boys in New Zealand showed that, between the ages of 11 and 15, about one third of the sample committed delinquent acts (Moffitt, 1991).

The good news is that the steep decline in offenders in early adulthood means that, for most delinquents, antisocial behavior is temporary and age-specific. T. E. Moffitt (1993) suggests that the pool of adolescent delinquents in society actually conceals two very distinct types of individuals: a very large group whose antisocial behavior is limited to adolescence and a much smaller group that persists in antisocial behavior over the life course, from childhood through adulthood. According to Moffitt (1991), these two types may be indistinguishable during adolescence: her New Zealand study found that the two types did not differ in the variety of laws they broke, the frequency of delinquency, or the number of times they appeared in juvenile court. But a look at the *preadolescent* history of the offenders does offer a way to distinguish between the persistent and temporary types.

From early childhood, persistent types are marked by continuity in antisocial behavior, which may have its origins in disruptions in neuropsychological functions. The antisocial child's aggressive behavior tends to create situations that only reinforce the antisocial tendencies, especially in unsupportive environments. Options for learning prosocial behavior narrow until the persistent antisocial behavior becomes fixed. The behavior may take different forms at different ages: The child who bites and hits at age 4 may be shoplifting at age 10, stealing cars at 16, robbing people at 22, and abusing a child at 30. This behavior takes place in all kinds of situations—at home, at school, at work, in shops (Patterson, 1993). The more stable and continuous the antisocial behavior, the more extreme the forms it takes.

Those whose delinquency is limited to adolescence differ from the persistent types in many important ways. Most significantly, their behavior is marked by *discontinuity*—their delinquent behavior tends to begin abruptly and end just as quickly. Moreover, unlike their persistent peers, they are discriminating: The temporary delinquents behave antisocially only in situations in which doing so seems rewarding to them; if prosocial behavior is more rewarding, they will engage in that. In other words, their antisocial behavior is adaptable and flexible rather than rigid and stable, as in the case of the persistent types. In addition, evidence now suggests another developmental pathway, more applicable to girls, that involves a delayed-onset trajectory (Frick, 1998). In essence, these girls meet the characteristics of the childhood-onset pathway but do not show the misbehaviors until adolescence.

The motivations of the two types differ. For persistent offenders, biological deficits combined with disadvantageous environmental factors produce antisocial behavior that is pathological and abnormal. By contrast, for the temporary types, delinquent behavior is normative. It is a matter of conformity to the group. Moffitt (1993) believes that most delinquents start behaving antisocially in adolescence when they feel the gap between their physical maturity and the social maturity they will not attain until adulthood. Delinquent acts appear to be a way to gain adult power and status. The crimes of the temporary delinquents tend to be those that symbolize adult privilege or release from parental control, such as vandalism, substance abuse, and theft, whereas persistent offenders are more likely to commit victim-oriented offenses, such as violence and fraud. As teenagers grow out of their maturity gap, most of them come to see that the negative consequences of their acts outweigh the rewards, and this realization gradually extinguishes the delinquent behavior.

Moffitt's theory of the two types of adolescent delinquents, if true, indicates that it is futile to study the peak period of delinquent activity in order to learn more about the antisocial individual who will go on to lead a life of crime. Rather, we should single out cases that begin in childhood, even infancy, and follow these antisocial individuals in longitudinal studies. Her theory also suggests that we should learn more about what effects biological age, attitudes about maturity, and access to antisocial peer models have on nondelinquent teenagers.

may simply be doing what was done to them. It is also possible that boys are more subject to prenatal disruptions or genetic influences that may lead to the disorders, especially ADHD. Finally, it has been suggested that natural selection programmed males and females differently—because they are responsible for bearing and rearing children, females are subject to selective pressure for gentleness and empathy, while males are selected for lesser sensitivity, the better to protect the family. Thus, women became "worriers"; men, "warriors" (Dawkins, 1976; Zahn-Waxler, 1993).

Whatever the truth of these hypotheses, there is no question that socioeconomic factors also play a part in conduct disorders. Parental unemployment, family disruption, inadequate schools, and subcultural approval of criminal acts—in other words, all the correlates of poverty—are also correlates of conduct disorder (Frick, 1998).

In addition, child maltreatment is closely related to the development of disruptive behavior disorders: Many youngsters who have been maltreated begin to act out, become defiant or noncompliant, get into fights at school, or lie. In fact, recent longitudinal studies indicate that a history of maltreatment in childhood is strongly predictive of antisocial behavior in adolescence and adulthood. Two studies found that child maltreatment is associated with later arrests, violence, and diagnoses of conduct disorder (Fergusson, Horwood, & Lynskey, 1996; Widom & Maxfield, 1996).

Prevention programs for disruptive behavior problems have successfully reduced aggression and oppositional behavior by focusing on early intervention to improve peer relations, self-control, social problem-solving ability, and early school achievement (Lochman, Coie, Underwood et al., 1993; Schweinhart & Weikart, 1988; Spivak & Shure, 1989). Prevention programs in this area take a parent- and family-training approach, teaching families how to reinforce desirable behavior, use appropriate discipline strategies, and communicate effectively. These are often integrated with classroom behavior management strategies (O'Donnell, Hawkins, Catalano, et al., 1995; Sheeber & Johnson, 1994; Webster-Stratton, 1994). Multicomponent approaches concentrate on parent training, home visits, social-skills training, academic tutoring, and classroom behavior management (Conduct Problems Prevention Research Group, 1992).

Disorders of Emotional Distress

In contrast to the acting out involved in the disruptive behavior disorders, the disorders of emotional distress are less easily observed. The conflict is turned inward; the major victim is the child. Disorders of emotional distress are difficult to diagnose in the younger age groups because children lack the verbal and conceptual skills to tell us what they are feeling. Their emotions have to be guessed at on the basis of their behavior. If a child refuses to go to school, for example, we may infer "school phobia"— and we may be wrong. School-avoidant children may not fear school; they may just find staying at home more rewarding (Kearney, 2001). Nevertheless, in the absence of advanced verbal skills, children's behavior is still the best clue to their emotions.

The accurate assessment of anxiety and depression becomes far easier by adolescence, when children are capable of talking about their feelings. Indeed, the high prevalence of disorders of emotional distress in adolescents, relative to younger children, may be due simply to the fact that adolescents are capable of verbalizing these problems. In any case, there is no doubt that both young children and adolescents experience severe emotional distress, in the forms of anxiety and depression.

Anxiety Disorders

Anxiety disorders in childhood and adolescence are often underrecognized problems, but they can be as common and as debilitating as disruptive behavior disorders. All of the anxiety disorders except separation anxiety disorder can also apply to adults, but children often show their own unique anxiety patterns. The symptoms of panic disorder and agoraphobia, for example, tend to be more physical and less cognitive in children than in adults (e.g., children are less worried about the potential seriousness of the symptoms). Many youths who suffer maltreatment at the hands of their parents or other adults are diagnosed with posttraumatic stress disorder. And many children tend to be perfectionistic about their schoolwork, a behavior that can evolve over time into formal obsessive-compulsive disorder.

Separation Anxiety Disorder

Matt, an eight-year-old boy, was brought into treatment by his mother because of his fears of being separated from her. Matt refused to be left at home alone. He was afraid that he would be kidnapped or that his parents would be killed in a car accident. He also refused to be left alone in his room at night and was demanding that his parents let him sleep in their bed.

Matt usually went to school, but on protest, and he often turned up at the nurse's office complaining of headaches and stomachaches. During the school day he would use the nurse's phone to call his mother several times a day at her office. Matt had friends and enjoyed playing with them, but only if his mother was in close proximity.

When she brought Matt in, the mother reported that she was very frustrated by her inability to quiet the boy's fears. She also said that she was utterly exhausted by him. (Eisen, Fairleigh Dickinson University, 1997, personal files)

Separation anxiety—intense fear and distress upon being separated from parents (or other caregivers)—is seen in almost all children toward the end of the first year of life. It peaks at about 12 months and then gradually disappears. In some children, however, it does not disappear but persists well into the school years. Or, in the more typical pattern, it disappears on schedule and then reappears, at full intensity, later in childhood, usually after the child has undergone some kind of stress, such as the death of a pet or a move to a new school or new neighborhood. This condition, essentially a phobia of being parted from parents, is known as **separation anxiety disorder.** It is the one childhood anxiety syndrome that is still listed separately in *DSM-IV-TR,* under "disorders of childhood and adolescence."

In extreme cases, children with this disorder cannot be separated from their parents by so much as a wall and will shadow them from room to room. In most cases, however, all that the child asks is to be allowed to stay at home, with the parent in the house. But, even with their parents present, children with this disorder may be haunted by fears of horrible things—kidnapping or murder—that may befall them or their parents if they are separated. They generally have sleeping problems as well, since sleep means separation; consequently, they may reappear night after night to crawl into bed with the parents. If banished from the parents' bedroom, they are likely to camp outside the door.

Children with this disorder are typically clinging and demanding, putting considerable strain on their parents. Parent-child conflicts, then, are common with separation anxiety disorder and they exacerbate it, because the parents' annoyance makes the child all the more fearful of abandonment. In addition to experiencing family conflicts, these children also suffer in other areas. They may refuse to attend school; consequently, their academic progress comes to a halt. Furthermore, because they cannot go to school or to other children's houses, they make no friends or they lose the friends they had.

The estimated prevalence of separation anxiety disorder is between 2 and 5 percent of children and adolescents (Silove & Manicavasagar, 2001). By definition, it appears before age 18, generally before puberty, and lasts for several years, with fluctuating intensity. Indeed, it may last beyond age 18. Adults with separation anxiety disorder either refuse to move out of their childhood home or, if they succeed in establishing a new family, are as anxious about separating from their spouses and children as they formerly were about being parted from their parents.

Social Phobia **Social phobia,** or fear of social or performance situations in which embarrassment may occur, was discussed in Chapter 7. As we saw, it tends to have its onset in adolescence, but it may also begin in childhood, at which time it typically takes the form of a paralyzing fear of strangers—peers as well as adults. This disorder affects between 2.4 and 13.3 percent of children and adolescents. (Kessler, McGonagle, Zhao, et al., 1994; Schneier, Johnson, Hornig, et al., 1992).

Like separation anxiety, fear of strangers is normal in very young children, beginning around 8 months. But most children grow out of it by age $2\frac{1}{2}$. Older children may still be standoffish with people they don't know—averting their gaze, pretending not to hear questions, and so forth—but eventually they warm up to the new person and resume their normal behavior. Children with social phobia, on the other hand, do not warm up. When addressed by a stranger, they may be struck mute. When a new person enters the room, they typically take refuge at the side of a familiar adult. When pushed into a situation with many new people, they simply withdraw into a corner, blushing and tongue-tied, until rescued, or, depending on their age, they may burst into tears or even throw a tantrum (Vasey, 1995). As in adults, however, social phobia in children is not necessarily generalized to all social situations. It may be restricted to one or two circumstances or greatly heightened by them. In children, the most common fear is public speaking—reading aloud or giving an oral report, for example.

Children with social phobia, unlike those with separation anxiety disorder, are often well adjusted at home and have normal relationships with their parents. But at school they are painfully withdrawn. This usually interferes with their academic progress, and it prevents them from making friends. Social phobia is possibly more painful for children than for adults, because children do not have the option of avoiding feared situations altogether. (They are required to go to school.) Furthermore, they may not understand the source of their anxiety, and usually they do not know, as adult social phobics do, that it is excessive.

Generalized Anxiety Disorder According to *DSM-IV-TR,* most people with **generalized anxiety disorder** claim that they have been anxious all their lives. In children and adolescents, the disorder often takes the form of anticipatory anxiety about performance situations. Will they pass the test? Will they be picked for the baseball team? If so, will they get hurt playing ball?

As these worries suggest, such children tend to have severe doubts about their own capabilities—doubts that lead them to constantly seek approval. This complex of worry and self-doubt may be the result of family dynamics. There is some evidence that children with generalized anxiety disorder tend to

Children with social phobia fear strangers and new situations, leading them to cling to a parent or familiar adult.

come from families in which parental love is made conditional on consistently "good" behavior.

Whatever its cause, the pervasive anxiety of these children causes significant impairment in their lives. Because anticipatory anxiety robs behavior of its spontaneity, it often creates the very problems that were anticipated. Terrified lest they fail a test or be excluded from a classmate's birthday party, anxious children run a higher risk of failing and being excluded. Such failures tend to lead to further anxiety and further failure—the familiar vicious cycle (Eisen & Engler, 1995).

Childhood Depression

For years the fact that children suffered depression was overlooked or misdiagnosed. Still today, parents and teachers often fail to notice depression in children, even children who report severe depressive feelings, including suicidal thoughts (Tarullo, Richardson, Radke-Yarrow, et al., 1995). Physicians, too, commonly fail to spot suicidal intent in young people (Slap, Vorters, Khalid, et al., 1992). Now, however, psychologists recognize the existence of **childhood depression,** though there is disagreement as to its manifestations. According to some research, the symptoms are similar to those of adult depression: a sad or hopeless mood, a negative view of life, concentration problems, and so on (Prieto, Cole, & Tageson, 1992). But, as developmental psychologists have pointed out, children express these symptoms differently than adults do—by clinging to their parents, refusing to go to school, or expressing exaggerated fears (of their parents' deaths, for example). Older children may sulk, withdraw from family activities, and retreat to their rooms. They may have trouble in school, become slovenly, or engage in delinquent acts. In both children and adolescents, depression may appear as merely one symptom of another emotional disorder or of conduct disorder (Compas, Ey, & Grant, 1993).

Still, clear-cut depressions are not rare in the underage population. Community surveys of children and adolescents have found the prevalence of clinical depression to be between 2 and 5 percent (Cohen, Cohen, Kasen, et al., 1993; Kashani, Carlson, Beck, et al., 1990; Lewinsohn, Hops, Roberts, et al., 1993). Adolescents may be somewhat more vulnerable than younger children. In school-age children in general, 1 percent are depressed enough to express clearly suicidal thoughts (Larsson & Melin, 1992), but adolescents are more likely to contemplate, attempt, and complete a suicide. As we saw in Chapter 10, adolescent suicides have increased alarmingly in recent years. Follow-up studies of people diagnosed as depressed in childhood indicate that they are also at risk for mood disorders as adults. Therefore, they could probably benefit from early detection and treatment (Rao, Ryan, Birmaher, et al., 1995).

❖ Groups at Risk for Disorders of Emotional Distress

Girls are more likely to experience separation anxiety disorder, social phobia, and generalized anxiety disorder (Eisen, Kearney, & Schaefer, 1995). Young boys are more vulnerable to depression. In the early years, the differences between the genders in risk for anxiety and mood disorders are not striking. By adolescence, however, the picture changes. Teenage girls are twice as likely as teenage boys to experience disorders of emotional distress (Cohen, Cohen, Kasen, et al., 1993). Perhaps by this time the genders have been socialized into their "worrier" and "warrior" roles and express their problems accordingly. In fact, a review (Schwartz, Gladstone,

& Kaslow, 1998) indicates that the main reasons for the different vulnerability of boys and girls are these differences in gender-role socialization as well as differences in cognitive styles, negative life events in early adolescence, and hormonal changes.

Several studies indicate that child maltreatment is closely related to the development of anxiety disorders, especially posttraumatic stress disorder. The experience of trauma, like child maltreatment, may trigger dual vulnerabilities for PTSD and other anxiety disorders (Famularo, Fenton, Kinscherff, et al., 1994; Fletcher, 1996; McLeer, Dixon, Henry, et al., 1998; McNally, 1996; Wolfe, Sas, & Wekerle, 1994). In addition, maltreatment is closely related to the development of childhood depression, as children who have been maltreated often feel betrayed, alone, guilty, worthless, suicidal, and morose (Dykman, McPherson, Ackerman, et al., 1997; Famularo, Kinscherff, & Fenton, 1992; Merry & Andrews, 1994; Wolfe & McEachran, 1997).

Gymnast Christy Henrich, pictured here with her boyfriend, developed anorexia after being told she was too heavy to make the United States Olympic squad. She died in 1994, at age 22, from multiple organ failure caused by her eating disorder.

Eating Disorders

Since Freud's time, psychologists have interpreted eating as a crucial part of development, because children's feelings about eating are bound up with their feelings about those who feed and sustain them—their parents and others. For the same reason, experts tend to view eating disorders as a reflection of emotional conflicts. We will discuss three conditions: anorexia nervosa, bulimia nervosa, and childhood obesity.

Anorexia Nervosa

Defined as a severe restriction of food intake caused by a fear of gaining weight, **anorexia nervosa** is overwhelmingly a disorder of adolescent girls and young women. From 85 to 95 percent of people with anorexia are female, and in most cases the onset is between ages 12 and 18, though it may also occur in prepuberty or as late as age 30. Anorexia is a rare disorder, but it is apparently becoming more common. Joergensen (1992) found incidence rates of 9.2 females per 100,000 in 10- to 14-year-olds and 11.9 females per 100,000 in 15- to 19-year-olds. Lucas and colleagues (Lucas, Beard, O'Fallon, et al., 1991) found incidence rates of 14.6 per 100,000 in 10- to 14-year-olds (25.7 females and 3.7 males) and 43.5 per 100,000 in 15- to 19-year-olds (69.4 females and 7.3 males). Unlike most psychological disorders, it is physically dangerous. About one third of people with anorexia remain chronically ill, and an estimated 5 percent die (Steinhausen, 1994).

Predictably, the most dramatic physical sign of anorexia is emaciation. Bliss and Branch (1960) cite the case of a woman whose weight dropped from 180 to 60 pounds. Not all cases are that severe, however, and not all involve a *loss* of weight. The cutoff line in the *DSM-IV-TR* criteria is a body weight less than 85 percent of what is normal for the patient's age and height, whether that condition is the result of the patient's losing weight or simply not gaining weight as she grew. Aside from low weight, the other criteria are an intense fear of becoming fat, an unrealistic body image, and, in girls, *amenorrhea,* or suspension of menstrual periods. All these symptoms must be present for the person to be diagnosed as anorexic.

In behavioral terms, people with anorexia usually follow one of two patterns. In the *restricting type,* they simply refuse to eat (and perhaps overexercise as well). In the *binge-eating/purging type,* they eat, sometimes voraciously, but compensate by making themselves vomit or by using laxatives or other purgatives. Some patients report that they are so repelled by food that they never experience normal sensations of hunger, but they are the exceptions. Most people with anorexia clearly have normal appetites, at least in the early stages of the disorder (Marrazzi & Luby, 1986). Indeed, they may become preoccupied with food, collecting cookbooks, preparing elaborate meals for others, and so forth.

Apart from low weight, fear of obesity is perhaps the most typical feature of anorexia. Despite overwhelming evidence to the contrary—clawlike hands, skull-like faces, protruding ribs—people with anorexia insist that they are too fat and need to lose weight. This distorted body image, together with an iron determination to correct the supposed fatness, is critical to the development of the disorder. Some women with anorexia have a history of obesity (Rastam, 1992), and anorexia often follows a period of dieting, as in the following case:

> At 15, Alma had been healthy and well-developed, had menstruated at age 12, was five feet six inches tall, and weighed one hundred twenty pounds. At that time her mother urged her to change to a school with higher academic standing, a change she resisted; her father suggested that she should watch her weight, an idea that she took up with great eagerness, and she began a rigid diet. She lost rapidly and her menses ceased. That she could be thin gave her a sense of pride, power, and accomplishment. She also began a frantic exercise program, would swim by the mile, play tennis for hours, or do calisthenics to the point of exhaustion. Whatever low point her weight reached, Alma feared that she might become "too fat" if she regained as little as an ounce. . . .
>
> When she came for consultation [at age twenty] she looked like a walking skeleton, scantily dressed in shorts and a halter, with her legs sticking out like broomsticks, every rib showing, and her shoulder blades standing up like little wings. . . . Alma insisted that she looked fine and that there was nothing wrong with being so skinny. (Bruch, 1978, pp. 1–2)

Bulimia Nervosa

People who engage in uncontrolled binge-eating and then compensate for it but who do not meet the other criteria for anorexia, such as low body weight or amenhorrea, are said to have **bulimia nervosa.** People with bulimia regularly go on binges, during which they consume extraordinary amounts of food, often sweet, high-calorie food—a whole cake, a quart of ice cream—until they are uncomfortably, even painfully, full. Then, in 9 out of 10 cases, they make themselves vomit by sticking their fingers or another instrument down the throat to stimulate the gag reflex. Some people with bulimia, instead of vomiting, use laxatives, diuretics (drugs that induce urination), or enemas. Still others do not purge themselves but try to compensate by fasting or exercising.

Like people with anorexia, people with bulimia base their self-esteem in large measure on their body shape. (This is one of the diagnostic criteria.) Consequently, their binges are surrounded by shame. Most of them binge alone, in secret, and try to hide the traces from their families or roommates. Binges are often triggered by stress or unhappiness and are followed by greater unhappiness. Bulimia can also have physical consequences—not only unstable weight but amenorrhea, electrolyte imbalance, and rotted teeth. (Repeated vomiting overexposes the teeth to stomach acid.)

Bulimia resembles anorexia not just in symptomatology but in other ways as well: It usually has its onset in late adolescence or early adulthood; it tends to appear after or during a period of dieting; and it is overwhelmingly a female disorder. In clinic and population samples, at least 90 percent of people with bulimia are female. But bulimia is far more common than anorexia, affecting 1 to 3 percent of adolescent girls and young women (Weltzin, Starzynski, Santelli, et al., 1993). The disorder tends to persist for several years, appearing and disappearing. Evidence indicates that people with bulimia fluctuate between improvement and relapse over time; and, even after treatment, many continue to show low-level eating disturbances such as extensive dieting, laxative use, and exercise (Mizes, 1995). For years a part of campus pathology, bulimia has only recently begun to be seriously studied.

Childhood Obesity

Obesity in children has not generated the alarm that anorexia and bulimia have in recent years, yet it is a far more common problem. The estimated prevalence of obesity in children and adolescents is 15 percent (National Center for Health Statistics, 2002). In children, as in adults, excess weight can contribute to physical disorders, but a special concern with children is the psychological consequences. Adults have ways of coping with the shame that our society attaches to being overweight. For a child, on the other hand, teasing by peers and humiliating visits to the "husky" department of clothing stores may be crushing to self-esteem. This problem is especially acute for girls. In boys, low self-esteem is more likely to be associated with being too thin than with being overweight (Pierce & Wardle, 1993).

Obesity in children can have negative physical and psychological consequences. Studies have shown that parental involvement and modification of family routines can positively affect the success of a child's treatment.

As we pointed out in Chapter 9, obesity is probably due to a combination of physiological factors—metabolic rate and exercise patterns—and psychological variables such as responsiveness to food cues. This is as true for children as for adults. But a factor that experts on childhood obesity take very seriously is the family routine: the balance of physical exercise *versus* television watching in their leisure time, the balance of broiled fish *versus* macaroni and cheese at the dinner table. Parents are usually brought into the child's treatment right away, and their cooperation has great influence on the child's success in returning to and maintaining a normal weight (Foreyt & Goodrick, 1993; Israel, Guile, Baker, et al., 1994).

❖ Groups at Risk for Eating Disorders

As we have pointed out, anorexia and bulimia are, for the most part, female disorders; they are as much the specialty of girls as conduct disorders are the specialty of boys. Why should females be so anxious about weight? Many experts blame the culture and, above all, the fashion and advertising industries. Over the past few decades, cultural ideals of female attractiveness, as reflected in magazine advertisements, have increasingly favored thinness, and it is in that same period that anorexia and, above all, bulimia have emerged as major public health problems (Killen, Taylor, Hayward, et al., 1996; Williamson, Kahn, Remington, et al., 1990). The recent increase in the incidence of these disorders may be due in part to greater public awareness and, hence, increased reporting, but it is surely due also to the fact that most of the fashion models on whom American girls base their notions of beauty are extremely underweight.

The risk for eating disorders now seems to be spreading to preteenage groups. In one study, almost a third of the 9-year-old girls reported a fear of being fat, and almost half said they were dieting or trying to control their food intake (Mellin, Irwin, & Scully, 1992). The fact that such attitudes and behaviors correlate with psychological problems—lower self-esteem, greater depression—has only increased alarm over the eating disorders (Killen, Hayward, Wilson, et al., 1994).

As a result, experts are now trying to identify girls who are at risk. This includes those with "partial syndromes"—that is, those who meet some of the criteria for anorexia or bulimia but not enough to receive the diagnosis. Between 35 and 50 percent of girls referred for treatment of eating disorders have only partial syndromes (Shisslak, Crago, & Estes, 1995). Others who may be vulnerable are those who report being worried about their weight, skipping meals, experiencing a loss of control while eating, feeling guilty after eating, and believing that others see them as overweight (Lask, 2000). The hope is that, by pinpointing such factors, programs—for example, nutritional education in schools—can be instituted to prevent full-syndrome eating disorders from developing. Prevention programs for eating disorders are very few, but those that exist have focused on educating people about the general characteristics of eating disorders and appropriate physical development, teaching about the effects of extreme weights, and promoting healthy weight regulation (Killen, Taylor, Hammer, et al., 1993; Moreno & Thelen, 1993).

Elimination Disorders

Like eating, toilet training can be an arena of intense conflict for a child. Toilet training is one of the first points in development at which children have to comply with demands that run counter to their natural impulses. Sometimes these demands are extreme, for our society insists that children achieve control over elimination at an early age. When children fail to pass this developmental milestone, they are diagnosed as having either enuresis (lack of bladder control) or encopresis (lack of bowel control).

Enuresis

Enuresis usually is defined as a lack of bladder control past the age when such control is usual. In this country, most children achieve daytime control between the ages of 2 and 3 and nighttime control a year later, but many are much slower. Most children who fall behind in bladder control have trouble with nighttime control—bed-wetting. Daytime wetting is much less common and may be the sign of a more serious psychological problem.

As for the age that separates normal "accidents" from enuresis, this varies with the clinician making the decision. *DSM-IV-TR* specifies only a minimum age: no child under the age of 5 may be given this diagnosis. In addition, the child must be wetting his or her pants or bed at least twice a week or, if the frequency is less, must be suffering serious distress or impaired functioning (e.g., humiliations at school) as a result of the wetting. According to *DSM-IV-TR,* the prevalence of enuresis is around 5 to 10 percent for 5-year-olds and 3 to 5 percent for 10-year-olds.

Enuresis may be primary or secondary. Children with *primary enuresis* have never achieved bladder control; whenever they have to urinate, day or night, they wet their pants. Primary enuresis may last until middle childhood, and in rare cases it persists well beyond that point. (At age 18, the prevalence of enuresis is still 1 percent for males.) Some authorities have suggested that the condition may stem from organic, possibly genetic, abnormalities (Ondersma & Walker, 1998). By contrast, children with *secondary enuresis* achieve bladder control and then lose it, almost always as a result of stress. The birth of a baby brother or sister, with the insecurity this often provokes, is probably the most common cause. Whether treated or not, secondary enuresis is usually temporary.

Most enuretic children are not emotionally disturbed (Christophersen & Edwards, 1992). When an emotional problem is present, it is usually a consequence, not a cause, of the wetting. When the enuresis occurs in isolation—that is, not as part of a larger problem—it usually responds well to treatment. Treatment may be warranted, for enuresis can cause problems. Children who wet their pants are likely to be ridiculed by their schoolmates. They may also have problems with their parents, who typically begin to resent being awakened in the night to change wet sheets. Rejecting or ridiculing the child only adds to the child's problems. Reassurance is a better tactic. Another is to keep a clean set of sheets and nightclothes next to the child's bed. Even a 6-year-old can be taught, when the bed is wet, to change pajamas, sheets, and rubber pad. This preserves the parents' peace and the child's self-respect.

Bed-wetting almost always clears up, but it may clear up slowly. Many normal children are still wetting their beds at age 12, and, as noted, the causes may be organic. About three quarters of enuretic children have a first-degree relative who was also enuretic, and the concordance rate is higher in MZ twins than in DZ twins (American Psychiatric Association, 2000).

Encopresis

When the elimination problem is lack of bowel control rather than of bladder control, the condition is called **encopresis.** Encopresis and enuresis may occur together—about one quarter of children with encopresis also manifest enuresis—and in some ways the two syndromes are alike. Encopresis, too, is classified as either primary (control is never achieved) or secondary (control is mastered and then lost). In the primary form, it may have an organic basis. It is more common in boys than in girls. Finally, even more than enuresis, encopresis can earn a child mockery from peers and wrath from parents, compounding whatever problems he or she has.

However, encopresis is far rarer. Its prevalence—1 percent of 5-year-olds (Doleys, 1989)—is one fifth that of enuresis. And it is a more serious problem. It rarely appears in isolation; usually, it occurs as part of a larger disorder, such as a disruptive behavior disorder, or in the context of severe family problems. It may be that some children with encopresis are maltreated children, though, again, this may be a result rather than, or as well as, a cause of the encopresis.

Childhood Sleep Disorders

Of the sleep disorders listed in *DSM-IV-TR,* the ones that are most common in children are insomnia, nightmares, night terrors, and sleepwalking.

Insomnia

Probably the most common response to stress in early childhood is insomnia, usually in the form of difficulties falling asleep or staying asleep. (Difficulty staying asleep is sometimes referred to as *night waking.*) We have already discussed insomnia in Chapter 9, and

Night terrors are a rare and puzzling sleep disorder. The child awakens in a state of panic, but has no memory of the incident the next day.

much of what was said there applies to children as well as adults. Childhood insomnia is special, however, in that, as with other childhood disorders, it is not the person with the problem but his or her parents who decide if treatment is needed. Some parents dismiss a child's insomnia as attention-getting behavior. (As a result, many cases of true childhood insomnia probably go unreported.) The sleeping problem may, in fact, have physiological causes—for example, sleep apnea, a breathing disorder, or a digestive problem such as colic. On the other hand, it is most often related to worries (Horne, 1992), particularly worries attendant on beginning school. Insomnia is endemic in children who are starting school, and it generally clears up by itself. Researchers have found that 65 percent of 3-month-olds and 28 percent of 9- to 12-month-olds have interruptions in their sleep at night (Michelsson, Rinne, & Paajanen, 1990). Other studies indicate that 20 to 30 percent of toddlers awaken during the night (Jenkins, Owen, Bax, et al., 1994) and that about one third of 4- and 5-year-olds—but only 15 percent of 6-year-olds and 8 percent of 10-year-olds—wake up repeatedly during the night (Klackenberg, 1982).

Nightmares and Night Terrors

Another common complaint is **nightmares,** which seem to occur more frequently in childhood than in the later years. Between 10 and 50 percent of children aged 3 to 5 have nightmares often enough to concern their parents (American Sleep Disorders Association, 1990). Less prevalent, but more disturbing for parents, are **sleep terrors,** also called *night terrors,* which occur in 1 to 6 percent of children and are very rare in adults (Anders & Eiben, 1997). Children having nightmares show no particular physiological arousal, and they may or may not be awakened by the dream. When they do wake up, they are usually able to describe the dream in detail—how big the monster was, what its cave looked like. By contrast, children in the throes of a sleep terror show intense physiological arousal (sweating, hyperventilation, racing heart), but when they wake up, they often don't recall the terror and will usually go right back to sleep. The next morning, they have no memory of the episode. While nightmares are thus more harrowing for children because they remember the dreams when they wake up, for parents sleep terrors are far more harrowing, because they see all of the child's behavior. Sleep terrors are timed differently, because they arise out of a different stage of sleep (slow-wave sleep) than do nightmares (REM sleep). Sleep terrors occur during the first few hours of sleep; nightmares, closer to morning (Bootzin, Manber, Perlis, et al., 1993; Mindell & Cashman, 1995).

Sleepwalking

Sleepwalking, or somnambulism, is another sleep disturbance that is much more common in the young. Less than 1 percent of adults sleepwalk, but about 15 percent of healthy children have at least 1 episode of sleepwalking, and about 1 to 6 percent have several episodes a week (Anders & Eiben, 1997), with prevalence peaking at about age 12. Children who sleepwalk typically fall asleep, and then, without waking up, they get out of bed an hour or two later and perform a complex action such as making a sandwich or even dressing and leaving the house. (They rarely go far, however.) Their eyes are open, and they do not bump into things. The episode may last anywhere from 15 seconds to 30 minutes, after which the sleepwalker usually returns to bed (Aldrich, 1989). Contrary to popular belief, sleepwalkers are not acting out their dreams. Like night terrors, sleepwalking occurs during non-REM sleep, which is not a period of dreaming.

Most experts do not regard sleepwalking in children as a serious problem. Generally, they advise parents to make sure the front door is locked and, if they find their children sleepwalking, not to wake them up—this often frightens them—but just to guide them back to bed (Bootzin, Manber, Perlis, et al., 1993).

Learning and Communication Disorders

Learning Disorders

When a person's skill in reading, writing, or mathematics is substantially below what would be expected for his or her age, education, and intelligence and when this interferes with the person's adjustment, the problem is said to be one of the three **learning disorders.** Children with *reading disorder* (also known as *dyslexia*) read slowly and with poor comprehension, and, when reading aloud, they drop, substitute, or distort words. Children with *disorder of written expression* typically have a number of writing problems: poor paragraph organization; faulty spelling, grammar, and punctuation; illegible handwriting. In *mathematics disorder,* the child may fail to understand concepts, to recognize symbols, or to remember operations (e.g., to "carry" a number). In any case, the answer comes out wrong.

A review by the American Academy of Child and Adolescent Psychiatry (1998) indicates that 10 to 20 percent of children have a language and/or learning disorder. The prevalence of reading disorder is estimated at 4 percent, mathematics disorder at 1 to 6 percent, and written expression disorder at 2 to 8 percent. However, prevalence figures are probably not accurate, because clinicians disagree on the definition of this syndrome. Mentally retarded children and children with impaired vision or hearing are usually excluded from the category, but that still leaves an extremely heterogeneous group. As many as one quarter of children with conduct disorders, ADHD, and depression also have diagnosable learning disorders (Durrant, 1994). Various medical conditions, such as lead poisoning and fetal alcohol syndrome, involve learning disorders. And, while *DSM-IV-TR* specifies that children whose school problems stem from lack of opportunity, poor teaching, and "cultural factors" should not receive this diagnosis, many of them do. At present, the diagnostic group probably runs the gamut from brain-damaged children to children with no quiet place to do their homework.

Though children with impaired vision and hearing are supposed to be excluded from the category, it is clear that most children with learning disorders do have perceptual (organization of information) problems. Thus, a child could have unimpaired eyesight, but could still have perceptual problems, such as difficulty recognizing words in a sentence, breaking down a new word into its parts (for example, *man* as *m-a-n*), and understanding the relationship between the sound of a word and its printed form. In fact, disturbed visual perception is the most common problem of children in this category. Many have trouble focusing on lines of type on a page. Some cannot copy words from the chalkboard correctly. Some cannot tell *mop* from *map,* *N* from *M,* or a circle from a triangle.

As for problems of auditory perception, children with learning disorders often have to struggle to distinguish the sounds of different words or to make simple associations between the words they hear (Hulme & Roodenrys, 1995). Some may not be able to identify the sound of, for example, a car horn honking or a dog barking. When perceptual problems accompany a learning disorder, they usually occur in more than one system—visual, auditory, and haptic (touch and movement). It is the prevalence of such perceptual difficulties that has led many experts to believe that learning disorders are neurologically based.

Some children with learning disorders also show disturbances in memory and other cognitive functions. Many cannot recall from one day to the next what they have learned in school—a problem that is painfully frustrating to them and to their teachers. They may also have difficulties with sequential thinking and with organizing their thoughts. The cognitive aspects of learning disorders have been the subject of much research in recent years.

The memory lapses associated with learning disorders may be related to attention deficits. As noted, some children with learning disorders also have ADHD, but even those who don't often have short attention spans. While children with learning disorders do worse than normal children at recalling important information, they do better at recalling irrelevant information (Felton & Wood, 1989). This suggests that their problem may lie not with remembering things but with paying attention to things that they will be expected to remember. Like other children, children with learning disorders get better at focusing attention as they grow

Focus On... Recognizing Learning Disorders: Some Signs

Starting school can be difficult for young children. It's even harder for the up to 20 percent of school-aged children who may have a neurological deficit (mild to severe) that makes it difficult to read and write (Fletcher, Shaywit, Shankweiler, et al., 1994). Fortunately, in the United States parents have a right to have public schools evaluate their children for learning disabilities after age 3. There are no absolute signs of learning disability; they vary with age and the individual. However, if a child seems to lag in comparison with the child's peers, an evaluation should be considered.

In preschool, children with learning disabilities may have problems with language or concentration. These children may start talking later than their peers and have slow-growing vocabularies. They may also have trouble learning lists of words like number words, the alphabet, or the days of the week. Sounds of words can be confusing, and many of these children have trouble pronouncing and rhyming words. In addition, these children are often restless and distractible, and they have problems following directions. They may avoid tasks that require sitting still or concentrating, such as solving puzzles, drawing, or cutting (Lyon, 1996).

When children with learning disabilities reach kindergarten, their symptoms begin to show up in their schoolwork. Students up to the fourth grade make consistent language errors in their spelling and reading classes, such as reversing letters (*p/q*) or inverting them (*u/n*), and they may have trouble learning which letters represent which sounds. Some children cannot hold a pencil well, which only makes their writing worse. Attention problems may express themselves as impulsiveness, or an inability to follow directions or learn about time. The children may have poor recall and trouble learning any new skill (Lyon, 1996).

Of course, not all children who have a hard time in school have a learning disability. Poor hearing, eyesight, and muscular diseases can all interfere with learning as well. Children who may be learning disabled also need to be screened for psychological problems, including anxiety, depression, and attention deficit hyperactivity disorder. Distractible, impulsive children may simply be having problems at home—problems that can affect schoolwork but that need to be solved outside the classroom (Bryan & Bryan, 1990).

older, but they lag two to four years behind. Some experts believe that learning disorders are fundamentally a problem of delayed development, and findings such as these support that theory. The signs of a learning disorder vary with each child and with the child's age (see the box above).

Because children with learning disorders do poorly in school, they are often seen as failures by their teachers, parents, and peers. In consequence, they usually show low self-esteem and low motivation by age 9 (Bjorkland & Green, 1992; Heavey, Adelman, & Smith, 1989), a problem which then worsens with time and with further failures. (According to *DSM-IV-TR*, their school dropout rate is 40 percent. They also tend to have employment problems as adults.) Children with learning disorders, especially girls, are usually less popular with their peers than are other children, a disadvantage that is probably due to a number of factors. On the one hand, frustration and anxiety may cause these children to act in ways that alienate people. On the other hand, their social success may be undermined by the same cognitive problems that impede their academic success. A child who can't remember the rules of a game tends to be left out of games.

❖ Groups at Risk for Learning Disorders

Boys are more likely than girls to develop learning disorders, though reading disorder occurs at equal rates in both sexes (*DSM-IV-TR*). Poverty, low socioeconomic status, and membership in a minority group also put children at a higher risk for learning disorders (Barona & Faykus, 1992; Council for Exceptional Children, 1994; McDermott, 1994).

Historically, learning disorders have been a middle-class disorder. In the 1970s and 1980s, White, middle-class children were disproportionately placed in classes for children with learning disorders, while Black children were disproportionately placed in classes for people with mental retardation (Kessler, 1988). In 1971, the student body in classes for children with learning disabilities was 96.8 percent White and 3.2 percent Black, while classes for people with mental retardation were 34.2 percent White, 65.2 percent Black (Barona & Faykus, 1992).

More recently, schools have recognized that many standardized tests discriminate against certain groups and that being labeled "mentally retarded" can be a stigma. As educators have tried to move more children into school placements that optimize learning, the class and ethnic differences between children with learning disorders and children with mental retardation have diminished. However, they have not disappeared; as of 1990, minorities made up 32 percent of the school-age population, 47 percent of the students in classes for children with mental retardation, and 30 percent of students enrolled in programs for children with learning disabilities (Council for Exceptional Children, 1994).

The cause of learning disorders is still a mystery, but its linkage to some dysfunction in the central nervous system remains a popular theory. In particular, children with learning disorders may have differences in certain key brain areas such as the parietal-occipital cortex or the planum temporale—the latter is often responsible for language and reading. Children without learning disorders often show asymmetry in the planum temporale, but this is not always the case for children with learning disorders. Learning disorders have also been linked to possible alterations on chromosomes 6 and 15.

Treatment for children with learning disorders focuses a great deal on educational practice and tutoring. Children with learning disorders often attend special resource rooms during the day to practice fundamental concepts of reading, spelling, writing, and arithmetic. Children with problems reading, for example, are often taught to review a particular book passage, identify and practice difficult words, read the passage with the teacher's help, and then read the passage alone until few errors are made. In doing so, children practice word recognition and awareness of phonemes, both of which are core deficits in a reading disability.

Successful prevention programs for the learning disorders focus on preschool learning initiatives like Head Start that concentrate on academic readiness skills such as speaking clearly, sitting in one's seat, taking turns, and following directions (Boocock, 1995; Yoshikawa, 1995) and include assistance to parents, social support, and health services. At the school-age level, prevention of learning disorders involves a heavy emphasis on tutoring, proactive classroom functioning, parent participation, and making schools more effective (Slavin, Karweit, & Wasik, 1994; Stevens & Slavin, 1995).

Communication Disorders

Delayed Speech and Other Gaps in Communication Most children say their first words within a few months after their first birthday, and by 18 to 24 months they put together 2- and 3-word sentences. A few months' delay in this schedule rarely signals a problem, but a prolonged delay is reason for worry. It may be an early sign of an organic disorder, such as deafness, autism, or mental retardation (Chapter 17), or it may stem from environmental causes.

In other cases, speech develops on time, but there are gaps in the child's communication skills. Some children have problems with *articulation:* They do not enunciate clearly, or they go on talking baby talk long after it is normally abandoned. Others have difficulties with *expressive language*—that is, with putting their thoughts into words—either because their vocabularies are limited or because they have a hard time formulating complete sentences. Both these patterns can cause a child to be treated "like a baby." The child may also become very frustrated when he or she is not understood. But both patterns tend to clear up by themselves during the grade-school years.

More serious and typically longer-lasting are delays in *receptive language*—that is, in understanding the language of others. This type of disability can be disastrous for a child in school. Surrounded by fast-paced verbal messages that others are obviously understanding while he or she is not, the child may become overwhelmed with frustration. Special education techniques are usually necessary for children with receptive language deficits.

Stuttering The interruption of fluent speech through blocked, prolonged, or repeated words, syllables, or sounds is called **stuttering.** Hesitant speech is common in young children. Therefore, as with so many other childhood disorders, it is often difficult to decide when stuttering is a serious problem. Persistent stuttering occurs in about 1 percent of the population and in about 4 times as many boys as girls. It is most likely to appear between the ages of 2 and 7 (with peak onset at around age 5) and seldom appears after age 11.

Many children outgrow stuttering as their motor skills and confidence increase. About 40 percent of stutterers are estimated to overcome the problem before they start school, and 80 percent overcome it by late adolescence. Even those who do not fully outgrow it stutter less, or only in stressful situations, as they grow older (Couture & Guitar, 1993).

Organic theories of stuttering are popular in some quarters. One hypothesis is that stuttering stems from a problem with the physical articulation of sounds in the mouth and larynx (Agnello, 1975; Kerr & Cooper, 1976). But many psychologists today think that stuttering is genetic. Indeed, one major study found that the heritability of stuttering is 71 percent (Andrews, Morris-Yates, Howie, et al., 1991) and that people who stutter tend to use more of their right hemispheres when they speak.

Disorders of Childhood and Adolescence: Theory and Therapy

Many people feel that treating childhood disorders is a matter of special urgency, not only to reduce the suffering of the children in question, but also in the hope of averting later problems, such as delinquency, and preventing difficulties that might otherwise persist into adulthood. Behavioral and cognitive-behavioral approaches have been found to be the most effective in treatment, so they are emphasized here.

The Behavioral Perspective

Inappropriate Learning From the behavioral point of view, childhood disorders usually stem from either inadequate learning or inappropriate learning. For example, inadequate learning—that is, a failure to learn relevant cues for performing desired behaviors—may play a role in primary enuresis: The child may never have learned to identify the physiological cues associated with a full bladder. In support of this idea, some researchers have found that enuresis can be successfully treated by teaching the child to recognize those cues (Houts, Berman, & Abramson, 1994). As for the development of problems through inappropriate learning—that is, the reinforcement of undesirable behavior—the behaviorist's prime example is the conduct disorders. Children with conduct disorders often come from homes where the parents constantly pay attention to their children when they are aggressive or disruptive or noncompliant and tend to ignore more prosocial behavior. In addition, there is little doubt that modeling plays a role in the conduct disorders. Parents may themselves be models of antisocial behavior, especially through indifferent or abusive treatment of the child.

In Chapters 4 and 5, we discussed the importance of avoidance learning—the reinforcement of avoidance behavior by the removal of an aversive stimulus such as anxiety—in the development of phobias. Behaviorists believe that this same mechanism—together with direct reinforcements associated with staying home (parental attention, home cooking, television)—may also explain separation anxiety disorder and social phobia.

Relearning To replace the child's maladaptive responses with adaptive behaviors, behavior therapists use the entire behavioral repertoire: reinforcement, extinction, punishment (usually in the form of the withdrawal of rewards), modeling, respondent conditioning, and so on. To begin with the simplest technique, respondent conditioning, a classic example is the treatment of nocturnal enuresis by means of the so-called Mowrer pad. This device, invented by psychologist O. H. Mowrer, is a liquid-sensitive pad connected by a battery to an alarm. Any moisture on the pad sounds the alarm, awakening the child (Mowrer & Mowrer, 1938; Houts, Berman, & Abramson, 1994). Although theoretically the child should learn to awaken in anticipation of the alarm, many children learn instead to sleep throughout the night, neither awakening nor wetting. Researchers have found that the urine alarm system, used over a 5- to 12-week period, is effective for 75 percent of children, although many relapse and require additional treatment (Christophersen & Mortweet, 2001; Doleys, 1977).

In treating anxiety disorders in children, as in adults, behaviorists have used systematic desensitization (Silverman & Treffers, 2001) and exposure techniques. An early example of exposure therapy was Mary Cover Jones' famous treatment of the boy Peter's fear of furry animals by bringing a rabbit closer and closer to him while he was eating candy.

Modeling has also proved very valuable in the treatment of phobias. The child watches the therapist or another person play with a dog, handle a snake, or deal in a relaxed manner with whatever it is that the child fears. Then, in successive steps, the child tries it, and the phobia gradually extinguishes (Barrios & O'Dell, 1997).

Operant-conditioning programs have been successful in the treatment of ADHD. One classroom program, for example, combined extinction of problem behaviors, such as the distracting of one's schoolmates, with reinforcement of more positive behaviors, such as remaining seated long enough to finish a task (Patterson, 1976). Such operant techniques have proven as effective as drugs in controlling the disruptiveness of children with ADHD (Barkley, 1998). Operant conditioning has also been used in the treatment of anorexia nervosa: When patients with anorexia are hospitalized and their privileges are made contingent upon eating, they almost invariably gain weight. But, once they are released from hospital treatment programs, they tend to relapse unless programs involving the family are also developed (Honig & Sharman, 2000). Parents, teachers, and other adults are a critical part of most behavioral programs. In fact, given the theory that parents may inadvertently reward a child's misbehavior (Patterson, Reid, & Dishion, 1992), parent training is a widely accepted form of behavior therapy for children. To break the cycle of attending to misbehavior through bribery or giving in to demands, therapists help parents reward positive behaviors, provide alternatives to misbehavior, use specific and clear commands that children can understand, and seek relief when they need it. In essence, parents learn to reward prosocial behavior and to be actively and positively involved in their children's lives.

One application of operant conditioning that has proved useful for certain behavior disorders is the token economy, a technique that we have discussed in relation to schizophrenia (Chapter 14). With children, it is used just as with adults. Desirable behavior is rewarded with stars, points, or a token that the child can save and later exchange for candy, a turn with a special toy, or another coveted reward. Token systems have proven successful in institutions for delinquent children and in schoolrooms (Kazdin, 1993).

Prevention The FRIENDS Program for Preventing Childhood Disorders

A promising prevention program by Barrett, Lowry-Webster, and Holmes (1999) concentrates on educating children about anxiety. The FRIENDS program teaches children to relax, challenge and change their own negative statements, cope with troublesome situations, reward themselves for positive behavior, and practice these steps in real-life situations. FRIENDS is an acronym for

- **F**eeling worried
- **R**elax and feel good
- **I**nner thoughts
- **E**xplore plans
- **N**ice work so reward yourself
- **D**on't forget to practice
- **S**tay cool

Research indicates that FRIENDS does reduce the prevalence of anxiety disorders in children compared to controls (Dadds, Holland, Barrett, et al., 1999; Dadds, Spence, Holland, et al., 1997; Spence, 1994). In one study, for example, children aged $6\frac{1}{2}$ to 10 years old with anxiety disorders were randomly assigned either to a family-based cognitive-behavioral treatment group or to a control group (Short, Barrett, & Fox, 2001). At posttreatment, more than 66 percent of the treatment group no longer met criteria for an anxiety disorder, compared to just 6 percent in the control group. Remarkably, even at 1-year follow-up, the treatment results were largely maintained. Lowry-Webster and Barrett (2001) also found that a 10-session FRIENDS intervention was useful for preventing the development of anxiety and depressive symptoms in children aged 10 to 13 years old.

These studies indicate that a cognitive-behavioral program involving family members and the child in question is effective for treating and preventing emotional distress in children. Such an approach could be useful in school settings to identify children at risk for emotional distress, allow for quick and effective intervention, and prevent further problems from occurring.

The Cognitive Perspective

Negative Cognitions in Children Cognitive theorists argue that in children, as in adults, problem behaviors can stem from negative beliefs, faulty attributions, poor problem solving, and other cognitive factors. Depression offers a good example. Depression in a child is usually precipitated by disruption in family life—for example, parental separation. But, according to cognitive theory, the real trigger is not the event but the cognitive factors that come into play around it. When parents separate, the children need to be reassured that this is for the best. Often, however, they get the opposite message, as one parent succumbs to depression and, by modeling depressive cognitive strategies—helplessness, hopelessness, self-blame—inadvertently teaches the children to adopt the same way of thinking. Many children of recently separated parents believe that they are responsible for the breakup. And, in general, depressed children tend to have at least one depressed parent.

Changing Children's Cognitions Cognitive therapy is now being used for a wide range of childhood disorders. In the early 1970s, Meichenbaum and Goodman (1971) pioneered cognitive therapy for children with ADHD, the goal being to teach them to modify their impulsiveness through self-control skills and reflective problem solving. This was accomplished by means of **self-instructional training,** whereby the person is taught to modify his or her self-statements before, during, and after a given action. The therapist models appropriate self-statements in the face of a task: defining the problem ("What do I have to do?"), focusing attention ("Keep working at it"), guiding performance ("Now I have to add the numbers in the right column and carry the first digit"), evaluating performance ("Did I do it right?"), correcting errors ("That's wrong—let's go back"), and rewarding oneself for good performance ("I did a good job"). Then the child attempts the task, using the same or similar self-statements as a guide.

Self-instructional training has now been used by many therapists working with children with ADHD. A review of 23 studies (Abikoff, 1985; Kendall & Braswell, 1993) indicates that the method works well for specific tasks and for a while, though the child's newly learned skills do not generalize as widely as was hoped and can vanish if not carefully reinforced. The technique is still being experimented with, however, and has served as a model for similar therapies aimed at improving the reading, writing, penmanship, and arithmetic skills of children with learning disorders (Lloyd, Hallahan, Kauffman, et al., 1991).

An important focus of cognitive therapy for depressed children is attribution retraining: teaching children to make attributions that are less internal ("It wasn't my fault"), less stable ("It won't always be this way"), and less global ("Not everything is bad"). Cognitive therapists also teach depressed children—and often their parents—how to increase their activity levels, how to solve problems effectively, and how to improve their affective communication—in other words, how to share their feelings. Social-skills training may also be used with a depressed child.

The usefulness of cognitive therapy depends greatly on the child's age. For most children under 7 or 8, cognitive retraining cannot be used, because the child cannot understand the technique. For older groups, too, the procedures have to be adapted in such a way

Cognitive therapists sometimes use cartoons with empty thought and speech bubbles, like the one pictured here, to help children express and combat fearful thoughts.

as to interest the child. Cognitive therapists have used cartoons with empty thought and speech bubbles to induce children to identify fearful thoughts and to combat them through self-talk (Kendall, 1990). Another technique is the so-called STOP acronym: *S* stands for "scared"; *T* stands for "thoughts," which the patients identify; *O* is for "other thoughts," coping thoughts, which they substitute; *P* is for "praise," which they then give themselves for mastering their fears (Silverman, Kurtines, Ginsburg, et al., 1999). Using these methods, Eisen and Silverman (1998) have successfully treated generalized anxiety disorder in young children.

As with adult disorders, cognitive techniques are often combined with behavioral strategies. Cognitive-behavioral treatment has had considerable success with bulimia (Wilson & Fairburn, 1993). In addition, treatment that combines social-skills training and empathy and perspective taking has been advocated as a treatment for children who are socially withdrawn.

The Interpersonal Perspective

The family system approach is the main interpersonal method of therapy used to treat childhood disorders. This approach sees the family as a miniature social system in which each member plays a critical role. According to this view, a childhood disorder is a signal of a disturbance in this system. The child may have the symptoms, but it is the family that requires intervention (Bailey, 2000; Briesmeister & Schaefer, 1998).

Consider the case of one highly intelligent boy of 14, who was referred for treatment because he was doing poorly in school. When the family was seen together, it soon became clear that there were problems between the mother and father. The mother repeatedly belittled the father, comparing him unfavorably with the son. The father, in turn, was gruff with his wife; and, despite his apparent concern about his son's academic difficulties, he made it clear that he doubted the virility of any boy who spent too much time with books. The boy, then, was caught in a struggle between his parents. He wanted to do well in order to please his mother, yet by succeeding academically, he would become a sissy in his father's eyes. Worse yet, he would give his mother a reason to prefer him to his father, thus further straining the father-son relationship: hence the boy's academic problems.

According to family therapists, such family psychopathology underlies many childhood disorders and must be dealt with if the child's problems are to be relieved. This is not to suggest that other therapists ignore family dynamics. (We have just seen how cognitive therapists implicate parent-child relations in childhood depression.) The difference is one of emphasis. The behavioral therapist, for example, might emphasize the reinforcement patterns of the one-to-one relationship between father and child and between mother and child rather than exploring the complex triangular interaction among the three family members.

Anorexia is one disorder that has been treated successfully through family therapy. Minuchin and his colleagues, who have been working with patients with anorexia for years, claim that these girls' families tend to share the same characteristics: overprotectiveness, rigidity, and a superficial "closeness," covering a good deal of unexposed anger and resentment. The girl's anorexia, then, serves an important function for the family. It gives them a "safe" target for the expression of frustration and thus makes it possible for them to avoid open conflict over their true grievances. Because it performs this essential service, the anorexia is subtly and unwittingly encouraged by the family (Minuchin & Fishman, 1981).

In order to relieve the anorexia, the family problems must first be relieved. To this end, the researchers propose "family therapy lunch sessions." Minuchin (1974) describes one such session with a hospitalized teenager with anorexia and her parents. First, the therapist allows both parents to try to get their daughter to eat. Inevitably, they fail, and the therapist points out to them why, in terms of intrafamily struggles, the child is responding in this way. Then the therapist, who interprets the girl's refusal to eat as a fight for independence within the family, tells the patient she has triumphed over the parents and can savor that triumph, but to stay alive she must eat. After a time, this strategy begins to work; the patient begins eating surreptitiously. Once the patient is released from the hospital, the parents are instructed to use behavior-modification techniques at home. The girl must eat enough to gain a certain amount of weight each week. If she falls short of the goal, she must remain in bed.

Approximately 85 percent of those on whom this method has been tried show a lasting recovery (Minuchin & Fishman, 1981)—a far better outcome than other therapies have achieved. Family therapy is now widely used for childhood disorders and has had some remarkable successes.

The Sociocultural Perspective

Can cultural patterns determine the shape that a childhood disorder will take? Weisz and his colleagues, pursuing this question, compared the records from mental health clinics in Thailand and the United States. These are two very different cultures. Americans place a high value on independence and open expression, whereas Thais, in keeping with Buddhist principles, value spontaneity less than the ability to maintain harmonious relations with others. And the American and Thai children in the Weisz team's sample conformed to these principles. The American children were more likely to have disorders of "undercontrolled behavior"—disruptiveness, fighting, temper tantrums—while the Thai children tended to have "overcontrolled-behavior" disorders such as anxiety, sleeping problems, and somatic complaints, particularly headaches (Weisz, Suwanlert, Chaiyasit, et al., 1987b).

This sample, however, was limited to children who had used mental health clinics. To find out if the same principles applied to the general population, Weisz and his colleagues later interviewed parents of school-age children in the two countries (Weisz, Suwanlert, Chaiyasit, et al., 1987a, 1993). They found a slightly different pattern. Again, problems of overcontrol—"sulks a lot," "has dizzy spells"—were more common in the Thai children than in the American children, but there was no difference in the incidence of undercontrol problems. Interestingly, though, the Thai children's undercontrol was more controlled than the American children's. They tended to show more subtle and indirect forms of acting out—attention problems, cruelty to animals—whereas the American children used more direct forms, such as cruelty to other children. Thus, the principle still applied: Even when they are violating norms, children heed norms.

What this suggests with regard to childhood disorders is the same point that sociocultural theorists have repeatedly made regarding adult disorders: To find the cause (and the cure), we should look to the culture as well as to the individual. Particularly in the case of the conduct disorders, sociocultural theorists are impatient with purely psychological explanations. Risk for conduct disorders correlates strongly with poverty-related factors: parental unemployment, family disruption, bad schools, and gang subcultures. In addressing the disorder, therefore, the society should attend to those matters. Another factor that may contribute to conduct disorder is the degree of violence in today's movies and on television. Children imitate aggressive acts that they see on television (Heath, Bresdin, & Rinaldi, 1989), and horror movies have been implicated in a number of serious crimes committed by children. For nearly 3 million children, exposure to violence happens in their own homes. Child maltreatment has been linked to a host of serious emotional problems in children.

Two other syndromes to which cultural norms probably contribute are anorexia and bulimia—a matter we have discussed. Very few experts would argue that anorexia and bulimia are wholly due to cultural influence, but it is worth noting that anorexia is far rarer among the Chinese (Lee & Chiu, 1989) and among African Americans (Dolan, 1991)—two groups that, in general, do not subscribe to the hyperthin female ideal—than it is among European Americans.

The Psychodynamic Perspective

The psychodynamic perspective is not widely used with children today, and it has little real value in our understanding, assessment, and treatment of childhood disorders. However, psychodynamic theorists (and others) sometimes use a very popular technique, **play therapy**, to treat children. Here, instead of asking young patients what the problem is, the therapist provides them with drawing materials and toys, on the assumption that whatever is troubling them will be expressed in their drawings and games. Typically, the therapist's office looks something like a small-scale nursery schoolroom, with blocks, crayons, and clay. Other essentials are toys for expressing aggression and dolls and puppets for play-acting family conflicts. The main goals of play therapy include allowing a child to communicate his or her feelings,

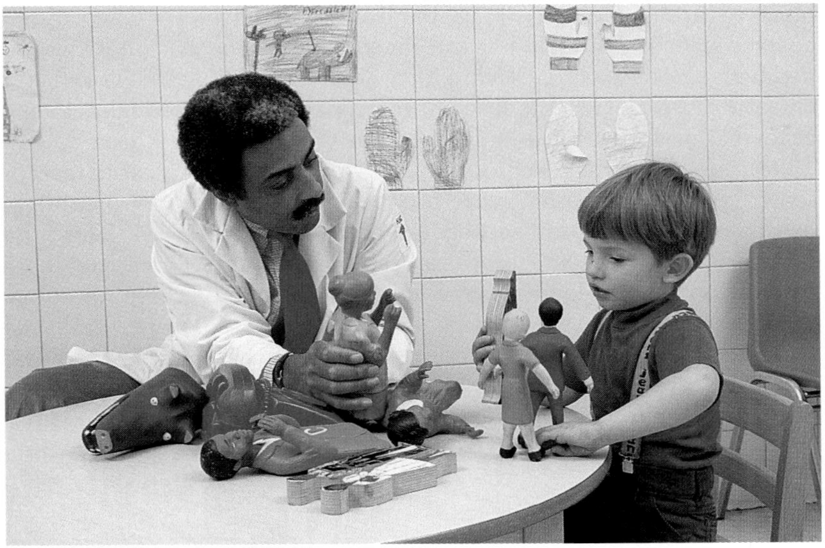

Very young children lack the ability to articulate what is troubling them. Through play therapy, they can express themselves nonverbally.

heal externalizing conflicts, master anxiety, take a respite from internal pressure, and exercise new solutions of problems (Kaduson & Schaefer, 2000).

Therapists treating children usually have a good deal of contact with parents. In some cases, the parents may be drawn in as "cotherapists," adopting at home techniques taught to them by the therapist. In other cases, all members of the family may be involved in therapy. Whatever the techniques used, the therapist's conversations with the parents may help to resolve family conflicts that have been maintaining the child's problem.

While such methods are generally characteristic of psychodynamic treatment of children, the specific approach varies with the tastes of the therapist, the age of the child, and the nature of the problem. Play therapy is good for young children who have experienced some type of trauma or who are unable or unwilling to speak in therapy. In treating a preschooler, the therapist may have regular contact with the parents; in treating an adolescent at war with her parents, the therapist may limit conversations with the parents, so as not to forfeit the child's trust. In all cases, the technique depends on the child's needs.

The Neuroscience Perspective

There have been a number of heated disputes between biogenic and psychogenic theorists in the area of childhood disorders. Neurological causes have been proposed for encopresis and enuresis. (As noted, three fourths of enuretic children have a first-degree relative who was also enuretic.) Likewise, it has been proposed that anorexia may be due to a disturbance in the neurological hunger response. With anorexia, however, recent research points to both neurological and psychological causes. The cerebrospinal fluid of severely underweight anorexics has been found to contain abnormally high levels of neuropeptide Y, a neurochemical that is known to signal the hunger response. Furthermore, when these anorexics regain their normal weight, their neuropeptide Y levels also return to normal. Thus, it seems that anorexics *are* physiologically hungry—indeed, very hungry. However, psychological factors (such as fear of gaining weight) appear to override this physical need (Kaye, Berrettini, Gwirtsman, et al., 1990; Leibowitz, 1991).

Virtually all of the disorders that we have discussed in this chapter have been found to have some genetic, hormonal, neurotransmitter, or other biological component. ADHD, for example, is believed to be caused by certain brain changes that are set in motion by genetic predispositions. Many children with ADHD respond to stimulant medications that increase activity in those areas of the brain most responsible for self-regulation and self-control of behavior. These stimulants work with both the inattentive types, increasing their powers of concentration, and the hyperactive types, reducing their fidgetiness and impulsiveness. Studies have found that as many as three fourths of ADHD children who are put on stimulants show dramatic improvements in attention span, social behavior, and self-control (DuPaul & Barkley, 1990; Gillberg, Melander, Liis von Knorring, et al., 1997).

Many children with ADHD are now on daily doses of amphetamines, usually either Dexedrine or Ritalin. Indeed, 3 to 5 percent of the school population takes Ritalin (Crossette, 1996). Some experts have strongly objected to this. For one thing, the drugs may have adverse side effects, including weight loss, insomnia, and high blood pressure. Second, they do not actually cure the disorder. General behavior may improve, but academic performance usually does not (Goldstein, 1998), and the prognosis for the child remains the same. No drug can compensate for the accumulated deficits in the child's problem-solving skills. Such skills must be taught after attention has been improved by medication, thus requiring a combination of approaches (Arnold, Abikoff, Cantwell, et al., 1997; DuPaul & Barkley, 1993). Third, if parents, schools, and physicians become accustomed to using drugs for "problem children," the possibilities for abuse are frightening. It is all too easy to imagine medication being administered to *all* problem children, including those whose disruptive behavior is a response to family conflicts or simply to a boring school program. Finally, there is the danger of the possible sale of the drug to other children and the incompatibility of drug therapy with anti-drug messages to combat substance abuse.

These objections are important, and it is generally agreed that drugs must be prescribed with great caution. And, as mentioned earlier, some behavioral programs have been as effective as drug therapy (Barkley, 1998). Nevertheless, because amphetamines do, in general, have beneficial effects on the adjustment of ADHD children, they are still widely used, often in conjunction with behavior therapy.

Key Terms

anorexia nervosa, 469
attention deficit hyperactivity disorder (ADHD), 461
bulimia nervosa, 470
childhood depression, 468
conduct disorder, 463
disruptive behavior disorders, 461
encopresis, 472
enuresis, 472
generalized anxiety disorder, 467
learning disorders, 474
nightmares, 473
play therapy, 480
self-instructional training, 478
separation anxiety disorder, 467
sleep terrors, 473
sleepwalking, 473
social phobia, 467
stuttering, 476

Summary

- The disorders of childhood and adolescence include a wide range of problems. Many of them have no parallel to adult disorders, and those that do (such as depression) may manifest themselves differently in children. Disorders of childhood are fairly common, become more prevalent with age, and are more common in boys up to adolescence.
- Empirical studies identify several general classes of childhood disorders: disruptive behavior disorders, involving impulsive, aggressive, acting-out behaviors; disorders of emotional distress, such as anxiety and depression; the disruption of habits such as eating, elimination, and sleeping; and learning and communication disorders.
- Childhood disorders may affect adult adjustment. A disorder may simply persist into adulthood in a similar form, as in the case of antisocial behavior, or a child's disorder may set him or her on a path that becomes a maladaptive pattern. Finally, childhood disturbances may create a reactivity to stressors, leaving the child at risk for problems later in life. Treatment (and prevention) of childhood disorders may help to prevent adult disorders.
- Two common disruptive behavior disorders are attention deficit hyperactivity disorder (ADHD) and conduct disorder. Children with ADHD lack the ability to focus their attention for more than a brief period and exhibit a variety of impulsive and disruptive behaviors. Some children with ADHD show more inattentiveness, and some, more hyperactivity, but most of them combine the two.
- A preadolescent or adolescent child who persistently violates social norms—stealing, lying, running away from home, destroying property, and so on—is said to have a conduct disorder. The younger the age of onset, the more serious the problem, both in childhood and adulthood.
- Boys are at a far higher risk than girls for developing disruptive behavior disorders. The genders also express conduct disorders differently. Boys are more physically aggressive and are prone to fighting, stealing, and vandalism, while girls choose less violent behaviors such as lying, being truant, running away from home, and shoplifting. These differences may be an artifact of reporting, a side effect of socialization, or the result of natural selection. For both genders, socioeconomic factors, such as parental unemployment, that correlate with poverty are also associated with a higher risk of conduct disorder.

- Disorders of emotional distress are less easily observed than the disruptive behavior disorders: The child turns the conflict inward and becomes depressed or anxious. Children may suffer from many of the same anxiety disorders as adults, such as social phobias and generalized anxiety disorder; in addition, young children may experience separation anxiety disorder when having to part from their parents, however briefly. Depression in childhood may manifest itself like adult depression, or it may show up as problems at school, delinquency, or exaggerated fears. By adolescence, girls are twice as likely as boys to experience disorders of emotional distress.
- Eating disorders tend to be prompted by a distorted body image. They include anorexia nervosa, involving severely restricted food intake and substantial weight loss; bulimia nervosa, a pattern of binge-eating followed by induced vomiting or elimination; and obesity. Far more girls than boys are diagnosed with eating disorders.
- Elimination disorders include enuresis (lack of bladder control) and, more rarely, encopresis (lack of bowel control). Among the childhood sleep disorders are insomnia, nightmares, sleep terrors, and sleepwalking.
- Learning disorders involve inadequate development of learning skills, such as reading, writing, or mathematics. Children with these problems may have abnormal visual or auditory perception or memory problems. Boys with learning disorders outnumber girls. Historically, learning disorders have been overdiagnosed in White, middle-class children and underdiagnosed in minorities.
- Communication disorders include delayed speech and stuttering. Sometimes speech develops on time but with gaps in skills such as articulation, expressive language, and the ability to understand others.
- Behaviorists focus on actual problem behaviors and the environmental variables that have conditioned them. They believe that children's behavioral problems usually stem from either inadequate or inappropriate learning. The behavioral treatment for both conduct and anxiety disorders makes use of the entire behavioral repertoire: reinforcement, extinction, withdrawal of rewards, modeling, respondent conditioning, and systematic desensitization.
- Cognitive theorists believe that some children's disorders may be caused by negative beliefs, faulty attributions, poor problem solving, and other cognitive factors. Cognitive therapy often focuses on teaching the child to make more positive and functional attributions. Self-instructional training may also be provided. Cognitive therapy is generally practiced with older children and adults, as most children under 7 cannot understand the techniques used.
- The interpersonal perspective views the family as a miniature social system, in which each person plays a critical role. One branch of this perspective, family theory, holds that a child may manifest a disorder, but it is the family that needs treatment. Treatment involves an exploration of the interaction among all family members.
- From the sociocultural perspective, cultural patterns help to determine the shape a disorder will take. Treatment and prevention entail tackling social problems, such as inadequate schools, poverty, family disruption, unemployment, and exposure to violence or to unrealistic ideals of beauty.
- The psychodynamic perspective is not widely used with children today, although play therapy, which assumes children will express in drawings and games what they are unable to communicate otherwise, is a popular treatment for young children.
- The neuroscience perspective ascribes some developmental disorders to neurological factors. Because ADHD has responded to medical treatment, it is assumed to be the developmental disorder most likely to have neurological causes. Even so, there are strong arguments against using drugs to treat children's psychological disturbances.

CHAPTER

17

Mental Retardation
- Levels of Mental Retardation
- Genetic Factors
- Environmental Factors
- Mental Retardation in Adults

Autism
- Symptoms of Autism
- Theories of Autism

Society and People with Developmental Disorders
- Public Policy
- Community Integration
- Quality of Life
- Support for the Family
- Employment

Prevention and Therapy
- Primary Prevention
- Secondary Prevention
- Behavioral Therapy
- Cognitive Therapy
- Pharmacological Therapy
- Psychotherapy

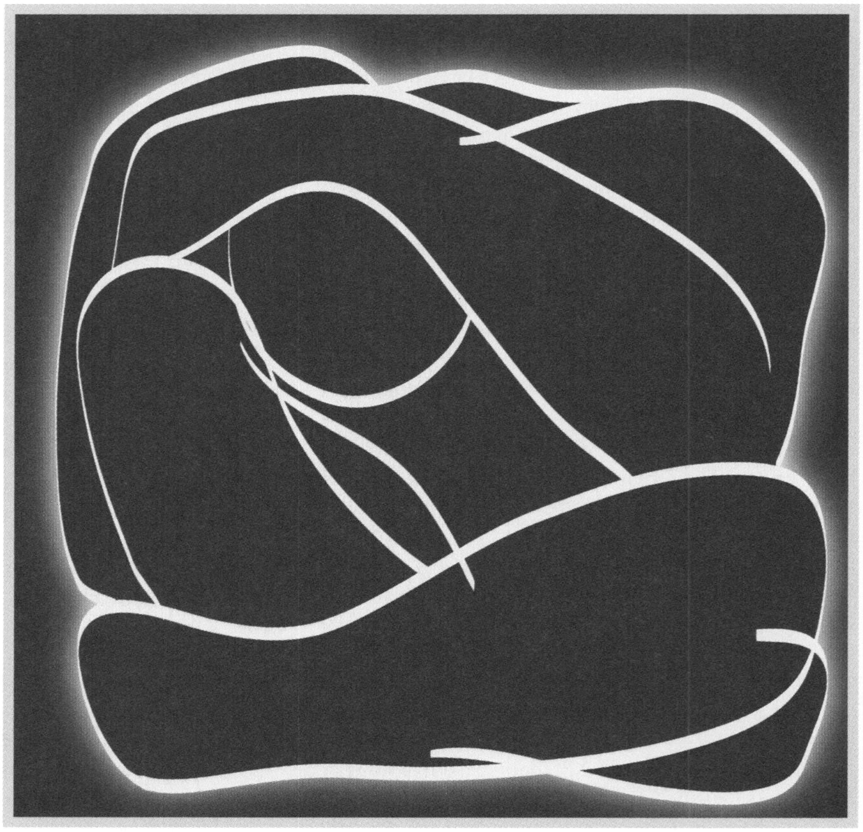

Mental Retardation and Autism

John P. is a 28-year-old Caucasian male who lives in a group home for people with developmental disorders. John was transferred to the facility four years ago following a stay at a large developmental center. During the day, John works in a sheltered workshop loading crates and folding cardboard boxes. At night and on the weekends, John is usually at home or out on supervised trips to the mall, supermarket, park, or other recreational activity.

During childhood, John was diagnosed with moderate mental retardation. He was unable to attend regular school because he could not read, write, or communicate well. In addition, he had many difficulties taking care of himself, and often needed help with eating, using the restroom, and bathing. John also liked to be by himself much of the time, and physical contact with others often seemed to be painful to him. He rarely associated with other people and had few friends.

Growing up, John often seemed depressed and would occasionally hurt himself or others if frustrated. His parents had cared for him for much of his life but were now older and unable to do so. John seems content with his life now, but still has trouble communicating to others and developing friendships. During his private time, after work and his educational programs, John often sits alone in his room and looks at books for hours. (Kearney, University of Nevada–Las Vegas, personal files)

Developmental disorders refer to conditions of impaired intelligence and adaptive functioning, and represent various problems with different causes. The causes may be due to genetic abnormalities, to damage to the brain before or at birth, or to deprivation in early childhood. The manifestations are as varied as the causes.

In this country, people with developmental disorders range from those who grow up, marry, and live on their own, going to work during the week and to the movies on Saturday night, to those who cannot learn, speak, or care for themselves in any way.

In this chapter, we discuss two main forms of developmental disorder, mental retardation and autism, and the definition and causes of each. Finally, we will look at the social issues surrounding mental retardation and autism, together with methods of prevention and therapy.

Mental Retardation

As defined by *DSM-IV-TR,* **mental retardation** involves three criteria:

1. Significantly subaverage general intellectual functioning, determined by standardized intelligence tests (criterion A)
2. Significant limitations in adaptive functioning in at least 2 of 11 adaptive skills areas (criterion B)
3. Onset before 18 years of age (criterion C)*

In criterion B, the term *adaptive functioning* refers to the person's ability to cope with life's demands and live independently, according to the standards of his or her age group, community, social class, and culture. To meet this criterion, the person must show limitations in at least two of the following adaptive skill areas: communication, self-care, home living, social/interpersonal skills, use of community resources, self-direction, functional academic skills, work, leisure, health, and safety (American Psychiatric Association, 2000). Several things should be noted about this definition. First, it requires that any person diagnosed with mental retardation show serious deficits in *both* intellectual and adaptive functioning. A child who scores low on an IQ test but who functions well in his or her community is not a candidate for this diagnosis. Second, mental retardation by definition manifests itself in childhood, and it is by judging the child in comparison with his or her peers that the diagnosis is made. Finally, the definition says nothing about cause. In many cases, mental retardation is due to a deficit or dysfunction of the nervous system, but in other cases the exact cause cannot be shown, and diagnosis does not depend on its being shown.

*Reprinted with permission from the *Diagnostic and Statistical Manual of Mental Disorders,* Fourth Edition, Text Revision. Copyright © 2000 American Psychiatric Association.

Although there are no absolute statistics on the prevalence of mental retardation, it affects approximately 2 percent of the U.S. population (Hodapp & Dykens, 1996). However imprecise this estimate, it signifies an enormous problem for society.

Levels of Mental Retardation

Intelligence test scores have an approximately normal distribution, generally with 100 as the mean and 15 as the standard deviation (a measure of the dispersion of scores above and below the mean). In diagnosing mental retardation, the cutoff point between normal and "significantly subaverage intellectual functioning" is about 2 standard deviations below the mean—that is, an IQ of about 70. People whose scores fall below that line may be diagnosed with mental retardation if their adaptive skills are also impaired. In addition, it has been traditional in the past few decades to specify the person's level of retardation: mild, moderate, severe, or profound. The following descriptions of these four levels are based on Harris (1995).

1. *Mild Retardation* About 85 percent of all cases of retardation are classified as mild retardation—a condition that, because it is mild, is often not recognized until the person enters school. In terms of criterion A, this level of retardation is equated with an IQ of 50–55 to 70. As young children, people with mild mental retardation develop more slowly and need help longer with self-care tasks such as eating, dressing, and toilet training. By adolescence, though, they can function independently in most areas of life. They speak fluently and can usually read easy material and do simple arithmetic. As adults, they may need someone who can act as an adviser, particularly with regard to money management. Most can hold a job and have friends; some can also marry and have children.

2. *Moderate Retardation* Moderate retardation is usually evident by age 2 or 3 years; it is equated with an IQ of 35–40 to 50–55. By about age 6, such children can feed themselves with cup and spoon, cooperate with dressing, begin toilet training, and use some words and recognize shapes. By adolescence, they have good self-care skills and can carry on simple conversations, read a few words, and do simple tasks. In the past, people with moderate retardation were often institutionalized, but today many live in community-based group homes or with their families.

3. *Severe Retardation* Severe retardation is equated with an IQ of 20–25 to 35–40. People with severe mental retardation can learn some self-care

Roughly 85 percent of people with mental retardation have a mild form of the disorder. These men with mild retardation in Amman, Jordan, are learning woodworking skills that will help them live productively and independently.

skills and, with proper training, can perform jobs in a sheltered workshop or daytime activity center. Training is especially valuable at this level, because it can make the difference between institutionalization and a more productive and happy life in a family or group home. People with severe mental retardation do, however, require considerable supervision. They can understand language, but many have trouble speaking, and their reading and number skills are not sufficient for independent living.

4. *Profound Retardation* Profound retardation is equated with an IQ below 20 or 25. People with profound mental retardation can carry out some self-care activities and can sometimes perform tasks in a daytime activity center, but they require extensive supervision and help. Language is a severe problem; they may understand a simple communication, but they have little or no ability to speak. Many people with profound mental retardation remain institutionalized, usually because of severe behavior problems or multiple physical handicaps. Because of increased susceptibility to disease, people in this category often die prematurely.

It should be added that these descriptions of the four levels of retardation are only broad generalizations. Even as generalizations, their value has been questioned. *DSM-IV-TR* lists them, but the American Association on Mental Retardation (AAMR) manual argues against these groups because they are based partly on IQ, which is only one measure of functioning. Furthermore, they assume more consistency between IQ scores and adaptive behavior than many people show. Two people with IQs of 60 may differ as much in their coping ability as two people with IQs of 100. In sum, these descriptions give too much weight to IQ.

The AAMR recommends that diagnosticians not apply the IQ criterion until deficits in adaptive behavior have been established. Instead, the association recommends a classification based on levels of required support or assistance. According to these guidelines, mild retardation may be indicated by the need for "intermittent" assistance and/or successful functioning in work and marital relationships. Moderate retardation may be associated with "limited" assistance and/or success in elementary school. Severe mental retardation may be indicated by the need for extensive assistance and/or the acquisition of only basic communication, work, and self-help skills. Finally, profound retardation may be associated with the need for "pervasive" assistance and/or the achievement of only basic self-care skills under close supervision (Schalock, Stark, Snell, et al., 1994). In many clinical settings, the strict use of IQ and adaptive behavior to define mental retardation is being replaced by treatment-friendly terms like these and more specific descriptions of neurological impairment.

Genetic Factors

In some cases, particularly the severest cases, mental retardation can be attributed to a specific biological factor. In fact, more than 300 organic or genetic anomalies are associated with retardation. But the mechanism by which that factor produces retardation is seldom understood. Furthermore, two people may have the same medical diagnosis yet be at very different levels of retardation. Finally, there is the problem of differential diagnosis. It is not always clear whether a diagnosis of retardation, autism, emotional disturbance, or learning disability is appropriate in any given case. All four conditions may result in generally impaired or deficient behavior and development, and the conditions are not mutually exclusive. Mental retardation and emotional disturbance, for example, may be present in the same person. Here, we discuss some of the more common and better-known syndromes that are associated with mental retardation.

Chromosomal Abnormalities Since the early twentieth century, it has been known that certain forms of mental retardation are "X-linked"—that is, they are genetically inherited via the X chromosome, which also determines sex. But it was not until 1969 that H. A. Lubs, a researcher at the University of Miami School of Medicine, described the cause. In certain individuals, Lubs noted, the X chromosome shows a weak spot, where it appears to be bent or broken. This condition, which is called **fragile X syndrome,** occurs in about 1 out of every 1,250 to 2,500 births (Hagerman & Lampe, 1999). People with fragile X syndrome have certain pronounced physical characteristics—large, prominent ears; an elongated face; and, in males, enlarged testicles. Many are hyperactive and may also show characteristics of autism: hand biting, limited speech, and poor eye contact. (Accordingly, some are diagnosed with autism.) In men, because they have only one X chromosome, this syndrome is more likely to have severe consequences; almost all males with fragile X experience some impairment in cognitive function, with the majority falling into the moderate-retardation category. In women, because there are two X chromosomes, with the possibility that a normal one may mask the effects of the abnormal one, the risk of mental retardation is less (Sherman, 1996).

About as common as fragile X syndrome is **Down syndrome,** which occurs in approximately 1.5 out of every 1,000 births (Simonoff, Bolton, & Rutter, 1996). This condition is named after Langdon Down, the British physician who first described it in 1866. Typical traits of Down syndrome are slanting eyes; a flat nose; a small, round head; an extra fold of skin on the upper eyelids; a small mouth with drooping corners; a thickened, protruding tongue; short, stubby fingers; poor muscle tone; and, in almost all cases, mental retardation. Most people with Down syndrome have moderate mental retardation. They are also susceptible to serious cardiac and respiratory diseases, with the result that their life expectancy is shorter than average. With advances in medicine, however, a child with Down syndrome who survives the first few months has a good chance of living into adulthood (Carr, 1994).

While Down syndrome was described in the mid-nineteenth century, its genetic basis was not discovered until the mid-twentieth century. In 1959, French geneticist Jerome Lejeune and his colleagues reported that people with Down syndrome almost always have an extra chromosome in pair 21, or **trisomy 21** (Figure 17.1). This extra chromosome is thought to be caused by an error in cell division in the mother's ovum.

Together, fragile X and Down syndrome account for one fourth of all cases of mental retardation, though their incidence—and that of the many other chromosomal abnormalities that can cause retardation—may eventually be reduced through genetic counseling. Because fragile X is inherited, those at risk are people with a family history of X-linked retardation. As for Down syndrome, the risk is directly related to the mother's age: For women aged 20 to 24, the chances are about 1 in every 1,400 births; for women aged 30, 1 in every 900 births; for women aged 40, 1 in every 100; and, for women over the age of 45, about 1 in 25 (Thompson, McInnes, & Willard, 1991). In genetic counseling, high-risk prospective parents are advised

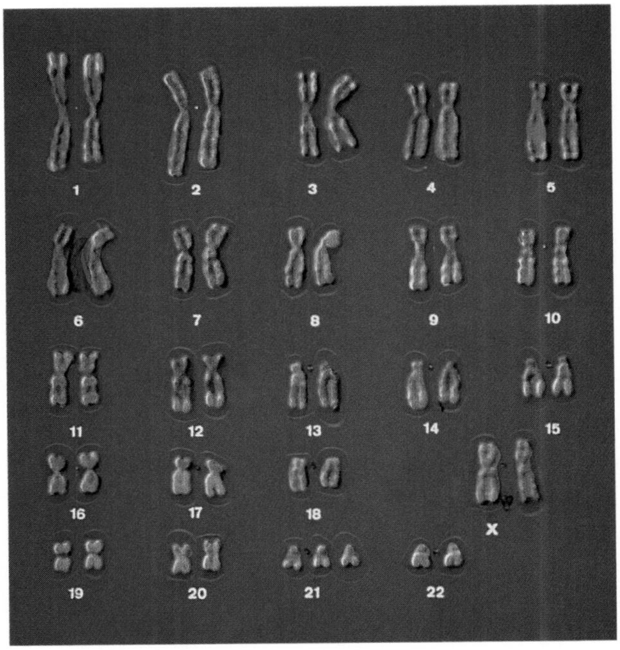

FIGURE 17.1 This false-color karyotype shows the pairs of chromosomes in a female with Down syndrome. Note the presence of an extra chromosome in pair 21, or trisomy 21.

as to the chances of an abnormal birth. If the woman is already pregnant, chromosomal abnormalities in the developing fetus can often be identified through a clinical procedure called **amniocentesis,** which involves extracting and analyzing a portion of the amniotic fluid in which the fetus is growing. Amniocentesis is now routinely recommended for pregnant women over 35, to screen for Down syndrome. When the tests reveal abnormalities, many couples are faced with difficult decisions about maintaining the pregnancy.

Metabolic Disturbances Another form of genetic defect results in metabolic disturbances. One of the best known is **phenylketonuria (PKU),** which occurs in about 1 in every 10,000 to 15,000 live births (Waisbren, 1999). The cause of PKU appears to be a defective recessive gene, which leaves the child deficient in phenylalanine 4-hydroxylase, a liver enzyme that is needed to metabolize the amino acid phenylalanine. In consequence, phenylalanine and its derivatives accumulate in the body and eventually damage the developing central nervous system. The result is usually severe retardation, hyperactivity, and erratic and unpredictable behavior. Fortunately, this disorder can be detected soon after birth. Most states require that newborns be tested for PKU. A special, low-phenylalanine diet from infancy to at least age 6 can often prevent or at least minimize neurological damage (Mazzoco, Nord, van Doorninck, et al., 1994).

Another metabolic disorder is **Tay-Sachs disease.** This disorder, transmitted by a recessive gene, is a defect of lipid metabolism, due to the absence of the enzyme hexosominidase A in the brain tissues. It is usually detected between 4 and 8 months and is confined largely to children of Eastern European Jewish ancestry. It is characterized by progressive deterioration to the point of complete immobility, with isolated episodes of convulsions. Tay-Sachs disease is untreatable. Even under intensive hospital care, only 17 percent of afflicted infants survive beyond 4 years, and death is virtually certain before the age of 6 (Sloan, 1991).

Environmental Factors

Genes are one factor that can cause retardation. The other crucial influence on the developing brain is the environment, both prenatal—the environment of the uterus—and postnatal—the physical and social world surrounding the child in his or her early years.

Prenatal Environment The prenatal environment allows for the safe development of a fetus, but its barriers can be breached; and when they are, mental retardation is one possible effect.

Congenital Disorders Mental retardation can be caused by **congenital disorders,** disorders acquired during prenatal development but not transmitted genetically (Shannon, 2000). Until recently, three common congenital causes of mental retardation were rubella (German measles), syphilis, and a hormonal imbalance called thyroxine deficiency. Children affected by congenital rubella may be born with various impairments, including brain lesions, which usually result in mental retardation. Congenital syphilis, under certain circumstances, causes hydrocephalus, or excessive cerebrospinal fluid, which results in retardation. Thyroxine deficiency causes **cretinism,** a condition marked by serious mental retardation and physical disabilities. If a pregnant woman's diet lacks iodine, or if the thyroid of the fetus is damaged during birth, thyroxine deficiency will result. Thanks to widespread immunization for rubella, premarital and prenatal blood tests for syphilis (which responds to penicillin), and the availability of iodized table salt, these congenital diseases are now rare.

More common today are congenital disorders that result from the transmission of the HIV virus from an infected mother to her unborn child. Encephalopathy (the degeneration of brain tissue), meningitis, and lymphoma are among the congenital disorders that can result from in utero HIV infections (Belfer & Munir, 1997). These disorders lead to developmental declines, including cognitive delays and delays in the development of language and motor skills, as well as to declines in adaptive functioning (Pearson, Doyle, Pickering, et al., 1996). Ultimately, they produce mental retardation. The National Institutes of Health estimate that in utero transmission of the HIV virus can be reduced from about 25 percent to as low as 8 percent of at-risk children if HIV-positive mothers are given a drug called zidovudine during pregnancy and delivery, and their newborn infants are treated with the drug for the first six weeks of life (Belfer & Munir, 1997).

Drugs In the early 1960s, a new drug, thalidomide, was introduced in Europe and Canada to relieve morning sickness in pregnant women. Thalidomide did help with morning sickness; unfortunately, it had other effects as well. Many of the women who took the drug gave birth to babies with mental retardation and severely malformed limbs. Thalidomide was swiftly removed from the market, but it had far-reaching effects, and not just for the families of these unfortunate children. The thalidomide scandal helped to raise worldwide consciousness as to the potentially damaging effect that any drug taken during pregnancy can have on the developing fetus.

Babies born to drug-addicted mothers show a variety of ill effects, which often include low birth weight, irritability, and mental retardation. The child shown here displays the facial features typical of fetal alcohol syndrome, including a flattened bridge, missing indentation below the nose, and a barely formed upper lip.

As many studies have shown, that includes alcohol. When a pregnant woman takes a drink, the alcohol enters the fetus's bloodstream almost immediately, slowing down the workings of the central nervous system. Repeated exposure to this experience can damage the fetus (Stratton, Howe, & Battaglia, 1996). Even women who are only "social drinkers" are more likely than nondrinkers to have babies of lowered birth weight. These babies' growth, IQ, motor skills, attention, and social performance may later suffer (Niccols, 1994). As for women with alcoholism, their babies are at high risk for a complex of physical and behavioral defects known as **fetal alcohol syndrome, or FAS.** FAS involves distinctive facial characteristics (short eye slits, drooping eyelids, short nose, narrow upper lip), retarded physical growth, and, frequently, mental retardation. In fact, the majority of people of any age with fetal alcohol syndrome have IQs between 40 and 80 (Niccols, 1994). Approximately 1 to 3 out of every 1,000 babies born in the United States shows FAS (Niccols, 1994). If children with less severe impairments are included, the incidence may rise to 1 in every 300 (Harris, 1995).

Illegal drugs have equally profound effects on the fetal brain, as has been seen in the "crack babies"—babies prenatally addicted to cocaine—that have been born since crack cocaine entered the illegal drug market in the mid-1980s. These babies are likely to show retarded growth at birth (Hadeed & Siegel, 1989). Their brain development may also be affected (Hurt, Brodsky, Betancourt, et al., 1995). They tend to be either overexcited or depressed; they develop language more slowly (van Baar, 1990); and they are less responsive to toys (Rodning, Beckwith, & Howard, 1989). The extent of retardation among children of crack-using mothers is not yet fully understood; more research is needed. There is no shortage of potential subjects, however. It has been estimated that, in the United States, among women aged 18 to 25, roughly 1 out of 5 uses illicit drugs; every year, half a million or more unborn children may be exposed to cocaine, marijuana, or some other substance (Harris, 1995).

Whatever damage these babies suffer is probably the result not just of prenatal environment but also of a subtle interaction of prenatal and postnatal disadvantages. Cocaine-exposed babies tend to be born into families that are poor and unstable and that lack adequate health services (Mayes, Granger, Bornstein, et al., 1992; Zuckerman & Frank, 1992). Their mothers are more likely to be clinically depressed (Hawley & Disney, 1992), not to mention cocaine-addicted and, therefore, unlikely to offer the kind of stimulating interaction required for adequate brain development. In addition, such babies, because of the effects of the cocaine, are harder to care for—they are often overexcited or depressed—and this probably does not endear them to their mothers. In one study, substance-abusing women were observed with their babies at 3 months and then 9 months after birth. In general, these women were less responsive to their babies' needs than were women who did not take drugs (Rodning, Beckwith, & Howard, 1992).

Malnutrition Another prenatal factor that can contribute to retardation is maternal malnutrition. A number of studies conducted in poorer countries have shown that prenatal malnutrition due to vitamin and mineral deficiencies later affects both a child's physical and behavioral development (Barrett & Frank, 1987). This is bad news; among poor families in the United States, 20 to 24 percent of African American and Latino babies may be affected by iron-deficiency anemia (Pollitt, 1994). Such dietary deficiencies can stunt physical growth (Tanner, 1990), cause delays in motor and intellectual development, and contribute to behavioral problems such as anxiety (Valenzuela, 1990), irritability, inattentiveness, listlessness, and lethargy.

Several recent studies have shown that, to overcome prenatal nutritional deficits, a combination of dietary supplements and social or intellectual stimulation is required. In one study, the progress of severely malnourished children who participated in a 3-year home-visiting program was compared with that of children of similar nutritional status who were not visited. At 14 years of age, the children who had participated in the program scored significantly higher on the WISC verbal scale than those who had not (Grantham-McGregor, Powell, Walker, et al., 1994). In another study, fetally malnourished infants who were placed in an intellectually supportive environment for the first 3 years of life did significantly better on measures of intellectual, behavioral, and social development than another group raised in a nonsupportive environment (Zeskind & Ramey, 1981). And, in a study of Colombian infants at risk for malnutrition, a combination of food supplements and home visitation proved effective in reducing the number of children whose growth was severely retarded, compared with that of a control group (Super, Herrera, & Mora, 1990).

Malnutrition probably does not operate alone, however, for it is often seen in conjunction with other retardation-associated factors. Drug-addicted mothers, for example, also tend to suffer from malnutrition, thus placing their babies at a double risk.

Postnatal Environment

Toxins Various substances, if they enter the child's bloodstream during infancy or childhood, can cause neurological damage resulting in retardation. A sad example is the DPT vaccine, which is routinely given to children to protect them from diphtheria, pertussis, and tetanus. In a very small number of children, the pertussis component in the vaccine causes adverse reactions, including brain damage.

A far higher risk of retardation is posed by lead poisoning (Chapter 15). Lead-based paint, though its use is now prohibited, is still to be found on the walls of older housing, particularly in low-income housing projects. If paint chips, or particles of household dust or soil that contain lead, are eaten by a child on a regular basis, lead deposits accumulate in the tissues and interfere with brain-cell metabolism, resulting in permanent damage. The developmental effects of low-level prenatal exposure to lead may be subtle and transient (Bellinger, 1994). In addition, children exposed to high levels of lead postnatally generally experience an IQ point drop in the 7- to 9-point range (Dietrich, Berger, Succop, et al., 1993).

Physical Trauma Another potential cause of mental retardation is trauma to the brain as a result of accidents or child maltreatment. Children who are repeatedly beaten may suffer irreversible brain damage. Shaking a baby, a form of abuse, can result in serious brain damage and mental retardation. The brain can also be harmed during birth. If labor is rapid and the baby's head compresses and reexpands so quickly that it hemorrhages, or if labor is slow and delivery by forceps injures the brain, retardation can occur. Another birth hazard is hypoxia, or insufficient oxygenation of the baby's blood. If anesthetic is improperly administered, if the mother is hypertensive, if labor is prolonged, or if the umbilical cord ruptures, hypoxia can result; even if it occurs only for a short period, it can cause mental retardation.

The Effects of Deprivation Lead-based paint, as we just saw, is more common in poor neighborhoods. So are malnutrition and drug abuse. Furthermore, children who are at risk for retardation are less likely to receive appropriate treatment if they are poor. These facts alone might account for the disproportionately high incidence of mental retardation among children from disadvantaged backgrounds. At the same time, it has been proposed that, in the absence of an identifiable physical cause, some cases of mild retardation may be due to the psychological handicaps of growing up in a deprived setting. According to this view, children who lack a stable home, proper parental care, intellectual stimulation, and adequate language models and who are exposed to low expectations for life advancement and feelings of hopelessness suffer a kind of mental impoverishment that is not organic but that is measurable with intelligence tests (Garber & McInerney, 1982). Such impoverishment is sometimes called environmentally based cultural/familial mental retardation, a form of mental retardation linked more to poor parenting practices, lack of adequate language and other stimulation, and lower parental intelligence (Hodapp & Dykens, 1996). Although every aspect of poverty, including substandard housing, inferior education, and discrimination, can contribute to emotional disturbance and, thus, to impaired learning, it is the decreased level of stimulation—of varied sensory experiences; of verbal communication; of one-on-one, parent-child interaction—that is thought to be most closely associated with poor intellectual development.

This hypothesis stresses psychological, as opposed to organic, factors. However, a report issued by the Carnegie Corporation (1994) suggests that what begin as psychological factors *become* physical factors. As we saw in Chapter 9, the long-held distinction between mind and body has become increasingly blurred as advances in neuroscience have permitted

Studies have shown that an infant's sensory environment is critical to his or her brain development. A positive, stimulating sensory environment builds a more complex and efficient brain.

researchers to observe the physical processes involved in "mental" events and vice versa. The research summarized by the Carnegie report constitutes a further stage in the collapse of the mind-body distinction. It also supports the concept of **brain plasticity,** that experiences can alter the structure and function of the brain. The research indicates that what infants learn, and don't learn, from their environments has a substantial effect on the physical development of their brains.

At birth, the formation of the neurons, or brain cells, is virtually complete. What is not finished is the *organization* of the neurons, the wiring up of one neuron to the next, via the synapses (Chapter 6), to create the brain's intricate structure. (A neuron may have up to 15,000 synapses.) Broadly speaking, the newborn brain consists of an immense tangle of neurons. Then, in the period after birth, this mass is "sculpted." Some neurons die; others remain. Those that remain develop synaptic connections to some cells and not to others. Through this process, the brain develops the circuitry that will allow it to process environmental stimuli for the rest of its life.

What is most critical about this process is that it seems to occur very early. In the first few months after birth, the number of synapses between neurons increases, twentyfold, from 50 trillion to 1,000 trillion (Kolb, 1989). By the time children are walking, they may have developed most of the neural connections they will ever have. PET studies have shown that the biochemical patterns of a 1-year-old's brain are qualitatively similar to those of a young adult's brain (Chugani, 1993). The second crucial point is that the formation of the neural synapses is heavily influenced by the environment, and this includes not only long-recognized biological factors such as nutrition but also psychological factors—above all, sensory experience. "The brain uses information about the outside world to design its architecture" (Carnegie Corporation, 1994, p. 8). A rich, stimulating, and benign sensory environment builds a more complex and efficient brain (Nelson & Bosquet, 2000). A barren environment produces a less efficient brain. Furthermore, environmental stress seems to activate hormones that impede brain functioning (Gunnar, 1998).

The consequences of these findings for disadvantaged children are grimly stated by the Carnegie report: "Studies of children raised in poor environments —both in this country and elsewhere—show that they have cognitive deficits of substantial magnitude by eighteen months of age" (Carnegie Corporation, 1994, p. 8). Those studies, so far, have consisted of observational and cognitive tests, but their findings seem to be on the verge of confirmation by brain scan technology. If they are confirmed, this will be bad news indeed, for such cognitive deficits, the report adds, may not be fully reversible. On the contrary, they may be cumulative. One study, for example, tracked the progress of two groups of inner-city children, one that had been exposed since early infancy to good nutrition, toys, and playmates versus a second group that had been raised in a less stimulating environment. By age 12 these factors had had a measurable impact on brain functioning, and by age 15 the difference between the groups was even greater (Campbell & Ramey, 1994).

Most of these findings are quite recent and difficult to apply definitively to mental retardation. Cognitive deficits are not necessarily retardation. Nevertheless, the research does suggest that children raised in poverty are at high risk.

Teenage Mothers In recent years, a factor that has placed the children of the poor at greater risk for developmental delays is the increase in teenage pregnancy. Among the industrialized nations, the United States has one of the highest rates of adolescent pregnancy (Newberger, Melnicore, & Newberger, 1986)—twice as high as England's, seven times higher than that of the Netherlands. Every year, in this country, more than a million adolescent girls become pregnant, and half of these pregnancies go to term.

Children themselves, these girls are rarely equipped to raise children. To begin with, most are unmarried (Williams & Pratt, 1990) and therefore bear the burdens of parenthood alone—or oblige their own parents (or, frequently, their mothers) to share the burden. Furthermore, they are usually poor and, as a result of their premature motherhood, become poorer. Almost half of all teenage mothers—in the case of unmarried teenage mothers, three quarters—go on welfare within four years of the birth of the child (Carnegie Corporation, 1994). In addition, teenage mothers, because they are caught up in the developmental struggles of adolescence, are unlikely to have the psychological stability and attentiveness that underlie parental competence—a fact that has been borne out by observations of these girls in interaction with their children. According to a number of studies, adolescent mothers, compared with adult mothers, are less sensitive to their children's cues, less likely to interact with their children verbally, less likely to praise them, and more likely to criticize and punish them (Borkowski, Whitman, Passino, et al., 1992; Brooks-Gunn & Chase-Lansdale, 1995).

At the same time that they receive lesser care, the children of adolescent mothers suffer greater exposure to factors associated with developmental disorders. Maternal use of drugs and alcohol, poor prenatal care, poor nutrition, low birth weight, maternal ignorance regarding child development, low maternal IQ—all these factors, known to predispose children to developmental delays, are more common with teenage motherhood. To take only the last factor, the average IQ of teen mothers who choose to raise their children has been estimated at 85 (Borkowski, Whitman, Passino, et al., 1992).

It should come as no surprise, then, that mild mental retardation turns up more frequently—according to one estimate, three times more frequently—in the children of adolescent mothers (Borkowski, Whitman, Passino, et al., 1992; Broman, Nichols, Shaughnessy, et al., 1987). The question is to what extent is this attributable to the mother's age alone, as opposed to the problems so often seen in the lives of teen mothers, such as poverty, single parenthood, and interrupted education?

Mental Retardation in Adults

Many people with mental retardation grow up to lead relatively happy and useful adult lives, but many others do not, for retardation involves an increased susceptibility both to further brain disorders and to emotional disturbance.

Down Syndrome and Alzheimer's Disease In years past, people with Down syndrome rarely lived beyond middle age, with the result that their aging process was little studied. Today, however, more and more people with this disorder are surviving into middle and even old age. One of the consequences of this development has been the discovery of a link between Down syndrome and Alzheimer's disease. In people with Down syndrome, furthermore, Alzheimer's strikes unusually early. To quote a recent review of research on this subject, "Virtually all adults with Down syndrome over 40 years of age have Alzheimer's disease" (Zigman, Schupf, Zigman, et al., 1993, p. 63). This is clearly the result of their abnormal genetic endowment, though the biochemistry of the connection is not yet fully understood.

In some respects, Alzheimer's in a person with Down syndrome is no different from Alzheimer's in other people. However, because of Down-related behavioral deficits, Alzheimer's may be harder to diagnose. In general, the onset of Alzheimer's in people with Down syndrome is marked by behavioral regression; that is, the skills they have learned, often with great difficulty—gross motor skills, toileting, dressing and grooming, eating, speaking—begin to crumble, often necessitating their removal from home or from relatively open residential programs into more restricted living arrangements. Some proceed to dementia. In any case, this is a cruel burden overlaid on an already difficult life (Prasher & Chung, 1996).

Mental Retardation and Other Mental Disorders People with mental retardation are also at risk for a variety of other mental disorders, including attention deficit hyperactivity disorder, disruptive behavior disorders, feeding and eating disorders, schizophrenia and other psychotic disorders, bipolar disorder, and anxiety disorders (Szymanski & Kaplan, 1997). They are also at greater risk for drug abuse today than in the past, due to increased contact with the general population (Christian & Poling, 1997). In addition, adults with mental retardation are vulnerable to depression (Szymanski & Kaplan, 1997). When the person's IQ is over 50, the symptoms of emotional disturbance are much like those of people with normal intelligence. Depressed people with mild retardation report sadness, self-blame, and sleeping and eating problems, just like those without retardation. When IQ is lower, emotional disturbance is harder to detect, but there are special scales for diagnosing psychopathology in people with mental retardation (e.g., Reiss, 1992; Reiss & Valenti-Hein, 1990).

Why are people with mental retardation more subject to depression than people without mental retardation? Researchers have noted that depression or dysthymia in people with mental retardation is often due to specific stressors such as loss of an important, supportive relationship, change in living settings, hospitalization, deprivation or abuse, and inability to communicate (Day, 1990; Jancar & Gunaratne, 1994). Another likely reason is simply their social position (Reiss, 1994): the fact that many people avoid them, that they must watch others succeed where they themselves fail, that they cannot have the same privileges as others. The day when a teenager with mental retardation sees his younger brother come home with a driver's license—something that he himself will never have—can be a bitter one, and the cumulative impact of these small, day-to-day sorrows can have serious emotional consequences.

Though treatment is available and effective, most people with mental retardation do not get to make use of treatment. In many cases, the emotional difficulties of people with mental retardation are not even diagnosed—a problem that is due in part to "diagnostic overshadowing": because the intellectual deficit is so obvious, the emotional dysfunction is ignored (Reiss & Rojahn, 1994). Another problem is that people with mental retardation who have emotional disturbances fall through a crack in the service-delivery system—between agencies that serve people with mental retardation and those that serve the mentally ill. Recognizing this situation, researchers and clinicians are now trying to recast their thinking about mental retardation in terms of the "whole person." In recent years, several model mental health programs have been set up for persons with mental retardation, but many more are needed.

❖ Groups at Risk for Mental Retardation

There are several risk factors for mental retardation. One of the most significant is gender: males tend to outnumber females by approximately 1.6 to 1, due largely to the prevalence of fragile X syndrome, which affects boys more dramatically than girls. However, other gender-linked disorders also have a disproportionate effect on males. Another risk factor is age. The prevalence of mental retardation appears to peak at age 5 to 6 years, due primarily to increased cognitive testing and a need for intellectual capability in school. Mental retardation is not usually diagnosed later in life, because a person's adaptive behavior generally increases over time.

A third important risk factor is socioeconomic status. In general, mild mental retardation is somewhat more prevalent in families with low incomes than in families with high incomes. This risk factor is related to parental intelligence and the amount of intellectual stimulation the child receives. However, socioeconomic status does not seem to be related to the more severe forms of mental retardation. A related risk factor may be minority group status. For example, compared with other ethnic groups, African Americans have a higher incidence of mild mental retardation. Factors such as testing bias and environmental and cultural background may help to explain this phenomenon.

Finally, prenatal and perinatal variables are major risk factors for mental retardation. As we saw, maternal age is closely related to the prevalence of Down syndrome. In addition, exposure to disease, drugs, toxins, incompatible blood types, maternal emotions, anoxia, and malnutrition can affect the development of a child's central nervous system before or during birth. Many different genetic and metabolic disorders can also contribute to mental retardation (Hodapp & Dykens, 1996; Szymanski & Kaplan, 1997).

Autism

Another developmental disorder that deserves special attention, by virtue both of its fame and its severity, is autism. Some children are so profoundly disturbed from early infancy that they withdraw from social contact, even from their parents, and have difficulty learning to communicate verbally and nonverbally. Many of these children also hurt themselves or engage in repeated motor behaviors for hours at a time. Although traditionally known as **infantile autism** (from the Greek *autos*, "self"), researchers now understand this disorder to be lifelong in nature. Here we discuss the primary characteristics of this bizarre developmental disorder.

Prevalence figures for autism vary, largely because there is a great deal of variation in symptoms and therefore considerable disagreement as to what should be called autism as opposed to "autistic-like" conditions. Strictly defined, autism occurs in about 5 out of every 10,000 births (American Psychiatric Association, 2000).

Dustin Hoffman's protrayal of Raymond Babbitt, a man with autism and savant syndrome, in the movie Rain Man *earned him an Academy Award.*

Symptoms of Autism

Despite the broad range of behaviors covered by the term *autism,* there are four symptoms that are almost invariably present: social isolation, mental retardation, language deficits, and stereotyped behavior.

Social Isolation

> A beautiful, enigmatic child tiptoes into your waiting room, his gaze averted from you. Instead of a toy, he clutches a strange, dirty, dangling string which he twirls from time to time. When you start to examine him, he shrinks from your touch, particularly disturbed by your hands touching his head. He stares out the window instead of noticing you or your office. He seems alone, totally self-preoccupied. (Coleman, 1989, p. 1)

One striking abnormality common to all people diagnosed with autism is impaired social behavior (Rapin, 1991; Waterhouse, 1994; Mesibov, Adams, & Klinger, 1997)—a problem implied, as we saw, in the very name of the syndrome. Many children with autism withdraw from all social contact into a state of what has been called "extreme autistic aloneness." As infants, they do not demand attention from others—a rare trait in a baby—and are difficult to hold and cuddle because they stiffen or go limp when they are picked up. The recoil from personal contact is even sharper in older children, who may behave as though other people simply do not exist. As with other characteristics of autism, however, the degree of social isolation varies. Many toddlers with autism show an attachment to their mothers; they cling to the mother and, when strangers are present, hover near her (Capps, Sigman, & Mundy, 1994; Sigman & Mundy, 1989). Furthermore, even when social isolation is extreme, this does not mean that the child shows no emotion. Children with autism may exhibit rage, panic, or inconsolable crying, but often in response to things that an observer cannot identify.

Partly on the basis of their social variability, Lorna Wing (Wing & Attwood, 1987; Wing & Gould, 1979) has proposed that children with autism can be subclassified into three types. In the *aloof* type, the child rarely makes a spontaneous social approach, except to get something he or she wants, and rejects approaches from others. In the *passive* type, the child does not initiate contact, but he or she responds if someone else makes the contact and structures the interaction. In the *active-but-odd* type, the child approaches others but in a peculiar, naive, or one-sided way. According to Wing and her colleagues, other characteristics of children with autism vary consistently with these social types: Aloof types move, play, and communicate in certain ways, passive types in other ways, and so on—a claim that has been at least partially validated (Castelloe & Dawson, 1993). It is possible that what we call autism is not one disorder but several. Subclassification schemes such as Wing's are an effort to make some sense out of the diversity of symptoms and, if different disorders are involved, to assemble the research groups necessary to find that out.

Mental Retardation Most children with autism have mental retardation. About 76 to 89 percent have an IQ of less than 70 (Bryson, Clark, & Smith, 1988; Gillberg, 1991; Steffenburg & Gillberg, 1986). But children with autism differ from other children with mental retardation in the nature of their cognitive deficits. Children with autism do quite a bit better, for example, on tests of sensorimotor ability, such as finding hidden figures, than on tests of social understanding and language; children with mental retardation tend to perform more evenly on all such tests (Shah & Frith, 1983). When children with

Focus On... Savant Syndrome

In rare cases, a person with greatly diminished mental skills shows extraordinary proficiency in one isolated skill—a phenomenon known as **savant syndrome.** Until recently, savant syndrome was thought to be associated with retardation, but it is likely that savants actually have autism, not mental retardation. The abilities of savants are often so wildly exaggerated by the press that the phenomenon is often regarded with some skepticism. However, scientists, too, have observed and described savants (e.g., Gillberg & Coleman, 2000).

How do these remarkable skills develop? Perhaps by way of compensation. Just as the blind may develop particularly keen hearing, so a child with autism may compensate by becoming "overproficient" in one salvaged skill. Alternatively, the source of savants' abilities may be purely biological; that is, one area of the brain may be rendered abnormally efficient by the same structural change that rendered the rest of the brain abnormally inefficient. Another possibility is that, when such abilities appear in association with autism, they are produced by the intense concentration typical of children with autism. Whatever its source, the savant phenomenon makes an enigmatic disorder, autism, seem even more enigmatic.

In almost all reported cases, the skill in question is based on memory or calculation. There have been several reports of children who, if given a date, could say immediately what day of the week it fell on. Others can recite columns of numbers from the telephone book after one reading. Raymond (played by Dustin Hoffman), the hero of the movie *Rain Man,* was a "calculator savant." There have also been several reports of musical savants—not surprising, because music, like numbers, involves intricate systems. Some years ago, an English psychiatrist, Lorna Selfe (1978), reported a truly unusual case—a drawing savant.

Nadia, the second of three children born to a Ukrainian couple living in England, was clearly abnormal from an early age. She did not speak, and she did not seem even to notice other people, with the exception of her mother and a few others. Most of her days were spent tearing paper into thin strips or performing some other ritualistic activity. Her diagnosis was autism.

When Nadia was 3, her mother had to be hospitalized for several months. When the mother returned, the child was overjoyed. Inexplicably, she began to draw. What she drew was equally inexplicable—figures of astonishing beauty and sophistication. For the next three years, Nadia produced drawing after drawing. She refused to use color; only a ballpoint pen would do. She drew on any kind of paper she could find, including boxes. She sketched with the utmost concentration, then sat back, surveyed the result, and wiggled her hands and knees with pleasure.

A rooster drawn by Nadia when she was about $3\frac{1}{2}$.

At the same time, Nadia was being taken on the round of clinics and special schools. She was enrolled in several programs but made no progress. Then, around age $6\frac{1}{2}$, she began speaking and stopped drawing. At the time when this case was written up, Nadia was 10 years old. She had acquired a small vocabulary, was responsive to a limited circle of people, and could even handle simple mathematics. When asked to draw a picture, she could produce one, but it had none of the genius of her earlier work. As mysteriously as it had appeared, her remarkable artistic talent had vanished.

Recent research on savant drawing ability has shown that children like Nadia can construct patterns from segmented components at the same level as children of high intelligence (Pring, Hermelin, & Heavey, 1995). Researchers have also found that savant abilities sometimes decline as the symptoms of autism improve (Bailey, Phillips, & Rutter, 1996). Perhaps these findings help to explain the changes in Nadia's savant abilities over time.

autism receive therapy to improve their social relationships, their mental retardation does *not* improve as well (Klinger & Dawson, 1996; Rutter, 1983). Therefore, in children with autism, mental retardation is a primary cognitive problem, not merely a result of their social withdrawal.

In some cases, however, people with autistic features show average or above-average intelligence. Sometimes this is expressed in one limited area, such as mathematics, art, or music (see the box on savant syndrome, above). In other cases, a person may show the social impairments inherent in autism but without any language problems or mental retardation. For these people, often diagnosed with Asperger's disorder, long-term prognosis is much brighter than for those diagnosed with formal autism.

Asperger's Disorder: A Mild Form of Autism?

The MindMAP video "Asperger's Disorder" presents two children diagnosed with Asperger's disorder, a condition some researchers believe to be a less severe form of autism. What symptoms of autism, in milder form, can you identify on the video? Why might it be more difficult to diagnose Asperger's disorder than autism?

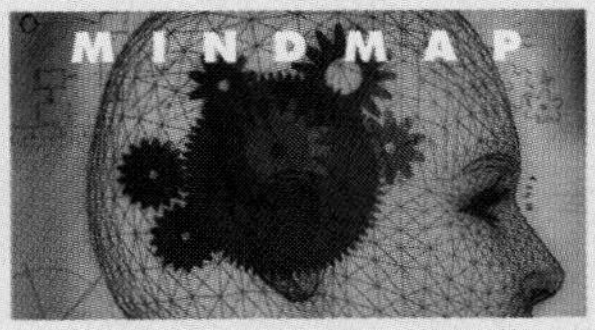

Language Deficits More than half of all children with autism do not speak at all. Others babble, whine, scream, or show **echolalia**—that is, they simply echo what other people say. Some children with autism aimlessly repeat snatches of songs, television commercials, or other bits of overheard language. Those who do speak can communicate only in a limited way (Bailey, Phillips, & Rutter, 1996). Some use pronouns strangely, referring to themselves in the second person ("you") or third person ("he," "she"). Still others speak extremely literally. In essence, children with autism cannot communicate *reciprocally,* cannot engage in the usual give-and-take of conversation.

The severity of language problems in children with autism is an excellent indicator of prognosis. Children most likely to benefit from treatment have developed some meaningful speech by the age of 5 years (Werry, 1996; Kobayashi, Murata, & Yoshinaga, 1992; Venter, Lord, & Schopler, 1992). A child's intellectual development is another excellent indicator of his or her prognosis. Children with autism who do not have mental retardation (about one fourth of those with autism) also tend to be those who have begun to speak meaningfully by age 5 years and who adjust better as adults.

Stereotyped Behavior Many children with autism tend to repeat a limited number of movements endlessly, ritualistically, and without any clear goal. These self-stimulating movements—twirling, tiptoeing, flapping the hands, rocking, tensing parts of the body—may involve the fine or gross muscles of the hands, face, trunk, arms, and legs. Left to themselves, many children with autism, especially those who are institutionalized, spend a great deal of time in these bizarre forms of self-stimulation.

Some of these repetitive movements cause physical harm. Head banging and hand biting are not uncommon. Children with autism have also been known to pull out their hair, bite off the ends of their fingers, and scratch themselves until they bleed, often crying out in pain as they do so. Why do children with autism engage in such self-stimulatory and self-injurious behaviors? According to Durand (1990, 1993), children with developmental disabilities, especially those with mental retardation and without language, often engage in maladaptive behavior to communicate desires to others or to obtain certain kinds of reinforcement. Specifically, these children often seek sensory reinforcement, escape from aversive situations (such as a boring educational routine), attention from others, and/or positive tangible reinforcement, such as food or a toy.

Motor mannerisms are not the only area in which children with autism show an intense and narrow focus. They may have a favorite activity—tearing paper, spinning the wheels on a toy car—in which they lose themselves for hours every day. With toys and other objects, they tend to interest themselves in the part rather than the whole—not the car, for example, but just the wheels. They are also likely to resist any change in their surroundings and routines. Toys must always be put in the same place on the same shelves. Breakfast must be an unvarying ritual of egg first, vitamin pill second, and then toast. If the child senses that any step has been skipped, he or she may respond with a tantrum. Clinicians have noted that many normal children, when they are about $2\frac{1}{2}$ years old, insist on sameness in routines. They have suggested, therefore, that the development of children with autism may stall at this point.

All these problems—the ritual behaviors, the self-absorption and bizarreness, the intellectual and social deficits—appear in the following case:

I first observed Jennie when she was 7 years old, in a small classroom at a school for children with severe disabilities. An uncommunicative and unresponsive child, Jennie rarely made eye contact with anyone. If left alone she would put her hands over her throat, stick out her tongue, and make strange noises. Unless her attention was diverted, she would continue this way for hours, standing or rocking back and forth in her chair. If someone got too close to Jennie, she might grab the person's jewelry or eyeglasses and fling them across the room. Jennie did not like new experiences. One day she slapped a new intern who had approached her shortly after entering the room.

Though Jennie did not speak, she did understand and comply with simple requests to get her lunch or use the bathroom. She had a picture book with photographs of items she might want or need—a lunch box, a cookie, a glass of water, a favorite toy, or the toilet—and used it to communicate when she was asked to. But Jennie seemed unable or unwilling to discriminate between colors, to understand the concept of yes versus no, or to follow commands that included more than one step (for example, "Clap your hands and touch your nose"). Her former teachers reported that, though she could learn the difference between red and blue in the classroom, she could not transfer her learning to a different setting.

Despite her poor cognitive skills, Jennie's life skills were relatively good. She could put on her winter jacket with help and could use the toilet without difficulty, as long as she was reminded to put her clothes on again afterward. Still, Jennie needed constant supervision, mostly for her own safety. She tended to be oblivious of danger and could not be trusted to leave alone a hot stove.

Jennie's parents told me that she "had always been like this." They had noticed that Jennie was different when as an infant she resisted being held, and later when she failed to talk by the age of 3 years. At first they had thought she was deaf, but medical tests indicated that her hearing was normal. They had enrolled Jennie in her current school at age 4 years and reported that her behavior had improved greatly since then. Limited psychological testing and extensive observations over the past three years had largely confirmed Jennie's impaired cognitive and social skills. Jennie was diagnosed with both autism and mental retardation. (Adapted from Kearney, 2002.)

Some children with autism improve enough by the time they are grown to hold down jobs and even live alone, though they are still aloof and still have language problems and poor social judgment. As for the remainder—that is, the vast majority of children with autism—most do improve with treatment but rarely enough to allow them to live outside a special residence when they reach adulthood, let alone on their own (Gillberg, 1991; Kobayashi, Murata, & Yoshinaga, 1992; Venter, Lord, & Schopler, 1992).

Theories of Autism

Explanations of autism have changed radically in the past few decades. Popular in the 1950s and 1960s was the psychodynamic view that autism was caused by cold, rejecting parents (e.g., Bettelheim, 1967)—a theory that, after adding grief and guilt to the lives of parents already coping with a difficult situation, has now been repudiated by research. Researchers are now focusing on brain dysfunction, investigating what factors may be involved, and on the cognitive perspective, examining the consequences of the presumed physical flaw.

The Neuroscience Perspective

Genetic Research As we noted in Chapter 14, a great deal of sophisticated and productive research has been carried out on the genetics of schizophrenia. In recent years, similar studies of autism have been done, despite the difficulty of finding large samples of twins. Researchers who scoured Great Britain, for example, found 11 pairs of monozygotic (MZ) twins and 10 pairs of dizygotic (DZ) twins in which at least 1 twin had autism (Folstein & Rutter, 1977). Of the MZ group, 4 of 11 were concordant. Of the DZ group, none was concordant. Even when a subject with an MZ twin who had autism was *not* diagnosed with autism, he or she was likely to be markedly impaired in language or cognition.

Three additional twin studies have essentially replicated these findings. A study based on a nationwide survey of clinics, schools, and parent organizations in Great Britain found a concordance rate of 50 percent for MZ twins and 0 percent for DZ twins. The concordance rates for cognitive/social disorder in this sample were 86 percent and 9 percent, respectively (Rutter, Macdonald, Le Couteur, et al., 1990). A follow-up study based on an earlier twin sample plus a new sample showed a concordance rate of 60 percent for MZ twins and 0 percent for DZ twins (Bailey, Le Couteur, Gottesman, et al., 1995). And a study done in the Nordic countries found a concordance rate of 91 percent for MZ twins and 0 percent for DZ twins. Concordance rates for cognitive disorder in this sample were 91 percent and 30 percent, respectively (Steffenburg, Gillberg, Hellgren, et al., 1989).

Even in nontwin siblings of children with autism, the rate of autism is about 3 to 7 percent (Bailey, Phillips, & Rutter, 1996). Findings differ with respect to the incidence of milder impairments among siblings of children with autism, however. In one study, 12 percent of the siblings of children with autism showed impairments in social interaction, compared with 0 percent of the siblings of children with Down syndrome (Bolton & Rutter, 1990). But, in another study, no difference was found between the rate of social or cognitive problems in siblings of children with autism and the rate in siblings of children with Down syndrome or low birth weight (Szatmari, Jones, Tuff, et al., 1993).

Whatever the genetic components that are involved, they are likely to differ with differing kinds of autism. One family study found that the patients with autism who were most likely to have siblings with autism or mental retardation were the ones who had the most severe retardation (Baird & August, 1985). Another study indicates that patients with autism who show the best functioning tend to come from families with a history of mood disorder (DeLong, 1992). In fact, several studies have found that major affective disorder is three times as common among parents of children with autism as among parents of children with tuberous sclerosis or epilepsy. Though the hardship of caring for a child with autism might be suspected as a contributing factor in major affective disorder, in nearly two thirds of such parents, onset of the disorder precedes the birth of a child with autism (Bailey, Phillips, & Rutter, 1996).

Chromosome Studies As was pointed out earlier, fragile X syndrome is associated not just with mental retardation but also with autism. Two recent studies have found that the prevalence rate among patients with autism is 2.5 to 7 percent (Bailey, Phillips, & Rutter, 1996; Hagerman, 1992). Other abnormalities, such as tuberous sclerosis and anomalies on chromosome 15, are also associated with autism, though none so strongly as fragile X (Bailey, Phillips, & Rutter, 1996). Cases of autism have now been linked to aberrations on all chromosomes except number 14 (Gillberg & Coleman, 2000).

Biochemical Studies In autism, as in schizophrenia (Chapter 14), a major focus of research today is the role of neurotransmitters. But researchers have found that children with autism do not necessarily have abnormally high levels of serotonin and dopamine, as was once thought (Tsai & Ghaziuddin, 1997). Chugani and associates found serotonin depletion in 30 children with autism, and other researchers found low levels of dopamine (Chugani, Muzik, Behen, et al., 1999; Ernst, Zametkin, Matochik, et al., 1997). Whatever their role in the development of autism, these two neurotransmitters may play a role in its treatment. When children with autism receive stimulants such as the amphetamines, which increase dopamine, their symptoms of hyperactivity, ritualistic behavior, and self-stimulation get worse (Young, Kavanagh, Anderson, et al., 1982). Dopamine-inhibiting drugs such as the phenothiazines mitigate many of the symptoms of autism, including self-mutilation and repetitive motions, although they are less effective with autism than with schizophrenia (Campbell, Overall, Small, et al., 1989; Tsai, 1992). In a recent study of risperidone, an atypical antipsychotic, 8 of 14 adults with autism experienced less repetitive behavior, aggression, and other behavior problems (McDougle, Homes, Carlson, et al., 1998).

Congenital Disorders and Birth Complications While genetic factors are implicated in many cases of autism, this does not rule out nongenetic factors. Several birth complications appear to be related to autism, including pregnancy at an advanced age, bleeding after the first trimester, the use of medication during pregnancy, and the presence of meconium in the amniotic fluid (Gillberg & Coleman, 2000; Tsai, 1987). According to Tsai and Ghaziuddin (1997), rubella, depressed immune function, autoimmune mechanisms, and problematic immune regulation may also be related to autism, though not necessarily in a cause-and-effect manner. But, in most cases of autism, congenital disorders and birth complications probably are not the primary causes of the disorder. Furthermore, congenital disorders may be related to genetic factors.

Neurological Research Most researchers believe that whatever its ultimate cause, autism results from a range of deficits in the brain. In the first place, most of the characteristic signs of autism—impaired language development, mental retardation, bizarre motor behavior, underreactivity and overreactivity to sensory input, responsiveness to touch and movement as opposed to auditory and visual stimuli—are related to the functioning of the central nervous system. Second, as many as 25 percent of persons with autism, particularly adolescents, develop seizure disorders, which are known to originate in the central nervous system (Klin & Volkmar, 1997; Volkmar & Nelson, 1990). Third, neurological examinations of children with autism sometimes reveal abnormalities such as poor muscle tone, poor coordination, drooling, and hyperactivity.

A fourth line of evidence has to do with neurophysiology. Two general types of research have been conducted: *EEG* and *ERP* studies. Electroencephalograms of people with autism are difficult to obtain, for the test requires more cooperation than many such people can give. Nevertheless, Minshew (1991) has reported that about 50 percent of persons with autism display abnormal EEGs. A recent study showed that children with autism show reduced EEG activity in the frontal and temporal regions of the brain, compared with that of normal children (Dawson, Klinger, Panagiotides, et al., 1995). Another study found that 23.6 percent of 106 patients with autism had EEG abnormalities and 18.9 percent had actual clinical seizures (Rossi, Parmeggiani, Bach, et al., 1995). ERP studies are concerned with event-related potentials: how the brain waves of people show patterns of reaction to various sensory stimuli. ERP studies of people with autism have shown abnormalities of attention to both novel stimuli and language stimuli (Courchesne, Townsend, Akshoomoff, et al., 1994; Dunn, 1994). Taken together, EEG and ERP studies strongly suggest a neurological impairment in people with autism.

Fifth, autopsies of the brains of people with autism have revealed certain abnormalities in the cerebellum and in the limbic system, which is known to be involved in cognition, memory, emotion, and behavior. Specifically, the neurons in the limbic system appear to be smaller and more tightly packed. In some areas, their dendrites—the branching arms through which they receive signals from adjacent neurons—are shorter and less complex (Figure 17.2). Both these conditions are typical of earlier stages of prenatal brain maturation (Bauman & Kemper, 1994). In other cases, an abnormally low density of Purkinje cells, which are responsible for inhibiting the action of other brain cells, has been found. Such an abnormality may explain the stereotyped and overactive behavior sometimes seen in persons with autism.

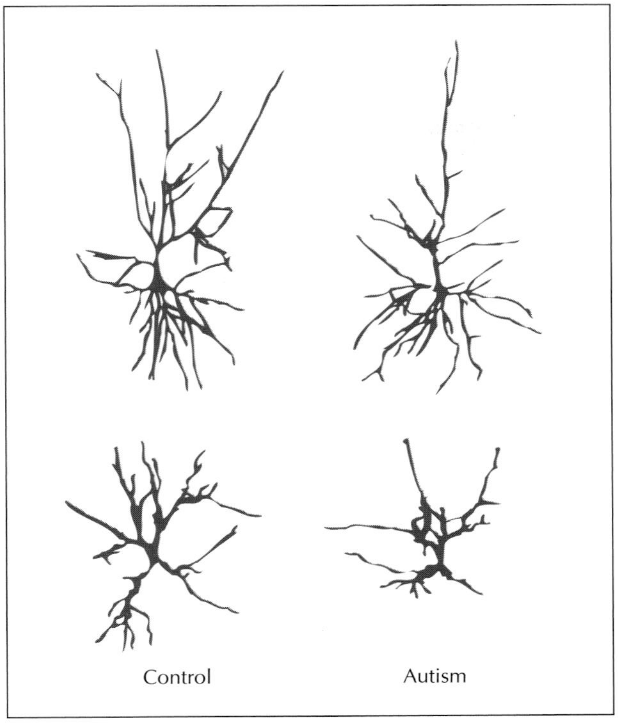

FIGURE 17.2 Photographic reproductions of neurons in a normal (control) brain and in the brain of a person with autism. In the upper pair, note the difference in the number of dendrites. In the lower pair, note the difference in dendrite length. (Adapted from Bauman & Kemper, 1994.)

Finally, some researchers have found a greater incidence of *megalencephaly* (an overly large brain size) in people with autism (Bailey, Luthert, Dean, et al., 1998; Kemper & Bauman, 1998).

Another hopeful line of investigation has to do with brain-imaging techniques, such as MRI and PET scans. Although the results of many such studies conflict, researchers have identified some possible causal influences in autism, including enlarged ventricles in the brain (Bailey, Luthert, Dean, et al., 1998; Minshew & Dombrowski, 1994). Scientists are now using brain-imaging techniques to develop interesting new hypotheses about causes of autism.

The Cognitive Perspective No one denies that children with autism have problems affecting their capacity to imitate and comprehend, to be flexible and inventive, to form and apply rules, and to use information—in other words, to cope with the world. Cognitive theories hold that the cognitive problems of children with autism are primary and cause their social problems (Rutter, Bailey, Bolton, et al., 1994).

Recent investigations have focused on four broad areas of cognitive function: executive function, categorization and memory, social understanding, and theory of mind. With respect to executive function, many researchers have noted that people with autism have great trouble solving problems, planning initiatives, controlling their impulses, maintaining attention, monitoring their performance, and inhibiting inappropriate behavior (Ozonoff, 1995).

Studies of categorization and memory have shown that people with autism also have difficulty forming new concepts and understanding new information based on those concepts. In particular, they have difficulty forming prototypes with which to categorize objects, so they tend to overrely on rules. Like people with amnesia, people with autism tend to show deficits in short- and long-term memory, which may be linked to dysfunctions in the amygdala and hippocampus (Bachevalier, 1994; DeLong, 1992; Klinger & Dawson, 1996).

The social understanding of children with autism is hampered by the fact that they do not attend to other people's emotional or attentional cues. In essence, their ability to comprehend gestures such as pointing or looking is severely impaired. They also have trouble understanding others' emotions and facial expressions (Hobson, 1993; Sigman, 1995).

A final cognitive hypothesis is that the fundamental problem of children with autism is that they have no **theory of mind**—that is, they cannot appreciate the existence of purely mental states, such as beliefs or desires, and therefore cannot predict or understand behavior based on such states. In one study, for example, normal children and children with autism or mental retardation were given the following task concerning two dolls, Sally and Anne (Baron-Cohen, 1995). Sally, they were shown, put her marble in her basket and left. While Sally was gone, Anne took the marble out of the basket and hid it. When Sally returned, the children were asked where Sally would look for the marble. Over 80 percent of the children both with and without retardation answered, "In the basket," but only 20 percent of the children with autism gave the obviously correct answer. It was not that they could not remember, but they could not take another person's point of view. The lack of this critical skill undoubtedly contributes to the social isolation of children with autism.

Children with autism vary in their success with theory of mind tasks. Normal children develop a theory of mind at around 18 months; about 20 percent of cases of autism have their onset at that time. Fein and Waterhouse (1990) have suggested that the theory of mind explanation may apply to that subgroup—their development becomes abnormal at that point—but that it is less likely to apply to children with autism who show abnormal social development in their first year of life. Another study has suggested that, in people with autism, the ability to solve theory of mind problems may be related to verbal ability (Yirmiya, Solomonica-Levi, Schulman, et al., 1996). Finally, some data suggest that the ability to solve this type of problem can be taught to persons with autism who are of normal intelligence (Ozonoff & Miller, 1995). It should be noted that although theory of mind is a fascinating psychological explanation for autism, researchers examining theory of mind have yet to design broad etiological, biological models to explain why theory of mind occurs in the first place.

❖ Groups at Risk for Autism

Socioeconomic status and ethnocultural background are *not* major risk factors for autism. Gender *is* a significant risk factor, however, for males with autism generally outnumber females by a 3 or 4 to 1 margin. This finding may be related to the risk factors for mental retardation. Specifically, females with autism generally have more severe forms of mental retardation, and more severe symptoms of autism, than males with autism. Conversely, though, females with autism but not mental retardation have fewer problems than males with autism but not mental retardation (Klin & Volkmar, 1999).

Another risk factor for autism is the presence of the disorder in siblings. The prevalence of autism in siblings of children with autism is estimated at 2 to 5 percent (Gillberg & Coleman, 2000), a rate that is substantially higher than that of the general population. This finding, in addition to the much higher rates of concordant autism in monozygotic but not dizygotic twins, raises the specter of genetic influences as a substantial risk factor for autism (Hodapp & Dykens, 1996; Klinger & Dawson, 1996; Szymanski & Kaplan, 1997).

Society and People with Developmental Disorders

Our society is designed for people with at least average coping skills, people who can park a car, pay a bill, fill out an income tax form. Most people with mental retardation and autism cannot handle such tasks. Indeed, most cannot care for themselves on their own. Some remain at home with their families, which is usually to their advantage, but many families cannot cope with a person with a developmental disorder, and those that are willing are generally hard-pressed. People with mental retardation need special schooling, special jobs (if they can hold jobs), special psychological supports. If the family cannot provide such things, should it be the responsibility of the society to do so? Our discussion of these social issues will cover developmental disorders as a whole, including mental retardation and autism.

Public Policy

In the past 30 years, there have been tremendous changes in the field of mental retardation. To begin with, parent groups—above all, the Association for Retarded Citizens (ARC)—have vigorously lobbied federal and state governments and have obtained not only large increases in funding but also legislation guaranteeing the right of people with mental retardation to a free education geared to their abilities. Second, these same parent organizations, along with other advocacy groups, have increasingly taken their grievances to the federal and state courts, whose decisions have substantially altered the treatment of people with retardation in this country. Finally, the number of professionals in the field of mental retardation has expanded greatly, a reflection of the discovery that people with mental retardation respond well to behavior therapy. This finding has generated a new mood of hope, attracting to the field a large number of young clinical psychologists. At the same time, several university-affiliated centers for training and research have been established to train these professionals and to teach them to work in interdisciplinary teams.

This new activism has brought about sweeping changes in public policy toward people with mental retardation. Whereas society once all but ignored them, today certain principles have been established. Although by no means fully implemented, these principles are guiding public institutions toward the granting of full citizens' rights to people with mental retardation. There are five basic principles:

1. *Free and appropriate education.* Public schools must create educational programs for people with retardation, so that they can learn with the maximum independence consistent with their abilities.
2. *Individualization.* Services should not be based on textbook descriptions of people with retardation; they should be tailored to the person—what he or she needs and can do.
3. *Timely progress reviews.* People with mental retardation, once placed in a program, should not be left there indefinitely but should have their progress reviewed regularly, with at least one comprehensive annual evaluation.
4. *Community integration.* Services for people with mental retardation should be provided in

Ideally, the mainstreaming of children with mental retardation into regular public school classrooms has educational and social benefits for the normal children as well as for those with retardation.

the least restrictive environment consistent with the person's disabilities.

5. *Human rights.* The law should protect people with mental retardation from abuse in residential programs and facilitate lawsuits to obtain needed services. In keeping with this principle, the federal government has established a protection and advocacy commission in each state to provide legal help for people with retardation.

For many years, children with mental retardation were essentially excluded from the public school system. Then, in the early 1970s, decisions in a number of class-action suits required that local school systems provide special education for children with retardation. Finally, in 1975, this requirement became effective nationwide when Congress passed Public Law 94-142, guaranteeing to every citizen aged 3 to 21 years a free public education appropriate to his or her needs. One consequence of excluding people under age 3 is that screening and intervention for very young children is not always available. This is especially unfortunate for children with severe developmental disorders, who tend to do better with very early and intensive intervention. Nevertheless, P.L. 94-142 has been responsible for a great increase in special education programs since the late 1970s. These programs are carefully tailored to the person, in keeping with the requirement that public education be appropriate to each child's needs. Typically, the school system has what is called an individualized education program (IEP). The school holds a multidisciplinary conference to identify the handicaps of children requesting special education and to review the progress of those already receiving such services. The committee then formulates, in writing, an IEP for each child, and the appropriate services are provided.

The law has stimulated some highly innovative programs. One concept, for example, is the "cascade system." Nine educational programs, beginning with a regular classroom in a regular school and ending with a hospital setting, are designed to accommodate individual needs and to provide for progression from one level to another. Upward mobility is the goal, and it is to be achieved by constant periodic evaluation, so that assignment to a particular cascade level does not become a life sentence. Many children with mental retardation have been integrated, or mainstreamed, into regular classes. (They are usually given modified tasks.) Other children may spend part of the school day in the regular class and part in a special class. Children who need more help and guidance may attend a special day school or live in a residential school. Such programs, however, are by no means the norm. Though P.L. 94-142 mandates special education for all children with disabilities, Congress has not provided full funding for the implementation of the law, and many communities have been unable or unwilling to find the necessary funds.

In the case of children with autism, designing an appropriate education program may be a harder task, because of these children's special disabilities. Their need for an unvarying routine is not easy to meet in a classroom, even a special classroom, and their ritualistic movements may leave little room in their attentional field for what the teacher is trying to say. Furthermore, as noted earlier, they tend not to respond to social reinforcement (e.g., the teacher's approval), which is the usual form of classroom reinforcement (Harris & Handleman, 1997; Schreibman, 1994).

Community Integration

Some of the most important changes in recent years have been those under the heading "community integration." As recently as 1970, virtually all services for people with retardation were segregated from services for people without mental retardation. Children with mild and moderate retardation attended special education classes separate from the classes for other children. People with severe and profound retardation were sent off to large institutions, which, because they were outside the community, provided their own educational, medical, and psychological services. The effect of this segregation was to deprive people with mental retardation of any real participation in the life of the society. The principle of community integration holds that people with retardation should be educated in the public schools and, when they get sick, they should go to the same hospitals as everyone else. They should be able to go to the same movie theaters, the same bowling alleys, the same restaurants as everybody else.

In some measure, this is now being achieved. Not only are children with mental retardation being educated in their local schools, but many in the mild-retardation category have been mainstreamed into regular education classes. As for residential facilities, community planning has shifted from a model of institutional care to deinstitutionalization, or residence within the community (Lynch, Kellar, & Willson, 1997; Stancliffe & Lakin, 1998; Polloway, Smith, Patton, et al., 1996). There has been considerable debate over the question of deinstitutionalization, and many researchers have examined the changes in behavior associated with the movement from institutional to community living. Recently, Kim, Larson, and Lakin (2001) reviewed all of the studies published between 1980 and 1999 that had to do with deinstitutionalization of people with intellectual disabilities. They found that most studies report statistically significant improvement in overall adaptive behavior when people with mental retardation move from institutions to smaller community settings. Most studies also report reductions in maladaptive behavior following deinstitutionalization, with the most consistent improvements in self-care/domestic skills and social skills. However, for some people with very severe developmental disorders, residence in large facilities with extensive medical and supervisory personnel may be desirable.

A wide range of assisted-living arrangements is now available, from supported living arrangements, in which supervision is generally provided only in the evening, to community living facilities—small- to medium-sized residential centers with round-the-clock supervision—and intermediate-care facilities, or medium-sized residences for groups of about six people. Each type of community living facility can care for people who function on several different levels. For example, someone with severe mental retardation but no major medical or behavioral problems might be successful in an intermediate-care facility, while someone with only moderate mental retardation but severe physical problems and self-injurious behavior might not be able to live there. Large state institutions still care for those who cannot function satisfactorily in community settings. But as increasing numbers of community living centers are being established, more and more people are being moved out of the state institutions. This is an extremely heartening development. Large institutions, as we saw in previous chapters, can have damaging effects on the people they are supposed to care for, not only because so many of them offer dreary and even cruel living conditions but because they do not allow patients to use the skills they have. Consequently, those skills tend to disappear. The great virtue of community living centers is that they challenge residents to use and develop their coping abilities.

Quality of Life

Over the past 10 years, one of the most intensely researched and discussed topics in the field of developmental disabilities has been the quality of life of people with disabilities. What is quality of life? Felce and Perry (1995) have suggested that it is a multidimensional concept that includes physical, material, social, and emotional well-being, as well as personal development and activity. Though these five dimensions are general enough to apply to almost anyone, individual differences should inform any assessment of quality of life.

Research shows that the size of a person's residential setting is not as important as the quality of life of the people who live within that setting. Because one key measure of quality of life is choice, some of the new research has focused on the choices people with developmental disabilities are allowed to make within their living arrangements. In one study, the degree of choice residents enjoyed was found to be correlated with adaptive, and to some extent maladaptive, behavior (Kearney, Durand, & Mindell, 1995b). Providing residents with some choice in their activities can affect the degree to which they participate in activities, the way they behave during the activities, and their perceptions of them (Harchik, Sherman, Sheldon, et al., 1993; McKnight & Kearney, 2001).

Given the difficulty of communicating with many people who have developmental disabilities, how can the degree of choice that is offered to them be measured? There are several methods, including interviews, questionnaires, pictures, and direct observation (Kearney & McKnight, 1997). For use in group homes for people with severe disabilities, Kearney, Durand, and Mindell (1995a) have developed the Resident Choice Assessment Scale. Ways have also been developed to implement or enhance the opportunity to make choices in programs and residences for those with developmental disabilities. Residents can be taught choice-making skills, and staff members can learn to facilitate their choice making (Kearney & McKnight, 1997).

Support for the Family

When a child is diagnosed with mental retardation or autism, the parents usually suffer terrible grief. In the past, the diagnosis was usually accompanied by a recommendation that a child be institutionalized. Today, even in the case of children with profound retardation, the recommendation is likely to be the opposite: that the parents try to care for the child at home. If they do so, however, they need supportive training and counseling (Day & Dosen, 2001; Dunst, Johanson, Trivette, et al., 1991).

Children with mental retardation, of course, have many of the same needs as normal children. They need to be fed, to be loved and held, to be given structure and discipline. Like normal children, they need to interact with other children and with adults to develop social skills, and they must be encouraged to be as independent as possible. But children with retardation also have special needs. They may be physically handicapped. They are often teased or shunned by other children. They learn more slowly. In recent years, efforts have been made to teach parents simple behavioral techniques for dealing with these problems (Harris, Alessandri, & Gill, 1991; Schreibman & Koegel, 1996). Through reinforcement, parents can help children with retardation to develop speech. Through shaping, they can help them master complex behaviors such as self-feeding and using the toilet. Such home training not only increases the child's skills; it also tightens the parent-child bond by making the parents feel that they can actually do something concrete to help the child.

The adolescent with mental retardation presents additional concerns to the family and community. Parents must walk a narrow line between the child's need for independence and his or her lack of maturity. They must help the child to deal with physical changes, with sexual feelings, with threats to self-esteem (an especially difficult task if the child is aware of being "different"), and with a peer group that is outgrowing him or her. The extent to which these problems become an issue depends, of course, on the level of retardation. They are of greatest concern for parents of teenagers with mild and moderate retardation.

As the adolescent nears adulthood, the family and community must consider carefully the extent to which he or she will be able to live independently. Although parents may be confident of their ability to provide for a young child with mental retardation, they become uneasy when they think about the stresses and demands placed on the adult with mental retardation. One of the most complex issues is that of sex and marriage.

Historically, attitudes toward the sexual development of people with mental retardation have favored complete desexualization, physically and emotionally. Relationships between men and women with mental retardation were discouraged, and involuntary sterilization was common. Today, a more humane approach is taken. The trend is toward the belief that people with mental retardation, like normal people, have a right to sexual development and that they can be taught sexual behavior appropriate to their level of functioning. Programs exist to teach social and relationship skills to young adults with mental retardation and to educate them about AIDS and HIV risk reduction (Scotti, Nangle, Masia, et al., 1997; Whitehouse & McCabe, 1997). With some assistance from families or social agencies, many people with mild retardation can marry and maintain regular social functioning. When sterilization is considered, usually only as a last resort, a great deal of thought is given to the ethical issues involved in the decision (Elkins & Andersen, 1992).

Employment

Federal and state laws provide that people with mental retardation must have opportunities for useful employment, whether or not in the types of jobs other people hold. In practice, this means that, whatever their residential placement, people with mental retardation must be offered planned daytime programs or supported employment (Wehman & Kregel, 1995). In the case of people with severe or profound retardation, such daytime activities may be very simple, but many people with mild and some with moderate retardation do hold paying jobs, some in ordinary work environments, others in special work centers, called **sheltered workshops**, tailored to their needs.

It has long been assumed that people with retardation belong to America's socioeconomic surplus population—that most of them either can't or don't want to work or, if they do work, that they are the first to lose their jobs when the payroll is being cut. But this is no longer the case. Many, if not most, people with mental retardation do want to work (Test, Hinson, Solow, et al., 1993). Furthermore, when properly placed, they make good employees and consequently are not necessarily the first to be fired when jobs become scarce (Nietupski, Hamre-Nietupski, VanderHart, et al., 1996). Interestingly, research also indicates that, when they are fired, it is often not because of a failure to do the job but because of a lack of social skills. The obvious conclusion is that vocational training for people with mental retardation must cover social skills as well as vocational skills—and training programs now tend to include them.

Prevention and Therapy

One of the most significant developments in the field of developmental disorders is the idea that treatment can make a decisive difference in the lives of people with developmental disorders. Whereas early detection of chromosomal and congenital abnormalities is available to help couples at risk and expectant parents, who may then seek counseling about the pregnancy, the new hope in the therapeutic community is to improve the quality of life of children and adults with developmental disorders (Campbell, Schopler, Cueva, et al., 1996; Kearney & McKnight, 1998).

Primary Prevention

A major breakthrough in the prevention of developmental disorders has been the advent of genetic analysis and counseling. Couples at risk for abnormal births can be identified, informed of the risk, and advised how to proceed. Tay-Sachs disease, for example, is a recessive genetic disorder, so both parents must contribute the gene for the disorder to occur. If one carrier marries another, their chances of having a child with the disease are 1 in 4. A simple blood test can identify carriers, who can then get advice from a genetic counselor. Genetic analysis can also identify abnormalities in the developing fetus. If fragile X, Down syndrome, or another abnormality is detected, the parents may choose to terminate the pregnancy.

Secondary Prevention

When a child is at risk for a condition that could lead to developmental disorders, secondary prevention, or early intervention, can do much to minimize its effects. We have already described several medical procedures that fall under this heading, including low-phenylalanine diets for PKU children and thyroid treatments for infants with missing or damaged thyroid glands. There are also psychological therapies. For example, babies with Down syndrome may be intensively taught for several hours a day to stimulate language acquisition, social and problem-solving skills, and achievement motivation. Parents do most of the teaching, aided and guided by a special education teacher and other child development specialists who observe the child periodically at home or at school and suggest and demonstrate activities to be added to the child's regimen. The key to these children's development is the amount of stimulation, exercise, and encouragement they receive as they strive to master the skills that come more easily to youngsters without developmental disorders. Teaching infants may be as simple as mothers talking to and making eye contact with their babies. Mothers can encourage use of the long muscles, helping the babies to sit up and lift their heads. (Children with Down syndrome are often strikingly "loose jointed" and have poor muscle tone.) Activities and equipment become more sophisticated as the child progresses. Many "graduates" of early intervention programs are able to feed and dress themselves, talk fluently, and participate in most children's activities. Some have learned to read and have acquired other academic skills (Hanson, 1987; Pines, 1982a; Gath, 2001; Seifer, Clark, & Sameroff, 1991).

Education programs have been expanded to include children whose only apparent risk factor is poverty. If it is true, as the research assembled by the Carnegie report suggests, that the conditions associated with poverty can lead to mild retardation, could helping poor families early lessen the risk? This has been the goal of family-support programs instituted in various American cities in the 1980s and 1990s. In one such program, called Avance, that serves 2,000 Mexican American families yearly in and around San Antonio, Texas, parents are given special help with their infants for 2 years. Evaluations of Avance have shown that mothers who have been in the program are more affectionate and positive with their children, encourage the children's speech more, and provide a more stimulating environment than mothers who have received no special services (Johnson, Walker, & Rodriguez, 1993). The Carnegie report also calls for a broad range of other reforms—promotion of family planning; inclusion of child development courses in high school curricula; and improvement of prenatal-care services, parental-leave benefits, and child-care facilities—to help break the link between poverty and developmental delay.

Behavioral Therapy

Of all the services for people with developmental disorders, almost none has generated more enthusiasm than the application of learning principles to training and behavior management. Behavioral techniques are being used extensively and with good success in the home, in schools and workshops, in institutional settings, and with both children and adults. They can be taught to parents, teachers, therapists, and hospital staffs, and they can be used for a variety of purposes.

The three basic techniques of behavior therapy are shaping (reinforcing successive approximations of desirable behavior), chaining (teaching the person to finish the task and then gradually expanding the number of steps required to finish), and using stimulus control (teaching that a behavior should occur in some situations but not in others). These methods have proved successful in the training of people with developmental disorders in many areas, including self-help and adaptive skills, language and communication skills, and leisure and community skills, as well as in the replacement of maladaptive behaviors.

Self-Help and Adaptive Skills Training in self-help and adaptive skills is designed to teach daily living skills such as feeding, dressing, and toileting. This type of training involves (1) breaking the task into small steps, (2) backward or forward chaining, and (3) substantial feedback and reinforcement. In addition, in daytime programs, behavior therapists have been able to teach adults with developmental disorders the skills necessary for holding a job.

For people with severe developmental disorders, especially those confined to institutions, behavior therapy is considered one of the most appropriate and effective techniques for teaching self-help skills (Reid, Wilson, & Faw, 1991; Sulzer-Azaroff & Mayer, 1991). The results, for both patients and staff, can be startling. Incontinence, for example, is a persistent problem in institutions for people with severe developmental disorders. Cleaning up not only consumes most of the staff's time but makes assignment to these institutions undesirable, so patients receive little friendly attention from the staff. Furthermore, patients who are incontinent generally cannot leave the ward. Toilet training not only improves patients' hygiene and promotes positive interactions with the staff but also opens new worlds; toilet-trained people can go out of the ward to other parts of the building or onto the grounds for outdoor recreation (McCartney & Holden, 1981).

Language and Communication Skills In early childhood, one of the most important applications of behavior therapy has been in language acquisition (Koegel & Koegel, 1995). Research into patterns of language acquisition by both normal children and children with developmental disorders has yielded information that has allowed for the construction of step-by-step behavioral sequences to teach both speech and comprehension. Shaping and verbal imitation are typically used to train people who are mute. Sign language and picture books, through which people with receptive language can communicate by pointing, are also useful. Finally, caregivers can be taught to recognize the communicative body movements of those they care for. Such training in communication is designed to enhance language skills, to improve the prognosis for those with developmental disabilities, and to reduce behavior problems.

Leisure and Community Skills Training in leisure and community skills is designed to improve the quality of life of people with developmental disorders and to help them adapt to new surroundings. This type of training typically involves modeling, prompting, giving feedback, and using reinforcement. Examples include guided social contact in recreational settings, game-playing, use of the telephone, money management, skills in choosing clothes, and cooking skills. Vocational, social-skills, and assertiveness training procedures are sometimes used as well (Kohler & Strain, 1997).

Procedures for developing appropriate responses, whether in leisure pursuits, communication, or self-help, depend first and foremost on conquering children's insensitivity to social reinforcement. To learn from others, children must regard others as important. In some cases, however, maladaptive behaviors must be extinguished using other means before positive behaviors can be taught.

Replacement of Maladaptive Behaviors Treatments for maladaptive behaviors such as aggression and self-injury include time-outs, differential reinforcement of other behavior, and differential reinforcement of incompatible behavior. Children may also be taught sign language to reduce the need to communicate using maladaptive behaviors. For instance, they can learn to sign for a drink rather than to push someone to get his or her attention. Punishment-oriented treatments such as response cost, aversives, and overcorrection may also be used (Didden, Duker, & Korzilius, 1997; Harris, 1996; Lovaas & Buch, 1997).

The effectiveness of such techniques seems to depend on what behavior is being eliminated, as well as its function. Self-mutilating responses such as head banging may eventually extinguish if social attention

Participating in social and recreational activities such as the Special Olympics can be an important part of therapy for individuals with mental retardation.

is withdrawn when they occur. But some behaviors seem to be maintained by internal rather than external rewards, in which case withdrawing social attention will have little if any effect. For example, ritualistic motor behaviors motivated by sensory reinforcement are highly resistant to extinction.

For therapeutic changes to be maintained, the environment must support them. Follow-up reports indicate that responses learned in the treatment laboratory often do not generalize to the school or the home (Sulzer-Azaroff & Mayer, 1991). And some children, especially those who are returned to institutions after their treatment, relapse completely. There is no question that institutions foster such relapses, because in many institutional settings patients are expected to act inappropriately and no rewards are given for acting otherwise.

Most behavior therapists have no illusion that they are transforming children with developmental disorders into normal children. Rather, their aim is to provide these children with enough adaptive responses so that they can graduate from custodial care to a more useful and fulfilling existence, albeit in a "special" class. Critics argue, however, that behavior therapy does not help youths with developmental disorders generalize their skills to other settings. For example, one child, when asked, "What did you have for breakfast?" would tell you that she had had "eggs, toast, jelly, juice, and milk" even on days when she had had no breakfast at all. In short, she had no understanding of the concept; she was simply responding with a programmed answer. In many other instances, however, behavioral treatment has resulted in the development of responses that are spontaneous as well as appropriate. Substantial gains have been made in eliminating self-mutilating and bizarre motor behavior and in developing language, self-help, and social skills.

Cognitive Therapy

Cognitive therapy for people with developmental disorders focuses on five primary areas: self-instructional training, correspondence training, self-management and self-monitoring, self-control, and problem solving. These therapies usually supplement behavior therapy.

Self-instructional training involves the development of self-regulatory speech that is useful in academic, leisure, and vocational skills. To get through routine tasks and difficulties, students are trained to control their actions by controlling what they say to themselves before, during, and after the action. One group of researchers (Rusch, Martin, & White, 1985), for example, reported on the use of self-instructional training with two women with developmental disorders who had jobs as kitchen helpers in a university dormitory. Both these women enjoyed their jobs, but both had received feedback that they were doing certain things wrong. Specifically, they were forgetting to wipe the counters and to check and restock supplies. Thus, they were taught to make a series of statements to themselves on the job: first a question ("What does the supervisor want me to do?"), then an answer to that question ("I am supposed to wipe the counters, check the supplies, and restock the supplies"), then a performance-guiding statement ("Okay, I need to wipe the counter," etc.), then a self-reinforcement ("I did that right"). The statements, together with the accompanying actions, were first modeled for the women by a therapist. Then the women copied the therapist's performance, first saying the statements out loud, then whispering them, then instructing themselves covertly, without speaking. Both women improved and kept their jobs.

Variations on self-instructional training have been used to teach children with developmental disorders to do arithmetic problems (Johnston, Whitman, & Johnson, 1980), to help mothers with developmental disorders to handle their babies (Tymchuk, Andron, & Rahbar, 1988), to teach dating skills to adults with developmental disorders (Muesser, Valenti-Hein, & Yarnold, 1987), and to teach a janitor with developmental disorders to control his anger on the job (Benson, 1986). Not surprisingly, in all these reports, the subjects were in the mild-retardation category. The technique seems simple, but it is often just such simple skills—knowing what to do when a baby has a fever, knowing not to yell at one's boss—that people with developmental disorders need to remain in normalizing situations (a mother-child relationship, a job) rather than be relegated to the fringes of society.

Correspondence training involves the use of rewards for action-oriented verbal statements. For instance, students are rewarded for completing tasks they have promised to do or for telling the truth about a task just completed. The idea is to encourage students to associate their verbal statements with their past and future actions. Correspondence training may be used to promote both academic and social behaviors.

Training in self-management and self-monitoring involves teaching students to regulate their own behavior, to decide whether their performance has been adequate or inadequate, and to reward themselves accordingly. This type of training can be used to bolster leisure activities, control stereotypic behavior, and improve on-task behavior.

Training in self-control involves delayed gratification of impulses—for example, giving large rewards for waiting and small rewards for immediate gratification. To cope with the waiting, students learn to make appropriate self-statements.

Finally, training in problem solving is a generic process that involves learning to define a problem, develop possible solutions, choose the best of these solutions, implement it, and decide whether the solution was effective. The procedure may be enhanced with visual prompts and imagery (Whitman, 1994; Whitman, Scherzinger, & Sommer, 1991).

Pharmacological Therapy

Pharmacotherapy is commonly used for people with developmental disorders. Major drug therapies for treating people with developmental disorders include psychotropic drugs, which are useful in managing disruptive or aggressive behavior, and anticonvulsive medications, which are used to control seizures. Aman and Singh (1991) estimate that 50 to 67 percent of people with developmental disorders are receiving medication for these types of problems; 30 to 50 percent take psychotropic drugs; and 25 to 35 percent take anticonvulsants. Psychotropic medications are also increasingly used for persons with developmental disorders to treat comorbid conditions such as attention deficit hyperactivity disorder and anxiety and mood disorders (Handen, 1998).

Other drugs have been tried to treat autism. In view of the fact that some people with autism show abnormally high levels of serotonin, it was hoped that they might be helped by serotonin-reducing drugs. Werry and Aman (1999) summarized the major studies on the effects of one such drug, fenfluramine, on children with autism. Nearly all studies report substantial reductions, usually around 50 percent, in whole-blood serotonin. Although IQ and adaptive behavior changes were found in some early reports, well-controlled studies show little support for these findings. Fenfluramine may improve stereotypic and ritualistic behaviors and social interaction, and often significantly improves overactivity, inattention, and distractability; it has little or no effect on speech, communication, and other language deficits.

Psychotherapy

For years it was believed that people with mental retardation could not benefit from psychotherapy because they lacked the intellectual sophistication to discuss their problems in psychodynamic terms. But, with the development of less insight-oriented therapies, there are now many forms of psychological treatment that can help people with mental retardation: supportive psychotherapy (Sinason, 2000), group psychotherapy (Hollins, 1990), family therapy, and a modified form of Carl Rogers' client-centered therapy (Prouty, 1994). Group therapy is often used in inpatient settings, to help clients gain insight into their problems and to enhance their social supports. Family therapy may also be useful with parents who are raising children with mental retardation; procedures such as contingency management and token economies can be taught. In addition, family therapy can focus on educating family members about a person's condition, changing family dynamics that curtail development, and building social support networks for family members. For someone with mental retardation who is considering raising a family, marital counseling and parent training may be helpful (Barrett, Walters, Mercurio, et al., 1992; Kearney & McKnight, 1998).

Key Terms

amniocentesis, 488
brain plasticity, 491
congenital disorders, 488
cretinism, 488
Down syndrome, 487
echolalia, 496
fetal alcohol syndrome (FAS), 489
fragile X syndrome, 487
infantile autism, 493
mental retardation, 485
phenylketonuria (PKU), 488
savant syndrome, 495
sheltered workshops, 503
Tay-Sachs disease, 488
theory of mind, 499
trisomy 21, 487

Summary

- Mental retardation, which affects about 2 percent of the U.S. population, is defined as involving significantly subaverage general intellectual functioning, determined using standardized intelligence tests; significant limitations in adaptive functioning in at least 2 of 11 adaptive skill areas; and onset before age 18 years. Four levels of retardation are generally recognized: mild, moderate, severe, and profound.
- About 85 percent of people diagnosed with mental retardation fall into the category of mild retardation. As adults they can often lead relatively independent lives. People with moderate mental retardation can learn to care for themselves but do not become independent. People with severe or profound retardation require considerable supervision.
- Many physical or genetic anomalies are associated with retardation, including chromosomal abnormalities, such as fragile X syndrome and Down syndrome, and metabolic disturbances, such as phenylketonuria.
- Environmental factors also contribute to mental retardation. In the prenatal environment, congenital disorders (such as rubella), drugs (such as cocaine and alcohol), and maternal malnutrition can cause retardation. In the postnatal environment, important causal factors include reactions to toxins, physical trauma, and the psychological handicaps of growing up in a deprived setting. The last may cause, or at least foster, cultural-familial retardation, a condition for which children of teenage mothers are especially at risk. Research suggests that what begin as psychological factors may become physical factors through effects on the developing brain. Institutionalization can also have profound effects on intellectual functioning.
- As adults, people with mental retardation are susceptible to other organic brain disorders (such as Alzheimer's disease) and emotional disturbance. Many forms of psychological treatment can help those with retardation, if they can find access to the treatment.
- Groups most at risk for mental retardation are males, young people, and people of low socioeconomic status. Males with mental retardation outnumber females with mental retardation by about 1.6 to 1, due largely to the greater prevalence of gender-linked disorders such as fragile X syndrome in males. The diagnosis of mental retardation peaks at age 5 to 6 years, around the time children enter the primary grades and encounter increased cognitive demands. Mild retardation is more prevalent in families with low incomes than in those with high incomes. Statistically, African Americans are at greater risk for mild mental retardation than are other ethnic groups, though testing bias and environmental and cultural factors may explain their higher incidence rate.
- Autism, normally recognizable in early childhood, is a profound disturbance with four basic symptoms: social isolation, mental retardation, language deficits, and stereotyped, ritualistic behavior. Many children with autism insist on preserving the sameness of their environment. Only a small percentage make a good adjustment as adults.
- Autism may have a genetic component; it has been associated with fragile X syndrome. It almost certainly has a biochemical component, for many children with autism show abnormally high levels of serotonin and dopamine. Congenital disorders and complications in pregnancy and birth are closely associated with autism. Neurological studies suggest that the basic deficit in autism lies in the limbic system or in the frontal and temporal regions of the brain. An abnormally low density of Purkinje cells, enlarged ventricles, and megalencephaly, or an enlarged brain, are also suspected as causes of autism.
- Cognitive researchers argue that cognitive abnormalities are the primary problem in autism. Recent investigations have focused on four broad areas of cognitive function: executive function, categorization and memory, social understanding, and theory of mind. Some researchers suspect that children with autism have no theory of mind, or appreciation of the existence of purely mental states, such as beliefs or desires; therefore, they cannot predict or understand others' behavior.

- Gender is a significant risk factor for autism: males with autism outnumber females with autism by 3 or 4 to 1. The high prevalence of the disorder among males may be related to the risk factors for mental retardation. Another risk factor for autism is the presence of the disorder in siblings. Socioeconomic status and ethnocultural background are *not* risk factors for autism.
- Opportunities for people with mental retardation have expanded greatly in recent years. Five principles have been established: (1) people with mental retardation are entitled to free and appropriate education; (2) services for them should be individualized; (3) their progress should be evaluated regularly; (4) their lives should be integrated into the community, not segregated from it; and (5) the law should protect them from abuse and deprivation. The education of children with mental retardation has been upgraded, but children with autism are difficult to educate because of their ritualistic behaviors and lack of response to social reinforcement.
- Parents today are normally urged to try to care for a child with mental retardation at home, though they need support in order to handle the problems involved. In the child's early years, parents can use behavioral techniques to teach self-care, self-discipline, and academic skills. In adulthood, some people with mental retardation may be able to live on their own or in assisted living arrangements, and some may marry. Many can also work, either in ordinary jobs or in sheltered workshops. Their quality of life, especially the degree of choice they enjoy, is an important influence on their adjustment.
- Efforts are being made to prevent mental retardation through genetic counseling and improved prenatal care and to minimize the effect of retardation when it occurs (e.g., through stimulation programs). Mental retardation can also be treated through behavior therapy, cognitive therapy, pharmacological therapy, and psychotherapy. Behavior therapy includes training in self-help and adaptive skills, language and communication skills, and leisure and community skills; it is also used to replace maladaptive behaviors. One form of cognitive therapy, self-instructional training, is especially helpful; it involves teaching people with mental retardation to deal with routine tasks and difficulties by talking themselves through the process step-by-step. Self-rewards, self-management, self-monitoring, and problem-solving techniques can also be taught through cognitive therapy. Pharmacological therapy involves the use of psychotropic drugs to manage disruptive or aggressive behavior and anticonvulsants to control seizures. Psychotherapy for people with mental retardation includes supportive therapy, group therapy, family therapy, and a modified form of client-centered therapy.

CHAPTER

18

Psychological Disturbance and Criminal Law

The Insanity Defense

Competency to Stand Trial

Civil Commitment

Procedures for Commitment

Standards for Commitment

Patients' Rights

The Right to Treatment

The Right to Refuse Treatment

The Right to a Humane Environment

Behavior Therapy and Patients' Rights

Ethics and the Mental Health Profession

Confidentiality in Psychotherapy

Informed Consent for Psychotherapy

Multiple and Exploitative Relationships in Psychotherapy

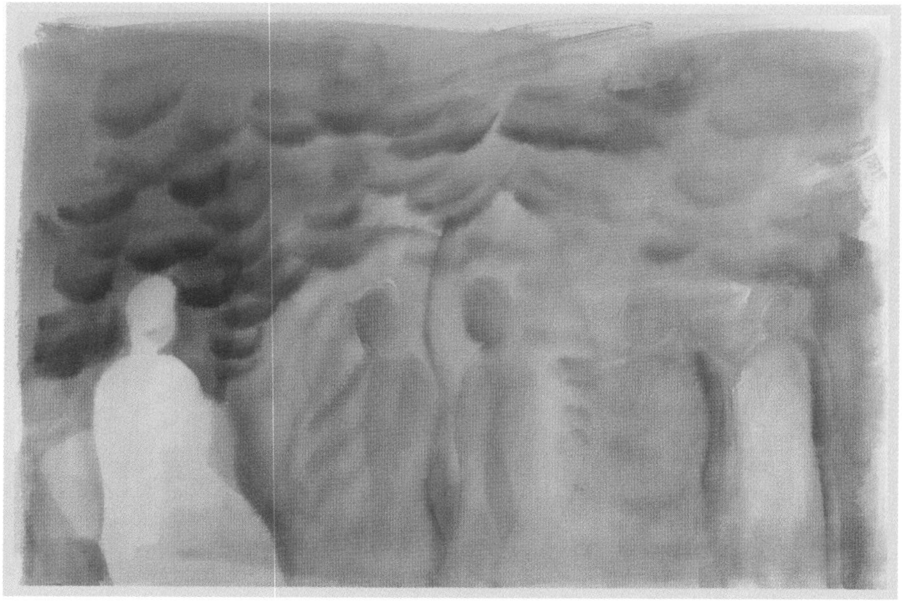

Legal and Ethical Issues in Abnormal Psychology

Andrea Yates, a 37-year-old housewife and mother, had to save her children from Satan. She believed that Satan was inside her and that the only way to be rid of Satan was to kill her children so that she could then be executed. Yates believed that Satan was guiding her actions on the morning of June 20, 2001, when she drowned all five of her children, aged 6 months to 7 years old, in the bathtub of their home in suburban Houston, Texas.

The defense sought a "not guilty by reason of insanity" verdict for Yates, based on a diagnosis of postpartum psychosis. At her trial, experts for the defense testified that Yates had obviously been psychotic and delusional at the time of the murders. There was little dispute that she was a person with serious psychiatric problems: two past suicide attempts, confirmed previous psychosis, four previous psychiatric hospitalizations, recurring hallucinations, delusional thoughts at the time of the killings. However, the insanity defense in Texas is quite restrictive. If Yates could differentiate between right and wrong at the time of the murders, then she was guilty, no matter how disturbed she was. The prosecution argued just that: Andrea Yates knew that what she was doing was wrong, and could tell good from evil. Experts called by the prosecution argued that Yates' psychosis became severe only the day after the killings, when she was in jail. Although hundreds, if not thousands, of people a year are found not to be criminally responsible for acts no one denies that they did, in this case the jury did not believe that the defendant did not know what she was doing. Amid stunned cries of anger from a nation that had watched this trial intently, Andrea Yates was found guilty of murder. The prosecutor sought the death penalty. The jury decided to spare Yates' life and voted to sentence her to life in prison. She will be eligible for parole in 2042.

The Yates case is a dramatic illustration of the overlap between mental health and the law. By now, the issues generated by that overlap are familiar to the public. When we read newspaper accounts of bizarre crimes, we take it for granted that a psychiatrist or psychologist will be called on to make judgments about the defendant's sanity and possibly to give "expert testimony" at the trial. In other

The Andrea Yates case was a shocking example of the kinds of controversies that arise when issues of mental health and the law intersect. Despite the defense's contention that she was legally insane when she killed her five children, the jury convicted Andrea Yates of murder.

widely publicized court cases—such as the 1975 case of Kenneth Donaldson, who successfully sued officials of the state of Florida for wrongfully keeping him in a mental institution for 14 years—the public saw the mental health system itself on trial.

These court cases are only the most obvious examples of the fact that decisions about people's mental health have important legal implications. For one thing, under some circumstances, an individual can be considered not guilty under the law because he or she did not intend to commit a crime, due to a mental disorder, regardless of whether his or her actions were illegal. For another thing, if individuals are institutionalized for their own or for society's protection, they may also be relieved of many of their constitutional rights.

Mental health law, the branch of law that deals with such matters, has been changing at a rapid pace. Since 1970, nearly all states have substantially revised their laws regarding the commitment and treatment of the psychologically disturbed (Frost & Bonnie, 2001), and more changes can be expected. These new laws attempt to settle three issues:

1. *Psychological disturbance and criminal law.* Can psychologically disturbed people be held guilty of breaking the law? Can such people be given a fair trial? If they are not tried or are acquitted by reason of insanity, what should the state then do with them?
2. *Civil commitment.* Under what circumstances can a person who has committed no crime but appears to be severely disturbed be involuntarily institutionalized by the state?
3. *Patients' rights.* Once a person is institutionalized, what are his or her rights concerning living conditions, mental health treatment, and so forth?

Most of this chapter is devoted to an examination of these three issues. Then, in the last section of the chapter, we address a related issue—the ethical obligations of mental health professionals to their clients.

Psychological Disturbance and Criminal Law

Abnormal behavior, as we saw in Chapter 1, can be defined as a violation of the society's norms. Many social norms, however, are not just standards of behavior but legal requirements. Hence, abnormal behavior may also be illegal behavior, ranging from drug abuse to murder. Many people agree that when deeply disturbed people commit crimes, they should not be treated in the same way as ordinary lawbreakers. But how they should be treated is a matter of great controversy.

The Insanity Defense

Though psychologists may question the concept of free will, criminal law does not. The business of criminal law is to fix blame for and to penalize morally and socially intolerable conduct. For the law to carry out these functions, it must assume that human beings freely choose their actions. (If they don't, how can we justifiably blame them?) Thus, when a court pronounces someone guilty, it is making both a judgment of fact *and* a moral judgment: The defendant not only committed the crime but is also morally responsible for it and can therefore be punished for it.

However, the law does acknowledge that certain people commit crimes not out of free choice but because mental disturbance has somehow deprived them of free choice. Such people may employ what is known in legal terms as the **insanity defense,** whereby the defendant admits to having committed the crime but pleads not guilty, stating that because of mental disturbance he or she was not morally responsible at the time of the crime. Though guilty in fact, the defendant claims to be innocent in moral terms and therefore exempt from punishment. This stems from the "fault principle" of criminal responsibility (Morse, 1999): Moral fault must be present in order to hold people accountable and to punish them.

The insanity defense, then, is intended to protect certain mentally disturbed persons from the penalties that we impose on the mentally sound. At the same time, it serves to protect the moral prestige of the law (Meehl, 1991). By making exceptions of people who cannot be held responsible for their actions, the insanity defense implies that every other defendant does have the capacity to choose "between good and evil."

Legal Tests of Insanity If the defendant pleads insanity, how is the finder of fact (jury or judge) to decide whether that plea is justifiable? In other words, what is the legal test of insanity? This question has haunted the courts for many years and has been answered in a variety of ways.

For the purposes of modern law, the first important ruling on this matter was the so-called M'Naghten rule, handed down by an English court in 1843. The defendant in this case, Daniel M'Naghten, claimed that he had been commanded by the voice of God to kill the English prime minister, Sir Robert Peel. Numerous medical witnesses agreed that he had heard such voices. He then killed Peel's secretary by mistake. In acquitting M'Naghten, the court ruled that defendants are legally insane and, therefore, not criminally responsible if, as a result of a "disease of the mind" and consequent impairment of reason, they either (1) did not know the nature and quality of the act they were doing or (2) did not know that what they were doing was wrong (hence, the commonly heard question "Did the defendant know right from wrong?"). Thus, the M'Naghten test singles out one aspect of self-control, cognition, and makes the test of insanity rest on that.

Critics of this test (e.g., Bromberg, 1965; Weihofen, 1957) argue that cognitive activity cannot be separated from emotion or from any other mental activity; the mind is an integrated whole, not a collection of separate compartments. Spring (1998) points out that M'Naghten was controversial at the time for relying on obsolete medicine; also, the judges in M'Naghten did not intend their ruling to be a general test for insanity or to apply beyond the instance of "insane delusions"—in fact, they explicitly warned against this. Legal scholars have responded that while the mind may be integrated, it is not an undifferentiated blob; almost all psychological theories recognize the existence of distinguishable mental processes. Furthermore, the M'Naghten rule has the virtue of limiting the insanity defense to those who are perceived by the public as truly insane. All of us have difficulty, in varying degrees, with resisting impulses, but very few of us commit misdeeds because we do not know what we are doing or because we do not know that they are wrong. By reserving the insanity defense for people who are in this extreme situation and who therefore cannot reasonably be expected to comply with the law, the M'Naghten test, in the eyes of some legal scholars (e.g., Livermore & Meehl, 1967), serves the purpose of excusing the truly excusable and preserving the moral authority of the law.

According to Morse (2001), the cognitive prong of the insanity defense, as captured by the M'Naghten test, reflects the truly important concept of criminal responsibility: the capacity to reason. Morse notes that the law defines humans as "practical reasoners" (1999, pp. 151–52) who, because of their ability to grasp and be guided by reason, are able to follow laws. When humans are no longer rational, it would be unfair to hold them morally accountable (Morse, 2001).

Another test, known as the Durham test, states that the defendant is not criminally responsible "if his unlawful act was the product of mental disease or mental defect." This test is also known as the "product test." As is obvious from the wording, this test forces the jury to rely on expert testimony, for how is a jury of ordinary citizens to determine whether the defendant has a mental disease or defect? But in American courts people are supposed to be tried by their peers, not by the mental health profession. Actually, the rules preceding the Durham test also involve this problem. How can a jury decide whether the defendant was under the sway of an irresistible impulse or knew right from wrong? But the Durham test, because of its wording, more or less *requires* expert judgment, and partly for this reason it has been replaced in most jurisdictions that had adopted it (Melton, Petrila, Poythress, et al., 1997), although it had never gained widespread use.

The most recent formulation of the insanity defense is that adopted by the American Law Institute (ALI) in its Model Penal Code of 1962:

1. A person is not responsible for criminal conduct if at the time of such conduct as a result of mental disease or defect he lacks substantial

> capacity either to appreciate the criminality of his conduct or to conform his conduct to the requirements of law.
>
> 2. As used in the Article [of the code], the terms "mental disease or defect" do not include an abnormality manifested only by repeated criminal or otherwise antisocial conduct (sec. 4.01).

Many legal scholars feel that the ALI test is the best that can be hoped for. To a degree, it incorporates the irresistible-impulse criterion, or volitional prong ("conform his conduct to the requirements of law") and the M'Naghten criterion, or cognitive prong ("appreciate the criminality of his conduct"). At the same time, however, it states these criteria in broader terms and adds the phrase "substantial capacity." The result is a test that *can* be applied without expert knowledge. In effect, the ALI rule asks the jury, "Can the defendant be justly blamed for his or her misbehavior?" In the opinion of many legal scholars, this is the question that should be asked—and of the jury, not of the mental health profession. The ALI test has been adopted by many states. However, many states repealed the volitional aspect of the law in response to John Hinckley's acquittal by reason of insanity for his attempted assassination of President Ronald Reagan (see the next section) (Reisner & Slobogin, 1990). Other states are still using the M'Naghten test, with or without a supplemental irresistible-impulse test. Only New Hampshire uses the Durham test. In 1984, again largely as a result of the Hinckley acquittal, Congress adopted an insanity test for federal courts that is highly similar to the M'Naghten test (Perlin, 1996).

After all this discussion, it must be added that the verbal formula used to define legal insanity may have little practical significance. While some studies have shown that the definition may affect the verdict (Melton, Petrila, Poythress, et al., 1997), other research indicates that the verdict will often be the same under any of the insanity tests now in use (Steadman, McGreevy, Morrisey, et al., 1993). This may be because jury instructions are too hard to understand (Lymburner & Roesch, 1999). A study by Wheatman and Shaffer (2001) found that instructions to mock jurors had no impact on the verdicts, unless jurors were told the disposition of the verdict—which real jurors are not. Under Texas law, for instance, the jury on the Andrea Yates trial was not informed that an insanity acquittal does not mean the defendant simply goes free. The judge in that case denied a defense request that the jurors be told Yates would likely be confined to a mental hospital if acquitted.

A New Verdict—Guilty but Mentally Ill Several scholars have expressed concern that, as the concept of mental illness has expanded from encompassing only the grossly psychotic to embracing what is potentially a very substantial fraction of the population, many defendants may escape responsibility for their crimes. This situation may weaken the deterrent effect of criminal law (Wilson, 1997). The deterrent effect is not compromised when an obviously psychotic person is found not guilty by reason of insanity; but when someone who appears to be sane is found to lack criminal responsibility, the authority of criminal law may seem to be diminished. (See the box on page 514.) A case often cited in this regard is that of John Hinckley, who in 1982 was acquitted on grounds of insanity after he tried to assassinate President Ronald Reagan. Hinckley claimed that he did this in order to "gain [the] love and respect" of movie actress Jodie Foster, whom he had never met.

Hinckley's trial focused not on whether he had committed the assassination attempt—clearly, he had—but on his sanity at the time. The jury was presented with vast amounts of conflicting evidence from expert witnesses called by both sides. The defense witnesses portrayed Hinckley as driven by a delusion of achieving a "magical union" with Jodie Foster and as suffering from a severe form of schizophrenia, as well as numerous other mental problems. The psychiatrists called by the prosecution testified that Hinckley made a conscious choice to shoot Reagan and had no "compelling drive" to do so. They depicted Hinckley as selfish and manipulative and suffering from only some minor personality disorders.

The jury's verdict of not guilty by reason of insanity stunned the courtroom, including the judge and Hinckley himself, who had fully expected conviction. Law professor Charles Nesson (1982) expressed the feelings of many when he wrote, "For anyone who experiences life as a struggle to act responsibly in the face of various temptations to let go, the Hinckley verdict is demoralizing, an example of someone who let himself go and who has been exonerated because of it" (p. A19).

This concern has led to consideration of a new verdict of "guilty but mentally ill" (GBMI) to serve as an intermediate between "guilty" and "not guilty by reason of insanity." It would be appropriate in cases in which the defendant knew what he or she was doing and that it was wrong but, nonetheless, had some form of mental illness. A defendant convicted by this verdict would serve time within the penal system but would also receive psychological treatment. Michigan was the first state to adopt the "guilty but mentally ill" verdict (in 1975). More than a dozen states

Focus On... Evolution, Misfortune, and Criminal Responsibility

Wania-6672 was the name given to a neurologically impaired young macaque monkey observed by primatologists among a group of macaques in an enclosed setting in Texas in 1972. He would stumble around, bumping into bushes and cacti, among other things. Because of his obvious impairment, other monkeys in effect exempted him from the monkey version of the criminal law. Older, stronger monkeys that routinely responded aggressively to other monkeys that bumped into them responded passively when Wania-6672 collided with them. It was as if they knew it wasn't his fault, so there was no point in punishing him (de Waal, 1996). That such a phenomenon can be observed in monkeys suggests that the moral intuitions that underlie the insanity defense may have deep roots in our evolutionary history.

To the extent that such evolutionary origins affect the content of our moral intuitions, they may apply to current problems in mental health law. Because the effectiveness of the criminal law is dependent on its congruence with our moral intuitions (Robinson & Darley, 1997)—in other words, dependent on its making moral sense to people—those who are not conspicuously crazy may undermine the effectiveness of the criminal law.

To sort out those whose condition *should* excuse them from criminal responsibility, psychologist Paul E. Meehl (1991) has proposed that criminal statutes be revised to include a list of specific psychiatric diagnoses that would have to be established in order for an insanity defense to succeed. These include major mood disorders and paranoid and catatonic schizophrenia. Meehl explains:

> Nothing else goes so you can't plead not guilty by reason of mental illness on the grounds that you had a battle-ax mother or a pick-pocket uncle or a poverty-stricken childhood or whatever. . . .
>
> The point is that mere intensity of motivation, of whatever character and origin, is not an excuse for predatory conduct. (p. 488)

In other words, Meehl would require that an insanity acquittee be as conspicuously impaired in our eyes as Wania-6672 was in the eyes of his fellow monkeys. Morse (2001), a highly respected legal scholar, has a wildly different point of view, arguing that conditions other than mental illess (stress, fatigue) should be permissible triggering conditions as long as they deprive people of rationality.

This dispute is not limited to the insanity defense. Various "abuse excuse" defenses are increasingly offered either to reduce the severity of the crime charged (e.g., from murder to manslaughter) or to justify a more lenient sentence for the crime. The response of the courts has been mixed. Some courts have given these defenses a sympathetic hearing; others have been far more skeptical (Wilson, 1997; Slobogin, 2001).

A recent decision by the United States Court of Appeals for the Seventh Circuit illustrates the more skeptical response. A defendant named Doss Pullen had been convicted of armed robbery and sentenced to over 15 years in prison. He appealed his sentence on the ground that the maltreatment he had suffered as a child warranted a more lenient sentence. Although the court did not deny that he had suffered serious abuse, it did not believe that the abuse should affect the length of his sentence:

> The defendant's father was a drunkard and a gambler. He beat his wife and children and threatened them with guns and knives. When the defendant was five years old, his father abused him sexually over a period of several months. His parents divorced and the defendant lived with his mother, but when he was 15, and drinking, smoking marijuana, and having scrapes with the law, his mother could no longer control him and the juvenile court sent him to live with his father. The two would go out drinking together and once after a bout of drinking, his father raped him. He ran away. His troubles with the law escalated. At the age of nineteen, he committed his first bank robbery. . . .
>
> A psychologist evaluated the defendant and concluded that as a result of the history of abuse that we have sketched, the defendant "has a need to punish himself, hence his illegal acts and the relative ease with which he is caught." The psychologist also found that the defendant suffers from "schizoid disorder" and "borderline personality disorder," and that these conditions too are both "clinically linked to the history of abusive treatment by his father" and causative of his criminal activity because they "reduce impulse and behavioral controls" and impair "his ability to think and act clearly."
>
> In emphasizing the causal history of Pullen's crimes, his lawyer overlooks the gap between cause and responsibility. The existence of the one does not cancel the other. The male violent-crime rate is roughly ten times the female. . . . This means that being male is a predisposing characteristic to violent crime; it is a "cause" of such crime in the same sense in which Pullen's history of being abused as a child may be a cause of his violent crimes. Would anyone argue that men are therefore less responsible for their violent crimes than women and so should be punished less severely? (*United States v. Pullen*, 1996, pp. 369–370, 372)

have since followed suit. It appears, however, that this new verdict has not reduced the number of insanity acquittals (Steadman, McGreevy, Morrissey, et al., 1993), although one study of mock jurors found that the availability of the "guilty but mentally ill" verdict reduced both guilty verdicts and insanity verdicts (Poulson, Wuensch, & Brondino, 1998). Furthermore, some legal scholars find the "guilty but mentally ill" verdict senseless and have called for its repeal. In the words of one expert, "The mental illness component of the verdict adds nothing to a simple guilty verdict except a diagnosis of the defendant at the time

The successful use of the insanity defense by John W. Hinckley, Jr., following his attempt to assassinate President Ronald Reagan set off a storm of controversy. The uproar obscured the fact that very few defendants are found not guilty by reason of insanity.

of the crime. It's no different than rendering a verdict of guilty, but suffering from influenza" (Morse, 1997, p. A19).

Leblanc-Allman (1998) questions the constitutionality (even though courts have upheld the law) of the "guilty but mentally ill" verdict on the grounds that it interferes with a defendant's rights to equal protection and a fair trial. He also argues that this verdict option shows little confidence in jurors' abilities to understand the insanity defense properly. Some (Robinson, 2002) have argued that the GBMI verdict subverts the insanity defense and results in the conviction and punishment of morally blameless offenders. Robinson also points out that this verdict runs the risk of confusing jurors, who must be able to distinguish between "mental illness" and "insanity," both of which are on the table when trying to determine GBMI versus a verdict for the insanity defense. Furthermore, as Borum and Fulero (1999) reported, there has been no clear empirical evidence that the GBMI verdict option actually reduces insanity verdicts (most states that have adopted the GBMI option also have retained the insanity defense). Moreover, there is rather clear evidence that persons found GBMI are *not* more likely to receive treatment for their mental health problems.

Procedural Aspects of the Insanity Defense The John Hinckley case stirred interest in two procedural aspects of the insanity defense. First, whose responsibility is it to prove the defendant's insanity (or sanity)? Second, if the defendant is acquitted, how do we determine whether he or she should be committed to a mental hospital or released back into the community?

As a general rule, the prosecution must prove beyond a reasonable doubt all elements of a criminal offense—including both the physical act and the requisite mental state, which in a murder case is the intent to kill (LaFave & Scott, 1986). When defendants raise the insanity defense, must they prove that they were insane at the time of the crime, or must the prosecution instead prove that they were sane?

Before the Hinckley verdict, a majority of states placed the burden on the prosecution to prove sanity, and prove it beyond a reasonable doubt, once the defense had presented evidence, such as psychiatric testimony, suggesting insanity. This is the rule under which Hinckley was tried. But, in 1984, partly because of the outcome of that case, the federal rules were changed to place the burden of proving insanity on the defendant, and about three quarters of the states now do so as well (Perlin, 1994). This shift has substantially reduced the number of insanity acquittals, which are now more likely to involve people with serious mental illnesses, such as schizophrenia or major mood disorders (Lymburner & Roesch, 1999; Steadman, McGreevy, Morrissey, et al., 1993).

What is to be done with defendants who are acquitted by reason of insanity? Prior to the 1970s, they were usually subjected to long-term confinement in a mental hospital, often a high-security hospital that seemed much like a prison. Then, in the 1970s, the field of mental health law was swept by a wave of reform, drawing on the antiestablishment politics of the 1960s (Bonnie, 2001). Law after law was changed, almost always in the direction of protecting civil rights, and this included laws governing defendants acquitted on the grounds of insanity. In many states, such acquittals were no longer automatically followed by commitment. The person might be placed briefly in a mental health facility for evaluation, but prolonged hospitalization was permitted only under standards of ordinary civil commitment ("Commitment Following," 1981). As we will see later, these standards typically require a finding that the person is *currently* mentally ill and dangerous. Because a great deal of time may have elapsed between the commission of the offense and the acquittal, the defendant's mental condition may have changed. Thus, under the new rules of the 1970s, it was entirely possible that a defendant might not meet commitment criteria at the postacquittal commitment hearing.

This possibility alarmed many people, including a majority of U.S. Supreme Court justices, and in *Jones v. United States* (1983) the Court ruled that it is permissible to commit insanity acquittees automatically. The acquittees could then be hospitalized until they proved themselves either no longer mentally ill or no longer dangerous. Further, the Court ruled that they could be hospitalized for longer than they could have been imprisoned had they been convicted. The year of this decision is significant: 1983, a year after the Hinckley verdict. In the wake of the Hinckley trial, a majority of states also tightened up postacquittal procedures so as to make release more difficult (Perlin, 1994; Steadman, McGreevy, Morrissey, et al., 1993). Linhorst (1999) studied a sample of 1,000 insanity acquittees and found that 85 percent remained institutionalized 5 years after disposition, and 76 percent were still institutionalized after 10 years. For less serious crimes (misdemeanors, Class C and D felonies), half or more remain institutionalized for longer than their criminal sentence would have been had they received the maximum (5 to 7 years for C and D felonies).

Criticism of the Insanity Defense In the abstract, it seems only fair to provide an insanity defense for people who violate the law as a result of psychological disturbance. In reality, however, the insanity defense poses thorny problems, both practical and moral.

For one thing, how can a jury accurately determine whether the case conforms to the court's definition of insanity? (Some would ask how a jury can accurately understand many other legal constructs that have nothing to do with mental illness.) To rule on a person's sanity is to arrive at a subjective judgment that is extremely difficult to make. Furthermore, the jury must make that judgment *retrospectively.* The question is not the defendant's current mental state, which the jury might at least guess at by observing his or her courtroom behavior, but the defendant's mental state at the time of the crime.

In most cases, the jury must rely on testimony of psychological professionals, but this is only a partial solution. Psychiatrists and psychologists sometimes have as much difficulty making retrospective diagnoses as other people do. They sometimes produce diametrically opposed diagnoses, thus producing a "battle of the shrinks" in the courtroom (Meehl, 1991), although this issue seems to have been overblown by the media (Lymburner & Roesch, 1999). Perlin (1996) notes that in the majority of cases, experts actually agree. Sometimes, however, even experts who are called by the same side contradict each other. And, as we have already mentioned, the opinions of expert witnesses are at best only partially relevant in criminal proceedings. The court is there not to make a scientific judgment but to make a legal judgment—whether the defendant should be held legally responsible for the crime. This is a judgment that only the fact-finder, not the mental health profession, is empowered to make, although mental health professionals can assist in the decision. But, because the jury has so little concrete information to go on, that judgment may be wrong.

A second criticism of the insanity defense is that those who successfully plead it sometimes end up in a worse situation than if they had been convicted of their crimes. As we pointed out earlier, people who are found not guilty by reason of insanity are usually not set free, like others who are acquitted of crimes. Rather, they are often committed to mental hospitals and are kept there until, on periodic review required by law, experts testify that they are no longer dangerous. Thus, while people convicted of crimes are deprived of their liberty for a specific period of time—after which, by law, they are free—many people acquitted by reason of insanity are in effect given **indeterminate sentences,** sentences with no limit. They could (although it would be very rare) languish for the rest of their lives in a mental hospital before a staff member decides that they are no longer dangerous. In fact, Linhorst (1999) found that the average time of institutionalization in Missouri was 7.3 to 12.7 years; Lymburner & Roesch (1999) report that although there are interstate differences, other studies have found the mean length of confinement to be less than 3 years. Of greater concern is the finding that the severity of the offense has more bearing on release decisions than mental illness does: Insanity acquittees are being punished, even though they were found not to be responsible by reason of insanity, and even though crime severity is not known to be predictive of future crime (Lymburner & Roesch, 1999).

These considerations, among others, have led to widespread criticism of the insanity defense. Some scholars recommend that mental illness be used not to form the basis of an insanity defense, but simply to negate the element of *mens rea* ("guilty mind," or the knowledge of wrongdoing) (Goldberg, 2000). As of 2003, four states—Idaho, Kansas, Montana, and Utah—have actually abolished the insanity defense. Nevada attempted to as well, in *Finger v. State,* but the effort was held unconstitutional by the Nevada Supreme Court. As Morse (1999) wrote, "unless the criminal justice system is willing to convict people who lack moral agency, legal insanity must be retained" (p. 163).

It should be added that, statistically speaking, the insanity defense is much less important than other questions linking law and psychology. Because it is sometimes involved in especially notorious cases, such as those of Yates and Hinckley, and because it touches on the elemental question of free will, the insanity defense receives a great deal of public attention, yet it is invoked in less than 1 percent of felony cases, and it is successful in less than one quarter of the cases in which it is raised (Melton, Petrila, Poythress, et al., 1997).

Competency to Stand Trial

The number of people confined in mental hospitals as a result of successful insanity pleas is small compared with the number who are there because they are judged mentally unfit even to be tried (American Bar Association, 1989). In all states, defendants, in order to stand trial, must be competent to stand trial. This usually means that they understand the nature of the proceedings against them and must be able to assist counsel in their own defense. When a defendant does not meet these requirements, the trial is delayed, and the person is sent to a mental health facility in hope of restoring competency. As with the insanity defense, the purpose is to protect the defendant and at the same time to preserve the court's reputation for justice. The courts would not inspire public trust if they tried people who were obviously out of touch with reality.

Incompetency to stand trial must not be confused with legal insanity. The insanity defense has to do with the defendant's mental state *at the time of the crime;* competency to stand trial has to do with the defendant's mental state *at the time of the trial.* Furthermore, while the insanity defense concerns the defendant's mental condition at the time of the crime, competency to stand trial is merely a question of ability to understand the charges and to confer fairly reasonably with one's attorney. Thus, a person who is judged competent to stand trial can still successfully assert an insanity defense. Even people diagnosed as psychotic may be competent to stand trial. Many are lucid enough to meet the competency requirements (Melton, Petrila, Poythress, et al., 1997).

Incompetency, then, is a limited concept. The rule is often applied in a loose fashion, however. Both prosecutors and defense attorneys have been accused of abusing the competency issue (American Bar Association, 1989). Prosecutors who fear that their cases are too weak can use it to keep the defendant locked up, thus accomplishing the same purpose that would be gained by a conviction. On the other hand, defense attorneys may use the competency proceedings in order to delay the trial, either in the hope that some of the prosecutor's witnesses may become unavailable to testify or simply in order to convince the defendant that they are doing all they can. This type of misuse may decrease with the publication and testing of reliable and valid measures for assessing competence to stand trial (Otto, Poythress, Nicholson, et al., 1998) and solid theoretical bases for competency (Bonnie, 1992).

For the defendants, the consequences used to be grave. Once ruled incompetent, they were often denied bail; cut off from their jobs, friends, family, and other social supports; and confined in a hospital for the criminally insane, when in fact they might never have committed the crimes they were charged with. They often remained in the hospital for years, because there was often no means of restoring their competency (Morris & Meloy, 1993). However, this particular abuse was ruled unconstitutional by the U.S. Supreme Court in the case of *Jackson v. Indiana* (1972). The defendant in this case was a mentally retarded deaf-mute who had been charged with robbery. Judged incompetent to stand trial, he was being held in a state hospital indefinitely, because there was no way to render him competent to stand trial. The court ruled that when a person is detained solely on the grounds of incompetency to stand trial, the detention can last only as long as it takes to determine whether the defendant is likely to become competent to stand trial in the foreseeable future. If the likelihood is poor or nil, the defendant must be either released or committed to an institution according to the state's ordinary civil commitment procedures. (Civil commitment is discussed later.) According to Hawk & Fitch (2001), most competence evaluations today are conducted in the community, and the turnaround time is shorter than in the past.

One controversy surrounding the competency issue has to do with antipsychotic drugs. If defendants fulfill the competency requirements only when under the influence of antipsychotic drugs, are they competent to stand trial? On the one hand, it seems almost unfair not to try such patients if the drugs render them lucid enough to be tried. On the other hand, these drugs, as we have seen, often render people groggy and passive—an inappropriate state in which to attend one's own trial. Furthermore, antipsychotic medication might well affect the defendant's chances of successfully pleading the insanity defense. The "crazier" the defendant seems during the trial, the more likely it is that the jury will accept the insanity plea. But whatever crazy behavior the defendant normally exhibits may well be reduced by the medication. Should we then allow defendants to undergo trial without medication, so that the jury can see them in their "true" state? But even if this were the most direct route to justice (which is questionable), many defendants could not be tried because they would not be competent to stand trial without the medication. This catch-22 has not yet been fully resolved, but in *Riggins v. Nevada* (1992) the Supreme Court ruled that people being tried for a crime could not be forced to take psychotropic (mind-affecting) medication unless the trial court specifically found this necessary to a fair trial.

Civil Commitment

Criminal commitment accounts for only a small percentage of those committed involuntarily to mental hospitals. The remainder are there as a result of **civil commitment;** that is, they have been committed not because they were charged with a crime but because the state decided that they were disturbed enough to require hospitalization. About 55 percent of admissions to public mental hospitals are involuntary (Brakel, 1985). Because it does not involve interesting crimes, civil commitment receives far less public attention than criminal commitment, yet the legal questions it involves are equally difficult and directly affect far more people.

Procedures for Commitment

The U.S. Constitution provides that the government may not deprive a person of life, liberty, or property without "due process of law." Involuntary commitment to a mental hospital is clearly a deprivation of liberty. What in the way of due process, or legal procedures, is required before a person may be subjected to involuntary commitment? This is a question that the Supreme Court has not fully considered. Many lower courts have addressed it, but the answers they have given vary from jurisdiction to jurisdiction.

A useful way to approach the problem is to consider the rights that a defendant has in a criminal trial and then to ask whether a person faced with the possibility of involuntary civil commitment should have the same rights. Among other things, the following are guaranteed to people accused of serious crimes: (1) a jury trial, (2) the assistance of counsel, (3) a right not to be compelled to incriminate themselves, and (4) the requirement that guilt be proved "beyond a reasonable doubt." Should these rights also apply to involuntary civil commitment?

The Right to a Jury Trial Today, states typically require a formal judicial hearing before commitment (though the hearing may follow a brief period of emergency commitment). In many states, the defendant has a right to have a jury at such a hearing. Other states make no provision for a jury but require that the decision be rendered by an impartial judge or a lower judicial officer, rather than by a clinician.

The argument against a jury trial is that juries are expensive and time-consuming and, furthermore, that it is not in the best interests of mentally distressed people to have their psychological condition formally debated before a jury. The argument for a jury trial is that, distressed or otherwise, these people stand to lose their liberty and that, in a matter so serious, the judgment must come from the citizenry, just as in a criminal trial, for this is the best protection against oppression. (Keep in mind that many civil libertarians feel that involuntary mental patients are akin to prisoners.) However, because the Supreme Court has ruled that jury trials are not required in juvenile cases, it is unlikely that the court will require them in commitment cases (Brakel, 1985).

The Right to the Assistance of Counsel A central feature of the wave of reform in mental health law in the 1970s was the provision of court-appointed lawyers for people faced with involuntary-commitment proceedings. Prior to the 1970s, commitments were often made on physicians' certifications alone, with little due process (Turkheimer & Parry, 1992). Now, in almost all jurisdictions, people facing involuntary-commitment proceedings are provided with lawyers to protect their rights (Melton, Petrila, Poythress, et al., 1997).

At the same time, there is considerable disagreement about what lawyers are supposed to do for their clients at such hearings (Leavitt & Maykuth, 1989). In criminal trials, defense attorneys have a clear role: They are the adversaries of the prosecutor, and they are supposed to do everything they legally can to get their clients acquitted. It is not their job to worry about the legal question of the defendant's guilt or innocence.

Should lawyers at commitment hearings behave in the same way—that is, as advocates for their clients' wishes? Or should they act, instead, as "guardians," pursuing their clients' best interests as they, the lawyers, see them? If we assume that some people are too disturbed to know what their best interests are, then lawyers who take the advocate role run the risk of acting against their clients' best interests. If, on the other hand, they take the guardian role, they may well act in direct opposition to the clients' wishes, deferring instead to the judgment of expert witnesses who claim hospitalization is necessary. Apparently, most lawyers at commitment hearings do precisely that (Turkheimer & Parry, 1992)—a practice that is bitterly criticized by those who feel that clients should be allowed to decide what their best interests are. Winick (2001) argues that civil commitment hearings do not meet due process requirements and should be conducted in ways that respect patients and give them the opportunity to be heard. Such hearings would increase the therapeutic nature of the commitment process and make patients feel less coerced and more likely to be open to hospitalization and treatment.

The Right Against Self-Incrimination Under the Fifth Amendment to the U.S. Constitution, defendants at criminal trials have the right to remain silent, and their silence may not be used against them. Should the same rule apply at a commitment hearing? Some people would say yes, that people threatened with commitment should have the same protections as those threatened with imprisonment, for they have as much, if not more, to lose. Others would say that, because silence may be a symptom of mental disturbance, it is inappropriate to exclude it from the evidence. Should psychiatrists, for example, be barred from testifying that their diagnosis of psychotic depression is based in part on the patient's muteness? However others decide this question, it seems likely that the Supreme Court would not apply Fifth Amendment rights to civil commitment (Melton, Petrila, Poythress, et al., 1997), although courts have been split sharply on the issue (Perlin, 1994).

The Standard of Proof Finally, in a criminal trial, a jury can convict only if the prosecution has proved guilt "beyond a reasonable doubt." The degree of certainty is called the **standard of proof.** The *beyond-a-reasonable-doubt* standard is a very high one—perhaps a 90 to 95 percent certainty. Should this requirement also apply to commitment hearings? There are other possibilities. In most civil proceedings (e.g., lawsuits), the standard of proof is the *preponderance of evidence*—in other words, "more likely than not," or at least 51 percent certainty (Strong, 1992). A third option is *clear and convincing evidence,* which is in between the other two options. And a final possibility is the far lower standard of proof used in medical diagnosis, in which any evidence whatsoever—theoretically, even a 5 to 10 percent certainty—may lead to diagnosis of illness. Which of these standards should apply in the case of involuntary commitment?

To answer this question, we must consider the seriousness of two possible errors: (1) a **false positive,** or an unjustified commitment, and (2) a **false negative,** or a failure to commit when commitment is justified and necessary.* In a criminal trial, a false positive—that is, the conviction of an innocent person—is considered a far more serious error than a false negative—that is, the acquittal of a guilty person. In the famous words of eighteenth-century English jurist William Blackstone, "It is better that ten guilty persons escape than one innocent suffer," hence the extremely high standard of proof in criminal trials: "When in doubt, acquit."

In a civil proceeding, a false positive (the complainant's unjustifiably winning the lawsuit) is considered approximately as serious as a false negative (the complainant's unjustifiably losing the lawsuit). Therefore, the standard of proof falls in the middle: 51 percent certainty. In medical diagnosis, on the other hand, a false positive (a false diagnosis of illness) is considered a negligible error, compared with the extremely serious mistake of a false negative (a false diagnosis of no illness). Imagine, for example, that a person is being tested for cancer and the physician finds only a few slightly suspicious cell changes. If the diagnosis is a false positive, this fact will emerge in the course of further testing, and the diagnosis will be changed, with no harm done except for the patient's suffering a few nights of worry. But a false-negative diagnosis may well eliminate the chance of the cancer's being treated at an early and perhaps curable stage. In other words, a great deal of harm will have been done and hence the extremely low standard of proof in medicine: "When in doubt, diagnose illness."

Which standard we should apply at a commitment hearing depends on what we see as the purpose of commitment. Generally, the law recognizes two justifications for involuntary commitment: the good of the patient and the good of society. At first glance, it would seem that when commitment is undertaken for the good of society (i.e., to protect people from harm by the patient), the criminal standard of proof should be used because the issue in both cases is the same:

*These terms are taken from the medical diagnostic vocabulary. A *false positive* is an incorrect diagnosis of illness; a *true positive,* a correct diagnosis of illness; a *false negative,* an incorrect diagnosis of no illness; a *true negative,* a correct diagnosis of no illness.

Prevention The Mental Health Court

While it is difficult to speak of true prevention by the time a case has come before the law, nevertheless the term *prevention* can be used to refer to efforts to reduce the incidence of repeated criminal offenses by the mentally ill. Mentally disordered individuals appear frequently in court for offenses that are primarily an expression or function of their mental illness. Persons with serious and persistent mental illness often end up in prison because of relatively minor offenses that occur as a result of their illness. Today, the number of persons with mental illness in jails and prisons is high (about 2 million), and mental health care in these settings is generally inadequate.

The Mental Health Court (MHC) is an innovation at the intersection of mental illness and the law. The MHC is intended to prevent the frequent cycling of the mentally ill between jail and community. By directing such persons to treatment resources, rather than finding them guilty of crimes and sentencing them to jail, where they will not receive adequate mental health care, and hence to which they are likely to return shortly after release, the MHC offers an escape from "revolving door justice." The MHC features a therapeutic aspect not normally found in the courtroom, to help mentally ill persons stop the cycle.

The first Mental Health Court in the United States was established in Broward County, Florida, in 1997. This MHC was an outgrowth of the increasing arrests of individuals for nonviolent psychiatric behavior rather than for clear criminal behavior. Police found it easier to arrest and book individuals who were acting out, rather than to connect them to crisis centers or outpatient facilities. Moreover, the services that might serve the mentally ill of the community, such as public psychiatric hospitals, drop-in centers, or psychiatric residency programs, were no longer in existence or else were fragmented, ill-equipped, and inadequate.

The Broward County MHC was established to improve legal advocacy for mentally ill defendants, to prevent the mentally ill from languishing in jail, to recommend appropriate remedies that balance public safety with defendants' rights, to provide evaluation and treatments for mentally disabled defendants, to provide follow-up for defendants released to the community, and to resolve a defendant's criminal problem with the defendant's active participation (Lerner-Wren & Appel, 2001). At the same time, the MHC relieves the criminal courts of the growing caseload of nonviolent misdemeanors by mentally ill individuals and places the resolution of these cases in a less expensive, more effective, and more just setting.

Unlike a criminal court, a Mental Health Court "sentences psychological care rather than jail time" (Rabasca, 2000, p. 56). The MHC is structured differently from regular courts. In addition to a judge, prosecutor, and public defender, the Court's treatment emphasis also involves the presence of mental health monitors, clinicians, and community resource liaisons in the courtroom. The court rarely uses punitive sanctions for noncompliance, but defendants must voluntarily agree to have their cases resolved in a Mental Health Court. The adequacy of informed consent is a significant question in MHC procedure because an "agreement to participate in the court may often mean the waiver of speedy trial or other rights available in a criminal context" (Poythress, Petrila, McGaha, et al., 2001, p. 14). In all events, central to the success of the Mental Health Court model is the emphasis on the active participation and responsibility of the individual with a mental disability.

The MHC is based on principles of therapeutic jurisprudence, and attempts

public safety versus individual liberty. By the same token, it would seem that, when commitment is sought for the good of the patient (e.g., so that he or she can be treated), the medical standard of proof should be applied.

Critics of civil commitment (e.g., Ennis & Emery, 1978; La Fond, 1996; Burt, 2001) argue, however, that the medical standard should never be used, because commitment cases, no matter what their stated purpose, are not analogous to medical diagnosis. According to these writers, so-called good-of-the-patient commitments are often undertaken more for the sake of others—usually, the patient's family—than for the sake of the patient. Moreover, unlike medical diagnosis, a decision to commit cannot be disproved, deprives the patient of liberty, stigmatizes the patient, and does not necessarily lead to treatment. For these reasons, among others, critics of commitment insist that, no matter what the reason for commitment, the beyond-a-reasonable-doubt standard should be used. It should be added that, in general, civil libertarians are extremely skeptical of procedures that are said to be for the good of the patient. Their skepticism extends beyond the lowered standard of proof to the nonjury hearing, the guardian lawyer, and the lack of protection against self-incrimination. In their opinion, an expressed attitude of concern for patients assumes that they are guilty and leads directly to a violation of their civil rights. If these people are threatened with loss of liberty as a result of socially offensive behavior, then they are in the same position as alleged criminals and should be given the same rights.

Unlike the other three procedural questions we have discussed, the standard of proof at commitment hearings *has* been dealt with by the Supreme Court. In the case of *Addington v. Texas* (1979), the defendant was a man whose mother had filed a petition to have him committed. The commitment was approved by a Texas court according to the preponderance-of-evidence standard. The defendant then appealed the

The Broward County Mental Health Court, established in 1997, was the first such institution in the United States.

to have the law act in a manner that has positive effects on individuals' mental health (i.e., in a therapeutic manner). Attention is given to the view and wishes of defendants, and a special point is made to treat them respectfully (i.e., to give them "voice"), an approach commensurate with principles of procedural justice. Poythress and colleagues (2002) found that individuals who go through the MHC perceive greater autonomy, control, choice, and freedom than persons involved in regular legal proceedings; that is, they report the experience to be less coercive than persons undergoing other legal proceedings, such as civil commitment. Persons in the MHC also perceive a greater amount of procedural justice (i.e., perception of being treated fairly, of being listened to, of being treated respectfully) (Poythress, Petrila, McGaha, et al., 2002) compared to persons in regular misdemeanor court. Elsewhere, Cascardi, Poythress, and Hall (2000) note that higher procedural justice scores are associated with statements of patients that they would be more receptive to treatment.

Today, there are a dozen or more MHCs in the United States, with plans to create many more. Evaluation is still in an early phase, but preliminary data suggest that MHCs are a promising intervention and that persons who go through the Mental Health Court receive increased access to services and spend less time in jail.

decision, arguing that the need for hospitalization should be proved "beyond a reasonable doubt." The Supreme Court quickly rejected the preponderance-of-evidence standard (and by implication any less stringent standard) because of the liberty interest at stake, yet the Court also failed to demand the criminal beyond-a-reasonable-doubt standard, for several reasons. The Court observed that, unlike the wrongfully convicted criminal defendant, who would languish in prison until his or her sentence had been served, the person who was wrongfully civilly committed would probably be discharged, as doctors would recognize that hospitalization was unwarranted. Thus, the false positive is less serious in the civil context than in the criminal context because of the greater opportunity to correct the error. The consequences of a false-negative error were also seen as different in the two contexts. A truly guilty criminal defendant benefits from a wrongful acquittal, whereas a truly mentally ill person who is not ordered to get treatment suffers from the absence of the needed treatment.

The Court thus used some of the notions underlying the medical decision rule as grounds for rejecting the beyond-a-reasonable-doubt standard. The Court held that an intermediate standard of proof, called *clear and convincing evidence,* was the minimum permissible standard for commitment hearings. It corresponds to approximately "75 percent sure"—higher than the ordinary civil standard but lower than the criminal one. This decision is, to some extent, a victory for the proponents of the criminal standard in that it at least rules out the civil and medical standards and moves the required degree of certainty that much closer to the criminal standard. Moreover, a number of states actually do use the beyond-a-reasonable-doubt standard because their state constitutions require it (Perlin, 1994). But it remains to be seen how jurors and judicial officers will interpret this standard of proof.

Standards for Commitment

So far, we have dealt only with the procedures for commitment; we must now consider the *standards* for commitment. What must be proved in order to justify involuntary commitment?

Until the early 1970s, mental illness alone or mental illness and "need for treatment" were sufficient grounds for involuntary commitment in many states. Then came the reform movement of the 1970s. Not just the general public but also judges and legislators read Szasz's *Myth of Mental Illness* (1961), as well as Erving Goffman's *Asylums* (1961), which were critical of the concept of mental illness and, above all, of involuntary hospitalization. As a result, there was a trend throughout the 1970s toward changing laws in such a way as to require evidence not just of mental illness but also of dangerousness to self and others as grounds for involuntary commitment (Perlin, 1994; Melton, Petrila, Poythress, et al., 1997).

Involuntary Commitment: Is a Beautiful Mind a Dangerous One? Part 2

In The MindMAP video "Beautiful Minds: An Interview with John Nash and Son," John Nash, Jr., a winner of the Nobel Prize in Economics, describes his involuntary hospitalization. After being diagnosed with paranoid schizophrenia in 1959, Nash was committed against his will to various psychiatric hospitals for treatment. Do you think having a mental illness was itself a sufficient ground for his commitment? What do you think are the advantages and disadvantages of involuntary commitment? Why?

The Definition of Dangerousness How do we define *dangerousness?* Should it be confined to the threat of physical harm to oneself or others? What about emotional harm, such as schizophrenic parents may inflict on their children? What about economic harm, such as people in a manic episode may bring down upon their families by spending their life savings on new Cadillacs? What about harm to property? Various courts and legislatures have taken different positions on this matter, with most requiring bodily harm to others and self, but some states consider a threat of harm to property sufficient for commitment (La Fond & Durham, 1992; Melton, Petrila, Poythress, et al., 1997).

The Determination of Dangerousness Whatever the definition of dangerousness, determining it is a difficult matter. To say that someone is dangerous is to predict future behavior. The rarer an event, the harder it is to predict accurately. Hence, if dangerousness is defined as homicide or suicide, both of which are rare events, the prediction of dangerousness inevitably involves many unjustified commitments as well as justified ones. Consider, for example, the following hypothetical case:

> A man with classic paranoia exhibits in a clinical interview a fixed belief that his wife is attempting to poison him. He calmly states that on release he will be forced to kill her in self-defense. The experts agree that his condition is untreatable. Assume that statistical data indicate an eighty percent probability that homicide will occur. (Livermore, Malmquist, & Meehl, 1968)

What should the court do? Instinctively, it would seem correct to "play it safe" and commit the patient (see the box on page 523). However, as the authors of this case point out, even accepting an 80 percent probability of homicide as sufficient to commit means committing 20 nonhomicidal people for every 80 homicidal ones.

Perhaps society could accept such a ratio. But the fact is that an 80 percent probability is unrealistically high. Despite public alarm over violence, murder is statistically rare: In any year, only 1 person in 10,000 in the United States commits homicide (U.S. Department of Justice, 2000), and mental patients without arrest records are no more likely than the general public to commit murder (Monahan, 1981). Further, very few patients threatened with commitment will calmly state in a clinical interview that they intend to commit murder upon release. In many cases, for example, the evidence for possible future homicide is simply a report from a family member that in the past the patient has threatened homicide, perhaps in a moment of extreme anger. In such a case, the probability of homicide would be very low—probably less than 1 percent. Is this a ratio that society can accept? If in criminal law it is better that 10 guilty people go free than that 1 innocent person suffer, how can we say that in cases of civil commitment it is better for 99 harmless people to be locked up than for 1 dangerous person to go free?

Although some extreme types of legally relevant violence, such as homicide, are rare, other legally relevant violence is not. Steadman and colleagues reported a base rate of 27.5 percent acts of violence over 1 year among a sample of approximately 1,000 mental patients (Steadman, Mulvey, Monahan, et al., 1998). Lidz, Mulvey, and Gardner (1993) studied 714 patients released from a psychiatric unit and

Focus On... The Limits of Confidentiality

On October 27, 1969, a student at the University of California at Berkeley named Prosenjit Poddar killed a young woman named Tatiana Tarasoff. Two months earlier, Poddar had told his therapist that he intended to commit the crime. Although the therapist then notified the police—who detained Poddar briefly but released him upon finding him "rational"—neither Tatiana Tarasoff nor her family was informed of Poddar's threat. After the murder, the young woman's parents brought suit against the therapist and the university that employed him, charging that they should have been warned about the man's intentions. The California Supreme Court agreed, holding that "when a therapist determines . . . that a patient presents a serious danger of violence to another, he incurs an obligation to use reasonable care to protect the intended victim against such danger" (*Tarasoff v. Regents of California,* 1976).

In effect, this ruling meant that psychotherapists in California have obligations to the society at large that override their obligations to their own patients. Traditionally, the relationship between therapist and patient has been considered privileged: Information supplied by the patient is held in strict confidence by the therapist. According to this ruling, however, the therapist must divulge such information if the patient is "dangerous"; the police and the family of the threatened victim must be warned. As the court stated in its opinion, "the protective privilege ends where the public peril begins." Many other states have similiar precedents or laws, and APA's ethical principles reflect this study. However, at least a few states have limited the reach of *Tarasoff.* For instance, under Florida statutory law the "duty" is permissive, meaning that therapists *may* breach confidentiality under such circumstances, although they do not have an affirmative duty to do so.

But where does the public peril begin? The prediction of dangerousness is a difficult task. As a dissenting opinion in this case pointed out, psychotherapists find it difficult enough to diagnose mental illness itself, without also having to predict whether a patient will or will not be dangerous at some time in the future.

The *Tarasoff* decision was widely denounced by mental health professionals. Psychiatrist Alan Stone (1976), for example, wrote that "the imposition of a duty to protect, which may take the form of a duty to warn threatened third parties, will imperil the therapeutic alliance and destroy the patient's expectation of confidentiality, thereby thwarting effective treatment and ultimately reducing the public safety" (p. 368). Under circumstances of reduced confidentiality, a patient who feels a compulsion to do violence might well be reluctant to confide it to a therapist. Potentially dangerous patients might be unwilling to seek therapy at all, for fear that the police would ultimately deal with them. On the other side, therapists, to avoid lawsuits, would be encouraged to report all threats of violence to potential victims and to the police—or even to seek the commitment of "dangerous" patients to avoid possible harm to others and to themselves.

In fact, the impact of the *Tarasoff* decision has not been noticeably negative (Appelbaum, 1994). McNiel, Binder, and Fulton (1998) studied the effects of the law on actual reporting behavior and found that *Tarasoff* did not have much, if any, impact: Many clinicians, for better or worse, seemed to ignore it (McNiel, Binder, & Fulton, 1998). According to surveys of psychotherapists, it has not seriously affected the way they handle threats, for they were accustomed to taking some protective measures already, simply on ethical grounds (Givelber, Bowers, & Blitch, 1985). The duty to report threats has been contracting in recent years through the combination of statute and case law (Walcott, Cerundolo, & Beck, 2001). Some jurisdictions, such as Florida, for example, simply have legislated that no such duty exists, but that clinicians *may* (rather than must) report imminent violence risk if they choose to.

Law professor David Wexler (1981) has pointed out that *Tarasoff* could even have a positive impact on treatment. Because 80 to 90 percent of people threatened by patients in therapy are family members or lovers (MacDonald, 1967), the prospective victim could be encouraged to participate in family or couple therapy with the patient. Direct discussion of the patient's anger and the potential victim's role in precipitating violence might serve to reduce the likelihood of such violence. In any event, the need to breach confidentiality sometimes in order to protect third parties is now so widely accepted that the Supreme Court acknowledged it without discussion in a recent decision establishing psychotherapist-patient privilege in federal courts (*Jaffee v. Redmond,* 1996).

reported a base rate of 47 percent acts of physical violence or threats of violence over a 6-month period. Both studies used archival records, patient self-reports, and reports from people who knew the patients well. Finally, Douglas and colleagues reported a base rate of 19 percent for physical violence over a 2-year follow-up among mental patients using archival records alone (Douglas, Ogloff, Nicholls, et al., 1999).

Several factors tend to make unstructured clinical predictions of dangerousness difficult to carry out effectively (Melton, Petrila, Poythress, et al., 1997). These factors include

1. *Variability in the legal definition.* From state to state, and sometimes from judge to judge, the definition of *dangerousness* may change, so the clinician may be aiming at a moving target.
2. *Complexity of the literature.* The research literature on the prediction of dangerousness is

both vast and of uneven quality, making it hard to identify the best methods.

3. *Judgment biases.* Clinicians sometimes rely on unproven assumptions about the relationship between particular diagnoses and the likelihood of dangerousness.
4. *Differential consequences to the predictor.* While false positives suffer in obscurity, false negatives create very bad publicity. When a person who has been spared or released from commitment kills somebody, the names of those who set him or her free are splashed all over the newspapers.

These factors encourage mental health professionals to err in the direction of overpredicting dangerousness. Do they, in fact, do so? Studies of unaided clinical predictions of dangerousness have yielded more false positives than false negatives (Grisso, 1991). Unstructured, impressionistic clinical predictions of violence (or of any behavior) are of little utility (Borum, 1996; Douglas, Cox, & Webster, 1999; Douglas & Kropp, 2002; Monahan et al., 2001; Otto, 2000). Today we know much more about the factors affecting the accuracy of violence-risk predictions. For instance, evaluations of the link between violence-risk factors, which typically are organized into *violence risk assessment schemes,* among psychiatric patients have shown fairly strong predictive accuracy (Douglas, Ogloff, Nicholls, et al., 1999; Douglas & Webster, 1999; Monahan et al., 2001; Webster, Douglas, Eaves, et al., 1997). These risk assessment instruments help specify risk factors to take into account and structure the decision-making task.

The basic problem is that any kind of prediction can be validated only after the fact. Mental health professionals are called upon to predict real-world behavior on the basis of reports of the patient's prior real-world behavior and of interviews with the patient. But we have little means of determining the validity of such predictions. It is not feasible to have mental health professionals evaluate the dangerousness of a large number of people threatened with commitment and then release all those people and keep track of them to find out whether the predictions have come true. The knowledge to be gained from such an experiment would not justify the hazard to society (Litwack, 2001).

Research has provided clear evidence that there is a connection between mental illness and violence (Douglas & Webster, 1999; Hodgins, Mednick, Brennan, et al., 1996). Persons experiencing psychotic symptoms commit violent acts at a rate several times higher than that of the general population. But this higher risk likely exists mainly during the presence of psychotic symptoms, and in any event it is modest compared with other risk factors such as substance abuse or psychopathy (Monahan, 1992). We also know from recent research that when persons with mental disorders also have substance abuse problems, risk is increased even more (Monahan et al., 2001). So, compared to the general population, symptoms of mental

Michael Laudor, a Yale Law School graduate who suffers from schizophrenia, was arrested and committed to a New York State mental institution for stabbing and killing his pregnant fiancee in 1998 after he had stopped taking his medication. Although the risk of violence by people experiencing psychotic symptoms is several times higher than it is for the population as a whole, it is lower than for individuals suffering from substance abuse disorders or psychopathy.

disorder likely are a risk factor for violence, but compared to these other factors, they are not. Violent acts associated with mental illness clearly account for a small—though disproportionate—portion of the violence in our society. Epidemiological research suggests that approximately 15 percent of persons with major mental disorders will act violently at some point, compared to 6 percent of persons without major mental disorders (Hodgins, Mednick, Brennan, et al., 1996). Research on near-exhaustive samples of homicide offenders shows that approximately 6 percent have schizophrenia—a figure much higher than that found in the general population (Eronen, Tiihonen, & Hakola, 1996). Accordingly, some experts seriously question the wisdom of tying commitment criteria to predictions of dangerousness.

Expert Testimony in Civil Commitment Whatever the standard for involuntary commitment, expert testimony will continue to be called for. As we saw earlier, many legal scholars feel that criminal courts rely too much on the opinions of mental health professionals. The same issue exists at commitment hearings. To say what mental health professionals should and should not rule upon in commitment cases requires certain fine distinctions, but they are distinctions that must be made. At commitment hearings, psychologists and psychiatrists may be asked, "How dangerous is this patient?" Though this is a difficult question, it is not an improper question to put to them. However, expert witnesses are frequently asked not only how dangerous patients are but whether they are *too dangerous to be released,* and this is not a proper question for the expert witness to answer. How dangerous a person must be in order to be deprived of his or her freedom is not a mental health question but a legal and moral question (although mental health professionals can assist the finder of fact in coming to a decision). It involves weighing the person's interest in liberty against the society's interest in public safety, and any judgment about these competing interests is the business not of the mental health profession but of the court (Morse, 1978).

Making Commitment Easier During the 1970s, as we saw, nearly all states tightened their standards for civil commitment. Then in the 1980s several states decided they had gone too far, and they amended their laws to make commitment easier. For example, threats to engage in violent conduct would not have qualified a person for commitment under a typical 1970s statute. But in the 1980s some state legislatures determined that such threats alone did justify commitment. In other states, danger to property was insufficient for commitment in the 1970s but was added to commitment criteria in the 1980s (Melton, Petrila, Poythress, et al., 1997).

Despite the controversies that commitment criteria often generate, most research reveals little long-term effect of changes in commitment criteria on the type or number of persons committed (Appelbaum, 1994). Here, as with the definition of insanity in criminal law, decisions seem to be made intuitively, with official definitions and standards having only a small effect.

Issues in Commitment Three issues in civil commitment have been the subject of recent research and debate: inpatient commitment for sexually violent predators, involuntary outpatient commitment, and the effectiveness of coerced commitment. We discuss them briefly here.

Commitment of Sexually Violent Predators Laws concerning sexually violent predators are controversial because they allow sex offenders to be civilly committed at the end of their prison sentences if they are deemed likely to reoffend sexually. About 15 states have such laws, which have so far survived constitutional challenge in the U.S. Supreme Court (*Kansas v. Hendricks,* 1997). Traditionally, an individual is subject to civil commitment only when his or her mental disorder is serious. Under these laws, however, sex offenders may be civilly committed for less serious mental abnormalities, such as personality disorders or paraphilias. This is at odds with the definition of mental illness under legal insanity provisions,

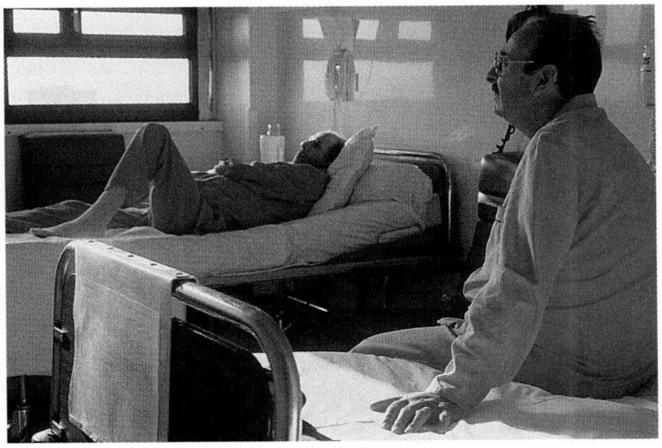

Although states have changed their standards for involuntary commitment, first tightening and then relaxing them, there has been little change in the type or number of people committed.

which tend specifically to exclude some personality disorders.

Critics of these laws argue that the government is using civil commitment to confine and punish. They claim that these laws expand the power of the state beyond reason, that these laws define mental illness so broadly as to permit the commitment of anyone on a mere pretext. As precedent, critics say, such laws could be used to justify commitment of any group of offenders argued to pose a threat to society (La Fond, 2000).

Another objection is that these laws confuse and obscure what is and is not mental illness under the law: A person can be found criminally sane but can then be civilly committed because of "mental abnormality" (Erickson, 2002). Critics claim that these laws send an incoherent message that certain categories of persons (i.e., psychopaths) both are and are not mentally ill and therefore are and are not moral agents (Schopp & Slain, 2000). Finally, Janus (2000) notes that these laws misdirect scarce treatment resources, rely on unvalidated predictions about sex offender recidivism, and confuse the functions of the criminal justice system and the mental health system.

Involuntary Outpatient Commitment Recently, the use of outpatient commitment has increased, as has research on the practice. Outpatient commitment legally requires patients to comply with treatments that are carried out in the community. Outpatient commitment gives more liberty to people who would otherwise have been committed to inpatient care; thus, some view the increase in outpatient commitment as a positive development. A counterargument is that the availability of this option will place more and more people under the compulsion of social control. People who would otherwise not have been committed will now be subject to community-based restrictions on their liberty.

Scholars argue that this alternative is appropriate for patients who would jeopardize their health by not complying with medication regimens (Swartz & Monahan, 2001). The APA's Council on Law and Psychiatry has recommended involuntary outpatient commitment for patients with persistent mental illness who are noncompliant with treatment and otherwise subject to the "revolving door" effect of multiple hospitalizations (Gerbasi, Bonnie, & Binder, 2000). It is especially recommended for people with severe psychiatric disorders (Torrey & Zdanowicz, 2001; Swartz, Swanson, Hiday, et al., 2001). The APA Council has also recommended that involuntary outpatient commitment may be applied not only to people who meet criteria for inpatient commitment but also to nondangerous people as well. Furthermore, the APA recommends that it may apply to competent as well as incompetent persons.

Evidence supports the effectiveness of outpatient commitment, though the question has not been settled conclusively (Appelbaum, 2001). Some researchers have found that the treatment people receive during outpatient commitment reduces the number of arrests and violence (Swanson, Borum, Swartz, et al., 2001). Intensive or long-lasting outpatient commitment increases the odds of treatment compliance and reduces the frequency of inpatient commitments and incidents of being victimized (Swartz et al., 2001). Other research, however, has found no differences in these outcomes (Steadman, Gounis, Dennis, et al., 2001) or insufficient evidence of its effectiveness (Allen & Smith, 2001).

Arguments against involuntary outpatient commitment include questions about its constitutionality, because it curtails liberties without the presence of dangerousness (simply the threat of psychiatric deterioration can be sufficient) (Allen & Smith, 2001). Some argue that outpatient commitment does not succeed in keeping persons with mental illness out of jail (as criminal diversion programs that integrate mental health and the justice system would; see box on page 520) and that outpatient commitment will fail for lack of funds to community programs (Mattison, 2000). Stein and Diamond (2000) argue that separate laws for outpatient and inpatient commitment further confuse an already disjointed collection of laws dealing with mental health care. They argue that a more integrated system would prevent people from falling through the cracks. They also doubt research findings that tout the effectiveness of outpatient commitment. Finally, Zonana (2000) cautions that outpatient commitment is not a solution for random acts of violence.

Can Coerced Treatment Be Effective? Involuntary commitment (whether inpatient or outpatient) is coerced treatment. But can forced mental health treatment be effective? Scholars have argued that patients' perceptions of coercion vary depending on how they are treated and that these perceptions affect the success of treatment. Whether coerced treatment can work, whether feelings of coercion vary in the contexts of inpatient or outpatient commitment, and what determines feelings of coercion are important questions.

Research reveals no particular correlation between coercion and benefit from hospitalization or adjustment level at discharge (Nicholson, Ekenstam, & Norwood, 1996), suggesting that coercion is as beneficial as less coercive treatment. Prendergast and colleagues found that coerced treatment works in the context of prison drug treatment as well (Prendergast, Farabee, Cartier, et al., 2002). The apparent effectiveness of coerced treatment likely stems from the fact that perceived coercion and perceived treatment needs are independent; that is, people can be coerced and still see themselves as needing treatment (Farabee, Shen, & Sanchez, 2002).

Nevertheless, Cascardi, Poythress, and Hall (2000) report that psychiatric patients indicate that they would be more receptive to treatment under less coercive admission contexts, and scholars believe that increased procedural justice (i.e., being listened to, treated with dignity and respect, and being meaningfully involved in the process) would enhance treatment by decreasing perceived coercion (Winick, 2001). However, the findings by Cascardi and colleagues are based on an analogue study in which patients rated reenactments of admission procedures as high or low on perceived coercion and procedural justice, and so the findings await confirmation from an actual experiment, which might not happen for ethical reasons (i.e., it would not be ethical to treat some patients disrespectfully in an actual treatment context just for the purpose of research; Cascardi, Poythress, & Hall, 2000).

Research has found that the patient's perception of coercion in the context of involuntary commitment has more to do with the presence of procedural justice than with actual negative pressures such as threats, which nevertheless remain important. These factors are also important to family members' perceptions of whether patients were coerced (Hoge, Lidz, Eisenberg, et al., 1998). This has implications for whether family members will support the treatment that patients receive, which can in turn have an impact on its effectiveness. Among the negative pressures, shows of force, legal force, and threats correlated most with perceived coercion (Lidz, Mulvey, Hoge, et al., 1998).

The Case Against Involuntary Commitment Just as some people have argued against the insanity plea, some argue that civil commitment itself should be abolished (Morse, 1982; Szasz, 1963). They maintain that people who commit criminal acts should be dealt with by the criminal justice system; those who do not should simply be left alone. "Disturbed" people who truly were dangerous would ultimately find themselves subject to the criminal justice system. This, the proponents argue, would be a benefit—both because of the greater procedural safeguards of the criminal process (trial by jury, etc.) and because of the fixed sentences of the criminal system (in contrast to the indeterminate sentences of the mental health system).

Those who want to abolish involuntary commitment are in the minority, however, and their arguments are disputable, particularly in regard to the comparison between commitment and imprisonment. Although the criminal justice system would seem to offer more protection to individual rights, the widespread practice of plea bargaining often negates these legal safeguards. Any procedural protections a defendant has may mean little in a system in which over 90 percent of all defendants plead guilty in exchange for a reduced sentence (Uviller, 1996). The distinction between fixed sentences for criminal defendants and indeterminate sentences for those involuntarily committed is also not completely compelling. Modern commitment statutes often put limits on involuntary commitment, though these limits are usually subject to extension through further judicial review (Brakel, 1985).

Nevertheless, the argument against involuntary commitment has gained a certain measure of support, particularly among civil libertarians. In their view, innocent people should never be confined in institutions against their will, no matter how "crazy" their behavior in some eyes or how convincingly it can be argued that they need therapy.

Patients' Rights

Until recently, people who were deprived of their liberty on the grounds that they were mentally ill and dangerous were usually deprived of most of their other civil rights as well. Once institutionalized, they were largely at the mercy of the institution, which decided for them what privileges and duties they should have and what treatments, if any, they should undergo (Appelbaum, 1994; Perlin, 1994; Melton, Petrila, Poythress, et al., 1997). Today there is a strong trend toward guaranteeing patients certain basic rights, especially the right to treatment, the right to refuse certain types of treatment, and the right to decent living conditions.

The Right to Treatment

For decades, the need for treatment has served as a justification, explicit or implicit, for involuntary commitment. However, it was not until the 1960s that the courts suggested that involuntary mental patients had a constitutional *right* to treatment. And it was not until the following decade that this right was spelled out, by an Alabama federal court in the seminal case of *Wyatt v. Stickney* (1972). In this case, the state of Alabama was accused of failure to provide adequate treatment for those confined in its hospitals for mentally disabled and retarded people. As it turned out, treatment was not all that these hospitals failed to provide. In the two institutions where the case originated, the wards were filthy, dark, and chaotic. The food was barely edible. (The state at that time spent less than 50 cents a day on food for each patient.) As for treatment, both of the institutions had well over a thousand patients for every psychologist. Needless to say, no treatment was being given under these conditions. As an expert witness put it, these were neither treatment facilities nor even facilities for "care" or "custody," because these words imply safekeeping. Rather, they were storage facilities.

In deciding the case against the state, the court ruled that it was a violation of due process to deny people their liberty on the grounds that they needed treatment and then to provide no treatment. The court went on to state that all Alabama mental institutions must provide (1) an individualized treatment program for each patient, (2) skilled staff in sufficient numbers to administer such treatment, and (3) a humane psychological and physical environment. This decision, then, established the right to treatment, and although it was binding only in Alabama, it has influenced mental health procedures across the country. Several states have passed revised mental health codes that incorporate most aspects of the *Wyatt* decision.

The next major case to touch upon the right-to-treatment issue was the highly publicized case of *O'Connor v. Donaldson* (1975), mentioned earlier. Kenneth Donaldson had been institutionalized involuntarily in 1957 on the petition of his father. The father claimed that Donaldson had delusions that people were poisoning his food. This testimony, along with the fact that Donaldson had been institutionalized for 3 months 13 years earlier, led the judge to conclude that Donaldson should be committed. He was sent to a Florida state mental hospital, and there he remained for 14 years. During this time, he was given no treatment that could realistically be expected to improve his "condition." He petitioned repeatedly for his release. Finally, under threat of a lawsuit, the hospital authorities discharged him. He then sued them for damages and ultimately settled for $20,000. The Supreme Court ruled that "a finding of mental illness alone cannot justify a State's locking a person up against his will and keeping him indefinitely in simple custodial confinement."

Though it has been hailed as a victory for right-to-treatment advocates, the *Donaldson* ruling, strictly speaking, has to do with the right to liberty rather than the right to treatment. (And even on the right to liberty it is somewhat vague. For example, if a person is found to be dangerous as well as mentally ill, can he or she then be subjected to simple custodial confinement?) In fact, then Chief Justice Burger claimed that he could "discern no basis" for a right to treatment. In other words, the Court flatly rejected the notion that such a right exists. While some early commentators argued that *Donaldson* at least lends indirect support to the view that involuntary patients have a constitutional right to treatment (Ennis & Emery, 1978), more recent commentary has noted a judicial conservatism in the right-to-treatment case law, concluding that there is little more than a right to be safe and receive basic necessities such as food and shelter, minimally adequate or reasonable training, and medical care (Petrila & Douglas, 2002).

The Supreme Court did not directly address the right-to-treatment issue until the case of *Youngberg v. Romeo* (1982). The lawsuit had been initiated on behalf of Nicholas Romeo, a resident of a state institution for the retarded in Pennsylvania. Romeo had been repeatedly injured, both by himself and by other residents. On several occasions, he was placed in physical restraints to prevent harm to himself and others. The Supreme Court held that involuntarily committed mentally retarded people—and presumably mentally ill people as well—have a constitutional right to "conditions of reasonable care and safety, reasonably non-restrictive confinement conditions, and such training as may be required by these interests," but that such training need only be "minimally adequate or reasonable." The Court emphasized, however, that treatment decisions made by professionals are "presumptively valid" and that courts should not second-guess the judgment of professionals responsible for the care of patients. Further, the Court seemed to limit the duty to the prevention of deterioration of a person's condition, rather than ameliorative treatment per se. Thus, this decision provided a subtle shift in emphasis from absolute patient right to support for decisions made by mental health professionals. In *United States v. Pennsylvania* (1995), the Court decided that the professional judgment standard to be used falls somewhere between negligence and intentional misconduct, suggesting a strict test to be used in determining whether mental health professionals provided reasonable care.

The Court did not decide whether there is a constitutional right to treatment per se, apart from any impact such treatment may have on safety and freedom from restraints. This is a question that remains to be addressed in a future Supreme Court decision, although the tenor of these cases has been increasingly conservative, and some commentators have claimed that "it is unlikely that we will see significant new right to treatment litigation" (Petrila & Douglas, 2002, p. 467).

The Right to Refuse Treatment

If mental patients have a right to treatment, do they also have a right to refuse treatment? This question was addressed in a 1990 case involving a man, Walter Harper, serving a prison sentence for robbery in the state of Washington. Harper was sometimes violent—a condition the prison doctors said was due to bipolar disorder. At times, Harper took the antipsychotic medication the doctors prescribed for him. At other times, he refused. The prison had a policy whereby medication could be administered over a prisoner's objection if a panel consisting of a psychiatrist, a psychologist, and a prison administrator held a hearing and determined that the prisoner was likely, without the medication, to do serious harm to himself or others as a result of mental illness. Harper claimed that this procedure was not sufficient to protect his constitutional rights in light of the recognized health risks involved in antipsychotic drugs. He therefore sued the state of Washington, arguing that medication over his objection should not be permitted unless a *judge* determined it was necessary.

Harper's suit ultimately reached the Supreme Court (*Washington v. Harper,* 1990), which upheld the constitutionality of the prison's policy on the grounds that decisions regarding the necessity of medication should be made by doctors, not judges. Thus, again, as in *Youngberg,* the court affirmed the "presumptive validity" of treatment decisions made by mental health professionals.

It remains to be seen how this decision will affect lower courts, which generally take a more limited view of the authority of doctors. In any case, the right to refuse treatment is still an open question. As we have seen in earlier chapters, the history of psychological treatment is replete with unpleasant surprises. When iproniazid was introduced as a treatment for depression, no one knew that it caused liver damage. When chlorpromazine was put on the market, no one knew that it could cause tardive dyskinesia. (In the case of Walter Harper, the risk of tardive dyskinesia was the primary grounds for refusal of treatment.) Thus, there is no reason to assume that when patients refuse treatment, they are refusing something that will truly work for their good. Furthermore, as civil rights advocates have pointed out, to deprive mental patients of any control over treatment is to make them vulnerable to a wide range of abuses.

But what if a patient's refusal does, in fact, seem grossly irrational? Or what if it is not grossly irrational but nevertheless infringes on the rights of others? Assume that a depressed, suicidal woman, involuntarily hospitalized, refuses electroconvulsive therapy (ECT), insisting instead on antidepressant drugs, which may not be as effective. Should the hospital assign one of its staff members to watch over the patient day and night to make sure she doesn't commit suicide? If so, what about the rights of the other patients, who are then deprived of that staff member's services? One might answer at this point that, because the woman made the choice, she should not be given special treatment; if she commits suicide, that is her decision. But surely the hospital has the duty to prevent suicides on its premises, particularly because it cannot be therapeutic for other patients to watch people kill themselves. Should the patient be coerced into receiving a particular treatment because less elaborate security measures would then be required?

State statutes and regulations regarding the right to refuse treatment vary considerably (Reisner, 1985), but the general rule is that involuntary patients may be required to undergo "routine" treatment, which may include psychotropic medication—a rule that will no doubt be strengthened by the Supreme Court's decision in the *Harper* case. More controversial forms of treatment, such as ECT, are usually regulated more closely, and consent from the patient or next of kin or, in some states, a court order may be required.

The Right to a Humane Environment

As we saw, the decision in the case of *Wyatt v. Stickney* affirmed not only the right to treatment but also the right to a humane environment. What the court meant by a humane environment is spelled out in the decision. The following is only a partial list of the minimum requirements, some of which are now reflected in statutes:

1. Patients have a right to privacy and dignity.
2. An opportunity must exist for religious worship on a nondiscriminatory basis.
3. Dietary menus must be satisfying and nutritionally adequate to provide the recommended daily allowances. Nutritionally adequate meals must not be withheld as punishment.
4. Within multipatient sleeping rooms, screens or curtains must be provided to ensure privacy. Each patient must be furnished with a

Focus On... Sex, Lives, and Mental Patients: The Hospital's Dilemma in the Age of AIDS

The federal court's decision in *Wyatt v. Stickney* (1972) stipulates that mental patients have the right to interact with the other sex. How far should interaction go? Before the AIDS epidemic, little was said about this question, nor was it felt that anything needed to be said. Now and then, a hospitalized patient was found to be pregnant or to have a sexually transmitted disease—usually curable—and these problems were handled somehow. But, as long as patients conducted their sex lives in private, hospitals had little incentive (or, many thought, legal or ethical justification) to prevent consensual sexual contact between patients. Especially in state mental hospitals, where patients were often shut in for years, sometimes decades, efforts to prevent sexual behavior in private have often been thought cruel.

But that was before AIDS. What now? Are hospitalized mental patients competent to accept the risk of HIV infection? If the hospital knows a particular patient to be HIV-infected, should the staff warn the other patients or just warn them about AIDS and make condoms available?

The problem with these approaches is that the assume that the patients are competent to assess the risks of HIV infection and to act appropriately if properly informed. Recent court cases strongly suggest that, for most patients, this assumption is unfounded. While there are only a few cases that explicitly address the competence of mentally disabled people to consent to sex, two recent decisions, one from Idaho and one from the state of Washington, require a high degree of understanding before the legal standard for competence is satisfied. The Idaho case, *State v. Soura* (1990), involved a mentally retarded woman (IQ of 71) living with her husband. She had sexual relations with another man, who was then charged with and convicted of rape on the grounds that the woman was not competent to consent. The Supreme Court of Idaho upheld the conviction, explaining that, even though the woman was competent to engage in marital sex, she was not competent to engage in extramarital sex, because the former is safe while the latter is dangerous. One of the dangers mentioned was AIDS. The Washington case, *State v. Summers* (1993), involved a mentally ill woman living in a group home. She, too, was found incompetent to consent to sex. The conviction of her sex partner was upheld on the grounds that, although she "had a basic understanding of the mechanical act of sexual intercourse," she did not understand its "nature and consequences," including the risk of AIDS.

The issue of sex between mental patients remains virtually undiscussed (Perlin, 1993–1994) and unlitigated, but, in view of these decisions, it will have to be addressed soon. If mental hospitals are to maintain conditions of reasonable safety for their patients, they will probably have to take measures to limit the sexual opportunities of their HIV-positive patients.

comfortable bed, a closet or locker for personal belongings, a chair, and a bedside table.

5. Toilets must be installed in separate stalls to ensure privacy. If a central bathing area is provided, showers must be separated by curtains to ensure privacy.
6. Patients have a right to wear their own clothes and to keep and use their own personal possessions.*
7. Patients have the same rights to visitation and telephone communications as patients at other public hospitals.*
8. Patients have an unrestricted right to send and receive mail.*
9. Patients have a right to regular physical exercise several times a week, as well as a right to be out of doors at regular and frequent intervals.
10. An opportunity must exist for interaction with members of the opposite sex (*Wyatt v. Stickney,* 1972, pp. 379–393). (Apropos of this last right, see the box above.)

Youngberg subsequently held that patients have the right to adequate food, clothing, shelter, and medical care and to freedom from undue restraint. In addition, the *Wyatt* decision addressed the matter of work requirements imposed on institutionalized patients. For years, mental institutions have used patients as a supplementary work force. Throughout the country, mental patients clear tables, wash dishes, scrub floors, feed other patients, and otherwise help to maintain the institutions in which they live. For their work, they often receive some reward—perhaps a small allowance or special privileges—but this reward in no way approximates the compensation they would receive for such work in the outside world. The *Wyatt* ruling declared this practice unconstitutional. The court ruled that patients may not be required to do any work aimed at maintaining the institution in which they live. If, however, they volunteer for such work, they must be given at least minimum-wage compensation for it. The point is that involuntary patients, by definition, do not ask to be committed to an institution. If the society chooses to commit them and then compels them to work without pay, their position is essentially that of slaves. (Indeed, this practice has been referred to as "institutional peonage.") Subsequent rulings by other courts have reaffirmed the

*The asterisks indicate rights that may be abridged if, in the judgment of a mental health professional, their exercise is detrimental to the patient's safety or welfare.

Wyatt position on this matter. And, though in some states mental patients are still assigned unpaid jobs in the hospital kitchen or laundry, the practice may be on its way out.

Behavior Therapy and Patients' Rights

Almost every issue raised in this chapter is the subject of intense debate between those concerned primarily with the constitutional rights of mental patients and those concerned primarily with what they consider the "best interests" of such patients. The issue of a humane environment is no exception. On the one hand, it seems indisputable that, if a society confines people to mental hospitals against their will, either to protect itself or to help them, then the people in question should be free from forced labor and should be provided with simple amenities that the rest of us take for granted—a comfortable bed, nourishing meals, privacy in the bathroom, and so forth. To treat them otherwise would seem improper. On the other hand, the guarantee of these rights may directly conflict with a mode of therapy that has proved most effective with long-term institutionalized patients: behavior therapy.

As we saw in earlier chapters, behavioral techniques for chronic patients tend to be contingency-management techniques, the most widespread and useful being the token economy. The principle on which these techniques work is that patients are given reinforcers as rewards for socially desirable behaviors. In many cases, however, these reinforcers are the same items and activities that such decisions as *Wyatt* have affirmed are absolute rights. If patients have an absolute right to stall showers or to curtains around their beds, you cannot offer them these things in return for completing a reading program, for example. They are entitled to them no matter what they do. A related problem arises with the ban on compulsory labor. Many token economies have used institution-maintaining work as a target response that earns reinforcers. If such work must be compensated by the minimum wage, then institutions may prefer to hire nonpatient labor rather than encourage patients to acquire work skills. In sum, "patients' rights" may make contingency management within institutions more difficult (Wexler, 1981).

Another aspect of behavior therapy that is now being carefully restricted is the use of aversive techniques. Aversive techniques are not widely used either inside or outside institutions, but in extreme cases therapists have used hand slapping, and even electric shock to suppress severely self-injurious behavior. Such practices are coming under increasing legal regulation. In the *Wyatt* decision, for example, the court ruled that electric shock could be used only "in extraordinary circumstances to prevent self-mutilation, leading to repeated and possibly permanent physical damage to the resident and only after alternative techniques have failed" (*Wyatt v. Stickney,* 1972, pp. 400–401).

Many behavior therapists feel that their techniques have been unfairly singled out by the courts. To some extent, this may be true. In the past decade, there have been a couple of notorious cases in which mental patients have been cruelly abused in programs masquerading as behavioral aversion therapy. In one case, mentally ill prisoners at the Iowa Security Medical Facility were punished for minor rule violations by injections of apomorphine, a drug that induces continuous vomiting for about 15 minutes (*Knecht v. Gillman,* 1973). The supposed justification for this program was that an aversion to antisocial behavior was being conditioned. However, the rule infractions that resulted in this treatment—failing to get out of bed, giving cigarettes against orders, talking, swearing, lying—are not serious antisocial actions that threaten society. What the hospital administrators were doing, in fact, was using punishment to terrify mental patients into cooperating with rules. Such procedures do not constitute behavior therapy; behaviorists find them as appalling as anyone else would. Nevertheless, because this and other abusive programs have been defended by their administrators as applications of behavioral psychology, the courts have cast an extremely suspicious eye on behavioral techniques in general.

There are other reasons for the emphasis on behavior therapy in patients' rights decisions. First, behavior therapy is highly specific and concrete. It is far easier to weigh the dangers of a procedure in which identifiable actions are taken and concrete things are given or withheld than it is to evaluate a process such as insight therapy. Second, while much less intrusive than medication, electroconvulsive therapy, or psychosurgery, behavior therapy may cause patients distress. They may have to do things that are difficult for them, or in rare cases they may actually experience physical pain. This makes behavior therapy easier to criticize, no matter how positive its results. By contrast, psychodynamic therapy may be of no help to chronic patients, but it is hard to say how such therapy could cause them pain, either.

If in fact the courts severely limit behavior therapy for institutionalized patients, they may be working against these patients' best interests. As we saw in Chapter 14, there is good evidence that, at least for people with chronic schizophrenia, a token economy in combination with individualized behavioral programs results in a greater increase in adaptive behavior, a greater decrease in bizarre and violent behavior, and a higher rate of release than either of the other two treatments available to such patients, *milieu therapy* (a type of treatment in which the patient's social environment is manipulated to effect behavioral changes) and traditional custodial care (Paul & Lentz, 1977).

Could contingency-management procedures be modified in such a way as to conform to decisions such as *Wyatt*? For example, instead of making breakfast contingent upon bedmaking, you might provide a very plain breakfast noncontingently and then offer a fancy breakfast as a reward for bedmaking (Wexler, 1981). It remains to be seen, however, whether chronic patients would appreciate such gradations. Often it is primary reinforcers—breakfast, not enhancements of breakfast—that are most effective with chronic mental patients.

Another possibility is that the superior effectiveness of behavior therapy, at least with chronic patients, will eventually encourage the courts to ease some restrictions. So far the courts have been concerned primarily with the adequacy of treatment. When they start to focus on the results of treatment—establishing the right to *effective* treatment—the courts may find that previous patients' rights decisions have severely restricted the effective treatments. Should this happen, some of those restrictions may have to be eased.

Ethics and the Mental Health Profession

In addition to the many laws and statutes that may affect the practice of psychology, members of the American Psychological Association adhere to its Ethical Principles of Psychologists and Code of Conduct (APA, 2002). The Ethics Code covers a broad range of behaviors and is intended to inspire psychologists to act according to the highest ideals of the profession. The five general principles are

1. Beneficence and nonmaleficence. "Psychologists strive to benefit those with whom they work and take care to do no harm" (p. 1062).
2. Fidelity and responsibility. "Psychologists establish relationships of trust with those with whom they work. They are aware of their professional and scientific responsibilities to society and to the specific communities in which they work" (p. 1062).
3. Integrity. "Psychologists seek to promote accuracy, honesty, and truthfulness in the science, teaching, and practice of psychology" (p. 1062).
4. Justice. "Psychologists recognize that fairness and justice entitle all persons to access to and benefit from the contributions of psychology and to equal quality in the processes, procedures, and services being conducted by psychologists" (pp. 1062–1063).
5. Respect for people's rights and dignity. "Psychologists respect the dignity and worth of all people. . . . Psychologists are aware that special safeguards may be necessary to protect the rights and welfare of persons or communities whose vulnerabilities impair autonomous decision making" (p. 1063).

The general principles set a high bar for ethical behavior among mental health professionals. For a thorough discussion of the general principles and ethical standards and a number of case vignettes related to them, see Nagy (2000).* Here, we will limit our discussion to confidentiality, informed consent, and multiple and exploitative relationships in psychotherapy.

Confidentiality in Psychotherapy

Confidentiality is one of the most important aspects of clinical practice, just as in research. Psychologists are obligated to protect private and sensitive information obtained during professional contact with clients; this is a necessary condition for the atmosphere of trust that is essential to effective psychotherapy. Typically, such information can be released only on the signed, written consent of the client or his or her legal guardian. However, there are limitations to this protection, as was apparent by the ruling of the California Supreme Court regarding duty to warn in *Tarasoff* (see box on page 523). Other limitations include laws that mandate psychologists and other health professionals to report instances of child abuse to appropriate agencies. Therefore, one of the most important activities that a psychologist can undertake at the beginning of a therapy relationship is to thoroughly discuss confidentiality, what kinds of information are protected, what kinds are not, and in what circumstances confidentiality may be breached.

Several ethical issues may arise if, for example, a client reports in psychotherapy that he or she is HIV+ and intends to continue a sexually active lifestyle. This is especially the case if the person does not plan to inform potential sexual partners of his or

*The Ethics Code was revised after Nagy's book, which focuses on the previous version (APA, 1992), was published. However, there is much to learn in this book for someone interested in a career in psychology.

Confidentiality is an essential condition for an atmosphere of trust between a therapist and client. Protected to some degree by law, this bond is necessary for effective treatment.

her HIV status. How do we resolve the conflict between the right to privacy and the duty to warn? Morrison (1999) describes the case of an HIV-positive man who was engaged to be married but feared losing the relationship if his fiancée learned of his condition. Certainly, this is a possible outcome if the therapist were to inform the client's fiancée, and the damage to the therapeutic relationship could be extreme. Furthermore, the fiancée, under no ethical constraints regarding confidentiality, might tell any number of other people, causing harm to the client. However, there is risk to the fiancée and her future children as well as to other, future sexual partners of either the client or fiancée. In addition to the obvious ethical dilemmas here, there is also a substantial legal issue, as the therapist could be sued for wrongful disclosure, on the one hand, or failure to warn, on the other, depending on the laws of the particular state. What is the therapist to do?

Morrison (1999) suggests that the ideal course of action would be to quickly persuade the client to inform his fiancée about the results of his HIV test. If that fails, the client might be convinced to practice safe sexual behavior while continuing to discuss the issue in therapy. Finally, the therapist should consult with medical and legal advisers before taking action. If the therapist decides to breach confidentiality, the client should be informed first and the legal and ethical basis for the decision discussed. Clearly, this is an area of great importance, and much work remains to be done in terms of ethics, case law, and statute.

Another area of concern is suicide. The average psychologist involved in direct client services has a greater than 20 percent chance of losing a client at some time during his or her professional career (Bongar, 1999). Bongar (1999) asserts that psychologists have a professional duty to prevent clients from harming themselves. This may necessitate communicating with family members as well as mobilizing support among the client's family and significant others. Morrison (1999), in a discussion of suicide among persons with AIDS, notes that suicide may be motivated by thoughts and emotions that are temporary, whereas suicide itself is permanent. Furthermore, although an argument can be made that individuals have the right to make a rational decision to choose suicide, this capacity may be compromised by the progressive dementia (similar to Alzheimer's disease) that is present in many people prior to a definitive diagnosis of AIDS. The Ethics Code allows the psychologist to breach confidentiality to protect the client from harm. In addition, there are a number of legal considerations. Morrison (1999) notes that recent reviews of research have found no successful lawsuits against psychologists who breached confidentiality to protect the life of a suicidal client. However, in failure to act, the psychologist may risk a wrongful death action, especially in inpatient settings.

The Ethics Code stipulates that psychologists disclose in written and oral communications only information that is germane to the reason for the communication and necessary to provide needed services; obtain appropriate consultation; protect the client, psychologist, or others from harm; or obtain payment for services. Thus, the need to communicate information to a third party does not empower the psychologist to say or write anything he or she chooses about the client, even if it is accurate and significant. The importance of this point is brought home in Nagy's (2000) description of a psychologist who ran the human resources office for a police department.

The psychologist was involved in decisions to hire, promote, and terminate officers' employment, and he often helped to mediate disputes within the department. He was thus in possession of much sensitive personal information. A police officer was referred by his supervisor for help with panic attacks. In talking with the psychologist, the police officer revealed that he was gay (which was a secret at work) and had recently learned that he was HIV-positive. The officer reported that he was able to carry out his police duties but that his anxiety and depression were beginning to impair his ability to concentrate. The psychologist referred the officer for outside treatment of his panic and depression, but he was not sufficiently guarded in his communications with the referring supervisor: The psychologist revealed in a written memo the officer's HIV-positive status. This information traveled rapidly through the department, and several other officers either avoided or harassed their comrade. The work environment became so negative that the police officer felt compelled to quit his job.

In the twenty-first century, it is also prudent to be concerned about the privacy of communication by e-mail and the confidentiality of electronic records, and this area of ethics and law is not yet well developed. The recently enacted Health Insurance Portability and Accountability Act will certainly have an impact on how these matters are handled.

Informed Consent for Psychotherapy

As in research, informed consent is a critical issue in psychotherapy. The Ethics Code describes three aspects of informed consent to therapy. First, psychologists should inform clients as early as possible about the nature and anticipated course of the therapy, fees, involvement of third parties, and limits of confidentiality and should provide the client with ample opportunity for questions and discussion of these issues.

Second, when obtaining informed consent, it is important to discuss the evidence for the effectiveness of the proposed therapy. Many (although by no means all) psychologists believe that it is best to conduct psychotherapy consistent with the scientific evidence for its efficacy (Chambless & Hollon, 1998; DeRubeis & Crits-Cristoph, 1998), and discussion of efficacy data may help clients know what to expect and give them hope for a positive outcome. However, the Ethics Code stipulates that when obtaining informed consent for new treatments, for which there are as yet no generally recognized procedures, psychologists must discuss with their clients the developing nature of the treatment, the risks involved, alternative treatments that may be available, and the voluntary nature of the client's participation. Smith (2003) adds that the Ethics Code does not prohibit the use of new treatments as long as they are based on scientific or professional knowledge.

Third, the Ethics Code says that if psychotherapy is being provided by a trainee and the legal responsibility for the treatment is the supervisor's, informed consent must include notification that the therapist is a trainee; the client must also be given the name of the supervisor.

Although not strictly related to informed consent for psychotherapy, a few additional issues are worth noting here. One has to do with the nature of group psychotherapy. The Ethics Code states that psychologists must describe at the outset of group treatment the roles and responsibilities of all parties and the limits of confidentiality. Heimberg and Becker (2002) discuss a number of these issues in relation to their cognitive-behavioral group therapy for persons with social phobia. After discussing the importance of keeping information divulged within the group confidential and the therapists' ethical obligation to maintain clients' confidentiality, all clients and group therapists sign a confidentiality contract. Clients may also run into other clients or the group therapists in the community, and options for handling these situations are discussed. Without this information, it is hard to give one's truly informed consent to participate in group treatment.

Psychologists frequently provide services to people who are related to each other in some way—for example, spouses in marital counseling, parents and children with behavior problems, and families in family therapy. The Ethics Code directs psychologists to clarify at the outset which of the individuals are clients, which are not, and the relationship that the psychologist will have with each of them. This discussion should include the psychologist's role and the probable uses of the services provided or the information obtained in therapy session. Such discussions are critical in setting the stage for effective treatment and for trusting relationships between the psychologist and the clients. What will be the psychologist's stance if a husband in marital therapy reveals to the psychologist that he is in an extramarital affair and does not intend to reconcile with the wife? In the treatment of a troubled teenager, will the psychologist provide reports to the parents about how therapy is going, or will he or she ask the parents to respect the confidential nature of the communication between their child and the therapist? Answers to these questions can have a huge impact on the success of psychological treatment.

Multiple and Exploitative Relationships in Psychotherapy

According to the Ethics Code, a multiple relationship exists when a psychologist has a professional relationship with a person—his or her client—and, at the same time, has another type of relationship with that client. Multiple relationships also exist when the psychologist is simultaneously in a relationship with a person closely associated with his or her client or if the psychologist promises that such a relationship might develop in the future. Multiple relationships pose an ethical risk if they could reasonably be expected to impair the psychologist's objectivity, competence, or effectiveness or otherwise harm the client.

Multiple relationships that would not reasonably be expected to cause impairment or risk exploitation or harm are not unethical, but the psychologist must always be on guard for their potential negative impact. Smith (2003) asks whether it is ethical to volunteer at your daughter's softball team fund-raiser if you know that a client is likely to be there. She further asks if it is acceptable to buy a car from a client who owns the only dealership in a small, rural town and speculates that deciding to buy a car elsewhere may, in fact, signal to the community that the dealer is in therapy with the psychologist! In fact, rural psychologists may find it very difficult to practice if they limit their client base only to persons they do not otherwise know, and townspeople who are acquainted with the psychologist may be unreasonably denied access to psychological treatment in that circumstance.

Multiple relationships can occur in a number of ways. Nagy (2000) describes a psychology professor who offered psychotherapy to his graduate student advisees. One student revealed in psychotherapy that she had plagiarized part of her doctoral dissertation and altered some of her data. The psychologist was placed in a conflict between his role of psychotherapist, in which maintaining confidentiality is crucial, and his role as professor, an important part of which is enforcing ethical conduct among students. The graduate student also enrolled in one of the psychotherapist's classes. He was concerned that she would have an unfair advantage because he might have difficulty maintaining enough objectivity to assign an appropriate grade.

Supervisor-supervisee, teacher-student, employer-employee, and therapist-client relationships involve a significant differential in power. Multiple relationships in these circumstances are inherently exploitative because psychologists may use their power to influence clients to do things that they may find objectionable, or the clients may fear negative consequences if they do not comply. Nagy (2000) describes a psychologist who prided himself on his good relationships with graduate students at a professional school of psychology. However, he exploited these relationships by asking his students to babysit, do his grocery shopping, and bring him coffee. He required his students to find journal articles for him. The psychologist also exploited his relationships with his clients, often using part of the therapy hour to consult on legal matters or investments. One wonders how these clients felt about their financial investment in therapy, as they were paying for the right to provide consultation to their therapist!

One type of multiple relationship that is *never* appropriate is sexual intimacy with current therapy clients. It is also a violation of the Ethics Code to engage in intimate sexual behavior with close relatives, guardians, or significant others of current clients. Furthermore, it is not acceptable to terminate a therapy relationship so that sexual relationships may be pursued and this standard circumvented. Coming at this from another direction, it is not appropriate for psychologists to accept persons with whom they have been sexually intimate as therapy clients.

Sexual intimacies with former clients are not prohibited by the Ethics Code if two or more years have elapsed since the termination of therapy. However, this is a slippery slope, and psychologists should not engage in sexual intimacies with former clients except under the most unusual circumstances. The psychologist who does so bears the burden of demonstrating that there has been no exploitation of the former client in light of all relevant factors, including (but not limited to) the former client's mental state, the likelihood of adverse impact on the client, and any statement of action taken by the therapist before the termination of therapy suggesting post-termination romantic or sexual involvement with the client. It is also important for the therapist to keep in mind that the end of an episode of therapy may not signal the end of the client's need for therapeutic assistance. What is the possible negative effect on a client who later suffers a recurrence of psychological difficulty and wishes to return to his or her previous therapist, if their relationship has become a sexual one in the interim?

Each year the Ethics Committee of the APA reports on the number and type of ethical complaints investigated. In 2001, the most common reason for opening a new ethics investigation was loss of one's license to practice psychology (American Psychological Association Ethics Committee, 2002). In 70 percent of cases, the underlying reason for loss of licensure was sexual misconduct. Of all cases involving multiple relationships, 80 percent involved sexual misconduct. Although the absolute number of investigations of sexual misconduct opened in 2001 was not large ($N = 10$), sexual misconduct was the single largest reason for termination from membership in APA in 2001 (8 of 17 cases, or 47 percent).

If the APA Ethics Code is so absolutely clear about the inappropriateness of sexual contact with current clients, why does it continue to occur? Pope (1999) discusses types of self-justification for multiple relationships in psychotherapy. These include directing one's attention away from thinking about the difficulties being caused by one's behavior, telling oneself or others that this is a common practice and therefore acceptable, and claiming that it was inevitable or unavoidable. Another self-justificational strategy is to assert that the multiple relationship was beneficial to the client:

> The addition of the sexual relationship was said to provide the patient with a more nurturantly human, warmer professional relationship; to provide the patient with a more complete sense of acceptance; to help the patient develop—under the watchful eye of the therapist—a more healthy view of his or her own sexuality and a more varied and complete array of sexual responses; to provide the patient with sexually corrective experiences that would help the patient recover from dysfunction caused by prior sexual trauma. (Pope, 1999, pp. 232–233)

Thinking in this way may maintain the therapist's belief that he or she is doing the right thing. However, the Ethics Code is clear that this is not the case.

Key Terms

civil commitment, 518
false negative, 519
false positive, 519
indeterminate sentences, 516
insanity defense, 512
standard of proof, 519

Summary

- Mental health law deals with both the legal responsibility and the constitutional rights of people judged to be mentally disturbed. These rapidly changing laws address three major issues: psychological disturbance and criminal law, involuntary civil commitment, and patients' rights.
- Abnormal behavior may also be illegal behavior. The insanity defense is designed to protect those who are not morally responsible for committing crimes because of mental disturbance. The test of insanity is based on the M'Naghten rule, handed down by a British court in 1843, and on the Durham test. The American Law Institute's formulation of the insanity defense places the burden of deciding a defendant's competency on the jury rather than on mental health professionals.
- After the Hinckley case, several states adopted a new verdict of "guilty but mentally ill" to serve as an intermediate between "guilty" and "not guilty by reason of insanity." The Hinckley case was also largely responsible for shifting the burden of proof in insanity cases from the prosecution to the defense.
- There are two major criticisms of the insanity defense. First, the jury is asked to make a judgment that is both subjective and retrospective and that often relies on conflicting testimony. A second criticism contends that for those who successfully plead insanity, commitment to a mental hospital is, in essence, an indeterminate sentence, having no limit.
- Competency is another legal issue in criminal trials. Defendants must be judged mentally competent to stand trial; that is, they must understand the nature of the proceedings against them and be able to assist counsel in their own defense.
- One controversy surrounding competency is whether incompetent defendants should be detained in jail. Another is whether defendants are competent who only fulfill the competency requirement when under the influence of antipsychotic drugs.
- Involuntary civil commitment to a mental hospital raises serious legal questions. The U.S. Supreme Court has failed to establish specific legal procedures necessary before a person may be involuntarily committed, and lower courts have differed on the issue. As a result, a person faced with involuntary civil commitment may not have the same legal rights that a criminal defendant has.
- The Supreme Court has held that a person cannot be involuntarily committed to a mental institution without "clear and convincing" evidence that he or she is committable. Typically, statutes require that, to be committable, a person must be found mentally ill and dangerous. The standard of "dangerous" behavior, however, is open to interpretation, and predictions of such behavior are shaky at best.
- Whatever the standard for commitment, distinctions must be made between mental health questions, which

psychologists and psychiatrists are qualified to answer, and legal and moral questions, which should be left to the courts.

- Patients' rights include the right to treatment, the right to refuse treatment, and the right to a humane environment. These rights may conflict with some techniques used in behavior therapy. Legally guaranteed rights and amenities can no longer be withheld to reinforce desired behavior. Also, it is now questionable whether certain behavioral techniques are legal.
- The Ethics Code of the American Psychological Association holds mental health professionals to the highest ideals. Ethical guidelines include striving to benefit clients and to do no harm; upholding standards of trust and responsibility; acting with integrity; treating all clients justly and with equal access to services; and respecting clients' dignity and rights. Among the most important aspects of the Ethics Code are obligations about confidentiality, informed consent, and multiple and exploitative relationships in psychotherapy.

GLOSSARY

Note: The number following the definition indicates the chapter in which the term is discussed.

ABAB design An experimental research design that seeks to confirm a treatment effect by showing that behavior changes systematically with alternate conditions of no treatment (A) and treatment (B). 3

abreaction An intense reexperiencing of an event in memory retrieval. 8

absence seizures Brief generalized epileptic seizures during which patients, usually children, seem to absent themselves from their surroundings. 15

acquired brain disorders Damage to a normally developed or developing brain. The damage can result in cognitive, behavioral, and emotional dysfunction. 15

acquired dysfunction A sexual dysfunction that develops after at least one episode of normal functioning. 13

acquired immune deficiency syndrome (AIDS) A disease caused by the human immunodeficiency virus (HIV), which attacks the immune system, making patients susceptible to infection. 9

acrophobia The fear of high places. 6

active phase The second stage of schizophrenia, during which the patient begins showing prominent psychotic symptoms. 14

acute confusional state The state of disorientation that a patient suffering from a brain contusion may experience upon awakening from the coma. 15

addiction Condition traditionally defined as physiological need for a drug, wherein drug use altered the body's chemistry to the point where the body required the drug to feel normal. 12

agitated depression A form of depression characterized by incessant activity and restlessness. 10

agnosia A disturbance in the ability to recognize familiar objects. 15

agoraphobia An anxiety disorder characterized by fear of being in any situation from which escape might be difficult and in which help would be unavailable in the event of panic symptoms. 6

alienation An existentialist concept; a condition of modern life that results from a failure to choose an authentic life; a kind of spiritual death, a sense of the meaninglessness of life and terror over what comes with death. 5

alters In dissociative identity disorder patients, the secondary or multiple identities the person adopts. 8

Alzheimer's disease An organic brain disorder characterized by cognitive deficits such as failure of concentration and memory. The disease can occur as early as age 40, but its prevalence increases with age. 15

amnesia The partial or total forgetting of past experiences. It can be associated with organic brain syndromes or with psychological stress. 8, 15

amniocentesis A clinical procedure that can identify abnormal chromosomes in a developing fetus. 17

amphetamines A group of synthetic stimulants—the most common of which are Benzedrine, Dexedrine, and Methedrine—which reduce feelings of boredom or weariness. 12

anal stage In psychodynamic theory, the second stage of psychosocial development, in which the child's focus is on the pleasurable feelings of retaining and expelling the feces; occurs in the second year of life. 5

analogue experiment An experimental situation that attempts to reproduce, under controlled conditions, the essential features of naturally occurring psychopathology or its treatment. 3

anhedonia A mood abnormality among schizophrenics in which the person's experience of pleasure is reduced. Often experienced by people during major depressive episodes, the inability to enjoy accustomed activities leads to a lack of interest in those activities. 10, 14

anorexia nervosa Chronic failure to eat for fear of gaining weight. Occurring usually among adolescent girls and young women, the disorder results in severe malnutrition, semistarvation, and sometimes death. 16

antidepressant drugs Drugs used to elevate mood in depressed patients. 10

antimanic drugs Drugs, principally lithium, used to prevent and treat manic episodes. 10

antipsychotic drugs Drugs used to relieve symptoms such as confusion, withdrawal, hallucinations, and delusions in psychotic patients. Also called *major tranquilizers* or *neuroleptics*. 14

antisocial behavior Behavior that violates the rights of others; usually associated with antisocial personality. 11

antisocial personality disorder (APD) A disorder marked by chronic indifference to and violation of the rights of others. 11

anxiety A state of fear that affects many areas of functioning and that involves three basic components: subjective reports of tension and dread, behavioral inhibitions and impairments, and certain physiological responses. 5, 6

anxiety disorders Disturbances characterized either by manifest anxiety or by behavior patterns aimed at warding off anxiety. 6

aphasia A language impairment generally attributable to damage in the left hemisphere of the brain. 15

apraxia Impairment of the ability to perform voluntary movements. 15

attachment theory Theory holding that people who had close, caring bonds with a caregiver while growing up are more apt to develop an adaptive, interpersonal style of relating to others (i.e., a "secure" attachment style). 10

attention deficit hyperactivity disorder (ADHD) A childhood disorder characterized by incessant restlessness and an extremely short attention span, leading to impulsive and disorganized behavior. 16

attribution One form of cognitive appraisal concerning beliefs about the causes of life events; how people explain events to themselves will affect their emotional state. 4

autism *See* **infantile autism.**

autogynephilia Sexual arousal created by the fantasy of being a female or having a female body. This arousal underlies most transvestism and much cross-dressing. 13

autonomic nervous system (ANS) The part of the nervous system that governs the smooth muscles, the heart muscle, the glands, and the viscera and controls their functions, including physiological responses to emotion. It has two divisions, the sympathetic and parasympathetic. 6

avoidant personality disorder A disorder in which the individual withdraws from social contact out of fear of rejection. 11

barbiturates A group of powerful sedative drugs used to alleviate tension and bring about relaxation and sleep. 12

behavioral experiments Cognitive technique by which clients are urged to "reality test" their predictions and assumptions, looking for evidence much as is done in science. 4

behavior genetics A subfield of psychology concerned with determining the extent to which behavior, including abnormal behavior, is influenced by genetics. 6

behavior therapy A method of treatment for specific problems that uses the principles of learning theory. 4

behavioral high-risk design A research design in which high-risk subjects are selected on the basis of behavioral traits thought to be associated with the disorder in question. 3, 14

behavioral perspective A theoretical approach that departs from psychodynamic theory in viewing all behavior as a result of learning. 4

benzodiazepines A group of anti-anxiety drugs that reduce anxiety by activating the inhibitory neurotransmitter, GABA. 6

biofeedback training A technique by which subjects, with the help of various machines, can monitor and control their own biological processes such as pulse, blood pressure, and brain waves. 8

biogenic A term used to describe abnormal behavior that results from malfunction within the body. According to biogenic theory, mental disturbance is due to organic disorders. 1

bipolar disorder A mood disorder involving both manic and depressive episodes. 10

blood alcohol level The amount of alcohol in the bloodstream, expressed in terms of the number of milligrams of alcohol per 100 milliliters of blood. 12

blunted affect A mood abnormality among schizophrenics in which the person shows little emotion. 14

body dysmorphic disorder A preoccupation with an imagined or a grossly exaggerated defect in one's appearance. 8

borderline personality disorder A disorder marked by an unstable sense of self, distrust, impulsive and self-destructive behavior, and difficulty in controlling anger and other emotions. 11

brain plasticity The brain's ability, during infancy, to be altered by environmental stimulation. 17

brain tumors Abnormal growths within the brain, classified as either **metastatic** or **primary.** 15

bulimia nervosa Excessive overeating or uncontrolled binge-eating followed by self-induced vomiting. 16

case-control design A research design in which *cases,* people diagnosed as having a mental disorder, are compared with *controls,* people who have not been diagnosed as having the disorder. 3

case study A research design that focuses on a single individual for description and analysis. 3

castration anxiety In psychodynamic theory, the male child's fear that his penis will be cut off as punishment for his sexual desire for his mother. 5

catatonic schizophrenia A form of schizophrenia characterized by a marked disturbance in motor behavior: decreases in motion, complete immobility, cessation of speech, or alternating periods of immobility and extreme agitation. 14

catatonic stupor An extreme form of withdrawal in which the individual retreats into a completely immobile state, showing a total lack of responsiveness to stimulation. 14

catecholamine hypothesis The biochemical theory that increased levels of the neurotransmitter norepinephrine produce mania, while decreased levels produce depression. 10

categorical classification The sorting of patients into qualitatively distinct categories, as in the *DSM.* 2

central nervous system (CNS) The part of the nervous system made up of the brain and spinal cord. 6

cerebral abscess A brain infection that becomes encapsulated by connective tissue. 15

cerebral cortex Outermost part of the brain. 6

cerebrovascular accident (CVA) A blockage of or break in the blood vessels in the brain, resulting in injury to brain tissue. Commonly called *stroke.* 15

childhood depression A disorder of emotional distress with symptoms similar to those of adult depression (sadness, hopelessness, etc.) but expressed differently by children (e.g., by clinging to their parents) and by adolescents (e.g., by engaging in delinquent acts). 16

chromosomes Threadlike structures in all the cells of the body that carry genes in a linear order. 6

civil commitment The commitment of a person to a mental institution because the state has decided that he or she is disturbed enough to require hospitalization. 18

clanging In schizophrenia, the pairing of words that have no relation to one another beyond the fact that they rhyme or sound alike. 14

claustrophobia The fear of enclosed places. 6

client-centered therapy Style of therapy that creates a warm and accepting atmosphere for the patient by offering respect and approval, mirroring the patient's feelings, and attempting to perceive the patient's world as he or she does. 5

clinical psychologist A Ph.D. or Psy.D. who spent four to six years in graduate school and completed a one-year clinical internship. Clinical psychology programs emphasize training in psychological assessment and therapeutic intervention, as well as research. 1

clinical significance A statistical effect that has practical value or importance. 3

clinical trials Studies of the effectiveness of treatments, involving randomized comparisons between two or more forms of therapy. 3

clinicians Therapists who work with people with mental health problems. 3

cocaine A natural stimulant, made from the coca plant, that produces feelings of euphoria and omnipotence. 12

coconscious In dissociative identity disorder, the term used to refer to a subordinate personality that is fully aware of the dominant personality's thoughts and actions. 8

cognition The act of knowing, including mental processes such as emotion, thought, expectation, and interpretation. 4

cognitive appraisal According to cognitive behaviorists, the process by which a person evaluates a stimulus in accordance with his or her memories, beliefs, and expectations before responding. It accounts for the wide variation in responses to the same stimulus. 4

cognitive behaviorism An alliance between cognitive theory and behavioral theory which claims that people's actions are often responses not so much to external stimuli as to their own individual mental processing of those stimuli. 4

cognitive case conceptualization Process by which therapist and client gather information about the client's problems and the situational triggers for the client's feelings, thought patterns, and responses. It leads to an understanding of the interrelationships among developmental experiences, core beliefs, and faulty coping patterns. This conceptualization is used to coordinate, plan, and guide all aspects of the treatment. 4

cognitive distortion A bias in information processing, patterns of faulty or distorted thinking. 4

cognitive perspective The view of abnormal behavior as the product of mental processing of environmental stimuli (cognition). 4

cognitive restructuring A variety of cognitive therapy techniques that help clients increase coping skills, develop problem-solving skills, and change the way they perceive and interpret their worlds. 4

communication deviance (CD) A measurement of parental deviant or idiosyncratic verbal responses; used to predict the potential for their children's future schizophrenic behaviors. 14

community mental health centers Facilities designed to provide a variety of psychological services for everyone within a specified area. 1

community psychology The branch of psychology that deals with human-environment interactions and the ways society affects individual and community functioning; focuses on social issues, social institutions, and other settings and their interaction with individuals, groups, and organizations. 1

comorbidity A condition in which a patient meets the criteria for more than one *DSM-IV* Axis I disorder. 2, 10

complex partial seizure A partial epileptic seizure in which cognitive functioning is interrupted. 15

compulsion An action that a person feels compelled to repeat again and again in a stereotyped fashion, though he or she has no conscious desire to do so. 6

computerized tomography (CT) A technique for mapping brain structure in which X rays are passed through cross sections of the brain, measuring the density of the tissue in each section. 6

concordant Refers to sharing the same disorder. 6

concussion A head injury caused by a blow to the head that jars the brain and momentarily disrupts its function. 15

conditioned reflex A basic mechanism of learning; if a neutral stimulus is paired with a nonneutral stimulus, the organism will eventually respond to the neutral stimulus as it does to the nonneutral stimulus. 4

conditioned reinforcers Stimuli or needs that one learns to respond to by associating them with primary reinforcers. Also called *secondary reinforcers*. 4

conditioned response A simple response to a neutral stimulus that is the result of repeatedly pairing the neutral stimulus with a nonneutral stimulus that would have naturally elicited the response. 4

conditioned stimulus The neutral stimulus that elicits a particular response as a result of repeated pairings with a nonneutral or unconditioned stimulus that naturally elicits that response 4

conditions of worth Extraneous values imposed on children; strings attached to positive regard that dictate which self-experiences are "good" and which are "bad." 5

conduct disorder A childhood disorder in which a preadolescent or an adolescent persistently violates social norms through aggression against people or animals, destruction of property, deceitfulness or theft, and/or other serious violations of rules. 16

confounding In a research study, a phenomenon that occurs when two or more causal factors are operating on the same thing simultaneously, interfering with accurate measurement of the causal role of either factor. 3

congenital disorders Disorders acquired during prenatal development but not transmitted genetically. 17

contingency In operant conditioning, a perceived association between action and consequence which, once learned, directs behavior: An individual will repeat a behavior or cease it in order to obtain or avoid the consequence. 4

contingency management An operant-conditioning technique in which the consequences of a response are manipulated in order to change the frequency of that response. 4

continuity hypothesis Theory resting on the idea that depression appears to be an exaggerated form of everyday sadness. 10

control The ability to manipulate or change a phenomenon. 3

control groups Groups that do not receive the experimental treatment or manipulation. 3

control techniques The three methods by which the independent variable in an experiment can be controlled: manipulating, holding conditions constant, and balancing. 3

contusion A head injury in which the brain is shifted out of its normal position and pressed against one side of the skull, thus bruising the neural tissue. 15

conversion disorder The loss or impairment of some motor or sensory function for which there is no organic cause; formerly known as "hysteria" or "hysterical neurosis." 8

coronary heart disease A disease brought about by atherosclerosis, the buildup of fatty deposits on the inside walls of the coronary arteries, and manifested as heart attack or sudden cardiac death. 8

corpus callosum A band of nerve fibers connecting the two hemispheres of the brain. 6

correlational research Research studies that seek to find the relationships between subjects' characteristics and their performance. Such studies effectively meet two of the objectives of the scientific method—description and prediction—but the results of correlational studies should not be used to make causal inferences. 3

correlation coefficient A numerical measure of the linear relationship between two variables. 3

covariation of events The first condition to be met before causality can be demonstrated: Two events must vary together; when one changes, the other must also change. 3

crack cocaine A cheaper and more powerful and highly addictive form of freebased cocaine, sold in small chunks or "rocks." 12

cretinism A congenital disorder marked by serious mental retardation and physical disabilities; caused by lack of iodine in the pregnant woman's diet or damage to the thyroid during birth. 17

cyclothymic disorder A chronic mood disorder in which, for years, the person goes no longer than a few months without a phase of hypomanic or depressive behavior. 10

decatastrophizing A strategy used in cognitive therapy whereby clients are helped to realize that their fears are exaggerated by being asked to consider what would actually happen if their worst fears were realized. 4

defense mechanism Any psychic stratagem that reduces anxiety by concealing the source of anxiety from the self and the world. 5

deficit symptoms Negative symptoms of schizophrenia that are primary and endure across the prodromal, active, and residual phases. 14

degenerative disorders Organic brain syndromes characterized by a general deterioration of intellectual, emotional, and motor functioning as a result of progressive pathological change in the brain. 15

deinstitutionalization The widespread discharge of mental patients from the hospital into the community. 1

delirium A global disorder of cognition and attention that begins suddenly and remits quickly, leaving most patients unharmed. Symptoms include confusion, hallucinations, and emotional lability. 15

delusional disorder A psychosis in which the delusional system is the basic or even the only abnormality, and in all other respects the person seems quite normal. 14

delusions False beliefs that have no basis in reality. 10

demand characteristics A methodological problem in which a subject's response is strongly determined by the expectations of the subject or the researchers. 3

dementia Severe mental deterioration. 15

dementia praecox A syndrome identified by Kraepelin and marked by delusions, hallucinations, attention problems, and bizarre motor behavior. Now called **schizophrenia.** 14

dependent personality disorder A disorder marked by extreme dependence on others. 11

dependent variable In a research study, the factor (in psychology, a particular behavior) that will be affected by the experimenter's manipulation of the independent variable, and whose changes the researcher wishes to measure. 3

depersonalization A sense of strangeness or unreality in oneself. 8

depersonalization disorder A disruption of personal identity that is characterized by a sense of strangeness or unreality in oneself, e.g., feeling that one is viewing oneself from the outside or is functioning like a robot. 8

depressant A drug that acts on the central nervous system to reduce pain, tension, and anxiety, to relax and disinhibit, and to slow intellectual and motor reactivity. 12

depression An emotional state characterized by the exaggeration of negative feelings. The person becomes inactive and dejected and thinks nothing is worthwhile. 10

depth hypothesis Freud's view that almost all mental activity takes place unconsciously. 5

derealization A feeling of strangeness about the world. Other people, and the self, seem robotic, dead, or somehow unreal. 8

derived stimulus relations The learning that occurs because the mind learns to group sets of different stimuli (e.g., pictures and objects for the same objects), called stimulus equivalence. This learning mechanism helps to explain why people learn to respond to symbols (e.g., the word *money*) much as they do to the actual object (e.g., dollar bills). 4

description (1) The first objective of the scientific method: the procedure by which events and their relationships are defined, classified, catalogued, or categorized. (2) The first goal of psychological assessment: the rendering of an accurate portrait of personality, cognitive functioning, mood, and behavior. 3

descriptive validity The degree to which an assessment device provides significant information about the current behavior of the people being assessed. 2

detoxification A medical treatment for alcoholism that consists of getting the alcohol out of the alcoholic's system and seeing him or her through the withdrawal symptoms. 12

dexamethasone suppression test (DST) A laboratory test used to identify people suffering from endogenous depression. In nondepressed individuals, dexamethasone suppresses cortisol secretion for at least 24 hours. Cortisol secretion of individuals with endogenous depression returns to high levels within 24 hours despite administration of dexamethasone. 10

diagnosis The classification and labeling of a patient's problem within one of a set of recognized categories of abnormal behavior. 2

dialectical behavior therapy A form of therapy developed to treat borderline personality disorder, integrating acceptance with change. 11

diathesis A genetic predisposition toward an abnormal or diseased condition. 6

diathesis-stress model The belief that certain genes or gene combinations may lead to a diathesis, or predisposition, toward a disorder and that, if this is combined with certain kinds of environmental stress, abnormal behavior will result. In schizophrenia research, this approach holds that a predisposition to schizophrenia is inherited but that the disorder must be triggered by environmental stresses. 6

differential deficits Deficits that are specific to the disorder in question (as opposed to other disorders) and that are presumably central to it. 14

dimensional classification The assignment of patients to scores on quantitative dimensions, such as personality, course, and functioning. 2

discrimination The process of learning to distinguish among similar stimuli and to respond only to the appropriate one. 4

disorder-specific biases The idea that there is a specific mental processing bias associated with each disorder (e.g., social anxiety, depression). It is reflected in different typical thoughts associated with each disorder and can involve different patterns of selective attention, memory, interpretation, etc. 4

disorganized schizophrenia A form of schizophrenia characterized by pronounced incoherence of speech, childlike disturbed affect such as giggling wildly and assuming absurd postures, and disorganized behavior, or lack of goal orientation. Also called hebephrenic schizophrenia. 14

disruptive behavior disorders Childhood disorders characterized by poorly controlled, impulsive, acting-out behavior in situations where self-control is expected. 16

dissociative amnesia Memory loss without any apparent physiological cause, as a response to psychological stress. Dissociative amnesia tends to be anterograde, blotting out a period of time after the precipitating stress. 8

dissociative disorders Disorders resulting from the splitting off of some psychological function—such as identity or memory—from the rest of the conscious mind. 8

dissociative fugue A condition related to amnesia in which a person not only forgets most or all of his or her past but also takes a sudden, unexpected trip away from home. 8

dissociative identity disorder (DID) A condition in which the personality breaks apart into two or more distinct personalities, each well integrated and well developed, which then take turns controlling the person's behavior. Also known as *multiple personality.* 8

dizygotic twins Twins who develop from two eggs fertilized by two different sperm; they have 50 percent of their genes in common. 6

dopamine hypothesis The theory that schizophrenia is associated with excess activity of the parts of the brain that use dopamine as a neurotransmitter. 14

double-blind A procedure in scientific research that seeks to minimize the influence of subjects' and experimenters' expectations. Both the subject and the experimenter are unaware of what treatment is being administered—that is, whether the subject is in the experimental group or the control group. 3

down-regulation Process where postsynaptic receptors decrease in number or become less sensitive to the neurotransmitter in response to too much neurotransmitter being released into the synapse. 6

Down syndrome A form of mental retardation caused by an extra chromosome. Individuals with this condition usually have IQs of 50 or less and distinctive physical characteristics, such as an extra fold of skin on the upper eyelid, a flat nose, and poor muscle tone. 17

DSM-IV-TR The most recent revision of the *Diagnostic and Statistical Manual,* the handbook that classifies the symptoms and types of mental disorders. 2

dyspareunia A sexual dysfunction characterized by pain during intercourse. 13

dysthymic disorder A chronic mood disorder involving a mild, persistent depression. Symptoms are similar to those of a major depressive episode, but they are not as severe or as numerous. 10

echolalia A speech deficit, characteristic of autistic children and some catatonic schizophrenics, in which the child aimlessly repeats what other people say. 14, 17

ego According to Freud, the psychic component that mediates between the id and the forces that restrict the id's satisfactions. 5

ego psychology School of psychology that sees the development of the personality as involving the formation of mental models of the world and how the world works; it focuses on the ego and the interplay between its conflict-solving functions and its conflict-free functions, particularly cognitive processes. 5

Electra complex Freud's concept, complementary to the Oediupus complex, which holds that a very young girl reorients her sexual interests toward her father, because she experiences penis envy and wishes to obtain the organ vicariously. 5

electroconvulsive therapy (ECT) The administering of an electric shock to a patient, thus inducing a convulsion; used in the treatment of serious depression. 10

electroencephalogram (EEG) A brain test in which electrodes, attached to the head with tape, pick up electrical activity within the brain and measure it in oscillating patterns known as brain waves. 2

electromyogram (EMG) A polygraph recording of the changes in the electrical activity of muscles. 2

elimination of plausible alternative causes The third condition to be met before causality can be demonstrated: The proposed causal relationship can be accepted only after other likely causes have been ruled out. 3

embolism The obstruction of a blood vessel by a ball of a substance such as fat, air, or clotted blood, thus cutting off the blood supply; a common cause of infarction. 15

encephalitis Any acute infection of the brain. 15

encopresis A lack of bowel control past the age when such control is normally achieved. 16

endocrine glands Glands responsible for the production of hormones that, when released into the bloodstream, affect various bodily mechanisms such as physical growth and development. 15

endocrine system The system of endocrine, or ductless, glands—such as the hypothalamus and the pituitary—that is closely integrated with the central nervous system and is responsible for the production of hormones. 6

endogenous In depression, the term used to describe patients whose symptoms are primarily physical. 10

endorphins Brain chemicals, similar to morphine, that may underlie one's natural control of pain and natural experience of pleasure. 12

enuresis A lack of bladder control past the age when such control is normally achieved. Children with *primary enuresis* have never achieved bladder control. Those with *secondary enuresis* have lost the control they once had. 16

epidemiology The study of the frequency and distribution of disorders within specific populations. 3

epilepsy A generic term for a variety of organic disorders characterized by irregularly occurring disturbances in consciousness in the form of seizures or convulsions. The seizures seem to be caused by a disruption in the electrical and physiochemical activity of the discharging cells of the brain. 15

episodic memory Memory of personal experience. 8

essential hypertension Chronically high blood pressure for which no organic cause can be found. 9

event-related potentials An EEG that measures changes in brain activity as a consequence of specific sensory, cognitive, or motor stimuli. 6

exhibitionism Sexual gratification through displaying one's genitals to an involuntary observer. 13

exorcism The practice of expelling evil spirits from a person believed to be possessed by such demons. 1

experimenter effects A methodological problem in which researchers inadvertently influence the subject's responses or perceive the subjects' behavior in terms of their own biases. 3

explicit memories Memories we are aware of, which may disappear in amnesia. *Cf.* **implicit memories.** 8

exposure A behavioral treatment for anxiety in which the client is confronted (suddenly or gradually) with his or her feared stimulus. 4

expressed emotion (EE) A measurement of key relatives' level of criticism and emotional overinvolvement, used in determining the family type of a hospitalized schizophrenic. 14

external validity The degree to which research results can be generalized, or applied, to different populations, settings, and conditions. 3

extinction A process in which a conditioned response is reduced to its preconditioned level. Previously reinforced responses are no longer reinforced. 4

false negative In commitment hearings, a failure to commit a person when commitment is justified and necessary. 18

false positive In commitment hearings, an unjustified commitment. 18

female orgasmic disorder A recurrent, lengthy delay or absence of orgasm in a woman. 13

female sexual arousal disorder In women, the absence or weakness of the physiological changes or feelings of sexual excitement that normally occur in the arousal phase of sexual response. 13

fetal alcohol syndrome (FAS) A complex of physical and behavioral defects found in many children of alcoholic women. The defects include distinctive facial characteristics, retarded physical growth, and, frequently, mental retardation. 17

fetishism Sexual gratification via inanimate objects or some part of the partner's body to the exclusion of the person as a whole. 13

flat affect A mood abnormality among schizophrenics in which the person shows no emotion. 14

flooding A method of imagined exposure in which the person is confronted with the feared stimulus for long periods of time. 7

fragile X syndrome A condition in which an individual's X chromosome shows a weak spot; the most common genetic cause of mental retardation. 17

free association A psychoanalytic technique in which the patient verbalizes whatever thoughts come to mind, without structuring or censoring the remarks. 1

frontal lobe Largest and anterior division of each cerebral hemisphere. Involved in motor function, language, memory, impulse control, and many other functions. 6

frontotemporal dementia A dementia that occurs in middle-aged people and results from progressive deterioration of the frontal and temporal lobes of the brain; it is characterized by a profound change in behavior. 15

frotteurism Sexual gratification through touching and rubbing against a nonconsenting person. 13

functional MRI Variation of MRI that measures the magnetic action of blood oxygen and thus produces images of brain metabolism. 6

galvanic skin response (GSR) A polygraphic recording of the changes in the electrical resistance of the skin, an indication of sweat gland activity. There is an intimate relationship between emotion and physiological functioning; when a person's anxiety level rises, so may the activity of the sweat glands. 2

gender dysphoria The symptom of being unhappy with one's assigned gender; one of the components of gender identity disorder. 13

gender identity disorder (GID) A condition in which people identify with the opposite sex so completely that they feel that they belong to that sex and that their own gender is simply a mistake. Also called *transsexualism*. 13

gender reassignment The process of changing one's gender to the other gender, usually through adopting the dress, manner, appearance, and physical characteristics of the other gender. This may include hormonal treatment and gender reassignment surgery. 13

general paresis A final stage of syphilis, involving the gradual and irreversible breakdown of physical and mental functioning. 1, 15

generalizability The ability of research results to be applied to different populations, settings, and conditions. 3

generalization The process by which an organism, conditioned to respond in a certain way to a particular stimulus, will respond to other, similar stimuli in the same way. 4

generalized anxiety disorder A chronic state of diffuse anxiety characterized by excessive worry, over a period of at least six months, about several life circumstances (most often family, money, work, and health). 6, 16

generalized dysfunction A sexual dysfunction that occurs in all sexual situations. 13

generalized seizures Epileptic seizures that either involve the entire brain at the outset (primary) or soon spread from one part to the whole brain (secondary). *Cf.* **partial seizure.** 15

genes The units of heredity on a chromosome that carry the instructions, inherited from the parents at conception, about the proteins that the body should produce. The proteins, in turn, determine the hereditary characteristics of the person—height, hair and eye color, and so on. 6

genetic high-risk design A research design in which high-risk subjects are selected on the basis of genetic factors associated with the disorder in question. 3, 14

genetic marker A gene with a known location on the human chromosome set; provides a clue to the location of a gene controlling a disorder. 6

genital stage According to Freud, the final phase of mature sexuality, by which he meant heterosexual genital mating. 5

genotype The unique combination of genes that represents one's biological inheritance from one's parents. 6

genotype-environment correlation The tendency for individuals' genetic predispositions for a trait or disorder to be associated with environmental experiences that also influence the trait or disorder. 6

good-poor premorbid dimension A dimension describing a patient's adaptive functioning prior to the onset of a disorder. 14

group therapy Treatment of up to 8 or 10 clients at a time by a single therapist. 5

hallucinations Sensory perceptions that occur in the absence of any appropriate external stimulus. 10, 14

hallucinogens A class of drugs that acts on the central nervous system in such a way as to cause distortions in sensory perception. 12

hashish A "minor hallucinogen" derived from the resin of cannabis, a hemp plant. It is five times stronger than marijuana, another cannabis derivative. 12

health psychology A research discipline that focuses on the relationship between mental and physical health. Also called *behavioral medicine*. 9

helplessness-hopelessness syndrome A thought process characteristic of deeply depressed persons in which they regard their condition as irreversible, believing that they are both unable to help themselves and unlikely to be helped by external forces. 10

hemorrhage A cerebrovascular accident in which a blood vessel in the brain ruptures, causing blood to spill out into the brain tissue. 15

heroin An addictive opiate derived from morphine. 12

hierarchy of fears A list of anxiety-producing situations in order of their increasing horror to the client (ascending from least to most frightening), established by a patient and therapist as a part of systematic desensitization. 4

hierarchy of needs Concept originating with Abraham Maslow, a series of needs that must be met in the process of development before the adult can begin to pursue self-actualization. 5

high-risk design A form of longitudinal research that involves the study of people who have a high probability of developing a disorder. 3

histrionic personality disorder A disorder involving the exaggerated display of emotion. 11

hormones Chemical messengers that are released directly into the bloodstream by the endocrine gland and that affect sexual functioning, physical growth and development, and emotional responses. 6

host In dissociative identity disorder patients, the personality corresponding to who the person was before the onset of the disorder. 8

human immunodeficiency virus (HIV) The virus that attacks and breaks down the human immune system and causes AIDS. It is transmitted by blood, semen, vaginal secretions, or breast milk of an infected person through unsafe sex, the sharing of hypodermic needles, a contaminated blood transfusion, or passage to a child in the womb of an infected mother. 9

humanistic existential perspective View taken by a group of thinkers, many trained as psychoanalysts, who rejected the pessimistic determinism of the psychodynamic approach and emphasized the positive, optimistic aspects of human potential for health, creativity, and constructive living. 5

humors In Hippocrates' view, the four vital fluids possessed by humans: phlegm, blood, black bile, and yellow bile. The balance of these humors in each individual was thought to influence personality. 1

Huntington's chorea A fatal organic brain disorder that is transmitted genetically. Symptoms include spasmodic jerking of the limbs, bizarre behavior, and mental deterioration. 15

hypertension Chronic elevation of blood pressure due to constriction of the arteries; a stress-related physical disorder. Also called *high blood pressure.* 9

hypnosis An artificially induced trance, or sleeplike state, in which the subject is highly susceptible to suggestion. 1

hypoactive sexual desire disorder A chronic lack of interest in sex. 13

hypochondriasis A disorder in which a person converts anxiety into a chronic fear of disease. The fear is maintained by the constant misinterpretation of physical signs and sensations as abnormal. 8

hypomanic episode Briefer and less severe manic episode. 10

hypothesis A tentative explanation for behavior that attempts to answer the questions "How?" and "Why?" Scientific research often begins with a hypothesis. 3

hypothesis testing A strategy used in cognitive therapy whereby clients are urged to test their assumptions in the real world. 4

hysteria A psychogenic disorder that mimics a biogenic disorder. 1, 8

iatrogenic A type of symptom brought about as a consequence of therapy or treatment. 8

id According to Freud, the basic psychic structure, consisting of primitive biological drives toward sex and aggression. 5

idiopathic epilepsy A convulsive disorder for which there is no known cause. 15

immune system The body's system of defense against infectious disease and cancer. 9

implicit memories Memories that a person with amnesia cannot call into conscious awareness but that still affect his or her behavior. *Cf.* **explicit memories.** 8

impulse-control disorders Patterns of impulsive behavior that seem to exist not as part of another major syndrome but independently. Their essential feature is the inability to resist the impulse to act in ways harmful to oneself or to others. 11

inappropriate affect A mood abnormality among schizophrenics in which the person's emotional responses seem unsuitable to the situation. 14

incest Sexual relations between family members. 13

informed consent An individual's agreeing to participate in a research study based on an understanding of the purpose, procedures, risks, and benefits of the study. 3

incidence The number of new cases of a disorder reported during a specific time period. 3

independent variable In a research study, a factor that has been determined before the experiment and may be manipulated by the experimenters in order to measure its effect. 3

indeterminate sentences Periods of incarceration with no limit, often given to defendants acquitted by reason of insanity. 18

individual response specificity The principle that people seem to have characteristic patterns of autonomic nervous system response which carry over from one kind of stress to another. 9

infantile autism A disorder in children in which the primary symptom, apparent from infancy, is the inability to relate to anyone outside of oneself. 17

infarction A cerebrovascular accident in which the supply of blood to the brain is cut off, resulting in the death of brain tissue fed by that source. 15

inpatient A mental patient who is hospitalized. 1

insanity defense A legal plea in which the defendant admits to having committed the crime but pleads not guilty, stating that because of mental disturbance he or she was not morally responsible at the time of the crime. 18

insomnia The chronic inability to sleep. The condition can stem from both physical and psychological factors. 9

intelligence quotient (IQ) The subject's final score on an adult version of the Stanford-Binet Intelligence scale, a test that measures a child's ability to perform a range of intellectual tasks. IQ tests play an important part in the diagnosis of mental retardation and brain damage. 2

intelligence tests Psychological assessment techniques effective in predicting success in school but questionable as a valid measure of intelligence. 2

interjudge reliability A criterion for judging the reliability of a psychological test: The test should yield the same results when scored or interpreted by different judges. 2

internal consistency A criterion for judging the reliability of a psychological test: Different parts of the test should yield the same result. 2

internal validity The extent to which the results of an experiment can be confidently attributed to the effects of the independent variable. 3

interpersonal psychotherapy (IPT) Short-term therapy for depression that looks for solutions and strategies to deal with interpersonal problems rather than spending time on interpretation and analysis. 10

interpretation Freud's primary tool for revealing hidden, intrapsychic motives; it involves going beyond observing surface behavior to uncover its latent content. 5

interview An assessment method consisting of a face-to-face conversation between subject and examiner. 2

knockouts Genes that are deleted to learn what they do—through observation of what the deletion does to behavior. 6

Korsakoff's psychosis An irreversible nutritional deficiency due to vitamin B_1 deficiency associated with alcoholism; characterized by anterograde amnesia and confabulation. 15

la belle indifférence A response often seen in conversion disorder in which the person does not seem at all disturbed by his or her disability. 8

latency The dormancy of a particular behavior or response. 5

lateralization The differences in structure and function between the right and the left hemispheres of the brain. 6

law of effect Thorndike's formulation of the importance of reward in the learning process which states that responses that lead to satisfying consequences are strengthened and, therefore, are likely to be repeated, while responses with unsatisfying consequences are weakened and, therefore, unlikely to be repeated. 4

lead encephalopathy Toxic brain disorder caused by excessive ingestion of lead, in which fluid accumulates in the brain, causing extreme pressure. 15

learned helplessness In behavioral theory, the depressed person's inability to initiate adaptive responses, possibly due to a helplessness conditioned by earlier, inescapable trauma. 10

learning The process whereby behavior changes in response to the environment. 4

learning disorders Three conditions characterized by reading, writing, or mathematical skills that are substantially below what would be expected for the person's age, education, and intelligence and by a resulting interference with the person's adjustment. The three conditions are reading disorder (dyslexia), disorder of written expression, and mathematics disorder. 16

Lewy body disease A relatively common form of dementia produced by the presence of Lewy bodies in neurons in the brain. The disease may produce Parkinson's symptoms, visual hallucination, and deficits in attention, concentration, and visual-perceptual skills. 15

libido Freud's term for a basic sexual drive, which he saw as the major source of psychic energy. 5

lifelong dysfunction A sexual dysfunction that has existed, without relief, since the person's earliest sexual experiences. 13

lithium A mood-altering drug used to control manic episodes. 10

longitudinal studies Scientific research designs in which a group of subjects is studied several different times over an extended period of time. Also called *prospective studies.* 3

loosening of associations The rambling, disjointed quality that is characteristic of schizophrenic speech. 14

LSD (lysergic acid diethylamide) A hallucinogen derived from a fungus; it interferes with the processing of information in the nervous system, causing perceptual distortions. 12

Lyme disease Tickborne disease that can affect the central nervous system; if untreated, it can lead to encephalitis or meningitis. 15

mad cow disease A spongiform brain disease of cows that results in neurological impairment and eventually death. The disease may be related to Creutzfeldt-Jakob disease, which causes similar results in humans. 15

magnetic resonance imaging (MRI) The use of magnetic fields to produce a highly precise picture of the brain. 6

major depressive disorder A condition characterized by one or more major depressive episodes with no intervening periods of mania. 10

major depressive episode An extended period of intense depression that usually begins and ends gradually and causes a radical change in most aspects of the individual's functioning. 10

male erectile disorder In the second phase of sexual arousal, a failure of the tissues in a man's penis to become congested with blood. 13

male orgasmic disorder A recurrent, lengthy delay or absence of ejaculation and orgasm in a man. 13

malingering The conscious faking of disease symptoms in order to avoid responsibility. 8

managed behavioral health care Managed care for mental health. *See* **managed care.**

managed care Umbrella term for the varied organizational structures, insurance benefits, and regulations that provide for and control the cost of health care. 1

mania An emotional state characterized by the exaggeration of positive feelings. The person becomes feverishly active and excited and feels capable of accomplishing anything. 10

manic episode An extended period of intense mania that usually begins and ends suddenly and causes a radical change in an individual's social functioning. 10

MAO inhibitors The first important class of antidepressants. Although named on the assumption that they block the action of monoamine oxidase (MAO), their mechanism has not been established. 6, 10

marijuana A "minor hallucinogen" derived from the dried, crushed leaves of cannabis, a hemp plant. 12

masochism Sexual gratification through pain and/or humiliation inflicted on oneself. 13

matching In alcohol treatment, directing the patient to a treatment program best suited to his or her personal characteristics. 12

MDMA Hallucinogenic drug commonly known as Ecstasy, associated with high-risk sexual behaviors; users may suffer paranoia, panic attacks, and depression as well as long-term impairment in memory with prolonged use. 12

medical model The conceptualization of psychological abnormality as a group of diseases analogous to physical diseases. 1

meningitis A cerebral infection characterized by acute inflammation of the meninges, the membrane covering of the brain and spinal cord. 15

mental retardation A condition that is characterized by subaverage intellectual functioning, by serious deficits in adaptive skills, and by onset before age 18. 17

mental status exam The mental status exam is a set of mental tests used to detect dementia (severe mental deterioration) and other organic brain disorders. The diagnostician evaluates the patient on appearance, speech, mood, perception, thought content, and cognitive processes (e.g., memory). 2

metastatic brain tumors Brain tumors that originate in some other part of the body and then metastasize, or spread, to the brain. 15

methadone A synthetic opiate that satisfies the craving for narcotics but does not produce narcotic euphoria. 12

migraine headache A severe form of chronic headache that is usually localized on one side of the head, is sometimes preceded by perceptual distortion, and is typically accompanied by other symptoms such as nausea or confusion; a stress-related disorder. 9

mind-body problem The issue of the relationship between the psychic and somatic aspects of human functioning. 6

mini mental status exam A shorter version of the mental status exam. 2

Minnesota Multiphasic Personality Inventory-2 (MMPI-2) The most widely used self-report personality inventory, the purpose of which is to simplify differential diagnosis by comparing self-descriptive statements endorsed by new patients to statements endorsed by groups of people already diagnosed with a particular condition. 2

minor tranquilizers Drugs taken to reduce anxiety or tension. 6

mixed episode An episode of mania that also meets the criteria for a major depressive disorder. 10

monozygotic twins Twins who develop from the same fertilized egg and have exactly the same genotype. 6

mood disorders Emotional conditions in which feelings of depression or mania become so extreme and prolonged that the person's life is completely disrupted. Also called *affective disorders.* 10

moral therapy A nineteenth-century approach to treatment that involved providing an environment in which the mentally ill would be treated humanely and could discuss their difficulties, live in peace, and engage in some useful employment. 1

morphine A dangerously addictive depressant drug, derived from one of the most powerful ingredients in opium; used as a painkiller. 12

motivational interviewing In drug and alcohol rehabilitation, a question-and-answer method of interviewing aimed at increasing the patient's motivation to change, leading to discontinuing substance abuse. 12

multiple-baseline design An experimental research design in which treatment is introduced at different intervals across subjects, behaviors, or situations. 3

narcissistic personality disorder A disorder characterized by a grandiose sense of self-importance, often combined with periodic feelings of inferiority. 11

negative reinforcement A conditioning procedure in which a response is followed by the removal of an aversive event or stimulus, thereby promoting the response. 4

negative symptoms In schizophrenia, the absence of something that is normally present; poverty of speech, flat affect, withdrawal, apathy, and attentional impairment. 14

neologisms Words and phrases used in schizophrenic speech, but not found in dictionaries, sometimes formed by combining parts of two or more regular words. 14

nervous system The vast electrochemical conducting network that extends from the brain through the rest of the body and carries information, in the form of electrical impulses, from the brain to the rest of the body and back to the brain. 6

neurons The cells of the nervous system, which connect motor and receptor cells and transmit information throughout the body. 6

neuroscience perspective A theory of abnormal behavior that concentrates on the physical aspects of a disorder in an effort to understand its characteristics. 1, 6

neuroses Conditions in which maladaptive behaviors serve as a protection against a source of unconscious anxiety. 5

neurosyphilis The deterioration of brain tissue as a result of syphilis. 15

neurotransmitter One of a group of chemicals that facilitate the transmission of electrical impulses between nerve endings in the brain. 6

nightmares Frightening dreams, which do not cause physiological arousal and do not necessarily awaken the dreamer. During early childhood, nightmares are distinguished from *sleep terrors,* which are both more physically arousing and more harrowing. 16

norms The rules in any society that define "right" and "wrong." Norms guide most of our actions and are an important standard for defining abnormality. 1

null hypothesis The assumption that the independent variable had no effect on the differences between experimental groups. 3

object relations In psychodynamic terminology, "objects" are the people to whom one is attached by strong emotional ties. According to object-relations theorists, the most powerful determinant of psychological development is the child's interaction with the primary caregiver, the child's chief object. 5

obsession A thought or an image that keeps unwillingly intruding into a person's consciousness, though the person may consider it senseless or even unpleasant. 6

obsessive-compulsive disorder Involuntary dwelling on an unwelcome thought (*obsession*) and/or involuntary repetition of an unnecessary action (*compulsion*). 6

obsessive-compulsive personality disorder A disorder marked by excessive preoccupation with trivial details, at the cost of both spontaneity and effectiveness. 11

occipital lobe Posterior lobe of each cerebral hemisphere; contains the visual center. 6

Oedipus complex According to Freud, the desire that all male children have during the phallic stage to do away with the parent of the same sex in order to take sexual possession of the parent of the opposite sex; a crucial stage of development which determines the child's future sexual adjustment. 5

operant conditioning The process by which an organism learns to associate certain consequences with certain actions it has taken. Also called *instrumental conditioning.* 4

operational definitions The definitions of concepts involved in a hypothesis in terms of operations that can be observed and measured, so that the hypothesis can be tested. 3

opiates A class of drugs that induces relaxation and reverie and provides relief from anxiety and pain. 12

opium A depressant derived from the opium poppy. 12

oral stage In psychodynamic theory, the first stage of psychosocial development, in which the mouth is the primary focus of libidinal impulses and pleasure; occurs in the first year of life. 5

outpatient A mental patient who receives treatment outside of the hospital. 1

pain disorder A syndrome characterized by chronic pain that is more severe or persistent than can be explained by medical causes. 8

panic attack An attack of almost unbearable anxiety, beginning suddenly and unexpectedly and usually lasting several minutes, though possibly continuing for hours. 6

panic disorder A disorder characterized by recurrent panic attacks followed by psychological or behavioral problems. 6

paranoid personality disorder A disorder defined by suspiciousness in almost all situations and with almost all people. 11

paranoid schizophrenia A form of schizophrenia characterized by consistent delusions and/or hallucinations, often related to themes of persecution and grandeur. 14

paranoid-nonparanoid dimension The classification of schizophrenics according to the presence (paranoid) or absence (nonparanoid) of delusions of persecution and/or grandeur. 14

paraphilias Sexual patterns—such as fetishism and transvestism—that deviate from the standard of normal sexuality as consisting of a nondestructive interplay between consenting adults. 13

parasympathetic division The division of the autonomic nervous system that decreases physical arousal and is usually dominant under less emotional conditions. It regulates breathing, heart rate, blood pressure, stomach and intestinal activity, and elimination. *Cf.* **sympathetic division.** 6

parietal lobe Middle division of each cerebral hemisphere; involved in sensation, perception, and integrating sensory input. 6

Parkinson's disease An organic brain disorder involving damage to the basal ganglia. Symptoms include tremors, a masklike countenance, a stiff gait, and psychological disturbances such as a general mental deficit and social withdrawal. 15

partial seizures Epileptic seizures that originate in one part of the brain rather than in the brain as a whole. May be either **simple** or **complex.** *Cf.* **generalized seizures.** 15

passive avoidance learning Learning to stop making certain behavioral responses to stimuli when those responses will result in punishment. 11

PCP (phencyclidine) Also called "angel dust," a hallucinogen widely used in the 1970s that poses the risk for users of harming themselves through burns, falls, or accidents, or harming others as a result of perceptual distortions and paranoia. 12

pedophilia Child molesting—that is, sexual gratification, on the part of an adult, through sexual contact with children. 13

penetrating head injury Potentially, the most serious form of brain trauma, in which a foreign object, such as a bullet or piece of metal, enters the skull and directly ruptures and destroys brain tissue. 15

peripheral nervous system The network of nerve fibers that leads from the central nervous system to all parts of the body and carries out the commands of the CNS. It has two branches: the somatic nervous system and the autonomic nervous system. 6

person variables A person's stable traits. Adherents of the psychometric approach hold that personality issues mainly from person variables. 2

personality disorder An enduring pattern of inner experience and behavior that deviates markedly from the expectations of the individual's culture, that is pervasive and inflexible, that has an onset in adolescence or early adulthood, that is stable over time, and that leads to distress or impairment. 11

phallic stage In psychodynamic theory, the third stage of psychosocial development, in which pleasure is derived from masturbation, the stroking and handling of the genitals; occurs from the third to the fifth or sixth year of life. 5

phenomenological approach Therapy method in which the therapist tries to see the world through clients' own perceptions and subjective experience. 5

phenothiazines A group of antipsychotic drugs that relieve symptoms such as confusion, withdrawal, hallucinations, and delusions. 14

phenotype The unique combination of observable characteristics that results from the combination of a person's genotype with the environment. 6

phenylketonuria (PKU) A genetic defect caused by a deficiency in a liver enzyme, phenylalanine 4-hydroxylase, which results in severe retardation, hyperactivity, and erratic behavior. 17

phobia An intense and persistent fear of an object or a situation that poses no real threat. 7

placebo An inert substance used in research, which may manifest some effects of the drug it has been substituted for. 3

play therapy A psychodynamic technique in which the therapist provides young patients with drawing materials and toys, rather than asking them questions, on the assumption that whatever is troubling them will be expressed in their drawings and games. 16

polygenic Refers to traits that are the products of the interaction of many genes. 6

polygraph A recording device equipped with sensors, which, when attached to the body, can pick up subtle physiological changes in the form of electrical impulses. The changes are recorded on a moving roll of paper. 2

positive-negative symptoms dimension A dimension describing a schizophrenic patient's symptoms. *Cf.* **negative symptoms; positive symptoms.** 14

positive psychology Movement that focuses on helping people to live more fulfilling lives; sees psychology as a study of strength and virtue, not just disease, weakness, and damage. 5

positive regard Affection and approval. 5

positive reinforcement A situation in which a response is followed by a positive event or stimulus, thereby increasing the probability that the response will be repeated. 4

positive symptoms In schizophrenia, the presence of something that is normally absent, including hallucinations, delusions, bizarre behavior, and incoherent thought patterns. 14

positron emission tomography (PET) A means of examining the brain. The patient is injected with a radioactively labeled sugar solution, and the path of the radioactive particles through the brain is traced. 6

postsynaptic receptors Special proteins on the surface of neurons that bind with neurotransmitters squirted into the synapse from the dendrites of adjoining neurons. Molecules in the neurotransmitter fit into the receptor like a key into a lock. 6

posttraumatic stress disorder A severe psychological reaction to intensely traumatic events, including assault, rape, natural disasters, and wartime combat. Victims may reexperience the traumatic event in recollections or in nightmares, show diminished responsiveness to their present surroundings, and suffer physical symptoms and intense irritability. Generally appearing shortly after the trauma, the symptoms usually disappear within six months, but some may last for years. 6

poverty of content A characteristic of schizophrenic speech in which words are used correctly but communication is poor. 14

prediction (1) The second objective of the scientific method: the ability to predict the relationship between events. (2) The second goal of psychological assessment: the development of hypotheses about future behavior, treatment, and statistical likelihoods. 3
predictive validity The degree to which a test's findings are consistent with the subject's future performance. 2
prefrontal lobotomy A psychosurgical procedure for severely disturbed patients in which some of the connections between the frontal lobe and the lower parts of the brain are severed; very rarely performed today. 1
premature ejaculation A sexual disorder in which the rapidity of ejaculation interferes with the couple's enjoyment. 13
prevalence The percentage of a population that has a particular disorder at a particular time. 3
prevention The process of keeping psychological disorders from beginning in the first place by changing the environment, the family, or the individual. 1
primary brain tumors Tumors that originate either within the brain or outside the brain but inside the skull. 15
primary gain In conversion disorder, the relief from anxiety that is experienced by the person as a result of the conversion symptom, which blocks the person's awareness of internal conflict. 8
primary prevention The first level of prevention of psychological disorder, the goal of which is to prevent disorders from developing. 1
primary reinforcer A stimulus or need that one responds to instinctively, without learning. 4
procedural memory Memory for skills. 8
process-reactive dimension The classification of people with schizophrenia according to whether the onset of symptoms is gradual (process) or abrupt and precipitated by a traumatic event (reactive). 14
prodromal phase The initial stage of schizophrenia, during which the person generally becomes withdrawn and socially isolated. 14
projective personality tests Assessment techniques used to draw out, indirectly, individuals' true conflicts and motives by presenting them with ambiguous stimuli and allowing them to project their private selves into their responses. 2
prospective studies Longitudinal studies in which the hypothesized predictors or causes of a phenomenon are measured or manipulated prior to the onset of the phenomenon. 3
psychiatric social worker Someone who has earned an M.S.W. (master of social work), with special courses and training in psychological counseling. 1
psychiatrist An M.D. who specializes in diagnosing and treating mental disorders. Because of their medical degree, psychiatrists can also prescribe psychoactive drugs. 1
psychoactive drug A drug that alters one's psychological state. 12
psychoanalysis The psychodynamic therapy method that relies heavily on the techniques of free association, dream interpretation, and analysis of resistance and transference. The aim is to give patients insight into their unconscious conflicts, impulses, and motives. 1, 5
psychoanalyst Someone who has had postgraduate training at a psychoanalytic institute and has undergone psychoanalysis him- or herself. (Most psychoanalysts are psychiatrists, but other mental health professionals may undertake this training.) 1
psychodynamic perspective A school of thought united by a common concern with the dynamics, or interaction, of forces lying deep within the mind. Almost all psychodynamic theorists agree on three basic principles: Much human behavior is determined by intrapsychic forces; such forces generally operate unconsciously; and the form taken by these forces is deeply affected by developmental factors, especially by family relationships. 5
psychogenic theory The theory that psychological disturbance is due primarily not to organic dysfunction but to emotional stress. 1
psychological assessment The collection, organization, and interpretation of information about a person and his or her situation. 2
psychological dependence The nonphysiological dimension of drug abuse, characterized by the abuser's growing tendency to center his or her life on the drug. 12
psychological test An assessment technique in which the subject is presented with a series of stimuli to which he or she is asked to respond. 2
psychometric approach A method of psychological testing that aims at locating and measuring stable underlying traits. 2
psychoneuroimmunology (PNI) The subspecialty of health medicine that studies the interaction between psychological factors and the immune system, mediated by the central nervous system. 9
psychopathology Abnormal psychology. 1
psychopharmacology Study of the drug treatment of psychological disorders. 6
psychoses. *See* **psychosis.**
psychosexual development Freud's theory that personality development takes place in a series of stages, in each of which the child's central motivation is to gratify the drive for pleasure in a different zone of the body. 5
psychosis A condition in which adaptive functioning is drastically curtailed and the person may be out of touch with reality. 5, 13, 14
psychosurgery Surgery aimed at reducing abnormal behavior in the absence of any signs of organic brain pathology. 6
punishment The process in which an organism, in order to avoid (or, less often, obtain) a consequence, stops performing a behavior. 4

radical behaviorism The form of behaviorism developed by B. F. Skinner that proposes that everything a person does, says, or feels constitutes behavior and, even if unobservable, is subject to experimental analysis. 4
random assignment A balancing control technique that involves assigning subjects randomly to the different groups in an experiment. 3
random sample A sample in which every element of a population has an equal likelihood of being included. 3
rape Sexual intercourse with a nonconsenting partner. 13
rational-emotive therapy Albert Ellis' approach to cognitive therapy, which sees emotional disturbances as the result of irrational beliefs that guide people's interpretation of events. Clients are helped to appraise their situations realistically and develop new ways of interpreting experience. 4
reactive In depression, the term used to describe patients whose symptoms are primarily emotional and cognitive. 10
reattribution training A strategy used in cognitive therapy whereby the client is helped to change distorted ideas of cause and effect and to attribute

events to their causes in a realistic manner. 4

reinforcement The process by which behavior is increased or maintained by rewarding consequences. Operant conditioning depends on reinforcement: Most people would not go to work if it weren't for the paycheck. 4

relapse prevention In alcohol rehabilitation, an approach aimed at reducing the likelihood of "slipping" and preventing an escalation of usage if "slips" do occur; in the treatment of rapists, an approach that trains rapists how to avoid situations that place them at risk for repeating the crime and how to resist the impulse to commit the offense. 12

relaxation training A technique that behaviorists have used in stress-relief programs in which the subject alternately tenses, then relaxes, groups of muscles. The goal is to teach the patient to distinguish between tension and relaxation and ultimately achieve the latter. 9

reliability (1) In the scientific method, the degree to which a description remains stable over time and under different testing conditions. (2) The degree to which a measurement device yields consistent results under varying conditions. 2

replicate To repeat aspects of a research study with some changes in certain variables in order to show whether a previous study's results are found under similar circumstances. 3

representativeness The degree to which a research sample's characteristics match those of the population under study. 3

repression A defense mechanism in which unacceptable id impulses are pushed down into the unconscious, thereby rendered unable to disturb the person consciously. 5

residual phase The third phase of schizophrenia, during which behavior is similar to that seen during the prodromal phase. 14

respondent conditioning The process of learning a conditioned response. Also called *classical conditioning.* 4

response sets Test-taking attitudes that lead subjects to distort their responses, often unconsciously. 2

retarded depression A type of depression in which there is little spontaneous motor activity. Movement is slow and deliberate, with a minimum number of gestures and little verbalization. 10

Rorschach Psychodiagnostic Inkblot Test The most well-known projective personality test, in which subjects are asked to interpret 10 cards, each showing a symmetrical inkblot design. 2

sadism Sexual gratification through infliction of pain and/or humiliation on others. 13

sadomasochistic The term applied to sexual partners in which either a sadist and a masochist pair up to satisfy their complementary needs, or both partners enjoy both sadism and masochism and switch between the two. 13

savant syndrome A disorder in which a person with greatly diminished mental skill shows extraordinary proficiency in one, isolated skill. 17

schema An organized structure of information about a particular domain in life; it is stored in the mind and helps a person to organize and process newly learned information. 4

schizoaffective disorder Diagnosis made when an individual has a manic or major depressive episode while at the same time exhibiting the symptoms of schizophrenia. 14

schizoid personality disorder A disorder marked by social withdrawal and isolation. 11

schizophrenia A group of psychoses marked by severe distortion of thought, perception, and mood; by bizarre behavior; and by social withdrawal. 14

schizotypal personality disorder A disorder marked by odd speech, behavior, thinking, and/or perception. 11

seasonal affective disorder (SAD) A mood disorder characterized by depression that occurs only during the winter. 10

secondary gain In conversion disorder, the "benefit," of being excused from responsibilities and of attracting sympathy and attention, which accrue to the person as a result of the conversion symptom. 8

secondary prevention The second level of prevention of psychological disorder, the goal of which is to detect and treat disorders at an early stage, so that minor disorders do not develop into major ones. 1

selective attention An adaptive mechanism by which human beings take in and process only some of the information bombarding their senses at any given moment. 4

selective serotonin reuptake inhibitors (SSRIs) A class of antidepressants that work by blocking the reuptake of the neurotransmitter serotonin. 6, 10

self-actualization The process of exploring and fulfilling one's potential—not only by staying alive but also by testing and fulfilling their vision of their highest capabilities. 5

self-instructional training A cognitive therapy technique that teaches people to control their behavior by controlling what they say to themselves before, during, and after their actions. 16

self-report personality inventories Psychological tests which, unlike projective tests such as the Rorschach and TAT, ask the subjects direct questions about themselves. 2

semantic memory General knowledge. 8

separation anxiety disorder A childhood disorder characterized by intense fear and distress upon being separated from parents or other caretakers. 16

sexual aversion disorder Active avoidance of sex as a result of feelings of disgust or fear about it. 13

sexual dysfunctions Disorders involving either a disruption of the sexual response cycle or pain during intercourse. 13

sheltered workshops Special work centers designed to meet the needs of mentally retarded people employed in them. 17

simple partial seizure A partial epileptic seizure in which cognitive functioning remains intact. 15

single-case experiment A research design that focuses on behavior change in one person but, unlike the *case study,* methodically varies the conditions surrounding the person's behavior and monitors the behavior under the changing conditions. 3

single photon emission computed tomography (SPECT) Technique of brain imaging used to measure blood flow and glucose metabolism in the brain. 6

situational dysfunction A sexual dysfunction that occurs only in certain situations or with certain partners. 13

situational variables The environmental stimuli that precede and follow any given action by a person. 2

sleep terrors Sleep disorder with harrowing dreams arising out of slow-wave sleep, in which a child shows intense psychological arousal but then has no memory of the event. 16

sleepwalking A dissociative disorder in which the person walks and performs some complex action while asleep. It is much more common in children than in adults. Also called *somnambulism.* 6

social phobia A phobic disorder in which the person's anxiety is aroused by one or more social situations and is related to the person's fear of being humiliated or criticized. In childhood, this disorder typically takes the form of a paralyzing fear of strangers—peers as well as adults. 6, 16

social-skills training A behavioral therapy that teaches depressed or schizophrenic people basic techniques for engaging in satisfying interactions with others. 10, 14

sociocultural perspective The theory that abnormal behavior is the product of broad social forces and conditions such as poverty, urbanization, and inequality. 4

Socratic questioning Technique by which the cognitive therapist asks a series of questions designed to get the client to look more objectively at the truth of thoughts, assumptions, and beliefs, and to think about whether they are adaptive. 4

somatic nervous system The part of the peripheral nervous system that senses and acts on the external world, relaying to the brain information picked up by the sense organs and transmitting the brain's messages to the skeletal muscles, which move the body. 6

somatization disorder A syndrome characterized by numerous and recurrent physical complaints, persisting for several years, for which no medical basis can be found. 8

somatoform disorders Conditions in which psychological conflicts take on a somatic or physical form. These disorders include hypochondriasis, somatization disorder, and conversion disorder. 8

source-monitoring deficit theory Theory that proposes that patients with dissociative identity disorder do not retrieve a sufficient number or a proper configuration of features that would allow them to identify past experiences as memories. 8

specific phobia A phobic disorder with a particular stimulus, such as heights, enclosed places, injury, or a certain type of animal. 6

spectator role A sexual dysfunction in which a person is constantly watching and judging his or her sexual performance and is not able to relax and experience pleasure. This worry often causes the much-feared failure, because the tension blunts response to sexual stimuli. 13

standard of proof In commitment hearings, the degree of certainty required in order to commit someone to a mental institution. There must be "clear and convincing evidence" that the person is mentally ill and dangerous. 18

state-dependent memory Phenomenon where knowledge obtained in a certain state (e.g., under the influence of drugs) may not be retained when the person is no longer in that state. 8

statistical inference A technique used by researchers to try to determine whether differences between experimental groups are due to the independent variable. It begins by assuming the *null hypothesis* and then using probability theory to determine the likelihood of having obtained the experimental results if the independent variable had had no effect. If the likelihood is small, the result is judged to be statistically significant, and the independent variable is assumed to have had an effect. 3

stereotypy The act of engaging in purposeless behaviors repetitively for hours, sometimes manifested by schizophrenics. 14

stigma A label identified with a certain characteristic, usually negative—such as the stigma of being mentally ill. 4

stimulants A class of drugs that provides energy, alertness, and feelings of confidence. 12

stimulus equivalence The learning of stimulus response connections without direct learning or mere physical similarities between stimuli. People can transfer stimulus-response connections learned for a set of pictures of animals to a new set of stimuli, such as words that symbolically represent the same stimuli (e.g., the words *dog* and *horse*). 4

stimulus specificity The principle that different kinds of stress produce different kinds of physiological response. 8

stress Variously defined as environmental stimulus of the body, as the body's response to the demands of the environment, and as the interaction between an environmental stimulus and the body's appraisal of it. 9

stroke *See* **cerebrovascular accident (CVA).**

structural hypothesis Freud's belief that the mind can be divided into three broad forces: the id, the ego, and the superego. 5

stuttering The interruption of fluent speech through blocked, prolonged, or repeated words, syllables, or sounds. 16

substance abuse A pattern of maladaptive drug use that has not progressed to full-blown dependence. It is determined by the appearance of any one of the following symptoms: recurrent drug-related failure to fulfill major role obligations (e.g., absenteeism from school or work, neglect of children); recurrent drug use in physically dangerous situations (e.g., drunk driving); drug-related legal problems; and continued drug use despite social or interpersonal problems caused by the effects of the drug. *Cf.* **substance dependence.** 12

substance dependence The diagnostic category to which a drug user is assigned who fulfills any three of these seven criteria: preoccupation with the drug; unintentional overuse; tolerance; withdrawal; persistent desire or efforts to control drug use; the abandonment of important social, occupational, or recreational activities for the sake of drug use; and continued drug use despite serious drug-related problems. *Cf.* **substance abuse.** 12

superego According to Freud, the part of the mind that represents the moral standards of the society and parents, as internalized by the child. 5

sympathetic division The division of the autonomic nervous system which becomes dominant in times of stress and which heightens the body's arousal, causing blood pressure, heart rate, perspiration, and adrenaline to increase, pupils to dilate, and salivation and digestive functions to diminish. *Cf.* **parasympathetic division.** 6

symptomatic epilepsy The label applied to convulsions that are a function of brain damage caused by pathologies such as neurosyphilis, alcohol or drug intoxication, tumors, encephalitis, trauma, or strokes. 15

synapse The gap between two neurons across which nerve impulses pass. 6

syndrome The distinct cluster of symptoms that tends to occur in a particular disease. 1

synergistic effect The combined impact of two drugs, which is greater than the effect of either drug when taken alone. 12

systematic desensitization A behavior therapy technique in which the patient, while in a relaxed state, imagines his or her anxiety-provoking stimuli or is presented with the actual stimuli. Progressing from the least to the most feared situations, the patient learns to remain relaxed—a response that should carry over to real-life situations. 4, 6

tardive dyskinesia A muscle disorder that causes uncontrollable grimacing and lip smacking; caused by antipsychotic drugs. 14

Tay-Sachs disease A genetic disorder of lipid metabolism marked by the absence of the enzyme hexosominidase A in brain tissues; causes mental retardation, muscular deterioration, convulsions, and death before the age of six. 17

temporal lobe Large lobe of each cerebral hemisphere that is located in front of the occipital lobe and contains the sensory center associated with hearing. Also involved in organization of sensory input. 6

test-retest reliability A criterion for judging the reliability of a psychological test: The test should yield the same results when administered to the same person at different times. 2

Thematic Apperception Test (TAT) A frequently used projective personality test in which the subject is presented with a series of pictures showing one, two, or three people doing something. The scenes are ambiguous enough to allow for a variety of interpretations, yet they nudge the subject in the direction of certain kinds of associations, unlike the Rorschach test. For example, a picture of a man in a business suit might tap a subject's feelings about his or her father. 2

theory of mind The ability, lacking in autistic children, to appreciate the existence of purely mental states, such as beliefs or desires, and to predict or understand behavior based on such states. 17

third-variable problem In scientific research, an alternative factor, not considered by the researchers, that may be causing the covariation of the two factors being investigated. 3

three-term contingency A description including a discriminating stimulus, a response, and the consequence of the response. 4

thrombosis The obstruction of a blood vessel by a buildup of fatty material coating the inside of the vessel, thus blocking the flow of blood; a common cause of infarction. 15

time-order relationship The second condition to be met before causality can be demonstrated: the presumed cause must occur before the presumed effect. 3

token economy A behavior modification procedure, based on operant-conditioning principles, in which patients are given a conditioned reinforcer such as tokens for performing target behaviors. The patients can exchange the tokens for backup reinforcers such as snacks or special privileges. 14

tolerance The physiological condition in which the usual dosage of a drug no longer produces the desired effect. 12

tonic-clonic seizures Generalized epileptic seizures that typically begin with a tonic, or rigid, extension of the arms and legs, followed by a clonic, or jerking, movement throughout the body. 15

traits Stable underlying characteristics that presumably exist in differing degrees in everyone. 2

tranquilizers A group of drugs that produce mild calm and relaxation. They can be addictive and have side effects. 12

transsexual *See* **gender identity disorders (GID).**

transvestism Sexual gratification through dressing in the clothes of the opposite sex. 13

traumatic brain injury Injury to brain tissue as a result of jarring, bruising, or cutting. 15

tricyclics A class of drugs widely used to treat depression, which generally works by blocking the reuptake of the neurotransmitter norepinephrine by the presynaptic neuron. 6, 10

trisomy 21 A condition in which there is an extra chromosome in pair 21 in the human cell; the genetic basis of Down syndrome. 17

Type A A personality characterized by pressure to achieve, impatience, high standards of self-evaluation, and hostility. 9

Type I schizophrenia A dimension of schizophrenia characterized by positive symptoms. 14

Type II schizophrenia A dimension of schizophrenia characterized by negative symptoms. 14

unconditioned response A natural, unlearned response to a stimulus. 4

unconditioned stimulus A stimulus that elicits a natural, or unconditioned, response. 4

unconscious In Freudian theory, the level of consciousness that contains all memories not readily available to the perceptual conscious, because they have been either forgotten or repressed. 5

understanding The identification of the cause or causes of a phenomenon. 3

up-regulation Process where postsynaptic receptors increase in number or become more sensitive when presynaptic neurons are not releasing enough neurotransmitter to carry the impulse. 6

vaginismus A sexual dysfunction in which the muscles surrounding the entrance to the vagina undergo involuntary spasmodic contractions, making intercourse either impossible or painfully difficult. 13

validity The degree to which a description or test measures what it is supposed to measure. 2

valuing process Part of process of self-actualization whereby experiences perceived as enhancing to oneself are valued as good and sought after whereas experiences perceived as not enhancing are valued as bad and are avoided. 5

vascular dementia The impairment of many of the brain's faculties as the cumulative result of many infarctions. 15

voyeurism Sexual gratification through clandestine observation of other people's sexual activities or sexual anatomy. 13

vulnerability-stress models Models that identify which persons might be vulnerable to developing clinical disorders (individuals with a particular cognitive style), when (after a stress), and even which disorders they are vulnerable to (depression, eating disorder, etc.). 4

withdrawal Temporary psychological and physiological disturbances resulting from the body's attempt to readjust to the absence of a drug. 6, 12

word salad A schizophrenic speech pattern in which words and phrases are combined in a disorganized fashion, seemingly devoid of logic, meaning, and even associational links. 14

REFERENCES

Abbey, A., Zawacki, T., Buck, P. O., Clinton, A. M., & McAuslan, P. (2001). Alcohol and sexual assault. *Alcohol Health and Research World, 25,* 43–51.

Abed, R. T., Vaidya, G., & Baker, I. (2000). Suicide in schizophrenia: A fourteen-year survey in an English health district. *International Journal of Psychiatry in Clinical Practice, 4,* 143–146.

Abel, G. G., Becker, J. V., Cunningham-Rathner, J., Mittelman, M., et al. (1988). Multiple paraphilic diagnoses among sex offenders. *Bulletin of the American Academy of Psychiatry and the Law, 16,* 153–168.

Abel, G. G., Gore, D. K., Holland, C. L., Camp, N., Becker, J. V., & Rathner, J. (1989). The measurement of cognitive distortions in child molesters. *Annals of Sex Research, 2,* 135–153.

Abel, G. G. & Harlow, N. (2001). *The Stop Child Molestation Book: What ordinary people can do in their everyday lives to save 3 million children.* Xlibris/Random House.

Abel, G. G., Lawry, A. S., Karlstrom, K., Osborn, C. A., & Gillespie, C. F. (1994). Screening tests for pedophilia. *Criminal Justice and Behavior, 21,* 115–131.

Abel, G. G., Osborn, C., Anthony, D., & Gardos, P. (1992). Current treatment of paraphilias. In J. Bancroft, C. Davis, & H. Ruppel (Eds.), *Annual Review of Sex Research,* 255–290.

Abel, G. G., Rouleau, J., & Cunningham-Rathner, J. (1984). Sexually aggressive behavior. In W. Curran, A. L. McGarry, & S. A. Shah (Eds.), *Modern legal psychiatry and psychology.* Philadelphia: Davis.

Abel-Aty, M. A. & Abdelwahab, H. T. (2000). Exploring the relationship between alcohol and the driver characteristics in motor vehicle accidents. *Accident Analysis and Prevention, 32,* 473–482.

Abelson, J. L., Curtis, G. C., & Cameron, O. G. (1996). Hypothalamic-pituitary-adrenal axis activity in panic disorder: Effects of alprazolam on 24 h secretion of adrenocorticotropin and cortisol. *Journal of Psychiatric Research, 30,* 79–93.

Abikoff, H. (1985). Efficacy of cognitive training interventions in hyperactive children: A critical review. Special Issue: Attention deficit disorder: Issues in assessment and intervention. *Clinical Psychology Review, 5,* 479–512.

About SMART Recovery. (2003). Retrieved July 9, 2003, from www.smartrecovery.com/about.html.

Abraham, H. D. (1983). Visual phenomenology of the LSD flashback. *Archives of General Psychiatry, 40,* 518–520.

Abraham, H. D. & Wolf, E. (1988). Visual function in past users of LSD: Psychophysical findings. *Journal of Abnormal Psychology, 97,* 443–447.

Abraham, K. (1948a). The first pregenital stage of the libido. In *Selected papers of Karl Abraham, M.D.* (D. Bryan & A. Strachey, Trans.). London: Hogarth Press. Original work published 1916.

Abraham, K. (1948b). Notes on psychoanalytic investigation and treatment of manic-depressive insanity and applied conditions. In *Selected papers of Karl Abraham, M.D.* (D. Bryan & A. Strachey, Trans.). London: Hogarth Press. Original work published 1911.

Abramowitz, J. S. (1996). Effectiveness of psychological and pharmacological treatments for obsessive-compulsive disorder: A quantitative review. *Journal of Consulting and Clinical Psychology, 65,* 44–52.

Abramowitz, S. I. (1986). Psychosocial outcomes of sex reassignment surgery. *Journal of Consulting and Clinical Psychology, 54,* 183–189.

Abramson, L. Y. & Alloy, L. B. (2002). *BAS and bipolar spectrum: Biopsychosocial integration.* National Institute of Mental Health grant proposal.

Abramson, L. Y., Alloy, L. B., Hankin, B. L., Haeffel, G. J., MacCoon, D. G., & Gibb, B. E. (2002). Cognitive-vulnerability stress models of depression in a self-regulatory and psychobiological context. In I. H. Gotlib & C. L. Hammen (Eds.), *Handbook of depression* (3rd ed., pp. 268–294). New York: Guilford Press.

Abramson, L. Y., Alloy, L. B., Hogan, M. E., Whitehouse, W. G., Cornette, M., Akhavan, S., & Chiara, A. (1998). Suicidality and cognitive vulnerability to depression among college students: A prospective study. *Journal of Adolescence, 21,* 473–487.

Abramson, L. Y., Alloy, L. B., Hogan, M. E., Whitehouse, W. G., Gibb, B. E., Hankin, B. L., & Cornette, M. M. (2000). The hopelessness theory of suicidality. In T. E. Joiner & M. D. Rudd (Eds.), *Suicide science: Expanding boundaries* (pp. 17–32). Boston: Kluwer Academic.

Abramson, L. Y., Alloy, L. B., & Metalsky, G. I. (1995). Hopelessness depression. In G. Buchanan & M. E. P. Seligman (Eds.), *Explanatory style.* Hillsdale, NJ: Erlbaum.

Abramson, L. Y., Metalsky, G. I., & Alloy, L. B. (1989). Hopelessness depression: A theory-based subtype of depression. *Psychological Review, 96,* 358–372.

Achenbach, T. M. (1991). *Manual for the Child Behavior Checklist/4-18 and 1991 profile.* Burlington, VT: University of Vermont Department of Psychiatry.

Achenbach, T. M. & McConaughy, S. H. (1996). Relations between *DSM-IV* and empirically based assessment. *School Psychology Review, 25,* 329–341.

Ackard, D. M. & Neumark-Sztainer, D. (2002). Date violence and date rape among adolescents: Associations with disordered eating behaviors and psychological health. *Child Abuse & Neglect, 26,* 455–473.

Ackenheil, M. (2001). Neurotransmitters and signal transduction processes in bipolar affective disorders: A synopsis. *Journal of Affective Disorders, 62,* 101–111.

Addington v. Texas, 99 S.Ct. 1804 (1979).

Adler, N. E., Boyce, T., Chesney, M. A., Folkman, S., & Syme, L. (1993). Socioeconomic inequalities in health: No easy solution. *Journal of the American Medical Association, 269,* 3140–3145.

Adler, R. H., Zamboni, P., Hofer, T., Hemmeler, W., Hurny, C., Minder, C., Radvila, A., & Zlot, S. I. (1997). How not to miss a somatic needle in the haystack of chronic pain. *Journal of Psychosomatic Research, 42,* 499–506.

Agency for Health Care Policy and Research. (1993). *Depression in primary care: Treatment of major depression.* Rockville, MD: Author. (DHHS, AHCPR Publication No. 93–0551).

Aggleton, J. P. & Young, A. W. (2000). The enigma of the amygdala: On its contribution to human emotion. In R. D. Lane & L. Nadel (Eds.), *Cognitive neuroscience of emotion* (pp. 106–128). New York: Oxford University Press.

Agnello, J. G. (1975). Voice onset and voice termination features of stutters. In L. M. Webster & L. C. Furst (Eds.), *Vocal tract dynamics and dysfluency.* New York: Speech and Hearing Institute.

Ainsworth, M. D. S. (1967). *Infancy in Uganda: Infant care and the growth of love.* Baltimore: Johns Hopkins University Press.

Ainsworth, M. D. S. (1982). Attachment: Retrospect and prospect. In C. M. Parkes & J. Stevenson-Hinde (Eds.), *The place of attachment in human behavior* (pp. 3–30). New York: Basic Books.

Ainsworth, M. D. S. & Bowlby, J. (1991). An ethological approach to personality development. *American Psychologist, 46,* 331–341.

Ainsworth, M. D. S. & Wittig, B. A. (1969). Attachment and the exploratory behavior of one-year-olds in a strange situation. In B. M. Foss (Ed.), *Determinants of infant behavior* (Vol. 4, pp. 113–136). London: Methuen.

Akbarian S., Kim, J. J., Potkin, S. G., Hetrick, W. P., Bunney, W. E., Jr., & Jones, E. G. (1996). Maldistribution of interstitial neurons in prefrontal white matter of the brains of schizophrenic patients. *Archives of General Psychiatry, 53,* 425–436.

Akiskal, H. S. & Casano, G. B. (Eds.). (1997). *Dysthymia and the spectrum of chronic depressions.* New York: Guilford Press.

Akiskal, H. S., Judd, L. L., Lemmi, H., & Gillin, J. C. (1997). Subthreshold depressions: Clinical and sleep EEG, validation of dysthymic, residual and masked forms. *Journal of Affective Disorders, 45,* 53–63.

Alarcon, R. D. (1995). Culture and psychiatric diagnosis: Impact on *DSM-IV* and *ICD-10. Psychiatric Clinics of North America, 18,* 449–465.

Albee, G. (1959). *Mental health manpower trend.* New York: Basic Books.

Albers, G. W. (1997). Rationale for early intervention in acute stroke. *American Journal of Cardiology, 80,* 4D–10D.

Aldrich, M. S. (1989). Cardinal manifestations of sleep disorders. In M. H. Kryger, T. Roth, & W. C. Dement (Eds.), *Principles and practice of sleep medicine* (pp. 351–357). Philadelphia: Saunders.

Alessandri, S. (1991). Play and social behavior in maltreated preschoolers. *Development and Psychopathology, 3,* 191–205.

Alexander, B. K. & Hadaway, P. F. (1982). Opiate addiction: The case for an adaptive orientation. *Psychological Bulletin, 92,* 367–381.

Alford, B. A. & Beck, A. T. (1997). *The integrative power of cognitive therapy.* New York: Guilford Press.

Allderidge, P. (1979). Hospitals, madhouses and asylums: Cycles in the care of the insane. *British Journal of Psychiatry, 134,* 321–334.

Allderidge, P. (1985). Bedlam: Fact or fantasy? In W. F. Bynum, R. Porter, & M. Shepherd (Eds.), *The anatomy of madness: Essays in the history of psychiatry* (Vol. 2). New York: Tavistock.

Allen, J. J. B. & Iacono, W. G. (2001). Assessing the validity of amnesia in dissociative identity disorders: A dilemma for the *DSM* and the courts. *Psychology, Public Policy, and Law, 7,* 311–344.

Allen, J. J., Chapman, L. J., Chapman, J., Vuchetich, J. P., & Frost, L. A. (1987). Prediction of psychoticlike symptoms in hypothetically psychosis-prone college students. *Journal of Abnormal Psychology, 96,* 83–88.

Allen, J. P., Hauser, S. T., & Borman-Spurrell, E. (1996). Attachment theory as a framework for understanding sequelae of severe adolescent psychopathology: An 11-year follow-up study. *Journal of Consulting and Clinical Psychology, 64,* 254–263.

Allen, M. G. (1976). Twin studies of affective illness. *Archives of General Psychiatry, 33,* 1476–1478.

Allen, M. & Smith, V. (2001). Opening Pandora's box: The practical and legal dangers of involuntary outpatient commitment. *Psychiatric Services, 52,* 342–346.

Alloy, L. B. & Abramson, L. Y. (1979). The judgment of contingency in depressed and nondepressed students: Sadder but wiser? *Journal of Experimental Psychology: General, 108,* 441–485.

Alloy, L. B. & Abramson, L. Y. (1988). Depressive realism: Four theoretical perspectives. In L. B. Alloy (Ed.), *Cognitive processes in depression* (pp. 223–265). New York: Guilford Press.

Alloy, L. B. & Abramson, L. Y. (1999). The Temple-Wisconsin Cognitive Vulnerability to Depression Project: Conceptual background, design, and methods. *Journal of Cognitive Psychotherapy: An International Quarterly, 13,* 227–262.

Alloy, L. B. & Abramson, L. Y. (2000). Cyclothymic personality. In W. E. Craighead & C. B. Nemeroff (Eds.), *The Corsini encyclopedia of psychology and behavioral science.* (3rd ed., Vol. 1, pp. 417–418). New York: Wiley.

Alloy, L. B. & Clements, C. M. (1992). Illusion of control: Invulnerability to negative affect and depressive symptoms after laboratory and natural stressors. *Journal of Abnormal Psychology, 101,* 234–245.

Alloy, L. B. & Clements, C. M. (1998). Hopelessness theory of depression: Tests of the symptom component. *Cognitive Therapy and Research, 22*(4), 303–335.

Alloy, L. B. & Riskind, J. H. (Eds.). (in press). *Cognitive vulnerability to emotional disorders.* Mahwah, NJ: Erlbaum.

Alloy, L. B., Abramson, L. Y., Hogan, M. E., Whitehouse, W. G., Rose, D. T., Robinson, M. S., Kim, R. S., & Lapkin, J. B. (2000). The Temple-Wisconsin Cognitive Vulnerability to Depression project: Lifetime history of Axis I psychopathology in individuals at high and low cognitive risk for depression. Conceptual background, design, and methods. *Journal of Abnormal Psychology, 109,* 403–418.

Alloy, L. B., Abramson, L. Y., Murray, L. A., Whitehouse, W. G., & Hogan, M. E. (1997). Self-referent information-processing in individuals at high and low cognitive risk for depression. *Cognition and Emotion, 11,* 539–568.

Alloy, L. B., Abramson, L. Y., Raniere, D., & Dyller, I. (1999). Research methods in adult psychopathology. In P. C. Kendall, J. N. Butcher, & G. N. Holmbeck (Eds.), *Handbook of research methods in clinical psychology* (2nd ed.). New York: Wiley.

Alloy, L. B., Abramson, L. Y., Safford, S. M., & Gibb, B. E. (in press). The cognitive vulnerability to depression (CVD) project: Current findings and future directions. In L. B. Alloy & J. H. Riskind, *Cognitive vulnerability to emotional disorders.* Mahwah, NJ: Erlbaum.

Alloy, L. B., Abramson, L. Y., Tashman, N. A., Berrebbi, D. S., Hogan, M. E., Whitehouse, W. G., Crossfield, A. G., & Morocco, A. (2001). Developmental origins of cognitive vulnerability to depression: Parenting, cognitive, and inferential feedback styles of the parents of individuals at high and low cognitive risk for depression. *Cognitive Therapy and Research, 25,* 397–424.

Alloy, L. B., Abramson, L. Y., Whitehouse, W. G., Hogan, M. E., Panzarella, C., & Rose, D. T. (2003). *Prospective incidence of first onsets and recurrences of depression in individuals at high and low cognitive risk for depression.* Manuscript under editorial review.

Alloy, L. B., Abramson, L. Y., Whitehouse, W. G., Hogan, M. E., Tashman, N. A., Steinberg, D. L., Rose, D. T., & Donovan, P. (1999). Depressogenic cognitive styles: Predictive validity, information processing and personality characteristics, and developmental origins. *Behaviour Research and Therapy, 37,* 503–531.

Alloy, L. B., Just, N., & Panzarella, C. (1997). Attributional style, daily life events, and hopelessness depression: Subtype validation by prospective variability and specificity of symptoms. *Cognitive Therapy and Research, 21,* 321–344.

Alloy, L. B., Kelly, K. A., Mineka, S., & Clements, C. M. (1990). Comorbidity of anxiety and depressive disorders: A helplessness-hopelessness perspective. In J. D. Maser & R. C. R. Cloninger (Eds.), *Comorbidity of mood and anxiety disorders* (pp. 499–543). Washington, DC: American Psychiatric Press.

Alloy, L. B., Lipman, A. J., & Abramson, L. Y. (1992). Attributional style as a vulnerability factor for depression: Validation by past history of mood disorders. *Cognitive Therapy and Research, 16,* 391–407.

Alloy, L. B., Reilly-Harrington, N. A., Fresco, D. M., & Flannery-Schroeder, E. (in press). Cognitive styles and life events as vulnerability factors for bipolar spectrum disorders. In L. B. Alloy & J. H. Riskind (Eds.), *Cognitive vulnerability to emotional disorders.* Mahwah, NJ: Erlbaum.

Alloy, L. B., Reilly-Harrington, N. A., Fresco, D. M., Whitehouse, W. G., & Zechmeister, J. S. (1999). Cognitive styles and life events in subsyndromal unipolar and bipolar disorders: Stability and prospective prediction of depressive and hypomanic mood swings. *Journal of Cognitive Psychotherapy: An International Quarterly, 13,* 21–40.

Alpher, V. S. (1996). Identity and introject in dissociative disorders. *Journal of Consulting and Clinical Psychology, 6,* 1238–1244.

Alterman, A. I., O'Brien, C. P., McLellan, A. T., August, D. S., et al. (1994). Effectiveness and costs of inpatient versus day hospital cocaine rehabilitation. *Journal of Nervous and Mental Disease, 182,* 157–163.

Altshuler, L. I., Bauer, M., Frye, M. A., Gitlin, M. J., Mintz, J., Szuba, M. P., Leight, K. I., & Whybrow, P. C. (2001). Does thyroid supplementation accelerate tricyclic antidepressant response? A review and meta-analysis of the literature. *American Journal of Psychiatry, 158,* 1617–1622.

Amador, X. F., Friedman, J. H., Kasapis, C., Yale, S. A., Flaum, M., & Gorman, J. M. (1996). Suicidal behavior in schizophrenia and its relationship to awareness of illness. *American Journal of Psychiatry, 153,* 1185–1188.

Aman, M. G. & Singh, N. N. (1991). Pharmacological intervention. In J. L. Matson & J. A. Mulick (Eds.), *Handbook of mental retardation* (2nd ed.) (pp. 347–372). New York: Pergamon Press.

American Academy of Child and Adolescent Psychiatry. (1998). Practice parameters for the assessment and treatment of children and adolescents with language and learning disorders. *Journal of the American Academy of Child and Adolescent Psychiatry, 37*(Suppl.), 46–62.

American Bar Association. (1989). *Criminal justice mental health standards.* Washington, DC: American Bar Association.

American Cancer Society. (2003). Cancer facts and figures—2003. Retrieved April 17, 2003, from http://www.cancer.org/downloads/STT/CAFF2003PWSecured.pdf.

American Psychiatric Association. (1974, April 9). Membership upholds decision of trustees bid to drop homosexuality from list of mental disorders. *The New York Times,* p. 12.

American Psychiatric Association. (1987). *Diagnostic and statistical manual of mental disorders (DSM-III-R)* (3rd ed. rev.). Washington, DC: Author.

American Psychiatric Association. (1994). *Diagnostic and statistical manual of mental disorders* (4th ed.). Washington, DC: Author.

American Psychiatric Association. (1997). Practice guideline for the treatment of patients with schizophrenia. *Supplement to American Journal of Psychiatry, 154,* 1–63.

American Psychiatric Association. (2000). *Diagnostic and statistical manual of mental disorders (4th ed., Text Revision).* Washington, DC: Author.

American Psychological Association. (1992). Ethical principles of psychologists and code of conduct. *American Psychologist, 47,* 1597–1611.

American Psychological Association. (2002). Ethical principles of psychologists and code of conduct. *American Psychologist, 57,* 1060–1073.

American Psychological Association Ethics Committee. (2002). Report of the Ethics Committee, 2001. *American Psychologist, 57,* 646–653.

American Sleep Disorders Association. (1990). *The international classification of sleep disorders: Diagnostic and coding manual.* Rochester, MN: Diagnostic Classification Steering Committee.

Amir, N., Stafford, J., Freshman, M. S., & Foa, E. B. (1998). Relationship between trauma narratives and trauma pathology. *Journal of Traumatic Stress, 11,* 385–392.

Anders, T. F. & Eiben, L. A. (1997). Pediatric sleep disorders: A review of the past 10 years. *Journal of the American Academy of Child and Adolescent Psychiatry, 36,* 9–20.

Andersen, A. E. (1999). Eating disorders in gay males. *Psychiatric Annals, 29*(4), 206–212.

Andersen, S. M. (1992). Toward a psychodynamically relevant empirical science. *Psychological Inquiry, 3,* 14–21.

Andersen, S. M., Reznik, I., & Manzella, L. M. (1996). Eliciting facial affect, motivation, and expectancies in transference: Significant-other representations in social relations. *Journal of Personality and Social Psychology, 71,* 1108–1129.

Anderson, E. M. & Lambert, M. J. (1995). Short-term dynamically oriented psychotherapy: A review and meta-analysis. *Clinical Psychology Review, 15,* 503–514.

Anderson, N. B. (1989). Racial differences in stress-induced cardiovascular reactivity and hypertension: Current status and substantive issues. *Psychological Bulletin, 105,* 89–105.

Anderson, N. B. & Armstead, C. A. (1995). Toward understanding the association of socioeconomic status and health: A new challenge for the biopsychosocial approach. *Psychosomatic Medicine, 57,* 213–225.

Anderson, V. E. & Hauser, W. A. (1991). Genetics. In M. Dam & L. Gram. (Eds.), *Comprehensive epileptology* (pp. 57–76). New York: Raven Press.

Andreasen, N. C., McDonald-Scott, P., Grove, W. M., Keller, M. B., Shapiro, R. W., & Hirschfeld, R. (1982). Assessment of reliability in multicenter collaborative research with a videotape approach. *American Journal of Psychiatry, 139,* 876–882.

Andreason, N. C. (1999). A unitary model of schizophrenia: Bleuler's "fragmented phrene" as schizencephaly. *Archives of General Psychiatry, 56,* 781–787.

Andrews, B., Brewin, C. R., Rose, S., & Kirk, M. (2000). Predicting PTSD symptoms in victims of violent crime: The role of shame, anger, and childhood abuse. *Journal of Abnormal Psychology, 109,* 69–73.

Andrews, G., Morris-Yates, A., Howie, P., & Martin, N. G. (1991). Genetic factors in stuttering confirmed. *Archives of General Psychiatry, 48,* 1034–1035.

Aneshensel, C. S., Phelan, J. C., et al., (Eds.). (1999). Handbook of sociology of mental health. In *handbook of sociology and social research* (pp. 167–182). New York: Kluwer Academic/Plenum.

Angst, J. & Merikangus, K. (1997). The depressive spectrum: Diagnostic classification and course. *Journal of Affective Disorders, 45,* 31–40.

Annegers, J. F. (1993). The epidemiology of epilepsy. In E. Wyllie (Ed.), *The treatment of epilepsy: Principles and practice* (pp. 157–164). Philadelphia: Lea & Febiger.

Annis, H. M., Schober, R., & Kelly, E. (1996). Matching addiction outpatient counseling to client readiness to change: The role of structured relapse prevention counseling. *Experimental and Clinical Psychopharmacology, 4,* 37–45.

Anthony, J. C. & Escheagaray-Wagner, F. (2000). Epidemiologic analysis of alcohol and tobacco use. *Alcohol Health & Research World, 24,* 201–208.

Antoni, M. H., Baggett, L., Ironson, G., LaPerriere, A., August, S., Klimas, N., Schneiderman, N., & Fletcher, M. A. (1991). Cognitive-behavioral stress management intervention buffers distress responses and immunologic changes following notification of HIV-1 seropositivity. *Journal of Consulting and Clinical Psychology, 59,* 906–915.

Antoni, M. H., Cruess, D. G., Klimas, N., Maher, K., Cruess, S., Kumar, M., Lutendorf, S., Ironson, G., Schneiderman, M., & Fletcher, M. A. (2002). Stress management and immune system reconstitution in symptomatic HIV-infected gay men over time: Effects on transitional naive T cells (CD4(+)CH45RA(+)CD29(+)). *American Journal of Psychiatry, 159,* 143–145.

Antoni M. H., Lehman, J. M., Kilbourn, K. M., Boyers, A. E., Culver, J. L., Alferi, S. M., Yount, S. E., McGregor, B. A., Arena, P. L., Harris, S. D., Price, A. A., & Carver, C. S. (2001). Cognitive-behavioral stress management intervention decreases the prevalence of depression and enhances benefit finding among women under treatment for early-stage breast cancer. *Health Psychology, 20,* 20–32.

Antony, M. M. & Barlow, D. H. (2001). *Handbook of assessment and treatment planning for psychological disorders.* New York: Guilford Press.

Antony, M. M., Downie, F. F., & Swinson, R. P. (1997). *Age of onset for individuals with obsessive-compulsive disorder.* Unpublished data.

Antony, M. M., Downie, F., & Swinson, R. P. (1998). Diagnostic issues and epidemiology in obsessive-compulsive disorder. In Swinson, R. P., Antony, M. M., Rachman, S., & Richter, M. A. (Eds.), *Obsessive-compulsive disorder: Theory, research, and treatment.* London: Guilford Press.

Appelbaum, P. (2001). Thinking carefully about outpatient commitment. *Psychiatric Services, 52,* 347–350.

Appelbaum, P. A. (1994). *Almost a revolution: Mental health law and the limits of change.* New York: Oxford University Press.

Appelbaum, P. S. (2000). "I vote. I count": Mental disability and the right to vote. *Psychiatric Services, 51,* 849–850, 863.

Arango, V. & Underwood, M. D. (1997). Serotonin chemistry in the brain of suicide victims. In R. W. Maris, M. M. Silverman, & S. S. Canetto (Eds.), *Review of suicidology* (pp. 237–250). New York: Guilford Press.

Arnold, L. E., Abikoff, H. B., Cantwell, D. P., Connors, C. K., Elliot, G., Greenhill, L. L., Hechtman, L., Hinshaw, S. P., Hoza, B., Jensen, P. S., Kraemer, H. C., March, J. S., Newcorn, J. H., Pelham, W. E., Richters, J. E., Schiller, E., Severe, J., Swanson, J. M., Vereen, D., & Wells, K. C. (1997). National Institute of Mental Health collaborative multimodal treatment study of children with ADHD (the MTA): Design challenges and choices. *Archives of General Psychiatry, 54,* 865–870.

Arntz, A. (1999). Do personality disorders exist? On the validity of the concept and its cognitive-behavioral formulation and treatment. *Behavior Research and Therapy, 37*(Suppl. 1), 97–134.

Aromacki, A. S. & Lindman, R. E. (2001). Alcohol expectancies in convicted rapists and child molesters. *Criminal Behaviour and Mental Health, 11,* 94–101.

Aronson, E. (1994). *The social animal* (7th ed.). New York: W. H. Freeman.

Artiges, E., Martinot, J. L., Verdys, M., Attar-Levy, D., Mazoyer, B., Tzourio, N., Giraud, M. J., & Paillere-Martinot, M. L. (2000). Altered hemispheric functional dominance during word generation in negative schizophrenia. *Schizophrenia Bulletin, 26,* 709–721.

Ashe, J., Rosen, S. A., McArthur, J. C., & Davis, L. E. (1993). Bacterial, fungal and parasitic causes of dementia. In P. J. Whitehouse (Ed.), *Dementia* (pp. 276–306). Philadelphia: F. A. Davis.

Asmundson, G. J., Norton, P. J., & Norton, G. R. (1999). Beyond pain: The role of fear and avoidance in chronicity. *Clinical Psychology Review, 19,* 97–119.

Assalian, P. & Margolese, H. C. (1996). Treatment of antidepressant-induced sexual side effects. *Journal of Sex and Marital Therapy, 22,* 218–224.

Asuni, T. (1986). African and Western psychiatry: A comparison. In J. L. Cox (Ed.), *Transcultural psychiatry* (pp. 306–321). London: Croom-Helm, Ltd.

Atchison, M. & McFarlane, A. C. (1994). A review of dissociation and dissociative disorders. *Australian and New Zealand Journal of Psychiatry, 28, 591–599.*

Baare, W. F. C., van Oel, C. J., Hulshoff Pol, H. E., Schnack, H. G., Durston, S., Sitshoorn, M. M., & Kahn, R. S. (2001). Volumes of brain structures in twins discordant for schizophrenia. *Archives of General Psychiatry, 58,* 33–40.

Bach, A. K., Brown, T. A., & Barlow, D. H. (1999). The effects of false negative feedback on efficacy expectancies and sexual arousal in sexually functional males. *Behavior Therapy, 30*(1), 79–95.

Bachevalier, J. (1994). Medial temporal lobe structures and autism: A review of clinical and experimental findings. *Neuropsychologia, 32,* 627–648.

Baer, J. S., Kivlahan, D. R., & Marlatt, G. A. (1995). High-risk drinking across the transition from high school to college. *Alcoholism: Clinical & Experimental Research, 19*(1), 54–61.

Baer, L. (1995). High-risk drinking across the transition from high school to college. *Alcoholism: Clinical and Experimental Research, 19,* 54–61.

Bahrke, M. S., Yesalis, C. E., & Brower, K. J. (1998). Anabolic-androgenic steroid abuse and performance-enhancing drugs among adolescents. *Child & Adolescent Psychiatric Clinics of North America, 7,* 821–838.

Bailey, A., LeCouteur, A., Gottesman, I., Bolton, P., Simonoff, E., Yuzda, E., & Rutter, M. (1995). Autism as a strongly genetic disorder: Evidence from a British twin study. *Psychological Medicine, 25,* 63–78.

Bailey, A., Luthert, P., Dean, A., Harding, B., Janota, I., Montgomery, M., Rutter, M., & Lantos, P. (1998). A clinicopathological study of autism. *Brain, 121,* 889–905.

Bailey, A., Phillips, W., & Rutter, M. (1996). Autism: Towards an integration of clinical, genetic, neuropsychological, and neurobiological perspectives. *Journal of Child Psychology and Psychiatry, 37,* 89–126.

Bailey, C. E. (2000). *Children in therapy: Using the family as a resource.* New York: W. W. Norton.

Bailine, S. H., Rifkin, A., Kayne, E., Selze, J. A., Vital-Herne, J., Blieka, M., & Pollack, S. (2000). Comparison of bifrontal and bitemporal ECT for major depression. *American Journal of Psychiatry, 157,* 121–123.

Baird, T. D. & August, G. J. (1985). Familial heterogeneity in infantile autism. *Journal of Autism and Developmental Disorders, 15,* 315–321.

Baker, B. & Merskey, H. (1982). Parental representations of hypochondriacal patients from a psychiatric hospital. *British Journal of Psychiatry, 141,* 233–238.

Baldessarini, R. J. & Tondo, L. (2000). Does lithium treatment still work? Evidence of stable responses over three decades. *Archives of General Psychiatry, 57,* 187–190.

Baldessarini, R. J., Tondo, L., & Viguera, A. C. (1999). Discontinuing lithium maintenance treatment in bipolar disorders: Risks and implications. *Bipolar Disorders, 1,* 17–24.

Ballenger, J. C., Davidson, J. R. T., Lecrubier, Y., Nutt, D. J., Borkovec, T. D., Stein, D. J., Rickels, K., & Wittchen, H. U. (2001). Consensus statement on generalized anxiety disorder. *Journal of Clinical Psychiatry, 62*(Suppl.) 53–58.

Ballinger, D., Leviton, A., Waternaux, C., Needleman, H., & Rabinowitz, M. (1987). Longitudinal analyses of prenatal and postnatal lead exposure and early cognitive development. *New England Journal of Medicine, 316,* 1037–1043.

Bandura, A. (1977). Self-efficacy: Toward a unifying theory of behavioral change. *Psychological Review, 84,* 191–215.

Bandura, A. (1986). *Social foundations of thought and action.* Englewood Cliffs, NJ: Prentice-Hall.

Bandura, A., Taylor, C. B., & Williams, S. L. (1985). Catecholamine secretion as a function of perceived coping self-efficacy. *Journal of Consulting and Clinical Psychology, 53,* 406–414.

Bandura, A. & Walters, R. H. (1963). *Social learning and personality development.* New York: Ronald Press.

Bandura, A. & Walters, R. (1963). *Social learning and personality development.* New York: Holt, Rinehart & Winston.

Barbaree, H. E. & Seto, M. C. (1997). Pedophilia: Assessment and treatment. In R. D. Laws and W. O'Donohue (Eds.), *Sexual deviance: Theory, assessment, and treatment.* New York: Guilford Press.

Barber, J. P. & DeRubeis, R. J. (1989). On second thought: Where the action is in cognitive therapy for depression. *Cognitive Therapy and Research, 13,* 441–457.

Barch, D. M. & Berenbaum, H. (1996). Language production and thought disorder in schizophrenia. *Journal of Abnormal Psychology, 105,* 81–88.

Barch, D. M. & Carter, C. S. (1998). Selective attention in schizophrenia: Relationship to verbal working memory. *Schizophrenia Research, 33,* 53–61.

Barch, D. M., Carter, C. S., Braver, T. S., Sabb, F. W., MacDonald, A., Noll, D. C., & Cohen, J. D. (2001). Selective deficits in prefrontal cortex function in medication-naive patients with schizophrenia. *Archives of General Psychiatry, 58,* 280–288.

Bargh, J. A. & Ferguson, M. J. (2000). Beyond behaviorism: On the automaticity of higher mental processes. *Psychological Bulletin, 126*(6), 925–945.

Barkley, R. A. (1998). *Attention-deficit hyperactivity disorder: A handbook for diagnosis and treatment* (2nd ed.). New York: Guilford Press.

Barkley, R. A., DuPaul, G. J., & McMurray, M. B. (1990). A comprehensive evaluation of attention-deficit disorder with and without hyperactivity defined by research criteria. *Journal of Consulting and Clinical Psychology, 58,* 775–789.

Barkley, R. A., Fischer, M., Edelbrock, C. S., & Smallish, L. (1990). The adolescent outcome of hyperactive children diagnosed by research criteria: An eight-year prospective follow-up study. *Journal of the American Academy of Child and Adolescent Psychiatry, 29,* 546–557.

Barlow, D. H. (1993). Covert sensitization for paraphilia. In J. R. Cantela & A. J. Kearney (Eds.), *Covert conditioning casebook* (pp. 187–198). Pacific Grove, CA: Brooks/Cole.

Barlow, D. H., Gorman, J. M., Shear, M. K., & Woods, S. W. (2000). Cognitive-behavioral therapy, imipramine, or their combination for panic disorder: A randomized controlled trial. *Journal of the American Medical Association, 283,* 2529–2536.

Barona, A. & Faykus, S. (1992). Differential effects of sociocultural variables on special education eligibility categories. *Psychology in the Schools, 29,* 313–320.

Baron-Cohen, S. (1995). *Mind blindness: An essay on autism and theory of mind.* Cambridge, MA: MIT Press.

Barondes, S. H. (1994). Thinking about Prozac. *Science, 263,* 1102–1103.

Barrash, J., Tranel, D., & Anderson, S. W. (2000). Acquired personality disturbances associated with bilateral damage to the ventromedial prefrontal region. *Developmental Neuropsychology, 18,* 355–381.

Barratt, E. S., Standford, M. S., Kent, T. A., & Felthous, A. (1997). Neuropsychological and cognitive psychophysiological substrates of impulsive aggression. *Biological Psychiatry, 41,* 1045–1061.

Barrett, D. E. & Frank, D. A. (1987). *The effects of undernutrition on children's behavior.* New York: Gordon & Breach.

Barrett, P., Lowry-Webster, H., & Holmes, J. (1999). *The FRIENDS anxiety prevention program.* Bowen Hills, Queensland, Australia: Australian Academic Press.

Barrett, R. P., Walters, A. S., Mercurio, A. F., Klitzke, M., & Feinstein, C. (1992). Mental retardation and psychiatric disorders. In V. B. Van Hasselt & D. J. Kolko (Eds.), *Inpatient behavior therapy for children and adolescents* (pp. 113–149). New York: Plenum Press.

Barrios, B. A. & O'Dell, S. (1997). Fears and anxieties. In E. J. Mash & L. G. Terdal (Eds.), *Behavioral assessment of childhood disorders.* (3rd ed.). New York: Guilford Press.

Barrows, K. A. & Jacobs, B. P. (2002). Mind-body medicine. An introduction and review of the literature. *Medical Clinics of North America, 86,* 11–31.

Barry, M. (1991). The influence of the U.S. tobacco industry on the health, economy, and environment of developing countries. *New England Journal of Medicine, 342,* 917–920.

Barsky, A. J. (1992a). Amplification, somatization, and the somatoform disorders. *Psychosomatics, 33,* 28–34.

Barsky, A. J. (1992b). Hypochondriasis and obsessive compulsive disorder. *Psychiatric Clinics of North America, 15,* 791–801.

Barsky, A. J. (1996). Hypochondriasis: Medical management and psychiatric treatment. *Psychosomatics, 37,* 48–56.

Barsky, A. J., Bailey, E. D., Fama, J. M., & Ahern, D. K. (2000). Predictors of remission in *DSM* hypochondriasis. *Comprehensive Psychiatry, 41,* 179–183.

Barsky, A. J., Brener, J., Coeytaux, R. R., & Cleary, P. D. (1995). Accurate awareness of heartbeat in hypochondriacal and non-hypochondriacal patients. *Journal of Psychosomatic Research, 39,* 489–497.

Barsky, A. J., Wool, C., Barnett, M. C., & Cleary, P. D. (1994). Histories of childhood trauma in adult hypochondriacal patients. *American Journal of Psychiatry, 151,* 397–401.

Barta, P. E., Pearlson, G. D., Brill, L. B., II, Royall, R., McGilchrist, I. K., Pulver, A. E., Powers, R. E., Casanova, M. F., Tien, A. Y., Frangou, S., & Petty, R. G. (1997). Planum temporale asymmetry reversal in schizophrenia: Replication and relationship to gray matter abnormalities. *American Journal of Psychiatry, 154,* 661–667.

Bartrop, R. W., Luckhurst, E., Lazarus, L., Kiloh, L. G., & Penny, R. (1977). Depressed lymphocyte function after bereavement. *Lancet,* 834–836.

Basco, M. R. (2000). Cognitive-behavioral therapy for bipolar I disorder. *Journal of Cognitive Psychotherapy: An International Quarterly, 14,* 287–304.

Bateman, A. & Fonagy, P. (2001). Treatment of borderline personality disorder with psychoanalytically oriented partial hospitalization: An 18-month follow-up. *American Journal of Psychiatry, 158,* 36–42.

Bateson, G., Jackson, D., Haley, J., & Weakland, J. (1956). Toward a theory of schizophrenia. *Behavioral Science, 1,* 251–264.

Battle, Y. I., Martin, B. C., Dorfman, J. H., & Miller, L. S. (1999). Seasonality and infectious disease in schizophrenia: The birth hypothesis revisited. *Journal of Psychiatric Research, 33,* 501–509.

Baumann, B. & Bogerts, B. (2001). Neuroanatomical studies on bipolar disorder. *British Journal of Psychiatry, 178,* S142–S147.

Baumeister, R. F. (1997). *Evil: Inside human violence and cruelty.* New York: W. H. Freeman.

Baumeister, R. F. & Butler, J. L. (1997). Sexual masochism: Deviance without pathology. In D. R. Laws, W. T. O'Donohue, et al. (Eds.), *Sexual deviance: Theory, assessment, and treatment* (pp. 225–239). New York: Guilford Press.

Baumeister, R. F., Dale, K., & Sommer, K. L. (1998). Freudian defense mechanisms and empirical findings in modern social psychology: Reaction formation, projection, displacement, undoing, isolation, sublimation, and denial. *Journal of Personality, 66,* 1081–1124.

Beach, F. A. (1975). Hormonal modification of sexually dimorphic behavior. *Psychoneuroendocrinology, 1*(1), 3–23.

Beautrais, A. L., Joyce, P. R., & Mulder, R. T. (1996). Risk factors for serious suicide attempts among youths aged 13 through 24 years. *Journal of the American Academy of Child and Adolescent Psychiatry, 35,* 1174–1182.

Bebbington, P. & Ramana, R. (1995). The epidemiology of bipolar affective disorder. *Social Psychiatry and Psychiatric Epidemiology, 30,* 279–292.

Beck, A. T. (1967). *Depression: Clinical, experimental, and theoretical aspects.* New York: Harper & Row.

Beck, A. T. (1976). *Cognitive therapy and the emotional disorders.* New York: International Universities Press.

Beck, A. T. (1987). Cognitive models of depression. *Journal of Cognitive Psychotherapy, 1,* 5–37.

Beck, A. T. (1999). Prisoners of hate: The cognitive basis of anger, hostility, and violence. New York: HarperCollins.

Beck, A. T. & Clark, D. A. (1997). An information processing model of anxiety: Automatic and strategic processes. *Behaviour Research and Therapy, 35,* 49–58.

Beck, A. T. & Freeman, A. (1990). *Cognitive therapy of personality disorders.* New York: Guilford Press.

Beck, A. T. & Rector, N. A. (2000). Cognitive therapy of schizophrenia: A new therapy for the new millennium. *American Journal of Psychotherapy, 54*(3), 291–300.

Beck, A. T., Brown, G., Berchick, R. J., Stewart, B. L., & Steer, R. A. (1990). Relationship between hopelessness and ultimate suicide: A replication with psychiatric outpatients. *American Journal of Psychiatry, 147,* 190–195.

Beck, A. T., Emery, G., & Greenberg, R. L. (1985). *Anxiety disorders and phobias: A cognitive perspective.* New York: Basic Books.

Beck, A. T., Freeman, A., Pretzer, J., Davis, D., Fleming, B., Ottaviani, R., Beck, J., Simon, K. M., Padesky, C., Meyer, J., & Trexler, L. (1990). *Cognitive therapy of personality disorders.* New York: Guilford Press.

Beck, A. T., Rush, A. J., Shaw, B. F., & Emery, G. (1979). *Cognitive theory of depression.* New York: Guilford Press.

Beck, J. G. (1995). Hypoactive sexual desire disorder: An overview. *Journal of Consulting and Clinical Psychology, 63,* 919–927.

Beck, J. S. (1995). *Cognitive therapy: Basics and beyond.* New York: Guilford Press.

Beck, R. & Perkins, T. S. (2001). Cognitive content-specificity for anxiety and depression: A meta-analysis. *Cognitive Therapy and Research, 25,* 651–663.

Beeder, A. B. & Millman, R. B. (1997). Patients with psychopathology. In J. H. Lowinson, P. Ruiz, R. B. Millman, & J. G. Langrod (Eds.), *Substance abuse: A comprehensive textbook* (pp. 551–563). Baltimore: Williams & Wilkins.

Beghi, E., Spagnoli, P., Airoldi, L., Fiordelli, E., Appollonio, I., Bogliun, G., Zardi, A., Paleari, F., Gamba, P., Frattola, L., & Da Prada, L. (2002). Emotional and affective disturbances in patients with epilepsy. *Epilepsy & Behavior, 3*(3), 255–261.

Beitchman, J. H. & Young, A. R. (1997). Learning disorders with a special emphasis on reading disorders: A review of the past 10 years. *Journal of the American Academy of Child and Adolescent Psychiatry, 36,* 1020–1032.

Bekker, M. H. J. (1996). Agoraphobia and gender: A review. *Clinical Psychology Review, 16,* 129–146.

Belanoff, J. K., Kalehzan, M., Sund, B., Fleming Ficek, S. K., & Schatzberg, A. F. (2001). Cortisol activity and cognitive changes in psychotic major depression. *American Journal of Psychiatry, 158,* 1612–1616.

Belfer, M. L. & Munir, K. (1997). Acquired immune deficiency syndrome. In J.M. Weiner (Ed.), *Textbook of child and adolescent psychiatry* (pp. 711–725). Washington, DC: American Psychiatric Association.

Bell, D. S. (1973). The experimental reproduction of amphetamine psychosis. *Archives of General Psychiatry, 39*(1), 35–40.

Bell, J. (1995). Generalized anxiety disorders. In J. L. Jacobson & A. M. Jacobson, (Eds.), *Psychiatric Secrets* (pp. 88–91). Philadelphia: Hanley & Belfus.

Bell, N. S., Amoroso, P. J., Yore, M. M., Senier, L., Williams, J. O., Smith, G. S., & Theriault, A. (2001). Alcohol and other risk factors for drowning among male active duty U.S. army soldiers. *Aviation, Space & Environmental Medicine, 72,* 1086–1095.

Bellack, A. S., Gearon, J. S., & Blanchard, J. J. (2000). Schizophrenia: Psychopathology. In M. Hersen & A. S. Bellack (Eds.), *Psychopathology in adulthood* (pp. 305–325). Boston: Allyn & Bacon.

Bellinger, D. (1994). Teratogen update: Lead. *Teratology, 50,* 367–373.

Belluck, P. (1997, November 6). "Memory" therapy leads to a lawsuit and big settlement. *New York Times,* pp. A1, A13.

Belsher, G. & Costello, C. G. (1988). Relapse after recovery from unipolar depression: A critical review. *Psychological Bulletin, 104,* 84–96.

Bemporad, J. R. (1988). Psychodynamic models of depression and mania. In A. Georgotas and R. Cancro (Eds.), *Depression and mania.* New York: Elsevier Science.

Benazzi, F. (2000). Depression with *DSM-IV* atypical features: A marker for bipolar II disorder. *European Archives of Psychiatry and Clinical Neuroscience, 250,* 53–55.

Benazzi, F. (2001). The clinical picture of bipolar II outpatient depression in private practice. *Psychopathology, 34,* 81–84.

Benca, R. M., Obermeyer, W. H., Thisted, R. A., & Gillin, J. C. (1992). Sleep and psychiatric disorders: A meta-analysis. *Archives of General Psychiatry, 49,* 651–668.

Bender, D. S., Dolan, R. T., Skodel, A. E., Sanislow, C. A., Dyck, I. R., et al. (2001). Treatment utilization by patients with personality disorders. *The American Journal of Psychiatry, 158,* 295–302.

Bender, L. (1938). A visual motor gestalt test and its clinical use. *Research Monograph of the American Orthopsychiatric Association, 3,* xi, 176.

Benioff, L. (1995). What is it like to have schizophrenia? In S. Vinogradov (Ed.), *Treating schizophrenia* (pp. 81–107). San Francisco: Jossey-Bass.

Benjamin, H. (1964). Nature and management of transsexualism: With a report of thirty-one operated cases. *Western Journal of Surgery, Obstetrics and Gynecology,* 105–111.

Benson, B. A. (1986). Anger management training. *Psychiatric Aspects of Mental Retardation Reviews, 5*(10), 51–55.

Benson, B. W., Rose, M. S., & Meeuwisse, W. H. (2002). The impact of face shield use on concussions in ice hockey: A multivariate analysis. *British Journal of Sports Medicine, 36,* 27–32.

Bentall, R. P., Corcoran, R., Howard, R., Blackwood, N., & Kinderman, P. (2001). Persecutory delusions: A review and theoretical integration. *Clinical Psychology Review, 21,* 1143–1192.

Bentler, P. M. & Prince, C. (1970). Psychiatric symptomology in transvestites. *Journal of Clinical Psychology, 26*(4), 434–455.

Bentler, P. M., Shearman, R. W., & Prince, C. (1970). Personality characteristics of male transvestites. *Journal of Clinical Psychology, 26,* 287–291.

Berenbaum, H. & Oltmanns, T. F. (1992). Emotional experience and expression in schizophrenia and depression. *Journal of Abnormal Psychology, 101,* 37–44.

Bergler, E. (1947). Analysis of an unusual case of fetishism. *Bulletin of the Menninger Clinic, 2,* 67–75.

Berlin, I., Payan, C., Corruble, E., & Puech, A. J. (1999). Serum thyroid stimulating hormone concentration as an index of severity of major depression. *International Journal of Neuropsychopharmacology, 2,* 105–110.

Berliner, L., Schram, D., Miller, L. L., & Milloy, C. D. (1995). A sentencing alternative for sex offenders: A study of decision making and recidivism. *Journal of Interpersonal Violence, 10,* 487–502.

Berman, A. L. (1988). Fictional depiction of suicide in television films and imitation effects. *American Journal of Psychiatry, 145,* 982–986.

Berman, J. R., Berman, L. A., Werbin, T. J., & Goldstein, I. (1999). Female sexual dysfunction; anatomy, physiology, evaluation, and treatment options. *Current Opinion in Urology, 9,* 563–568.

Berman, R. M., Narasimhan, M., Miller, H. L., Anand, A., Cappiello, A., Oren, D. A., Heninger, G. R., & Charney, D. S. (1999). Transient depressive relapse induced by catecholamine depletion: Potential phenotypic vulnerability marker? *Archives of General Psychiatry, 56,* 395–403.

Bernstein, A. S. (1987). Orienting response research in schizophrenia: Where we have come and where we might go. *Schizophrenia Bulletin, 13,* 623–641.

Bernstein, A., Newman, J. P., Wallace, J. F., & Lau, K. E. (2000). Left-hemisphere activation and deficient response modulation in psychopaths. *Psychological Science, 11,* 414–419.

Berrettini, W. H., Ferraro, T. N., Goldin, L. R., Detera-Wadleigh, S. D., Choi, H., Muniec, D., Guroff, J. J., Kazuba, D. M., Nurnberger, J. I., Hsieh, W. T., Hoehe, M. R., & Gershon, E. S. (1997). A linkage study of bipolar illness. *Archives of General Psychiatry, 54,* 27–35.

Berrios, D. C., Hearst, N., Coates, T. J., Stall, R., Hudes, E. S., Turner, H., Eversley, R., & Catania, J. (1993). HIV antibody testing among those at risk for infection: The national AIDS behavioral surveys. *Journal of the American Medical Association, 270,* 1576–1580.

Bersoff, D. M. & Bersoff, D. N. (1999). Ethical perspectives in clinical research. In P. C. Kendall, J. N. Butcher, & G. N. Holmbeck (Eds.), *Handbook of research methods in clinical psychology* (2nd ed., pp. 31–53). New York: Wiley.

Bettelheim, B. (1967). *The empty fortress.* New York: Free Press.

Beutler, L. E., Kim, E. J., Davison, E., Karno, M., & Fisher, D. (1996). Research contributions to improving managed health care outcomes. *Psychotherapy, 33,* 197–206.

Biederman, J., Faraone, S. V., Milberger, S., Curtis, S., Chen, L., Marrs, A., Ouellette, C., Moore, P., & Spencer, T. (1996). Predictors of persistence and remission of ADHD into adolescence: Results from a four-year prospective follow-up study. *Journal of the American Academy of Child and Adolescent Psychiatry, 35,* 343–351.

Biederman, J., Hirshfeld-Becker, D. R., Rosenbaum, J. F., Herot, C., Friedman, D., Snidman, N., Kagan, J., & Faraone, S. V. (2001a). Further evidence of association between behavioral inhibition and social anxiety in children. *American Journal of Psychiatry, 158*(10), 1673–1679.

Biederman, J., Hirshfeld-Becker, D. R., Rosenbaum, J. F., Perenick, S. G., Wood, J., & Faraone, S. V. (2001b).

Lack of association between parental alcohol or drug addiction and behavioral inhibition in children. *American Journal of Psychiatry, 158*(10), 1731–1733.

Biederman, J., Newcorn, J., & Sprich, S. (1991). Comorbidity of attention deficit hyperactivity disorder with conduct, depressive, anxiety, and other disorders. *American Journal of Psychiatry, 148,* 564–577.

Bigler, E. D., Yeo, R. A., & Turkheimer, E. (Eds.) (1989). *Neuropsychological function and brain imaging.* New York: Plenum.

Bilder, R. M., Goldman, R. S., Volavka, J., Czobor, P., Hoptman, M., Sheitman, B., Lindenmayer, J., Citrome, L., McEvoy, J., Kunz, M., Chakos, M., Cooper, T. B., Horowitz, T. L., & Lieberman, J. A. (2002). Neurocognitive effects of clozapine, olanzapine, risperidone, and haloperidol in patients with chronic schizophrenia or schizoaffective disorder. *American Journal of Psychiatry, 159,* 1018–1028.

Billings, D. W., Folkman, S., Acree, M., & Moskowitz, J. T. (2000). Coping and physical health during care-giving: The roles of positive and negative affect. *Journal of Personality and Social Psychology, 79,* 131–142.

Bini, L. (1938). Experimental researches on epileptic attacks induced by the electric current. *American Journal of Psychiatry* (Suppl. 94), 172–183.

Binik, Y. M., Bergeron, S., & Khalife, S. (2000). Dyspareunia. In S. R. Leiblum & R. C. Rosen (Eds.), *Principles and practice of sex therapy* (3rd ed., pp. 154–180). New York: Guilford Press.

Birmaher, B., Kaufman, J., Brent, D. A., Dahl, R. E., Perel, J. M., Al-Shabbout, M., Nelson, B., Stull, S., Rao, U., Waterman, G. S., Williamson, D. E., & Ryan, N. D. (1997). Neuroendocrine response to 5-Hydroxy-L-Tryptophan in prepubertal children at high risk of major depressive disorder. *Archives of General Psychiatry, 54,* 1113–1119.

Birnbaum, K. (1914). *Die psychopathischen verbrecker* (2nd ed.). Leipzig: Thieme.

Bishop, G. D. & Robinson, G. (2000). Anger, harassment, and cardiovascular reactivity among Chinese and Indian men in Singapore. *Psychosomatic Medicine, 62,* 684–692.

Bjorkland, D. F. & Green, B. L. (1992). The adaptive nature of cognitive immaturity. *American Psychologist, 47,* 46–54.

Black, D. W. (1998). Recognition and treatment of obsessive-compulsive spectrum disorders. In R. P. Swinson, M. M. Antony, S. Rachman, & M. A. Richter (Eds.), *Obsessive-compulsive disorder: Theory, research, and treatment.* New York: Guilford Press.

Black, D. W., Noyes, R., Jr., Pfohl, B., Goldstein, R. B., & Blum, N. (1993). Personality disorder in obsessive-compulsive volunteers, well comparison subjects, and their first-degree relatives. *American Journal of Psychiatry, 150,* 1226–1232.

Blackburn, I. M. & Moorhead, S. (2000). Update in cognitive therapy for depression. *Journal of Cognitive Psychotherapy: An International Quarterly, 14,* 305–336.

Blair, C. D. & Lanyon, R. I. (1981). Exhibitionism: Etiology and treatment. *Psychological Bulletin, 89*(3), 439–463.

Blanchard, E. B. & Andraski, F. (1985). *Management of chronic headaches: A psychological approach.* New York: Pergamon Press.

Blanchard, J. J. & Neale, J. M. (1992). Medication effects: Conceptual and methodological issues in schizophrenia research. *Clinical Psychology Review, 12,* 345–361.

Blanchard, R. (1989). The concept of autogynephilia and the typology of male gender dysphoria. *Journal of Nervous and Mental Disease, 177,* 616–623.

Blane, L. & Roth, R. H. (1967). Voyeurism and exhibitionism. *Perceptual and Motor Skills, 24,* 391–400.

Blashfield, R. K. & Draguns, J. G. (1976). Evaluative criteria for psychiatric classification. *Journal of Abnormal Psychology, 85,* 140–150.

Blatt, S. J. & Homann, E. (1992). Parent-child interaction in the etiology of dependent and self-critical depression. *Clinical Psychology Review, 12,* 47–91.

Blazer, D. G., Kessler, R. C., McGonagle, K. A., & Swartz, M. S. (1994). The prevalence and distribution of major depression in a national community sample: The national comorbidity survey. *American Journal of Psychiatry, 151,* 979–986.

Bleuler, E. (1950). *Dementia praecox or the group of schizophrenias* (J. Zinkin, Trans.). New York: International Universities Press. Original work published 1911.

Bliss, E. L. (1984). A symptom profile of patients with multiple personalities—with MMPI results. *Journal of Nervous and Mental Disease, 172,* 197–202.

Bliss, E. W. & Branch, C. H. (1960). *Anorexia nervosa: Its history, psychology, and biology.* New York: Hoeber Medical Book.

Bliss, R. E., Garvey, A. J., Heinold, J. W., & Hitchcock, J. L. (1989). The influence of situation and coping on relapse crisis outcomes after smoking cessation. *Journal of Consulting and Clinical Psychology, 57,* 443–449.

Blumberg, H. P., Stern, E., Ricketts, S., Martinez, D., de Asis, J., White, T., Epstein, J., Isenberg, N., McBride, P. A., Kemperman, I., Emmerich, S., Dhawan, V., Eidelberg, D., Kocsis, J. H., & Silbersweig, D. A. (1999). Rostral and orbital prefrontal cortex dysfunction in the manic state of bipolar disorder. *American Journal of Psychiatry, 156,* 1986–1988.

Bobes, J. (1999). Social anxiety disorder/social phobia—The course of illness prior to treatment. *International Journal of Psychiatry in Clinical Practice, 3*(Suppl. 3), S21–S23.

Bockoven, J. S. (1963). *Moral treatment in American psychiatry.* New York: Springer.

Bodlund, O. & Kullgren, G. (1995). *Transsexualism: General outcome and prognostic factors.* Paper presented at the XIVth International Symposium on Gender Dysphoria, Kloster Irsee, Germany.

Bohman, M., Cloninger, C. R., von Knorring, A., & Sigvardsson, S. (1984). An adoption study of somatoform disorders: III. Cross-fostering analysis and genetic relationship to alcoholism and criminality. *Archives of General Psychiatry, 41,* 872–878.

Bohus, M., Haaf, B., Stiglmayr, C., et al. (2000). Evaluation of inpatient dialectical-behavior therapy for borderline personality disorder—A prospective study. *Behavior Research & Therapy, 38,* 875–887.

Boll, T. J., Heaton, R., & Reitan, R. M. (1974). Neuropsychological and emotional correlates of Huntington's chorea. *Journal of Nervous and Mental Disease, 158,* 61–69.

Bolling, M., Kohlenberg, R. J., & Parker, C. (2000). Depression: A radical behavioral analysis and treatment approach. In M. Dougher, (Ed.), *Clinical behavior analytic approaches to treatment.* Reno: Context Press.

Bolton, P. & Rutter, M. (1990). Genetic influences in autism. *International Review of Psychiatry, 2,* 67–80.

Bongar, B. (1999). The ethical issue of competence in working with the suicidal patient. In D. N. Bersoff (Ed.), *Ethical conflicts in psychology* (2nd ed., pp. 356–358). Washington, DC: American Psychological Association.

Bonnie, R. J. (1992). The competence of criminal defendants: A theoretical reformulation. *Behavioral Sciences and the Law, 10,* 291–316.

Bonnie, R. J. (2001). Three strands of mental health law: Developmental mileposts. In L. E. Frost & R. J. Bonnie (Eds.), *The evolution of mental health law* (pp. 31–54). Washington, DC: American Psychological Association.

Bonomo, Y., Coffey, C., Wolfe, R., Lynskey, M., Bowes, G., & Patto, G. (2001). Adverse outcomes of alcohol use in adolescents. *Addiction, 96,* 1485–1496.

Boocock, S. S. (1995). Early childhood programs in other nations: Goals and outcomes. *The Future of Children, 5,* 94–114.

Boon, S. & Draijer, N. (1993). Multiple personality disorder in the Netherlands: A clinical investigation of 71 patients. *American Journal of Psychiatry, 150,* 489–494.

Booth, G. K. (1995). Outcome and treatment strategies. In S. Vinogradov (Ed.), *Treating schizophrenia* (pp. 166–169). San Francisco: Jossey-Bass.

Booth-Kewley, S. & Friedman, H. S. (1987). Psychological predictors of heart disease: A quantitative review. *Psychological Bulletin, 101,* 343–362.

Bootzin, R. R., Manber, R., Perlis, M. L., Salvia, M., & Wyatt, J. K. (1993). Sleep disorders. In P. B. Sutker & H. E. Adams (Eds.), *Comprehensive handbook of psychopathology* (2nd ed., pp. 531–561). New York: Plenum Press.

Bootzin, R. R. & Perlis, M. L. (1992). Nonpharmacological treatments for insomnia. *Journal of Clinical Psychiatry.*

Borkovec, T. D. & Costello, E. (1993). Efficacy of applied relaxation and cognitive-behavioral therapy in the treatment of generalized anxiety disorder. *Journal of Consulting and Clinical Psychology, 61,* 611–619.

Borkovec, T. D. & Inz, J. (1990). The nature of worry in generalized anxiety disorder: A predominance of thought activity. *Behaviour Research and Therapy, 28,* 153–158.

Borkovec, T. D., Lane, T. W., & VanOot, P. H. (1981). Phenomenology of sleep among insomniacs and good sleepers: Wakefulness experience when cortically asleep. *Journal of Abnormal Psychology, 90,* 607–609.

Borkovec, T. D., Ray, W. J., & Stoeber, J. (1998). Worry: A cognitive phenomenon intimately linked to affective, physiological, and interpersonal behavioral processes. *Cognitive Therapy & Research, 22,* 561–576.

Borkowski, J. G., Whitman, T. L., Passino, A. W., Rellinger, E. A., Sommer, K., Keogh, D., & Weed, K. (1992). Unraveling the "new morbidity": Adolescent parenting and developmental delays. In N. W. Bray (Ed.), *International review of research in mental retardation* (Vol. 18, pp. 159–196). San Diego, CA: Academic Press.

Bornstein, R. F. (1992). The dependent personality: Developmental, social, and clinical perspectives. *Psychological Bulletin, 112,* 3–23.

Bornstein, R. F. (1993). *The dependent personality.* New York: Guilford Press.

Bornstein, R. F. (1998). Depathologizing dependency. *Journal of Nervous & Mental Disease, 186*(2), 67–73.

Bornstein, R. F. (1999). Histrionic personality disorder, physical attractiveness, and social adjustment. *Journal of Psychopathology and Behavioral Assessment, 21,* 79–94.

Bornstein, R. F. & Cecero, J. J. (2000). Deconstructing dependency in a five-factor world: A meta-analytic review. *Journal of Personality Assessment, 74,* 324–343.

Borum, R. (1996). Improving the clinical practice of violence risk assessment: Technology, guidelines, and training. *American Psychologist, 51,* 945–956.

Borum, R. & Fulero, S. M. (1999). Empirical research on the insanity defense and attempted reforms: Evidence toward informed policy. *Law and Human Behavior, 23,* 117–135.

Boscarino, J. A. & Chang J. (2001). PTSD and coronary heart disease. *Annals of Behavioral Medicine.*

Boscarino, J. A. & Chang, J. 1999. Electrocardiogram abnormalities among men with stress-related psychiatric disorders: Implications for coronary heart disease and clinical research. *Annals of Behavioral Medicine, 21*(3), 227–234.

Bosma, H., Marmot, M. G., Hemingway, H., Nicholson, A. C., Brunner, E., & Stansfield, S. A. (1997). Low job control and risk of coronary heart disease in Whitehall II (prospective cohort) study. *British Medical Journal, 314,* 558–565.

Botzer, M. C. & Vehrs, B. (1997). *Self-integrative traits and pathways to gender transition.* Paper presented at the XVth Harry Benjamin International Gender Dysphoria Association Symposium, Vancouver, Canada.

Bouchard, T. J. & Pedersen, N. (1999). Twins reared apart: Nature's double experiment. In M. C. LaBuda & E. L. Grigorenko (Eds.), *On the way to individuality: Current methodological issues in behavioral genetics* (pp. 71–93). Huntington, NY: Nova Science.

Bouchard, T. J., Jr., Lykken, D. T., McGue, M., Segal, N.L., et al. (1990). Sources of human psychological differences: The Minnesota study of twins reared apart. *Science, 250,* 223–250.

Bourin, M., Fiocco, A. J., & Clenet, F. (2001). How valuable are animal models in defining antidepressant activity? *Human Psychopharmacology: Clinical and Experimental, 16,* 9–21.

Bourne, P. G. (1974). *Addiction.* New York: Academic Press.

Bouton, M. E., Mineka, S., & Barlow, D. H. (2001). A modern learning theory perspective on the etiology of panic disorder. *Psychological Review, 108*(1), 4–32.

Boutros, N. N. & Bowers, M. B., Jr. (1996). Chronic substance-induced psychotic disorders: State of the literature. *Journal of Neuropsychiatry & Clinical Neurosciences, 8,* 262–269.

Bovjberg, D. H., Redd, W. H., Maier, L. A., Holland, J. C., Lesko, L. M., Niedzwiecki, D., Rubin, S. C., & Hakes, T. B. (1990). Anticipatory immune suppression and nausea in women receiving cyclic chemotherapy for ovarian cancer. *Journal of Consulting and Clinical Psychology, 58,* 153–157.

Bower, G. H. (1992). How might emotions affect learning? In S. A. Christianson (Ed.), *Handbook of emotion and memory* (pp. 3–31). Hillsdale, NJ: Erlbaum.

Bower, G. H. (1994). Temporary emotional states act like multiple personalities. In R. M. Klein & B. K. Doane (Eds.), *Psychological concepts and dissociative disorders* (pp. 207–234). Hillsdale, NJ: Erlbaum.

Bowers, K. S. & Farvolden, P. (1996). Revisiting a century-old Freudian slip: From suggestion disavowed to the truth repressed. *Psychological Bulletin, 119,* 355–380.

Bowlby, J. (1951). *Maternal care and mental health.* World Health Organization Monograph. (Serial No. 2).

Bowlby, J. (1969). *Attachment and loss, Vol. 1: Attachment.* New York: Basic Books.

Bowlby, J. (1973). *Attachment and loss, Vol. 2: Separation.* New York: Basic Books.

Bowlby, J. (1977). The making and breaking of affectional bonds: I. Aetiology and psychopathology in the light of attachment theory. *British Journal of Psychiatry, 130,* 201–210.

Bowlby, J. (1980). *Attachment and loss, Vol. 3: Loss, sadness and depression.* New York: Basic Books.

Bowlby, J. (1988). Developmental psychiatry comes of age. *American Journal of Psychiatry, 145,* 1–10.

Bowman, E. S. & Markand, O. N. (1996). Psychodynamics and psychiatric diagnoses of pseudoseizure subjects. *American Journal of Psychiatry, 153,* 57–63.

Boyd, J. H., Rae, D. S., Thompson, J. W., Burns, B. J., Bourdon, K., Locke, B. Z., & Regier, D. A. (1990). Phobia: Prevalence and risk factors. *Social Psychiatry and Psychiatric Epidemiology, 25,* 314–323.

Boysen, G. (1993). Prevention of stroke. In J. P. Whisnant (Ed.), *Stroke, populations, cohorts, and clinical trials.* Boston: Butterworth-Heinemann.

Bradford, J. M. W. (1990). The antiandrogen and hormonal treatment of sex offenders. In W. L. Marshall, D. R. Laws, & H. E. Barbaree (Eds.), *Handbook of sexual assault* (pp. 297–310). New York: Plenum Press.

Bradford, J. M. W. & Greenberg, D. M. (1996). Pharmacological treatment of deviant sexual behaviour. *Annual Review of Sex Research, 6,* 283–306.

Bradford, J. M. W. & Pawlak, A. (1993). Double-blind placebo crossover study of cyproterone acetate in the treatment of paraphilias. *Archives of Sexual Behavior, 22,* 383–402.

Brady, J. V. (1958). Ulcers in "executive" monkeys. *Scientific American, 199,* 95–100.

Braff, D. L. (1993). Information processing and attention dysfunctions in schizophrenia. *Schizophrenia Bulletin, 19,* 233–259.

Brakel, S. J. (1985). Involuntary institutionalization. In S. J. Brakel, J. Parry, & B. A. Weiner (Eds.), *The mentally disabled and the law* (3rd ed.). Chicago: American Bar Foundation.

Brand, B. (2001). Establishing safety with patients with dissociative identity disorder. *Journal of Trauma and Dissociation, 2,* 133–155.

Brandenburg, N. A., Friedman, R. M., & Silver, S. E. (1990). The epidemiology of childhood psychiatric disorders: Prevalence findings from recent studies. *Journal of the American Academy of Child and Adolescent Psychiatry, 29,* 76–83.

Brantley, P. J. & Garrett, V. D. (1993). Psychobiological approaches to health and disease. In P. B. Sutker & H. E. Adams (Eds.), *Comprehensive handbook of psychopathology* (2nd ed., pp. 647–670). New York: Plenum Press.

Brantley, P. J. & Jones, G. N. (1993). Daily stress and stress-related disorders. *Annals of Behavioral Medicine, 15,* 17–25.

Bray, G. A. (1984). The role of weight control in health promotion and disease prevention. In J. D. Matarazzo, S. M. Weiss, J. A. Herd, & N. E. Miller (Eds.), *Behavioral health: A handbook of health enhancement and disease prevention* (pp. 632–656). New York: Wiley.

Brebion, G., Amador, X., David, A., Malaspina, D., Sharif, Z., & Gorman, J. M. (2000). Positive symptomatology and source-monitoring failure in schizophrenia—An analysis of symptom-specific effects. *Psychiatry Research, 95,* 119–131.

Brebion, G., Smith, M. J., Amador, X., Malaspina, D., & Gorman, J. M. (1997). Clinical correlates of memory in schizophrenia: Differential links between depression, positive and negative symptoms, and two types of memory impairment. *American Journal of Psychiatry, 154,* 1538–1543.

Brecklin, L. R. & Ullman, S. E. (2000). The role of offender alcohol use in rape attacks: An analysis of national crime victimization survey data. *Journal of Interpersonal Violence, 16,* 3–21.

Brehm, N. M. & Khantzian, E. J. (1997). Psychodynamics. In J. H. Lowinson, P. Ruiz, R. B. Millman, & J. G. Langrod (Eds.), *Substance abuse: A comprehensive textbook* (pp. 90–100). Baltimore: Williams & Wilkins.

Bremner, J. D., Innis, R. B., Salomon, R. M., Staib, L. H., Ng, C. K., Miller, H. L., Bronen, R. A., Krystal, J. H., Duncan, J., Rich, D., Price, L. H., Malison, R., Dey, H., Soufer, R., & Charney, D. S. (1997). Positron emission tomography measurement of cerebral metabolic correlates of tryptophan depletion-induced depressive relapse. *Archives of General Psychiatry, 54,* 364–374.

Bremner, J. D., Krystal, J. H., Charney, D. S., & Southwick, S. M. (1996). Neural mechanisms in dissociative amnesia for childhood abuse: Relevance to the current controversy surrounding the "false memory syndrome." *American Journal of Psychiatry, 153,* 71–82.

Bremner, J. D., Krystal, J. H., Southwick, S. M., & Charney, D. S. (1995). Functional neuroanatomical correlates of the effects of stress on memory. *Journal of Traumatic Stress, 8,* 527–553.

Bremner, J. D., Narayan, M., Anderson, E. R., Staib, L. H., Miller, H. L., & Charney, D. S. (2000). Hippocampal volume reduction in major depression. *American Journal of Psychiatry, 157,* 115–117.

Brennan, K. A. & Shaver, P. R. (1998). Attachment styles and personality disorders: Their connections to each other and to parental divorce, parental death, and perceptions of parental caregiving. *Journal of Personality, 66,* 835–878.

Brennan, P. A. & Walker, E. F. (2001). Vulnerability to schizophrenia: Risk factors in childhood and adolescence. In R. E. Ingram & J. M. Price (Eds.), *Vulnerability to psychopathology: Risk across the lifespan* (pp. 329–354). New York: Guilford Press.

Brenneis, C. B. (1996). Multiple personality: Fantasy proneness, demand characteristics, and indirect communication. *Psychoanalytic Psychology, 13,* 367–387.

Brenner, C. (1982). *The mind in conflict.* Madison, CT: International Universities Press.

Brenner, H. D., Roder, V., Hodel, B., Kienzie, N., Reed, D., & Liberman, R. P. (1995). *Integrated psychological therapy for schizophrenic patients.* Bern, Switzerland: Hogrefe & Huber.

Brenner, I. (1996). The characterological basis of multiple personality. *American Journal of Psychotherapy, 50,* 154–166.

Brent, D. A., Bridge, J., Johnson, B. A., & Connolly, J. (1996). Suicidal behavior runs in families: A controlled family study of adolescent suicide victims. *Archives of General Psychiatry, 53,* 1145–1152.

Breslau, N., Davis, G. C., Andreski, P., & Peterson, E. (1991). Traumatic events and posttraumatic stress disorder in an urban population of young adults. *Archives of General Psychiatry, 48,* 218–228.

Breslau, N., Kessler, R. C., Chilcoat, H. D., Schultz, L. R. Davis, G. C., & Andreski, P. (1998). Trauma and posttraumatic stress disorder in the community: The 1996 Detroit Area Survey of Trauma. *Archives of General Psychiatry, 55,* 626–632.

Brewin, C. R., Andrews, B., & Valentine, J. D. (2000). Meta-analysis of risk factors for posttraumatic stress disorder in trauma-exposed adults. *Journal of Consulting and Clinical Psychology, 68,* 748–766.

Brewin, C. R., MacCarthy, B., Duda, K., & Vaughn, C. E. (1991). Attribution and expressed emotion in the relatives of patients with schizophrenia. *Journal of Abnormal Psychology, 100,* 546–554.

Briesmeister, J. M. & Schaefer, C. E. (1998). *Handbook of parent training: Parents as co-therapists for children's behavior problems* (2nd ed.). New York: Wiley.

Bright, J. I., Baker, K. D., & Neimeyer, R. A. (1999). Professional and paraprofessional group treatments for depression: A comparison of cognitive-behavioral and mutual support interventions. *Journal of Consulting and Clinical Psychology, 67,* 491–501.

Brinkley, C. A., Bernstein, A., & Newman, J. P. (1999). Coherence in the narratives of psychopathic and nonpsychopathic criminal offenders. *Personality and Individual Differences, 27,* 519–530.

Brion, S. (1969). Korsakoff's syndrome: Clinico-anatomical and physiopathological considerations. In G. A. Talland & N. C. Waugh (Eds.), *The pathology of memory.* New York: Academic Press.

Broadwell, S. D. & Light, K. C. (1999). Family support and cardiovascular responses in married couples during conflict and other interactions. *International Journal of Behavioral Medicine, 6,* 40–63.

Brockington, I. (2001). Suicide in women. *International Clinical Psychopharmacology, 16*(Suppl.), S7–S19.

Brodaty, H., Peters, K., Boyce, P., Hickie, I., Parker, G., Mitchell, P., & Wilhelm, K. (1991). Age and depression. *Journal of Affective Disorders, 23,* 137–149.

Brody, A. L., Saxena, S., Stoessel, P., Gillies, L. A., Fairbanks, L. A., Alborzian, S., Phelps, M. E., Huang, S. C., Wu, H. M., Ho, M. L., Ho, M. K., Au, S. C., Maidment, K., & Baxter, L. R., Jr. (2001). Regional brain metabolic changes in patients with major depression treated with either paroxetine or interpersonal therapy: Preliminary findings. *Archives of General Psychiatry, 58,* 631–640.

Broman, S., Nichols, P. L., Shaughnessy, P., & Kennedy, W., et al. (1987). *Retardation in young children.* Hillsdale, NJ: Erlbaum.

Bromberg, W. (1965). *Crime and the mind.* New York: Macmillan.

Bron, B., Strack, M., & Rudolph, G. (1991). Childhood experiences of loss and suicide attempts: Significance in depressive states of major depressed and dysthymic or adjustment disordered patients. *Journal of Affective Disorders, 23,* 165–172.

Brookoff, D., O'Brien, K. K., Cook, C. S., Thompson, T. D., & Williams, C. (1997). Characteristics of participants in domestic violence: Assessment at the scene of a domestic assault. *Journal of the American Medical Association, 277,* 1369–1373.

Brooks, P. J. (2000). Brain atrophy and neuronal loss in alcoholism: A role for DNA damage? *Neurochemistry International, 37,* 403–412.

Brooks-Gunn, J. (1988). Antecedents and consequences of variations in girls' maturational timing. *Journal of Adolescent Health Care, 9,* 365–373.

Brooks-Gunn, J. & Chase-Lansdale, P. L. (1995). Adolescent parenthood. In M. H. Bornstein (Ed.), *Handbook of parenting: Vol. 3. Status and social conditions of parenting* (pp. 113–150). Mahwah, NJ: Erlbaum.

Broskowski, A. & Baker, F. (1974). Professional, organizational, and social barriers to primary prevention. *American Journal of Orthopsychiatry, 44,* 707–719.

Brown, G. P., Hammen, C. L., Craske, M. G., & Wickens, T. D. (1995). Dimensions of dysfunctional attitudes as vulnerabilities to depressive symptoms. *Journal of Abnormal Psychology, 104,* 431–435.

Brown, G. W. & Harris, T. O. (1978). *Social origins of depression.* London: Tavistock.

Brown, G. W., Harris, T. O., & Hepworth, C. (1994). Life events and endogenous depression: A puzzle reexamined. *Archives of General Psychiatry, 51,* 525–534.

Brown, G. W., Harris, T. O., & Eales, M. J. (1996). Social factors and comorbidity of depressive and anxiety disorders. *British Journal of Psychiatry. 168* (Suppl. 30), 50–57.

Brown, H. N. & Vaillant, G. E. (1981). Hypochondriasis. *Archives of Internal Medicine, 141,* 723–726.

Brown, L. S. (1992). A feminist critique of the personality disorders. In L. S. Brown & M. Ballou (Eds.), *Personality and psychopathology: Feminist reappraisals* (pp. 206–228). New York: Guilford Press.

Brown, P. (1997). The risk of bovine spongiform encephalopathy ("Mad Cow Disease") to human health. *Journal of the American Medical Association, 278,* 1008–1011.

Brown, S. A., Goldman, M. S., & Christiansen, B. A. (1985). Do alcohol expectancies mediate drinking patterns of adults? *Journal of Consulting and Clinical Psychology, 53,* 512–519.

Brown, S. A., Goldman, M. S., Inn, A., & Anderson, L. R. (1980). Expectations of reinforcement from alcohol: Their domain and relation to drinking patterns. *Journal of Consulting and Clinical Psychology, 48,* 419–426.

Brown, S. A., Vik, P. W., Patterson, T. L., Grant, I., & Schuckit, M. A. (1995). Stress, vulnerability, and adult alcohol relapse. *Journal of Studies on Alcohol, 56,* 538–545.

Brown, T. A., Chorpita, B. R., & Barlow, D. H. (1998). Structural relationships among dimensions of the *DSM-IV* anxiety and mood disorders and dimensions of negative affect, positive affect, and autonomic arousal. *Journal of Abnormal Psychology, 107*(2), 179–192.

Brown, T. A., Marten, P. A., & Barlow, D. H. (1995). Discriminant validity of the symptoms constituting the *DSM-III-R* and *DSM-IV* associated symptom criterion of generalized anxiety disorder. *Journal of Anxiety Disorders, 4,* 317–328.

Browne, A. & Finkelhor, D. (1986). Impact of child sexual abuse: A review of the research. *Psychological Bulletin, 99,* 66–77.

Brownell, K. D. (1986). Public health approaches to obesity and its management. *Annual Review of Public Health, 7,* 521–533.

Brownell, K. D. (1993). Whether obesity should be treated. *Health Psychology, 12,* 339–341.

Brownell, K. D. (1999). The central role of lifestyle change in long-term weight management. *Clinical Cornerstone, 2,* 43–51.

Brownell, K. D. & Wadden, T. A. (1992). Etiology and treatment of obesity: Understanding a serious, prevalent, and refractory disorder. *Journal of Consulting and Clinical Psychology, 60,* 505–517.

Bruce, M. L. & Kim, K. M. (1992). Differences in the effects of divorce on major depression in men and women. *American Journal of Psychiatry, 149,* 914–917.

Bruch, H. (1978). *The golden cage: The enigma of anorexia nervosa.* Cambridge, MA: Harvard University Press.

Bruch, M. A. & Heimberg, R. G. (1994). Differences in perceptions of parental and personal characteristics between generalized and nongeneralized social phobics. *Journal of Anxiety Disorders, 8,* 155–168.

Bruder, G. E., Stewart, J. W., Tenke, C. E., McGrath, P. J., Leite, P., Bhattacharya, N., & Quitkin, F. M. (2001). Electroencephalographic and perceptual asymmetry differences between responders and nonresponders to an SSRI antidepressant. *Biological Psychiatry, 49,* 416–425.

Bryan, T. & Bryan, J. (1990). Social factors in learning disabilities. In H. L. Swanson & B. Keogh (Eds.), *Learning disabilities: Theoretical and research issues.* Hillsdale, NJ: Erlbaum.

Bryant, R. A. & Harvey, A. G. (1995). Processing threatening information in posttraumatic stress disorder. *Journal of Abnormal Psychology, 104,* 537–541.

Bryant, R. A. & Harvey, A. G. (1998). Relationship between acute stress disorder and posttraumatic stress disorder following mild traumatic brain injury. *American Journal of Psychiatry, 155*(5), 625–629.

Bryant, R. A. & McConkey, K. M. (1989). Visual conversion disorder: A case analysis of the influence of visual information. *Journal of Abnormal Psychology, 98,* 326–329.

Bryson, S. E., Clark, B. S., & Smith, I. M. (1988). First report of a Canadian epidemiological study of autistic syndromes. *Journal of Child Psychology and Psychiatry, 29,* 433–445.

Buchanan, G. M., Gardenswartz, C. A. R., & Seligman, M. E. P. (1999). Physical health following a cognitive-behavioral intervention. *Prevention & Treatment, 2.*

Buchanan, R. W., Strauss, M. E., Breier, A., Kirkpatrick, B., & Carpenter, W. T. (1997). Attentional impairments in deficit and nondeficit forms of schizophrenia. *American Journal of Psychiatry, 154,* 363–370.

Buckner, R. L. & Logan, J. M. (2001). Functional neuroimaging methods: PET and fMRI. In R. Cabeza & A. Kingstone (Eds.), *Handbook of functional neuroimaging of cognition* (pp. 27–48). Cambridge, MA: MIT Press.

Buka, S. L., Tsuang, M. T., Torrey, E. F., Klebanoff, M. A., Bernstein, D., & Yolken, R. H. (2001). Maternal infections and subsequent psychosis among offspring. *Archives of General Psychiatry, 58,* 1032–1037.

Bulik, C. M., Epstein, L. H., & Kaye, W. (1990). Treatment of laxative abuse in a female with bulimia nervosa using an operant extinction paradigm. *Journal of Substance Abuse, 2,* 381–388.

Bullock, R. (2002). New drugs for Alzheimer's disease and other dementias. *British Journal of Psychiatry, 180,* 135–139.

Bullough, V. L. & Bullough, B. (1993). *Cross-dressing, sex, and gender.* Philadelphia: University of Pennsylvania Press.

Burbridge, J. A. & Barch, D. M. (2002). Emotional valence and reference disturbance in schizophrenia. *Journal of Abnormal Psychology, 111,* 186–191.

Burgess, A. W., Groth, A. N., & McCausland, M. P. (1981). Child sex initation rings. *American Journal of Orthopsychiatry, 51,* 110–119.

Burke, J. D., Jr., Burke, K. C., & Rae, D. S. (1994). Increased rates of drug abuse and dependence after onset of mood or anxiety disorders in adolescence. *Hospital and Community Psychiatry, 45,* 451–455.

Burke, K. C., Burke, J. D., Jr., Regier, D. A., & Rae, D. S. (1990). Age at onset of selected mental disorders in five community populations. *Archives of General Psychiatry, 47,* 511–518.

Burke, K. C., Burke, J. D., Rae, D. S., & Regier, D. A. (1991). Comparing age at onset of major depression and other psychiatric disorders by birth cohorts in five U. S. community populations. *Archives of General Psychiatry, 48,* 789–795.

Burns, D. D. & Spangler, D. L. (2001). Do changes in dysfunctional attitudes mediate changes in depression and anxiety in cognitive-behavioral therapy? *Behavior Therapy, 21,* 337–370.

Burt, R. A. (2001). Promises to keep, miles to go: Mental health law since 1972. In L. E. Frost & R. J. Bonnie (Eds.), *The evolution of mental health law* (pp. 11–30). Washington, DC: American Psychological Association.

Bushman, B. (1993). Human aggression while under the influence of alcohol and other drugs: An integrative research review. *Current Directions in Psychological Science, 2,* 148–152.

Butcher, J. N. (1999). Research design in objective personality assessment. In P. C. Kendall, J. N. Butcher, & G. N. Holmbeck (Eds.), *Handbook of research methods in clinical psychology* (2nd ed., pp. 155–182). New York: Wiley.

Butler, L. D., Duran, R. E. F., Jasiukaitis, P., Koopman, C., & Spiegel, D. (1996). Hypnotizability and traumatic experience: A diathesis-stress model of dissociative symptomatology. *American Journal of Psychiatry, 153,* 42–63.

Butow, P. N., Hiller, J. E., Price, M. A., Thackway, S. V., Kricker, A., & Tennant, C. C. (2000). Epidemiological evidence for a relationship between life events, coping style, and personality factors in the development of breast cancer. *Journal of Psychosomatic Research, 49*(3), 169–181.

Butzlaff, R. L. & Hooley, J. M. (1998). Expressed emotion and psychiatric relapse: A meta-analysis. *Archives of General Psychiatry, 55,* 547–552.

Buvat, J., Buvat-Herbaut, M., Lemaire, A., Marcolin, G., & Quittelier, E. (1990). Recent developments in the clinical assessment and diagnosis of erectile dysfunction. *Annual Review of Sex Research, 2,* 265–308.

Buysse, D. J. & Kupfer, D. J. (1993). Sleep disorders in depressive disorders. In J. J. Mann & D. J. Kupfer (Eds.), *Biology of depressive disorders: Part A. A systems perspective* (pp. 123–154.). New York: Plenum.

Byrne, M., Hodges, A., Grant, E., Owens, D. C., & Johnstone, E. C. (1999). Neuropsychological assessment of young people at high genetic risk for developing schizophrenia compared with controls: Preliminary findings of the Edinburgh High Risk Study (EHRS). *Psychological Medicine, 29,* 1161–1173.

Caballo, V. E. (Ed.) (1998). *International handbook of cognitive and behavioural treatments for psychological disorders.* New York: Pergamon Press.

Cadoret, R. J., Troughton, E., O'Gorman, T. W., & Heywood, E. (1986). An adoption study of genetic and environment factors in drug abuse. *Archives of General Psychiatry, 43,* 1131–1136.

Caetano, R. & Rasperry, K. (2000). Drinking and *DSM-IV* alcohol and drug dependence among White and Mexican-American DUI offenders. *Journal of Studies on Alcohol, 61,* 420–426.

Cain, J. W. (1992). Poor response to fluoxetine: Underlying depression, serotonergic overstimulation, or a "therapeutic window"? *Journal of Clinical Psychiatry, 53,* 272–277.

Calderon, R., Jr., Schneider, R. H., Alexander, C. N., Myers, H. F., Nidich, S. I., & Haney, C. (1999). Stress, stress reduction and hypercholesterolemia in African Americans: A review. *Ethnicity and Disease, 9,* 451–462.

Calhoun, G. B., Glaser, B., Stefurak, T., & Bradshaw, C. P. (2001). Preliminary validation of the Narcissistic Personality Inventory-Juvenile Offender. *International Journal of Offender Therapy and Comparative Criminology, 44,* 564–580.

Callahan, L. A. & Silver, E. (1998). Revocation of conditional release: A comparison of individual and program characteristics across four U.S. states. *International Journal of Law and Psychiatry, 21,* 177–186.

Cameron, L. D. & Nicholls, G. (1998). Expression of stressful experiences through writing: Effects of a self-regulation manipulation for pessimists and optimists. *Health Psychology, 17,* 84–92.

Campbell, F. & Ramsey, C. T. (1994). Effect of early intervention on intellectual and academic achievement: A follow-up study of children from low-income families. *Child Development, 65,* 684–698.

Campbell, M., Overall, J. E., Small, A. M., Sokol, M. S., Spencer, E. K., Adams, P., Foltz, R. L., Monti, K. M., Perry, R., Nobler, M., & Roberts, E. (1989). Naltrexone in autistic children: An open dose range tolerance trial. *Journal of the American Academy of Child and Adolescent Psychiatry, 28,* 200–206.

Campbell, M., Schopler, E., Cueva, J. E., & Hallin, A. (1996). Treatment of autistic disorder. *Journal of the American Academy of Child and Adolescent Psychiatry, 35,* 134–143.

Campbell, W. K. (1999). Narcissism and romantic attraction. *Journal of Personality and Social Psychology, 77,* 1254–1270.

Canada Newswire. (2001, March 28). Patient visits for depression rise for sixth consecutive year. Retrieved March 28, 2001, from http://www.newswire.ca.

Candilis, P. J., McLean, R. Y., Otto, M. W., Manfro, G. G., Worthington, J. J., 3rd, Penava, S. J., Marzol, P. C., & Pollack, M. H. (1999). Quality of life in patients with panic disorder. *Journal of Nervous and Mental Disease, 187,* 429–434.

Cannon, T. D. (1998). Genetic and perinatal influences in the etiology of schizophrenia: A neurodevelopmental model. In M. Lenzenweger & B. Dworkin (Eds.), *Origins and development of schizophrenia* (pp. 67–92). Washington, DC: American Psychological Association.

Cannon, T. D., Rosso, I. M., Bearden, C. E., Sanchez, L. E., & Hadley, T. (1999). A prospective cohort study of neurodevelopmental processes in the genesis and epigenesis of schizophrenia. *Development & Psychopathology, 11,* 467–485.

Cannon, T. D., van Erp, T. G. M., Rosso, I. M., Huttunen, M., Lonnqvist, J., Pirhola, T., Salonen, O., Valanne, L., Poutanen, V. P., Standertskjold-Nordenstam, C. G. (2002). Fetal hypoxia and structural brain abnormalities in schizophrenic patients, their siblings, and controls. *Archives of General Psychiatry, 59,* 35–41.

Cannon, W. B. (1936). *Bodily changes in pain, hunger, fear, and rage.* New York: Appleton-Century.

Capitano, J. P. & Lerche, N. W. (1998). Social separation, housing relocation, and survival in simian AIDS: A retrospective analysis. *Psychosomatic Medicine, 60,* 235–244.

Capps, L., Sigman, M., & Mundy, P. (1994). Attachment security in children with autism. *Development and Psychopathology, 6,* 249–261.

Carels, R. A., Blumenthal, J. A., & Sherwood, A. (2000). Emotional responsivity during daily life: relationship to psychosocial functioning and ambulatory blood pressure. *International Journal of Psychophysiology, 36,* 25–33.

Carels, R. A., Sherwood, A., Babyak, M., Gullette, E. C., Coleman, R. E., Waugh, R., Jiang, W., & Blumenthal, J. A. (1999). Emotional responsivity and transient myocardial ischemia. *Journal of Consulting and Clinical Psychology, 67,* 605–610.

Carey, G. & Goldman, D. (1997). The genetics of antisocial behavior. In D. M. Stoff, J. Breiling, & J. D. Maser (Eds.), *Handbook of antisocial behavior* (pp. 243–254). New York: Wiley.

Carey, M. P. & Johnson, B. T. (1996). Effectiveness of yohimbine in the treatment of erectile disorder: Four meta-analytic integrations. *Archives of Sexual Behavior, 25,* 341–360.

Carlsson, A. (2001). Neurotransmitters—Dopamine and beyond. In A. Breier, P. V. Tran, F. Bymaster, & C. Tollefson (Eds.), *Current issues in the psychopharmacology of schizophrenia* (pp. 3–11). Philadelphia: Lippincott Williams & Wilkins.

Carlsson, A., Waters, N., Waters, S., & Carlsson, M. L. (2000). Network interactions in schizophrenia—therapeutic implications. *Brain Research Reviews, 31,* 342–349.

Carnegie Corporation of New York. (1994). *Starting points: Meeting the needs of our youngest children* (Report of the Carnegie Task Force on Meeting the Needs of Young Children).

Carr, J. (1994). Annotation: Long term outcome for people with Down syndrome. *Journal of Child Psychology and Psychiatry, 35,* 425–439.

Carroll, K. M. (1996). Relapse prevention as a psychosocial treatment. *Experimental and Clinical Psychopharmacology, 4,* 40–54.

Carroll, M. E. & Comer, S. D. (1996). Animal models of relapse. *Experimental and Clinical Pharmacology, 4,* 11–18.

Carroll, R. A. (1997). *The diversity of psychosocial outcomes of treatment of gender dysphoria.* Paper presented at the XVth Harry Benjamin International Gender Dysphoria Association Symposium, Vancouver, Canada.

Carson, R. C. (1996). Aristotle, Galileo, and the DSM taxonomy: The case of schizophrenia. *Journal of Consulting and Clinical Psychology, 64,* 1133–1139.

Carter, C. S., Mintun, M., Nichols, T., & Cohen, J. D. (1997). Anterior cingulate gyrus dysfunction and selective attention deficits in schizophrenia: $[^{15}O]H_2O$ PET study during single-trial Stroop task performance. *American Journal of Psychiatry, 154,* 1670–1675.

Carter, M. M., Hollon, S. D., Carson, R., & Shelton, R. C. (1995). Effects of a safe person on induced distress following a biological challenge in panic disorder with agoraphobia. *Journal of Abnormal Psychology, 104,* 156–163.

Carter, R. M., Wittchen, H. U., Pfister, H., et al. (2001). One-year prevalence of subthreshold and threshold *DSM-IV* generalized anxiety disorder in a nationally representative sample. *Depression and Anxiety, 3,* 78–88.

Cascardi, M., Poythress, N. G., & Hall A. (2000). Procedural justice in the context of civil commitment: An analogue study. *Behavioral Sciences and the Law, 18,* 731–740.

Casey Family Programs and the U.S. Department of Health and Human Services. (2001). *Starting Early, Starting Smart: Summary of Early Findings.* Washington, DC: Casey

Family Programs and the U.S. Department of Health and Human Services, Substance Abuse and Mental Health Services Administration.

Cassidy, J. & Shaver, P. R. (1999). *Handbook of attachment: Theory, research, and clinical applications.* New York: Guilford Press.

Casson, I. R., Seigel, O., Sham, R., Campbell, E. A., Tarlau, M., & DiDomenico, A. (1984). Brain damage in modern boxers. *Journal of the American Medical Association, 251,* 2663–2667.

Castelloe, P. & Dawson, G. (1993). Subclassification of children with autism and pervasive developmental disorder. A questionnaire based on Wing's subgrouping scheme. *Journal of Autism and Developmental Disorders, 23.*

Castillo, R. J. (1997a). *Culture & mental illness: A client-centered approach.* Pacific Grove, CA: Brooks/Cole.

Castillo, R. J. (1997b). Dissociation. In W. S. Tseng & J. Streltzer (Eds.), *Culture and psychopathology: A guide to clinical assessment* (pp. 101–123). New York: Brunner/Mazel.

Castillo-Richmond, A., Schneider, R. H., Alexander, C. N., Cook, R., Myers, H., Nidich, S., Haney, C., Rainforth, M., & Salerno, J. (2000). Effects of stress reduction on carotid atherosclerosis in hypertensive African Americans. *Stroke, 31, 568–573.*

Castle, D. J., Abel, K., Takei, N., & Murray, R. M. (1995). Gender differences in schizophrenia: Hormonal effect or subtypes? *Schizophrenia Bulletin, 21,* 1–12.

Castle, D. J. & Murray, R. M. (1993). The epidemiology of late-onset schizophrenia. *Schizophrenia Bulletin, 19,* 691–700.

Catts, S.V., Shelley, A. M., Ward, P. B., Liebert, B., McConaghy, N., Andrews, S., & Michie, P. T. (1995). Brain potential evidence for an auditory sensory memory deficit in schizophrenia. *American Journal of Psychiatry, 152,* 213–219.

Cautela, J. R. (2000). Rationale and procedures for covert conditioning. *Psicoterapia Cognitiva e Comportamentale, 6,* 194–205.

Cavallin, H. (1966). Incestuous fathers: A clinical report. *American Journal of Psychiatry, 122*(10), 1132–1138.

Cecil, K. M., Lenkinski, R. E., Gur, R. E., & Gur, R. C. (1999). Proton magnentic resonance spectroscopy in the frontal and temporal lobes of neuroleptic naive patients with schizophrenia. *Neuropsychopharmacology, 20,* 131–140.

Centers for Disease Control and Prevention. (1997). Smoking-attributable mortality and years of potential life lost—United States, 1984, and Editorial Note. *Morbidity and Mortality Weekly Report, 46,* 444–451.

Centers for Disease Control and Prevention. (2002). State-specific mortality from sudden cardiac death—United States, 1999. *Morbidity and Mortality Weekly Report, 51,* 123–126.

Centers for Disease Control and Prevention. (2003a). Preventing and controlling cancer: the nation's second leading cause of death—2003. Retrieved April 17, 2003, from http://www.cancer.org/downloads/STT/CAFF2003PWSecured.pdf.

Centers for Disease Control and Prevention. (2003b). *HIV/AIDS update.* Retrieved April 17, 2003, from http://www.cdc.gov/nchstp/od/news/At-a-Glance.pdf.

Cercy, S. P. & Bylsma, F. W. (1997). Lewy bodies and progressive dementia: A critical review and meta-analysis. *Journal of the International Neuropsychological Society, 3,* 179–194.

Chabot, R. J., diMichele, F., Prichep, L., & John, E. R. (2001). The clinical role of computerized EEG in the evaluation and treatment of learning and attention disorders in children and adolescents. *Journal of Neuropsychiatry and Clinical Neurosciences, 13,* 171–186.

Chadwick, P. D. J., Lowe, C. F., Horne, P. J., & Higson, P. J. (1994). Modifying delusions: The role of empirical testing. *Behavior Therapy, 25,* 35–49.

Chambless, D. L. & Hollon, S. D. (1998). Defining empirically supported therapies. *Journal of Consulting and Clinical Psychology, 66,* 7–18.

Chambless, D. L. & Ollendick, T. H. (2000). Empirically supported psychological interventions: Controversies and evidence. *Annual Review of Psychology, 52,* 685–716.

Chambless, D. L., Baker, M. J., Baucom, D. H., Beutler, L., Calhoun, K. S., Crits-Christoph, P., Daiuto, A., DeRebuis, R., Detweier, J., Haiga, D. A. F., Bennett Johnson, S., McCurry, S., Mueser, K. T., Pope, K. S., Sanderson, W. C., Shoham, V., Stickle, T., Williams, D. A., & Woddy, S. A. (1998). Update on empirically validated therapies, II. *The Clinical Psychologist, 51,* 3–16.

Chantarujikapong, S. I., Scherrer, J. R., Xian, H., Eisen, S. A., Lyons, M. J., Golberg, J., Tsuang, M., & True, W. R. (2001). A twin study of generalized anxiety disorder symptoms, panic disorder symptoms, and post-traumatic stress disorder in men. *Psychiatry Research, 102*(2–3), 133–146.

Chaplin, S. L. (1997). Somatization. In W. S. Tseng & J. Streltzer (Eds.), *Culture and psychopathology: A guide to clinical assessment* (pp. 67–86). New York: Brunner/Mazel.

Chapman, L. J. & Chapman, J. P. (1973). *Disordered thought in schizophrenia.* New York: Appleton-Century-Crofts.

Chapman, L. J. & Chapman, J. P. (1985). Psychosis proneness. In M. Alpert (Ed.), *Controversies in schizophrenia* (pp. 157–172). New York: Guilford Press.

Chapman, L. J., Chapman, J. P., Kwapil, T. R., Eckblad, M., & Zinser, M. C. (1994). Putatively psychosis-prone subjects 10 years later. *Journal of Abnormal Psychology, 103,* 171–183.

Characteristics of the recovering compulsive gambler: A survey of 150 members of Gamblers Anonymous. Paper presented at the fourth annual Conference on Gambling, Reno, NV.

Charcot, J. & Marie, P. (1892). On hystero-epilepsy. In D. H. Tuke (Ed.), *A dictionary of psychological medicine* (Vol. 1). Philadelphia: Blakiston.

Chemtob, C. M., Hamada, R. S., Roitblat, H. L., & Muraoka, M. Y. (1994). Anger, impulsivity, and anger control in combat-related posttraumatic stress disorder. *Journal of Consulting and Clinical Psychology, 62,* 827–832.

Chen, C. C., David, A. S., Nunnerley, H., Michell, M., Dawson, J. L., Berry, H., et al. (1995). Adverse life events and breast cancer: A case control study. *British Medical Journal, 311,* 1527–1530.

Chen, J., Mabjeesh, N. J., & Greenstein, A. (2001). Sildenafil versus the vacuum erection device: Patient preference. *Journal of Urology, 166,* 1779–1781.

Chen, Y. C., Lu, R. B., Peng, G. S., Wang, M. F., Wang, H. K., Ko, H. C., Lu, J. J., Li, T. K., & Yin, S. I. (1999). Alcohol metabolism and cardiovascular response in an alcoholic patient homozygous for the ALDH2*2 variant gene allele. *Alcoholism: Clinical and Experimental Research, 23,* 1853–1860.

Chodorow, N. (1978). *The reproduction of mothering: Psychoanalysis and the sociology of gender.* Berkeley: University of California Press.

Chorpita, B. E. & Barlow, D. H. (1998). The development of anxiety: The role of control in the early environment. *Psychological Bulletin, 124,* 3–21.

Christenson, G. A., Pyle, R. I., & Mitchell, J. E. (1991). Estimated lifetime prevalence of trichotillomania in college students. *Journal of Clinical Psychology, 52,* 415–417.

Christian, L. & Poling, A. (1997). Drug abuse in persons with mental retardation: A review. *American Journal of Mental Retardation, 102,* 126–136.

Christiansen, B. A., Smith, G. T., Roehling, P. V., & Goldman, M. S. (1989). Using alcohol expectancies to predict adolescent drinking behavior after one year. *Journal of Consulting and Clinical Psychology, 57,* 93–99.

Christoffel, H. (1956). Male genital exhibitionism. In S. Lorand & M. Bolint (Eds.), *Perversions: Psychodynamics and therapy.* New York: Random House.

Christophersen, E. R. & Edwards, K. J. (1992). Treatment of elimination disorders. State of the art. *Applied and Preventive Psychology, 1,* 15–22.

Christophersen, E. R. & Mortweet, S. L. (2001). *Treatments that work with children: Empirically supported strategies for managing childhood problems.* Washington, DC: American Psychological Association.

Chugani, D. C., Muzik, O., Behen, M., Rothermel, R., Janisse, J. J., Lee, J., & Chugani, H. T. (1999). Developmental changes in brain serotonin synthesis capacity in autistic and nonautistic children. *Annals of Neurology, 45,* 287–295.

Chugani, H. (1993). Positron emission tomography scanning in newborns. *Clinics in Perinatology, 20*(2), 398.

Clancy, S. A., Schacter, D. L., McNally, R. J., & Pitman, R. K. (2000). False recognition in women reporting recovered memories of sexual abuse. *Psychological Science, 11,* 26–31.

Clark, D. A., Beck, A. T., & Alford, B. A. (1999). *Scientific foundations of cognitive theory and therapy of depression.* New York: Wiley.

Clark, D. M. (1977). Cognitive mediation of panic attacks induced by biological challenge tests. *Behaviour Research and Therapy, 15,* 75–84.

Clark, D. M. (1988). A cognitive model of panic attacks. In S. Rachman and J. Maser (Eds), *Panic: Psychological perspectives.* Hillsdale, NJ: Erlbaum.

Clark, D. M. (1991, September 23–25). *Cognitive therapy for panic disorder.* Paper presented at the NIH Consensus Development Conference on the Treatment of Panic Disorders, Bethesda, MD.

Clark, D. M. (1993). Cognitive mediation of panic attacks induced by biological challenge tests. *Advances in Behaviour Research and Therapy, 15,* 75–84.

Clark, D. M., Salkovskis, P. M., Hackmann, A., et al. (1998). Two psychological treatments for hypochondriasis: A randomised controlled trial. *British Journal of Psychiatry, 173,* 218–225.

Clark, D. M. & Wells, A. (1995). A cognitive model of social phobia. In R. Heimberg, M. Liebowitz, D. A. Hope, & F. R. Schneier (Eds.), *Social phobia: Diagnosis, assessment, and treatment.* New York: Guilford Press.

Clark, L. A. (1999). Dimensional approaches to personality disorder assessment and diagnosis. In C. R. Cloninger (Ed.), *Personality and psychopathology* (pp. 219–246). Washington, DC: American Psychiatric Press.

Clark, L., Iversen, S. D., & Goodwin, G. M. (2001). A neuropsychological investigation of prefrontal cortex involvement in acute mania. *American Journal of Psychiatry, 158,* 1605–1611.

Clarke, G. N., Hornbrook, M., Lynch, F., Polen, M., Gale, J., Beardslee, W., O'Connor, E., & Seeley, J. (2001). A randomized trial of a group cognitive intervention for preventing depression in adolescent offspring of depressed parents. *Archives of General Psychiatry, 58,* 1127–1136.

Clarkin, J. F., Marziali, E., & Monroe-Blum, H. (1991). Group and family treatments for borderline personality disorder. *Hospital and Community Psychiatry, 42,* 1038–1043.

Classen, C., Koopman, C., Hales, R., & Spiegel, D. (1998). Acute stress disorder as a predictor of posttraumatic stress symptoms. *American Journal of Psychiatry, 155,* 620–624.

Claussen, B. (1999). Alcohol disorders and re-employment in a 5-year follow-up of long-term unemployed. *Addiction, 94,* 133–138.

Cleckley, H. M. (1976). *The mask of sanity.* St. Louis: Mosby.

Cleghorn, J. M., Franco, S., Szechtman, B., Kaplan, R. D., Szechtman, H., Brown, G. M., Nahmias, C., & Garnett, E. S. (1992). Toward a brain map of auditory hallucinations. *American Journal of Psychiatry, 149,* 1062–1069.

Clementz, B. A., Geyer, M. A., & Braff, D. L. (1998). Multiple site evaluation of P50 suppression among schizophrenia and normal comparison subjects. *Schizophrenia Research, 30,* 70–80.

Clementz, B. A., McDowell, J. E., & Zisook, S. (1994). Saccadic system functioning among schizophrenia patients and their first-degree biological relatives. *Journal of Abnormal Psychology, 103,* 277–287.

Clinthorne, J. K., Cisin, I. H., Balter, M. B., Mellinger, G. D., & Uhlenhuth, E. H. (1986). Changes in popular attitudes and beliefs about tranquilizers: 1970–1979. *Archives of General Psychiatry, 43,* 527–532.

Cloninger, C. R. (1987a). Neurogenetic adaptive mechanisms in alcoholism. *Science, 236,* 410–416.

Cloninger, C. R. (1987b). A systematic method of clinical description and classification of personality variants: A proposal. *Archives of General Psychiatry, 44,* 573–588.

Cloninger, C. R., Bayon, C., & Przybeck, T. R. (1997). Epidemiology and axis I comorbidity of antisocial personality. In D. M. Stoff, J. Breiling, & J. D. Maser (Eds.), *Handbook of antisocial behavior* (pp. 12–21). New York: Wiley.

Cloninger, C. R., Bohman, M., & Sigvardsson, S. (1981). Inheritance of alcohol abuse: Cross-fostering analysis of adopted men. *Archives of General Psychiatry, 38*(8), 861–868.

Cloninger, C. R., Sigvardsson, S., von Knorring, A., & Bohman, M. (1984). An adoption study of somatoform disorders: II. Identification of two discrete somatoform disorders. *Archives of General Psychiatry, 41,* 863–871.

Clum, G. A. & Knowles, S. L. (1991). Why do some people with panic disorders become avoidant? A review. *Clinical Psychology Review, 11*(3), 295–313.

Cobb, S. C. & Rose, R. M. (1973). Hypertension, peptic ulcer, and diabetes in air traffic controllers. *Journal of the American Medical Association, 224,* 489–492.

Coccaro, E. F. (1993). Psychopharmologic studies in patients with personality disorders: Review and perspective. *Journal of Personality Disorders, 7,* 181–192.

Cohen, B. D., Nachmani, G., & Rosenberg, S. (1974). Referent communication disturbances in acute schizophrenia. *Journal of Abnormal Psychology. 83*(1), 1–13.

Cohen, D., Taieb, O., Flament, M., Benoit, N., Chevret, S., Corcos, M.,

Fossatti, P., Jeammet, P., Allilaire, J. F., & Basquin, M. (2000). Absence of cognitive impairment at long-term follow-up in adolescents treated with ECT for severe mood disorder. *American Journal of Psychiatry, 157,* 460–462.

Cohen, J. D., Barch, D. M., Carter, C., & Servan-Schreiber, D. (1999). Context-processing deficits in schizophrenia: Converging evidence from three theoretically motivated cognitive tasks. *Journal of Abnormal Psychology, 108,* 120–133.

Cohen, K., Auld, F., & Brooker, H. (1994). Is alexithymia related to psychosomatic disorder and somatizing? *Journal of Psychosomatic Research, 38,* 119–127.

Cohen, M. & Seghorn, T. (1969). Sociometric study of the sex offender. *Journal of Abnormal Psychology, 74,* 249–255.

Cohen, N. L. (2000). Mental health services in New York City. *International Journal of Mental Health, 28,* 48–53.

Cohen, P., Cohen, J., Kasen, S., Velez, C. N., Hartmark, C., Johnson, J., Rojas, M., Brook, J., Streuning, E. L. (1993). An epidemiological study of disorders in late childhood and adolescence: I. Age- and gender-specific prevalence. *Journal of Child Psychology and Psychiatry and Allied Disciplines, 34,* 851–867.

Cohen, S. (1986). Effects of long-term marijuana use. *Alcohol, Drugs, & Driving, 2*(3–4), 155–163.

Cohen, S. & Lichtenstein, E. (1990). Partner behaviors that support quitting smoking. *Journal of Consulting and Clinical Psychology, 58,* 304–309.

Cohen, S., Doyle, W. J., Skoner, D. P., Rabin, B. S., & Gwaltney, J. M. (1997). Social ties and susceptibility to the common cold. *Journal of the American Medical Association, 24,* 1940–1944.

Cohen, S., Tyrrell, D. A. J., & Smith, A. P. (1991). Psychological stress and susceptibility to the common cold. *New England Journal of Medicine, 325,* 606–612.

Cole, C. M., O'Boyle, M., Emory, L. E., & Meyer, W. (1997). Comorbidity of gender dysphoria and other major psychiatric diagnoses. *Archives of Sexual Behavior, 26,* 13–27.

Cole, D. A. & Turner, J. E., Jr. (1993). Models of cognitive mediation and moderation in child depression. *Journal of Abnormal Psychology, 102,* 271–281.

Cole, S. W., Kemeny, M. E., Taylor, S. E., & Visscher, B. R. (1996). Elevated physical health risk among gay men who conceal their homosexual identity. *Health Psychology, 15,* 243–251.

Coleman, M. (1989). Medical evaluation of individuals with an autistic disorder. *Forum Medicum.*

Coleman, M. J., Levy, D. L., Lenzenweger, M. F., & Holzman, P. S. (1996). Thought disorder, perceptual aberrations, and schizotypy. *Journal of Abnormal Psychology, 105,* 469–473.

Coles, E. M. & Veiel, H. O. F. (2001). Expert testimony and pseudoscience: How mental health professionals are taking over the courtroom. *International Journal of Law and Psychiatry, 24,* 607–625.

Collins, R. L., Koutsky, J. R., Morsheimer, E. T., & MacLean, M. G. (2001). Binge drinking among underage college students: A test of a restraint-based conceptualization of risk for alcohol abuse. *Psychology of Addictive Behaviors, 15,* 333–340.

Combs, B. J., Hales, D. R., & Williams, B. K. (1980). *An invitation to health: Your personal responsibility.* Menlo Park, CA: Benjamin/ Cummings.

Comment. (2001). *People v. Lloyd:* Michigan's guilty but mentally ill verdict created with intention to help is not really a benefit at all. *University of Detroit Mercy Law Review, 79,* 75–95.

Commitment following an insanity acquittal. (1981). *Harvard Law Review, 94,* 604–625.

Committee on Ethical Guidelines for Forensic Psychologists. (1991). Specialty guidelines for forensic psychologists. *Law and Human Behavior, 15,* 655–665.

Compas, B. E., Ey, S., & Grant, K. E. (1993). Taxonomy, assessment, and diagnosis of depression during adolescence. *Psychological Bulletin, 114,* 323–344.

Conacher, G. N. & Fleming, R. L. The extreme regressive reactions of a psychopath. *Psychiatric Quarterly, 1996, 67,* 1–10.

Conduct Problems Prevention Research Group. (1992). A developmental and clinical model for the prevention of conduct disorder: The FAST Track Program. Special Issue: Developmental approaches to prevention and intervention. *Development and Psychopathology, 4,* 509–527.

Cone, J. D. (1999). Observational assessment: Measure development and research issues. In P. C. Kendall, J. N. Butcher, & G. N. Holmbeck (Eds.), *Handbook of research methods in clinical psychology* (2nd ed., pp. 183–223). New York: Wiley.

Conger, J. J. (1951). The effects of alcohol on conflict behavior in the albino rat. *Quarterly Journal of Studies on Alcohol, 12,* 1–29.

Conklin, H. M. & Iacono, W. G. (2002). Schizophrenia: A neurodevelopmental perspective. *Current Directions in Psychological Sciences, 11,* 33–37.

Conner, K. R., Cox, C., Duberstein, P. R., Tian, L., Nisbet, P. A., & Conwell, Y. (2001). Violence, alcohol, and completed suicide: A case-control study. *American Journal of Psychiatry, 158,* 1701–1705.

Conte, J. R. & Berliner, L. (1981). Sexual abuse of children: Implications for practice. *Social Casework, 62,* 601–606.

Cook, M., Mineka, S., Wolkenstein, B., & Laitsch, K. (1985). Observational conditioning of snake fear in unrelated rhesus monkeys. *Journal of Abnormal Psychology, 94,* 591–610.

Cooke, D. J. & Michie, C. (1999). Psychopathy across cultures: North America and Scotland compared. *Journal of Abnormal Psychology, 1999,* 58–68.

Coolidge, F. L., Thede, L. L., & Jang, K. L. (2001). Heritability of personality disorders in childhood: A preliminary investigation. *Journal of Personality Disorders, 15,* 33–40.

Cools, J., Schotte, D. E., & McNally, R. J. (1992). Emotional arousal and overeating in restrained eaters. *Journal of Abnormal Psychology, 101,* 348–351.

Coons, P. M. (1986). Treatment progress in 20 patients with multiple personality disorder. *Journal of Nervous and Mental Disease, 174,* 715–721.

Coons, P. M. (1991). Iatrogenesis and malingering of multiple personality disorder in the forensic evaluation of homicide defendants. *Psychiatric Clinics of North America, 14,* 757–768.

Coons, P. M. (1994). Confirmation of childhood abuse in child and adolescent cases of multiple personality disorder and dissociative disorder not otherwise specified. *Journal of Nervous and Mental Disease, 182,* 461–464.

Coons, P. M. (1999). Psychogenic or dissociative fugue: A clinical investigation of five cases. *Psychological Reports, 84,* 881–886.

Coons, P. M. & Milstein, V. (1992). Amnesia: A clinical investigation of 25 cases. *Dissociation, 5,* 73–79.

Cooper, J. E., Kendell, R. E., Gurland, B. J., Sharp, L., Copeland, J. R. M., & Simon, R. (1972). *Psychiatric diagnosis in New York and London: A comparative study of mental hospital admissions.* New York: Oxford University Press.

Cooper, J. & Hall, J. (2000). Reaction of mock jurors to testimony of a court appointed expert. *Behavioral Sciences and the Law, 18,* 719–729.

Cooper, J. & Neuhaus, I. M. (2000). The "hired gun" effect: Assessing the effect of pay, frequency of testifying, and credentials on the perception of expert testimony. *Law and Human Behavior, 24,* 149–171.

Cooper, L. M. & Orcutt, H. K. (1997). Drinking and sexual experience on first dates among adolescents. *Journal of Abnormal Psychology, 106,* 191–202.

Cooper, R. S. (2001). Social inequality, ethnicity and cardiovascular disease. *International Journal of Epidemiology, 30,* S48–S52.

Cooper, S. H. (1998). Changing notions of defense within psychoanalytic theory. *Journal of Personality, 66,* 947–992.

Copeland, J., Swift, W., Roffman, R., & Stephens, R. (2001). A randomized controlled trial of brief cognitive-behavioral interventions for cannabis use disorder. *Journal of Substance Abuse Treatment, 21,* 55–64.

Coplan, J. D., Andrews, M. W., Rosenblum, L. A., Owens, M. J., Friedman, S., Gorman, J. M., & Nemeroff, C. B. (1996). Persistent elevations of cerebrospinal fluid concentrations of corticotropin-releasing factor in adult nonhuman primates exposed to early-life stressors: Implications for the pathophysiology of mood and anxiety disorders. *Proceedings of the National Academy of Science, 93,* 1619–1623.

Corbitt, E. M. & Widiger, T. A. (1995). Sex differences among the personality disorders: An exploration of the data. *Clinical Psychology: Science and Practice, 2,* 225–238.

Corder, E. H., Saunders, A. M., Strittmatter, W. J., Schmechel, D. E., Gaskell, P. C., Small, G. W., Roses, A. D., Haines, J. L., & Pericak-Vance, M. A. (1993). Gene dose of apolipoprotein E type 4 allele and the risk of Alzheimer's disease in late onset families. *Science, 261,* 921–924.

Cornblatt, B. A. (2001). Predictors of schizophrenia and preventive intervention. In A. Breier, P. V. Tran, F. Bymaster, & C. Tollefson (Eds.), *Current issues in the psychopharmacology of schizophrenia* (pp. 389–406). Philadelphia: Lippincott Williams & Wilkins.

Cornblatt, B. A. & Keilp, J. G. (1994). Impaired attention, genetics, and the pathophysiology of schizophrenia. *Schizophrenia Bulletin, 20,* 31–46.

Cornblatt, B. A., Lencz, T., & Obuchowski, M. (in press). The schizophrenia prodrome: Treatment and high risk perspectives. *Schizophrenia Research.*

Cornblatt, B. A., Lenzenweger, M. F., Dworkin, R. H., & Erlenmeyer-Kimling, L. (1985). Positive and negative schizophrenic symptoms, attention, and information processing. *Schizophrenia Bulletin, 11,* 397–408.

Cornblatt, B. & Obuchowski, N. (1997). Update of high-risk research: 1987–1997. *International Review of Psychiatry, 9,* 437–447.

Cororve, M. B. & Gleaves, D. H. (2001). Body dysmorphic disorder: A review of conceptualizations, assessment, and treatment strategies. *Clinical Psychology Review, 21,* 949–970.

Corrigan, J. D. (1995). Substance abuse as a mediating factor in outcome from traumatic brain injury. *Archives of Physical Medicine and Rehabilitation, 76*(4), 302–309.

Coryell, W. (1996). Psychotic depression. *Journal of Clinical Psychiatry, 57,* 27–31.

Coryell, W., Akiskal, H. S., Leon, A. C., Winokur, G., Maser, J. D., Mueller, T. I., & Keller, M. B. (1994). The time course of nonchronic major depressive disorder: Uniformity across episodes and samples. *Archives of General Psychiatry, 51,* 405–410.

Coryell, W., Leon, A., Winokur, G., Endicott, J., Keller, M., Akiskal, H., & Solomon, D. (1996). Importance of psychotic features to long-term course in major depressive disorder. *American Journal of Psychiatry, 153,* 483–489.

Cossette, S., Frasure-Smith, N., & Lesperance, F. (2001). Clinical implications of a reduction in psychological distress on cardiac prognosis in patients participating in a psychosocial intervention program. *Psychosomatic Medicine, 63,* 257–266.

Costa, E. & Guidotti, A. (1985). Endogenous ligands for benzodiazepine recognition sites. *Biochemical Pharmacology, 34,* 3399–3403.

Costa, P. T. & McCrae, R. R. (1990). Personality disorders and the Five-Factor model of personality. *Journal of Personality Disorders, 4,* 362–371.

Costa, P. T. & McCrae, R. R. (1995). Primary traits of Eysenck's P-E-N system: Three- and five-factor solutions. *Journal of Personality & Social Psychology, 69*(2), 308–317.

Costa, P. T., McCrae, R. R., & Siegler, I. C. (1999). Continuity and change over the adult life cycle: Personality and personality disorders. In C. R. Cloinger (Ed.), *Personality and Psychopathology* (pp. 129–154). Washington, DC: American Psychiatric Press.

Costa, P. T. & Widiger, T. A. (Eds.). (1994). *Personality disorders and the five-factor model of personality.* Washington, DC: American Psychological Association.

Council for Exceptional Children. (1994). Statistical profile of special education in the United States. *Teaching Exceptional Children, 26,* Supplement.

Courchesne, E., Townsend, J., Akshoomoff, N. A., Saitoh, O., Yeung-Courchesne, R., Lincoln, A. J., James, H. E., Hass, R. H., Schreibman, L., & Lau, L. (1994). Impairment in shifting attention in autistic and cerebellar patients. *Behavioral Neuroscience, 108,* 848–865.

Couture, E. G. & Guitar, B. E. (1993). Treatment efficacy research in stuttering. *Journal of Fluency Disorders, 18,* 253–387.

Cowen, E. L. & Durlak, J. A. (2000). Social policy and prevention in mental health. *Development and Psychopathology, 12,* 815–834.

Cowley, G. (1992a, June 29). Poison at home and at work. *Newsweek,* p. 54.

Cowley, G. (1992b, April 6). A quit-now drive that worked. *Newsweek,* p. 54.

Cox, B. J. (1996). The nature and assessment of catastrophic thoughts in panic disorder. *Behaviour Research and Therapy, 34,* 363–374.

Cox, B. J. & Taylor, S. (1999). Anxiety disorders: Panic and phobias. In T. Millon, P. H. Blaney, et al. (Eds.), *Oxford textbook of psychopathology* (pp. 81–113). New York: Oxford University Press.

Coyne, J. C. (1976). Toward an interactional description of depression. *Psychiatry, 39,* 14–27.

Coyne, J. C. (1990). Interpersonal processes in depression. In G. I. Keitner (Ed.), *Depression and families* (pp. 31–54). Washington, DC: American Psychiatric Press.

Coyne, J. C. & Whiffen, V. E. (1995). Issues in personality as diathesis for depression: The case of sociotropy-dependency and autonomy-self-criticism. *Psychological Bulletin, 118,* 358–378.

Craighead, L. W. & Agras, W. S. (1991). Mechanisms of action in cognitive-behavioral and pharmacological interventions for obesity and bulimia nervosa. *Journal of Consulting and Clinical Psychology, 59,* 115–125.

Craighead, W. E. (1990) There's a place for us: All of us. *Behavior Therapy, 21,* 3–23.

Craighead, W. E., Ilardi, S. S., Greenberg, M. D., & Craighead, L. W. (1997). Cognitive psychology: Basic theory and clinical implications. In A. Tasman, J. Kay, & J. A. Lieberman (Eds.), *Psychiatry* (Vol. 1, pp. 350–370). Philadelphia: Saunders.

Cramer, P. (1998). Coping and defense mechanisms: What's the difference? *Journal of Personality, 66,* 919–946.

Craske, M. G. (1991). Phobic fear and panic attacks: The same emotional states triggered by different cues? *Clinical Psychology Review, 11,* 599–620.

Crews, F. T., Braun, C. J., Ali, R., & Knapp, D. J. (2001). Interaction of nutrition and binge ethanol treatment on brain damage and withdrawal. *Journal of Biomedical Science, 8,* 134–142.

Crick, N. R. & Dodge, K. A. (1996). Social information processing mechanisms in reactive and proactive aggression. *Child Development, 67,* 993–1002.

Crino, R. D. & Andrews, G. (1996). Personality disorder in obsessive compulsive disorder: A controlled study. *Journal of Psychiatric Research, 30,* 29–38.

Crits-Cristoph, P. (1992). The efficacy of brief dynamic psychotherapy: A meta-analysis. *American Journal of Psychiatry, 149*(2), 151–158.

Crits-Christoph, P., Siqueland, L., Blaine, J., Frank, A., Luborsky, L., Onken, L. S., Muentz, L., Thase, M. E., Weiss, R. D., Gastfiend, D. R., Woody, G., Barber, J. P., Butler, S. F., Daley, D., Bishop, S., Najavits, L. M., Lis, J., Mercer, D., Griffin, M. L., Moras, K., & Beck, A. T. (1997). The National Institute of Drug Abuse Collaborative Cocaine Treatment Study. *Archives of General Psychiatry, 54,* 721–726.

Cromwell, R. L. (1993). Searching for the origins of schizophrenia. *Psychological Science, 4,* 276–279.

Cronkite, R. C. & Moos, R. H. (1995). Life context, coping processes, and depression. In E. E. Beckham & W. R. Leber (Eds.), *Handbook of depression* (2nd ed., pp. 569–587). New York: Guilford Press.

Crossette, B. (1996, February 29). Agency sees risk in drug to temper child behavior. *New York Times,* p. A14.

Crow, T. J. (1989). A current view of the Type II syndrome: Age of onset, intellectual impairment, and the meaning of structural changes in the brain. *British Journal of Psychiatry, 155,* 15–20.

Crowe, R. R. (1991). Genetic studies of anxiety disorders. In M. T. Tsuang, K. S. Kendler, & M. T. Lyons (Eds.), *Genetic issues in psychosocial epidemiology* (pp. 175–190). New Brunswick, NJ: Rutgers University Press.

Cruess, D. G., Antoni, M. H., Gonzalez, J., Fletcher, M. A., Klimas, N., Duran, R., et al. (2003). Sleep disturbance mediates the association between psychological distress and immune status among HIV-positive men and women on combination antiretroviral therapy. *Journal of Psychosomatic Research, 54,* 185–189.

Cruz, J., Joiner, T. E., Johnson, J. G., Heisler, L., Spitzer, R. L., & Petit, J. W. (2000). Self-defeating personality disorder reconsidered. *Journal of Personality Disorders, 14,* 64–71.

Cuellar, I. (1998). Cross-cultural clinical psychological assessment of Hispanic Americans. *Journal of Personality Assessment, 70,* 71–86.

Cui, X. & Valliant, G. E. (1996). Antecedents and consequences of negative life events in adulthood: A longitudinal study. *American Journal of Psychiatry, 153,* 21–26.

Cummings, C., Gordon, J. R., & Marlatt, G. A. (1980). Relapse: Prevention and prediction. In W. R. Miller (Ed.), *The addictive disorders: Treatment of alcoholism, drug abuse, smoking, and obesity.* New York: Pergamon Press.

Cummings, J. L. (1985). *Clinical neuropsychiatry.* Orlando, FL: Grune & Stratton.

Cummings, J. L. (1987). Multi-infarct: Diagnosis and management. *Psychosomatics, 28,* 117–126.

Cummings, J. L. & Benson, D. F. (1992). *Dementia: A clinical approach* (2nd ed.). Boston: Butterworths.

Cunradi, C. B., Caetano, R., Clark, C. L., & Schafer, J. (1999). Alcohol-related problems and intimate partner violence among White, Black, and Hispanic couples in the U.S. *Alcoholism: Clinical and Experimental Research, 23,* 1492–1501.

Curry, S., Wagner, E. H., & Grothaus, L. C. (1990). Intrinsic and extrinsic motivation for smoking cessation. *Journal of Consulting and Clinical Psychology, 58,* 310–316.

Cushman, P. & Gilford, P. (2000). Will managed care change our way of being? *American Psychologist, 55,* 985–996.

Cusin, C., Serretti, A., Lattuada, E., Mandelli, L., & Smeraldi, E. (2000). Impact of clinical variables on illness time course in mood disorders. *Psychiatry Research, 97,* 217–227.

Cutting, L. P. & Docherty, N. M. (2000). Schizophrenia outpatients' perceptions of their parents: Is expressed emotion a factor? *Journal of Abnormal Psychology, 109,* 266–272.

Cyranowski, J. M., Frank, E., Young, E., & Shear, M. K. (2000). Adolescent onset of the gender difference in lifetime rates of major depression: A theoretical model. *Archives of General Psychiatry, 57,* 21–27.

Dadds, M. R., Holland, D. E., Barrett, P. M., Laurens, K. R., & Spence, S. H. (1999). Early intervention and prevention of anxiety disorders in children: Results at 2-year follow-up. *Journal of Consulting and Clinical Psychology, 67,* 145–150.

Dadds, M. R., Holland, D. E., Spence, S. H., Laurens, K. R., Mullins, M., & Barrett, P. M. (1999). Early intervention and prevention of anxiety disorder in children: Results at 2-year follow-up. *Journal of Consulting and Clinical Psychology, 67,* 145–150.

Dadds, M. R., Spence, S. H., Holland, D. E., Barrett, P. M., & Laurens, K. R. (1997). Prevention and early intervention for anxiety disorders: A controlled trial. *Journal of Consulting and Clinical Psychology, 65,* 627–635.

Dain, N. (1964). *Concepts of sanity in the United States, 1789–1895.* New Brunswick, NJ: Rutgers University Press.

Daley, S. E., Hammen, C., Burge, D., Davila, J., Paley, B., Lindberg, N., & Herzberg, D. S. (1997). Predictors of the generation of episodic stress: A longitudinal study of late adolescent women. *Journal of Abnormal Psychology, 106,* 251–259.

Dalton, S. O., Boesen, E. H., Ross, L., Schapiro, I. R., & Johansen, C. (2002). Mind and cancer: Do psychological factors cause cancer? *European Journal of Cancer, 38,* 1313–1323.

Dancu, C. V., Riggs, D. S., Hearst-Ikeda, D., Shoyer, B. G., & Foa, E. B. (1996). Dissociative experiences and posttraumatic stress disorder among female victims of criminal assault and rape. *Journal of Traumatic Stress, 9,* 253–267.

Danner, D. D., Snowdon, D. A., & Friesen, W. V. (2001). Positive emotions in early life and longevity: Findings from the Nun Study. *Journal of Personality and Social Psychology, 80,* 804–813.

Daoud, A. S., Batieha, A., Bashtawi, M., & El-Shanti, H. (2003). Risk factors for childhood epilepsy: A case-control study from Irbid, Jordan. *Seizure, 12*(3), 171–174.

Daskalakis, Z. J., Christensen, B. K., Chen, R., Fitzgerald, P. B., Zipursky, R. B., & Kapur, S. (2002). Evidence for impaired cortical inhibition in schizophrenia using transcranial magnetic stimulation. *Archives of General Psychiatry, 59,* 347–354.

Davey, G. C. L. (1995). Preparedness and phobias: Specific evolved associations or a generalized expectancy bias? *Behavioral and Brain Sciences, 106,* 289–325.

Davidson, J. R. T. & Foa, E. B. (1991). Diagnostic issues in posttraumatic stress disorder: Considerations for the *DSM-IV. Journal of Abnormal Psychology, 106,* 289–325.

Davidson, J. R. T., Smith, R. D., & Kudler, H. S. (1989). Familial psychiatric illness in chronic posttraumatic stress disorder. *Comprehensive Psychiatry, 30,* 339–345.

Davidson, J. R., Rothbaum, B. O., van der Kolk, B. A., Sikes, C. R., & Farfel, G. M. (2001). Multicenter, double-blind comparison of sertraline and placebo in the treatment of posttraumatic stress disorder. *Archives of General Psychiatry, 58,* 485–492.

Davidson, K., MacGregor, M. W., Stuhr, J., & Gidron, Y. (1999). Increasing constructive anger verbal behavior decreases resting blood pressure: A secondary analysis of a randomized controlled hostility intervention. *International Journal of Behavioral Medicine, 6,* 268–278.

Davidson, K. & Tyrer, P. (1996). Cognitive therapy for antisocial and borderline personality disorders: Single case study series. *British Journal of Clinical Psychology, 35,* 413–429.

Davidson, L. & McGlashan, T. H. (1997). The varied outcomes of schizophrenia. *Canadian Journal of Psychiatry, 42,* 34–43.

Davidson, R. J. (1992). Emotion and affective style: Hemispheric substrates. *Psychological Science, 3,* 39–43.

Davidson, R. J. (1993).The neuropsychology of emotion and affective style. In M. Lewis & J. M. Haviland (Eds.), *Handbook of emotions* (pp. 143–154). New York: Guilford Press.

Davidson, R. J. (1994). Asymmetric brain function, affective style, and psychopathology: The role of early experience and plasticity. *Development and Psychopathology, 6,* 741–758.

Davidson, R. J. (2000). The functional neuroanatomy of affective style. In R. D. Lane & L. Nadel (Eds.), *Cognitive neuroscience of emotion* (pp. 371–388). New York: Oxford University Press.

Davidson, R. J. & Fox, N. A. (1989). Frontal brain asymmetry predicts infants' response to maternal separation. *Journal of Abnormal Psychology, 98,* 127–131.

Davidson, R. J., Lewis, D., Alloy, L. B., Amaral, D., Bush, G., Cohen, J., Drevets, W., Farah, M., Kagan, J., McClelland, J., Nolen-Hoeksema, S., & Peterson, B. (2002). Neural and behavioral substrates of mood and mood regulation. *Biological Psychiatry, 52,* 478–502.

Davis, J. O. & Bracha, H. S. (1996). Prenatal growth markers in schizophrenia: A monozygotic co-twin control study. *American Journal of Psychiatry, 153,* 1166–1172.

Davis, J. O. & Phelps, J. A. (1995). Twins with schizophrenia: Genes or germs? *Schizophrenia Bulletin, 21,* 13–18.

Davis, K. L., Kahn, R. S., Ko, G., & Davidson, M. (1991). Dopamine in schizophrenia: Review and reconceptualization. *American Journal of Psychiatry, 148,* 1474–1486.

Davis, M. C., Mathews, K. A., & McGrath, C. E. (2000). Hostile attitudes predict elevated vascular resistance during interpersonal stress in men and women. *Psychosomatic Medicine, 62,* 17–25.

Davis, M. K. & Gidycz, C. A. (2000). Child sexual abuse prevention programs: A meta-analysis. *Journal of Clinical Child Psychology, 29,* 257–265.

Davis, P. J. & Gibson, M. G. (2000). Recognition of posed and genuine facial expressions of emotion in paranoid and nonparanoid schizophrenia. *Journal of Abnormal Psychology, 109,* 445–450.

Davis, R. T., Blashfield, R. K., & McElroy, R. A. (1993). Weighting criteria in the diagnosis of a personality disorder: A demonstration. *Journal of Abnormal Psychology, 102,* 319–322.

Dawkins, R. (1976). *The selfish gene.* Oxford: Oxford University Press.

Dawson, G., Klinger, L. G., Panagiotides, H., Lewy, A., & Castelloe, P. (1995). Subgroups of autistic children based on social behavior display distinct patterns of brain activity. *Journal of Abnormal Child Psychology, 23,* 569–583.

Dawson, M. E., Nuechterlein, K. H., & Schell, A. M. (1992). Electrodermal anomalies in recent-onset schizophrenia: Relationships to symptoms and prognosis. *Schizophrenia Bulletin, 18,* 295–311.

Day, K. (1990). Depression in mildly and moderately retarded adults. In A. Dosen & F. L. Menolascino (Eds.), *Depression in mentally retarded children and adults* (pp. 129–154). Leiden, Netherlands: Logon.

Day, K. & Dosen, A. (2001). Treatment: An integrative approach. In A. Dosen & K. Day (Eds.), *Treating mental illness and behavior disorders in children and adults with mental retardation* (pp. 519–528). Washington, DC: American Psychiatric Press.

Deakin, J. F. W. & Graeff, F. G. (1991) Critique. 5-HT and mechanisms of defence. *Journal of Psychopharmacology, 5,* 305–315.

Deakin, J. F. W. (1998). The role of serotonin in panic, anxiety, and depression. *International Clinical Psychopharmacology, 13*(Suppl. 4), S1–S5.

Debakey, S. F., Stinson, F. S., Grant, B. F., & Dufour, M. C. (1996). Liver cirrhosis mortality in the United States, 1970–1993. *Surveillance Report* No. 41. Washsington, DC: CSR.

DeCaria, C., Hollander, E., Grossman, R., Wong, C. M., Mosoich, S. A., & Cherasky, S. (1996). Diagnosis, neurobiology, and treatment of pathological gambling. *Journal of Clinical Psychiatry, 57*(Suppl. 8), 80–84.

De Castillo, J. (1970). The influence of language upon symptomatology in foreign-born patients. *American Journal of Psychiatry, 127,* 242–244.

Deckel, A. W., Hesselbrock, V., & Bauer, L. (1996). Antisocial personality disorder, childhood delinquency, and frontal brain functioning: EEG and neuropsychological findings. *Journal of Clinical Psychology, 52,* 639–650.

Deckersbach, T., Savage, C. R., Phillips, K. A., et al. (2000). Characteristics of memory dysfunction in body dysmorphic disorder. *Journal of the International Neuropsychology Society, 6,* 673–681.

DeHart, D. D. & Mahoney, J. M. (1994). The serial murderer's motivations: An interdisciplinary review. *Omega, 29,* 29–45.

Delanty, D. L., Heberman, H. B., Craig, K. J., Hayward, M. C., Ursano, R. J., & Baum, A. (1997). Acute and chronic posttraumatic stress disorder as a function of responsibility for serious motor vehicle accidents. *Journal of Consulting and Clinical Psychology, 65,* 560–567.

Delgado, P. L. & Moreno, F. A. (2000). Role of norepinephrine in depression. *Journal of Clinical Psychiatry, 61* (Suppl. 1), 5–12.

Delgado, P. L., Price, L. H., Heninger, G. R., & Charney, D. S. (1992). Neurochemistry. In E. S. Paykel (Ed.), *Handbook of affective disorders* (2nd ed., pp. 219–254). New York: Guilford Press.

DeLisi, L. E. (1999). Regional brain volume change over the life-time course of schizophrenia. *Journal of Psychiatric Research, 33,* 535–541.

DeLisi, L. E. (2001). Speech disorder in schizophrenia: Review of the literature and exploration of its relation to the uniquely human capacity for language. *Schizophrenia Bulletin, 27,* 481–496.

Delizonna, L. L., Wincze, J. P., Litz, B. T., Brown, T. A., & Barlow, D. H. (2001). A comparison of subjective and physiological measures of mechanically produced and erotically produced erections (Or, is an erection an erection?). *Journal of Sex & Marital Therapy, 27*(1).

Delong, R. G. (1992). Autism, amnesia, hippocampus, and learning. *Neuroscience and Biobehavioral Review, 16,* 63–70.

DeLongis, A. D., Coyne, J. C., Dakof, G., Folkman, S., & Lazarus, R. S. (1982). Relationship of daily hassles, uplifts and major life events to health status. *Health Psychology, 1,* 119–136.

DeRubeis, R. J. & Crits-Cristoph, P. (1998). Empirically supported individual and group psychological treatments for adult mental disorders. *Journal of Consulting and Clinical Psychology, 66,* 37–52.

DeRubeis, R. J., Gelfand, L. A., Tang, T. Z., & Simons, A. D. (1999). Medications versus cognitive behavior therapy for severely depressed outpatients: Mega-analysis of four randomized comparisons. *American Journal of Psychiatry, 156,* 1007–1013.

Desmond, J. E. & Annabel Chen, S. H. (2002). Ethical issues in the clinical application of fMRI: Factors affecting the validity and interpretation of activations. *Brain and Cognition 50*(3): 482–497.

D' Esposito, M. (2000). Functional imaging of neurocognition. *Seminars in Neurology, 20*(4), 487–498.

Dessureault, D., Cote, G., & Lesage, A. (2000). Impact of first contacts with the criminal justice or mental health systems on the subsequent orientation of mentally disordered persons toward either system. *International Journal of Law and Psychiatry, 23,* 79–90.

Destun, L. M. & Kuiper, N. A. (1996). Autobiographical memory and recovered memory therapy: Integrating cognitive, clinical, and individual difference perspectives. *Clinical Psychology Review, 16,* 421–450.

Deutsch, A. (1949). *The mentally ill in America* (2nd ed.). New York and London: Columbia University Press.

Devor, E. J., Abell, C. W., Hoffman, P. L., Tabakoff, B., & Cloninger, C. R. (1994). Platelet MAO activity in Type I and Type II alcoholism. *Annals of the New York Academy of Science, 708,* 119–128.

de Waal, F. (1996). *Good natured: The origins of right and wrong in humans and other animals.* Cambridge: Harvard University Press.

Dhabhar, F. S. (2002). Stress-induced augmentation of immune function—The role of stress hormones, leukocyte tracking, and cytokines. *Brain, Behavior, and Immunity, 16,* 785–798.

Dhabhar, F. S. & McEwen, B. S. (1996). Stress-induced enhancement of antigen-specific cell-mediated immunity. *Journal of Immunology, 156,* 2608–2615.

Dhabhar, F. S. & McEwen, B. S. (1997). Acute stress enhances while chronic stress suppresses immune function in vivo: A potential role for leukocyte tracking. *Brain, Behavior, and Immunity, 11,* 286–306.

Dhawan, S. & Marshall, W. L. (1996). Sexual abuse histories of sexual offenders. *Sexual Abuse: Journal of Research and Treatment, 8,* 7–15.

Di Cara, L. & Miller, N. (1968). Instrumental learning of vasomotor responses by rats: Learning to respond differentially in the two ears. *Science, 159,* 1485–1486.

Di Lorenzo, R., Tondelli, G., & Genedani, S. (2001). Effectiveness of clozapine and olanzapine: A comparison in severe, psychotically ill patients. *International Journal of Neuropsychopharmacology, 4,* 135–137.

Dick, D. D., Rose, R. J., Viken, R. J., Kaprio, J., & Koskenvuo, M. (2001). Exploring gene-environmental interactions: Socioregional moderation of alcohol use. *Journal of Abnormal Psychology, 110,* 625–632.

Dickey, B. (2000). Review of programs for persons who are homeless and mentally ill. *Harvard Review of Psychiatry, 8,* 242–250.

Didden, R., Duker, P. C., & Korzilius, H. (1997). Meta-analytic study on treatment effectiveness for problem behaviors with individuals who have mental retardation. *American Journal of Mental Retardation, 101,* 387–399.

Dietrich, K. N., Berger, O. G., Succop, P. A., Hammond, P. B., & Bornschien, R. L. (1993). The developmental consequences of low to moderate prenatal and postnatal lead exposure: Intellectual attainment in the Cincinnati Lead Study cohort following school entry. *Neurotoxicology and Teratology, 15,* 37–44.

Dikman, S., Temkin, N., Machamer, J., Holubkov, A., Fraser, R., & Winn, H. R. (1994). Employment following traumatic head injuries. *Archives of Neurology, 51,* 177–186.

DiLalla, D. L., Carey, G., Gottesman, I. I., & Bouchard, T. J. (1996). Heritability of MMPI personality indicators of psychopathology in twins reared apart. *Journal of Abnormal Psychology, 105,* 491–499.

Dilsaver, S. C., Chen, Y. R., Shoaib, A. M., & Swann, A. C. (1999). Phenomenology of mania: Evidence for distinct depressed, dysphoric, and euphoric presentations. *American Journal of Psychiatry, 156,* 426–430.

Dilts, S. L. (1998). On the Szaszian argument. *Journal of Psychiatry & Law, 26,* 311–325.

Dishion, T. J., Spracklen, K. M., Andrews, D. W., & Patterson, G. R. (1996). Deviancy training in male adolescent friendships. *Behavior Therapy, 27,* 373–390.

Dobson, K. S., Backs-Dermott, B. J., & Dozois, D. J. (2000). Cognitive and cognitive behavioral therapies. In C. R. Synder & R. E. Ingram (Eds.), *Handbook of psychological change: Psychotherapy processes and practices for the 21st century.* New York: Wiley.

Docherty, N. M. & Gordiner, S. W. (1999). Immediate memory, attention and communication disturbances in schizophrenia patients and their relatives. *Psychological Medicine, 29,* 189–197.

Docherty, N. M. & Gottesman, I. I. (2000). A twin study of communication disturbances in schizophrenia. *Journal of Nervous and Mental Disease, 188,* 395–401.

Docter, R. F. & Prince, V. (1997). Transvestism: A survey of 1032 cross-dressers. *Archives of Sexual Behavior, 26*(6), 589–605.

Dodge, K. A., Lochman, J. E., Harnish, J. D., Bates, J. E., & Pettit, G. S. (1997). Reactive and proactive aggression in school children and psychiatrically impaired chronically assaultive youth. *Journal of Abnormal Psychology, 106,* 37–51.

Dodge, K. H. & Schwartz, D. (1997). Social information processing mechanisms in aggressive behavior. In D. M. Stoff, J. Breiling, & J. D. Maser (Eds.), *Handbook of antisocial behavior* (pp. 171–180). New York: Wiley.

Dodrill, C. B. (1992). Neuropsychological aspects of epilepsy. *Psychiatric Clinics of North America, 15,* 383–394.

Dodrill, C. B. (1993). Neuropsychology. In J. Laidlaw, A. Richens, & D. Chadwick (Eds.), *A textbook of epilepsy* (pp. 459–473). Edinburgh: Churchill Livingstone.

Doering, S., Müller, E., Kopcke, W., Pietzcker, A., Gaebel, W., Linden, M., Muller, P., Muller-Spahn, F., Tegeler, J., & Schussler, G. (1998). Predictors of relapse and rehospitalization in schizophrenia and schizoaffective disorder. *Schizophrenia Bulletin, 24,* 87–98.

Dohrenwend, B. P., Levav, I., Shrout, P. E., Schwartz, S., Naveh, G., Link, B. G., Skodol, A. E., & Stueve, A. (1998). Ethnicity, socioeconomic status, and psychiatric disorders. A test of the social causation-social selection issue. In B. P. Dohrenwend et al. (Eds.), *Adversity, stress, and psychopathology* (pp. 285–318). New York: Oxford University Press.

Dolan, B. (1991). Cross-cultural aspects of anorexia nervosa and bulimia: A review. *International Journal of Eating Disorders, 10,* 67–79.

Dolberg, O. T., Iancu, I., Sasson, Y., & Zohar, J. (1996). The pathogenesis and treatment of obsessive-compulsive disorder. *Clinical Neuropharmacology, 19,* 129–147.

Doleys, D. M. (1989). Enuresis and encopresis. In T. H. Ollendick & M. Hersen (Eds.), *Handbook of child psychopathology* (2nd ed.). New York: Plenum Press.

Doleys, D. M. (1997). Behavioral treatments for nocturnal enuresis in children: A review of the recent literature. *Psychological Bulletin, 84,* 30–54.

Dorahy, M. J. (2001). Dissociative identity disorder and memory dysfunction: The current state of experimental research and its future directions. *Clinical Psychology Review, 21,* 771–795.

Dosajh, N. L. (1996). Projective techniques with particular reference to inkblot tests. *Journal of Projective Psychology and Mental Health, 3,* 59–68.

Douglas, K. S., Cox, D. N., & Webster, C. D. (1999). Violence risk assessment: Science and practice. *Legal and Criminological Psychology, 4,* 149–184.

Douglas, K. S. & Kropp, P. R. (2002). A prevention-based paradigm for violence risk assessment: Clinical and research applications. *Criminal Justice and Behavior, 29,* 617–658.

Douglas, K. S., Ogloff, J. R. P., Nicholls, T. L. & Grant, I. (1999). Assessing risk for violence among psychiatric patients: The HCR-20 violence risk assessment scheme and the Psychopathy Checklist: Screening Version. *Journal of Consulting and Clinical Psychology, 67,* 917–930.

Douglas, K. S. & Webster, C. D. (1999). Predicting violence in mentally and personality disordered individuals. In R. Roesch, S. D. Hart, & J. R. P. Ogloff (Eds.), *Psychology and law: The state of the discipline* (pp. 175–239). New York: Plenum Press.

Douglass, H. M., Moffitt, T. E., Dar, R., McGee, R., et al. (1995). Obsessive compulsive disorder in a birth cohort of 18-year-olds: Prevalence and predictors. *Journal of the American Academy of Child and Adolescent Psychiatry, 34,* 1424–1431.

Dozois, D. J. A. & Dobson, K. S. (2001). Information processing and cognitive organization in unipolar depression: Specificity and comorbidity issues. *Journal of Abnormal Psychology, 110,* 236–246.

Dreher, H. M. (2003). The effect of caffeine reduction on sleep quality and well-being in persons with HIV. *Journal of Psychosomatic Research, 54,* 191–198.

Dressler, W. W. (1999). Modernization, stress, and blood pressure: New directions in research. *Human Biology, 71,* 583–605.

Drukteinis, A. M. (1992). Serial murderer: The heart of darkness. *Psychiatric Annals, 22,* 532–538.

Druss, B. G., Rosenheck, R. A., & Sledge, W. H. (2000). Health and disability costs of depressive illness in a major U.S. corporation. *American Journal of Psychiatry, 157,* 1274–1278.

Dryden, W. & Ellis, A. (in press). Rational-emotive behavor therapy. In K. S. Dobson (Ed.), *Handbook of cognitive-behavioral therapies* (2nd ed.). New York: Guilford Press.

Dubovsky, S. L. & Thomas, M. (1995). Beyond specificity: Effects of serotonin and serotonergic treatments on psychobiological dysfunction. *Journal of Psychosomatic Research, 39,* 429–444.

Dulmus, C. N. & Rapp-Paglicci, L. A. (2000). The prevention of mental disorders in children and adolescents: Future research and public-policy recommendations. *Families in Society, 81,* 294–303.

Duman, R. S., Heninger, G. R., & Nestler, E. J. (1997). A molecular and cellular theory of depression. *Archives of General Psychiatry, 54,* 597–606.

Duncan, G. J., Brooks-Gunn, J., & Klebanov, P. K. (1994). Economic deprivation and early childhood development. *Child Development, 65,* 296–318.

Dunn, M. (1994). Neurophysiologic observations in autism. In M. L. Bauman & T. L. Kempner (Eds.), *The neurobiology of autism.* Baltimore: Johns Hopkins University Press.

Dunner, D. L. (1997). *Current psychiatric therapy II.* Philadelphia: Saunders.

Dunst, C. J., Johanson, C., Trivette, C. M., & Hamby, D. (1991, October–November). Family-oriented early intervention policies and practices: Family-centered or not? *Exceptional Children.*

DuPaul, G. J. & Barkley, R. A. (1990). Medication therapy. In R. A. Barkley (Ed.), *Attention-deficit hyperactivity disorder: A handbook for diagnosis and treatment* (pp. 573–612). New York: Guilford Press.

DuPaul, G. J. & Barkley, R. A. (1993). Behavioral contributions to pharmacotherapy: The utility of behavioral methodology in medication treatment of children with attention-deficit hyperactivity disorder. *Behavior Therapy, 24,* 47–65.

Durand, V. M. (1990). *Severe behavior problems: A functional communication training approach.* New York: Guilford Press.

Durand, V. M. (1993). Functional communication training using assistive devices: Effects on challenging behavior and affect. *Augmentative and Alternative Communication, 9,* 168–176.

Durkheim, E. (1951). *Suicide* (J. A. Spaulding & G. Simpson, Trans.). Glencoe, IL: Free Press. Original work published 1897.

Durrant, J. E. (1994). A decade of research on learning disabilities: A report card on the state of the literature. *Journal of Learning Disabilities, 27,* 25–33.

Duster, T. (1999). The social consequences of genetic disclosure. In R. A. Carson & M. A. Rothman (Eds.), *Behavioral genetics: The clash of culture and biology* (pp. 172–188). Baltimore, MD: Johns Hopkins University Press.

Dworkin, B. R. & Miller, N. E. (1986). Failure to replicate visceral learning in the acute curarized rat preparation. *Behavioral Neuroscience, 100,* 299–314.

Dworkin, R. H. & Lenzenweger, M. F. (1984). Symptoms and the genetics of schizophrenia: Implications for diagnosis. *American Journal of Psychiatry, 141,* 1541–1546.

Dykman, R. A., McPherson, B., Ackerman, P. T., Newton, J. E. O., Mooney, D. M., Wherry, J., Chaffin, M. (1997). Internalizing and externalizing characteristics of sexually and/or physically abused children. *Integrative Physiological and Behavioral Science, 32,* 62–74.

Eames, P. (1992). Hysteria following brain injury. *Journal of Neurology, Neurosurgery, and Psychiatry, 55,* 1046–1053.

Earnst, K. S. & Kring, A. M. (1997). Construct validity of negative symptoms: An empirical and conceptual review. *Clinical Psychology Review, 17,* 167–189.

Eaton, W. W., Anthony, J. C., Gallo, J., Cai, G., Tien, A., Romanoski, A., Lyketsos, C., & Chen, L. S. (1997). Natural history of diagnostic interview schedule/*DSM-IV* major depression: The Baltimore Epidemiologic Catchment Area follow-up. *Archives of General Psychiatry, 54,* 993–999.

Eaton, W. W., Kessler, R. C., Wittchen, H. U., & Magee, W. J. (1994). Panic and panic disorder in the United States. *American Journal of Psychiatry, 151,* 413–420.

Eaton, W. W. & Keyl, P. M. (1990). Risk factors for the onset of diagnostic interview schedule/*DSM-III* agoraphobia in a prospective, population-based study. *Archives of General Psychiatry, 47,* 819–824.

Eaton, W. W. & Muntaner, C. (1999). Socioeconomic stratification and mental disorder. In A.V. Horwitz, T. L. Scheid, et al. (Eds.), *A handbook for the study of mental health: Social contexts, theories, and systems* (pp. 259–283). New York: Cambridge University Press.

Edwards, B. K., Howe, H. L., Ries, L. A. G., Thun, M. J., Rosenberg, H. M., Yancik, R., et al. (2002). Annual report to the nation on the status of cancer, 1973-1999, featuring implications of age and aging on U.S. cancer burden. *Cancer, 94,* 2766–2792.

Edwards, C. L., Sudhakar, S., Scales, M. T., Applegate, K. L., Wester, W., & Dunn, R. H. (2000). Electromyographic (EMG) biofeedback in the comprehensive treatment of central pain and ataxic tremor following thalamic stroke. *Applied Psychophysiology and Biofeedback, 25,* 229–240.

Egeland, J. A., Gerhard, D. S., Pauls, D. L., Sussex, J. N., Kidd, K. K., Allen, C. R., Hostetter, A. M., & Housman, D. E. (1987). Bipolar affective disorders linked to DNA markers on chromosome 11. *Nature, 325,* 783–787.

Egeland, J. A. & Hostetter, A. M. (1983). Amish study: I. Affective disorders among the Amish. *American Journal of Psychiatry, 140,* 56–61.

Eggert, L. L., Thompson, E. A., Herting, J. R., & Nicholas, L. J. (1995). Reducing suicide potential among high-risk youth: Tests of a school-based prevention program. *Suicide and Life-Threatening Behavior, 25,* 276–296.

Ehlers, A. & Breuer, P. (1996). How good are patients with panic disorder at perceiving their heartbeats? *Biological Psychology, 42,* 165–182.

Ehlers, A. & Clark, D. M. (2000). A cognitive model of persistent posttraumatic stress disorder. *Behaviour Research and Therapy, 38,* 319–345.

Ehlers, A., Mayou, R. A., Bryant, B. (1998). Psychological predictors of chronic posttraumatic stress disorder after motor vehicle accidents. *Journal of Abnormal Psychology, 107,* 508–519.

Ehlers, C. L., Frank, E., & Kupfer, D. J. (1988). Social zeitgebers and biological rhythms. A unified approach to understanding the etiology of depression. *Archives of General Psychiatry, 45,* 948–952.

Eisen, A. R. & Engler, L. B. (1995). Chronic anxiety. In A. R. Eisen, C. A. Kearney, & C. E. Schaefer (Eds.), *Clinical handbook of anxiety disorders in children and adolescents.* Northvale, NJ: Aronson.

Eisen, A. R. & Silverman, W. K. (1998). Prescriptive treatment for generalized anxiety disorder in children. *Behavior Therapy, 29,* 105–121.

Eisen, A. R., Kearney, C. A., & Schaefer, C. E. (Eds.). (1995). *Clinical handbook of anxiety disorders in children and adolescents.* Northvale, NJ: Aronson.

Eisenberger, N. I., Kemeny, M. E., & Wyatt, G. E. (2003). Psychological inhibition and CD4 T-cell levels in HIV-seropositive women. *Journal of Psychosomatic Research, 54,* 213–224.

Elkin, I., Shea, T., Watkins, J. T., Imber, S. D., Sotsky, S. M., Collins, J. F., Glass, D. R., Pilkonis, P. A., Leber, W. R., Docherty, J. P., Fiester, S. J., & Parloff, M. B. (1989). National Institute of Mental Health treatment of depression collaborative research program. *Archives of General Psychiatry, 46,* 971–982.

Elkins, T. E. & Andersen, H. F. (1992). Sterilization of persons with mental retardation. *Journal of the Association for Persons with Severe Handicaps, 17,* 19–26.

Ellason, J. W. & Ross, C. A. (1997). Two-year follow-up of inpatients with dissociative identity disorder. *American Journal of Psychiatry 154,* 832–839.

Elliot, R. & Greenberg, L. S. (1995). Experiential therapy in practice: The process-experiential approach. In B. M. Bongar & L. E. Beutler (Eds.), *Comprehensive textbook of psychotherapy: Theory and practice* (pp. 123–139). New York: Oxford University Press.

Elliott, D. M. (1997). Traumatic events: Prevalence and delayed recall in the general population. *Journal of Consulting and Clinical Psychology, 65,* 811–820.

Elliott, D. S., Ageton, S. S., Huizinga, D., Knowles, B. A., & Canter, R. J. (1983). *The prevalence and incidence of delinquent behavior: 1976–1980* (National Youth Survey Report No. 26). Boulder, CO: Behavioral Research Institute.

Ellis, A. (1962). *Reason and emotion in psychotherapy.* New York: Lyle Stuart.

Ellis, A. (1980). An overview of the clinical theory of rational-emotive therapy. In R. Grieger & J. Boyd

(Eds.), *Rational-emotive therapy: A skills-based approach.* New York: Van Nostrand Reinhold.

Elmer-De Witt, P. (1994, October 17). Now for the truth about Americans and sex. *Time.*

Elzinga, B. M., van Dyck, R., & Spinhoven, P. (1998). Three controversies about dissociative identity disorder. *Clinical Psychology and Psychotherapy, 5,* 13–23.

Emmelkamp, P. M. G. (1994). Behavior therapy with adults. In A. E. Bergin & S. L. Garfield (Eds.), *Handbook of psychotherapy and behavior change* (4th ed., pp. 379–427). New York: Wiley.

Emslie, G. J., Armitage, R., Weinberg, W. A., Rush, A. J., Mayes, T. L., & Hoffmann, R. F. (2001). Sleep polysomnography as a predictor of recurrence in children and adolescents with major depressive disorder. *International Journal of Neuropsychopharmacology, 4,* 159–168.

Endicott, J. & Spitzer, R. A. (1978). A diagnostic interview: The Schedule for Affective Disorders and Schizophrenia. *Archives of General Psychiatry, 35,* 837–844.

Engel, B. T. (1960). Stimulus-response and individual-response specificity. *Archives of General Psychiatry, 2,* 305–313.

Engel, B. T. & Bickford, A. F. (1961). Response specificity: Stimulus response and individual response specificity in essential hypertension. *Archives of General Psychiatry, 5,* 478–489.

Engle-Friedman, M., Baker, E. A., & Bootzin, R. R. (1985). Reports of wakefulness during EEG identified states of sleep. *Sleep Research, 14,* 121.

Ennis, B. J. & Emery, R. D. (1978). *The rights of mental patients.* New York: Avon.

Enserink, M. (2001). Is the U.S. doing enough to prevent mad cow disease? *Science, 292*(5522), 1639–1641.

Epel, E. S., McEwen, B., Seeman, T., Matthews, K., Castellazzo, G., Brownell, K. D., Bell, J., & Ickovics, J. R. (2000). Stress and body shape: Stress-induced cortisol secretion is consistently greater among women with central fat. *Psychosomatic Medicine, 62,* 623–632.

Epps, J. & Kendall, P. C. (1995). Hostile attributional bias in adults. *Cognitive Therapy and Research, 19*(2), 159–178.

Epstein, R. L. (1997). The effect of overtime work on blood pressure. *Journal of Occupational and Environmental Medicine, 39,* 286.

Epstein, S. (1983). The stability of confusion: A reply to Mischel and Peake. *Psychological Review, 90,* 179–184.

Erdelyi, M. H. (1985). *Psychoanalysis: Freud's cognitive view.* New York: Freeman.

Erdelyi, M. H. & Goldberg, B. (1979). Let's not sweep repression under the rug: Toward a cognitive psychology of repression. In J. F. Kihlstrom & F. J. Evans (Eds.), *Functional disorders of memory.* Hillsdale, NJ: Erlbaum.

Erickson, P. E. (2002). The legal standard of volitional impairment: An analysis of substantive due process and the United States Supreme Court's decision in *Kansas v. Hendricks. Journal of Criminal Justice, 30,* 1–10.

Ernst, M., Zametkin, A. J., Matochik, J. A., Pascualvaca, D., & Cohen, R. M. (1997). Low medial prefrontal dopaminergic activity in autistic children [Letter]. *Lancet, 351,* 454.

Eron, L. D. (1997). The development of antisocial behavior from a learning perspective. In D. M. Stoff, J. Breiling, & J. D. Maser (Eds.), *Handbook of antisocial behavior* (pp. 140–147). New York: Wiley.

Eronen, M., Tiihonen, J., & Hakola, P. (1996). Schizophrenia and homicidal behavior. *Schizophrenia Bulletin, 22,* 83–89.

Erwin, R. J., Turetsky, B. I., Moberg, P., Gur, R. C., & Gur, R. E. (1998). P50 abnormalities in schizophrenia: Relationship to clinical and neuropsychological indices of attention. *Schizophrenia Research, 33,* 157–167.

Eslinger, P. J. & Damasio, A. R. (1985). Severe disturbance of higher cognition after bilateral frontal lobe ablation: Patient EVR. *Neurology, 35*(12), 1731–1741.

Evans, D. L., Leserman, J., Perkins, D. O., et al. (1997). Severe life stress as a predictor of early disease progression in HIV infection. *American Journal of Psychiatry, 154,* 630–634. (Cited in Balbin, E. G., Ironson, G. H., & Solomon, G. F. [1999]. Stress and coping: the psychoneuroimmunology of HIV/AIDS. *Baillière's Clinical Endocrinology and Metabolism, 13,* 615–633.)

Evans, J. D., Paulsen, J. S., Harris, M. J., Heaton, R. K., & Jeste, D. V. (1996). A clinical and neuropsychological comparison of delusional disorder and schizophrenia. *Journal of Neuropsychiatry and Clinical Neurosciences, 8,* 281–286.

Ewart, C. K. & Suchday, S. (2002). Discovering how urban poverty and violence affect health: Development and validation of a neighborhood stress index. *Health Psychology, 21,* 254–262.

Ewen, D. (1956). *Journey to greatness: The life and music of George Gershwin.* New York: Holt, Rinehart & Winston.

Exner, J. E. (1978). *The Rorschach: A comprehensive system* (Vol. 1). New York: Wiley.

Exner, J. E. (1982). *The Rorschach: A comprehensive system* (Vol. 2). New York: Wiley.

Exner, J. E. (1986). *The Rorschach: A comprehensive system* (Vol. 3). New York: Wiley.

Exner, J. E. (2002). A new nonpatient sample for the Rorschach Comprehensive System: A progress report. *Journal of Personality Assessment, 78,* 391–404.

Exner, J. E. & Weiner, I. B. (1995). *The Rorschach: A comprehensive system: Vol. 3. Assessment of children and adolescents* (2nd. ed.). New York: Wiley.

Eysenck, H. J. (Ed.). (1967). *The biological basis of personality.* Springfield, IL: Charles C Thomas.

Fabian, W. D., Jr. & Fishkin, S. M. (1981). A replicated study of self-reported changes in psychological absorption with marijuana intoxication. *Journal of Abnormal Psychology, 90,* 546–553.

Fairburn, C. G., Jones, R., Peveler, R. C., Hope, R. A., & O'Connor, M. E. (1993). Psychotherapy and bulimia nervosa: Long term effects of interpersonal psychotherapy, behavior therapy, and cognitive behavior therapy. *Archives of General Psychiatry, 50,* 419–428.

Fallon, B. A. & Feinstein, S. (2001). Hypochondriasis. In K. A. Phillips (Ed.), *Somatoform and factitious disorders* (pp. 27–65). Washington, DC: American Psychiatric Press.

Fallon, B. A., Qureshi, A. I., Laje, G., et al. (2000). Hypochondriasis and its relationship to obsessive-compulsive disorder. *Psychiatric Clinics of North America, 23,* 605–616.

Falloon, I. R. H., Boyd, J. L., McGill, C. W., et al. (1982). Family management in prevention of exacerbation of schizophrenia: A controlled study. *New England Journal of Medicine, 306* (24), 1437–1440.

Falloon, I. R. H., Boyd, J. L., McGill, C. W., Williamson, M., Razani, J., Moss, H. B., Gilderman, A. M., &

Simpson, G. M. (1985). Family management in the prevention of morbidity of schizophrenia. *Archives of General Psychiatry, 42,* 887–896.

Falloon, I. R. H., Kydd, R. R., Coverdale, J. H., & Laidlaw, T. M. (1996). Early detection and intervention for initial episodes of schizophrenia. *Schizophrenia Bulletin, 22,* 271.

Falsetti, S. A. & Resnick, H. S. (2000). Treatment of PTSD using cognitive and cognitive behavioral therapies. *Journal of Cognitive Psychotherapy, 14,* 261–285.

Fals-Stewart, W., Birchler, G. R., & O'Farrell, T. J. (1996). Behavioral couples therapy for male substance-abusing patients: Effects on relationship adjustment and drug-using behavior. *Journal of Consulting and Clinical Psychology, 64,* 959–972.

Famularo, R., Fenton, T., Kinscherff, R., Ayoub, C., & Barnum, R. (1994). Maternal and child posttraumatic stress disorder in cases of child maltreatment. *Child Abuse and Neglect, 18,* 27–36.

Famularo, R., Kinscherff, R., & Fenton, T. (1992). Psychiatric diagnoses of maltreated children. *Journal of the American Academy of Child and Adolescent Psychiatry, 31,* 863–867.

Fancher, R. E. (2000). Snapshots of Freud in America, 1899–1999. *American Psychologist, 55,* 1025–1028.

Fang, C. Y. & Myers, H. F. (2001). The effects of racial stressors and hostility on cardiovascular reactivity in African American and Caucasian men. *Health Psychology, 20,* 64–70.

Fanous, A., Gardner, C., Walsh, D., & Kendler, K. S. (2001). Relationship between positive and negative symptoms of schizophrenia and schizotypal symptoms in nonpsychotic relatives. *Archives of General Psychiatry, 58,* 669–673.

Farabee, D., Shen, H., & Sanchez, S. (2002). Perceived coercion and treatment need among mentally ill parolees. *Criminal Justice and Behavior, 29,* 76–86.

Farlow, M., Gracon, S. I., Hershey, L. A., Lewis, K. W., Sadowsky, C. H., & Dolan-Ureno, J. (1992). A controlled trial of tacrine in Alzheimer's disease. *Journal of the American Medical Association, 268,* 2523–2529.

Fauman, M. A. (1994). *Study guide to* DSM-IV. Washington, DC: American Psychiatric Press.

Faustman, W. O. (1995).What causes schizophrenia? In S. Vinogradov (Ed.), *Treating schizophrenia* (pp. 57–79). San Francisco: Jossey-Bass.

Fawzy, F. L., Fawzy, N. W., Hyun, C. S., Elashoff, R., Guthrie, D., Fahey, J. L., & Morton, D. L. (1993). Malignant melanoma: Effects of an early structured psychiatric intervention, coping, and affective state on recurrence and survival 6 years later. *Archives of General Psychiatry, 50,* 681–689.

Fear, C., Sharp, H., & Healy, D. (1996). Cognitive processes in delusional disorders. *British Journal of Psychiatry, 168,* 61–67.

Feeney, N. C., & Foa, E. B. (in press). Cognitive vulnerability to PTSD. In L. B. Alloy & J. H. Riskind (Eds.), *Cognitive vulnerability to emotional disorders.* Mahwah, NJ: Erlbaum.

Fein, D. & Waterhouse, L. (1990). Social cognition in infantile autism. *Forum Medicum.*

Feinberg, A. (2002). Forcible medication of mentally ill criminal defendants: The case of Russell Eugene Weston, Jr. *Stanford Law Review, 54,* 769–791.

Feingold, A. (1994). Gender differences in personality: A meta-analysis. *Psychological Bulletin, 116,* 429–456.

Felce, D. & Perry, J. (1995). Quality of life: Its definition and measurement. *Research in Developmental Disabilities, 16,* 51–74.

Feldman, M. D. & Feldman, J. M. (1998). *Stranger than fiction: When our minds betray us.* Washington, DC: American Psychiatric Press.

Feldman, R. S., Meyer, J. S., & Quenzer, L. F. (1997). *Principles of neuropsychopharmacology.* Sunderland, MA: Sinauer.

Felton, R. H. & Wood, F. B. (1989). Cognitive deficits in reading disability and attention deficit disorder. *Journal of Learning Disabilities, 22,* 3–13.

Fenichel, O. (1945). *The psychoanalytic theory of neurosis.* New York: W.W. Norton.

Fenton, W. S. & McGlashan, T. H. (1991). Natural history of schizophrenia subtypes: I. Longitudinal study of paranoid, hebephrenic, and undifferentiated schizophrenia. *Archives of General Psychiatry, 48,* 969–977.

Fenton, W. S., McGlashan, T. H., Victor, B. J., & Blyler, C. R. (1997). Symptoms, subtype, and suicidality in patients with schizophrenia spectrum disorders. *American Journal of Psychiatry, 154,* 199–204.

Ferguson, S. A. (2001). A review of rodent models of ADHD. In M. V. Solanto, A. F. T. Arnsten, et al. (Eds.), *Stimulant drugs and ADHD: Basic and clinical neuroscience* (pp. 209–220). New York: Oxford University Press.

Fergusson, D. M., Horwood, L. J., & Beautrais, A. L. (1999). Is sexual orientation related to mental health problems and suicidality in young people? *Archives of General Psychiatry, 56,* 876–880.

Fergusson, D. M., Horwood, L. J., & Lynskey, M. T. (1995). The stability of disruptive childhood behaviors. *Journal of Abnormal Child Psychology, 23,* 379–396.

Fergusson, D. M., Horwood, L. J., & Lynskey, M. (1996). Childhood sexual abuse and psychiatric disorder in young adulthood: II. Psychiatric outcomes of childhood sexual abuse. *Journal of the American Academy of Child and Adolescent Psychiatry, 35,* 1365–1374.

Ferster, C. B. (1973). A functional analysis of depression. *American Psychologist, 28,* 857–870.

Finch, J. R., Smith, J. P., & Pokorny, A. D. (1970, May). *Vehicular studies.* Paper presented at meetings of the American Psychiatric Association.

Fine, C. G. (1999). The tactical-integration model for the treatment of dissociative identity disorder and allied dissociative disorders. *American Journal of Psychotherapy, 53,* 361–376.

Fink, C. M., Turner, S. M., & Beidel, D. C. (1996). Culturally relevant factors in the behavioral treatment of social phobia: A case study. *Journal of Anxiety Disorders, 10,* 201–209.

Finkelhor, D. (1984). *Child sexual abuse: New theory and research.* New York: Free Press.

Finkelhor, D. (1994a). Current information on the scope and nature of child sexual abuse. *The Future of Children, 4*(2), 31–53.

Finkelhor, D. (1994b). The international epidemiology of child sexual abuse. *Child Abuse and Neglect, 18,* 409–411.

Finkelhor, D. & Araji, S. (1986). Explanations of pedophilia: A four factor model. *The Journal of Sex Research, 22,* 145–161.

Finkelson, L. & Oswalt, R. (1995). College date rape: Incidence and reporting. *Psychological Reports, 77,* 526.

Finkelstein, J. R. J., Cannon, T. D., Gur, R. E., Gur, R. C., & Moberg, P. (1997). Attentional dysfunctions in neuroleptic-naive and neuroleptic-withdrawn schizophrenic patients and their siblings. *Journal of Abnormal Psychology, 106,* 203–212.

Finn, C. T. & Smoller, J. W. (2001). The genetics of panic disorder. *Current Psychiatry Reports, 3*(2), 131–137.

Finn, P. R., Sharkansky, E. J., Brandt, K. M., & Turcotte, N. (2000). The effects of familial risk, personality and expectancies on alcohol use and abuse. *Journal of Abnormal Psychology, 109,* 122–133.

Finn, P. R., Sharkansky, E. J., Viken, R., West, T. L., Sandy, J., & Bufferd, G. M. (1997). Heterogeneity in the families of sons of alcoholics: The impact of familial vulnerability type on offspring characteristics. *Journal of Abnormal Psychology, 106,* 26–36.

Firoe, M. C., Novotny, T. E., Pierce, J. P., Hatziandreu, E. J., Patel, K. M., & Davis, R. M. (1989). Trends in cigarette smoking in the United States: The changing influence of gender and race. *Journal of the American Medical Association, 261,* 49–55.

Fischer, E. H., Dornelas, E. A., & Goethe, J. W. (2001). Characteristics of people lost to attrition in psychiatric follow-up studies. *Journal of Nervous and Mental Disease, 189,* 49–55.

Fischer, M. (1997). The persistence of ADHD into adulthood: It depends on whom you ask. *ADHD Report, 5,* 8–10.

Fisher, S. & Greenberg, R. P. (1977). *The scientific credibility of Freud's theories and therapy:* New York: Basic Books.

Fiske, S. T. & Taylor, S. E. (1991). *Social cognition* (2nd ed.). New York: McGraw-Hill.

Flaum, M., Arndt, S., & Andreasen, N. C. (1990). The role of gender in studies of ventricle enlargement in schizophrenia: A predominantly male effect. *American Journal of Psychiatry, 147,* 1327–1332.

Flaum, M. & Schultz, S. K. (1996). When does amphetamine-induced psychosis become schizophrenia? *American Journal of Psychiatry, 153,* 812–815.

Fletcher, J. M., Shaywitz, S. E., Shankweiler, D., Katz, L., Liberman, I. Y., Steubing, K. K., Francis, D. J., Fowler, A. F., & Shaywitz, B. A. (1994). Cognitive profiles of reading disability. Comparisons of discrepancy and low achievement definitions. *Journal of Educational Psychology, 86,* 6–23.

Fletcher, K. E. (1996). Childhood posttraumatic stress disorder. In E. J. Mash & R. A. Barkley (Eds.), *Child psychopathology* (pp. 242–276). New York: Guilford Press.

Flett, G. L., Vredenburg, K., & Krames, L. (1997). The continuity of depression in clinical and nonclinical samples. *Psychological Bulletin, 121,* 395–416.

Flint, A. J., Cook, M., & Rabins, P. V. (1996).Why is panic disorder less frequent in late life? *American Journal of Geriatric Psychiatry, 4,* 96–109.

Flor-Henry, P. (1987). Cerebral aspects of sexual deviation. In G. D. Wilson (Ed.), *Variant sexuality: Research and theory.* Baltimore: Johns Hopkins University Press.

Flor-Henry, P., Fromm-Auch, D., Tapper, M., & Schopflocher, D. (1981). A neuropsychological study of the stable syndrome of hysteria. *Biological Psychiatry, 16,* 601–626.

Flory, K., Lynam, D., Milich, R., Leukefeld, C., & Clayton, R. (2000). The relations among personality, symptoms of alcohol and marijuana abuse, and symptoms of comorbid psychopathology: Results from a community sample. *Experimental & Clinical Psychopharmacology, 10*(4), 425–434.

Foa, E. B. (2000). Psychosocial treatment of posttraumatic stress disorder. *Journal of Clinical Psychiatry, 61*(Suppl. 5), 43–48.

Foa, E. B., Ehlers, A., Clark, D., Tolin, D. F., & Orsillo, S. (1999). Posttraumatic cognitions inventory (PTCI): Development and comparison with other measures. *Psychological Assessment, 11,* 303–314.

Foa, E. B., Hearst-Ikeda, D., & Perry, K. J. (1995). Evaluation of a brief cognitive-behavioral program for the prevention of chronic PTSD in recent assault victims. *Journal of Consulting and Clinical Psychology, 63,* 948–955.

Foa, E. B. & Liebowitz, M. (1995). *Recent findings on the efficacy of behavior therapy and clomipromine for obsessive-compulsive disorder.* Paper presented at the annual meeting of the Psychiatric Research Society, February 1995, Park City, Utah.

Foa, E. B. & Rothbaum, B. O. (1998). *Treating the trauma of rape.* New York: Guilford Press.

Folkman, S., Lazarus, R., Dunkel-Schetter, C., DeLongis, A., & Gruen, R. (1986). The dynamics of a stressful encounter: Cognitive appraisal, coping, and encounter outcomes. *Journal of Personality and Social Psychology, 50,* 992–1003.

Follette, W. C. & Hayes, S. C. (2000). Contemporary behavior therapy. In C. R. Synder & R. E. Ingram (Eds.), *Handbook of psychological change: Psychotherapy processes and practices for the 21st century.* New York: Wiley.

Follette, W. C. & Houts, A. C. (1996). Models of scientific progress and the role of theory in taxonomy development: A case study of the DSM. *Journal of Consulting and Clinical Psychology, 64,* 1120–1132.

Folstein, S. & Rutter, M. (1977). Genetic influences and infantile autism. *Nature, 265,* 726–728.

Ford, C. V. (1995). Dimensions of somatization and hypochondriasis. *Neurologic Clinics, 13,* 241–253.

Foreyt, J. P. & Goodrick, G. K. (1993). Obesity in children. In R. T. Ammerman & M. Hersen (Eds.), *Handbook of behavior therapy with children and adults: A developmental and longitudinal perspective.* Boston: Allyn & Bacon.

Forness, S. R., Serna, L. A., Nielsen, E., Lambros, K., Hale, M. J., & Kavale, K. A. (2000). A model for early detection and primary prevention of emotional or behavioral disorders. *Education & Treatment of Children, 23,* 325–345.

Forsyth, R. P. (1974). Mechanisms of the cardiovascular responses to environmental stressors. In P. A. Obrist, A.H. Black, J. Brener, & L. U. Di Cara (Eds.), *Cardiovascular psychophysiology: Current issues in response mechanisms, biofeedback and methodology.* Hawthorne, NY: Aldine.

Fortmann, S. P. & Killen, J. D. (1995). Nicotine gum and self-help behavioral treatment for smoking relapse prevention: Results from a trial using population-based recruitment. *Journal of Consulting and Clinical Psychology, 63,* 460–468.

Foucault, M. (1965). *Madness and civilization.* New York: Random House.

Foulks, E. F. (1996). Culture and personality disorders. In J. E. Mezzich, A. Kleinman, H. Fabrega, & D. L. Parron (Eds.), *Culture and psychiatric diagnosis: A DSM-IV perspective* (pp. 243–252). Washington, DC: American Psychiatric Press.

Fountain, N. B. (2000). Status epilepticus: Risk factors and complications. *Epilepsia, 41*(Suppl. 2), S23–S30.

Fowles, D. C. (2001). Biological variables in psychopathology: A psychobiological perspective. In H. E. Adams & P. B. Sutker (Eds.), *Comprehensive handbook of psychopathology* (3rd edition, pp. 85–104). New York: Kluwer Academic/Plenum.

Fox, B. H. (1998). A hypothesis about Spiegel et al.'s 1989 paper on psychosocial intervention and breast cancer survival. *Psycho-Oncology, 7,* 361–370.

Fox, H. C., McLean, A., Turner, J. J. D., Parrott, A. C., Rogers, R., & Sahakian, B. J. (2002). Neuropsychological evidence of a relatively selective profile of temporal dysfunction in drug-free MDMA ("ecstasy") polydrug users. *Psychopharmacology, 162,* 203–214.

Frances, A., Docherty, J. P., & Kahn, D. A. (1996). The Expert Consensus Guideline Series: Treatment of schizophrenia. *Journal of Clinical Psychiatry, 57,* Supplement 12B, 1–58.

Frances, A., First, M. B., & Pincus, H. A. (1995). *DSM-IV guidebook.* Washington, DC: American Psychiatric Press.

Frances, A. & Ross, R. (1996). *DSM-IV case studies: A clinical guide to differential diagnosis.* Washington, DC: American Psychiatric Press.

Frank, E., Kupfer, D. J., Perel, T. M., Cornes, C. L., Jarrett, D. J., Mallinger, A., Thase, M. E., McEachran, A. B., & Grochocinski, V. J. (1990). Three-year outcomes for maintenance therapies in recurrent depression. *Archives of General Psychiatry, 47,* 1093–1099.

Frank, E., Swartz, H. A., & Kupfer, D. J. (2000). Interpersonal and social rhythm therapy: Managing the chaos of bipolar disorder. *Biological Psychiatry, 48,* 593–604.

Frankel, E. H. (1990). Hypnotizability and dissociation. *American Journal of Psychiatry, 147,* 823–829.

Frankl, V. E. (1962). *Man's search for meaning.* Boston: Beacon Press.

Freeman, A. & Leaf, R. (1989). Cognitive therapy applied to personality disorders. In A. Freeman, K. Simon, L. Beutler, & H. Arkowitz (Eds.), *Comprehensive handbook of cognitive therapy.* New York: Plenum Press.

Freeman, H. (1989). Relationship of schizophrenia to the environment. *British Journal of Psychiatry, 155,* 90–99.

Freeston, M. H., Ladouceur, R., Gagnon, F., Thibodeau, N., et al. (1997). Cognitive-behavioral treatment of obsessive thoughts: A controlled study. *Journal of Consulting and Clinical Psychology, 65,* 405–413.

French, S. A. & Jeffrey, R. W. (1994). Consequences of dieting to lose weight: Effects on physical and mental health. *Health Psychology, 13,* 195–212.

Fresco, D. M. & Heimberg, R. G. (2001). Empirically supported psychological treatments for social phobia. *Psychiatric Annals, 11*(8), 489–500.

Freud, A. (1946). *The ego and mechanisms of defense.* New York: International Universities Press.

Freud, S. (1953a). Three essays on sexuality. In J. Strachey (Ed.), *The standard edition of the complete psychological works of Sigmund Freud* (Vol. 3). London: Hogarth Press. Original work published 1905.

Freud, S. (1953b). The questioning of lay analysis. In J. Strachey (Ed.), *The standard edition of the complete psychological works of Sigmund Freud* (Vol. 20). London: Hogarth Press. Original work published 1926.

Freud, S. (1957). Mourning and melancholia. In J. Rickman (Ed.), *A general selection from the works of Sigmund Freud.* Garden City, NY: Doubleday. Original work published 1917.

Freud, S. (1962a). Analysis of a phobia in a five-year-old boy. In J. Strachey (Ed.), *The standard edition of the complete psychological works of Sigmund Freud* (Vol. 10). London: Hogarth Press. Original work published 1909.

Freud, S. (1962b). Studies on hysteria. In J. Strachey (Ed.), *The standard edition of the complete psychological works of Sigmund Freud* (Vol. 2). London: Hogarth Press. Original work published 1895.

Freud, S. (1974). Femininity. In J. Strachey (Ed.), *The standard edition of the complete psychological works of Sigmund Freud* (Vol. 22). London: Hogarth Press. Original work published 1932.

Freund, K. & Blanchard, R. (1989). Phallometric diagnosis of pedophilia. *Journal of Consulting and Clinical Psychology, 57,* 100–105.

Freund, K. & Watson, R. (1991). Assessment of the sensitivity and specificity of a phallometric test: An update of phallometric diagnosis of pedophilia. *Psychological Assessment, 3,* 254–260.

Frick, P. J. (1998). *Conduct disorders and severe antisocial behavior.* New York: Plenum Press.

Fried, D., Crits-Christoph, P., & Luborsky, L. (1992). The first empirical demonstration of transference in psychotherapy. *Journal of Nervous and Mental Disease, 180,* 326–331.

Friedman, A. S., Glassman, K., & Terras, A. (2001). Violent behavior as related to use of marijuana and other drugs. *Journal of Addictive Diseases, 20,* 49–72.

Friedman, M. & Rosenman, R. H. (1974). *Type A behavior and your heart.* New York: Knopf.

Frith, C. D. (1996). The role of the prefrontal cortex in self-consciousness: The case of auditory hallucinations. *Philosophical Transactions of the Royal Society of London, 351B,* 1505–1512.

Frith, C. & Dolan, R. J. (2000). The role of memory in the delusions associated with schizophrenia. In D. L. Schacter & E. Scarry (Eds.), *Memory, brain, and belief* (pp. 115–135). Cambridge, MA: Harvard University Press.

Fromm, Erich. (1980). *Greatness and limitations of Freud's thought.* New York: Harper & Row.

Frosch, W. A., Robbins, E. S., & Stern, M. (1965). Untoward reactions of lysergic acid diethylamide (LSD) resulting in hospitalization. *New England Journal of Medicine, 273*(23), 1236.

Frost, L. E. & Bonnie, R. J. (Eds.) (2001). *The evolution of mental health law.* Washington, DC: American Psychological Association.

Frost, R. O. (2000). People who hoard animals. *Psychiatric Times, 17*(4).

Frost, R. O. & Gross, R. C. (1993). The hoarding of possessions. *Behaviour Research and Therapy, 31*(4), 367–381.

Frost, R. O., Meager, B., & Riskind, J. H. (2001). Obsessive-compulsive features in pathological lottery and scratch ticket gamblers. *Journal of Gambling Studies, 17,* 5–19.

Fukuzako, H., Fukuzaki, S., Fukuzako, T., Jing, H., Ueyama, K., & Takigawa, M. (1999). P300 event-related potentials in probably dissociative generalized amnesia. *Progress in Neuro-Psychopharmacology & Biological Psychiatry, 23,* 1319–1327.

Furby, L., Weinrott, M. R., & Blackshaw, L. (1989). Sex offender recidivism: A review. *Psychological Bulletin, 105*(1), 3–30.

Fyer, A. J., Liebowitz, M. R., & Klein, D. F. (1990). Treatment trials, comorbidity, and syndromal complexity. In J. D. Maser and C.R. Cloninger (Eds.), *Comorbidity of mood and anxiety disorders.* Washington, DC: American Psychiatric Press.

Fyer, A. J., Mannuzza, S., Chapman, T. F., Martin, L. Y., & Klein, D. F. (1995). Specificity in familial aggregation of phobic disorders. *Archives of General Psychiatry, 52,* 564–573.

Fyer, A. J., Mannuzza, S., Chapman, T. F., Liebowitz, M. R., et al. (1993) A direct interview family study of social phobia. *Archives of General Psychiatry, 50*(4), 286–293.

Gabbard, G. O. (1994). *Psychodynamic psychiatry in clinical practice. The DSM-IV edition.* Washington, DC: American Psychiatric Press.

Gabriel, S. M., Haroutunian, V., Powchik, P., Honer, W. G., Davidson, M., Davies, P., & Davis, K. L. (1997). Increased concentrations of presynaptic proteins in the cingulate cortex of subjects with schizophrenia. *Archives of General Psychiatry, 54,* 559–566.

Gaebel, W., Janner, M., Frommann, N., Pietzcker, A., Kopcke, W., Linden, M., Muller, P., Muller-Spahn, F., & Tegeler, J. (2000). Prodromal states in schizophrenia. *Comprehensive Psychiatry, 41,* 76–85.

Gagnon, J. H., Rosen, R. C., & Leiblum, S. R. (1982). Cognitive and social aspects of sexual dysfunction: Sexual scripts in sex therapy. *Journal of Sex and Marital Therapy, 8,* 44–56.

Galderisi, S., Maj, M., Mucci, A., Cassano, G. B., Invernizzi, G., Rossi, A., Vita, A., Dell'Osso, L., Daneluzzo, E., & Pini, S. (2002). Historical, psychopathological, neurological, and neuropsychological aspects of deficit schizophrenia: A multicenter study. *American Journal of Psychiatry, 159,* 983–990.

Galen, L. W., Henderson, M. J., & Whitman, R. D. (1997). The utility of novelty seeking, harm avoidance, and expectancy in the prediction of drinking. *Addictive Behaviors, 22,* 93–106.

Gallo, W. T., Bradley, E. H., Siegel, M., & Kasl, S. V. (2000). Health effects of involuntary job loss among older workers: Findings from the health and retirement survey. *Journals of Gerontology Series B-Psychological Sciences & Social Sciences, 55B*(3), S131–S140.

Garb, H. N. (1998). *Studying the clinician: Judgment research and psychological assessment.* Washington, DC: American Psychological Association.

Garber, H. L. & McInerney, M. (1982). Sociobehavioral factors in mental retardation. In P. T. Legelka & H. G. Prehm (Eds.), *Mental retardation: From categories to people.* Columbus, OH: Charles E. Merrill.

Garber, J. & Flynn, C. (2001). Predictors of depressive cognitions in young adolescents. *Cognitive Therapy and Research, 25,* 353–376.

Garbutt, J. C., West, S. L., Carey, T. S., Lohr, K. N., & Crews, F. T. (1999). Pharmacological treatment of alcohol dependence: A review of the evidence. *Journal of the American Medical Association, 28*(14), 1318–1325.

Garcia, M. E., Schmitz, J. M., & Doerfler, L. A. (1990). A fine-grained analysis of the role of self-efficacy in self-initiated attempts to quit smoking. *Journal of Consulting and Clinical Psychology, 58,* 317–322.

Gardner, H. (1998). Are there additional intelligences? The case for naturalist, spiritual, and existential intelligences. In J. Kane (Ed.), *Education, information, and transformation.* Englewood Cliffs, NJ: Prentice-Hall.

Gardner, H. & Hatch, T. (1989). Multiple intelligences go to school: Educational implications of the theory of multiple intelligences. *Educational Research, 18*(8), 6.

Garety, P. A., Fowler, D., & Kuipers, E. (2000). Cognitive-behavioral therapy for medication-resistant symptoms. *Schizophrenia Bulletin, 26,* 73–86.

Garssen, B., De Beurs, E., Buikhuisen, M., van Balkom, A., Lange, A., & van Dyck, R. (1996). On distinguishing types of panic. *Journal of Anxiety Disorders, 10,* 173–184.

Gath, A. (2001). Working with families and caregivers of people with severe mental retardation. In A. Dosen & K. Day (Eds.), *Treating mental illness and behavior disorders in children and adults with mental retardation* (pp. 119–130). Washington, DC: American Psychiatric Press.

Gatz, M., Bengtson, V. L., & Blum, M. J. (1990). Caregiving families. In J. E. Birren & K. W. Schaie (Eds.), *Handbook of the psychology of aging* (3rd ed., pp. 405–426). New York: Academic Press.

Gatz, M., Lowe, B., Berg, S., Mortimer, J., & Pedersen, N. (1994). Dementia: Not just a search for the gene. *Gerontologist, 34,* 251–255.

Gawin, F. H. & Kleber, H. D. (1986). Abstinence symptomatology and psychiatric diagnosis in cocaine abusers. *Archives of General Psychiatry, 43,* 107–113.

Gaynor, S. T., Baird, S. C., & Nelson-Gray, R. O. (1999). Application of time-series (single-subject) designs in clinical psychology. In P. C. Kendall, J. N. Butcher, & G. N. Holmbeck (Eds.), *Handbook of research methods in clinical psychology* (2nd ed., pp. 297–329). New York: Wiley.

Gebhard, P. H., Gagnon, J. H., Pomeroy, W. B., & Christenson, C. V. (1965). *Sex offenders.* New York: Harper & Row.

Gelder, M. (1991). Psychological treatment for anxiety disorders: Adjustment disorder with anxious mood, generalized anxiety disorders, panic disorder, agoraphobia, and avoidant personality disorder. In W. Coryell & G. Winokur (Eds.), *The clinical management of anxiety disorders* (pp. 10–27). New York: Oxford University Press.

Gelenberg, A. J. (1991). Psychoses. In A. J. Gelenberg, E. L. Bassuk, & S. C. Schoonover (Eds.), *The practitioner's guide to psychoactive drugs* (3rd ed., pp. 125–215). New York: Plenum Press.

Geller, B. & Luby, J. (1997). Child and adolescent bipolar disorder: A review of the past 10 years. *Journal of the American Academy of Child and Adolescent Psychiatry, 36,* 1168–1176.

Geller, B., Zimerman, B., Williams, M., Bolhofner, K., & Craney, J. L. (2001a). Adult psychosocial outcome of prepubertal major depressive disorder. *Journal of the American Academy of Child and Adolescent Psychiatry, 40,* 673–677.

Geller, B., Zimerman, B., Williams, M., Bolhofner, K., & Craney, J. L. (2001b). Bipolar disorder at prospective follow-up of adults who had prepubertal major depressive disorder. *American Journal of Psychiatry, 158,* 125–127.

Geller, P. A., Klier, C. M., & Neugebauer, R. (2001). Anxiety disorders following miscarriage. *Journal of Clinical Psychiatry, 62,* 432–438.

Gelman, D. (1990, March 26). Drugs vs. the couch. *Newsweek,* pp. 42–43.

Gemar, M. C., Segal, Z. V., Sagrati, S., & Kennedy, S. J. (2001). Mood-induced changes on the implicit association test in recovered depressed patients. *Journal of Abnormal Psychology, 110,* 282–289.

Gentz, B. A. (2001). Alternative therapies for the management of pain in labor and delivery. *Clinical Obstetrics and Gynecology, 44,* 704–732.

George, M. S., Lisanby, S. H., & Sackeim, H. A. (1999). Transcranial magnetic stimulation: Applications in neuropsychiatry. *Archives of General Psychiatry, 56,* 300–311.

George, W. H. & Stoner, S. A. (2000). Understanding acute alcohol effects on sexual behavior. *Annual Review of Sex Research, 11,* 92–124.

Gerbasi, J. B., Bonnie, R. J., & Binder, R. L. (2000). Resource document on mandatory outpatient treatment. *Journal of the American Academy of Psychiatry and the Law, 28,* 127–144.

Gerin, W., Litt, M. D., Deich, J., & Pickering, T. G. (1995). Self-efficacy as a moderator of perceived control effects on cardiovascular reactivity: Is enhanced control always beneficial? *Psychosomatic Medicine, 57,* 390–397.

Gerlach, A. L., Wilhelm, F. H., Gruber, K., & Roth W. T. (2001). Blushing and physiological arousability in social phobia. *Journal of Abnormal Psychology, 10,* 247–258.

Gershuny, B. S. & Thayer, J. F. (1999). Relations among psychological trauma, dissociative phenomena, and trauma-related distress: A review and integration. *Clinical Psychology Review, 19,* 631–657.

Geyer S. (1991). Life events prior to manifestation of breast cancer: A limited prospective study covering eight years before diagnosis. *Journal of Psychosomatic Research, 35,* 355–363.

Giancola, P. R. & Zeichner, A. (1997). The biphasic effects of alcohol on human physical aggression. *Journal of Abnormal Psychology, 106,* 598–607.

Gibb, B. E., Abramson, L. Y., & Alloy, L. B. (in press). Emotional maltreatment from parents, peer victimization and cognitive vulnerability to depression. *Cognitive Therapy and Research.*

Gibb, B. E., Alloy, L. B., Abramson, L. Y., Rose, D. T., Whitehouse, W. G., Donovan, P., Hogan, M. E., Cronholm, J., & Tierney, S. (2001). History of childhood maltreatment, negative cognitive styles, and depression. *Cognitive Therapy and Research, 25,* 425–446.

Gibbs, N. A. (1996). Nonclinical populations in research on obsessive-compulsive disorder: A critical review. *Clinical Psychology Review, 16,* 729–773.

Giesler, R. B., Josephs, R. A., & Swann, W. B., Jr. (1996). Self-verification in clinical depression: The desire for negative evaluation. *Journal of Abnormal Psychology, 105,* 358–368.

Giles, D. E., Kupfer, D. J., Rush, A. J., & Roffwarg, H. P. (1998). Controlled comparison of electrophysiological sleep in families of probands with unipolar depression. *American Journal of Psychiatry, 155,* 192–199.

Gill, M., McKeon, P., & Humphries, P. (1988). Linkage analysis of manic depression in an Irish family using H-ras 1 and INS DNA markers. *Journal of Medical Genetics, 25,* 634–635.

Gillberg, C. (1991). Outcome in autism and autistic-like conditions. *Journal of the American Academy of Child and Adolescent Psychiatry, 30,* 375–382.

Gillberg, C. & Coleman, M. (2000). *The biology of the autistic syndromes* (3rd ed.). London: Cambridge University Press.

Gillberg, C., Melander, H., Liis von Knorring, A., Lars-Olof, J., Thernlund, G., Hagglof, B., Eidevall, W. L., Gustafsson, P., & Kopp, S. (1997). Long-term stimulant treatment of children with attention-deficit hyperactivity disorder symptoms. *Archives of General Psychiatry, 54,* 857–864.

Gillham, J. E. & Reivich, K. J. (1999). Prevention of depressive symptoms in school children: A research update. *Psychological Science, 10,* 461–462.

Gillham, J. E., Reivich, K. J., Jaycox, L. H., & Seligman, M. E. P. (1995). Prevention of depressive symptoms in schoolchildren: Two-year follow-up, *Psychological Science, 6,* 343–351.

Gillham, J. E. & Seligman, M. E. P. (1999). Footsteps on the road to a positive psychology. *Behaviour Research and Therapy, 37,* S163–S173.

Gilligan, C. (1982). *In a different voice.* Cambridge, MA: Harvard University Press.

Ginsberg, G. L. (1985). Psychiatric history and mental status examination. In H. I. Kaplan & B. J. Sadock (Eds.), *Comprehensive textbook of psychiatry, IV* (pp. 487–495). Baltimore: Williams & Wilkins.

Gitlin, M. J., Swendsen, J., Heller, T. L., & Hammen, C. (1995). Relapse and impairment in bipolar disorder. *American Journal of Psychiatry, 152,* 1635–1640.

Givelber, D. J., Bowers, W., & Blitch, C. (1985). The *Tarasoff* controversy: A summary of findings from an empirical study of legal, ethical and clinical issues. In J. Beck (Ed.), *The potentially violent patient and the* Tarasoff *decision in psychiatric practice* (pp. 36–57). Washington, DC: American Psychiatric Association.

Glantz, L. A. & Lewis, D. A. (1997). Reduction of synaptophysin immunoreactivity in the prefrontal cortex of subjects with schizophrenia: Regional and diagnostic specificity. *Archives of General Psychiatry, 54,* 943–952.

Glanz, L. M., Haas, G. L., & Sweeney, J. A. (1995). Assessment of hopelessness in suicidal patients. *Clinical Psychology Review, 15,* 49–64.

Glaser, R., Pearson, G. R., Bonneau, R. H., Esterling, B. A., Atkinson, C., & Kiecolt-Glaser, J. K. (1993). Stress and the memory T-cell response to the Epstein-Barr virus in healthy medical students. *Health Psychology, 12,* 435–442.

Glassman, A. H. (1993). Cigarette smoking: Implications for psychiatric illness. *American Journal of Psychiatry, 150,* 546–553.

Glassman, N. S. & Andersen, S. M. (1999). Activating transference without consciousness: Using significant-other presentations to go beyond what is subliminally given. *Journal of Personality and Social Psychology, 77,* 1146–1162.

Gleaves, D. H. (1996). The sociocognitive model of dissociative identity disorder: A reexamination of the evidence. *Psychological Bulletin, 120,* 42–59.

Glucksman, M. L. (1995). Psychodynamics and neurobiology. An integrated approach. *Journal of the American Academy of Psychoanalysis, 23,* 179–195.

Goedde, H. W., Agarwal, D. P., Fritze, G., Meier-Tackmann, D., Singh, S., Beckmann, G., Bhatia, K., Chen, L. Z., Fang, B., Lisker, R., Paik, Y. K., Rothhammer, F., Saha, N., Segal, B., Srivastava, L. M., & Czeizel, A. (1992). Distribution of ADH2 and ALD2 genotypes in different populations. *Human Genetics, 88,* 344–366.

Goffman, E. (1959). The moral career of the mental patient. *Psychiatry: Journal for the Study of Interpersonal Processes, 22,* 123–131.

Goffman, E. (1961). *Asylums: Essays on the social situation of mental patients and other inmates.* New York: Doubleday.

Gold, L. H. (2001). Clinical and forensic aspects of postpartum disorders. *Journal of the American Academy of Psychiatry and the Law, 29,* 344–347.

Goldberg, D. L. (2000). Unqualified acquittal versus insanity: mental disorder as an evidentiary issue, not an affirmative defense. *Journal of Psychiatry & Law, 28,* 49–75.

Goldberg, D. P. & Bridges, K. (1988). Somatic presentations of psychiatric illness in primary care settings. *Journal of Psychosomatic Research, 32,* 137–144.

Goldberg, J. F., Harrow, M., & Grossman, L. S. (1995). Course and outcome in bipolar affective disorder: A longitudinal follow-up study. *American Journal of Psychiatry, 152,* 379–384.

Goldberg, J. F., Harrow, M., & Whiteside, J. E. (2001). Risk for bipolar illness in patients initially hospitalized for unipolar depression. *American Journal of Psychiatry, 158,* 1265–1270.

Goldgaber, D., Lerman, M. I., McBride, O. W., Saffiotti, U., & Gajdusek, D. C. (1987). Characterization and chromosomal localization of a cDNA encoding brain amyloid of Alzheimer's disease. *Science 235,* 877–880.

Goldman, M. S., Brown, S. A., & Christiansen, B. A. (1987). Expectancy theory: Thinking about drinking. In H. T. Blane & K. E. Leonard (Eds.), *Psychological theories of drinking and alcoholism* (pp. 181–226). New York: Guilford Press.

Goldsmith, S. K., Shapiro, R. M., & Joyce, J. N. (1997). Disrupted pattern of D2 dopamine receptors in the temporal lobe in schizophrenia: A postmortem study. *Archives of General Psychiatry, 54,* 649–658.

Goldstein, A. (1976). Opioid peptides (endorphins) in pituitary and brain. *Science, 193,* 1081–1086.

Goldstein, A. (1994). *Addiction: From biology to drug policy.* New York: Freeman.

Goldstein, I., Lue, T. F., Padma-Nathan, H., Rosen, R. C., Steers, W. D., & Wicker, P. A. (1998). Pral sildenafil in the treatment of erectile dysfunction. Sildenafil Study Group. *New England Journal of Medicine, 338,* 1397–1404.

Goldstein, J. M., Faraone, S. V., Chen, W. J., Tolomiczencko, G. S., & Tsuang, M. T. (1990). Sex differences in the familial transmission of schizophrenia. *British Journal of Psychiatry, 156,* 819–826.

Goldstein, J. M. & Lewine, R. R. J. (2000). Overview of sex differences in schizophrehia: Where we have been and where do we go from here? In D. J. Castle, J. J. McGrath, & J. Kulkarni (Eds.), *Women and schizophrenia* (pp. 111–153). Cambridge, MA: Cambridge University Press.

Goldstein, J. M., Seidman, L. J., O'Brien, L. M., Horton, N. J., Kennedy, D. N., Makris, N., Caviness, V. S., Jr., Faraone, S. V., & Tsuang, M. T. (2002). Impact of normal sexual dimorphisms on sex difference in structural brain abnormalities in schizophrenia assessed by magnetic resonance imaging. *Archives of General Psychiatry, 59,* 154–164.

Goldstein, M. (1998). Medications for ADHD. In S. Goldstein & M. Goldstein (Eds.), *Managing attention deficit hyperactivity disorder in children* (pp. 459–532). New York: Wiley.

Goldstein, M. J. (1987). Family interaction patterns that antedate the onset of schizophrenia and related disorders: A further analysis of data from a longitudinal prospective study. In K. Hahlweg & M. J. Goldstein (Eds.), *Understanding major mental disorder: The contribution of family interaction research* (pp. 11–32). New York: Family Process Press.

Goldstein, M. J. & Miklowitz, D. J. (1995). The effectiveness of psychoeducational family therapy in the treatment of schizophrenia disorders. *Journal of Marital and Family Therapy, 21,* 361–375.

Goldstein, R. B., Black, D. W., Nasrallah, A., & Winokur, G. (1991). The prediction of suicide: Sensitivity, specificity, and predictive value of a multivariate model applied to suicide among 1906 patients with affective disorders. *Archives of General Psychiatry, 48,* 418–422.

Gomberg, E. S. (1997). Alcohol abuse: Age and gender differences. In R. W. Wilsnack & S. C. Wilsnack (Eds.), *General and alcohol: Individual and social perspectives* (pp. 39–84). New Brunswick, NJ: Alcohol Research Dissemination, Inc.

Goodkin, K., Blaney, N. T., Feasley, D., Fletcher, M. A., Baum, M. K., Mantero-Atienza, E., Klimas, N. G., Millon, C., Szapocznik, J., & Eisdorfer, C. (1992). Active coping style is associated with natural killer cell cytotoxicity in asymptomatic HIV-1 seropositive homosexual men. *Journal of Psychosomatic Research, 36,* 635–650.

Goodwin, D. W. & Gabrielli, W. F. (1997). Alcohol: Clinical aspects. In J. H. Lowinson, P. Ruiz, R. B. Millman, & J. G. Langrod (Eds.), *Substance abuse: A comprehensive textbook* (pp. 142–148). Baltimore: Williams & Wilkins.

Goodwin, D. W., Gabrielli, W. F., Jr., Penick, E. C., Nickel, E. J., Chhibber, S., Knop, J., Jensen, P., & Schulsinger, F. (1999). Breast-feeding and alcoholism: The Trotter Hypothesis. *American Journal of Psychiatry, 155,* 650–652.

Goodwin, D. W., Schulsinger, F., Hermansen, L., Guze, S. B., & Winokur, G. (1973). Alcohol problems in adoptees raised apart from alcoholic biological parents. *Archives of General Psychiatry, 28,* 238–243.

Goodwin, D. W., Schulsinger, F., Moller, N., Mednick, S., & Guze, S. (1977). Psychopathology in adopted and nonadopted daughters of alcoholics. *Archives of General Psychiatry, 34,* 1005–1009.

Goodwin, P. J., Leszcz, M., Ennis, M., Koopmans, J., Vincent, L., Guther, H., et al. (2001). The effect of group psychosocial support on survival in metastatic breast cancer. *New England Journal of Medicine, 345,* 1719–1726.

Goodyer, I. M. (1992). Depression in childhood and adolescence. In E. S. Paykel (Ed.), *Handbook of affective disorders* (2nd ed., pp. 585–600). New York: Guilford Press.

Goodyer, I. M., Herbert, J., Tamplin, A., Secher, S. M., & Pearson, J. (1997). Short-term outcome of major depression: II. Life events, family dysfunction, and friendship difficulties as predictors of persistent disorder. *Journal of the American Academy of Child and Adolescent Psychiatry, 36,* 474–480.

Gorman, J. M., Liebowitz, M. R., Fyer, A. J., & Stein, J. (1989). A neuroanatomical hypothesis for panic disorder. *American Journal of Psychiatry, 146,* 148–161.

Gorman, J. M., Liebowitz, M. R., & Shear, M. K. (1992). Panic and anxiety disorders. In R. Michels (Ed.), *Psychiatry* (chap. 32). Philadelphia: J. B. Lippincott.

Gortner, E. T., Gollan, J. K., Dobson, K. S., & Jacobson, N. S. (1998). Cognitive-behavioral treatment for depression: Relapse prevention. *Journal of Consulting and Clinical Psychology, 66,* 377–378.

Gotlib, I. A. & Schraedley, P. K. (2000). Interpersonal psychotherapy. In C. R. Synder & R. E. Ingram (Eds.), *Handbook of psychological change: Psychotherapy processes and practices for the 21st century.* New York: Wiley.

Gottesman, I. I. (1991). *Schizophrenia genesis: The origins of madness.* New York: Freeman.

Gottesman, I. I. (1996). Blind men and elephants: Genetic and other perspectives on schizophrenia. In L. L. Hall (Ed.), *Genetics and mental illness: Evolving issues for research and society* (pp. 51–77). New York: Plenum Press.

Gottesman, I. I. & Bertelsen, A. (1989). Confirming unexpressed genotypes for schizophrenia. *Archives of General Psychiatry, 46,* 867–872.

Gottesman, I. I. & Shields, J. (1982). *Schizophrenia: The epigenetic puzzle.* New York: Cambridge University Press.

Gottman, J. M., Jacobson, N. S., Rushe, R. H., Short, J. W., Babcock, J., La Taillade, J. J., & Waltz, J. (1995).

The relationship between heart rate reactivity, emotionally aggressive behavior and general violence in batterers. *Journal of Family Psychology, 9,* 227–248.

Gould, M. S., Fisher, P., Parides, M., Flory, M., & Shaffer, D. (1996). Psychosocial risk factors of child and adolescent completed suicide. *Archives of General Psychiatry, 53,* 1155–1162.

Gould, M. S. & Kramer, R. A. (2001). Youth suicide prevention. *Suicide and Life Threatening Behavior, 31*(Suppl.), 6–30.

Gould, M. S., Shaffer, D., Fisher, P., Kleinman, M., & Morishima, A. (1992). The clinical prediction of adolescent suicide. In R. W. Maris, A. L. Berman, J. T. Maltsberger, & R. I. Yufit (Eds.), *Assessment and prediction of suicide* (pp. 130–143). New York: Guilford Press.

Gould, R. A., Otto, M. W., Pollack, M. H. (1995). A meta-analysis of treatment outcome for panic disorder. *Clinical Psychology Review, 15*(8), 819–844.

Gould, R., Miller, B. L., Goldberg, M. A., & Benson, D. F. (1986). The validity of hysterical signs and symptoms. *Journal of Nervous and Mental Disease, 174,* 593–597.

Graham, D. T. (1967). Health, disease, and the mind-body problem: Linguistic parallelism. *Psychosomatic Medicine, 39,* 52–71.

Graham, J. R. (2000). *MMPI-2: Assessing personality and psychopathology* (3rd ed.). New York: Oxford University Press.

Graham, J. R., Ben-Porath, Y. S., & McNulty, J. L. (1999). *MMPI-2 correlates for outpatient mental health settings.* Minneapolis: University of Minnesota Press.

Gramzow, R. & Tangney, J. P. (1992). Proneness to shame and the narcissistic personality. *Personality and Social Psychology Bulletin, 18,* 369–376.

Granholm, E., Morris, S. K., Sarkin, A. J., Asarnow, R. F., & Jeste, D. V. (1997). Pupillary responses index overload of working memory resources in schizophrenia. *Journal of Abnormal Psychology, 106,* 458–467.

Grant, B. F. (2001). Estimates of US children exposed to alcohol abuse and dependence in the family. *American Journal of Public Health, 90,* 112–115.

Grant, I. & Martin, A. (1994). *Neuropsychology of HIV infection.* New York: Oxford University Press.

Grantham-McGregor, S., Powell, C., Walker, S., Chang, S., & Fletcher, P. (1994). The long-term follow-up of severely malnourished children who participated in an intervention program. *Child Development, 65,* 428–439.

Gray, J. A. (1994). Three fundamental emotions systems. In P. Ekman & R. J. Davidson (Eds.), *The nature of emotion: Fundamental questions* (pp. 243–247). New York: Oxford University Press.

Graziottin, A. (2001). Clinical approach to dyspareunia. *Journal of Sex & Marital Therapy, 27*(5), 489–501.

Green, M. F. (1996). What are the functional consequences of neurocognitive deficits in schizophrenia? *American Journal of Psychiatry, 153,* 321–330.

Green, M. F., Marshall, B. D., Jr., Wirshing, W. C., Ames, D., Marder, S. R., McGurk, S., Kern, R. S., & Mintz, J. (1997). Does risperidone improve verbal working memory in treatment-resistant schizophrenia? *American Journal of Psychiatry, 154,* 799–804.

Green, M. F., Nuechterlein, K. H., & Breitmeyer, B. (1997). Backward masking performance in unaffected siblings of schizophrenic patients: Evidence for a vulnerability indicator. *Archives of General Psychiatry, 54,* 465–472.

Green, R. (1987). *The "sissy boy syndrome" and the development of homosexuality.* New Haven: Yale University Press.

Green, R. & Fleming, D. T. (1990). Transsexual surgery follow-up: Status in the 1990s. *Annual Review of Sex Research, 1,* 163–174.

Greenwald, E. & Leitenberg, H. (1989). Long-term effects of sexual experiences with siblings and nonsiblings during childhood. *ASB, 18,* 389–400.

Greenwood, G. L., White, E. W., Page-Shafer, K., Bein, E., Osmond, D. H., Paul, J., & Stall, R. D. (2001). Correlates of heavy substance use among young gay and bisexual men: The San Francisco Young Men's Health Study. *Drug and Alcohol Dependence, 61,* 105–112.

Greist, J. H., Jefferson, J. W., Kobak, K. A., Katzelnick, D. J., & Serlin, R. C. (1995). Efficacy and tolerability of serotonin transport inhibitors in obsessive-compulsive disorder: A meta-analysis. *Archives of General Psychiatry, 21, 53–60.*

Grenyer, B. F. S. & Luborsky, L. (1996). Dynamic change in psychotherapy: Mastery of interpersonal conflicts. *Journal of Consulting and Clinical Psychology, 64,* 411–416.

Grewen, K., Girdler, S. S., West, S. G., Bragdon, E., Costello, N., & Light, K. C. (2000). Stable pessimistic attributions interact with socioeconomic status to influence blood pressure and vulnerability to hypertension. *Journal of Women's Health and Gender Based Medicine, 9,* 905–915.

Griffin, M. G., Resick, P. A., & Mechanic, M. B. (1997). Objective assessment of peritraumatic dissociation: Psychophysiological indicators. *American Journal of Psychiatry, 154,* 1081–1088.

Griffin, S. L., van Reekum, R., & Masanic, C. (2003). A review of cholinergic agents in the treatment of neurobehavioral deficits following traumatic brain injury. *Journal of Neuropsychiatry & Clinical Neurosciences, 15*(1).

Grigorenko, E. L. & Sternberg, R. J. (1998). Dynamic testing. *Psychological Bulletin,* 124, 75–111.

Grinspoon, L. (1977). *Marihuana reconsidered* (2nd ed.). Cambridge, MA: Harvard University Press.

Grinspoon, L. & Bakalar, J. B. (1994). The war on drugs—a peace proposal. *New England Journal of Medicine, 330,* 357–360.

Grinspoon, L. & Bakalar, J. B. (1997). Marihuana. In J. H. Lowinson, P. Ruiz, R. B. Millman, & J. G. Langrod (Eds.), *Substance abuse: A comprehensive textbook* (pp. 199–206). Baltimore: Williams & Wilkins.

Grisso, T. (1991). Clinical assessments for legal decision making. In S. A. Shah & B. D. Sales (Eds.), *Law and mental health: Major developments and research needs.* Rockville, MD: National Institute of Mental Health.

Gronwall, D., Wrightson, P., & Waddell, P. (1990). *Head injury: The facts. A guide for families and care-givers.* New York: Oxford University Press.

Gross, D. E. (2002). Presumed dangerous: California's selective policy of forcibly medicating state prisoners with antipsychotic drugs. *U.C. Davis Law Review, 35,* 483–517.

Gross, J. J. & Levenson, R. W. (1997). Hiding feelings: The acute effects of inhibiting negative and positive emotion. *Journal of Abnormal Psychology, 106,* 95–103.

Grossarth-Maticek, R., Eysenck, H. J., Pfeifer, A., Schmidt, P., & Koppel, G. (1997). The specific action of different personality risk factors on cancer of the breast, cervix, corpus uteri and other types of cancer: A prospective investigation. *Personality & Individual Differences, 23,* 949–960.

Groth, N. A. (1978). Guidelines for assessment and management of the offender. In A. Burgess, N. Groth, S. Holmstrom, & S. Sgroi (Eds.), *Sexual assault of children and adolescents* (pp. 25–42). Lexington, MA: Lexington Books.

Grove, W. M., et al. (1990). Heritability of substance abuse and antisocial behavior: A study of monozygotic twins reared apart. *Biological Psychiatry, 27,* 1293–1304.

Grove, W. M., Lebow, B. S., Clementz, B. A., Cerri, A., Medus, C., & Iacono, W. G. (1991). Familial prevalence and coaggregation of schizotype indicators: A multitrait family study. *Journal of Abnormal Psychology, 100,* 115–121.

Grubin, D. & Mason, D. (1997). Medical models of sexual deviance. In D. R. Laws, W. T. O'Donohue, et al. (Eds.), *Sexual deviance: Theory, assessment, and treatment.* New York: Guilford Press.

Grundman, M. & Thal, L. J. (2000). Treatment of Alzheimer's disease: Rationale and strategies. *Neurologic Clinics, 18,* 807–827.

Guerra, N. G., Attar, B., & Weissberg, R. P. (1997). Prevention of aggression and violence among inner-city youths. In D. M. Stoff, J. Breiling, & J. D. Maser (Eds.), *Handbook of antisocial behavior* (pp. 375–383). New York: Wiley.

Guggenheim, F. G. & Babigian, H. M. (1974). Catatonic schizophrenia—epidemiology and clinical course—7-year register study of 798 cases. *Journal of Nervous and Mental Disease, 158*(4), 291–305.

Guilette, E. C. D., Blumenthal, J. A., Babyak, M., Jiang, W., Waugh, R. A., Frid, D. J., O'Connor, C. M., Morris, J. J., & Krantz, D. S. (1997). Effects of mental stress on myocardial ischemia during daily life. *Journal of the American Medical Association, 277,* 1521–1526.

Gump, B. S., Matthews, K. A., & Räikkönen, K. (1999). Modeling relationships among socioeconomic status, hostility, cardiovascular reactivity, and left ventricular mass in African American and White children. *Health Psychology, 18,* 140–150.

Gunderson, J. G. (1984). *Borderline personality disorder.* Washington, DC: American Psychiatric Press.

Gunderson, J. G. (1992). Diagnostic controversies. In A. Tasman & M. B. Riba (Eds.), *Review of psychiatry* (Vol. 11, pp. 9–24). Washington, DC: American Psychiatric Press.

Gunderson, J. G. (1996). The borderline patient's intolerance of aloneness: Insecure attachments and therapist availability. *American Journal of Psychiatry, 153,* 752–758.

Gunderson, J. G. & Elliott, G. R. (1985). The interface between borderline personality disorder and affective disorder. *American Journal of Psychiatry, 147,* 277–287.

Gunderson, J. G. & Phillips, K. A. (1991). A current view of the interspace between borderline personality disorder and depression. *American Journal of Psychiatry, 148,* 967–975.

Gunderson, J. G. & Ronningstam, E. (2001). Differentiating narcissistic and antisocial personality disorders. *Journal of Personality Disorders, 15,* 103–109.

Gunnar, M. R. (1998). Quality of early care and buffering of neuroendocrine stress reactions: Potential effects on the developing human brain. *Preventive Medicine, 27,* 208–211.

Gur, R. E., Cowell, P. E., Latshaw, A., Turetsky, B. I., Grossman, R. I., Arnold, S. E., Bilker, W. B., & Gur, R. C. (2000). Reduced dorsal and orbital prefrontal gray matter volumes in schizophrenia. *Archives of General Psychiatry, 57,* 761–768.

Gur, R. E., Petty, R. G., Turetsky, B. I., & Gur, R. C. (1996). Schizophrenia throughout life: Sex differences in severity and profile of symptoms. *Schizophrenia Research, 21,* 1–12.

Gur, R. E., Turetsky, B. I., Cowell, P. E., Finkelman, C., Maany, V., Grossman, R. I., Arnold, S. E., Bilker, W. B., & Gur, R. C. (2000). Temporolimbic volume reductions in schizophrenia. *Archives of General Psychiatry, 57,* 769–775.

Guralnik, O., Schmeidler, J., & Simeon, D. (2000). Feeling unreal: Cognitive processes in depersonalization. *American Journal of Psychiatry, 157,* 103–109.

Gureje, O., Simon, G. E., Üstün, T. B., & Goldberg, D. P. (1997). Somatization in cross-cultural perspective: A World Health Organization study in primary care. *American Journal of Psychiatry, 154,* 989–995.

Gurevich, E.V., Bordelon, Y., Shapiro, R. M., Arnold, S. E., Gur, R. E., & Joyce, J. N. (1997). Mesolimbic dopamine D_3 receptors and use of antipsychotics in patients with schizophrenia: A postmortem study. *Archives of General Psychiatry, 54,* 225–232.

Gurland, B., Dean, L., Craw, P., & Golden, R. (1980). The epidemiology of depression and delirium in the elderly: The use of multiple indicators of these conditions. In J. O. Cole & J. E. Barrett (Eds.), *Psychopathology in the aged.* New York: Raven Press.

Gutheil, T. G. & Simon, R. I. (1999). Attorneys' pressures on the expert witness: Early warning signs of endangered honesty, objectivity, and fair compensation. *Journal of the American Academy of Psychiatry and the Law, 27,* 546–553.

Guze, S. B., Cloninger, C. R., Martin, R. L., & Clayton, P. J. (1986). A follow-up and family study of Briquet's syndrome. *British Journal of Psychiatry, 149,* 17–23.

Haaga, D. A. F. & Beck, A. T. (1995). Perspectives on depressive realism: Implications for cognitive theory of depression. *Behaviour Research and Therapy, 33,* 41–48.

Haaga, D. A. F., Dyck, M. J., & Ernst, D. (1991). Empirical status of cognitive theory of depression. *Psychological Bulletin, 110,* 215–236.

Haaga, D. A. F. & Stiles, W. B. (2000). Randomized clinical trials in psychotherapy research: Methodology, design, and evaluation. In C. R. Synder & R. E. Ingram (Eds.), *Handbook of psychological change* (pp. 14–39). New York: Wiley.

Haapasalo, J. & Kankkonen, M. (1997). Self-reported childhood abuse among sex and violent offenders. *Archives of Sexual Behavior, 26,* 421–431.

Haas, G. L. & Sweeney, J. A. (1992). Premorbid and onset features of first-episode schizophrenia. *Schizophrenia Bulletin, 18,* 373–386.

Haddock, G., Tarrier, N., Spaulding, W., Yusupoff, L., Kinney, C., & McCarthy, E. (1998). Individual cognitive-behavior therapy in the treatment of hallucinations and delusions: A review. *Clinical Psychology Review, 18(7),* 821–838.

Hadeed, A. & Seigel, S. (1989). Maternal cocaine use during pregnancy: Effect on the newborn infant. *Pediatrics, 84,* 205–210.

Haenen, M. A., de Jong, P. J., Schmidt, A. J. M., Stevens, S., & Visser, L. (2000). Hypochondriacs' estimation of negative outcomes: Domain-specificity and responsiveness to reassuring and alarming information. *Behaviour Research and Therapy, 38,* 819–833.

Hafner, H., Loffler, W., Maurer, K., Hambrecht, M., & van der Heiden, W. (1999). Depression, negative symptoms, social stagnation and social decline in the early course of schizophrenia. *Acta Psychiatrica Scandinavica, 100,* 105–118.

Hagerman, R. J. (1992). Annotation: Fragile X syndrome: Advances and controversy. *Journal of Child Psychology and Psychiatry, 33,* 1127–1139.

Hagerman, R. J. & Lampe, M. E. (1999). Fragile X syndrome. In S. Goldstein & C. R. Reynolds (Eds.), *Handbook of neurodevelopmental and genetic disorders in children* (pp. 298–316). New York: Guilford Press.

Hale, R. (1994). The role of humiliation and embarrassment in serial murder. *Psychology: A Journal of Human Behavior, 31,* 17–23.

Hall, C. C. I. (1997). Cultural malpractice: The growing obsolescence of psychology with the changing U. S. population. *American Psychologist, 52,* 642–651.

Hall, G. C. N. (1995). Sexual offender recidivism revisited: A meta-analysis of recent treatment studies. *Journal of Consulting and Clinical Psychology, 63,* 802–809.

Hall, G. C. N. & Barongan, C. (1997). Prevention of sexual aggression: Sociocultural risk and protective factors. *American Psychologist, 52,* 5–14.

Hall, S. M., Havassy, B. E., & Wasserman, D. A. (1990). Commitment to abstinence and acute stress in relapse to alcohol, opiates, and nicotine. *Journal of Consulting and Clinical Psychology, 58,* 175–181.

Hall, S. M., Havassy, B. E., & Wasserman, D. A. (1991). Effects of commitment to abstinence, positive moods, stress, and coping on relapse to cocaine use. *Journal of Consulting and Clinical Psychology, 59,* 526–532.

Halligan, P. W., Athwal, B. S., Oakley, D. A., & Frackowiak, R. S. J. (2000). The functional anatomy of a hypnotic paralysis: Implications for conversion hysteria. *Lancet, 355,* 986–987.

Halligan, P. W., Bass, C., & Wade, D. T. (2000). New approaches to conversion hysteria. *British Medical Journal, 320,* 1488–1489.

Halpern, J. H. & Farrison, G. P., Jr. (2001). Hallucinogens on the Internet: A vast new source of underground drug information. *American Journal of Psychiatry, 158,* 481–483.

Hamblin, M. W. (1997). Neuroreceptors and their place in psychiatry. In D. L. Dunner (Ed.), *Current psychiatric therapy II* (pp. 11–27). Philadelphia: Saunders.

Hamel, M., Shaffer, T. W., & Erdberg, P. (2000). A study of nonpatient preadolescent Rorschach protocols. *Journal of Personality Assessment, 75,* 280–294.

Hamrick, N., Cohen, S., & Rodriguez, M. S. (2002). Being popular can be healthy or unhealthy: Stress, social network diversity, and incidence of upper respiratory infection. *Health Psychology, 21,* 294–298.

Han, L., Wang, K., Du, Z., Cheng, Y., Simons, J. S., & Rosenthal, N. E. (2000). Seasonal variations in mood and behavior among Chinese medical students. *American Journal of Psychiatry, 157,* 133–135.

Handen, B. L. (1998). Mental retardation. In E. J. Mash & R. A. Barkley (Eds.), *Treatment of childhood disorders* (2nd ed., pp. 369–415). New York: Guilford Press.

Hankin, B. L. & Abramson, L. Y. (2001). Development of gender differences in depression: An elaborated cognitive vulnerability–transactional stress theory. *Psychological Bulletin, 127,* 773–796.

Hankin, B. L., Abramson, L. Y., Moffitt, T. E., et al. (1998). Development of depression from preadolescence to young adulthood: Emerging gender differences in a 10-year longitudinal study. *Journal of Abnormal Psychology, 107,* 128–140.

Hans, S. L., Marcus, J., Nuechterlein, K. H., Asarnow, R. F., Styr, B., & Auerbach, J. G. (1999). Neurobehavioral deficits at adolescence in children at risk for schizophrenia: The Jerusalem Infant Development Study. *Archives of General Psychiatry, 56,* 741–748.

Hansen, W. B. (1993). School-based alcohol prevention programs. *Alcohol, Health & Research World, 17*(1), 54–60.

Hanson, M. J. (1987). *Teaching the infant with Down syndrome* (pp. 23–30). Austin, TX: Pro-Ed.

Harada, S., Agarwal, D., Goedde, H., Takagi, S., & Ishikawa, B. (1982). Possible protective role against alcoholism for aldehyde dehydrogenase isozyme deficiency in Japan. *Lancet, 2,* 827.

Harburg, E. (1978). Skin color, ethnicity and blood pressure in Detroit blacks. *American Journal of Public Health, 68,* 1177–1183.

Harchik, A. E., Sherman, J. A., Sheldon, J. B., & Bannerman, D. J. (1993). Choice and control: New opportunities for people with developmental disabilities. *Annals of Clinical Psychiatry, 5,* 151–161.

Hardy, J. (1993, November). Genetic mistakes point the way for Alzheimer's disease. *Journal of NIH Research, 5,* 46–49.

Hare, E., Bulusu, L., & Adelstein, A. (1979). Schizophrenia and season of birth. *Population Trends, 17,* 9.

Hare, R. D. (1993). *Without conscience: The disturbing world of the psychopaths among us.* New York: Pocket Books.

Hare, R. D. (1996). Psychopathy: A clinical construct whose time has come. *Criminal Justice and Behavior, 23,* 25–44.

Hare, R. D. (1992). *The Hare Psychopathy Checklist-Revised.* Toronto: Multi-Health Systems.

Harlow, B. L., Cohen, L. S., Otto, M. W., Spiegelman, D., & Cramer, D. W. (1999). Prevalence and predictors of depressive symptoms in older premenopausal women: The Harvard Study of Moods and Cycles. *Archives of General Psychiatry, 56,* 418–424.

Harlow, J. (1868). Recovery from the passage of an iron bar through the head. *Publication of the Massachusetts Medical Society, 2,* 327–340.

Harmon-Jones, E., Abramson, L. Y., Sigelman, J., Bohlig, A., Hogan, M. E., & Harmon-Jones, C. (2002). Proneness to hypomania/mania symptoms or depression symptoms and asymmetrical frontal cortical responses to an anger-evoking event. *Journal of Personality and Social Psychology, 82,* 610–618.

Harmon-Jones, E. & Allen, J. J. B. (1997). Behavioral activation sensitivity and resting frontal EEG asymmetry: Covariation of putative indicators related to risk for mood disorders. *Journal of Abnormal Psychology, 106,* 159–163.

Harrington, R. (1993). Similarities and dissimilarities between child and adult disorders: The case of depression. In C. G. Costello (Ed.), *Basic issues in psychopathology* (pp. 103–124). New York: Guilford Press.

Harris, A. W. F., Bahramali, H., Slewa-Younan, S., Gordon, E., Williams, L., & Li, W. M. (2001). The topography of quantified electroencephalography in three syndromes of schizophrenia. *International Journal of Neuroscience, 107,* 265–278.

Harris, J. (1996). Physical restraint procedures for managing challenging behaviours presented by mentally retarded adults and children. *Research in Developmental Disabilities, 17,* 99–134.

Harris, J. C. (1995). *Developmental neuropsychiatry* (Vol. 2). New York: Oxford (see pages 97–99).

Harris, S. L., Alessandri, M., & Gill, M. J. (1991). Training parents of developmentally disabled children. In J. L. Matson & J. A. Mulick (Eds.), *Handbook of mental retardation* (2nd ed.) (pp. 373–381). New York: Pergamon Press.

Harris, S. L. & Handleman, J. S. (1997). Helping children with autism enter the mainstream. In D. J. Cohen & F. R. Volkmar (Eds.), *Handbook of autism and pervasive developmental disorders* (2nd ed.) (pp. 665–675). New York: Wiley.

Harris, T. O., Brown, G. W., & Bifulco, A. T. (1990). Depression and situational helplessness/mastery in a sample selected to study childhood parental loss. *Journal of Affective Disorders, 20,* 27–41.

Harris, W. S., Gowda, M., Kolb, J. W., Strychacz, C. P., Vacek, J. L., Jones, P. G., Forker, A., O'Keefe, J. H., & McCallister, B. D. (1999). A randomized, controlled trial of the effects of remote, intercessory prayer on outcomes in patients admitted to the coronary care unit. *Archives of Internal Medicine, 159,* 2273–2278.

Harrison, P. (1997). Suicidal behavior. In W. S. Tseng & J. Streltzer (Eds.), *Culture & psychopathology: A guide to clinical assessment* (pp. 157–172). New York: Brunner/Mazel.

Harry Benjamin International Gender Dysphoria Association. (1990). *Standards of care: The hormonal and surgical sex reassignment of gender dysphoric persons.* Palo Alto, CA: Author.

Hart, S. D. & Hare, R. D. (1989). Discriminant validity of the Psychopathy Checklist in a forensic psychiatric population. *Psychological Assessment: A Journal of Consulting and Clinical Psychology, 1,* 211–218.

Hart, S. D. & Hare, R. D. (1997). Psychopathy: Assessment and association with criminal conduct. In D. M. Stoff, J. Breiling, & J. D. Maser (Eds.), *Handbook of antisocial behavior*(pp. 22–35). New York: Wiley.

Harter, S. (1999). *The construction of the self: A developmental perspective.* New York: Guilford Press.

Hartlage, S., Alloy, L. B., Vázquez, C., & Dykman, B. (1993). Automatic and effortful processing in depression. *Psychological Bulletin, 113,* 247–278.

Hartmann, H. (1939). *Ego psychology and the problem of adaptation.* New York: International Universities Press.

Hartwell, S. (2001). An examination of racial differences among mentally ill offenders in Massachusetts. *Psychiatric Services, 52,* 234–236.

Harvey, A. G. & Bryant, R. A. (1998). The relationship between acute stress disorder and posttraumatic stress disorder: A prospective evaluation of motor vehicle accident survivors. *Journal of Consulting and Clinical Psychology, 66*(3), 507–512.

Harvey, A. G., Bryant, R. A., & Rapee, R. M. (1996). Preconscious processing of threat in posttraumatic stress disorder. *Cognitive Therapy and Research, 20,* 613–623.

Harvey, P. D., Lombardi, J., Leibman, M., Parrella, M., White, L., Powchik, P., Mohs, R. C., Davidson, M., & Davis, K. L. (1997). Age-related differences in formal thought disorder in chronically hospitalized schizophrenic patients: A cross-sectional study across nine decades. *American Journal of Psychiatry, 154,* 205–210.

Harwood, H. J., Fountain, D., & Livermore, G. (1998). Economic costs of alcohol abuse and alcoholism. In M. Galanter (Ed.), *Recent developments in alcoholism, Vol. 14: The consequences of alcoholism: Medical, neuropsychiatric, economic, cross cultural.* New York: Plenum Press.

Hathaway, S. R. & McKinley, J. C. (1943). *Minnesota Multiphasic Personality Inventory: Manual.* New York: Psychological Corporation.

Hathaway, S. R. & McKinley, J. C. (1989). *Manual for administration and scoring MMPI-2.* Minneapolis: University of Minnesota Press.

Hawk, G. & Fitch, W. L. (2001). Community forensic evaluation: Trends and reflections on the Virginia experience. In L. E. Frost & R. J. Bonnie (Eds.), *The evolution of mental health law* (pp. 213–226). Washington, DC: American Psychological Association.

Hawley, T. L. & Disney, E. R. (1992). Crack's children: The consequences of maternal cocaine abuse. *Social Policy Report of the Society for Research in Child Development, 6,* 1–22.

Hawton, K. (1992). Sex therapy research: Has it withered on the vine? *Annual Review of Sex Therapy, vol. 3,* 49–72.

Hay, D. P. & Hay, L. K. (1990). The role of ECT in the treatment of depression. In C.D. McCann & N. S. Endler (Eds.), *Depression: New directions in theory, research, and practice* (pp. 255–272). Toronto: Wall & Emerson.

Hayes, S. C. (1989). *Rule governed behavior: Cognition, contingencies and instructional control.* New York: Plenum Press.

Hayes, S. C., Jacobson, N. S., Follette, V., & Dougher, M. (1994). *Acceptance and change in psychotherapy.* Reno, NV: Context Press.

Hayes, S. C., Strosahl, K. D., & Wilson, K. O. (1999). *Acceptance and commitment therapy: An experiential approach to behavior change.* New York: Guilford Press.

Hayes, S. C., Wilson, K. G., Gifford, E. V., Follette, V. M., & Strosahl, K. (1996). Experiential avoidance and behavior disorders: A functional dimensional approach to diagnosis and treatment. *Journal of Consulting and Clinical Psychology, 64,* 1152–1168.

Hays, R. D., Wells, K. B., Sherbourne, C. D., Rogers, W., & Spritzer, K. (1995). Functioning and well-being outcomes of patients with depression compared with chronic general medical illnesses. *Archives of General Psychiatry, 52,* 11–19.

Hazlett, E. A., Dawson, M. E., Filion, D. L., Schell, A. M., & Nuechterlein, K. H. (1997). Autonomic orienting and the allocation of processing resources in schizophrenia patients and putatively at-risk individuals. *Journal of Abnormal Psychology, 106,* 171–181.

Heath, A. C. (1995). Genetic influences on drinking behavior in humans: In H. Begletter & B. Kissin (Eds.), *The genetics of alcoholism* (Vol. 1, pp. 82–131). New York: Oxford University Press.

Heath, A. C., Bucholz, K. K., Madden, P. A. F., Dinwiddie, S. H., Slutske, W. S., Bierut, L. J., Statham, D. J., Dunne, M. P., Whitfield, J. B., & Martin, N. G. (1997). Genetic and environmental contributions to alcohol dependence risk in a national twin sample: Consistency of findings in women and men. *Psychological Medicine, 27,* 1381–1396.

Heath, A. C., Slutske, W. S., & Madden, P. A. F. (1997). Gender differences in the genetic contribution to alcoholism and drinking patterns. In R. W. Wilsnack & S. C. Wilsnack (Eds.), *Gender and alcohol* (pp. 114–149). New Brunswick, NJ: Rutgers.

Heath, L., Bresdin, L. B., & Rinaldi, R. C. (1989). Effects of media violence on children: A review of the literature. *Archives of General Psychiatry, 46,* 376–379.

Heatherton, T. F., Herman, C. P., & Polivy, J. (1991). Effects of physical threat and ego threat on eating behavior. *Journal of Personality and Social Psychology, 60,* 138–143.

Heaton, J. A. & Wilson, N. L. (1998). Memory, media, and the creation of mass confusion. In S. J. Lynn & K. M. McConkey (Eds.), *Truth in memory* (pp. 349–371). New York: Guilford Press.

Heavey, C. L., Adelman, H. S., Nelson, P., & Smith, D. C. (1989). Learning problems, anger, perceived control and misbehavior. *Journal of Learning Disabilities, 22,* 46–50.

Hebert, M., Lavoie, F., Piche, C., & Poitras, M. (2001). Proximate effects of a child sexual abuse prevention program in elementary school children. *Child Abuse & Neglect, 25,* 505–522.

Hécaen, H. & Albert, M. C. (1978). *Human neuropsychology.* New York: Wiley.

Heckers, S. (1997). Neuropathology of schizophrenia: Cortex, thalamus, basal ganglia, and neurotransmitter-specific projection systems. *Schizophrenia Bulletin, 23,* 403–421.

Hedlund, S. & Rude, S. S. (1995). Evidence of latent depressive schemas in formerly depressed individuals. *Journal of Abnormal Psychology, 104,* 517–525.

Heffernan, K. & Cloitre, M. (2000). A comparison of posttraumatic stress disorder with and without borderline personality disorder among women with a history of childhood sexual abuse: Etiological and clinical characteristics. *Journal of Nervous and Mental Disease, 188,* 589–595.

Heiman, J. (2002). Psychologic treatments for female sexual dysfunction: Are they effective and do we need them? *Archives of Sexual Behavior, 31*(5), 445–450.

Heiman, J. R. (1997). *Empirically validated treatments of sexual dysfunction.* Paper presented at the Annual Meeting of the Society for Sex Therapy and Research, Chicago, IL.

Heiman, J. R., LoPiccolo, L., & LoPiccolo, J. (1981). The treatment of sexual dysfunction. In A. Gurma & D. Kniskern (Eds.), *Handbook of family therapy.* New York: Brunner/Mazel.

Heiman, J. R. & Meston, C. (1997). Empirically validated treatment for sexual dysfunctions. *Annual Review of Sex Research,* vol. 8.

Heimberg, R. G. & Becker, R. E. (2002). *Cognitive-behavioral treatment for social phobia: Basic mechanisms and clinical strategies.* New York: Guilford Press.

Heimberg, R. G., Liebowitz, M. R., Hope, D. A., Schneier, F. R., Holt, C. S., Welkowitz, L. A., Juster, H. R., Campeas, R., Bruch, M. A., Cloitre, M., Falon, B., & Klein, D. F. (1998). Cognitive behavioral group therapy vs. phenelzine therapy for social phobia: 12-week outcome. *Archives of General Psychiatry, 55,* 1133–1141.

Heindel, W. C. & Salmon, D. P. (2001). Cognitive approaches to the memory disorders of demented patients. In H. E. Adams & P. B. Sutker (Eds.), *Comprehensive handbook of psychopathology* (3rd edition, pp. 841–878). New York: Kluwer Academic/Plenum.

Heinz, A., Mann, K., Weinberger, D. E., & Goldman, D. (2001). Serotonergic dysfunction, negative mood states, and response to alcohol. *Alcoholism: Clinical & Experimental Research, 24*(4), 487–495.

Hellerstein, D. J., Kocsis, J. H., Chapman, D., Stewart, J. W., & Harrison, W. (2000). Double-blind comparison of sertraline, imipramine, and placebo in the treatment of dysthymia: Effects on personality. *American Journal of Psychiatry, 157,* 1436–1444.

Helmes, E. & Reddon, J. R. (1993). A perspective on developments in assessing psychopathology. A critical review of the MMPI and MMPI-2. *Psychological Bulletin, 113,* 453–471.

Helmstaedter, C. (2001). Behavioral aspects of frontal lobe epilepsy. *Epilepsy & Behavior, 2*(5), 384–395.

Helzer, J. E., Robins, L., & McEvoy, L. (1987). Posttraumatic stress disorder in the general population. *New England Journal of Medicine, 317,* 1630–1634.

Henggeler, S. W., Pickrel, S. G., Brondino, M. J., & Crouch, J. L. (1996). Eliminating treatment dropout of substance abusing or dependent delinquents through home-based multisystemic therapy. *American Journal of Psychiatry, 153,* 427–428.

Heninger, G. R. (1990). A biologic perspective on co-morbidity of major depressive disorder and panic disorder. In J. D. Maser & C. R. Cloninger (Eds.), *Comorbidity of mood and anxiety disorders.* Washington, DC: American Psychiatric Press.

Herbener, E. S. & Harrow, M. (2002). The course of anhedonia during 10 years of schizophrenic illness. *Journal of Abnormal Psychology, 111,* 237–248.

Herdt, G. & Stoller, R. J. (1990). *Intimate communications: Erotics and the study of culture.* New York: Columbia University Press.

Herman, C. P. & Mack, D. (1975). Restrained and unrestrained eating. *Journal of Personality, 43,* 647–660.

Herman, J. L. (1981). *Father-daughter incest.* Cambridge, MA: Harvard University Press.

Herman, J. L. (1992). *Trauma and recovery.* New York: Basic Books.

Hernandez-Peon, R., Chavez-Ibarra, G., & Aguilar-Figueroa, E. (1963). Somatic evoked potentials in one case of hysterical anaesthesia. *Electroencephalography and Clinical Neurophysiology, 15,* 889–892.

Hernandez-Serrano, R. (2001). Advances in the treatment of sexual disorders. *International Medical Journal, 8,* 83–89.

Herperts, S. C., Werth, U., Lukas, G., Qunaibi, M., Schuerkens, A., et al. (2001). Emotion in criminal offenders with psychopathy and borderline personality disorder. *Archives of General Psychiatry, 58,* 737–745.

Herrera, J. M., Lawson, W. B., Sramek, J. J., et al. (Eds.). (1999). *Cross cultural psychiatry.* Chichester, England: Wiley.

Hersen, M. & Turner, S. M. (1984). *DSM-III* and behavior therapy. In S. M. Turner & M. Hersen (Eds.), *Adult psychopathology and diagnosis.* New York: Wiley.

Herz, M. I., Lamberti, S., Mintz, J., Scott, R., O'Dell, S. P., McCartan, L., & Nix, G. (2000). A program for relapse prevention in schizophrenia: A controlled study. *Archives of General Psychiatry, 57,* 277–283.

Herzberg, D. S., Hammen, C., Burge, D., Daley, S. E., Davila, J., & Lindberg, N. (1999). Attachment cognitions predict perceived and enacted social support during late adolescence. *Journal of Adolescent Research, 14,* 387–404.

Heston, L. L. (1966). Psychiatric disorders in foster home reared children of schizophrenic mothers. *British Journal of Psychiatry, 112,* 819–825.

Hettema, J., Prescott, C. A., & Kendler, K. (2001) A population-based twin study of generalized anxiety disorder in men and women. *Journal of Nervous and Mental Disease, 189*(7), 413–420.

Hewitt, P. L., Flett, G. L., & Ediger, E. (1996). Perfectionism and depression: Longitudinal assessment of a specific vulnerability hypothesis. *Journal of Abnormal Psychology, 105,* 276–281.

Higgins, S. T. & Abbott, P. J. (2001). CRA and treatment of cocaine and opioid dependence. In R. J. Meyers & W. R. Miller (Eds.), *A community reinforcement approach to addiction treatment. International research monographs in the addictions* (pp. 123–146). New York: Cambridge University Press.

Higgins, S. T., Budney, A. J., Bickel, W. K., Foerg, F. E., Donham, R., & Badger, G. J. (1994). Incentives improve outcome in outpatient behavioral treatment of cocaine dependence. *Archives of General Psychiatry, 51,* 568–576.

Higgins, S. T., Delaney, D. D., Budney, A. J., Bickel, W. K., Hughes, J. R., Foerg, B. A., & Fenwick, J. W. (1991). A behavioral approach to achieving initial cocaine abstinence. *American Journal of Psychiatry, 148,* 1218–1224.

Hildebran, D. & Pithers, W. D. (1989). Enhancing offender empathy for sexual abuse victims. In D. R. Laws (Ed.), *Relapse prevention with sex offenders* (pp. 236–243). New York: Guilford Press.

Hilmert, C. J., Christenfeld, N., & Kulik, J. A. (2002). Audience status moderates the effects of social support and self-efficacy on cardiovascular reactivity during public speaking. *Annals of Behavioral Medicine, 24,* 122–131.

Hingson, R., Heeren, T., Levenson, S., Jamanka, A., & Voas, R. (2002). Age of drinking onset, driving after drinking, and involvement in alcohol related motor-vehicle crashes. *Accident Analysis and Prevention, 34,* 85–92.

Hlastala, S. A., Frank, E., Kowalski, J., Sherrill, J. T., Tu, X. M., Anderson, B., & Kupfer, D. J. (2000). Stressful life events, bipolar disorder, and the "kindling model." *Journal of Abnormal Psychology, 109,* 777–786.

Ho, A. P., Gillin, J. C., Buchsbaum, M. S., Wu, J. C., Abel, L., & Bunney, W. E., Jr. (1996). Brain glucose metabolism during non-rapid eye movement sleep in major depression: A positron emission tomography study. *Archives of General Psychiatry, 53,* 645–652.

Ho, B. T., Richard, D. W., & Chute, D. L. (Eds.). (1978). *Drug discrimination and state dependent learning.* New York: Academic Press.

Hobson, R. P. (1993). *Autism and the development of mind.* Hillsdale, NJ: Erlbaum (see chapter on "The growth of interpersonal learning").

Hodapp, R. M. & Dykens, E. M. (1996). Mental retardation. In E. J. Mash & R. A. Barkley (Eds.), *Child psychopathology* (pp. 362–389). New York: Guilford Press.

Hodgins, S., Mednick, S. A., Brennan, P. A., Schulsinger, F., & Engberg, M. (1996). Mental disorder and crime: Evidence from a birth cohort. *Archives of General Psychiatry, 53,* 489–496.

Hodgkinson, S., Sherrington, R., Gurling, H., Marchbanks, R., Reeders, S., Mallet, J., McInnis, M., Petursson, H., & Brynjolfsson, J. (1987). Molecular genetic evidence for heterogeneity in manic depression. *Nature, 325,* 805–806.

Hodkinson, H. M. (1976). *Common symptoms of disease in the elderly.* Oxford: Blackwell.

Hodson, J., Thompson, J., & al-Azzawi, F. (2000). Headache at menopause and in hormone replacement therapy users. *Climacteric, 3,* 119–124.

Hoek, H. W., Brown, A. S., & Susser, E. (1998). The Dutch famine and schizophrenia spectrum disorders. *Social Psychiatry and Psychiatric Epidemiology, 33,* 373–379.

Hoenig, J. (1985). Etiology of transsexualism. In B. W. Steiner (Ed.), *Gender dysphoria: Development, research, management.* New York: Plenum Press.

Hoffman, A. (1971). LSD discoverer disputes "chance" factor in finding. *Psychiatric News, 6*(8), 23–26.

Hoffman, J. H., Welte, J. W., & Barnes, G. M. (2001). Co-occurrence of alcohol and cigarette use among adolescents. *Addictive Behaviors, 26,* 63–78.

Hoffman, K. B., Cole, D. A., Martin, J. M., Tram, J., & Seroczynski, A. D. (2000). Are the discrepancies between self- and others' appraisals of competence predictive or reflective of depressive symptoms in children and adolescents: A longitudinal study, Part II. *Journal of Abnormal Psychology, 109,* 651–662.

Hogarty, G. E., Anderson, C. M., Reiss, D. J., Kornblith, S. J., Greenwald, D. P., Javna, C. D., & Madonia, M. J. (1986). Family psychoeducation, social skills training, and maintenance chemotherapy in the aftercare treatment of schizophrenia: I. One-year effects of a controlled study on relapse and expressed emotion. *Archives of General Psychiatry, 43,* 633–642.

Hogarty, G. E., Greenwald, D., Ulrich, R. F., Kornblith, S. J., DiBarry, A. L., Cooley, S., Carter, M., & Flesher, S. (1997). Three-year trials of personal therapy among schizophrenic patients living with or independent of family, II: Effects on adjustment of patients. *American Journal of Psychiatry, 154,* 1514–1524.

Hogarty, G. E., Kornblith, S. J., Greenwald, D., DiBarry, A. L., Cooley, S., Ulrich, R. F., Carter, M., & Flesher, S. (1997). Three-year trials of personal therapy among schizophrenic patients living with or independent of family, I: Description of study and effects on relapse rates. *American Journal of Psychiatry, 154,* 1504–1513.

Hoge, M. A. & Grottole, E. (2000). The case against outpatient commitment. *Journal of the American Academy of Psychiatry and the Law, 28,* 165–170.

Hoge, S. K., Lidz, C. W., Eisenberg, M., Monahan, J., Bennett N., Gardner, W., Mulvey, E. P., & Roth, L. (1998). Family, clinician, and patient perceptions of coercion in mental hospital admission: A comparative study. *International Journal of Law and Psychiatry, 21,* 131–146.

Holder-Perkins, V. & Wise, T. N. (2001). Somatization disorder. In K. A. Phillips (Ed.), *Somatoform and factitious disorders* (pp. 1–26). Washington, DC: American Psychiatric Press.

Holland, J. G. (1978). Behaviorism: Part of the problem or part of the solution? *Journal of Applied Behavior Analysis, 11,* 163–174.

Holland, J. G. & Tross, S. (1985). The psychosocial and neuropsychiatric sequelae of the acquired immunodeficiency syndrome and related disorders. *Annals of Internal Medicine, 103,* 760–764.

Hollander, E., Allen, A., Kwon, J., Aronowitz, B., Schmeidler, J., Wong, C., & Simeon, D. (1999). Clomipramine vs. desipramine crossover trial in body dysmorphic disorder. *Archives of General Psychiatry, 56,* 1033–1039.

Hollander, E., Stein, D. J., Kwon, J. H., Rowland, C., Wong, C. M., Broatch, J., et al. (1997). Psychosocial function and economic costs of obsessive-compulsive disorder. *CNS Spectr, 2,* 16–25.

Hollingshead, A. B. & Redlich, F. C. (1958). *Social class and mental illness.* New York: Wiley.

Hollins, S. (1990). Group analytic therapy with people with mental handicap. In A. Dosen, A. van Gennep, & G. J. Zwanikken (Eds.), *Treatment of mental illness and behavioral* *disorder in the mentally retarded* (pp. 81–89). Leiden, Netherlands: Logon.

Hollister, J. M., Mednick, S. A., Brennan, P., & Cannon, T. D. (1994). Impaired autonomic nervous system habituation in those at genetic risk for schizophrenia. *Archives of General Psychiatry, 51,* 552–558.

Hollister, L. E. (1998). Health aspects of cannabis: Revisited. *International Journal of Neuropsychopharmacology, 1,* 71–80.

Hollon, S. D. & Beck, A. T. (1994). Cognitive and cognitive-behavioral therapies. In A. E. Bergin & S. L. Garfield (Eds.), *Handbook of psychotherapy and behavior change* (4th ed., pp. 428–466). New York: Wiley.

Hollon, S. D., DeRubeis, R. J., & Evans, M. D. (1996). Cognitive therapy in the treatment and prevention of depression. In P. M. Salkovskis (Ed.), *Frontiers of cognitive therapy,* (pp. 293–317). New York: Guilford Press.

Hollon, S. D., DeRubeis, R. J., Evans, M. D., Wiemer, M. J., Garvey, M. J., Grove, W. M., & Tuason, V. B. (1992). Cognitive therapy and pharmacotherapy for depression: Singly and in combination. *Archives of General Psychiatry, 49,* 774–781.

Hollon, S. D., DeRubeis, R. J., Shelton, R. C., & Weiss, B. (2002). The emperor's new drugs. Effect size and moderation effects. *Prevention & Treatment, 5,* Article 28. Retrieved August 15, 2003, from http://www.journals.apa.org/prevention/volume5/pre0050028a.html.

Hollon, S. D., Shelton, R. C., & Davis, D. D. (1993). Cognitive therapy for depression: Conceptual issues and clinical efficacy. *Journal of Consulting and Clinical Psychology, 61,* 270–275.

Hollon, S. D., Shelton, R. C., & Loosen, P. T. (1991). Cognitive therapy and psychopharmacotherapy for depression. *Journal of Consulting and Clinical Psychology, 59,* 88–99.

Holmes, D. S. (1978). Projection as a defense mechanism. *Psychological Bulletin, 85,* 677–688.

Holmes, R. M. & DeBurger, J. E. (1985). Profiles in terror: The serial murderer. *Federal Probation, 49,* 29–34.

Holmes, T. H. & Rahe, R. H. (1967). The social readjustment rating scale. *Journal of Psychosomatic Research, 11,* 213–218.

Holsboer, F. (1992). The hypothalamic-pituitary-adrenocortical system. In E. S. Paykel (Ed.), *Handbook of affective disorders* (2nd ed., pp. 267–288). New York: Guilford Press.

Holsboer, F. (1995). Neuroendocrinology of mood disorders. In F. E. Bloom & D. J. Kupfer (Eds.), *Psychopharmacology: The fourth generation of progress* (pp. 957–970). New York: Raven Press.

Holsboer, F. (2001). Stress, hypercortisolism and corticosteroid receptors in depression: Implications for therapy. *Journal of Affective Disorders, 62,* 77–91.

Holtz, G. A., Cohn, S. M., Popkin, C., Ekeh, P., Duncan, R., Johnson, E. W., Pernas, F., & Selem, J. (2002). The impact of a repealed motorcycle helmet law in Miami-Dade County. *Journal of Trauma, 52,* 469–474.

Holzer, C. E., III., Tischler, G. L., Leaf, P. J., & Myers, J. K. (1984). An epidemiologic assessment of cognitive impairment in a community population. *Research in Community and Mental Health, 4,* 3–32.

Honig, P. & Sharman, W. (2000). Inpatient management. In B. Lask & R. Bryant-Waugh (Eds.), *Anorexia nervosa and related eating disorders in childhood and adolescence* (2nd ed., pp. 265–288). East Sussex, England: Psychology Press.

Hooker, E. (1957). The adjustment of the male overt homosexual. *Journal of Projective Techniques, 21*(1), 18–31.

Hooley, J. M. & Hiller, J. B. (1998). Expressed emotion and the pathogenesis of relapse in schizophrenia. In M. F. Lenzenweger & R. H. Dworkin (Eds.), *Origins and development of schizophrenia* (pp. 447–468). Washington, DC: American Psychological Association.

Horley, J. (2001). Frotteurism: A term in search of an underlying disorder? *Journal of Sexual Aggression, 7*(1), 51–55.

Horne, J. (1992). Sleep and its disorders in children. *Journal of Child Psychology and Psychiatry, 33,* 473–487.

Horney, K. (1937). *The neurotic personality of our time.* New York: W. W. Norton.

Horton, A. M. (1997). The Halstead-Reitan Neuropsychological Test Battery: Problems and prospects. In A. Horton & D. Wedding (Eds.), *The neuropsychology handbook: Vol. 1. Foundations and assessment* (pp. 221–254). New York: Springer.

Hough, M. S. (1990). Narrative comprehension in adults with right and left hemisphere brain damage: Theme organization. *Brain and Language, 38,* 253–277.

House, J. S., Landis, K. R., & Umberson, D. (1988). Social relationships and health. *Science, 241,* 540–545.

Houts, A. C., Berman, J. S., & Abramson, H. (1994). Effectiveness of psychological and pharmacological treatments for nocturnal enuresis. *Journal of Consulting and Clinical Psychology, 62,* 737–745.

Howells, K. (1981). Some meanings of children for pedophiles. In M. Cook & G. Wilson (Eds.), *Love and attraction* (pp. 57–82). London: Pergamon Press.

Huang, C., Liao, H., & Chang, S. H. (1998). Social desirability and the clinical self-report inventory: Methodological reconsideration. *Journal of Clinical Psychology, 54,* 517–528.

Hudson, S. M., Marshall, W. L., Ward, T., Johnston, D. W., et al. (1995). Kia Marama: A cognitive-behavioral program for incarcerated molesters. *Behaviour Change, 12,* 64–80.

Huesmann, L. R., Moise, J. F., & Podolski, C. (1997). The effects of media violence on the development of antisocial behavior. In D. M. Stoff, J. Breiling, & J. D. Maser (Eds.), *Handbook of antisocial behavior* (pp. 181–193). New York: Wiley.

Hughes, J. C. & Cook, C. C. H. (1997). The efficacy of disulfram: A review of outcome studies. *Addiction, 92,* 381–395.

Hull, J. G. & Bond, C. F., Jr. (1986). Social and behavioral consequences of alcohol consumption and expectancy: A meta-analysis. *Psychological Bulletin, 99,* 347–360.

Hulme, C. & Roodenrys, S. (1995). Practitioner review: Verbal working memory development and its disorders. *Journal of Child Psychology and Psychiatry, 36,* 373–398.

Hulshoff Pol, H. E., Schnack, H. G., Mandl, R. C. W., van Haren, N. E. M., Koning, H., Collins, D. L., Evans, A. C., & Kahn, R. S. (2001). Focal gray matter density changes in schizophrenia. *Archives of General Psychiatry, 58,* 1118–1125.

Hunt, M. (1979). *Sexual behavior in the 1970's.* Chicago: Playboy Press.

Hurley, R. A., Black, D. N., Stip, E., & Taber, K. H. (2000). Surgical treatment of mental illness: Impact of imaging. *Journal of Neuropsychiatry and Clinical Neurosciences, 12,* 421–424.

Hurt, H., Brodsky, N., Betancourt, L., Braitman, L. E., Malmud, E., & Gianetta, J. (1995). Cocaine-exposed children: Follow-up at 30 months. *Journal of Developmental and Behavioral Pediatrics, 16,* 29–35.

Huxley, N. A., Rendall, M., & Sederer, L. (2000). Psychosocial treatments in schizophrenia: A review of the past 20 years. *Journal of Nervous and Mental Disease, 188,* 187–201.

Iacono, W. G. & Beiser, M. (1992a). Are males more likely than females to develop schizophrenia? *American Journal of Psychiatry, 149,* 1070–1074.

Iacono, W. G. & Beiser, M. (1992b). Where are the women in the first-episode studies of schizophrenia? *Schizophrenia Bulletin, 18,* 471–480.

Iacono, W. G. & Grove, W. M. (1993). Schizophrenia revisited: Toward an integrative genetic model. *Psychological Science, 4,* 273–276.

Ickovics, J. R., Viscoli, C. M., & Horwitz, R. I., (1997). Functional recovery after myocardial infarction in men: The independent effects of social class. *Annuals of Internal Medicine, 127,* 518–525.

Iezzi, A. & Adams, H. E. (1993). Somatoform and factitious disorders. In P. B. Sutker & H. E. Adams (Eds.), *Comprehensive handbook of psychopathology* (2nd ed.). New York: Plenum Press.

Iezzi, T., Duckworth, M. P., & Adams, H. E. (2001). Somatoform and factitious disorders. In H. E. Adams & P. B. Sutker (Eds.), *Comprehensive handbook of psychopathology* (3rd ed., pp. 211–258). New York: Kluwer Academic/Plenum.

Ilardi, S. S., Craighead, W. E., & Evans, D. D. (1997). Modeling relapse in unipolar depression: The effects of dysfunctional cognitions and personality disorders. *Journal of Consulting and Clinical Psychology, 65,* 381–391.

Illegal drugs. (2002). *Public Agenda Online.* Retrieved July 12, 2002, from www.publicagenda.org.

Ingram, R. E., Miranda, J., & Segal, Z. V. (1998). *Cognitive vulnerability to depression.* New York: Guilford Press.

Ingram, R. E. & Ritter, J. (2000). Vulnerability to depression: Cognitive reactivity and parental bonding in high-risk individuals. *Journal of Abnormal Psychology, 109,* 588–596.

Iribarren, I. G. (1999). Pharmacological treatment of erectile dysfunction. *Current Opinion in Urology, 9,* 547–551.

Ironson, G., Solomon, G. F., Balbin, E. G., O'Cleirigh, C., George, A., Kumar, M., Larson, D., & Woods, T. E. (2002). The Ironson-Woods Spirituality/Religiousness Index is associated with long survival, health behaviors, less distress, and low cortisol in people with HIV/AIDS. *Annals of Behavioral Medicine, 24,* 34–48.

Ironson, G., Taylor, C. B., Boltwood, M., Bartzokis, T., Dennis, C., Chesney, M., Spitzer, S., & Segall, G. (1992). Effects of anger on left ventricular ejection fraction in coronary artery disease. *American Journal of Cardiology, 70,* 281–285.

Isacsson, G. & Rich, C. L. (1997). Depression, antidepressants, and suicide: Pharmaco-epidemiological evidence. In R. W. Maris, M. M. Silverman, & S. S. Canetto (Eds.), *Review of suicidology* (pp. 168–201). New York: Guilford Press.

Ishikawa, S., Raine, A., Lencz, T., Bihrle, S., & Lacasse, L. (2001). Autonomic stress reactivity and executive functions in successful and unsuccessful criminal psychopaths from the community. *Journal of Abnormal Psychology, 110,* 423–432.

Isometsä, E. T., Henriksson, M. E., Aro, H. M., Heikkinen, M. E., Kuoppasalmi, K. I., & Lonnqvist, J. K. (1994). Suicide in major depression. *American Journal of Psychiatry, 151,* 530–536.

Israel, A. C., Guile, C. A., Baker, J. E., & Silverman, W. K. (1994). An evaluation of enhanced self-regulation training in the treatment of childhood obesity. *Journal of Pediatric Psychology, 19,* 737–749.

Jablensky, A. (2000). Epidemiology of schizophrenia: The global burden of disease and disability. *European Archives of Psychiatry and Clinical Neuroscience, 250,* 274–285.

Jackson K., Sher, K. I., Gotham, H. J., & Wood, P. K. (2001). Transitioning into and out of large-effect drinking in young adulthood. *Journal of Abnormal Psychology, 110,* 378–391.

Jackson v. Indiana, 92 S. Ct. 1845 (1972).

Jackson, R. W., Treiber, F. A., Turner, J. R., Davis, H., & Strong, W. B. (1999). Effects of race, sex, and socioeconomic status upon cardiovascular stress responsivity and recovery in youth. *International Journal of Psychophysiology, 31,* 111–119.

Jacobsen, J. W., Mulick, J. A., & Schwartz, A. A. (1995). A history of facilitated communication: Science, pseudoscience, and antiscience. *American Psychologist, 50,* 750–765.

Jacobson, E. (1938). *Progressive relaxation.* Chicago: University of Chicago Press.

Jacobson, N. S. (1995). The overselling of therapy. *Family Therapy Networker, 19,* 41–47.

Jacobson, N. S. & Christensen, A. (1996). Studying the effectiveness of psychotherapy. How well can clinical trials do the job? *American Psychologist, 51,* 1031–1039.

Jacobson, N. S., Christensen, A., Prince, S. E., Cordova, J., & Eldridge, K. (2000). Integrative behavioral couple therapy: An acceptance-based, promising new treatment for couple discord. *Journal of Consulting & Clinical Psychology. 68,* 351–355.

Jacobson, N. S., Dobson, K. S., Truax, P. A., Addis, M. E., Koerner, K., Gollan, J. K., Gortner, E., & Prince, S. E. (1996). A component analysis of cognitive- behavioral treatment for depression. *Journal of Consulting and Clinical Psychology, 64,* 295–304.

Jacobson, N. S., Dobson, K. S., Truax, P. A., Addis, M. E., Koerner, K., Gollan, J. K., Gortner, E., & Prince, S. E. (1996). A component analysis of cognitive-behavioral treatment for depression. *Journal of Consulting and Clinical Psychology, 64,* 295–304.

Jacobson, N. S., Gottman, J. M., & Shortt, J. W. (1995). The distinction between type I and type II batterers—Further considerations: Reply to Ornduff et al. (1995), Margolin et al. (1995), and Walker (1995). *Journal of Family Psychology, 9,* 272–279.

Jacobson, N. S. & Hollon, S. D. (1996). Cognitive-behavior therapy versus pharmacotherapy: Now that the jury's returned its verdict, it's time to present the rest of the evidence. *Journal of Consulting and Clinical Psychology, 64,* 74–80.

Jacobson, N. S., Martell, C. R., & Dimidjian, S. (2001). Behavioral activation treatment for depression: Returning to contextual roots. *Clinical Psychology: Science and Practice, 8,* 255–270.

Jacobson, N. S., Roberts, L. J., Berns, S. B., & McGlinchey, J. B. (1999). *Journal of Consulting and Clinical Psychology, 67,* 300–307.

Jaffe, C., Clance, P. R., Nichols, M. F., & Emshoff, J. G. (2001). The prevalence of alcoholism and feelings of alienation in lesbian and heterosexual women. *Journal of Gay and Lesbian Psychotherapy, 3,* 25–35.

Jaffee v. Redmond, 116 S. Ct. 1923 (1996).

Jain, P., Rademaker, A. W., & McVary, K. T. (2000). Testosterone supplementation for erectile dysfunction: Results of a meta-analysis. *Journal of Urology,* 164, 371–375.

Jallon, P. (2002). Epilepsy and epileptic disorders: An epidemiological marker? Contribution of descriptive epidemiology. *Epileptic Disorders, 4*(1), 1–13.

James, L., Singer, A., Zurynski, Y., Gordon, E., Kraiuhin, C., Harris, A., Howson, A., & Meares, R. (1987). Evoked response potentials and regional cerebral blood flow in somatization disorder. *Psychotherapy and Psychosomatics, 47,* 190–196.

James, W. E., Mefford, R. B., & Kimbell, I. (1969). Early signs of Huntington's chorea. *Diseases of the Nervous System, 30,* 556–559.

Jamison, K. R. (1992). *Touched with fire: Manic-depressive illness and the artistic temperament.* New York: Free Press.

Janca, A., Isaac, M., Bennett, L. A., & Tacchini, G. (1995). Somatoform disorders in different cultures—a mail questionnaire survey. *Social Psychiatry and Psychiatric Epidemiology, 30,* 44–48.

Jancar, J. & Gunaratne, I. J. (1994). Dysthymia and mental handicap. *British Journal of Psychiatry, 164,* 691–693.

Janet, P. (1929). *The major symptoms of hysteria.* New York: Macmillan.

Jang, K. L., Lam, R. W., Livesley, W., & Vernon, P. A. (1997). Gender differences in the heritability of seasonal mood change. *Psychiatry Research, 70,* 145–154.

Janoff-Bulman, R. & Frantz, C. (1997). The impact of trauma on meaning. From meaningless world to meaningful life. In M. Power & C. Brewer (Eds.), *The transformation of meaning in psychological therapies* (pp. 91–106). London: Wiley.

Janssen, E. (1995). Understanding the rapist's mind. *Perspectives in Psychiatric Care, 31,* 9–13.

Janus, E. S. (2000). Sex predator commitment laws: Constitutional but unwise. *Psychiatric Annals, 30,* 411–420.

Jarrett, R. B., Kraft, D., Doyle, J., Foster, B. M., Eaves, G. G., & Silver, P. C. (2001). Preventing recurrent depression using cognitive therapy with and without a continuation phase: A randomized clinical trial. *Archives of General Psychiatry, 58,* 381–388.

Jaspers, J. P. C. (1996). The diagnosis and psychopharmacological treatment of trichotillomania: A review. *Pharmacopsychiatry, 29,* 115–120.

Javitt, D. C., Doneshka, P., Grochowski, S., & Ritter, W. (1995). Impaired mismatch negativity generation reflects widespread dysfunction of working memory in schizophrenia. *Archives of General Psychiatry, 52,* 550–558.

Javitt, D. C. & Silipo, G. S. (1997). Use of electroencephalograms and evoked potentials in psychiatry. In D. L. Dunner (Ed.), *Current psychiatric therapy II* (pp. 28–36). Philadelphia: W. B. Saunders.

Jefferson, J. W. (1996). Social phobia: Everyone's disorder? *Journal of Clinical Psychiatry, 57,* 28–32.

Jellineck, E. M. (1946). *Phases in the drinking history of alcoholics.* New Haven, CT: Hillhouse Press.

Jellinger, K. A., Paulus, W., Wrocklage, C., & Litvan, I. (2001). Effects of closed traumatic brain injury and genetic factors on the development of Alzheimer's disease. *European Journal of Neurology, 8,* 707–710.

Jenike, M. A. (1998). Neurosurgical treatment of obsessive-compulsive disorder. *British Journal of Psychiatry, 173,* 79–90.

Jenkins, S., Owen, C., Bax, M., & Hart, H. (1984). Continuities of common behavior problems in pre-school children. *Journal of Child Psychology and Psychiatry, 25,* 75–89.

Jernigan, T. L. (1990). Techniques for imaging brain structure: Neuropsychological applications. In A. A. Boulton, G. R. Baker, & H. Hiscock (Eds). *Neuromethods* (Vol. 17). Neuropsychology. Clifton, NJ: Humana Press.

Jeste, D. V., Gladsjo, J. A., Lindamer, L. A., & Lacro, J. P. (1996). Medical comorbidity in schizophrenia. *Schizophrenia Bulletin, 22,* 413–430.

Jeste, D. V., Heaton, S. C., Paulsen, J. S., Ercoli, L., Harris, M. J., & Heaton, R. K. (1996). Clinical and neuropsychological comparison of psychotic depression with nonpsychotic depression and schizophrenia. *American Journal of Psychiatry, 153,* 490–496.

Jiang, W., Babyak, M., Kranz, D. S., Waugh, R. A., Coleman, R. E., Hanson, M. M., Frid, D. J., McNulty, S., Morris, J. J., O'Connor, C. M., & Blumenthal, J. A. (1996). Mental stress-induced myocardial ischemia and cardiac events. *Journal of the American Medical Association, 275,* 1651–1656.

Joe, S. & Kaplan, M. S. (2001). Suicide among African American men. *Suicide and Life Threatening Behavior, 31*(Suppl.), 106–120.

Joergensen, J. (1992). The epidemiology of eating disorder in Fyn County, Denmark, 1977–1986. *Acta Psychiatrica Scandinavica, 85,* 30–34.

Joffe, R. T. & Marriott, M. (2000). Thyroid hormone levels and recurrence of major depression. *American Journal of Psychiatry, 157,* 1689–1691.

Joffe, R. T. & Sokolov, S. T. H. (2000). Thyroid hormone treatment of primary unipolar depression: A review. *International Journal of Neuropsychopharmacology, 3,* 143–147.

Johansson, B. & Zarit, S. H. (1995). Prevalence and incidence of dementia in the oldest old: A longitudinal study of a population-based sample of 84–90-year-olds in Sweden. *International Journal of Geriatric Psychology, 10.*

Johns, L. C., Rossell, S., Frith, C., Ahmad, F., Hemsley, D., Kuipers, E., & McGuire, P. K. (2001). Verbal self-monitoring and auditory verbal hallucinations in patients with schizophrenia. *Psychological Medicine, 31,* 705–715.

Johnson, D., Walker, T., & Rodriguez, G. (1993, March). *Teaching low-income mothers to teach their children.* Paper presented at the biennial meeting of the Society for Research in Child Development, New Orleans.

Johnson, J. G., Cohen, P., & Brook, J. S. (2000). Associations between bipolar disorder and other psychiatric disorders during adolescence and early adulthood: A community-based longitudinal study. *American Journal of Psychiatry, 157,* 1679–1681.

Johnson, J. G., Cohen, P., Brown, J., Smailes, E., & Bernstein, D. P. (1999). Childhood maltreatment increases risk for personality disorders during early childhood. *Archives of General Psychiatry, 56,* 600–606.

Johnson, J. G., Cohen, P., Dohrenwend, B. P., Link, B. G., Brook, J. S. (1999). A longitudinal investigation of social causation and social selection processes involved in the association between socioeconomic status and psychiatric disorders. *Journal of Abnormal Psychology, 109*(3), 490–499.

Johnson, J. G., Cohen, P., Skodol, A. E., Oldham, J. M., Kasen, S., & Brook, J. S. (1999). Personality disorders in adolescence and risk of major mental disorders and suicidality during adulthood. *Archives of General Psychiatry, 56,* 805–811.

Johnson, J. G., Cohen, P., Smailes, E. M., Skodol, A. E., Brown, J., & Oldham, J. M. (2001). Childhood verbal abuse and risk for personality disorders during adolescence and early adulthood. *Comprehensive Psychiatry, 42,* 16–23.

Johnson, L. D., O'Malley, P. M., & Bachman, J. G. (2000). Monitoring the future: National results on adolescent drug use. *National Institute on Drug Abuse.*

Johnson, M. R. & Lydiard, R. B. (1995). The neurobiology of anxiety disorders. *Psychiatric Clinics of North America, 18,* 681–725.

Johnson, S. L. & Kizer, A. (2002) Bipolar and unipolar depression: A comparison of clinical phenomenology and psychosocial predictors. In I. H. Gotlib & C. L. Hammen (Eds.), *Handbook of depression* (pp. 141–165). New York: Guilford Press.

Johnson, S. L. & Miller, I. (1997). Negative life events and time to recovery from episodes of bipolar disorder. *Journal of Abnormal Psychology, 106,* 449–457.

Johnson, S. L. & Roberts, J. E. (1995). Life events and bipolar disorder: Implications from biological theories. *Psychological Bulletin, 117,* 434–449.

Johnson, S. L., Sandrow, D., Meyer, B., Winters, R., Miller, I., Solomon, D., & Keitner, G. (2000). Increases in manic symptoms after life events involving goal attainment. *Journal of Abnormal Psychology, 109,* 721–727.

Johnston, L. D., O'Malley, P. M., & Bachman, J. G. (1987). *National trends in drug use and related factors among American high school students and young adults, 1975–1986.* Rockville, MD: National Institute on Drug Abuse.

Johnston, M. B., Whitman, T. L., & Johnson, M. (1980). Teaching addition and subtraction to mentally retarded children: A self-instruction program. *Applied Research in Mental Retardation, 1,* 141–160.

Joiner, T. E., Alfano, M. S., & Metalsky, G. I. (1992). When depression breeds contempt: Reassurance-seeking, self-esteem, and rejection of depressed college students by their roommates. *Journal of Abnormal Psychology, 101,* 165–173.

Joiner, T. E., Jr. (1995). The price of soliciting and receiving negative feedback: Self-verification theory as a vulnerability to depression theory. *Journal of Abnormal Psychology, 104,* 364–372.

Joiner, T. E., Jr. (2000). Depression's vicious scree: Self-propagating and erosive processes in depression chronicity. *Clinical Psychology: Science and Practice, 7,* 203–218.

Joiner, T. E., Jr. & Katz, J. (1999). Contagion of depressive symptoms and mood: Meta-analytic review and explanations from cognitive, behavioral, and interpersonal viewpoints. *Clinical Psychology: Science and Practice, 6,* 149–164.

Joiner, T. E., Jr. & Metalsky, G. I. (1995). A prospective test of an integrative interpersonal theory of depression: A naturalistic study of college roommates. *Journal of Personality and Social Psychology, 69,* 778–788.

Joiner, T. E., Jr., Metalsky, G. I., Katz, J., & Beach, S. R. H. (1999). Excessive reassurance-seeking and depression. *Psychological Inquiry, 10,* 269–278.

Joiner, T. E., Jr., Pettit, J. W., Walker, R. L., Voelz, Z. R., Cruz, J., Rudd, M. D., & Lester, D. (2002). Perceived burdensomeness and suicidality: Two studies on the suicide notes of those attempting and those completing suicide. *Journal of Social & Clinical Psychology, 21,* 531–545.

Joiner, T. E., Jr. & Schmidt, N. B. (1998). Excessive reassurance- seeking predicts depressive but not anxious reactions to acute stress. *Journal of Abnormal Psychology, 107,* 533–537.

Joiner, T. E., Jr. & Wagner, K. D. (1995). Attributional style and depression in children and adolescents: A meta-analytic review. *Clinical Psychology Review, 15,* 777–798.

Joiner, T. E., Jr., Steer, R. A., Abramson, L. Y., Alloy, L. B., Metalsky, G. I., & Schmidt, N. B. (2001). Hopelessness depression as a distinct dimension of depressive symptoms among clinical and nonclinical samples. *Behaviour Research and Therapy, 39,* 523–536.

Joiner, T. E., Jr., Steer, R. A., Beck, A. T., Schmidt, N. B., Rudd, M. D., & Catanzaro, S. J. (1999). Physiological hyperarousal: Construct validity of a central aspect of the tripartite model of depression and anxiety. *Journal of Abnormal Psychology, 2,* 290–298.

Jones v. United States, 103 S. Ct. 3043 (1983).

Jones, P. & Cannon, M. (1998). The new epidemiology of schizophrenia. *Psychiatric Clinics of North America, 21,* 1–25.

Jordan, J. C. (1995). First person account: Schizophrenia—adrift in an anchorless reality. *Schizophrenia Bulletin, 21,* 501–503.

Jorgensen, R. S., Johnson, B. T., Kolodziej, M. E., & Schreer, G. E. (1996). Elevated blood pressure and personality: A meta-analytic review. *Psychological Bulletin, 120,* 293–320.

Joseph, S., Williams, R., & Yule, W. (1995). Psychosocial perspectives on post-traumatic stress. *Clinical Psychology Review, 15,* 515–544.

Judd, L. L. (1997). The clinical course of unipolar major depressive disorders. *Archives of General Psychiatry, 54,* 989–991.

Judd, L. L., Akiskal, H. S., Zeller, P. J., Paulus, M., Leon, A. C., Maser, J. D., Endicott, J., Coryell, W., Kinovac, J. L., Mueller, T. I., Rice, J. P., & Keller, M. B. (2000). Psychosocial disability during the long-term course of unipolar major depressive disorder. *Archives of General Psychiatry, 57,* 375–380.

Jung, C. G. (1935). Fundamental psychological conceptions. In M. Baker & M. Game (Eds.), *A report of five lectures.* London: Institute of Medical Psychology.

Just, N. & Alloy, L. B. (1997). The response styles theory of depression: Tests and an extension of the theory. *Journal of Abnormal Psychology, 106,* 221–229.

Jutila, I., Immonen, A., Mervaala, E., Partanen, J., Partanen, K., Puranen, M., Kalviainen, R., Alafuzoff, I., Hurskainen, H., Vapalahti, M., & Ylinen, A. (2002). Long term outcome of temporal lobe epilepsy surgery: Analyses of 140 consecutive patients. *Journal of Neurology, Neurosurgery, and Psychiatry, 73*(5), 486–494.

Kachin, K. E., Newman, M.G., & Pincus, A. L. (2001). An interpersonal problem approach to the division of social phobia subtypes. *Behavior Therapy, 32*(3), 479–490.

Kaduson, H. G. & Schaefer, C. E. (2000). *Short-term play therapy for children.* New York: Guilford Press.

Kaelber, C. T., Moul, D. E., & Farmer, M. E. (1995). Epidemiology of depression. In E. E. Beckham & W. R. Leber (Eds.), *Handbook of depression* (2nd ed., pp. 3–35). New York: Guilford Press.

Kafka, M. P. & Pretky, R. (1992). Fluoxetine treatment on nonparaphilic sexual addictions and paraphilias in men. *Journal of Clinical Psychiatry, 53,* 351–358.

Kagan, J. (1989a). Commentary. *Human Development, 32* (2-3), 172–176.

Kagan, J. (1989b). The concept of behavioral inhibition to the unfamiliar. In R. J. Steven (Ed.), Perspectives on behavioral inhibition (pp. 1–23). Chicago: University of Chicago Press.

Kagan, J. (1989c). Temperamental contributions to social behavior. *American Psychologist, 44*(4), 668–674.

Kahn, M. W., Hannah, M., Hinkin, C., Montgomery, C., & Pitz, D. (1987). Psychopathology on the streets: Psychological measurement of the homeless. *Professional Psychology.*

Kalat, J. W. (2001). *Biological psychology* (7th ed.). Belmont, CA: Wadsworth.

Kalivas, P. W. (2003). Predisposition to addiction: Pharmacokinetics, pharmacodynamics, and brain circuitry. *American Journal of Psychiatry, 160*(1), 1–2.

Kalra, S., Bergeron, C., & Lang, A. E. (1996). Lewy body disease and dementia: A review. *Archives of Internal Medicine, 156,* 487–493.

Kamarck, T. W., Eranen, J., Jennings, J. R., Manuck, S. B., Everson, S. A., Kaplan, G. A., & Salonen, J. T. (2000). Anticipatory blood pressure responses to exercise are associated with left ventricular mass in Finnish men: Kuopio Ischemic Heart Disease Risk Factor Study. *Circulation, 102,* 1394–1399.

Kamarck, T. W., Everson, S. A., Kaplan, G. A., Manuck, S. B., Jennings, J. R., Salonen, R., & Salonen, J. T. (1997). Exaggerated blood pressure responses during mental stress are associated with enhanced carotid atherosclerosis in middle-aged Finnish men. *Circulation, 96,* 3842–3848.

Kandel, E. R. (1999). Biology and the future of psychoanalysis: A new intellectual framework for psychiatry revisited. *American Journal of Psychiatry, 156,* 505–524.

Kane, J. M., Marder, S. R., Schooler, N. R., Wirshing, W. C., Umbricht, D., Baker, R. W., Wirshing, D. A., Safferman, A., Ganguli, R., McMeniman, M., & Borenstein, M. (2001). Clozapine and haloperidol in moderately refractory schizophrenia: A 6-month randomized and double-blind comparison. *Archives of General Psychiatry, 58,* 965–972.

Kannel, W. B. & Higgins, M. (1990). Smoking and hypertension as predictors of cardiovascular risk in population studies. *Journal of Hypertension, 8,* S3-S8.

Kansas v. Hendricks, 117 S. Ct. 2072 (1997).

Kaplan, B. (Ed.). (1964). *The inner world of mental illness.* New York: Harper & Row.

Kaplan, H. I. & Sadock, B. J. (1991). *Synopsis of psychiatry: Behavioral sciences, clinical psychiatry* (6th ed.). Baltimore: Williams & Wilkins.

Kaplan, H. S. (1974). *The new sex therapy: Active treatment of sexual dysfunctions.* New York: Brunner/Mazel.

Kaplan, H. S. (1979). *Disorder of sexual desire.* New York: Brunner/Mazel.

Kaplan, J. R., Adams, M. R., Clarkson, T. B., & Koritnik, D. R. (1984). Psychosocial influences on female "protection" among cynomologus macaques. *Atherosclerosis, 53,* 283–295.

Kaplan, J. R. & Manuck, S. B. (1999). Status, stress, and atherosclerosis: The role of environment and individual behavior. *Annals of the New York Academy of Sciences, 896,* 145–161.

Kaplan, J. R., Manuck, S. B., Anthony, M. S., & Clarkson, T. B. (2002). Premenopausal social status and hormone exposure predict postmenopausal atherosclerosis in female monkeys. *Obstetrics and Gynecology, 99,* 381–388.

Kaplan, M. S. & Kreuger, R. B. (1997). Voyeurism: Psychopathology and theory. In D. R. Laws & W. O'Donohue (Eds.), *Sexual deviance: Theory, assessment, and treatment.* New York: Guilford Press.

Kaplan, R. M. (2000). Two pathways to prevention. *American Psychologist, 55,* 382–396.

Kaprio, J., Koskenvuo, M., Langinvainio, H., Romanov, K., Sarna, S., & Rose, R. J. (1987). Genetic influences on use and abuse of alcohol: A study of 5638 adult Finnish twin brothers. *Alcoholism: Clinical and Experimental Research, 11,* 349–356.

Kapur, S. & Remington, G. (1996). Serotonin-dopamine interaction and its relevance to schizophrenia. *American Journal of Psychiatry, 153,* 466–476.

Karasek, R., Baker, D., Marxer, F., Ahlbom, A., & Theorell, T. (1981). Job decision latitude, job demands, and cardiovascular disease: A prospective study of Swedish men. *American Journal of Public Health, 71,* 694–705.

Karlsson, P., Farde, L., Halldin, C., & Sedvall, G. (2002). PET study of D_1 dopamine receptor binding in neuroleptic-naive patients with schizophrenia. *American Journal of Psychiatry, 159,* 761–767.

Karoumi, B., Saoud, M., D'Amato, T., Rosenfeld, F., Densie, P., Gutknecht, C., Gaveau, V., Beaulieu. F. E., Dalery, J., & Rochet, T. (2001). Poor performance in smooth pursuit and antisaccadic eye-movement tasks in healthy siblings of patients with schizophrenia. *Psychiatry Research, 101,* 209–219.

Karper, L. P. & Krystal, J. H. (1997). Pharmacotherapy of violent behavior. In D. M. Stoff, J. Breiling, & J. D. Maser (Eds.), *Handbook of antisocial behavior* (pp. 436–444). New York: Wiley.

Karpman, B. (1954). *The sexual offender and his offenses.* New York: Julian Press.

Kashani, J. H., Carlson, G. A., Beck, N. C., et al. (1990). Depression, depressive symptoms, and depressed mood among a community sample of adolescents. *American Journal of Psychiatry, 144,* 931–934.

Kashner, T. M., Rost, K., Cohen, B., Anderson, M., & Smith, G. R. (1995). Enhancing the health of somatization disorder patients: Effectiveness of short-term group therapy. *Psychosomatics, 36,* 462–470.

Kass, D. J., Silver, F. M., & Abrams, G. M. (1972). Behavioral group treatment of hysteria. *Archives of General Psychiatry, 26,* 42–50.

Kassirer, J. P. (1997). Federal foolishness and marijuana. *New England Journal of Medicine, 336,* 366–367.

Katerndahl, D. A. (1996). Panic attacks and panic disorder. *Journal of Family Practice, 43,* 275–282.

Katsanis, J., Iacono, W. G., & Beiser, M. (1996). Eye-tracking performance and adaptive functioning over the short-term course of first-episode psychosis. *Psychiatry Research, 64,* 19–26.

Kaufman, J., Martin, A., King, R. A., & Charney, D. (2001). Are child-, adolescent-, and adult-onset depression one and the same disorder? *Biological Psychiatry, 49,* 980–1001.

Kaufman, J. & Zigler, E. (1987). Do abused children become abusive parents? *American Journal of Orthopsychiatry, 57,* 186–192.

Kaye, W. H., Berrettini, W., Gwirtsman, H., & George, D. T. (1990). Altered cerebrospinal fluid neuropeptide Y and peptide YY immunoreactivity in anorexia and bulimia nervosa. *Archives of General Psychiatry, 47,* 548–556.

Kazdin, A. E. (1999). Overview of research design issues in clinical psychology. In P. C. Kendall, J. N.

Butcher, & G. N. Holmbeck (Eds.), *Handbook of research methods in clinical psychology* (2nd ed., pp. 3–30). New York: Wiley.

Kazdin, A. E., Bass, D., Ayers, W. A., & Rodgers, A. (1990). Empirical and clinical focus of child and adolescent psychotherapy research. *Journal of Consulting and Clinical Psychology, 58,* 100–110.

Kazdin, A. E. & Wassell, G. (1999). Barriers to treatment participation and therapeutic change among children referred for conduct disorder. *Journal of Clinical Child Psychology, 28,* 160–172.

Kazdin, A. E. & Wilson, G. T. (1978). *Evaluation of behavior therapy: Issues, evidence and research strategies.* Cambridge, MA: Ballinger.

Kearney, C. A. (2001). *School refusal behavior in youth: A functional approach to assessment and treatment.* Washington, DC: American Psychological Association.

Kearney, C. A. (2002). *Casebook for childhood behavior disorders.* 2nd ed. Belmont, CA: Wadsworth.

Kearney, C. A., Durand, V. M., & Mindell, J. A. (1995a). Choice assessment in residential settings. *Journal of Developmental and Physical Disabilities, 7,* 203–213.

Kearney, C. A., Durand, V. M., & Mindell, J. A. (1995b). It's not where but how you live: Choice and adaptive/maladaptive behavior in persons with severe handicaps. *Journal of Developmental and Physical Disabilities, 7,* 203–213.

Kearney, C. A. & McKnight, T. J. (1997). Preference, choice, and persons with disabilities: A synopsis of assessments, interventions, and future directions. *Clinical Psychology Review, 17,* 217–238.

Kearney, C. A. & McKnight, T. J. (1998). Mental retardation. In C. Radnitz (Ed.), *Cognitive-behavioral interventions for persons with disabilities.* Northvale, NJ: Aronson.

Keefe, R. S. E., Silverman, J. M., Mohs, R. C., Siever, L. J., Harvey, P. D., Friedman, L., Roitman, S. E. L., DuPre, R. L., Smith, C. J., Schmeidler, J., & Davis, K. L. (1997). Eye tracking, attention, and schizotypal symptoms in nonpsychotic relatives of patients with schizophrenia. *Archives of General Psychiatry, 54,* 169–176.

Keller, M. B., Lavori, P. W., Mueller, T. I., Endicott, J., Coryell, W., Hirschfeld, R. M. A., & Shea, T. (1992). Time to recovery, chronicity, and levels of psychopathology in major depression. *Archives of General Psychiatry, 49,* 809–816.

Kellner, R. (1985). Functional somatic symptoms and hypochondriasis: A survey of empirical studies. *Archives of General Psychiatry, 42,* 821–833.

Kellner, R. (1990). Somatization. *Journal of Nervous and Mental Disease. 178,* 150–160.

Kelly, G. A. (1955). *The psychology of personal constructs.* New York: W. W. Norton.

Kemp, S. (1985). Modern myth and medieval madness: Views of mental illness in the European middle ages and renaissance. *New Zealand Journal of Psychology, 14,* 1–8.

Kemp, S. (1990). *Medieval psychology,* New York: Greenwood Press.

Kemper, T. L. & Bauman, M. (1998). Neuropathology of infantile autism. *Journal of Neuropathology and Experimental Neurology, 57,* 645–652.

Kendall, P. C. (1990). *Coping cat workbook.* Ardmore, PA: Workbook Publishing.

Kendall, P. C. (1992). Healthy thinking. *Behavior Therapy, 23,* 1–11.

Kendall, P. C. & Braswell, L. (1993). *Cognitive-behavioral therapy for impulsive children* (2nd ed.). New York: Guilford Press.

Kendall, P. C., Howard, B. L., & Hays, R. C. (1989). Self-referent speech and psychopathology: The balance of positive and negative thinking. *Cognitive Therapy and Research, 13,* 583–598.

Kendall, P. C., Marrs-Garcia, A., Nath, S. R., & Sheldrick, R. C. (1999). Normative comparisons for the evaluation of clinical significance. *Journal of Consulting and Clinical Psychology, 67,* 285–299.

Kendall, P. C. & Treadwell, K. R. (1996). Cognitive-behavioral treatment for childhood anxiety disorders. In E. D. Hibbs & P. S. Jensen (Eds.), *Psychosocial treatment research with children and adolescents* (pp. 23–41). Washington, DC: American Psychological Association.

Kendall-Tuckett, K. A., Williams, L. M., & Finkelhor, D. (1993). Impact of sexual abuse on children: A review and synthesis of recent empirical studies. *Psychological Bulletin, 113,* 164–180.

Kendler, K. S. (1996). Major depression and generalised anxiety disorder: Same genes, (partly) different environments–revisited. *British Journal of Psychiatry, 168,* 68–75.

Kendler, K. S. & Diehl, S. R. (1993). The genetics of schizophrenia: A current genetic-epidemiological perspective. *Schizophrenia Bulletin, 19,* 261–285.

Kendler, K. S., Eaves, L. J., Walters, E. E., Neale, M. C., Heath, A. C., & Kessler, R. C. (1996). The identification and validation of distinct depressive syndromes in a population-based sample of female twins. *Archives of General Psychiatry, 53,* 391–399.

Kendler, K. S., Gallagher, T. J., Abelson, J. M., & Kessler, R. C. (1996). Lifetime prevalence, demographic risk factors, and diagnostic validity of nonaffective psychosis as assessed in a US community sample. *Archives of General Psychiatry, 53,* 1022–1031.

Kendler, K. S., Gardner, C. O., Neale, M. C., & Prescott, C. A. (2001). Genetic risk factors for major depression in men and women: Similar or different heritabilities and same or partly distinct genes? *Psychological Medicine, 31,* 605–616.

Kendler, K. S., Karkowski, L. M., & Prescott, C. A. (1999). Causal relationship between stressful life events and the onset of major depression. *American Journal of Psychiatry, 156,* 837–841.

Kendler, K. S., Kessler, R. C., Neale, M. C., Heath, A. C., & Eaves, L. J. (1993). The prediction of major depression in women: Toward an integrated etiologic model. *American Journal of Psychiatry, 150,* 1139–1148.

Kendler, K. S., Kessler, R. C., Walters, E. E., MacLean, C., Neale, M. C., Heath, A. C., & Eaves, L. J. (1995). Stressful life events, genetic liability, and onset of an episode of major depression in women. *American Journal of Psychiatry, 152,* 833–842.

Kendler, K. S., McGuire, M., Gruenberg, A. M., & Walsh, D. (1994). Outcome and family study of the subtypes of schizophrenia in the west of Ireland. *American Journal of Psychiatry, 151,* 849–856.

Kendler, K. S., McGuire, M., Gruenberg, A. M., & Walsh, D. (1995). Examining the validity of *DSM-III-R* schizoaffective disorder and its putative subtypes in the Roscommon Family Study. *American Journal of Psychiatry, 152,* 755–764.

Kendler, K. S., Myers, J., Prescott, C. A., & Neal, M. C. (2001). The genetic epidemiology of irrational fears and phobias in men. *Archives of General Psychiatry, 58,* 257–265.

Kendler, K. S., Neale, M. C., Kessler, R. C., Heath, A. C., & Eaves, L. J. (1992a). Childhood parental loss and adult psychopathology in women: A twin study perspective. *Archives of General Psychiatry, 49,* 109–116.

Kendler, K. S., Neale, M. C., Kessler, R. C., Heath, A. C., & Eaves, L. J. (1992b). Generalized anxiety disorder in women: A population-based twin study. *Archives of General Psychiatry, 49,* 267–272.

Kendler, K. S., Neale, M. C., Kessler, R. C., Heath, A. C., & Eaves, L. J. (1992c). A population-based twin study of major depression in women: The impact of varying definitions of illness. *Archives of General Psychiatry, 49,* 257–266.

Kendler, K. S., Thornton, L. M., & Gardner, C. O. (2000). Stressful life events and previous episodes in the etiology of major depression in women: An evaluation of the "kindling" hypothesis. *American Journal of Psychiatry, 157,* 1243–1251.

Kent, D. A., Tomasson, K., & Coryell, W. (1995). Course and outcome of conversion and somatization disorders: A four-year follow-up. *Psychosomatics, 36,* 138–144.

Kernberg, O. F. (1975). *Borderline conditions and pathological narcissism.* New York: Aronson.

Kernberg, O. (1998). Narcissistic personality disorders. *Journal of European Psychoanalysis*, *7,* 7–18.

Kerns, J. G. & Berenbaum, H. (2002). Cognitive impairments associated with formal thought disorder in people with schizophrenia. *Journal of Abnormal Psychology, 111,* 211–224.

Kerr, S. H. & Cooper, E. B. (1976). *Phonatory adjustment times in stutterers and nonstutterers.* Unpublished manuscript.

Kessler, J. W. (1988). *Psychopathology of childhood.* Englewood Cliffs, NJ: Prentice-Hall.

Kessler, K. A. (1998). History of managed behavioral health care and speculations about its future. *Harvard Review of Psychiatry, 6,* 155–159.

Kessler, R. C. (2000). Posttraumatic stress disorder. The burden to the individual and to society. *Journal of Clinical Psychiatry, 61*(Supp. 5), 4–12.

Kessler, R. C. (in press). The effects of chronic medical conditions on work impairment. In A. S. Rossi (Ed.), *Caring and doing for others: Social responsibility in the domains of family, work, and community.* Chicago: University of Chicago Press.

Kessler, R. C., Avenevoli, S., & Merikangas, M. R. (2001). Mood disorders in children and adolescents: An epidemiological perspective. *Biological Psychiatry, 49,* 1002–1014.

Kessler, R. C., Borges, G., & Walters, E. E. (1999). Prevalence of and risk factors for lifetime suicide attempts in the National Comorbidity Survey. *Archives of General Psychiatry, 56,* 617–626.

Kessler, R. C., Foster, C., Joseph, J., Ostrow, D., Wortman, C., Phair, J., & Chmiel, J. (1991). Stressful life events and symptom onset in HIV infection. *American Journal of Psychiatry, 148,* 733–738.

Kessler, R. C., McGonagle, K. A., Zhao, S., Nelson, C. B., Hughes, M., Eshleman, S., Wittchen, H. U., & Kendler, K. S. (1994). Lifetime and 12-month prevalence of *DSM-III-R* psychiatric disoders in the United States: Results from the National Comorbidity Study. *Archives of General Psychiatry, 51,* 8–19.

Kessler, R. C., Sonnega, A., Bromet, E., Hughes, M., & Nelson, C. B. (1995). Posttraumatic stress disorder in the National Comorbidity Survey. *Archives of General Psychiatry, 52,* 1048–1060.

Kessler, R. C., Zhao, S., Blazer, D. G., & Swartz, M. (1997). Prevalence, correlates, and course of minor depression and major depression in the national comorbidity survey. *Journal of Affective Disorders, 45,* 19–30.

Kety, S. S. (1988). Schizophrenic illness in the families of schizophrenic adoptees: Findings from the Danish national sample. *Schizophrenia Bulletin, 14,* 217–222.

Kety, S. S. (1970). Genetic environment interactions in schizophrenia. In R. E. Jones (Ed.), *Transactions and studies of the College of Physicians of Philadelphia* (pp. 124–134). Baltimore: Waverly Press.

Kety, S. S., Rosenthal, D., Wender, P. H., & Schulsinger, F. (1968). The types and prevalence of mental illness in the biological and adoptive families of adopted schizophrenics. In D. Rosenthal & S. S. Kety (Eds.), *The transmission of schizophrenia.* Oxford: Pergamon Press.

Kety, S. S., Rosenthal, D., Wender, P. H., Schulsinger, F., & Jacobsen, B. (1975). Mental illness in the biological and adoptive families of adopted individuals who have become schizophrenic: A preliminary report based upon psychiatric interviews. In R. Fieve, D. Rosenthal, & H. Brill (Eds.), *Genetic research in psychiatry.* Baltimore: Johns Hopkins University Press.

Kety, S. S., Wender, P. H., Jacobsen, B., Ingraham, L. J., Jansson, L., Faber, B., & Kinney, D. K. (1994). Mental illness in the biological and adoptive relatives of schizophrenic adoptees: Replication of the Copenhagen study in the rest of Denmark. *Archives of General Psychiatry, 51,* 442–455.

Kiecolt-Glaser, J. K., Dura, J. R., Speicher, C. E., Trask, O. J., & Glaser, R. (1991). Spousal caregivers of dementia victims: Longitudinal changes in immunity and health. *Psychosomatic Medicine, 53,* 345–362.

Kiecolt-Glaser, J. K., Fisher, L., Ogrocki, P., Stout, J. C., Speicher, C. E., & Glaser, R. (1987). Marital quality, marital disruption, and immune function. *Psychosomatic Medicine, 46,* 7–14.

Kiecolt-Glaser, J. K. & Glaser, R. (1991). Stress and immune function in humans. In R. Ader, D. Felten, & N. Cohen (Eds.), *Psychoneuroimmunology II* (pp. 849–867). San Diego: Academic Press.

Kiecolt-Glaser, J. K., Glaser, R., Williger, D., Stout, J., Messick, G., Sheppard, S., Ricker, D., Romisher, S. C., Briner, W., Bonnell, G., & Donnerberg, R. (1985). Psychosocial enhancement of immunocompetence in a geriatric population. *Health Psychology, 4,* 25–41.

Kiecolt-Glaser, J. K., Malarkey, W. B., Chee, M., Newton, T., Cacioppo, J. T., Hsiao-Yin, M., & Glaser, R. (1993). Negative behavior during marital conflict is associated with immunological down-regulation. *Psychosomatic Medicine, 55,* 395–409.

Kiehl, K. A., Smith, A. M., Hare, R. D., & Liddle, P. F. (2000). An event-related potential investigation of response inhibition in schizophrenia and psychopathy. *Biological Psychiatry, 48*(3), 210–221.

Kiesler, C. A. (1982a). Mental hospitals and alternative care. *American Psychologist, 37,* 349–360.

Kiesler, C. A. (1982b). Public and professional myths about mental hospitalization. *American Psychologist, 37,* 1323–1339.

Kiesler, D. J. (1992). Interpersonal circle inventories: Pantheoretical applications to psychotherapy research and practice. *Journal of Psychotherapy Integration, 2,* 77–79.

Kihlstrom, J. F. (1987). The cognitive unconscious. *Science, 237,* 1445–1452.

Kihlstrom, J. F. (2001). Dissociative disorders. In H. E. Adams & P. B.

Sutker (Eds.), *Comprehensive handbook of psychopathology* (3rd ed., pp. 259–276). New York: Kluwer Academic/Plenum.

Kihlstrom, J. F., Barnhardt, T. M., & Tataryn, D. J. (1991). Implicit perception. In R. F. Bornstein & T. S. Pittman (Eds.), *Perception without awareness*. New York: Guilford Press.

Kihlstrom, J. F. & Schacter, D. L. (1995). Functional disorders of autobiographical memory. In A. D. Baddeley, B. A. Wilson, & F. N. Watts (Eds.), *Handbook of memory disorders* (pp. 337–364). New York: Wiley.

Kihlstrom, J. F., Tataryn, D. J., & Hoyt, I. P. (1993). Dissociative disorders. In P. B. Sutker & H. E. Adams (Eds.), *Comprehensive handbook of psychopathology* (2nd ed.). New York: Plenum Press.

Killen, J. D., Hayward, C., Wilson, C. B., Taylor, C. B., Hammer, L. D., Litt, T. N., Simmonds, B., & Haydel, F. (1994). Factors associated with eating disorder symptoms in a community sample of 6th and 7th grade girls. *International Journal of Eating Disorders, 15*, 357–367.

Killen, J. D., Taylor, C. B., Hammer, L. D., Litt, I., Wilson, D. M., Rich, T., Hayward, C., Simmonds, B., Kraemer, H., & Varady, A. (1993). An attempt to modify unhealthful eating attitudes and weight regulation practices of young adolescent girls. *International Journal of Eating Disorders, 13*, 369–384.

Killen, J. D., Taylor, C. B., Hayward, C., Haydel, K. F., Wilson, D. M., Hammer, L., Kraemer, H., Blair-Greiner, A., & Strachowski, D. (1996). Weight concerns influence the development of eating disorders: A 4-year prospective study. *Journal of Consulting and Clinical Psychology, 64*, 936–940.

Kim, P. Y. & Bailey, M. (1997). Sidestreets on the information superhighway: Paraphilias and sexual variations on the Internet. *Journal of Sex Education and Therapy, 32*, 35–43.

Kim, S., Larson, S. A., & Lakin, K. C. (2001). Behavioural outcomes of deinstitutionalisation for people with intellectual disability: A review of US studies conducted between 1980 and 1999. *Journal of Intellectual and Developmental Disability, 26*, 35–50.

Kimble, G. A. (2000). Behaviorism and unity in psychology. *Current Directions in Psychological Science, 9*, 208–212.

Kinderman, P. & Bentall, R. P. (1996). Self-discrepancies and persecutory delusions: Evidence for a model of paranoid ideation. *Journal of Abnormal Psychology, 105*, 106–113.

King, C. A. (1997). Suicidal behavior in adolescence. In R. W. Maris, M. M. Silverman, & S. S. Canetto (Eds.), *Review of suicidology* (pp. 61–95). New York: Guilford Press.

King, S. A. & Barak, A. (2000). Compulsive Internet gambling: A new form of an old clinical pathology. *Cyberpsychology and Behavior, 25*, 441–456.

Kinney, D. K. (2001). Prenatal stress and risk for schizophrenia. *International Journal of Mental Health, 29*, 62–72.

Kinney, D. K., Holzman, P. S., Jacobsen, B., Jansson, L., Faber, B., Hildebrand, W., Kasell, E., & Zimbalist, M. E. (1997). Thought disorder in schizophrenic and control adoptees and their relatives. *Archives of General Psychiatry, 54*, 475–479.

Kinsey, A. C., Pomeroy, W. B., & Martin, C. E. (1948). *Sexual behavior in the human male*. Philadelphia: Saunders.

Kinsey, A. C., Pomeroy, W. B., Martin, C. E., & Gebhard, P. H. (1953). *Sexual behavior in the human female*. Philadelphia: Saunders.

Kirch, D. G. (1993). Infection and autoimmunity as etiologic factors in schizophrenia: A review and reappraisal. *Schizophrenia Bulletin, 19*, 355–370.

Kirkpatrick, B., Buchanan, R. W., Ross, D. E., & Carpenter, W. T., Jr. (2001). A separate disease within the syndrome of schizophrenia. *Archives of General Psychiatry, 58*, 165–171.

Kirmayer, L. J. & Young, A. (1998). Culture and somatization: Clinical, epidemiological, and ethnographic perspectives. *Psychosomatic Medicine, 60*, 420–430.

Kirmayer, L. J. & Young, A. (1999). Culture and context in the evolutionary concept of mental disorder. *Journal of Abnormal Psychology, 108*, 446–452.

Kirmayer, L. J., Young, A., & Hayton, B. C. (1995). The cultural context of anxiety disorders. *Psychiatric Clinics of North America, 18*, 503–521.

Kirsch, I., Moore, T. J., Scoboria, A., & Nicholls, S. S. (2002). The emperor's new drugs. An analysis of antidepressant medication data submitted to the U.S. Food and Drug Administration. *Prevention & Treatment, 5*, Article 23. Retrieved August 15, 2003, from http://www.journals.apa.org/prevention/volume5/pre0050023a.html.

Kirsch, I. & Saperstein, G. (1998). Listening to Prozac but hearing placebo: A meta-analysis of antidepressant medication. *Prevention & Treatment, 1*, Article 0002a. Retrieved August 15, 2003, from http://www.journals.apa.org/prevention/volume1/pre0010002a.html.

Kisiel, C. L. & Lyons, J. S. (2001). Dissociation as a mediator of psychopathology among sexually abused children and adolescents. *American Journal of Psychiatry, 158*, 1034–1039.

Klackenberg, G. (1982). Sleep behavior studied longitudinally: Data from 4–16 years on duration, night-awakening and bed-sharing. *Acta Paediatrica Scandinavica, 71*, 501–506.

Klajner, R., Herman, C. P., Polivy, J., & Chhabra, R. (1981). Human obesity, dieting, and anticipatory salivation. *Physiology and Behavior, 27*, 195–198.

Klatka, L. A., Louis, E. D., & Schiffer, R. B. (1996). Psychiatric features in diffuse Lewy body disease: A clinicopathologic study using Alzheimer's disease and Parkinson's disease comparison groups. *Neurology, 47*, 1148–1152.

Klein, D. F. (1996a). Panic disorder and agoraphobia: Hypothesis hothouse. *Journal of Clinical Psychiatry, 57*, 21–27.

Klein, D. F. (1996b). Preventing hung juries about therapy studies. *Journal of Consulting and Clinical Psychology, 64*, 81–87.

Klein, D. F. (1998). Listening to meta-analysis but hearing bias. *Prevention & Treatment, 1*, Article 0006c. Retrieved August 15, 2003, from http://www.journals.apa.org/prevention/volume1/pre0010006c.html.

Klein, D. N., Kocsis, J. H., McCullough, J. P., Holzer, C. E., III, Hirschfeld, R. M. A., & Keller, M. B. (1996). Symptomatology in dysthymic and major depressive disorder. *Psychiatric Clinics of North America, 19*, 41–53.

Klein, D. N., Schatzberg, A. F., McCullough, J. P., Dowling, F., Goodman, D., Howland, R. H., Markowitz, J. C., Smith, C., Thase, M. E., Rush, A. J., LaVange, L., Harrison, W. M., & Keller, M. B. (1999). Age of onset in chronic major depression: Relation to demographic and clinical variables, family history, and treatment response. *Journal of Affective Disorders, 55*, 149–157.

Klein, D. N., Schwartz, J. E., Rose, S., & Leader, J. B. (2000). Five-year course and outcome of dysthymic disorder: A prospective, naturalistic follow-up study. *American Journal of Psychiatry, 157,* 931–939.

Klein, D. N., Taylor, E. B., Dickstein, S., & Harding, K. (1988). The early-late onset distinction in *DSM-III-R* dysthymia. *Journal of Affective Disorders, 14,* 25–33.

Klein, D. W. (2002). Trial rights and psychotropic drugs: The case against administering involuntary medications to a defendant during trial. *Vanderbilt Law Review, 55,* 165–218.

Klein, E., Kreinin, I., Chistyakov, A., Koren, D., Mecz, L., Marmur, S., Ben-Shachar, D., & Feinsod, M. (1999). Therapeutic efficacy of right prefrontal slow repetitive transcranial magnetic stimulation in major depression: A double-blind controlled study. *Archives of General Psychiatry, 56,* 315–320.

Klerman, G. L. (1988). The current age of youthful melancholia. *British Journal of Psychiatry, 152,* 4–14.

Klerman, G. L. (1990). Approaches to the phenomena of comorbidity. In J. D. Maser & C. R. Cloninger (Eds.), *Cormorbidity of mood and anxiety disorders.* Washington, DC: American Psychiatric Press.

Klerman, G. L., Lavori, P. W., Rice, J., Reich, T., Endicott, J., Andreasen, N. C., Keller, M. B., & Hirschfeld, R. M. A. (1985). Birth cohort trends in rates of major depressive disorder among relatives of patients with affective disorder. *Archives of General Psychiatry, 42,* 689–693.

Klerman, G. L., Weissman, M. M., Rounsaville, B. J., & Chevron, E. S. (1984). *Interpersonal psychotherapy of depression.* New York: Basic Books.

Klin, A. & Volkmar, F. R. (1997). Autism and the pervasive developmental disorders. In J. D. Noshpitz, S. Greenspan, S. Wieder, & J. Osofsky (Eds.), *Handbook of child and adolescent psychiatry* (Vol. 1; pp. 536–560). New York: Wiley.

Klin, A. & Volkmar, F. R. (1999). Autism and other pervasive developmental disorders. In S. Goldstein & C. R. Reynolds (Eds.), *Handbook of neurodevelopmental and genetic disorders in children* (pp. 247–274). New York: Guilford Press.

Klinger, L. G. & Dawson, G. (1996). Autistic disorder. In E. J. Mash & R. A. Barkley (Eds.), *Child psychopathology* (pp. 311–339). New York: Guilford Press.

Klitzman, R. L., Pope, H. G., & Hudson, J. I. (2000). MDMA ("Ecstasy") abuse and high risk sexual behaviors among 169 gay and bisexual men. *American Journal of Psychiatry, 157,* 1162–1164.

Kluft, R. P. (1984). Treatment of multiple personality disorder. A study of 33 cases. *Psychiatric Clinics of North America, 7,* 9–29.

Kluft, R. P. (1986). Personality unification in multiple personality disorder: A follow-up study. In B. G. Braun (Ed.), *Treatment of multiple personality disorder.* Washington, DC: American Psychiatric Press.

Kluft, R. P. (1988). Dissociative disorders. In J. A. Talbott, R. E. Hales, & S. C. Yudofsky (Eds.), *The American Psychiatric Press textbook of psychiatry* (pp. 557–586). Washington, DC: American Psychiatric Press.

Kluft, R. P. (1991). Clinical presentations of multiple personality disorder. *Psychiatric Clinics of North America, 14,* 605–629.

Kluft, R. P. (1992). A specialist's perspective on multiple personality disorder. *Psychoanalytic Inquiry, 12,* 139–171.

Kluft, R. P. (1999). An overview of the psychotherapy of dissociative identity disorder. *American Journal of Psychotherapy, 53,* 289–319.

Knecht v. Gillman, 488 F.2d 1136, 1140 (8th Cir. 1973).

Knecht, S., Deppe, M., Draeger, B., Bobe, L., Lohmann, H., Ringelstein, E. B., & Henningsen, H. (2000). *Brain, 123,* 74–81.

Knight, R. A. & Roff, J. D. (1985). Affectivity in schizophrenia. In M. Alpert (Ed.), *Controversies of schizophrenia* (pp. 280–313). New York: Guilford Press.

Knight, R. A. & Silverstein, S. M. (2001). A process-oriented approach for averting confounds resulting from general performance deficiencies in schizophrenia. *Journal of Abnormal Psychology, 110,* 15–30.

Knopp, F. H. (1976). *Instead of prisons.* Syracuse, NY: Safer Society Press.

Knutsson, A. & Boggild, H. (2000). Shiftwork and cardiovascular disease: Review of disease mechanisms. *Reviews on Environmental Health, 15,* 359–372.

Kobayashi, R., Murata, T., & Yoshinaga, K. (1992). A follow-up study of 201 children with autism in Kyushu and Yamaguchi areas, Japan. *Journal of Autism and Developmental Disorders, 22,* 395–411.

Kocsis, J. H., Friedman, R. A., Markowitz, J. C., Leon, A. C., Miller, N. L., Gniwesch, L., & Parides, M. (1996). Maintenance therapy for chronic depression: A controlled clinical trial of desipramine. *Archives of General Psychiatry, 53,* 769–774.

Koegel, R. L. & Koegel, L. K. (Eds.). (1995). *Teaching children with autism: Strategies for initiating positive interactions and improving learning opportunities.* Baltimore: Paul H. Brookes.

Koenig, H. G., George, L. K., Hays, J. C., Larson, D. B., Cohen, H. J., & Blazer, D. G. (1998). The relationship between religious activities and blood pressure in older adults. *International Journal of Psychiatry in Medicine, 28,* 189–213.

Kohlenberg, R. J. (1973). Behavioristic approach to multiple personality: A case study. *Behavior Therapy, 4,* 137–140.

Kohlenberg, R. J. & Tsai, M. (1992). *Functional analytic psychotherapy: Creating intense and curative therapeutic relationships.* New York: Plenum Press.

Kohler, F. W. & Strain, P. S. (1997). Procedures for assessing and increasing social interaction. In N. N. Singh (Ed.), *Prevention and treatment of severe behavior problems: Models and methods in developmental disabilities* (pp. 49–59). Pacific Grove, CA: Brooks/Cole.

Kohn, R., Dohrenwend, B. P., & Mirotznik, J. (1998). Epidemiological findings on selected psychiatric disorders in the general population. In B. P. Dohrenwend (Ed.), *Adversity, stress and psychopathology* (pp. 235–284.) New York: Oxford University Press.

Kohn, Y., Zislin, J., Agid, O., Hanin, B., Troudart, T., Shapira, B., Bloch, M., Gur, E., Ritsner, M., & Lerer, B. (2001). Increased prevalence of negative life events in subtypes of major depressive disorder. *Comprehensive Psychiatry, 42,* 57–63.

Kohut, H. (1966). Forms and transformations of narcissism. *Journal of the American Psychoanalytic Association, 14,* 243–272.

Kohut, H. (1972). Thoughts on narcissism and narcissistic rage. *Psychoanalytic Study of the Child, 27,* 360–400.

Kohut, H. (1977). *The restoration of the self.* New York: International Universities Press.

Kohut, H. & Wolf, E. S. (1978). The disorders of the self and their treatment: An outline. *International Journal of Psychoanalysis, 59,* 413–425.

Kokmen, E., Beard, C. M., O'Brien, P. C., Offord, K. P., & Kurland, L. T. (1993). Is the incidence of dementing illness changing? A 25-year time trend study in Rochester, Minnesota (1960–1984). *Neurology, 43,* 1887–1892.

Kokmen, K., Beard, C. M., Offord, K. P., & Kurland, L. T. (1989). Prevalence of medically diagnosed dementia in a defined United States population. *Neurology, 39,* 773–776.

Kolb, B. (1989). Brain development, plasticity, and behavior. *American Psychologist, 44,* 1203–1212.

Kolb, B. & Taylor, L. (2000). Facial expression, emotion, and hemispheric organization. In R. D. Lane & L. Nadel (Eds.), *Cognitive neuroscience of emotion* (pp. 62–81). New York: Oxford University Press.

Kolb, L. C. (1982). *Modern clinical psychiatry* (10th ed.). Philadelphia: Saunders.

Kolodny, R. C., Masters, W. H., Kolodner, R. M., & Gelson, T. (1974). Depression of plasma testosterone levels after chronic intensive marihuana use. *New England Journal of Medicine, 290*(16), 872–874.

Koopman, C., Classen, C., & Spiegel, D. (1994). Predictors of posttraumatic stress symptoms among Oakland/Berkeley firestorm survivors. *American Journal of Psychiatry, 151,* 888–894.

Kopelman, M. D., Reed, L. J., Marsden, P., Mayes, A. R., Jaldow, E., Laing, H., & Isaac, C. (2001). Amnesic syndrome and severe ataxia following the recreational use of 3,4-methylene-dioxymethamphetamine (MDMA, "ecstasy") and other substances. *Neurocase, 7,* 423–432.

Kopelman, M. D., Christensen, H., Puffett, A., & Stanhope, N. (1994). The great escape: A neuropsychological study of psychogenic amnesia. *Neuropsychologia, 32,* 675–691.

Kornreich, C., Blairy, S., Phillippot, P., Hess, U., Noel, X., Streel, E., Le Bon, O., Dan, B., Pele, I., & Verbanck, P. (2001). Deficits in recognition of emotional facial expression are still present in alcoholics after mid- to long-term abstinence. *Journal of Studies on Alcohol, 62,* 533–542.

Kornstein, S. G., Schatzberg, A. F., Thase, M. E., Yonkers, K. A., McCullough, J. P., Keitner, G. I., Gelenberg, A. J., Davis, S. M., Harrison, W., & Keller, M. B. (2000). Gender differences in treatment response to sertraline versus imipramine in chronic depression. *American Journal of Psychiatry, 157,* 1445–1452.

Koss, M. P. (1996). The measurement of rape victimization in crime surveys. *Criminal Justice and Behavior, 23,* 55–69.

Kostanski, M. & Gullone, E. (1998). Adolescent body image dissatisfaction: Relationships with self-esteem, anxiety, and depression controlling for body mass. *Journal of Child Psychology and Psychiatry, 39,* 255–262.

Kotrla, K. J. & Weinberger, D. R. (1995). Brain imaging in schizophrenia. *Annual Reviews of Medicine, 46,* 113–122.

Kovacs, M., Devlin, B., Pollock, M., Richards, C., & Mukerji, P. (1997). A controlled family history study of childhood-onset depressive disorder. *Archives of General Psychiatry, 54,* 613–623.

Kraepelin, E. (1923). *Textbook of psychiatry.* New York: Macmillan. Original work published 1883.

Kraepelin, E. (1968). *Lectures on clinical psychiatry* (T. P. Johnstone, Trans.). New York: Hafner. Original work published 1904.

Krafft-Ebing, R. von. (1900). *Textbook of psychiatry.* Original work published 1879.

Krafft-Ebing, R. von. (1965). *Psychopathia sexualis* (F. S. Klaf, Trans.). New York: Bell. Original work published 1886.

Kramer, P. D. (1993). *Listening to Prozac.* New York: Viking.

Krantz, D. S. & Manuck, S. B. (1984). Acute psychophysiologic reactivity and risk of cardiovascular disease: A review and methodologic critique. *Psychological Bulletin, 96,* 435–464.

Krantz, D. S. & McCeney, M. K. (2002). Effects of psychological and social factors on organic disease: A critical assessment of research on coronary heart disease. *Annual Review of Psychology, 53,* 341–369.

Kratzer, L. & Hodgins, S. (1997). Adult outcomes of child conduct problems: A cohort study. *Journal of Abnormal Child Psychology, 25,* 65–81.

Kravdal, O. (2001). The impact of marital status on cancer survival. *Social Science and Medicine, 52,* 357–368.

Kring, A. M. & Neale, J. M. (1996). Do schizophrenic patients show a disjunctive relationship among expressive, experiential, and psychophysiological components of emotion? *Journal of Abnormal Psychology, 105,* 249–257.

Kringlen, E. & Cramer, G. (1989). Offspring of monozygotic twins discordant for schizophrenia. *Archives of General Psychiatry, 46,* 873–877.

Kristiansson, M. (1995). Incurable psychopaths? *Bulletin of the American Academy of Psychiatry and the Law, 23,* 555–562.

Kroenke, K. & Spitzer, R. J. (1998). Gender differences in the reporting of physical and somatoform symptoms. *Psychosomatic Medicine, 60,* 150–155.

Kromhout, D., Menotti, A., Kesteloot, H., & Sans, S. (2002). Prevention of coronary heart disease by diet and lifestyle: Evidence from prospective cross-cultural, cohort, and intervention studies. *Circulation, 105,* 893–898.

Kubicki, M., Westin, C. F., Maier, S. E., Frumin, M., Nestor, P. G., Salisbury, D. F., Kikinis, R., Jolesz, F. A., McCarley, R. W., & Shenton, M. E. (2002). Uncinate fasciculus findings in schizophrehia: A magnetic resonance diffusion tensor imaging study. *American Journal of Psychiatry, 159,* 813–820.

Kubota, M., Nakazaki, S., Hirai, S., Saeki, N., Yamaura, A., & Kusaka, T. (2001). Alcohol consumption and frontal lobe shrinkage: Study of 1432 non-alcoholic subjects. *Journal of Neurology, Neurosurgery & Psychiatry, 71*(1), 104–106.

Kulka, R. A., Achlenger, W. E., Fairbank, J. A., Hough, R. L., Jordan, B. K., Marmar, C. R. & Weiss, D. S. (1990) *Trauma and the Vietnam War generation: Report of findings from the National Vietnam Veterans Readjustment Study.* Philadelphia: Brunner/Mazel.

Kulkarni, J. (1997). Women and schizophrenia: A review. *Australian and New Zealand Journal of Psychiatry, 31,* 46–56.

Kumanyika, S. (1987). Obesity in black women. *Epidemiological Review, 9,* 31–50.

Kunovac, J. L. & Stahl, S. M. (1995). Future directions in anxiolytic pharmacotherapy. *Psychiatric Clinics of North America, 18,* 895–909.

Kupfer, D. J. & Frank, E. (2001). The interaction of drug- and psychotherapy in the long-term treatment of depression. *Journal of Affective Disorders, 62,* 131–137.

Kupfer, D. J., Frank, E., Carpenter, L. L., Neiswanger, K. (1989). Family history in recurrent depression. *Journal of Affective Disorders, 17,* 113–119.

Kurtzke, J. F. (1980). Epidemiology of cerebrovascular disease. Cerebrovascular Survey Report for Joint Council Subcommittee on Cerebrovascular Disease. National Institute of Neurological and Communicative Disorders and Stroke and National Heart and Lung Institute. Rochester, MN: Whiting Press.

Lacks, P. & Morin, C. M. (1992). Recent advances in the assessment and treatment of insomnia. *Journal of Consulting and Clinical Psychology, 60,* 586–594.

La Fond, J. Q. (1996). The impact of law on the delivery of involuntary mental health services. In B. D. Sales & D. W. Shuman (Eds.). *Law, mental health, and mental disorder* (pp. 219–239). New York: Brooks/Cole.

La Fond, J. Q. (2000). The future of involuntary civil commitment in the U.S.A. after *Kansas v. Hendricks. Behavioral Sciences and the Law, 18,* 153–167.

La Fond, J. Q. & Durham, M. L. (1992). *Back to the asylum.* New York: Oxford University Press.

La Greca, A. M. & Fetter, M. (1995). Peer relations. In A. R. Eisen, C. A. Kearney, & C. E. Schaefer (Eds.), *Clinical handbook of anxiety disorders in children and adolescents.* Northvale, NJ: Aronson.

Lambert, G., Johansson, M., Agren, H., & Friberg, P. (2000). Reduced brain norepinephrine and dopamine release in treatment-refractory depressive illness. *Archives of General Psychiatry, 57,* 787–793.

Lampert, P. W. & Hardman, J. M. (1984). Morphological changes in brains of boxers. *Journal of the American Medical Association, 251,* 2676–2679.

Lang, P. J., Bradley, M. M., & Cuthbert, B. N. (1998). Emotion, motivation, and anxiety: Brain mechanisms and psychophysiology. *Biological Psychiatry, 44,* 1248–1263.

Langenbucher, J. W., Morgenstern, J., Labouvie, E., & Nathan, P. E. (1994). Lifetime *DSM-IV* diagnosis of alcohol, cannabis, cocaine and opiate dependence: Six month reliability in a multi-site clinical sample. *Addiction, 89,* 1115–1127.

LaPerriere, A., Klimas, N., Fletcher, M. A., Perry, A., Ironson, G., Perna, F., & Schneiderman, N. (1997). Change in CD4+ cell enumeration following aerobic exercise training in HIV-1 disease: Possible mechanisms and practical applications. *International Journal of Sports Medicine, 18*(Suppl. 1), S56–S61.

Lara, M. E. & Klein, D. N. (1999). Psychosocial processes underlying the maintenance and persistence of depression: Implications for understanding chronic depression. *Clinical Psychology Review, 19,* 553–570.

Lara, M. E., Leader, J., & Klein, D. N. (1997). The association between social support and course of depression: Is it confounded with personality? *Journal of Abnormal Psychology, 106,* 478–482.

Larimore, W. L., Parker, M., & Crowther, M. (2002). Should clinicians incorporate positive spirituality into their practices? What does the evidence say? *Annals of Behavioral Medicine, 24,* 69–73.

Larsson, B. & Melin, L. (1992). Prevalence and short-term stability of depressive symptoms in school children. *Acta Psychiatrica Scandinavica 85,* 17–22.

Lask, B. (2000). Aetiology. In B. Lask & R. Bryant-Waugh (Eds.), *Anorexia nervosa and related eating disorders in childhood and adolescence* (pp. 63–79). East Sussex, England: Psychology Press.

Latz, T. T., Kramer, S. I., & Hughes, D. L. (1995). Multiple personality disorder among female inpatients in a state hospital. *American Journal of Psychiatry, 152,* 1343–1348.

Laumann, E. O., Gagnon, J. H., Michael, R. T., & Michaels, S. (1994). *The social organization of sexuality: Sexual practices in the United States.* Chicago: University of Chicago Press.

Laumann, E. O., Paik, A., & Rosen, R. (1999). Sexual dysfunction in the United States: Prevalence and predictors. *The Journal of the American Medical Association, 281,* 537–544.

Lauriello, J., Bustillo, J., & Keith, S. J. (1999). A critical review of research on psychosocial treatment of schizophrenia. *Biological Psychiatry, 46,* 1409–1417.

Lawrie, S. M., Whalley, H. C., Abukmeil, S. S., Kestelman, J. N., Donnelly, L., Miller, P., Best, J. J., Owens, D. G., & Johnstone, E. C. (2001). Brain structure, genetic liability, and psychotic symptoms in subjects at high risk of developing schizophrenia. *Biological Psychiatry, 49,* 811–823.

Laws, D. R. & O'Donohue, W. (Eds.). (1997). *Sexual deviance: Theory, assessment, and treatment.* New York: Guilford Press.

Lawson, W. B. (1999). The art and science of ethnopharmacotherapy. In Herrera, J. M., Lawson, W., et al. (Eds.), *Cross cultural psychiatry* (pp. 67–73). Chichester, England: Wiley.

Lay, B., Blanz, B., Hartmann, M., & Schmidt, M. H. (2000). The psychosocial outcome of adolescent-onset schizophrenia: A 12-year followup. *Schizophrenia Bulletin, 26,* 801–816.

Lazarus, R. S. (1966). *Psychological stress and the coping process.* New York: McGraw-Hill.

Lazarus, R. S. (1980). The stress and coping paradigm. In C. Eisdorfer, D. Cohen, & A. Kleinman (Eds.), *Conceptual models for psychopathology.* New York: Spectrum.

Lazarus, R. S. & Folkman, S. (1984). *Stress, appraisal, and coping.* New York: Springer.

Lazarus, R. S., Kanner, A., & Folkman, S. (1980). Emotions: A cognitive-phenomenological approach. In R. Plutchik & H. Kellerman (Eds.), *Theories of emotion.* New York: Academic Press.

Leavitt, N. & Maykuth, P. L. (1989). Conformance to attorney performance standards: Advocacy behavior in a maximum security prison hospital. *Law and Human Behavior, 13,* 217–230.

Leblanc-Allman, R. J. (1998). Guilty but mentally ill: A poor prognosis. *South Carolina Law Review, 49,* 1095–1114.

LeDoux, J. (2000). Cognitive-emotional interactions: Listen to the brain. In R. D. Lane & L. Nadel (Eds.), *Cognitive neuroscience of emotion* (pp. 129–155). New York: Oxford University Press.

Lee, S. & Chiu, H. F. (1989). Anorexia nervosa in Hong Kong—Why not more in Chinese? *British Journal of Psychiatry, 154,* 683–688.

Lee, T. M., Blashko, C. A., Janzen, H. L., Paterson, J. G., & Chan, C. C. H. (1997). Pathophysiological mechanism of seasonal affective disorder. *Journal of Affective Disorders, 46,* 25–38.

Lehman, A. F., Steinwachs, D., and the Co-investigators of the PORT Project. (1998). At issue: Translating research into practice: The Schizophrenia Patient Outcomes Research Team (PORT) treatment recommendations. *Schizophrenia Bulletin, 24,* 1–10.

Leibenluft, E. (1996). Women with bipolar illness: Clinical and research issues. *American Journal of Psychiatry, 153,* 163–173.

Leibenluft, E. (2000). Women and bipolar disorder: An update. *Bulletin of the Menninger Clinic, 64,* 5–17.

Leibowitz, S. F. (1991). Brain neuropeptide Y: An integrator of endocrine, metabolic, and behavioral processes. *Brain Research Bulletin, 27,* 333–337.

Leigh, B. C. (1989). In search of the seven dwarves: Issues of measurement and meaning in alcohol expectancy research. *Psychological Bulletin, 105,* 361–373.

Lenox, R. H. & Hahn, C. G. (2000). Overview of the mechanism of action of lithium in the brain: Fifty-year update. *Journal of Clinical Psychiatry, 61*(Suppl. 9), 5–15.

Lensi, P., Cassano, G. B., Correddu, G., Ravagli, S., Kunovac, J. L., & Akiskal, H. S. (1996). Familial-developmental history, symptomatology, comorbidity, and course with special reference to gender-related differences. *British Journal of Psychiatry, 169,* 101–107.

Lenzenweger, M. F. (2001). Reaction time slowing during high-load, sustained-attention task performace in relation to psychometrically identified schizotypy. *Journal of Abnormal Psychology, 110,* 290–296.

Lenzenweger, M. F., Dworkin, R. H., & Wethington, E. (1989). Models of positive and negative symptoms in schizophrenia: An empirical evaluation of latent structures. *Journal of Abnormal Psychology, 98,* 62–70.

Lenzenweger, M. F. & Loranger, A. W. (1989). Detection of familial schizophrenia using a psychometric measure of schizotypy. *Archives of General Psychiatry, 46,* 902–907.

Leocani, L., Locatelli, M., Bellodi, L., Fornara, C., Henin, M., Magnani, G., Mennea, S., & Comi, G. (2001). Abnormal pattern of cortical activation associated with voluntary movement in obsessive-compulsive disorder: An EEG study. *American Journal of Psychiatry, 158,* 140–142.

Leon, A. C., Keller, M. B., Warshaw, M. G., Mueller, T. I., Solomon, D. A., Coryell, W., & Endicott, J. (1999). Prospective study of fluoxetine treatment and suicidal behavior in affectively ill subjects. *American Journal of Psychiatry, 156,* 195–201.

Lerner, H. D. & Ehrlich, J. (2001). Psychoanalytic model. In M. Hersen & V. B. Van Hasselt (Eds.), *Advanced abnormal psychology* (2nd ed., pp. 65–92). New York: Kluwer Academic/Plenum.

Lerner-Wren, G. & Appel, A. R. (2001). A court for the nonviolent defendant with a mental disability. *Psychiatric Annals, 31,* 453–458.

LeShan, L. (1966). An emotional life-history pattern associated with neoplastic disease. *Annals of New York Academy of Sciences, 125,* 780–793.

Leshner, A. I. (1999). Science-based views of drug addiction and its treatment. *Journal of the American Medical Association, 282*(14), 1314–1316.

Lesier, H. R. & Rosenthal, R. J. (1991). Pathological gambling: A review of the literature. *Journal of Gambling Studies, 7,* 5–39.

Lesperance, F., Frasure-Smith, N., Talajic, M., & Bourassa, M. G. (2002). Five-year risk of cardiac mortality in relation to initial severity and one-year changes in depression symptoms after myocardial infarction. *Circulation, 105,* 1049–1053.

Lester, D. (1994). Access to gambling opportunities and compulsive gambling. *The International Journal of the Addictions, 29,* 1611–1616.

Levenson, R. W., Oyama, O. N., & Meek, P. S. (1987). Greater reinforcement from alcohol for those at risk: Parental risk, personality risk, and sex. *Journal of Abnormal Psychology, 96,* 242–253.

Levine, J., Estrad, C. R., & Morgenthaler, A. (2001). Mechanical reliability and safety of, and patient satisfaction with, the AMBICOR Inflatable Penile Prosthesis. Results of a 2 center study. *Journal of Urology, 166,* 932–937.

Levine, S., Haltmeyer, G. C., Kaas, G. G., & Penenberg, V. H. (1967). Physiological and behavioral effects of infantile stimulation. *Physiology & Behavior, 2,* 55–63.

Levis, D. J. (1985). Implosive theory: A comprehensive extension of conditioning theory of fear/anxiety to psychology. In S. Reiss & R. R. Bootzin (Eds.), *Theoretical issues in behavior therapy.* New York: Academic Press.

Levitan, R. D., Lesage, A., Parikh, S.V., Goering, P., & Kennedy, S. H. (1997). Reversed neurovegetative symptoms of depression: A community study of Ontario. *American Journal of Psychiatry, 154,* 934–940.

Levy, D., Kimhi, R., Barak, Y., Demmer, M., Harel, M., & Elizur, A. (1996). Brainstem auditory evoked potentials of panic disorder patients. *Neuropsychobiology, 33,* 164–167.

Levy, D. L., Holzman, P. S., Matthysse, S., & Mendell, N. R. (1993). Eye tracking dysfunction and schizophrenia: A critical perspective. *Schizophrenia Bulletin, 19,* 461–536.

Levy, R. & Mushin, J. (1973). The somatosensory evoked response in patients with hysterical anaesthesia. *Journal of Psychosomatic Research, 17,* 81–84.

Lewinsohn, P. M. (1974). Clinical and theoretical aspects of depression. In K. S. Calhoun, H. E. Adams, & K. M. Mitchell (Eds.), *Innovative treatment methods of psychopathology.* New York: Wiley.

Lewinsohn, P. M., Allen, N. B., Seeley, J. R., & Gotlib, I. H. (1999). First onset versus recurrence of depression: Differential processes of psychosocial risk. *Journal of Abnormal Psychology, 108,* 483–489.

Lewinsohn, P. M. & Gotlib, I. H. (1995). Behavioral theory and treatment of depression. In E. E. Becker & W. R. Leber (Eds.), *Handbook of depression* (pp. 352–375). New York: Guilford Press.

Lewinsohn, P. M., Gotlib, I. H., & Hautzinger, M. (1998). Behavioral treatment of unipolar depression. In V. E. Caballo (Ed.), *International handbook of cognitive and behavioural treatments for psychological disorders* (pp. 441–488). Oxford: Pergamon/Elsevier Science.

Lewinsohn, P. M., Hoberman, H. M., & Rosenbaum, M. (1988). A prospective study of risk factors for unipolar depression. *Journal of Abnormal Psychology, 97,* 251–264.

Lewinsohn, P. M., Hoberman, H., Teri, L., & Hautzinger, M. (1985). An integrative theory of depression. In S. Reiss & R. R. Bootzin (Eds.), *Theoretical issues in behavior therapy* (pp. 331–359). New York: Academic Press.

Lewinsohn, P. M., Hops, H., Roberts, R. E., Seely, J. R., & Andrews, J. A. (1993). Adolescent psychopathology: I. Prevalence and incidence of depression and other *DSM-III-R* disorders in high school students. *Journal of Abnormal Psychology, 102,* 133–144.

Lewinsohn, P. M., Joiner, T. E., Jr., & Rohde, P. (2001). Evaluation of cognitive diathesis-stress models in predicting major depressive disorder in adolescents. *Journal of Abnormal Psychology, 110,* 203–215.

Lewinsohn, P. M., Roberts, R. E., Seeley, J. R., Rohde, P., Gotlib, I. H., & Hops, H. (1994). Adolescent psychopathology: II. Psychosocial risk factors for depression. *Journal of Abnormal Psychology, 103,* 302–315.

Lewinsohn, P. M., Rohde, P., Seeley, J. R., & Baldwin, C. L. (2001). Gender differences in suicide attempts from adolescence to adulthood. *Journal of the American Academy of Child and Adolescent Psychiatry, 40,* 427–434.

Lewinsohn, P. M., Rohde, P., Seeley, J. R., & Fischer, S. A. (1993). Age-cohort changes in the lifetime occurrence of depression and other mental disorders. *Journal of Abnormal Psychology, 102,* 110–120.

Lewinsohn, P. M., Rohde, P., Seeley, J. R., & Hops, H. (1991). Comorbidity of unipolar depression: I. Major depression with dysthymia. *Journal of Abnormal Psychology, 100,* 205–213.

Lewinsohn, P. M., Rohde, P., Seeley, J. R., Klein, D. N., & Gotlib, I. H. (2000). Natural course of adolescent major depressive disorder in a community sample: Predictors of recurrence in young adults. *American Journal of Psychiatry, 157,* 1584–1591.

Lewinsohn, P. M., Solomon, A., Seeley, J. R., & Zeiss, A. (2000). Clinical implications of "subthreshold" depressive symptoms. *Journal of Abnormal Psychology, 109,* 345–351.

Lewinsohn, P. M., Sullivan, J. M., & Grosscup, S. J. (1980). Changing reinforcing events: An approach to the treatment of depression. *Psychotherapy: Theory, Research, and Practice, 17,* 322–334.

Lewy, A. J., Bauer, V. K., Cutler, N. L., Sack, R. L., Ahmed, S., Thomas, K. H., Blood, M. L., & Latham Jackson, J. M. (1998). Morning vs. evening light treatment of patients with winter depression. *Archives of General Psychiatry, 55,* 890–896.

Lichtenstein, E. & Glasgow, R. E. (1992). Smoking cessation: What have we learned over the past decade? *Journal of Consulting and Clinical Psychology, 60,* 518–527.

Lidbeck, J. (1997). Group therapy for somatization disorders in general practice: Effectiveness of a short cognitive-behavioural treatment model. *Acta Psychiatrica Scandinavica, 96,* 14–24.

Lidz, C. W., Mulvey, E. P., & Gardner, W. (1993). The accuracy of predictions of violence to others. *Journal of the American Medical Association, 269,* 1007–1111.

Lidz, C. W., Mulvey, E. P., Hoge, S. K., Kirsch, B. L., Monahan, J., Eisenberg, M., Gardner, W., & Roth, L. H. (1998). Factual sources of psychiatric patients' perceptions of coercion in the hospital admission process. *American Journal of Psychiatry, 155,* 1254–1260.

Liebenluft, E. & Wehr, T. A. (1992). Is sleep deprivation useful in the treatment of depression? *American Journal of Psychiatry, 149,* 159–168.

Lieberman, J. A. & Koreen, A. R. (1993). Neurochemistry and neuroendocrinology of schizophrenia: A selective review. *Schizophrenia Bulletin, 19,* 371–429.

Lieberman, R. P., Wallace, C. J., Blackwell, G., Kopelowicz, A., Vaccaro, J. V., & Mintz, J. (1998). Skills training versus psychosocial occupational therapy for persons with persistent schizophrenia. *American Journal of Psychiatry, 155,* 1087–1091.

Liebowitz, M. R. (1992). Diagnostic issues in anxiety disorders. In A. Tasman & M. B. Riba (Eds.), *Review of psychiatry* (Vol. 11, pp. 247–259). Washington, DC: American Psychiatric Press.

Liebowitz, M. R., Heimberg, R. G., Scheier, F. R., et al. (1998). Congnitive-behavioral group therapy versus phenelzine in social phobia: Long term outcome. *Depression and Anxiety, 10,* 89–98.

Light, K. C., Girdler, S. S., Sherwood, A., Bragdon, E. E., Brownley, K. A., West, S. G., & Hinderliter, A. L. (1999). High stress responsivity predicts later blood pressure only in combination with positive family history and high life stress. *Hypertension, 33,* 1458–1464.

Liguori, A., Gatto, C. P., & Robinson, J. H. (1998). Effects of marijuana on equilibrium, psychomotor performance, and simulated driving. *Behavioural Pharmacology, 9,* 599–609.

Lilenfield, L. R., Kaye, W. H., Greeno, C. G., Merikangas, K. R., Plotnicov, K., Pollice, C., Rao, R., Strober, M., Bulik, C. M., & Naggy, L. (1998). A controlled family study of anorexia nervosa and bulimia nervosa: Psychiatric disorders in first-degree relatives and effects of proband cobmorbidity. *Archives of General Psychiatry, 66,* 603–610.

Lilienfeld, S. O. (1992). The association between antisocial personality and somatization disorders: A review and integration of theoretical models. *Clinical Psychology Review, 12,* 641–662.

Lilienfeld, S. O., Lynn, S. J., Kirsch, I., Chaves, J. F., Sarbin, T. R., Ganaway, G. K., & Powell, R. A. (1999). Dissociative identity disorder and the sociocognitive model: Recalling the lessons of the past. *Psychological Bulletin, 125,* 507–523.

Lilienfeld, S. O., Wood, J. M., & Garb, H. N. (2000). The scientific status of projective techniques. *Psychological Science in the Public Interest, 1,* 27–66.

Lim, K. O., Tew, W., Kushner, M., Chow, K., Matsumoto, B., & DeLisi, L. E. (1996). Cortical gray matter volume deficit in patients with first-episode schizophrenia. *American Journal of Psychiatry, 153,* 1548–1553.

Limpert, C. & Amador, X. F. (2001). Negative symptoms and the experience of emotion. In R. S. E. Keefe & J. P. McEvoy (Eds.), *Negative symptom and cognitive deficit treatment response in schizophrenia* (pp. 111–137). Washington, DC: American Psychiatric Press.

Lin, K. M. & Lin, M. T. (2001). Ethnic issues in schizophrenia. In A. Breier, P. V. Tran, F. Bymaster, & C. Tollefson (Eds.), *Current issues in the psychopharmacology of schizophrenia* (pp. 459–469). Philadelphia: Lippincott Williams & Wilkins.

Linden, W., Stossel C., & Maurice, J. (1996). Psychosocial interventions for patients with coronary artery disease: A meta-analysis. *Archives of Internal Medicine, 156,* 745–752.

Lindsay, K. A., Sankis, L. M., & Widiger, T. A. (2000). Gender bias in self-report personality disorder inventories. *Journal of Personality Disorders 14,* 218–232.

Linehan, M. M. (1987). Dialectical behavior therapy for borderline personality disorder. *Bulletin of the Menninger Clinic, 41*(3), 261–276.

Linehan, M. M. (1992). Behavior therapy, dialectics, and the treatment of borderline personality disorder. In D. Silver, M. Rosenbluth, et al. (Eds.), *Handbook of borderline disorders* (pp. 415–434). Madison, WI: International Universities Press.

Linehan, M. M. (1993). *Cognitive-behavioral treatment of borderline personality disorder.* New York: Guilford Press.

Linehan, M. M., Heard, H. L., & Armstrong, H. E. (1993). Naturalistic follow-up of a behavioral treatment for chronically parasuicidal borderline patients. *Archives of General Psychiatry, 50,* 971–974.

Linehan, M. M., Schmidt, H., III, Dimeff, L. A., Craft, J., Christopher, K. J., & Comtois, K. A. (1999). Dialectical behavior therapy for patients with borderline personality disorder and drug-dependency. *American Journal on Addictions, 8,* 279–292.

Linhorst, D. M. (1999). The unconditional release of mentally ill offenders from indefinite commitment: A study of Missouri insanity acquittees. *Journal of the American Academy of Psychiatry and the Law, 27,* 563–579.

Linszen, D. H., Dingemans, P. M., Nugter, M. A., Van der Does, A. J. W., Scholte, W. F., & Lenior, M. A. (1997). Patient attributes and expressed emotion as risk factors for psychotic relapse. *Schizophrenia Bulletin, 23,* 119–130.

Lipowsky, Z. J. (1989). Delirium in the elderly patient. *New England Journal of Medicine, 320,* 578–582.

Lisanby, S. H., Maddox, J. H., Prudic, J., Devanand, D. P., & Sackeim, H. A. (2000). The effects of electroconvulsive therapy on memory of autobiographical and public events. *Archives of General Psychiatry, 57,* 581–590.

Littlewood, R. & Lipsedge, M. (1986). The 'culture-bound syndromes' of the dominant culture: Culture, psychopathology, and biomedicine. In J. L. Cox (Ed.), *Transcultural psychiatry* (pp. 253–273). London: Croom-Helm.

Litwack, T. R. (2001). Actuarial versus clinical assessments of dangerousness. *Psychology, Public Policy, and Law, 7,* 409–443.

Livermore, J. M., Malmquist, C. P., & Meehl, P. E. (1968). On the justifications for civil commitment. *University of Pennsylvania Law Review, 117,* 75–96.

Livermore, J. M. & Meehl, P. E. (1967). The virtues of M'Naghten. *Minnesota Law Review, 51,* 789–856.

Livesley, W. J. (Ed.). (2001). *Handbook of personality disorders: Theory, research, and treatment.* New York: Guilford Press.

Lizardi, H., Klein, D. N., Ouimette, P. C., Riso, L. P., Anderson, R. L., & Donaldson, S. K. (1995). Reports of the childhood home environment in early-onset dysthymia and episodic major depression. *Journal of Abnormal Psychology, 104,* 132–139.

Lloyd, J. W., Hallahan, D. P., Kauffman, J. M., & Keller, C. E. (1991). Academic problems. In R. J. Morris & T. R. Kratochwill (Eds.), *The practice of child therapy* (2nd ed.). Elsmford, NY: Pergamon Press.

Lochman, J. E., Coie, J. D., Underwood, M. K., & Terry, R. (1993). Effectiveness of a social relations intervention program for aggressive and nonaggressive, rejected children. *Journal of Consulting and Clinical Psychology, 61,* 1053–1058.

Lockwood, R. (1994). The psychology of animal collectors. *Trends, 9,* 18–21.

Loeber, R. & Farrington, D. P. (2000). Young children who commit crime: Epidemiology, developmental origins, risk factors, early interventions, and policy implications. *Development and Psychopathology, 12,* 737–762.

Loeber, R., Green, S. M., Keenan, K., & Lahey, B. B. (1995). Which boys will fare worse? Early predictors of the onset of conduct disorder in a six-year longitudinal study. *Journal of the American Academy of Child and Adolescent Psychiatry, 34,* 499–509.

Loewenstein, R. J. (1991). Psychogenic amnesia and psychogenic fugue: A comprehensive review. *Annual Review of Psychiatry, 10,* 223–247.

Loewenstein, R. J. (1994). Diagnosis, epidemiology, clinical course, treatment, and cost effectiveness of treatment for dissociative disorders and MPD: Report submitted to the Clinton administration Task Force on Health Care Financing Reform. *Dissociation, 7,* 3–11.

Loewenstein, R. J., & Ross, D. R. (1992). Multiple personality and psychoanalysis: An introduction. *Psychoanalytic Inquiry, 12,* 3–48.

Loftus, E. F. (1993). The reality of repressed memories. *American Psychologist, 48,* 518–537.

Loftus, E. F., Feldman, J., & Dashiell, R. (1995). The reality of illusory memories. In D. L. Schacter (Ed.), *Memory distortions: How minds, brains, and societies reconstruct the past* (pp. 47–68). Cambridge, MA: Harvard University Press.

Loftus, J., DeLisi, L. E., & Crow, T. J. (1998). Familial associations of subsyndromes of psychosis in affected sibling pairs with schizophrenia and schizoaffective disorder. *Psychiatry Research, 80,* 101–111.

Lohr, J. M., Lilienfeld, S. O., Tolin, D. F., & Herbert, J. D. (1999). Eye movement desensitization and reprocessing: An analysis of specific versus nonspecific treatment factors. *Journal of Anxiety Disorders, 13,* 185–207.

Lopez, S. R. & Hernandez, P. (1986). How culture is considered in evaluations of psychopathology. *Journal of Nervous and Mental Disease, 176,* 598–606.

Lopez, S. R., Nelson, K. A., Snyder, K. S., & Mintz, J. (1999). Attributions and affective reactions of family members and course of schizophrenia. *Journal of Abnormal Psychology, 108,* 307–314.

LoPiccolo, J. (1985). Diagnosis and treatment of male sexual dysfunction. *Journal of Sex & Marital Therapy, 11*(4), 215–232.

LoPiccolo, J. (1992). Post-modern sex therapy for erectile failure. In R. C. Rosen & S. R. Leiblum (Eds.), *Erectile failure: Assessment and treatment.* New York: Guilford Press.

LoPiccolo, J. & Lobitz, W. C. (1973). Behavior therapy of sexual dysfunction. In L. A. Hammerlynck, L. C. Handy, & E. J. Mash (Eds.), *Behavior change: Methodology, concepts, and practice.* Champaign, IL: Research Press.

LoPiccolo, J. & Stock, W. E. (1986). Treatment of sexual dysfunction. *Journal of Consulting and Clinical Psychology, 54,* 158–167.

Lovaas, O. I. & Buch, G. (1997). Intensive behavioral intervention with young children with autism. In N. N. Singh (Ed.), *Prevention and treatment of severe behavior problems: Models and methods in developmental disabilities* (pp. 61–76). Pacific Grove, CA: Brooks/Cole.

Lovestone, S., Anderton, B., Betts, J., Dayanandan, R., Gibb, G., Ljungberg, C., & Pearce, J. (2001). Apolipoprotein E gene and Alzheimer's disease: Is tau the link? *Biochemical Society Symposia, 67,* 111–120.

Lowing, P. A., Mirsky, A. F., Pereira, R. (1983). The inheritance of schizophrenia spectrum disorders: A reanalysis of the Danish adoptee study data. *American Journal of Psychiatry, 140,* 1167–1171.

Lowry-Webster, H. M. & Barrett, P. M. (2001). A universal prevention trial of anxiety and depressive disorders in childhood: Preliminary data from an Australian study. *Behaviour Change, 18,* 36–50.

Luborsky, L. (1984). *Principles of psychoanalytic psychotherapy.* New York: Basic Books.

Luborsky, L. & Crits-Christoph, P. (1998). *Understanding transference: The CCRT method* (2nd ed.). Washington, DC: American Psychological Association.

Luborsky, L., Crits-Christoph, P., & Barber, J. (1991). University of Pennsylvania: The Penn Psychotherapy Research Projects. In L. E. Beutler & M. Crago (Eds.). *Psychotherapy research: An international review of programmatic studies* (pp. 133–141). Washington, DC: American Psychological Association.

Lucas, A. R., Beard, C. M., O'Fallon, W. M., & Kurlan, L. T. (1991). Fifty year trends in the incidence of anorexia nervosa in Rochester, Minnesota: A population-based study. *American Journal of Psychiatry, 148,* 917–922.

Luchins, A. S. (1993). Social control doctrines of mental illness and the medical profession in nineteenth-century America. *Journal of the History of the Behavioral Sciences, 29,* 29–47.

Ludwig, A. M. (1986). *Principles of clinical psychiatry.* New York: Free Press.

Luepnitz, R. R., Randolph, D. L., & Gutsch, K. W. (1982). Race and socioeconomic status as confounding variables in the accurate diagnosis of alcoholism. *Journal of Clinical Psychology, 38,* 665–669.

Luh, K. E. & Gooding, D. C. (1999). Perceptual biases in psychosis-prone individuals. *Journal of Abnormal Psychology, 108,* 283–289.

Luisada, P. V. (1977, August). *The PCP psychosis: A hidden epidemic.* Paper presented at the Sixth World Congress of Psychiatry, Honolulu, HI.

Lunetta, P., Penttilae, A., & Sarna, S. (2001). The role of alcohol in accidents and violent deaths in Finland. *Alcoholism: Clinical and Experimental Research, 25,* 1654–1661.

Lussier, I. & Stip, E. (2001). Memory and attention deficits in drug naive patients with schizophrenia. *Schizophrenia Research, 48,* 45–55.

Lydiard, L. R., Brawman, M. O., & Ballenger, J. C. (1996). Recent developments in the psychopharmacology of anxiety disorders. *Journal of Consulting and Clinical Psychology, 64,* 660–668.

Lykken, D. T. (1995). *The antisocial personalities.* Hillsdale, NJ: Erlbaum.

Lymburner, J. A. & Roesch, R. (1999). The insanity defense: Five years of research (1993–1997). *International Journal of Law and Psychiatry, 22,* 213–240.

Lynch, J. J. (1977). *The broken heart: The medical consequence of loneliness.* New York: Basic Books.

Lynch, P. S., Kellow, J. T., & Willson, V. L. (1997). The impact of deinstitutionalization on the adaptive behavior of adults with mental retardation: A research synthesis. *Education and Training in Mental Retardation and Developmental Disabilities, 32,* 255–261.

Lyon, G. R. (1996). Learning Disabilities. In E. J. Mash & R. A. Barkley (Eds.), *Child psychopathology* (pp. 390–435). New York: Guilford Press.

Lyon, H. M., Startup, M., & Bentall, R. P. (1999). Social cognition and the manic defense: Attributions, selective attention, and self-schema in bipolar affective disorder. *Journal of Abnormal Psychology, 108,* 273–282.

Lyon, L. S. (1985). Facilitating telephone number recall in a case of psychogenic amnesia. *Journal of Behaviour Therapy and Experimental Psychiatry, 16,* 147–149.

Lytton, H. & Romney, D. (1991). Parents' differential socialization of boys and girls: A meta-analysis. *Psychological Bulletin, 109,* 267–296.

Ma, G. X. & Shive, S. (2000). A comparative analysis of perceived risks and substance abuse among ethnic groups. *Addictive Behaviors, 25,* 361–371.

MacDonald, J. (1967). Homicidal threats. *American Journal of Psychiatry, 124,* 475.

MacFarlane, K. (1978). Sexual abuse of children. In J. R. Chapman & M. Gates (Eds.), *The victimization of women* (pp. 81–109). Beverly Hills, CA: Sage.

Mack, A. H., Forman, L., Brown, R., & Frances, A. (1994). A brief history of psychiatric classification: From the ancients to *DSM-IV. Psychiatric Clinics of North America, 17,* 515–523.

MacMahon, S., Peto, R., Cutter, J., Collins, R., Sorlie, P., Neaton, J., Abbott, R., Godwin, J., Dyer, A., & Stamler, J. (1990). Blood pressure, stroke, and coronary heart disease. *Lancet, 335,* 765–774.

MacMillan, H. L., Fleming, J. E., Trocme, N., Boyle, M. H., Wong, M., Racine, Y. A., Beardslee, R., & Offord, D. R. (1997). Prevalence of child physical and sexual abuse in the community—Results from the Ontario Health Supplement. *Journal of the American Medical Association, 278*(2), 131–135.

Macpherson, A. K. & Parkin, P. C. (2001). Mandatory helmet legislation and children's exposure to cycling. *Injury Prevention, 7*(3), 228–231.

Madden P. A. F., Heath, A. C., Rosenthal, N. E., & Martin, N. G. (1996). Seasonal changes in mood and behavior: The role of genetic factors. *Archives of General Psychiatry, 53,* 47–55.

Maddux, J. E. & Mundell, C. E. (1999). Disorders of personality: Diseases or individual differences. In V. J. Derlega, B. A. Winstead, et al. (Eds.), *Personality: Contemporary theory and research* (2nd ed., pp. 541–571). Chicago: Nelson-Hall.

Madge, N. & Harvey, J. G. (1999). Suicide among the young—the size of the problem. *Journal of Adolescence, 22,* 145–155.

Maes, M. (1995). Evidence for an immune response in major depression: A review and hypothesis. *Progress in Neuro-Psychopharmacology & Biological Psychiatry, 19,* 11–38.

Maes, M. (2001). Pedophilia: A biological disorder? *Current Opinion in Psychiatry, 14,* 571–573.

Maes, M., De Vos, N., Van Hunsel, F., Van West, D., Westenberg, H., Cosyns, P., & Neels, H. (2001). Pedophilia is accompanied by increased plasma concentrations of catecholamines, in particular, epinephrine. *Psychiatry Research, 103,* 43–49.

Magee, W. J., Eaton, W. W., Wittchen, H. U., McGonoagle, K. A., & Kessler, R. C. (1996). Agoraphobia, simple phobia, and social phobia in the National Comorbidity Survey. *Archives of General Psychiatry, 53,* 159–168.

Maher, B. A. (2001). Delusions. In P. B. Sutker & H. E. Adams (Eds.), *Comprehensive handbook of psychopathology* (3rd ed., pp. 309–340). New York: Kluwer Academic/Plenum.

Maher, B. A. & Deldin, P. J. (2001). Schizophrenias: Biopsychological aspects. In P. B. Sutker & H. E. Adams (Eds.), *Comprehensive handbook of psychopathology* (3rd ed., pp. 341–370). New York: Kluwer Academic/Plenum.

Maher, B. A. & Spitzer, M. (1993). Delusions. In P. B. Sutker & H. E. Adams (Eds.), *Comprehensive handbook of psychopathology* (2nd ed., pp. 263–293). New York: Plenum Press.

Maher, W. B. & Maher, B. A. (1985). Psychopathology: I. From ancient times to the eighteenth century. In G. A. Kimble & K. Schlesinger (Eds.), *Topics in the history of psychology* (Vol. 2). Hillsdale, NJ: Erlbaum.

Mahoney, M. J. (1991). *Human change process: The scientific foundations of psychotherapy.* New York: Basic Books.

Mahoney, M. J. (1995). The psychological demands of being a constructivist psychotherapist. In R. A. Neimeyer & M. J. Mahoney (Eds.), *Construc-*

tivism in psychotherapy (pp. 385–399). Washington, DC: American Psychological Association.

Maidenberg, E., Chen, E., Craske, M., Bohn, P., & Bystritsky, A. (1996). Specificity of attentional bias in panic disorder and social phobia. *Journal of Anxiety Disorders, 10,* 529–541.

Maier, S. F., Seligman, M. E. P., & Solomon, R. L. (1969). Pavlovian fear conditioning and learned helplessness. In B. A. Campbell & R. M. Church (Eds.), *Punishment.* New York: Appleton.

Maier, W., Lichtermann, D., Minges, J., & Heun, R. (1994). Personality disorders among the relatives of schizophrenia patients. *Schizophrenia Bulletin, 20,* 481–493.

Malamuth, N. M., Heavey, C. L., & Linz, D. (1993). Predicting men's antisocial behavior against women: The interaction model of sexual aggression. In C. C. Nagayama Hall, R. Hirschman, J. Graham, & M. Zaragoza (Eds.), *Sexual aggression: Issues and etiology, assessment and treatment (pp. 63–97).* Washington, DC: Taylor Francis.

Malamuth, N. M., Linz, D., Heavey, C. L., Barnes, G., et al. (1995). Using the confluence model of sexual aggression to predict men's conflict with women: A 10-year follow-up study. *Journal of Personality and Social Psychology, 69,* 353–369.

Malaspina, D., Harlap, S., Fennig, S., Heiman, D., Nahon, D., Feldman, D., & Susser, E. S. (2001). Advancing paternal age and the risk of schizophrenia. *Archives of General Psychiatry, 58,* 361–367.

Maldonado, J. R. & Spiegel, D. (2001). Conversion disorder. In K. A. Phillips (Ed.), *Somatoform and factitious disorders* (pp. 67–94). Washington, DC: American Psychiatric Press.

Malec, J. F. & Basford, J. S. (1996). Postacute brain injury rehabilitation. *Archives of Physical Medicine and Rehabilitation, 77,* 198–207.

Malgady, R. G. & Costantino, G. (1998). Symptom severity in bilingual Hispanics as a function of clinician ethnicity and language of interview. *Psychological Assessment, 10,* 120–127.

Malkoff-Schwartz, S., Frank, E., Anderson, B. P., Hlastala, S. A., Luther, J. F., Sherrill, J. T., et al. (2000). Social rhythm disruption and stressful life events in the onset of bipolar and unipolar episodes. *Psychological Medicine, 30,* 1005–1016.

Malkoff-Schwartz, S., Frank, E., Anderson, B., Sherrill, J. T., Siegel, L., Patterson, D., & Kupfer, D. J. (1998). Stressful life events and social rhythm disruption in the onset of manic and depressive bipolar episodes. *Archives of General Psychiatry, 55,* 702–707.

Malmberg, A., Lewis, G., David, A., & Allebeck, P. (1998). Premorbid adjustment and personality in people with schizophrenia. *British Journal of Psychiatry, 172,* 308–313.

Malmo, R. B. & Shagass, C. (1949). Physiologic study of symptom mechanisms in psychiatric patients under stress. *Psychosomatic Medicine, 11,* 25–29.

Mann, J. J., Huang, Y., Underwood, M. D., Kassir, S. A., Oppenheim, S., Kelly, T. M., Dwork, A. J., & Arango, V. (2000). A serotonin transporter gene promoter polymorphism (5-HTTLPR) and prefrontal cortical binding in major depression and suicide. *Archives of General Psychiatry, 57,* 729–738.

Mann, J. J. & Kapur, S. (1994). Elucidation of biochemical basis of the antidepressant action of electroconvulsive therapy by human studies, *Psychopharmacology Bulletin, 30,* 445–453.

Mann, J. J., Malone, K. M., Diehl, D. J., Perel, J., Cooper, T. B., & Mintun, M. A. (1996). Demonstration in vivo of reduced serotonin responsivity in the brain of untreated depressed patients. *American Journal of Psychiatry, 153,* 174–182.

Mann, J. J., McBride, A., Brown, R. P., Linnoila, M., Leon, A. C., DeMeo, M., Mieczkowski, T., Myers, J. E., & Stanley, M. (1992). Relationship between central and peripheral serotonin indexes in depressed and suicidal psychiatric inpatients. *Archives of General Psychiatry, 49,* 442–446.

Mann, K., Klingler, T., Noe, S., Roeschke, J., et al. (1996). Effects of yohimbine on sexual experiences and nocturnal penile tumescence and rigidity in erectile dysfunction. *Archives of Sexual Behavior, 25*(1), 1–16.

Manschreck, T. C. (1992). Delusional disorders: Clinical concepts and diagnostic strategies. *Psychiatric Annals, 22,* 241–251.

Mansueto, C. S., Stemberger, R. M. T., Thomas A. M., & Golomb, R. G. (1997). Trichotillomania: A comprehensive behavioral model. *Clinical Psychology Review, 17,* 567–577.

Manuck, S. B., Marsland, A. L., Kaplan, J. R., & Williams, J. K. (1995). The pathogenicity of behavior and its neuroendocrine mediation: An example from coronary artery disease. *Psychosomatic Medicine, 57,* 275–283.

Marcos, L. R., Alpert, M., Urcuyo, L., & Kesselman, M. (1973). The language barrier in evaluating Spanish-American patients. *Archives of General Psychiatry, 29,* 655–659.

Marcotte, T. D., Grant, I., Atkinson, J. H., & Heaton R. K. (2001). Neurobehavioral complications of HIV infection. In R. E. Tartar, M. Butters, & S. R. Beers (Eds.) *Medical neuropsychology* (2nd ed. pp. 285–331). New York: Kluwer Academic/Plenum.

Marder, S. R., Wirshing, W. C., Mintz, J., McKenzie, J., Johnston, K., Eckman, T. A., Lebell, M., Zimmerman, K., & Liberman, R. P. (1996). Two-year outcome of social skills training and group psychotherapy for outpatients with schizophrenia. *American Journal of Psychiatry, 153,* 1585–1592.

Margolese, H. C. & Assalian, P. (1996). Sexual side effects of anti- depressants: A review. *Journal of Sex & Marital Therapy, 22,* 209–218.

Maris, R. W. (1992). The relation of nonfatal suicide attempts to completed suicides. In R. W. Maris, A. L. Berman, J. T. Maltsberger, & R. I. Yufit (Eds.), *Assessment and prediction of suicide* (pp. 362–380). New York: Guildford Press.

Marlatt, G. A., Curry, S., & Gordon, J. R. (1988). A longitudinal analysis of unaided smoking cessation. *Journal of Consulting and Clinical Psychology, 56,* 715–720.

Marlatt, G. A. & Gordon, J. R. (1985). *Relapse prevention: Maintenance strategies in addictive behavior change.* New York: Guilford Press.

Marmot, M. G., Bosma, H., Memingway, H., Brunner, E., & Stansfeld, S. (1997). Contribution of job control and other risk factors to social variations in coronary heart disease incidence. *Lancet, 350,* 235–239.

Marrazzi, M. A. & Luby, E. D. (1986). An autoaddiction model of chronic anorexia nervosa. *International Journal of Eating Disorders, 5,* 191–208.

Marsh, L., Harris, D., Lim, K. O., Beal, M., Hoff, A. L., Minn, K., Csernansky, J. G., DeMent, S., Faustman, W. O., Sullivan, E. V., & Pfefferbaum, A. (1997). Structural magnetic resonance imaging abnormalities in men with severe chronic schizophrenia and an early age at clinical onset. *Archives of General Psychiatry, 54,* 1104–1112.

Marshall, D. S. (1971). Sexual behavior on Mangaia. In D. S. Marshall &

R. C. Suggs (Eds.), *Human sexual behavior.* New York: Basic Books.

Marshall, W. L. (1997). Pedophilia: Psychopathology and theory. In D. R. Laws & W. O'Donahue (Eds.), *Sexual deviance: Theory, assessment, and treatment* (pp. 152–174). New York: Guilford Press.

Marshall, W. L. & Hambley, L. S. (1996). Intimacy and loneliness, and their relationship to rape myth acceptance and hostility toward women among rapists. *Journal of Interpersonal Violence, 11,* 586–592.

Marshall, W. L., Hudson, S. M., Jones, R., & Fernandez, Y. M. (1995). Empathy in sex offenders. *Clinical Psychology Review, 15,* 99–113.

Marshall, W. L. & Pithers, W. D. (1994). A reconsideration of treatment outcome with sex offenders. *Criminal Justice and Behavior, 21,* 10–27.

Marsland, A. L., Cohen, S., Rabin, R. S., & Manuck, S. B. (2001). Associations between stress, trait negative affect, acute immune reactivity, and antibody response to hepatitis B injection in healthy young adults. *Health Psychology, 20,* 4–11.

Martens, W. H. J. (1997). Psychopathy and maturation. MD dissertation, Tilburg University, The Netherlands. Maastricht: Shaker.

Martens, W. H. J. (1999). Marcel—a case report of a violent sexual psychopath in remission. *International Journal of Offender Therapy and Comparative Criminology, 43,* 391–399.

Martens, W. H. J. (2002). The hidden suffering of the psychopath. *Psychiatric Times,* 19(1).

Martin, R. L. (1995). *DSM-IV* changes for the somatoform disorders. *Psychiatric Annals, 25,* 29–39.

Martinez-Taboas, A. & Rodriguez-Cay, J. R. (1997). Case study of a Puerto Rican woman with dissociative identity disorder. *Dissociation, 10,* 141–147.

Marx, B., Nichols-Anderson, C., Mesman-Moore, T., Miranda, R., Jr., & Porter, C. (2000). Alcohol consumption, outcome expectancies, and victimization status among female college students. *Journal of Applied Social Psychology, 30,* 1056–1070.

Maslow, A. H. (1987). *Motivation and personality* (3rd ed.). New York: Harper & Row.

Masserman, J. H. (1961). *Principles of dynamic psychiatry* (2nd ed.). Philadelphia: Saunders.

Masters, W. H. & Johnson, V. E. (1970). *Human sexual inadequacy.* Boston: Little, Brown.

Masters, W. H. & Johnson, V. E. (1996). *Human sexual response.* Boston: Little, Brown.

Mathalon, D. H., Sullivan, E. V., Lim, K. O., & Pfefferbaum, A. (2001). Progressive brain volume changes and the clinical course of schizophrenia in men: A longitudinal magnetic resonance imaging study. *Archives of General Psychiatry, 58,* 148–157.

Mathews, A. & MacLeod, C. (1994). Cognitive approaches to emotion and emotional disorders. *Annual Review of Psychology, 45,* 25–50.

Matthews, K. A. (1988). Coronary heart disease and Type A behaviors: Update on and alternative to the Booth-Kewley and Friedman (1987) quantitative review. *Psychological Bulletin, 104,* 373–380.

Matthews, K. A. (1989). Interactive effects of behavior and reproductive hormones on sex differences in risk for coronary heart disease. *Health Psychology, 8,* 373–387.

Mattison, E. (2000). Commentary: The law of unintended consequences. *Journal of the American Academy of Psychiatry and the Law, 28,* 154–158.

Maude-Griffin, P. M., Hohenstein, J. M., Humfleet, G. L., Reilly, P. M., Tusel, D. J., & Hall, S. M. (1998). Superior efficacy of cognitive-behavioral therapy for urban crack cocaine abusers: Main and matching effects. *Journal of Consulting & Clinical Psychology, 66,* 832–837.

Maugh, T. H. (1982). Marijuana "justifies serious concern." *Science, 215,* 1488–1489.

Maxmen, J. S. & Ward, N. G. (1995). *Psychotropic drugs: Fast facts* (2nd ed.). New York: W. W. Norton.

May, R. (1959). *The discovery of being. Writings in existential psychology.* New York: W. W. Norton.

May, R. (1990). Will, decision, and responsibility. In K. Hoeller et al. (Eds.). *Readings in existential psychology and psychiatry. Studies in existential psychology and psychiatry* (pp. 269–278). Atlantic Highlands, NJ: Humanities Press.

Mayberg, H. S., Liotti, M., Brannan, S. K., McGinnis, S., Mahurin, R. K., Jerabeck, P. A., Silva, J. A., Tekell, J. I., Martin, C. C., Lancaster, J. L., & Fox, P. T. (1999). Reciprocal limbiccortical function and negative mood: Converging PET findings in depression and normal sadness. *American Journal of Psychiatry, 156,* 675–682.

Mayer, J. D., Salovey, P., & Caruso, D. (2000). Models of emotional intelligence. In R. J. Sternberg (Ed.), *Handbook of intelligence* (pp. 396–420). Cambridge: Cambridge University Press.

Mayes, L. C., Granger, R. H., Bornstein, M. H., & Zuckerman, B. (1992). The problem of prenatal cocaine exposure: A rush to judgment. *Journal of the American Medical Association, 267,* 406–408.

Mayne, T. J., Acree, M., Chesney, M. A., & Folkman, S. (1998). HIV sexual risk behavior following bereavement in gay men. *Health Psychology, 17,* 403–411.

Mayville, S., Katz, R. C., Gipson, M. T., & Cabral, K. (1999). Assessing the prevalence of body dysmorphic disorder in an ethnically diverse group of adolescents. *Journal of Child and Family Studies, 8,* 357–362.

Mazure, C. M., Bruce, M. L., Maciejewski, P. K., & Jacobs, S. C. (2000). Adverse life events and cognitive-personality characteristics in the prediction of major depression and antidepressant response. *American Journal of Psychiatry, 157,* 896–903.

Mazzoco, M. M., Nord, A. M., van Doorninck, W., Greene, C. L., Kovar, C. G., & Pennington, B. F. (1994). Cognitive development among children with early-treated phenylketonuria. *Developmental Neuropsychology, 10,* 133–151.

McArdle, E. F. (2001). Advance directives and the treatment of patients with mental illness: Can an advance directive avert court intervention when the patient refuses the administration of antipsychotic medication? *Journal of Psychiatry & Law, 29,* 147–174.

McArdle, P., O'Brien, G., & Kolvin, I. (1995). Hyperactivity: Prevalence and relationship with conduct disorder. *Journal of Child Psychology and Psychiatry, 36,* 279–303.

McArthur, J. C., Cohen, B. A., Seines, O. A., Kumar, A. J., Cooper, K., McArthur, J. H., Soucy, G., Cronblath, D. R., Chmile, J. S., Wang, M. C., Starkleym, D. J., Ginzburg, H., Ostrow, D., Johnson, R. T., Phair, J. P., & Polk, B. F. (1989). Low prevalence of neurological and neuropsychological abnormalities in otherwise healthy HIV-1- infected individuals. Results from the Multicenter AIDS Cohort Study. *Annals of Neurology, 26,* 601–611.

McArthur, J. C., Hoover, D. R., Bacellar, H., Miller, E. N., Cohen, B. A., Becker, J. T., Graham, N. M. H., McArthur, J. H., Selnes, O. A., Jacobson, L. P., Visscher, B. R., Concha, M., & Saah, A. (1993).

Dementia in AIDS patients: Incidence and risk factors. *Neurology, 43,* 2245–2252.

McAuliffe, W. E. (1990). A randomized controlled trial of recovery training and self-help for opioid addicts in New England and Hong Kong. *Journal of Psychoactive Drugs, 22,* 197–209.

McCrae, R. R., Jang, K. L., Livesley, W. J., Riemann, R., & Angleitner, A. (2001). Sources of structure: Genetic, environmental, and artifactual influences on the covariation of personality traits. *Journal of Personality, 69,* 511–535.

McCarley, R. W., Salisbury, D. F., Hirayasu, Y., Yurgelun-Todd, D., Tohen, M., Zarate, C., Kikinis, R., Jolesz, F. A., & Shenton, M. E. (2002). Association between smaller left posterior superior temporal gyrus volume on magnetic resonance imaging and smaller left temporal P300 amplitude in first-episode schizophrenia. *Archives of General Psychiatry, 59,* 321–331.

McCartney, J. R. & Holden, J. C. (1981). Toilet training for the mentally retarded. In J. L. Matson & J. R. McCartney (Eds.), *Handbook of behavior modification with the mentally retarded.* New York: Plenum Press.

McClelland, G. M. & Teplin, L. A. (2001). Alcohol intoxication and violent crime. Implications for public health policy. *American Journal on Addictions, 10*(Suppl.), 70–85.

McCloskey, J., Quintero, G., Russell, S., & Vince, A. (1999). Alcohol dependence and conduct disorder among Navajo Indians. *Journal of Studies on Alcohol, 60,* 159–167.

McClure, R. K. & Weinberger, D. R. (2001). The neurodevelopmental hypothesis of schizophrenia: A review of the evidence. In A. Breier, P. V. Tran, F. Bymaster, & C. Tollefson (Eds.), *Current issues in the psychopharmacology of schizophrenia* (pp. 27–56). Philadelphia: Lippincott Williams & Wilkins.

McCubbin, J. A., Helfer, S. G., Switzer, F. S. 3rd, & Price, T. M. (2002). Blood pressure control and hormone replacement therapy in post-menopausal women at risk for coronary heart disease. *American Heart Journal, 143,* 711–717.

McDermott, P. A. & Weiss, R. V. (1995). A normative typology of healthy, subclinical, and clinical behavior styles among American children and adolescents. *Psychological Assessment, 7,* 162–170.

McDermott, S. (1994). Explanatory model to describe school district prevalence rates for mental retardation and learning disabilities. *American Journal of Mental Retardation, 99,* 175–185.

McDougle, C. J., Homes, J. P., Carlson, D. C., Pelton, G. H., Cohen, D. J., & Price, L. H. (1998). A double-blind, placebo-controlled study of risperidone in adults with autistic disorder and other pervasive developmental disorders. *Archives of General Psychiatry, 55,* 633–641.

McEachin, J. J., Smith, T., & Lovaas, O. I. (1993). Long term outcome for children with autism who received early intensive behavioral treatment. *American Journal of Mental Retardation, 97*(4), 359–372.

McElroy, S. L., Strakowski, S. M., West, S. A., Keck, P. E., Jr., & McConville, B. J. (1977). Phenomenology of adolescent and adult mania in hospitalized patients with bipolar disorder. *American Journal of Psychiatry, 154,* 44–49.

McFarlane, W. R., Lukens, E., Link, B., Dushay, R., Deakins, S. A., Newmark, M., Dunne, E. J., Horen, B., & Toran, J. (1995). Multiple-family groups and psychoeducation in the treatment of schizophrenia. *Archives of General Psychiatry, 52,* 679–687.

McGee, R. (1999). Does stress cause cancer? There's no good evidence of a relation between stressful events and cancer. *British Medical Journal, 319,* 1015–1016.

McGhie, A. & Chapman, J. (1961). Disorders of attention and perception in early schizophrenia. *British Journal of Medical Psychology, 34,* 103–116.

McGinnis, J. M. & Foege, W. H. (1999). Mortality and morbidity attributable to use of addictive substances in the United States. *Proceedings of the Association of American Physicians, 111,* 109–118.

McGlashan, T. H. & Hoffman, R. E. (2000). Schizophrenia as a disorder of developmentally reduced synaptic connectivity. *Archives of General Psychiatry, 57,* 637–648.

McGorry, P. D. (1995). The clinical boundaries of posttraumatic stress disorder: *Australian and New Zealand Journal of Psychiatry, 29,* 385–393.

McGrath, J., El-Saadi, O., Grim, V., Cardy, S., Chapple, B., Chant, D., Lieberman, D., & Mowry, B. (2002). Minor physical anomalies and quantitative measures of the head and face in patients with psychosis. *Archives of General Psychiatry, 59,* 458–464.

McGrath, P. J. (1999). Clinical psychology issues in migraine headaches. *Canadian Journal of Neurological Sciences, 26,* S33–S36.

McGrath, P. J., Stewart, J. W., Janal, M. N., Petkova, E., Quitkin, F. M., & Klein, D. F. (2000). A placebo-controlled study of fluoxetine versus imipramine in the acute treatment of atypical depression. *American Journal of Psychiatry, 157,* 344–350.

McGue, M., Pickens, R. W., & Svikis, D. S. (1992). Sex and age effects on the inheritance of alcohol problems. A twin study. *Journal of Abnormal Psychology, 101,* 3–17.

McGuffin, P., Katz, R., Watkins, S., & Rutherford, J. (1996). A hospital-based twin register to the heritability of *DSM-IV* unipolar depression. *Archives of General Psychiatry, 53,* 129–136.

McGuire, L., Junginger, J., Adams, S. G., Jr., Burright, R., & Donovick, P. (2001). Delusions and delusional reasoning. *Journal of Abnormal Psychology, 110,* 259–266.

Mclntyre, D. & Carr, A. (2000). Prevention of child sexual abuse: Implications of programme evaluation research. *Child Abuse Review, 9,* 183–199.

McKay, D. (1999). Two-year follow-up of behavioral treatment and maintenance for body dysmorphic disorder. *Behavior Modification, 23,* 620–629.

McKay, J. R., Alterman, A. I., McLellan, T., Snider, E. C., & O'Brien, C. P. (1995). Effects of random versus nonrandom assignment in a comparison of inpatient and day hospital rehabilitation for male alcoholics. *Journal of Consulting and Clinical Psychology, 63,* 70–78.

McKeith, I. G., Galasko, D., Kosaka, K., Perry, E. K., Dickson, D. W., Hansen, L. A., Salmon, D. A., Lowe, J., Mirra, S. S., Byrne, E. J., Lennox, G., Quinn, N. P., Edwardson, J. A., Ince, P. G., Bergeron, C., Burns, A., Miller, B. L., Lovestune, S., Collerton, D., Jansen, E. N. H., Ballard, C., de Vos, R. A. I., Wilcock, G. K., Jellinger, K. A., & Perry, R. H. (1996). Consensus guidelines for the clinical and pathologic diagnosis of dementia with Lewy bodies (DLB): Report of the consortium on DLB international workshop. *Neurology, 47,* 1113–1124.

McKeith, I. G. (2002). Dementia with Lewy bodies. *British Journal of Psychiatry, 180,* 144–147.

McKnight, T. J. & Kearney, C. A. (2001). Staff training regarding choice availability for persons with mental retardation: A preliminary analysis. *Journal of Developmental and Physical Disabilities, 13,* 1–10.

McLeer, S. V., Dixon, J. F., Henry, D., Ruggiero, K., Escovitz, K., Niedda, T., & Scholle, R. (1998). Psychopathology in non-clinically referred sexually abused children. *Journal of the American Academy of Child and Adolescent Psychiatry, 37,* 1326–1333.

McLellan, A. T., Alterman, A. I., Metzger, D. S., Grissom, G. R., Woody, G. E., Luborsky, L., & O'Brien, C. P. (1994). Similarity of outcome predictors across opiate, cocaine, and alcohol treatments: Role of treatment services. *Journal of Consulting and Clinical Psychology, 62,* 1141–1158.

McLeod, C. C. & Budd, M. A. (1997). Treatment of somatization in primary care: Evaluation of the Personal Health Improvement Program. *HMO Practice, 11,* 88–94.

McMahon, P. D., Alloy, L. B., & Abramson, L. Y. (2001). *Course of and recovery from depressive episodes: Role of cognitive vulnerability and negative life events.* Manuscript in preparation, Temple University, Philadelphia.

McNally, R. J. (1995). Automaticity and the anxiety disorders. *Behaviour Research and Therapy, 33,* 747–754.

McNally, R. J. (1996). Assessment of posttraumatic stress disorder in children and adolescents. *Journal of School Psychology, 34,* 147–161.

McNally, R. J. (2001). Vulnerability to anxiety disorders in adulthood. In R. E. Ingram & J. M. Price (Eds.), *Vulnerability to psychopathology: Risk across the lifespan* (pp. 304–321). New York: Guilford Press.

McNally, R. J., Clancy, S. A., & Schacter, D. L. (2001). Directed forgetting of trauma cues in adults reporting repressed or recovered memories of childhood sexual abuse. *Journal of Abnormal Psychology, 110,* 151–156.

McNally, R. J., Clancy, S. A., Schacter, D. L., & Pitman, R. K. (2000). Personality profiles, dissociation, and absorption in women reporting repressed, recovered, or continuous memories of childhood sexual abuse. *Journal of Consulting and Clinical Psychology, 68,* 1033–1037.

McNiel, D. E., Binder, R. L., & Fulton, F. M. (1998). Management of threats of violence under California's Duty-to-Protect Statute. *American Journal of Psychiatry, 155,* 1097–1101.

McWilliams, N. (1999). *Psychoanalytic case formulation,* New York: Guilford Press.

Meador, K. J. (2002). Cognitive outcomes and predictive factors in epilepsy. *Neurology, 53*(58; 8 Suppl. 5), S21–S26.

Meador-Woodruff, J. H., Haroutunian, V., Powchik, P., Davidson, M., Davis, K. L., & Watson, S. J. (1997). Dopamine receptor transcript expression in striatum and prefrontal and occipital cortex: Focal abnormalities in orbitofrontal cortex in schizophrenia. *Archives of General Psychiatry, 54,* 1089–1095.

Mechanic, D. (1962). The concept of illness behavior. *Journal of Chronic Diseases, 15,* 189–194.

Mednick, S. A. (1970). Breakdown in individuals at high risk for schizophrenia: Possible predispositional perinatal factors. *Mental Hygiene, 54,* 50–63.

Mednick, S. A. (1971). Birth defects and schizophrenia. *Psychology Today, 4,* 48–50.

Mednick, S. A., Machon, R. A., Huttunen, M. O., & Bonett, D. (1988). Adult schizophrenia following prenatal exposure to an influenza epidemic. *Archives of General Psychiatry, 45,* 189–192.

Meehl, P. E. (1991). The insanity defense. In C. A. Anderson & K. Gunderson (Eds.), *Paul E. Meehl: Selected philosophical and methodological papers.* Minneapolis: University of Minnesota Press.

Meesters, Y., Jansen, J. H. C., Beersma, D. G. M., Bouhuys, A. L., & van der Hoofdakker, R. H. (1993). Early light treatment can prevent an emerging winter depression from developing into a full-blown depression. *Journal of Affective Disorders, 29,* 41–47.

Meichenbaum, D. H. (1975). Self-instructional methods. In F. H. Kanfer & A. P. Goldstein (Eds.), *Helping people change: A textbook of methods.* New York: Pergamon Press.

Meichenbaum, D. H. (Ed.). (1977). *Cognitive behavior modification: An integrative approach.* New York: Plenum Press.

Meichenbaum, D. H. & Goodman, J. (1971). Training impulsive children to talk to themselves: A means of developing self control. *Journal of Abnormal Psychology, 77,* 115–126.

Meichenbaum, D. H. & Jaremko, M. E. (Eds.). (1983). *Stress reduction and prevention.* New York: Plenum Press.

Meinardi, H. & Pachlatko, C. (1991). Special centers for epilepsy. In M. Dam & L. Gram (Eds.), *Comprehensive epileptology* (pp. 769–779). New York: Raven Press.

Mellin, L. M., Irwin, C. E., & Scully, S. (1992). Prevalence of disordered eating in girls. A survey of middle-class children. *Journal of the American Dietetic Association, 92,* 851–853.

Melton, G. B., Petrila, J., Poythress, N. G., & Slobogin, C. (1997). *Psychological evaluation for the courts* (2nd ed.). New York: Guilford Press.

Melzack, R. (1988). The tragedy of needless pain: A call for social action. In R. Dubner, R. G. F. Gebhart, & M. R. Bond (Eds.), *Proceedings for the Fifth World Congress on Pain.* New York: Elsevier.

Mendel, W. M. (1976). *Schizophrenia: The experience and its treatment.* San Francisco: Jossey-Bass.

Mendlewicz, J. & Rainer, J. D. (1977). Adoption study supporting genetic transmission in manic-depressive illness. *Nature, 168,* 327–329.

Merckelbach, H., de Jong, P. J., Muris, P., & van den Hout, M. (1996). The etiology of specific phobias: A review. *Clinical Psychology Review, 16,* 337–361.

Merikangus, K. R. (1990). Comorbidity for anxiety and depression: Review of family and genetic studies. In J. D. Maser & C. R. Cloninger (Eds.), *Comorbidity of mood and anxiety disorders.* Washington, DC: American Psychiatric Press.

Merikangus, K. R. & Angst, J. (1995). Comorbidity and social phobia: Evidence from clinical, epidemiologic, and genetic studies. *European Archives of Psychiatry and Clinical Neuroscience, 244,* 297–303.

Merrill, L. L., Thomsen, C. J., Gold, S. R., & Milner, J. S. (2001). Childhood abuse and premilitary sexual assault in male navy recruits. *Journal of Consulting and Clinical Psychology, 69,* 252–261.

Merritt, H. H. (1967). *A textbook of neurology* (4th ed.), Philadelphia: Lea & Febiger.

Merry, S. & Andrews, L. K. (1994). Psychiatric status of sexually abused children 12 months after disclosure of abuse. *Journal of the American Academy of Child and Adolescent Psychiatry, 33,* 939–944.

Merskey, H. (1995). The manufacture of personalities: The production of multiple personality disorder. In L. M. Cohen, J. N. Berzoff, & M. R. Elin (Eds.), *Dissociative identity disorder:*

Theoretical and treatment controversies (pp. 3–32). Northvale, NJ: Aronson.

Mesibov, G. B., Adams, L. W., & Klinger, L. G. (1997). *Autism: Understanding the disorder.* New York: Plenum Press.

Messenger, J. C. (1971). Sex and repression in an Irish folk community. In D. Marshall & R. Suggs (Eds.), *Human sexual behavior.* New York: Basic Books.

Metalsky, G. I., Joiner, T. E., Jr., Hardin, T. S., & Abramson, L. Y. (1993). Depressive reactions to failure in a naturalistic setting: A test of the hopelessness and self-esteem theories of depression. *Journal of Abnormal Psychology, 102,* 101–109.

Metz, M. E., Pryor, J. L., Nesvacil, L. J., Abuzzhab, F., & Koznar, J. (1997). Premature ejaculation: A psychophysiological review. *Journal of Sex and Marital Therapy, 23,* 3–23.

Meyer, G. J. (1996). The Rorschach and MMPI: Toward a more scientifically differentiated understanding of cross-method assessment. *Journal of Personality Assessment, 67,* 558–578.

Meyer, G. J. (1997). On the integration of personality assessment methods: The Rorschach and MMPI. *Journal of Personality Assessment, 68,* 297–330.

Meyer, G. J., Finn, S. E., Eyde, L. D., Kay, G. G., Moreland, K. L., Dies, R. R., Eisman, E. J., Kubiszyn, T. W., & Reed, G. M. (2001). Psychological testing and psychological assessment: A review of evidence and issues. *American Psychologist, 56,* 128–165.

Meyer, J. H., Kapur, S., Houle, S., DaSilva, J., Owczarek, B., Brown, G. M., Wilson, A. A., & Kennedy, S. H. (1999). Prefrontal cortex 5-HT_2 receptors in depression: An [^{18}F] Setoperone PET imaging study. *American Journal of Personality, 156,* 1029–1034.

Meyer, J. M. (1979). The theory of gender identity disorders. *Journal of the American Psychoanalytic Association, 30,* 381–418.

Mezzacappa, E. S. & Katkin, E. S. (2002). Breast-feeding is associated with reduced perceived stress and negative mood in mothers. *Health Psychology, 21,* 187–193.

Mezzich, J. E., Fabrega, H., Coffman, G. A., & Haley, R. (1989). *DSM-III* disorders in a large sample of psychiatric patients: Frequency and specificity of diagnoses. *American Journal of Psychiatry, 146,* 212–219.

Michelson, L. K. & Marchione, K. (1991). Behavioral, cognitive, and pharmacological treatments of panic disorder with agoraphobia: Critique and synthesis. *Journal of Consulting and Clinical Psychology, 59,* 100–114.

Michelsson, K., Rinne, A., & Paajanen, S. (1990). Crying, feeding, and sleeping patterns in 1 to 12-month-old infants. *Child: Care, Health, and Development, 16,* 99–111.

Mick, M. A. & Telch, M. J. (1998). Social anxiety and history of behavioral inhibition in young adults. *Journal of Anxiety Disorders, 12,* 1–20.

Miklowitz, D. J., Goldstein, M. J., & Nuechterlein, K. H. (1995). Verbal interactions in the families of schizophrenic and bipolar affective patients. *Journal of Abnormal Psychology, 104,* 268–276.

Miklowitz, D. J., Strachan, A. M., Goldstein, M. J., Doane, J. A., Snyder, K. S., Hogarty, G. E., & Falloon, I. R. H. (1986). Expressed emotion and communication deviance in the families of schizophrenics. *Journal of Abnormal Psychology, 95,* 60–66.

Miklowitz, D. J., Velligan, D. I., Goldstein, M. J., Nuechterlein, K. H., & Gitlin, M. J. (1991). Communication deviance in families of schizophrenic and manic patients. *Journal of Abnormal Psychology, 100,* 163–173.

Mikulincer, M. & Solomon, Z. (1988). Attributional style and combat-related posttraumatic stress disorder. *Journal of Abnormal Psychology, 97,* 308–313.

Milberg, W. (1996). Issues in the assessment of cognitive function in dementia. *Brain and Cognition, 31,* 114–132.

Milgram, S. (1963). Behavioral study of obedience. *Journal of Abnormal and Social Psychology, 67,* 371–378.

Miller, G. E. & Cohen, S. (2001). Psychological interventions and the immune system: A meta-analytic review and critique. *Health Psychology, 20,* 47–63.

Miller, H. L., Delgado, P. L., Salomon, R. M., Berman, R., Krystal, J. H., Heninger, G. R., & Charney, D. S. (1996). Clinical and biochemical effects of catecholamine depletion on antidepressant-induced remission of depression. *Archives of General Psychiatry, 53,* 117–128.

Miller, M. B., Chapman, J. P., Chapman, L. J., & Collins, J. (1995). Task difficulty and cognitive deficits in schizophrenia. *Journal of Abnormal Psychology, 104,* 251–258.

Miller, N. E. (1969). Learning of visceral and glandular responses. *Science, 163,* 434–445.

Miller, N. E. (1972). Comments on strategy and tactics of research. In A. E. Bergin & H. H. Strupp (Eds.), *Changing frontiers in the science of psychotherapy.* New York: Aldine-Atherton.

Miller, S. M. (1995). Case Studies: Profiles of women recovering from drug addiction. *Journal of Drug Education, 25*(2), 139–148.

Miller, T. Q., Smith, T. W., Turner, C. W., Guijarro, M. L., & Hallet, A. J. (1996). A meta-analytic review of research on hostility and physical health. *Psychological Bulletin, 119,* 322–348.

Miller, W. R. & Rollnick, S. (2002). *Motivational interviewing: Preparing people for change* (2nd ed.). New York, NY: Guilford Press.

Miller, W. R., Walters, S. T., & Bennett, M. E. (2001). How effective is alcoholism treatment in the United States? *Journal of Studies on Alcohol, 62,* 211–220.

Millon, T. (1981). *Disorders of personality.* New York: Wiley.

Millon, T. (1994). *Millon Clinical Multiaxial Inventory—III Manual.* Minneapolis: National Computer Systems.

Millon, T. & Davis, R. D. (1996). *Disorders of personality: DSM IV and beyond.* New York: Wiley.

Millon, T. & Davis, R. D. (1998). Ten types of psychopathy. In T. Millon, E. Simonsen, et al. (Eds). *Psychopathy: Antisocial, criminal, and violent behavior* (pp. 1161–1170). New York: Guilford Press.

Min, S. K. & Lee, B. O. (1997). Laterality in somatization. *Psychosomatic Medicine, 59,* 236–240.

Mindell, J. A. & Cashman, L. (1995). Sleep disorders. In A. R. Eisen, C. A. Kearney, & C. E. Schaefer (Eds.), *Clinical handbook of anxiety disorders in children and adolescents.* Northvale, NJ: Aronson.

Mineka, S., Watson, D., & Clark, L. A. (1998). Comorbidity of anxiety and unipolar mood disorders. *Annual Review of Psychology, 49,* 377–412.

Minor, T. & Saade, S. (1997). Poststress glucose mitigates behavioral impairment in rats in the "learned helplessness" model of psychopathology, *Biological Psychiatry, 42,* 324–334.

Minshew, N. (1991). Evidence of neural function in autism: Clinical and biological implications. *Pediatrics, 87 (Supplement),* 774–780.

Minshew, N. J. & Dombrowski, S. M. (1994). In vivo neuroanatomy of autism: Neuroimaging studies. In M. L. Bauman & T. L. Kemper (Eds.), *The neurobiology of autism.* Baltimore: Johns Hopkins University Press.

Minuchin, S. (1974). *Families and family therapy.* Cambridge, MA: Harvard University Press.

Minuchin, S. & Fishman, H. C. (1981). *Family therapy techniques.* Cambridge, MA: Harvard University Press.

Mirsky, A. F. & Duncan, C. C. (1986). Etiology and expression of schizophrenia: Neurobiological and psychosocial factors. *Annual Review of Psychology, 37,* 291–319.

Mischel, W. & Shoda, Y. (1995). A cognitive-affective system of personality: Reconceptualizing situations, disposition, dynamics, and invariance in personality structure. *Psychological Review, 102,* 246–268.

Mitchell, B., Mitchell, D., & Berk, M. (2000). The role of genetics in suicide and the link with major depression and alcoholism. *International Journal of Psychiatry in Clinical Practice, 4,* 275–280.

Mitchell, D. & Blair, J. (2000). State of the art: Psychopathy. *Psychologist, 13,* 356–360.

Mitchell, S. (1988). *Relational concepts in psychoanalysis.* Cambridge, MA: Harvard University Press.

Mitchell, W. B., DiBartolo, P. M., Brown, T. A., & Barlow, D. H. (1998). Effects of positive and negative mood on sexual arousal in sexually functional males. *Archives of Sexual Behavior, 27*(2), 197–207.

Mittelman, M. S., Ferris, S. H., Shulman, E., Steinberg, G., & Levin, B. (1996). A family intervention to delay nursing home placement of patients with Alzheimer's disease. *Journal of the American Medical Association, 276,* 1725–1731.

Mittleman, M. A., Maclure, M., Sherwood, J. B., Mulry, R. P., Tofler, G. H., Jabobs. S. C., Friedman, R., Benson, H., & Muller, J. E. (1995). Triggering of acute myocardial infarction onset by episodes of anger. *Circulation, 92,* 1720–1725.

Mittleman, M., Ferris, S. H., Steinberg, G., Shulman, E., Mackell, J. A., Ambinder, A., & Cohen, J. (1993). An intervention that delays institutionalization of Alzheimer's disease patients: Treatment of spouse-caregivers. *Gerontologist, 33,* 730–740.

Mizes, J. S. (1995). Eating disorders. In M. Hersen & R. T. Ammerman (Eds.), *Advanced abnormal child psychology* (pp. 375–391). Hillsdale, NJ: Erlbaum.

Moffitt, T. E. (1991). *Juvenile delinquency: Seed of a career in violent crime, just sowing wild oats—or both?* Paper presented at the Science and Public Policy Seminars of the Federation of Behavioral, Psychological, and Cognitive Sciences, Washington, DC.

Moffitt, T. E. (1993). Adolescence-limited and life-course-persistent antisocial behavior: A developmental taxonomy. *Psychological Review, 100,* 674–701.

Mogg, K. & Bradley, B. P. (1998). A cognitive-motivational analysis of anxiety. *Behaviour Research and Therapy, 36,* 809–848.

Mogotsi, M., Kaminer, D., & Stein, D. J. (2000). Quality of life in the anxiety disorders, *Harvard Review of Psychiatry, 8,* 273–282.

Mohlman, J. & Zinbarg, R. E. (2000). What kind of attention is necessary for fear reduction? An empirical test of the emotional processing model. *Behavior Therapy, 31,* 113–133.

Mohr, J. W., Turner, R. E., & Jerry, M. B. (1964). *Pedophilia and exhibitionism.* Toronto. University of Toronto Press.

Mohs, R. C. (1995). Assessing cognitive function in schizophrenics and patients with Alzheimer's disease. *Schizophrenia Research, 17,* 115–121.

Monahan, J. (1981). *The clinical prediction of violent behavior.* Rockville, MD: National Institute of Mental Health.

Monahan, J. (1992). Mental disorder and violent behavior. *American Psychologist, 47,* 511–521.

Monahan, J. (1996). Violence prediction: The past twenty and the next twenty years. *Criminal Justice and Behavior, 23,* 107–120.

Monahan, J. & Steadman, H. (1994). Toward a rejuvenation of risk assessment research. In J. Monahan & H. Steadman (Eds.), *Violence and mental disorder: Developments in risk assessment.* Chicago: University of Chicago Press.

Money, J., Hampson, J. G., & Hampson, J. L. (1957). Imprinting and the establishment of the gender role. *Archives of Neurology and Psychiatry, 77,* 333–336.

Monnier, J., Resnick, H. S., Kilpatrick, D. G., & Seals, B. (2002). The relationship between distress and resource loss following rape. *Violence & Victims, 17,* 85–92.

Monroe, S. M., Rohde, P., Seeley, J. R., & Lewinsohn, P. M. (1999). Life events and depression in adolescence: Relationship loss as a prospective risk factor for first onset of major depressive disorder. *Journal of Abnormal Psychology, 108,* 606–614.

Monsen, K. & Havik, O. E. (2001). Psychological functioning and bodily conditions in patients with pain disorder associated with psychological factors. *British Journal of Medical Psychology, 74,* 183–195.

Moore, H., West, A. R., & Grace, A. A. (1999). The regulation of forebrain dopamine transmission: Relevance to the pathophysiology and psychopathology of schizophrenia. *Biological Psychiatry, 46,* 40–55.

Moore, P. M. & Baker, G. A. (1997). Non-epileptic attack disorder: A psychological perspective. *Seizure, 6*(6), 429–434.

Mora, G. (1980). Mind-body concepts in the middle Ages: Part II. The Moslem influence, the great theological systems and cultural attitudes toward the mentally ill in the late Middle Ages. *Journal of the History of the Behavioral Sciences, 16,* 58–72.

Moreno, A. B. & Thelen, M. H. (1993). A preliminary prevention program for eating disorders in a junior high school population. *Journal of Youth and Adolescence, 22,* 109–124.

Morey, L. C. (1991). *The Personality Assessment Inventory Professional Manual.* Odessa, FL: Psychological Assessment Resources, Inc.

Morgan, C. A., Hazlett, G., Wang, S., Richardson, E. G., Schnurr, P., & Southwick, S. M. (2001). Symptoms of dissociation in humans experiencing acute, uncontrollable stress: A prospective investigation. *American Journal of Psychiatry, 158,* 1239–1247.

Morgan, D. L. & Morgan, R. K. (2001). Single-participant research design: Bringing science to managed care. *American Psychologist, 56,* 119–127.

Morgan, G. D., Ashenberg, Z. S., & Fisher, E. B., Jr. (1988). Abstinence from smoking and the social environment. *Journal of Consulting and Clinical Psychology, 56,* 298–301.

Morgan, J. F. & Crisp, A. H. (2000). Use of leukotomy for intractable anorexia nervosa: A long-term follow-up study. *International Journal of Eating Disorders, 27,* 249–258.

Morgenstern, J., Labouvie, E., McCrady, B. S., Kahler, C. W., & Frey, R. M.

(1997). Affiliation with Alcoholics Anonymous after treatment: A study of therapeutic effects and mechanisms of action. *Journal of Consulting and Clinical Psychology, 65,* 768–777.

Morgenstern, J. & Longabaugh, R. (2000). Cognitive-behavioral treatment for alcohol dependence: A review of evidence for its hypothesized mechanisms of action. *Addiction, 95,* 1475–1490.

Morin, C. M., Hauri, P. J., Espie, C. A., Spielman, A. J., Buysse, D. J., & Bootzin, R. R. (1999). Nonpharmacologic treatment of chronic insomnia. An American Academy of Sleep Medicine review. *Sleep, 22,* 1134–1156.

Morris, E. L. (2001). The relationship of spirituality to coronary heart disease. *Alternative Therapies in Health and Medicine, 7,* 96–98.

Morris, G. H. & Meloy, J. R. (1993). Out of mind? Out of sight: The uncivil commitment of permanently incompetent criminal defendants. *University of California, Davis Law Review, 27,* 1–23.

Morrison, C. F. (1999). AIDS: Ethical implications for psychological intervention. In D. N. Bersoff (Ed.), *Ethical conflicts in psychology* (2nd ed., pp. 209–212). Washington, DC: American Psychological Association.

Morrison, R. L. (1991). Schizophrenia. In M. Hersen & S. M. Turner (Eds.), *Adult psychopathology and diagnosis* (2nd ed., pp. 149–169). New York: Wiley.

Morse, S. J. (1978). Law and mental health professionals: The limits of expertise. *Professional Psychology, 9,* 389–399.

Morse, S. J. (1982). A preference for liberty: The case against the involuntary commitment of the mentally disordered. *California Law Review, 70,* 55–106.

Morse, S. J. (1997, February 28). A verdict of guilty but mentally ill doesn't work medically or morally. *Philadelphia Inquirer,* p. A19.

Morse, S. J. (1999). Craziness and criminal responsibility. *Behavioral Sciences and the Law, 17,* 147–164.

Morse, S. J. (2001). From *Sikora* to *Hendricks:* Mental disorder and criminal responsibility. In L. E. Frost & R. J. Bonnie (Eds.), *The evolution of mental health law* (pp. 129–168). Washington, DC: American Psychological Association.

Mortensen, P. B., Pedersen, C. B., Westergaard, T., Wohlfahrt, J., Ewald, H., Mors, O., Andersen, P. K., & Melbye, M. (1999). Effects of family history and place and season of birth on the risk of schizophrenia. *New England Journal of Medicine, 340,* 603–608.

Moscicki, E. K. (1995). Epidemiology of suicide. *International Psychogeriatrics, 7,* 137–148.

Moser, C. & Levitt, E. E. (1987). An exploratory-descriptive study of a sadomasochistically oriented sample. *Journal of Sex Research, 23*(3), 322–337.

Mosher-Ashley, P. M., Henrikson, N., & French, E. (2000). Meeting the needs of the mentally ill homeless in Massachusetts-based emergency shelters. *Journal of Social Distress and the Homeless, 9,* 1–17.

Mosley, T. H., Jr., Penizen, D. B., Johnson, C. A., et al. (1991). Time-series analysis of stress and headache. *Cephalalgia, 11,* 306–307.

Moss, H. B. (1999). Pharmacotherapy. In M. Herson & A. S. Bellack (Eds.), *Handbook of comparative intervention for adult disorders* (2nd ed.). New York: Wiley.

Mowrer, O. H. (1948). Learning theory and the neurotic paradox. *American Journal of Orthopsychiatry, 18,* 571–610.

Mowrer, O. H. & Mowrer, W. M. (1938). Enuresis: A method for its study and treatment. *American Journal of Orthopsychiatry, 8,* 436–459.

Mrazek, P. J. & Haggerty, R. J. (1994). *Reducing risk for mental disorders: Frontiers for preventive intervention research.* Washington, DC: National Academy Press.

Mueller, T. I., Leon, A. C., Keller, M. B., Solomon, D. A., Endicott, J., Coryell, W., Warshaw, M., & Maser, J. D. (1999). Recurrence after recovery from major depressive disorder during 15 years of observational follow-up. *American Journal of Psychiatry, 156,* 1000–1006.

Mueser, K. T. (1998). Cognitive behavioral treatment of schizophrenia. In V. E. Caballo (Ed.), *International handbook of cognitive and behavioural treatments for psychological disorders* (pp. 551–570). New York: Pergamon Press.

Mueser, K. T., Salyers, M. P., & Mueser, P. R. (2001). A prospective analysis of work in schizophrenia. *Schizophrenia Bulletin, 27,* 281–296.

Mueser, K. T., Valenti-Hein, D., & Yarnold, P. R. (1987). Dating-skills groups for the developmentally disabled. *Behavior Modification, 11*(2), 200–228.

Mufson, L., Weissman, M. M., Moreau, D., & Garfinkel, R. (1999). Efficacy of interpersonal psychotherapy for depressed adolescents. *Archives of General Psychiatry, 56,* 573–579.

Mulvey, E. P. & Wooland, J. L. (1997). Themes for consideration in future research on prevention and intervention with antisocial behaviors. In D. M. Stoff, J. Breiling, & J. D. Maser (Eds.), *Handbook of antisocial behavior* (pp. 454–462). New York: Wiley.

Mundo, E., Walker, M., Cate, T., Macciardi, F., & Kennedy, J. L. (2001). The role of serotonin transporter protein gene in antidepressant-induced mania in bipolar disorder: Preliminary findings. *Archives of General Psychiatry, 58,* 539–544.

Munetz, M. R., Geller, J. L., & Frese, F. J., III. (2000). Commentary: Capacity-based involuntary outpatient treatment. *Journal of the American Academy of Psychiatry and the Law, 28,* 145–148.

Muris, P., Merckelbach, H., & Clavin, M. (1997). Abnormal and normal compulsions. *Behaviour Research and Therapy, 35,* 249–252.

Murphy, W. D. (1990). Assessment and modification of cognitive distortions in sex offenders. In W. L. Marshall, D. R. Laws, & H. E. Barbaree (Eds.), *The handbook of sexual assault: Issues, theories, and treatment of the offender* (pp. 331–342). New York: Plenum Press.

Murphy, W. D. (1997). Exhibitionism: Psychopathology and theory. In D. R. Laws & W. O'Donohue (Eds.), *Sexual deviance: Theory, assessment, and treatment.* New York: Guilford Press.

Murray, C. J. L. & Lopez, A. D. (Eds.). (1996). *The global burden of disease.* Geneva, Switzerland: The Harvard School of Public Health on behalf of The World Health Organization and The World Bank.

Murtagh, D. R. R. & Greenwood, K. M. (1995). Identifying effective psychological treatments for insomnia: A meta-analysis. *Journal of Consulting and Clinical Psychology, 63,* 79–89.

Mustafa, T., Sy, F. S., Macera, C. A., Thompson, S. J., Jackson, K. L., Selassie, A., & Dean, L. L. (1999). Association between exercise and HIV disease progression in a cohort of homosexual men. *Annals of Epidemiology, 9,* 27–31.

Myers, J. K. & Bean, L. L. (1968). *A decade later: A follow-up of social class and mental illness.* New York: Wiley.

Myin-Germeys, I., van Os, J., Schwartz, J. E., Stone, A. A., & Delespaul, P. A. (2001). Emotional reactivity to daily life stress in psychosis. *Archives of General Psychiatry, 58,* 1137–1144.

Nagayama, G. C. & Barongan, C. (1997). Prevention of sexual aggression: Sociocultural risk and protective factors. *American Psychologist, 52,* 5–14.

Nagy, T. F. (2000). *Ethics in plain English: An illustrative casebook for psychologists.* Washington, DC: American Psychological Association.

Nahas, G. G., Sutin, K. M., Harvey, D., Agurell, S., Pace, N., & Cancro, R. (Eds.) (1999a). *Marihuana and medicine.* Totowa, NJ: Humana Press.

Nathan, P. E. & Langenbucher, J. W. (1999). Psychopathology: Description and classification. *Annual Review of Psychology, 50,* 79–107.

Nathan, P. E., Marlatt, G. A., & Loberg, T. (Eds.). (1978). *Alcoholism: New directions in behavioral research and treatment.* New York: Plenum Press.

National Center for Health Statistics. (2002). *Prevalence of Overweight Among Children and Adolescents: United States, 1999-2000.* Retrieved August 15, 2003, from www.cdc.gov/nchs/products/pubs/pubd/hestats/overwght99.htm.

National Center for Injury Prevention and Control, Centers for Disease Control. 1999, United States suicide injury deaths and rates per 100,000. Retrieved May 31, 2002, from http://webapp.cdc.gov/cgi-bin/broker.exe.

National Highway Traffic Safety Administration. (January 1998). Research note: *Further analysis of motorcycle helmet effectiveness using CODES linked data.* Washington, DC: U.S. Department of Transportation.

National Highway Traffic Safety Administration. (2001). *Setting limits, saving lives.* Appendix A. Retrieved July 8, 2003, from http://www.nhtsa.dot.gov/people/injury/alcohol/setting%20limits%20saving%20lives%20/AppA.html.

National Hospital Discharge Survey. (1985). Bethesda; National Center for Health Statistics. Department of Health and Human Services, Publication No. 87.

National Institute on Alcohol Abuse and Alcoholism. (2000). *Updating Estimates of the Economic Costs of Alcohol Abuse in the United States.* Retrieved July 8, 2003, from http://www.niaaa.nih.gov/publications/economic-2000/index#updated.

National Institute on Alcohol Abuse and Alcoholism. (2001). Research refines alcoholism treatment options. *Alcohol Health and Research World, 24,* 53–61.

National Institute on Drug Abuse. (1989). *1988 National Household Survey on Drug Abuse.* Rockville, MD: NIDA.

National Institute on Drug Abuse. (1997). *National household survey on drug abuse: Population estimates.* Rockville, MD: NIDA.

National Institute on Drug Abuse. (2000). *Methamphetamine abuse and addiction.* Retrieved August 15, 2003, from http://165.112.78.61/ResearchReports/Methamph.html.

National Institute on Drug Abuse (NIDA). (2002). Economic costs of alcohol and drug abuse in the United States, 1992. http://www.nida.nih.gov/Economic Costs/Index.html.

Nayani, T. & David, A. S. (1996). The auditory hallucination: A phenomenological survey. *Psychological Medicine, 26,* 177–189.

Neary, D., Snowden, J. S., Gustafson, L., Passant, U., Stuss, D., Black, S., Freedman, M., Kertesz, A., Robert, P. H., Albert, M., Boone, K., Miller, B. L., Cummings, J., & Benson, D. F. (1998). Frontotemporal lobar degeneration: A consensus on clinical diagnostic criteria. *Neurology, 51,* 1546–1554.

Neimeyer, R. A. & Stewart, A. E. (2000). Constructivist and narrative psychotherapies. In C. R. Synder & R. E. Ingram (Eds.), *Handbook of psychological change: Psychotherapy processes & practices for the 21st century.* New York: Wiley.

Nelson, C. A. & Bosquet, M. (2000). Neurobiology of fetal and infant development: Implications for infant mental health. In C. H. Zeanah (Ed.), *Handbook of infant mental health* (2nd ed., pp. 37–59). New York: Guilford Press.

Nelson, J. C. & Davis, J. M. (1997). DST studies in psychotic depression: A meta-analysis. *American Journal of Psychiatry, 154,* 1497–1503.

Nemeroff, C. B. (1996). The corticotropin-releasing factor (CRF) hypothesis of depression: New finding and new directions. *Molecular Psychiatry, 1,* 326–342.

Nemeroff, C. B., Krishnan, R. R., Reed, D., Leder, R., Beam, C., & Dunnick, N. R. (1992). Adrenal gland enlargement in major depression: A computed tomographic study. *Archives of General Psychiatry, 49,* 384–387.

Nesse, R. (1998). Emotional disorders in evolutionary perspective. *British Journal of Medical Psychology, 71,* 397–415.

Nesson, C. (1982, July 1). A needed verdict: Guilty but insane. *The New York Times,* p. A19.

Nestor, P. G., Kimble, M. O., O'Donnell, B. F., Smith, L., Niznikiewicz, M., Shenton, M. E., & McCarley, R. W. (1997). Aberrant semantic activation in schizophrenia: A neurophysiological study. *American Journal of Psychiatry, 154,* 640–646.

Neugebauer, R. (1978). Treatment of the mentally ill in medieval and early modern England: A reappraisal. *Journal of the History of the Behavioral Sciences, 14,* 158–169.

Neumeister, A., Praschak-Rieder, N., NeBelmann, B., Rao, M. L., Gluck, J., & Kasper, S. (1997). Effects of tryptophan depletion on drug-free patients with seasonal affective disorder during a stable response to bright light therapy. *Archives of General Psychiatry, 54,* 133–138.

Newberger, C. M., Melnicore, L. H., & Newberger, E. H. (1986). *The American family at crisis: Implications for children* (Vol. 16, No. 12). Chicago: Year Book Medical.

Newcomer, J. W., Haupt, D. W., Fucetola, R., Melson, A. K., Schweiger, J. A., Cooper, B. P., & Selke, G. (2002). Abnormalities in glucose regulation during antipsychotic treatment of schizophrenia. *Archives of General Psychiatry, 59,* 337–345.

Newman, C. F., Leahy, R. L., Beck, A. T., Reilly-Harrington, N. A., & Gyulai, L. (2002). *Bipolar disorder: A cognitive therapy approach.* Washington, DC: American Psychological Association.

Newman, J. P. (1997). Conceptual models of the nervous system: Implications for antisocial behavior. In D. M. Stoff, J. Breiling, & J. D. Maser (Eds.), *Handbook of antisocial behavior* (pp. 324–335). New York: Wiley.

Newman, J. P. (1998). Psychopathic behavior: An information processing perspective. In D. J. Coke, A. F. Forth, & R. D. Hare (Eds.), *Psychopathy theory: Research and implications for society* (pp. 81–104). Dondrecht, Netherlands: Kluwer.

Newman, J. P., Schmitt, W. A., & Voss, W. D. (1997). The impact of motivationally neutral cues on psychopathic individuals: Assessing the generality of the response modulation hypothesis. *Journal of Abnormal Psychology, 106,* 563–575.

Nezu, A. M., Ronan, G. F., Meadows, E. A., & McClure, K. S. (Eds.). (2000). *Practitioner's guide to empirically based measures of depression.* New York: Kluwer Academic/Plenum.

Niccols, G. A. (1994). Fetal alcohol syndrome: Implications for psychologists. *Clinical Psychology Review, 14,* 91–111.

Nicholson, R. A., Ekenstam, C., & Norwood, S. (1996). Coercion and the outcome of psychiatric hospitalization. *International Journal of Law and Psychiatry, 19,* 201–217.

Nicolosi, A., Molinari, S., Musicco, M., Saracco, A., Ziliani, N., & Lazzarin, A. (1991). Positive modification of injecting behavior among intravenous heroin users from Milan and northern Italy, 1987–1989. *British Journal of Addiction, 86,* 91–102.

Nicolson, R. & Rapoport, J. L. (2000). Childhood onset in schizophrenia: What can it teach us? In J. L. Rapoport (Ed.), *Childhood onset of "adult" psychopathology: Clinical and research advances* (pp. 167–192). Washington, DC: American Psychiatric Press.

Nielson, P. E. (1960). A study in transsexualism. *Psychiatric Quarterly, 34,* 203–235.

Nierenberg, A. A., Farabaugh, A. H., Alpert, J. E., Gordon, J., Worthington, J. J., Rosenbaum, J. F., & Fava, M. (2000). Timing of onset of antidepressant response with fluoxetine treatment. *American Journal of Psychiatry, 157,* 1423–1428.

Nietupski, J., Hamre-Nietupski, S., VanderHart, N.S., & Fishback, K. (1996). Employer perceptions of the benefits and concerns of supported employment. *Education and Training in Mental Retardation and Developmental Disabilities, 31,* 310–323.

Nietzel, M. T. & Harris, M. J. (1990). Relationship of dependency and achievement/autonomy to depression. *Clinical Psychology Review, 10,* 279–297.

Nigg, J. T. & Goldsmith, H. H. (1994). Genetics of personality disorders: Perspectives from personality and psychopathology research. *Psychological Bulletin, 115,* 346–380.

NIH Consensus Development Panel on Rehabilitation of Persons with Traumatic Brain Injury. (1999). Rehabilitation of persons with traumatic brain injury. *Journal of the American Medical Association, 282,* 974–983.

NIH Consensus Statement (1998). Rehabilitation of persons with traumatic brain injury. Oct. 26–28, 16(1): 1–41.

NIH Technology Assessment Panel (1996). Integration of behavioral and relaxation approaches into the treatment of chronic pain and insomnia. *Journal of the American Medical Association, 276,* 313–318.

Nisbett, R. E. (1968). Taste, deprivation, and weight determinants of eating behavior. *Journal of Personality and Social Psychology, 10,* 107–116.

Nolen-Hoeksema, S. (1991). Responses to depression and their effects on the duration of depressive episodes. *Journal of Abnormal Psychology, 100,* 569–582.

Nolen-Hoeksema, S. (2001). Gender differences in depression. *Current Directions in Psychological Science, 10,* 173–176.

Nolen-Hoeksema, S. & Girgus, J. S. (1994). The emergence of gender differences in depression during adolescence. *Psychological Bulletin, 115,* 424–443.

Noonan, J. R. (2000). Dissociative identity disorder and criminal intent: An approach to determining responsibility. *American Journal of Forensic Psychology, 18,* 5–26.

Nopoulos, P., Flaum, M., & Andreason, N. C. (1997). Sex differences in brain morphology in schizophrenia. *American Journal of Psychiatry, 154,* 1648–1654.

Nopoulos, P., Torres, I., Flaum, M., Andreason, N. C., Ehrhardt, J. C., & Yuh, W. T. C. (1995). Brain morphology in first-episode schizophrenia. *American Journal of Psychiatry, 152,* 1721–1723.

Nordstrom, A. L., Farde, L., Nyberg, S., Karlsson, P., Halldin, C., & Sedvall, G. (1995). D_1, D_2, and 5-HT_2 receptor occupancy in relation to clozapine serum concentration: A PET study of schizophrenic patients. *American Journal of Psychiatry, 152,* 1444–1449.

Norem, J. K. (1998). Why should we lower our defenses about defense mechanisms? *Journal of Personality, 66,* 895–918.

Norman, R. M. & Malla, A. K. (1993a). Stressful life events and schizophrenia: I. A review of the research. *British Journal of Psychiatry, 162,* 161–166.

Norman, R. M. & Malla, A. K. (1993b). Stressful life events and schizophrenia: II. Conceptual and methodological issues. *British Journal of Psychiatry, 162,* 167–174.

Novick, D. M., Haverkos, H. W., & Teller, D. W. (1997). The medically ill substance abuser. In J. H. Lowinson, P. Ruiz, R. B. Millman, & J. G. Langrod (Eds.), *Substance abuse: A comprehensive textbook* (pp. 534–551). Baltimore: Williams & Wilkins.

Noyes, R., Jr., Kathol, R. G., Fisher, M. M., Phillips, B. M., Suelzer, M. T., & Woodman, C. L. (1994). Psychiatric comorbidity among patients with hypochondriasis. *General Hospital Psychiatry, 16,* 78–87.

Noyes, R., Jr., Woodman, C., Garvey, M. J., Cook, B. L., Suelzer, M., Clancy, J., & Anderson, D. J. (1992). Generalized anxiety disorder vs. panic disorder: Distinguishing characteristics and patterns of comorbidity. *Journal of Nervous and Mental Disease, 180,* 369–379.

Nuechterlein, K. H., Dawson, M. E., Gitlin, M., Ventura, J., Goldstein, M. J., Snyder, K. S., Yee, C. M., & Mintz, J. (1992). Developmental processes in schizophrenic disorders: Longitudinal studies of vulnerability and stress. *Schizophrenia Bulletin, 18,* 387–425.

Nunn, J. & Peters, E. (2001). Schizotypy and patterns of lateral asymmetry on hemisphere-specific language tasks. *Psychiatry Research, 103,* 179–192.

Nurnberger, J. I., Adkins, S., Lahiri, D. K., Mayeda, A., Hu, K., Lewy, A., Miller, A., Bowman, E. S., Miller, M. J., Rau, N. L., Smiley, C., & Davis-Singh, D. (2000). Melatonin suppression by light in euthymic bipolar and unipolar patients. *Archives of General Psychiatry, 57,* 572–579.

Nutt, D. J. (2000). The psychobiology of posttraumatic stress disorder. *Journal of Clinical Psychiatry, 61,* 24–29.

Nutt, D. J. (2001). Neurobiological mechanisms in generalized anxiety disorder. *Journal of Clinical Psychiatry, 62*(Suppl. 11), 22–27.

Nutt, D. (1992) Panic attacks: A neurochemical overview of models and mechanisms. *British Journal of Psychiatry, 160,* 165–178.

Nutt, D. & Lawson, C. (1992). Panic attacks: A neurochemical overview of models and mechanisms. *British Journal of Psychiatry, 160,* 165–178.

Oakley, D. A. (1999). Hypnosis and conversion hysteria: A unifying model. *Cognitive Neuropsychiatry, 4,* 243–265.

O'Brien, C. P., Volpicelli, L. A., & Volpicelli, J. R. (1996). Naltrexone in the treatment of alcoholism: A clinical review. *Alcohol, 13,* 35–39.

Obsessive Compulsive Cognitions Working Group. (1997). Cognitive assessment of obsessive-compulsive disorder. *Behaviour Research and Therapy, 35,* 667–681.

O'Cleirigh, C., Ironson, G., Antoni, M., Fletcher, M. A., McGuffey, L., Balbin, E., et al. (2003). Emotion expression and depth processing of trauma and their relation to long-term survival in patients with HIV/AIDS. *Journal of Psychosomatic Research, 54,* 225–235.

O'Connor v. Donaldson, 95 S. Ct. 2486 (1975).

O'Donnell, J., Hawkins, J. D., Catalano, R. F., Abbott, R. D., & Day, L. E. (1995). Preventing school failure, drug use, and delinquency among low-income children: Long-term intervention in elementary schools. *American Journal of Orthopsychiatry, 65,* 87–100.

O'Driscoll, G. A., Benkelfat, C., Florencio, P. S., Wolff, A. V. G., Joober, R., Lal, S., & Evans, A. C. (1999). Neural correlates of eye tracking deficits in first-degree relatives of schizophrenic patients: A positron emission tomography study. *Archives of General Psychiatry, 56,* 1127–1134.

Oehman, A., Flykt, A., & Esteves, F. (2001). Emotion drives attention: Detecting a snake in the grass. *Journal of Experimental Psychology: General, 130,* 466–478.

O'Farrell, T. J. & Fals-Stewart, W. (2000). Behavioral couples therapy for alcoholism and drug abuse. *Behavior Therapist, 23,* 49–54, 70.

O'Farrell, T. J., Van Hutton, V., & Murphy, C. M. (1999). Domestic violence after alcoholism treatment: A two-year longitudinal study. *Journal of Studies on Alcohol, 60,* 317–321.

Offord, D. R. (1997). Bridging development, prevention, and policy. In D. M. Stoff, J. Breiling, & J. D. Maser (Eds.), *Handbook of antisocial behavior* (pp. 357–364). New York: Wiley.

O'Leary, K. D. & Wilson, G. T. (1975). *Behavior therapy—application and outcome.* Englewood Cliffs, NJ: Prentice-Hall.

O'Sullivan, R. L., Phillips, K. A., Keuthen, N. J., et al. (1999). Near-fatal skin picking from delusional body dysmorphic disorder responsive to fluvoxamine. *Psychosomatics, 40,* 79–81.

Offord, D. R., Boyle, M. H., Fleming, J. E., Munroe-Blum, H., & Rae-Grant, N. I. (1989). The Ontario Child Health Study: Summary of selected results. *Canadian Journal of Psychiatry, 34,* 483–491.

Ohno, T., Ikebuchi, E., Henomatsu, K., Kasai, K., Nakagome, K., Iwanami, A., Hiramatsu, K. I., Hata, A., Fukuda, M., Honda, M., & Miyauchi, M. (2000). Psychophysiological correlates of social skills deficits in persons with schizophrenia. *Psychiatry Research: Neuroimaging Section, 100,* 155–167.

Okazaki, S. & Sue, S. (1995). Methodological issues in assessment research with ethnic minorities. *Psychological Assessment, 7,* 367–375.

Olbrich, R., Kirsch, P., Pfeiffer, H., & Mussgay, L. (2001). Patterns of recovery of autonomic dysfunctions and neurocognitive deficits in schizophrenics after acute psychotic episodes. *Journal of Abnormal Psychology, 110,* 142–150.

Oldehinkel, A. J., Ormel, J., & Neeleman, J. (2000). Predictors of time to remission from depression in primary care patients: Do some people benefit more from positive life change than others? *Journal of Abnormal Psychology, 109,* 299–307.

Olfson, M. & Mechanic, D. (1996). Mental disorders in public, private nonprofit, and proprietary general hospitals. *American Journal of Psychiatry, 153,* 1613–1619.

Olin, S. S. & Mednick, S. A. (1996). Risk factors of psychosis: Identifying vulnerable populations premorbidly. *Schizophrenia Bulletin, 22,* 223–240.

Olivardia, R., Pope, H. G., Jr., & Hudson, J. I. (2000). Muscle dysmorphia in male weightlifters: A case-control study. *American Journal of Psychiatry, 157,* 1291–1296.

Ollendick, T. H. (1995). Cognitive behavioral treatment of panic disorder with agoraphobia in adolescents: A multiple baseline design analysis. *Behavior Therapy, 26,* 517–531.

Olney, J. W. & Farber, N. B. (1995). Glutamate receptor dysfunction and schizophrenia. *Archives of General Psychiatry, 52,* 998–1007.

Ondersma, S. J. & Walker, C. E. (1998). Elimination disorders. In T. H. Ollendick & M. Hersen (Eds.), *Handbook of child psychopathology* (3rd ed., pp. 355–378). New York: Plenum Press.

Op den Velde, W., Hovens, J. E., Aarts, P. G. H., Frey-Wouters, E., Falger, P. R. J., Van Duijn, H., & De Groen, J. H. M. (1996). Prevalence and course of posttraumatic stress disorder in Dutch veterans of the civilian resistance during World War II: An overview. *Psychological Reports, 78,* 519–529.

Oquendo, M. A., Ellis, S. P., Greenwald, S., Malone, K. M., Weissman, M. M., & Mann, J. J. (2001). Ethnic and sex differences in suicide rates relative to major depression in the United States. *American Journal of Psychiatry, 158,* 1652–1658.

Oren, D. A. & Rosenthal, N. E. (1992). Seasonal affective disorders. In E. S. Paykel (Ed.), *Handbook of affective disorders.* (2nd ed., pps. 551–568). New York: Guilford Press.

Orth, D. N., Shelton, R. C., Nicholson, W. E., Beck-Peccoz, P., Tomarken, A. J., Persani, L., & Loosen, P. T. (2001). Serum thyrotropin concentrations and bioactivity during sleep deprivation in depression. *Archives of General Psychiatry, 58,* 77–83.

Orth-Gomér, K., Eriksson, I., Moser, V., Theorell, T., & Fredlund, P. (1994). Lipid lowering through work stress reduction. *International Journal of Behavioral Medicine, 1,* 204–214.

Osgood, C., Luria, Z., Jeans, R., & Smith, S. (1976). The three faces of Evelyn: A case report. *Journal of Abnormal Psychology, 85,* 247–286.

Otto, M. W., Pollack, M. H., Sachs, G. S., Reiter, S. R., Meltzer-Brody, S., & Rosenbaum, J. F. (1993). Discontinuation of benzodiazepine treatment: Efficacy of cognitive-behavioral therapy for patients with panic disorder. *American Journal of Psychiatry, 150,* 1485–1490.

Otto, R. K. (1992). Prediction of dangerous behavior: A review and analysis of "second-generation" research. *Forensic Reports, 5,* 103–133.

Otto, R. K. (2000). Assessing and managing violence risk in outpatient settings. *Journal of Clinical Psychology, 56,* 1239–1262.

Otto, R. K., Poythress, N. G., Nicholson, R. A., Edens J. F., Monahan, J., Bonnie, R. J., Hoge, S. K., & Eisenberg, M. (1998). Psychometric properties of the MacArthur Competence Assessment Tool—Criminal adjudication. *Psychological Assessment, 10,* 435–443.

Ouimette, P. C., Finney, J. W., & Moos, R. H. (1997). Twelve-step and cognitive behavioral treatment for substance abuse: A comparison of treatment effectiveness. *Journal of Consulting and Clinical Psychology, 65,* 220–240.

Overton, D. A. (1984). State dependent learning and drug discrimination. In J. L. Iverson, S. D. Iverson, & S. H. Snyder (Eds.), *Handbook of psychopharmacology* (Vol. 18, pp. 59–127). New York: Plenum Press.

Overweight, obesity threaten U.S. health gains. (2002). *FDA Consumer, 36*(2), 8.

Owen, H. M. (2001). Pharmacological aversion treatment of alcohol dependence: I. Production and prediction of conditioned alcohol aversion. *American Journal of Drug & Alcohol Abuse, 27,* 561–585.

Oxman, T. E., Freeman, D. H., Jr., & Manheimer, E. D. (1995). Lack of social participation or religious strength and comfort as risk factors for death after cardiac surgery in the elderly. *Psychosomatic Medicine, 57,* 5–15.

Ozonoff, S. (1995). Executive functions in autism. In E. Schopler & G. Mesibov (Eds.), *Learning and cognition in autism* (pp. 199–219). New York: Plenum Press.

Ozonoff, S. & Miller, J. N. (1995). Teaching theory of mind: A new approach to social skills training for individuals with autism. *Journal of Autism and Developmental Disorders, 25,* 415–433.

Paillere Martinot, M. L., Bragulat, V., Artiges, E., Dolle, F., Hinnen, F., Jouvent, R., & Martinot, J. L. (2001). Decreased presynaptic dopamine function in the left caudate of depressed patients with affective flattening and psychomotor retardation. *American Journal of Psychiatry, 158,* 314–316.

Pakenham, K. I. & Rinaldis, M. (2002). Development of the HIV/AIDS Stress Scale. *Psychology and Health, 17,* 203–219.

Palermo, G. B. & Martens, W. H. J. (in press). *Jeffrey Dahmer and Dennis Nilsen: A double portrait of two sadistic serial killers.* Thousand Oaks, CA: Sage.

Palermo-Neto, J., Massoco, C. O., & de Souza, W. R. (2003). Effects of physical and psychological stressors on behavior, macrophage activity, and Ehrlich tumor growth. *Brain, Behavior, and Immunity, 17,* 43–54.

Palfai, T. P., Monti, P. M., Colby, S. M., & Rohsennow, D. J. (1997). Effects of suppressing the urge to drink on the accessibility of alcohol outcome expectancies. *Behavior Research and Therapy, 35,* 59–65.

Palombo, J. (2001). *Learning disorders and disorders of the self in children and adolescents.* New York: W. W. Norton.

Panzarella, C., Alloy, L. B., & Whitehouse, W. G. (2003). *Expanded hopelessness theory of depression: On the mechanisms by which social support protects against depression.* Manuscript under editorial review.

Papero, D. V. (1995). Bowen family systems and marriage. In N. S. Jacobson, A. S. Gurman, et al. (Eds.), *Clinical handbook of couple therapy* (pp. 11–30). New York: Guilford Press.

Pardo, P. J., Knesevich, M. A., Vogler, G. P., Pardo, J. V., Towne, B., Cloninger, C. R., & Posner, M. I. (2000). Genetic and state variables of neurocognitive dysfunction in schizophrenia: A twin study. *Schizophrenia Bulletin, 26,* 459–477.

Pariante, C. M., Nemeroff, C. B., & Miller, A. H. (1997). In D. L. Dunner (Ed.), *Current psychiatric therapy II* (pp. 44–51). Philadelphia: Saunders.

Park, C. L., Folkman, S., & Bostrom, A. (2001). Appraisals of controllability and coping in caregivers and HIV+ men: Testing the goodness-of-fit hypothesis. *Journal of Consulting and Clinical Psychology, 69,* 481–488.

Parker, G. & Lipscombe, P. (1980). The relevance of early parental experiences to adult dependency, hypochondriasis and utilization of primary physicians. *British Journal of Medical Psychology, 53,* 355–363.

Parker, G., Johnston, P., & Hayward, L. (1998). Parental "expressed emotion" as a predictor of schizophrenic relapse. *Archives of General Psychiatry, 45,* 806–813.

Parker, G., Roy, K., Hadzi-Pavlovic, D., Mitchell, P., Wilhelm, K., Menkes, D. B., Snowdon, J., Loo, C., & Schweitzer, I. (2000). Subtyping depression by clinical features: The Australasian database. *Acta Psychiatrica Scandinavica, 101,* 21–28.

Parks, G. A., Anderson, B. K., & Marlatt, G. A. (2001). Relapse prevention therapy. In N. Heather & T. J. Peters (Eds.), *International handbook of alcohol dependence and problems* (pp. 575–592). New York: Wiley.

Parnas, J., Cannon, T. D., Jacobsen, B., Schulsinger, H., Schulsinger, F., & Mednick, S. A. (1993). Lifetime *DSM-III-R* diagnostic outcomes in the offspring of schizophrenic mothers: Results from the Copenhagen high-risk study. *Archives of General Psychiatry, 50,* 707–714.

Pasquier, F. & Delacourte, A. (1998). Non-Alzheimer degenerative dementias. *Current Opinions in Neurology, 11,* 417–427.

Patronek, G. J. (1999). Hoarding of animals: An under-recognized public health problem in a difficult-to-study population. *Public Health Reports, 114*(1), 81–87.

Patterson, G. R. (1976). *Living with children: New methods for parents and teachers.* Champaign, IL: Research Press.

Patterson, G. R. (1982). *A social learning approach: Vol. 3. Coercive family processes.* Eugene, OR: Castilia.

Patterson, G. R. (1993). Orderly change in a stable world: The antisocial trait as a chimera. *Journal of Consulting and Clinical Psychology, 61,* 911–919.

Patterson, G. R., Reid, J. B., & Dishion, T. J. (1992). *Antisocial boys.* Eugene, OR: Castalia.

Patton, R. B. & Sheppard, J. A. (1956). Intercranial tumors found at autopsy in mental patients. *American Journal of Psychiatry, 113,* 319–324.

Paul, G. L. & Lentz, R. J. (1977). *Psychosocial treatment of chronic mental patients: Milieu versus social-learning programs.* Cambridge, MA: Harvard University Press.

Paul, W. M., Gonsiorek, J. C., & Hotvedt, M. E. (Eds.). (1982). *Homosexuality.* Beverly Hills, CA: Sage.

Pauls, D. L., Alsobrook, J. P., II., Goodman, W., Rasmussen, S., & Leckman, J. F. (1995). A family study of obsessive-compulsive disorder. *American Journal of Psychiatry, 152,* 76–84.

Paykel, E. S. & Cooper, Z. (1992). Life events and social stress. In E. S. Paykel (Ed.), *Handbook of affective disorders.* (2nd ed., pp. 149–170). New York: Guilford Press.

Paykel, E. S., Scott, J., Teasdale, J. D., Johnson, A. L., Garland, A., Moore, R., Jenaway, A., Cornwall, P. L., Hayhurst, H., Abbott, R., & Pope, M. (1999). Prevention of relapse in residual depression by cognitive therapy: A controlled trial. *Archives of General Psychiatry, 56,* 829–835.

Pearlin, L. I., Mullan, J. T., Semple, S. J., & Skaff, M. M. (1990). Caregiving and the stress process: An overview of concepts and their measures. *Gerontologist, 30,* 583–594.

Pearlson, G. D. & Marsh, L. (1999). Structural brain imaging in schizophrenia: A selective review. *Biological Psychiatry, 46,* 627–649.

Pearson, D. A., Doyle, M. D., Pickering, L. K., & Ortegon, J. (1996). Pediatric HIV infection: A review of epidemiology, clinical manifestations, and current intervention. *Journal of Developmental and Physical Disabilities, 8,* 179–210. Public mental health issue. Risk-taking behavior and compulsive gambling. *American Psychologist, 41,* 461–465.

Pedersen, C. B. & Mortensen, P. B. (2001). Evidence of a dose-response relationship between urbanicity during upbringing and schizophrenia risk. *Archives of General Psychiatry, 58,* 1039–1046.

Pelham, W. E., Gnagy, E. M., Greenslade, K. E., & Milich, R. (1992). Teacher ratings of *DSM-III-R* symptoms for the disruptive behavior disorders. *Journal of the American Academy of Child and Adolescent Psychiatry, 31,* 210–218.

Penick, E. C., Powell, B. J., Campbell, J., Liskow-Barry, I., et al. (1996). Pharmacological treatment for antisocial personality disorder alcoholics: A preliminary study. *Alcoholism: Clinical and Experimental Research 20,* 477–484.

Penn, D. L. & Mueser, K. T. (1996). Research update on the psychosocial treatment of schizophrenia. *American Journal of Psychiatry, 153,* 607–617.

Penn, D. L., Combs, D. R., & Mohamed, S. (2001). Social cognition and social functioning in schizophrenia. In P. W. Corrigan & D. L. Penn (Eds.), *Social cognition and schizophrenia* (pp. 97–121). Washington, DC: American Psychological Association.

Penn, D. L., Combs, D. R., Ritchie, M., Francis, J., Cassisi, J., Morris, S., & Townsend, M. (2000). Emotion recognition in schizophrenia: Further investigation of generalized versus specific deficit models. *Journal of Abnormal Psychology, 109,* 512–516.

Penn, D. L., Kohlmaier, J. R., & Corrigan, P. W. (2000). Interpersonal factors contributing to the stigma of schizophrenia: Social skills, perceived attractiveness, and symptoms. *Schizophrenia Research, 45,* 37–45.

Pennebaker, J. W. (1990). *Opening up: The healing power of confiding in others.* New York: Morrow.

Pennebaker, J. W. (1993). Putting stress into words: Health, linguistic, and therapeutic implications. *Behavior Research and Therapy, 31,* 539–548.

Pennebaker, J. W. & Francis, M. (1996). Cognitive, emotional, and language processes in disclosure. *Cognition and Emotion, 10,* 601–626.

Pennebaker, J. W., Kiecolt-Glaser, J., & Glaser, R. (1988). Disclosure of traumas and immune function: Health implications for psychotherapy. *Journal of Consulting and Clinical Psychology, 56,* 239–245.

Pennebaker, J. W. & Seagal, J. D. (1999). Forming a story: The health benefits of narrative. *Journal of Clinical Psychology, 55,* 1243–1254.

Pennebaker, J. W. & Watson, D. (1991). The psychology of somatic symptoms. In L. J. Kirmayer & J. M. Robbins (Eds.), *Current concepts of somatization: Research and clinical perspectives* (pp. 21–35). Washington, DC: American Psychiatric Press.

Penninx, B. W. J. H., Beekman, A. T. F., Honig, A., Deeg, D. J. H., Schoevers, R. A., van Eijk, J. T. M., & van Tilburg, W. (2001). Depression and cardiac mortality: Results from a community-based longitudinal study. *Archives of General Psychiatry, 58,* 221–227.

Penninx, B. W. J. H., Geerlings, S. W., Deeg, D. J. H., van Eijk, J. T. M., van Tilburg, W., & Beekman, A. T. F. (1999). Minor and major depression and the risk of death in older persons. *Archives of General Psychiatry, 56,* 889–895.

Pericek-Vance, M. A., Bass, M. P., Yamaoka, L. H., Gaskell, P. C., Scott, W. K., Terwedow, H. A., Menold, M. M., Conneally, P. M., Small, G. W., Vance, J. M., Saunders, A. M., Roses, A. D., & Haines, J. L. (1997). Complete genomic screen in late-onset familial Alzheimer's disease. Evidence for a new locus on chromosome 12. *Journal of the American Medical Association, 278,* 1282–1283.

Perlin, M. L. (1993–1994). Hospitalized patients and the right to sexual interaction: Beyond the last frontier? *NYU Review of Law and Social Change, 20,* 517–547.

Perlin, M. L. (1994). *Law and mental disability.* Charlottesville: Michie.

Perlin, M. L. (1996). The voluntary delivery of mental health services in the community. In B. D. Sales & D. W. Shuman (Eds.), *Law, mental health, and mental disorder* (pp. 150–177). New York: Brooks/Cole.

Perlis, M., Aloia, M., Millikan, A., Boehmler, J., Smith, M., Greenblatt, D., & Giles, D. (2000). Behavioral treatment of insomnia: A clinical case series study. *Journal of Behavioral Medicine, 23,* 149–161.

Perls, F. S. (1970). Four lectures. In J. Fagan & I. I. Shepherd (Eds.) *Gestalt therapy now: Therapy techniques, applications.* Palo Alto, CA: Science and Behavior Books.

Perls, F. (1973). *The Gestalt approach.* Palo Alto, CA: Science Behavior.

Perry, S., Frances, A., & Clarkin, J. (1990). *A* DSM-III-R *casebook of treatment selection.* New York: Brunner/Mazel.

Perry, W. & Braff, D. L. (1994). Information-processing deficits and thought disorder in schizophrenia. *American Journal of Psychiatry, 151,* 363–367.

Perry, W., Geyer, M. A., & Braff, D. L. (1999). Sensorimotor gating and thought disturbance measured in close temporal proximity in schizophrenic patients. *Archives of General Psychiatry, 56,* 277–281.

Persons, J. B. & Davidson, J. (2001). Cognitive-behavioral case formulation. In K. Dobson (Ed.), *Handbook of cognitive-behavioral therapies* (2nd ed., pp. 86–110). New York: Guilford Press.

Peters, E. R., Pickering, A. D., Kent, A., Glasper, A., Irania, M., David, A. S., Day, S., & Hemsley, D. R. (2000). The relationship between cognitive inhibition and psychotic symptoms. *Journal of Abnormal Psychology, 109,* 386–395.

Peters, K. D. & Murphy, S. L. (1998). Deaths: Final data for 1996. *National Vital Statistics Report, 47*(9).

Peterson, C., Maier, S. F., & Seligman, M. E. P. (1993). *Learned helplessness: A theory for the age of personal control.* New York: Oxford University Press.

Peterson, G. & Putnam, F. W. (1994). Preliminary results of the field trial of proposed criteria for Dissociative Disorder of Childhood. *Dissociation, 7,* 212–220.

Petrila, J. & Douglas, K. S. (2002). Legal issues in maximum security institutions for people with mental illness: Liberty, security, and administrative discretion. *Behavioral Sciences and the Law, 20,* 463–480.

Petrila, J., Poythress, N. G., McGaha, A., & Boothroyd, R. A. (2001). Preliminary observations from an evaluation of the Broward County Mental Health Court. *Court Review,* Winter, 14–22.

Phillips, K. A. (1996a). *The broken mirror: Understanding and treating body* *dysmorphic disorder*. New York: Oxford University Press.

Phillips, K. A. (1996b). Pharmacologic treatment of body dysmorphic disorder. *Psychopharmacology Bulletin, 32,* 597–605.

Phillips, K. A. (2001). Body dysmorphic disorder. In K. A. Phillips (Ed.), *Somatoform and factitious disorders* (pp. 95–128). Washington, DC: American Psychiatric Press.

Phillips, K. A., Atala, K. D., & Albertini, R. S. (1995). Case study: Body dysmorphic disorder in adolescents. *Journal of the American Academy of Child and Adolescent Psychiatry, 34,* 1216–1220.

Phillips, K. A. & Diaz, S. F. (1997). Gender differences in body dysmorphic disorder. *Journal of Nervous and Mental Disease, 185,* 578–582.

Phillips, K. A., Dufresne, R. G., Jr., Wilkel, D., et al. (2000). Rate of body dysmorphic disorder in dermatology patients. *Journal of the American Academy of Dermatology, 42,* 436–441.

Phillips, K. A., Nierenberg, A. A., Brendel, G., et al. (1996). Prevalence and clinical features of body dysmorphic disorder in atypical major depression. *Journal of Nervous and Mental Disease, 184,* 125–129.

Pica, M. (1999). The evolution of alter personality states in dissociative identity disorder. *Psychotherapy, 36,* 404–415.

Pickering, T. (1999). Cardiovascular pathways: Socioeconomic status and stress effects on hypertension and cardiovascular function. *Annals of the New York Academy of Sciences, 896,* 262–277.

Pierce, J. W. & Wardle, J. (1993). Self-esteem, parental appraisal and body size in children. *Journal of Child Psychology and Psychiatry, 34,* 1125–1136.

Pierri, J. N., Volk, C. L. E., Auh, S., Sampson, A., & Lewis, D. A. (2001). Decreased somal size of deep layer 3 pyramidal neurons in the prefrontal cortex of subjects with schizophrenia. *Archives of General Psychiatry, 58,* 466–473.

Pigott, T. A. (1996). OCD: Where the serotonin selectivity story begins. *Journal of Clinical Psychiatry, 57,* 11–20.

Pilowsky, I. (1994). Abnormal illness behaviour: A 25th anniversary review. *Australian and New Zealand Journal of Psychiatry, 28,* 566–573.

Pincus, T. & Morley, S. (2001). Cognitive-processing bias in chronic pain: A review and integration. *Psychological Bulletin, 127,* 571–598.

Pinel, P. (1967). *A treatise on insanity* (D. D. Davis, Trans.). New York: Hafner. Original work published 1801.

Pines, M. (1982a, June). Infant-stim. It's changing the lives of handicapped kids. *Psychology Today,* pp. 48–52.

Pines, M. (1982b, April 16). Recession is linked to far-reaching psychological harm. *The New York Times,* p. C1.

Pini, S., Cassano, G. B., Simonini, E., Savino, M., Russo, A., & Montgomery, S. A. (1997). Prevalence of anxiety disorders comorbidity in bipolar depression, unipolar depression and dysthymia. *Journal of Affective Disorders, 42,* 145–153.

Piotrowski, C., Belter, R. W., & Keller, J. W. (1998). The impact of "managed care" on the practice of psychological testing: Preliminary findings. *Journal of Personality Assessment, 70,* 441–447.

Piper, A. (1997). *Hoax and reality: The bizarre world of multiple personality disorder*. Northvale, NJ: Jason Aronson.

Piper, A., Jr. (1994a). Multiple personality disorder. *British Journal of Psychiatry, 164,* 600–612.

Piper, A., Jr. (1994b). Treatment for multiple personality disorder: At what cost? *American Journal of Psychotherapy, 48,* 392–400.

Pithers, W. D. & Cumming, G. F. (1989). *Can relapse be prevented? Initial outcome data from the Vermont treatment program for sexual aggressors*. New York: Guilford Press.

Pitman, R. K. (1988). Post-traumatic stress disorder, conditioning, and network theory. *Psychiatric Annals, 18,* 182–189.

Pitman, R. K. (1989). Editorial: Post-traumatic stress disorder, hormones, and memory. *Biological Psychiatry, 26,* 221–223.

Plomin, R. & Crabbe, J. (2000). DNA. *Psychological Bulletin, 126,* 806–828.

Plomin, R., DeFries, J. C., McClearn, G. E., & McGuffin, P. (2001). *Behavioral genetics* (4th ed.). New York: W. H. Freeman.

Plomin, R. & Rende, R. (1991). Human behavioral genetics. *Annual Review of Psychology, 42,* 161–190.

Plotsky, P. M. & Meaney, M. J. (1993). Early, postnatal experience alters hypothalamic corticotropin-releasing factor (CRF) mRNA median eminence CRF content and stress-induced release in adult rats. *Brain Research: Molecular Brain Research, 18,* 195–200.

Polaschek, D. L. L., Ward, T., & Hudson, S. M. (1997). Rape and rapists: Theory and treatment. *Clinical Psychology Review, 17,* 117–144.

Poletiek, F. H. (2002). How psychiatrists and judges assess the dangerousness of persons with mental illness: An "expertise bias." *Behavioral Sciences and the Law, 20,* 19–29.

Polivy, J. & Herman, C. P. (1985). Dieting and binging: A causal analysis. *American Psychologist, 40,* 193–201.

Pollitt, E. (1994). Poverty and child development: Relevance of research in developing countries to the United States. *Child Development, 65,* 283–295.

Polloway, E. A., Smith, J. D., Patton, J. R., & Smith, T. E. C. (1996). Historic changes in mental retardation and developmental disabilities. *Education and Training in Mental Retardation and Developmental Disabilities, 31,* 3–12.

Pope, H. G. & Katz, D. L. (1990). *Journal of Clinical Psychology, 51.*

Pope, H. G., Oliva, P. S., Hudson, J. I., Bodkin, J. A., & Gruber, A. J. (1999). Attitudes toward *DSM-IV* dissociative disorders diagnoses among board-certified American psychiatrists. *American Journal of Psychiatry, 156,* 321–323.

Pope, H. G., Phillips, K. A., & Olivardia, R. (2000). *The Adonis complex: The secret crisis of male body obsession*. New York: Free Press.

Pope, K. S. (1999). Dual relationships in psychotherapy. In D. N. Bersoff (Ed.), *Ethical conflicts in psychology* (2nd ed., pp. 231–234). Washington, DC: American Psychological Association.

Porcerelli, J. H. & Sandler, B. A. (1998). Anabolic-androgenic steroid abuse and psychopathology. *Psychiatric Clinics of North America, 21,* 829–833.

Portenoy, R. K. & Payne, R. (1997). Acute and chronic pain. In J. H. Lowinson, P. Ruiz, R. B. Millman, & J. G. Langrod (Eds.), *Substance abuse: A comprehensive textbook* (pp. 563–591). Baltimore: Williams & Wilkins.

Porter, S., Birt, A. R., Yuille, J. C., & Herve, H. F. (2001). Memory for murder: A psychological perspective on dissociative amnesia in legal contexts. *International Journal of Law and Psychiatry, 24*, 23–42.

Portin, P. & Alanen, Y. O. (1997). A critical review of genetic studies of schizophrenia. I. Epidemiological and brain studies. *Acta Psychiatrica Scandinavica, 95*, 1–5.

Posener, J. A., DeBattista, C., Williams, G. H., Kraemer, H. C., Kalehzan, B. M., & Schatzberg, A. F. (2000). 24-hour monitoring of cortisol and corticotropin secretion in psychotic and nonpsychotic major depression. *Archives of General Psychiatry, 57*, 755–760.

Post, F. (1994). Creativity and psychopathology: A study of 291 world-famous men. *British Journal of Psychiatry, 165*, 22–34.

Potter, L. B. & Mercy, J. A. (1997). Public health perspective on interpersonal violence among youths in the United States. In D. M. Stoff, J. Breiling, & J. D. Maser (Eds.), *Handbook of antisocial behavior* (pp. 3–21). New York: Wiley.

Poulson, R. L., Wuensch, K. L., & Brondino, M. J. (1998). Factors that discriminate among mock jurors' verdict selections: Impact of the guilty but mentally ill verdict option. *Criminal Justice and Behavior, 25*, 366–381.

Powell, R. A. & Gee, T. L. (1999). The effects of hypnosis on dissociative identity disorder: A reexamination of the evidence. *Canadian Journal of Psychiatry, 44*, 914–916.

Poythress, N. G., Petrila, J., McGaha, A., & Boothroyd, R. (2002). Perceived coercion and procedural justice in the Broward mental health court. *International Journal of Law and Psychiatry, 5*, 517–533.

Prasher, V. P. & Chung, M. C. (1996). Causes of age-related decline in adaptive behavior of adults with Down syndrome: Differential diagnoses of dementia. *American Journal on Mental Retardation, 101*, 175–183.

Preisig, M., Bellivier, F., Fenton, B. T., et al. (2000). Association between bipolar disorder and monoamine oxidase A gene polymorphisms: Results of a multicenter study. *American Journal of Psychiatry, 157*, 948–955.

Prendergast, M. L., Farabee, D., Cartier, J., & Henkin, S. (2002). Involuntary treatment within a prison setting: Impact on psychosocial change during treatment. *Criminal Justice and Behavior, 29*, 5–26.

Prescott, C. A., Aggen, S. H., & Kendler, K. S. (2000). Sex-specific genetic influences on the comorbidity of alcoholism and major depression in a population-based sample of US twins. *Archives of General Psychiatry, 57*(8), 803–811.

Preu, P. W. (1944). The concept of the psychopathic personality. In J. McV. Hunt (Ed.), *Personality and the behavior disorders* (Vol. 2). New York: Ronald Press.

Price, J. & Hess, N. C. (1979). *Australian and New Zealand Journal of Psychiatry, 13*, 63–66.

Price, R. H. (1978). *Abnormal behavior: Perspectives in conflict* (2nd ed.). New York: Holt, Rinehart & Winston.

Prieto, S. L., Cole, D. A., & Tageson, C. W. (1992). Depressive self-schemas in clinic and nonclinic children. *Cognitive Therapy and Research, 16*, 521–534.

Prince, M. (1905). *The dissociation of personality*. New York: Longman.

Pring, L., Hermelin, B., & Heavey, L. (1995). Savants, segments, art and autism. *Journal of Child Psychology and Psychiatry, 36*, 1065–1076.

Project MATCH Research Group. (1997). Matching alcoholism treatments to client heterogeneity: Project MATCH posttreatment drinking outcomes. *Journal of Studies on Alcohol, 58*, 7–29.

Protheroe, D., Turvey, K., Horgan, K., Benson, E., Bowers, D., & House, A. (1999). Stressful life events and difficulties and onset of breast cancer: case-control study. *British Medical Journal, 319*, 1027–1030.

Prouty, G. (1994). *Theoretical evolutions in person-centered/experiential therapy: Applications to schizophrenic and retarded psychoses.* Westport, CT: Praeger.

Provins, K. A. (1997). Handedness and speech: A critical reappraisal of the role of genetic and environmental factors in the cerebral lateralization of function. *Psychological Review, 104*, 554–571.

Puhl, R. & Brownell, K. D. (2001). Bias, discrimination, and obesity. *Obesity Research, 9*, 788–805.

Purba, J. S., Hoogendijk, W. J. G., Hofman, M. A., & Swaab, D. F. (1996). Increased number of vasopressin- and oxytocin-expressing neurons in the paraventricular nucleus of the hypothalamus in depression. *Archives of General Psychiatry, 53*, 137–143.

Putnam, F. W. (1989). *Diagnosis and treatment of multiple personality disorder*. New York: Guilford Press.

Putnam, F. W. (1997). *Dissociation in children and adolescents: A developmental perspective*. New York: Guilford Press.

Putnam, F. W., Guroff, J. J., Silberman, E. K., Barban, L., & Post, R. M. (1986). The clinical phenomenology of multiple personality disorder: Review of 100 recent cases. *Journal of Clinical Psychiatry, 47*, 285–293.

Putnam, F. W. & Loewenstein, R. J. (1993). Treatment of multiple personality disorder: A survey of current practices. *American Journal of Psychiatry, 150*, 1048–1052.

Putnam, F. W. & Loewenstein, R. J. (2000). Dissociative identity disorder. In B. J. Sadock & V. A. Sadock (Eds.), *Kaplan and Sadock's comprehensive textbook of psychiatry* (7th ed., Vol. 1, pp. 1552–1564). Philadelphia: Lippincott Williams & Wilkins.

Pykett, I. L. (1982). NMR imaging in medicine. *Scientific American, 246*, 78–88.

Quitkin, F. M., Rabkin, J. G., Gerald, J., Davis, J. M., & Klein, D. F. (2000). Validity of clinical trials of antidepressants. *American Journal of Psychiatry, 157*, 327–337.

Rabasca, L. (2000). A court that sentences psychological care rather than jail time. *Monitor on Psychology*, July/August, 58–60.

Rabkin, J. G., Williams, J. B., Remien, R. H., Goetz, R., Kertzner, R., & Gorman, J. (1991). Depression, distress, lymphocyte subsets, and human immunodeficiency virus symptoms on two occasions in HIV-positive homosexual men. *Archives of General Psychiatry, 48*, 111–119.

Rachman, S. J. (1997). A cognitive theory of obsessions. *Behaviour Research and Therapy, 35*, 793–802.

Rachman, S. J. & de Silva, P. (1978) Abnormal and normal obsessions. *Behaviour Research and Therapy, 16*, 233–248.

Rachman, S. J. & Hodgson, R. J. (1980). *Obsessions and compulsions*. Englewood Cliffs, NJ: Prentice-Hall.

Rachman, S. J., Lopatka, C., & Levitt, K. (1988). Experimental analyses of panic—II. Panic patients. *Behaviour Research and Therapy, 26*, 33–40.

Rachman, S. J., Shafran, R., & Riskind, J. H. (in press). Cognitive vulnerability to obsessive-compulsive disorders (OCD). In L.B. Alloy & J. H. Riskind (Eds.), *Cognitive vulnerability to emotional disorders*. Mahwah, NJ: Erlbaum.

Ragland, D. R. & Brand, R. J. (1988). Type A behavior and mortality from coronary heart disease. *New England Journal of Medicine, 318,* 65–69.

Raguram, R., Weiss, M. G., Channabasavanna, S. M., & Devins, G. M. (1996). Stigma, depression, and somatization in South India. *American Journal of Psychiatry, 153,* 1043–1049.

Rahe, R. H., Taylor, C. B., Tolles, R. L., Newhall, L. M., Veach, T. L., & Bryson, S. (2002). A novel stress and workplace program reduces illness and healthcare utilization. *Psychosomatic Medicine, 64,* 278–286.

Raine, A. (1997). Antisocial behavior and psychophysiology: A biosocial perspective and a pre-frontal dysfunction hypothesis. In D. M. Stoff, J. Breiling, & J. D. Maser, (Eds.), *Handbook of antisocial behavior* (pp. 289–304). New York: Wiley.

Raine, A., Venables, P., & Mednick, S. A. (1997). Low resting heart rate at age 3 years predisposed to aggression at 11 years: Evidence from the Mauritius child health project. *Journal of the American Academy of Child Adolescent Psychiatry, 36.*

Raine, A., Venables, P., & Williams, M. (1995). High autonomic arousal and electrodermal orienting at age 15 years as protective factors against criminal behavior at age 29 years. *American Journal of Psychiatry, 152,* 1595–1600.

Ram, R., Bromet, E. J., Eaton, W. W., Pato, C., & Schwarz, J. E. (1992). The natural course of schizophrenia: A review of first admission studies. *Schizophrenia Bulletin, 18,* 185–207.

Ramirez, A., Craig, T. K. J., Watson, J. P., Fentiman, I. S., North, W. R. S., & Rubens, R. D. (1989). Stress and relapse of cancer. *British Medical Journal, 298,* 291–293.

Rao, U., Ryan, N. D., Birmaher, B., Dahl, R. E., Williamson, D. E., Kaufman, J., Rao, R., & Nelson, G. (1995). Unipolar depression in adolescents: Clinical outcome in adulthood. *Journal of the American Academy of Child and Adolescent Psychiatry, 34,* 566–578.

Rao, V. & Lyketsos, C. G. (2002). Psychiatric aspects of traumatic brain injury. *Psychiatric Clinics of North America, 25*(1), 43–69.

Rapaport, D., Gill, M., & Schaefer, R. (1968). *Diagnostic psychological testing*. New York: International Universities Press.

Rapee, R. M. & Heimberg, R. G. (1997). A cognitive-behavioral model of anxiety in social phobia. *Behaviour Research and Therapy, 35,* 741–756.

Rapin, I. (1991). Autistic children: Diagnosis and clinical features. *Pediatrics, 87* (Suppl.), 751–760.

Rashid, W. (2000). Testosterone abuse and affective disorders. *Journal of Substance Abuse Treatment, 18,* 179–184.

Raskin, N. H., Hosobuchi, Y., & Lamb, S. A. (1987). Headache may arise from perturbation of brain. *Headache, 27,* 416–420.

Rasmussen, S. A. & Tsuang, M. T. (1986). Clinical characteristics and family history of *DSM-III* obsessive–compulsive disorder. *American Journal of Psychiatry, 143,* 317–322.

Rastam, M. (1992). Anorexia nervosa in 51 Swedish adolecents. *Journal of the American Academy of Child and Adolescent Psychiatry, 31,* 819–829.

Rauschenberger, S. L. & Lynn, S. J. (1995). Fantasy proneness, *DSM-III-R* Axis I psychopathology, and dissociation. *Journal of Abnormal Psychology, 104,* 373–380.

Ray, O. S. (1983). *Drugs, society, and human behavior*. St. Louis: Mosby.

Ray, O. & Ksir, C. (1993). *Drugs, society, and human behavior.* St. Louis: Mosby.

Ray, W. A., Meredith, S., Thapa, P. B., Meador, K. G., Hall, K., & Murray, K. T. (2001). Antipsychotics and the risk of sudden cardiac death. *Archives of General Psychiatry, 58,* 1161–1167.

Recent Cases. (2001). Criminal procedure—Substantive due process—Circuit holds that the government may forcibly treat incompetent criminal defendants with antipsychotic medication to render them competent to stand trial. —*United States v. Weston,* 255 F.3D 873 (D.C. Cir. 2001), Petition for cert. Filed (U.S. Sept. 5, 2001) (No. 01-6161). *Harvard Law Review, 115,* 737–743.

Rector, N. A. & Beck, A. T. (2001). Cognitive behavioral therapy for schizophrenia: An empirical review. *Journal of Nervous and Mental Disease, 189,* 278–287.

Redding, R. E., Floyd, M. Y., & Hawk, G. L. (2001). What judges and lawyers think about the testimony of mental health experts: A survey of the courts and bar. *Behavioral Sciences and the Law, 19,* 583–594.

Redlich, F. C. & Freedman, D. X. (1966). *The theory and practice of psychiatry*. New York: Basic Books.

Reed, G. M., Kemeny, M. E., Taylor, S. E., & Visscher, B. R. (1999). Negative HIV-specific expectancies and AIDS-related bereavement as predictors of symptom onset in asymptomatic HIV-positive gay men. *Health Psychology, 18,* 354–363. (Cited in Kemeny, M. E. [2003]. An interdisciplinary research model to investigate psychosocial cofactors in disease: Application to HIV-1 pathogenesis. *Brain, Behavior, and Immunity, 17,* S62–S72).

Reed, G. M., Kemeny, M. E., Taylor, S. E., Wang, H. Y., & Visscher, B. R. (1994). Realistic acceptance as a predictor of decreased survival time in gay men with AIDS. *Health Psychology, 13,* 299–307. (Cited in Kemeny, M. E. [2003]. An interdisciplinary research model to investigate psychosocial cofactors in disease: Application to HIV-1 pathogenesis. *Brain, Behavior, and Immunity, 17,* S62–S72).

Rehm, L. P., Wagner, A., & Ivens-Tyndal, C. (2001). Mood disorders: Unipolar and bipolar. In P. B. Sutker & H. E. Adams (Eds.), *Comprehensive handbook of psychopathology* (3rd ed., pp. 277–308). New York: Kluwer Academic/Plenum.

Reich, J., Goldenberg, I., Vasile, R., Goisman, R., & Keller, M. A. (1994). A prospective follow-along study of the course of social phobia. *Psychiatry Research, 54,* 249–258.

Reid, D. H., Wilson, P., & Faw, G. (1991). Teaching self-help skills. In J. L. Matson & J. A. Mulick (Eds.), *Handbook of mental retardation* (2nd ed., pp. 436–450). New York: Pergamon Press.

Reid, J. B. & Eddy, J. M. (1997). The prevention of antisocial behavior: Some considerations in the search for effective interventions. In D. M. Stoff, J. Breiling, & J. D. Maser (Eds.), *Handbook of antisocial behavior* (pp. 343–356). New York: Wiley.

Reid, M. R., Drummond, P. D., & Mackinnon, L. T. (2001). The effect of moderate aerobic exercise and relaxation on secretory immunoglobulin A. *International Journal of Sports Medicine, 22,* 132–137.

Reilly-Harrington, N. A., Alloy, L. B., Fresco, D. M., & Whitehouse, W. G. (1999). Cognitive styles and life events interact to predict bipolar and unipolar symptomatology. *Journal of Abnormal Psychology, 108,* 567–578.

Reinecke, M. A. & Rogers, G. M. (2001). Dysfunctional attitudes and attachment style among clinically depressed adults. *Behavioral and Cognitive Psychotherapy, 29,* 129–141.

Reisner, R. (1985). *Law and the mental health system.* St. Paul, MN: West.

Reisner, R. & Slobogin, C. (1990). *Law and the mental health system: Civil and criminal aspects* (2nd ed.). St. Paul: West. With 1995 supplement.

Reiss, S. (1992). Assessment of psychopathology in persons with mental retardation. In J. L. Matson & R. P. Barrett (Eds.), *Psychopathology and mental retardation.* New York: Grune & Stratton.

Reiss, S. (1994). *Handbook of challenging behavior: Mental health aspects of mental retardation.* Worthington, OH: IDS Publications.

Reiss, S. & Rojahn, J. (1994). Joint occurrence of depression and aggression in children and adults with mental retardation. *Journal of Intellectual Disability Research, 37,* 287–294.

Reiss, S. & Valenti-Hein, D. (1990). *Reiss scales for children's dual diagnosis test manual.* Worthington, OH: International Diagnostic Systems.

Reite, M., Sheeder, J., Teale, P., Adams, M., Richardson, D., Simon, J., Jones, R. H., & Rojas, D. C. (1997). Magnetic source imaging evidence of sex differences in cerebral lateralization in schizophrenia. *Archives of General Psychiatry, 54,* 433–440.

Rescorla, R. A. (1988). Pavlovian conditioning: It's not what you think it is. *American Psychologist, 43,* 151–160.

Resnick, H., Monnier, J., Seals, B., Holmes, M., Nayak, M., Walsh, J., Weaver, T. L., Acierno, R., & Kilpatrick, D. G. (2002). Rape-related HIV risk concerns among recent rape victims. *Journal of Interpersonal Violence, 17,* 746–759.

Resnick, H. S., Kilpatrick, D. G., Dansky, B. S., Saunders, B. E., & Best, C. L. (1993). Prevalence of civilian trauma and PTSD in a representative national sample of women. *Journal of Consulting and Clinical Psychology, 61,* 984–991.

Reynolds, A. J., Temple, J. A., Robertson, D. L., & Mann, E. A. (2001). Long term effects of an early childhood intervention on educational achievement and juvenile arrest: A 15-year follow-up of low-income children in public schools. *Journal of the American Medical Association, 285,* 2339–2346.

Reynolds, A. L. & Caron, S. L. (2001). How intimate relationships are impacted when heterosexual men cross-dress. *Journal of Psychology and Human Sexuality, 12,* 63–77.

Reynolds, D. K. (1993). *Plunging through the clouds: Constructive living currents.* Albany: State University of New York Press.

Reynolds, W. M. & Mazza, J. J. (1994). Suicide and suicidal behaviors in children and adolescents. In W. M. Reynolds & H. F. Johnston (Eds.), *Handbook of depression in children and adolescents* (pp. 525–580). New York: Plenum Press.

Rhee, S. H., Feignon, S. A., Bar, J. L., Hadeishi, Y., & Waldman, I. D. (2001). Behavior genetic approaches to the study of psychopathology. In H. E. Adams & P. B. Sutker (Eds.), *Comprehensive handbook of psychopathology* (3rd ed., pp. 53–84). New York: Kluwer Academic/Plenum.

Rice, M. (1997). Violent offender research and implications for the criminal justice system. *American Psychologist, 53,* 414–423.

Rich, C. L., Warsradt, M. D., Nemiroff, R. A., Fowler, R. C., & Young, D. (1991). Suicide, stressors, and the life cycle. *American Journal of Psychiatry, 148,* 524–527.

Richards, R. L., Kinney, D. K., Lunde, I., et al. (1988). Creativity in manic-depressives, cyclothymes, their normal relatives and control subjects. *Journal of Abnormal Psychology, 97,* 281–288.

Richards, T. A., Acree, M., & Folkman, S. (1999). Spiritual aspects of loss among partners of men with AIDS: Postbereavement follow-up. *Death Studies, 23,* 105–127.

Richens, A. & Perucca, E. (1993). Clinical pharmacology and medical treatment. In J. Laidlaw, A. Richens, & D. Chadwick (Eds.), *A textbook of epilepsy* (pp. 495–559). Edinburgh: Churchill Livingstone.

Rickels, K., Schweizer, E., Case, W. G., & Greenblatt, D. J. (1990). Long-term therapeutic use of benzodiazepines: I. Effects of abrupt discontinuation. *Archives of General Psychiatry, 47,* 899–907.

Riether, A. M. & Stoudemire, A. (1988). Psychogenic fugue states: A review. *Southern Medical Journal, 81,* 568–571.

Rifkin, A., Ghisalbert, D. O., Dimatou, S., Jin, C., & Sethi, M. (1998). Dissociative identity disorder in psychiatric inpatients. *American Journal of Psychiatry, 155,* 844–845.

Riggins v. Nevada, 112, S. Ct. 1810 (1992).

Riggs, D. S., Rothbaum, B. O., & Foa, E. B. (1995) A prospective examination of symptoms of posttraumatic stress disorder in victims of nonsexual assault. *Journal of Interpersonal Violence, 10*(2), 201–214.

Rihmer, Z. (1996). Strategies of suicide prevention: Focus on health care. *Journal of Affective Disorders, 39,* 83–91.

Riley, T. A. & Fava, J. L. (2003). Stress and transtheoretical model indicators of stress management behaviors in HIV-positive women. *Journal of Psychosomatic Research, 54,* 245–252.

Rind, B., Tromovitch, P., and Bauserman, R. (1998). A meta-analytic examination of assumed properties of child sexual abuse using college samples. *Psychological Bulletin, 124*(1), 22–53.

Riskind, J. H. & Alloy, L. B. (in press). Cognitive vulnerability to emotional disorders: Theory, design, and methods. In L. B. Alloy & J. H. Riskind (Eds.), *Cognitive vulnerability to emotional disorders.* Mahwah, NJ: Erlbaum.

Riskind, J. H., Moore, R., & Bowley, L. (1995). The looming of spiders: The fearful perceptual distortion of movement and menace. *Behaviour Research and Therapy, 33,* 171–178.

Riskind, J. H. & Williams, N. L. (in press). A unique vulnerability common to all anxiety disorders: The looming maladaptive cognitive style. In L. B. Alloy & J. H. Riskind (Eds.), *Cognitive vulnerability to emotional disorders.* Mahwah, NJ: Erlbaum.

Riskind, J. H., Williams, N. L., Gessner, T., Chrosniak, L. D., & Cortina, J. (2000). The looming maladaptive style: Anxiety, danger, and schematic processing. *Journal of Personality and Social Psychology, 79,* 837–852.

Robbins, J. M. & Kirmayer, L. J. (1996). Transient and persistent hypochondriacal worry in primary care. *Psychological Medicine, 26,* 575–589.

Roberts, J., Gotlib, I., & Kassel, J. D. (1996). Adult attachment security and symptoms of depression: The mediating roles of dysfunctional attitudes and low self-esteem. *Journal of Personality and Social Psychology, 70*(2), 310–320.

Roberts, R. E., Kaplan, G. A., Shema, S. J., & Strawbridge, W. J. (1997). Does growing old increase the risk for depression? *American Journal of Psychiatry, 154,* 1384–1390.

Robins, L. N. (1991). Conduct disorder. *Journal of Child Psychology and Psychiatry and Allied Disciplines, 32,* 193–212.

Robins, L. N., Helzer, J. E., Croughan, J., & Ratcliff, K. S. (1981). National Institute of Mental Health diagnostic interview schedule. *Archives of General Psychiatry, 38,* 381–389.

Robins, L. N., Helzer, J. E., Weissman, M. M., Orvaschel, H., Gruenberg, E., Burke, J. D., & Regier, D. A. (1984.) Lifetime prevalence of specific psychiatric disorders in three sites. *Archives of General Psychiatry, 41,* 949–958.

Robins, L. N. & Price, R. K. (1991). Adult disorders predicted by childhood conduct problems: Results from the NIMH epidemiologic catchment area project. *Psychiatry, 54,* 116–132.

Robins, L. N., Tipp, J., & Przybeck, T. (1991). Antisocial personality. In L. N. Robins & D. A. Regier (Eds.), *Psychiatric disorders in America* (pp. 258–290). New York: Free Press.

Robinson, D., Woerner, M. G., Alvir, J. M. J., Bilder, R., Goldman, R., Geisler, S., Koreen, A., Sheitman, B., Chakos, M., Mayerhoff, D., & Lieberman, J. A. (1999). Predictors of relapse following response from a first episode of schizophrenia or schizoaffective disorder. *Archives of General Psychiatry, 56,* 241–247.

Robinson, N. S., Garber, J., & Hilsman, R. (1995). Cognitions and stress: Direct and moderating effects on depressive versus externalizing symptoms during the junior high school transition. *Journal of Abnormal Psychology, 104,* 453–463.

Robinson, P. H. & Darley, J. M. (1997). The utility of desert. *Northwestern University Law Review, 91,* 453–499.

Robinson, R. G. (1997). Neuropsychiatric consequences of stroke. *Annual Review of Medicine, 48,* 217–229.

Rodin, G. & Voshort, K. (1986). Depression in the medically ill: An overview. *American Journal of Psychiatry, 143,* 696–705.

Rodin, J. (1977). Bidirectional influences of emotionality, stimulus responsivity and metabolic events in obesity. In J. D. Maser & M. E. P. Seligman (Eds.), *Psychopathology: Experimental models.* San Francisco: Freeman.

Rodin, J. (1981). Current status of the internal-external hypothesis for obesity: What went wrong? *American Psychologist, 36,* 361–372.

Rodin, J. & Salovey, P. (1989). Health psychology. *Annual Review of Psychology, 40,* 533–579.

Rodning, C., Beckwith, L., & Howard, J. (1989). Characteristic of attachment organization and play organization in prenatally drug-exposed toddlers. *Development and Psychopathology, 1,* 277–289.

Rodning, C., Beckwith, L., & Howard, J. (1992). Quality of attachments and home environments in children prenatally exposed to PCP and cocaine. *Development and Psychopathology, 3,* 351–366.

Rodriguez, N., Ryan, S. W., Vande Kemp, H., & Foy, D. W. (1997). Posttraumatic stress disorder in adult female survivors of childhood sexual abuse: A comparison study. *Journal of Consulting and Clinical Psychology, 65,* 53–59.

Rogers, C. R. (1955). Persons or science? A philosophical question. *American Psychologist, 10,* 267–278.

Rogers, C. R. (1980). *A way of being.* Boston: Houghton Mifflin.

Rogers, J., Widiger, T. A., & Krupp, A. (1995). Aspects of depression associated with borderline personality disorder. *American Journal of Psychiatry, 152,* 268–270.

Rogers, S. L., Friedhoff, L. T., Apter, J. T., et al. (1996). The efficacy and safety of Donepezil in patients with Alzheimer's disease: Results of a US multicentre, randomized, double-blind, placebo-controlled trial. *Dementia, 7,* 293–303.

Rogler, L. H. (1999). Methodological sources of cultural insensitivity in mental health research. *American Psychologist, 54,* 424–433.

Rohsenow, D. J. (1983). Drinking habits and expectancies about alcohol's effects for self versus others. *Journal of Consulting and Clinical Psychology, 51,* 752–756.

Rojas, D. C., Teale, P., Sheeder, J., Simon, J., & Reite, M. (1997). Sex-specific expression of Heschl's Gyrus functional and structural abnormalities in paranoid schizophrenia. *American Journal of Psychiatry, 154,* 1655–1662.

Rokeach, M. (1964). *The three Christs of Ypsilanti.* New York: Random House.

Roos, R. (2001). Controlling new prion diseases. *New England Journal of Medicine, 344*(20), 1548–1551.

Rorschach, H. (1942). *Psychodiagnostics: A diagnostic test based on perception.* New York: Grune & Stratton.

Rose, J. E. (1996). Nicotine addiction and treatment. *Annual Review of Medicine, 47,* 493–507.

Rose, R. J. (1998). A developmental behavioral-genetic perspective on alcoholism risk. *Alcohol Health and Research World, 22,* 131–143.

Rose, R. J. & Chesney, M. A. (1986). Cardiovascular stress reactivity: A behavioral-genetic perspective. *Behavior Therapy, 17,* 314–323.

Rosen, J. C. & Ramirez, E. (1998). A comparison of eating disorders and body dysmorphic disorder on body image and psychological adjustment. *Journal of Psychosomatic Research, 44,* 441–449.

Rosen, R. C. & Leiblum S. R. (1995). *Disorders of sexual desire.* New York: Guilford Press.

Rosen, R. C., Lane, R. M., & Menza, M. (1999). Effects of SSRIs on sexual function: A critical review. *Journal of Clinical Psychopharmacology, 19,* 67–85.

Rosenbaum, J. F., Biederman, J., Pollock, R. A., & Hirshfeld, D. R. (1994). The etiology of social phobia. *Journal of Clinical Psychiatry, 55,* 10–16.

Rosenbaum, J. F. & Gelenberg, A. J. (1991). Anxiety. In A. J. Gelenberg, E. L. Bassuk, & S. C. Schoonover (Eds.), *The practitioner's guide to psychoactive drugs* (3rd ed.). New York: Plenum Press.

Rosenberg, D. R., Sweeney, J. A., Squires-Wheeler, E., Keshavan, M. S., Cornblatt, B. A., & Erlenmeyer-Kimling, L. (1997). Eye-tracking dysfunction in offspring from the New York High-Risk Project: Diagnostic specificity and the role of attention. *Psychiatry Research, 66,* 121–130.

Rosenblatt, A. (1984). Concepts of the asylum in the care of the mentally ill. *Hospital and Community Psychiatry, 35,* 244–250.

Rosenfarb, I. S., Goldstein, M. J., Mintz, J., & Nuechterlein, K. H. (1995). Expressed emotion and subclinical psychopathology observable within the transactions between schizophrenic patients and their family members. *Journal of Abnormal Psychology, 104,* 259–267.

Rosenfarb, I. S., Nuechterlein, K. H., Goldstein, M. J., & Subotnik, K. L. (2000). Neurocognitive vulnerability, interpersonal criticism, and the emergence of unusual thinking by schizophrenic patients during family transactions. *Archives of General Psychiatry, 57,* 1174–1179.

Rosenfeld, B. & Wall, A. (1998). Psychopathology and competence to stand trial. *Criminal Justice and Behavior, 25,* 443–462.

Rosenhan, D. L. (1973). On being sane in insane places. *Science, 179,* 250–258.

Rosenman, R. H., Brand, R. J., Jenkins, C. D., Friedman, M., Straus, R., & Wurm, M. (1975). Coronary heart disease in the Western Collaborative

Group study: Final follow-up experience in $8^1/_2$ years. *Journal of the American Medical Association, 8,* 872–877.

Rosenstein, D. S. & Horowitz, H. A. (1996). Adolescent attachment and psychopathology. *Journal of Consulting and Clinical Psychology, 64,* 244–253.

Rosenthal, D., Wender, P. H., Kety, S. S., Schulsinger, F., Welner, J., & Ostergaard, L. (1968). Schizophrenics' offspring reared in adoptive homes. In D. Rosenthal & S. S. Kety (Eds.), *The transmission of schizophrenia.* Oxford, England: Pergamon Press.

Rosenthal, T. & Bandura, A. (1978). Psychological modeling: Theory and practice. In S. L. Garfield & A. E. Bergin (Eds.), *Handbook of psychotherapy and behavior change: An empirical analysis* (2nd ed.). New York: Wiley.

Ross, C. A. (1997). *Dissociative identity disorder: Diagnosis, clinical features, and treatment of multiple personality,* 2nd ed. New York: Wiley.

Ross, C. A., Miller, S. D., Reagor, P., Bjornson, L., Fraser, G. A., & Anderson, G. (1990). Structured interview data on 102 cases of multiple personality disorder from four centers. *American Journal of Psychiatry, 147,* 596–601.

Ross, D. E., Thaker, G. K., Buchanan, R. W., Lahti, A. C., Medoff, D., Bartko, J. J., Moran, M., & Hartley, J. (1996). Association of abnormal smooth pursuit eye movements with the deficit syndrome in schizophrenic patients. *American Journal of Psychiatry, 153,* 1158–1165.

Rossi, P. G., Parmeggiani, A., Bach, V., Santucci, M., & Visconti, P. (1995). EEG features and epilepsy in patients with autism. *Brain Development, 17,* 169–174.

Rossi, P. H. (1990). The old homeless and the new homelessness in historical perspective. *American Psychologist, 45,* 945–959.

Roth, A. D., Fresco, D. M., & Heimberg, R. G. (in press). Cognitive phenomena in social anxiety disorder. A unique vulnerability common to all anxiety disorders: The looming maladaptive cognitive style. In L. B. Alloy & J. H. Riskind (Eds.), *Cognitive vulnerability to emotional disorders.* Mahwah, NJ: Erlbaum.

Rothbaum, B. O., Foa, E. B., Murdock, T., Riggs, D., & Walsh, W. (1990). *Post-traumatic stress disorder following rape.* Unpublished manuscript.

Rothbaum, B. O., Foa, E. B., Riggs, D. S., Murdock, T., & Walsh, W. (1992). A prospective examination of post-traumatic stress disorder in rape victims. *Journal of Traumatic Stress, 5,* 455–475.

Rotheram-Borus, M. J., Koopman, C., & Haignere, C. (1991). Reducing HIV sexual risk behaviors among runaway adolescents. *Journal of the American Medical Association, 266,* 1237–1241.

Rothstein, H. R., Haller, O. L., & Bernstein, D. (2000). Remarks and reflections on managed care: Analysis of comments by New Jersey psychologists. *Journal of Psychotherapy in Independent Practice, 1,* 73–82.

Rotunda, R. J., Alter, J. G., & O'Farrell, T. J. (2001). Behavioral couples therapy for comorbid substance abuse and psychiatric problems. In M. M. MacFarlane (Ed.), *Family therapy and mental health: Innovations in theory and practice* (pp. 289–309). Binghamton, NY: Haworth Clinical Practice Press.

Rovner, S. (1993, April 6). Anxiety disorders are real and expensive. *Washington Post,* p. WH5.

Rowe, D. C. & Jacobson, K. C. (1999). In the mainstream: Research in behavioral genetics. In R. A. Carson & M. A. Rothman (Eds.), *Behavioral genetics: The clash of culture and biology* (pp. 12–34). Baltimore, MD: Johns Hopkins University Press.

Roy, A., DeJong, J., Lamparski, D., Adinoff, B., George, T., Moore, V., Garnett, D., Kerich, M., & Linnoila, M. (1991). Mental disorders among alcoholics: Relationship to age of onset and cerebrospinal fluid neuropeptides. *Archives of General Psychiatry, 48,* 423–427.

Roy, M. A., Neale, M. C., Pedersen, N. L., Mathe, A. A., & Kendler, K. S. (1995). A twin study of generalized anxiety disorder and major depression. *Psychological Medicine, 25,* 1037–1049.

Roy-Byrne, P. P. (1996). Generalized anxiety and mixed anxiety-depression: Association with disability and health care utilization. *Journal of Clinical Psychiatry, 57,* 86–91.

Ruderman, A. J. (1986). Dietary restraint: A theoretical and empirical review. *Psychological Bulletin, 99,* 247–262.

Ruderman, A. J. & Wilson, G. T. (1979). Weight, restraint, cognitions, and counterregulation. *Behaviour Research and Therapy, 17,* 581–590.

Rudolph, K. D. & Hammen, C. (1999). Age and gender as determinants of stress exposure, generation, and reactions in youngsters: A transactional perspective. *Child Development, 70,* 660–677.

Rundell, J. R. & Ursano, R. J. (1996). Psychiatric responses to war trauma. In R. J. Ursano & A. E. Norwood (Eds.), *Emotional aftermath of the Persian Gulf War: Veterans, families, communities, and nations* (pp. 43–81). Washington, DC: American Psychiatric Press.

Rusch, F. R., Martin, J. E., & White, D. M. (1985). Competitive employment: Teaching mentally retarded employees to maintain their work behavior. *Education and Training of the Mentally Retarded, 20,* 182–189.

Ruscio, J. & Ruscio, A. M. (2000). Informing the continuity controversy: A taxometric analysis of depression. *Journal of Abnormal Psychology, 109,* 473–487.

Rush, A. J. & Weissenburger, J. E. (1994). Melancholic symptom features and *DSM-IV. American Journal of Psychiatry, 151,* 489–498.

Russell, C. J. & Keel, P. K. (2002). Homosexuality as a specific risk factor for eating disorders in men. *International Journal of Eating Disorders, 31*(3), 300–306.

Russell, D. E. H. (1986). *The secret trauma: Incest in the lives of girls and women.* New York: Basic Books.

Rutenfanz, J., Haider, M., & Koller, M. (1985). Occupational health measures for nightworkers and shiftworkers. In S. Folkard & T. W. Monk (Eds.), *Hours of work: Temporal factors in work scheduling* (pp. 199–210). New York: Wiley.

Rutter, M. (1983). Cognitive deficits in the pathogenesis of autism. *Journal of Child Psychology and Psychiatry, 24,* 513–531.

Rutter, M. & Bailey, A. (1994). Thinking and relationships: Mind and brain (some reflections on theory of mind and autism). In S. Baron-Cohen, H. Tager-Flusberg, & D. Cohen (Eds.), *Understanding other minds: Perspectives from autism* (pp. 481–504). Oxford: Oxford University Press.

Rutter, M., Bailey, A., Bolton, P., & Le Couteur, A. (1994). Autism and known medical conditions: Myth and substance. *Journal of Child Psychology and Psychiatry, 35,* 311–322.

Rutter, M., Macdonald, H., LeCouteur, A., Harrington, R., Bolton, P., & Bailey, A. (1990). Genetic factors in child psychiatric disorders: II. Empirical findings. *Journal of Child Psychology and Psychiatry, 31,* 39–83.

Rutter, M. L. (1997). Nature-nurture integration: The example of antisocial behavior. *American Psychologist, 52,* 390–398.

Saccuzzo, D. S., Cadenhead, K. S., & Braff, D. L. (1996). Backward versus forward masking deficits in schizophrenic patients: Centrally, not peripherally, mediated? *American Journal of Psychiatry, 153,* 1564–1570.

Sachs, G. S., Baldassano, C. F., Truman, C. J., & Guille, C. (2000). Comorbidity of attention deficit hyperactivity disorder with early- and late-onset bipolar disorder. *American Journal of Psychiatry, 157,* 469–471.

Sachs, G. S., Prinz, D. J., Kahn, D. A., Carpenter, D., & Docherty, J. P. (2000). The expert consensus guideline series: Medication treatment of bipolar disorder 2000. *Postgraduate Medicine,* Spec. No: 1-104.

Sachs-Ericsson, N. (2000). Gender, social roles, and suicidal ideation and attempts in a general population sample. In T. E. Joiner, Jr. & M. D. Rudd (Eds.), *Suicide science: Expanding the boundaries* (pp. 201–220). Boston: Kluwer Academic.

Sackeim, H. A. & Devanand, D. P. (1991). Dissociative disorders. In M. Hersen & S. M. Turner (Eds.), *Adult psychopathology and diagnosis* (2nd ed., pp. 279–322). New York: Wiley.

Sackeim, H. A., Prudic, J., Devanand, D. P., Nobler, M. S., Lisanby, S. H., Peyser, S., Fitzsimons, L., Moody, B. J., & Clark, J. (2000). A prospective, randomized, double-blind comparison of bilateral and right unilateral electroconvulsive therapy at different stimulus intensities. *Archives of General Psychiatry, 57,* 425–437.

Sacks, O. (1985). *The man who mistook his wife for a hat and other clinical tales.* New York: Summit Books.

Sadowski, C. & Kelley, M. L. (1993). Social problem solving in suicidal adolescents. *Journal of Consulting and Clinical Psychology, 61,* 121–127.

Safford, S. M., Alloy, L. B., Crossfield, A. G., Morocco, A. M., & Wang, J. C. (in press). The relationship of cognitive style and attachment style to depression and anxiety in young adults. *Journal of Cognitive Psychotherapy: An International Quarterly.*

Safran, J. D. & Muran, J. C. (2000). *Negotiating the therapeutic alliance: A relational treatment guide.* New York: Guilford Press.

Safran, J. D. & Segal, Z. V. (1990). *Interpersonal process in cognitive therapy.* New York: Basic Books.

Saghir, M. T. & Robins, E. (1969). Homosexuality: I. Sexual behavior of the female homosexual. *Archives of General Psychiatry, 20,* 192–201.

Saghir, M. T., Robins, E., & Walbran, B. (1969). Homosexuality: II. Sexual behavior of the male homosexual. *Archives of General Psychiatry, 21,* 219–229.

Salekin, R. T. (2002). Psychopathy and therapeutic pessimism: Clinical lore or clinical reality? *Clinical Psychology Review, 22,* 79–112.

Salkovskis, P. M. (1985). Obsessional-compulsive problems: A cognitive-behavioural analysis. *Behaviour Research and Therapy, 23*(5), 571–583.

Salkovskis, P. M. & Clark, D. M. (1993). Panic disorder and hypochondriasis. *Advances in Behaviour Research and Therapy, 15,* 23–48.

Salkovskis, P. M., Clark, D. M., & Gelder, M. G. (1996). Cognition-behaviour links in the persistence of panic. *Behaviour Research and Therapy, 34,* 453–458.

Salkovskis, P. M. & Harrison, J. (1984). Abnormal and normal obsessions—a replication. *Behaviour Research and Therapy, 22,* 549–552.

Salkovskis, P. M. & Kirk, J. (1997). Obsessive-compulsive disorder. In D. M. Clark & C. G. Fairburn (Eds.), *Science and practice of cognitive behaviour therapy* (pp. 179–208). Oxford: Oxford University Press.

Salkovskis, P. M. & Warwick, H. M. C. (1986). Morbid preoccupations, health anxiety and reassurance: A cognitive-behavioural approach to hypochondriasis. *Behaviour Research and Therapy, 24,* 597–602.

Salmon, P. & Calderbank, S. (1996). The relationship of childhood physical and sexual abuse to adult illness behavior. *Journal of Psychosomatic Research, 40,* 329–336.

Salzman, C., Goldenberg, I., Bruce, S. E., & Keller, M. B. (2001). Pharmacologic treatment of anxiety disorders in 1989 versus 1996: Results from the Harvard/Brown Anxiety Disorders Research Program. *Journal of Clinical Psychiatry, 62,* 149–152.

Samson, J. A., Mirin, S. M., Hauser, S. T., Fenton, B. T., & Schildkraut, J. J. (1992). Learned helplessness and urinary MHPG levels in unipolar depression. *American Journal of Psychiatry, 149,* 806–809.

San Jose, B., van Oers, H. A. M., van de Mheen, H. D., Garretsen, H. F. L., & Mackenback, J. P. (2000). Stressors and alcohol consumption. *Alcohol & Alcoholism, 35,* 307–312.

Sana, M., Ernesto, C., Thomas, R. G., Klauber, M. R., Schafer, K., Grundman, M., Woodbury, P., Growdon, J., Cotman, C. W., Pfeiffer, E., Schneider, L. S., & Thal, L. J. (1997). A controlled trial of selegiline, alpha-tocopherol, or both as treatment for Alzheimer's disease. *New England Journal of Medicine, 336,* 1216–1247.

Sander, J. W. (2003). The epidemiology of epilepsy revisited. *Current Opinion in Neurology 16*(2), 165–170.

Sanders, B. (1992). The imaginary companion experience in multiple personality disorder. *Dissociation: Progress-in-the-Dissociative Disorders, 5,* 159–162.

Sanderson, W. C. & Rego, S. A. (2000). Empirically supported treatment for panic disorder: Research, theory, and application for cognitive behavioral therapy. *Journal of Cognitive Psychotherapy, 14,* 219–244.

Sandnabba, N. K. & Niklas, P. S. (1999). Sexual behavior and social adaptation among sadomasochistically-oriented males. *Journal of Sex Research, 36*(3), 273.

Sandnabba, N. K., Santtila, P., & Nordling, N. (1999). Sexual behavior and social adaptation among sadomasochistically-oriented males. *Journal of Sex Research, 36*(3), 273–282.

Sanfilipo, M., Lafargue, T., Rusinek, H., Arena, L., Loncragan, C., Lautin, A., Feiner, D., Rotrosen, J., & Wolkin, A. (2000). Volumetric measure of the frontal and temporal lobe regions in schizophrenia: Relationship to negative symptoms. *Archives of General Psychiatry, 57,* 471–480.

Sanislow, C. A. & Carson, R. C. (2001). Schizophrenia: A critical examination. In P. B. Sutker & H. E. Adams (Eds.), *Comprehensive handbook of psychopathology* (3rd ed., pp. 403–444). New York: Kluwer Academic/Plenum.

Sapolsky, R. M. (1998). *Why zebras don't get ulcers: An updated guide to stress, stress-related diseases and coping.* New York: W. H. Freeman.

Sapolsky, R. M., Alberts, S. C., & Altmann, J. (1997). Hypercortisolism associated with social subordinance or social isolation among wild baboons. *Archives of General Psychiatry, 54,* 1137–1143.

Sar, V., Yargic, L. I., & Tutkun, H. (1996). Structured interview data on 35 cases of dissociative identity disorder in Turkey. *American Journal of Psychiatry, 153,* 1329–1333.

Sarbin, T. R. (1997). On the futility of psychiatric diagnostic manuals (DSMs) and the return of personal agency. *Applied Preventive Psychology, 6,* 233–243.

Sarrel, P. (1977). Biological aspects of sexual functioning. In R. Gemene & C. C. Wheeler (Eds.), *Progress in sexology* (pp. 227–244). New York: Plenum Press.

Sartorius, N., Üstün, B., Korten, A., Cooper, J. E., & van Drimmelen, J. (1995). Progress toward achieving a common language in psychiatry, II: Results from the international field trials of the ICD-10 Diagnostic Criteria for Research for Mental and Behavioral Disorders. *American Journal of Psychiatry, 152,* 1427–1437.

Sarwer, D. B. & Durlak, J. A. (1997). A field trial of the effectiveness of behavioral treatment for sexual dysfunctions. *Journal of Sex & Marital Therapy, 23* (2), 87–97.

Satel, S. L. & Edell, W. S. (1991). Cocaine-induced paranoia and psychosis proneness. *American Journal of Psychiatry, 148,* 1708–1711.

Sax, K. W., Strakowski, S. M., Zimmerman, M. E., DelBellow, M. P., Keck, P. E., Jr., & Hawkins, J. M. (1999). Frontosubcortical neuroanatomy and the continuous performance test in mania. *American Journal of Psychiatry, 156,* 139–141.

Saxena, S. & Prasad, K. (1989). *DSM-III* subclassifications of dissociative disorders applied to psychiatric outpatients in India. *American Journal of Psychiatry, 146,* 261–262.

Sbrocco, T. & Barlow, D. H. (1996). Conceptualizing the cognitive component of sexual arousal: Implications for sexuality research and treatment. In P. M. Salkovskis, et al. (Eds.), *Frontiers of cognitive therapy* (pp. 419–449). New York: Guilford Press.

Schachter, S. (1971). Eat, eat. *Psychology Today,* pp. 44–47, 78–79.

Schachter, S. (1982). Recidivism and self-cure of smoking and obesity. *American Psychologist, 37,* 436–444.

Schachter, S. & Gross, L. (1968). Manipulated time and eating behavior. *Journal of Personality and Social Psychology, 10,* 98–106.

Schacter, D. L. (1999). The seven sins of memory: Insights from psychology and cognitive neuroscience. *American Psychologist, 54,* 182–203.

Schaeffer, J., Andrysiak, T., & Ungerleider, J. T. (1981). Cognition and long-term use of ganja (cannabis). *Science, 213*(4506), 465–466.

Schalock, R. L., Stark, J. A., Snell, M. E., Coulter, D. L., Polloway, E. A., Luckasson, R., Reiss, S., & Spitalnik, D. M. (1994). The changing conception of mental retardation: Implications for the field. *Mental Retardation, 32,* 181–193.

Scharff, D. E. & Scharff, J. S. (1991). *Object relations couple therapy.* Northvale, NJ: Aronson.

Scharff, L. (1997). Recurrent abdominal pain in children: A review of psychological factors and treatment. *Clinical Psychology Review, 17,* 145–166.

Schatzberg, A. F. (2000). Pros and cons of Prozac and its relatives. *American Journal of Psychiatry, 157,* 323–325.

Scheele, L. A., Maravilla, K. R., & Dager, S. R. (1997). Neuroimaging of medical disorders in clinical psychiatry. In D. L. Dunner (Ed.), *Current psychiatric therapy II* (pp. 37–44). Philadelphia: Saunders.

Scheerer, M., Rothmann, E., & Goldstein, K. (1945). A case of "idiot savant": An experimental study of personality organization. *Psychology Monograph, 58,* 1–63.

Scheff, T. J. (1966). *Being mentally ill: A sociological theory.* Chicago: Aldine.

Scheff, T. J. (1975). *Labeling madness.* Englewood Cliffs, NJ: Prentice-Hall.

Scheff, T. J. (1998). Shame in the labeling of mental illness. In P. Gilbert & B. Andrews (Eds.), *Shame: Interpersonal behavior, psychopathology, and culture.* (Series in affective science, pp. 191–205). New York: Oxford University Press.

Scheiffelin, E. (1984). *The cultural analysis of depressive affect: An example from New Guinea.* Unpublished manuscript. University of Pennsylvania, Philadelphia.

Schildkraut, J. (1965). The catecholamine hypothesis of affective disorders: A review of supporting evidence. *American Journal of Psychiatry, 122,* 509–522.

Schleifer, S. J., Keller, S. E., Bartlett, J. A., Eckholdt, H. M., & Delaney, B. R. (1996). Immunity in young adults with major depressive disorder. *American Journal of Psychiatry, 153,* 477–482.

Schmidt, N. B. (1999). Panic disorder: Cognitive behavioral and pharmacological treatment strategies. *Journal of Clinical Psychology in Medical Settings, 6*(1), 89–111.

Schmidt, N. B., Lerew, D. R., & Jackson, R. L. (1997). The role of anxiety sensitivity in the pathogenesis of panic: Prospective evaluation of spontaneous panic attacks during acute stress. *Journal of Abnormal Psychology, 106,* 355–364.

Schmidt, N. B., Lerew, D. R., & Trakowski, J. H. (1997). Body vigilance in panic disorder: Evaluating attention in bodily perturbations. *Journal of Consulting and Clinical Psychology, 65,* 214–220.

Schmidt, N. B., Telch, M. J., & Jaimez, T. L. (1996). Biological challenge of PCO-sub-2 levels: A test of Klein's (1993) suffocation alarm theory of panic. *Journal of Abnormal Psychology, 105,* 446–454.

Schmidt, N. B. & Woolaway-Bickel, K. (in press). Cognitive vulnerability to panic disorder. In L. B. Alloy & J. H. Riskind (Eds.), *Cognitive vulnerability to emotional disorders.* Mahwah, NJ: Erlbaum.

Schmitt, W. A. & Newman, J. P. (1999). Are all psychopathic individuals low-anxious? *Journal of Abnormal Psychology, 108,* 351–358.

Schmitz, J. M., Schneider, N. G., & Jarvik, M. E. (1997). Nicotine. In J. H. Lowinson, P. Ruiz, R. B. Millman, & J. G. Langrod (Eds.), *Substance abuse: A comprehensive textbook* (pp. 276–294). Baltimore: Williams & Wilkins.

Schneider, F. & Deldin, P. J. (2001). Genetics and schizophrenia. In P. B. Sutker & H. E. Adams (Eds.), *Comprehensive handbook of psychopathology* (3rd ed., pp. 371–402). New York: Kluwer Academic/Plenum.

Schneider, F., Gur, R. E., Alavi, A., Seligman, M. E. P., Mozley, L. H., Smith, R. J., Mozley, P. D., & Gur, R. C. (1996). Cerebral blood flow changes in limbic regions induced by unsolvable anagram tasks. *American Journal of Psychiatry, 153,* 206–212.

Schneider, L. S. (1996). Overview of generalized anxiety disorder in the elderly. *Journal of Clinical Psychiatry, 57,* 34–45.

Schneider, R. H., Nidich, S. I., & Salerno, J. W. (2001). The Transcendental Meditation program: Reducing the risk of heart disease and mortality and improving quality of life in African Americans. *Ethnicity and Disease, 11,* 159–160.

Schneier, F. R., Johnson, J., Hornig, C. D., Liebowitz, M. R., & Weissman, M. M. (1992). Social phobia: Comorbidity and morbidity in an epidemiologic sample. *Archives of General Psychiatry, 49,* 282–288.

Schooler, N. R., Keith, S. J., Severe, J. B., Matthews, S. M., Bellack,

A. S., Glick, I. D., Hargreaves, W. A., Kane, J. M., Ninan, P. T., Frances, A., Jacobs, M., Lieberman, J. A., Mance, R., Simpson, G. M., & Woerner, M. G. (1997). Relapse and rehospitalization during maintenance treatment of schizophrenia: The effects of dose reduction and family treatment. *Archives of General Psychiatry, 54,* 453–463.

Schopp, R. F. & Slain, A. J. (2000). Psychopathy, criminal responsibility, and civil commitment as a sexual predator. *Behavioral Sciences and the Law, 18,* 247–274.

Schou, M. (1997). Forty years of lithium treatment. *Archives of General Psychiatry, 54,* 9–13.

Schover, L. R. & LoPiccolo, J. (1982). Treatment effectiveness for dysfunctions of sexual desire. *Journal of Sex and Marital Therapy, 8*(3), 179–197.

Schreiber, F. (1974). *Sybil.* New York: Warner.

Schreiber, W., Lauer, C. J., Krumrey, K., Holsboer, F., & Krieg, J. C. (1996). Dysregulation of the hypothalamic-pituitary-adrenocortical system in panic disorder. *Neuropsychopharmacology, 15,* 7–15.

Schreibman, L. (1994). Autism. In L. W. Craighead, W. E. Craighead, A. E. Kazdin, & M. J. Mahoney (Eds.), *Cognitive and behavioral interventions: An empirical approach to mental health problems* (pp. 335–358). Boston: Allyn & Bacon.

Schreibman, L. & Koegel, R. L. (1996). Fostering self-management: Parent-delivered pivotal response training for children with autistic disorder. In E. D. Hibbs & P. S. Jensen (Eds.), *Psychosocial treatments for child and adolescent disorders: Empirically based strategies for clinical practice* (pp. 525–552). Washington, DC: American Psychological Association.

Schroder, M. & Carroll, R. A. (1996). *Psychosexual outcome in 19 male-to-female post-operative transsexuals.* Paper presented at the Annual Meeting of the Society for Sex Therapy and Research, Miami Beach, FL.

Schuckit, M. A. (1995). A long-term study of sons of alcoholics. *Alcohol Health & Research World, 19*(3), 172–175.

Schuckit, M. A., Tsuang, J. W., Anthenelli, R. M., Tipp, J. E., et al. (1996). Alcohol challenges in young men from alcoholic pedigrees and control families: A report from the COGA project. *Journal of Studies on Alcohol, 57*(4), 368–377.

Schuldberg, D. (1999). Creativity, bipolarity, and dynamics of style. In S. W. Russ (Ed.), *Affect, creative experience, and psychological adjustment* (pp. 221–237). Philadelphia: Brunner/Mazel.

Schulman, J., Sacks, J., & Provenzano, G. (2002). State level estimates of the incidence and economic burden of head injuries stemming from non-universal use of bicycle helmets. *Injury Prevention, 8*(1), 47–52.

Schultz, S. K., Nopoulous, P. C., & Andreasen, N. C. (2001). Neuroanatomy: A regional understanding. In A. Breier, P. V. Tran, F. Bymaster, & C. Tollefson (Eds.), *Current issues in the psychopharmacology of schizophrenia* (pp. 12–26). Philadelphia: Lippincott Williams & Wilkins.

Schulz, S. C., Schulz, P. M., & Wilson, W. H. (1988). Medication treatment of schizotypal personality disorder. *Journal of Personality Disorders, 2,* 1–13.

Schwartz, G. E. (1977). Psychosomatic disorders and biofeedback: A psychobiological model of disregulation. In J. D. Maser & M. E. P. Seligman (Eds.), *Psychopathology: Experimental models.* San Francisco: Freeman.

Schwartz, G. E. (1978). Psychobiological foundations of psychotherapy and behavior change. In S. L. Garfield & A. E. Bergin (Eds.), *Handbook of psychotheraphy and behavior change.* New York: Wiley.

Schwartz, G. E., Weinberger, D. A., & Singer, J. A. (1981). Cardiovascular differentiation of happiness, sadness, anger, and fear following imagery and exercise. *Psychosomatic Medicine, 43,* 343–364.

Schwartz, J. A., Gladstone, T. R., & Kaslow, N. J. (1998). Depressive disorders. In T. H. Ollendick & M. Hersen (Eds.), *Handbook of child psychopathology* (3rd ed., pp. 269–289). New York: Plenum Press.

Schwartz, P. J., Brown, C., Wehr, T. A., & Rosenthal, N. E. (1996). Winter seasonal affective disorder: A follow-up study of the first 59 patients of the National Institute of Mental Health seasonal studies program. *American Journal of Psychiatry, 153,* 1028–1036.

Schwarz, J. R. (1981). *The Hillside strangler: A murderer's mind.* New York: New American Library.

Schweinhart, L. J. & Weikart, D. B. (1988). The High/Scope Perry Preschool Program. In R. H. Price, E. L. Cowen, R. P. Lorion, & J. Ramos-McKay (Eds.), *Fourteen ounces of prevention: A casebook for practitioners* (pp. 53–65). Washington, DC: American Psychological Association.

Schweizer, E., Rickels, K., Case, W. G., & Greenblatt, D. J. (1990). Long-term therapeutic use of benzodiazepines: II. Effects of gradual taper. *Archives of General Psychiatry, 47,* 908–916.

Scott, J. (1996). Cognitive therapy of affective disorders: A review. *Journal of Affective Disorders, 37,* 1–11.

Scott, J. E. & Dixon, L. B. (1995). Psychological interventions for schizophrenia. *Schizophrenia Bulletin, 21,* 621–630.

Scott, J., Garland, A., & Moorhead, S. (2001). A pilot study of cognitive therapy in bipolar disorders. *Psychological Medicine, 31,* 459–467.

Scott, J., Stanton, B., Garland, A., & Ferrier, I. N. (2000). Cognitive vulnerability in patients with bipolar disorder. *Psychological Medicine, 30,* 467–472.

Scotti, J. R., Nangle, D. W., Masia, C. L., Ellis, J. T., Ujcich, K. J., Giacoletti, A. M., Vittimberga, G. L., & Carr, R. (1997). Providing an AIDS education and skills training program to persons with mild developmental disabilities. *Education and Training in Mental Retardation and Developmental Disabilities, 32,* 113–128.

Scull, A. (1993). *The most solitary of afflictions: Madness and society in Britain, 1700–1900.* New Haven, CT: Yale University Press.

Seeley, S. M. F. (1997). In R. W. Maris, M. M. Silverman, & S. S. Canetto (Eds.), *Review of suicidology* (pp. 251–270). New York: Guilford Press.

Seeman, P. & Kapur, S. (2001). The dopamine receptor basis of psychosis. In A. Breier, P. V. Tran, F. Bymaster, & C. Tollefson (Eds.), *Current issues in the psychopharmacology of schizophrenia* (pp. 73–84). Philadelphia: Lippincott Williams & Wilkins.

Segal, D. L. (2000). Levels of knowledge about suicide facts and myths among younger and older adults. *Clinical Gerontologist, 22,* 71–80.

Segal, G. (1991). *A primer on brain tumors* (5th ed.). Des Plaines, IL: American Brain Tumor Association.

Segal, Z. V., Gemar, M., Truchon, C., Guirguis, M., & Horowitz, L. M. (1995). A priming methodology for studying self-representation in major depressive disorder. *Journal of Abnormal Psychology, 104,* 205–213.

Segal, Z. V., Gemar, M., & Williams, S. (1999). Differential cognitive response to a mood challenge following successful cognitive therapy or pharmacotherapy for unipolar depression. *Journal of Abnormal Psychology, 108,* 3–10.

Segraves, R. T. & Althof, S. (1998). Psychotherapy and pharmacotherapy of sexual dysfunctions. In P. Nathan & J. Gorman (Eds.), *A guide to treatments that work* (pp. 447–471). New York: Oxford University Press.

Segrin, C. & Abramson, L. Y. (1994). Negative reactions to depressive behaviors: A communication theories analysis. *Journal of Abnormal Psychology, 103,* 655–668.

Seifer, R. D., Clark, G. N., & Sameroff, A. J. (1991). Positive effects of interaction coaching on infants with developmental disabilities and their mothers. *American Journal of Mental Retardation, 96,* 1–11.

Sekuler, R. & MacArthur, R. D. (1977). Alcohol retards visual recovery from glare by hampering target acquisition. *Nature, 270,* 428–429.

Selfe, L. (1978). *Nadia: A case of extraordinary drawing ability in an autistic child.* New York: Academic Press.

Seligman, M. E. P. (1971). Phobias and preparedness. *Behavior Therapy, 2,* 307–320.

Seligman, M. E. P. (1975). *Helplessness: On depression, development, and death.* San Francisco: Freeman.

Seligman, M. E. P. (1988). Research in clinical psychology: Why is there so much depression today? *G. Stanley Hall Lecture Series, 9,* 79–96.

Seligman, M. E. P. (1998). Building human strength: Psychology's forgotten mission. *APA Monitor, 29*(1).

Seligman, M. E. P. & Csikszentmihalyi, M. (2000). Positive psychology: An introduction. *American Psychologist, 55,* 5–14.

Seligman, M. E. P., Schulman, P., DeRubeis, R. J., & Hollon, S. D. (1999). The prevention of depression and anxiety. *Prevention & Treatment, 2,* 1–25.

Selling, L. S. (1940). *Men against madness.* New York: Greenberg.

Seltzer, A. (1994). Multiple personality: A psychiatric misadventure. *Canadian Journal of Psychiatry, 39,* 442–445.

Selye, H. (1956). *The stress of life.* New York: McGraw-Hill.

Selye, H. (1974). *Stress without distress.* Philadelphia: Lippincott.

Selye, H. (1976). *Stress in health and disease.* Woburn, MA: Butterworths.

Selye, H. (1978). *The stress of life* (2nd ed.). New York: McGraw-Hill.

Semans, J. H. (1956). Premature ejaculation: A new approach. *Southern Medical Journal, 49,* 353–357.

Servan-Schreiber, D., Cohen, J. D., & Steingard, S. (1996). Schizophrenic deficits in the processing of context: A test of a theoretical model. *Archives of General Psychiatry, 53,* 1105–1112.

Seymour, G. (1986). Acute and chronic confusional states in the elderly surgical patients. In: *Medical assessment of the elderly surgical patient* (pp. 229–239). Kent, England: Croom Helm.

Shader, R. I. & Greenblatt, D. J. (1993). Use of benzodiazepines in anxiety disorders. *New England Journal of Medicine, 328,* 1398–1405.

Shader, R. I., Greenblatt, D. J., & Balter, M. B. (1991). Appropriate use and regulatory control of benzodiazepines. *Journal of Clinical Pharmacology, 31,* 781–784.

Shaefi, S. & Harkness, W. (2003). Current status of surgery in the management of epilepsy. *Epilepsia, 44*(Suppl. 1), 43–47.

Shaffer, D., Gould, M. S., Fisher, P., Trautman, P., Moreau, D., Kleinman, M., & Flory, M. (1996). Psychiatric diagnosis in child and adolescent suicide. *Archives of General Psychiatry, 53,* 339–348.

Shah, A. & Frith, U. (1983). An islet of ability in autistic children: A research note. *Journal of Child Psychology and Psychiatry, 24,* 613–620.

Shannon, J. B. (2000). *Mental retardation sourcebook.* Detroit, MI: Omnigraphics.

Shapiro, D. & Goldstein, I. B. (1982). Biobehavioral perspectives on hypertension. *Journal of Consulting and Clinical Psychology,* 841–858.

Shapiro, P. J. (2001). *Creativity and bipolar diathesis: Relationships between trait and state affect, creative cognition, and clinical diagnosis of affective disorder.* Unpublished doctoral dissertation, Temple University, Philadelphia.

Shapiro, P. J. & Weisberg, R. W. (1999). Creativity and bipolar diathesis: Common behavioural and cognitive components. *Cognition and Emotion, 13,* 741–762.

Shapiro, T. (1989). Our changing science. *Journal of the American Psychoanalytic Association, 37,* 3–6.

Sharf, R. S. (1996). *Theories of psychotherapy and counseling: Concepts and cases.* Pacific Grove, CA: Brooks/Cole.

Shea, M. T., Elkin, I., Imber, S. D., Sotsky, S. M., Watkins, J. T., Collins, J. F., Pilkonis, P. A., Beckham, E., Glass, D. R., Dolan, R. T., & Parloff, M. B. (1992). Course of depressive symptoms over follow-up. *Archives of General Psychiatry, 49,* 782–787.

Shear, M. K. (1996). Factors in the etiology and pathogenesis of panic disorder: Revisiting the attachment-separation paradigm. *American Journal of Psychiatry, 153,* 125–136.

Shear, M. K. & Barlow, D. H. (1998). "Cognitive behavioral treatment compared with nonprescriptive treatment of panic disorder": Reply. *Archives of General Psychiatry, 5,* 665–666.

Shear, M. K., Cooper, A. M., Klerman, G. L., Busch, F. N., & Shapiro, T. (1993). A psychodynamic model of panic disorder. *American Journal of Psychiatry, 150,* 859–866.

Shear, M. K., Pilkonis, P. A., Clotre, M., & Leon, A. C. (1994). Cognitive behavioral treatment compared with nonprescriptive treatment of panic disorder. *Archives of General Psychiatry, 51,* 395–401.

Shear, M. K. & Weiner, K. (1997). Psychotherapy for panic disorder. *Journal of Clinical Psychiatry, 58*(Suppl. 2), 38–45.

Sheeber, L. B. & Johnson, J. H. (1994). Evaluation of a temperament- focused, parent-training program. *Journal of Clinical Child Psychology, 23,* 249–259.

Sheehan, S. (1982). *Is there no place on earth for me?* Boston: Houghton Mifflin.

Shelton, R. C. & Brown, L. L. (2001). Mechanisms of action in the treatment of anxiety. *Journal of Clinical Psychiatry, 62*(Suppl. 12), 10–15.

Shepherd, M., Cooper, B., Brown, A., & Kalton, C. W. (1996). *Psychiatric illness in general practice.* London: Oxford University Press.

Sheps, D. S., McMahon, R. P., Becker, L., Carney, R. M., Freedland, K. E., Cohen, J. D., Sheffield, D., Goldberg, A. D., Ketterer, M. W., Pepine, C. J., Raczynski, J. M., Light, K., Krantz, D. S., Stone, P. H., Knatterud, F. L., & Kaufmann, P. G. (2002). Mental stress-induced ischemia and all-cause mortality in patients with coronary artery disease: Results from the Psychophysiological Investigations of Myocardial Ischemia study. *Circulation, 105,* 1780–1784.

Shergill, S. S., Brammer, M. J., Williams, S. C. R., Murray, R. M., & McGuire, P. K. (2000). Mapping auditory hallucinations in schizophrenia using functional magnetic resonance imaging. *Archives of General Psychiatry, 57,* 1033–1038.

Sherman, S. (1996). Epidemiology. In R. J. Hagerman & A. C. Silverman (Eds.), *The fragile X syndrome:*

Diagnosis, treatment, and research (2nd. ed., pp. 165–192). Baltimore, MD: Johns Hopkins University Press.

Shiffman, S. (1982). Relapse following smoking cessation: A situational analysis. *Journal of Consulting and Clinical Psychology, 50,* 71–86.

Shiffman, S., Paty, J. A., Gnys, M., Kassel, J. A., & Hickcox, M. (1996). First lapses to smoking: Within-subjects analysis of real-time reports. *Journal of Consulting and Clinical Psychology, 64,* 366–379.

Shihabuddin, L., Buchsbaum, M. S., Hazlett, E. A., Silverman, J., New, A., Brickan, A. M., Mitropoula, V., Nunn, M., & Fleishman, M. B. (2001). Striatal size and relative glucose metabolic rate in schizotypal personality disorder and schizophrenia. *Archives of General Psychiatry, 58,* 877–884.

Shilony, E. & Grossuman, F. K. (1993). Depersonalization as a defense mechanism in survivors of trauma. *Journal of Traumatic Stress, 6,* 119–128.

Shipherd, J. C. & Beck, J. G. (1999). The effects of suppressing trauma-related thoughts on women with rape-related posttraumatic stress disorder. *Behavior Research and Therapy, 37,* 99–112.

Shisslak, C. M., Crago, M., & Estes, L. S. (1995). The spectrum of eating disturbances. *International Journal of Eating Disorders, 18,* 209–219.

Shneidman, E. S. (1992). A conspectus of the suicidal scenario. In R. W. Maris, A. L. Berman, J. T. Maltsberger, & R. I. Yufit (Eds.), *Assessment and prediction of suicide* (pp. 50–64). New York: Guilford Press.

Shneidman, E. S. & Farberow, N. L. (1970). Attempted and completed suicide. In E. S. Shneidman, N. L. Farberow, & R. E. Litman (Eds.), *The psychology of suicide.* New York: Science House.

Shorter, E. (1995). The borderland between neurology and history: Conversion reactions. *Neurologic Clinics, 13,* 229–239.

Shortt, A., Barrett, P., & Fox, T. (2001). A family-based cognitive behavioural group treatment for anxious children: An evaluation of the FRIENDS program. *Journal of Clinical Child Psychology.*

Shulman, I. D., Cox, B. J., Swinson, R. P., Kuch, K., & Reichman, J. T. (1994). Precipitating events, locations, and reactions associated with initial unexpected panic attacks. *Behaviour Research and Therapy, 32,* 17–20.

Shulman, R. G. (2001). Functional imaging studies: Linking mind and basic neuroscience. *American Journal of Psychiatry, 158,* 11–20.

Siegel, B. V., Buchsbaum, M. S., Bunney, W. E., Jr., Gottschalk, L. A., Haier, R. J., Lohr, J. B., Lottenberg, S., Najafi, A., Nuechterlein, K. H., Potkin, S. G., & Wu, J. C. (1993). Cortical-striatal-thalamic circuits and brain glucose metabolic activity in 70 unmedicated male schizophrenic patients. *American Journal of Psychiatry, 150,* 1325–1336.

Siever, L. J. (1992). Schizophrenia spectrum disorders. In A. Tasman & M. B. Riba (Eds.), *Review of psychiatry* (Vol. 11, pp. 25–42). Washington, DC: American Psychiatric Press.

Siever, L. J. & Davis, K. L. (1991). A psychobiological perspective on personality disorders. *American Journal of Psychiatry, 148,* 1647–1658.

Siever, L. J., Friedman, L., Moskowitz, J., Mitropoulou, V., Keefe, R., Roitman, S. L., Merhige, D., Trestman, R., Silverman, J., & Mohs, R. (1994). Eye movement impairment and schizotypal psychopathology. *American Journal of Psychiatry, 151,* 1209–1215.

Sigman, M. (1995). Behavioral research in childhood autism. In M. Lenzenweger & J. Haugaard (Eds.), *Frontiers of developmental psychopathology* (pp. 190–206). New York: Springer/Verlag.

Sigman, M. & Mundy, P. (1989). Social attachments in autistic children. *Journal of the American Academy of Child and Adolescent Psychiatry, 28,* 74–81.

Silove, D. & Manicavasagar, V. (2001). Early separation anxiety and its relationship to adult anxiety disorders. In M. W. Vasey & M. R. Dadds (Eds.), *The developmental psychopathology of anxiety* (pp. 459–480). New York: Oxford University Press.

Silove, D., Manicavasagar, V., Curtis, J., & Blaszczynski, A. (1996). Is early separation anxiety a risk factor for adult panic disorder?: A critical review. *Comprehensive Psychiatry, 37,* 167–179.

Silverman, K., Svikis, D., Robles, E., Stitzer, M. L., & Bigelow, G. E. (2001). A reinforcement-based therapeutic workplace for the treatment of drug abuse: Six-month abstinence outcomes. *Experimental & Clinical Psychopharmacology, 9*(1), 14–23.

Silverman, M. M. (1997). Introduction: Current controversies in suicidology. In R. W. Maris, M. M. Silverman, & S. S. Canetto (Eds.), *Review of suicidology* (pp. 1–21). New York: Guilford Press.

Silverman, W. K., Kurtines, W. M., Ginsburg, G. S., Weems, C. F., Lumpkin, P. W., & Carmichael, D. H. (1999). Treating anxiety disorders in children with group cognitive-behavior therapy: A randomized clinical trial. *Journal of Consulting and Clinical Psychology, 67,* 995–1003.

Silverman, W. K. & Treffers, P. D. A. (2001). *Anxiety disorders in children and adolescents: Research, assessment, and intervention.* Cambridge, England: Cambridge University Press.

Simeon, D., Gross, S., Guralnik, O., Stein, D. J., Schmeidler, J., & Hollander, E. (1997). Feeling unreal: 30 cases of *DSM-III-R* depersonalization disorder. *American Journal of Psychiatry, 154,* 1107–1113.

Simeon, D., Guralnik, O., Hazlett, E. A., Spiegel-Cohen, J., Hollander, E., & Buchsbaum, M. S. (2000). Feeling unreal: A PET study of depersonalization disorder. *American Journal of Psychiatry, 157,* 1782–1788.

Simeon, D., Guralnik, O., Schmeidler, J., Sirof, B., & Knutelska, M. (2001). The role of childhood interpersonal trauma in depersonalization disorder. *American Journal of Psychiatry, 158,* 1027–1033.

Simeon, D. & Hollander, E. (1993). Depersonalization disorder. *Psychiatric Annals, 23,* 382–388.

Simeon, D., Stein, D. J., & Hollander, E. (1995). Depersonalization disorder and self-injurious behavior. *Journal of Clinical Psychiatry, 56,* 36–39.

Simonoff, E., Bolton, P., & Rutter, M. (1996). Mental retardation: Genetic findings, clinical implications and research agenda. *Journal of Child Psychology and Psychiatry, 37,* 259–280.

Simpson, J. A., Rholes, W. S., et al. (Eds.). (1998). *Attachment theory and close relationships.* New York: Guilford Press.

Sinason, V. (2000). Psychotherapeutic work with disabled individuals: The past is alive in the present. *Psychotherapy Review, 2,* 325–382.

Singleton, L. & Johnson, K. A. (1993). *The black health library guide to stroke.* New York: Holt.

Sinha, R. (2001). How does stress increase risk of drug abuse and relapse? *Psychopharmacology, 158,* 343–359.

Siqueland, L., Crits-Christoph, P., Gallop, R., Barber, J. P., Griffin, M. L., Thase, M. E., Daley, D., Frank, A., Gastfriend, D. R., Blaine,

J., Connolly, M. B., & Gladis, M. (2002). Retention in psychosocial treatment of cocaine dependence: Predictors and impact on outcome. *American Journal on Addictions, 11,* 24–40.

Sirey, J. A., Bruce, M. L., Alexopoulos, G. S., Perlick, D. A., Raue, P., Friedman, S. J., & Meyers, B. S. (2001). Perceived stigma as a predictor of treatment discontinuation in young and older outclients with depression. *American Journal of Psychiatry, 158,* 479–481.

Sivec, H. J. & Lynn, S. J. (1995). Dissociative and neuropsychological symptoms: The question of differential diagnosis. *Clinical Psychology Review, 15,* 297–316.

Skinner, B. F. (1953). *Science and human behavior.* New York: Macmillan.

Skinner, B. F. (1965). *Science and human behavior.* New York: Free Press.

Skinner, B. F. (1990). Can psychology be a science of mind? *American Psychologist, 45*(11), 1206–1210.

Sklar, L. S. & Anisman, H. (1979). Stress and coping factors influence tumor growth. *Science, 205,* 513–515.

Skre, I., Onstad, S., Torgersen, S., Lygren, S., & Kringlen, E. (1993). A twin study of *DSM-III-R* anxiety disorders. *Acta Psychiatrica Scandinavica, 88,* 85–92.

Slaghuis, W. L. & Curran, C. E. (1999). Spatial frequency masking in positive- and negative-symptom schizophrenia. *Journal of Abnormal Psychology, 108,* 42–50.

Slap, G. B., Vorters, D. F., Khalid, N., Margulies, S. R., et al. (1992). Adolescent suicide attempters: Do physicians recognize them? *Journal of Adolescent Health, 13,* 286–292.

Slavin, R. E., Karweit, N. L., & Wasik, B. A. (1994). *Preventing early school failure.* Needham Heights, MA: Allyn & Bacon.

Sloan, D. M., Strauss, M. E., & Wisner, K. L. (2001). Diminished response to pleasant stimuli by depressed women. *Journal of Abnormal Psychology, 110,* 488–493.

Sloan, H. R. (1991). Metabolic screening methods. In J. L. Matson & J. A. Mulick (Eds.), *Handbook of mental retardation* (2nd. ed., pp. 292–307). New York: Pergamon.

Slobogin, C. (2001). Psychiatric evidence in criminal trials: A 25-year retrospective. In L. E. Frost & R. J. Bonnie (Eds.), *The evolution of mental health law* (pp. 245–276). Washington, DC: American Psychological Association.

Slovenko, R. (1999). The mental disability requirement in the insanity defense. *Behavioral Sciences and the Law, 17,* 165–180.

Slutske, W. S., Eisen, S. A., True, W. R., Lyons, M. J., Goldberg, J., & Tsuang, M. T. (2000). Common genetic vulnerability for pathological gambling and alcohol dependence in men. *Archives of General Psychiatry, 57,* 666–673.

Slutske, W. S., Heath, A. C., Dinwiddie, S. H., Madden, P. A. F., Bucholz, K. K., Dunne, M. P., Statham, D. J., & Martin, N. G. (1997). Modeling genetic and environmental influences in the etiology of conduct disorder: A study of 2,682 adult twin pairs. *Journal of Abnormal Psychology, 106,* 266–279.

Slutske, W. S., Heath, A. C., Dinwiddie, S. H., Madden, P. A. F., Bucholz, K. K., Dunne, M. P., Statham, D. J., & Martin, N. G. (1998). Common risk factors for conduct disorder and alcohol dependence. *Journal of Abnormal Psychology, 107,* 363–374.

Small, D. M., Zatorre, R. J., Dagher, A., Evans, A. C., & Jones-Gotman, M. (2001). Changes in brain activity related to eating chocolate: From pleasure to aversion. *Brain, 124,* 1720–1733.

Small, J. G., Klapper, M. H., Milstein, V., Kellams, J. J., Miller, M. J., Marhenke, J. D., & Small, I. F. (1991). Carbamazepine compared with lithium in the treatment of mania. *Archives of General Psychiatry, 48,* 915–921.

Smeets, G., de Jong, P. J., & Mayer, B. (2000). If you suffer from a headache, then you have a brain tumour: Domain-specific reasoning "bias" and hypochondrias. *Behaviour Research and Therapy, 38,* 763–776.

Smith, D. (2003, January). 10 ways practitioners can avoid frequent ethical pitfalls, *Monitor on Psychology, 34, 50–55.*

Smith, G. S., Keyl, P. M., Hadley, J. A., Bartley, C. L., Foss, R. D., Tolbert, W. G., & McNight, J. (2001). Drinking and recreational boating fatalities: A population-based case-control study. *Journal of the American Medical Association, 286,* 2974–2980.

Smith, L. C., Friedman, S., & Nevid, J. (1999). Clinical and sociocultural differences in African American and European American patients with panic disorder and agoraphobia. *Journal of Nervous and Mental Disease, 187,* 549–560.

Smith, T. E., Bellack, A. S., & Liberman, R. P. (1996). Social skills training for schizophrenia: Review and future directions. *Clinical Psychology Review, 16,* 599–617.

Smith, T. W. & Brown, P. C. (1991). Cynical hostility, attempts to exert social control, and cardiovascular reactivity in married couples. *Journal of Behavioral Medicine, 14,* 581–592.

Smyth, J. M., Stone, A. A., Hurewitz, A., & Kaell, A. (1999). Effects of writing about stressful experiences on symptom reduction in patients with asthma or rheumatoid arthritis. *Journal of the American Medical Association, 281,* 1304–1309.

Snowden, J. S., Bathgate, D., Varma, A., Blackshaw, Z. C., Gibbons, Z. C., & Neary, D. (2001). Distinct behavioural profiles in frontotemporal dementia and semantic dementia. *Journal of Neurology, Neurosurgery, and Psychiatry, 70,* 323–332.

Snowden, J. S., Neary, D., & Mann, D. M. A. (2002). Frontotemporal dementia. *British Journal of Psychiatry, 180,* 140–143.

Snowdon, D. A., Greiner, L. H., & Markesbery, W. R. (2000). Linguistic ability in early life and the neuropathology of Alzheimer's disease and cerebrovascular disease: Findings from the Nun Study. *Annals of the New York Academy of Sciences, 903,* 34–38.

Snyder, C. R. (1958). *Alcohol and the Jews.* New York: Free Press.

Snyder, S. H. (1979). The true speed trip: Schizophrenia. In D. Goleman & R. J. Davidson (Eds.), *Consciousness: Brain, states of awareness, and mysticism.* New York: Harper & Row.

Soares, J. C. & Mann, J. J. (1997). The anatomy of mood disorders—Review of structural neuroimaging studies. *Biological Psychiatry, 41,* 86–106.

Sobell, L. C., Toneatto, A., & Sobell, M. B. (1990). Behavior therapy (alcohol and other substance abuse). In A. S. Bellack & M. Hersen (Eds.), *Handbook of comparative treatments for adult disorders* (pp. 479–505). New York: Wiley.

Solomon, A., Haaga, D. A. F., & Arnow, B. A. (2001). Is clinical depression distinct from subthreshold depressive symptoms? A review of the continuity issue in depression research. *Journal of Nervous and Mental Disease, 189,* 498–506.

Solomon, D. A., Keller, M. B., Leon, A. C., Mueller, T. I., Shea, M. T., Warshaw, M., Maser, J. D., Coryell,

W., & Endicott, J. (1997). Recovery from major depression: A 10-year prospective follow-up across multiple episodes. *Archives of General Psychiatry, 54,* 1001–1006.

Solomon, S. D. & Davidson, R. T. (1997). Trauma: Prevalence, impairment, service use, and cost. *Journal of Clinical Psychiatry, 58*(Suppl. 9), 5–11.

Solomon, Z., Ginzburg, K., Mikulincer, M., Neria, Y., & Ohry, A. (1998). Coping with war captivity: The role of attachment style. *European Journal of Personality, 12,* 271–285.

Solomon, Z., Iancu, I., & Tyano, S. (1997). World assumptions following disaster. *Journal of Applied Social Psychology, 27,* 1758–1798.

Solomon, Z., Laor, N., & McFarlane, A. C. (1996). Acute posttraumatic reactions in soldiers and civilians. In B. A. van der Kolk, A. C. McFarlane, & L. Weisaeth (Eds.), *Traumatic stress: The effects of overwhelming experience on mind, body, and society* (pp. 102–114). New York: Guilford Press.

Sommer, I., Aleman, A., Ramsey, N., Bouma, A., & Kahn, R. (2001). Handedness, language lateralisation and anatomical asymmetry in schizophrenia. *British Journal of Psychiatry, 178,* 344–351.

Sonnerborg, A. B., Ehrnst, A. C., Bergdahl, S. K., Pehronson, P. O., Skoldenberg, B. R., & Strannegard, O. O. (1988). HIV isolation from cerebrospinal fluid in relation to immunological deficiency and neurological symptoms. *AIDS, 2,* 89–93.

Southern-Gerow, M. A. & Kendall, P. C. (1997). Parent-focused and cognitive-behavioral treatments of antisocial youth. In D. M. Stoff, J. Breiling, & J. D. Maser (Eds.), *Handbook of antisocial behavior* (pp. 384–394). New York: Wiley.

Spanos, N. P. (1994). Multiple identity enactments and multiple personality disorder: A sociocognitive perspective. *Psychological Bulletin, 116,* 143–165.

Spanos, N. P. (1996). *Multiple identities and false memories: A sociocognitive perspective.* Washington, DC: American Psychological Association.

Spanos, N. P., Weekes, J. R., & Bertrand, L. D. (1985). Multiple personality: A social psychological perspective. *Journal of Abnormal Psychology, 94,* 362–376.

Sparrow, S. S. & Davis, S. M. (2000). Recent advances in the assessment of intelligence and cognition. *Journal of Child Psychology and Psychiatry, 41,* 117–131.

Spasojevic, J. & Alloy, L. B. (2002). *Dependency reconceptualized: Is neediness a vulnerability factor for depression?* Manuscript under editorial review, Temple University, Philadelphia.

Spaulding, W. D., Reed, D., Sullivan, M., Richardson, C., & Weiler, M. (1999). Effects of cognitive treatment in psychiatric rehabilitation. *Schizophrenia Bulletin, 25,* 657–676.

Spector, I. P. & Carey, M. P. (1990). Incidence and prevalence of the sexual dysfunctions: A critical review of the empirical literature. *Archives of Sexual Behavior, 19,* 389–408.

Spence, S. H. (1994). Preventative strategies. In T. H. Ollendick, N. J. King, & W. Yule (Eds.), *International handbook of phobic and anxiety disorders in children and adolescents* (pp. 453–474). New York: Plenum Press.

Spencer, S. M., Lehman, J. M., Wynings, C., Arena, P., Carver, C. S., Antoni, M. H., et al. (1999). Concerns about breast cancer and relations to psychosocial well-being in a multiethnic sample of early-stage patients. *Health Psychology, 18,* 159–168.

Spiegel, D. (2001). Mind matters—group therapy and survival in breast cancer. *New England Journal of Medicine, 345,* 1767–1768.

Spiegel, D., Bloom, J. R., Kraemer, H. C., & Gottheil, E. (1989). Effect of psychosocial treatment on survival of patients with metastatic breast cancer. *Lancet,* 888–891.

Spirito, A., Overholser, J. C., & Stark, L. J. (1989). Common problems and coping strategies: II. Findings with adolescent suicide attempters. *Journal of Abnormal Child Psychology, 17,* 213–221.

Spitzer, C., Spelsberg, B., Grabe, H., Mundt, B., & Freyberger, H. J. (1999). Dissociative experiences and psychopathology in conversion disorders. *Journal of Psychosomatic Research, 46,* 291–294.

Spitzer, R. L. (1976). More on pseudoscience in science and the case for psychiatric diagnosis. A critique of D. L. Rosenhan's "On being sane in insane places" and "The contextual nature of psychiatric diagnosis." *Archives of General Psychiatry, 33,* 459–470.

Spitzer, R. L. & Fleiss, J. L. (1974). A reanalysis of the reliability of psychiatric diagnosis. *British Journal of Psychiatry, 125,* 341–347.

Spitzer, R. L., Gibbon, M., Skodol, A. E., Williams, J. B. W., & First, M. B. (Eds.). (1994). *DSM-IV casebook: A learning companion to the diagnostic and statistical manual of mental disorders, fourth edition.* Washington, DC: American Psychiatric Press.

Spitzer, R. L., Skodol, A. E., Gibbon, M., & Williams, J. B. W. (1983). *Psychopathology: A case book.* New York: McGraw-Hill.

Spitzer, R. L. & Wakefield, J. C. (1999). *DSM-IV* diagnostic criterion for clinical significance: Does it help solve the false positives problem? *American Journal of Psychiatry, 156,* 1856–1864.

Spivak, G. & Shure, M. B. (1989). Interpersonal cognitive problem solving (ICPS): A competence-building primary prevention program. *Prevention in Human Services, 6,* 151–178.

Spring, R. L. (1998). The return to *Mens Rea:* Salvaging a reasonable perspective on mental disorder in criminal trials. *International Journal of Law and Psychiatry, 21,* 187–196.

Squire, L. R. & Slater, P. C. (1978). Bilateral and unilateral ECT: Effects on verbal and nonverbal memory. *American Journal of Psychiatry, 135,* 1316–1320.

Stacy, A. W. (1997). Memory activation and expectancy as prospective predictors of alcohol and marijuana use. *Journal of Abnormal Psychology, 106,* 61–73.

Stacy, A. W., Newcomb, M. D., & Bentler, P. M. (1991). Cognitive motivation and drug use: A 9-year longitudinal study. *Journal of Abnormal Psychology, 100,* 502–515.

Stahl, S. M. (1996). *Essential psychopharmacology: Neuroscientific basis and practical applications.* Cambridge: Cambridge University Press.

Staines, G. L., Magura, S., Foote, J., Deluca, A., & Kosanke, N. (2001). Polysubstance abuse among alcoholics. *Journal of Addictive Disease, 20,* 53–69.

Stancliffe, R. J. & Lakin, K. C. (1998). Analysis of expenditures and outcomes of residential alternatives for persons with developmental disabilities. *American Journal of Mental Retardation, 102,* 552–568.

Stanton, M. D. & Shadish, W. R. (1997). Outcome, attrition, and family-couples treatment for drug abuse. *Psychological Bulletin, 122,* 170–191.

State v. Soura, 796 P. 2d 109 (Idaho 1990).

State v. Summers, 853 P. 2d 953 (Wash. App. 1993).

Steadman, H., Gounis, K., Dennis, D., Hopper, K., Roche, B., Swartz, M., & Robbins, P. (2001). Assessing the New York City involuntary outpatient commitment pilot program. *Psychiatric Services, 52,* 330–336.

Steadman, H., McGreevy, M. A., Morrissey, J. P., et al. (1993). *Before and after Hinckley: Evaluating insanity defense reform.* New York: Guilford Press.

Steadman, H. J., Mulvey, E., Monahan, J., Robbins, P. C., Appelbaum, P. S., Grisso, T., Roth, L. H., & Silver, E. (1998). Violence by people discharged from acute psychiatric inpatient facilities and by others in the same neighborhoods. *Archives of General Psychiatry, 55,* 393–401.

Steege, J. F., Stout, A. L., & Culley, C. C. (1986). Patient satisfaction in Scott and Small-Carrion penile implant recipients: A study of 52 patients. *Archives of Sexual Behavior, 15*(5), 393–399.

Steere, A. C. (2001). Lyme disease. *New England Journal of Medicine, 345*(2), 115–125.

Stefanek, M. & McDonald, P. G. (2003). Biological mechanisms of psychosocial effects on disease: Implications for cancer control. *Brain, Behavior, and Immunity, 17,* S1–S4.

Steffen, P. R., Hinderliter, A. L., Blumenthal, J. A., & Sherwood, A. (2001). Religious coping, ethnicity, and ambulatory blood pressure. *Psychosomatic Medicine, 63,* 523–530.

Steffenburg, S. & Gillberg, C. (1986). Autism and autistic-like conditions in Swedish rural and urban areas: A population study. *British Journal of Psychiatry, 149,* 81–87.

Steffenburg, S., Gillberg, C., Hellgren, L., Andersson, L., Gillberg, I. C., Jakobssen, G., & Bohman, M. (1989). A twin study of autism in Denmark, Finland, Iceland, Norway, and Sweden. *Journal of Child Psychology and Psychiatry, 30,* 405–416.

Steil, R. & Ehlers, A. (2000). Dysfunctional meaning of posttraumatic intrusions in chronic PTSD. *Behaviour Research and Therapy, 38,* 537–558.

Stein, E. A., Prankiewicz, J., Hanch, H. H., Cho, J., Fuller, S. A., Hoffman, R. G., Hawkins, M., Rao, S. M., Banderettint, P. A., & Bloom, A. S. (1998). Nicotine-induced limbic cortical activation in the human brain: A functional MRI study. *American Journal of Psychiatry, 155,* 1009–1015.

Stein, L. I. & Diamond, R. J. (2000). Commentary: A "systems"-based alternative to mandatory outpatient treatment. *Journal of the American Academy of Psychiatry and the Law, 28,* 159–164.

Stein, M. A., Szumowski, E., Blondis, T. A., & Roizen, N. (1995). Adaptive skills dysfunction in ADD and ADHD children. *Journal of Child Psychology and Psychiatry, 36,* 663–670.

Stein, M. B. & Kean, Y. M. (2000). Disability and quality of life in social phobia: Epidemiologic findings. *American Journal of Psychiatry, 157,* 1606–1613.

Stein, M. B., Kirk, P., Prabhu, V., Grott, M., & Terepa, M. (1995). Mixed anxiety-depression in a primary-care clinic. *Journal of Affective Disorders, 34,* 79–84.

Stein, M. B., Walker, J. R., & Forde, D. R. (2000). Gender differences in susceptibility to posttraumatic stress disorder. *Behaviour Research and Therapy, 38,* 619–628.

Steinberg, L. & Meyer, R. (1995). *Childhood.* New York: McGraw-Hill.

Steinhausen, H. C. (1994). Anorexia and bulimia nervosa. In M. Rutter, E. Taylor, & L. Hersov (Eds.), *Child and adolescent psychiatry.* Oxford, England: Blackwell.

Steketee, G. & Pruyn, N. A. (1998). Families of individuals with obsessive-compulsive disorder. In R. P. Swinson, M. M. Antony, S. Rachman, & M. A. Richter (Eds.), *Obsessive-compulsive disorder: Theory, research, and treatment.* London: Guilford Press.

Stemberger, R. T., Turner, S. M., Beidel, D. C., & Calhoun, K. S. (1995). Social phobia: An analysis of possible developmental factors. *Journal of Abnormal Psychology, 104,* 526–531.

Stern, Y., Gurland, B., Tatemichi, T. K., Tang, M. X., Wilder, D., & Mayeux, R. (1994). Influence of education and occupation on the incidence of Alzheimer's disease. *Journal of the American Medical Association, 271,* 1004–1010.

Sternberg, R. J. & Kaufman, J. C. (1998). Human abilities. *Annual Review of Psychology, 49,* 479–502.

Stetson, B. A., Rahn, J. M., Dubbert, P. M., Wilner, B. I., & Mercury, M. G. (1997). Prospective evaluation of the effects of stress on exercise adherence in community-residing women, *16,* 515–520.

Stevens, R. J. & Slavin, R. E. (1995). The cooperative elementary school: Effects on students' achievement, attitudes, and social relations. *American Educational Research Journal, 32,* 321–351.

Stewart, S. H., Taylor, S., Jang, K. L., Cox, B. J., Watt, M. C., Fedoroff, I. C., & Borger, S. C. (2001). Causal modeling of relations among learning history, anxiety sensitivity, and panic attacks. *Behaviour Research and Therapy, 39* (4), 443–456.

Stoller, R. J. (1975). *Sex and gender: The transsexual experiment.* London: Hogarth Press.

Stone, A. A. (1976). The *Tarasoff* decision: Suing psychotherapists to safeguard society. *Harvard Law Review, 90,* 358.

Stone, A. A., Bovbjerg, D. M., Neale, J. M., & Napoli, A. (1992). Development of cold symptoms following experimental rhinovirus infection is related to prior stressful life events. *Behavioral Medicine, 18,* 115–120.

Stone, A. A., Valdimarsdottir, H. B., Katkin, E. S., Burns, J., & Cox, D. S. (1993). Effects of mental stressors on mitogen-induced lymphocyte responses in the laboratory. *Psychology and Health, 8,* 269–284.

Stone, M. H. (1993). *Abnormalities of personality. Within and beyond the realm of treatment.* New York: W. W. Norton.

Stoney, C. M., Davis, M. C., & Matthews, K. A. (1987). Sex differences in physiological responses to stress and in coronary heart disease: A causal link? *Psychophysiology, 24,* 127–131.

Stoney, C. M., Hughes, J. W., Kuntz, K. K., West, S. G., & Thornton, L. M. (2002). Cardiovascular stress responses among Asian Indian and European American women and men. *Annals of Behavioral Medicine, 24,* 113–121.

Stoney, C. M., Owens, J. F., Guzick, D. S., & Matthews, K. A. (1997). A natural experiment on the effects of ovarian hormones on cardiovascular risk factors and stress reactivity: Hysterectomy with or without bilateral oophorectomy. *Health Psychology, 16,* 349–358.

Stoney, C. M., West, S. G., Hughes, J. W., Lentino, L. M., Finney, M. L., Falko, J., & Bausserman, L. (2002). Acute psychological stress reduces plasma triglyceride clearance. *Psychophysiology, 39,* 80–85.

Strain, E. C. (1995). Antisocial personality disorder, misbehavior, and drug abuse. *Journal of Nervous and Mental Disease, 183,* 162–165.

Strakowski, S. M., Flaum, M., Amador, X., Bracha, H. S., Pandurangi, A. K.,

Robinson, D., & Tohen, M. (1996). Racial differences in the diagnosis of psychosis. *Schizophrenia Research, 21,* 117–124.

Stratton, K., Howe, C., & Battaglia, F. (1996). *Fetal alcohol syndrome: Diagnosis, epidemiology, and treatment.* Washington, DC: National Academy Press.

Strauss, M. E. (1993). Relations of symptoms to cognitive deficits in schizophrenia. *Schizophrenia Bulletin, 19,* 215–231.

Strauss, M. E. (2001). Demonstrating specific cognitive deficits: A psychometric perspective. *Journal of Abnormal Psychology, 110,* 6–14.

Streltzer, J., Eliashof, B. A., Kline, A. E., & Goebert, D. (2000). Chronic pain disorder following physical injury. *Psychosomatics, 41,* 227–234.

Strong, J. W. (1992). *McCormick on evidence* (4th ed.). St. Paul, MN: West.

Stroop, J. R. (1935). Studies of interference in serial verbal reactions. *Journal of Experimental Psychology, 18,* 643–661.

Strote, J., Lee, J. E., & Wechsler, H. (2002). Increasing MDMA use among college students: Results of a national survey. *Journal of Adolescent Health, 30,* 64–72.

Strupp, H. & Binder, J. L. (1984). *Psychotherapy in a new key: A guide to time-limited dynamic psychotherapy.* New York: Basic Books.

Stunkard, A. J. & Koch, C. (1964). The interpretation of gastric motility: I. Apparent bias in the reports of hunger by obese persons. *Archives of General Psychiatry, 11,* 74–82.

Sturgis, E. T. (1993). Obsessive-compulsive disorders. In P. B. Sutker & H. E. Adams (Eds.), *Comprehensive handbook of psychopathology* (2nd ed., pp. 129–144). New York: Plenum Press.

Suarez, E. C. & Harralson, T. L. (1999). Hostility-related differences in the associations between stress-induced physiological reactivity and lipid concentrations in young healthy women. *International Journal of Behavioral Medicine, 6,* 190–203.

Substance Abuse and Mental Health Services Administration. (1996). *National household survey on drug abuse: Population estimates 1993.* Rockville, MD: DHHS Publication no. (SMA), 1994:94–3017.

Sullivan, G., Burnam, A., & Koegel, P. (2000). Pathways to homelessness among the mentally ill. *Social Psychiatry and Psychiatric Epidemiology, 35,* 444–450.

Sullivan, G. M., Hatterer, J. A., Herbert, J., Chen, X., Roose, S. P., Attia, E., Mann, J. J., Marangell, L. B., Goetz, R. R., & Gorman, J. M. (1999). Low levels of transthyretin in the CSF of depressed patients. *American Journal of Psychiatry, 156,* 710–715.

Sullivan, P. F., Neale, M. C., & Kendler, K. S. (2000). Genetic epidemiology of major depression. Review and meta-analysis. *American Journal of Psychiatry, 157,* 1552–1562.

Sulzer-Azaroff, B., & Mayer, R. G. (1991). *Behavior analysis for lasting change.* New York: Holt, Rinehart & Winston.

Summerfeldt, L., Antony, M. M., Downie, F., Richter, M. A., & Swinson, R. P. (1997). *Prevalence of particular obsessions and compulsions in a clinic sample.* (Unpublished, cited in Antony, Downie, & Swinson, 1998).

Suomi, S. J. (2000). A biobehavioral perspective on developmental psychopathology: Excessive aggression and serotonergic dysfunction in monkeys. In A. J. Sameroff, M. Lewis, et al. (Eds.), *Handbook of developmental psychopathology* (2nd ed., pp. 237-256). New York: Kluwer Academic/Plenum.

Super, C. M., Herrera, M. G., & Mora, J. O. (1990). Long-term effects of food supplementation and psychosocial intervention on the physical growth of Columbian infants at risk of malnutrition. *Child Development, 61,* 29–49.

Suppes, T., Dennehy, E. B., & Gibbons, E. W. (2000). The longitudinal course of bipolar disorder. *Journal of Clinical Psychiatry, 61*(Suppl.), 23–30.

Sushinsky, L. (1970). An illustration of a behavioral therapy intervention with nursing staff in a therapeutic role. *Journal of Psychiatric Nursing and Mental Health Services, 8*(5), 24–26.

Sutker, P. B. & Allain, A. N., Jr. (1996). Assessment of PTSD and other mental disorders in World War II and Korean conflict POW survivors and combat veterans. *Psychological Assessment, 8,* 18–25.

Sutton, S. K. & Davidson, R. J. (1997). Prefrontal brain asymmetry: A biological substrate of the behavioral approach and inhibition systems. *Psychological Science, 8,* 204–210.

Suvisaari, J. M., Haukka, J. K., Tanskanen, A. J., & Lonnqvist, J. K. (1999). Decline in the incidence of schizophrenia in Finnish cohorts born from 1954 to 1965. *Archives of General Psychiatry, 56,* 733–740.

Suzuki, L. A. & Valencia, R. R. (1999). Race—ethnicity and measured intelligence: Educational implications. *American Psychologist, 52,* 1103–1114.

Swados, E. (1991, August 18). The story of a street person. *The New York Times Magazine,* pp. 16–18.

Swan, W. B., Jr., Stein-Seroussi, A., & Giesler, R. B. (1992). Why people self-verify. *Journal of Personality and Social Psychology, 62,* 392–401.

Swann, W. B., Jr., Wenzlaff, R. M., Krull, D. S., & Pelham, B. W. (1992). Allure of negative feedback: Self-verification strivings among depressed persons. *Journal of Abnormal Psychology, 101,* 293–306.

Swanson, J. W., Borum, R., Swartz, M. S., Hiday, V. A., Wagner, H. R., & Burns, B. J. (2001). Can involuntary outpatient commitment reduce arrests among persons with severe mental illness? *Criminal Justice and Behavior, 28,* 156–189.

Swartz, M. S. & Monahan, J. (2001). Special section on involuntary outpatient commitment: Introduction. *Psychiatric Services, 52,* 323–350.

Swartz, M. S., Swanson, J. W., Hiday, V. A., Wagner, H. R., Burns, B. J., & Borum, R. (2001). A randomized controlled trial of outpatient commitment in North Carolina. *Psychiatric Services, 52*(3), 325–329.

Swedish Research Council. (2002). Unique research finding: Majority of heroin addicts can be treated. Retrieved August 15, 2002, from www.AlphaGalileo(2).htm.

Sweeney, J., Hass, G., & Nimgaonkar, V. (2000). Schizophrenia: Etiology. In M. Hersen & A. S. Bellack (Eds.), *Psychopathology in adulthood* (pp. 278–304). Boston, MA: Allyn & Bacon.

Swendsen, J., Heller, T. L., & Hammen, C. (1995). Relapse and impairment in bipolar disorder. *American Journal of Psychiatry, 152,* 1635–1640.

Swerdlow, N. R., Braff, D. L., Taaid, N., & Geyer, M. A. (1994). Assessing the validity of an animal model of deficient sensorimotor gating in schizophrenic patients. *Archives of General Psychiatry, 51,* 139–154.

Szasz, T. S. (1961). *The myth of mental illness.* New York: Harper & Row.

Szasz, T. S. (1963). *Law, liberty, and psychiatry.* New York: Macmillan.

Szasz, T. S. (1977). *Psychiatric slavery.* New York: Free Press.

Szatmari, P., Jones, M. B., Tuff, L., Bartolucci, G., Fisman, S., & Mahoney, W. (1993). Lack of cognitive impairment in first-degree relatives of children with pervasive developmental disorders. *Journal of the American Academy of Child and Adolescent Psychiatry, 32,* 1264–1273.

Szymanski, L. S. & Kaplan, L. C. (1997). Mental retardation. In J. M. Weiner (Ed.), *Textbook of child and adolescent psychiatry* (pp. 183–218). Washington, DC: American Psychiatric Association.

Szymanski, S., Lieberman, J. A., Alvir, J. M., Mayerhoff, D., Loebel, A., Geisler, S., Chakos, M., Koreen, A., Jody, D., Kane, J., Woerner, M., & Cooper, T. (1995). Gender differences in onset of illness, treatment response, course, and biologic indexes in first-episode schizophrenic patients. *American Journal of Psychiatry, 152,* 698–703.

Taber, K. H., Lewis, D. A., & Hurley, R. A. (2001). Schizophrenia: What's under the microscope? *Journal of Neuropsychiatry and Clinical Neuroscience, 13,* 1–4.

Takei, N., Lewis, S., Jones, P., Harvey, I., & Murray, R. M. (1996). Prenatal exposure to influenza and increased cerebrospinal fluid spaces in schizophrenia. *Schizophrenia Bulletin, 22,* 521–534.

Takeshita, J. (1997). Psychosis. In W. S. Tseng & J. Streltzer (Eds.), *Culture and psychopathology: A guide to clinical assessment* (pp. 124–138). New York: Brunner/Mazel.

Taller, A. M., Asher, D. M., Pomeroy, K. L., Eldadah, B. A., Godec, M. S., Falkai, P. G., Bogerts, B., Kleinman, J. E., Stevens, J. R., & Torrey, E. F. (1996). Search for viral nucleic acid sequences in brain tissues of patients with schizophrenia using nested polymerase chain reaction. *Archives of General Psychiatry, 53,* 32–40.

Tam, W. C. & Sewell, K. W. (1995). Seasonality of birth in schizophrenia in Taiwan. *Schizophrenia Bulletin, 21,* 117–127.

Tamminga, C. A. (1997). The promise of new drugs for schizophrenia treatment. *Canadian Journal of Psychiatry, 42,* 265–273.

Tancer, M. E. (1993). Neurobiology of social phobia. *Journal of Clinical Psychiatry, 54,* 26–30.

Tanner, J. M. (1990). *Fetus into man: Physical growth from conception to maturity*. Cambridge, MA: Harvard University Press.

Tanzi, R. E., Gusella, J. F., Watkins, P. C., Bruns, G. A. P., St George-Hyslop, P., Van Keuren, M. L., Patterson, D., Pagan, S., Kurnitt, D. M., & Neve, R. L. (1987). Amyloid beta protein gene: cDNA, mRNA distribution, and genetic linkage near the Alzheimer locus. *Science, 235,* 880–884.

Tarasoff v. Regents of California, 17 Cal. 3d 425, 131 Cal. Rptr. 14 (1976).

Tarrier, N., Barrowclough, C., Porceddu, K., et al. (1988). The assessment of psychophysiological reactivity to the expressed emotion of the relatives of schizophrenic patients. *British Journal of Psychiatry, 152,* 618–624.

Tarrier, N., Harwood, S., Yusopoff, L., Beckett, R., & Baker, A. (1990). Coping strategy enhancement (CSE): A method of treating residual schizophrenic symptoms. *Behavioural Psychotherapy, 18,* 283–293.

Tarullo, L. B., Richardson, D. T., Radke-Yarrow, M., & Martinez, P. E. (1995). Multiple sources in child diagnosis: Parent-child concordance in affectively ill and well families. *Journal of Clinical Child Psychology, 24,* 173–183.

Tauscher, J., Kapur, S., Verhoeff, P. I. G., Hussey, D. F., Daskalakis, Z. J., Tauscher-Wisniewski, S., Wilson, A. A., Houle, S., Kasper, S., & Zipursky, R. B. (2002). Brain serotonin 5-HT_{1A} receptor binding in schizophrenia measured by positron emissions tomography and $[^{11}C]$ WAY-100635. *Archives of General Psychiatry, 59,* 514–520.

Taylor, E. (2000). Psychotherapeutics and the problematic origins of clinical psychology in America. *American Psychologist, 55,* 1029–1033.

Taylor, G. J., Bagby, R. M., & Parker, J. D. A. (1997). *Disorders of affect regulation: Alexithymia in medical and psychiatric illness*. Cambridge: Cambridge University Press.

Taylor, L. & Ingram, R. E. (1999). Cognitive reactivity and depressotypic information processing in children of depressed mothers. *Journal of Abnormal Psychology, 108,* 202–210.

Taylor, L. A., Kreutzer, J. S., Demm, S. R. (2003). Traumatic brain injury and substance abuse: A review and analysis of the literature. *Neuropsychological Rehabilitation, 13,* (1–2.)

Taylor, S. E., Kemeny, M. E., Reed, G. M., Bower, J. E., Gruenewald, T. L. (2000). Psychological resources, positive illusions, and health. *American Psychologist, 55*(1), 99–109.

Taylor, S. & Koch, W. J. (1995). Anxiety disorders due to motor vehicle accidents: Nature and treatment. *Clinical Psychology Review, 15*(8), 721–738.

Taylor, S., Kuch, K., Koch, W. J. Crockett, D. J., & Passey, G. (1998). The structure of posttraumatic stress symptoms. *Journal of Abnormal Psychology, 107,* 154–160.

Taylor, S. & McLean, P. (1993). Outcome profiles in the treatment of unipolar depression. *Behaviour Research and Therapy, 31,* 325–330.

Taylor, S., Woody, S., Koch, W. J., McLean, P. D., et al. (1996). Suffocation false alarms and efficacy of cognitive behavioral therapy for panic disorder. *Behavior Therapy, 27,* 115–126.

Teachman, B. A., Gregg, A. P., Woody, S. R. (2001). Implicit associations for fear-relevant stimuli among individuals with snake and spider fears. *Journal of Abnormal Psychology, 110,* 226–235.

Teasdale, J. D., Taylor, M. J., Cooper, Z., Hayhurst, H., & Paykel, E. S. (1995). Depressive thinking: Shifts in construct accessibility or in schematic mental models? *Journal of Abnormal Psychology, 104,* 500–507.

Teicher, M. H., Glod, C. A., Magnus, E., Harper, D., Benson, G., Krueger, K., & McGreenery, C. E. (1997). Circadian rest-activity disturbances in seasonal affective disorder. *Archives of General Psychiatry, 54,* 124–130.

Tek, C., Kirkpatrick, B., & Buchanan, R. W. (2001). A five-year study of deficit and nondeficit schizophrenia. *Schizophrenia Research, 49,* 253–260.

Tellegen, A., Lykken, D. T., Bouchard, T. J., Wilcox, K. J., Segal, N. L., & Rich, S. (1988). Personality similarity in twins reared apart and together. *Journal of Personality and Social Psychology, 54,* 1031–1039.

Temoshok, L., Heller, B. W., Sagebiel, R. W., Blois, M. S., Sweet, D. M., DiClemente, R. J., et al. (1985). The relationship of psychosocial factors to prognostic indicators in cutaneous malignant melanoma. *Journal of Psychosomatic Research, 29,* 139–153.

Templeton, B. (1997). Alcohol-impaired driving: The family's tragedy and the public's health. *Journal of the American Medical Association, 277,* 1279.

Terént, A. (1993). Stroke mortality. In J. P. Whisnant (Ed.), *Stroke, populations, cohorts, and clinical trials* (pp. 37–58). Boston: Butterworth-Heinemann.

Terman, J. S., Terman, M., Lo, E. S., & Cooper, T. B. (2001). Circadian time of morning light administration and therapeutic response in winter depression. *Archives of General Psychiatry, 58,* 69–75.

Test, D. W., Hinson, K. B., Solow, J., & Keul, P. (1993). Job satisfaction of persons in supported employment. *Education and Training in Mental Retardation, 28,* 39–46.

Test, M. A. & Stein, L. I. (1978). Training in community living: Research design and results. In L. I. Stein & M. A. Test (Eds.), *Alternatives to mental hospital treatment.* New York: Plenum Press.

Thase, M. E. (2002). Antidepressant effects: The suit may be small, but the fabric is real. *Prevention & Treatment, 5,* Article 32. Retrieved August 15, 2003, from http://www.journals.apa.org/prevention/volume5/pre0050032a.html.

Thase, M. E., Dube, S., Bowler, K., Howland, R. H., Myers, J. E., Friedman, E., & Jarrett, D. B. (1996). Hypothalamic-pituitary-adrenocortical activity and response to cognitive-behavior therapy in unmedicated, hospitalized depressed patients. *American Journal of Psychiatry, 153,* 886–891.

Thase, M. E., Fava, M., Halbreich, U., Kocsis, J. H., Koran, L., Davidson, J., Rosenbaum, J., & Harrison, W. (1996). A placebo-controlled, randomized clinical trial comparing sertraline and imipramine for the treatment of dysthymia. *Archives of General Psychiatry, 53,* 777–784.

Thase, M. E., Frank, E., & Kupfer, D. J. (1985). Biological processes in major depression. In E. E. Beckham & W. R. Leber (Eds.), *Handbook of depression* (pp. 816–913). Homewood, IL: Dorsey Press.

Thase, M. E., Greenhouse, J. B., Frank, E., Reynolds, C. F., III., Pilkonis, P. A., Hurley, K., Grochocinski, V., & Kupfer, D. J. (1997). Treatment of major depression with psychotherapy or psychotherapy-pharmacotherapy combinations. *Archives of General Psychiatry, 54,* 1009–1015.

Thase, M. E. & Kupfer, D. J. (1996). Recent developments in the pharmacotherapy of mood disorders. *Journal of Consulting and Clinical Psychology, 64,* 646–659.

Thase, M. E., Simons, A. D., & Reynolds, C. F., III. (1996). Abnormal electroencephalographic sleep profiles in major depression: Association with response to cognitive behavior therapy. *Archives of General Psychiatry, 53,* 99–108.

Thayer, J. F., Friedman, B. H., & Borkovec, T. D. (1996). Autonomic characteristics of generalized anxiety disorder and worry. *Biological Psychiatry, 39,* 255–266.

Thayer, J. F., Friedman, B. H., Borkovec, T. D., Johnsen, B. H., & Molina, S. (2000). Phasic heart period reactions to cued threat and nonthreat stimuli in generalized anxiety disorder. *Psychophysiology, 37,* 361–368.

Theodore, W. H. (Ed.) (1988a). *Clinical neuroimaging (Vol. 7) Frontiers in neuroscience.* New York: Alan R. Liss.

Theodore, W. H. (1988b). Introduction. In W. H. Theodore (Ed.), *Clinical neuroimaging (Vol. 7). Frontiers in neuroscience.* New York: Alan R. Liss.

Thigpen, C. H. & Cleckley, H. (1957). *The three faces of Eve.* New York: McGraw-Hill.

Thomas, V. S. & Rockwood, K. J. (2001). Alcohol abuse, cognitive impairment, and mortality among older people. *Journal of the American Geriatrics Society, 49,* 415–420.

Thompson, M. G., McInnes, R. R., & Willard, H. F. (1991). *Genetics in medicine* (5th ed.). Philadelphia: Saunders.

Thomson, N., Fraser, D., & McDougall, A. (1974). The reinstatement of speech in near-mute chronic schizophrenics by instructions, imitative prompts, and reinforcement. *Journal of Behavior Therapy and Experimental Psychiatry, 5,* 83–89.

Thoresen, C. E. (1999). Spirituality and health: Is there a relationship? *Journal of Health Psychology, 4,* 291–300.

Thoresen, C. E. & Harris, A. H. S. (2002). Spirituality and health: What's the evidence and what's needed? *Annals of Behavioral Medicine, 24,* 3–13.

Thornberry, T. P. & Krohn, M. D. (1997). Peers, drug use, and delinquency. In D. M. Stoff, J. Breiling, & J. D. Maser (Eds.), *Handbook of antisocial behavior* (pp. 218–233). New York: Wiley.

Thorpe, S. J. & Salkovskis, P. M. (1997). The effect of one-session treatment for spider phobia on attentional bias and beliefs. *British Journal of Clinical Psychology,* 36(2), 225–241.

Thorton, C. C., Gottheil, E., Weinstein, S. P., & Kerachsky, R. S. (1998). Patient-treatment matching in substance abuse: Drug addiction severity. *Journal of Substance Abuse Treatment,* 15(6), 505–511.

Tichenor, V., Marmar, C. R., Weiss, D. S., Metzler, T. J. & Ronfeldt, H. M. (1996). The relationship of peritraumatic dissociation and posttraumatic stress: Findings in female Vietnam theater veterans. *Journal of Consulting and Clinical Psychology, 64*(5), 1054–1059.

Tiefer, L., Pedersen, B., & Melman, A. (1988). Psychosocial follow-up of penile prosthesis implant patients and partners. *Journal of Sex and Marital Therapy, 14,* 184–201.

Tienari, P., Wynne, L. C., Moring, J., Lahti, I., Naarala, M., Sorri, A., Wahlberg, K. E., Saarento, O., Seitamaa, M., Kaleva, M., & Laksy, K. (1994). The Finnish Adoptive Family Study of Schizophrenia: Implications for family research. *British Journal of Psychiatry, 164,* 20–26.

Tiller, J. M., Sloane, G., Schmidt, U., Troop, N., Power, M., & Tresure, J. L. (1997). Social support in patients with anorexia nervosa and bulimia nervosa. *International Journal of Eating Disorders, 21,* 31–38.

Tillfors, M., Furmark, T., Ekselius, L., & Fredrikson, M. (2001). Social phobia and avoidant personality disorder as related to parental history of social anxiety: A general population study. *Behaviour Research and Therapy, 39,* 289–298.

Timio, M., Verdecchia, P., Venanzi, S., Gentili, S., Ronconi, M., Francucci, B., Montanari, M., & Bichisao, E. (1988). Age and blood pressure changes: A 20-year follow-up study in nuns in a secluded order. *Hypertension, 12,* 457–461.

Tinklenberg, J. R. (1971). A clinical view of the amphetamines. *American Family Physician,* (5), 82–86.

Tinklenberg, J. R. (1974). What a physician should know about marihuana. *Rational Drug Therapy* (American Pharmacology and Experimental Therapeutics).

Titone, D., Holzman, P. S., & Levy, D. L. (2002). Idiom processing in schizophrenia: Literal implausibility saves the day for idiom priming. *Journal of Abnormal Psychology, 111,* 313–320.

Titone, D., Levy, D. L., & Holzman, P. S. (2000). Contextual insensitivity in schizophrenic language processing: Evidence from lexical ambiguity. *Journal of Abnormal Psychology, 109,* 761–767.

Tolan, P. H. & Thomas, P. (1995). The implications of age of onset for delinquency risk II: Longitudinal data. *Journal of Abnormal Child Psychology, 23,* 157–181.

Tolman, E. C. (1948). Cognitive maps in rats and men. *Psychological Review, 55,* 189–208.

Tolman, E. C. & Honzig, C. H. (1930). "Insight" in rats. *University of California Publications in Psychology, 4,* 215–232.

Tomarken, A. J. (1995). A psychometric perspective on psychophysiological measures. *Psychological Assessment, 7,* 387–395.

Tomarken, A. J. (1999). Methodological issues in psychophysiological research. In P. C. Kendall, J. N. Butcher, & G. N. Holmbeck (Eds.), *Handbook of research methods in clinical psychology* (2nd ed., pp. 251–275). New York: Wiley.

Tomarken, A. J., Sutton, S. K., & Mineka, S. (1995). Fear-relevant illusory correlations: What types of associations promote judgmental bias? *Journal of Abnormal Psychology, 104,* 312–326.

Tonigan, J. S., Toscova, R., & Miller, W. R. (1996). Meta-analysis of the literature on Alcoholics Anonymous: Sample and study characteristics moderate findings. *Journal of Studies on Alcohol, 57,* 65–72.

Toomey, R., Kremen, W. S., Simpson, J. C., Samson, J. A., Seidman, L. J., Lyons, M. J., Faraone, S. V., & Tsuang, M. T. (1997). Revisiting the factor structure for positive and negative symptoms: Evidence from a large heterogeneous group of psychiatric patients. *American Journal of Psychiatry, 154,* 371–377.

Torgersen, S. (1983). Genetic factors in anxiety disorders. *Archives of General Psychiatry, 40,* 1085–1089.

Torgersen, S. (1986). Genetics of somatoform disorders. *Archives of General Psychiatry, 43,* 502–505.

Torgersen, S., Kringlen, E., & Cramer, V. (2001). The prevalence of personality disorders in a community sample. *Archives of General Psychiatry, 58,* 590–596.

Torrey, E. F., Miller, J., Rawlings, R., & Yolken, R. H. (1997). Seasonality of births in schizophrenia and bipolar disorder: A review of the literature. *Schizophrenia Research, 28,* 1–38.

Torrey, E. F. & Peterson, M. R. (1976). The viral hypothesis of schizophrenia, *Schizophrenia Bulletin, 2,* 136–145.

Torrey, E. F. & Zdanowicz, M. (2001). Outpatient commitment: What, why, and for whom. *Psychiatric Services, 52,* 337–341.

Trenerry, M. R., Jack, C. R., Jr., Cascino, G. D., Sharbrough, F. W., & Ivnik, R. J. (1995). Gender differences in post-temporal lobectomy verbal memory and relationships between MRI hippocampal volumes and preoperative verbal memory. *Epilepsy Research, 20,* 69–76.

Trenerry, M. R., Jack, C. R., Jr., Cascino, G. D., Sharbrough, F. W., & Ivnik, R. J. (1996). Sex differences in the relationship between visual memory and MRI hippocampal volumes. *Neuropsychology, 10,* 343–351.

True, W. R., Xian, H., Scherrer, J. F., Madden, P. A. F., Bucholz, K. K., Heath, A. C., Eisen, S. A., Lyons, M. J., Goldberg, J., & Tsuang, M. (1999). Common genetic vulnerability for nicotine and alcohol dependence in men. *Archives of General Psychiatry, 56,* 655–661.

Trull, T. J., Sher, K. J., Minka-Brown, C., Durbin, J., & Burr, R. (2000). Borderline personality disorder and substance abuse disorders: A review and integration. *Clinical Psychology Review, 20,* 235–253.

Trull, T. J., Widiger, T. A., Useda, J. D., Holcomb, J., Doa, B-T., & Axelrod, S. R. (1998). A structured interview for the assessment of the five-factor model of personality. *Psychological Assessment, 10,* 229–240.

Tsai, L. Y. (1987). Pre-, peri-, and neonatal factors in autism. In E. Schopler & G. B. Mesibov (Eds.), *Neurobiological issues in autism* (pp. 179–189). New York: Plenum Press.

Tsai, L. Y. (1992). Medical treatment in autism. In D. E. Berkell (Ed.), *Autism: Identification, education, and treatment* (pp. 151–184). Hillsdale, NJ: Erlbaum.

Tsai, L. Y. & Ghaziuddin, M. (1997). Autistic disorder. In J. M. Weiner (Ed.), *Textbook of child and adolescent psychiatry* (pp. 219–254). Washington, DC: American Psychiatric Association.

Tsuang, M. (2000). Schizophrenia: Genes and environment. *Biological Psychiatry, 47,* 210–220.

Tsuang, M. T., Lyons, M. J., Meyer, J. M., Doyle, T., Eisen, S. A, Goldberg, J., True, W., Lin, N., Toomey, R., & Eaves, L. (1998). Co-occurrence of abuse of different drugs in men. *Archives of General Psychiatry, 55,* 967–972.

Tsuang, M. T., Stone, W. S., & Faraone, S. V. (2001). Genes, environment and schizophrenia. *British Journal of Psychiatry, 178*(Suppl. 40), S18–S24.

Tucker, J. S., Friedman, H. S., Wingard, D. L., & Schwartz, J. E. (1996). Marital history at midlife as a predictor of longevity: Alternative explanations to the protective effect of marriage. *Health Psychology, 15,* 94–101.

Tue, G. C. & Israel, Y. (1995). Alcohol consumption by Orientals in North America is predicted largely by a single gene. *Behavior Genetics, 25,* 59–65.

Tulsky, D. S. & Ledbetter, M. F. (2000). Updating to the WAIS-III and WMS-III: Considerations for research and clinical practice. *Psychological Assessment, 12,* 253–262.

Turkat, I. D. & Levin, R. A. (1984). Formulation of personality disorders. In H. E. Adams & P. B. Sutker (Eds.), *Comprehensive handbook of psychopathology*. New York: Plenum Press.

Turkheimer, E. & Parry, C. D. H. (1992). Why the gap? Practice and policy in civil commitment hearings. *American Psychologist, 47,* 646–655.

Turner, S. M., Beidel, D. C., Stanley, M. A., & Heiser, N. (2001). Obsessive-compulsive disorder. In H. E. Adams & P. B. Sutker (Eds.), *Comprehensive handbook of psychopathology* (3rd ed., pp. 155–182). New York: Kluwer Academic/Plenum.

Tyler, T. R. (2001). Public trust and confidence in legal authorities: What do majority and minority groups members want from the law and legal institutions? *Behavioral Sciences and the Law, 19,* 215–235.

Tymchuk, A. J., Andron, L., & Rahbar, B. (1988). Effective decision-making/problem-solving training with mothers who have mental retardation. *American Journal on Mental Retardation, 92*(6), 510–516.

Uchino, B. N., Cacciopo, J. T., & Kiecolt-Glaser, J. K. (1996). The relationship between social support and physiological processes: A review with emphasis on underlying mechanisms and implications for health. *Psychological Bulletin, 119,* 488–531.

Ullman, S. E. & Brecklin, L. R. (2000). Alcohol and adult sexual assault in a national sample of women. *Journal of Substance Abuse, 11,* 405–420.

Ullmann, L. P. & Krasner, L. (1975). *A psychological approach to abnormal behavior* (2nd ed.). Englewood Cliffs, NJ: Prentice-Hall.

Ullmann, L. P. & Krasner, L. (Eds.). (1965). *Case studies in behavior modification.* New York: Holt, Rinehart and Winston.

Ullrich, P. M., Lutgendorf, S. K., & Stapleton, J. T. (2003). Concealment of homosexual identity, social support and CD4 cell count among HIV-seropositive gay men. *Journal of Psychosomatic Research, 54,* 205–212.

Umbricht, D., Schmid, L., Koller, R., Vollenweider, F. X., Hell, D., & Javitt, D. C. (2000). Ketamine-induced deficits in auditory and visual context-dependent processing in health volunteers: Implications for models of cognitive deficits in schizophrenia. *Archives of General Psychiatry, 57,* 1139–1147.

Unger, J. B., Li, U., Johnson, A., Gong, J., Chen, X., Li, C. Y., Trinidad, D. R., Tran, N. T., & Lo, A. T. (2001). Stressful life events among adolescents in Wuhan, China: Associations with smoking, alcohol use, and depressive symptoms. *International Journal of Behavioral Medicine, 8,* 1–18.

Ungless, M. A., Whistler, J. L., Malenka, R. C., & Bonci, A. (2001). Single cocaine exposure in vivo induces long-term potentiation in dopamine neurons. *Nature, 411,* 563–587.

United States v. Pennsylvania, 902 F. Supp. 565 (WD Pa.) (1995).

United States v. Pullen, 89 F. 3d 368 (7th Cir. 1996).

Unnewehr, S., Schneider, S., Margraf, J., Jenkins, M., & Florin, I. (1996). Exposure to internal and external stimuli: Reactions in children of patients with panic disorder or animal phobia. *Journal of Anxiety Disorders, 10,* 489–508.

U.S. Bureau of the Census. (1995). *Statistical abstracts of the U. S.* (115th ed.). Washington, DC: Author.

U.S. Bureau of the Census. (1997). Statistical abstract of the United States (117th ed.). Washington, DC: U.S. Government Printing Office.

U.S. Bureau of the Census. (2001). Profiles of general demographic characteristics: 2000 census of population and housing. Washington, DC: Author.

U.S. Department of Health and Human Services. (1991). *Health status of minorities and low-income groups.* Hyattsville, MD.

U.S. Department of Health and Human Services. (1997). *Preliminary results from the 1996 National Household Survey on Drug Abuse.* Rockville, MD: Author.

U.S. Department of Health and Human Services. (1999). Mental Health: A Report of the Surgeon General. Rockville, MD: National Institute of Mental Health.

U.S. Public Health Service. (1964). *Smoking and health* (Report of the Advisory Committee to the Surgeon General of the Public Health Service). Washington, DC: Department of Health, Education, and Welfare.

Üstün, T. B. (2001). The worldwide burden of depression in the 21st century. In M. M. Weissman (Ed.), *Treatment of depression: Bridging the 21st century* (pp. 35–45). Washington, DC: American Psychiatric Press.

Üstün, T. B., Bertelsen, A., Dilling, H., vanDrimmelen, J., Pull, C., Okasha, A., Sartorius, N., et al. (1996). *ICD-10 casebook: The many faces of mental disorders—Adult case histories according to ICD-10* (pp. 67–69). Washington, DC: American Psychiatric Press.

Uviller, H. R. (1996). *Virtual justice.* New Haven: Yale University Press.

Vaca, F. & Berns, S. D. (2001). Commentary: motorcycle helmet law repeal—a tax assessment for the rest of the United States? *Annals of Emergency Medicine 37*(2), 230–232.

Vaillant, G. (1976). Natural history of male psychological health: V. The relation of choice of ego mechanisms of defense to adult adjustment. *Archives of General Psychiatry, 33,* 535–545.

Vaillant, G., & Drake, R. (1985). Maturity of defenses in relation to *DSM-III* Axis II personality disorders. *Archives of General Psychiatry, 42,* 597–601.

Vakoch, D. A. & Strupp, H. H. (2000). Psychodynamic approaches to psychotherapy: Philosophical and theoretical foundations of effective practice. In C. R. Snyder & R. E. Ingram (Eds.), *Handbook of psychological change: Psychotherapy processes and practices for the 21st century.* New York: Wiley.

Valenzuela, M. (1990). Attachment in chronically underweight young children. *Child Development, 61,* 1984–1996.

Valleni-Basile, L. A., Garrison, C. Z., Waller, J. L., Addy, C. L., et al. (1996). Incidence of obsessive-compulsive disorder in a community sample of young adolescents. *Journal of the American Academy of Child and Adolescent Psychiatry, 35,* 898–906.

van Baar, A. (1990). Development of infants of drug dependent mothers. *Journal of Child Psychology and Psychiatry, 31,* 911–920.

Van der Does, A. J. W., Antony, M. M., Ehlers, A., & Barsky, A. J. (2002). Heartbeat perception in panic disorder: A reanalysis. *Behaviour Research and Therapy, 38(1),* 47–62.

Van der Pompe, G., Antoni, M. H., Duivenvoorden, H. J., deGraeff, A., Simonis, R. F., van der Vegt, S. G., & Heijnen, C. J. (2001). An exploratory study into the effect of group psychotherapy on cardiovascular and immunoreactivity to acute stress in breast cancer patients. *Psychotherapy and Psychosomatics, 70,* 307–318.

Van Italli, J. B. (1985). Health implications of overweight and obesity in the United States. *Annals of Internal Medicine, 103,* 983–988.

Van Noppen, B., Steketee, G., McCorkle, B. H., & Pato, M. (1997). Group and family behavioral treatment for obsessive compulsive disorder: A pilot study. *Journal of Anxiety Disorders, 11,* 431–446.

van Os, J., Hanssen, M., Bijl, R. V., & Vollebergh, W. (2001). Prevalence of psychotic disorder and community level of psychotic symptoms: An urban-rural comparison. *Archives of General Psychiatry, 58,* 663–668.

Vanable, P. A., Ostrow, D. G., McKirnan, D. J. (2003). Viral load and HIV treatment attitudes as correlates of sexual risk behavior among HIV-positive gay men. *Journal of Psychosomatic Research, 54,* 263–269.

Vasey, M. W. (1995). Social anxiety disorder. In A. R. Eisen, C. A. Kearney, & C. E. Schaefer (Eds.), *Clinical handbook of anxiety disorders in children and adolescents* (pp. 131–168). Northvale, NJ: Aronson.

Vaughan, S. C. & Roose, S. P. (1995). The analytic process: Clinical and research definitions. *International Journal of Psycho-Analysis, 76,* 343–356.

Veale, D. (2000). Outcome of cosmetic surgery and "DIY" surgery in patients with body dysmorphic disorder. *Psychiatric Bulletin, 24,* 218–221.

Veale, D., Gournay, K., Dryden, W., Boocock, A., Shah, F., Willson, R., & Walburn, J. (1996). Body dysmorphic disorder: A cognitive behavioural model and pilot randomised controlled trial. *Behaviour Research and Therapy. 34,* 717–729.

Vega, W. A., Kolody, B., Aguilar-Gaxiola, S., & Catalano, R. (1999). Gaps in service utilization by Mexican Americans with mental health problems. *American Journal of Psychiatry, 156,* 928–934.

Velakoulis, D., Pantelis, C., McGorry, P. D., Dudgeon, P., Brewer, W., Cook, M., Desmond, P., Bridle, N., Tierney, P., Murrie, V., Singh, B., & Copolov, D. (1999). Hippocampal volume in first-episode psychoses and chronic schizophrenia: A high-resolution magnetic resonance imaging study. *Archives of General Psychiatry, 56,* 133–140.

Velligan, D. I., Mahurin, R. K., Eckert, S. L., Hazleton, B. C., & Miller, A. (1997). Relationship between specific types of communication deviance and attentional performance in patients with schizophrenia. *Psychiatry Research, 70,* 9–20.

Velting, D. M. & Gould, M. S. (1997). Suicide contagion. In R. W. Maris, M. M. Silverman, & S. S. Canetto (Eds.), *Review of suicidology* (pp. 96–137). New York: Guilford Press.

Venables, P. H. (1996). Schizotypy and maternal exposure to influenza and to cold temperature: The Mauritius Study. *Journal of Abnormal Psychology, 105,* 53–60.

Venter, A., Lord, C., & Schopler, E. (1992). A follow-up study of high-functioning autistic children. *Journal of Child Psychology and Psychiatry, 33,* 489–507.

Vernon, P. (1941). Psychological effects of air raids. *Journal of Abnormal and Social Psychology, 36,* 457–476.

Viederman, M. (1995). Metaphor and meaning in conversion disorder: A brief active therapy. *Psychosomatic Medicine, 57,* 403–409.

Vinogradov, S., Willis-Shore, J., Poole, J. H., Marten, E., Ober, B. A., & Shenaut, G. K. (1997). Clinical and neurocognitive aspects of source monitoring errors in schizophrenia. *American Journal of Psychiatry, 154,* 1530–1537.

Virkkunen, M., Goldman, D., Nielsen, D., & Linnoila, M. (1995). Low brain serotonin turnover rate (Low CSF5-HIAA) and impulsive violence. *Journal of Psychiatry and Neuroscience, 20,* 271–275.

Visintainer, M. A., Volpicelli, J. R., & Seligman. M. E. P. (1982). Tumor rejection in rats after inescapable or escapable shock. *Science, 216*(23), 437–439.

Visser, S. & Bouman, T. K. (2001). The treatment of hypochondriasis: Exposure plus response prevention vs. cognitive therapy. *Behaviour Research and Therapy, 39,* 423–442.

Voas, R. B., Holder, H. D., & Gruenewald, P. J. (1997). The effect of drinking and driving interventions on alcohol-involved traffic crashes within a comprehensive community trial. *Addiction, 92,* Supplement 2, S221–S236.

Volk, D. W., Austin, M. C., Pierri, J. N., Sampson, A. R., & Lewis, D. A. (2000). Decreased glutamic acid decarboxylase$_{67}$ messenger RNA expression in a subset of prefrontal cortical γ-aminobutyric acid neurons in subjects with schizophrenia. *Archives of General Psychiatry, 57,* 237–245.

Volkmar, F. R. & Nelson, D. S. (1990). Seizure disorders in autism. *Journal of the American Academy of Child and Adolescent Psychiatry, 29,* 127–129.

Volkow, N., Chang, L., Wang, G., Fowler, J., Ding, Y., Sedler, M., Logan, J., Franceschi, D., Gatlev, J., Hitzemann, R., Gifford, A., Wong, C., & Pappas, N. (2001). Low level of brain dopamine D-sub-2 receptors in methamphetamine abusers: Association with metabolism in the orbitofrontal cortex. *American Journal of Psychiatry, 158*(12), 2015–2021.

Volpicelli, J. R., Rhines, K. C., Rhines, J. S., Volpicelli, L. A., Alterman, A. I., & O'Brien, C. P. (1997). Naltrexone and alcohol dependence. *Archives of General Psychiatry, 54,* 737–742.

Voth, E. A. & Schwartz, R. H. (1997). Medicinal applications of delta-9-tetrahydrocannabinol and marijuana. *Annals of Internal Medicine, 1997,* 791–798.

Wachtel, P. L. (1997). *Psychoanalysis, behavior therapy, and the relational world.* Washington, DC: American Psychological Association.

Waddington, J. L., Clifford, J. J., McNamara, F. N., Tomiyama, K., Koshikawa, N., & Croke, D. T. (2001). The psychopharmacology-molecular biology interface: Exploring the behavioural roles of dopamine receptor subtypes using targeted gene deletion ("knockout"). *Progress in Neuro-Psychopharmacology & Biological Psychiatry, 25,* 925–964.

Waggoner, R. W. & Bagchi, B. K. (1954). Initial masking of organic brain changes by psychic symptoms. *American Journal of Psychiatry, 110,* 904–910.

Wagner, B. M. (1997). Family risk factors for child and adolescent suicidal behavior. *Psychological Bulletin, 121,* 246–298.

Wagner, R. K. (2000). Practical intelligence. In R. J. Sternberg (Ed.), *Handbook of intelligence* (pp. 380–395). Cambridge: Cambridge University Press.

Wahl, O. F. (1999). *Telling is risky business: Mental health consumers confront stigma.* New Brunswick, NJ: Rutgers University Press.

Wahlberg, K. E., Wynne, L. C., Keskitalo, P., Nieminen, P., Moring, J., Laksy, K., Sorri, A., Koistinen, P., Tarvainen, T., Miettunen, J., & Tienari, P. (2001). Long-term stability of communication deviance. *Journal of Abnormal Psychology, 110,* 443–448.

Wahlberg, K. E., Wynne, L. C., Oja, H., Keskitalo, P., Pykalainen, L., Lahti, I., Moring, J., Naarala, M., Sorri, A., Seitamaa, M., Laksy, K., Kolassa, J., & Tienari, P. (1997). Gene-environment interaction in vulnerability to schizophrenia: Findings from the Finnish Adoptive Family Study of Schizophrenia. *American Journal of Psychiatry, 154,* 355–362.

Waisbren, S. E. (1999). Phenylketonuria. In S. Goldstein & C. R. Reynolds (Eds.), *Handbook of neurodevelopmental and genetic disorders in children* (pp. 433–458). New York: Guilford Press.

Wakefield, J. C. (1999). Evolutionary versus prototype analyses of the concept of disorder. *Journal of Abnormal Psychology, 108,* 374–399.

Walcott, D. M., Cerundolo, P., & Beck, J. C. (2001). Current analysis of the *Tarasoff* duty: An evolution towards the limitation of the duty to protect. *Behavioral Sciences and the Law, 19,* 325–343.

Waldinger, M. D., Hengeveld, M. W., Zwinderman, A. H., & Olivier, R. (1998). Randomized, placebo-controlled study with fluoxetine, fluvoxamine, paroxetine, and setraline. *Journal of Clinical Pharmacology, 18,* 274–281.

Waldinger, R. J. & Gunderson, J. G. (1987). *Effective psychotherapy with borderline patients: Case studies.* New York: Macmillan.

Waldo, T. G. & Merritt, R. D. (2000). Fantasy proneness, dissociation, and *DSM-IV* Axis II symptomatology. *Journal of Abnormal Psychology, 109,* 555–558.

Waldron, I., Lye, D., & Brandon, A. (1991). Gender differences in teenage smoking. *Women and Health, 17*(2), 65–90.

Walker, E. F., Grimes, K. E., Davis, D. M., & Smith, A. J. (1993).

Childhood precursors of schizophrenia: Facial expressions of emotion. *American Journal of Psychiatry, 150,* 1654–1660.

Wall, T. L., Shea, S. H., Chan, K. K., & Can, L. G. (2001). A genetic association with the development of alcohol and other substance use behavior in Asian Americans. *Journal of Abnormal Psychology, 110,* 173–178.

Wallace, J. M., Jr., Forman, T. A., Guthrie, B. J., Bachman, J. G., O'Malley, P. M., & Johnston, L. D. (1999). The epidemiology of alcohol, tobacco, and other drug use among Black youth. *Journal of Studies on Alcohol, 60,* 800–809.

Waller, N. G., Putnam, F. W., & Carlson, E. B. (1996). Types of dissociation and dissociative types: A taxometric analysis of dissociative experiences. *Psychological Methods, 1,* 300–321.

Waller, N. G. & Ross, C. A. (1997). The prevalence and biometric structure of pathological dissociation in the general population: Taxometric and behavior genetic findings. *Journal of Abnormal Psychology, 106,* 499–510.

Walsh, R. (1999). Asian contemplative disciplines: Common practices, clinical applications, and research findings. *The Journal of Transpersonal Psychology, 31,* 83–107.

Ward, K. E., Friedman, L., Wise, A., & Schulz, S. C. (1996). Meta-analysis of brain and cranial size in schizophrenia. *Schizophrenia Research, 22,* 197–213.

Ward, T., Hudson, S. M., Johnston, L., & Marshall, W. I. (1997). Cognitive distortions in sex offenders: An integrative review. *Clinical Psychology Review, 17,* 479–507.

Ward, T., Hudson, S. M., & Marshall, W. L. (1996). Attachment style in sex offenders: A preliminary study. *Journal of Sex Research, 33,* 17–26.

Ward, T., McCormack, J., & Hudson, S. M. (1997). Sexual offenders' perceptions of their intimate relationships. *Sexual Abuse: Journal of Research and Treatment, 9,* 57–74.

Warda, G. & Bryant, R. (1998). Cognitive bias in acute stress disorder. *Behaviour Research and Therapy, 36,* 1177–1183.

Wardle, J. (1980). Dietary restraint and binge eating. *Behavioral Analysis and Modification, 4,* 201–209.

Warner, L., Canino, G., & Colon, H. M. (2001). Prevalence and correlates of substance use disorders among older adolescents in Puerto Rico and the United States: A cross-cultural comparison. *Drug & Alcohol Dependence, 63,* 229–243.

Warren, J. L., Hazelwood, R. R., & Dietz, P. E. (1996). The sexually sadistic serial killer. *Journal of Forensic Sciences, 41,* 970–974.

Warwick, H. M. C. (1995). Assessment of hypochondriasis. *Behaviour Research and Therapy, 33,* 845–853.

Warwick, H. M. C., Clark, D. M., Cobb, A. M., & Salkovskis, P. M. (1996). A controlled trial of cognitive-behavioural treatment of hypochondriasis. *British Journal of Psychiatry, 169,* 189–195.

Warwick, H. M. C. & Marks, I. M. (1988). Behavioural treatment of illness phobia and hypochondriasis: A pilot study of 17 cases. *British Journal of Psychiatry. 152,* 239–241.

Washington v. Harper, 110 S. Ct. 1028 (1990).

Waterhouse, L. (1994). Severity of impairment in autistic spectrum disorders. In S. H. Broman & J. Grafman (Eds.), *Atypical cognitive deficits in developmental disorders: Implications for brain function* (pp. 159–182). Hillsdale, NJ: Erlbaum.

Waters, E., Merrick, S., Treboux, D., Crowell, J., & Albersheim, L. (2000). Attachment security in infancy and early adulthood: A twenty-year longitudinal study. *Child Development, 71,* 684–689.

Watkins, C. E., Campbell, V. L., Nieberding, R., & Hallmark, R. (1995). Contemporary practice of psychological assessment by clinical psychologists. *Professional Psychology: Research and Practice, 26,* 54–60.

Watkins, M. J. (1990). Mediationism and the obfuscation of memory. *American Psychologist, 45,* 328–335.

Watson, J. B. (1913). Psychology as the behaviorist views it. *Psychological Review, 20,* 158–177.

Watson, J. B. & Rayner, R. (1920). Conditioning emotional responses. *Journal of Experimental Psychology, 3,* 1–14.

Weardon, A. J., Tarrier, N., Barrowclough, C., Zastowny, T. R., & Rahill, A. A. (2000). A review of expressed emotion research in health care. *Clinical Psychology Review, 20,* 633–666.

Webster-Stratton, C. (1994). Advancing videotape parent training: A comparison study. *Journal of Consulting and Clinical Psychology, 62,* 583–593.

Webster-Stratton, C. & Hammond, M. (1997). Treating children with early-onset conduct problems: A comparison of child and parent training interventions. *Journal of Consulting and Clinical Psychology, 65,* 91–109.

Wechsler, D. (1958). *The measurement and appraisal of adult intelligence* (4th ed.). Baltimore: Williams & Wilkins.

Wechsler, H., Dowdall, G. W., Davenport, A., Rimm, E. B. (1995). A gender-specific measure of binge drinking among college students. *American Journal of Public Health, 85*(7), 982–985.

Wegner, D. M., Erber, R., & Zanakos, S. (1993). Ironic processes in the mental control of mood and mood-related thought. *Journal of Personality and Social Psychology, 65,* 1093–1104.

Wegner, D. M., Schneider, D. J., Carter, S. R., & White, T. L. (1987). Paradoxical effects of thought suppression. *Journal of Personality and Social Psychology, 53,* 5–13.

Wehman, P. & Kregel, J. (1995). At the crossroads: Supported employment a decade later. *Journal of the Association for Persons with Severe Handicaps, 20,* 286–299.

Wehr, T. A., Duncan, W. C., Jr., Sher, L., Aeschbach, D., Schwartz, P. J., Turner, E. H., Postolache, T. T., & Rosenthal, N. E. (2001). A circadian signal of change of season in patients with seasonal affective disorder. *Archives of General Psychiatry, 58,* 1108–1114.

Weihofen, H. (1957). *The urge to punish.* London: Gollancz.

Weiner, B. & Kukla, A. (2000). An attributional analysis of achievement motivation. In E. T. Higgins & A. W. Kruglanski. (Eds.), *Motivational science: Social and personality perspectives. Key reading in social psychology* (pp. 380–393). Philadelphia: Taylor & Francis/Psychology Press.

Weiner, H. (1994). The revolution in stress theory and research. In R. P. Liberman & J. Yager (Eds.), *Stress in psychiatric disorders* (pp. 1–36). New York: Springer.

Weiner, I. B. (1999). What the Rorschach can do for you: Incremental validity in clinical applications. *Assessment, 6,* 327–338.

Weingarten, S. M., & Cummings, J. L. (2001). Psychosurgery of frontal-subcortical circuits. In D. G. Lichter & J. L. Cummings (Eds.), *Frontal-subcortical circuits in psychiatric and neurological disorders* (pp. 421–435). New York: Guilford Press.

Weinstock, L. S. (1999). Gender differences in the presentation and management of social anxiety disorder.

Journal of Clinical Psychiatry, 60, 9–13.

Weinstock, M. (2000). Behavioral and neurohormonal sequelae of prenatal stress: A suggested model of depression. In M. S. Myslobodsky & I. Weiner (Eds.), *Contemporary issues in modeling psychopathology: Neurobiological foundation of aberrant behaviors* (pp. 45–54). Norwell, MA: Kluwer Academic.

Weisberg, R. B., Brown, T. A., Wincze, J. P., & Barlow, D. H. (2001). Causal attributions and male sexual arousal: The impact of attributions for a bogus erectile difficulty on sexual arousal, cognitions, and affect. *Journal of Abnormal Psychology. 110,* 324–334.

Weisman, A. G., Nuechterlein, K. H., Goldstein, M. J., & Snyder, K. S. (2000). Controllability perceptions and reactions to symptoms of schizophrenia: A within-family comparison of relatives with high and low expressed emotion. *Journal of Abnormal Psychology, 109,* 167–171.

Weiss, E. L., Longhurst, J. G., & Mazure, C. M. (1999). Childhood sexual abuse as a risk factor for depression in women: Psychosocial and neurobiological correlates. *American Journal of Psychiatry, 156,* 816–828.

Weiss, G. & Hechtman, L. (1993). *Hyperactive children grown up.* New York: Guilford Press.

Weiss, J. M. (1997). Psychosomatic disorders. In J. D. Maser & M. E. P. Seligman (Eds.), *Psychopathology: Experimental models.* San Francisco: Freeman.

Weissberg, R. P. & Bell, D. N. (1997) A meta-analytic review of primary prevention in programs for children and adolescents: Contributions and caveats. *American Journal of Community Psychology, 25,* 207–214.

Weissman, M. M. (1990). Evidence for comorbidity of anxiety and depression: Family and genetic studies of children. In J. D. Maser & C. R. Cloninger (Eds.) *Comorbidity of mood and anxiety disorders.* Washington, DC: American Psychiatric Press.

Weissman, M. M. (1993). Family genetic studies of panic disorder. *Journal of Psychiatric Research, 27,* 69–78.

Weissman, M. M., Bland, R. C., Canino, G. J., et al. (1997). The cross-national epidemiology of panic disorder. *Archives of General Psychiatry, 54,* 305–309.

Weissman, M. M., Bland, R. C., Canino, G. J., Greenwald, S., Hwu, H. G., Lee, C. K., Newman, S. C., Oakley-Browne, M. A., Rubio-Stipec, M., Wickramaratne, P. J., Wittchen, H. U., & Yeh, E. K. (1994). The cross national epidemiology of obsessive compulsive disorder: The Cross National Collaborative Group. *Journal Of Clinical Psychiatry, 55,* 5–10.

Weissman, M. M., Warner, V., Wickramaratne, P., & Prusoff, B. A. (1988). Early-onset major depression in parents and their children. *Journal of Affective Disorders, 15,* 269–277.

Weissman, M. M., Wolk, S., Wickramaratne, P., Goldstein, R. B., Adams, P., Greenwald, S., Ryan, N. D., Dahl, R. E., & Steinberg, D. (1999). Children with prepubertal-onset major depressive disorder and anxiety grown up. *Archives of General Psychiatry, 56,* 794–805.

Weisz, J. R., Chaiyasit, W., Weiss, B., Eastmen, K. L., & Jackson, E. W. (1995). A multimethod study of problem behavior among Thai and American children in school: Teacher reports versus direct observations. *Child Development, 66,* 402–415.

Weisz, J. R., Donenberg, G. R., Han, S. S., & Weiss, B. (1995). Bridging the gap between laboratory and clinic in child and adolescent psychotherapy. *Journal of Consulting and Clinical Psychology, 63,* 688–701.

Weisz, J. R., Southam-Gerow, M. A., & McCarty, C. A. (2001). Control-related beliefs and depressive symptoms in clinic-referred children and adolescents: Developmental differences and model specificity. *Journal of Abnormal Psychology, 110,* 97–109.

Weisz, J. R., Suwanlert, S., Chaiyasit, W., & Walter, B. (1987a). Epidemiology of behavioral and emotional problems among Thai and American children: Parent reports for ages 6–11. *Journal of the American Academy of Child and Adolescent Psychiatry, 26,* 890–897.

Weisz, J. R., Suwanlert, S., Chaiyasit, W., & Walter, B. (1987b). Over- and undercontrolled referral problems among children and adolescents from Thailand and the United States: The *Wat* and *Wai* of cultural differences. *Journal of Consulting and Clinical Psychology, 55,* 719–726.

Weisz, J. R., Suwanlert, S., Chaiyasit, W., Weiss, B., Achenbach, T. M., & Eastman, K. I. (1993). Behavioral and emotional problems among Thai and American adolescents: Parent reports for ages 12–16. *Journal of Abnormal Psychology, 102,* 395–403.

Wekstein, L. (1979). *Handbook of suicidology: Principles, problems, and practice.* New York: Brunner/Mazel.

Wells, A. (1999). *Cognitive therapy of anxiety disorders: A scientific manual and conceptual guide.* Chichester Englands: Wiley.

Wells, A. & Clark, D. M. (1997). Social phobia: A cognitive approach. In D. C. L. Davey (Ed.), *Phobias: A handbook of description, treatment and theory.* Chichester England: Wiley.

Wells, K. B. & Sherbourne, C. D. (1999). Functioning and utility for current health of patients with depression or chronic medical conditions in managed, primary care practices. *Archives of General Psychiatry, 56,* 897–904.

Weltzin, T. E., Starzynski, J., Santelli, R., & Kaye, W. H. (1993). Anorexia and bulimia nervosa. In R. T. Ammerman, C. G. Last, & M. Hersen (Eds.), *Handbook of prescriptive treatments for children and adolescents* (pp. 214–239). Boston: Allyn & Bacon.

Wender, P. H., Kety, S. S., Rosenthal, D., Schulsinger, F., Ortmann, J., & Lunde, I. (1986). Psychiatric disorders in the biological and adoptive families of adopted individuals with affective disorders. *Archives of General Psychiatry, 43,* 923–929.

Wenzlaff, R. M. & Wegner, D. M. (2000). Thought suppression. *Annual Review of Psychology, 51,* 59–91.

Werry, J. S. (1996). Pervasive developmental, psychotic, and allied disorders. In L. Hechtman (Ed.), *Do they grow out of it? Long-term outcomes of childhood disorders* (pp. 195–223). Washington, DC: American Psychiatric Press.

Werry, J. S. & Aman, M. G. (1999). *Practitioner's guide to psychoactive drugs for children and adolescents* (2nd ed.). New York: Plenum Press.

Wesson, D. R. & Smith, D. E. (1971, December 15). *Barbiturate use as an intoxicant: A San Francisco perspective.* Testimony presented at the subcommittee to investigate juvenile delinquency.

Westen, D. (2000). Integrative psychotherapy: Integrating psychodynamic and cognitive-behavioral theory and technique. In C. R. Snyder, & R. E. Ingram (Eds.), *Handbook of psychological change: Psychotherapy processes and practices for the 21st century* (pp. 217–242). New York: Wiley.

Wexler, D. B. (1981). *Mental health law: Major issues.* New York: Plenum Press.

Wexler, D. B. (2001). The development of therapeutic jurisprudence: From theory to practice. In L. E. Frost & R. J. Bonnie (Eds.), *The evolution of mental health law* (pp. 279–290). Washington, DC: American Psychological Association.

Wheatman, S. R. & Shaffer, D. R. (2001). On finding for defendants who plead insanity: The crucial impact of dispositional instructions and opportunity to deliberate. *Law and Human Behavior, 25,* 167–183.

Whisman, M. A. (1993). Mediators and moderators of change in cognitive therapy of depression. *Psychological Bulletin, 114,* 248–265.

Whisnant, J. P. (1993). Natural history of transient ischemic attack and ischemic stroke. In J. P. Whisnant (Ed.), *Stroke, populations, cohorts, and clinical trails* (pp. 135–153). Boston: Butterworth-Heinemann.

White, J. (1991). *Drug dependence.* Englewood Cliffs, NJ: Prentice-Hall.

Whitehouse, M. A. & McCabe, M. P. (1997). Sex education programs for people with intellectual disability: How effective are they? *Education and Training in Mental Retardation and Developmental Disabilities, 32,* 229–240.

Whitlatch, C. J., Zarit, S. H., & von Eye, A. (1991). Efficacy of interventions with caregivers: A reanalysis. *Gerontologist, 31,* 9–14.

Whitman, T. L. (1994). Mental retardation. In L. W. Caraighead, W. E. Craighead, A. E. Kazdin, & M. J. Mahoney (Eds.), *Cognitive and behavioral interventions: An empirical approach to mental health problems* (pp. 313–333). Boston: Allyn & Bacon.

Whitman, T. L., Scherzinger, M. F., & Sommer, K. S. (1991). Cognitive instruction and mental retardation. In P. C. Kendall (Ed.), *Child and adolescent therapy: Cognitive-behavioral procedures* (pp. 276–315). New York: Guilford Press.

Wichstrom, L. (1999). The emergence of gender differences in depressed mood during adolescence: The role of intensified gender socialization. *Developmental Psychology, 35,* 232–245.

Widiger, T. A. (1995). Detection of self-defeating and sadistic personality disorder diagnoses. In W. J. Livesley (Ed.), *The* DSM-IV *personality disorders* (pp. 359–373). New York: Guilford Press.

Widiger, T. A. (2001). Social anxiety, social phobia, and avoidant personality. In R. Crozier & L. E. Alden (Eds.), *International handbook of social anxiety: Concepts, research and interventions relating to the self and shyness* (pp. 336–356). New York: Wiley.

Widiger, T. A., Cadoret, R., Hare, R., Robins, L., Rutherford, M., Zanarini, M., Alterman, A., Apple, M., Corbitt, E., Forth, A., Hart, S., Kultermann, J., Woody, G., & Frances, A. (1996). *DSM-IV* Antisocial Personality Disorder field trial. *Journal of Abnormal Psychology, 105,* 3–16.

Widiger, T. A. & Costa, P. T. (1994). Personality and personality disorders. *Journal of Abnormal Psychology, 103,* 78–91.

Widiger, T. A., Mangine, S., Corbitt, E. M., Ellis, C. G., & Thomas, G. V. (1995). *Personality Disorder Interview-IV. A semistructured interview for the assessment of personality disorders.* Odessa, FL: Psychological Assessment Resources.

Widiger, T. A. & Sanderson, C. J. (1997). Personality disorders. In A. Tasman, J. Kay, & J. A. Lieberman (Eds.), *Psychiatry* (Vol. 2, pp. 1291–1317). Philadelphia: W. B. Saunders.

Widiger, T. A. & Trull, T. J. (1991). Diagnosis and clinical assessment. *Annual Review of Psychology, 41,* 109–135.

Widiger, T. A. & Trull, T. J. (1993). Borderline and narcissistic personality disorders. In P. B. Sutker & H. E. Adams (Eds.), *Comprehensive handbook of psychopathology* (2nd ed.) (pp. 181–201). New York: Plenum Press.

Widom, C. S. & Maxfield, M. G. (1996). A prospective examination of risk for violence among abused and neglected children. *Annals of the New York Academy of Sciences, 794,* 224–237.

Wielgus, M. S. & Harvey, P. D. (1988). Dichotic listening and recall in schizophrenia and mania. *Schizophrenia Bulletin, 14,* 689–700.

Wiersma, D., Nienhuis, F. J., Slooff, C. J., & Giel, R. (1998). Natural course of schizophrenic disorders: A 15-year followup of a Dutch incidence cohort. *Schizophrenia Bulletin, 24,* 75–85.

Wilcox, H. C., Wagner, F. A., & Anthony, J. C. (2002). Exposure opportunity as a mechanism linking youth marijuana use to hallucinogen use. *Drug and Alcohol Dependence, 66,* 127–135.

Wilhelm, S. (2000). Cognitive therapy for obsessive-compulsive disorder. *Journal of Cognitive Psychotherapy, 14,* 245–260.

Wilhem, S., Keuthen, N. J., Deckesback, T., Engelhard, I. M., Forker, A. E., Baer, L., O'Sullivan, R. J., & Jenike, M. A. (1999). Self-injurious skin picking: Clinical characteristics and comorbidity. *Journal of Clinical Psychiatry, 60,* 454–459.

Willerman, L. & Cohen, D. B. (1990). *Psychopathology.* New York: McGraw-Hill.

William, F., Birchler, G. R., & O'Farrell, T. J. (1996). Behavioral couples therapy for male substance-abusing patients. *Journal of Consulting and Clinical Psychology, 64,* 959–972.

Williams, J. M. G., Mathews, A., & MacLeod, C. (1996). The emotional Stroop task and psychopathology. *Psychological Bulletin, 120,* 3–24.

Williams, J. M. G., Watts, F. N., MacLeod, C., & Mathews, A. (1997). *Cognitive psychology and emotional disorders* (2nd ed.). Chichester, England: Wiley.

Williams, L. M. (1994). Recall of childhood trauma: A prospective study of women's memories of child sexual abuse. *Journal of Consulting and Clinical Psychology, 62,* 1167–1176.

Williams, L. M. (1995). Recovered memories of abuse in women with documented child sexual victimization histories. *Journal of Traumatic Stress. 8,* 649–673.

Williams, N. L. & Riskind, J. H. (in press). Adult romantic attachment and cognitive vulnerabilities to anxiety and depression: Examining the interpersonal basis of vulnerability models. *Journal of Cognitive Psychotherapy: An International Quarterly.*

Williams, R. B., Barefoot, J. C., Califf, R. M., Haney, T. L., Saunders, W. B., Pryor, D. B., Hlatky, M. A., Siegler, I. C., & Mark, D. B. (1992). Prognostic importance of social and economic resources among medically treated patients with angiographically documented coronary artery disease. *Journal of the American Medical Association, 267,* 520–524.

Williamson, D. F., Kahn, H. S., Remington, P. L., & Anda, R. F. (1990). The 10-year incidence of overweight and weight gain in U.S. adults. *Archives of Internal Medicine. 150,* 665–672.

Willson, P., McFarlane, J., Malecha, A., Watson, K., Lemmey, D., Schultz, P., Gist, J., & Fredland, N. (2000). Severity of violence against women by intimate partners and associated use of alcohol and/or illicit drugs by the perpetrator. *Journal of Interpersonal Violence, 15*(9), 996–1008.

Wilson, G. D. (1987). An ethological approach to sexual deviation. In G. D. Wilson (Ed.), *Variant sexuality: Research and theory.* Baltimore: Johns Hopkins University Press.

Wilson, G. T. & Fairburn, C. G. (1993). Cognitive treatments for eating disorders. *Journal of Consulting and Clinical Psychology, 61,* 261–269.

Wilson, J. J. & Gil, K. M. (1996). The efficacy of psychological and pharmacological interventions for the treatment of chronic disease-related and non-disease-related pain. *Clinical Psyschology Review, 16,* 573–597.

Wilson, J. Q. (1997). *Moral Judgment.* New York: Basic Books.

Wilson, M. (1984). Female homosexuals' need for dominance and endurance. *Psychological Reports, 55,* 79–82.

Wincze, J. P. (1989). Assessment and treatment of atypical sexual behavior. In S. R. Leiblum & R. C. Rosen (Eds.), *Principles and practice of sex therapy.* New York: Guilford Press.

Wincze, J. P., Bansal, S., & Malamud, M. (1986). Effects of medroxyprogesterone acetate on subjective arousal, arousal to erotic stimulation, and nocturnal penile tumescence in male sex offenders. *Archives of Sexual Behavior. 15*(4), 293–305.

Windholz, G. (1997). Ivan P. Pavlov: An overview of his life and psychological work. *American Psychologist, 52*(9), 941–946.

Wing, L. (1993). The definition and prevalence of autism: A review. *European Child and Adolescent Psychiatry, 2,* 61–74.

Wing, L. & Attwood, A. (1987). Syndromes of autism and atypical development. In D. J. Cohen & A. Donnelan (Eds.), *Handbook of autism* (pp. 3–17). New York: Wiley.

Wing, L. & Gould, J. (1979). Severe impairments of social interaction and associated abnormalities in children: Epidemiology and classification. *Journal of Autism and Developmental Disorders, 9,* 11–29.

Winick, B. J. (1997). *The right to refuse mental health treatment.* Washington, DC: American Psychological Association.

Winick, B. J. (2001). The civil commitment hearing: Applying the law therapeutically. In L. E. Frost & R. J. Bonnie (Eds.), *The evolution of mental health law* (pp. 291–308). Washington, DC: American Psychological Association.

Winokur, G., Coryell, W., Endicott, J., & Akiskal, H. (1993). Further distinctions between manic-depressive illness (bipolar disorder) and primary depressive disorder (unipolar depression). *American Journal of Psychiatry, 150,* 1176–1181.

Winokur, G., Coryell, W., Keller, M., Endicott, J., & Leon, A. (1995). A family study of manic-depressive (Bipolar I) disease: Is it a distinct illness separable from primary unipolar depression? *Archives of General Psychiatry, 52,* 367–373.

Wise, R. A. (1988). The neurobiology of craving: Implications for the understanding and treatment of addiction. *Journal of Abnormal Psychology, 97,* 118–132.

Wise, R. A. (1996). Neurobiology of addiction. *Current Opinions in Neurobiology, 6,* 243–251.

Wittchen, H. U., & Essau, C. A. (1993). Epidemiology of panic disorder: Progress and unresolved issues. *Journal of Psychiatric Research, 27,* 47–68.

Wittchen, H. U. & Hoyer, J. (2001). Generalized anxiety disorder: Nature and course. *Journal of Clinical Psychiatry, 62,* 15–21.

Wittchen, H. U., Schuster, P., & Lieb, R. (2001). Comorbidity and mixed anxiety-depressive disorder: Clinical curiosity or pathophysiological need? *Human Psychopharmacology, 16,* S21–S30.

Witzig, J. S. (1968). The group treatment of male exhibitionists. *American Journal of Psychiatry, 25,* 75–81.

Wolf, S. (2000). Schizoid personality in childhood and Asperger syndrome. In A. Klin, F. R. Volkmar, et al. (Eds.). *Asperger syndrome* (pp. 278–305). New York: Guilford Press.

Wolf, S. & McGuire, R. J. (1995). Schizoid personality in girls: A follow-up study: What are the links with Asperger's syndrome? *Journal of Child Psychology and Psychiatry & Allied Disciplines, 36,* 793–817.

Wolf, S. & Wolff, H. G. (1947). *Human gastric functions.* New York: Oxford University Press.

Wolfe, D. A. & McEachran, A. (1997). Child physical abuse and neglect. In E. J. Mash & L. G. Terdal (Eds.), *Assessment of childhood disorders* (pp. 523–568). New York: Guilford Press.

Wolfe, D. A., Sas, L., & Wekerle, C. (1994). Factors associated with the development of posttraumatic stress disorder among child victims of sexual abuse. *Child Abuse and Neglect, 18,* 37–50.

Wolpe, J. (1958). *Psychotherapy by reciprocal inhibition.* Stanford, CA: Stanford University Press.

Wolpe, J. (1969). *The practice of behavior therapy.* New York: Pergamon Press.

Wolpe, J. (1973). *The practice of behavior therapy* (2nd ed.). New York: Pergamon Press.

Wolpe, J. (1976). *Theme and variations: A behavior therapy casebook*. Elmsford, NY: Pergamon Press.

Wolpe, J. & Rowan, V. C. (1988). Panic disorder: A product of classical conditioning. *Behaviour Research and Therapy, 26,* 441–450.

Wolpe, J. & Wolpe, D. (1981). *Our useless fears,* Boston: Houghton Mifflin.

Wong, D. F., Gjedde, A., Wagner, H. N., Jr., Tune, L. E., Dannals, R. F., Pearlsson, G. D., Links, J. M., Tamminga, C. A., Broussolle, E. P., Ravert, H. T., Wilson, A. A., Toung, J. K. T., Malat, J., Williams, F. A., O'Touma, L. A., Snyder, S. H., Kuhar, M. J., & Gjedde, A. (1986). Positron emission tomography reveals elevated D2 dopamine receptors in drug-naive schizophrenics. *Science, 234,* 1558–1563.

Wood, J. M., Garb, H. N., Lilienfeld, S. O., & Nezworski, M. T. (2002). Clinical assessment. *Annual Review of Psychology, 53,* 519–543.

Wood, J. M., Nezworski, M. T., Garb, H. N., & Lilienfeld, S. O. (2001). The misperception of psychopathology: Problems with the norms of the Comprehensive System for the Rorschach. *Clinical Psychology: Science and Practice, 8,* 350–373.

Wood, J. M., Nezworski, M. T., & Stejskal, W. J. (1996). The Comprehensive System for the Rorschach: A critical examination. *Psychological Science, 7,* 3–10.

Woodruff, P. W. R., Wright, I. C., Bullmore, E. T., Brammer, M., Howard, R. J., Williams, S. C. R., Shapleske, J., Rossel, S., David, A. S., McGuire, P. K., & Murray, R. M. (1997). Auditory hallucinations and the temporal cortical response to speech in schizophrenia: A functional magnetic resonance imaging study. *American Journal of Psychiatry, 154,* 1676–1682.

Woods, J. H., Katz, J. L., & Winger, G. (1987). Abuse liability of benzodiazepines. *Pharmacological Reviews, 39,* 251–413.

Woods, S. W., Money, R., & Baker, C. B. (2001). Does the manic/mixed episode distinction in bipolar disorder patients run true over time?

American Journal of Psychiatry, 158, 1324–1325.

Woody, G. E., McLellan, A. T., Luborsky, L., & O'Brien, C. P. (1995). Psychotherapy in community methadone programs. *American Journal of Psychiatry, 152,* 1302–1308.

Woolson, A. M. & Swanson, M. G. (1972). The second time around: Psychotherapy with the "hysterical woman." *Psychotherapy: Theory, Research, and Practice, 9,* 168–173.

World Health Organization. (1996). *The global burden of disease.* Cambridge, MA: Harvard School of Public Health.

Wright, E. R., Gronfein, W. P., Owens, T. J. (2000). Deinstitutionalization, social rejection, and the self-esteem of former mental patients. *Journal of Health & Social Behavior, 41,* 68–90.

Wright, L. (1994). *Remembering Satan.* New York: Knopf.

Wright, P., Takie, N., Rifkin, L., & Murray, R. M. (1995). Maternal influenza, obstetric complications, and schizophrenia. *American Journal of Psychiatry. 152,* 1714–1720.

Wuerker, A. K., Haas, G. L., & Bellack, A. S. (2001). Interpersonal control and expressed emotion in families of persons with schizophrenia: Change over time. *Schizophrenia Bulletin, 27,* 671–686.

Wulfert, E., Greenway, D. E., & Dougher, M. J. (1996). A logical functional analysis of reinforcement-based disorders: Alcoholism and pedophilia. *Journal of Consulting and Clinical Psychology, 64,* 1140–1151.

Wurtele, S. K. & Miller-Perrin, C. L. (1992). *Preventing child sexual abuse—sharing the responsibility.* Lincoln: University of Nebraska Press.

Wyatt v. Stickney, (1972). 1974 AL. 503 Fed 1305. U.S. Court of Appeals, 5th Circuit.

Wykes, T. & van der Gaag, M. (2001). Is it time to develop a new cognitive therapy for psychosis—Cognitive Remediation Therapy (CRT)? *Clinical Psychology Review, 21,* 1227–1256.

Wylie, K. R. (1997). Treatment outcome of brief couple therapy in psychogenic erectile disorder. *Archives of Sexual Behavior, 26,* 527–545.

Wyllie, E. (Ed.). (2001). *The treatment of epilepsy: Principles and practice* (3rd ed.). Philadelphia: Lippincott Williams & Wilkins.

Wynne, L. C. & Singer, M. T. (1963). Thought disorder and family relations of schizophrenics: I. A research strategy. *Archives of General Psychiatry, 9,* 191–198.

Xian, H., Chantarujikapong, S. I., Scherrer, J. F., Eisen, S. A., Lyons, M. J., Golberg, J., Tsuagn, M., & True, W. R. (2000). Genetic and environmental influences on posttraumatic stress disorder, alcohol and drug dependence in twin pairs. *Drug and Alcohol Dependence, 61*(1), 95–102.

Yamada, N., Nakajima, S., & Noguchi, T. (1998). Age at onset of delusional disorder is dependent on the delusional theme. *Acta Psychiatrica Scandinavica, 97,* 122–124.

Yang, B. & Clum, G. A. (1996). Effects of early negative life experiences on cognitive functioning and risk for suicide: A review. *Clinical Psychology Review. 16,* 177–195.

Yang, J., McCrae, R. R., Costa, P. T., Yao, S., Dai, X., Gait, T., & Gao, B. (2000). The cross-cultural generalizability of Axis-II constructs: An evaluation of two personality assessment instruments in the People's Republic of China. *Journal of Personality Disorders, 14,* 249–263.

Yatham, L. N., Liddle, P. F., Shiah, I. S., Scarrow, G., Lam, R. W., Adam, M. J., Zis, A. P., & Ruth, T. J. (2000). Brain serotonin$_2$ receptors in major depression: A positron emission tomography study. *Archives of General Psychiatry, 57,* 850–858.

Yehuda, R., Levengood, R. A., Schmeidler, J., Wilson, S., Guo, L. S., & Gerber, D. (1996). Increased pituitary activation following metyrapone administration in post-traumatic stress disorder. *Psychoneuroendocrinology, 21,* 1–16.

Yehuda, R., Teicher, M. H., Trestman, R. L., Levengood, R. A., & Siever, L. J. (1996). Cortisol regulation in posttraumatic stress disorder and major depression: A chronobiological analysis. *Biological Psychiatry, 40,* 79–88.

Yetman, N. R. (1994). Race and ethnic inequality. In C. Calhoun & G. Ritzer (Eds.), *Social problems.* New York: McGraw-Hill/Primis.

Yirmiya, N., Solomonica-Levi, D., Schulman, C., & Pilowsky, T. (1996). Theory of mind abilities in individuals with autism, Down syndrome, and mental retardation of unknown etiology. The role of age and intelligence. *Journal of Child Psychology and Psychiatry, 37,* 1003–1014.

Yonkers, K. A. & Gurguis, G. (1995). Gender differences in the prevalence and expression of anxiety disorders. In M. V. Seeman (Ed.), *Gender and psychopathology* (pp. 113–130). Washington, DC: American Psychiatric Press.

Yonkers, K. A., Zlotnick, C., Allsworth, J., et al. (1998). Is the course of panic disorder the same in women and men? *American Journal of Psychiatry, 155*(5), 596–602.

Yoshikawa, H. (1995). Long-term effects of early childhood programs on social outcomes and delinquency. *The Future of Children, 5,* 51–75.

Young, A. S., Klap, R., Sherbourne, C. D., & Wells, K. B. (2001). The quality of care for depressive and anxiety disorders in the United States. *Archives of General Psychiatry, 58,* 55–61.

Young, D. M. (1997). Depression. In W. S. Tseng & J. Streltzer (Eds.), *Culture & psychopathology: A guide to clinical assessment* (pp. 28–45). New York: Brunner/Mazel.

Young, J. E., Beck, A. T., & Weinberger, A. (1993). Depression. In D. H. Barlow (Ed.), *Clinical handbook of psychological disorders: A step-by-step treatment manual* (pp. 240–277). New York: Guilford Press.

Young, M. A., Meaden, P. M., Fogg, L. F., Cherin, E. A., & Eastman, C. I. (1997). Which environmental variables are related to the onset of seasonal affective disorder? *Journal of Abnormal Psychology, 106,* 554–562.

Youngberg v. Romeo, 102 S. Ct. 2452, 2462, 2463 (1982).

Zagon, I. K. (1995). Psychopathy: A viable alternative to antisocial personality disorder? *Australian Psychologist, 30,* 11–16.

Zahn-Waxler, C. (1993) Warriors and worriers: Gender and psychopathology. *Development and Psychopathology, 5,* 79–89.

Zaidel, D. W., Esiri, M. M., & Harrison, P. J. (1997). Size, shape, and orientation of neurons in the left and right hippocampus: Investigation of normal asymmetries and alterations in schizophrenia. *American Journal of Psychiatry, 154,* 812–818.

Zanarini, M. C., Frankenburg, F. R., Dubo, E. D., Sickel, A. E., Trikha, A., Levin, A., & Reynolds, V. (1998). Axis I combordidity of borderline personality disorder. *The American Journal of Psychiatry, 155,* 1733–1739.

Zarit, S. H. (1992). Concepts and measures in family caregiving research. In

B. Bauer (Ed.), *Conceptual and methodological issues in family caregiver research* (pp. 1–19). Toronto, Canada: University of Toronto Press.

Zarit, S. H. (1994). Research perspectives on family caregiving. In M. Cantor (Ed.), *Family caregiving: Agenda for the future* (pp. 9–24). San Francisco: American Society on Aging.

Zeskind, P. S. & Ramey, C. T. (1981). Preventing intellectual and interactional sequelae of fetal malnutrition: A longitudinal, transactional, and synergistic approach to development. *Child Development, 52,* 213–218.

Zhang, A. & Snowden, L. R. (1999). Ethnic characteristics of mental disorders in five U. S. communities. *Cultural Diversity and Ethnic Minority Psychology, 5,* 134–146.

Zhang, X. L., Cohen, H. L., Porjesz, B., & Begleiter, H. (2001). Mismatch negativity in subjects at high risk for alcoholism. *Alcoholism: Clinical & Experimental Research, 25*(3), 330–337.

Zhang-Wong, J., Beiser, M., Bean, G., & Iacono, W. G. (1995). Five-year course of schizophreniform disorder. *Psychiatry Research, 59,* 109–117.

Zigler, E. (1994). Reshaping early childhood intervention to be a more effective weapon against poverty. *American Journal of Community Psychology, 22,* 37–46.

Zigman, W. M., Schupf, N., Zigman, A., et al. (1993). Aging and Alzheimer disease in people with mental retardation. *International Review of Research in Mental Retardation, 19,* 63.

Zilboorg, G. & Henry, G. W. (1941). *A history of medical psychology.* New York: W. W. Norton.

Zimbardo, P. (1971). *The psychological power and pathology of imprisonment* (a statement prepared for the U. S. House of Representatives Committee on the Judiciary; subcommittee No. 3, Hearings on Prison Reform, San Francisco, Calif., October 25th, p. 3.

Zimmerman, M., McDermut, W., & Mattia, J. I. (2000). Frequency of anxiety disorders in psychiatric outpatients with major depressive disorder. *American Journal of Psychiatry, 157,* 1337–1340.

Zinbarg, R. E. (1998). Concordance and synchrony in measures of anxiety and panic reconsidered: A hierarchical model of anxiety and panic. *Behavior Therapy, 29,* 301–323.

Zinbarg, R. E., Barlow, D. H., Liebowitz, M., Street, L., Broadhead, E., Katon, W., Roy-Byrne, P., Lepine, J. P., Teherani, M., Richards, J., Brantley, P. J., & Kraemer, H. (1994). The *DSM-IV* field trial for mixed anxiety-depression. *American Journal of Psychiatry, 151,* 1153–1162.

Zobel, A. W., Yassouridis, A., Frieboes, R. M., & Holsboer, F. (1999). Prediction of medium-term outcome by cortisol response to the combined dexamethasone-CRH test in patients with remitted depression. *American Journal of Psychiatry, 156,* 949–951.

Zoccolillo, M. (1993). Gender and the development of conduct disorder. *Development and Psychopathology, 5,* 65–78.

Zoccolillo, M. & Rogers, K. (1991). Characteristics and outcome of hospitalized adolescent girls with conduct disorder. *Journal of the American Academy of Child and Adolescent Psychiatry, 30,* 973–981.

Zonana, H. (2000). Mandated outpatient treatment: A quick fix for random violence?—Not likely. *Journal of the American Academy of Psychiatry and the Law, 28,* 124–126.

Zubieta, J. K., Huguelet, P., Ohl, L. E., Koeppe, R. A., Kilbourn, M. R., Carr, J. M., Giordani, B. J., & Frey, K. A. (2000). High vesicular monoamine transporter binding in asymptomatic bipolar I disorder: Sex differences and cognitive correlates. *American Journal of Psychiatry, 157,* 1619–1628.

Zucker, K. J. & Bradley, S. J. (1995). *Gender identity disorder and psychosexual problems in children and adolescents.* New York: Guilford Press.

Zuckerman, B. & Frank, D. A. (1992). "Crack kids": Not broken. *Pediatrics, 89,* 337–339.

Zuckerman, M. (1998). *Vulnerability to psychopathology: A biosocial model.* Washington, DC: American Psychological Association.

CREDITS

PHOTOGRAPHS

CHAPTER 1

Opener: © Archivo Iconografico, S.A./Corbis Images; **2:** © Paul Conklin/PhotoEdit; **4:** © James Marshall/Image Works; **7:** © Bettmann/Corbis Images; **9:** © Spencer Grant/PhotoEdit; **10:** © S. Agricola/Image Works; **11:** © Sandved B. Kjell/Visuals Unlimited; **12:** © Scala/Art Resource, NY; **14:** © Bettmann/Corbis Images; **15 top:** Stock Montage; **15 bottom:** © Bettmann/Corbis Images; **18:** © Eunice Harris/Photo Researchers; **20:** © The Wellcome Institute Collection; **22:** © Bettmann/Corbis Images

CHAPTER 2

Opener: © Images.com/Corbis Images; **27:** © Victor Habbick Visions/SPL/Photo Researchers; **29:** © AP/Wide World Photos; **36:** © Alan Carey/Image Works; **40 left:** © Dan McCoy/Rainbow; **40 right:** © Bob Daemmrich/Image Works; **42:** © Hogrefe & Huber Publishers; **43:** Simulated items similar to those in the Thematic Apperception Test (TAT). © 1971 by Henry A. Murray. Reproduced with permission of Mrs. Caroline C. Murray.; **49:** © Richard Nowitz/Photo Researchers; **50:** © James Shaffer/PhotoEdit; **51:** © Phil McCarten/PhotoEdit

CHAPTER 3

Opener: © Images.com/Corbis Images; **57:** © Chuck Savage/Corbis Images; **60:** © Erich Hartmann/Magnum Photos; **67:** © Donna DeCesare; **69 left:** © John A. Giordano/Corbis Images; **69 right:** © John A. Giordano/Corbis Images

CHAPTER 4

Opener: © Diana Ong/Superstock; **76:** © Granger Collection; **77 top:** © Archives of the History of American Psychology; **77 bottom:** © Joe McNally; **81:** © Spencer Grant/Stock Boston; **89:** Courtesy Beck Institute for Cognitive Therapy; **90 bottom:** © Tim Pannell/ Corbis Images; **90 top:** Courtesy Albert Ellis; **98:** © Chuck Painter/Stanford News Service; **101:** © Kirk Condyles

CHAPTER 5

Opener: © Images.com/Corbis Images; **107:** © Lynne J. Weinstein/Woodfin Camp; **109:** © Mary Evans Picture Library; **110:** © Tom McCarthy/PhotoEdit; **113:** © Bettmann/Corbis Images; **114:** © Sarah Putnam/Index Stock Imagery; **115 top:** © Alan Carey/Image Works; **115 bottom:** © Margaret S. Mahler Papers, Manuscripts and Archives, Yale University Library; **117:** © Freud Museum, London; **118:** © Rousseau, Henri. The Dream. 1910. Oil on canvas, 6′8 1/2″ x 9′9 1/2″. The Museum of Modern Art, New York. Gift of Nelson A. Rockefeller. Photograph © 1995 The Museum of Modern Art, New York; **124:** National Library of Medicine; **127:** © Jose Luis Pelaez/Corbis Images

CHAPTER 6

Opener: © Digital Art/Corbis Images; **132:** © Bob Daemmrich/Image Works; **133:** © Bob Sacha; **136:** © CNRI/SPL/Photo Researchers; **142:** © Wellcome Dept. of Cognitive Neurology/SPL/Photo Researchers; **143:** © A. Glauberman/Photo Researchers; **147:** © John Ficara/Woodfin Camp

CHAPTER 7

Opener: © Images.com/Corbis Images; **152:** © AP/Wide World Photos; **155:** © Michael Newman/PhotoEdit; **158:** © AP/Wide World Photos; **159 top:** © Jeffrey D. Smith/Woodfin Camp; **159 bottom:** © AP/Wide World Photos; **163:** © Barbara Stitzer/PhotoEdit; **165:** © Gerhard Steiner/Corbis Images; **166:** © AP/Wide World Photos; **171 left:** © Will & Deni McIntyre/Photo Researchers; **171 right:** © Richard T. Nowitz/Photo Researchers; **175:** © Damien Lovegrove/SPL/Photo Researchers

CHAPTER 8

Opener: © Diana Ong/Superstock; **181:** © Bettmann/Corbis Images; **185:** © Kobal Collection; **190:** © AP/Wide World Photos; **193:** © Tony Freeman/PhotoEdit; **194:** © Susan Ragan/Corbis Images; **196:** © Bettmann/Corbis Images; **198:** © Corbis; **199:** © Gerry Goodstein/Hartman Theatre Company; **205:** © Mary Evans Picture Library/Photo Researchers; **207:** © Gary Conner/Index Stock Imagery/PictureQuest

CHAPTER 9

Opener: © Images.com/Corbis Images; **213:** © Brian Brake/Photo Researchers; **217:** © A. Liepins /Photo Researchers; **218:** © David Young-Wolff/PhotoEdit; **220:** © Superstock; **223:** © Mark Godfrey/Image Works; **225:** © Keith Bernstein/Gamma Press; **229:** © Alon Reininger/WoodFin Camp; **231:** © Scala/Art Resource; **234:** © Ed Young/SPL/Photo Researchers; **238:** © David Sacks/Getty Images; **241:** © Mark Peterson/Corbis Images

CHAPTER 10

Opener: © Images.com/Corbis Images; **246:** © Bettmann/Corbis Images; **249:** © David Young-Wolff/PhotoEdit; **251:** © AP/Wide World Photos; **254 left:** © Sylvia Beach Collection/Photo Researchers; **254 right:** © Bettmann/Corbis Images; **256:** © Kathy McLaughlin/Image Works; **260:** © Steve Goldberg; **261:** © 1990 The Muskegon Chronicle. All rights reserved. Reprinted with permission; **274:** © David Strickler/Index Stock Imagery; **276:** © Erik Hill/Anchorage Daily News; **278:** © Wellcome Dept. of Cognitive Neurology/SPL/Photo Researchers; **282:** © Stephen Frisch

CHAPTER 11

Opener: © Images.com/Corbis Images; **288:** © Tim Brown/Getty Images; **295:** © Kobal Collection; **297:** © Superstock; **298:** © M. Bridwell/PhotoEdit; **306:** © Nancy Richmond/Image Works; **309:** © Gary Conner/PhotoEdit

CHAPTER 12

Opener: © Images.com/Corbis Images; **314:** © Dan McCoy; William McCoy/Rainbow/PictureQuest; **315:** © Bettmann/Corbis Images; **318:** © A. Glauberman/Photo Researchers; **320:** © Nathan Benn/Stock, Boston/PictureQuest; **321 top left:** © S.I.N./Corbis Images; **321 top center:** © Fashion Wire Daily/Wide World Photos; **321 top right:** © Lynn Goldsmith/Corbis Images; **321 bottom left:** © AP/Wide World Photos; **321 bottom center:** © Neal Preston/Corbis Images; **321 bottom right:** © Karen Mason Blair/Corbis Images; **324:** © Mary Kate Denny/PhotoEdit; **328:** © Larry Mulvehil/Image Works; **331:** © Bettmann/Corbis Images; **335:** © Ralph Steadman/www.ralphsteadman.com; **337:** © PhotoDisc; **342:** © Comnet LTD/eStock Photo/PictureQuest; **344, 347:** © PhotoDisc; **350:** Hanson, L., Deere, D., Lee, C., Lewin, A., and Seval. C. (2001) Key Principles in providing integrated behavioral health services for young children and their families: The starting early starting smart experience. Washington, DC; Casey Family Programs and the U.S. Department of Health and Human Services, Substance Abuse and Mental Health Services Administration.; **351:** © D. Crawford/ Image Works; **354:** © Reunion des Musees Nationaux/Art Resource, NY

CHAPTER 13

Opener: © Images.com/Corbis Images; **355:** © AP/Wide World Photos; **366:** © Rick Rappaport/Corbis Images; **368:** © Theo Westenberger/Getty Images; **370:** AMS 700™ Penile Prosthesis. Courtesy of American Medical Systems, Inc. Minnetonka, Minnesota. www.AmericanMedicalSystems.com; **371:**

© Rommel Pecson/Image Works; **373:** © Reuters NewMedia Inc./Corbis Images; **375:** © Bettmann/Corbis Images; **379 left:** © Rob Crandall/Stock Boston; **379 right:** © Rob Crandall/Image Works; **384:** © AP/Wide World Photos

CHAPTER 14

Opener: © Images.com/Corbis Images; **393 left:** Photo: A. Bert, Print by L. Rosen, Courtesy of the Roger Pryor Dodge Collection; Dance Collection, The New York Public Library for the Performing Arts, Astor, Lenox and Tilden Foundations; **393 right:** From "The Diary of Vaslav Nijinsky," edited by Romila Nijinksy, Simon & Schuster, NY, 1936; **397:** Courtesy Camarillo State Hospital; **398:** © Peter Southwick/Stock Boston; **400 (both):** © National Institutes of Health; **401:** © Grunitas/Photo Researchers; **408:** Courtesy, The Genain Quadrulplets; **414 left:** © Tim Beddow/SPL/Photo Researchers; **414 right:** © Tim Beddow/SPL/Photo Researchers; **420:** © David J. Deluhery; **423 left:** © AP/Wide World Photos; **423 right:** © Dreamworks/Universal/The Kobal Collection/Reed, Eli; **424:** © PhotoDisc; **426:** © Joel Gordon

CHAPTER 15

Opener: © Jane Sterrett/janesterrett.com; **433:** © Bettmann/Corbis Images; **436:** © Zephyr/SPL/Photo Researchers; **438 top:** © Biophoto Associates/SPL/Photo Researchers; **438 center:** © Ralph Eagle, Jr./Photo Researchers; **441:** From Damasio H, Grabowski, T, Frank R, Galaburda AM, Damasio AR: The return of Phineas Gage: Clues about the brain from the skull of a famous patient. Science, 264:1102–1105, 1994. Department of Neurology and Image Analysis Facility, University of Iowa; **443:** © PhotoDisc; **446, 448:** © AP/Wide World Photos; **452:** © Sybil Shackman; **454:** © Archivo Iconografico, S.A./Corbis Images

CHAPTER 16

Opener: © Collier Campbell Lifeworks/Corbis Images; **460:** © Richard Hutchings/PhotoEdit; **462:** © Jose Azell/Aurora Photos; **468:** © Tom McCarthy/Southern Stock/PictureQuest; **469:** © Kansas City Star; **471:** © Bob Daemmrich/Stock Boston; **473:** © Dan McCoy/Rainbow; **479:** © Kendall, P.C. (1990). "Coping Cat Workbook," Ardmore, PA: Workbook Publishing. Reproduced by permission of Philip C. Kendall and Peter Mikulka; **481:** ©Michal Heron

CHAPTER 17

Opener: © Images.com/Corbis Images; **486:** © Bill Lyons/Photo Researchers; **487:** © CNRI/SPL/Photo Researchers; **489:** © George Steinmetz/National Geographic Society; **491:** © Sybil Shackman; **494:** © Shooting Star; **501:** © Jeff Greenberg/Image Works; **506:** © Bob Daemmrich/Image Works

CHAPTER 18

Opener: © Diana Ong/Superstock; **511:** © Reuters/Richard Carson/Corbis Images; **515:** © AP/Wide World Photos; **521:** Courtesy Honorable Ginger Lerner-Wren; **524:** © AP/Wide World Photos; **525:** © Superstock; **533:** © Jose Luis Pelaez, Inc./Corbis Images.

TEXT AND LINE ART

CHAPTER 1

5 Case Study: From *Culture and Mental Illness: A Client-Centered Approach*, 1st edition, by Richard Castillo. Copyright © 1997 Wadsworth. Reprinted with permission of Wadsworth, a division of Thomson Learning: www.thomsonrights.com. Fax 800-730-2215; **17 Figure 1.3:** From Halgin & Whitbourne, *Abnormal Psychology*, Fourth Edition. Copyright © 2003 The McGraw-Hill Companies. Reproduced with permission of The McGraw-Hill Companies; **23 Case Study:** From "African and Western Psychiatry: A Comparison," by T. Asuni, in *Transcultural Psychiatry*, p. 313, by J.L. Cox (ed.), 1986. London: Croom-Helm. Adapted with permission.

CHAPTER 2

30 Box: Reprinted with permission from D.L. Rosenhan, "On Being Sane in Insane Places," 1973, *Science*, 179, p. 253. Copyright © 1973 by the American Association for the Advancement of Science; **31-32 Quote:** Reprinted with permission from the *Diagnostic and Statistical Manual of Mental Disorders*, Text Revision, Copyright © 2000 American Psychiatric Association; **33 Figure 2.1:** From W.C. Follette & A.C. Houts, "Models of Scientific Progress and the Role of Theory in Taxonomy Development: A Case Study of the DSM," 1996, *Journal of Consulting and Clinical Psychology*, 64, pp. 1120–1132. Copyright © 1996 by the American Psychological Association. Reprinted with permission; **38 Box:** From M.B. First, R.L. Spitzer, M. Gibbon & J.B.W. Williams, *Structured Clinical Interview for DSM-IV Axis I Disorders (SCID-I)*, p. A1. Biometrics Department, New York State Psychiatric. Reprinted by permission; **39 Box:** From C.E. Holzer, III, G.L. Tischler, P.J. Leaf, and J.K. Myers, "An Epidemiologic Assessment of Cognitive Impairment in a Community Population," 1984, *Research in Community and Mental Health*, 4, pp. 3–32. Reprinted with permission from Marshall Folstein, M.D.; **43 Figure 2.4:** Reprinted by permission of the publisher from *The Thematic Apperception Test* by Henry A. Murray, Cambridge: MA: Harvard University Press. Copyright © 1943 by the President and Fellows of Harvard College; **47 Table 2.1:** From G.J. Meyer, "On the Integration of Personality Assessment Methods: The Rorschach and MMPI," 1997, *Journal of Personality Assessment*, 68, p. 299. Copyright © 1997 Lawrence Erlbaum Associates. Reprinted by permission; **48 Figure 2.5:** From "A Visual Motor Gestalt Test and its Clinical Use," by L. Bender, 1938, *Research Monographs of the American Orthopsychiatric Association*, 3, xi, p. 176. Copyright © 1938 by the American Orthopsychiatric Association. Reprinted by permission of Riverside Publishing; **51 Case Study:** Case Study from J. Del Castillo, "The Influence of Language Upon Symptomatology in Foreign-Born Patients," 1970, *American Journal of Psychiatry*, 127, p. 161. Reprinted with permission from the *American Journal of Psychiatry*. Copyright © 1970 American Psychiatric Association.

CHAPTER 3

71 Figure 3.3: Reprinted from *Journal of Substance Abuse*, 2, C.M. Bulik, L.H. Epstein & W. Kaye, "Treatment of Laxative Abuse in a Female with Bulimia Nervosa Using an Operant Extinction Paradigm," pp. 384–385. Copyright © 1990, with permission from Elsevier; **72 Figure 3.4:** From T.H. Ollendick, "Cognitive Behavioral Therapy of Panic Disorder with Agoraphobia in Adolescents: A Multiple Baseline Design Analysis," *Behavior Therapy*, 26, p. 524. Reprinted with permission from the Association for the Advancement of Behavior Therapy.

CHAPTER 4

84 Quote: From J. Wolpe & D. Wolpe, *Our Useless Fears*. 1981, New York: Houghton Mifflin; **96, 97 Case Study:** Case Study from the files of Robert Leahy, American Institute for Cognitive Therapy. Reprinted by permission.

CHAPTER 6

135 Figure 6.1: From Santrock, *Psychology*, 7th Edition. Copyright © 2003 The McGraw-Hill Companies. Reproduced with permission of The McGraw-Hill Companies; **138 Figure 6.3:** From Nolen-Hoeksema, *Abnormal Psychology*, 3rd Edition. Copyright © 2004 The McGraw-Hill Companies. Reproduced with permission of The McGraw-Hill Companies; **141 Figure 6.6:** From Halgin & Whitbourne, *Abnormal Psychology*, 4th Edition. Copyright © 2003 The McGraw-Hill Companies. Reproduced with permission of The McGraw-Hill Companies.

CHAPTER 7

153 Case Study: Copyright © 1999 from *International Journal of Psychiatry in Clinical Practice*, by J. Bobes. Reproduced by permission of Routledge/Taylor & Francis Books, Inc.; **156 Case Study:** From S. Wilhelm, 2000, "Cognitive Therapy for Obsessive-Compulsive Disorder," *Journal of Cognitive Psychotherapy*, 14, 245–260. Copyright © 2000 Springer Publishing Company, Inc., New York 10012; **158 Case Study:** From S.A. Falsetti &

H.S. Resnick, 2000, "Treatment of PSD Using Cognitive and Cognitive Behavioral Therapies," *Journal of Cognitive Psychotherapy*, 14, 261–285. Copyright © 2000 Springer Publishing Company, Inc., New York 10012; **162 Case Study:** From W.C. Sanderson & S.A. Rego, 2000, "Empirically Supported Treatment for Panic Disorder: Research, Theory, and Application for Cognitive Behavioral Therapy, *Journal of Cognitive Psychotherapy*, 14, 219–244. Copyright © 2000 Springer Publishing Company, Inc., New York 10012; **167 Case Study:** From W.C. Sanderson & S.A. Rego, 2000, "Empirically Supported Treatment for Panic Disorder: Research, Theory, and Application for Cognitive Behavioral Therapy, *Journal of Cognitive Psychotherapy*, 14, 219–244. Copyright © 2000 Springer Publishing Company, Inc., New York 10012; **166 Figure 7.2:** Reprinted from *Behavior Research and Therapy*, 24, D.M. Clark, "A Cognitive Approach to Panic," p. 463. Copyright © 1986, with permission from Elsevier; **173 Figure 7.3:** From Rita Carter, 1998, *Mapping the Mind*, Weidenfeld & Nicolson Publishing. Reproduced with permission from Moonrunner Design.

CHAPTER 8

180 Case Study: Reprinted from *Journal of Behavior Therapy and Experimental Psychiatry*, 16, L.S. Lyon, "Facilitating Telephone Number Recall in a Case of Psychogenic Amnesia," pp. 147–149. Copyright © 1985, with permission from Elsevier; **184 Case Study:** From J.H. Masserman, 1961, *Principles of Dynamic Psychiatry*, Second Edition, pp. 35–37. Copyright © 1961, with permission from Elsevier; **185, 186 Case Study:** From A. Martinez-Taboas & J.R. Rodriguez-Cay, 1997, "Case Study of Puerto Rican Woman with Dissociation Identity Disorder," *Dissociation*, 10, 141–147. Reprinted by permission; **189 Case Study:** Case Study from D. Simeon, S. Gross, O. Guralnik, D.J. Stein, J. Schmeidler & E. Hollander, 1997, "Feeling Unreal: 30 Cases of DSM-III-R Depersonalization Disorder," *American Journal of Psychiatry*, 154, pp. 1107–1113. Reprinted with permission from the *American Journal of Psychiatry*. Copyright © 1997 American Psychiatric Association; **194 Quote:** From J.R. Schwarz, 1981, *The Hillside Strangler: A Murderer's Mind*. Copyright © 1981 by Ralph B. Allison, M.D. and Ted R. Schwarz; **199 Case Study:** Reprinted with permission from *Somatoform and Factitious Disorders*. Copyright © 2001 American Psychiatric Association; **202 Case Study:** Copyright © 1997 from *Culture and Psychopathology: A Guide to Clinical Assessment*, by S.L. Chaplin, W.S. Tseng, & J. Streltzer (Eds.). Reproduced by permission of Routledge/Taylor & Francis Books, Inc.

CHAPTER 9

221, 222 Case Study: Case Study from J. Haythornthwaite, Johns Hopkins University, personal files. Reprinted by permission; **242 Figure 9.1:** From S. Cohen & G.M. Williamson, 1991, "Stress and Infectious Disease in Humans," *Psychological Bulletin*, 109, p. 8. Copyright © 1991 by the American Psychological Association. Reprinted with permission; **243 Figure 9.3:** From S. Cohen & G.M. Williamson, 1991, "Stress and Infectious Disease in Humans," *Psychological Bulletin*, 109, p. 8. Copyright © 1991 by the American Psychological Association. Reprinted with permission.

CHAPTER 10

245 Case Study: From Spitzer, R.L., Skodol, A.E., Gibbon, M., & Williams, J.B.W., 1983, *Psychopathology: A Case Book*. Copyright © 1983 The McGraw-Hill Companies. Reproduced with permission of The McGraw-Hill Companies; **246, 247 List:** Reprinted with permission from the *Diagnostic and Statistical Manual of Mental Disorders*, Text Revision, Copyright © 2000 American Psychiatric Association; **247, 248 List:** Reprinted with permission from the *Diagnostic and Statistical Manual of Mental Disorders*, Text Revision, Copyright © 2000 American Psychiatric Association; **248 Case Study:** From Spitzer, R.L., Skodol, A.E., Gibbon, M., & Williams, J.B.W., 1983, *Psychopathology: A Case Book*. Copyright © 1983 The McGraw-Hill Companies. Reproduced with permission of The McGraw-Hill Companies; **252 Case Study:** From Lawrence C. Kolb, *Modern Clinical Psychiatry*, Tenth Ed.; **262 List:** From E.S. Shneidman, 1992, "A Conspectus of the Suicidal Scenario," *Assessment and Prediction of Suicide*, R.W. Maris, A.L. Berman, & J.T. Maltsberger, & R.I. Yufit (Eds.), pp. 50–64. Copyright © 1992 by Guilford Publications, Inc. Reprinted by permission; **267, 268 Quote:** From J.E. Young, A.T. Beck & A. Weinberger, 1993, "Depression," in *Clinical Handbook of Psychological Disorders: A Step-by-Step Treatment Manual*, D.H. Barlow (Ed.), pp. 240–277. Copyright © 1993 by Guilford Publications, Inc. Reprinted by permission; **268 Figure 10.5:** From J.E. Young, A.T. Beck, & A. Weinberger, 1993, *Clinical Handbook of Psychological Disorders: A Step-by-Step Treatment Manual*, D.H. Barlow (Ed.), p. 250. Copyright © 1993 by Guilford Publications, Inc. Reprinted by permission; **270 Figure 10.6:** From B.L. Hankin, L.Y. Abramson, T.E. Moffitt, et al., 1998, "Development of Depression from Preadolescence to Young Adulthood: Emerging Gender Differences in a 10-Year Longitudinal Study," *Journal of Abnormal Psychology*, 107, pp. 128–140. Copyright © 1998 by the American Psychological Association. Reprinted with permission; **275 Figure 10.8:** From *Biological Psychiatry*, Vol. 48, by E. Frank, H.A. Swartz, & D.J. Kupfer, "Interpersonal and Social Rhythm Therapy: Managing the Chaos of Bipolar Disorder," p. 598. Copyright © 2000 with permission from the Society of Biological Psychiatry; **271 Figure 10.7:** From J.E. Gillham, L.H. Jaycox, K.J. Reivich, & M.E.P. Seligman, 1995, "Prevention of Depressive Symptoms in Schoolchildren: Two-Year Follow-Up," *Psychological Science*, 6, pp. 343–351. Reprinted by permission from Blackwell Publishing.

CHAPTER 11

286, 287 Case Study: Case Study from T.A. Widiger & C.J. Sanderson, 1997, "Personality Disorders," in *Psychiatry*, A. Tasman, J. Kay, & J.A. Lieberman (Eds.), Vol. 2, pp. 1304. Copyright © 1997 by the American Psychological Association. Reprinted with permission; **289 Case Study:** From A. Frances and R. Ross (Eds.). 1996, *DSM-IV Case Studies: A Clinical Guide to Differential Diagnosis*, pp. 288–289. Reprinted with permission from American Psychiatric Publishing, Inc. Copyright © 1996; **287, 290 List:** Reprinted with permission from the *Diagnostic and Statistical Manual of Mental Disorders*, Text Revision, Copyright © 2000 American Psychiatric Association; **293 Case Study:** Case Study from G.N. Conacher & R.L. Fleming, 1996, "The Extreme Regressive Reaction of Psychopath," *Psychiatric Quarterly*, 67, pp. 1–10; **298, 299 Case Study:** Copyright © 1990 from *DSM-III R Casebook of Treatment Selection*, by S. Perry, A. Francis, & J. Clarkin. Reproduced by permission of Routledge/Taylor & Francis Books, Inc.; **299, 301 Case Study:** Reprinted with permission from American Psychiatric Publishing, Inc. Copyright © 1994 American Psychiatric Association.

CHAPTER 12

312 Case Study: Case Study from S.M. Miller, 1995, "Case Studies: Profiles of Women Recovering from Drug Addiction," *Journal of Drug Education*, *25*(2), 139–148; **314 List:** Reprinted with permission from the *Diagnostic and Statistical Manual of Mental Disorders*, Text Revision, Copyright © 2000 American Psychiatric Association; **314 List:** Reprinted with permission from the *Diagnostic and Statistical Manual of Mental Disorders*, Text Revision, Copyright © 2000 American Psychiatric Association; **343 Case Study:** Case Study from S.W. Henggeler, S.G. Pickrel, M.J. Brondino, & J.L. Crouch, 1996, "Eliminating Treatment Dropout of Substance Abusing or Dependent Delinquents Through Home-Based Multisystemic Therapy," *American Journal of Psychiatry*, 153, 427–428. Reprinted with permission from the *American Journal of Psychiatry*. Copyright © 1996 American Psychiatric Association; **316 Table 12.1:** From O. Ray & C. Ksir, *Drugs, Society & Human Behavior*. Copyright © 1993 The McGraw-Hill Companies. Reproduced with permission of The McGraw-Hill Companies; **327 Figure 12.2:** Data from David Briscoe, "Cigarettes Losing Grip, Survey Finds," *Seattle Times* online edition, May 22, 2000. Reprinted with permission of The Associated Press; **334 Figure 12.4:** From F.H. Gawin & H.D. Kleber, 1986, "Abstinence Symptomatology and Psychiatric Diagnosis in Cocaine Abusers," *Archives of General Psychiatry*, *43*, pp. 107–113. Copyright © 1986 by the American Medical Association. Reprinted by permission.

CHAPTER 13

355 From *DSM-IV Casebook: A Learning Companion to the DSM-IV* (pp. 266–267), by R. L. Spitzer, M. Gibbon, A. E. Skodol, et al. (Eds.), 1994, Washington: D.C. American Psychiatric Press, Inc. Copyright © 1994 by American Psychiatric Association. Reprinted by permission; **360 Case Study:** Case Study from unpublished composite and altered clinical case histories from the files of Dr. Richard Carroll, Northwestern University Medical School, Chicago, Illinois; **362 Case Study:** Case Study from unpublished composite and altered clinical case histories from the files of Dr. Richard Carroll, Northwestern University Medical School, Chicago, Illinois; **363 Table 13.1:** Reprinted with permission from E.O. Laumann, et al., *The Social Organization of Sexuality: Sexual Practices in the United States*. Copyright ©1994 University of Chicago Press, Chicago, Illinois; **364 Table 13.2:** Reprinted with permission from E.O. Laumann, et al., *The Social Organization of Sexuality: Sexual Practices in the United States*. Copyright © 1994 University of Chicago Press, Chicago, Illinois; **364 Figure 13.1:** Reprinted with permission from E.O. Laumann, et al., *The Social Organization of Sexuality: Sexual Practices in the United States*. Copyright © 1994 University of Chicago Press, Chicago, Illinois; **372, 373 Case Study:** Reprinted with permission from American Psychiatric Publishing, Inc. Copyright © 1994 American Psychiatric Association; **386 Case Study:** Case Study from unpublished composite and altered clinical case histories from the files of Dr. Richard Carroll, Northwestern University Medical School, Chicago, Illinois.

CHAPTER 14

391 Case Study: Excerpt from *Is There No Place on Earth for Me?* By Susan Sheehan. Copyright © 1982 by Susan Sheehan. Reprinted by permission of Houghton Mifflin Company. All rights reserved; **394 Letter:** From M.E. Bleuler, 1950, *Dementia Praecox or the Group of Schizophrenia*, trans. J. Zinkin, p. 17. Madison CT: International Universities Press. Original work published in 1911. Reprinted by permission of International Universities Press; **395 Case Study:** From the clinical files of Dr. Richard L. Hagen, Florida State University. Reprinted by permission; **398 Case Study:** From the clinical files of Dr. Richard L. Hagen, Florida State University. Reprinted by permission; **400, 401 Case Study:** From G.K. Booth, 1995, "Outcome and Treatment Strategies," in *Treating Schizophrenia*, S. Vinogradov (Ed.), pp. 166–169. Copyright © 1995 John Wiley & Sons, Inc. This material is used by permission of John Wiley & Sons, Inc.; **402 Case Study:** From *ICD-10 Casebook: The Many Faces of Mental Disorders – Adult Case Histories According to ICD-10*, pp. 67–69, by T.B. Üstün, A. Bertelsen, H. Dilling, J. vanDrimmelen, C. Pull, A. Okasha, N. Sartorius, et al., 1996, Switzerland: World Health Organization. Copyright © 1996 by World Health Organization. Reprinted with permission; **402 Case Study:** Case Study from M. Flaum & S.K. Schultz, 1996, "When Does Amphetamine-Induced Psychosis Become Schizophrenia?" *American Journal of Psychiatry*, 106, pp. 812–813. Reprinted with permission from the *American Journal of Psychiatry*. Copyright © 1996 American Psychiatric Association; **405, 406 Case Study:** From *The Lanahan Cases and Readings in Abnormal Behavior*, Second Edition, by Kayla F. Bernheim. Copyright © 1997, 2004 by Lanahan Publishers, Inc. Reprinted by permission of Lanahan Publishers, Inc., Baltimore; **408 Figure 14.1:** From *Schizophrenia Genesis: The Origins of Madness*, by Irving I. Gottesman. Copyright © 1991 by Irving I. Gottesman. Used with permission of W.H. Freeman and Company; **412 List:** Reprinted with permission from *Psychology Today* magazine. Copyright © 1971 Sussex Publishers, Inc.; **415 Figure 14.2:** From "Schizophrenia and Season of Birth," by E. Hare, L. Bulusu, & A. Adelstein, 1979, *Population Trends*, 17. Adapted with permission of Office for National Statistics, London. © Crown Copyright; **425 Case Study:** From L. Sushinsky, 1970, "An Illustration of a Behavioral Therapy Intervention with Nursing Staff in a Therapeutic Role," *Journal of Psychiatric Nursing and Mental Health Services*, 8(5), p. 24. Reprinted with permission from Slack, Inc.; **431, 432 Case Study:** From the personal files of Dr. Glenn Smith, The Mayo Clinic. Reprinted by permission; **435 Case Study:** Reprinted with the permission of Simon & Schuster Adult Publishing Group from *The Man Who Mistook His Wife for a Hat and Other Clinical Tales*, by Oliver Sacks. Copyright © 1970, 1981, 1983, 1984, 1985 by Oliver Sacks. Reprinted with the permission of the Wylie Agency, Inc.; **437 Case Study:** Reprinted with permission from American Psychiatric Publishing, Inc. Copyright © 1994 American Psychiatric Association; **440 Figure 15.1:** From "The Worst Case," by M. Farber, December 1994, *Sports Illustrated*. Illustration by Paragraphics. Copyright © 1994 by Paragraphics; **450 Case Study:** From S.H. Zarit, 1992, "Concepts and Measures in Family Caregiving Research," in *Conceptual and Methodological Issues in Family Caregiver Research*, B. Bauer (Ed.), pp. 1–19. Reprinted by permission of the Faculty of Nursing, University of Toronto.

CHAPTER 16

448 Case Study: Reprinted by permission of the publisher from *The Golden Cage: The Enigma of Anorexia Nervosa*, by Hilde Bruch, Cambridge, MA: Harvard University Press, Copyright © 1978, 2001 by the President and Fellows of Harvard College; **458 Case Study:** Reprinted with permission from Dr. Christopher A. Kearney; **461 Case Study:** Reprinted with permission from Dr. Andrew R. Eisen; **463 Case Study:** Case Study from C.A. Kearney, 2003, *Casebook in Child Behavior Disorders*. Copyright © 2003 by Wadsworth Publishing Company, a division of Thomson Learning: www.thomsonrights.com. Fax 800-730-2215; **466 Case Study**: Reprinted with permission from Dr. Andrew R. Eisen.

CHAPTER 17

484 Case Study: Reprinted with permission from Dr. Christopher A. Kearney; **485 List:** Reprinted with permission from the *Diagnostic and Statistical Manual of Mental Disorders*, Text Revision, Copyright © 2000 American Psychiatric Association; **496, 497 Case Study:** Case Study from C.A. Kearney, 2003, *Casebook in Child Behavior Disorders*. Copyright © 2003 by Wadsworth Publishing Company, a division of Thomson Learning: www.thomsonrights.com. Fax 800-730-2215; **499 Figure 17.2:** From T.L. Kemper & M.L. Bauman, 1992, "Neuropathology of Infantile Autism," in *Neurobiology of Infantile Autism*, H. Naruse & E.M. Ornitz (Eds.), pp. 43–57. Reprinted by permission.

NAME INDEX

Aarts, P. G. H., 158
Abbott, P. J., 342
Abdelwahab, H. T., 316
Abed, R. T., 399
Abel, G. G., 374, 376, 379, 380, 381, 382, 383
Abel-Aty, M. A., 316
Abell, C. W., 345
Abelson, J. M., 390
Abikoff, H., 478
Abikoff, H. B., 482
Abraham, H. D., 336
Abraham, K., 269
Abramowitz, J. S., 168
Abramowitz, S. I., 385, 386
Abrams, G. M., 306
Abramson, A. Y., 263
Abramson, H., 477
Abramson, L. Y., 64, 65, 66, 91, 92, 144, 148, 250, 253, 255, 257, 261, 265, 266, 267, 270
Abukmeil, S. S., 413
Achenbach, T. M., 31, 459
Ackard, D. M., 378
Ackenheil, M., 279
Ackerman, P. T., 469
Acree, M., 219
Adams, H. E., 200, 201, 203, 204, 205, 206
Adams, L. W., 494
Adams, M. R., 235
Adams, S. G., Jr., 391
Adelman, H. S., 475
Adelstein, A., 415
Adkins, S., 276
Adler, A., 113
Adler, N. E., 236
Adler, R. H., 201
Agarwal, D. P., 345, 346
Agency for Health Care Policy and Research, 280, 281
Ageton, S. S., 465
Aggen, S. H., 317
Aggleton, J. P., 141
Agid, O., 67
Agnello, J. G., 476
Agras, W. S., 232
Agren, H., 277–278
Aguilar-Figueroa, E., 209
Aguilar-Gaxiola, S., 101
Ainsworth, M. D. S., 116
Airoldi, L., 455
Akbarian, S., 415
Akiskal, H. S., 246, 249, 252, 253
Akshoomoff, N. A., 498
Alavi, A., 265
al-Azzawi, 230–231
Albee, George, 17, 19
Albers, G. W., 444
Albert, M. C., 435
Alberts, S. C., 277
Aldrich, M. S., 474
Aleman, A., 414
Alessandri, M., 503
Alexander, B. K., 332
Alexander, C. N., 237
Alexopoulos, G. S., 99
Alfano, M. S., 92, 127
Alford, B. A., 88, 91, 94, 98, 266
Allderidge, P., 13, 14
Allen, A., 209
Allen, J. J., 413
Allen, J. J. B., 148, 188, 191
Allen, J. P., 117
Allen, M., 526
Allen, M. G., 273
Allen, N. B., 255, 256
Alloy, L. B., 64, 65, 66, 88, 91, 92, 140, 148, 247, 253, 255, 257, 261, 265, 266, 267, 270, 271
Allsworth, J., 163
Aloia, M., 88
Alpert, J. E., 279, 280
Alpert, M., 51
Alpher, V. S., 192
Alsobrook, J. P., III, 171, 173
Alter, J. G., 342
Alterman, A. I., 324, 340
Althof, S., 362
Altmann, J., 277
Altshuler, L. I., 277
Alvir, J. M. J., 399, 403
Amador, X. F., 397, 399
Aman, M. G., 507
American Academy of Child and Adolescent Psychiatry, 474
American Association on Mental Retardation (AAMR), 486
American Bar Association, 517
American Cancer Society, 225, 227
American Psychiatric Association, 6, 7, 29, 51, 198, 201, 212, 283, 287, 303, 329, 335, 357, 376, 383, 390, 472, 485, 493, 526
American Psychological Association, 62, 532, 535
American Sleep Disorders Association, 473
Amoroso, P. J., 316
Anders, T., 473
Andersen, H. F., 503
Andersen, N. B., 224
Andersen, S. M., 119, 120
Anderson, B. K., 325, 329
Anderson, B. P., 275
Anderson, C. M., 425
Anderson, E. M., 120
Anderson, E. R., 276–277
Anderson, N. B., 236
Anderson, S. W., 444
Anderson, V. E., 453
Anderton, B., 448
Andreasen, N. C., 37, 405, 413, 414
Andreski, P., 160
Andrews, B., 159, 161
Andrews, G., 476
Andrews, L. K., 469
Andron, L., 507
Andrysiak, T., 338
Aneshensel, C. S., 101, 102
Angst, J., 255
Anisman, H., 226
Annegers, J. F., 453
Annis, H. M., 325
Anthenelli, R. M., 347
Anthony, D., 379, 380, 381, 382
Anthony, J. C., 320, 338
Anthony, M. S., 222
Antoni, M. H., 230, 239
Antony, M. M., 47, 154, 155, 157
Appel, A. R., 520
Appelbaum, P., 526
Appelbaum, P. A., 523, 525, 527
Apter, J. T., 451
Araji, S., 376
Arango, V., 279
Armitage, R., 274
Armstead, C. A., 236
Arndt, S., 413
Arnold, L. E., 482
Arntz, A., 308
Aro, H. M., 260
Aromacki, A. S., 316
Aronson, E., 98, 99
Arrow, B. A., 255
Artiges, E., 247, 413
Ashe, J., 439
Ashenberg, Z. S., 329
Asmundson, G. J., 201
Assalian, P., 370
Asuni, T., 22–23
Atchison, M., 186, 188, 192
Athwal, B. S., 209
Atkinson, J. H., 437, 438
Attwood, A., 494
August, G. J., 497
Auh, S., 414
Austin, M. C., 417
Avenevoli, S., 250

Baare, W. F. C., 413
Babigian, H. M., 402
Babyak, M., 224
Bacellar, H., 437
Bach, V., 498
Bachevalier, J., 499
Bachman, J. G., 313, 326, 327
Backs-Dermott, B. J., 94, 95, 97
Baer, J. S., 322
Bagby, R. M., 207
Bagchi, B. K., 432
Baggett, L., 239
Bahramali, H., 142
Bahrke, M. S., 339
Bailey, A., 495, 496, 497, 498, 499
Bailey, C. E., 479
Bailey, E. D., 207
Bailey, M., 371
Bailine, S. H., 283
Baird, S. C., 70, 71
Baird, T. D., 497
Bakalar, J. B., 337, 338
Baker, B., 200, 222
Baker, C. B., 248
Baker, E. A., 233
Baker, F., 19
Baker, I., 399
Baker, J. E., 471
Baker, M. J., 98
Baldassano, C. F., 252
Baldessarini, R. J., 282
Ballenger, J. C., 167, 176
Balter, M. B., 174, 234, 333
Bandura, Albert, 81, 93, 238, 380
Bansal, S., 383
Bar, J. L., 131, 132, 134
Barbaree, H. E., 382
Barber, J. P., 97
Barch, D. M., 394, 395, 420
Bargh, J. A., 93, 120, 121
Barkley, R. A., 461, 462, 463, 477, 481, 482
Barlow, D. H., 47, 151, 168, 169, 171, 257, 380
Barnett, M. C., 200
Barnhardt, T. M., 202, 203
Baron, D., 322
Barona, A., 475
Baron-Cohen, S., 499
Barondes, S. H., 280, 281
Barongan, C., 378
Barrash, J., 444
Barratt, E. S., 292
Barrett, D. E., 489
Barrett, P., 478
Barrett, P. M., 478
Barrett, R. P., 508
Barrios, B. A., 477
Barrowclough, C., 422, 423, 424
Barrows, K. A., 213
Barry, M., 329
Barsky, A. J., 200, 207, 208
Barta, P. E., 414
Bartlett, J. A., 249
Bartrop, R. W., 218
Basco, M. R., 269
Basford, J. S., 441
Bashtawi, M., 455
Bass, E., 191
Bass, M. P., 446
Bateman, A., 304
Bateson, G., 127, 423
Bathgate, D., 447
Batieha, A., 455
Battaglia, F., 489
Battle, Y. I., 415
Baucom, D. H., 98
Bauer, M., 277
Bauer, V. K., 276
Bauman, M., 498, 499
Baumann, B., 276
Baumeister, R. F., 120, 294, 375
Bauserman, R., 187
Bax, M., 473
Bayon, C., 290
Beach, F. A., 385
Bean, L. L., 99
Beard, C. M., 445, 449, 469
Bearden, C. E., 412
Beautrais, A. L., 154
Beck, A. T., 60, 88, 90, 91, 94, 94–95, 98, 151, 164, 261, 266, 267, 268, 269, 306, 307, 422
Beck, J. C., 523
Beck, J. G., 95, 167, 360
Beck, N. C., 468
Beck, R., 168
Becker, J. V., 376
Becker, L., 216, 223
Becker, R. E., 534
Beckwith, L., 489
Beeder, A. B., 340
Beekman, A. T. F., 249
Beersma, D. G. M., 276
Beghi, E., 455
Behen, M., 498
Beidel, B. D., 143
Beiser, M., 405, 411
Bekker, M. H. J., 162, 163

Belanoff, J. K., 255
Belfer, M. L., 488
Bell, D. S., 334
Bell, J., 154
Bell, N. S., 316
Bellack, A. S., 399, 404, 405, 422, 426
Bellinger, D., 490
Bellivier, F., 273
Bellodi, L., 141
Belluck, P., 188, 190
Belsher, G., 249
Belter, R. W., 45
Belusu, L., 415
Bemporad, J. R., 269
Benazzi, F., 252
Benca, R. M., 274
Bender, D. S., 287, 296
Bender, L., 48
Bengston, V. L., 450
Benioff, L., 396
Benjamin, H., 383
Benkelfat, C., 411
Bennett, L. A., 204
Bennett, M. E., 323
Ben-Porath, Y. S., 46
Benson, B. A., 507
Benson, B. W., 442
Benson, D. F., 444, 445, 448, 451
Bentall, R. P., 267, 402
Bentler, P. M., 343, 372
Berchick, R. J., 261
Berenbaum, H., 392, 395, 397
Berg, S., 447
Bergdahl, S. K., 437
Berger, O. G., 490
Bergeron, C., 447, 449
Bergeron, S., 362
Bergler, E., 372
Berk, M., 273
Berlin, I., 146
Berliner, L., 376
Berman, A. L., 273
Berman, J. R., 360, 361
Berman, J. S., 477
Berman, L. A., 360, 361
Berman, R. M., 278
Bernheim, Hippolyte-Marie, 21
Berns, S. B., 62
Berns, S. D., 442
Bernstein, A., 292, 293
Bernstein, A. S., 420
Bernstein, D., 20
Berrettini, W., 481
Berrios, D. C., 228
Bersoff, D. M., 62, 63, 64
Bersoff, D. N., 62, 63, 64
Bertelsen, A., 402, 409
Bertrand, L. D., 195
Betancourt, L., 489
Bettelheim, B., 497
Betts, J., 448
Beutler, L. E., 27
Bianchi, K., 183, 194
Bickford, A. F., 215
Biederman, J., 172, 462, 463
Bifulco, A. T., 270
Bigler, E. D., 436
Bijl, R. V., 405
Bilder, R. M., 417
Billings, D. W., 219
Binder, R. L., 523, 526
Binet, A., 39
Bini, L., 283
Binik, Y. M., 362
Birchler, G. R., 343
Birmaher, B., 279, 468
Birnbaum, K., 291
Birt, A. R., 182, 183, 191
Bishop, G. D., 236
Bjorkland, D. F., 475
Black, D. N., 143
Black, D. W., 156, 260
Blackburn, I. M., 268, 269
Blackshaw, L., 381
Blackstone, W., 519
Blackwell, G., 426
Blaine, J., 341
Blair, C. D., 374
Blair, J., 292
Blairy, S., 317
Blanchard, E. B., 237
Blanchard, J. J., 399, 404, 405, 407
Blanchard, R., 373, 383
Bland, R. C., 156, 163
Blane, L., 374
Blaney, N. T., 229
Blanz, B., 403, 405
Blashfield, R. K., 33, 37
Blashko, C. A., 276
Blatt, S. J., 269
Blazer, D. G., 249, 272
Bleuler, E., 390, 392, 394, 396, 403, 407, 417
Bliss, E. L., 201
Bliss, E. W., 469
Bliss, R. E., 329
Blitch, C., 523
Blondis, T. A., 462
Bloom, J. R., 212
Blum, M. J., 450
Blumberg, H. P., 277
Blumenthal, J. A., 224, 240
Bobbitt, L., 182
Bobes, J., 153
Bockoven, J. S., 15, 16
Bodlund, O., 386
Boesen, E. H., 226
Bogerts, B., 276
Boggild, H., 220, 222, 234
Bohman, M., 208, 345
Bohus, M., 306
Boll, T. J., 448
Bolton, P., 487, 497, 499
Boltwood, M., 224
Bond, C. F., Jr., 317
Bongar, B., 533
Bonneau, R. H., 216, 219
Bonnie, R. J., 511, 515, 517, 526
Bonomo, Y., 316
Boocock, S. S., 476
Boon, S., 187
Booth, G. K., 400–401
Booth-Kewley, S., 223
Bootzin, R. R., 233, 234, 235, 473, 474
Borges, G., 257, 258, 259, 262
Borkovec, T. D., 154, 164, 165, 233
Borkowski, J. G., 492
Borman-Spurrell, E., 117
Bornstein, M. H., 489
Bornstein, R. F., 120, 269, 296, 299, 301
Borum, R., 515, 524, 526
Boscarino, J., 151, 158
Bosma, H., 222, 236
Bosquet, M., 491
Bostrum, A., 238
Botzer, M. C., 386
Bouchard, T. J., 134, 308
Bouman, T. K., 206
Bourassa, M. G., 212
Bourin, M., 69
Bourne, P. G., 332
Bouton, M. E., 169
Boutros, N. N., 338
Bovjberg, D. H., 237
Bower, G. H., 196
Bowers, M. B., Jr., 338
Bowers, W., 523
Bowlby, J., 116, 170, 269
Bowler, K., 277
Bowley, L., 164
Bowman, E. S., 201, 204
Boyce, P., 251
Boyce, T., 236
Boyd, J. H., 152
Boyd, J. L., 425
Boysen, G., 444
Bracha, H. S., 415, 428
Bradford, J. M. W., 382
Bradley, B. P., 93
Bradley, M. M., 150
Bradley, S. J., 384
Brady, J. V., 56
Braff, D. L., 93, 419, 420, 421
Bragulat, V., 247
Brakel, S. J., 518, 527
Brammer, M. J., 414
Branch, C. H., 469
Brand, B., 196
Brand, R. J., 223
Brandenburg, N. A., 459
Brandon, A., 329
Brandt, K. M., 317
Brannan, S. K., 277
Brantley, P. J., 220, 230, 231
Braswell, L., 478
Braver, T. S., 394
Brawman, M. O., 176
Bray, G. A., 231
Brebion, G., 397
Brecklin, L. R., 316
Brehm, N. M., 340
Breier, A., 404
Bremner, J. D., 197, 276–277, 279
Brendel, G., 199
Brener, J., 200
Brennan, K. A., 116, 117
Brennan, P., 412
Brennan, P. A., 413, 414, 524, 525
Brenner, C., 119
Brenner, C. B., 192
Brent, D. A., 279
Bresdin, L. B., 480
Breslau, N., 67, 158, 160
Breuer, J., 22, 204
Breuer, P., 165
Brewin, C. R., 159, 161, 422
Bridges, K., 206
Briesmeister, J. M., 479
Brill, L. B., 414
Brinkley, C. A., 292–293
Brion, S., 451
Broadwell, K. C., 242
Broadwell, S. D., 242
Brockington, I., 257, 258
Brodaty, H., 251
Brodsky, N., 489
Brody, A. L., 142, 277
Broman, S., 492
Bromberg, W., 512
Bromet, E., 161
Bromet, E. J., 399
Bron, B., 270
Brondino, M. J., 343, 514
Brook, J. S., 257
Brookoff, D., 342
Brooks, P. J., 317
Brooks-Gunn, J., 492
Broskowski, A., 19
Brower, K. J., 339
Brown, A., 151
Brown, A. S., 415
Brown, G., 261
Brown, G. W., 91, 92, 255, 270
Brown, H. N., 204
Brown, J., 302
Brown, L. L., 174
Brown, L. S., 308
Brown, P., 438
Brown, P. C., 235
Brown, R. P., 279
Brown, S. A., 343, 344
Brown, T. A., 151, 367
Browne, A., 377
Brownell, K. D., 88, 231, 232, 344
Browning, Elizabeth Barrett, 205
Bruce, M. L., 64, 99, 266–267
Bruce, S. E., 175
Bruch, H., 470
Bruch, M. A., 153
Bruder, G. E., 142
Bryan, J., 475
Bryan, T., 475
Bryant, B., 159, 161
Bryant, R. A., 161, 167, 180
Bryson, S. E., 494
Buch, G., 505
Buchanan, R. W., 404, 405, 411
Buchbaum, M. S., 290
Bucholz, K. K., 346
Buchsbaum, M. S., 274, 414
Buckner, R. L., 142, 143
Budd, M. A., 208
Budney, A. J., 85, 342
Buikhuisen, M., 162
Buka, S. L., 412
Bulik, C. M., 70
Bullmore, E. T., 397
Bullock, R., 451
Bullough, B., 383
Bullough, V. L., 383
Bundy, Ted, 294
Bunney, W. E., Jr., 414
Burge, D., 116, 249
Burgess, A. W., 376
Burgus, P., 188, 190
Burke, J. D., Jr., 151, 157, 249, 250, 340
Burke, K. C., 151, 157, 249, 250, 340
Burnam, A., 18
Burns, D. D., 97
Burt, R. A., 520
Bush, Barbara, 452
Bush, George H. W., 452
Bushman, B., 317
Bustillo, J., 425, 427
Butcher, J. N., 46, 47
Butler, J. L., 375
Butler, L. D., 186, 187
Butzlaff, R. L., 264
Buvat, J., 360
Buvat-Herbaut, M., 360
Buydens-Branchey, 346
Buysse, D. J., 274
Bylsma, F. W., 447, 449

Byrne, M., 412
Byron, Lord, 254

Caballo, V. E., 369
Cadenhead, K. S., 421
Cadoret, R., 291, 293
Cadoret, R. J., 345
Caesar, Julius, 454
Caetano, R., 319–320
Cain, J. W., 280
Calderbank, S., 200
Calderon, R., Jr., 237
Calhoun, G. B., 297
Califf, R. M., 236
Cameron, L. D., 240
Campbell, F., 491
Campbell, M., 498, 504
Campbell, V. L., 45
Campbell, W. K., 297
Candilis, P. J., 162
Canino, G. J., 156, 163
Cannon, M., 414
Cannon, T. D., 412, 413, 421
Cannon, W. B., 214, 217
Cantwell, D. P., 482
Capitano, J. P., 230
Capps, L., 494
Carels, R. A., 224
Carey, G., 134
Carey, M. P., 368
Carey, T. S., 323
Carlson, D. C., 498
Carlson, G. A., 468
Carlsson, A., 137, 416
Carnegie Corporation, 490, 491, 492
Caron, S. L., 372
Carpenter, L. L., 256
Carr, A., 187
Carr, J., 487
Carroll, K. M., 325
Carroll, M. E., 345
Carroll, R. A., 385
Carson, R. C., 29, 400, 402, 403, 404, 405, 409, 416, 424
Carter, C. S., 394, 413, 420
Carter, R. M., 154
Carter, S. R., 68
Cartier, J., 527
Caruso, D., 41
Cascardi, M., 521, 527
Cascino, G. D., 455
Case, W. G., 174, 174–175
Cashman, L., 473
Cassano, G. B., 157, 252, 257
Cassidy, J., 270
Casson, I. R., 440
Castelloe, P., 494
Castillo, Richard J., 5, 7, 192
Castillo-Richmond, A., 237
Castle, D. J., 404, 405
Catalano, R. F., 466
Cate, T., 273
Catts, S. V., 421
Cautela, J. R., 341
Cavallin, H., 377
Cecero, J. J., 301
Cecil, K. M., 413
Centers for Disease Control and Prevention, 216, 225, 228, 259
Cercy, S. P., 447, 449
Cerundolo, P., 523
Chabot, R. J., 142
Chadwick, P. D. J., 422
Chaiyasit, W., 2, 480
Chambless, D. L., 98, 163, 534
Chan, K. K., 346
Chang, J., 151, 158
Chang, L., 333, 348
Chang, S. H., 46
Channabasavanna, S. M., 206
Chantarujikapong, S. I., 171, 172
Chaplin, S. L., 202, 204
Chapman, D., 280
Chapman, J., 396
Chapman, Jean P., 407, 413
Chapman, Loren J., 407, 413
Chapman, T. F., 171
Charcot, J., 197
Charcot, Jean-Martin, 21, 203
Charney, D. S., 197
Chase-Lansdale, P. L., 492
Chavez-Ibarra, G., 209
Chee, M., 220
Chemtob, C. M., 159
Chen, Annabel, 436
Chen, C. C., 226
Chen, Desmond, 436
Chen, R., 420
Chen, W. J., 405
Chen, Y. C., 346
Chen, Y. R., 248
Chesney, M. A., 219, 236, 242
Chiarugi, Vincenzo, 14
Chilcoat, H. D., 67, 158
Chistyakov, A., 283
Chiu, H. F., 480
Chodorow, Nancy, 112
Christenfeld, N., 238
Christensen, A., 86, 87, 88
Christensen, B. K., 420
Christensen, H., 182
Christenson, G. A., 300
Christian, L., 492
Christiansen, B. A., 343, 344
Christoffel, H., 374
Christophersen, E. R., 472, 477
Chugani, D. C., 498
Chugani, H., 491
Chung, M. C., 492
Chute, D. L., 176
Cisin, I. H., 333
Clance, P. R., 319
Clancy, S. A., 190, 193, 195
Clark, B. S., 494
Clark, D. A., 88, 91, 164, 266
Clark, D. M., 164, 165, 166, 167, 168, 206, 208
Clark, G. N., 504
Clark, L., 248
Clark, L. A., 257
Clarke, G. N., 271
Clarkin, J. F., 295, 299
Clarkson, T. B., 222, 235
Classen, C., 161
Claussen, B., 319
Clavin, M., 156
Cleckley, H. M., 290–291, 292, 293
Cleghorn, J. M., 396
Clements, C. M., 266, 267
Clementz, B. A., 411, 413, 420
Clenet, F., 69
Clifford, J. J., 135
Clinthorne, J. K., 333
Cloitre, M., 296, 302
Cloninger, C. R., 148, 208, 290, 345, 349
Clotre, M., 171
Clum, G. A., 166
Coates, T. J., 228
Cobb, A. M., 208
Cobb, S. C., 224
Coccaro, E. F., 309
Coeytaux, R. R., 200
Coffey, C., 316
Coffman, G. A., 34
Cohen, B., 205
Cohen, B. A., 437
Cohen, B. D., 393–394
Cohen, D., 283
Cohen, D. B., 395
Cohen, H. L., 347
Cohen, J., 464, 468
Cohen, J. D., 394
Cohen, L. S., 249
Cohen, M., 380
Cohen, N. L., 16, 17
Cohen, P., 99, 257, 287, 302, 464, 468
Cohen, S., 212, 215, 216, 241, 329, 338
Cohen, Sheldon, 211, 215, 243
Cohn, S. M., 442
Coie, J. D., 466
Colby, S. M., 344
Cole, C. M., 384
Cole, D. A., 266, 267, 468
Cole, S. W., 239
Coleman, M., 494, 495, 498, 500
Coleman, M. J., 413
Columbus, Christopher, 437
Combs, B. J., 332
Combs, D., 398
Combs, D. R., 397
Comer, S. D., 345
Compas, B. E., 468
Conacher, G. N., 293
Conduct Problems Prevention Research Group, 466
Cone, J. D., 50
Conger, J. J., 341
Conklin, H. M., 410
Conner, K. R., 261
Conte, J. R., 376
Cook, C. S., 342
Cook, Frederick, 275
Cook, M., 163, 169
Cooke, D. J., 303
Coolidge, F. L., 308
Cools, J., 232
Coons, P. M., 182, 184, 188, 192, 193
Cooper, B., 151
Cooper, E. B., 476
Cooper, J. E., 36
Cooper, R. S., 236
Cooper, S. H., 120
Cooper, Z., 255
Copeland, J., 345
Corbitt, E. M., 296, 298, 302
Corcoran, R., 402
Corder, E. H., 447
Cornblatt, Barbara A., 418, 419, 420
Cororve, M. B., 199, 208
Correddu, G., 157
Corrigan, J. D., 441
Corrigan, P. W., 399
Corruble, E., 146
Coryell, W., 203, 205, 246, 252, 255, 273
Cossette, S., 212
Costa, E., 172
Costa, P. T., 83, 287, 303
Costantino, G., 51
Costello, C. G., 249
Council for Exceptional Children, 475
Courchesne, E., 498
Couture, E. G., 476
Coverdale, J. H., 419
Cowell, P. E., 413
Cowen, E. L., 19
Cowley, G., 326, 329
Cox, B. J., 152, 162
Cox, C., 261
Cox, D. N., 524
Coyne, J. C., 127, 216, 263, 267, 270
Crabbe, J., 135
Crago, M., 471
Craighead, L. W., 232
Craighead, W. E., 88, 89, 93–94, 266
Cramer, G., 409
Cramer, P., 120
Cramer, V., 302
Craske, M. G., 162
Craw, P., 433
Crick, N. R., 464
Crisp, A. H., 143
Crits-Christoph, P., 120, 121, 170, 341, 534
Cromwell, R. L., 411
Cronkite, R. C., 255
Crossette, B., 481
Crossfield, A. G., 271
Croughan, J., 37
Crow, T. J., 404
Crowe, R. R., 171
Cruess, D. G., 228, 230
Csikszentmihalyis, M., 36, 124
Cuellar, I., 51
Cueva, J. E., 504
Cullen, William, 151
Culley, C. C., 370
Cumming, G. F., 381
Cummings, C., 344
Cummings, J. L., 143, 435, 444, 445, 448, 449, 451
Cunningham-Rathner, J., 374, 376
Curran, C. E., 421
Curry, S., 329
Curtis, J., 170
Cushman, P., 19
Cusin, C., 252
Cuthbert, B. N., 150
Cutler, N. L., 276
Cutter, J., 224
Cutting, L. P., 423
Cyranowski, J. M., 250

Dadds, M. R., 168, 478
Dager, S. R., 142
Dagher, A., 348
Dahmer, Jeffrey, 294, 375
Dain, N., 16
Dakof, G., 216
Dale, K., 120
Daley, S. E., 249
Dalton, S. O., 226
Damasio, A. R., 444
d'Amato, T., 411
Danner, D. D., 124
Dansky, B. S., 158, 160
Daoud, A. S., 455
Darley, J. M., 514
Darwin, Charles, 110
Dashiell, R., 191
Daskalakis, Z. J., 420
Davenport, A., 322
Davey, G. C. L., 169

David, A., 397, 398
David, A. S., 226, 396
Davidson, J., 95
Davidson, J. R., 176
Davidson, J. R. T., 161, 167
Davidson, K., 239, 308
Davidson, L., 397, 399
Davidson, R. J., 140, 144, 148, 215
Davidson, R. T., 160, 167
Davis, D. D., 268
Davis, D. M., 412
Davis, G. C., 160
Davis, J. M., 277
Davis, J. O., 409, 415, 428
Davis, K. L., 295, 308, 416
Davis, Laura, 191
Davis, M. C., 223, 235
Davis, M. K., 187
Davis, P. J., 402
Davis, R. D., 297, 298, 305
Davis, R. T., 37
Davis, S. M., 40
Davison, E., 27
Dawkins, R., 465
Dawson, G., 494, 495, 498, 499, 500
Dawson, M. E., 419
Dawson, M. F., 421
Day, K., 493, 503
Deakin, J. F. W., 172–173
Dean, A., 499
Dean, B., 433
Dean, L., 433
Debakey, S. F., 317
DeBattista, C., 277
DeBeurs, E., 162
Debomoy, D. K., 276
DeBurger, J. E., 294
DeCaria, C., 300
De Castillo, J., 51
Deckersbach, T., 198
Deeg, D. J. H., 249
DeFries, J. C., 131, 132, 133
DeHart, D. D., 294
Deich, J., 238
DeJong, J., 317
de Jong, P. J., 169, 207
Delacourte, A., 448
Delaney, D. D., 85, 342
Delanty, D. L., 167
Deldin, P. J., 408, 411, 414, 416, 421
Delgado, P. L., 138, 278, 279
DeLisi, L. E., 393, 395, 404, 413
DeLong, R. G., 497, 499
DeLongis, A. D., 216
Demeff, L. A., 306
Demm, S. R., 441
Dennehy, E. B., 251, 252, 257
Dennis, D., 526
Deppe, M., 144
DeRubeis, R. J., 97, 168, 268, 269, 271, 280, 281, 534
de Sade, Marquis, 375
Descartes, René, 213
de Silva, P., 156
de Souza, W. R., 226
D' Esposito, M., 433
Destun, L. M., 191, 193
Deutsch, A., 13
Devanand, D. P., 181, 197, 283
Devor, E. J., 345
De Vos, N., 382
de Waal, F., 514
Dhabhar, F. S., 215
Dhawan, S., 377
Diamond, R. J., 526
Diaz, S. F., 204
Di Cara, L., 237
Dick, D. D., 346
Dickey, B., 17, 18
Dickstein, S., 256
Didden, R., 505
Diehl, S. R., 408, 410
Dietrich, K. N., 490
Dietz, P. E., 294
Dikman, S., 439
DiLalla, D. L., 134
Dilling, H., 402
Dilsaver, S. C., 248
Dimatou, S., 189
Dimeff, L. A., 88, 342
di Michele, F., 142
Dimidjian, S., 263, 264
Dingemans, P. M., 422
Dishion, T. J., 463, 477
Disney, E. R., 489
Dix, Dorothea, 15–16
Dixon, J. F., 469
Dixon, L. B., 427
Dobson, K. S., 94, 95, 97, 264, 266, 269
Docherty, J. P., 417
Docherty, N. M., 393, 394, 420, 423
Docter, R. F., 372
Dodge, K. A., 464
Dodge, K. H., 307
Dodrill, C. B., 455
Doerfler, L. A., 329
Doering, S., 405
Dohrenwend, B. P., 6, 99
Dolan, B., 480
Dolan, R. J., 392
Dolan, R. T., 287, 296
Dolberg, O. T., 173
Doleys, D. M., 472, 477
Dombrowski, S. M., 499
Donaldson, Kenneth, 511
Donenberg, G. R., 461
Dorahy, M. J., 184, 185, 195, 196
Dorfman, J. H., 415
Dornelas, E. A., 67
Dosajh, N. L., 41
Dosen, A., 503
Dostoyevsky, Fyodor, 454
Douglas, K. S., 523, 524, 528, 529
Dowdall, G. W., 322
Down, Langdon, 487
Downie, F., 154, 155, 157
Doyle, J., 269
Doyle, M. D., 488
Doyle, W. J., 241
Dozois, D. J. A., 94, 95, 97, 266
Draeger, B., 144
Draguns, J. G., 33
Draijer, N., 187
Drake, R., 120
Dreher, H. M., 228
Dreser, Heinrich, 330–331
Dressler, W. W., 224
Drukteinis, A. M., 294
Drummond, P. D., 237
Druss, B. G., 249
Dryden, W., 207
Du, Z., 276
Dubbert, P. M., 221
Dube, S., 277
Duberstein, P. R., 261
Dubo, E. D., 296
Dubovsky, S. L., 138
Duckworth, M. P., 200, 201, 203, 204, 205, 206
Duda, K., 422
Dufresne, R. G., Jr., 203
Duker, P. C., 505
Dulmus, C. N., 11
Duman, R. S., 278, 279
Duncan, C. C., 428
Duncan, W. C., Jr., 276
Dunkel-Schetter, C., 238
Dunn, M., 498
Dunner, D. L., 135
Dunst, C. J., 503
DuPaul, G. J., 462, 481, 482
Dura, J. R., 218, 450
Duran, R. E. F., 186, 187
Durand, V. M., 496, 502, 503
Durham, M. L., 522
Durkheim, Emile, 272
Durlack, J. A., 19
Durrant, J. E., 474
Duster, T., 146
du Toit, 300
Dworkin, B. R., 237
Dworkin, R. H., 404, 409, 419, 420
Dyck, M. J., 267
Dykens, E. M., 485, 490, 493, 500
Dykman, R. A., 469

Eales, M. J., 91
Eames, P., 209
Earnst, K. S., 404
Eaton, W. W., 99, 152, 153, 163, 399
Eaves, L. J., 247
Echeagaray-Wagner, F., 320
Eckert, S. L., 423, 424
Edell, W. S., 334
Edwards, B. K., 226
Edwards, C. L., 237
Edwards, K. J., 472
Egeland, J. A., 272, 273
Ehlers, A., 159, 161, 165, 167
Ehlers, C. L., 274
Ehrnst, A. C., 437
Eiben, L. A., 473
Eisen, A. R., 468, 479
Eisen, S. A., 347
Eisenberg, M., 527
Eisenberger, N. I., 228
Ekenstam, C., 526
Ekselius, L., 298
Eliashopf, B. A., 201
Elkin, I., 272, 281
Elkins, T. E., 503
Ellason, J. W., 193
Elliot, G. R., 295
Elliott, D. M., 190
Elliott, D. S., 465
Elliott, R., 126
Ellis, Albert, 89, 91, 94, 95, 365
Ellis, S. P., 249
Elmer-De Witt, P., 359
El-Saadi, O., 414
Elzinga, B. M., 187
Emerson, Ralph Waldo, 163
Emery, R. D., 520, 528
Emmelkamp, P. M. G., 88
Emory, L. E., 384
Emslie, G. J., 274
Endicott, J., 37, 252
Engel, B. T., 215
Engle-Friedman, M., 233
Engler, L. B., 468
Ennis, B. J., 520, 528
Enserink, M., 438
Epel, E. S., 232
Epstein, L. H., 70
Epstein, R. L., 224
Eranen, J., 216, 223
Erber, R., 167
Erdberg, P., 44
Erdelyi, M. H., 109, 120
Erickson, P. E., 526
Erikson, Erik, 113, 114–115
Eriksson, I., 237
Erlich, J., 106
Ernesto, C., 451
Ernst, D., 267
Ernst, M., 498
Eronen, M., 525
Erwin, R. J., 420
Eslinger, P. J., 444
Espie, C. A., 237
Esquirol, Jean, 14
Essau, C. A., 163
Estes, L. S., 471
Esteves, F., 164, 172
Estrad, C. R., 370
Evans, D. D., 266
Evans, D. L., 229
Evans, J. D., 406
Evans, Margiad, 455
Evans, M. D., 97, 268
Everson, S. A., 223
Ewart, C. K., 236
Ewen, D., 433
Exner, J. E., 41, 44
Ey, S., 468
Eyde, L. D., 27
Eysenck, H. J., 172, 226

Fabian, W. D., Jr., 337
Fabrega, H., 34
Fairburn, C. G., 127, 479
Fallon, B. A., 200, 209
Falloon, I. R. H., 419, 425
Falsetti, S. A., 158, 168
Fals-Stewart, W., 342, 343
Fama, J. M., 207
Famularo, R., 469
Fancher, R. E., 22
Fanous, A., 404
Farabaugh, A. H., 279, 280
Farabee, D., 527
Faraone, S. V., 405, 410, 463
Farberow, N. L., 258, 262
Farde, L., 416
Farlow, M., 449
Farmer, M. E., 5
Farrington, D. P., 10
Farrison, G. P., Jr., 335
Fauman, M. A., 373, 437
Faustman, W. O., 416
Fava, J. L., 229
Fava, M., 280
Faw, G., 505
Fawzy, F. L., 227, 239, 240–241
Fawzy, N. W., 227, 239, 240–241
Faykus, S., 475
Feasley, D., 229
Feeney, N. C., 159, 160, 167
Feigon, S. A., 131, 132, 134
Fein, D., 499
Feingold, A., 303
Feinstein, S., 200, 209
Felce, D., 502
Feldman, J., 191
Feldman, J. M., 187
Feldman, M. D., 187
Feldman, R. S., 136, 137, 138, 140, 144, 145

Felton, R. H., 474
Fenichel, Otto, 269, 364–365, 379
Fennig, S., 410
Fenton, B. T., 273
Fenton, T., 469
Fenton, W. S., 399, 400, 402, 405
Ferguson, M. J., 93, 120, 121
Ferguson, S. A., 69
Fergusson, D. M., 154, 464, 466
Ferris, S. H., 450
Ferster, C. B., 263
Fetter, M., 460
Filion, D. L., 421
Finch, J. R., 257
Fine, C. G., 197
Finkelhor, D., 187, 376, 377
Finkelson, L., 378
Finkelstein, J. R. J., 421
Finn, C. T., 171
Finn, P. R., 317
Finn, S. E., 27
Finney, J. W., 325
Fiocco, A. J., 69
Firoe, M. C., 329
First, M. B., 34
Fischer, E. H., 67
Fischer, M., 463
Fisher, E. B., Jr., 329
Fisher, L., 238
Fisher, M. M., 162, 205
Fisher, P., 258, 260, 261
Fisher, S., 121
Fishkin, S. M., 337
Fishman, H. C., 479, 480
Fiske, S. T., 92, 94
Fitch, W. L., 517
Flament, M., 283
Flaum, M., 402–403, 405, 413
Fleiss, J. L., 33
Fleming, D. T., 385, 386
Fleming, J. E., 187
Fleming, R. L., 293
Fletcher, J. M., 475
Fletcher, K. E., 469
Fletcher, M. A., 237
Flint, A. J., 163
Florencio, P. S., 411
Flor-Henry, P., 209, 379
Flory, K., 300
Flykt, A., 164, 172
Flynn, C., 266, 270
Foa, E. B., 159, 160, 161, 167, 170, 176
Foege, W. H., 212
Fogg, L. F., 276
Folkman, S., 120, 214, 219, 238
Follette, V., 87
Follette, W. C., 28, 32, 33, 34, 81, 82, 87, 88, 97
Folstein, S., 497
Fonagy, P., 304
Foote, J., 313
Ford, C. V., 204
Forde, D. R., 161
Foreyt, J. P., 471
Forman, L., 27
Forman, R., 27
Forness, S. R., 87
Forsyth, R. P., 224
Fortmann, S. P., 328
Foster, C., 229
Foucault, M., 13, 16
Fountain, N. B., 455
Fowler, D., 422
Fowles, D. C., 148
Fox, B. H., 227
Fox, H. C., 336
Fox, N. A., 215
Fox, T., 478
Frances, A., 34, 289, 299, 417
Francis, M., 240
Franco, S., 396
Frank, D. A., 489
Frank, E., 250, 256, 268, 272, 274, 275, 278, 280, 281
Frankel, E. H., 186
Frankenburg, F. R., 296
Frankl, Viktor, 9, 126
Franklin, George, 190
Frantz, C., 167
Fraser, D., 426
Frasure-Smith, N., 212
Freedman, D. X., 16, 451
Freeman, A., 306, 307
Freeman, D. H., Jr., 241
Freeman, H., 307
Freeston, M. H., 168
French, E., 18
French, S. A., 232
Fresco, D. M., 152, 153, 164, 167, 255, 267
Freud, Anna, 108, 109
Freud, Sigmund, 22, 58, 106, 107, 108, 109, 110, 111–113, 114, 117, 118, 121, 122, 176, 192, 201, 204, 205, 269, 281, 364, 379
Freund, K., 383
Frick, P. J., 465, 466
Frieboes, R. M., 277
Fried, D., 120
Friedhoff, L. T., 451
Friedman, A. S., 316
Friedman, B. H., 154, 164
Friedman, H. S., 223, 242
Friedman, J. H., 399
Friedman, L., 411, 413
Friedman, M., 223
Friedman, R. M., 459
Friedman, S., 163
Friesen, W. V., 124
Frith, C., 392, 397
Frith, U., 494
Fritze, G., 345, 346
Fromm, Erich, 122
Frommann, N., 399
Fromm-Auch, D., 209
Frosch, W. A., 336
Frost, L. E., 511
Frost, R. O., 155, 156
Frye, M. A., 277
Fucetola, R., 417
Fukuzaki, S., 182
Fukuzako, H., 182
Fukuzako, T., 182
Fulero, S. M., 515
Fulton, F. M., 523
Furby, L., 381
Furmark, T., 298
Fyer, A. J., 171, 173, 257

Gabbard, G. O., 304
Gabrielli, W. F., Jr., 340
Gacy, John Wayne, 294
Gaebel, W., 399
Gage, Phineas P., 440–441
Gagnon, F., 168
Gagnon, J. H., 359, 360, 361, 362, 363, 364, 365, 377
Galasko, D., 447
Galderisi, S., 405
Galen, L. W., 344
Galilei, Galileo, 213
Gallagher, T. J., 390
Gallop, R., 341
Garb, H. N., 35, 36, 37, 44, 45, 51
Garber, H. L., 490
Garber, J., 266, 270
Garbutt, J. S., 323
Garcia, M. E., 329
Gardner, C., 404
Gardner, C. O., 250, 256
Gardner, Howard, 40
Gardner, W., 522
Garety, P. A., 422
Garland, A., 269
Garland, Judy, 332
Garrett, V. D., 220, 231
Garrison, C. Z., 157
Garssen, B., 162
Garvey, A. J., 329
Garvey, M. J., 162
Gath, A., 504
Gatto, C. P., 337
Gatz, M., 447, 450
Gawin, F. H., 334
Gaynor, S. T., 70, 71
Gearon, J. S., 399, 404, 405
Gebhard, P. H., 377
Gee, T. L., 187, 191, 193
Geerlings, S. W., 249
Gelder, M., 85
Gelenberg, A. J., 175, 417
Gelfand, L. A., 269, 281
Geller, B., 250
Geller, P. A., 157
Gelman, D., 281
Gemar, M. C., 93, 266
Gentz, B. A., 237
George, L. K., 241
George, M. S., 283, 284
George, W. H., 317
Gerald, J., 279
Gerbasi, J. B., 526
Gerhard, D. S., 273
Gerin, W., 238
Gerlach, A. L., 153
Gershuny, B. S., 180, 189
Gershwin, George, 432–433
Gessner, T., 91, 93, 164, 168
Geyer, M. A., 419, 420
Ghaziuddin, M., 498
Ghisalbert, D. O., 189
Giancola, P. R., 317
Gibb, B. E., 266
Gibbon, M., 245, 248, 301, 355
Gibbons, E. W., 251, 252, 257
Gibbs, N. A., 154, 156
Gibson, M. G., 402
Gidycz, C. A., 187
Giesler, R. B., 92, 94, 263–264
Gil, K. M., 200, 207, 208, 209
Giles, D. E., 274
Gilford, P., 19
Gill, M., 43, 273
Gill, M. J., 503
Gillberg, C., 481, 494, 495, 497, 498, 500
Gillham, J. E., 124, 270, 271
Gilligan, Carol, 112
Gillin, J. C., 274
Ginsberg, G. L., 37
Ginsburg, G. S., 479
Ginzburg, K., 164
Gipson, M. T., 204
Girdler, S. S., 225, 236, 242
Girgus, J. S., 250
Gitlin, M. J., 252
Givelber, D. J., 523
Gjedde, A., 416
Gladsjo, J. A., 399
Gladstone, T. R., 468
Glantz, L. A., 414
Glanz, L. M., 265
Glaser, B., 297
Glaser, R., 212, 216, 219, 240
Glasgow, R. E., 328
Glassman, A. H., 329
Glassman, K., 316
Glassman, N. S., 119
Gleaves, D. H., 187, 188, 199, 208
Glod, C. A., 276
Glucksman, M. L., 118
Gnagy, E. M., 463
Gnys, M., 329
Goedde, H., 345
Goedde, H. W., 345, 346
Goethe, J. W., 67
Goffman, Erving, 16, 522
Gold, S. R., 316
Goldberg, B., 120
Goldberg, D. L., 517
Goldberg, D. P., 206
Goldberg, J. F., 255
Goldberg, M. A., 203
Goldenberg, I., 153, 175
Goldgaber, D., 446
Goldman, M. S., 343, 344
Goldman, R. S., 417
Goldsmith, H. H., 288, 290, 308
Goldsmith, S. K., 416
Goldstein, A., 347
Goldstein, I., 370
Goldstein, I. B., 224
Goldstein, J. M., 405
Goldstein, M. J., 127, 419, 422, 423, 424
Goldstein, R. B., 260
Goldstin, M., 482
Gollan, J. K., 264, 269
Gomberg, E. S., 319
Gonsiorek, J. C., 358
Gooding, D. C., 413
Goodkin, K., 229
Goodman, J., 478
Goodman, W., 171, 173
Goodrick, G. K., 471
Goodwin, 227, 273
Goodwin, D. W., 320, 340, 345, 346
Goodwin, G. M., 248
Goodwin, P. J., 227
Goodyer, I. M., 250, 460
Gordiner, S. W., 393
Gordon, J. R., 325, 329, 344
Gore, D. K., 381
Gorman, J. M., 168, 173
Gortner, E. T., 264, 269
Gotham, H. J., 346
Gotlib, I., 164
Gotlib, I. A., 127
Gotlib, I. H., 88, 264
Gottesman, I., 497
Gottesman, I. I., 134, 393, 394, 408, 409, 410, 420, 427
Gottheil, E., 227
Gottman, J. M., 57
Gould, J., 494
Gould, M. S., 258, 259, 260, 261, 262, 263, 272
Gould, R., 203
Gounis, K., 526
Gournay, K., 207
Gowda, M., 240, 241
Grabe, H., 180
Grace, A. A., 416

Gracon, S. I., 449
Graham, D. T., 214
Graham, J. R., 45, 46, 47
Gramzow, R., 297
Granger, R. H., 489
Granholm, E., 421
Grant, B. F., 314, 317
Grant, E., 412
Grant, I., 437, 438, 439
Grant, K. E., 468
Grantham-McGregor, S., 490
Gray, J. A., 148
Graziottin, A., 362
Green, B. L., 475
Green, M. F., 399, 417
Green, R., 384, 385, 386
Greenberg, L. S., 126
Greenberg, M. D., 88, 93–94
Greenberg, R. P., 121
Greenblatt, D. J., 174, 234
Greenhouse, J. B., 281
Greenslade, K. E., 463
Greenwald, D., 427
Greenwald, E., 377
Greenwald, S., 249
Greenwood, G. L., 313, 319
Greenwood, K. M., 234
Gregg, A. P., 164
Greiner, L. H., 124
Greist, J. H., 176
Grenyer, B. F. S., 120
Grewen, K., 236
Griffin, M. G., 189
Griffin, S. L., 441
Grigorenko, E. L., 40
Grim, V., 414
Grimes, K. E., 412
Grinspoon, L., 337, 338
Grisso, T., 524
Gronfein, W. P., 99
Gronwall, D., 439
Gross, J. J., 225
Gross, L., 232
Gross, R. C., 155
Gross, S., 189, 192
Grossarth-Maticek, R., 226
Grosscup, S. J., 267
Grossman, F. K., 189
Grossman, R., 300
Groth, A. N., 376
Groth, N. A., 377
Grothaus, L. C., 329
Grove, W. M., 37, 411, 413
Gruber, K., 153
Grubin, D., 382
Gruenberg, A. M., 402
Grundman, M., 449, 451
Guggenheim, F. G., 402
Guidotti, A., 172
Guile, C. A., 471
Guilette, E. C. D., 224
Guitar, B. E., 476
Gullone, E., 250
Gump, B. S., 236
Gunaratne, I. J., 493
Gunderson, J. G., 295, 296, 297–298, 299, 304
Gunnar, M. R., 491
Gur, R. E., 265, 405, 413, 421
Guralnik, O., 189, 192
Gureje, O., 201, 204, 205, 206
Gurenewald, P. J., 315
Gurguis, G., 157
Gurland, B., 449
Gurland, B. J., 36
Gurling, H., 273
Guroff, J. J., 185, 186, 192
Gustafson, L., 448
Gutsch, K. W., 101
Guze, S. B., 208
Guzick, D. S., 235
Gwirtsman, H., 481

Haaf, B., 306
Haaga, D. A. F., 60, 67–68, 255, 267
Haapasalo, J., 378
Haas, G., 409
Haas, G. L., 265, 405, 422
Hackmann, A., 206, 208
Hadaway, P. F., 332
Haddock, G., 91, 98
Hadeed, A., 489
Hadley, J. A., 316
Hadson, 230–231
Hadzi-Pavlovic, D., 255
Haenen, M. A., 207
Häfner, H., 399
Hagerman, R. J., 487, 498
Haggerty, R. J., 19
Haguelet, P., 278
Hahn, C. G., 282
Haider, M., 220
Haignere, C., 229
Hakola, P., 525
Halbreich, U., 280
Hale, Robert, 294
Hales, D. R., 332
Hales, R., 161
Haley, J., 127, 423
Hall, A., 521, 527
Hall, C. C. I., 62
Hall, G. C. N., 378
Hall, S. M., 345
Hallahan, D. P., 478
Halldin, C., 416
Haller, O. L., 20
Halligan, P. W., 209
Halpern, J. H., 335
Hamada, R. S., 159
Hambley, L. S., 378
Hamblin, M. W., 137
Hamel, M., 44
Hammen, C., 116, 249, 250
Hammer, L. D., 471
Hammond, M., 305
Hampson, J., 385
Hamre-Nietupski, S., 504
Hamrick, N., 241
Han, L., 276
Han, S. S., 461
Hanch, H. H., 328
Handen, B. L., 507
Handleman, J. S., 501
Hankin, B. L., 148, 250, 270
Hans, S. L., 412
Hansen, W. B., 320, 321, 322
Hanson, M. J., 504
Hanssen, M., 405
Harada, S., 345
Harburg, E., 225
Harchik, A. E., 502
Hardin, T. S., 266
Hardman, J. M., 440
Hardy, J., 446
Hare, E., 415
Hare, R. D., 291, 292, 293
Harkness, W., 455
Harlap, S., 410
Harlow, B. L., 249
Harlow, J., 441
Harlow, N., 382
Harmon-Jones, E., 144, 148
Harnish, J. D., 464
Haroutunian, V., 416
Harper, Walter, 529
Harralson, T. L., 223
Harrington, R., 250
Harris, A. H. S., 240
Harris, A. W. F., 142
Harris, J., 505
Harris, J. C., 485, 489
Harris, M. J., 266, 406
Harris, S. L., 501, 503
Harris, T. O., 91, 92, 255, 270
Harris, W. S., 240, 241
Harrison, J., 156
Harrison, P., 257
Harrow, M., 255, 397
Harry Benjamin International Gender Dysphoria Association (HBIGDA), 385
Hart, S. D., 293
Harter, S., 250
Hartlage, S., 247
Hartmann, Heinz, 113, 114
Hartmann, M., 403, 405
Hartwell, S., 101
Harvey, A. G., 161, 167
Harvey, D., 338
Harvey, J. G., 257
Harvey, P. D., 420
Harwood, S., 422
Hatch, T., 40
Hathaway, S. R., 45
Hatterer, J. A., 277
Haukka, J. K., 390
Haupt, D. W., 417
Hauri, P. J., 237
Hauser, S. T., 117, 265
Hauser, W. A., 453
Hautzinger, M., 88
Havassy, B. E., 345
Haverkos, H. W., 340
Havik, O. E., 201
Hawk, G., 517
Hawkins, J. D., 466
Hawley, T. L., 489
Hawton, K., 368, 369
Hay, D. P., 283
Hay, L. K., 283
Hayes, S. C., 81, 82, 87, 88, 97
Hays, J. C., 241
Hays, R. C., 47
Haythornthwaite, J., 222
Hayton, B. C., 163
Hayward, C., 471
Hayward, L., 422
Hazelwood, R. R., 294
Hazlett, E. A., 189, 290, 421
Hazlett, G., 181
Hearst, N., 228
Heath, A. C., 346, 347
Heath, L., 480
Heatherton, T. F., 232
Heaton, J. A., 190
Heaton, R., 448
Heavey, C. L., 378, 381, 475
Heavey, L., 495
Heberman, H. B., 167
Hebert, M., 187
Hécaen, H., 435
Hechtman, L., 463
Heckers, S., 413
Heeren, T., 320
Heffernan, K., 296, 302
Heiman, J., 366
Heiman, J. R., 368, 369
Heimberg, F. R., 167
Heimberg, R. G., 68, 152, 153, 164, 167, 534
Heinold, J. W., 329
Heinz, A., 349
Helfer, S. G., 235
Heller, B. W., 226
Heller, T. L., 252
Hellerstein, D. J., 280
Hellgren, L., 497
Helmes, E., 46
Helmstaedter, C., 454
Helzer, J. E., 37, 161, 272
Hemingway, H., 222, 236
Henderson, M. J., 344
Hengeveld, M. W., 362
Henggeler, S. W., 343
Heninger, G. R., 257, 278, 279
Henomatsu, K., 399
Henrich, Christy, 469
Henrikson, N., 18
Henriksson, M. E., 260
Henry, D., 469
Henry, G. W., 12
Henry VIII, 437
Hepworth, C., 255
Herbener, E. S., 397
Herbert, J., 277, 460
Herdt, G., 356
Herman, C. P., 232
Herman, J. L., 193, 377
Hermansen, I., 345, 346
Hermelin, B., 495
Hernandez, P., 51–52
Hernandez-Peon, R., 209
Hernandez-Serrano, R., 366, 369, 370
Herperts, S. C., 292
Herrera, J. M., 101
Herrera, M. G., 490
Hersen, M., 83
Hershey, L. A., 449
Herz, M. I., 419
Herzberg, D. S., 116
Hess, N. C., 195
Heston, L. L., 409
Hettema, J., 171
Hiday, V. A., 526
Higgins, M., 225
Higgins, S. T., 85, 342
Hildebran, D., 381
Hilmert, C. J., 238
Hinckley, John, 513, 515, 516
Hinderliter, A. L., 240
Hingson, R., 320
Hinson, K. B., 504
Hippocrates, 12, 26–27, 201, 275
Hirai, S., 317
Hirayasu, Y., 414
Hirschfeld, Magnus, 356
Hirshfeld-Becker, D. R., 172
Hlastala, S. A., 256
Ho, A. P., 274
Ho, B. T., 176
Hoberman, H., 83
Hobson, R. P., 499
Hodapp, R. M., 485, 490, 493, 500
Hodges, A., 412
Hodgins, S., 460, 464, 524, 525
Hodgkinson, S., 273
Hodgson, R. J., 85, 154–155
Hodkinson, H. M., 434
Hoek, H. W., 415
Hoenig, J., 385
Hofer, T., 201
Hoffman, Albert, 335
Hoffman, K. B., 267
Hoffman, P. L., 345
Hoffman, R. E., 414

Hofman, M. A., 277
Hogan, M. E., 66, 91, 261, 265
Hogarty, G. E., 425, 427
Hoge, S. K., 527
Hohenstein, J. M., 345
Holden, J. C., 505
Holder, H. D., 315
Holder-Perkins, V., 200, 201, 204, 206, 208
Holland, C. L., 381
Holland, D. E., 168, 478
Holland, J. G., 308, 437
Hollander, E., 156, 189, 197, 209, 300
Hollingshead, A. B., 99
Hollins, S., 507
Hollister, J. M., 412
Hollister, L. E., 338
Hollon, S. D., 97, 268, 280, 281, 534
Holmes, D. S., 120
Holmes, J., 478
Holmes, R. M., 294
Holmes, T. H., 214, 216
Holsboer, F., 146, 277
Holtz, G. A., 442
Holzer, C. E., III, 39
Holzman, P. S., 393, 394, 411
Homann, E., 269
Homes, J. P., 498
Honig, A., 249
Honig, P., 477
Honzig, C. H., 89
Hoogendijk, W. J. G., 277
Hooker, E., 358
Hooley, J. M., 264
Hoover, D. R., 437
Hope, D. A., 68
Hops, H., 468
Horgan, K., 226
Horley, J., 376
Hornbrook, M., 271
Horne, J., 473
Horne, P. J., 422
Horney, Karen, 112, 113–114
Hornig, C. D., 467
Horowitz, H. A., 117
Horton, A. M., 48
Horwitz, R. I., 236
Horwood, L. J., 154, 464, 466
Hosobuchi, Y., 230
Hostetter, A. M., 272
Hotvedt, M. E., 358
Hough, M. S., 144
Houle, S., 279
House, J. S., 241
Houts, A. C., 28, 32, 33, 34, 477
Hovens, J. E., 158
Howard, B. L., 47
Howard, J., 489
Howard, R., 402
Howe, C., 489
Howe, H. L., 226
Howells, K., 376
Howie, P., 476
Hoyer, J., 154
Hoyt, I. P., 183
Huang, C., 46
Huang, Y., 279
Hudson, J. I., 198, 336
Hudson, J. L., 188
Hudson, S. M., 378, 380, 381
Hughes, J. W., 223, 236
Huizinga, D., 465
Hull, J. G., 317
Hulme, C., 474
Hulshoff Pol, H. E., 413
Humfleet, G. L., 345
Humphries, P., 273
Hunt, M., 377
Hurewitz, A., 240
Hurley, R. A., 143
Hurt, H., 489
Huttunen, M. O., 415
Huxley, N. A., 425, 427
Hyun, C. S., 227, 239, 240–241

Iacono, W. G., 188, 191, 405, 410, 411
Iancu, I., 167, 173
Ickovics, J. R., 236
Iezzi, A., 201
Iezzi, T., 200, 201, 203, 204, 205, 206
Ikebuchi, E., 399
Ilardi, S. S., 88, 93–94, 266
Imber, S. D., 272, 281
Immonen, A., 455
IMS Health Canada, 249
Ingram, Paul, 191
Ingram, R. E., 266
Inn, A., 343
Innis, R. B., 279
Institute of Medicine, 332
Inz, J., 165
Iribarren, I. G., 369
Ironson, G., 224, 239, 240
Irwin, C. E., 471
Isaac, M., 204
Isacsson, G., 257
Ishikawa, S., 292
Isometsä, E. T., 260
Israel, A. C., 471
Israel, Y., 346
Ivens-Tyndal, C., 251, 255
Iversen, S. D., 248

Jablensky, A., 390, 399, 405
Jack, C. R., Jr., 455
Jackson, D., 127, 423
Jackson, K., 346
Jackson, R. W., 224
Jacob, B. P., 213
Jacobsen, B., 394, 410, 412
Jacobson, Edmund, 237
Jacobson, K. C., 131, 132
Jacobson, N. S., 57, 62, 87, 88, 263, 264, 268, 269
Jaffe, C., 319
Jaimez, T. L., 173
Jain, P., 370
Jallon, P., 455
James, L., 209
James, W. E., 448
James, William, 22
Jamison, Kay Redfield, 253, 254
Janal, M. N., 279
Janca, A., 204
Jancar, J., 493
Janet, Pierre, 192
Jang, K. L., 166, 276, 308
Janner, M., 399
Janoff-Bulman, R., 167
Jansen, J. H. C., 276
Janssen, E., 378
Janus, E. S., 526
Janzen, H. L., 276
Jaremko, M. E., 238
Jarrett, R. B., 269
Jarvik, M. E., 326
Jasiukaitis, P., 186, 187
Jaspers, J. P. C., 300
Jaycox, L. H., 270
Jeans, R., 185
Jefferson, J. W., 173, 176
Jeffrey, R. W., 232
Jellinek, E. M., 318
Jellinger, K. A., 440
Jenike, M. A., 143
Jenkins, C. D., 223
Jenkins, S., 473
Jennings, J. R., 216, 223
Jernigan, T. L., 436
Jerry, M. B., 374
Jeste, D. V., 399
Jiang, W., 224
Joe, S., 259
Joergensen, J., 469
Joffe, R. T., 146, 277
Johanson, C., 503
Johansson, B., 445
Johansson, M., 277–278
Johns, L. C., 397
Johnson, A., 236
Johnson, Ben, 339
Johnson, B. T., 225
Johnson, C. A., 231
Johnson, D., 504
Johnson, J., 467
Johnson, J. G., 99, 257, 287, 302
Johnson, J. H., 466
Johnson, K. A., 444
Johnson, L. D., 313, 326, 327
Johnson, M., 507
Johnson, M. R., 172
Johnson, S. L., 148, 255
Johnson, Virginia, 358, 365, 366–367, 368, 369, 374
Johnston, L., 381
Johnston, M. B., 507
Johnston, P., 422
Joiner, T. E., 92, 127
Joiner, T. E., Jr., 151, 249, 262, 263, 264, 266
Jones, G. N., 230
Jones, Mary Cover, 477
Jones, M. B., 497
Jones, P., 414, 415
Jones, R., 127, 378
Jorgensen, R. S., 225
Joseph, J., 229
Josephs, R. A., 263–264
Joyce, J. N., 416
Judd, L. L., 249, 253
Jung, Carl Gustav, 113
Junginger, J., 391
Just, N., 266
Jutila, I., 455

Kachin, K. E., 153
Kaduson, H. G., 481
Kaelber, C. T., 5
Kafka, M. P., 383
Kagan, J., 172
Kahn, D. A., 282, 417
Kahn, H. S., 471
Kahn, R. S., 416
Kalat, J. W., 323, 346
Kalehzan, M., 255
Kalivas, P. W., 314, 348
Kalra, S., 447, 449
Kamarck, T. W., 216, 223
Kaminer, D., 151, 153, 156
Kandel, E. R., 121, 122, 147
Kane, J. M., 417
Kankkonen, M., 378
Kannel, W. B., 225
Kanner, A., 214
Kaplan, B., 455
Kaplan, G. A., 223, 250
Kaplan, Helen Singer, 361, 365, 367, 368
Kaplan, H. I., 333, 335, 336, 390, 396
Kaplan, J. R., 222, 235
Kaplan, L. C., 492, 493, 500
Kaplan, M. S., 259, 374
Kaplan, R. M., 10
Kaprio, J., 346
Kapur, S., 279, 283, 416, 417
Karasek, R., 222
Karkowski, L. M., 255
Karlsson, P., 416
Karlstrom, K., 376, 383
Karoumi, B., 411
Karpman, 376
Karweit, N. L., 476
Kasapis, C., 399
Kasen, S., 464, 468
Kashani, J. H., 468
Kashner, T. M., 205
Kaslow, N. J., 468
Kass, D. J., 306
Kassel, J. D., 164
Kaszniak, 182
Katerndahl, D. A., 162
Kathol, R. G., 162, 205
Katkin, E. S., 219
Katsanis, J., 411
Katz, David L., 339
Katz, D. L., 339
Katz, J., 263, 264
Katz, J. L., 174
Katz, R. C., 204
Kauffman, J. M., 478
Kaufman, J., 251, 279
Kaye, W., 70
Kaye, W. H., 481
Kayne, E., 283
Kazdin, A. E., 56, 57, 69, 84, 88, 477
Kean, Y. M., 153
Kearney, 458, 484
Kearney, C. A., 463, 466, 468, 496–497, 502, 503, 504, 508
Keefe, R. S. E., 411
Keith, S. J., 425, 427
Keller, J. W., 45
Keller, M., 273
Keller, M. B., 249, 280
Keller, S. E., 249
Kelley, M. L., 263
Kellner, R., 200, 205, 206
Kellow, J. T., 502
Kelly, E., 325
Kelly, K. A., 257
Kemeny, M. E., 94, 124, 228, 229, 239
Kemp, S., 12, 13, 26
Kemper, 498, 499
Kemper, T. L., 499
Kendall, P. C., 47, 62, 168, 478, 479
Kendall-Tuckett, K. A., 377
Kendell, R. E., 36
Kendler, 410
Kendler, K. S., 152, 162, 171, 247, 250, 255, 256, 270, 273, 279, 317, 390, 402, 408, 410
Kent, A., 420
Kent, D. A., 203, 205
Kent, T. A., 292
Kernberg, Otto F., 293, 295, 297, 298, 304
Kerns, J. G., 392
Kerr, S. H., 476

Keskitalo, P., 423, 424
Kessler, J. W., 475
Kessler, K. A., 17, 20
Kessler, R. C., 35, 67, 94, 99, 153, 154, 158, 161, 163, 171, 229, 249, 250, 251, 253, 257, 258, 259, 262, 270, 272, 273, 279, 290, 467
Kesteloot, H., 221
Kety, S. S., 410, 427
Kety, S. S., 273, 409
Keuthen, N. J., 198
Keyl, P. M., 163, 316
Khalid, N., 468
Khalife, S., 362
Khantzian, E. J., 340
Kiecolt-Glaser, J. K., 212, 216, 218, 219, 220, 238, 450
Kiehl, K. A., 292
Kiesler, C. A., 16
Kiesler, D. J., 128
Kihlstrom, J. F., 121, 180, 181, 182, 183, 186, 189, 202, 203
Killen, J. D., 328, 471
Kilpatrick, D. G., 158, 160, 378
Kim, E. J., 27
Kim, J. J., 415
Kim, K. M., 64
Kim, P. Y., 371
Kim, S., 502
Kimbell, I., 448
Kimble, G. A., 87
Kimble, M. O., 394
King, C. A., 259, 260, 262
King, R. A., 251
Kinney, D. K., 254, 394, 414
Kinscherff, R., 469
Kinsey, Alfred C., 357, 359, 377
Kirch, D. G., 415
Kirk, J., 167
Kirk, P., 257
Kirkpatrick, B., 404, 405
Kirmayer, L. J., 163, 200, 204, 205, 206
Kirsch, I., 186, 188, 195, 280
Kirsch, P., 421
Kisïel, C. L., 186
Kivlahan, D. R., 322
Kizer, A., 255
Klackenberg, G., 473
Klajner, R., 232
Klap, R., 249
Klapper, M. H., 282
Klatka, L. A., 449
Kleber, H. D., 334
Klein, D. F., 173, 257, 268, 280
Klein, D. N., 252–253, 256, 270
Klein, E., 283
Klein, Melanie, 113, 115
Klerman, G. L., 127, 249, 271, 272
Klier, C. M., 157
Klimas, N., 230, 237
Klin, A., 498, 500
Kline, A. E., 201
Klinger, L. G., 494, 495, 498, 499, 500
Klingler, T., 369–370
Klitzman, R. L., 336
Kluft, R. P., 192, 193
Knecht, S., 144
Knight, R. A., 397, 407
Knopp, F. H., 380
Knowles, S. L., 166
Knutsson, A., 220, 222, 234
Ko, G., 416
Koback, K. A., 176
Kobayashi, R., 496, 497
Koch, C., 232
Koch, W. J., 157, 158, 160, 173
Kocsis, J. H., 280
Koegel, L. K., 505
Koegel, P., 18
Koegel, R. L., 503, 505
Koenig, H. G., 241
Kohlenberg, Robert J., 60, 61, 195
Kohler, F. W., 505
Kohlmaier, J. R., 399
Kohn, R., 6
Kohn, Y., 67
Kohut, Heinz, 113, 116, 297, 298, 304
Kokmen, E., 449
Kokmen, K., 445
Kolb, B., 144, 491
Kolb, J. W., 240, 241
Kolb, L. C., 252, 453
Koller, M., 220
Koller, R., 417
Kolodner, R. M., 338
Kolodny, R. C., 338
Kolody, B., 101
Kolodziej, M. E., 225
Kolvin, I., 461, 462
Koopman, C., 161, 229
Köpcke, W., 405
Kopelman, M. D., 182
Koreen, A. R., 416
Kornblith, S. J., 427
Kornreich, C., 317
Kornstein, S. G., 279, 280
Korzilius, H., 505
Kosaka, K., 447
Koskenvuo, M., 346
Koss, M. P., 378
Kostanski, M., 250
Kowalski, J., 256
Kraemer, H. C., 212
Kraepelin, Emil, 20–21, 28, 389–390, 396, 403, 407
Krafft-Ebing, Richard von, 21, 356, 372, 375
Kraft, D., 269
Kramer, Peter, 281
Kramer, R. A., 259, 260, 261, 262, 263, 272
Krantz, D. S., 216, 222, 224
Krasner, L., 205, 206, 425
Krasner, Leonard, 58
Kratzer, L., 460, 464
Kravdal, O., 227
Kregel, J., 503
Kreinin, I., 283
Kremen, W. S., 404
Kresevich, M. A., 421
Kreutzer, J. S., 441
Kring, A. M., 397, 404
Kringlen, E., 302, 409
Krishnan, R. R., 277
Kroenke, K., 204
Kromhout, D., 221
Kropp, P. R., 524
Krueger, R. B., 374
Krull, D. S., 264
Krupp, A., 295
Krystal, J. H., 197
Ksir, C., 338
Kubicki, M., 414
Kubota, M., 317
Kuch, K., 157
Kudler, H. S., 161
Kuiper, N. A., 191, 193
Kuipers, E., 422
Kukla, A., 91
Kulik, J. A., 238
Kulka, R. A., 160
Kulkarni, J., 405
Kullgren, G., 386
Kumanyika, S., 236
Kunovac, J. L., 175
Kuntz, K. K., 236
Kupfer, D. J., 256, 268, 272, 274, 275, 278, 280, 281, 282
Kurtines, W. M., 479
Kurtzke, J. F., 444
Kwapil, T. R., 413
Kwon, J., 156, 209
Kydd, R. R., 419

Labouvie, E., 33, 324
Lacks, P., 234
Ladouceur, R., 168
Lafargue, T., 404
La Fond, J. Q., 520, 522, 526
La Greca, A. M., 460
Laing, R. D., 9
Laje, G., 200
Lakin, K. C., 502
Lam, R. W., 276
Lamb, S. A., 230
Lambert, G., 277–278
Lambert, M. J., 120
Lamberti, S., 419
Lamparski, D., 317
Lampe, M. E., 487
Lampert, P. W., 440
Landis, K. R., 241
Lane, R. M., 280
Lane, T. W., 233
Lang, A. E., 447, 449
Lang, P. J., 150
Langenbucher, J. W., 28, 29, 31, 33, 34
Langinvainio, H., 346
Lanyon, R. I., 374
Laor, N., 161
LaPerierre, A., 237
Lara, M. E., 256, 270
Larson, S. A., 502
Larsson, B., 468
Lask, B., 471
Latshaw, A., 413
Lattuada, E., 252
Laumann, E. O., 359, 360, 361, 362, 363, 364
Lauriello, J., 425, 427
Lavori, P. W., 249, 272
Lawrie, S. M., 413
Lawry, A. S., 376, 383
Laws, D. R., 383
Lawson, C., 166, 172
Lawson, W. B., 101
Lay, B., 403, 405
Lazarus, L., 218
Lazarus, Richard S., 120, 214, 216, 238
Leader, J., 256
Leaf, P. J., 39
Leaf, R., 307
Leahy, R. L., 269
Leavitt, N., 518
Leblanc-Allman, R. J., 515
Lebow, B. S., 413
LeCouteur, A., 497
Lecrubier, Y., 167
Ledbetter, M. F., 39, 40
LeDoux, J., 140, 141
Lee, B. O., 209
Lee, J. E., 313
Lee, S., 480
Lee, T. M., 276
Lehman, A. F., 417
Lehman, J. M., 227
Leibenluft, E., 251, 275
Leiblum, S. R., 358, 365
Leibowitz, M. R., 68
Leibowitz, S. F., 481
Leigh, B. C., 344
Leitenberg, H., 377
Lejeune, Jerome, 487
Lemaire, A., 360
Lemmi, H., 253
Lencz, T., 292
Lenkinski, R. E., 413
Lenox, R. H., 282
Lensi, P., 157
Lentz, R. J., 426, 532
Lenzenweger, M. F., 404, 409, 413, 419, 420
Leocani, L., 141
Leon, A. C., 246, 249, 280
Lerche, N. W., 230
Lerew, D. R., 166
Lerman, M. I., 446
Lerner, H. D., 106
Lerner-Wren, G., 520
Leserman, J., 229
LeShan, L., 241
Leshner, A. I., 314
Lesier, H. R., 300
Lesperance, F., 212
Lester, D., 300
Levav, I., 99
Levenson, R. W., 225, 347
Levenson, S., 320
Levin, R. A., 305
Levine, J., 370
Levine, S., 147
Levis, D. J., 85
Levitt, E. E., 375
Levy, D. L., 393, 394, 411, 413
Levy, R., 209
Lewine, R. R. J., 405
Lewinsohn, P. M., 83, 88, 249, 255, 256, 259, 263, 264, 266, 267, 272, 295, 468
Lewis, D. A., 143, 414
Lewis, G., 398
Lewis, S., 415
Lewy, A. J., 276
Li, U., 236
Liao, H., 46
Liberman, R. P., 426
Lichtenstein, E., 328, 329
Lichteran, D., 288, 290
Lidbeck, J., 208
Liddle, P. F., 279
Lidz, C. W., 522, 527
Lieb, R., 257
Liébault, Ambrose-Auguste, 21
Liebenluft, E., 275
Lieberman, J. A., 416
Lieberman, R. P., 426
Liebowitz, M., 176, 257
Liebowitz, M. R., 167, 173, 257, 309
Light, K. C., 225, 242
Liguori, A., 337
Liis von Knorring, A., 481
Lilienfeld, S. O., 37, 44, 45, 170, 186, 188, 195, 208
Lim, K. O., 413
Limpert, C., 397
Lin, K. M., 390, 405
Lin, M. T., 390, 405

Lincoln, Abraham, 246
Lindamer, L. A., 399
Linden, W., 239
Lindman, R. E., 316
Lindsay, K. A., 302
Linehan, M. M., 88, 306, 342
Linhorst, D. M., 516
Link, B., 425
Linszen, D. H., 422
Linz, D., 378, 381
Liotti, M., 277
Lipowsky, Z. J., 434
Lipscombe, P., 200
Lipsedge, M., 7
Lipsker, Eileen Franklin, 190
Lisanby, S. H., 283, 284
Litt, M. D., 238
Littlewood, R., 7
Litwack, T. R., 524
Livermore, J. M., 512, 522
Livesley, W., 276, 308
Lloyd, J. W., 478
Lo, E. S., 276
Loberg, T., 88
Lobitz, W. C., 366
Locatelli, M., 141
Lochman, J. E., 464, 466
Lockwood, R., 155
Loeber, R., 10
Loewenstein, R. J., 182, 186, 187, 189
Löffler, W., 399
Loftus, E. F., 191
Loftus, J., 404
Logan, J. M., 142, 143
Lohr, J. M., 170
Longhurst, J. G., 250, 277
Loosen, P. T., 281
Lopez, A. D., 249
Lopez, S. R., 51–52, 422
LoPiccolo, J., 361, 366, 368, 369, 380
LoPiccolo, L., 368
Loranger, A. W., 413
Lord, C., 496, 497
Louis, E. D., 449
Lovaas, O. I., 88, 505
Lovestone, S., 448
Lowe, B., 447
Lowe, C. F., 422
Lowing, P. A., 410
Lowry-Webster, H. M., 478
Lu, R. B., 346
Luborsky, L., 120, 121, 340, 349
Lubs, H. A., 487
Luby, E. D., 470
Lucas, A. R., 469
Luchins, A. S., 16
Luckhurst, E., 218
Ludwig, A. M., 396
Lue, T. F., 370
Luepnitz, R. R., 101
Luh, K. E., 413
Luisada, P. V., 336
Lukas, G., 292
Lukens, E., 425
Lunde, L., 254
Lunetta, P., 316
Luria, Z., 185
Lussier, I., 396
Lutgendorf, S. K., 228
Luthert, P., 499
Lydiard, L. R., 176
Lydiard, R. B., 172
Lye, D., 329
Lyketsos, C. G., 441
Lykken, D. T., 134, 291, 308
Lyman, D., 300
Lymburner, J. A., 513, 515, 516
Lynch, F., 271
Lynch, J. J., 218, 241
Lynch, P. S., 502
Lynn, S. J., 180, 181, 186, 188, 195, 197
Lynskey, M., 464, 466
Lyon, G. R., 475
Lyon, H. M., 267
Lyons, J. S., 186
Lyons, M. J., 313
Lytton, H., 465

Ma, G. X., 319
MacArthur, R. D., 315
MacCarthy, B., 422
Macdonald, H., 497
MacDonald, J., 523
Macera, C. A., 237
MacFarlane, K., 377
MacGregor, M. W., 239
Machamer, J., 439
Machon, R. A., 415
Maciejewski, P. K., 266–267
Mack, A. H., 27
Mack, D., 232
MacKinnon, L. T., 237
MacLeod, C., 88, 91, 266
Maclure, M., 224
MacMahon, S., 224
MacMillan, H. L., 187
Madden, P. A. F., 346, 347
Maddox, J. H., 283
Madge, N., 257
Maes, M., 382
Magee, W. J., 152, 153
Magnus, E., 276
Magura, S., 313
Maher, B. A., 4, 20, 391, 392, 420, 421
Maher, W. B., 4, 20
Mahler, Margaret, 112, 113, 115–116, 304
Mahoney, J. M., 294
Mahoney, Michael J., 95, 97
Mahurin, R. K., 423, 424
Maier, L. A., 237
Maier, S. E., 414
Maier, S. F., 69, 265
Maier, W., 288, 290
Maj, M., 405
Malamud, M., 383
Malamuth, N. M., 378, 381
Malarkey, W. B., 220
Malaspina, D., 410
Maldonado, J. R., 201, 202, 203, 204, 205, 206
Malec, J. F., 441
Malecha, A., 316
Malenka, R. C., 348
Malgady, R. G., 51
Malkoff-Schwartz, S., 275
Malla, A. K., 399, 428
Malmberg, A., 398
Malmo, R. B., 215
Malmquist, C. P., 522
Manber, R., 235, 473, 474
Mandl, R. C. W., 413
Mangine, S., 298
Manheimer, E. D., 241
Manicavasagar, V., 170, 467
Mann, D. M. A., 447, 448, 451
Mann, J. J., 279, 283
Mann, K., 349, 369–370
Mannuzza, S., 171
Manschreck, T. C., 406
Mansueto, C. S., 300
Manuck, S. B., 222
Maravilla, K. R., 142
Marchione, K., 174
Marcos, L. R., 51
Marcotte, T. D., 437, 438
Marcus, J., 412
Marder, S. R., 417
Margolese, H. C., 370
Margraf, J., 169
Marie, P., 197
Maris, R. W., 260
Markand, O. N., 201, 204
Markesbery, W. R., 124
Marks, I. M., 206
Marlatt, G. A., 88, 322, 325, 329, 344
Marmot, M. G., 222, 236
Marrazzi, M. A., 470
Marriott, M., 277
Marrs-Garcia, A., 62
Marsden, P., 336
Marsh, L., 141, 143
Marshall, B. D., Jr., 417
Marshall, D. S., 357
Marshall, W. L., 376, 377, 378, 380, 381
Marsland, A. L., 216, 222
Martell, C. R., 263, 264
Marten, P. A., 151
Martens, W. H. J., 294
Martens, Willem H. J., 294, 308
Martin, A., 251, 439
Martin, B. C., 415
Martin, C. E., 357, 377
Martin, J. E., 506
Martin, J. M., 267
Martin, R. L., 204, 208
Martinez-Taboas, A., 186
Martinot, J. L., 413
Marxer, F., 222
Marziali, E., 295
Masanic, C., 441
Masia, C. L., 503
Maslow, Abraham, 9, 123, 125–126
Mason, D., 382
Masserman, J. H., 184
Massoco, C. O., 226
Masters, W. H., 338
Masters, William, 358, 365, 366–367, 368, 369, 374
Mathalon, D. H., 413
Mathews, A., 88, 91
Matochik, J. A., 498
Matthews, K. A., 223, 235, 236
Matthysse, S., 411
Mattia, J. I., 257
Mattison, E., 526
Maude-Griffin, P. M., 345
Maugh, T. H., 338
Maurer, K., 399
Maurice, J., 239
Maxfield, M. G., 466
Maxmen, J. S., 174, 175, 233
May, Rollo, 9, 122, 123, 126, 150
Mayberg, H. S., 277
Mayer, B., 207
Mayer, J. D., 41
Mayer, R. G., 505, 506
Mayes, L. C., 489
Maykuth, P. L., 518
Mayne, T. J., 219
Mayou, R. A., 159, 161
Mayville, S., 204
Mazure, C. M., 250, 266–267, 277
Mazza, J. J., 259
Mazzoco, M. M., 488
McArdle, E. F., 461, 462
McArthur, J. C., 437, 439
McAuliffe, W. E., 344
McBride, A., 279
McCabe, M. P., 503
McCarley, R. W., 414
McCarthy, C. A., 265
McCartney, J. R., 505
McCausland, M. P., 376
McCeney, M. K., 216, 222
McClearn, G. E., 131, 132, 133
McClelland, G. M., 316
McCloskey, J., 320
McClure, R. K., 415
McConaughy, S. H., 31
McConkey, K. M., 180
McCrady, B. S., 324
McCrae, R. R., 287, 303, 308
McCubbin, J. A., 235
McCullough, J. P., 256
McDermott, P. A., 459
McDermott, S., 475
McDermut, W., 257
McDonald-Scott, P., 37
McDougall, A., 426
McDougle, C. J., 498
McDowell, J. E., 411
McEachin, J. J., 88
McEachran, A., 469
McElroy, R. A., 37
McEvoy, L., 161
McEwen, B., 232
McFarlane, A. C., 161, 186, 188, 192
McFarlane, J., 316
McFarlane, W. R., 425
McGaha, A., 520, 521
McGee, R., 226
McGhie, A., 396
McGill, C. W., 425
McGinnis, J. M., 212
McGlashan, T. H., 397, 399, 400, 402, 405, 414
McGonagle, K. A., 35, 94, 99, 153, 154, 163, 249, 251, 253, 272, 290, 467
McGorry, P. D., 161, 413
McGrath, C. E., 223
McGrath, J., 414
McGrath, P. J., 237, 279
McGreevy, M. A., 513, 514, 515, 516
McGue, M., 134, 346
McGuire, L., 391
McGuire, M., 402
McGuire, R. J., 290
McInerney, M., 490
McInnes, R. R., 487
McIntyre, D., 187
McKay, D., 206
McKay, J. R., 324
McKeith, I. G., 447, 451
McKeon, P., 273
McKinley, J. C., 45
McKirnan, D. J., 229
McKnight, T. J., 502, 503, 504, 508
McLaren-Hume, 232
McLean, A., 336
McLean, R. Y., 162
McLeer, S. V., 469
McLellan, A. T., 324, 340, 349
McLellan, T., 324
McLeod, C. C., 208
McMahon, P. D., 266

McMahon, R. P., 216, 223
McMurray, M. B., 462
McNally, R. J., 93, 163, 190, 193, 195, 232, 469
McNamara, F. N., 135
McNiel, D. E., 523
McNulty, J. L., 46
McPherson, B., 469
McVary, K. T., 370
McWilliams, N., 119
Meador, K. J., 455
Meador-Woodruff, J. H., 416
Meadows, E. A., 47
Meager, B., 156
Meaney, M. J., 147
Mechanic, D., 205, 248
Mechanic, M. B., 189
Mednick, S. A., 66, 308, 412
Mednick, Sarnoff A., 66, 411–412, 415, 524, 525
Meehl, Paul E., 512, 514, 522
Meek, P. S., 347
Meesters, Y., 276
Meeuwisse, W. H., 442
Mefford, R. B., 448
Meichenbaum, Donald H., 91, 94, 238, 478
Meinardi, H., 453
Melander, H., 481
Melin, L., 468
Mellin, L. M., 471
Melman, A., 370
Melnicore, L. H., 492
Melroy, J. R., 517
Melton, G. B., 512, 513, 517, 518, 519, 522, 523, 525, 527
Melzack, R., 332
Mendel, W. M., 390–391
Mendlewicz, J., 273
Menotti, A., 221
Menza, M., 280
Merckelbach, H., 156, 169
Mercurio, A. F., 508
Meredith, S., 417
Merikangas, M. R., 250
Merikangus, K., 255
Merikangus, K. R., 257
Merrick, S., 116
Merrill, L. L., 316
Merritt, H. H., 443
Merritt, R. D., 186, 187, 195
Merry, S., 469
Merskey, H., 188, 200
Mervaala, E., 455
Mesibov, G. B., 494
Mesmer, Franz Anton, 21
Messenger, J. C., 356
Meston, C., 369
Metalsky, G. I., 92, 127, 263, 264, 265, 266
Metz, M. E., 362
Metzger, D. S., 340
Meyer, Adolph, 22
Meyer, B., 148
Meyer, G. J., 27, 47
Meyer, J. H., 279
Meyer, J. M., 313, 385
Meyer, J. S., 136, 137, 138, 140, 144, 145
Mezzich, J. E., 34
Michael, R. T., 359, 360, 361, 362, 363, 364
Michaels, Stuart, 359
Michelson, L. K., 174
Michelsson, K., 473
Michie, C., 303
Mick, M. A., 153
Miklowitz, D. J., 127, 424
Mikulincer, M., 167
Milberg, W., 48
Milberger, S., 463
Milgram, S., 98
Milich, R., 300
Miller, B. L., 203
Miller, G. E., 212
Miller, H. L., 278
Miller, J., 415
Miller, N. E., 237
Miller, Neal, 57, 237
Miller, S. D., 186
Miller, S. M., 312
Miller, T. Q., 223
Miller, W. R., 323, 324
Miller-Perrin, C. L., 187
Milligan, William Stanley, 183
Millikan, A., 88
Millman, R. B., 340
Millon, T., 297, 298, 305
Milstein, V., 182, 282
Min, S. K., 209
Mindell, J. A., 473, 502, 503
Mineka, S., 169, 257
Minges, J., 288, 290
Minka-Brown, C., 296
Minor, T., 265
Minshew, N. J., 499
Mintun, M., 413
Mintz, J., 419
Minuchin, S., 479, 480
Miranda, J., 266
Mirin, S. M., 265
Mirotznik, J., 6
Mirsky, A. F., 410, 428
Mitchell, B., 273
Mitchell, D., 273, 292
Mitchell, J. E., 300
Mitchell, S., 119
Mittelman, M. S., 450
Mittleman, M. A., 224
Mizes, J. S., 470
Moberg, P., 420
Moffitt, T. E., 250, 270, 465
Mogg, K., 93
Mogotsi, M., 151, 153, 156
Mohamed, S., 398
Mohlman, J., 165
Mohr, J. W., 374
Mohs, R. C., 38, 411
Molière, 199
Molinari, S., 88
Monahan, J., 522, 524, 526
Money, John, 385
Money, R., 248
Monnier, J., 378
Monroe, Marilyn, 332
Monroe, S. M., 255
Monroe-Blum, H., 295
Monsen, K., 201
Monti, P. M., 344
Moore, H., 416
Moore, R., 164
Moore, T. J., 280
Moorhead, S., 268, 269
Moos, R. H., 255, 325
Mora, G., 13
Mora, J. O., 490
Moreau, D., 272
Moreno, A. B., 471
Moreno, F. A., 138, 278, 279
Morey, L. C., 295
Morgan, C. A., 181
Morgan, D. L., 70, 71
Morgan, G. D., 329
Morgan, J. F., 143
Morgan, R. K., 70, 71
Morgenstern, J., 33, 324
Morgenthaler, A., 370
Morin, C. M., 234, 237
Moring, J., 410
Morley, S., 201
Morris, E. L., 221
Morris, G. H., 517
Morris, S. K., 421
Morrisey, J. P., 513, 514, 515, 516
Morrison, C. F., 533
Morrison, R. L., 401
Morris-Yates, A., 476
Morse, S. J., 512, 514, 515, 517, 525, 527
Mortensen, P. B., 405, 415
Mortweet, S. L., 477
Moser, C., 375
Moser, V., 237
Mosher-Ashley, P. M., 18
Moskowitz, J., 411
Mosley, T. H., Jr., 231
Moss, H. B., 323
Moul, D. E., 5
Mowrer, O. H., 168, 477
Mowrer, W. M., 477
Mrazek, P. J., 19
Mucci, A., 405
Mueller, T. I., 249
Mueser, K. T., 399, 422, 426, 507
Mueser, P. R., 399
Mufson, L., 272
Mullan, J. T., 450
Müller, E., 405
Mulvey, E. P., 522, 527
Mundo, E., 273
Mundy, P., 494
Munir, K., 488
Muntaner, C., 99
Murata, T., 496, 497
Murdock, T., 161
Muris, P., 156, 169
Murphy, C. M., 343
Murphy, S. L., 257, 259
Murphy, W. D., 374, 381
Murray, C. J. L., 249
Murray, L. A., 266
Murray, R. M., 404, 405
Murtagh, D. R. R., 234
Mushin, J., 209
Musicco, M., 88
Mustafa, T., 237
Muzik, O., 498
Myers, J., 152, 162, 171
Myers, J. K., 99
Myin-Germeys, I., 428

Nachmani, G., 393–394
Nagy, T. F., 532, 533, 535
Nahas, G. G., 338
Nakajima, S., 406
Nakazaki, S., 317
Nangle, D. W., 503
Narasimhan, M., 278
Narayan, M., 276–277
Nash, John, 423
Nasrallah, A., 260
Nath, S. R., 62
Nathan, P. E., 28, 29, 31, 33, 34, 88
National Center for Health Statistics, 259, 470
National Center for Injury Prevention and Control, 257
National Highway Traffic Safety Administration, 315, 442
National Hospital Discharge Survey, 360
National Institute of Mental Health, 258
National Institute on Alcohol Abuse and Alcoholism, 315, 322–323
National Institute on Drug Abuse, 333, 334, 336
National Institutes of Health, 441
Nayani, T., 396
Neale, J. M., 215, 397, 407
Neale, M. C., 171, 250, 270, 273, 279
Neary, D., 447, 448, 451
Neeleman, J., 256
Neimeyer, R. A., 95, 97
Nelson, C. A., 491
Nelson, D. S., 498
Nelson, J. C., 277
Nelson, K. A., 422
Nelson, P., 475
Nelson-Gray, R. O., 70, 71
Nemeroff, C. B., 146, 147, 277
Nemiroff, R. A., 261
Nesse, R., 150
Nesson, Charles, 513
Nestler, E. J., 278, 279
Nestor, P. G., 394
Nesvacil, L. J., 362
Neugebauer, R., 12, 157
Neumark-Sztainer, D., 378
Nevid, J., 163
Newberger, C. M., 492
Newberger, E. H., 492
Newcomb, M. D., 343
Newcomer, J. W., 417
Newcorn, J., 462
Newman, C. F., 269
Newman, J. P., 91, 292, 292–293
Newman, M. G., 153
Newton, Isaac, 213
Nezu, A. M., 47
Nezworski, M. T., 44
Niccols, G. A., 489
Nicholls, G., 240
Nicholls, T. L., 523, 524
Nichols, M. F., 319
Nichols, P. L., 492
Nichols, T., 413
Nicholson, R. A., 517, 526
Nicholson, W. F., 275
Nicolosi, A., 88
Nicolson, R., 290
NIDH, 313
Nidich, S. I., 237
Nieberding, R., 45
Niehaus, 300
Nielsen, E., 87
Nielson, P. E., 379
Nienhuis, F. J., 399, 403
Nierenberg, A. A., 199, 279, 280
Nietupski, J., 504
Nietzel, M. T., 266
Nigg, J. T., 288, 290, 308
NIH Consensus Development Panel on Rehabilitation of Persons with Traumatic Brain Injury, 439, 441, 442
Nijinsky, Vaslav, 393
Niklas, P. S., 375
Nilsen, Dennis, 294
Nimgaonkar, V., 409
Nisbett, R. E., 232
Noe, S., 369–370
Noguchi, T., 406
Nolen-Hoeksema, Susan, 249, 250
Noonan, J. R., 183

Nopoulos, P., 405
Nopoulos, P. C., 413
Nord, A. M., 488
Nordström, A. L., 416
Norem, J. K., 120
Norman, R. M., 399, 428
Norris, James, 14
Norton, G. R., 201
Norton, P. J., 201
Norwood, S., 526
Novick, D. M., 340
Novotny, T. E., 329
Noyes, R., Jr., 205
Nuechterlein, K. H., 412, 419, 422, 423
Nugter, M. A., 422
Nunnerley, H., 226
Nurnberger, J. L., 276
Nutt, D. J., 172, 173
Nyberg, S., 416

Oakley, D. A., 209
Obermeyer, W. H., 274
O'Boyle, M., 384
O'Brien, C. P., 324, 349
O'Brien, G., 461, 462
O'Brien, K. K., 342
O'Brien, L. M., 405
O'Brien, P. C., 449
Obsessive Compulsive Cognitions Working Group, 167
Obuchowski, N., 412
O'Cleirigh, C., 228
O'Dell, S., 477
O'Donnell, B. F., 394
O'Donnell, J., 466
O'Donohue, W., 383
O'Driscoll, G. A., 411
Oehman, A., 164, 172
O'Fallon, W. M., 469
O'Farrell, T. J., 342, 343
Offord, K. P., 445
Ofshe, Richard, 191
Ogloff, J. R. P., 523, 524
O'Gorman, T. W., 345
Ogrocki, P., 238
Ohi, L. E., 278
Ohno, T., 399
Oja, H., 410
Okazaki, S., 51
Olbrich, R., 421
Oldehinkel, A. J., 256
O'Leary, K. D., 328
Olfson, M., 248
Olin, S. S., 66, 412
Oliva, P. S., 188
Olivardia, R., 198
Ollendick, T. H., 71, 163
Oltmanns, T. F., 397
O'Malley, P. M., 313, 326, 327
Ondersma, S. J., 472
Onstad, S., 171
Op den Velde, W., 158
Oquendo, M. A., 249
Oren, D. A., 276
Ormel, J., 256
Orth, D. N., 275
Orth-Gomér, K., 237
Osborn, C., 379, 380, 381, 382
Osgood, C., 185
Ostrwo, D. G., 229
O'Sullivan, R. L., 198
Oswalt, R., 378
Otto, M. W., 162, 175, 249
Otto, R. K., 517, 524
Ouimette, P. C., 325
Overall, J. E., 498
Overholser, J. C., 263
Overton, D. A., 176
Owen, C., 473
Owen, H. M., 341
Owens, J. F., 235
Owens, T. J., 99
Oxman, T. E., 241
Oyama, O. N., 347
Ozonoff, S., 499, 500

Paajanen, S., 473
Pachlatko, C., 453
Padma-Nathan, H., 370
Page-Shafer, K., 313, 319
Paik, A., 363
Paillere Martinot, M. L., 247
Pakenham, K. I., 230
Palermo, G. B., 294
Palermo-Neto, J., 226
Palfai, T. P., 344
Panagiotides, H., 498
Pantelis, C., 413
Panzarella, C., 255, 266
Pardo, P. J., 421
Parides, M., 260
Park, C. L., 238
Parker, G., 200, 255, 422
Parker, J. D. A., 207
Parkinson, James, 448
Parks, G. A., 325, 329
Parmeggiani, A., 498
Parnas, J., 412
Parry, C. D. H., 518, 519
Pasquier, F., 448
Passino, A. W., 492
Pasteur, Louis, 213
Pato, M., 156
Patronek, G. J., 155
Patterson, G. R., 79, 463, 465, 477
Patterson, T. L., 344
Patton, J. R., 502
Patton, R. B., 432
Paty, J. A., 329
Paul, G. L., 426, 532
Paul, W. M., 358
Pauls, D. L., 171, 173, 273
Paulsen, J. S., 406
Paulus, W., 440
Pavlov, Ivan, 76, 78
Pawlak, A., 382
Payan, C., 146
Paykel, E. S., 255, 269
Payne, R., 340
Pearlin, L. I., 450
Pearlson, G. D., 141, 143, 414
Pearson, D. A., 488
Pearson, G. R., 216, 219
Pedersen, B., 370
Pedersen, C. B., 405, 415
Pedersen, N., 134
Pelham, W. E., 463
Peng, G. S., 346
Penick, E. C., 340
Penizen, D. B., 231
Penn, D. L., 397, 398, 399, 422
Pennebaker, J. W., 207, 240
Penninx, B. W. J. H., 249
Pennsylvania Hospital, 15
Penttilae, A., 316
Pereira, R., 410
Perel, T. M., 272
Pericek-Vance, M. A., 446
Perkins, D. O., 229
Perkins, T. S., 168
Perlin, M. L., 513, 515, 516, 519, 521, 522, 527, 530
Perlis, M. L., 233, 234, 235, 473, 474
Perls, F. S., 123
Perry, J., 502
Perry, S., 299
Perry, W., 93, 419
Persons, J. B., 95
Perucca, E., 455
Peters, E. R., 420
Peters, K. D., 257, 259
Peterson, C., 69, 265
Peterson, G., 192
Peterson, Mark, 183
Peterson, M. R., 415
Peto, R., 224
Petrila, J., 512, 513, 517, 518, 519, 520, 521, 522, 523, 525, 527, 528, 529
Pettit, J. W., 262
Petty, R. G., 405
Peveler, R. C., 127
Pfeifer, A., 226
Pfeiffer, H., 421
Pfister, H., 154
Phelan, J. C., 101, 102
Phelps, J. A., 409
Phillippot, P., 317
Phillips, K. A., 198, 199, 203, 204, 205, 207, 209, 295
Phillips, W., 495, 496, 497, 498
Pica, M., 192, 193
Pickens, R. W., 346
Pickering, A. D., 420
Pickering, L. K., 488
Pickering, T., 236
Pickrel, S. G., 343
Pierce, J. P., 329
Pierce, J. W., 470
Pierri, J. N., 414, 417
Pigott, T. A., 173
Pilkonis, P. A., 171
Pilowsky, I., 205
Pincus, A. L., 153
Pincus, H. A., 34
Pincus, T., 201
Pinel, Philippe, 14, 15, 16, 246
Pines, M., 504
Pini, S., 257
Piotrowski, C., 45
Piper, A., 186, 187
Piper, A., Jr., 193
Pithers, W. D., 381
Pitman, R. K., 173
Plato, 213
Plomin, R., 131, 132, 133, 135, 242
Plotsky, P. M., 147
Poddar, Prosenjit, 523
Pokorny, A. D., 257
Polaschek, D. L. L., 378
Poling, A., 492
Polivy, J., 232
Pollack, M. H., 175
Pollack, R. A., 172
Pollitt, E., 489
Polloway, E. A., 502
Pomeroy, W. B., 357, 377
Pope, Harrison G., 188, 198, 336, 339
Pope, H. G., Jr., 198
Pope, K. S., 536
Popkin, C., 442
Porceddu, K., 423
Porcerelli, J. H., 339
Porjesz, B., 347
Portenoy, R. K., 340
Porter, S., 182, 183, 191
Posener, J. A., 277
Post, F., 253
Potkin, S. G., 415
Poulson, R. L., 514
Powchik, P., 416
Powell, C., 490
Powell, R. A., 187, 191, 193
Poythress, N. G., 512, 513, 517, 518, 519, 520, 521, 522, 523, 525, 527
Prabhu, V., 257
Prankiewicz, J., 328
Prasad, K., 34
Prasher, V. P., 492
Preisig, M., 273
Prendergast, M. L., 527
Prescott, C. A., 152, 162, 171, 255, 317
Pretky, R., 383
Pretzer, J., 306, 307
Preu, P. W., 291
Price, J., 195
Price, R. H., 8
Prichard, J. C., 291
Prichep, L., 142
Prieto, S. L., 468
Prince, C., 372
Prince, M., 185
Prince, Morton, 20, 22, 184
Prince, S. E., 88
Prince, V., 372
Pring, L., 495
Prinz, D. J., 282
Prinze, Freddie, 273
Project MATCH Research Group, 326
Protheroe, D., 226
Prouty, G., 507
Provenzano, G., 442
Provins, K. A., 144
Prudic, J., 283
Pruyn, N. A., 156
Pryor, J. L., 362
Przybeck, T. R., 290
Puffett, A., 182
Puhl, R., 231
Pullen, Doss, 514
Purba, J. S., 277
Pussin, Jean-Baptiste, 14, 16
Putnam, F. W., 184, 185, 186, 187, 189, 192, 196
Putnam, James Jackson, 22
Pykett, I. L., 436
Pyle, R. I., 300

Quenzer, L. F., 136, 137, 138, 140, 144, 145
Quereshi, A. I., 200
Quintero, G., 320
Quitkin, F. M., 279

Rabasca, L., 520
Rabin, R. S., 216
Rabins, P. V., 163
Rabkin, J. G., 229, 279
Rachman, S., 156, 167, 169
Rademaker, A. W., 370
Radke-Yarrow, M., 468
Rae, D. S., 151, 152, 249, 340
Ragland, D. R., 223
Raguram, R., 206
Rahbar, B., 507
Rahe, R. H., 214, 216, 239
Rahn, J. M., 221
Räikkönen, K., 236
Raine, A., 292, 308
Rainer, J. D., 273
Ram, R., 399

Ramey, C. T., 490
Ramirez, A., 226
Ramirez, E., 199
Ramsey, C. T., 491
Ramsey, N., 414
Randolph, D. L., 101
Raniere, D., 64, 65, 66, 91
Rao, U., 468
Rao, V., 441
Rapaport, D., 43
Rapee, R. M., 164
Rapin, I., 494
Rapoport, J. L., 290
Rapp-Paglicci, L. A., 11
Rashid, W., 339
Raskin, N. H., 230
Rasmussen, S. A., 155, 157
Rasperry, K., 319–320
Rastam, M., 470
Rauschenberger, S. L., 180
Rawlings, R., 415
Ray, O. S., 331
Ray, W. A., 417
Ray, W. J., 164, 165
Rayner, Rosalie, 77
Reagor, P., 186
Rector, N. A., 88, 91, 98, 422
Redd, W. H., 237
Reddon, J. R., 46
Redich, F. C., 99
Redlich, F. C., 16, 451
Reed, D., 277, 421
Reed, G. M., 94, 124, 229
Reed, L. J., 336
Regier, D. A., 157, 250
Rego, S. A., 162, 167, 168
Rehm, L. P., 251, 255
Reich, J., 153
Reid, D. H., 505
Reid, J. B., 463, 477
Reid, M. R., 237
Reilly-Harrington, N. A., 255, 267
Reinecke, M. A., 117, 164
Reisner, R., 513, 529
Reiss, D. J., 425
Reiss, S., 493
Reitan, R. M., 448
Reivich, K. J., 270, 271
Remien, R. H., 229
Remington, G., 417
Remington, P. L., 471
Rendall, M., 425, 427
Rende, R., 242
Resick, P. A., 189
Resnick, H. S., 158, 160, 168, 378
Reynolds, A. J., 305
Reynolds, A. L., 372
Reynolds, D. K., 23
Reynolds, W. M., 259
Rhee, S. H., 131, 132, 134
Rhines, J. S., 349
Rhines, K. C., 349
Rholes, W. S., 117
Rice, J., 272
Rich, C. L., 257, 261
Richard, D. W., 176
Richards, Renee, 384
Richards, R. L., 254
Richards, T. A., 219
Richardson, D. T., 468
Richens, A., 455
Rickels, K., 174, 174–175
Ricketts, S., 277
Ries, L. A. G., 226
Riether, A. M., 183
Rifkin, A., 189, 283
Rifkin, L., 415
Riggs, D. S., 160
Riley, T. A., 229
Rinaldi, R. C., 480
Rinaldis, M., 230
Rind, B., 187
Rinne, A., 473
Riskind, J. H., 88, 91, 93, 117, 156, 164, 167, 168
Ritchie, M., 397
Ritter, J., 266
Robbins, E. S., 336
Robbins, J. M., 200, 205
Roberts, J., 164
Roberts, L. J., 62
Roberts, R. E., 250, 468
Robertson, D. L., 305
Robins, E., 358
Robins, L., 161
Robins, L. N., 37, 272, 290, 464
Robinson, D., 399, 403
Robinson, G., 236
Robinson, P. H., 514
Robinson, R. G., 443
Robles, E., 88
Rockwood, K. J., 317
Rodin, G., 212
Rodin, J., 231, 232, 238
Rodning, C., 489
Rodriguez, G., 504
Rodriguez, M. S., 241
Rodriguez-Cay, J. R., 186
Roehling, P. V., 343
Roesch, R., 513, 515, 516
Roff, J. D., 397
Roffman, R., 345
Rogers, Carl, 9, 123, 124–125, 507
Rogers, G. M., 117, 164
Rogers, J., 295
Rogers, K., 464
Rogers, S. L., 451
Rogler, L. H., 5, 7
Rohde, J. R., 249, 259, 295
Rohde, P., 249, 255, 259, 266, 272, 295
Rohsenow, D. J., 343
Roitblat, H. L., 159
Rojahn, J., 493
Rollnick, S., 324
Romney, D., 465
Ronan, G. F., 47
Ronningstam, E., 297–298
Roodenrys, S., 474
Roose, S. P., 117
Rorschach, H., 41
Rose, M. S., 442
Rose, R. J., 242, 346
Rose, R. M., 224
Rose, S., 161, 252–253
Rosen, J. C., 199
Rosen, R. C., 280, 358, 365
Rosen, S. A., 439
Rosenbaum, J. F., 172, 175
Rosenberg, S., 393–394
Rosenblatt, A., 16
Rosenfarb, I. S., 419, 423
Rosenhan, D. L., 29–30, 31
Rosenheck, R. A., 249
Rosenman, R. H., 223
Rosenstein, D. S., 117
Rosenthal, D., 273, 409, 410
Rosenthal, N. E., 276
Rosenthal, R. J., 300
Rosenthal, T., 81
Ross, C. A., 186, 187, 188, 193
Ross, D. E., 405, 411
Ross, D. R., 186
Ross, L., 226
Ross, R., 289
Rossell, S., 397
Rossi, P. G., 498
Rosso, I. M., 412, 413
Rost, K., 205
Roth, A. D., 152, 153, 164
Roth, R. H., 374
Rothbaum, B. O., 160, 161, 167, 176
Rotheram-Borus, M. J., 229
Rothstein, H. R., 20
Rotunda, R. J., 342
Rouleau, J., 374
Rounsaville, B. J., 127, 271
Rovner, S., 151
Rowan, V. C., 169
Rowe, D. C., 131, 132
Roy, A., 317
Roy, K., 255
Ruderman, A. J., 232
Rudolph, G., 270
Rudolph, K. D., 250
Rusch, F. R., 506
Ruscio, A. M., 255
Ruscio, J., 255
Rush, A. J., 98, 255, 268, 274
Rushe, R. H., 57
Rusinek, H., 404
Russell, D. E. H., 377
Russell, S., 320
Rutenfranz, J., 220
Rutter, M., 487, 495, 496, 497, 498, 499
Ryan, N. D., 468

Saade, S., 265
Saccuzzo, D. S., 421
Sachs, G. S., 175, 252, 282
Sachs-Ericsson, N., 258
Sackeim, H. A., 181, 197, 283
Sackheim, H. A., 283, 284
Sacks, J., 442
Sacks, Oliver, 58, 435
Sadock, B. J., 333, 335, 336, 390, 396
Sadowski, C., 263
Safford, S. M., 271
Sagebiel, R. W., 226
Saghir, M. T., 358
Sagrati, S., 266
Salerno, J. W., 237
Salisbury, D. F., 414
Salkovskis, P. M., 156, 164, 167, 206, 207, 208
Salmon, P., 200
Salomon, R. M., 279
Salovey, P., 41, 238
Salyers, M. P., 399
Salzman, C., 175
Sameroff, A. J., 504
Samson, J. A., 265
Sana, M., 451
Sanchez, S., 527
Sander, J. W., 453
Sanders, B., 192
Sanderson, C. J., 287, 297
Sanderson, W. C., 162, 167, 168
Sandler, B. A., 339
Sandnabba, N. K., 375
Sandrow, D., 148
Sanfilipo, M., 404
Sanislow, C. A., 400, 402, 403, 404, 405, 409, 416, 424
San Jose, B., 319, 332
Sankis, L. M., 302
Santelli, R., 470
Saoud, M., 411
Saperstein, G., 280
Sapolsky, Robert M., 146, 215, 277
Sar, V., 192
Sarbin, T. R., 28, 29
Sarkin, A. J., 421
Sarna, S., 316
Sarrel, P., 369
Sas, L., 469
Sasson, Y., 173
Satel, S. L., 334
Saunders, A. M., 447
Savage, C. R., 198
Sax, K. W., 277
Saxena, S., 34, 142, 277
Scales, M. T., 237
Schachter, S., 232, 328
Schacter, D. L., 190, 193, 195
Schaefer, C. E., 468, 479, 481
Schaeffer, J., 338
Schalock, R. L., 486
Scharff, D. E., 365
Scharff, J. S., 365
Scharff, L., 201
Schatzberg, A. F., 256, 279, 280
Scheele, L. A., 142
Scheff, Thomas J., 16, 29, 99
Scheiffelin, E., 272
Schell, A. M., 419
Scherrer, J. F., 171, 172, 346
Scherrer, J. R., 171, 172
Scherzinger, M. F., 507
Schiffer, R. B., 449
Schildkraut, J., 278
Schleifer, S. J., 249
Schmeidler, J., 173, 189
Schmeidler, R. A., 173
Schmid, L., 417
Schmidt, A. J. M., 207
Schmidt, H., III, 88, 306, 342
Schmidt, N. B., 165, 166, 173, 176, 264
Schmidt, U., 127
Schmitt, W. A., 91, 292
Schmitz, J. M., 326, 329
Schnack, H. G., 413
Schneider, D. J., 68
Schneider, F., 265, 408, 411, 414, 416
Schneider, N. G., 326
Schneider, R. H., 237
Schneider, S., 169
Schneier, F. R., 467
Schober, R., 325
Schooler, N. R., 417, 425
Schopler, E., 496, 497, 504
Schopp, R. F., 526
Schotte, D. E., 232
Schou, M., 280, 282
Schover, L. R., 368
Schraedley, P. K., 127
Schreiber, F., 184
Schreibman, L., 501, 503
Schuckit, M. A., 318, 332, 347
Schuldberg, D., 253
Schulman, C., 500
Schulman, J., 442
Schulman, P., 97, 168, 271
Schulsinger, F., 345, 346
Schultz, S. K., 402–403, 413
Schulz, P. M., 290
Schulz, S. C., 290
Schupf, N., 446, 492
Schuster, P., 257
Schwartz, D., 307

Schwartz, G. E., 213, 214, 224
Schwartz, J. A., 468
Schwartz, J. E., 252–253, 428
Schwartz, R. H., 338
Schweinhart, L. J., 466
Schweizer, E., 174, 174–175
Scoboria, A., 280
Scott, J., 269
Scott, J. E., 427
Scotti, J. R., 503
Scull, A., 13
Scully, S., 471
Seagal, J. D., 240
Seals, B., 378
Sederer, L., 425, 427
Seeley, J. R., 255, 256, 272
Seeman, P., 416
Seeman, T., 232
Segal, D. L., 260
Segal, G., 444
Segal, Z. V., 93, 266
Seghorn, T., 380
Segraves, R. T., 362
Segrin, C., 263
Seidman, L. J., 405
Seifer, R. D., 504
Seines, O. A., 437
Sekuler, R., 315
Selfe, Lorna, 495
Seligman, Martin E. P., 36, 69, 88, 97, 124, 168, 169, 264–265, 265, 271, 272
Seligman, M. E. P., 226, 238
Selling, L. S., 21
Seltzer, A., 194
Selye, Hans, 214, 215, 216
Semans, J. H., 366
Semple, S. J., 450
Serna, L. A., 87
Serretti, A., 252
Severe, J. B., 425
Seymour, G., 434
Shader, R. I., 174, 234
Shadish, W. R., 343
Shaefer, R., 43
Shaefi, S., 455
Shaffer, D., 258, 260, 261
Shaffer, D. R., 513
Shaffer, T. W., 44
Shafran, R., 167
Shagass, C., 215
Shah, A., 494
Sham, R., 440
Shankweiler, D., 475
Shannon, J. B., 488
Shapiro, D., 224
Shapiro, P. J., 253
Shapiro, R. M., 416
Shapiro, T., 281
Sharf, R. S., 23
Sharkansky, E. J., 317
Sharman, W., 477
Shaughnessy, P., 492
Shaver, P. R., 116, 117, 270
Shaw, B. F., 98, 268
Shaywitz, S. E., 475
Shea, M. T., 272, 281
Shea, S. H., 346
Shea, T., 272
Shear, M. K., 168, 170, 171
Shearman, R. W., 372
Sheeber, L. B., 466
Sheehan, S., 391
Sheldon, J. B., 502
Shelley, A. M., 421
Shelton, R. C., 174, 268, 275, 280, 281
Shema, S. J., 250
Shen, H., 527
Shepherd, M., 151
Sheppard, J. A., 432
Sheps, D. S., 216, 223
Sher, K. I., 346
Sher, K. J., 296
Sher, L., 276
Sherbourne, C. D., 249
Shergill, S. S., 414
Sherman, J. A., 502
Sherman, S., 487
Sherrington, R., 273
Sherwood, A., 224, 225, 242
Sherwood, J. B., 224
Shiah, I. S., 279
Shields, J., 410
Shiffman, S., 329, 345
Shihabuddin, L., 290
Shilony, E., 189
Shipherd, J. C., 167
Shisslak, C. M., 471
Shive, S., 319
Shneidman, E. S., 258, 262
Shoaib, A. M., 248
Shortt, A., 478
Shortt, J. W., 57
Shrout, P. E., 99
Shulman, I. D., 162
Shulman, R. G., 142
Shure, M. B., 466
Siegel, B. V., 414
Siegel, S., 489
Siegler, I. C., 287
Siever, L. J., 295, 308, 309, 411
Sigelman, J., 144
Sigman, M., 494, 499
Sigvardsson, S., 208, 345
Silberman, E. K., 185, 186, 192
Silove, D., 170, 467
Silver, F. M., 306
Silver, S. E., 459
Silverman, J. M., 411
Silverman, K., 88
Silverman, M. M., 259
Silverman, W. K., 477, 479
Silverstein, S. M., 407
Simeon, D., 189, 192, 197
Simon, G. E., 201, 204, 205, 206
Simonini, E., 257
Simonoff, E., 487
Simpson, J. A., 117
Simpson, J. C., 404
Sinason, V., 507
Singer, A., 209
Singer, J. A., 214
Singer, M. T., 423
Singh, N. N., 507
Singleton, L., 444
Sinha, R., 221
Siqueland, L., 341
Sirey, J. A., 99
Sirhan Sirhan, 196
Sivec, H. J., 181, 197
Skinner, B. F., 75, 76, 77–78, 79, 87, 97
Sklar, L. S., 226
Skodol, A. E., 245, 248, 287, 301, 355
Skoner, D. P., 241
Skre, I., 171
Slaghuis, W. L., 421
Slain, A. J., 526
Slap, G. B., 468
Slavin, R. E., 476
Sledge, W. H., 249
Slewa-Younan, S., 142
Sloan, D. M., 247
Sloan, G., 127
Sloan, H. R., 488
Slobogin, C., 513, 514
Slooff, C. J., 399, 403
Slutske, W. S., 346, 347
Smailes, E. M., 302
Small, A. M., 498
Small, D. M., 348
Small, J. G., 282
Smeets, G., 207
Smith, A. M., 292
Smith, A. P., 212, 215
Smith, D., 534
Smith, D. E., 332
Smith, G. S., 316
Smith, G. T., 343
Smith, I. M., 494
Smith, J. D., 502
Smith, J. P., 257
Smith, L. C., 163
Smith, R. D., 161
Smith, T., 88
Smith, T. E., 426
Smith, T. W., 223, 235
Smith, V., 526
Smoller, J. W., 171
Smyth, J. M., 240
Snell, M. E., 486
Snowden, J. S., 447, 448, 451
Snowden, L. R., 5, 249
Snyder, C. R., 320
Snyder, K. S., 422
Snyder, S. H., 334
Sobell, L. C., 341
Sobell, M. B., 341
Sokolov, S. T. H., 146
Solomon, A., 255
Solomon, D. A., 249
Solomon, R. L., 265
Solomon, S. D., 160, 167
Solomon, Z., 161, 164, 167
Solomonica-Levi, D., 500
Solow, J., 504
Sommer, I., 414
Sommer, K. L., 120
Sommer, K. S., 507
Sonnega, A., 161
Sonnerborg, A. B., 437
Southam-Gerow, M. A., 265
Southwick, S. M., 197
Spagnoli, P., 455
Spangler, D. L., 97
Spanos, N. P., 13, 188, 194, 195
Sparrow, S. S., 40
Spasojevic, J., 270
Spaulding, W. D., 421
Spector, I. P., 368
Speicher, C. E., 218, 450
Spelsberg, B., 180
Spence, S. H., 168, 478
Spencer, S. M., 227
Spiegel, D., 201, 202, 203, 204, 205, 206, 212, 227, 228
Spinhoven, P., 187
Spirito, A., 263
Spitzer, C., 180
Spitzer, R. A., 37
Spitzer, R. J., 204
Spitzer, R. L., 29, 30, 31, 33, 245, 248, 301, 355
Spivak, G., 466
Sprich, S., 462
Spring, R. L., 512
Sramek, J. J., 101
Stacy, A. W., 343, 344
Stahl, S. M., 137, 175, 328
Staines, G. L., 313
Stancliffe, R. J., 502
Standford, M. S., 292
Stanley, M. A., 143
Stanton, M. D., 343
Stapleton, J. T., 228
Stark, J. A., 486
Stark, L. J., 263
Startup, M., 267
Starzynski, J., 470
Steadman, H., 513, 514, 515, 516, 526
Steadman, H. J., 522
Steege, J. F., 370
Steer, R. A., 151, 266
Steere, A. C., 438, 439
Steffen, P. R., 240
Steffenburg, S., 494, 497
Stefurak, T., 297
Steil, R., 167
Stein, D. J., 151, 153, 156, 197
Stein, E. A., 328
Stein, L. I., 427, 526
Stein, M. A., 462
Stein, M. B., 153, 161, 257
Steinberg, E., 450
Steinhausen, H. C., 469
Stein-Seroussi, A., 92, 94
Steinwaches, D., 417
Stejskal, W. J., 44
Steketee, G., 156
Stemberger, R. M. T., 300
Stern, E., 277
Stern, M., 336
Stern, Y., 449
Sternberg, R. J., 40
Stetson, B. A., 221
Stevens, R. J., 476
Stewart, A. E., 95, 97
Stewart, J. W., 142, 279
Stewart, S. H., 166
St. George-Hyslop, P. H., 446
Stiglmayr, C., 306
Stiles, W. B., 60, 67–68
Stinson, F. S., 317
Stip, E., 143, 396
Stock, W. E., 366
Stoeber, J., 164, 165
Stoessel, P., 142, 277
Stoller, R. J., 356
Stone, A. A., 215, 219, 240
Stone, Alan, 523
Stone, M. H., 306
Stone, W. S., 410
Stoner, S. A., 317
Stoney, C. M., 223, 235, 236
Stossel, C., 239
Stoudemire, A., 183
Stout, A. L., 370
Strachan, A. M., 424
Strack, M., 270
Strain, E. C., 293
Strain, P. S., 505
Strakowski, S. M., 277, 405
Stratton, K., 489
Strauss, M. E., 247, 402, 404, 407
Streltzer, J., 201
Stricker, 292
Strittmatter, W. J., 447
Strong, J. W., 519
Strosahl, K. D., 87
Strote, J., 313
Strupp, H. H., 110, 114, 115, 122
Stuhr, J., 239
Stunkard, A. J., 232
Sturgis, E. T., 157

Suarez, E. C., 223
Succop, P. A., 490
Suchday, S., 236
Sudhakar, S., 237
Sue, S., 51
Sullivan, E. V., 413
Sullivan, G., 18
Sullivan, G. M., 277
Sullivan, Harry Stack, 113, 127, 128, 271
Sullivan, J. M., 267
Sullivan, M., 421
Sullivan, P. F., 273
Sulzer-Azaroff, B., 505, 506
Summerfeldt, L., 154
Sund, B., 255
Suomi, S. J., 68, 69
Super, C. M., 490
Suppes, T., 251, 252, 257
Sushinsky, L., 425
Susser, E., 415
Suten, K. M., 338
Sutton, S. K., 148, 169
Suvisaari, J. M., 390
Suwanlert, S., 480
Suzuki, L. A., 40
Svikis, D. S., 346
Swann, W. B., Jr., 92, 94, 263–264, 264
Swanson, J. W., 526
Swanson, M. G., 306
Swartz, H. A., 274, 275
Swartz, M. S., 526
Sweeney, J. A., 265, 405
Swendsen, J., 252
Swerdlow, N. R., 420
Swift, W., 345
Swinson, R. P., 155, 157, 162
Switzer, F. S., III, 235
Sy, F. S., 237
Szasz, T. S., 8, 28, 522, 527
Szatmari, P., 497
Szechtman, B., 396
Szumowski, E., 462
Szymanski, L., 492, 493, 500

Taaid, N., 420
Taber, K. H., 143
Tageson, C. W., 468
Taieb, O., 283
Takei, N., 415
Takeshita, J., 405
Talajic, M., 212
Tamminga, C. A., 416, 417
Tamplin, A., 460
Tancer, M. E., 173
Tang, T. Z., 269, 281
Tangney, J. P., 297
Tanner, J. M., 489
Tanskanen, A. J., 390
Tapper, M., 209
Tarrier, N., 91, 98, 422, 423, 424
Tarullo, L. B., 468
Tashman, N. A., 266, 270
Tataryn, D. J., 183, 202, 203
Tatemichi, T. K., 449
Tauscher, J., 416
Taylor, C. B., 224, 238, 239, 471
Taylor, E., 20, 22
Taylor, E. B., 256
Taylor, G. J., 207
Taylor, L., 144, 266
Taylor, L. A., 441
Taylor, S., 152, 157, 158, 160, 166, 173
Taylor, S. E., 92, 94, 124, 229, 239
Teachman, B. A., 164
Teasdale, J. D., 269
Teicher, M. H., 276
Tek, C., 404
Telch, M. J., 153, 173
Tellegen, A., 308
Teller, D. W., 340
Temkin, N., 439
Temoshok, L., 226
Temple, J. A., 305
Tenke, C. E., 142
Teplin, L. A., 316
Terént, A., 443
Teri, L., 83
Terman, J. S., 276
Terman, Lewis, 39
Terman, M., 276
Terras, A., 316
Test, D. W., 504
Test, M. A., 427
Thaker, G. K., 411
Thal, L. J., 449, 451
Thapa, P. B., 417
Thase, M. E., 277, 278, 279, 280, 281, 282
Thayer, J. F., 154, 164, 180, 189
Thede, L. L., 308
Thelen, M. H., 471
Theodore, W. H., 436
Thigpen, C. H., 184
Thisted, R. A., 274
Thomas, A. M., 300
Thomas, M., 138
Thomas, P., 464
Thomas, R. G., 451
Thomas, V. S., 317
Thompson, J. W., 152
Thompson, M. G., 487
Thomsen, C. J., 316
Thomson, N., 426
Thoresen, C. E., 240, 241
Thorndike, Edward Lee, 76, 77, 78, 79
Thornton, L. M., 256
Thorpe, S. J., 164
Tiefer, L., 370
Tienari, P., 410
Tiihonen, J., 525
Tiller, J. M., 127
Tillfors, M., 298
Timio, M., 224
Tinklenberg, J. R., 333, 337
Tipp, J., 290
Tischler, G. L., 39
Titone, D., 393, 394
Tofrey, E. F., 412
Tolan, P. H., 464
Tolin, D. F., 170
Tolles, R. L., 239
Tolman, Edward C., 88–89
Tomarken, A. J., 49, 169
Tomasson, K., 203, 205
Tondo, L., 282
Toneatto, A., 341
Tonigan, J. S., 324
Toomey, R., 404
Torgersen, S., 171, 172, 208, 302
Torrey, E. F., 415, 526
Toscova, R., 324
Townsend, J., 498
Trakowski, J. H., 166
Tranel, D., 444
Treadwell, K. R., 168
Treboux, D., 116
Treffers, P. D. A., 477
Treiber, F. A., 224
Trenerry, M. R., 455
Trivette, C. M., 503
Trocme, N., 187
Tromovitch, P., 187
Tross, S., 437
Trotter, Thomas, 340
Troughton, E., 345
Truax, P. A., 264, 269
Truchon, C., 266
True, W. R., 346, 347
Trull, T. J., 31, 287, 296, 302
Truman, C. J., 252
Tsai, L. Y., 498
Tsai, M., 60, 498
Tsuang, J. W., 347
Tsuang, M. T., 155, 157, 313, 410, 412
Tucker, J. S., 242
Tue, G. C., 346
Tuff, L., 497
Tuke, William, 14, 16
Tulsky, D. S., 39, 40
Turetsky, B. I., 405, 413, 420
Turkat, I. D., 305
Turkheimer, E., 436, 518, 519
Turner, C. W., 223
Turner, J. E., Jr., 266
Turner, J. J. D., 336
Turner, J. R., 224
Turner, R. E., 374
Turner, S. M., 83, 143
Turvey, K., 226
Tutkun, H., 192
Twain, Mark, 328
Tyano, S., 167
Tymchuk, A. J., 507
Tyrer, P., 308
Tyrrell, D. A. J., 212, 215

Ullman, S. E., 316
Ullmann, L. P., 205, 206, 425
Ullrich, P. M., 228
Ulrich, R. F., 427
Umberson, D., 241
Umbricht, D., 417
Underwood, M. D., 279
Underwood, M. K., 466
Unger, J. B., 236
Ungerleider, J. T., 338
Ungless, M. A., 348
Unnewehr, S., 169
Urcuyo, L., 51
U.S. Census Bureau, 17, 62, 464
U.S. Department of Health and Human Services, 319, 320, 336
Useda, J. D., 287
U.S. Public Health Service, 326
Üstün, T. B., 201, 204, 205, 206, 248, 402
Uviller, H. R., 527

Vaca, F., 442
Vaidya, G., 399
Vaillant, G., 120, 204
Vakoch, D. A., 110, 114, 115, 122
Valavka, J., 417
Valdimarsdottir, H. B., 219
Valencia, R. R., 40
Valenti-Hein, D., 493, 507
Valentine, J. D., 159, 161
Valenzuela, M., 489
Valleni-Basile, L. A., 157
Vanable, P. A., 229
van Baar, A., 489
van de Mheen, H. D., 319, 332
van der Gaag, M., 421
VanderHart, N. S., 504
van der Kolk, B. A., 176
van Doorninck, W., 488
van Dyck, R., 187
Van Erp, T. G. M., 413
Van Hunsel, F., 382
Van Hutton, V., 343
Van Italli, J. B., 225
van Kradenburg, 300
Van Ness, 455
Van Noppen, B., 156
van Oel, C. J., 413
van Oers, H. A. M., 319, 332
VanOot, P. H., 233
van Os, J., 405, 428
van Reekum, R., 441
Varma, A., 447
Vasey, M. W., 467
Vasile, R., 153
Vaughan, S. C., 117
Vázquez, C., 247
Veale, D., 198, 207
Vega, W. A., 101
Vehrs, B., 386
Velakoulis, D., 413
Velligan, D. I., 423, 424
Velting, D. M., 272
Venables, P. H., 308, 415
Venanzi, S., 224
Venter, A., 496, 497
Verdecchia, P., 224
Verdys, M., 413
Verhoeff, P. I. G., 416
Vernon, P., 238
Viederman, M., 201, 205
Viguera, A. C., 282
Vik, P. W., 344
Viken, R., 317, 346
Viscoli, C. M., 236
Visintainer, M. A., 226, 238
Visscher, B. R., 229
Visser, S., 206
Voas, R. B., 315
Vogler, G. P., 421
Volk, C. L. E., 414
Volk, D. W., 417
Volkmar, F. R., 498, 500
Volkow, N., 333, 348
Volpicelli, J. R., 226, 238, 349
Volpicelli, L. A., 349
von Eye, A., 450
von Knorring, A., 208
Vorters, D. F., 468
Voshort, K., 212
Voss, W. D., 91
Voth, E. A., 338

Wachtel, P. L., 121
Waddell, P., 439
Wadden, T. A., 88
Waddington, J. L., 135
Waggoner, R. W., 432
Wagner, A., 251, 255
Wagner, B. M., 258, 260
Wagner, E. H., 329
Wagner, F. A., 338
Wagner, H. N., 416
Wagner, K. D., 265
Wagner, R. K., 41
Wahl, O. F., 100
Wahlberg, K. E., 410, 418, 423, 424
Waisbren, S. E., 488
Wakefield, J. C., 29
Walbran, B., 358

Walcott, D. M., 523
Waldinger, M. D., 362
Waldinger, R. J., 304
Waldo, T. G., 186, 187, 195
Waldron, I., 329
Walker, C. E., 472
Walker, E. F., 412, 413, 414
Walker, J. R., 161
Walker, M., 273
Walker, R. L., 262
Walker, S., 490
Walker, T., 504
Wall, T. L., 346
Wallace, C. J., 426
Wallace, J. F., 293
Waller, J. L., 157
Waller, N. G., 180
Walsh, D., 404
Walsh, R., 23
Walters, A. S., 508
Walters, E. E., 247, 257, 258, 259, 262, 273
Walters, R. H., 81
Walters, S. T., 323
Wang, G., 333, 348
Wang, K., 276
Wang, S., 181
Ward, K. E., 413
Ward, N. G., 174, 175, 233
Ward, P. B., 421
Ward, T., 378, 380, 381
Warda, G., 167
Wardle, J., 232, 470
Warner, V., 256
Warren, J. L., 294
Warshaw, M. G., 280
Warsradt, M. D., 261
Warwick, H. M. C., 206, 207, 208
Wasik, B. A., 476
Wassell, G., 88
Wasserman, D. A., 345
Waterhouse, L., 494, 499
Waters, E., 116
Waters, N., 137
Waters, S., 137
Watkins, C. E., 45
Watkins, J. T., 272
Watkins, M. J., 97
Watson, D., 207, 257
Watson, John B., 76–77, 78
Watson, J. P., 226
Watson, R., 383
Watts, F. N., 266
Weardon, A. J., 422, 424
Webster, C. D., 524
Webster-Stratton, C., 305, 466
Wechsler, David, 39, 40
Wechsler, H., 313
Weekes, J. R., 195
Wegner, D. M., 68, 167
Wehman, P., 503
Wehr, T. A., 275, 276
Weihofen, H., 512
Weikart, D. B., 466
Weinberg, W. A., 274
Weinberger, A., 267, 268
Weinberger, D. A., 214
Weinberger, D. E., 349
Weinberger, D. R., 415
Weiner, B., 91
Weiner, H., 214
Weiner, I. B., 41, 44
Weiner, K., 171
Weingarten, S. M., 143
Weinrott, M. R., 381
Weinstock, L. S., 153
Weinstock, M., 146
Weisberg, R. B., 367
Weisberg, R. W., 253
Weisman, A. G., 422
Weiss, B., 2
Weiss, E. L., 250, 277
Weiss, G., 463
Weiss, J. M., 56
Weiss, M. G., 206
Weiss, R. V., 459
Weissenburger, J. E., 255
Weissman, M. M., 127, 156, 163, 250, 256, 257, 271, 272
Weisz, J. R., 2, 265, 461, 480
Wekerle, C., 469
Wekstein, L., 272
Wells, A., 164, 165
Wells, K. B., 249
Weltzin, T. E., 470
Wender, Paul, 281
Wender, P. H., 273, 409, 410
Wenzlaff, R. M., 68, 264
Werbin, T. J., 360, 361
Werry, J. S., 496, 507
Werth, U., 292
Wesson, D. R., 332
West, A. R., 416
West, S. G., 223, 236
West, S. L., 323
Westen, D., 121, 122
Westergaard, T., 415
Westin, C. F., 414
Wethington, E., 404
Wexler, David, 523
Wexler, D. B., 531, 532
Whalley, H. C., 413
Wheatman, S. R., 513
Whiffen, V. E., 267, 270
Whisman, M. A., 97
Whisnant, J. P., 443
Whistler, J. L., 348
White, D. M., 506
White, E. W., 313, 319
White, J., 328
Whitehouse, M. A., 503
Whitehouse, W. G., 66, 255, 265, 266
Whiteside, J. E., 255
Whitlach, C. J., 450
Whitman, R. D., 344
Whitman, T. L., 492, 507
Wichstrom, L., 250
Wickramaratne, P., 250, 256
Widiger, T. A., 31, 83, 287, 291, 293, 295, 296, 297, 298, 302
Widom, C. S., 466
Wielgus, M. S., 420
Wiersma, D., 399, 403
Wilcox, H. C., 338
Wilhelm, F. H., 153
Wilhelm, S., 156
Wilkel, D., 203
Willard, H. F., 487
Willerman, L., 395
Williams, B. K., 332
Williams, G. H., 277
Williams, J. B., 229
Williams, J. C., 236
Williams, J. M. G., 266
Williams, L. M., 190, 377
Williams, M., 250
Williams, N. L., 91, 93, 117, 164, 168
Williams, R. B., 236
Williams, S., 93, 266
Williams, S. C. R., 414
Williams, S. L., 238
Williamson, D. F., 471
Williamson, Gail, 243
Willson, P., 316
Willson, V. L., 502
Wilson, C. B., 471
Wilson, G. D., 379
Wilson, G. T., 84, 232, 328, 479
Wilson, J. J., 200, 207, 208, 209
Wilson, J. Q., 513, 514
Wilson, K. O., 87
Wilson, M., 358
Wilson, N. L., 190
Wilson, P., 505
Wilson, W. H., 290
Wincze, J. P., 367, 381, 383
Wing, Lorna, 494
Wingard, D. L., 242
Winger, G., 174
Winick, B. J., 519, 527
Winokur, G., 252, 273
Wirshing, W. C., 417
Wise, A., 413
Wise, R. A., 348
Wise, T. N., 200, 201, 204, 206, 208
Wisner, K. L., 247
Wittchen, H. U., 152, 153, 154, 163, 257
Wittig, B. A., 116
Witzig, J. S., 374
Woerner, M. G., 399, 403
Wolf, E., 336
Wolf, Hugo, 254
Wolf, S., 214, 290
Wolfe, D. A., 469
Wolfe, R., 316
Wolff, H. G., 214
Wolk, S., 250
Wolkenstein, B., 169
Wolpe, D., 84
Wolpe, Joseph, 84, 169, 365
Wong, D. F., 416
Wood, F. B., 474
Wood, J. M., 37, 44, 45
Woodman, C., 162
Woodruff, P. W. R., 397
Woods, J. H., 174
Woods, S. W., 248
Woody, G. E., 349
Woody, S. R., 164
Wool, C., 200
Woolaway-Bickel, K., 165, 166
Woolf, Virginia, 254
Woolson, A. M., 306
Wright, E. R., 99
Wright, I. C., 397
Wright, L., 191
Wright, P., 415
Wrightson, P., 439
Wrocklage, C., 440
Wuensch, K. L., 514
Wuerker, A. K., 422
Wundt, Wilhelm, 20
Wurtele, S. K., 187
Wyatt, G. E., 228
Wykes, T., 421
Wylie, K. R., 368
Wyllie, E., 453
Wynings, C., 227
Wynne, L. C., 410, 418, 423, 424

Xian, H., 171, 172, 346

Yamada, N., 406
Yamaoka, L. H., 446
Yang, J., 303
Yargic, L. I., 192
Yarnold, P. R., 507
Yassouridis, A., 277
Yates, Andrea, 510, 511
Yatham, L. N., 279
Yehuda, R., 173
Yeo, R. A., 436
Yesalis, C. E., 339
Yesalis, Charles, 339
Yetman, N. R., 320
Yirmiya, N., 500
Yonkers, K. A., 157, 163
Yore, M. M., 316
Yoshikawa, H., 476
Yoshinaga, K., 496, 497
Young, A., 163, 204, 206
Young, A. S., 249
Young, A. W., 141
Young, E., 250
Young, J. E., 267, 268
Young, M. A., 276
Young, P. M., 276
Yuille, J. C., 182, 183, 191
Yusopoff, L., 422

Zagon, I. K., 291, 293
Zahn-Waxler, C., 459, 464, 465
Zamboni, P., 201
Zametkin, A. J., 498
Zanakos, S., 167
Zanarini, M. C., 296
Zarit, S. H., 445, 450
Zatorre, R. J., 348
Zdanowicz, M., 526
Zeichner, A., 317
Zeller, P. J., 249
Zeskind, P. S., 490
Zhang, A., 249
Zhang, A. V., 5
Zhang, X. L., 347
Zhao, S., 35, 94, 99, 153, 154, 163, 251, 253, 290, 467
Zigman, W. N., 446, 492
Zigman, Z., 446, 492
Zilboorg, G., 12
Zimbardo, P., 98–99
Zimbarg, R. E., 165
Zimmerman, B., 250
Zimmerman, M., 257
Zimmerman, M. E., 277
Zinbarg, R. E., 151, 257
Zislin, J., 67
Zisook, S., 411
Zlotnick, C., 163
Zobel, A. W., 277
Zoccolillo, M., 464
Zonana, H., 526
Zubieta, J. K., 278
Zucker, K. J., 384
Zuckerman, B., 489
Zuckerman, M., 91
Zurynski, Y., 209
Zwinderman, A. H., 362

SUBJECT INDEX

AA (Alcoholics Anonymous), 323–324
ABAB (reversal) design, 70, 71
abnormal behavior
definitions, 2–6
extent of, 35
multiperspective approach, 23–24
non-Western approaches, 22–23
theory overview, 6, 8–9
abreaction, 193
absence (petit mal) seizures, 454
abstinence violation effect (AVE), 325, 344
acamprosate, 349
acceptance-based behavior therapy, 85–87
accidents
and acquired brain disorders, 441, 442
and alcohol abuse/dependence, 315–316
and psychopharmacology, 174
acetylcholine, 137, 449, 451
acquaintance rape, 378
acquiescence response set, 46
acquired brain disorders, 432–455
brain tumors, 444, 453
caregiving, 450
cerebral infections, 436–439
dementia overview, 444–451
diagnosis, 432–436
and endocrine disorders, 451–452
epilepsy, 197, 453–455
groups at risk, 439, 443–444, 449, 455
and malnutrition, 451
and mental retardation, 490
stroke, 441–444, 449, 453
and substance abuse/dependence, 317, 441, 443, 451, 453
and syphilis, 21, 437
toxic disorders, 452–453
traumatic brain injuries, 439–441, 442, 453, 490
acquired immune deficiency syndrome. *See* AIDS/HIV
acquired sexual dysfunctions, 362
acquired sociopathy, 444
acrophobia, 152
ACT (assertive community treatment), 427
active-but-odd autism, 494
active phase of schizophrenia, 399
acute confusional state, 440
acute stress disorder, 181
adaptive functioning, 3–4, 485, 486, 505
addiction, 313. *See also* substance abuse/dependence
Addington v. Texas, 520–521
Addison's disease, 452
ADHD. *See* attention deficit hyperactivity disorder
adjustment disorders, 161
adolescence
and anxiety disorders, 153
and developmental disorders, 503
and mood disorders, 250
and paraphilias, 383
and substance abuse/dependence, 326–327, 340, 343–344
and suicide, 259–260, 262, 263
teenage pregnancy, 491–492
See also age; childhood/adolescent disorders
adoption studies, 133–135, 409–410
adrenal syndromes, 452
advertising. *See* media
affectionless control, 270
Africa, 22–23. *See also* cultural variations
African Americans. *See* race/ethnicity
age
and acquired brain disorders, 434, 445, 447, 449
and anxiety disorders, 154, 160–161, 163
and delusional disorder, 406
and dissociative disorders, 192
and mental retardation, 493
and mood disorders, 250–251
and schizophrenia, 405
and sexual disorders, 360
and sleep disorders, 234–235
and substance abuse/dependence, 320–321, 332
and suicide, 257, 259, 261
aggression/violence
domestic violence, 342–343, 377, 399
psychodynamic perspective, 107
and sexuality, 374–375, 378, 379
and substance abuse/dependence, 316, 317, 333, 339, 342–343
and suicide, 261
agnosia, 435
agoraphobia
behavioral perspective, 169
childhood/adolescent forms, 466
as culture-bound syndrome, 7
and panic disorder, 162–163
psychodynamic perspective, 170
AIDS/HIV
and acquired brain disorders, 437–438, 439
and confidentiality, 532–533
and mental retardation, 488
and patients' rights, 530
and sexual assault, 378
and stress, 217, 228–230, 237, 239
and substance abuse/dependence, 349, 351, 352
alcohol abuse/dependence, 314–326
and acquired brain disorders, 441, 451
cognitive perspective, 325, 343–344
development of, 318
groups at risk, 319–321
and mental retardation, 489
personal costs of, 316–318
prevalence, 313
and sexual disorders, 360
social cost of, 315–316
and synergistic effects, 332
treatment, 322–326
See also substance abuse/dependence
alcohol expectancies, 343–344
Alcoholics Anonymous (AA), 323–324, 345
alienation, 126
ALI test, 512–513
aloof autism, 494
alprazolam (Xanax), 174
alternating personality, 184
alter personalities, 184–185. *See also* dissociative identity disorder
Alzheimer's disease, 141
and Down syndrome, 446, 492
groups at risk, 449
overview, 445–447
and stress, 218
and traumatic brain injuries, 440
treatment, 449, 451
Ambien (zolpidem), 234
American Law Institute (ALI) test, 512–513
American Psychological Association Ethics Code, 532–536
amitriptyline (Elavil), 175
amnesia
and acquired brain disorders, 434, 451
and dissociative disorders, 181–182, 183–184, 193
and recovered memory controversy, 190, 191
amniocentesis, 488
amok syndrome, 7
amotivational syndrome, 338
amphetamines, 333–334, 416, 481–482, 498
amygdala, 141, 168, 292
amyloid-cascade hypothesis, 446–447
anabolic steroids, 339
Anafranil (clomipramine), 156, 175, 176
analogue experiments, 68–69
anal stage, 110
ancient societies, 11, 26
aneurysms, 443
angel dust (PCP), 336
anhedonia, 247, 289
animal experimentation, 68–69
animal hoarding, 155
anorexia nervosa
behavioral perspective, 477
as culture-bound syndrome, 7
interpersonal perspective, 479–480
neuroscience perspective, 481
overview, 469–470
sociocultural perspective, 480
and stress, 231
ANS (autonomic nervous system), 144–146, 216–217
Antabuse (disulfiram), 323
anterograde amnesia, 181, 451
An Anthropologist on Mars (Sacks), 58
antiandrogen drugs, 382–383
anticipatory anxiety, 233
antidepressant drugs
and anxiety disorders, 156, 172, 173, 175–176
and dissociative disorders, 197
and impulse-control disorders, 300
and mood disorders, 172, 253, 279–280
and personality disorders, 309
and sexual dysfunctions, 361, 370
and somatoform disorders, 199, 209
and substance abuse/dependence, 329
table, 139
antimanic medication, 139, 280, 282
antipsychotic drugs
and autism, 498
and competency to stand trial, 517–518
and personality disorders, 296
and schizophrenia, 416, 417–418
table, 139
See also psychopharmacology
antismoking movement, 326–327
antisocial personality disorder (APD)
cognitive perspective, 307
and comorbidity, 35
and conduct disorder, 464
gender differences, 302
and narcissistic personality disorder, 297–298
neuroscience perspective, 308
overview, 290–293
and rape, 378
and serial killers, 294
and somatoform disorders, 208
and substance abuse/dependence, 293, 317
anxiety
and autonomic nervous system, 144
defined, 151

anxiety—*Cont.*
and dissociative disorders, 192
and paraphilias, 379
and sexual dysfunctions, 358, 360, 363, 365, 366
and sleep disorders, 233
and somatoform disorders, 201, 204–205
See also anxiety disorders; psychodynamic perspective
anxiety disorders, 150–176
behavioral perspective, 85, 168–170
and borderline personality disorder, 295–296
childhood/adolescent forms, 466–468, 477, 478, 479
cognitive perspective, 163–168
and culture-bound syndromes, 7
generalized anxiety disorder overview, 153–154
groups at risk, 152, 153, 154, 156–157, 160–161, 163
and mood disorders, 153, 168, 172, 257
neuroscience perspective, 156, 171–176
obsessive-compulsive disorder overview, 154–157
panic disorder overview, 161–163
phobia overview, 152–153
posttraumatic stress disorder overview, 157–161
psychodynamic perspective, 151, 170–171
and substance abuse/dependence, 153, 317, 333
anxiety sensitivity, 166
anxious/fearful personality disorders, 298–301. *See also* avoidant personality disorder; dependent personality disorder; obsessive-compulsive personality disorder
APD. *See* antisocial personality disorder
aphasia, 435, 443
apomorphine, 370
apraxia, 434–435
archetypes, 113
Aricept, 449, 451
arousal phase of sexual response, 360–361
articulation, 476
Asia, 23. *See also* cultural variations
Asian Americans. *See* race/ethnicity
Asperger's disorder, 495
assertive community treatment (ACT), 427
assessment. *See* psychological assessment
assisted living, 502
Association for Retarded Citizens (ARC), 500
astrology, 26, 27, 35
asylums, 13–16
atherosclerosis, 221
athletes, 339
Ativan (lorazepam), 174, 181, 197
Attachment (Bowlby), 116
attachment theory
and anxiety disorders, 164, 170
and mood disorders, 270–271
and neuroscience perspective, 147–148
overview, 116–117
attention
and acquired brain disorders, 434
and anxiety disorders, 164
cognitive perspective, 93
and dissociative disorders, 189
and learning disorders, 474–475
and mood disorders, 252, 266
and schizophrenia, 296, 396, 397, 399, 412, 418–421
attention deficit hyperactivity disorder (ADHD)
behavioral perspective, 477
cognitive perspective, 478
and learning disorders, 474
and mood disorders, 252
neuroscience perspective, 481
overview, 461–463
attribution styles
and mood disorders, 265, 266, 478
overview, 92
and personality disorders, 307
and sexual dysfunctions, 367
authenticity, 123
autism, 493–500
behavioral perspective, 505–506
cognitive perspective, 499–500, 506–507
groups at risk, 500
neuroscience perspective, 497–499, 500, 507
and personality disorders, 290
social issues, 501, 503
symptoms, 494–497
autogynephilia, 373
automatic information processing, 93
Automatic Thoughts Questionnaire—Revised (ATQ-R), 47
autonomic nervous system (ANS), 144–146, 206, 216–217, 236
Avance, 504
AVE (abstinence violation effect), 325, 344
aversion conditioning, 341, 531
avoidance (escape) learning, 79, 168–169, 292, 477
avoidant personality disorder, 298–299, 306, 309
axes of diagnosis, 32
axon, 136
axon terminals, 136

BA (behavioral activation) therapy, 264, 267–268
backward-masking paradigm, 421
barbiturates
and dissociative disorders, 181, 193, 197
and sleep disorders, 234
and substance abuse/dependence, 332
basal ganglia, 141
and acquired brain disorders, 448
and anxiety disorders, 173
and mood disorders, 276
and schizophrenia, 413, 416
BAS (Behavioral Approach System; Behavioral Activation System), 148
A Beautiful Mind, 423
bed-wetting, 472
behavioral activation. *See* Behavioral Approach System
behavioral activation (BA) therapy, 264, 267–268
Behavioral Approach System (Behavioral Activation System) (BAS), 148
behavioral couple therapy, 342–343
behavioral experiments, 95–96
behavioral high-risk studies, 66, 412–413
behavioral inhibition, 172
Behavioral Inhibition System (BIS), 148
behavioral medicine. *See* health psychology
behavioral perspective, 8, 75–88
anxiety disorders, 85, 168–170
assumptions of, 78
background of, 76–78
childhood/adolescent disorders, 477
contemporary approaches, 83
developmental disorders, 503, 505–506
dissociative disorders, 193–194, 195
evaluation of, 87–88
gender identity disorders, 385
on learning mechanisms, 78–82
mood disorders, 263, 264
and neuroscience perspective, 148
paraphilias, 380–381
and patients' rights, 531–532
personality disorders, 298, 305–306
and psychological assessment, 50
and sleep disorders, 234
somatoform disorders, 205–207
stress-related illness, 236–237
substance abuse/dependence, 325, 327–328, 341–342
treatment overview, 83–87
See also cognitive-behavioral therapy
behavior genetics, 131–135
la belle indifférence, 202, 204, 205
Bender Visual-Motor Gestalt Test, 48
Benzedrine (amphetamine), 333
benzodiazepines
and anxiety disorders, 172, 173, 174–175
and dissociative disorders, 181, 193, 197
and sleep disorders, 233–234
bereavement, 218–219
beriberi, 451
Bethlem (Bedlam) Hospital, 13–14
beyond-a-reasonable-doubt standard of proof, 519, 520–521
bias
experimenter effects, 59–60
and interviews, 37
See also cultural bias
binge drinking, 322
binge eating, 470
biofeedback, 212, 213, 234, 237
biogenic theories of abnormal behavior, 6, 8, 19, 20–21. *See also* medical model; neuroscience perspective
biological clock, 274
bipolar disorder
and anxiety disorders, 257
cognitive perspective, 267, 269
and creativity, 254
neuroscience perspective, 146, 273–274, 275, 277, 278
overview, 251–252
See also mood disorders
BIS (Behavioral Inhibition System), 148
bleeding, 12, 15
blocking, 392
blood alcohol level, 315
blunted affect, 397
body dysmorphic disorder
cognitive perspective, 207, 208
groups at risk, 203–204
neuroscience perspective, 209
overview, 198–199
psychodynamic perspective, 205
borderline personality disorder
behavioral perspective, 305, 306
and dependent personality disorder, 299
gender differences, 302
groups at risk, 302
neuroscience perspective, 308, 309
overview, 293, 295–296
boys. *See* gender differences
brain
anatomy of, 139–141
lateralization, 143–144, 209
measurement, 141–143
and mood disorders, 276–277
plasticity of, 146–147, 491
See also acquired brain disorders; neuroscience perspective
brain abscesses. *See* cerebral abscesses
brain-derived neurotrophic factor, 279
brain stem, 141
brain tumors, 444, 453
brief psychotic disorder, 391
Buddhism, 23
bulimia nervosa, 141, 470, 480
buprenorfin, 349
bupropion (Wellbutrin), 280
BuSpar (buspirone), 175, 349
buspirone (BuSpar), 175, 349
B-values, 125, 126

California equine encephalitis, 439
cancer, 225–228, 236–237, 239
carbon monoxide poisoning, 453

cardiovascular reactivity, 222–224, 242
caregiving, 450
cascade system, 501
case-control designs, 64
case studies, 58, 70
Case Studies in Behavior Modification (Ullmann & Krasner), 58
castration anxiety, 111, 379
catastrophic thoughts, 161–162, 207
catatonic negativism, 401–402
catatonic rigidity, 401
catatonic schizophrenia, 401–402
catatonic stupor, 398, 401
catecholamine hypothesis, 278
categorical classification, 30
catharsis, 240–241
causality, 56, 64–65. *See also* theories of abnormal behavior
CBT. *See* cognitive-behavioral therapy
cell body, 136
central nervous system (CNS), 135–144
  brain anatomy, 139–141
  brain lateralization, 143–144, 209
  brain measurement, 141–143
  neurons, 136–137
  See also neurotransmitters
cerebellum, 141, 413, 498
cerebral abscesses, 436
cerebral artieriosclerosis, 453
cerebral cortex, 139, 208–209, 308, 414–415
cerebral infections, 436–439
cerebrovascular accident (CVA). *See* stroke
chaining, 505
character disorders. *See* personality disorders
Chicago Child-Parent Center (CPC), 305
child abuse
  and acquired brain disorders, 441, 490
  and childhood disruptive behavior disorders, 466, 477, 480
  and childhood emotional distress disorders, 466, 469
  and dissociative disorders, 186–187, 188, 189, 192–193, 197
  and elimination disorders, 472
  and mood disorders, 266, 277
  and pedophilia, 373–374, 376–377, 379, 381
  and personality disorders, 296, 302
  prevention, 187
  and rape, 378
  recovered memory controversy, 190–191
  and sexual dysfunctions, 360, 362
  and somatoform disorders, 200, 201, 204
  and substance abuse/dependence, 317
  and suicide, 258
childhood/adolescent disorders, 458–482
  behavioral perspective, 477
  cognitive perspective, 478–479
  diagnosis, 459–460
  disruptive behavior disorders overview, 459, 461–466
  dissociative disorders, 192
  eating disorders overview, 469–471
  elimination disorders, 471–472, 481
  emotional distress disorders overview, 250, 251, 466–469
  groups at risk, 464–466, 468–469, 471, 475–476
  interpersonal perspective, 479–480
  learning/communication disorders, 460, 474–476
  neuroscience perspective, 475–476, 481–482, 491
  personality disorders, 302
  and predictability, 460–461
  prevalence, 459
  psychodynamic perspective, 480–481
  sleep disorders, 472–474
  sociocultural perspective, 480
childhood depression, 250, 251, 468, 469, 474, 478
childhood disruptive behavior disorders
  behavioral perspective, 477
  cognitive perspective, 478
  and learning disorders, 474
  and mood disorders, 252
  neuroscience perspective, 481
  overview, 459, 461–466
  sociocultural perspective, 480
childhood emotional distress disorders, 250, 251
  behavioral perspective, 477
  cognitive perspective, 478, 479
  and learning disorders, 474
  overview, 459, 466–469
  prevention, 478
  and suicide, 259–260, 262, 263
child maltreatment. *See* child abuse
child molestation. *See* child abuse; pedophilia
chlorazepate (Tranxene), 174, 332
chlorpromazine (Thorazine), 417
cholinesterase inhibitors, 441
chromosomes, 131
chrono-therapy, 235
cingulotomy, 143
circadian rhythm disorders, 234–235, 276
cirrhosis of the liver, 317
civil commitment, 516, 518–527
  issues in, 525–527
  procedural issues, 518–521
  standards for, 522–525
clanging, 395
class differences. *See* sociocultural perspective; socioeconomic status
classical (respondent) conditioning
  and anxiety disorders, 168–169
  and childhood/adolescent disorders, 477
  overview, 78–79, 83–84
  and paraphilias, 380
  and sexual dysfunctions, 365
  and shaping, 80–81
  and somatoform disorders, 206
  and stress-related illness, 236–237
classification. *See Diagnostic and Statistical Manual of Mental Disorders*; psychological assessment
clear and convincing evidence standard of proof, 519, 521
client-centered therapy, 125
clinical psychologists, 10
clinical trials, 67–68
clinicians, 57–58
clomipramine (Anafranil), 156, 175, 176
clozapine (Clozaril), 416, 417
Clozaril (clozapine), 416, 417
CNS. *See* central nervous system
cocaine, 334–335, 351, 489
coconscious alters, 185
Cognex (tacrine), 449
cognitive appraisal, 90–93
cognitive-behavioral questionnaires, 47
cognitive-behavioral therapy (CBT), 60
  and anxiety disorders, 167, 168, 170–171, 175, 176
  and childhood/adolescent disorders, 478
  and dissociative disorders, 196–197
  and mood disorders, 267–269
  and sexual disorders, 368–369, 381
  and somatoform disorders, 206, 207–208
  and stress-related illness, 229, 234, 239
  and substance abuse/dependence, 325, 341–342, 344–345
  See also behavioral perspective; cognitive perspective
cognitive behaviorism, 89–90. *See also* cognitive-behavioral therapy
cognitive case conceptualization, 95
cognitive distortions, 90
cognitive perspective, 8, 88–98
  anxiety disorders, 163–168
  background of, 88–89
  childhood/adolescent disorders, 478–479
  cognitive appraisal, 90–93
  cognitive behaviorism, 89–90
  developmental disorders, 499–500, 506–507
  dissociative disorders, 195–197
  evaluation of, 97–98
  information processing, 93–94
  mood disorders, 92, 264–269, 270–271
  and neuroscience perspective, 148
  paraphilias, 381
  personality disorders, 292–293, 306–308
  and psychodynamic perspective, 121
  and psychological assessment, 47
  schizophrenia, 418–422
  somatoform disorders, 207–208
  stress-related illness, 214, 238–239
  substance abuse/dependence, 325, 343–345
  suicide, 261–262
  and transference, 119
  treatment overview, 94–97, 98
cognitive rehabilitation, 421
cognitive restructuring, 95, 207, 208
cognitive vulnerability, 91–92
collectivism, 22
combined ADHD, 462
commitment. *See* civil commitment
communication deviance (CD), 423–424
communication disorders, 476
community integration, 502
community mental health centers, 16, 17
Community Mental Health Centers Act (1963), 16, 19
community psychology, 19
community reinforcement, 342
community skills, 505
comorbidity, 34, 35
  and mood disorders, 257
  and personality disorders, 301–302
  and somatoform disorders, 198
competency to stand trial, 517–518
complex partial seizures, 453–454
compulsions, 154. *See also* obsessive-compulsive disorder
compulsive gambling, 156, 300, 318
computerized tomography (CT), 48, 142–143
concordance, 133
concussion, 440
conditioned reflexes, 76
conditioned response (CR), 78
conditioned (secondary) reinforcers, 79
conditioned stimulus (CS), 78
conditions of worth, 125
conduct disorder
  behavioral perspective, 477
  and learning disorders, 474
  overview, 463–464
  sociocultural perspective, 480
  types, 465
confabulation, 451
confidentiality, 63, 523, 532–534
conflict-resolution theory of conversion disorder, 201–202, 204–205
confounding, 56, 59
congenital disorders, 488, 498
conservation of energy, 204
constructivism, and cognitive perspective, 97
constructivist cognitive therapy, 95
contextual model, 19
contingencies, 79, 83

contingency management, 85
  and childhood/adolescent disorders, 477
  and patients' rights, 531–532
  and schizophrenia, 426
  and somatoform disorders, 206–207
  and substance abuse/dependence, 342
continuity hypothesis of mood disorders, 255
continuous amnesia, 181–182
control
  and behavioral perspective, 78, 87–88
  and research, 56, 58–62
  and stress-related illness, 238
control groups, 63, 68, 70
controlled information processing, 93
contusion, 440
conversion disorder
  behavioral perspective, 205, 206–207
  groups at risk, 204
  historical perspective, 180, 201
  neuroscience perspective, 208–209
  overview, 201–203
  psychodynamic perspective, 204, 205
coping skills
  and psychodynamic perspective, 120
  and somatoform disorders, 206
  and stress-related illness, 238–239
  and substance abuse/dependence, 329, 341, 344–345
coronary heart disease, 221–224, 235, 236, 239
corpus callosum, 139
correlational research designs, 64–66
correlation coefficient (r), 65
corticotropion-releasing factor (CRF), 146
cortisol, 251, 277, 278
counsel, right to, 518–519
couple therapy, 86, 342–343, 366–367, 368, 369
The Courage to Heal (Bass & Davis), 191
couvade, 201
covariation of events, 56, 64–65
covert sensitization, 341, 380
crack cocaine, 313, 334, 351, 489
CR (conditioned response), 78
creativity, and mood disorders, 253, 254
cretinism, 488
Creutzfeldt-Jakob disease, 438, 439
CRF (corticotropion-releasing factor), 146
crime
  and antisocial personality disorder, 290, 291, 292, 294
  and childhood/adolescent disorders, 464, 465
  and dissociative disorders, 182, 183
  and paraphilias, 373–374, 376–378, 379
  prevention, 520
  and schizophrenia, 399
  and substance abuse/dependence, 316, 351
  See also child abuse; legal issues; sexual assault
criminal responsibility. *See* legal issues
cross-dressing, 372–373
CS (conditioned stimulus), 78
CT (computerized tomography), 48, 142–143
cued panic attacks, 162
cultural bias
  and personality disorders, 303
  and psychodynamic perspective, 122
  and psychological assessment, 40, 46, 50–52
cultural variations
  and childhood/adolescent disorders, 480
  and definitions of abnormal behavior, 2, 5
  and dissociative disorders, 192
  non-Western approaches, 22–23
  and panic disorder, 163
  and personality disorders, 303
  and research, 62
  and schizophrenia, 405
  and sexuality, 356–357
  somatoform disorders, 201, 204, 206
  suicide, 258
  See also race/ethnicity
Culture and Mental Illness (Castillo), 5
culture-bound syndromes, 7, 51
Cushing's syndrome, 452
CVA (cerebrovascular accident). *See* stroke
cyclothymic disorder, 253

Dalmane (flurazepam), 233, 332, 333
dangerousness, 522–524
date rape, 378
DBT (dialectical behavior therapy), 85–86, 306, 341–342
debriefing, 64
decatastrophizing, 95
deception, 63
declarative (explicit) memory, 147, 182
defect model, 19
defense mechanisms, 108, 120, 170
deficit symptoms, 404, 405
degenerative disorders. *See* dementia
deinstitutionalization, 16–17, 18
déjà vu, 189
delinquency. *See* conduct disorder
delirium, 434, 440
delirium tremens (DTs), 318
delusional disorder, 288, 405–406
delusions, 253, 391–392, 402
  and delusional disorder, 405–406
  treatment for, 421–422
demand characteristics, 59–60
dementia
  and age, 445
  caregiving, 450
  diagnosis, 433, 434, 435–436
  and HIV, 437–438, 439
  overview, 444–451
  and substance abuse/dependence, 317
  See also acquired brain disorders
dementia praecox, 390
dementia pugilistica (punch-drunk syndrome), 440
dendrites, 136
denial, 109, 120
Depakote, 455
dependency, 269–270
dependent personality disorder
  behavioral perspective, 305, 306
  gender differences, 302, 308
  overview, 299, 301
dependent variables, 58–59
depersonalization, 161, 188–189
depersonalization disorder, 188–189, 192, 197
depressants, 330–333. *See also* alcohol abuse/dependence
depression
  and acquired brain disorders, 443
  and anxiety disorders, 153, 168, 172
  and attribution styles, 92, 478
  childhood/adolescent forms, 250, 251, 468, 469, 474, 478
  and endocrine system, 146
  and mental retardation, 492–493
  neuroscience perspective, 144, 172
  and somatoform disorders, 199, 201
  and substance abuse/dependence, 316, 317, 329
  See also mood disorders
depth hypothesis, 106
derealization, 161, 189
derived stimulus relations, 82
description, 55–56
descriptive validity, 34
desensitization, 165
desire phase of sexual response, 358, 360
determinism, 87
detoxification, 322
developmental adaptation continuity, 460
developmental disorders, 484–485, 500–508
  behavioral perspective, 503, 505–506
  cognitive perspective, 499–500, 506–507
  neuroscience perspective, 486–488, 497–499, 507
  prevention, 488, 504
  social issues, 500–504
  treatment, 505–508
  See also autism; mental retardation
dexamethasone suppression test (DST), 277
Dexedrine, 481
Dexedrine (dextroamphetamine), 333
dextroamphetamine (Dexedrine), 333
diagnosis, 28–32
  acquired brain disorders, 432–436
  anxiety disorders, 161
  and behavioral perspective, 83
  childhood/adolescent disorders, 459–460
  dissociative disorders, 187–188
  learning disorders, 475
  and psychopharmacology, 309
  sexual dysfunctions, 362–363
  somatoform disorders, 203
  See also Diagnostic and Statistical Manual of Mental Disorders
Diagnostic and Statistical Manual of Mental Disorders (APA)
  on acquired brain disorders, 435, 447
  on antisocial personality disorder, 290–291, 293
  and assessor interference, 36, 37
  on childhood/adolescent disorders, 459, 460
  on childhood anxiety disorders, 467
  on childhood disruptive behavior disorders, 461, 462, 463, 464
  criticisms of, 29, 30, 31
  and cultural bias, 51, 52
  on cultural variations, 6, 101
  on culture-bound syndromes, 7, 51
  on definitions of abnormal behavior, 4
  on delusional disorder, 406
  and diagnosis, 28
  on dissociative disorders, 188
  on eating disorders, 469
  on elemination disorders, 472
  on generalized anxiety disorder, 153
  on histrionic personality disorder, 303
  on impulse-control disorders, 300
  on learning/communication disorders, 474, 475
  on mental retardation, 485, 486
  on mood disorders, 246–248, 252, 253, 255, 257, 276
  on narcissistic personality disorder, 297, 304
  on neurosis, 151
  on panic disorder, 162, 163
  on paraphilias, 371, 372, 375–376, 378–379
  on personality disorders, 287, 309
  on posttraumatic stress disorder, 157, 161
  and reliability, 33
  revisions of, 31–32
  on schizophrenia, 391, 400
  on schizotypal personality disorder, 289
  on sexual disorders, 356, 357, 358
  on sexual dysfunctions, 358, 362
  on somatoform disorders, 198, 200
  on stress-related illness, 212
  on substance abuse/dependence, 313, 316, 326
  and validity, 34
Diagnostic Interview Schedule (DIS), 37
dialectical behavior therapy (DBT), 85–86, 306, 341–342
diathesis-stress (vulnerability-stress) model, 128
  and cognitive perspective, 91, 98
  and developmental disorders, 490–491

diathesis-stress (vulnerability-stress) model—*Cont.*
and neuroscience perspective, 131, 146–147, 172
and schizophrenia, 407, 418, 427–428
diazepam (Valium), 172, 174, 332
DID. *See* dissociative identity disorder
dieting, 232
differential deficits, 407
Dilantin, 455
dimensional classification, 30–31, 101, 287
Discovery of Witchcraft (Weyer), 13
discrimination learning, 80
disease model. *See* medical model
disorder-specific biases, 91
disorganized-nondisorganized dimension of schizophrenia, 404
disorganized schizophrenia, 400–401
displacement, 109
disregulation model of stress, 220, 224, 231, 232
disruptive behavior disorders. *See* childhood disruptive behavior disorders
dissociative amnesia, 181–182, 193
dissociative disorders, 179–197
behavioral perspective, 193–194, 195
and borderline personality disorder, 296
cognitive perspective, 195–197
depersonalization disorder, 188–189, 192, 197
dissociative amnesia, 181–182, 193
dissociative fugue, 182–184, 192, 193, 194
dissociative identity disorder overview, 184–188
groups at risk, 189, 192
neuroscience perspective, 189, 197
and posttraumatic stress disorder, 161, 181, 188, 189
psychodynamic perspective, 192–193, 197
vs. schizophrenia, 184, 390
sociocultural perspective, 194–195
and somatoform disorders, 201
dissociative fugue, 182–184, 192, 193, 194
dissociative identity disorder (DID)
cognitive perspective, 196–197
and crime, 183
groups at risk, 189, 192
neuroscience perspective, 197
overview, 184–188
psychodynamic perspective, 192–193, 197
vs. schizophrenia, 184, 390
sociocultural perspective, 194–195
disulfiram (Antabuse), 323
diversity. *See* cultural variations; gender differences
dizygotic (DZ) twins, 133
domestic violence, 342–343, 377, 399
dopamine, 137
and acquired brain disorders, 451
and autism, 498
and schizophrenia, 404, 416–417, 420
and substance abuse/dependence, 328, 333, 348
double-bind communication, 423
double-blind procedures, 60–61
double depression, 280
down-regulation, 137
Down syndrome, 487, 488, 504
and Alzheimer's disease, 446, 492
doxepin (Sinequan), 175
DPT vaccine, 490
dramatic/emotional personality disorders, 290–298. *See also* antisocial personality disorder; borderline personality disorder; histrionic personality disorder; narcissistic personality disorder
dream interpretation, 117–118
drug abuse. *See* substance abuse/dependence
drug-induced insomnia, 333
drug treatment. *See* psychopharmacology
DST (dexamethasone suppression test), 277
DTs (delirium tremens), 318
dualism, 213
due process, 518–521
duration, 66–67
Durham test, 512, 513
dynamic intelligence tests, 40
dyslexia (reading disorder), 474
dyspareunia, 362, 369
dysthymic disorder, 252–253, 280
DZ (dizygotic) twins, 133

early intervention, 350
eating disorders
behavioral perspective, 477
and borderline personality disorder, 296
and culture-bound syndromes, 7
interpersonal perspective, 479–480
neuroscience perspective, 141, 146, 481
overview, 469–471
sociocultural perspective, 480
and stress, 231
echolalia, 496
echopraxia, 401
Ecstasy (MDMA), 313, 336
ECT (electroconvulsive therapy), 282–283
education, 500, 501, 502, 504
EE (expressed emotion), 422–423, 424
EEG. *See* electroencephalography
Effexor (venlafaxine), 280
EFT (emotion-focused treatment), 171
ego, 107, 304
ego psychology, 114
Ego Psychology and the Problem of Adaptation (Hartmann), 114
Elavil (amitriptyline), 175
elderly people. *See* age
Electra complex, 111, 112
electroconvulsive therapy (ECT), 282–283
electroencephalography (EEG), 48, 49, 141–142, 144, 498
electromyography (EMG), 49
elimination disorders, 471–472, 481
elimination of plausible alternative causes, 56, 64, 65
embolism, 442
EMDR (Eye Movement Sensitization and Reprocessing) therapy, 170
EMG (electromyography), 49
emotional distress disorders. *See* childhood emotional distress disorders
emotional lability, 443
emotion-focused treatment (EFT), 171
empathic joining, 86
empirical classification method, 459
employment
and confidentiality, 533–534
and mental retardation, 503–504
encephalitis, 436–437
encephalopathy, 488
encopresis, 472, 481
endocrine disorders, 451–452
endocrine system, 146
endogenous-reactive dimension of mood disorders, 255–256
endorphins, 347–348
enkephalins, 137, 347–348
enuresis, 472, 477, 481
epidemic encephalitis (sleeping sickness), 436–437
epidemics, 415
epidemiological studies, 66–67
epilepsy, 197, 453–455
episodic memory, 182
Epstein-Barr virus, 439
erectile disorder. *See* male erectile disorder
erotomanic type of delusional disorder, 406
ERPs (event-related potentials), 142, 182, 420, 498
escape (avoidance) learning, 79, 168–169, 292, 477
ESPACE program, 187
essential hypertension, 224–225
ethics, 532–536
and animal experimentation, 69
and behavioral perspective, 87–88, 426
confidentiality, 63, 523, 532–534
informed consent, 62–63, 534
and mental retardation, 503
and neuroscience perspective, 146
and psychological assessment, 50
and research, 62–64, 67, 68, 70, 534
ethnicity. *See* cultural variations; race/ethnicity
event-related potentials (ERPs), 142, 182, 420, 498
evolutionary theory, 169, 514
executive functions, 435
exercise, 232, 237
exhaustion, 215
exhibitionism, 7, 373–374
existentialism, 126. *See also* humanistic-existential perspective
exorcism, 11
expectancy theory, 265, 343–344
expectations, 59–60, 317
experimental designs, 67–69
experimenter effects, 59–60
expert testimony, 525
explicit cognition, 93
explicit (declarative) memory, 147, 182
exploitative relationships, 535–536
exposure therapy
and anxiety disorders, 170, 477
overview, 84–85, 86
and somatoform disorders, 206
expressed emotion (EE), 422–423, 424
expressive language, 476
external validity, 56, 69, 71
extinction
and developmental disorders, 505–506
and mood disorders, 263, 264, 265
overview, 80, 83, 84
extracerebral brain tumors, 444
Eye Movement Sensitization and Reprocessing (EMDR) therapy, 170
eye tracking, 411

faking. *See* malingering
family dynamics
and anxiety disorders, 153, 170, 467–468
and childhood/adolescent disorders, 463, 467–468, 472, 477, 478, 479
and gender identity disorders, 384–385
and incest, 377
and mental retardation, 492, 503
and mood disorders, 266, 270
and neuroscience perspective, 147–148
and personality disorders, 303–304, 305, 307
and schizophrenia, 419, 422–425
and somatoform disorders, 200, 201, 206
and stress-related illness, 239
and substance abuse/dependence, 343
and suicide, 260
See also attachment theory; child abuse; psychodynamic perspective; social support
family studies, 132, 407–408
family system approach, 479–480
family therapy
and childhood/adolescent disorders, 479–480, 481
and developmental disorders, 507–508
and substance abuse/dependence, 343
FAP-enhanced CBT (FECT), 60–61
FAS (fetal alcohol syndrome), 474, 489

Fatal Attraction, 295
FECT (FAP-enhanced CBT), 60–61
feedback, 220
female orgasmic disorder, 361, 365, 366, 368, 370
female sexual arousal disorder, 360, 368
fenfluramine, 507
fetal alcohol syndrome (FAS), 474, 489
fetishism, 371–372
Fifth Amendment, 519
Finger v. State, 517
5-Factor model of personality, 287, 301, 308
flashbacks, 157, 336
flashing (exhibitionism), 7, 373–374
flat affect, 397
flooding, 85, 170
fluent aphasia, 435
fluoxetine (Prozac), 173, 176, 197, 209, 280
flurazepam (Dalmane), 233, 332, 333
fMRI (functional MRI), 142, 143
fractionated abreaction, 193
fragile X syndrome, 487, 493, 497–498
FRAMES, 325
free association, 22, 117, 118
Freudian theory. *See* psychodynamic perspective
FRIENDS program, 478
frontal lobes, 139–140, 173, 276, 317, 348, 413–414
frontotemporal dementia, 447–448, 449, 451
frotteurism, 376
fugue, 182–184, 192, 193, 194
functional analysis psychotherapy (FAP), 60
functional MRI (fMRI), 142, 143

GABA (gamma-amino-butyric acid), 138, 172, 173, 349
galvanic skin response (GSR), 49
Gamblers Anonymous, 300
gambling, 156, 300, 318
gay/lesbian people, 319, 375. *See also* homosexuality
gaze discrimination, 398
GBMI (guilty but mentally ill), 513–515
gender differences
  and acquired brain disorders, 449, 455
  and anxiety disorders, 152, 153, 154, 157, 161, 163
  and autism, 500
  and childhood disruptive behavior disorders, 461, 464–465
  and childhood emotional distress disorders, 468–469
  and culture-bound syndromes, 7
  and definitions of abnormal behavior, 6
  and delusional disorder, 406
  and dissociative disorders, 189, 192, 197
  and eating disorders, 469, 470, 471
  and headache, 230
  and impulse-control disorders, 300
  and mental retardation, 493
  and mood disorders, 250, 253, 276, 279, 280
  and paraphilias, 378–379
  and pedophilia, 376
  and personality disorders, 296, 297, 301, 302–303, 308
  and psychodynamic perspective, 111, 112, 114
  and schizophrenia, 405
  and sexual dysfunctions, 360, 361, 363–364
  and somatoform disorders, 198, 204, 208
  and stress-related illness, 221, 235, 242
  and stroke, 444
  and substance abuse/dependence, 315, 318, 319, 329
  and suicide, 257–258
gender dysphoria, 383
gender identity disorders (GID), 373, 383–386
gender reassignment, 383, 385–386
general adaptation syndrome, 214, 215
generalizability, 56–57, 71
generalization, 80
generalized amnesia, 181, 182
generalized anxiety disorder
  childhood/adolescent forms, 467–468, 479
  cognitive perspective, 164–165, 167
  neuroscience perspective, 172, 176
  overview, 153–154
  psychodynamic perspective, 170
generalized sexual dysfunctions, 362
general paresis, 21, 437
genes, 131
genetic counseling, 487–488, 504
genetic high-risk studies, 66, 410–412
genetic markers, 135, 410, 411
genetics, 131–135
  and acquired brain disorders, 446, 448, 449
  and anxiety disorders, 171–172
  and developmental disorders, 486–488, 497–498, 500, 504
  ethical issues, 146
  and learning disorders, 476
  and mood disorders, 273–274
  and personality disorders, 308
  and schizophrenia, 290, 407–413
  and somatoform disorders, 208
  and stress-related illness, 226, 242
  and stuttering, 476
  and substance abuse/dependence, 345–347
genital stage, 111
genotype-environment correlation, 131–132
genotypes, 131
German measles (rubella), 488
GID. *See* gender identity disorders
girls. *See* gender differences
glove anesthesia, 203
glue sniffing, 453
glutamate, 417
glutomate system, 172
good-of-the-patient commitment, 520
good-poor premorbid dimension of schizophrenia, 403
graded exposure, 85
grandiose type of delusional disorder, 406
grand mal (tonic-clonic) seizures, 454
Graves' disease (hyperthyroidism), 451–452
groups at risk, 4–5
  acquired brain disorders, 439, 443–444, 449, 455
  anxiety disorders, 152, 153, 154, 156–157, 160–161, 163
  autism, 500
  body dysmorphic disorder, 203–204
  childhood/adolescent disorders, 464–466, 468–469, 471, 475–476
  delusional disorder, 406
  dissociative disorders, 189, 192
  mental retardation, 493
  mood disorders, 249–251
  paraphilias, 378–379
  personality disorders, 301–303
  schizophrenia, 405
  sexual dysfunctions, 363–364
  somatoform disorders, 203–204
  stress-related illness, 235–236
  substance abuse/dependence, 319–321, 340
  suicide, 257–260
group therapy
  ethical issues, 534
  and paraphilias, 379–380
  and somatoform disorders, 205, 208
  and stress-related illness, 227
GSR (galvanic skin response), 49
guilt, and psychodynamic perspective, 122
guilty but mentally ill (GBMI), 513–515
gyri, 139
habit disorders, 460
Halcion (triazolam), 233, 234, 332
halfway houses, 17
hallucinations, 253, 396–397, 402, 421–422
hallucinogens, 335–336, 338
Halstead-Reitan Neuropsychological Battery, 48
harm-reduction policies, 351–352
Harrison Act (1914), 329
hashish, 336–338, 340
headache, 197, 230–231, 237, 242
Head Start, 476
Health Insurance Portability and Accountability Act, 534
health psychology, 212
hearing impairments, 474
heart disease, 158, 174, 216, 221–224, 239
helmets, 442
helplessness-hopelessness syndrome, 246, 264–266
hemorrhage, 442–443
heroin, 331–332, 349, 351
herpes simplex virus, 439
hierarchy of fears, 84
hierarchy of needs, 125–126
high blood pressure, 224–225
high-risk design, 66
Hillside Recognition and Prevention Program (RAPP), 418–419
Hinduism, 23
hippocampus, 141, 148
  and dissociative disorders, 197
  and epilepsy, 455
  and mood disorders, 276, 279
Hispanic Americans. *See* race/ethnicity
historical perspectives, 11–22
  ancient societies, 11, 26
  antisocial personality disorder, 291
  asylum reorm, 14–16
  deinstitutionalization, 16–17, 18
  early asylums, 13–14
  gender identity disorders, 383
  homosexuality, 356, 357–358
  hospitalization, 16
  late nineteenth-century approaches, 20–22
  managed care, 19–20
  mind-body problem, 213
  prevention movement, 17, 19
  psychological assessment, 20–21, 26–27
  schizophrenia, 390–391
  somatoform disorders, 180, 201
histrionic personality disorder, 296, 297, 302, 306
HIV. *See* AIDS/HIV
HIV dementia, 437–438, 439
hoarding, 155
holistic thinking, 212
homelessness, 17, 18
homosexuality
  and gender identity disorders, 384
  historical perspectives, 356, 357–358
  See also gay/lesbian people
hopelessness, 246, 261, 264–266, 272
hormones, 235
  and acquired brain disorders, 451–452
  and anxiety disorders, 173
  and gender identity disorders, 385
  and mood disorders, 146, 277–278
  and sexual dysfunctions, 370
  and substance abuse/dependence, 338, 339
  See also neuroscience perspective
hostility, 223, 239
host personality, 184–185. *See also* dissociative identity disorder
humane environment, right to, 529–531
Human Genome Project, 274
human immunodeficiency virus (HIV), 228. *See also* AIDS/HIV
humanistic-existential perspective, 9, 123–126

Human Sexual Inadequacy (Masters & Johnson), 358, 365
Human Sexual Response (Masters & Johnson), 358
Huntington's chorea, 448, 449
hydrocephalus, 488
hyperactivity. *See* attention deficit hyperactivity disorder
hypertension, 224–225, 242, 442, 449
hyperthyroidism (Graves' disease), 451–452
hypnosis, 21
  and dissociative disorders, 187, 193, 194
  and recovered memory controversy, 191
hypoactive sexual desire disorder, 358, 360, 368–369
hypochondriasis
  behavioral perspective, 205, 206
  cognitive perspective, 207
  neuroscience perspective, 209
  overview, 199–200
  psychodynamic perspective, 204, 205
hypoglycemia, 209
hypomanic episodes, 248
hypothalamus, 140–141, 146, 277
hypotheses, 57–58, 60–61
hypothesis testing, 95–97
hypothyroidism (myxedema), 452
hypoxia, 209
hysteria, 21, 106, 180, 201

iatrogenic (therapy-induced) disorders, 186, 188
IBCT (integrative behavioral couple therapy), 86
id, 107, 111, 379
idioms of distress, 303
idiopathic epilepsy, 453
IEP (individualized education program), 501
illness phobia, 206
The Imaginary Invalid (Molière), 199
imipramine (Tofranil), 175
imitation. *See* modeling
immigrants, 16
immune system, 217–220, 229, 338
implicit cognition, 93
implicit (procedural) memory, 147, 182, 184, 196
impotence. *See* male erectile disorder
imprinting, 385
impulse-control disorders, 156, 300, 301, 318
In a Different Voice (Gilligan), 112
inappropriate affect, 397
incest, 377
incidence, 66–67
independent variables, 58–59
indeterminate sentences, 516
individualism, 22
individualized education program (IEP), 501
individual response specificity, 214–215, 225
infarction, 442
inferential style, 265–266
inferiority complex, 113
influenza, 415
information processing, 93–94, 292, 307
informed consent, 62–63, 534
inkblot (Rorschach) test, 41–42, 44, 45
inpatient care, 16–17
insanity defense, 511–517
insomnia, 233–234, 472–473
instrumental (operant) conditioning, 79–81, 85, 206, 477
integrative behavioral couple therapy (IBCT), 86
intellectualization, 110
intelligence tests, 38–41
interjudge reliability, 33
intermittent explosive disorder, 300
internal consistency, 33
internal validity, 56, 59, 69
International Classification of Diseases (ICD) (WHO), 28, 257
interpersonal and social rhythm therapy (IPSRT), 275
interpersonal perspective, 8, 127
  childhood/adolescent disorders, 479–480
  mood disorders, 263–264
  schizophrenia, 422–425
  sexual dysfunctions, 368
  stress-related illness, 241–242
  substance abuse/dependence, 342–343
interpersonal therapy (IPT), 127, 271–272
interpretation, 106
interviews, 37–38
intoxication delirium, 316
intracerebral brain tumors, 444
intuition, 57
involuntary outpatient commitment, 526
iodine deficiency, 452
IPSRT (interpersonal and social rhythm therapy), 275
IPT (interpersonal therapy), 127, 271–272
IQ tests. *See* intelligence tests
ischemia, 221
isolation, as defense mechanism, 109–110, 120

Jackson v. Indiana, 517
Jafee v. Redmond, 523
jamais vu, 189
jealous type of delusional disorder, 406
Jones v. United States, 516
Journal of Abnormal Psychology, 20
Journal of the American Psychoanalytic Association, 281
jury trial, right to, 518

Kansas v. Hendricks, 525
kindling model of mood disorders, 256
kleptomania, 156, 300
Knecht v. Gillman, 531
knockouts, 135
koro syndrome, 7
Korsakoff's psychosis, 317, 451

labeling, 99, 100, 102
laboratory tests, 48–49
Lancet, 227
language
  and acquired brain disorders, 434, 447–448
  and brain lateralization, 144
  and developmental disorders, 496, 505
  and schizophrenia, 391–396
language differences, 51. *See also* race/ethnicity
latency period, 111
lateralization, 143–144, 209
Latinos/Latinas. *See* race/ethnicity
lead poisoning, 452, 474, 490
learned helplessness, 264–265
learning
  and anxiety disorders, 168–169, 176
  behavioral perspective overview, 76, 78–82
  cognitive perspective overview, 88–89
  and dissociative disorders, 193–194
  and paraphilias, 380
  and personality disorders, 298, 307
  and substance abuse/dependence, 327–328
  See also behavioral perspective; cognitive perspective; learning/communication disorders
learning/communication disorders, 460, 474–476
legal issues, 510–532
  competency to stand trial, 517–518
  insanity defense, 511–517
  patients' rights, 527–532
  and sexual assault, 378
  See also civil commitment
leisure skills, 505
Lewy body disease, 447, 449, 451
libido, 107, 110, 113
lifelong sexual dysfunctions, 362
light therapy, 276
light treatment, 235
limbic structures, 141
  and autism, 498
  and dissociative disorders, 197
  and mood disorders, 277
  and personality disorders, 292
  and schizophrenia, 413
linkage analysis, 135
lithium, 280, 282
localized amnesia, 181
locus ceruleus, 173
longitudinal studies, 66, 411
looming maladaptive style, 164, 168
loosening of associations, 392–393
lorazepam (Ativan), 174, 181, 197
Loss (Bowlby), 116
LSD (lysergic acid diethylamide), 335–336
Lyme disease, 438–439
lymphocytes, 217
lymphoma, 488
lysergic acid diethylamide (LSD), 335–336

mad cow disease, 438
magical thinking, 288
magnetic resonance imaging (MRI), 48, 142–143, 432
magnification, 90
major depressive disorder, 248–249. *See also* depression; mood disorders
major depressive episodes, 246–247. *See also* depression; mood disorders
maladaptive behavior, 3–4
male erectile disorder
  behavioral perspective, 366
  multifaceted treatment, 368
  neuroscience perspective, 369
  overview, 360–361
  psychodynamic perspective, 364–365
male orgasmic disorder, 361–362
malingering, 183, 188, 203
malnutrition, 451, 489–490
managed behavioral health care (MBHC), 19–20, 27
manganese poisoning, 452–453
manic episodes, 247–248. *See also* bipolar disorder; mood disorders
The Man Who Mistook His Wife for a Hat and Other Clinical Tales (Sacks), 435
MAO (monoamine oxidase) inhibitors, 175, 279, 280
marijuana, 197, 336–338, 340
marriage. *See* social support
The Mask of Sanity (Cleckley), 291
masochism, 374–376, 378–379, 380
masturbation, 361, 366, 380
matching, 65–66, 325–326
mathematics disorder, 474
MBHC (managed behavioral health care), 19–20, 27
MDMA (Ecstasy), 313, 336
media
  and conduct disorder, 480
  and eating disorders, 471
  and recovered memory controversy, 191
  and sexuality, 358, 359
  and somatoform disorders, 199
  and substance abuse/dependence, 321, 326, 329, 335, 352
  and suicide, 272–273
medical marijuana use, 338, 340
medical model, 6, 8
  and behavioral perspective, 83
  and civil commitment, 519–520

medical model—*Cont.*
and diagnosis, 28
historical perspectives, 21
meditation, 23, 237, 306
medulla, 141
megalencephaly, 499
melatonin, 276
Mellaril, 417
memory
and Alzheimer's disease, 445–446
and autism, 499
and depersonalization disorder, 189
and dissociative disorders, 181–182, 189, 190–191, 195–197
and electroconvulsive therapy, 283
and epilepsy, 454
and learning disorders, 474
and psychodynamic perspective, 147
and psychopharmacology, 174
recovered memory controversy, 190–191
and schizophrenia, 393, 421
See also amnesia
men. *See* gender differences
meningitis, 437, 488
mens rea, 517
Mental Health Court (MHC), 520–521
mental health law. *See* legal issues
Mental Health Manpower Trends (Albee), 17
mental retardation, 485–493
adult, 492–493
and autism, 494–495
behavioral therapy, 505–506
defined, 485
environmental factors, 488–492
genetic factors, 486–488
groups at risk, 493
levels of, 485–486
prevention, 488, 504
and psychotherapy, 507–508
social issues, 500–504
mental status exam (MSE), 37–38, 39
mercury poisoning, 452–453
mesolimbic system, 328
metabolic disorders, 488
metastatic brain tumors, 444
metaworry, 165
methadone, 331, 349
methamphetamine (Methedrine), 333
Methedrine (methamphetamine), 333
methylphenidate, 416
MHC (Mental Health Court), 520–521
Middle Ages, 6, 12–13
migraine headaches, 197, 230, 237, 242
milieu therapy, 532
MI (motivational interviewing), 324–325
mind-body problem, 131, 212–214, 490–491
mindfulness, 306
mini mental status exam (MMS), 37–38, 39
Minnesota Multiphasic Personality Inventory–2 (MMPI–2), 45–47
minority group status. *See* race/ethnicity
minor tranquilizers, 139, 174–175
mixed anxiety-depression, 257
mixed episodes, 248
MMPI–2 (Minnesota Multiphasic Personality Inventory–2), 45–47
MMS (mini mental status exam), 37–38, 39
M'Naghten test, 512, 513
modal suicide attempter, 258
modal suicide committer, 258
modeling, 81
and childhood/adolescent disorders, 477, 478
and paraphilias, 380
and personality disorders, 305, 307
and substance abuse/dependence, 343
molecular genetics, 135
monoamine oxidase (MAO) inhibitors, 175, 279, 280
monozygotic (MZ) twins, 132–133
mood disorders, 245–284
and acquired brain disorders, 443
and anxiety disorders, 153, 168, 172, 257
and attribution styles, 92, 478
and autism, 497
behavioral perspective, 263, 264
bipolar disorder overview, 251–252
and borderline personality disorder, 295, 308
childhood/adolescent forms, 250, 251, 259–260, 262, 263, 468, 469, 474, 478
cognitive perspective, 92, 264–269, 270–271
and comorbidity, 257
and creativity, 253, 254
cyclothymic disorder, 253
dimensions of, 253–256
dysthymic disorder, 252–253
episodes, 246–248
groups at risk, 249–251
interpersonal perspective, 263–264
major depressive disorder overview, 248–249
and mental retardation, 492–493
prevention, 270–271
psychodynamic perspective, 269–272
vs. schizophrenia, 397
sociocultural perspective, 272–273
and somatoform disorders, 199, 201
and substance abuse/dependence, 316, 317, 329
and suicide, 247, 257–263
treatment, 264, 267–269, 271–272, 279–284
See also childhood emotional distress disorders; neuroscience perspective on mood disorders
moral insanity, 291
moral therapy, 14–15, 16
Morita therapy, 23
morphine, 330, 340
motivational interviewing (MI), 324–325
"Mourning and Melancholia" (Freud), 269
Mowrer pad, 477
MRI (magnetic resonance imaging), 48, 142–143, 432
MSE (mental status exam), 37–38, 39
multimodal treatments, 9, 85, 323
multiple-baseline design, 70–71, 72
multiple personality disorder. *See* dissociative identity disorder
multiple relationships, 534–536
muscle-contraction headaches, 230
muscle dysmorphia, 198
mutism, 401
myelin sheath, 136
The Myth of Mental Illness (Szasz), 8
myxedema (hypothyroidism), 452
MZ (monozygotic) twins, 132–133

Naikan therapy, 23
naltrexone (Revia), 348, 349
Nancy school, 21–22
narcissistic personality disorder, 116, 297–298, 302, 304
Narcotics Anonymous, 345
Nardil (phenelzine), 175, 176, 309
National Comorbidity Survey (NCS), 35
National Institue of Mental Health (NIMH), 60
Native Americans. *See* race/ethnicity
needle-exchange programs, 351, 352
nefazodone (Serzone), 280
negative feedback, 220
negative reinforcement, 79–80
negative self-schema model, 266–267
negative spiral, 79
negative symptoms of schizophrenia, 404–405, 414, 417
negative triad, 90, 95
Nembutal (pentobarbital), 332
neologisms, 395
nervios syndrome, 7
neuroleptics. *See* antipsychotic drugs
neurological impairment, 47–48, 203. *See also* acquired brain disorders
neurons, 136–137
neuropsychological disorders. *See* acquired brain disorders
neuroscience perspective, 8, 130–148
anxiety disorders, 156, 171–176
childhood/adolescent disorders, 475–476, 481–482, 491
and cognitive-behavioral perspectives, 148
developmental disorders, 486–488, 497–499, 507
dissociative disorders, 189, 197
eating disorders, 141, 146, 481
endocrine system, 146
evaluation of, 146–147
gender identity disorders, 385
genetics overview, 131–135
nicotine dependence, 328
obsessive-compulsive disorder, 141, 171, 173, 176
paraphilias, 381–383
peripheral nervous system, 144–146
personality disorders, 290, 292, 308–309
and psychodynamic perspective, 147–148
sexual dysfunctions, 369–370
somatoform disorders, 208–209
stress-related illness, 145–146, 242–243
substance abuse/dependence, 345–349
See also central nervous system; genetics; neuroscience perspective on mood disorders; neuroscience perspective on schizophrenia
neuroscience perspective on mood disorders, 273–284
antidepressant medication, 172, 253, 279–280
antimanic medication, 280, 282
brain lateralization, 144
electroconvulsive therapy, 282–283
genetics, 273–274
hormone imbalance theory, 146, 277–278
and learned helplessness, 265
neuroimaging research, 276–277
neurotransmitter imbalance theory, 273, 278–279
vs. psychotherapy, 281
and seasonal affective disorder, 275–276
and sleep disorders, 274–275
transcranial magnetic stimulation, 283–284
neuroscience perspective on schizophrenia, 407–418
and antipsychotic drugs, 416, 417–418
brain imaging studies, 140, 141, 413–415, 416
dopamine hypothesis, 404, 416–417, 420
genetic studies, 290, 407–413
viral hypothesis, 415
neurosis, 151, 170
neurosyphilis, 21, 437
neurotransmitters
and acquired brain disorders, 449, 451
and anxiety disorders, 172–176
and autism, 498, 507
and dissociative disorders, 197
and headache, 197, 230, 237
and impulse-control disorders, 300
and mood disorders, 265, 273, 278–279, 283
overview, 137–138
and paraphilias, 381–382
and schizophrenia, 404, 416–417, 420
and sexual dysfunctions, 369
and somatoform disorders, 209
and substance abuse/dependence, 328, 333, 347–348, 349

New England Journal of Medicine, 212, 227
nicotine dependence, 326–329
nightmares, 473
night terrors (sleep terrors), 473
night waking, 472
nocturnal penile tumescence (NPT), 369
nonbarbiturate sedatives, 233, 234, 332–333
nondeficit symptoms, 404–405
nonfluent aphasia, 435
norepinephrine (NE), 138
  and anxiety disorders, 172, 173, 175
  and mood disorders, 265, 278, 283
  and sexual dysfunctions, 369
  and somatoform disorders, 209
norms, 2, 6, 8, 99
not otherwise specified (NOS) diagnoses, 34
NPT (nocturnal penile tumescence), 369
null hypothesis, 61

obesity, 141, 231–232, 470–471
objectification, 381
object relations, 115, 304, 365
observation, 49–50
observational learning, 169
obsessions, 154. *See also* obsessive-compulsive disorder
obsessive-compulsive disorder (OCD)
  behavioral perspective, 85, 169
  childhood/adolescent forms, 466
  cognitive perspective, 166–167, 168
  groups at risk, 302
  and impulse-control disorders, 156, 300
  neuroscience perspective, 141, 171, 173, 176
  overview, 154–157
  psychodynamic perspective, 170
  and somatoform disorders, 199, 200
obsessive-compulsive personality disorder, 301, 306–308
occipital lobe, 140
OCD. *See* obsessive-compulsive disorder
O'Connor v. Donaldson, 528
odd/eccentric personality disorders, 287–290. *See also* paranoid personality disorder; schizoid personality disorder; schizotypal personality disorder
Oedipus complex, 111, 112, 364–365, 379
onset dimension of mood disorders, 256
operant (instrumental) conditioning, 79–81, 85, 206, 477
operational definitions, 58
opiate receptors, 347, 349
opiates, 330–331
opium, 329, 330
oral stage, 110, 340
organ neuroses, 239
organ transplants, 217
orgasmic disorders, 361–362, 363, 365, 366, 368, 370
orienting response, 420–421
oscillating system model of stress, 220
outpatient counseling, 16
overgeneralization, 90
oversimplification, 87
oxazepam (Serax), 322

pain disorder, 201, 206–207, 208, 209
panic attacks, 151, 167. *See also* panic disorder
panic disorder
  behavioral perspective, 169
  childhood/adolescent forms, 466
  cognitive perspective, 165–166, 167–168, 176
  and culture-bound syndromes, 7
  neuroscience perspective, 171, 172, 174, 175, 176
  overview, 161–163
  psychodynamic perspective, 170, 171
paradoxical instruction, 366
paranoid-nonparanoid dimension of schizophrenia, 405
paranoid personality disorder, 287–288, 302
paranoid schizophrenia, 288, 333–334, 402–403, 406
paraphilias, 370–383
  behavioral perspective, 380–381
  and civil commitment, 525–526
  cognitive perspective, 381
  and culture-bound syndromes, 7
  groups at risk, 378–379
  neuroscience perspective, 381–383
  psychodynamic perspective, 379–380
  types, 371–378
parasympathetic division, 145–146, 217
parenting. *See* family dynamics
parent training, 305, 477, 503
parietal lobe, 140
parietal-occipital cortex, 476
Parkinson's disease, 333, 416, 447, 448–449, 451
Parnate (tranylcypromine), 175
paroxetine (Paxil), 176, 280
partialism, 372
partial seizures, 453
passive autism, 494
passive avoidance learning, 292
pathological gambling, 300, 318
patients' rights, 527–532
Paxil (paroxetine), 176, 280
PCP (phencyclidine), 336
pedophilia, 373–374, 376–377, 379, 381. *See also* child abuse
peeping Toms, 374
pellagra, 451
penetrating head injuries, 440–441
penile plethysmography, 383
penile prostheses, 370
penis envy, 111, 112, 379
Penn Optimism Project, 270–271
Pennsylvania, United States v., 528
Pennsylvania Hospital, 15
pentobarbital (Nembutal), 332
perceptual conscious, 106
perfectionism, 301, 307
performance anxiety, 360, 363, 365
peripheral nervous system, 144–146
persecutory type of delusional disorder, 406
personal discomfort approach to abnormal behavior, 3
personality disorders, 286–309
  antisocial personality disorder overview, 290–293
  avoidant personality disorder, 298–299, 306, 309
  behavioral perspective, 298, 305–306
  borderline personality disorder overview, 293, 295–296
  cognitive perspective, 292–293, 306–308
  dependent personality disorder, 299, 301, 302, 305, 306, 308
  groups at risk, 301–303
  histrionic personality disorder, 296, 297, 302, 306
  narcissistic personality disorder, 116, 297–298, 302, 304
  neuroscience perspective, 290, 292, 308–309
  obsessive-compulsive personality disorder, 301, 306–308
  paranoid personality disorder, 287–288, 302
  prevention, 305
  psychodynamic perspective, 116, 298, 303–305
  schizoid personality disorder, 289–290
  schizotypal personality disorder, 288–289, 308, 309, 411, 412
  and serial killers, 294
  sociocultural perspective, 302–303, 308
personality inventories, 45–47
personal therapy, 427
person-centered approach. *See* client-centered therapy
person variables, 50
pessimism, 267. *See also* hopelessness
petit mal (absence) seizures, 454
PET (positron emission tomography), 48, 142–143
phallic stage, 110–111
phencyclidine (PCP), 336
phenelzine (Nardil), 175, 176, 309
phenobarbital, 455
phenomenological approach, 123
phenothiazines, 16, 309, 416, 417, 498
phenotypes, 131
phenylketonuria (PKU), 488, 504
phobias
  behavioral perspective, 169–170
  childhood/adolescent forms, 466, 467, 468, 477
  cognitive perspective, 164, 165
  and culture-bound syndromes, 7
  neuroscience perspective, 171, 172, 173, 175, 176
  overview, 152–153
  and panic disorder, 162–163
  and personality disorders, 298
  psychodynamic perspective, 170
  and somatoform disorders, 199
physical attractiveness, 296
pibloktoq syndrome, 7
pituitary gland, 146, 277
PKU (phenylketonuria), 488, 504
placebos, 59–60, 206, 348
planum temporale, 476
play therapy, 480–481
pleasure principle, 107
PNI (psychoneuroimmunology), 218, 242–243
polygraph, 49
pons, 141
poor laws, 13
positive-negative symptoms dimension of schizophrenia, 404–405, 414, 417
positive regard, 125
positive reinforcement, 79, 81
positive symptoms of schizophrenia, 404–405, 414, 417
positron emission tomography (PET), 48, 142–143
possession, 11, 26, 192
posterior cortex, 189
postmodernism, 95
postsynaptic receptors, 137
posttraumatic stress disorder (PTSD)
  behavioral perspective, 169, 170
  and borderline personality disorder, 296
  childhood/adolescent forms, 466, 469
  cognitive perspective, 167, 168
  and dissociative disorders, 161, 181, 188, 189
  neuroscience perspective, 171, 172, 173–174, 176
  overview, 157–161
  and rape, 378
poverty
  and anxiety disorders, 153
  and conduct disorder, 480
  and mental retardation, 489, 490, 491, 504
  and substance abuse/dependence, 349, 351
  See also sociocultural perspective; socioeconomic status
poverty of content, 394
prayer, 240–241
predictability, 238, 460–461
prediction, 34–35, 56, 78

predictive validity, 34–35
predominantly attentive ADHD, 462
predominantly hyperactive/impulsive ADHD, 462
preferential molesters, 376
prefrontal cortex, 277, 283
prefrontal lobotomy, 16, 143
prejudice, and moral therapy, 16
premature ejaculation, 362, 363, 366, 368, 370
premorbid adjustment, 249
prenatal environment
  and mental retardation, 488–490, 493
  and schizophrenia, 414–415
preponderance of evidence standard of proof, 519, 520, 521
prevalence, 66–67
prevention
  acquired brain disorders, 442
  anxiety disorders, 168, 478
  behavioral perspective, 87
  child abuse, 187
  childhood/adolescent disorders, 466, 478
  cognitive perspective, 97, 168, 270–271
  crime, 520
  developmental disorders, 488, 504
  eating disorders, 471
  and health psychology, 212
  historical perspectives, 17, 19
  learning disorders, 476
  mental retardation, 488, 504
  mood disorders, 270–271
  overview, 9–11
  personality disorders, 305
  schizophrenia, 418–419
  and sociocultural perspective, 101–102
  stress-related illness, 240–241
  substance abuse/dependence, 350, 352
  suicide, 262–263
prevention science, 11
primary brain tumors, 444
primary enuresis, 472
primary gain, 201
primary prevention, 10, 19, 504
primary reinforcers, 79
procedural (implicit) memory, 147, 182, 184, 196
process-experiential approach, 126
process-reactive dimension of schizophrenia, 403
process schizophrenia, 403
prodromal phase of schizophrenia, 399, 418–419
progressive nonfluent dementia, 448
progressive relaxation, 237
projection, 109, 120
projective personality tests, 41–45, 47
Project MATCH, 325–326
Prolixin, 417
prospective studies, 66, 411
Prozac (fluoxetine), 173, 176, 197, 209, 280
psychiatric social workers, 10
psychiatrists, 10
psychoactive drugs, 312–313. *See also* substance abuse/dependence
psychoanalysis
  defined, 106
  historical perspectives, 22
  overview, 117–120
  practitioners, 10
  See also psychodynamic perspective; treatment
psychodynamic perspective, 8, 105–122
  anxiety disorders, 151, 170–171
  basic concepts of, 106–111
  childhood/adolescent disorders, 480–481
  and cognitive perspective, 97
  dissociative disorders, 192–193, 197
  evaluation of, 120–122
  gender identity disorders, 384–385
  and humanistic-existential perspective, 123–124
  mood disorders, 269–272
  and neuroscience perspective, 147–148
  paraphilias, 379–380
  personality disorders, 116, 298, 303–305
  post-Freudian approaches, 111–117
  and psychological assessment, 41
  sexual dysfunctions, 364–365
  somatoform disorders, 201–202, 204–205
  stress-related illness, 239–241
  substance abuse/dependence, 340–341
  suicide, 269, 272
  treatment overview, 117–120
psychogenic theory, 21–22, 49
psychological assessment
  childhood/adolescent disorders, 458–459
  and cultural bias, 40, 46, 50–52
  defined, 26
  and diagnosis, 28–32
  goals of, 27
  historical perspectives, 20–21, 26–27
  interviews, 37–38
  laboratory tests, 48–49
  observation, 49–50
  problems in, 35–37
  and psychodynamic perspective, 122
  reliability, 32–34, 44
  and sexual dysfunctions, 365
  validity, 34–35, 44, 47, 69
  See also psychological tests
psychological dependence, 313
psychological tests, 38–48
  intelligence tests, 38–41
  and neurological impairment, 47–48
  projective personality tests, 41–45, 47
  self-report personality inventories, 45–47
psychological theories of abnormal behavior, 8–9
"Psychology as the Behaviorist Views It" (Watson), 76
psychometric approach, 38, 49–50
psychoneuroimmunology (PNI), 218, 242–243
Psychopathia Sexualis (Krafft-Ebing), 21, 356, 375
psychopathology, 20
psychopathy, 291–293, 294, 308
psychopharmacology
  and acquired brain disorders, 441, 449, 451, 455
  and anxiety disorders, 156, 172, 173, 174–176
  and attention deficit hyperactivity disorder, 481
  and autism, 498
  and competency to stand trial, 517–518
  and developmental disorders, 507
  and diagnosis, 309
  and dissociative disorders, 181, 193, 197
  ethical issues, 146
  and impulse-control disorders, 300
  and mood disorders, 253, 278, 279–284
  overview, 18, 137, 139
  and paraphilias, 382–383
  and personality disorders, 296, 309
  practitioners, 10
  and schizophrenia, 416, 417–418
  and sexual dysfunctions, 361, 369–370
  and sleep disorders, 174, 233–234
  and somatoform disorders, 199, 209
  and substance abuse/dependence, 329
psychophysiological (psychosomatic) disorders, 212, 213
psychosexual development, 110–111
psychosexual therapy, 368
psychosocial development, 114–115
psychosocial vulnerability, 344
psychosomatic (psychophysiological) disorders, 212, 213
psychosurgery, 16, 143
psychotherapy. *See* treatment
psychotic-nonpsychotic dimension of mood disorders, 253, 255
PTSD. *See* posttraumatic stress disorder
Public Law, 94–142, 501
Pullen, United States v., 514
punch-drunk syndrome (dementia pugilistica), 440
punishment, 79–80, 505
Purkinje cells, 498
pyromania, 300

quality of life, 502–503

race/ethnicity
  and acquired brain disorders, 449
  and anxiety disorders, 152, 157, 163
  and eating disorders, 480
  and hypertension, 224–225
  and learning disorders, 475
  and malnutrition, 489
  and mental retardation, 493
  and mood disorders, 249
  and psychological assessment, 50–51
  and research, 62
  and schizophrenia, 405
  and sexual disorders, 363
  sociocultural perspective, 101
  and somatoform disorders, 204
  and stress-related illness, 235, 235–236, 242
  and substance abuse/dependence, 319–320, 345, 346, 349
  and suicide, 259
  See also cultural variations
racism, 349, 351. *See also* race/ethnicity; sociocultural perspective
radical behaviorism, 77–78, 83, 85–86
random assignment, 59
random sampling, 57, 59, 66, 67
rape, 374, 378. *See also* sexual assault
rapid-cycling type bipolar disorder, 251
RAPP (Hillside Recognition and Prevention Program), 418–419
rational-emotive therapy, 89, 94
rationalization, 109
reaction formation, 110, 120
reactive mood disorders, 255–256
reactive schizophrenia, 403
reactivity, 460
reading disorder (dyslexia), 474
rebound, 157, 174
receptive language, 476
reconstructive memory, 196
recovered memory controversy, 190–191
regression, 110, 205
reinforcement, 79, 88–89
  and developmental disorders, 505–506
  and dissociative disorders, 194, 195
  and mood disorders, 263
  and personality disorders, 305
  and schizophrenia, 425–426
  and somatoform disorders, 206
relapse prevention (RP) model, 325, 344–345, 381
relationships. *See* family dynamics; social support
relaxation training, 84
  and anxiety disorders, 167, 169
  and personality disorders, 306
  and somatoform disorders, 206–207
  and stress-related illness, 212, 234, 237
reliability, 32–34, 44, 55
religion
  and alcohol abuse/dependence, 320
  and cultural variations, 22, 23
  and dualism, 213
  and incest, 377

and sexuality, 356
and stress-related illness, 240–241
and suicide, 260
See also spirituality; supernatural theories
Renaissance, 6, 13
representativeness, 56, 57, 67
repression, 106, 108–109, 192
The Reproduction of Motherhood (Chodorow), 112
research, 54–72
designs for, 64–71
and diagnosis, 28, 31
ethical issues, 62–64, 67, 68, 70, 534
scientific method, 55–62
Resident Choice Assessment Scale, 503
residual phase of schizophrenia, 399
resistance, 118
respondent conditioning. *See* classical (respondent) conditioning
response sets, 46
Restoril (temazepam), 233
retarded ejaculation. *See* male orgasmic disorder
reticular activating system, 141
retrograde amnesia, 181
reversal (ABAB) design, 70, 71
Revia (naltrexone), 348, 349
revolving door syndrome, 17
Riggins v. Nevada, 518
risk, 63
Risperdal (risperidone), 417, 498
risperidone (Risperdal), 417, 498
Ritalin, 481–482
rivastigmine, 451
Rocky Mountain spotted fever, 439
role-playing, 86
role reversal, 381
Rorschach Psychodiagnostic Inkblot Test, 41–42, 44, 45
RP (relapse prevention) model, 325, 344–345, 381
rubella (German measles), 488

sadism, 374–376, 379, 380
sadomasochism, 375
SAD (seasonal affective disorder), 275–276
SADS (Schedule for Affective Disorders and Schizophrenia), 37
sampling, 57, 59, 66, 67, 121–122
savant syndrome, 495
SCD (sudden cardiac death), 216
Schedule for Affective Disorders and Schizophrenia (SADS), 37
schemas
and mood disorders, 266–267
overview, 93–94
and personality disorders, 306–308
and substance abuse/dependence, 343
and transference, 119
schematic camouflage, 307–308
schizoaffective disorder, 397
schizoid personality disorder, 289–290
schizophrenia, 389–405
cognitive perspective, 418–422
course of, 399
vs. delusional disorder, 406
dimensions, 403–405
vs. dissociative identity disorder, 184, 390
groups at risk, 405
historical perspectives, 390–391
interpersonal perspective, 422–425
mood symptoms, 397–398
motor symptoms, 398
perception symptoms, 396–397
and personality disorders, 287, 288, 290, 308
prevalence, 390
prevention, 418–419
problems in study of, 406–407
and social withdrawal, 398–399
sociocultural perspective, 427
and substance abuse/dependence, 333–334, 338
subtypes, 400–403
thought/language symptoms, 391–396
unitary theories, 427–428
See also neuroscience perspective on schizophrenia
schizophreniform disorder, 391
schizotypal personality disorder, 288–289, 308, 309, 411, 412
SCID (Structured Clinical Interview for *DSM-IV*), 37, 38
scientific method, 55–62
objectives of, 55–57
procedures, 57–62
and skepticism, 55
seasonal affective disorder (SAD), 275–276
secobarbital (Seconal), 332
Seconal (secobarbital), 332
secondary (conditioned) reinforcers, 79
secondary enuresis, 472
secondary gain, 201–202
secondary prevention, 10, 19, 504
sedative-hypnotic drugs, 139
seizures, 453–454
selective abstraction, 90
selective amnesia, 181
selective attention, 93, 266, 396, 397, 419–420
selective serotonin reuptake inhibitors (SSRIs)
and acquired brain disorders, 451
and anxiety disorders, 156, 173, 175–176
and dissociative disorders, 197
and mood disorders, 279–280
and sexual dysfunctions, 361, 370
and somatoform disorders, 209
self-actualization, 124–126
self-care skills, 340–341
self-concept, 124–125
self-dramatization, 296
self-efficacy, 93, 238, 329
self-help groups, 300, 323–324, 345
self-help skills, 505
self-incrimination, 519
self-instructional training (SIT), 94, 478, 506–507
self-medication, 340, 347, 349
self-report personality inventories, 45–47
self-talk, 94
self-verification, 92, 94
semantic dementia, 447
semantic memory, 182
sensate focus exercises, 366, 381
Sentence Completion Test, 43–44
separation anxiety disorder, 250, 466–467, 468, 477
Separation (Bowlby), 116
separation-individuation process, 115–116, 304
September 11, 2001 terrorist attacks, 157, 160, 319
Serax (oxazepam), 322
serial killers, 294
serotonin, 138
and anxiety disorders, 172–173, 175–176
and autism, 498, 507
and dissociative disorders, 197
and impulse-control disorders, 300
and migraine headache, 197, 230, 237
and mood disorders, 273, 278–279, 283
and paraphilias, 382
and schizophrenia, 416–417
and somatoform disorders, 209
and substance abuse/dependence, 349
sertraline (Zoloft), 176, 209, 280
Serzone (nefazodone), 280
SES. *See* socioeconomic status
SE/SS (Starting Early/Starting Smart), 350
sexology, 356
sexual abuse. *See* child abuse
sexual arousal disorders, 360–361, 368. *See also* male erectile disorder
sexual assault
and exhibitionism, 374
and frotteurism, 376
offenders, 371, 525–526
overview, 378
and schizophrenia, 399
and sexual dysfunctions, 360, 362, 378
and substance abuse/dependence, 316
See also child abuse; pedophilia
sexual aversion disorder, 360, 366
sexual desire disorders, 358, 360, 366, 368–369
sexual disorders, 355–358
classification, 356–358
gender identity disorders, 383–386
See also paraphilias; sexual dysfunctions
sexual dysfunctions, 358–370
behavioral/cognitive perspectives, 365–367
diagnosis, 362–363
forms of, 358, 360–362
groups at risk, 363–364
multifaceted treatment, 367–369
neuroscience perspective, 361, 369–370
psychodynamic perspective, 364–365
and sexual assault, 360, 362, 378
and substance abuse/dependence, 317, 338
sexuality
and developmental disorders, 503
and ethical issues, 535–536
myths about, 359, 361, 363
and patients' rights, 530
psychodynamic perspective, 107, 110–111, 112, 113
and somatoform disorders, 204
and substance abuse/dependence, 336
sexual offenders, 371, 525–526. *See also* child abuse; exhibitionism; sexual assault; voyeurism
sexual pain disorders, 362, 368, 369
sexual trauma. *See* child abuse; sexual assault
shaken-baby syndrome, 441
shame aversion therapy, 380–381
shaping, 80–81, 385, 505
sheltered workshops, 503
shoplifting, 7
shyness, 153
sick role, 205–206
sign language, 505
sildenifil (Viagra), 370
silent strokes, 442
simple partial seizures, 453
Sinequan (doxepin), 175
single-case experiments, 69–72
single photon emission computer tomography (SPECT), 142
SIT (self-instructional training), 94, 478, 506–507
situational molesters, 376
situational sexual dysfunctions, 362
situational variables, 49
skepticism, 55
sleep disorders
and AIDS/HIV, 228
childhood/adolescent forms, 472–474
and mood disorders, 247, 248, 274–275, 276
and psychopharmacology, 174, 233–234
and stress, 233–235
and substance abuse/dependence, 332–333
sleep-state misperception, 233
sleep terrors (night terrors), 473
sleepwalking, 473–474
SMART Recovery, 324

smokeless tobacco, 327
smooth-pursuit eye tracking, 411
social desirability response set, 46
social isolation, 241, 494
social phobia
  and avoidant personality disorder, 298
  childhood/adolescent forms, 467, 468, 477
  cognitive perspective, 164, 165
  neuroscience perspective, 172, 173, 175, 176
  overview, 152–153
  and somatoform disorders, 199
social-skills training
  and anxiety disorders, 167
  and mental retardation, 504
  and mood disorders, 264, 478
  and paraphilias, 381
  and personality disorders, 306, 308
  and schizophrenia, 426–427
  and somatoform disorders, 206
  and substance abuse/dependence, 341
social support
  and mood disorders, 255, 256
  and stress-related illness, 227–228, 241–242
  and substance abuse/dependence, 329, 345
social zeitgebers, 274–275
sociocultural perspective, 8, 98–102
  childhood/adolescent disorders, 480
  and diagnosis, 29
  dissociative disorders, 194–195
  evaluation of, 102
  mood disorders, 272–273
  personality disorders, 302–303, 308
  schizophrenia, 427
  somatoform disorders, 206
  stress-related illness, 242
  substance abuse/dependence, 340, 349–352
socioeconomic status (SES), 99–101
  and alcohol abuse/dependence, 319
  and anxiety disorders, 153
  and childhood disruptive behavior disorders, 465–466, 480
  and learning disorders, 474, 475
  and mental retardation, 489, 490, 491, 493, 504
  and mood disorders, 251
  and personality disorders, 302
  and sexual disorders, 363
  and somatoform disorders, 204, 206
  and stress-related illness, 236
  and substance abuse/dependence, 345, 349, 351
  and suicide, 272
  See also sociocultural perspective
Socratic questioning, 95, 96
sodium amytal, 181, 197
somatic nervous system, 144
somatic type of delusional disorder, 406
somatization disorder
  behavioral perspective, 205
  cognitive perspective, 207, 208
  groups at risk, 204
  neuroscience perspective, 208
  overview, 200–201
somatoform disorders, 197–209
  behavioral perspective, 205–207
  body dysmorphic disorder, 198–199, 203–204, 205, 207, 208, 209
  cognitive perspective, 207–208
  conversion disorder, 180, 201–203, 204, 205, 206–207, 208–209
  groups at risk, 203–204
  hypochondriasis, 199–200, 204, 205, 206, 207, 209
  neuroscience perspective, 208–209
  pain disorder, 201, 206–207, 208, 209
  psychodynamic perspective, 201–202, 204–205
  sociocultural perspective, 206
  somatization disorder, 200–201, 204, 205, 207, 208
  types, 198–203
somnambulism (sleepwalking), 473–474
Soura, State v., 530
source amnesia, 190
source-monitoring deficit theory, 196
specific phobias, 152, 164, 169–170, 176
spectator role, 365
SPECT (single photon emission computer tomography), 142
Spellbound, 181
spirituality, 219, 240–241. *See also* religion
split personality. *See* dissociative identity disorder
spongiform encephalopathies, 438
SSRIs. *See* selective serotonin reuptake inhibitors
stability, 460
standard of proof, 519–521
Stanford-Binet Intelligence Scale, 39
Starting Early/Starting Smart (SE/SS), 350
state-dependent memory, 196
statistical inference, 61–62
statistical-rarity approach to abnormal behavior, 3
Stelazine, 417
stereotactic subcaudate tractotomy, 143
stereotyped behavior, 496
steroids, 339
stigma, 99, 100, 146
stimulant medications, 481–482, 498
stimulants, 333–335
stimulus control, 505
stimulus equivalence, 81–82
stimulus satiation, 380
stimulus specificity, 214, 215
St. Louis encephalitis, 439
stress, 214–221
  acute vs. chronic, 215
  and autonomic nervous system, 144
  defined, 214
  and dissociative disorders, 180–181, 184, 197
  effects on illness, 215–220
  and high-risk behavior, 220–221
  individual response specificity, 214–215, 225
  and mood disorders, 255–256
  and psychogenic theory, 21
  as result of illness, 212
  and schizophrenia, 412
  sociocultural perspective, 99
  stimulus specificity, 214, 215
  and substance abuse/dependence, 319, 328, 331–332, 333, 345
  and suicide, 261
  See also stress-related illness
stress-management therapy, 206, 229–230, 238–239
stress-related illness, 211–243
  AIDS/HIV, 217, 228–230, 237, 239
  behavioral perspective, 236–237
  cancer, 225–228, 236–237, 239
  cognitive perspective, 214, 238–239
  coronary heart disease, 221–224, 235, 236, 239
  groups at risk, 235–236
  headache, 230–231, 237, 242
  and high-risk behavior, 220–221
  hypertension, 224–225, 242
  interpersonal perspective, 241–242
  and mind-body problem, 212–214
  neuroscience perspective, 145–146, 242–243
  obesity, 231–232
  and posttraumatic stress disorder, 161
  psychodynamic perspective, 239–241
  sleep disorders, 233–235
  sociocultural perspective, 242
  stress-illness connections, 215–220
  stress response variables, 214–215
stroke, 441–444, 449, 453
stroke syndrome, 442
Stroop color-word test, 219
structural hypothesis, 107–108
Structured Clinical Interview for *DSM-IV* (SCID), 37, 38
Studies in Hysteria (Breuer & Freud), 22
stuttering, 476
sublimation, 110
substance abuse, 314. *See also* substance abuse/dependence
substance abuse/dependence, 312–352
  and acquired brain disorders, 317, 441, 443, 451, 453
  anabolic steroids, 339
  and antisocial personality disorder, 293, 317
  and anxiety disorders, 153, 317, 333
  behavioral perspective, 325, 327–328, 341–342
  and borderline personality disorder, 296
  cognitive perspective, 325, 343–345
  and comorbidity, 35
  definitions, 313–314
  depressants, 330–333
  and dissociative disorders, 182
  groups at risk, 319–321, 340
  hallucinogens, 335–336, 338
  interpersonal perspective, 342–343
  marijuana/hashish, 336–338, 340
  and mental retardation, 488–489
  neuroscience perspective, 345–349
  nicotine dependence, 326–329
  psychodynamic perspective, 340–341
  and sexual disorders, 338, 360
  sociocultural perspective, 340, 349–352
  stimulants, 333–335
  and suicide, 258, 259
  See also alcohol abuse/dependence
substantia nigra, 448, 451
sudden cardiac death (SCD), 216
suffocation false alarm hypothesis, 173
suicide, 257–263
  and alcohol abuse/dependence, 315
  and anxiety disorders, 153
  and barbiturates, 332
  childhood/adolescent forms, 259–260, 262, 263, 468
  cognitive perspective, 261–262
  and confidentiality, 533
  groups at risk, 257–260
  and mood disorders, 247, 257–263
  myths about, 260
  neuroscience perspective, 279
  prediction, 260–262
  prevention, 262–263
  psychodynamic perspective, 269, 272
  and schizophrenia, 399
  sociocultural perspective, 272–273
  and somatoform disorders, 198–199
sulci, 139, 276
Summers, State v., 530
superego, 107–108
supernatural theories, 6, 11, 12–13
supportive-expressive therapy, 340–341
Surgeon General's Report (U.S. Public Health Service), 326
susto syndrome, 7
Sybil (Schreiber), 184
sympathetic division, 144–145, 216–217, 222
symptomatic epilepsy, 453
synapse, 136–137
synaptic vesicles, 137
syndromes, 20–21
synergistic effects, 332
syphilis, 21, 437, 488

systematic desensitization, 84, 169–170, 366, 477
systematized amnesia, 182

tacrine (Cognex), 449
tactical-integration therapy, 196–197
Tarasoff v. Regents of California, 523, 532
tardive dyskinesia, 416, 417, 529
TAT (Thematic Apperception Test), 42–43, 45
Tay-Sachs disease, 488
TBIs. *See* traumatic brain injuries
teenage pregnancy, 491–492
teenagers. *See* adolescence
Tegretol, 455
temazepam (Restoril), 233
temporal lobe, 140, 141, 385, 413, 414, 416
temporal-lobe seizures. *See* complex partial seizures
tension-reduction hypothesis of substance abuse/dependence, 341
tertiary prevention, 10
testosterone, 338, 339, 370
test-retest reliability, 33
Textbook of Psychiatry (Kraepelin), 20
Textbook of Psychiatry (Krafft-Ebing), 21
thalamus, 141
thalidomide, 488–489
Thematic Apperception Test (TAT), 42–43, 45
theories of abnormal behavior, 6, 8–9
  and diagnosis, 32
  integration, 127–128
theories of abnormal behavior *(continued)*
  See also behavioral perspective; cognitive perspective; interpersonal perspective; medical model; neuroscience perspective; psychodynamic perspective; sociocultural perspective
theory of mind, 499–500
therapy. *See* treatment
therapy-induced (iatrogenic) disorders, 186, 188
third-variable problem, 65
Thorazine (chlorpromazine), 417
The Three Faces of Eve (Thigpen & Cleckley), 184, 185
three-term contingencies, 80, 83
threshold model of Alzheimer's disease, 447
thrombosis, 442
thrombus, 221
thyroid, 277
thyroid syndromes, 451–452
thyroxine deficiency, 488, 504
time-order relationships, 56, 64
TMS (transcranial magnetic stimulation), 283–284
tobacco, 326–329
Tofranil (imipramine), 175
toilet training, 471–472, 505
token economies, 426, 477, 531–532
tolerance, 314, 332
tonic-clonic (grand mal) seizures, 454
Touched with Fire: Manic-Depressive Illness and the Artistic Temperament (Jamison), 254
Tourette's syndrome, 156, 173
toxins, 452–453, 490
traits, 38, 287. *See also* personality disorders
tranquilizers, 139, 174–175, 332–333, 451
transcranial magnetic stimulation (TMS), 283–284
transference, 118, 119
transsexuals, 383–386
transvestism, 372–373, 379
Tranxene (chlorazepate), 174, 332
tranylcypromine (Parnate), 175
traumatic brain injuries (TBIs)
  and epilepsy, 453
  and mental retardation, 490
  overview, 439–441
  prevention, 442
traumatic life events
  and anxiety disorders, 168–169
  and dissociative disorders, 181, 182, 184, 189, 192–193
  and mood disorders, 255, 256, 269
  and stress-related illness, 218–219
  and substance abuse/dependence, 319
  See also child abuse; posttraumatic stress disorder; stress
treatment
  acquired brain disorders, 439, 441, 444, 449, 451, 455
  anxiety disorders, 167–168, 169–171, 174–176
  autism, 498
  behavioral perspective overview, 83–87
  childhood/adolescent disorders, 461, 477, 478–481
  and civil commitment, 526–527
  and clinical trials, 67–68
  cognitive perspective overview, 94–97, 98
  developmental disorders, 505–508
  dissociative disorders, 193, 195, 196–197
  elimination disorders, 472
  gender identity disorders, 385–386
  and humanistic-existential perspective, 125, 126
  and hypothesis generation, 57–58, 60–61
  interpersonal perspective overview, 127
  learning disorders, 476
  mood disorders, 264, 267–269, 271–272, 279–284
  neuroscience perspective overview, 174–176
  non-Western approaches, 22–23
  overview, 9
  paraphilias, 379–381, 382–383
  personality disorders, 304–305, 306, 307–308
  practitioners, 10
  and prevention, 10–11
  psychodynamic perspective overview, 117–120
  right to, 527–529
  right to refuse, 529
  schizophrenia, 416, 417–418, 421–422, 424–427
  sexual dysfunctions, 365–368
  sleep disorders, 233–234
  and sociocultural perspective, 101, 195
  somatoform disorders, 205, 206–208, 209
  stress-related illness, 233–234, 237, 238–239, 240–241
  substance abuse/dependence, 322–326, 328–329, 331, 340–343, 344–345, 349
  See also historical perspectives; psychopharmacology
tremor, 449
trephination, 11
triazolam (Halcion), 233, 234, 332
trichotalomania, 156
trichotillomania, 300
tricyclic antidepressants, 175, 176, 209, 278, 279
trisomy 21, 487
L-tryptophan, 279
twin studies, 132–133, 134, 408–409
Type A Behavior and Your Heart (Friedman & Rosenman), 223
Type A personality, 223, 239, 242
UCR (unconditioned response), 78
UCS (unconditioned stimulus), 78
unconditioned response (UCR), 78
unconditioned stimulus (UCS), 78
unconscious, 106, 120, 147, 201
uncued panic attacks, 162
understanding, 56
undoing, 110, 120
unified detachment, 86
United States v. Pullen, 514
up-regulation, 137

vaginal orgasm myth, 361
vaginismus, 362, 368
validity, 34–35, 44, 47
  and research, 55–57, 59, 69, 71
Valium (diazepam), 172, 174, 332
valley fever, 439
valuing process, 124
variables, 58–59
vascular dementia, 447, 449
vasodilation, 369
venlafaxine (Effexor), 280
ventricles, 141, 276, 413, 415, 499
Viagra (sildenifil), 370
vicious cycles, 92, 317, 468
victim awareness training, 381
violence. *See* aggression/violence
violence risk assessment schemes, 524
viral hypothesis of schizophrenia, 415
vision impairments, 474
vitamin E, 451
voyeurism, 374
vulnerability-stress model. *See* diathesis-stress (vulnerability-stress) model

Washington v. Harper, 529
waxy flexibility, 401
Wechsler Intelligence Scales, 39, 40, 41
Wellbutrin (bupropion), 280
western equine encephalitis, 439
West Nile virus encephalitis, 437
Why Zebras Don't Get Ulcers (Sapolsky), 215
witch hunts, 13
withdrawal, 174, 314
  and alcohol, 318
  and barbiturates, 332
  and cocaine, 334–335
  and endorphins, 348
  and heroin, 331
  and nicotine, 328
  and substance abuse/dependence treatment, 345
women. *See* gender differences
word salad, 395–396
World Health Organization (WHO), 28
worry, 164–165
written expression disorder, 474
Wyatt v. Stickney, 527–528, 529, 530, 531, 532

Xanax (alprazolam), 174

yohimbine, 369–370
York Retreat, 14
Youngsberg v. Romeo, 528, 530

zeitgebers, 274–275
zidovudine, 488
Zoloft (sertraline), 176, 209, 280
zolpidem (Ambien), 234

Shared Psychotic Disorder
Psychotic Disorder Due to a General Medical Condition
Substance-Induced Psychotic Disorder

- **MOOD DISORDERS**

Depressive Disorders
Major Depressive Disorder
Dysthymic Disorder

Bipolar Disorders
Bipolar I Disorder
Bipolar II Disorder
Cyclothymic Disorder
Mood Disorder Due to General Medical Condition
Substance-Induced Mood Disorder

- **ANXIETY DISORDERS**

Panic Disorder without Agoraphobia
Panic Disorder with Agoraphobia
Agoraphobia without History of Panic Disorder
Specific Phobia
Social Phobia
Obsessive-Compulsive Disorder
Posttraumatic Stress Disorder
Acute Stress Disorder
Generalized Anxiety Disorder
Anxiety Disorders Due to General Medical Condition
Substance-Induced Anxiety Disorder

- **SOMATOFORM DISORDERS**

Somatization Disorder
Undifferentiated Somatoform Disorder
Conversion Disorder
Pain Disorder
Hypochondriasis
Body Dysmorphic Disorder

- **FACTITIOUS DISORDERS**

- **DISSOCIATIVE DISORDERS**

Dissociative Amnesia
Dissociative Fugue
Dissociative Identity Disorder
Depersonalization Disorder

- **SEXUAL AND GENDER IDENTITY DISORDERS**

Sexual Dysfunctions
Sexual Desire Disorders
Hypoactive Sexual Desire Disorder
Sexual Aversion Disorder

Sexual Arousal Disorders
Female Sexual Arousal Disorder
Male Erectile Disorder

Orgasmic Disorders
Female Orgasmic Disorder
Male Orgasmic Disorder
Premature Ejaculation

Sexual Pain Disorders
Dyspareunia
Vaginismus

Sexual Dysfunction Due to a General Medical Condition
Substance-Induced Sexual Dysfunction

Paraphilias
Exhibitionism
Fetishism
Frotteurism
Pedophilia
Sexual Maso
Sexual Sadis
Transvestic F
Voyeurism

Gender Identi

- **EATING DISO**

Anorexia N
Bulimia Ne

- **SLEEP DISO**

Primary Sleep

Dyssomnias
Primary Ins
Primary Hy
Narcolepsy
Breathing-
Circadian Disorder

Parasomnias
Nightmare
Sleep Terro
Sleepwalk

Sleep Disord
Mental Diso
Other Sleep

- **IMPULSE-C**
NOT ELSE

Intermittent Explosive Disorder
Kleptomania
Pyromania
Pathological Gambling
Trichotillomania

- **ADJUSTMENT DISORDERS**

- **PERSONALITY DISORDERS (AXIS II)**

Paranoid Personality Disorder
Schizoid Personality Disorder
Schizotypal Personality Disorder
Antisocial Personality Disorder
Borderline Personality Disorder
Histrionic Personality Disorder
Narcissistic Personality Disorder
Avoidant Personality Disorder
Dependent Personality Disorder
Obsessive-Compulsive Personality Disorder

- **OTHER CONDITIONS THAT MAY BE A FOCUS OF CLINICAL ATTENTION**

Psychological Factors Affecting Medical Condition
Medication-Induced Movement
duced

Related to a
r General

onal Problem
Problem
Problem
Abuse or

Child
ild

Adult
dult
ns That May
l Attention
th Treatment

ehavior
t Antisocial

tual
s II)
itive Decline

lem

ual Problem
blem
lem

- **ADDITIONAL CODES**

Unspecified Mental Disorder (Nonpsychotic)
No Diagnosis or Condition on Axis I
Diagnosis or Condition Deferred on Axis I
No Diagnosis on Axis II
Diagnosis Deferred on Axis II